# THE
★
# GROWTH
★
# OF
★
# AMERICAN
★
# THOUGHT

# SOCIAL & MORAL THOUGHT SERIES

*Abraham Edel and Elizabeth Flower, series editors*

An age of vast technical and institutional changes calls for a focus on basic social and moral ideas. This series makes accessible past works of serious import deserving renewed attention in the contemporary world for present moral decision and social policy. Books in this series are drawn not only from general social science, but also from philosophy, education, law, history, anthropology, and psychology. Each volume has an introductory essay prepared especially for the series by a contemporary scholar in the particular field.

# THE GROWTH OF AMERICAN · THOUGHT ·

## Third Edition

## · Merle Curti ·

### With a New Preface by the Author

Transaction Books
New Brunswick (U.S.A.) and London (U.K.)

Library of Congress Catalog Number: 81-3433
ISBN: 0-87855-879-9 (paper)
Printed in the United States of America

**Library of Congress Cataloging in Publication Data**

Curti, Merle Eugene, 1897-
  The growth of American thought.

  (Social and moral thought series)
  Reprint. Originally published: 3rd ed. New York:
Harper & Row, 1964.
  Bibliography: p.
  Includes index.
  1. United States—Intellectual life. 2. United
States—Civilization. I. Title. II. Series.
E169.1.C87  1982      973      81-3433
ISBN: 0-87855-879-9 (pbk.)    AACR2

# Preface to the Transaction Edition

*The Growth of American Thought* (1943, new editions 1951 and 1964) was generously greeted as a pioneer achievement. With one exception the many reviews in periodicals intended for informed readers were warm in praise. Appreciation, and frequently enthusiastic commendation, characterized the reviews in scholarly journals. In 1952 Professor John Caughey, after canvassing historians of the national experience, reported that this was the most admired of books on American history published between 1936 and 1950.

Several factors explained the book's appeal. In view of the interest Vernon L. Parrington and Arthur M. Schlesinger, Sr., had stimulated in a social and intellectual interpretation of the Republic's past, the time was ripe for a comprehensive social history of American thought. After World War II the rapid spread of the American Studies movement also explained the usefulness and popularity of the first real synthesis. The vogue of American Studies in Western and Central Europe and in Japan accounted for the early translations into German, French, Italian, Spanish, and Japanese.

Some historians question the advisability of attempting a synthesis of an emerging or even a fairly well developed field when gaps in knowledge and uncertainty about methods present all but impossible obstacles. This was particularly relevant in 1943. Recognizing its validity, the preface to the 1943 edition of *The Growth of American Thought* suggested that "to wait until scholars have completed all the requisite special studies is to postpone wider considerations on the assumption that these studies will in fact be completed; such an assumption may or may not be warranted. So to wait is to deprive even particular inquiries of the thought about the problem as a whole, which is available at the present stage in the development of the theme."

The conceptualization of *The Growth of American Thought* emphasized the influence of the European heritage of religion, philosophy, law, and science and the modification of the ideas and values associated with this heritage by distinctive conditions and experiences in America. In time the interaction took form in the gospel of nationalism, progress, and democracy. The heritage and its modifications have resulted in American perceptions of the nature and origin of the universe, of human nature, and of social relations.

Since the appearance of *The Growth of American Thought* hundreds of articles and monographs have developed various aspects of the broad canvas it presented. The specialized studies have deepened the understanding of many aspects of American intellectual history. Some of this rich, new material has contributed important knowledge about ideas, movements of thought, attitudes, and the institutions of cultural life which *The Growth* specified as "work needed." Scholars in American Studies carried much further the analysis of symbols, myths, and images. Some of the recent work on popular culture, a theme which *The Growth of American Thought* only sketched, reflects considerable sophistication and also raises stimulating questions about the interrelations of "high" and "low" culture.

Some scholars have developed aspects of American intellectual history unanticipated by *The Growth of American Thought*. Neil Harris and others in showing the significance of visual forms for an understanding of intellectual history have broadened and enriched an appreciation of the esthetic component in the nation's cultural development. Among others Warren Susman has illustrated the explanatory usefulness of the concept of personality and culture. Various psychological models have been offered in the new psychohistory.

In the last two decades important developments have influenced work in intellectual history. The spirited contribution of "the new left" has given added importance to the role of the less articulate and to protest and conflict of ideas. The much more influential new social history has, while displacing intellectual history in prestige, pushed to the fore the contextual approach to the study of ideas. Demographic studies of small communities have shed new light on changing attitudes toward the shifting character of the family, child-rearing, sex roles, and career choices. The reciprocal relations of social change and ideas have thus often been clarified. While closely related to the new social history, ethnohistory, including black studies, has achieved virtual autonomy. These interests were not ignored in *The Growth of American Thought*, but their development has revolutionized the study of this aspect of the field.

Most practitioners of intellectual history have shunned anything approaching a comprehensive synthesis. The only real exception was Stow Persons' admirable *American Minds* (1958, 1975), which is no longer in print. To be sure, Paul K. Conkin's *Puritans and Pragmatists: Eight Eminent Thinkers* (1968), Charles A. Barker's *American Convictions: Cycles of Public Thought 1600-1850* (1970), to be followed by a second volume, and Henry F. May's *The Enlightenment in America* (1976) on a limited chronological scale, and a few other titles stand out in contrast with the formidable number of specialized monographs. It is also true, however, that scholars in religious, educational, legal, and medical history in the United States have given us notable syntheses of these aspects of intellectual development.

Problems associated with scope, definition, and methods in the study of intellectual history have continued to trouble scholars. Concern with the precise and often changing meaning of words and language and with the structure, logic, and character of ideas and concepts, attitudes, and movements of thought has been reinforced Lovejoy, Ralph Henry Gabriel, and Stow Persons, but by the emphasis on rigor and precision in philosophical and linguistic analysis. While recognizing the validity of this approach and not entirely neglecting it, *The Growth of American Thought* emphasized the contextual setting and convergence of ideas and "interests" broadly understood. Identified in 1943 as the exterior or social history of ideas in contrast with logical analysis and antecedent ideas, labeled "the interior" of ideas, this functional and instrumental view of concepts, attitudes, and movements of thought has been reenforced by the growing interest in the sociology of knowledge as well as by the pressure of public crises. This approach has won increasing favor. A recent example is *New Directions in American Intellectual History* (1979), a volume of essays, mainly by younger scholars, planned and edited by John Higham and Paul K. Conkin. Some of these essays, like other work in the field, advocate or approximate a combination of the two leading ways of viewing intellectual history that *The Growth of American Thought* recommended as a desirable goal.

In trying to work out specific and verifiable ways of discovering the precise ways in which ideas and the social context interacted, some have espoused the paradigm concept as developed by Thomas S. Kuhn in *The Nature of Scientific Revolutions* (1962, 1970). Others have experimented on a limited scale with quantification in examining the kinds of printed material in early New England and the availability and circulation of leading expositions of the French Enlightenment. The exact relationships between ideas and context continues, however, to be a major challenge sharpened by the recognition of the importance of rigorous methods in formulating generalizations.

It is an honor to have *The Growth of American Thought* made available in Transaction's Social and Moral Thought Series. I hope a book that played an important part in the development of a new field and that has been widely read for well over three decades will be useful until a new synthesis appears which makes use of all that has been learned since the first edition of this book. Perhaps even then it may have some interest for students of the interdisciplinary trend in American historiography.

*Merle Curti*

*March, 1981*

# Contents

### Part IV. Democratic Upheaval

### Part V. Triumph of Nationalism

### Part VI. Individualism in a Corporate Age

### Part VII. Diversion, Criticism, and Contraction

# Preface to the Third Edition

Conceived and largely written in the 1930s, the original edition of *The Growth of American Thought* assumed that ideas could best be understood in terms of their social context and social utility. Because it also assumed that the life of the mind depends in large measure on the existence and activity of the agencies of culture, it emphasized the role of the church, government, and business, the development of schools, publishing, and libraries, the impact of wars and economic crises. I was well aware that another approach was possible and desirable: one that systematically analyzed ideas in terms of their philosophical foundations, internal structure, and interrelationships. In *The Growth* and in other writings I tried my hand at this approach and urged others, with better training, to probe deeply and systematically into what I called "the interior of ideas." I thought at the time, and still think, that a combination of these two main approaches is highly desirable.

Since the appearance of the second edition of *The Growth of American Thought* in 1951, some scholars have carried the functional approach much further than I did. This has been particularly true of intellectual historians who have been sensitive to the role of American ideas and values in the contest with totalitarianism. But the main emphasis in scholarship has been on the systematic inner analysis of ideas. The only general synthesis that has been largely governed by this approach is Stow Persons' *American Minds* (1958). But a long list of essays and monographs, cited in the new bibliographical note of the present edition, has greatly enriched the literature of American intellectual history through the internal analysis approach. The reaction against the study of movements of thought in social context and in terms of social uses reflects dissatisfaction with the assumption that the instrumentality of ideas is a valid and useful key to understanding them. The reaction also reflects the vogue of the consensus interpretation of American historical experience, that is, the thesis that conflicts of interest have been less real and important than we commonly believed in the 1930s.

Loss of faith in the role of reason as a major factor in men's experience and potentialities has been natural, if not inevitable, in a world of war, revolution, and violence, a world which testifies to the power of emotion and irrationality. It is not surprising that scholars have recently attached considerable importance to legends, myths, and symbols. The work of Charles Feidlerson, Henry Nash Smith, John Ward, R. W. B. Lewis, and Marvin Meyers, to cite only a few, reflects this concern, a concern heightened by the fashionableness of Freudian and neo-Freudian theories and by the teachings of many social psychologists. As yet, however, no scholar has made this approach the governing frame of reference of a systematic, comprehensive history of American intellectual and emotional life. Preoccupation with symbols and myths, with rhetoric and appearances, with the need for greater precision in the analysis of units of thought and emotional currents, is reflected in the vocabulary of many younger scholars. One meets again and again such terms as tension, irony, tragedy, search for identity, and alienation.

Although the institutional embodiment of ideas has not been neglected by scholars in the last ten or fifteen years, the main emphasis in recent accounts of American religious, political, economic, philosophical, legal, and scientific thought, has been analytical rather than functional. The latest scholarship has added new, rich, and significant dimensions to the work of pioneers in the field.

In preparing this new edition of *The Growth of American Thought* I considered the possibility and desirability of a drastic reorganization within an essentially different framework. To my surprise I found that in the original edition I had taken into account, however briefly and inadequately, many ideas, approaches, and emphases that have since become popular. The emotional content of culture, as expressed in myths, legends, and folklore, received attention in my earlier work. So too did anti-intellectualism and the related problem of the status and role of intellectuals in American society. Preceding editions also helped to call attention to another theme that has become a major interest—the "image" of America in foreign lands.

Yet it would be immodest and inaccurate to suggest that recent scholarship on these and other subjects has changed our understanding of American intellectual history only slightly. In the present edition I have tried to take into account the new scholarship and fresh points of view. I have also added a chapter on the intellectual and cultural interests of the 1950s. Whatever its shortcomings, this chapter has profited from the criticisms of my seminars and of friends, particularly Irvin G. Wyllie, Kendall Birr, Fulmer Mood, and Louis C. Hunter, and of my daughter, Martha Wohlforth.

I want to express my appreciation to Gail Bremer, who did tedious checking, and to Mildred Lloyd, who typed and retyped portions of the present edition of *The Growth*. But my main debt is to Raymond J. Wilson who, as my research assistant, carefully analyzed the text of the 1951 edition in relation to the recent monographic and interpretative literature.

Many basic books, old and new, are available to scholars, teachers, and students of intellectual history, often in inexpensive paperback form. Despite this rich supply, I dare to hope that the comprehensive synthesis of *The Growth of American Thought*, together with its revised discussion of specific problems, will guarantee its future usefulness. I hope, too, that the book may continue to suggest themes and problems for investigation.

*Merle Curti*

*January, 1964*

# Introduction

An account of the growth of American thought involves, in the first place, a study of the growth on American soil of *knowledge* of the physical universe, of human nature, and of social relationships. Since man's precise and tested knowledge of his environment, physical and social, and of himself has been at every point in time subject to varying limitations, he has *speculated* on that which he did not know. These speculative operations, sometimes casual, random, and entirely unorganized, have been transmitted from generation to generation as superstitions and folklore; sometimes they have been systematized as theology and philosophy. In either case such informal notions and beliefs, or organized ideas, properly belong to intellectual history. To knowledge and ideas must be added the values which men and women have held and cherished. The history of knowledge, of speculation and ideas, and of values cannot easily be traced without reference to the institutions especially concerned with making accretions to knowledge and thought and disseminating these. Thus the growth in America of schools, colleges, libraries, the press, laboratories, foundations, and research centers becomes an important condition for the growth of American thought.

Bodies of exact knowledge, patterns of thought, and all the agencies of intellectual life developed in America in relation to their counterparts in Europe. Each generation of Europeans who came to America brought prevailing or dissenting European ideas, brought in greater or less degree special intellectual techniques and the command of bodies of knowledge, brought concepts of the good and the desirable. All these played essential roles in the growth of American thought. Americans, old and new, familiarized themselves with newer intellectal currents in the Old World through travel and study abroad and through reading in the original or in translation reports of scientific discoveries and emerging systems of thought. But even in the seventeenth century, and increasingly with the passage of time, Americans also contributed both knowledge and ideas to Europe.

If the history of the growth of knowledge, thought, values, and the agencies of intellectual life is not to be a mere chronicle, it is necessary to explain, as far as possible, how this growth took place. The factors that have aided and the factors that have retarded it must be considered. The status of knowledge, the tissue of thought, the cluster of values are all at any particular time affected by the physical environment and economy, polity, and social arrangements, all more or less in the process of change. Because the American environment, physical and social, differed from that of Europe, Americans, confronted by different needs and problems, adapted the European intellectual heritage in their own way. And because American life came increasingly to differ from European life, American ideas, American agencies of intellectual life, and the use made of knowledge likewise came to differ in America from their European counterparts. The interrelationships between the growth of thought and the whole social milieu seem to be so close and have been so frequently neglected that this study of American life has tried consistently to relate that growth to the whole complex environment. It is thus not a history of American thought but a social history of American thought, and to some extent a socioeconomic history of American thought.

This emphasis on the relationships between developing ideas and bodies of knowledge on the one hand and other phases of American life on the other imposes certain limitations, if the account is to be encompassed in a single volume. An effort has been made throughout to describe in broad outline the nature of the dominant ideas and to indicate the major contributions made by Americans to exact knowledge. But this study does not purport to provide an exhaustive analysis of the "interiors" of the ideas and systems of thought chosen for consideration. Such analyses, in the manner of Bury's *History of the Idea of Progress* or Lovejoy's *Great Chain of Being*, would indeed be valuable, but they are not a part of the plan of this book. The emphasis chosen has also precluded a full discussion of the development of each of the intellectual disciplines in America. The study is primarily a social history of American thought.

This study of American intellectual life is organized in chronological periods according to ideas which may be thought of as characteristic of the successive eras in that history. Complex and long though the colonial era was, different though American life and thought on the eve of the Revolution were from life and thought in the seventeenth century, the colonial period nevertheless presents a certain unity. In that period Europeans adapted their heritage of thought and knowledge to the conditions of colonization and to a new physical and social environment. The heritage of Christian thought, of the polite learning of the Renais-sance, and of a vast body of folklore was supplemented by that of the Enlightenment which began to make its impact on America in the seventeenth century. The next general period, extending from the rise of the Revolution to the end of the eighteenth century, was marked by the growth of the idea of Americanism. Cultural nationalism, the expanding Enlightenment, and the conservative reaction all contributed to and were in turn affected by the concept of Americanism. The first third of the nineteenth century, roughly, was marked by patrician leadership in thought. This, however, was challenged by the frontier in those decades, and the nationalism inherited from the revolutionary shift in emphasis was challenged by both cosmopolitan and regional ideas and interests. The period extending approximately from 1830 to 1850 was dominated by the democratic upheaval that profoundly affected intellectual life; this was an era in which new currents of equalitarian thought made themselves felt. This was also the golden day of progress and optimism, in which science and technology made great advances, in which knowledge was popularized, and in which patriotic and nationalistic ideas were assimilated to democratic theory.

The period extending roughly from 1850 to 1870 was marked by the triumph of nationalism and business ideology in social and political thought. The cultural regionalism of the Old South was paralleled in the decade prior to the Civil War by the intellectual defense of commerce and industry in the North; these patterns of thought and feeling were opposed as their associated interests were in the Civil War. Appomattox was followed by an upsurge of business ideology and a new nationalism in thought and feeling.

From 1870 or thereabouts to the end of the century the dominant idea was the assertion of individualism in a corporate age of applied science. Science advanced on supernaturalism, and evolutionary thought affected and was affected by the utilitarian ideas and interests that prevailed. At the same time the earlier democratic movement toward the popularization of knowledge continued; the corporate character of the age was reflected in the new emphasis on the professionalization of many areas and levels of intellectual life. At the same time, in the name of individualism and reform, ideas and systems of thought reflected the challenge implicit in the application of science to life, and these reform and protest ideas stimulated a counterdefense in the name of conservative interests.

In the twentieth century optimism has been subject to diversion, criticism, and contraction. The imperialistic adventure of 1898 and subsequent years and the crusade of 1917 to make the world safe for democracy were followed by disillusionment, criticism, and complacency, and then by renewed optimism in the decade of the 'twenties. But the breakdown in economy during the 'thirties eventuated in new intellectual searches, and the world crisis intensified the widespread pessimism and uncertainty.

No brief is held for the superiority of the organization of this study. With a different set of purposes a different organization would be natural. The fact that a treatment based on leading social attitudes is combined with a chronological division of the subject matter means that a particular person or group, or a given conception or attitude, is often dealt with in different connections in different parts of this book. But this is unavoidable in a work departing as this does from a strictly chronological treatment.

The problem of emphasis, of selection and rejection of materials, and that of chronology have not been the only difficulties encountered. The sources for a study of American intellectual history are abundant —formal treatises by theologians, philosophers, scientists, and social scientists; autobiographies and letters of scholars, published and unpublished; novels, tales, poems, essays, critical reviews in periodicals; records of the agencies of intellectual life, schools, colleges, foundations, learned societies, publishing houses, newspapers, and the like; collections of folklore, folk songs, ballads, and proverbs; literature written and published for the masses—these are only some of the materials available. In some measure this study rests on such materials. But the scope of this undertaking is so vast that by necessity monographic literature bulks large. Of this there is an impressive amount, in spite of the fact that students of American history have long been primarily concerned with political, military, economic, and social activities and institutions.

Even from the start, however, intellectual interests were in some measure represented in historical writing. Edward Johnson, one of

New England's first historians, included in his *Wonder-Working Providence of Zion's Saviour in New-England* (1654) an account of the founding of the churches in Massachusetts Bay and of the religious ideas and controversies that both harassed the founders and added zest to life. A half century later Cotton Mather's *Magnalia Christi Americana* chronicled in detail the lives of the divines, the "afflictive disturbances," and the fortunes of Harvard College. Nor did other colonies lack historians to relate intellectual interests and achievements, or the absence of them. Hugh Jones' *The Present State of Virginia* (1724) is still a valuable source for our knowledge of the agencies of intellectual life in the Old Dominion. Other historians throughout the eighteenth century included in their narratives fragments of intellectual history.

The first monumental work devoted solely to this field appeared in 1803, when the Reverend Samuel Miller, a Presbyterian clergyman of New York, published his two-volume *Retrospect of the Eighteenth Century*. This series of essays on virtually every phase of the intellectual life of Europe in the eighteenth century included surveys of the state of knowledge in the United States and of American contributions to knowledge. With all its shortcomings it was a notable effort and is still useful to the student of the growth of American thought.

The historians of the first half of the nineteenth century were above all else concerned with political and institutional history. In consequence our intellectual past fared badly at their hands. The neglect that it suffered in formal historical writings was in part compensated for by the appearance, beginning in 1829, of a series of anthologies of American literature and by an unbroken interest in the history of American letters. Moreover, in such informal histories as academic orators often provided at the meetings of literary societies or at commencements, our intellectual glory was a favored theme. But the circumstance that Americans had actually created a notable political record, that sectional and party controversies were so absorbing, that our intellectual life was so largely subordinated to other matters, tended to keep that aspect of our past subordinate. The tendency to emphasize political events was subsequently confirmed by the political and institutional interests of scholars trained in the German historical seminars and influenced by such English historians as E. A. Freeman.

The last two decades of the nineteenth century witnessed significant departures from this pattern. John Bach McMaster's first volume of the *History of the People of the United States* (1883) devoted refreshing attention to intellectual developments and interests, and this emphasis was sustained in subsequent volumes. Eight years after the appearance of McMaster's first volume Henry Adams, in his *History of the United States during the Administrations of Jefferson and Madison*, made an effort to fathom the "American mind" of the early nineteenth century. Edward Eggleston called attention to the need for studying the cultural development of the American people. He did not carry out his full plans, but the appearance in 1901 of *The Transit of Civilization from England to America in the Seventeenth Century* broke new ground. About this time Moses Coit Tyler was bringing to a close his scholarly and comprehensive literary history of the colonial and revolutionary periods, the first volume of which had appeared in 1878.

New European emphases in the historical studies of European development were not without their influence. In England, Green's *Short History of the English People* carried still further the tradition of Macaulay and others in devoting some attention to the social and cultural chapters of the nation's past, and historians of France were following in the same course. The visit to America in 1904 of the German historian, Karl Lamprecht, did much to focus attention on cultural history, broadly conceived. Taking up the work of Dr. John Draper of New York University, who had published in 1863 *The Intellectual Development of Europe*, James Harvey Robinson of Columbia University called the attention of students of American history as well as those in the European field to the history of man's mind as an important means of determining how the past gave way to the present. Evarts B. Greene, Frederick J. Turner, Edward Channing, and, on the Pacific coast, Herbert E. Bolton, all gave attention to the development of intellectual interests.

In the period since the First World War great strides have been made in the study of our intellectual past and this aspect of our history has begun to come into its own. The publication in 1917 and the following years of the *Cambridge History of American Literature* was significant by reason of its scope and scholarship. When the *History of American Life* under the editorship of Dixon Ryan Fox and Arthur M. Schlesinger began to appear in 1927, it was clear beyond doubt that our intellectual history is both richer than anyone had supposed it to be and, furthermore, susceptible of the same scholarly treatment that other aspects of the national life have received.

Yet in view of the emphasis given by historians to political, military, and economic activities, it is still correct to say that intellectual life in the United States, especially in its relation to other phases of history, has been, comparatively speaking, sadly neglected in detail and in general. Only in 1940 was our first history of American democratic ideas made available; and admirable though Ralph Gabriel's study is, it does not cover the whole sweep of democratic thought in America. We have recently had from the hands of Charles and Mary Beard a history of the idea of civilization in the United States, but we are virtually without histories of such ideas as liberty, progress, security, militarism, individualism, and collectivism—ideas now in tumultuous and heated use. It is impossible at present to say with what meanings they have been employed, or what changes in meaning they have undergone in the course of their American experience.

The situation is only slightly better in the area of systematic thought. It is true that we have histories of American philosophic thought, of educational thought, and of political thought; and that we shall presently have from Joseph Dorfman a systematic history of American economic thought. Religious and theological thought in America have also been studied and reported on for certain periods. But these histories of American systems of thought, despite their merits, are not comprehensive. Furthermore, there are no general histories of scientific and technological thought, or of esthetic thought, or of American social thought.

Even more striking is the dearth of studies of the ideas or fragments of larger bodies of thought present in the minds of the great mass of common people or implicit in their behavior. The vast majority of plain people do not, of course, write books or make public addresses or focus their attention in any sustained way on the objects of intellectual interest. Yet popular thought is certainly a phase of American life that bears profoundly on the nature of American democracy and on American destiny itself. A people commonly believed to be noted for its common sense deserves studies indicating what each generation from the beginning has regarded as practical, as common sense. To what extent have the assumptions of what is regarded as common sense been implicit in the behavior of ordinary men and women, and to what extent have they been made explicit by their spokesmen or by writers, orators, and artists?

We have at our command few adequate histories of specific disciplines in the United States—progress of knowledge in the natural sciences, for example, or in geography, history, or psychology. The studies that do exist are for the most part lacking in comprehensiveness.

Nor have all the histories of knowledge, of thought, and of speculation related the subject matter to changing social, economic, and cultural conditions. In a few cases, it is true, efforts to do so have been made. In this field Vernon L. Parrington was a pioneer. *Main Currents in American Thought* (1927, 1930) related the writings of American men of letters, political leaders, orators, and other figures to the social and economic conflicts in American life, especially to agrarianism on the one hand and to capitalism on the other. Bernard Smith's *Forces in American Criticism* (1939) carried this approach further. In the chapters in *The Rise of American Civilization* and *America in Midpassage* dealing with American cultural interests, the Beards have achieved notable success in the integration of ideas and interests, of cultural values, systems of thought, and bodies of knowledge with the context of which all these are part.

Some may contend that the history of intellectual life in America cannot be written now for the reason that adequate special studies on which a general synthesis must rest have not yet been made. According to one widely held view, efforts to grasp the whole or any part, even in thought, are useless until preliminary inquiries have been completed. In fact, however, monographic studies made without thought about the relations of the special to the general are likely to be arid.

Actually it is not possible, of course, for specialized research and writing to proceed without some reference to thought, however stray and surreptitious such thought may be, about the wider relationships. Since particulars do bear relations to the general, preliminary thought about the problem of these relations, based of course on the knowledge available, can aid in the production of monographs that will be useful as the higher and higher generalizations are reached. To wait until scholars have completed all the requisite special studies is to postpone wider consideration on the assumption that these studies will in fact be completed; such an assumption may or may not be warranted. So to wait is to deprive even particular inquiries of the thought about the problem of the whole, which is available at the present stage in the development of the theme.

The task of writing a social history of American thought may be undertaken, meantime, in the light of present thought and knowledge.

It is a task of such magnitude that the author has no idea that his labors are definitive. He hopes only that they may furnish some suggestions to other historians who will explore this field, and that they may help some readers to achieve a fuller appreciation of our country's past.

M. C.

*June, 1943*

# Acknowledgments

I wish to thank the following publishers for permission to quote from books or periodicals bearing their imprint: Little, Brown and Co. (Oliver Wendell Holmes, Jr., *The Common Law*); Charles Scribner's Sons (William N. Clark, *Sixty Years with the Bible*); Harper & Row ( Hamlin Garland, *Main Travelled Roads* and *The Public Papers of Woodrow Wilson*); The Chautauqua Institution (John H. Vincent, *The Chautaqua Movement*); McFadden Publications, Inc., (*True Story*), the Essex Institute (Harriet S. Tapley, *Salem Imprints, 1768-1825*); the University of Maine Studies (Laura G. M. Pedder, ed., *The Letters of Joseph Dennie*); and Constable and Co. (*The Works of Herman Melville*). I also appreciate permission to quote from the *Secret Diary of William Byrd II*, edited by Louis B. Wright and Marion Tinling.

It is impossible to express my specific indebtedness to everyone who has in one way or another contributed to this book. I am indebted to Louis C. Hunter, Charles A. Barker, Richard Hofstadter, William Miller, Thomas C. Cochran, John and LaWanda Cox, and Howard K. Beale for reading the manuscript and for making valuable detailed suggestions and stimulating general criticisms. Charles A. Beard has read the whole manuscript and given it a searching criticism, for which I am very grateful. Guy Stanton Ford has encouraged me throughout the undertaking and has made many helpful suggestions. One or more chapters were read by Clement Eaton, Theodore Hornberger, Theodore Brameld, Fulmer Mood, Erling M. Hunt, Richard Thursfield, Norris F. Hall, and Harold U. Faulkner. I should also like to thank for their comments on the outline or on certain problems which I posed, Kenneth W. Porter, Robert E. Riegel, and Harold J. Laski; my former colleagues at Columbia University, especially Marjorie H. Nicolson, J. Montgomery Gambrill, Arthur E. Bestor, Jr., and George S. Counts; and my colleagues at the University of Wisconsin, especially Curtis P. Nettels and Paul A. Knaplund. As a former student of Arthur M. Schlesinger, I should like to express my appreciation of the work he has done in this field and to acknowledge the indebtedness which I, with all other students of American intellectual history, owe to him for the high standards he has set. Above all, I am deeply grateful to my wife, Margaret Wooster Curti, who has given the entire manuscript detailed criticisms.

Livia Appel aided in the stylistic revision of part of the manuscript, and Royce Moch and William Hermann checked the quotations in several chapters.

Several libraries have extended unusual courtesies, particularly the Dartmouth College Library, the Wisconsin Historical Society, and the Columbia University Library. I wish to thank Max Farrand, former director of research at the Huntington Library, and the trustees of that institution, for making it possible for me to spend a year at San Marino as Visiting Scholar and Research Associate. Like all other scholars who have worked at the Huntington, I am indebted to the staff for patient, helpful, and intelligent assistance in my researches.

Bernard Gronert helped me in the collection of materials for Chapter 29; I am also indebted to Richard Hofstadter, John Higham, David Fellman, and Robert Riegel, and John Barton for reading this chapter and for making helpful suggestions.

*June, 1951*

# PART
# I

*Adaptation*
*of the*
*European*
*Heritage*

# 1 ✳✳✳✳✳✳✳✳ The Christian Heritage

*The Old Spirit of New England hath been sensibly going out of the world, as the old saints in whom it hath gone; and instead the return of the spirit of the world with a lamentable neglect of strict piety has crept in upon the rising generation.*

—COTTON MATHER, 1702

*I was not only taught patience, but also made thankful to God who thus led me about and instructed me, that I might have a quick and lively feeling of the Afflictions of my fellow-Creatures, whose Situation in life is difficult.*

—JOHN WOOLMAN, 1774

The Christian tradition, introduced by the first comers, reinforced by nearly all their European successors, and perpetuated by conscious effort, was the chief foundation stone of American intellectual development. No intellectual interest served so effectively as Christian thought to bring some degree of unity to the different classes, regions, and ethnic groups. Whatever differences in ways of life and whatever conflicts of interest separated the country gentry and great merchants from the frontiersmen, poor farmers, artisans, and small shopkeepers, all nominally subscribed to Christian tenets and at least in theory accepted Christianity as their guide. However much French Huguenots, Dutch and German Calvinists, German and Swedish Lutherans, German and Swiss Baptists differed in creed and culture from one another and from the English-speaking Calvinists, Quakers, Anglicans, Baptists, and Catholics, all adhered to a core of common beliefs and values. However widely all

3

these social and ethnic groups differed in doctrine and form of worship, they all, with certain notable exceptions, shared a common Christian conception of human nature, of social relationships, and of the nature of knowledge and beauty; and all were substantially agreed on the supernatural origin and destiny of man and the supernatural basis of the universe itself.

There were, to be sure, minorities which did not share fully in the Christian heritage: the great majority of the Indians, who were always on the fringe of colonial life rather than part and parcel of it, and the newcomers among the Africans. The latter, though they clung to many of their own religious ideas and though many masters were opposed or indifferent to their Christianization, tended to accept Christianity and to make it in their own way their own religion.

The Jews alone of those who lived in the heart of colonial society clung steadfastly to a non-Christian faith. Yet the tiny Jewish minority that had established synagogues by the end of the colonial era in Newport, New York, Philadelphia, Charleston, and Savannah shared many of the ideas and values of Christians. Christianity had been derived from Judaism, a fact that was greatly emphasized in Puritan thought. All branches of Christianity shared with the Jews the Old Testament, the teachings of which at that time occupied a large place in Christian ideology.

The traditional Christian prejudice toward Jews did not disappear in colonial thought, but it became less marked than in the Old World. The Swedish traveler Peter Kalm saw Jews as possessing equal political privileges with Christians. This was not actually the case. But they usually did enjoy a status superior to that of the Jews in Europe, a situation explained by several factors. The generally tolerant position of Roger Williams and of the Quakers provided oases for the Jews in Rhode Island and Pennsylvania. No doubt their improved status owed something to the fact that they contributed to commercial prosperity in a society in which capital was scarce. The jealousy frequently occasioned by such success was offset in part by the common assumption in a rapidly expanding economy that there was room for everyone to get ahead. More valid than these explanations, however, is the fact that the Jews were so small a minority as to be inconspicuous. Nevertheless they introduced a distinctive element into colonial life.

## Clerical Support of Intellectual Life

In the early decades of American experience the clergy, whose duties were multiple and pressing, were the leading representatives of intellectual interests. Some acted as physicians and legal advisers, others taught the young. A surprising number found time to write theological tracts or treatises that stimulated the development of printing presses in the colonies and frequently elicited praise from their colleagues in the Old World. In the later seventeenth century and especially in the eighteenth, when the colonial population became more numerous and society more complex, intellectual functions were more frequently divided and specialized. But even at the end of the colonial era the clergy continued to be a force as intellectual leaders.

This leadership was well exemplified by the role of the clergy in the development of the colonial colleges. Anglican, Lutheran, and Calvinist churches alike insisted on a trained clergy, and hence provision had to be made for their higher education. Harvard and Yale provided the necessary facilities for the New England Congregationalists; the College of New Jersey (Princeton) and the "log colleges" that sprang up in the mid-eighteenth century in the Middle Colonies existed for the Presbyterians, Queens College (Rutgers) for the Dutch Reformed churches, and the College of William and Mary and King's College (Columbia) for the Anglicans. It is true that in Philadelphia, where the Quakers repudiated the need for a trained clergy, a college was launched in 1741 that in some measure represented secular interests; but the other colonial colleges were all founded to give ecclesiastical training. The clergy provided these colleges, including the College of Philadelphia, with the main body of their faculties; and even at the end of the colonial period, when secular interests were stronger than they were a hundred years earlier, many college students were planning a ministerial career.

Intellectual leadership of the clergy was also evident in the support they gave to higher learning outside college halls. The Calvinist, Lutheran, and Anglican clergy in the Middle and Southern Colonies frequently befriended natural science and almost always supported classical knowledge and culture. The learning of the New England clergy is proverbial. In his erudite study, *The New England Mind*, Perry Miller has demonstrated that the first three generations of Puritan clergymen had immense appetite for learning in almost every field. The intellectual giants of Puritan New England were masters of a profound synthesis of ancient and modern knowledge of the universe, a synthesis tied together by the now all but forgotten Ramist logic. Even after this synthesis of knowledge had begun to crumble, the New England clergyman was regarded as sufficiently learned to instruct college students in all branches of the curriculum. The practice of "rustication," or the residence of a delinquent undergraduate with a country parson who acted as his tutor, survived even in the nineteenth century.

The clergy not only supported higher learning but did much to disseminate knowledge. The conception of a learned clergy capable of expounding the Bible in the light of scholarship and reason implies a sufficiently well-educated laity to follow theological discussions. It is this fact that helps to explain why New England led in supporting secondary education. The New England minister generally continued to supervise the town schools. When the town could not or did not support a Latin grammar school, the minister prepared bookish or ambitious youth for college. In New York the Dutch Reformed church continued its early interest in schools; among the German Pennsylvanians both Henry Melchior Mühlenberg, the Lutheran leader, and Michael Schlätter, the Swiss-born patriarch of the German Reformed sect, devoted much time to establishing and improving church schools. The Moravian bishops at Bethlehem and Nazareth enjoyed wide renown for the excellence of their schools. Nor was the Scotch-Irish Presbyterian clergy negligent in regard to education; in Pennsylvania, New Jersey, and the Carolinas they too were leaders in founding and maintaining elementary and secondary schools. Many Anglican parsons in Maryland and Virginia either conducted schools or taught boys in the rectory. The Quakers had no specially trained clergy; they insisted that, however unlearned and ignorant, any soul could commune directly with the Holy Spirit. Thus they put somewhat less emphasis on secondary education than other Christian groups. But they did not neglect it, and they supported elementary schools.

As promoters of adult education the clergy helped to break down some of the barriers between the learned classes and their less lettered fellows. In founding libraries for the lower and middle classes the Anglican Society for the Promotion of Christian Knowledge spread not only religious literature but books on mathematics, history, and agriculture. In this connection the pioneer work of Dr. Thomas Bray and his "associates" in Maryland and Virginia is memorable. In New England the custom of printing sermons contributed to public instruction and enlightenment. The sermon dealt not only with matters of faith and morals. The funeral sermon retailed and interpreted news of shipwrecks and other calamities. The ordination sermon was weighted with theological learning, and the election day sermon aimed to advance political understanding and, of course, to influence political action. Finally, the stimulus the weekly sermon provided for household discussion enlarged the mental horizons of many plain people who thus found an intellectual interest in Christianity as well as comfort, support, and social outlet.

### The Sources of Christian Truth

No function of the trained clergy was regarded as of equal importance with the exposition of God's Word, for in the last analysis each branch of Christianity fell back on revelation as the only sure path to knowledge and truth. God had spoken and His Word, contained in the Bible, was holy, absolute, and final.

The profound differences in doctrine, worship, and church government that separated the various branches of Christendom were overshadowed by the importance every Christian group attached to the Bible, the Book of Books. Catholics and Anglicans put less emphasis on individual Bible reading than other Christians, but the Bible was their final authority on matters of doctrine and the ultimate source of God's revelation. As such it occupied an indispensable place in church services. The early Puritan prejudice against reading the Scriptures in church services because it smacked of Catholic and Anglican liturgy had begun to disappear before the end of the seventeenth century. The Bible was to be found in almost every Calvinist household that possessed any books at all, and it was read not only once but over and over again. The obligation to read it was the chief reason for universal elementary education in communities dominated by Calvinism. Children sometimes learned their first letters from its pages; and even when they got their start in a catechism, a book of piety, or the highly Biblical *New England Primer*, they were soon graduated to the Testaments. The Bible constituted the chief reading matter in the German schools maintained in the Middle Colonies by the German Reformed and Lutheran bodies. The children of many Calvinist and Lutheran households could repeat by heart an impressive number of Scripture verses. Among Quakers and Mennonites the Bible or Pastorius' *New Primer*, a thoroughly scriptural handbook, were the mainstays when the young were instructed in the art of reading. The German population could read the Bibles that in 1743 began to issue from the Pennsylvania press of the Dunker Christopher Sower. Anglo-Americans had to depend on imported Bibles until 1777, when the first American edition of the New Testament in the English version was printed.

In the interpretation of the Bible there were wide differences. The historical conception of one true church as the guardian and expounder of God's word governed not only the Catholics and Anglicans but in some measure the Calvinists and Lutherans as well. These churches, either in the Old World or in some part of the New, had enjoyed the prestige and authority of being "established" by law. All emphasized the creed and the catechism or "confession" as the necessary and proper distillation of God's meaning in Holy Writ. These faiths therefore had to set great store on a properly trained clergy capable of using reason and logic in an authoritative way to expound the creeds, the traditions peculiar to the given church, and the Bible itself. But the concept of an historical church and an authoritative clergy as the custodians and interpreters of sacred truth was not universal.

The idea that the individual could determine religious truth on the compulsion of his own subjective intuitions rather than on the authority of a clergy or the traditions of a church was a significant and logical outcome in the seventeenth and eighteenth centuries of the Protestant revolt itself. The teachings of the Cambridge Platonists and much in the Puritan movement were an expression of this general current of thought and feeling. But the Quakers, Mennonites, and related "plain sects" provided the most clear-cut and consistent example of this position. Accepting the Bible as God's revealed word, these groups dispensed with creeds, clergy, and liturgy. They emphasized rather direct, subjective communication of every individual with the Holy Spirit as the authentic way of arriving at the truth.

This aspect of Quakerism reached its highest level in the writings of John Woolman, a simple farmer, tailor, and teacher. Woolman did not reject sensory experience and natural knowledge as important instruments for understanding human nature and human relations. But he believed that direct personal communication with God enabled man to test, supplement, and revise what he learned by the outward and more obvious processes of knowledge and what he received through others, no matter how authoritatively they might speak, whether on secular or on spiritual matters. Woolman wrote in his *Journal* that "as the mind was moved by an inward principle to love God as an invisible, incomprehensible being, by the same principle it was moved to love Him in all His manifestations in the visible world."[1] The fact that Woolman and his fellow Quakers did not feel the need of learned ministers to interpret religious truths and that he believed in the power of even the most humble among them to speak the tongue of the Spirit, tended to break down the prevailing barriers between the learned and the untutored at the same time that authoritative creeds and priests were rejected as sources of Christian truth.

The emphasis on the religious feelings and intuitions of the individual layman as a source of divine truth, as the way of illuminating the meaning of Scripture, made inroads on churches that attached importance to tradition, a trained clergy, and ecclesiastical authority. Belief in the inspiration of laymen by the Holy Spirit found exponents in early Massachusetts Bay; Anne Hutchinson and Roger Williams defied the theocracy by insisting on the inalienable, God-given right of every individual to search for the Lord's truth in his own soul. Anne Hutchinson's antinomianism was peculiarly subversive of a society founded on orthodoxy and hierarchy. She insisted, in somewhat the same fashion as the Quakers, that God's love was communicated immediately to the regenerate, and that this love served the saint as a guide to action. Thus, no mediation of the clergy was necessary, either for salvation or for right conduct. The theocracy of Massachusetts Bay was able to banish Anne Hutchinson and Roger Williams. But their ideas were not so easily stilled. In the eighteenth century Jonathan Edwards fostered anew the development of the emotional, intuitive, and personal strains in Puritanism. At about the same time the Middle Colonies witnessed the impact of German Pietism on the Lutheran and German Reformed churches, a movement which subordinated intellectualistic theology to personal fervor and piety. In both the Middle and Southern Colonies Presbyterian

[1] Amelia M. Gummere (ed.), *The Journal and Essays of John Woolman* (The Macmillan Co., 1922), 156.

ranks were broken by the rise of a group that emphasized the leadership of the emotionally fervent and redeemed Christian irrespective of his theological training and ordination. Meantime the Baptists and the Methodist group within the Anglican church were making headway in their emphasis on personal feeling as the key to an understanding of God's Word and Will.

These tendencies were all related to the Great Awakening or wave of revivals that swept the colonies in the 1740s. From Maine to Georgia the revivals were preached by men of great feeling and eloquence, many of whom had been inspired by German Pietism or English evangelicalism. The social significance of the Great Awakening will be clarified in a subsequent discussion of the democratic aspects of Christian social thought. Here it is important to emphasize the fact that the Awakening counteracted the growing secularism, rationalism, and skepticism of the eighteenth century on the one hand and on the other challenged the traditionally dominant intellectualistic and authoritarian expositions of Christianity. In kindling the religion of the heart in the great mass of plain people the revivals gave a broader base to the Christian heritage.

Christians differed considerably, and at times vindictively, in their interpretations of the Bible and especially in what they considered the most effective way to salvation. The Great Awakening, which in some respects cut across denominational lines and weakened the hold of sectarian dogma, by no means dispelled sectarian differences and bitterness. In fact, it multiplied sectarian cleavages by leading to new splits within such groupings as the Congregationalists and the Presbyterians—one group favored the Great Awakening, another opposed it. Sectarian differences cannot be entirely explained on the doctrinal level alone; religious affiliations in part followed social stratification. All religious organizations, to be sure, included both humble and substantial folk; but some, especially the Anglicans and the Congregationalists and Presbyterians in at least the more settled communities, tended to attract the better-educated and better-established classes. On the other hand the Baptists and the Methodist group within the Anglican organization tended to appeal to the less lettered and poorer people.

The Protestant churches, thus held apart by class as well as by doctrinal differences, believed firmly in the absolute correctness of their own interpretation of Scripture. Sectarianism was bitter, and this fact had and continued to have a marked effect on education. It meant that sects regarded education as of first importance in the maintenance of sectarianism: the education of children was to be controlled either in sectarian schools or, as in New England, in public schools whose policies and practices were determined by the orthodox in the community. It also meant that the development of higher education was generally regarded as the business of the various sects.

Sectarianism also exerted an unmeasurable yet nevertheless positive influence on intellectual habits. It resulted from and tended to strengthen naïve and absolutistic ways of thinking: if one steadfastly adhered to the principles of his own sect, he must believe not only in the superiority of its creed but also in the inferiority of every other. Thus Baptists were convinced that the immersion of adults rested on Scriptural authority and was thus immensely preferable to the baptism of infants by sprinkling.

Bitter though the rivalry among Protestant groups was, they all shared a common hatred of Catholics. This had its roots in the rancor that most seventeenth-century Anglo-Americans felt toward "popery"; a rancor shared by the Huguenots who settled in South Carolina and other colonies, by the Scotch-Irish Presbyterians in the back country of Pennsylvania, Virginia, and the Carolinas, and by the German-speaking Lutherans and Calvinists in Pennsylvania, Maryland, and Virginia. The relative proximity to Catholic foes during the French and Indian War still further accentuated anti-Catholicism. Calvinist clergy denounced the papacy; the colleges closed their doors to adherents of Rome; and with few exceptions provincial governments either excluded Catholics or discriminated against them.

## The Origin of the Universe

From the point of view of intellectual history the most distinguishing feature of Christianity was its acceptance of a particular type of supernaturalism. In one way or another this dictated the Christian view of the origins of the physical universe, the character of human nature, social relationships, and esthetic values.

To all but the most liberal Christians—whose number to be sure was growing—the area in which the supernatural agency of God constantly exerted itself was very large. Orthodox Christians of all sects regarded the universe as God's handiwork, something He had created and which was separate from Him. The book of Genesis told the story. According to sacred chronology, some four thousand years had elapsed since the Creator, existing prior to and independent of the universe, had created the world in six days by His absolute fiat. Fashioned from nothing, the earth was destined to return to nothing. The phenomena of its surface and those immediately beneath its surface might teach man something of its true history and character, but on the whole the earth concealed rather than revealed God's nature. The enigma of creation could be understood only through revelation.

While liberal Christians were accommodating their thought to the findings of natural scientists, the orthodox tended to discount as utterly worthless the opinions of these scientists on such issues as the origins of the earth. In 1798 Ebenezer Marsh of Yale, presently to be named to an instructorship in Hebrew, illustrated in his commencement oration, "On the Truth of the Mosaic History of the Creation," the inherited opinion of the orthodox educated clergy of New England. Upholding the literal Biblical account of the creation of land, water, mountains, and light, Marsh concluded that "the expression of Moses, 'In the beginning God created the Heaven and the earth,' exhibits a more rational idea on this subject than all the opinions of . . . philosophers."[2]

All who were counted as orthodox Christians continued to believe in divine intervention in the phenomena of nature and in the affairs of men. It is true that by the end of the eighteenth century miracles had come to be regarded as exceptional rather than as normal occurrences. The general view of educated orthodox Christians at the end of the colonial period was expressed in an article in the *New Haven Gazette and Connecticut Magazine*. The author of this piece upheld the validity of miracles but discouraged the faithful from looking for daily signs of God's miraculous intervention. According to common belief God intervened also in the affairs of nations. His justice brought disaster to wicked rulers and peoples and rejoicing to those deserving of His benovolence.

## Christian Concepts of the Origin, Nature, and Destiny of Man

All orthodox Christians subscribed to the doctrine that, while God had created man in His image, His favored creatures had fallen from

---

[2] Ebenezer Grant Marsh, *An Oration on the Truth of the Mosaic History of the Creation* (Hartford, 1798), 43.

grace when the devil tempted Eve. In consequence the sons and daughters of man had thereafter been born in sin. All likewise subscribed to the doctrine of personal immortality and to the idea that man might, directly or indirectly, enlist divine aid in meeting worldly trials. Save for the Calvinists all entertained the possibility of personal salvation for every man, woman, and child.

The Calvinist conception of human nature, shared by New England Puritans, the Dutch and German Reformed churches, and the Presbyterians, did not make a mere automaton of man; he had limited free will, but this did not essentially lessen the base and weak character that was his. Whatever virtue, whatever rationality a man might have was a mere vestige of his creation in God's image. The Fall had almost completely corrupted the faculties of man's soul—his memory, his imagination, his reason, his will—and only God's grace could cleanse the soul and return the faculties to balance and order. One of the leading Puritan thinkers, Thomas Hooker, placed the central difficulty in the corruption of the imagination, which in turn defiled all other faculties. "A man's imaginations," Hooker wrote, "are the forge of villainy, where it's all framed, the warehouse of wickedness, the magazine of all mischief and iniquity, whence the sinner is furnished to the commission of all evil . . . the sea of abominations, which overflows into all the senses, and they are polluted into all the parts of the body, and they are defiled and carried aside with many noisome corruptions."[3]

This pessimistic view of human nature, with its expectation of eternal punishment for all save the elect few, cut deep and left many marks. One of the most popular poems in New England continued to be Michael Wigglesworth's "Day of Doom." In this grim seventeenth-century description of judgment day the Calvinistic God of wrath and justice spared none of the damned the fullness of torment:

> For day and night, in their despite
> Their torment's smoke ascendeth,
> Their pain and grief have no relief,
> Their anguish never endeth,
> There must they be and never die,
> There must they dying, ever lie,
> And not consume away.

[3] Quoted in Perry Miller, *The New England Mind: The Seventeenth Century* (Harvard University Press, 1953), 258.

Moreover, the theology in even the revised hymnbooks toward the end of the eighteenth century clung to tradition. Hymns of death and perdition were amply represented. Joel Barlow's collection of Watts's hymns (1785) omitted the joyous "When I survey the Wondrous Cross" but included "My Thoughts on Awful Subjects Roll":

> Hark, from the tombs a doleful sound,
> Mine ears attend the cry—
> Ye living men, come, view the ground
> Where you must shortly lie.

Divine wrath and a grim hereafter entered at least on Sundays into the minds of those who sang such words as:

> Far in the deep where darkness dwells,
> The land of horror and despair;
> Justice has built a dismal hell,
> And laid her stores of vengence there.
> Eternal plagues and heavy chains,
> Tormenting racks and fiery coals,
>    And darts t'inflict immortal pains,
>    Dipped in the blood of damned souls.

Disparaging views of human kind were illustrated in prevalent notions of child nature. "Infants," declared Jonathan Edwards, "are not looked upon by God as sinless. They are by nature children of wrath, seeing this terrible evil comes so heavily on mankind in infancy." On another occasion the great New England theologian referred to children as "vipers." But Calvinist thought not only regarded child nature as depraved, unregenerate, and corrupt; it also imbued the child with all the qualities of mature adults. Thus Edwards described the religious experiences of four-year-old Phebe Bartlet in almost exactly the same terms that he used to portray the emotions and conflicts of a hardened sinner. Sermons and books for children continued to hold that the young were susceptible to the same disciplinary training as adults. Such a conception of child nature favored appeals to emulation in the training of youth. In a society that was marked by a hard struggle for existence if not by an increasing competitiveness, emulation in character training was useful in promoting a successful adjustment to social environment.

But in no denomination was the Christian view of human nature entirely dark. Even within the Puritan fold itself human nature was often regarded as good in so far as the true and the divine entered into a given regenerate individual; and in the early eighteenth century several New England clergymen, under the influence of the rationalistic element in Puritanism and the rising deism, looked on human nature with some measure of optimism. It will be remembered that Anne Hutchinson, Roger Williams, and the Quakers, while admitting that the flesh is weak, nevertheless regarded it as the vehicle through which the Holy Spirit moves. Anglicans, notwithstanding their emphasis on piety and morals, seem in practice to have viewed human nature more charitably than the Calvinists, in any case they were less concerned with private morals if the forms of the church were decently observed. Catholic doctrine also emphasized the divine spark in every human being. Nor was the grim Calvinistic conception of child nature shared by all religious men. A Lutheran synod in 1760 took a realistic and humane view of child nature in declaring that the Bible must be so presented in religious instruction that children "may feel in their youthful sensuousness as if a box of sugar or something of that sort had been opened for distribution." The German Mennonite schoolmaster, Christopher Dock, observed in his *Schulordnung* (1750) that because of the humanitarian sentiments prevailing in America, schoolmasters could not treat children as strictly as custom in the Old World prescribed. Dock's conception of child nature was revealed in his insistence that the cause of moral infractions on the part of some children must be patiently and intelligently inquired into, and in his emphasis on the principle of loving understanding as the basis of all discipline.

## Esthetics in Christian Thought and Expression

The subordinate role that Americans have frequently given to beauty has often been attributed to the horror with which Quakers and Calvinists regarded any appeal to the senses in worship and to their tendency to deprecate sensuous beauty in everyday life. It is indeed true that seventeenth-century Puritans limited music in church to a dismal and unmelodious psalmody, and that Quakers justified their exclusion of it altogether on the score that, in Penn's words, "to bewitch the heart with temporal delight by playing upon the instruments and singing, was to forget God." Nor can it be denied that both Calvinists and Quakers shrank from decoration in everyday life and that both frowned on such vehicles for esthetic expression as the theater. That these prevailing attitudes had some effect in subordinating the concept of beauty to religion and subsequently to utilitarianism is probably true. But in view of certain elements in both Puritanism and Quakerism such a position can easily be pushed too far.

Even on the religious level the attitude of Puritans and Quakers toward esthetic experience was not altogether one of mere negation. Puritans expressed some feeling for design on their tombstones and in the eighteenth century gave increasing scope to elements of beauty in both church music and church architecture. In religious literature Puritanism made room for a beauty of imagery and expression that achieved esthetic heights in the writings of the greatest of the latter-day Puritans, Jonathan Edwards. The spiritually exalted, serenely contemplative, and socially sensitive writings of some Quakers were also evidence of the relation of religious mysticism to esthetic form and feeling.

In their everyday lives Puritans and Quakers did not stifle every esthetic impulse. If they did not, like the German sects of Pennsylvania, decorate clocks, chests, and furniture with gaily colored and exquisitely designed geometrical figures, unicorns, flowers, and fruits, they frequently expressed their feelings for line and proportion in their furniture and their homes. In making these truly functional, even the most rigidly ascetic Christian sects achieved an austere but pleasing dignity and quiet beauty. Both Quakers and Puritans inherited and developed the great medieval shop or craft tradition in which simple dignity and grace were achieved through proportion and line, and this accounts for the genuine beauty of many Quaker and Puritan homes and everyday utensils. What is more, the well-known tendency of both Puritans and Quakers to deplore worldly vanities did not prevent them from having their portraits painted when they could afford to do so. Indeed, the first American artist to achieve European distinction, Benjamin West, was born of simple Quaker parents.

The religious groups in Pennsylvania contributed positively to the development of music and the minor arts on American soil. Johann Kelpius, deeply versed in the mysticism of Jacob Boehme, not only wrote theosophical tracts on doctrine and prayer at the hermit's retreat on the Wissahickon but composed hymns rich in symbolism. At the Ephrata Community Conrad Beissel, of the Seventh-Day Baptist persuasion, contributed many highly figurative hymns to a volume entitled *Zionitic Hill of Incense or Mountain of Myrrh, wherein are to be found all sorts of lovely and sweet-smelling odors, prepared according to the apothecary's art. Consisting of all sorts of Love-operations in divinely sanctified souls, which has expressed itself in many various spiritual and lovely Hymns.* It was not only in *The Song of the Solitary and Deserted Turtle Dove* that Beissel's religious mysticism found esthetic expression. He invented a new system of harmony emphasizing peculiar arrangements in the falsetto, and trained the Cloister Sisters to celebrate in picturesque song the awakening of God's kingdom at the setting of the sun and the midnight appearance of the Bridegroom. At the Moravian colony in Bethlehem great emphasis was put on choral work, orchestration, and composition. In 1742 the Collegium Musicum not only enriched the Moravian liturgy but presented in concert form the great music of the Old World. Among many of the Pennsylvania Germans love of beauty also found expression in illuminated manuscripts. At Ephrata this form of esthetic expression was carried to a high level.

The view that esthetic appeals to the senses had their value not only colored the attitude of Anglicans and Catholics toward form and ritual in worship but in some measure affected their outlook on the everyday world. This was in part true also of the Swedish and German Lutherans. Adherents to these liturgical faiths preserved, so far as circumstances permitted, the grand tradition of beauty in church architecture and the use of the organ in worship. As wealth increased, church structures of dignity and beauty appeared in the larger cities. To cite only a few examples, Christ Church in Philadelphia, which was built in 1724 in the Sir Christopher Wren style, installed an organ in 1728 and chimes a few years later; the lovely Rhode Island church presided over by Dean Berkeley was another pioneer in the use of organ music; and the Anglican churches in Charleston exemplified the simplicity, proportion, and stateliness of the architecture of the Georgian renaissance in the mother country. St. Barnabas (Episcopal) Church in St. Anne's parish in Maryland employed the Swedish artist Hesselius to decorate the altar with a "last supper." In Philadelphia St. Peter's Church, noted for its fenestration and the general beauty of its interior, embodied the Catholic conception of esthetics in worship. In 1774 John Adams, after attending services in St. Mary's Church in Philadelphia, wrote to his wife that "the music, consisting of an organ and a choir of singers, went all the afternoon except at sermon time, and the assembly chanted most sweetly and exquisitely. Here is everything which can charm and bewitch the simple and ignorant. I wonder how Luther ever broke the spell."

Even the Calvinists of John Adams' Boston had gradually modified their early prevailing views regarding the role of music in church worship. The Puritans had always drawn a sharp distinction between music in church and music in the home. The use of instrumental and melodious music in church they had condemned on the score that it distracted from true worship. Vocal and instrumental music in the home and at social gatherings they had approved unless it violated their sense of decency. Gradually, however, their attitude toward church music itself had changed. The dismal and grim metrical versions of the Psalms in the *Bay Psalm Book* (1640, 1651) aimed to reflect as closely as possible the meaning of the Hebrew text. "Lined out" by the church sexton and intoned rather than sung by note, psalm singing at best was on a low esthetic level; by the end of the seventeenth century, with the passing of the old generation and the exigencies of frontier conditions, the quality of intoning had deteriorated markedly. In the early decades of the eighteenth century dissatisfaction with the "old style" of church singing prompted clerical discourses advocating better church singing and encouraged the formation of singing schools. By the middle of the eighteenth century the Psalms had begun to lose their hold in the Calvinistic churches. The *Bay Psalm Book* was modernized, and as a result of the Great Awakening, the hymns of the English Nonconformist, Dr. Isaac Watts, became familiar even in churches that had not opened their doors to the evangelical revivalists. The increasing vogue of Anglicanism, with its use of the organ, also strengthened the desire for more melodious music within the orthodox New England churches.

Marked improvement in church singing resulted from the labors of men gifted in music. Josiah Flagg's *A Collection of the Best Psalm Tunes* (1764) marked an important step in the process by which psalmody was modified in the direction of the more harmonious traditions of church music. William Billings, a lame tanner, popularized fugues and included in *The New England Psalm Singer* (1770) the newer hymns as well as paraphrases of the Psalms adapted to the times. During the last two decades of the century several greatly improved hymnbooks appeared, the most notable ones being those arranged by Joel Barlow, Timothy Dwight, and Nathan Strong. Another popular hymnal was that sponsored by the well-known printer of Boston and Worcester, Isaiah Thomas. The first edition of the *Laus Deo* (1786) included the Hallelujah Chorus and many familiar and popular religious songs. Most of the newer books also included a few hymns composed by Americans, the most celebrated of which were Samuel Davies' "Lord I am Thine, Entirely Thine" and Timothy Dwight's austere choral "I love Thy Kingdom, Lord." Francis Hopkinson, the Philadelphian whose original song *My Days Have Been so Wondrous Free* (1759) is regarded as colonial America's earliest secular composition, achieved a wide reputation as a psalmodist by virtue of his adaptation of the Psalms of David for the Dutch Reformed church in New York. This work, together with James Lyon's *Urania* (1761), which likewise marked an achievement in psalmody, indicated that in the Middle Colonies as well as in New England Calvinistic religion was responding to the demand for new and better musical standards in church services.

Calvinist church architecture as well as its church music improved greatly during the eighteenth century. This was partly due to the fact that in the larger and richer communities more means were available for church structures. The spread of Anglicanism and the new architectural fashions in England represented by Sir Christopher Wren and his school also played a part in this development. If the greater emphasis put on ecclesiastical architecture among Calvinists did not consciously reflect the growing idea that objects of beauty might properly turn man's thoughts and feelings toward God, it nevertheless must have enhanced the esthetic experience of the worshiper.

### Christian Doctrines and Social Attitudes

Whatever their persuasion, Christians shared certain social ideas. Yet, here, as in conceptions of human nature and esthetics, there was much variety and even considerable contradiction. The Dutch Calvinists, and even more the Swedish and German Lutherans, refrained from applying religious doctrines to political issues. When political authority was seriously challenged, Anglicans tended to emphasize the doctrine of passive obedience to divinely constituted political powers; but they by no means always made a religious duty of political obedience. The Quakers, Mennonites, Dunkers, and other related sects carefully defined the degree of obedience due the state and in consequence were somewhat suspect among other Christians. Within the Puritan fold itself there were various leaders and groups who failed to see eye to eye. The social and political theory of John Winthrop was not that of Roger Williams. The former regarded church and state as two aspects of an organic unity. The latter believed in the separation of religious and political functions and denied the right of the state to dictate the beliefs and forms of worship of any individual. Finally, the evangelical party, largely identified with the more humble social groups and embodying many of the earlier dissenting traditions within Puritanism, still further complicated the social implications of Protestant Christianity. Nevertheless, it is possible to name a common authority to which almost all Christians, Protestants and Catholics alike, appealed: the Bible was in general regarded as a guide in all human relations.

Thus the Biblical condemnation of witches was invoked not only in New England but in Pennsylvania and Virginia. If social and psychological conditions were favorable, as was the case in the New England of the last quarter of the seventeenth century, the Biblical command, suffer ye not a witch to live, could be invoked to persecute eccentric women—and men—against whom other members of the community had some grudge. The belief in witchcraft did not entirely disappear after the Salem hangings, but long before the end of the colonial period the execution of witches in the name of God had become merely a memory.

The general Biblical prescription for family relationships continued to be taken more or less seriously in most quarters. Scripture taught that the primary social unit was the patriarchal family. Children were enjoined to give absolute obedience as well as their labor to their parents; woman, in accordance with St. Paul's teaching, was in her original nature weaker than man and therefore subordinate to him in all things. Such a pattern of thought, which was generally accepted in Christian circles save among Quakers and related sects, provided little experience within the family in democratic living. Yet this general conception of family relations served human needs fairly well in a new society. The Biblical command to multiply and replenish the earth and the stipulation that a youth's labor belonged to his father were congenial precepts in view of the economic value of children in a new land where labor was scarce.

The Christian's duty to accept his worldly lot was illustrated in many sermons. Representative of these was one by the Reverend Joseph Morgan. In 1732 this spokesman of the Lord argued that the poor should be content with their station and that the rich should be sustained in theirs. The poor, Morgan went on, have in general "a more comfortable Life here, and far less danger as to the next Life. . . . A Rich Man has a *miserable* Life; for he is always full of Fear and Care. . . . Whereas a man that has but Food and Raiment with honest Labour, is free from these fears and Cares. . . . We need to *pity* and *love* Rich Men." But, Morgan hastened to add, the accumulation of riches is a public good: "Thus God in his *Wisdom* and *Mercy* turns our Wickedness to Publick Benefits."[4]

The Christian's obligation cheerfully to accept his station was an idea transmitted to the young Republic. Noah Webster, the author of the widely used *Spelling Book* (1783), is only one of many well-known Americans who entertained social beliefs similar to those expressed in such colonial sermons as that of Joseph Morgan. Webster noted in his diary that the Christian must show patient submission to "the evils of life and calm acquiescence in the disposition of divine providence which suffers no more evils to take place in the system than are necessary to produce the greatest possible good." The poor were to submit to poverty with faith that they might better their lot through the practice of frugality, industry, and obedience to the moral teachings of God.

Most colonial Americans recognized that they had as great an obligation to obey civil authorities as to respect their social and economic superiors. British patriotism was a Christian duty which at least the English-speaking Calvinists and Anglicans preached from their pulpits. The fact that the Empire's chief enemies, France and Spain, were Catholic in faith merely served to deepen the patriotic zeal of English-speaking clergymen whose hatred of Rome remained intense. The Dutch and German-speaking Calvinists and Lutherans felt less enthusiasm for Britain. But as Protestants who hated Romanism and as advocates of the doctrine of obedience to civil authority, they tended to go along with their English-speaking Protestant brethren. In the minds of the orthodox it was not only a Christian duty to obey the state but it was the patriotic obligation of civil authorities in turn to support religion.

By and large, Christian doctrine was used to reinforce an economy

---

[4] Joseph Morgan, *The Nature of Riches, Shewed from the Natural Reasons of the Use and Effects Thereof* . . . (Philadelphia, 1732), 14, 15, 17, 21.

based on the sanctity of private property and the value of individual enterprise and profit. But it also sanctioned controls over the use of private property and was even invoked to justify communism. Kelpius, Beissel, and the early Moravian leaders found in Scripture warrant for the religious communism with which they experimented in Pennsylvania. The Pauline and Thomistic conceptions of the rich man as the steward of possessions to be used for the benefit of the needy continued to have at least theoretical importance in general Christian thought. In the early seventeenth century Massachusetts Puritan leaders, well read in St. Thomas Aquinas and aware that a Bible commonwealth involved "the integrity of the community," endeavored to enforce the medieval practices of regulated wages, prices, and profits. But the opportunities provided by cheap and abundant lands and business enterprise deflected men's minds from the ideal of a regulated economy in which profits and the acquisition of property should be subordinated to community well-being. Survivals of the early doctrine, to be sure, were found in the careful regulations provided for the market places in New England towns and elsewhere, and in New England town planning.

The less conservative social teachings of Christianity were expressed in still other ways. Implicit in Puritan doctrine was the idea of the covenant or compact: God and man, men and men, were united by covenant or compact, the terms of which were a sacred guide to conduct. It is true that Puritans in authority tended to interpret the idea of the covenant or compact to their own advantage. Yet it provided a powerful instrument to such dissenters from oligarchic control as Roger Williams, Thomas Hooker, John Wise, and Jonathan Mayhew. In the true spirit of the dissenter these and other men made bold to defy authority, both in England and in Massachusetts, and to defend the principle that authority is limited by compact in both civil and ecclesiastical relationships.

The Puritans were not the only group that opposed authority whenever it clearly overran its "just bounds" by ruling against the word of God and the "common interest." The duty of resisting the evil actions of secular authority was so central in Quaker and Mennonite doctrine that the members of these sects frequently suffered. This was particularly true of the Friends, who during their early career in non-Quaker colonies paid heavy penalties for disobeying the law of religious and civil conformity. The Quaker and Mennonite conviction that war is an instrument of evil which the faithful should not use led to "sufferings" when provinces in which they were in a minority engaged in war. Many preferred harsh punishment to the betrayal of their conscience. In Pennsylvania, where the Quakers long controlled the colonial government, the peace policy that was pursued served fairly well the economic interests of the Friends, many of whom profited from the Indian fur trade. Moreover, unlike the Scotch-Irish on the frontier, seaboard Quakers did not face the immediate danger of Indian attack. Yet the Friends surrendered control of the Pennsylvania government during the French and Indian War rather than take the responsibility for conducting war.

The limitation of authority also owed much to the minority groups struggling for religious freedom. Such struggles were unnecessary in four colonies—Rhode Island, Pennsylvania, New Jersey, and Delaware— where, for the first time in modern history, church and state were entirely separated. Elsewhere, however, the situation was different. The seventeenth-century Maryland Catholics and the eighteenth-century New England Anglicans alike contributed to the growth of religious freedom, not because they believed in it as a Christian principle of universal application, but rather because without it their own position was hardly endurable. Opportunism played a part, too, in the eighteenth-century struggles of Presbyterians, Baptists, and Methodists in colonies where Anglicanism or Congregationalism was established. But some among these groups, especially the Baptists, were also ardent believers in religious freedom as a basic Christian principle; in this they were disciples of Roger Williams and the seventeenth-century Quakers, Mennonites, and other quietistic sects, who had taken the same position. Since minority religious groups could not enjoy full civil rights in provinces where an established church existed, every contest for religious freedom was likewise one for political democracy. Thus Christianity could lend itself to the support of democratic as well as undemocratic political and social practices.

The struggle of the dissenting sects for religious freedom was not their only contribution to democratic ideas and practices. In asserting the importance of a common humanity in contradistinction to a class society, evangelical religion still further charted the road to freedom. Lesser folk who resented political and social domination by the ruling strata in society saw in the revivals one means of protest, one way to defy the well-educated professional groups and privileged merchants and planters.

The religious enthusiasm engendered by the Great Awakening did for a time divert attention from political struggles between the more and the less democratic forces, but it also prepared the way for the advance of democratic forces. By materially augmenting the dissenting strength in colonies with established churches the Great Awakening hastened the separation of church and state. It also resulted in a greater parity between the untutored laity and a clergy that was frequently far less well trained than that which the established churches insisted on having.

Great numbers of plain people were aroused during the revivals to a religious enthusiasm and a conception of their significance in the eyes of God. Domine Theodorus Frelinghuysen and Jonathan Edwards prepared the ground for the later revivalists, for George Whitefield, Gilbert Tennent, Samuel Davies, and Devereux Jarratt. These men, impassioned preachers, dispensed with manuscript notes and erudite sermons and spoke from their hearts to the hearts of the plain people. In promoting new educational agencies, especially the "log colleges," the evangelists helped to democratize learning.

The opposition of the well educated and the well-to-do to the Great Awakening merely accentuated the democratic character of the movement. The opposition of so many among the well-to-do classes may be partly ascribed to the natural distaste of cultivated men and women for the emotional and physical excesses associated with the revivals, excesses especially marked in meetings conducted by such Scotch Presbyterians as the Tennents. But the established classes also opposed the Great Awakening because it threatened, or seemed to threaten, the prevailing political and social arrangements. The vehemence with which certain evangelists, notably James Davenport, denounced the well born, the rich, and the educated was plainly a matter of concern to these classes; the extravagances of Davenport led to his imprisonment. The Anglican doctrine that one must accept his station in life, and the Calvinist emphasis on the idea that the few were to be saved and the many condemned, were in many respects more appropriate to a class society than the evangelical stress on a common humanity in which each soul, however humble, communed directly with God on the same equal plane with everyone else.

Humanitarianism as well as democratic resistance to authority and status also drew strength from Christian thought and feeling. The revivalists promoted missionary enterprises and humanitarian activities.

But general concern for the less fortunate colonial Americans seems first clearly to have appeared among the Friends and Mennonites. In the latter part of the seventeenth century Pastorius urged Friends in Pennsylvania to free their slaves. From 1754, when John Woolman wrote *Some Considerations on the Keeping of Negroes*, until his death in 1772, this Quaker teacher tried to persuade Friends to emancipate their slaves. In 1776 the Philadelphia Meeting excluded those who refused to free their bondsmen. Woolman, whose conception of a compassionate religion with disinterested service to the lowly was so concretely expressed by his life and in his imperishable *Journal*, also preached the Christian virtue of a just distribution of man's worldly goods. In his eyes excessive riches and abject poverty flooded the land with endless ills. Although even Quakers who had achieved wealth and worldly position in some measure shared his spiritual and social values, Woolman was outstanding for the emphasis he put on the social implications of Quakerism. When the philosophers of the European Enlightenment idealized the Pennsylvania Quakers for their humanitarianism, their condemnation of excessive riches and vanity, their pacifism, and their simple morality, they could have pointed to John Woolman as the outstanding model for their picture.

But Quakerism had no monopoly of Christian humanitarianism. The Puritan concern for the well-being of everyone in the group, particularly in matters of morals and faith, could be extended to humanitarian and charitable action, as the "friendly societies" of Cotton Mather proved. Franklin confessed that the *Essays to do Good* of this erudite divine inspired in him devotion to the ideals of neighborly cooperation, service, and humanitarianism. Moreover, the Puritan concern for the degraded was not limited to their own culture group. John Eliot, the Mayhews, and others tried, it will be recalled, to educate and uplift the Indian of New England; and Judge Samuel Sewall of Boston published in 1700 a tract, *The Selling of Joseph*, in which the slave trade and slavery itself were condemned as un-Christian. "There is no proportion," observed Sewall, "between Twenty Pieces of Silver and LIBERTY."

Such Christian sentiments were to develop, under proper social pressures, into wider protests against the status quo. And to the Quaker and Puritan appreciation of the hardships of the less fortunate must be added that of the Anglicans, whose missionary and educational efforts reached from New York to Georgia. Evangelistic preachers in the slave communities drew inspiration in their stand against slavery from their colleagues in England, who by the mid-century were beginning their notable campaign against the slave trade.

## The Cultivation of Theological Thought

The clergy naturally laid special emphasis upon theology as the most important field of speculation and knowledge. American clergymen continued to follow closely the work of their colleagues abroad, and the theological developments in the eighteenth-century colonies paralleled in many respects those in the Old World. Henry Melchior Mühlenberg, the patriarch of the Lutheran church, had studied at Göttingen and Halle and possessed sound and extensive scholarship. In 1763 three of his sons set off for Halle to prepare for the ministry. Fresh recruits from the German theological centers, such as J. H. C. Helmuth who arrived in Pennsylvania in 1769 and published devotional and theological writings, kept Lutherans in touch with the theological scholarship and speculation of the fatherland. Similarly the German Reformed church continued throughout the first three-quarters of the eighteenth century to send well-trained theologians to Pennsylvania and to German settlements in other provinces, and these clerics—J. A. C. Helffenstein, for example—published their sermons and theological reflections. The Dutch Reformed church in New York also sent its sons to Holland for theological study and received well-trained clergymen from Leyden, Groningen, and other university centers. English-speaking clergymen likewise, through books and sojourns in England and Scotland, kept in close touch with the theological interests of their fellows abroad. Occasionally English leaders, such as Fox, Whitefield, the Wesleys, and John Murray, the Universalist, came to America in person.

But the streams did not all flow down one side of the mountain. American theologians addressed not only their fellow Americans but an audience in Europe as well. By the middle of the eighteenth century two fairly well-defined groups were developing one or the other of the two major traditions in early Puritan thought and enjoying a European response to their writings. One, which emphasized the rational and the humanistic elements in the Puritan tradition, can best be considered subsequently in relation to the rise of the Enlightenment. The other developed in a systematic way, and with much intellectual skill, the de-terministic and mystical or emotional elements in the Puritan tradition.

Several factors explain the tendency to systematize the deterministic and mystical in the Calvinist New England tissue of thought. The evangelical emphasis on free will and grace demanded a counterdefense of election and predestination. The deistical implications of the rationalistic position of the liberals invited orthodox refutations. The rising tide of secularism could not go unchallenged. This had advanced so far that there was no longer a question of building God's kingdom, a Bible commonwealth, here and now; it was necessary to deal in terms of universals, to emphasize the relation of man's temporary sojourn in an evil world to the nature of evil, the essence of God, the eternal verities. To strengthen their position New England theologians of the conservative school reasserted in more systematic form the essentials of the Calvinistic position as it had been modified by the seventeenth-century Puritans. By tying together loosened knots and by straightening out snarls in the theological argument, they sought to give a renewed strength to the fabric of New England theology. At the same time its champions made certain compromises with the enemy. As yet they were reluctant to meet the rationalistic challenge of the Enlightenment—that was to be largely reserved for a later generation. But they did try to square somewhat the harshest and the most rigorous aspects of Calvinism with the new sentiments of humanity and reason. And the growing challenge of evangelicism, which conservatives had belittled and derided, they met by taking it to their own bosom. Jonathan Edwards, a leading evangelist and a great theologian, did far more than point the way to such a synthesis.

Although Edwards died in 1758, his influence persisted. Two of his works were published posthumously in 1788, and long after that his metaphysical and theological writings, especially his great *On the Freedom of the Will*, inspired many a student. What gives Edwards a highly significant place in the history of our thought is that he made many concessions to the newer currents challenging Calvinism, and yet in his final synthesis he subordinated all of these to an amazingly logical defense of the essentials of the Genevan master as they had been developed by subsequent Calvinists. To rationalism and even to materialism he made certain bows; Locke's theory of knowledge, with modifications, he partly, but only partly, incorporated. Accepting with unquestioning loyalty the truth and rationality of the Scriptures, Edwards like the rationalists saw no conflict at all between the Bible and reason. In maintaining that philosophy and science are one and in taking some heed of the growing spirit of scientific discovery, Edwards in a sense fortified Calvinism against the onslaughts of new and hostile forces. To those who emphasized the feelings and sentiments rather than reason, he also held out a warm hand. His own poetic nature led him to give an important if secondary place to esthetics, and his conviction that emotions bulk large in the makeup of the human mind lay at the basis of his bold acceptance of revivalism.

Nor was Edwards, be it remembered, deaf to the claims of intuitionalism. He did not accept Woolman's doctrine of the "inner light"; but in a simple figure of speech he compared the relation between the "divine and supernatural light" and the human mind to the sun's illumination of the visible universe. It was this divine light, Edwards taught, that rewarded the true believer for gladly and willingly accepting the seemingly harsh determinism of Calvinism. The great theologian of Geneva had seemed to deny to man the sense of freedom for which he yearned; but Edwards assured the faithful that freedom was to be obtained by accepting as beautiful and reasonable the divine necessity of which he was a part. Thus, to some extent, he disarmed the critics of Calvinism and provided its followers with less uncomfortable quarters.

Jonathan Edwards was one of America's most gifted intellectuals. He chose to spend his genius in the service of a sternly Calvinistic piety, but new intellectual paths lay before his countrymen. The materialistic, humane, and progressive ethics of the Enlightenment eventually replaced Edwardsean piety; an optimistic view of human nature superseded Edwards' conviction of man's timeless and crushing imperfections. Some of Edwards' successors tried to hold his lofty position, but the history of New England theology in the latter part of the eighteenth century is the history of Calvinism's retreat before its critics whom Edwards had not stilled. After his death—whether as evangelists, rationalists, or universalists—they continued to gnaw away at the surviving framework of his thought.

The most distinguished of Edwards' followers was the learned editor of his literary remains, Samuel Hopkins, pastor of the church in Great Barrington, Massachusetts until 1769, when he removed to a Congregational pulpit in Newport, Rhode Island. In his *System of Doctrine Contained in Divine Revelation* (1793), a work incorporating the results of more than two decades of thinking and writing, Hopkins developed the New Divinity theology associated with his name. Hopkins attempted to hold to the essentials of Edwards' theology, but he slipped into compromise with the new ethic of worldly reform. For Edwards, God's plan for the world was an objective good, whether it made for human happiness or for worldly misery. To Hopkins, on the other hand, God's universe was a stage on which progress toward the greatest happiness of the whole was enacted. To this conception of the greatest happiness of the whole, Hopkins coupled the doctrine of general atonement, the idea that Christ died for everyone, for Negroes, Indians, and the disinherited generally, as well as for the godly and substantial classes. Hopkins' ideas of the happiness of the whole and general atonement led him to take an active missionary interest in the unfortunate, especially the slaves. He vigorously attacked slavery, in spite of the interest of Newport merchants in the slave trade.

Hopkins tried to maintain that his reformist attitude was consonant with Edwards' determinism by emphasizing that all benevolence must be completely disinterested. Edwards had asserted that all selfishness is sin. Hopkins, shifting the emphasis, insisted that all sin is selfishness. Any interest in the self, apart from the objective order of creation, is sinful. Thus the antidote to sin, the supreme human goal, is to become "disinterested" in the self, to become truly benevolent. Hopkins' New Divinity was an attempt to defend Calvinism by incorporating into it the elements of the more humane morality of the eighteenth century. But Hopkins, and Edwards' other followers, failed to achieve a compromise or a synthesis that would restore unity to the religious life of New England.

Thus the intellectual life of the colonists—their views of the universe, of human nature, and of esthetics, their social and political ideas—was shaped in large measure by Christian patterns of thought. The Great Awakening brought Christian doctrine and Christian experience to the great body of plain people, who in many instances had previously been affected by the Christian heritage in only a general way. Within the patterns of Christian thought, of course, still other intellectual values and perspectives found a place and formed a part of the intellectual legacy from the colonial age.

# 2 Legacies to the New Nation

> What then is the American, this new man? He is
> either an European, or the descendant of an Euro-
> pean; hence that strange mixture of blood, which
> you will find in no other country.
> —DE CRÈVECŒUR,
> Letters from an American Farmer, 1782

By the end of the eighteenth century the young American nation possessed a distinctive intellectual life. The ideas and agencies of thought and opinion in the newly launched republic were no mere replica of those in the Old World. This resulted in the first instance from the fact that the American physical environment provided a unique stage on which colonial life developed. The unique nature of intellectual life in the young nation was also related to the fact that a company of many-tongued actors played their parts on that stage.

The colonial legacy to the United States was the contribution of many peoples each influencing the others—a process that inevitably modified the ideas and cultural institutions imported from the Old World by each of these varied groups. Although the influence of non-English-speaking peoples of the seventeenth and eighteenth centuries on subsequent intellectual life in America has often been underestimated, it is nonetheless true that the ideas and agencies of intellectual life bequeathed by the colonial era owed far more to Great Britain than to any other land, for English-speaking peoples made up the dominant element in colonial society.

## The Unique Legacy of the English-Speaking Colonial Americans

The English-speaking colonists contributed, from their own heritage, all-important vehicles for the communication of knowledge, ideas, and attitudes. Modified though it was by accretions from other culture groups and by colonial conditions, the English language was yet the dominant one in the new nation—a fact of profound significance. It meant, among other things, that the Americans shared with Great Britain the ballads and the more formal literature of the motherland. But the literary legacy was greater than this, for it was through English and Scotch channels that the Graeco-Roman classics and the literature of the Renaissance were transmitted to the American people. The better-educated colonial Americans might and did read in the original the writings of the great French thinkers, but for the most part eighteenth-century Continental thought was introduced to the colonies through translations made in Great Britain and through British interpretations. The British news-paper, pamphlet, broadside, and magazine likewise provided colonial Americans with models. Colonial colleges were patterned after the British colleges, and the Latin grammar schools closely followed British prototypes. Even the dame schools and charity schools had their English precedents.

The Atlantic seaboard was a stage on which the bitter conflicts of the entire Protestant Reformation and the Catholic Counter-Reformation were reenacted. The dominant religious patterns, however, came from Great Britain and Ireland. Catholicism, Anglicanism, Calvinism in its Congregational and Presbyterian forms, and Quakerism were all derived from Great Britain. British Independents, Baptists, and Quakers contributed to America their distinctive religious doctrines, including the significant idea of the separation of church and state. The ideas of religious toleration and freedom expounded in Great Britain by Quakers, by certain Puritan groups and individuals, and by the Cambridge Plato-nists and Latitudinarians provided the necessary seeds for the growth of these ideas in American soil, which proved to be even more fertile ground for them than that of the motherland.

British social and economic ideas, modified by the colonial environment, bulked large in the legacy to the new nation. Conceptions of class, including the remnants of such feudal ideas as benefit of clergy and the laws of land inheritance, were brought over during the time of settlement, and the English ideal of the gentleman took firm root in early America. More consequential were the British middle-class conceptions of comfort, individual success, and usefulness. The Irish and Scotch-Irish contributed the ideas of clan loyalty and opposition to landlordism. Remnants of English medieval economic ideas, such as control of the market place, also took root in the colonies. The mercantilistic doctrine of integrated control of the Empire's economic life increasingly ran counter to many colonial interests; but a mercantilistic philosophy, modified to promote the interests of American merchants, was enlisting support on the eve of the Revolution. Above all, the growing idea of free economic enterprise figured in the British-derived legacy.

In the field of legal and political ideas the heritage from the motherland was of paramount significance. English-speaking colonial Americans had the same respect for law as the British, as well as the same inclination to protest against it or against its administrators when it seemed to be incompatible with local self-interests. The doctrine of the higher law, or the supremacy of the law of God and Nature over all human law, though of course not exclusively English in origin, was transmitted to the new American nation through British channels. The common law, modified though it was in some respects by colonial conditions, was of English derivation. The British Americans brought with them and nourished on colonial soil the characteristically British concepts of local self-government and representation, of written constitutions, and of judicial supremacy. The seventeenth-century doctrines espoused by the English Puritans in their struggles with the King also migrated to America and were refurbished in conflicts between the colonists and the mother country and even in tussles between the more and the less privileged groups within the colonies themselves. In this arsenal of ideas were included the conviction that the relationship between ruler and ruled is a contractual one, the doctrine of the supremacy of the higher law over human authority, the right of revolution, and the conception, unforgettably formulated by Milton, of the civil liberties. The antithetical political ideas of passive obedience to constituted authority also survived among English-speaking colonial Americans, who cited British precedents and treatises in support of their contentions.

The full significance of the British heritage of ideas and patterns for the agencies of intellectual life will become more clear in subsequent discussions.

## The Culture of Non-English-Speaking Groups on the Atlantic Seaboard

The Dutch, Germans, Swedes, Welsh, and French Huguenots scattered along the Atlantic coast from New England to Georgia resembled the heirs of British culture in that they possessed much of the same knowledge, many common values, and a similar outlook on nature, man, and society. This similarity was related to the fact that the non-English-speaking groups, as well as the English, Scottish, and Scotch-Irish, were affected by certain great processes that were profoundly altering the civilization of all western Europe: the process of maritime expansion and colonization on the one hand, and the religious conflicts of the Reformation and Counter-Reformation on the other. Whatever the land of their origin, the lives of the migrants had been affected by economic and social changes incident to the expansion of trade, overseas activities, and internal readjustments, especially the dislocation of agriculture. In consequence of these social and economic changes and conditions in Europe, it was largely artisans, peasants, and small traders who left their homelands for America. With few exceptions, these peoples also subscribed to one or another form of Protestantism. These facts, together with the common life which they more or less shared in the New World, made it all the more natural for them, regardless of differences of speech, national culture, and creed, to think alike on many matters. At the same time, however, the Dutch, Swedes, Huguenots, Germans, and other peoples differed from one another and from their English-speaking neighbors in many respects and made each his own contribution.

The century between the British conquest of New Netherlands in 1664 and the outbreak of the American Revolution had been marked by the waning role of the Dutch element in New York. Certain ideas and customs prevalent during the Dutch rule, such as the use of judicial torture and easy divorce, had disappeared altogether. The beginnings of an indigenous literature had, except in the field of theology, been forgotten. No one read the early seventeenth-century treatise of Domine Johannes Megapolensis on the Indians, in which he confessed his mystification at the Mohawk dialect. The verses of Jacob Steendam and Domine Henricas Selyns, as well as the political and descriptive tracts written in the early years of the colony by such men as Van der Donck, a university-bred physician, apparently lay collecting dust on the shelves of a few great houses. Indeed, the vigorous intellectual life in Holland had occasioned few echoes in New Netherlands even at the height of Dutch rule.

Nevertheless, some remnants of the old Dutch culture survived and even affected the intellectual life of the province a hundred years after the British took over in 1664. The use of arbitration as a means of administering justice and the quasi-feudal ideas that governed the relations of patroons and tenants had left their traces in the Hudson valley. As Protestants and traders the Dutch attached considerable importance to literacy; a majority of the ten thousand people in the colony at the time of the British conquest could apparently read and write, and the tradition of elementary education survived in the schools maintained by the Dutch Reformed church. The church itself, with its peculiar polity and architecture, was no doubt the most significant intellectual survival of the Dutch era. The theological, philosophical, and classical writings imported by ministers and schoolmasters during the Dutch regime continued to find readers in the Dutch-speaking settlements. Even more significant was the fact that the ministers of the Dutch Reformed church still wrote and published books; more than fifty books in the Dutch language, chiefly of a religious nature, were published between 1708 and 1794.

The picturesque body of folklore and tradition bequeathed by the Dutch-Americans was hardly less significant as an intellectual legacy than the Dutch Reformed church. Early in the intellectual life of the new American nation a group of New York writers created, from memories of doughty burghers, irascible governors, lordly but indecisive and quaintly phlegmatic patroons, together with the folklore and legends of a simple, fun-loving, and superstitious people, distinctively American specimens of literature that have a permanent place in our culture. Washington Irving's[*Knickerbocker's*] *History of New York* (1809) and Hudson valley legends are, of course, the best-known examples.

On the eve of the Revolution the presence of German-speaking groups provided another element in the intellectual heritage of the new nation, and their culture displayed more vitality than that of the Dutch. From the three counties in eastern Pennsylvania largely dominated by Germans, these people had spread into southern New York, into western Maryland and Virginia, and even into the Carolinas. German-speaking groups from the Rhineland and Switzerland had also settled in the Southern Colonies. Only recently, in fact, has the importance of the German contribution to the cultural life of the colonial South been fully appreciated.

Although the German groups included skilled artisans and even learned scholars, the peasant element predominated. In many respects the plain folk among the Germans resembled the untutored men and women in other cultural groups: they feared God, labored hard, cherished their families, resorted to weird remedies when ailing, and took but little interest in the affairs of the larger world. Yet the unusually thrifty, family-centered, pious, and industrious peasants and artisans of German stock possessed certain skills, values, and ideas that gave a singular flavor to their culture. Combining a love of beauty with utilitarianism, the German peasant and craftsman introduced the great medieval tradition of folk art; the sturdy barns with their decorative effects, the carefully designed and colorful household utensils and furniture, the fine-line drawings often found on baptismal and marriage certificates, rich in religious symbolism and folklore, added variety and picturesqueness to the intellectual and artistic heritage of the young American nation. The Pennsylvania Germans also cherished religious music. The 500-odd hymns composed at the Anabaptist community at Ephrata in Pennsylvania utilized every known measure and stanzaic form. These did not become the nucleus of a permanent and significant musical tradition, but the auspicious beginnings of music among the Moravians had a more permanent influence on the development of esthetic ideas and values. Outsiders frequently visited Bethlehem, the principal Moravian center, to hear original compositions in the Bach tradition and to become familiar with the scores of the great European composers.

In still other ways did the skills and values of the plain German folk exert an influence beyond their own communities. The peasant stock's superior knowledge of agriculture found expression both in practice and in discussions in eighteenth-century German newspapers and almanacs, and fostered an interest in scientific agriculture among Americans of other national backgrounds. As pioneers in the manufacture of paper and in the foundry skills on which printing rests, German artisans helped to provide one of the basic agencies of intellectual life.

Like other culture groups, the Germans included a small number of learned men whose knowledge stood in striking contrast to the intellectual unsophistication of the main body of the people. The founder of Germantown, Pennsylvania, Francis Daniel Pastorius, was known throughout the eighteenth century by his writings, which included *Description of Pennsylvania, Disputation, Missive to the Pietists, Letters, Tractates*, and *New Primer*. The great erudition of Pastorius is even more evident in his *Beehive*, an encyclopedia for his children which was not published until after his death. Another layman, far less learned, did much to disseminate religious knowledge and practical information among the Germans. This was Christopher Sower, the founder of the German-language press in America.

It was in the religious field that the German intellectual leaders contributed most to the foundations of American thought. True, the theosophical writings and songs of Johann Kelpius and Conrad Beissel were not destined to have as much influence on the subsequent development of mysticism in America as did the mystical elements in Quakerism and Puritanism. But German Pietism was a considerable element in the legacy from the colonial era. Pietism was a reaction against the formalism of Lutheranism and the intellectualism of Calvinism. It emphasized the subordination of theology and doctrinal controversy to the religion of the heart and appealed to the ideal of personal piety; it made much of the importance of applying Christian ethics and morals to everyday living. German Pietism influenced American evangelicalism both directly and indirectly. The first contact between German Pietists and Anglo-American Christian leaders seems to have been established by the Lutheran court minister in London who put Cotton Mather in touch with A. H. Francke, the Pietist leader at the University of Halle. In the Middle Colonies Theodorus J. Frelinghuysen and Henry Melchior Mühlenberg, who were sympathetic to Pietism, helped pave the way for the Great Awakening of the mid-eighteenth century. The most telling contribution of German Pietism to colonial evangelicalism was, to be sure, an indirect one: George Whitefield, the English evangelist who had been stimulated by the Halle movement, was the chief agent of the Great Awakening in America.

Other national groups in colonial America made some impact on intellectual life without exerting anything like the influence of the Germans. The Swedes on the Delaware, for example, wrote pioneer descriptions of the topography, flora, fauna, and meteorology of that region. They produced a philological treatise on the Lenape dialect in connection with their efforts to convert the tribe. In Gustav Hesselius the Swedes possessed an organ-builder and artist of distinction who became well known outside Swedish-American circles. Swedish parsons and Swedish religious literature were both imported from the mother-land throughout the colonial period. Yet the Swedes were too few in number to resist cultural absorption.

Similarly the French Huguenots had largely been absorbed by their neighbors before the American Revolution. In South Carolina they had contributed to the knowledge of the culture of the grape, rice, indigo, and silk; and in Charleston, in New Rochelle near New York City, and in other centers they had established schools for young women, contributed to the graces of everyday life, and provided nuclei for the subsequent reception of French ideas and customs.

Collectively the large strains of non-English-speaking stocks exerted an imponderable but nonetheless real influence on the intellectual life of the colonial era. The non-English-speaking groups did not subscribe to the Anglican form of religion, and their opposition to the payment of taxes for its maintenance in certain of the colonies strengthened the growing movement for separation of church and state. The mere presence of so many non-British people likewise gave force to the idea that America was an asylum for the oppressed of all the world.

It was in laying a foundation stone for American nationality that the non-English-speaking groups along the Atlantic seaboard made one of their most significant contributions. In Europe new peoples or nationalities had arisen when one conquered and assimilated or was assimilated by another. But in colonial America a distinctive people emerged partly because of a naturalization policy more liberal than that in Europe and partly because the mutual aloofness of the British and non-British cultural groups gradually decreased and gave way to intimate daily association and intermarriage. The fusion of many peoples into a distinctive one was evident in the modification of the English language by the accretion of words from the Dutch, German, and French. And having no British ties and feeling little or no intellectual subserviency to England, these non-British stocks helped pave the way for, and gave reality to, the intellectual declarations of independence from England during the revolutionary period. Their contribution to the development of the idea of American nationality was pointed out by that shrewd French husbandman, Crèvecœur. "I could point out to you," he wrote in his *Letters of an American Farmer* (1782), "a man whose grandfather was an Englishman, whose wife was Dutch, whose son married a French woman, and whose present four sons have now four wives of different nations." In America, he continued, "individuals of all nations are melted into a new race of men," new in part because of that "strange mixture of blood, which you will find in no other country," but new also by reason of the fact that, having left behind all his ancient prejudices and manners, the immigrant had received "new ones from the new mode of life he has embraced, the new government he obeys, and the new rank he holds."[1]

Significant as were the contributions, separate and collective, of the non-English-speaking groups on the Atlantic seaboard, their influence on the ideas and agencies of intellectual life during the colonial period was less marked than that of the English-speaking peoples. The fact that the Dutch, Swedes, and Germans, especially during the early period of colonization, lived more or less by themselves in relatively contiguous neighborhoods explains in part why their influence was overshadowed by that of the British and their offspring. Moreover, it should be remembered, in estimating the influence of the non-English stocks on the development of intellectual life, that the non-English were probably at no time in a majority in any province. Indeed, the Swedes, Finns, and Huguenots were tiny minorities. Even in Pennsylvania, where Franklin once feared that the German language and culture might supplant the English, the Germans dominated only a few counties. Moreover, the Germans had come not from a united nation but from a variety of separate states. Having fled from persecution, famine, and war, they had little motive for maintaining any close ties with the fatherland, save the religious one. Without political experience and having no desire to participate in politics, the Germans in general willingly surrendered political leadership to the English-speaking groups who represented the governing nation, Great Britain. The political dominance of the English-speaking groups, together with the fact that they maintained closer associations

[1] J. Hector St. John de Crèvecœur, *Letters from an American Farmer* (Philadelphia, 1793), 46.

with their motherland than did the non-English-speaking groups with theirs, explains in large part the more influential role of the British-derived heritage of ideas and cultural agencies.

## Legacies of the French and Spanish Borderlands

The American stage received its actors from different Old World backgrounds, but these backgrounds were not unrelated; the French and Spanish on the borderlands in America were basically related to the English, Swedish, Dutch, and German colonists on the Atlantic seaboard by virtue of their common venture in overseas enterprise, economic and religious. That is to say, the French and Spanish in the interior and on the southern and western rims of the present domain of the United States shared with the Europeans on the eastern coast the cultural dynamics of European maritime expansion and the conflicting forces of the Reformation and Counter-Reformation. The differences between the cultural patterns of the Protestant colonists from Great Britain, Sweden, Holland, and Germany and those of the Catholic French and Spanish in the borderlands should not obscure the common tie between them.

Thus it was natural that the thought and feeling of the Atlantic seaboard colonists should have been affected by the presence of the Catholic Spaniards in Florida and of the Catholic French in the trans-Appalachian hinterland. It is true that the Atlantic coast peoples gained little or no actual knowledge from the French and Spanish colonists. But the Latin outskirts of their world were a part of their own setting and inevitably affected their thinking. For one thing New France and New Spain aroused the hostility of those engaged in building a civilization on the Atlantic coast not only because they were Catholic but also because they were the seat of activities that threatened the fur-trading and agricultural ambitions of the seaboard colonists. Moreover, the Dutch and British colonists further inherited the deeply rooted hostility of their homelands to Spaniards and French. With such ideas and interests the seaboard colonists entered into the wars waged by Great Britain against the Spanish and French, and even toyed with the plan of an intercolonial union, the better to defend themselves or even to conquer their economic, political, and religious foes. Thus the presence of the Spanish and French in the borderlands occasioned, as a legacy to the new American nation, a feeling of suspicion, distrust, and bitterness toward these people.

But the Spanish and French contributions were not merely negative. The pockets of French and Spanish culture that existed at the time of the American Revolution within the present confines of the United States were, sooner or later, to enrich the intellectual life of the nation by increasing the heterogeneous character of its legacies of ideas and values bequeathed by the Old World.

When the Atlantic seaboard colonists began their revolt against England, islands of French culture existed at Mobile and New Orleans and dotted the vast wilderness of the Mississippi valley and the remote regions of the Great Lakes. Although they had faced the vicissitudes of wilderness and imperial struggle, these islands of French life were no longer held together and dominated by military and administrative officials. In 1763, when France surrendered the trans-Appalachian country to England, the French Jesuits were expelled, and the small farmers or *habitants* in the Illinois country, the fur traders, and the merchants were virtually without leadership.

Despite their heroic efforts to convert the Indian, the French religious orders had little permanent influence on the aborigines. But in the course of their missionary efforts they did introduce some part of intellectual culture into the forest. The Jesuits established a college at Kaskaskia in 1721, and a half century later some of the rare volumes from its library graced the private collections of the aristocracy of St. Louis. Father Meurin, who had come to the Illinois country in 1742 and who had received special permission to return after the expulsion of his order, had studied the dialects of the Illinois Indians and prepared a dictionary. In view of the supreme difficulties involved in the effort to convert the red men and to exert some vigilance over the scattered *coureurs de bois* and farming communities, it was impossible for the religious orders to sustain intellectual life save as the most pressing requirements of the Catholic faith dictated.

In the more settled villages, such as Vincennes, St. Charles, and St. Louis, intellectual culture had made some advances among the well-to-do fur merchants, physicians, and other substantial citizens. Impressive private libraries could still be found on the baronial estates with their seignorial traditions. In 1800, when the population of St. Louis numbered only 669 souls, fifty-six heads of families owned books—a total of 1350 volumes. Among them was a good representation of standard French works on engineering, medicine, science, and the classics. What is more surprising, several of the well-to-do merchants owned the writings of the great exponents of the Enlightenment. The library of Auguste Chouteau of St. Louis, for example, included the works of Voltaire, Diderot, Rousseau, Beccaria, Locke, Descartes, Buffon, Montesquieu, and the Abbé Raynal. Dr. Antoine François Saugrain, pioneer in the use of smallpox vaccine in the western country, owned copies of Goethe's works, the writings of Molière and Beaumarchais, and a number of books on medicine. As late as 1818 a Protestant missionary in Missouri complained that every Frenchman "of any intelligence and importance" with whom he formed an acquaintance was of the school of French Liberalists—"an infidel to Bible Christianity."[2] However true this may have been of the upper group, the rank and file of small merchants, fur trappers, and *habitants* clung to the Catholic faith. Nor did much learning grace this picturesque folk; in 1796 two-thirds of the population of Vincennes did not even know how to read.

New Orleans and, to a much smaller extent, Mobile were the only French centers destined to exert an important and persistent influence on the life and thought of the nation of which they were ultimately to become a part. In 1766, when the Spanish took over New Orleans, it was a village of little more than three thousand people, a third of whom were slaves. Yet its impressive ecclesiastical and public architecture displayed civic and esthetic values. The Jesuits and Ursulines had made it possible for many youth to obtain an elementary Catholic education. There is, indeed, some evidence that by the end of the century the writings of the French *philosophes* were known in New Orleans. The urbane social amenities and gaiety of the substantial citizens did not, however, encourge serious intellectual endeavors. Apart from a few official reports and memoirs, the only literary production of any note seems to have been an epic poem written by a wealthy planter in 1779.

Yet Louisiana transmitted a definite intellectual legacy to the nation that purchased it in 1803. The Siete Partidas, an amalgamation of Roman-French-Spanish law, continued to influence Louisiana law. Creoles clung to the French language and customs and even maintained

---

[2] Rufus Babcock (ed.), *Memoir of John Mason Peck, D.D.* (Philadelphia, 1864), 87.

cultural supremacy in New Orleans until almost the middle of the nineteenth century. The cosmopolitan admixtures of French, Spanish, and other peoples provided a grace of life, a light-hearted, pleasure-loving spirit, a strong feeling of caste, and a picturesque, dreamy sense of the past. At length French-speaking Louisiana was to become conscious of this past and interpret it to the nation in histories and legends. In time a local-color school of literature, of which George Cable and Grace King were representative, was to present a faint but charming silhouette of this lingering Latin culture.

To some of the lands they conquered and attempted to colonize the Spaniards left little more than a legacy of place names and faded memories. On others they had significant and enduring influence. Only a few converts, churches, and ruined garrisons, and the names of places testified to the long Spanish occupation of Florida which in 1763 came under the British flag. In 1776 the Spanish impact on Texas promised to be lasting. The dozen Franciscan missions that had been established by 1731 had introduced among the Indians a knowledge of textiles, stock raising, and Spanish agriculture in general. The vocational training that the natives received went hand in hand with the main purpose of the fathers—the Christianization of the aborigines. In 1778 Fray Juan Augustin Morfi wrote that "these Indians are today well instrumented and civilized. Many play the harp, the violin, and the guitar, sing well." The Indian neophytes painted frescoes and altarpieces that fused primitive and Spanish concepts of color, design, and imagery, and they carved figures of saints and cherubim striking in effect. Yet the promise was not fulfilled. The future of Texas was not to lie with the Spaniards. Only in place names, in traditions, and in land law was the Spanish influence to survive the migration from the United States in the 1820s and 1830s.

Under the leadership of the remarkable Franciscan, Junipero Serra, the missions of California were entering on a golden age when the eastern seaboard colonies struck for independence from England. But the labors of the friars of California bore little fruit so far as the Indians were concerned. The paternalistic mission regime failed to teach the Indians how to preserve and develop the civilization of Spain without clerical direction. Thus when the missions declined and finally became secularized in the nineteenth century, the Indians generally reverted to their primitive way of life.

In the New Mexico country a sufficient number of Spaniards, lay and clerical, took root to provide lasting foundations of Spanish culture. The Pueblo Indians, differing as they did in their culture from the aborigines of Texas and California, accepted and retained Catholicism, which they blended with their own religious rites and doctrines. The mixture of Spanish and Indian blood in the mesas, canyons, and deserts of New Mexico and Arizona provided another basis for the permanent survival of Spanish Catholic culture. Indeed, Santa Fé, with its garrison, trading post, churches, and convents, reproduced on a small scale some of the glories of the Spanish-American culture of Mexico City.

Although the efforts of the Jesuits and Franciscans in the Southwest nowhere fully achieved their dream of narrowing the gulf between the Spaniard and the native, the missionaries did carry their own learning into the Southwest and in the course of their labors made significant contributions to knowledge. To the chain of sturdy and beautiful mission structures that stretched from the Rio Grande to San Francisco Bay, Junipero Serra, Father Kino, and other friars brought theological and devotional volumes of intellectual and artistic merit. In quest of souls, the Franciscans and Jesuits did not come as scientists, ethnologists, historians, geographers, and teachers, although they were to some extent all of these. Their reports to their superiors, sometimes made available to a larger public, contained valuable maps and descriptions of the physical environment and of the languages and cultures of the Indians themselves. In the Arizona country the Jesuit missionary Father Kino, after formulating necessary vocabularies, translated catechism and prayers into native tongues. His *Historical Memoirs of Pimeria Alta* describes with accuracy and insight the customs, character, and topography of the regions visited by this tireless and devoted missionary. For a century and a half Father Kino's map, which discredited the prevailing theory that California was an island, was the principal map of the Arizona-California country. Between the years 1745 and 1763 three Franciscan fathers in the Texas missions wrote books on missionary methods and on the philology and character of the native peoples.

The Spanish missionary era came to an end in the first quarter of the nineteenth century, but its influence survived among the Spanish-speaking Californians and New Mexicans, and to a lesser extent among the Pueblo Indians. At length English-speaking America, after its conquest of these regions in the middle of the nineteenth century, was to discover the survivals of architecture, the crude but fascinating and often moving decorative arts of the Spanish-Indian culture, and the folklore of those who had come under Spanish influence. Archeologists and anthropologists enlarged the horizons of their respective fields and contributed to a general awareness, especially in the Southwest, of the antiquity and achievements of the earlier cultures and their lingering traces. The Spanish past provided materials for California writers of the local-color school that emerged after the Civil War. Thanks to Helen Hunt Jackson, Mary Austin, Willa Cather, and others, the reading public both in the Southwest and in the country at large have become increasingly aware of the romantic and primitive glow of the mesa and pueblo land and of the mission past. The discovery of all these traditions and survivals came too late to be a dominant or shaping influence in American intellectual life. Yet in the Southwest the Spanish left a permanent impress, and the Spanish bequest to American thought and feeling has been colorful and enriching.

### The Indian, the Negro, and the Atlantic Seaboard Legacy

The colonists on the Atlantic seaboard knew relatively little about the French and Spanish achievements with the Indian and distrusted what was commonly supposed to be a Machiavellian alliance. But their own experience with the Indians in the coastal region and hinterland shaped their ideas about the red men. Indeed, the presence of the Indian was a telling factor in the emotional and intellectual heritage passed on by the colonists. The ever-felt nearness of the red man explains many differences in ideas and attitudes between the colonial Americans and their European fathers and brothers.

The fact that the English, Dutch, and Germans did not achieve the same measure of racial and cultural fusion with the Indian as did the Spanish and the French had far-reaching consequences. For one thing, it prevented the seaboard newcomers from understanding what great differences existed in the cultural levels and characteristics of the various tribes; in their eyes all red men were alike. Thus the white man's ideas of the Indians were warped by much misinformation, fancy, and prejudice. The Indian concept of the collective character of landownership, for instance, did not make sense to a people rapidly becoming more conscious of individual property rights and beginning to show a competitive spirit in agriculture as in other forms of economic enterprise. By and large the whites understood little of Indian nature worship, of the poetical Indian love of the land as it was rather than as it might become under cultivation, or of the Indian fondness for symbolizing memorable communal experiences in rituals and ceremonials. Neither did the whites fully understand the Indian concept of passive submission to an irresistible fate, or the curiously dual behavior of the red man when he was with his own kind and when he was with the whites. The stoicism, the sober gloom, and the dignity attributed by the whites to the Indian did not always correspond to his actual behavior when he was with Indians.

These misconceptions tended to be corrected as traders and missionaries among the Dutch, German Moravians, and English made contacts with the Indians. From the material culture of the red men the whites learned lessons in forest lore, in agriculture, and in medicine; they also learned the advantages in forest fighting of the open or deployed order under protection of ambushes—a tactic that contrasted with the close order of the Europeans. Forest diplomacy likewise occasioned the Indian treaty, a new literary form born of the contacts of the two races. Some fifty of these treaties found their way into print. Constance Rourke has emphasized the highly dramatic character of this form of "practical letters," and has called attention to the rich episodes, the bold portraiture, the sly humor, the high quality of poetry, and the epic proportions of these treaties, the prototypes of the later stage plays of Indian life.

The interplay of action between the whites and Indians required explanations and vindications of the white men's behavior and of the Indian responses to that behavior. Being unable to enslave the Indian, the whites worked out a theory of the red men as quasi-sovereign peoples to be won as allies in the contests with French and Spanish rivals. When the Indians blocked the agricultural advance of the white frontier they were killed or pushed farther into the hinterland or confined to reservations. It was this process that set the major intellectual problems for the whites in their relations with the Indians.

The practical nature of the problems posed did not prevent the whites from cloaking their ideas about the Indians in religious terms, for the age was an intensely religious one and religious assumptions underlay much of its thinking. It was incumbent on the whites, in the first instance, to explain in terms of Genesis and Exodus the existence of the

Indians on the western hemisphere, a problem that was generally answered by regarding the Indian as a descendant of the African Phoenicians or the Asiatic Tartars.

More important, of course, was the idea, widely held, that Christian duty demanded the salvation of the Indian from the devil, whose peculiar creature he was. The early Virginians endeavored, sporadically and half-heartedly to be sure, to Christianize the red man; the Swedish Lutherans along the Delaware sent out missionaries to the Indians and translated the catechism into the Lenape dialect; the Moravians entered into the work with genuine devotion. Puritan divines preached the duty of rescuing aboriginal souls from hellfire; the Mayhews, David Brainard, Jonathan Edwards, and Eleazar Wheelock followed in the footsteps of John Eliot, the pioneer Puritan missionary whose work had included the translation of the Bible into an Algonquin dialect. In devotion to faith and empire, the Anglican Society for the Propagation of the Gospel in Foreign Parts maintained missions among the Indians of central New York. The fact that so little success attended the efforts to bring the Indian into the Christian fold has sometimes been attributed to the Protestant emphasis on an ability to read the Bible, an emphasis that made the labors of Protestant missionaries far more difficult than those of French and Spanish Catholics in the Ohio and Mississippi valleys and on the distant plateaus of the Spanish Southwest. In a larger measure the relative failure of the Protestant missionary efforts may be attributed to the basic conflict between the economy of the Indians and that of the English. The fact that the Atlantic seaboard settlers pushed westward in search of farms jeopardized the Indians' hunting grounds and made conflict inevitable.

When the conflict became particularly bloody, when the white men, hysterically fearful for their lives and for those of their women and children, indulged in brutal recriminations and even in massacres, they found it necessary to justify their actions on moral and rational grounds. In their efforts to enslave the Indians the whites had already elaborated a rationale of white superiority. This rationale was now extended. The Indian was condemned as a savage incapable of becoming civilized and Christianized. He was, in the words of Cotton Mather, a rabid animal, perfidious, bloody, cruel, a veritable devil in the flesh, an agent employed by Satan himself to overcome God's chosen people. If such vituperations were less necessary in periods of equilibrium, it was still easy to regard the Indian as an inferior species to be forced onto a reservation or pushed farther into the wilderness when the land hunger of the whites pressed too heavily on his preserves.

Such rationalizations of white superiority were of course a far cry from the picture of the Noble Savage that had gradually emerged in the drawing rooms of European philosophers and poets for whom, at a safe distance, the savage Indian possessed great romantic charm. Educated eighteenth-century Americans gradually became familiar with the romanticized conception of the Indian as a stoical, dignified, unspoiled child of nature, or with the rationalistic idea that he was an innately good creature, conditioned by his peculiar environment and susceptible of quickly taking on the white man's virtues.

The African cultural pattern, like that of the Indian, stood out in stark contrast to those derived from western Europe. But by reason of their intimate association with the whites the Africans were to influence American intellectual life to a greater extent than the Indians. This was true in spite of the fact that the Negro was a minority element in the seventeenth century and that, even at the end of the colonial period, it was only in the Southern Colonies that he made up a considerable part of the population. There was also the consideration that African culture did not come to America intact. Carried to the Atlantic seaboard against their will, thrown abruptly into an utterly unfamiliar way of life, and held to an abject status, the Negroes retained only portions of their primitive African culture.

It is no easy task to estimate even roughly the extent to which African culture survived among the Negroes and directly influenced the whites. Some anthropologists hold that the Negro retained large portions of his African culture and that these had great power of survival. There can be little doubt that the culture which the African did bring with him affected his selection of certain elements in the white culture; yet it seems to be stretching a point to assume, as one authority has, that the Negro fondness for the Baptist faith resulted from the presence among the slaves of many priests of the African river-cults. But in any case, the African-born Negroes did not entirely abandon all their religious rites. It may be that in some instances these reinforced comparable culture traits among the whites; the Reverend Samuel Parris, whose credulous view of the testimony of the bewitched was heightened when members of his family became afflicted during the Salem outbreak, may have been influenced by, and may well in turn have influenced, his Barbados slave woman, Tituba, who was wise in the ways of voodooism and a confessed witch. Whether or not African rhythms survived to any appreciable extent in the dance, in work songs, and ultimately in the religious music or spirituals of evangelical revivals is a disputed point; but there is no question regarding the transmission by the Negroes of such African "day names" as Cudjo, Quashy, and Cuffee, and of a considerable body of folklore, including the tar-baby and rabbit stories.

It would be easy to overemphasize the importance of formal education, whether secular or religious, in the acculturation of the Negroes. The dominant white view regarding formal instruction of Negroes crystallized only slowly. In the interest of efficiency masters early began to teach Africans the English language, vocational skills, and concepts of obedience and subordination. As the slave status of the Negro servant became generally accepted and legally insured, masters were reluctant to Christianize colored people lest conversion work manumission. But the Bishop of London made it clear that conversion need not affect slave status. Thus the way was opened to formal efforts in the Anglican colonies to instruct Negroes in Christian doctrine. The Anglican Society for the Propagation of the Gospel in Foreign Parts outshone any other group in its services to Negro education. The Reverend Thomas Bray and his "associates" promoted the establishment of schools and taught hundreds of slaves and free Negroes not only Christian doctrine but reading, writing, and simple arithmetic. Puritan slaveowners in New England gave religious instruction to their household servants, and the Quakers as early as 1693 began to advocate religious training as a preparation for emancipation. By the third quarter of the eighteenth century such Quakers as Anthony Benezet were instructing Negroes in schools established for that purpose.

In spite of these efforts progress was slow, partly because of the Negroes' unfamiliarity with the English language, their disinclination to accept a new religion in place of their own rites unless they clearly saw an advantage in doing so, and the great differences between African conceptions of morality, truthfulness, and property rights and those of Christians. In addition, many slaveowners continued, despite official pronouncements, to fear that Christianization, especially if accompanied by the knowledge of reading, might promote Negro unrest and make white control more difficult. Born of such fears was the law South Carolina enacted in 1740 forbidding whites to instruct Negroes in reading and writing. Yet in the course of time, and especially as a result of the religious revivals of the eighteenth century, increasing numbers of Negroes were gathered to the fold. With its emphasis on humility, equality before God, and salvation in the future world, Christian faith made more and more appeal to the slaves, who tended, in some cases against the wishes of their masters, to make the Christian religion their own.

Instruction in reading for Christian uplift gave some Negroes a considerable body of the white man's knowledge. Advertisements for the sale of Negroes or for the return of fugitives included such informative statements as "he can read print," "can write a pretty good hand and has probably forged a pass," "could read, write, and speak both French and Spanish pretty well," and "has some knowledge of medicine." Exceptional members of the race achieved distinction in the white man's realm of the mind. The poems of Phyllis Wheatley (1773) and of Jupiter Hammon (1761) may be cited for their feeling and versification, and the almanacs of Benjamin Banneker for the mathematical skill they displayed. Before the end of the colonial period at least a few Negroes were sufficiently well trained, or on the way to becoming sufficiently well trained, to instruct the sons of the white gentry in the higher as well as in the elementary branches of knowledge. The mass of the black race, however, remained largely ignorant of the intellectual arts of the whites.

While the Negroes were slowly becoming familiar with some of the white man's ideas and even his intellectual skills, the whites were being influenced by the Negroes. In areas where their numbers were considerable, the Africans influenced the folklore, idiom, pronunciation, and food habits, and possibly the music and dance, of the whites.

The indirect influence of the Negro on American intellectual life was an even greater factor in the colonial legacy to the new nation than any direct influence. In the South the presence of a host of abjectly ignorant slaves deepened the traditional Old World gulf between the classes who shared the great body of humane and scientific knowledge and the masses whose world of thought and feeling was governed largely by lore and superstition. In creating the problem of slavery and a related race issue, the presence of the Negro bequeathed a stubborn legacy to the new nation. The slave system gave rise in the South to a greater emphasis on the idea of social class than would otherwise have been the case. The concept of the dignity of manual labor, which was to become a characteristically American idea, was largely lacking in the slaveholding communities of the Old South, where physical toil was associated with slavery. In the later seventeenth century, as the whites slowly crystallized their ideas about the slave status of the Negroes (these had at first been regarded as servants in more or less temporary bondage), it became necessary to rationalize the dominant position of the white race. The blacks were looked upon as "accursed" and "inferior." The repressive and brutal punishments sometimes meted out to slaves, especially to those who resisted their fate by engaging in revolts, were justified on similar grounds. At the same time the pitiful condition of the blacks fed the springs of Christian and humanitarian sentiment and thus gave rise to the idea that the Negroes must be freed and enlightened.

The ideas and attitudes represented by so many cultures—indigenous, African, and European—not only were modified by interaction with one another. They were still further modified by factors that resulted from the physical environment. The two intimately related forces—cultural interaction and environmental selection and modification—were changing the ideas and attitudes of all the peoples living in America, were creating a new civilization.

# 3 The Old World Heritage Modified

*January 27, 1711 I rose at 5 o'clock and read two chapters in Hebrew and some Greek in Lucian. I said my prayers and ate boiled milk for breakfast. I danced my dance. It rained all night but held up about 8 o'clock this morning. My sick people were all better, thank God Almighty. I settled several accounts; then I read some English which gave me great light into the nature of spirit. I ordered Tom to plant some (l-c-s) seed. I ate goose giblets for dinner. In the afternoon my wife and I took a little walk and then danced together. Then I read some more English. At night I read some Italian and then played at piquet with my wife. . . . I said my prayers and had good health, good thoughts, and good humor, thank God Almighty.*

—The Secret Diary of
William Byrd of Westover, 1711

Intellectual life in colonial America was much like that of the Old World from which in so large a measure it was derived; on both sides of the Atlantic there were always the fundamental postulates and categories of civilized western thought. But one cannot understand the intellectual equipment of the rising American nation without taking into account how the American physical environment and the new social environment modified the Old World intellectual agencies. It would be a great mistake to assume that the intellectual life of Great Britain, Holland, France, Germany, and other lands was transferred to the New World *in toto* and developed here in the same way as in Europe. Here the first colonists, after trying and perilous voyages, encountered a physical environment that often differed strikingly from that of their homeland; at once they were confronted with pressing problems of survival and of adjustment to their fellow men, problems they had never met before. Here their descendants continued their conquest of the wilderness; they had to work out new ways of dealing with the people, savage and civilized, of their own and of different nationalities with whom they were thrown in contact or whose company they needed. New problems beget new thoughts, and in the long-drawn-out process of learning to live in America the colonists found that their habits of living, their attitudes and hopes, and, along with these, their systematized ideas were altered in many ways.

Whatever the differences between the areas comprised in the thirteen original states—and these environmental differences were indeed considerable—all had certain common features that differentiated them from the Old World. In all the colonies natural resources were abundant as compared with the homelands; in all of them the population was not only varied in ethnic makeup but relatively sparse. These facts, together with the related one that colonial economy was predominantly extractive in character and hence predominantly rural, exerted a selective influence on the survival and modification of Old World ideas.

A few examples must serve to illustrate the general theme. The effort to transplant the declining feudal institutions and ideas of Great Britain was largely futile because of the easy accessibility of free lands. The plan for establishing a titled aristocracy, whether in Massachusetts or the Carolinas, failed chiefly because humble folk could not be kept in a position of quasi-serfdom on vast landed estates when an abundance of land enabled them to become freeholders. Even the feudal ideas of land inheritance, primogeniture and entail, were difficult to sustain and were in fact declining as a result of frontier influences long before the American Revolution struck them a death blow. To take another example, the great distances, the scarcity of population, and the primacy of economic tasks in a new country made it impossible to reproduce in totality the specialized intellectual functions of a mature society. Even if Latin grammar schools, colleges resting on medieval foundations, and richly endowed libraries had been immediately needed and pressingly demanded in the relatively simple colonial societies they simply could not have been maintained as in the Old World. Nor, even had there been the desire, could literary and scientific patronage in all its fullness, or the Inns of Court, or the scientific institutions of Holland and Germany have been duplicated. In time various agencies of intellectual life did indeed develop according to Old World patterns; but the colonists in adjusting themselves to the new conditions of colonial life modified these institutions in more than one respect.

The colonies not only differed from Europe in physical environment and social conditions, they differed from one another; and each colony was further divided into regions, some of which had much in common with similar regions in neighboring provinces. The differences between the settled districts along the seacoast and the less populated inland or frontier country were no less striking. He who swung an axe in the back country had a different outlook from the merchant, the artisan, or the planter in the coastal regions. The varied economies that developed as a result of differences in soil, climate, and natural resources in New England, the Middle Colonies, the Southern Colonies, and the back country in all these sections affected the number and character of schools, libraries, colleges, newspapers, and indirectly the more basic attitudes toward nature and society.

The complex economy of New England, for example, encouraged the growth of compact communities which, in contrast to the far-flung isolated homesteads in the South, could maintain schools fairly easily and could foster training useful to the town-meeting type of local government and to rising commercial pursuits. The bountiful provisions of nature in the South, so different from the sparse endowment of New England, encouraged the Southerners to concentrate on agriculture—a fact that profoundly affected intellectual life. The Southerner, too, was less careful in his attitude toward the exploitation of the soil than the New Englander, and more inclined to develop out-of-doors recreational habits. Economic conditions springing out of the physical environment made large slaveholding unprofitable in the northern colonies and materially affected thought respecting that social relationship, just as the profitableness of slavery in the tobacco and rice colonies inclined Southerners toward the justification of slavery and toward an agricultural aristocracy. These examples will be multiplied as the story of American intellectual development unfolds.

How the agencies of intellectual life and patterns of thought and feeling were modified by the common features that differentiated all the colonies from Europe, and by the peculiar local conditions in the colonies, can be illustrated by reference to the varied problems and needs of men and women in the country and in the towns, whether in New England, the Middle Colonies, or the South.

## The Intellectual Interests of Country Gentlemen

Whether of English gentry or trading background, the substantial Narragansett planters of Rhode Island, the lords of estates in eastern New York and Pennsylvania, and the more numerous great planters in the Southern Colonies inherited and aspired to realize the ideal of the English country gentleman. Land was too abundant, too easily accessible to enable them to establish a feudal aristocracy by completely identifying political privileges with the holding of great estates. But if they could not entirely succeed in reproducing the English feudal estates, they lived and thought in a way that set them apart from their indentured servants, their poorer neighbors, and the rough and ready hunters and pioneer farmers on the frontier. They cherished the conviction of their own natural right and destiny to leadership in civil and social affairs, and of consequent responsibility for those beneath them in the social order; they thought of themselves as guardians of courteous manners, hospitality, fortitude, prudence, moderation, and justice; they assumed the utility of religion both to individuals and to the decent foundations of society; and they respected learning both as a practical tool and as a badge of gentility. These ideals, which in some degree governed the planter wherever he lived, can be illustrated by reference to Virginia.

The planting aristocrats of Virginia, convinced that one was "better never born than ill-bred," spared no effort to acquire learning and culture and to provide it for their sons. The culture of a gentleman approximated the Renaissance ideal of versatility; it included a general rather than a specialized knowledge of the Greek and Roman classics, an acquaintance with French and with the great writers in the English tongue, and some familiarity with the Bible and Christian doctrine, history, philosophy, law and political thought and practice, medicine, music, architecture, painting, and natural science. In order to introduce their sons to this culture Virginia gentlemen customarily employed tutors— sometimes educated young men who came to America as indentured servants or as employees, sometimes neighboring parsons. The tutor prepared the young Virginian for college by grounding him in Lilly's *Latin Grammar,* the *English Rudiments, Goldmine on the French Tongue,* Hodder's *Arithmetic,* and *Euclid.* In the natural course of things sons were sent either to one of the colonial colleges or to the great public schools and universities of the mother country or, in the case of the Catholic planters of Maryland, to a Jesuit college in France. The daughters of these country families often learned their French and occasionally other subjects from family tutors; from their mothers they acquired the finish and social graces appropriate to ladies. The planters themselves possessed the means, leisure, and inclination to buy and read newspapers, magazines, and books, to travel to the provincial capital on matters of business and politics, and there to attend concerts and dramatic pieces and to exchange talk with college professors, clergymen, and officials who had recently been in London or at Cambridge, Oxford, or Edinburgh. At the provincial capital the planter also displayed his remarkable knowledge of political theory and practice, the one field of knowledge in which the professional rather than the amateur standard was acceptable.

The versatile intellectual equipment of a gentleman planter not only was a badge of social status but was designed to be useful in the practical concerns of everyday life. The Virginia planter, like his Elizabethan forebear and his New England contemporary, did much "purposeful" reading; even the books on religion and piety which the planters read in greater measure than is commonly supposed were presumably useful preparations for leading a good life and for the next world. The classics themselves were considered useful in providing lessons of patriotism and statesmanship, models of pure taste in writing, and personal solace and inspiration. The Virginia planter also acquainted himself with Blackstone, Coke, the Virginia statutes, and A *Perfect Guide for Studious Young Lawyers,* the more effectively to adjudicate local disputes involving points of law. He sometimes read the classical treatises on medicine and always had at hand at least one practical book of advice on the epidemic diseases that struck at his slaves and his livestock. He studied the best English architectural guides when the time came to design and build a new house or garden. Aroused by the ill effects that prevalent methods of farming had on the soil, planters and substantial farmers responded to the British agricultural reform movement and read the imported *Mystery of Husbandry Discovered* by John Worlidge or some other treatise on scientific agriculture even though the best British guides were of little use to cultivators of such indigenous staples as tobacco and corn. As the scientific movement associated with the Enlightenment became felt in America, planters occasionally supplemented their reading and practical experience by planned experiments with soil and breeding. Some, motivated by practical needs or by a desire for distinction in the great world of learning or perhaps merely by an unusual curiosity, diligently collected and classified flora, fauna, and other natural phenomena in their neighborhood and sent descriptions of their labors to the American Philosophical Society in Philadelphia or the Royal Society in London. William Byrd and John Clayton are examples of planters whose amateur work in science won them recognition abroad as well as at home; and in South Carolina a planter's daughter, Eliza Lucas Pinckney, added to the existing knowledge of rice and indigo culture.

There was, no doubt, some truth in the remark of the Reverend Hugh Jones of the College of William and Mary that early eighteenth-century Virginia planters were "generally diverted, by business or inclination, from profound study and prying into the depth of things" and "more inclinable to read men by business and conversation, than to dive into books."[1] Yet in many cases the depth of book learning possessed by planting gentlemen was considerable. William Byrd the second, for example, began every day by reading a chapter in Hebrew, or the Greek Testament, or Homer, Lucian, Thucydides, or the Anacreon, or one or another of the Latin classical writers. Book lists, diaries, letters, and wills indicate that many planters sustained a lifelong and genuine interest in the wide range of books deemed important in the equipment of a gentleman and useful in carrying on the many activities of the plantation.

The intellectual qualities and talents of southern planters were seldom communicated to the public and transmitted to posterity through the

[1] Hugh Jones, *The Present State of Virginia* (London, 1724), 44.

printed page. For this there were several reasons. The code of the gentle-man, emphasizing as it did versatile accomplishments rather than a specialized knowledge, partly explains why contributions to the trans-actions of scientific societies were the exception rather than the rule. Partly it was due to the necessity planters felt for expressing their intel-lectual skill in the practice of politics, amateur medicine and law, archi-tecture and landscape gardening, and partly to the lack of publishing facilities and of close contacts in a rural society.

Yet as letters, diaries, and other unpublished materials testify, many planters had literary gifts. William Byrd's diaries, penned in shorthand, reveal versatile and ingenious qualities of mind, pungent wit and keen insight, that were probably not untypical of his class. His *History of the Dividing Line*, which circulated in manuscript form in England, reflects not only the elegant style of the eighteenth century but an earthy humor and a sophisticated urbanity. The qualities of mind of which William Byrd was so excellent a representative became part of the legacy which the ruling class of the plantation South bestowed upon the intellectual life of the new nation.

At the end of the colonial period the values and intellectual interests of the planting gentry closely resembled those of the English country gentleman. But colonial conditions had in some respects modified the heritage. In the first place, it was easier in Virginia, as it was in Mary-land and the Carolinas, for self-made men to enter the ranks of the country gentry because land was so much more abundant and accessible than in England. Granted that pride of family became a pronounced trait in the psychology of the rural gentry, the planting aristocracy was by no means a closed caste. The values and attitudes of the colonial planter were more practical than those of many of his English forebears and contemporaries. Having to attend to the direct export of his produce and to the import of his luxuries, he disparaged commerce and trade less than did the English country gentry; indeed, planters seldom objected to hav-ing their sons become merchants. Furthermore, the colonial planter could succeed only through shrewdness and careful attention to the prac-tical and business details of a great plantation; in this respect his per-spectives and values differed in some measure from those of his English model.

Planters were aware that special efforts needed to be made in a rural, isolated, and provincial society if the younger generation was not to become one of ignorant boors, if their sons were to have the courteous manners, graces, and polite acquaintance with the classics that distinguished a gentleman. Thus planters frequently put even more emphasis than their English contemporaries on the importance of their own education and that of their children.

Finally, slavery introduced a new note in the code and behavior of the American planter. It tended to reinforce and give reality to the attenuated feudal ideal, including pride in the feeling of being a lord of creation. If some achieved the gentlemanly ideal of restraint and liberality in dealing with slaves and other inferiors, many acquired an arrogance and a belief that physical violence was necessary to control such childish people. Thus the American southern gentleman resembled his English cousin, but he was, as the studies of Louis B. Wright and others show, definitely American.

## The Intellectual Interests of the Plain People in the Country

The plain people in the country generally did not share the intellectual interests of the local gentry, but the lower classes in the Middle and Southern Colonies included a certain number of indentured servants with some claims to education. In these colonies the demand for family tutors and teachers was frequently met by obtaining an indentured servant deemed capable of providing instruction to the young. In 1773 the Reverend Jonathan Boucher of Maryland testified that "not a ship arrives with either redemptioners or convicts, in which schoolmasters are not as regularly advertised for sale, as weavers, tailors, or any other trade with little other difference, that I can hear of, excepting perhaps that the former do not usually fetch so good a price as the latter."[2] Advertisements in newspapers informed the public that such and such a ship captain would sell a white servant who knew Latin, or French, or mathematics, or accounts. The indentured servants that bound themselves out as tutors or teachers frequently included well-trained Scotsmen and even occasional university men anxious to make a start in the New World. In general, however, the talents of most of the indentured servant teachers

[2] Jonathan Boucher, A View of the Causes and Consequences of the American Revolution: In Thirteen Discourses . . . (London, 1797), 184.

were meager; the evidence is fairly clear that many drank to excess and even had criminal records. Although in some instances an indentured teacher might enjoy the respect of his master and the community, for the most part these men were treated as servants. Thus the scarcity of schools for the sons of the planters introduced a factor in the intellectual life of rural American communities less frequently found in the English country-side—the educated or semi-educated servant or near-servant.

The great body of farmers throughout the colonies did not, of course, possess either the leisure or the economic means to develop their minds in the degree and manner possible among substantial planters. The grim tasks of everyday existence absorbed most of their mental and physical energy. Nor did they have either the time or the money to buy many books or to make prolonged visits in the towns and cities. Yet from the very experiences that tied them to their farms they and their children learned much about the seasons and elements, about animals, plants, and trees. They learned the skills associated with husbandry and the household arts. This knowledge was related to their main concern in a way which that acquired from books could not have been.

Handicapped though small farmers were in matters of book learning, they were not entirely cut off from the world of ideas expressed in the printed page. As boys most of them had learned to read and write, meager though school opportunities were in rural America, especially in the Middle and Southern Colonies. Even in New York, Pennsylvania, New Jersey, and Delaware the churches maintained some schools in rural districts; and in the Southern Colonies these were supplemented by "old field" schools supported by neighboring farm families. Toward the end of the colonial period these slender facilities in the Middle and Southern Colonies were enlarged by the rise of "log colleges." Founded by Cal-vinist clergymen, these institutions made it possible for the sons of ordinary farmers to acquire some part of the classical education regarded as necessary for the ministry. In New England the sons of plain farmers mastered the rudiments of reading, writing, and arithmetic during short winter terms at the district schools sustained by the community. Boys too frail to endure the rigors of farm life or gifted with intellectual talents often managed to prepare for college in the home of the village parson or to attend a Latin grammar school in a neighboring town. Farm girls everywhere generally fared less well in schooling than boys, but it was often customary, especially in New England and in the church schools of Pennsylvania, to admit girls; elsewhere they sometimes learned to read without benefit of school attendance.

Religion offered some intellectual stimulus to farmers in almost every region of the colonies save the frontier. In many village churches, both in New England and in the provinces to the south, farmers often listened to sermons on theology and ethics that were of high intellectual caliber. From the middle of the eighteenth century to the eve of the Revolution farmers as well as townsmen heard well-trained ministers expound the political teachings of Sidney, Milton, Harrington, and Locke. Some farmers no doubt applied these writers' doctrine of political contract to the local political area and were thereby fortified in demanding from the ruling groups a larger participation in legislative matters. Anglican clergymen in the Southern Colonies sometimes displayed less zeal for learning than their Calvinist colleagues, but such men as Commissary James Blair and the Reverend Thomas Bray of Virginia cherished high standards of scholarship and stimulated parsons, professional men, and farmers alike to read books in the parish libraries that they founded. Above all, farmers obtained much intellectual stimulus from reading and especially from discussing and "chewing over" the Bible and books on piety.

The almanac was another source of intellectual stimulus to the farmer. Read and reread, enjoyed for the jokes and humor and for the engraved embellishments as well as for the information their pages contained, the almanacs were frequently saved for many years, and provided eager boys and girls with a wide variety of reading material during the long winter evenings. Probably few farmers questioned the accuracy of the almost encyclopedic information found in the almanacs. Yet if these popular pamphlets did not do much to foster a critical attitude toward what was contained in their pages, the best almanacs struck straight blows at superstition and folklore, and introduced to many a country lad the Copernican and Newtonian conceptions of the universe.

From the almanacs the farm family secured practical advice on health and medicine, the planting and harvesting of crops, the position of heavenly bodies in different seasons, household arts and lore, and political information. Under the influence of the two outstanding almanac makers, Dr. Nathaniel Ames and Benjamin Franklin, the better almanacs also provided esthetic satisfactions through quotations and selections from some of the great Continental writers as well as from such eighteenth-century English essayists and poets as Addison, Steele, Thomson, and Pope.

In the almanacs there was much sprightly and homely wisdom; and from these proverbial expressions it is possible to guess at the social attitudes and general values that farmers held or that the editors of these pamphlets desired them to hold. In accordance with the needs of colonial life the farmer was advised to be enterprising, painstaking, frugal, and industrious. *An idle man is a Burden to himself, to his Family, and to the Publick. . . . God gives all things to Industry. . . . A fat Kitchen makes a lean Will. . . . Industry and frugality make a Poor Man Rich. . . .*

Numberless maxims made virtues of self-help and self-reliance: *If you would thrive, first contrive & then Strive. . . . Many complain of bad Times, but take no care to become better themselves. . . . Adversity makes a Man Wise. . . .*

Contentment with one's lot found frequent expression: *Let the Poor be Content with their present Lot, for when they come to make Brick without Straw, their case will be yet Worse. . . . Pain's our Inheritance; Pleasure is lent to Man upon Hard Usury. . . . All men are by nature equal, But differ greatly in the sequel. . . . 'Tis as truly Folly for the Poor to ape the Rich, as for the Frog to swell, in order to equal the Ox.* But the advice to accept one's fate was tempered with the admonition to acquire what one could: *Get what you can, and what you get hold; 'Tis the Stone that will turn all your Lead into Gold.* Besides such maxims the folk wisdom of the almanacs included among the roster of virtues obedience to parents and a proper neighborly cooperation in practical matters.

Because the farmers read little and wrote less, it is difficult even with the aid of the almanacs to reconstruct their social attitudes and intellectual presuppositions. A study of the ballads and folk songs that farm people sang throws some light on their sentiments and ideas. While it is true that indentured servants and even slaves sang these songs, they belonged in a peculiar sense to the yeomanry or small freeholders.

The ballads and folk songs that the colonists brought with them from England, Ireland, Scotland, and other countries became subject to the changes of oral transmission and to the impact of new experiences. Innumerable variants of such famous Scotch and English ballads as "The Maid Freed from the Gallows" and "Lord Randall" reflect rural crimes and sensations. But since there are no written versions of these ballads and folk songs as they were sung in the colonial period it is not possible to say with certainty to what extent and in just what respects they were modified. It is reasonable to suppose, however, that some of the modifications that occurred gradually during the American career of these Old World ballads began in the colonial period itself. Thus supernatural elements no doubt began to be discarded, high-born personages tended to shed some of their aristocratic peculiarities. In addition to the Old World songs and ballads which were modified as they took root in American soil, rural folk sometimes composed new songs to express new experiences. From the colonial period, however, relatively few songs have come down to us in their eighteenth-century form; "Springfield Mountain," the trivial ditty of a young man "bitten by a pison sarpent" while mowing hay, and several songs celebrating the French and Indian War are among those that did become part of the American heritage.

The ballads and folk songs sung by rural people during the colonial period portrayed vigorously, swiftly, and concretely universal problems of the human heart. Grim warfare, disappointments in love, the harshness of parents, gentleness toward women, mercy toward the poor, and justice for the oppressed—these were themes of many of the gloomy and somewhat fatalistic songs in which both evil and good stood out starkly without qualification. Poignant and simple, these romantic songs were charged with values admirably summarized in an evaluation attributed to Sidney Lanier. "I know that he who walks in the way that these ballads point will be manful in necessary fight, fair in trade, loyal in love, generous to the poor, tender in the household, prudent in living, plain in speech, merry upon occasion, simple in behavior and honest in all things." The songs lived because they helped those who sang them to meet the vicissitudes of rural life in a new country. In answering the need for beauty, in providing emotional outlets, and in upholding as a moral value resignation to frustration and tragedy, the ballads and folk songs were useful to the bold, unsophisticated people confronted by strange new problems as well as by the traditional ones.

The limited formal intellectual interests and many of the attitudes of the farmers, who at the end of the colonial period formed a majority of the Americans, stood in direct contrast not only with the culture of the well-to-do planter but also with that of the frontiersman who had pushed into the raw land to the west of settled areas. Even in New England, where the frontier was advancing more largely by town groups than by individuals, the process often lowered intellectual standards. An example was the division of the New England town school into local or "district" schools that were smaller and accordingly inferior but which were the best that sparsely settled areas of the newly laid-out township could maintain. Beyond the thin line of settled communities the frontier diluted such intellectual culture as the farmer and his family possessed. The hunters, trappers, adventurers, and first wave of pioneer farmers seldom had either the opportunity or the need to indulge in what commonly passes for the life of the mind. Churches and schools, the two chief agencies of intellectual life in the more settled rural areas, were at first nonexistent in the remote hinterlands. Communication was so inadequate that broadsides, newspapers, almanacs, and the Bible itself could be obtained only by chance. In any case conditions of life on the farthermost frontier were such that these agencies of intellectual life were of little use in the immediate tasks at hand.

Yet even life on the frontier was not one of entire mental and emotional torpor. We may be almost certain that Scotch and English ballads were sung and adapted to new experiences and needs in the wilderness. And a new kind of education was achieved in the very struggle with the primitive forces of nature, which often sharpened practical inventiveness and promoted self-sufficiency, versatility, and independence of mind. Nor should the educational value of exploring new terrains, new phenomena in nature, and new tribes of aborigines be forgotten in any effort to balance the intellectual gains and losses incidental to pushing back the frontier.

The most significant idea that both ordinary country people and frontiersmen possessed was that of the value and dignity of their way of life. Toil on the farm was hard, but the American farmer was not a peasant. He had come to regard the cultivation of the soil not only as a dignified calling but as the most important element in the economy. He did not need to have the Physiocrats tell him that. The farmer and even the frontiersman in the wilderness had also come to realize that, to protect or advance his interests, he must participate to some extent in public life. He bequeathed a legacy of individualism and of democratic inclinations —these constituted his chief intellectual gift to the new republic.

## Colonial Towns as Intellectual Centers

Wherever towns sprang up and flourished, intellectual life differed markedly from that in rural areas. When measured on the same cultural scale as the larger provincial towns of Great Britain the more consider-able colonial towns made an excellent showing in cultural opportunities and achievements. But similar though American towns were in many respects to provincial British towns, they differed in various ways. New ideas and new books reached America from England only at irregular and often at long-delayed intervals; apparently one of the first copies of Newton's *Principia*, published in England in 1687, to arrive in the colo-nies was that which James Logan obtained in 1708. English intellectuals had sometimes qualified or even abandoned given ideas before the colonists had received and assimilated them. Isolation was consequently even more marked in some respects than in the provincial towns of the mother country. In addition, almost every American seaport of any size numbered among its residents people of various ethnic backgrounds, a fact which made American towns and their intellectual life unique.

In considering the legacy of colonial towns to the intellectual life of the nation it is of some importance to keep in mind the fact that at the end of the colonial era no town was sufficiently larger than the others or was so situated as to become the dominant cultural center. Boston and New York each numbered scarcely more than 20,000 people in 1770, and Philadelphia had only 30,000. Charleston with its 10,000 population and Newport with 7000 were themselves centers of considerable importance. Each colony or group of colonies looked in the first instance to the largest town in a given stretch of the Atlantic seaboard. After that Lon-don was naturally regarded as the center of thought. This was true in spite of the preeminence of Boston and Philadelphia in certain cultural activities, and notwithstanding the growing habit among artists, scholars, clergymen, and printers of developing contacts in cities other than their own. The fact that the new nation began with several intellectual cen-ters no one of which enjoyed cultural hegemony was to be a telling factor in its subsequent intellectual history.

The growth of towns in the eighteenth century—one person in thirty lived in a town at the end of the colonial era—profoundly affected the development of intellectual life. Besides the larger towns, smaller ones, such as Annapolis, Lancaster, Providence, Hartford, Albany, New Haven, and Lynn were centers of communication, exchange, and to some extent of intellectual activity. The seaboard cities were in relatively close touch with England, and all the towns were centers of communication for sur-rounding areas. Annapolis and Williamsburg, although little more than villages, were frequented by the more consequential Maryland and Virginia planters who enjoyed the social life as well as the advantages offered by the theater and concerts, and, in the case of Virginia's capital, the College of William and Mary. Although Williamsburg and in greater measure Charleston shared the characteristics of northern towns, urban life developed chiefly in the colonies north of the Potomac. Thus the rise of towns still further differentiated the northern from the southern provinces, intellectually as well as economically and socially.

The towns were the chief centers of intellectual activity because they enjoyed closer relations with Europe and because they offered great opportunities for social contacts and the discussion of events and ideas. They also contained the great majority of the men for whom professional and intellectual interests were the main concern. It was in the larger towns that printers published the greatest number of the broadsides, almanacs, newspapers, sermons, and books that appeared with increasing frequency in each successive decade of the eighteenth century. It was also there that the chief collections of books were to be found, if the great libraries on a relatively small number of plantations and estates be excepted. The towns, too, were for the most part seats of the provincial colleges, whose faculties took a leading part in the intellectual activities. The cities also attracted the most distinguished figures in law, in medicine, and, with notable exceptions, in theology, and they were the homes of the official and merchant classes, whose role in the development of intellectual life was considerable.

### Intellectual Interests of the Official and Merchant Classes

The intellectual and cultural life of the capital towns occasionally profited from the presence of royal governors or proprietors' agents interested in learning and culture. These men were often the product of the English universities and the Inns of Court. Many of them stimulated interest in schools and colleges and even contributed to educational institutions from their own funds. Thus Governor Nicholson gave valuable support to William and Mary and to other institutions; Gabriel Johnston of North Carolina encouraged the establishment of a printing press and of schools; and James Hamilton of Pennsylvania took an active interest in the College of Philadelphia and became the patron of Benjamin

West, the first colonial American to achieve distinction in painting. Governor Dinwiddie and Lieutenant Governor de Lancey were both patrons of the theater.

A few representatives of proprietors and of the crown contributed to the intellectual life of the colonies by their own writings. James Logan, agent of the Penns, experimented with Indian maize in an effort to determine sex relationships in plants, and corresponded with the great naturalists of the Old World. Governor Hamilton published literary and scientific papers, and Governor Robert Hunter of New York wrote a political farce, the first play printed in the English-speaking colonies. Governor Hutchinson of Massachusetts compiled a relatively accurate *History of the Massachusetts Bay Colony* (1764). The contribution of Cadwallader Colden, lieutenant governor of New York, to mathematics, physics, botany, and medicine was the most notable enrichment of Anglo-American cultural life by a member of the official class.

The intellectual life of the colonial towns was even more closely dependent upon the merchant aristocracy. In spite of risks and losses incident to business and commerce and the necessity in a new and rapidly developing society of reinvesting a great portion of capital in enterprise, the eighteenth century saw the emergence of a considerable number of men with fortunes resulting from land speculation, the Indian fur trade, lumbering and shipbuilding, fishing, the lending of money, and, above all, trade and commerce. This merchant aristocracy was chiefly confined to the towns of New England and the Middle Colonies, but it was also represented in Charleston, where planters frequently combined agriculture with commerce. These well-to-do merchants, like the planters, tended to imitate in their manners the way of life of the English aristocracy. However demanding their practical affairs were, some among the merchant aristocracy found occasional leisure for intellectual and cultural pursuits. Although few may have specifically recognized it, class distinctions were maintained by a type of education in which the mind of the future lordly merchant was disciplined by the classics, the esthetic sense developed by belles-lettres and the arts, and the social graces supplemented by considerable acquaintance with polite learning. Subscription concerts, limited for the most part to exclusive social circles, enabled him to hear some of the best chamber and symphonic music, including that of Handel and his contemporaries.

The merchants also had to acquaint themselves with more practical subjects. It was desirable to have some knowledge of navigation, geography, and current economic conditions in the larger world as well as in the colonies themselves. Merchants had to be familiar with the law, modern languages, accounting, and mathematics. Their sons, when they did not go abroad for cultural or professional training, often studied at the colonial colleges. Partly in response to the needs of this group, some of the newer colleges established in the eighteenth century broadened the traditionally classical and theologically weighted curriculum by offering more work in the modern languages and sciences which were useful to the nonclerical professions and in the training of leaders in civil life.

The merchant class thus influenced intellectual life by emphasizing the knowledge useful for their business interests and for the maintenance of their social status. Its members encouraged the provincial colleges by making gifts of scientific apparatus, and, occasionally, funds. Sometimes they contributed to well-planned astronomical observations and other scientific investigations. Along with professional men and a few planters, merchants participated in the activities of the "academy" established by Franklin in 1744 and reorganized 25 years later as the American Philosophical Society. They also had the means to attend the theater which, especially after the fourth decade of the eighteenth century, in some cities presented the plays of the classical English dramatists including Shakespeare, Congreve, Steele, Addison, and Goldsmith. Well-to-do merchants and their ladies had their portraits painted while on visits to England; others patronized such local portrait painters as Robert Feke of Newport and a half dozen others. A Philadelphia merchant, William Allen, made it possible for young Benjamin West to study in Italy; John Singleton Copley's portraits of the merchants of Boston and other cities bear witness to their patronage of this subsequently distinguished artist. Silversmiths, pewterers, glassmakers, and engravers likewise drew support from the merchant aristocracy whose mansions they embellished with their handicraft, much of which was of high merit.

The support given by merchants to printers and bookdealers was an even more notable contribution to intellectual life. A few merchants collected rare and costly books on a wide variety of subjects for their private libraries. The library assembled at Newport by the prosperous merchant Abraham Redwood was rich in the classics, theology, philosophy, and science. The library, like that of James Logan, Penn's representative in Philadelphia, was made accessible to a limited number of readers. Other merchants supported the proprietary libraries that developed in almost all the larger towns. Some of these libraries were ostensibly open to the public, but in practice they seem to have been used chiefly by the professional and merchant groups that established and supported them. Now and then books were included in the donations made by merchants to the colleges; the college libraries were open to cultivated gentlemen. Sometimes a wealthy merchant subsidized the publication of the writings of less well-to-do fellow colonists. Merchants also helped in the support of the dozen ephemeral magazines which enterprising printers launched in the years between 1741 and 1776. They were also subscribers to such British periodicals as the *Gentleman's Magazine*. All in all, the growth of intellectual life in the colonies was greatly furthered by the merchants.

## The Intellectual Opportunities of the Lower Ranks in the Towns

Not every urban dweller, of course, shared in the intellectual life that the cities offered. Children of mechanics, artisans, small shopkeepers, and tradesmen did often profit from the town-supported elementary schools in New England and from the sectarian schools elsewhere, but they seldom attended the Latin grammar schools or the provincial colleges. Franklin's father, for instance, could not send his more intellectually inclined sons to Harvard. Only in exceptional cases did poorer town boys of special promise receive sufficient aid to prepare for college and to continue their studies until graduation.

Thanks in part to the fact that the European guild system, with its regimented restrictions over artisans, was never transplanted to America, mechanics and artisans were able, after their long day's toil, to supplement the training they received in school and apprenticeship. New agencies arose which enabled them to satisfy their natural curiosity and improve their status. In the eighteenth century almost every colonial town advertised private evening schools where one might learn mathematics, accounting, modern languages, and other subjects useful to those seeking to climb in the ranks of commerce. In the two or three decades preceding independence some artisans extended their knowledge of natural science by attending the lectures on electricity, mechanics, geography, and astronomy which men like Ebenezer Kinnersley of Philadelphia and Christopher Colles of New York gave in their own and in other cities.

The lower social orders did not enjoy equal opportunities with those above them in the matter of libraries, but they did have certain facilities for obtaining and reading books. The intellectually ambitious artisan or tradesman might occasionally profit from the goodly supply of standard authors in proprietary libraries by virtue of the custom enabling impecunious aspirants to become members through payment of the stipulated fees in kind. Until the Town House in Boston burned in 1747, its reading room, well stocked with theological tomes, could be consulted. In the decades preceding the Revolution private circulating libraries, such as that of John Mein the Boston bookseller, were open to anyone able to pay the required fee—one pound eight shillings in the case of Mein's establishment. Most mechanics and artisans probably found this too steep, but they could and did follow the example of Benjamin Franklin, who organized his fellow tradesmen and artisans in Philadelphia into mutual improvement societies in which practical and philosophical questions were debated and collections of books acquired. The intellectually curious or ambitious artisan found in these libraries ample opportunities for pursuing a wide variety of literary and scientific interests.

The mechanic or artisan or tradesman often profited from the increasing number of newspapers that were launched to meet the needs of merchants for more frequent and systematic reports; twenty-two papers were established between 1713 and 1745. Enterprising lads from the mechanic class sometimes enjoyed remarkable educational opportunities as printers' devils and journeymen in publishing shops. The papers were fairly expensive, but they could be perused at the neighboring taverns. In these journals the man of humble station might read shipping news, stories of crime and accidents, poems, moral advice, essays, and bits of curious and useful information. More important, the papers carried political letters on current issues in the colonies and in the mother country. The newspaper reader was, in fact, profiting from the growing freedom of the press, a freedom of significance to the more humble classes in their tussles with the privileged groups. If a plain citizen were sufficiently ambitious and gifted he might even find in these papers a vehicle for his own thoughts, since the newspaper, by printing contributors' letters, became a sort of public forum. A milepost on the road to free political discussion was passed in 1735 when John Peter Zenger, a German printer in New York, was upheld by a jury in his claim that a newspaper might, contrary to English practice, criticize an official by printing a statement of fact.

The intellectual life of the sailors, longshoremen, fishermen, indentured servants, and Negro slaves was narrower than that of small shopkeepers and artisans, but even the least favored orders in the towns were not cut off from all chances for schooling. In New England the children of such people could learn the rudiments of book knowledge in the town schools. Elsewhere some of the young of this class learned how to read, write, and "figure" in schools maintained by various religious organizations, the most active of which was the Anglican Society for the Propagation of the Gospel and its allied societies. The laws governing the responsibilities of men to whom children were bound out as apprentices required that the boys, and even the girls, be given a minimum of instruction, and these laws, in spite of frequent violation, accomplished some part of their purpose. Offspring of the Negro slaves in the towns fared less well. But even an occasional black youngster, if his master was indulgent or unusually pious, might learn the catechism, along with respect for his superiors, from the missionaries of the Anglican philanthropic and proselyting societies, or the elements of Christian ethics from Quaker teachers. Notwithstanding the great inequality of opportunity to pursue knowledge in the colonial towns there was, according to European travelers, less illiteracy than in the towns of the Old World.

Those from the lower ranks who knew their letters could find suitable reading matter in the cheap and popular broadsides that could be purchased for a pittance or read in the tavern. These single sheets contained spirited "news ballads" of Indian encounters, patriotic accounts of the French wars, and lurid descriptions of earthquakes and other catastrophes.

The hostility of the "inferior sort" toward "pretentious and haughty aristocrats" was more frequently expressed in political and social tensions than in literary output. But an almanac rhymster's lines "To Spring" betray the resentment of the poor toward the rich:

> Now the pleasant time approaches;
> Gentlemen do ride in coaches;
> But poor men they don't regard
> That labor to maintain them hard.

Such expressions also implied the "lowbrow's" jealousy and compensatory disdain for the effete "culture" of the "better folk." Thus the cleavage in the intellectual life of townspeople was already raising problems bound to become important with the gradual democratization of life.

If the lower classes disliked the cultured aristocracy it is clear that the educated rich in turn looked down on the "lesser folk," who appeared to them incapable of light and culture. The indifference of the "riffraff" to the learned sermons of the clergy and their hearty response to the emotional appeals of the revivalists during the Great Awakening of the 1740s was, in the eyes of the elite, only one proof of the intellectual shortcomings of the masses. Their "foolish," convivial, gay street songs, adaptations no doubt of current London music hall ditties, also betokened in the minds of cultured and pious leaders a lack of taste and propriety.

On the eve of the Revolution the seventeenth-century sumptuary legislation was largely a memory. But the established classes had by no means abandoned all types of social control. The criminal code was harsh. The church and the schools, as upholders of law and order, made use of broadsides to promote obedience, respect for authority and rank, and upright living. Descriptions of earthquakes were accompanied by solemn warnings sometimes directed specifically to the lowly wicked to repent lest similar visitations of God's wrath utterly destroy them. The execution of criminals charged with offenses against society was similarly made the occasion for hortatory warnings frequently put into the alleged "last confession" of the culprit:

> Let servants all in their own Place
> The masters serve with Faith.
> Lest God should leave them to themselves
> As these poor Creatures were.
>
> Shun vain and idle Company;
> They'll lead you soon astray;
> From ill-famed Houses ever flee,
> And keep yourselves away.
> With honest Labor earn your Bread,
> While in your youthful Prime;
> Nor come you near the Harlot's Bed;
> Nor idly waste your Time.

The gulf between the intellectual and cultural attitudes of the lowest and highest ranks was wide, but some hoped that a bridge might be thrown across it. Cotton Mather took his own group to task for failing to provide the street folk with pious and uplifting songs in place of the foolish ditties in which they delighted, and his neighborhood clubs endeavored to provide light as well as virtue to the poor and degraded. Particularly in the period just before the Revolution, a humane, enlightened, and democratic representative of the favored classes occasionally admonished the lesser folk to oppose the detestable "European" policy which condemned the common people, "three-quarters of the world," to be kept in ignorance "that they may be slaves to the other quarter who live in magnificence."[3] However inadequate were the facilities for teaching the children of the poor, these facilities in some measure justified the hope that the social and cultural ladder was within the reach of those at the very bottom. Indentured servants sometimes won places of prominence in the intellectual life of the later colonial and revolutionary era— an achievement not altogether surprising when it is recalled that many teachers and well-educated men came to America as indentured servants. Yet the gulf between the intellectually favored upper classes and the ignorant poor remained wide indeed.

### The Growth of Colonial Self-Consciousness

Neither the wide divergences between the intellectual life of the various social groups in the city and country nor the isolation of many rural districts prevented the gradual growth of an intercolonial culture. From the mid-eighteenth century to the eve of the Revolution the needs of a more settled society and of a growing trade promoted the improvement of roads and other facilities for communication. Inns multiplied, and the postrider with his pouch of letters, newspapers, and official documents became a more frequent visitor even in the remoter rural areas. As deputy postmaster for the colonial post, Franklin during the years between 1753 and 1755 introduced shorter and better postal routes, lower rates, and the regularization of the practice of sending newspapers through the government post office. As a result of these improvements the communication of ideas was greatly facilitated.

[3] Samuel Briggs, *The Essays, Humor and Poems of Nathaniel Ames, Father and Son, of Dedham, Massachusetts from their Almanacks, 1726–1775* (Scott and Forman, Cleveland, 1891), 382–383.

At the same time the growth of a newspaper press with the increase of population and of commerce facilitated the development of intercolonial self-consciousness. Journalists and printers traveled from colony to colony; even if a newspaper found few readers outside a given community, the events and opinions expressed in any one were frequently copied in others. In somewhat the same way the emergence of colonial magazines was a symptom of a growing self-consciousness.

The lower schools were still too decentralized and autonomous to provide any great stimulus to an intercolonial consciousness, but the colleges promoted that end. Students from one province sometimes studied at the learned institutions of another, and scholars interested in a particular field naturally corresponded with and visited colleagues elsewhere with similar interests.

During the eighteenth century a group consciousness developed not only among college students and scholars but also among physicians, lawyers, clergymen, and Masonic Lodge men. These personal as well as business and professional intercolonial contacts furthered the idea that the colonies should develop a culture different from that of the mother country. With the rise of intercolonial political problems, especially those of defense against the French, the idea of union found expression. As early as 1722 Daniel Coxe, a wealthy and influential resident of New Jersey, anticipated Franklin's famous plan and plea for a union of the colonies.

One mark of this emerging provincial culture was an increasing concern with the colonial past. This was evidenced in part in the efforts of Franklin to purchase Americana in London for the Philadelphia Library Society, and of the Reverend Thomas Prince of Boston to collect the records of New England's past. The development of historical interest in America's past was also expressed in the gradual growth of American historiography. Whereas many histories had been written, like Cotton Mather's *Magnalia Christi Americana* (1702), to glorify God and to demonstrate His particular concern with America and its people, the historical writing in the two or three decades preceding the Revolution was noteworthy for its secular outlook on the colonial past. The Reverend Thomas Prince wrote with surprisingly little of the didacticism that was prevalent in the eighteenth century; and the histories by the Reverend William Stith of Virginia and by Governor Thomas Hutchinson of Massachusetts showed pride in the colonial past without sacrificing the existing canons of historical scholarship. Such books were read in the various colonies.

But the developing pattern of colonial culture envisioned a bright future as well as a glorious past. Many shared Jonathan Edwards' conviction that Providence had singled America out as "the glorious renovator of the world." Although John Adams, writing in 1765, did not have in mind exactly the same kind of renovation, his words bear quoting. "I always consider," he wrote, "the settlement of America with reverence and wonder, as the opening of a grand scheme and design in Providence for the illumination and the emancipation of the slavish part of mankind all over the earth." In 1730 when Philadelphia was still a small town a local enthusiast predicted that

> Europe shall mourn her ancient fame declined
> And Philadelphia be the Athens of Mankind.

Others noted the deviation of American English from the mother tongue. Some pointed to the greater diffusion of knowledge in America, and others to the pronounced mechanical ingenuity of the people, as tokens of an emerging and different American culture. Expansiveness, self-sufficiency, and visions of "imperial grandeur" likewise marked the growing colonial self-consciousness, but the dream of a great American culture had, of course, to remain almost wholly in the realm of aspiration until social conditions permitted more specialization among those most interested in the life of the mind.

# 4 Diffusion of the Arts and Sciences

*All intended for divinity should be taught Latin and Greek; for physic the Latin, Greek and French; for law the Latin and French; merchants, the French, German and Spanish; and though all should not be compelled to learn Latin, Greek, or the modern foreign languages, yet none that have an ardent desire to learn them should be refused.*

*—BENJAMIN FRANKLIN, 1749*

*Hypotheses may be of use to put us upon further enquiry, and a more critical examination, but are never to be received, any further than they are supported by proper evidence.*

*—SAMUEL WILLIAMS, 1785*

Physical distance did not break the intellectual ties between the New World and the Old. The American colonists brought with them from Europe a vast store of polite learning and a rapidly developing body of scientific knowledge. Throughout the colonial period Americans worked to preserve this inheritance. The practical demands of life in America and the separation from European centers of learning made it extremely difficult for any thinker to do more than merely transmit literature and science. But in spite of adverse conditions, a number of Americans did make original contributions to the development of their intellectual heritage. Above all, colonial scholars and scientists made it possible for Americans to participate in the vigorous intellectual life of seventeenth- and eighteenth-century Europe.

The mass of the colonial population was only slightly touched, if at all, by the body of polite learning and scientific interests which developed in the colonies and which was a precious part of the legacy to the new nation. In a sense, to be sure, Christianity had assimilated much classical learning, and ordinary men and women did hear frequent allusions to the ancient writers in the learned sermons of some of their clergy. Here and there among the lowly an indentured teacher-servant was well versed in the classics. In rare instances an ambition to master natural science led the son of an artisan to study Latin; Thomas Godfrey, a Pennsylvania glazier, learned the language in order to read Newton's *Principia*. But on the whole the plain people had little use for Latin, Greek, and Hebrew, or indeed for the classics of the Renaissance literature. The idea that even the common people might derive esthetic satisfactions and mental stimulus from the classics was still practically unheard of. To the people themselves such studies doubtless seemed a useless luxury. Only as the offspring of humble folk sought entrance into the professions or the world of culture and social status did knowledge of the classics and of modern polite learning become essential.

### The Transmission of the Ancient Classics

The classics of Greece and Rome might well have been entirely neglected in the busy New World had they not ministered to many needs. In the first place they served the requirements of professional interests. Law and medicine both assumed a familiarity with Latin. The Catholic, Anglican, Lutheran, and Calvinistic faiths all set much store on a clergy that could read Scriptures in the original Hebrew and Greek and had some acquaintance with the vast theological literature in the Latin tongue. If the Christian faith was to be perpetuated in the New World, provision had to be made in schools and colleges for the training of youth in the ancient classics.

That educated Americans in the colonial period enjoyed a firsthand knowledge of classical literature was also the result of the medieval conception that associated command of Latin with status and of the

Renaissance ideal that associated gentility with classical learning. Yet the classics were never regarded merely as a superficial badge of the gentleman. The ancient languages, valued as the repositories of a timeless wisdom and truth, had trained great leaders in the past, and it was assumed that they still had the power to do so in a later day. More than that, the cultured class believed that the truth and wisdom in classical literature were bound to solace the human spirit.

The merchant or planter who regarded himself and was regarded by others as a gentleman thus possessed a knowledge of the classics and saw to it that his sons learned their Latin and Greek at an early age. However much he was occupied with interests allied to his business or occupation, he was likely to maintain a genuine interest in the classics. It is probably true that many a planter who as a lad had learned his Latin and Greek from a family tutor or from the neighboring parson failed to make much personal use of the beautifully bound classical tomes in his library. But classical knowledge was by no means rare among planters, even if most of them were less assiduous in reading the classics than the second William Byrd, whose library included 394 volumes of the ancient classics. In polite conversation in the drawing room, in private letters, and in political orations classical allusions were frequent. Nor was it deemed odd when Richard Lee of Virginia had inscribed in Latin on his tombstone the words: "He was very skillful in the Greek and Latin languages. . . ."

Local parsons and private tutors in the homes of the well-to-do aided in transmitting classical learning to succeeding generations of favored youth, but the task was largely shouldered by the schools and colleges. Thanks to the Puritan zeal for learning and the fact that New England settlement followed the township organization of closely settled communities, Latin grammar schools were established by legislation and in part supported from the public funds of the towns themselves. Thus almost from the start New England had more schools in which a classical training might be obtained than did the planting colonies that boasted a mere handful of preparatory schools endowed by private philanthropy. In the eighteenth century, when well-trained Presbyterian clergymen from Scotland and Ireland settled in the Southern and Middle Colonies, these regions came to enjoy much better opportunities for the pursuit of classical scholarship.

Since the colonial colleges, in the manner of the English and Scotch universities, specified the admission requirements in the classical languages, the type of training provided in the preparatory schools or at the hand of private tutors was essentially the same everywhere. Masters were almost always themselves products of the Old World universities or the colonial colleges. The best of these teachers, such as Ezekiel Cheever of New Haven and Boston, the Reverend William Tennent of Pennsylvania, and Dr. David Caldwell of North Carolina, commanded a thorough knowledge of Latin and Greek. Their pupils, boys from seven to fourteen, were subjected to a rigorous training in Latin grammar, composition, and reading. In the better schools Latin was also used as a medium of communication. The present use of Latin in commencement exercises is a survival of the colonial view that the language of the Romans was the proper vehicle for academic communication. During the course of Latin studies boys read Juvenal, Corderius, Ovid, Vergil, Caesar, Cicero, and Horace. Greek grammar was also begun, and the higher classes dipped into Xenophon and Homer. In accordance with tradition and the prevailing belief in mental discipline through drill, the emphasis was put primarily on an acquisition of the languages themselves. But the products of the best Latin grammar schools enjoyed no mean acquaintance with some of the greatest masterpieces of classical literature.

The colleges, in contrast to the Latin grammar schools, admitted into the curriculum a number of studies other than the ancient languages, particularly logic, mathematics, and metaphysics. But the classics dominated the four-year course of study in all nine of the colonial colleges. The curriculum included Cicero, Terence, Ovid, Sallust, Vergil, Horace, and Martial, and not infrequently Livy and Tacitus among Roman writers; among those of Greece, Homer, Demosthenes, Aristotle, Hesiod, and Theocritus supplemented the New Testament. The private libraries of college students indicate that it was not uncommon for undergraduates also to read Euripides, Sophocles, and other writers. There is ample evidence that while the classics were regarded as indispensable tools in the study of divinity, they were also cherished for their humanistic value. Samuel Eliot Morison has shown that at seventeenth-century Harvard the undergraduates were manifestly appreciative of the literary and esthetic qualities of the great masterpieces of the ancient world. In the eighteenth century, when so much emphasis was put on elegance of style, the humanistic and literary value of the classics received even greater attention.

It is true that the eighteenth century also saw a tendency to give some-what less emphasis to the classics in the curriculum of both secondary schools and institutions of higher learning. Many of the disciples of the Enlightenment desired to have them largely replaced by modern languages and the natural and social sciences. Yet in spite of this, and not-withstanding the impatience of many in the rising middle class with the emphasis on the classics in the secondary schools, Latin and Greek maintained their dominant position. Franklin, himself the leading spirit in the movement to give the utilitarian studies a larger place in the Academy of Philadelphia, observed in 1773 that "it has been of late too much the mode to slight the learning of the ancients." Nor did the academies that began to replace or supplement the Latin grammar schools in the late colonial era subordinate Latin and Greek to non-classical studies. On the eve of the Revolution a group of tutors and undergraduates at Yale demanded that more attention be given to English letters, but the classics continued to dominate the curriculum. Inventories of books and lists of holdings in libraries bear witness to their continued vogue. Thus in spite of growing criticisms the classics held their own in institutions of learning.

That many men grounded in the great books of the Greeks and Romans continued after college to read and to draw inspiration from them in their everyday lives is clear from the wealth of classical allusions in oratory, in polite letters, and even in journalism. The argument has been made that the classics broadened the mental horizons of the men who led the Revolution and instilled in their hearts the Greek concept of honor and the Roman ideal of virtue. In point of fact, both conservatives and radicals drew support for their views from the classics. The distrust of human nature and the traditionalism in much classical literature no doubt strengthened men of a conservative and skeptical temper. On the other hand, liberals with rationalistic leanings no doubt derived support from the classical ideal that reason should control emotion and from the ancients' concept of natural law. During the discussions that preceded the Revolution and in the struggle itself, Aristotle and other classical authorities were cited on the superiority of the law of God and nature to that of human enactment. John Dickinson of Pennsylvania appealed to the *Antigone* as proof of the danger involved in violating the im-mutable law of nature. Demosthenes, Thucydides, Polybius, Plutarch, Cicero, and Tacitus were invoked to justify colonial resistance, and classi-cal writers were quoted in support of the republican ideal.

## Contributions to Classical Scholarship

The eighteenth century was witnessing in Europe the publication of new and improved texts of most of the ancient writers, a series of superior lexicons and grammars, and a number of notable translations, which contributed not only to an understanding of the Greek and Latin classics themselves but to the modern tongues as well. Americans participated little in this development, but they were not altogether inactive. Even against the odds of the first terrible years in Jamestown, George Sandys labored there on his poetical translation of Ovid's *Metamorphoses* (London, 1626), a translation praised by both Dryden and Pope. Although not actually published until 1709, Ezekiel Cheever's *Accidence, A Short Introduction to the Latin Tongue*, was in reality a product of the seventeenth century. This manual, remarkable for its simplicity, comprehensiveness, and exactness, reached its twentieth edition in 1785. While in part based on existing English manuals, Cheever's *Accidence* contained much that was derived from his own greatness as a teacher, a greatness that led Cotton Mather to write

> Do but name Cheever, and the Echo straight
> Upon that Name, Good Latin, will repeat.

Preoccupied though the American press was with the publication of sermons, almanacs, broadsides, and official documents, it also paid its respects to the classics. In 1729 a translation of the *Morals* of Epictetus issued from a Philadelphia press. With the appearance in Philadelphia of James Logan's translations of Dionysius Cato's *Moral Distichs* (1735) and Cicero's *De Senectute* (1744) with notes of explanation, it was clear that American classical scholarship could be productive as well as thorough. When, in 1760, James Otis of Boston printed his *Rudiments of Latin Prosody*, it became apparent that no single colony was monopolizing the publication of classical studies.

Nor was American interest in Hebrew, Chaldee, and Syriac entirely lacking. Regarded as the parents of all western tongues, these ancient Oriental languages were valued as a philological tool. But it was principally as a key to the Old Testament that they were so greatly respected not only in Puritan New England but wherever a learned clergy was regarded as indispensable to Christian worship. Judah Monis, a Christianized Jew, set a high standard of scholarship in the field of Hebraic studies at Harvard. His successor, Stephen Sewall, prepared a Hebrew grammar. Sewall's example was followed by other Hebraists, especially by the erudite president of King's College, Dr. Samuel Johnson, and by the Reverend Dr. Kunze of the University of Pennsylvania, who announced that his grammar was based upon an "improved plan." Although interest in Hebrew waned in the colleges during the later colonial period, the rich scholarship that Ezra Stiles, subsequently president of Yale, possessed in this field testified to the high standards that were still maintained. The proficiency that an exceptional scholar trained in the late colonial period might achieve in Arabic is illustrated by the correspondence the Reverend William Bentley of maritime Salem conducted with Arabic chiefs in their own tongue, and by the references in Bentley's diary, one of the great documents in the intellectual history of late eighteenth-century America.

## The Reception of Modern Literature

On the eve of the Revolution the private and quasi-public libraries of the American colonies included not only the writings of the ancient poets, historians, orators, and philosophers, but virtually all the works in Italian, French, and English of the leading figures of the Renaissance and succeeding centuries. Many of these urbane products of the Renaissance period had come from the libraries of seventeenth-century planters and clergymen, who had brought or imported them along with books on agriculture, mineralogy, medicine, law, theology, and piety. Planters favored Castiglione's *The Book of the Courtier* and comparable books in French and English, particularly *The Compleat Gentleman, The English Gentleman, The Gentleman's Calling*, and the like. But, as the studies of Louis B. Wright show, seventeenth-century planters also owned the works of Erasmus, Montaigne, Sir Thomas More, Bacon, Machiavelli, Guicciardini, Bodin, Hobbes, Descartes, Locke, Grotius, Butler, Burton, and many another known today only to specialists but highly regarded in that century.

Despite fires and other mishaps, many books from the seventeenth-century libraries of New England parsons were still in existence on the eve of the Revolution to testify to the broad interests of the erudite leaders of the Puritan church. For these men read not only ponderous Latin tomes of theologians, Catholic and Protestant, but most of the writers included in the libraries of Virginia planters. In addition, New England libraries gave space to such poets as Herbert, Donne, and Milton; and at least some Harvard students were familiar with the "Venus and Adonis" of Shakespeare, the worldly verse of Herrick, the richly imaginative and urbane poetry of Spenser, and the Renaissance *Arcadia* of Sidney.

As the eighteenth century advanced planters, merchants, lawyers, physicians, clergymen, and even rising mechanics continued to import from abroad books by the leading writers of the time. To cite an example, on the eve of the Revolution the Philadelphia Library Association possessed not only the ancient and modern classics and works on science and practical affairs, but such contemporary writers as Fielding, Steele, Richardson, and Thomson. On the shelves of other libraries in the City of Brotherly Love were the leading contemporary writings as well as rare volumes representing the secular culture of earlier centuries in England and on the Continent. Philadelphia publishers brought out reprints of Defoe, Goldsmith, Gray, Locke, Pope, Samuel Johnson, Blackstone, Lord Kames, Robertson, Sterne, and Young, among others. But only an analysis of the reception that was accorded the Enlightenment in America can reveal the full richness of colonial acquaintance with eighteenth-century secular thought.

## The Colonial Interest in Natural Science

The colonial legacy of classical scholarship cannot be easily over-emphasized, but the legacy of natural science was from some points of view even more significant. Scientific inquiry not only accumulated a body of reasonably accurate knowledge of the natural world. It also diminished the authority of superstition, of classical tradition, and of religion itself. When the Republic was founded the great majority of the people, including many learned men, doubtless still cherished traditional superstitions and supernatural beliefs, but these were far less general than they had been at the end of the seventeenth century. In view of the small number of persons concerned with scientific inquiry and the obstacles confronting them, and considering the preoccupation of most of these men with other concerns as well, their achievements seem truly remarkable.

It has already been noted that occasional planters, farmers, and merchants engaged in scientific pursuits along with their other activities, or in other ways supported them. The interest in mathematics, astronomy, navigation, map making, and surveying sprang partly from the fact that these studies had practical value for men engaged in commerce, industry, and land promotion. John Winthrop, Jr., the seventeenth-century industrial promoter and governor of Connecticut, pursued his studies in astronomy, botany, chemistry, and metallurgy largely in the hope of achieving economic independence for himself and New England through the establishment of mines and industries. The interest of Philadelphia merchants in northern maritime routes led to their support of a project, premature to be sure, for arctic exploration. Only the scarcity of capital, it seems, prevented prospective entrepreneurs from acting on the suggestion of a Pennsylvania scientist for a geological survey.

In response to the stimulus of agricultural reformers in England, planters and farmers often engaged in scientific observation and experiment. But they were also influenced to do so by the exhaustion of their soil and by a desire to discover new or improved varieties of staples and stocks. The experiments of John Winthrop, II, with Indian corn, Jared Eliot's studies of husbandry, John Clayton's botanical observations, William Byrd's exploration of the economic and curative value of Virginia's plants, and Eliza Pinckney's experiments with indigo and rice are illustrative of the utilitarian motive of much scientific inquiry. So is the work of the Virginia planter, William Fitzhugh, who studied mineralogy in the hope of discovering precious metals on his estate. To emphasize this is not to deny that in some instances, notably in the case of John Bartram, the Quaker farmer of Pennsylvania, sheer love of nature itself or genuine scientific curiosity was a stronger motive than any utilitarian consideration.

Artisans with an unusual flair for mechanical manipulation also contributed to the advance of science. Thus navigation profited from the invention of the quadrant, to which the Philadelphia glazier Thomas Godfrey seems to have as good a claim as the Englishman Hadley for whom it was named. David Rittenhouse, self-taught astronomer, began his scientific work as a clock maker; and Amos Whittemore, subsequent inventor of a textile machine, was trained as a gunsmith. The greatest of colonial scientists, Benajmin Franklin, came from the artisan class and pursued the printing trade for much of his life.

The professions made the major contribution to the development of natural history. Lawyers such as Paul Dudley of Massachusetts; clergymen such as the Mathers, Benjamin Colman, Thomas Prince, and Samuel Williams; physicians such as William Douglass of Boston, Cadwallader Colden of New York, John Mitchell of Virginia, and Alexander Garden of South Carolina are representative examples. These men, for whom scientific inquiry was an avocation, were motivated by a variety of considerations. With some the pursuit of science was a hobby, an expression of an unusually strong curiosity about the flora, fauna, and other phenomena of a strange new world. Some of them doubtless also set store on the prestige to be won by contributing papers to the Royal Society in London and corresponding with the great naturalists in the Old World, who were generous in their recognition of the contributions of American scientific workers. Physicians hoped to obtain effective cures from some of the native herbs in their neighborhoods. Some clergymen, like the Mathers, hoped to demonstrate through their observations of natural phenomena the reality of the supernatural world of spirits. Others believed that the study of nature might enable them to understand rationally some of God's mysteries and to demonstrate His hand in every phenomenon and occurrence in the natural world. Thus the Reverend Samuel Lee, an important figure in the Royal Society, did much after his migration to New England in 1686 to familiarize the local clergy with the idea that the new science magnified God's glory. In the eighteenth century this view came to be increasingly accepted.

Only a handful of men devoted themselves solely to science and derived their livelihood from it. Perhaps Isaac Greenwood of Boston was the first colonist to support himself by teaching natural science. His successor at Harvard, John Winthrop, who taught natural philosophy from 1738 until his death in 1779, was, after Franklin, colonial America's most distinguished scientist. William Small, a professor at William and Mary in the later colonial period, also made science his main concern, and in other colleges scholars gave at least part of their talent and energy to that discipline. Surveying and instrument making, applications of scientific knowledge, enabled Rittenhouse to pursue his investigations. John Bartram supported himself in part by selling seeds and plants to other gardeners and naturalists.

Material support for scientific activity in the colonial period was scanty and for the most part unorganized; in general, American naturalists depended on their own resources. They found a vehicle for the publication of their work in the transactions of the Royal Society. Occasionally a well-to-do English friend of science contributed funds for the support of scientific investigations in the colonies. The action of the crown in appointing John Bartram royal botanist and allocating to him a small annual stipend was exceptional. The provincial legislature of Massachusetts helped finance the first astronomical expedition undertaken by Professor John Winthrop in 1761, when he observed in Nova Scotia the transit of Venus across the sun, and the Pennsylvania assembly contributed to the construction of telescopes and observatories for the study of the transit of Venus in 1769. Greatest of all boons was the establishment of the American Philosophical Society, which aided in the astronomical observations in 1769, promoted facilities for cooperative investigations on other occasions, and provided an outlet for publication.

The chief institutional support for colonial science came from the colleges. Instruction in the sciences, especially in the Copernican astronomy and in mathematics, was well established before the end of the seventeenth century. At Harvard Thomas Brattle observed and computed lunar eclipses and Halley's comet (1680). The data he thus assembled, together with his precise observations of the variations of the magnetic needle, were utilized by Newton in his *Principia*. Such recruits from the mother country as Charles Morton, who joined the Harvard staff in 1692, and especially Isaac Greenwood, did much to lessen the vogue of Aristotelian authoritarianism in college science.

Other colleges gradually assembled sufficient apparatus to give students some acquaintance with the experimental method of studying astronomy, physics, and chemistry. In his *General Idea of the College of Mirania* (1753) Provost William Smith of the College of Pennsylvania visioned the triumph of scientific knowledge over error, superstition, and the physical obstacles imposed by the wilderness. The first instruction in non-Aristotelian botany given in an American college was that provided at the Philadelphia institution over which he presided. In 1768 Adam Kuhn, a student of Linnaeus, began his lectures in botany. The following year Dr. Benjamin Rush became, at the same institution, the first American professor of chemistry. At King's College special attention was also given to the study of natural phenomena.

On the popular level the magazines and especially the almanacs contributed to the diffusion of scientific knowledge. *The American Magazine* (1757–1758) found space for original problems in mathematics and for scientific papers. Horticulture and mechanics also received attention in the short-lived colonial magazines. The almanac, it is true, frequently confirmed astrological lore by encouraging farmers to think of the planets as the words of life, death, growth, and decay, and to plant their crops according to the phases of the moon. So marked, indeed, was the impact of tradition that it was possible for the Reverend Dr. Samuel Deane, respected and moderate pastor of the First Church in Portland, to advance, as late as 1790, the theory that the moon put a larger amount of spirit into fruit when the heavenly bodies exerted their greatest attraction. Still it is also important to remember that in the hands of enlightened compilers the almanac was a scientific educator of importance. The first colonial account of the Copernican system appeared in an almanac for 1659 published at Cambridge by a young Harvard graduate, Zechariah Bridgen. In the words of Theodore Hornberger, Franklin's *Poor Richard* in 1753 "began an account of modern astronomy, which ran for two years and amounted practically to a popular textbook on that subject." In New England Nathaniel Ames also popularized in his famous almanac the Copernican and Newtonian theories of the universe.

Nor should it be forgotten that many clergymen familiarized their flocks with current scientific theories. Increase Mather in 1683 organized the first scientific society to effect "Improvements in Philosophy and Additions to the Stores of Natural History." With his son, Cotton, he also supported, against the opposition of some of Boston's leading physicians, the new movement for inoculation against smallpox. Benjamin Colman and Professor John Winthrop of Harvard not only popularized Newtonian theories but, as their writings on earthquakes, droughts, and rains reveal, were also well informed in both natural history and natural philosophy.

Although such clergymen promoted the spread of the newer scientific theories of the universe and of natural phenomena, many of their colleagues clung to the cruder supernaturalism. Notwithstanding the naturalistic explanations of earthquakes advanced by Professor Winthrop in 1755 and 1759, educated clergymen as well as untutored laymen were quite willing, when darkness descended at midday on May 19, 1790, to attribute it to supernatural agencies. The prevailing distress over God's anger suggested that a naturalistic conception of the heavens had made less headway among the semieducated than might have been expected in view of the fact that Calvinism with its doctrine of special interpositions of the Deity had long been on the wane.

## Methods, Assumptions, and Theories in Colonial Science

In looking at the growing body of scientific knowledge accumulated during the colonial period one is struck by many features that differenti-ate it from science today. What we think of as science was then divided into two fields: natural philosophy, which included physics, chemistry, and mathematics; and natural history, comprising geology, botany, and zoology. But there was so little specialization that most investigators were as much at home in natural philosophy as in natural history. Dr. John Mitchell of Virginia won a reputation in physics, medicine, scien-tific agriculture, and cartography, and also found time to assemble more than a thousand specimens of native plants. James Logan, a Philadelphia merchant and agent for the Penn family, stole time from his labors to study mathematics, botany, and optics.

Cadwallader Colden was a physician, an anthropoligist, a botanist, a physicist, and a mathematician. Professor Winthrop worked in the fields of mathematics, geography, physics, electricity, and astronomy. Franklin concerned himself with mathematics, mechanics, physics, geology, and oceanography. The greatest degree of specialization was achieved by John Bartram and his son William, whose activities were largely confined to botany.

Any discussion of scientific method in the colonial period must take as its point of departure the status of mathematical knowledge, for the study of astronomy and physics especially was closely dependent on mathematics. Although the relatively simple economy of the seventeenth century did not generally require widespread use of anything except the most elementary arithmetic, a few scholars, chief of whom was Thomas Brattle of Harvard, displayed in their calculations for the almanacs accu-rate knowledge of certain branches of higher mathematics. Such mathe-matics as Harvard taught was largely subordinated to astronomy; in considerable measure this remained true of all the colleges in the eighteenth century.

As commerce, navigation, and surveying enlisted ever stronger interest in the later colonial period, knowledge of mathematics became more widespread. Bishop Berkeley's presence in New England and the evolu-tion of the American Philosophical Society also contributed to the grow-ing interest in this subject. In 1728, when Isaac Greenwood became Hollis professor of mathematics and natural science at Harvard, the course of study included, besides arithmetic, a subject almost entirely neglected in the preparatory schools, the elements of algebra, with the principles of algebraic conic sections, plain and spherical trigonometry, the doctrine of spheres, the use of globes, and the principles of mensuration. Calculus, the Newtonian system of "fluxions," was slower to gain currency. James Logan mastered Newton's *Principia*, as did his friends Cadwallader Colden and Thomas Godfrey. But Calculus was not taught in the colleges until 1746, after John Winthrop succeeded Isaac Greenwood as Hollis professor at Harvard. At about the same time, President Clap of Yale was invigorating the study of mathematics. With the foundation of the College of Philadelphia mathematics was, at least in theory, given an honored place; but in general there was no very significant advance in the mathematical curriculum until the last two decades of the century.

The character of mathematics instruction is revealed by the textbooks of the period. In 1729 Professor Greenwood produced an "arithmetic," the first textbook by an American wholly devoted to the subject. Although it marked an improvement on existing English textbooks, it reached only a limited audience. The most popular textbook throughout most of the century was that of the Englishman, Thomas Dilworth. His *Schoolmaster's Assistant* excluded demonstration and reasoning and gave much attention to difficult and ambiguous rules and definitions based on the principle of memorization. Nevertheless, much of the instruction must have been able. Jefferson, for example, acquired at William and Mary not only a taste for, but considerable skill in, mathematics, which he put to good use in his formula for constructing the moldboard of a plow on mathematical principles.

Mathematics enabled colonial scientists to prepare almanacs and especially after the introduction of Copernican and Newtonian science at Harvard in the second half of the seventeenth century, to make astronomical calculations of practical value. Skill in mathematics and a firm grasp of Newtonian physics enabled Professor Winthrop of Harvard to put to excellent account his observations of the transits of Venus over the sun. His studies of these transits from various vantage points enabled him to determine with surprising exactness the number of degrees of longitude between Cambridge and London and to demonstrate the accuracy of Newton's laws of motion.

Mathematical knowledge figured no less in the astronomical work of

David Rittenhouse, who was likewise a disciple of Newton. Self-taught though he was, handicapped by ill health and straitened means, suspected by many orthodox Quakers, Rittenhouse nonetheless developed sufficient competency in both mathematics and astronomy to contribute to these fields work that was significant if not as original as Winthrop's paper on comets (1759). In his calculations of the transit of Venus in 1769 Rittenhouse corrected an error made by the more learned Winthrop and, according to good authority, observed certain features that escaped all other observers. His part in fixing the disputed boundaries of his state also testified to his skill in mathematics.

But what most endeared Rittenhouse to his contemporaries was his construction in 1767 of the orrery. This machine, which simulated the motions of the planets and their satellites and lunar and solar eclipses at any point in time backward or forward for 5000 years, provided spectators with a remarkable picture of the solar system and the precision of its movements. Jefferson with pardonable pride and exaggeration wrote of him in his *Notes on the State of Virginia:* "He has not indeed made a world; but he has by imitation approached nearer its Maker than any man who has lived from the creation to this day."[1] His improvements in the telescope constituted another practical service to astronomy for which Rittenhouse was much applauded.

Not only did mathematics assist scientists in constructing precision instruments; it enabled them to manipulate the "philosophical apparatus" in the "cabinets" that gradually took shape in college halls. Instructors resorted to mathematics to test and demonstrate hypotheses in the fields of gravitation, electricity, heat, and pneumatics. This was all the more important in view of the fact that some of the current textbooks, such as Benjamin Martin's *Philosophical Grammar,* lent sanction to many views that were accepted on mere authority. Dr. Alexander Garden of Charleston admired the use to which Linnaeus put mathematics in his studies of botany and zoology, but the time had not yet come for its wide application in biology.

Colonial naturalists, largely concerned as they were with the collection and classification of specimens, made only occasional use of the microscope and of experimental techniques. Cotton Mather was impressed by the microscope's wondrous powers, and Edward Bromfield of Boston

---

[1] Thomas Jefferson, *Notes on the State of Virginia* (University of North Carolina Press, 1955), 64.

later used a powerful magnifying glass to study "the strong workings of the bowels of a louse." John Bartram also made use of microscopic observations "upon the male and female parts in vegetables." The Bartrams found time to experiment with hybridization, but most investigators of flora, fauna, and rocks confined their work largely to assiduous collecting and classification. This specimen gathering greatly extended knowledge of the animal and vegetable realms and enabled Gronovius, Linnaeus, and other European leaders in the field to work out their systematic classifications. The value of some of the studies of American naturalists was increased by the remarkably faithful drawings that accompanied them, the work of such talented craftsmen as Mark Catesby, an English visitor who studied southern plants, birds, fishes, shells, and serpents, and Jane Colden, the daughter of the lieutenant governor of New York.

Students of the medicinal properties of flora and fauna were sometimes handicapped by basic theological assumptions related to the ancient doctrine of correspondence. According to this theory, God had placed a "signature" on each substance so that, by reason of a symbolical correspondence between its outer appearance and a given condition or ailment, it acted as a cure. The Creator, it was believed, had made nothing in vain; hence the whole world was a great cosmic pharmacy to be explored and utilized.

Assuming in advance that God's purpose was revealed in every minute aspect of His handiwork, naturalists did not make their observations with entire objectivity. Thus Dr. John Mitchell, one of the most distinguished colonial naturalists of the eighteenth century, remarked, in describing the pouch of the Virginia opossum: "How often, then are we obliged, in discovering and prying into the works of nature, to acknowledge the Almighty has not only given being to, but has likewise provided for the well-being of this, as well as other creatures!"[2] The Biblical doctrine that man had been created in the image of God tended to set human kind apart from the animals, with the result that medicine was insufficiently grounded on animal pathology and physiology. Scientific classification based on the relationship of various created objects was also hampered by the conviction that God had created fixed species. What was more, the scholastic method of discussing scientific questions

[2] Herbert Thatcher, "Dr. Mitchell, M.D., F.R.S., of Virginia," in *Virginia Magazine of History and Biography*, XL (January, April, July, October, 1932), 345–346.

persisted. In 1769 a Harvard disputation on the question whether the reptiles of America originated from those preserved by Noah was decided in the affirmative.

Authoritarian and traditional barriers to scientific advance nevertheless did give way. Many a time-honored myth sanctioned by the authority of a distinguished name was dispelled by the shrewd observations of a people who had to adjust themselves to a new environment. Even the untutored pioneer, seeking his food in stream and forest, rejected the notion that migrating birds flew to the moon in winter. While a Philadelphia naturalist maintained as late as 1800 that swallows hibernated in mud and while ideas of fantastic animals persisted in some quarters, such concepts were exceptional among a people who had from necessity rubbed close elbows with nature.

Colonial scientists were generally more concerned with amplifying and supporting the theories of European scientists, Newton in natural philosophy and Linnaeus in natural history, than in advancing hypotheses of their own. For the most part American naturalists contented themselves with filling in the gaps which the strange phenomena in their own vicinity invited them to explore. In this they showed good judgment, for at best they were ill equipped to advance theoretical explanations or to make imposing syntheses of scientific knowledge.

Cadwallader Colden, the versatile lieutenant governor of New York, was an exception. He was interested in the larger issues of synthesis and made bold to grapple with the stiffest problems implicit in Cartesianism and Newtonianism. Trained at the University of Edinburgh, Colden corresponded with the leading scientists and thinkers in England and on the Continent. He differed with Bishop Berkeley's analysis of Newton's theories and ventured to criticize and make practical applications of the theories of fluxions and gravitation. In his *Principles of Action in Matter* (1751) he disavowed materialism. Nevertheless, he himself came close to taking a materialist position; what he did was to resolve matter into the mechanics of force by holding that the properties of things are merely their various modes of activity. In 1778 another physicist, Benjamin Thompson, provided experimental evidence in his work on heat in support of this theory of matter. But in taking an even more comprehensive position Colden made a pioneer contribution toward a mature phase of scientific materialism which deserves to be remembered.

Colden was not the only one to advance scientific hypotheses in explanation of natural phenomena. The appearance of earthquakes in New England in 1727 and 1755 posed fundamental questions concerning the cause of this extraordinary phenomenon. While most of the clergy saw in them the hand of God, Paul Dudley, trained in law and honored by the Royal Society for his investigations in natural history, advanced the theory that the earthquake resulted from the motion of the earth's crust. But the first really scientific explanation of the earthquake was that advanced in 1759 by Professor Winthrop of Harvard. Using the inductive method, Winthrop concluded that the disturbance of the earth's crust seemed to be waves of motion which transmitted a pendulum-like movement to houses and barns. Applying computation to the phenomenon, he drew an analogy between musical vibrations and seismic motions. In 1785 Winthrop's pupil and successor, Samuel Williams, developed his teacher's seismic theories, maintaining that the earth's undulations resulted from a strong elastic vapor which moved along the under surface of the earth, producing fire in the bowels of the earth as it advanced. However crude these explanations now seem, they were at the time in accord with the most advanced scientific theories; and what is of greater significance, they were at least in part arrived at by empirical observations and mathematical calculations, and advanced with some degree of tentativeness. The fact that was most important was that earthquakes were accounted for by natural rather than by supernatural agencies.

Often standing on the verge of original work in the field of thermodynamics, Winthrop supplied Benjamin Franklin with aid in his studies of atmospheric electricity. It was of course Franklin's work in this field that established American science in the eyes of European contemporaries. Only slightly familiar with the emerging European literature on electricity, Franklin conducted a thorough analysis of the Leyden jar and in consequence revised the first general theory of electricity, that of Dufay. Franklin advanced the single-fluid theory of electricity and contributed the language ("plus" and "minus") for its description. His theory enabled him to make measurements, therein proving its superiority to the two-fluid theory, and to explain adequately the condenser and the phenomena of repulsion and attraction. A true scientist, Franklin devised various ways for testing his theory, one of which was the famous kite experiment. Unfamiliar, apparently, with the theories of certain French savants which identified electricity and lightning, in his identification Franklin depended on his own previous analyses of the

Leyden jar and on his own theory concerning the nature of electricity. The kite experiment, the date of which is somewhat obscure, confirmed his thesis that machine-made or frictional electricity was identical with atmospheric electricity. The significance of his experiment has been popularly overemphasized, but it did make his original contributions to electrical theory better known. His hypothesis and theories, advanced first in letters to an English correspondent and presented by him to the Royal Society, were published in 1751 as *Experiments and Observations on Electricity made at Philadelphia in America*, a book rightly regarded as one of the most important treatises in the history of man's knowledge of electricity. French scientists confirmed his findings, but Franklin's honor remains that of an original mind.

Because of the great popularity it achieved, Franklin's work had a double significance. It contributed to an explanation of the phenomenon of lightning, one of nature's wildest spectacles. But it also increased the respect of the popular mind for natural philosophy. Lightning, like earthquakes, comets, violent storms, and other awesome displays of nature, had always been a principal source of dread and speculation about the supernatural. Franklin helped tame the thunderbolt, and by doing so helped foster a more empirical and less fearful attitude toward the world. Franklin also discovered a way of controlling lightning. In hitting on the fact that "points have a property by which they can draw on as well as throw off the electrical fluid at a greater distance than blunt bodies can," and that atmospheric electricity could be drawn from the skies through a wet string and passed off in visible sparks through a key, he took the easy next step to the invention of the lightning rod.

The invention of the lightning rod was only one illustration of Franklin's conviction that science should promote general well-being. His practical interest did not stop with experimentation and theory; he illustrated the relationship between science and its application to everyday life for the increase of comfort and well-being by inventing a stove that vastly improved the heating of houses, and by suggesting bifocal lenses, daylight saving, and air bathing. Out of a concern for sailing vessels on the high seas and for man's good in other situations, Franklin provided proof of the movement of cyclonic storms, constructed a pioneer map of the Gulf Stream, studied the behavior of oil in water, and investigated many other phenomena in natural history, chemistry, geology, mathematics, and physics.

While utilitarianism governed Franklin's conception of science—he once apologized for spending time in a mathematical exercise which could have no useful bearing—it did not exclude a larger vision. To the criticism that the new experiments in balloon flights were utterly useless Franklin rejoined by asking. "Of what use are new born babies?" With unusual honesty he admitted his own lack of patience with the indispensable process of verification and willingly heard all he could against his favorite theories. Thus he achieved in remarkable degree the true scientist's ideal in preferring to have truth prevail, even if over his most cherished hypotheses. And his groping realization of the relative rather than the absolutistic character of truth was in itself of great potential value to scientific theory.

Franklin, then, with Colden and Winthrop, demonstrated that American scientists could on occasion concern themselves with larger theories and general principles. Yet his interest in the utilization of scientific knowledge for man's good was characteristic of the humane inventor, the utilitarian. In the field of mechanics the utilitarian motive which American soil nourished found many illustrations. In a pioneer country labor-saving expedients were particularly necessary; before the middle of the seventeenth century an important improvement in a sawmill was patented. German mechanics in Lancaster, Pennsylvania, perfected the "Kentucky rifle," an asset alike to the patriots in the Revolution and to pioneers in the wilderness. The names of at least two inventors should not be lost from the record of our intellectual history. Christopher Colles built the first steam engine in the colonies; and before the Revolution the principle of an improvement in flour milling was simmering in the mind of Oliver Evans, pioneer in many fields of invention.

## The Status of Medical Knowledge

An equally utilitarian application of scientific knowledge was found in the practice of medicine. The effort to cure the sick also illustrates well the conflict between superstitious traditionalism and scientific procedure. Not only in America but in Europe itself the status of medical knowledge at the end of our colonial period seems primitive from the standpoint of today. That germs were the cause of many diseases was not yet suspected; and in the absence of clinical thermometers and stethoscopes diagnosis was naturally very faulty. Anesthetics were not in use, and many important agents in materia medica, such as ergot, iodine, morphia, and strychnine, were not yet in vogue. Almost all physicians were prone to use excessive drugs, both in quantity and in kind. Even worse in its effects on therapeutics was the doctrine of correspondence. The best physicians accepted, a priori, general theories of the cause of disease and then applied the specific that seemed logical. Thus blood-letting was carried to incredible lengths on the assumption that it was the proper means, with blistering and emetics, of relieving the system of "morbid acrimonies, and other matters in the blood."

In colonial America certain social and economic conditions still further handicapped the advance of professional medicine. Not until the second quarter of the eighteenth century did many young men go to Edin-burgh, London, and other medical centers for their training; the great majority of the physicians on the eve of the Revolution were trained as apprentices to established practitioners. The fact that only in the larger towns could physicians devote their entire time to medicine, since in most communities the practitioner had to supplement his meager income by farming or some other vocation, put yet another check on professional development. Specialization was frowned upon; it made faltering head-way even in the largest towns only after the mid-century. With popula-tion widely dispersed, with few and bad roads, with little ready cash in the pockets of great numbers of the common people, much reliance was put on self-treatment. George Fisher's *The American Instructor, to which is added The Poor Planter's Physician,* and John Wesley's *Primi-tive Physick, or An Easy and Natural Method of Curing Most Diseases,* are examples of popular books of home medicine.

Although trained physicians did not themselves continue generally to employ folk notions such as administering drugs according to the phases of the moon, and using manure for poulticing sores, spider webs for treating fever, and rattlesnake poison mixed with cheese for rheuma-tism, they had to contend against such practices. Matters were not helped by the fact that quacks abounded. The poverty of great numbers of people, together with their credulity, made them, then as now, easy prey to unscrupulous vendors of miraculous cure-alls.

In still other ways popular prejudice stood in the way of medical advance. Although autopsies were occasionally performed in the seven-teenth century, religious prejudices against such practices made it almost impossible for physicians to use cadavers in teaching anatomy. Angry crowds opposed such attempts, and Dr. William Shippen, who announced a course of lectures in 1762 in Philadelphia, found it necessary on one occasion to hide from an enraged citizenry. The generally held belief that epidemics were visitations of an angry God likewise halted empirical inquiries into the occasion of such catastrophes.

On the other hand the scientific attitude did make definite advance, especially after the first quarter of the eighteenth century. This followed partly from the fact that a larger number of young men received their training in European medical centers. The growth of rationalism in religious circles further facilitated the use of empirical methods and provided encouragement for concerted efforts to discover natural causes and natural remedies for diseases. The establishment of a hospital in Philadelphia in 1752, and of medical schools in the same city and in New York in the 1760s, was a milestone. Although the great body of practitioners remained unorganized, three medical associations had been established before the outbreak of the Revolution, and legislative provisions for the regulation and improvement of practice were making progress in the larger towns.

With increasing frequency individual physicians conducted experiments which heralded a new spirit. Thus, Dr. Lining of Charleston investigated the spread of "noninfectious epidemic diseases" and in a series of pioneer experiments in human metabolism studied the relation of the weight of food to bodily exertions and fluctuations in perspiration. Yellow fever was the subject of interest and scientific observation; the studies of Dr. John Mitchell of Virginia were to play a subsequent role of importance in Philadelphia at the end of the century. Cadwallader Colden's *Treatise on Wounds and Fevers* and his extensive contributions to materia medica helped to establish his European reputation. In 1736 Dr. William Douglass of Boston published the first adequate clinical description of scarlet fever, a significant contribution. But in many respects the most memorable pioneer and hero in the annals of eighteenth-century American medicine was Dr. Zabdiel Boylston of Boston. In opposition to the European-trained leaders of the profession, Boylston experimented with inoculation against smallpox and was ultimately rewarded by the Royal Society. The time was still far in the future when American medicine would enjoy a reputation for originality as well as competency, but the record was not altogether blank.

In accepting, modifying, and extending the venerable classical tradition and the rising body of scientific knowledge colonial Americans once more showed that in spite of their isolation at least their intellectual leaders belonged to the western community of knowledge. While the classics and polite literature, which were regarded as indispensable to the training of a learned clergy and the education of gentlemen, continued as in Europe to set the social classes apart, science promised to close somewhat the gulf between the learned few and the uncultivated many. Many clergymen welcomed science as an additional support for theology. But it was also welcomed because it was useful in helping colonists to conquer the wilderness, to advance their social status, and to achieve wealth and comfort.

The development of a body of scientific knowledge regarding the universe and the application of parts of this knowledge to the increase of man's worldly goods and the improvement of his physical health had other consequences. It tended to promote secularism and faith in the ability of human reason to find the truth and to use it to improve the human lot. At the same time that man's faith in supernaturalism, whether in matters of cosmology or of therapeutics, was diminished, his conception of human nature, of social relations, and of the Deity became more rational, that is, he viewed such matters as more subject to investigation in terms of reason and nature. But this is another story.

# 5 The Rise of the Enlightenment

*The Prime Immunity in Mans State, is that he is most properly the Subject of the Law of Nature. . . . The Second Great Immunity of Man is an Original Liberty Instampt upon his Rational Nature. He that intrudes upon this Liberty, Violates the Law of Nature. . . . The Third Capital Immunity belonging to Mans Nature, is an equality amongst Men. . . .*

—JOHN WISE, 1717

Among the legacies transmitted to the new nation the pattern of thought known as the Enlightenment was one of the most important. In Kant's celebrated words, the Enlightenment was "the liberation of man from his self-caused state of minority." It was a protest against traditional reliance on authority in religious and secular life. It asserted man's ability to understand the universe without supernatural revelation and without the authoritative guidance of earthly superiors. It assumed the original worth and dignity of all men, and challenged the comfortable to alleviate the harsh lot of the poverty-stricken and ignorant masses and the victims of irrational and inhumane social conditions.

The apostles of the Enlightenment were under the spell of the Newtonian conception of a harmonious, law-governed universe, a rational

98

system ruled by the mathematical law of cause and effect. The assumption was that man, as a part of this rational universe, could understand it through his own reason; it was no longer necessary to view the universe as a mystery only partially explained by divine revelation. Religious doctrines must consequently be tested by reason and accepted only if found to be in accord with the great rational design of the universe as comprehended by man's mind. To the true son of the Enlightenment the only religion validated by mathematics, logic, and scientific observation and experiment was deism—a philosophy conceiving of the Deity as an architect who had planned and set in motion a harmonious and self-regulating universe.

According to the philosophy of the Enlightenment, human nature was not predetermined by an arbitrary deity; it was the natural result of the environment that molded it. Man possessed no innate ideas; his mind was the product of his experiences, good and bad. Total depravity and predestination were mere religious fictions invented by the priests to reinforce their control over the credulous. If human nature contained large elements of evil, these were simply the result of natural causes—irrational conditions and an authoritative type of training. Man had the power to improve his own nature by improving his environment through science and education so it would accord with reason and natural law. Thus the Enlightenment conceived of human nature in optimistic terms.

Political, social, and economic theories no longer rested on supernatural revelation, but on natural law. The ancient theory of contract under natural law was invoked to explain the procedure by which man had forged society from the original state of nature in which individuals existed like so many atoms. Thus the state and society were not organic but mechanistic; they were merely an artificial entity. The only ultimate reality was the individual, whose natural rights to life, liberty, property, and the pursuit of happiness could not rightfully be alienated by the state. If the state did violate the natural law of the universe by alienating these rights, then in the interest of reason and justice men could and should resort to revolution. Since man could in any case test institutions by reason and reform them according to its light, the world was infinitely perfectible. The heavenly city was here on this earth, and man was to achieve it through his own rational powers. Belief in these powers constituted, as Carl Becker has maintained, a new religious faith.

These basic ideas of the Enlightenment were deeply rooted in the growth of secularism and the science that had been transforming western Europe since the late Middle Ages and especially since the Renaissance. The great popularity of the Enlightenment in the late seventeenth and eighteenth centuries can be only partly explained, however, by the scientific progress of the period and the consequent delimitation of the area in which supernaturalism flourished.

The ideas of the Enlightenment answered new needs resulting from new ways of life. The rising middle classes needed ideas quite different from those that had served the priestly and feudal classes. Natural science was a more useful instrument in guiding them in their mercantile enterprise than the revealed word. The pursuit of commerce called for religious toleration, the civil liberties, respect for property, and security of property from arbitrary taxation. The middle classes needed individual freedom for enterprise. They needed to be released from the hampering economic doctrines that a religious and feudal society had imposed against taking interest and "undue" profits. They required not an organic, regulatory state, but one invested with mere police powers. An environment allowing for personal freedom, so necessary to commerce and trade, came to be regarded as the natural environment, the one in accord with the great harmonious mathematical laws of the universe itself. A philosophy of free will rather than of predestination, one which assumed that reason and natural law enabled man to control his environment and mold his destiny, seemed plausible to men with such requirements. Optimism and faith in progress stood high in the scale of values of the middle classes. Thus the doctrines of the Enlightenment provided these classes, especially the trading folk, with ideas congenial to their interests.

It might appear that colonial society was an uncongenial soil for the growth of the Enlightenment. Colonial thought was dominated by religion, and though trade prospered, agriculture with its long feudal past formed the primary basis of the economy. But certain considerations offset these facts. Agriculture was not, as in Europe, glutted with feudal remains. It was largely an agriculture of the small independent farmer or of the planter who as an exporter of staple crops was something of a business man or at least in close touch with merchants. Then, too, the religion that dominated colonial life contained, as we shall see, elements favorable to an emphasis on reason and on a humanity operative in this world. Thus not only among the leaders of the trading class but among the clergy and the landed proprietors were to be found ardent disciples of the new faith.

Commerce and trade and the urban life, which grew rapidly along the Atlantic seacoast throughout the eighteenth century, provided fertile soil for the growth of ideas characteristic of the Enlightenment. The fact that many peoples with conflicting religious ideas were living together helped to break down religious authoritarianism; some degree of toleration was a practical necessity if order and prosperity were to be realized. These peoples had come to America to be free from authority—in many cases from the authority of a particular kind of religion or from that of a landed gentry or a restrictive trade guild system. They had come here to realize a fuller life as individuals, and in the belief that America had a future which human effort might shape. Colonial conditions—above all, the existence of free or cheap lands and other natural resources—proved that they were not entirely wrong.

The predominantly agricultural and religious character of colonial society and thought and its remoteness from European centers of intellectual life explain in part why the Enlightenment developed later in America than in Europe. But conditions favorable to it did exist, and it did develop. Its rise and growth provided the most exciting intellectual experience of the men and women who looked with increasing favor on the "great truths" which were congenial to their physical and spiritual needs.

## Rationalism in Religion

Recent scholarship has emphasized the place that Puritanism made for the exercise of reason in the solution of both daily problems and theological mysteries. Roger Williams, it will be recalled, was a true precursor of the Enlightenment in his opposition to external compulsion in matters of faith and belief—in his insistence that all men, and not merely priestly scholars, were capable of understanding truth. And Roger Williams' imperishable pleas for religious freedom were not the only elements in Puritan thought that foreshadowed the rationalism of the Enlightenment. Even the most orthodox Puritans believed that the truth of Scripture was to be upheld by means of "right reason." In according prominence to the humanistic logic of the great French Protestant thinker, Petrus Ramus, New England Puritans modified the Aristotelian and scholastic logic and the metaphysics of Calvin. Many shared with Ramus the conviction that the inherently rational universe was comprehensible by man's reason. Thus the way was open for Puritans to extend hospitality to Copernican and Newtonian science, when it promised a better key to the universe than did Aristotelianism and scholastic physics.

The favor accorded the new science by many Puritan divines was probably not a deviation from Puritanism but an expression of the rational element in the Ramean interpretation of it. Charles Morton's *Compendium Physicae,* a traditional work in some respects, nevertheless gave a place to much of the newer science and paved the way for the full introduction of Newtonianism in the 1730s and 1740s by such men as Isaac Greenwood and John Winthrop. Even Cotton Mather and Jonathan Edwards responded to the implications of the rational element in Puritanism and attempted to meet the challenge of the new science to theology.

Anglicanism reserved a large compartment for rationalism. Holding that the Bible did not specify every minute detail of the workings of God, many Anglicans regarded Scripture as a general guide rather than a complete code of laws. It was not difficult for them, therefore, to give large scope to natural rather than to supernatural processes in everyday matters. In putting less emphasis than Puritanism on the depravity of man and more on God's grace, Anglicanism made it relatively easy for its adherents to give a considerable role to reason. Thus the Reverend William Smith, provost of the College of Philadelphia, contended that the God-given faculties of reason and understanding must be improved in the interest of truth and happiness, and insisted that young men would be more receptive to the truth and value of Christianity if its accord with reason and natural law were clearly demonstrated. Samuel Johnson, a New England Puritan, in reacting against the grim bearings of the Calvinism he had known among the Yale theologians, went straight over to the Anglican camp and to Bishop Berkeley's philosophical idealism. Calvinism, Johnson declared, "reflects dishonour upon the Best of Beings." All beings, he continued, whatever their race or age, have the capacity to comprehend God's beneficent purposes and plans through intellectual light. However tenaciously Johnson clung to Berkelian idealism in order to support his faith against the onslaughts of a more thoroughgoing rationalism, he nevertheless marks a halfway point between the older Calvinism and the more rationalistic religious position of the deists. As president of King's College he was in a position to influence important groups in New York as well as the youth under his charge.

As Newton's exposition of the rational nature of the universe was more widely accepted, a group of New England clergymen carried further the rationalistic implications in Puritanism itself. Newton's influence accounts in part for the rationalistic tone in the writings of Benjamin Colman of Boston, who declared for the principle of rationality both in the Deity and in His human creatures. The reading of such seventeenth- and early eighteenth-century English latitudinarian and rationalistic theologians as Herbert of Cherbury, Chillingworth, Locke, Taylor, Clarke, and Tillotson further strengthened Puritan divines in their new views, for these English theologians had absorbed, among many streams of thought, the teachings of the Dutch Arminius, who had emphasized man's cooperation in salvation as well as God's grace. The Puritan doctrine that God had given man his reason to use in pursuit of the truth influenced such New England parsons as Lemuel Briant, Ebenezer Gay, Solomon Stoddard, and Peter Bulkeley to apply the test of reason to some of the chief problems of religion.

The shift away from revealed religion to natural religion is illustrated by the theology of John Wise. This Ipswich minister, whose father was an indentured servant and who himself had gone to jail for protesting against the regime of Governor Andros, declared that "right reason, that great oracle in human affairs, is the soul of man so formed and endowed by creation with a certain sagacity or acumen whereby man's intellect is enabled to take up the true idea or perception of things agreeable with and according to their natures." In a subsequent book this champion of democracy in church and in secular government argued for reason and revelation as equally valid.

During this period the rationalistic emphasis in theological thought led to modifications of the doctrines of predestination and Trinitarianism. Jonathan Mayhew of the West Church in Boston expounded his belief in rational liberty and in man's capacity to determine his fate. In his discussion of theological problems he applied the rational method; the light of nature and the law of Moses pointed, he urged, to the same duties of man. In Mayhew's insistence on the unity of the Deity and in his conception of the subordinate nature of Christ he was close to the Unitarian position, a significant outcome of rationalistic theology. The rationalistic interest in the nature of Christ led to the republication in

Boston in 1756 of *The Humble Inquiry into the Scripture Account of Jesus Christ*, whose author, Thomas Emlyn, was the first minister in England to call himself a Unitarian. Mayhew's own successor at West Church, the Reverend Simon Howard, rejected on rational grounds the Calvinistic tenet of predestination and total depravity and virtually denied the doctrine of the Trinity.

The positive corollary of the protest against the Calvinistic conception of a harsh and omnipotent Deity who had predestined the greater part of mankind to eternal damnation was the conception of God as a divine father whose entire relations with all His creatures reflected His beneficence and their divinity. This was the position of Charles Chauncy of the First Church in Boston. Although it was not published until 1784, his *Beneficence of the Deity* was actually written in 1755. This treatise marked the systematic exposition of the ideas Chauncy had been expounding from the pulpit ever since 1739, when he preached a sermon in favor of religious toleration. Sickened at the horrors pictured by the itinerant evangelists of the Great Awakening, Chauncy taught that God is a rational being who gives evidence of His essential goodness in the creation and the endowment of man, who partakes of the same nature as Himself. Total depravity and the constant intervention of the Deity in man's daily affairs had no place in his thought. The general position of Mayhew and Chauncy anticipated the Unitarianism and Universalism that became explicit and institutionally expressed in the last decades of the eighteenth century.

## The Spread of Rationalism and Deism

By 1740 the rationalistic theology of the more liberal New England clergymen had made considerable headway among the upper classes in the larger towns. Deism itself, a logical development of rationalism in theology, was also winning recognition. Deism had been formulated by such seventeenth-century and early eighteenth-century English writers as Blount, Tindal, Shaftesbury, Collins, and others. They deduced from Newton's picture of the universe as a law-governed machine the corollary of God as First Cause, as a supreme architect who, having created a perfect self-regulating machine, was no longer concerned with His creation. With an alarm perhaps unwarranted by the facts, the English

revivalist Whitefield reported that the writings of such deists as Tillotson and Clarke enjoyed great popularity among Harvard students. He
was no less exercised over the fact that the library which Bishop Berkeley
bequeathed to Yale contained some thirty volumes written by exponents
of rationalism in religion. At Newport the painter Robert Feke was the
center of a group that read and discussed deistic writings. It was also
from Newport that the freethinking printer, Theophilus Cossart, traveled about the colonies, no doubt spreading his unorthodox wares. At
Philadelphia a circle of which Franklin was in a sense the center imbibed
the new ideas. The Library Company of Pennsylvania's capital was
amply supplied with the writings of the great rationalists and deists.
According to the Reverend Jonathan Dickinson, Philadelphia coffee-
houses were by mid-century the scene of considerable deistic talk. Whitefield preached in that city for the special benefit of "Reasoning Unbeliev-
ers." Some of Virginia's gentry were exposed to such advanced doctrines
at William and Mary, and many planters read deistic literature in
their own libraries and more than half accepted its teachings. At Savannah in 1737 John Wesley discovered an avowed deist! Presently the
great evangelist declared that deism was a greater menace to the colony
than popery itself.

The spread of the ideas of British and French deists and rationalists
was facilitated not only by the importation of their books but by the
discussion of their theories in colonial periodicals. Although editors
generally pictured Voltaire as a devil and a brilliant wit, Jeremy Gridley, learned Boston lawyer and a leading contributor to the *American
Magazine and Historical Chronicle*, showed the "great philosopher"
proper respect. Voltaire's *Treatise on Tolerance* and his *Philosophical
Dictionary* were frequently referred to, and long extracts from his tales,
historical writings, and essays appeared in the periodical press. The
poetical versions of rationalism and deism in the writings of Pope and
other English poets likewise gained fragmentary admittance to the pages
of colonial magazines in the years following the mid-century.

Newspaper readers also began to get glimmerings of the new approach
to religion and the universe. Some journals included deistic pieces and
others printed articles written to refute these heresies. In 1739 the
*Charleston Gazette* discussed rationalism and deism, and the spread of
"infidelity" was deplored by Alexander Graham, another South Carolina
writer. Certain New York journals opened their columns to the new

dispensation. William Livingston, himself a liberal member of the Dutch Reformed church, founded his *Independent Reflector* in 1752 to oppose, among other "ogres," superstition, priestcraft, and bigotry. The same year saw the appearance in James Parker's *New York Gazette* of an allegorical polemic against revealed religion. Although Parker was threatened with legal action, Franklin urged Governor Colden to stay the prosecution on the ground that publicity would give even greater effectiveness to the article. Parker in any case subsequently recanted.

It is difficult to estimate the extent to which deistic ideas had spread by the eve of the American Revolution. John Adams testified that "the principles of Deism had made considerable progress" in the outlying towns of Massachusetts. It is probable that deism was largely confined to the better educated, for newspaper readers made up only a small proportion of the population, and it was only an occasional almanac that incorporated any part of Voltaire's creed. In any case, certainly the mass of the people read very little. Explicit evidence points in the same direction. Dr. William Douglass of Boston declared that "the wise and thinking" part of the population had learned by the mid-century to regulate itself by natural religion (a religion which squared with reason and science). On the eve of the Revolution Joseph Clarke, a prominent citizen of Northampton, Massachusetts, felt it necessary in ordering certain works on natural religion from a Boston bookdealer to take great precautions for secrecy lest people in their "bigoted attachment" to orthodoxy cast infamy on him because he was known to be interested in unorthodox volumes.

Between the rationalistic outlook on theology and cosmology and deism itself in its concrete and fully developed form there was no sharp dividing line. In general, the cultivated man who espoused the rationalistic or moderately deistic position elevated reason to a position on a par with revelation; only a few went so far as to repudiate revelation altogether, and fewer still subscribed to a definitely "materialistic" or "atheistic" position. Joseph Hawley, a lawyer of Northampton, Massachusetts, and John Adams did embrace skepticism for a time. To these representatives of the advance guard Franklin must be added. Although in his youth he went so far as to reduce God to a machine, to deny His providence and man's free will, to question the conception of sin and of personal immortality, he presently retreated to the moderate deistic position which stopped considerably short of such extremes. Other prominent men, including Virginians who were to play leading parts in the Revolution, continued to maintain nominal affiliations with churches and avoided open espousals of deism in its advanced forms.

Further investigation may yield a more complete and satisfactory explanation for the acceptance of a moderate form of deism by many among the fortunate classes. Where authority is concentrated in a military or political or religious aristocracy and the masses are ignorant and poor, faith in an arbitrary God would naturally prevail more widely, and the need for mercy and for divine intervention be more widely felt, than in a society where a relatively prosperous and less ignorant middle class was beginning to be important and in which business men and successful farmers could attain both money and learning. Many such men, one might suppose, would not need the comforts of the old religion and would be equipped to understand the new. Very likely many thoughtful men were influenced to entertain the new doctrines by such excesses as those of the witchcraft delusion and the Great Awakening.

However one may account for the appeal of the rationalistic and deistic ideas to many educated men, the reasons for their failure to spread widely among the common people in this period can more easily be understood. One factor, perhaps a minor one, was the attitude of many among the favored classes who regarded religion as an important device for maintaining order and discipline among the "meaner sort" of folk. In 1745 a writer in the *American Magazine* urged reasonable men to hold "infidels" in contempt because they tended to become the "Idols of the Mob." Religious teachings, this writer continued, kept the "Rabble" orderly; deism might well promote social upheaval. Many among the substantial classes probably agreed with Franklin that even if the more extreme form of deism was valid, it could not be useful. As Franklin put it, "talking against religion is unchaining a tiger; the beast let loose may worry his liberator." Franklin and those who agreed with him feared that attacks on religion might, in short, sap morality among the feeble and ignorant. In holding that religion was justified by its moral utility and its value in social control of the masses, the humane and generally liberal Franklin probably represented the point of view of the class into which he had moved since the days of his apprenticeship in the printing trade.

The opposition of such men as Franklin to the spread of deism among the plain people was by no means the most important reason for the relatively slight headway it made in popular thought. Not many ordinary folk read books on the intellectual level of rationalism and deism, or periodicals, or even newspapers. The rationalism of the minority of liberal New England ministers was overshadowed by the orthodoxy of the great majority of clergymen who reached the plain people. When secularism and religious indifference had begun to make headway among the humble ranks of society, the Great Awakening checked these tendencies. The doctrine of repentance or hellfire aroused exciting emotions as rationalistic religion did not. It is also possible that many small farmers, shopkeepers, artisans, and longshoremen saw no advantage in espousing deism, associated as it was in their minds with the upper classes, the very classes that were unpopular for their unwillingness to concede political privileges or to grant economic measures, such as paper money, which the lower classes desired. Under revolutionary conditions. however, rationalism and deism were to become instruments by which the militant common man defied the authority both of the churches and of the established classes.

## Social and Economic Theory

Just as European formulations of rationalism and deism found American sympathizers, so did the social and economic thought of the Enlightenment. The emergence in Europe of this body of thought was related on the one hand to the tendency to apply the Newtonian formulations of the physical universe to social and economic relationships, to substitute a rational and secular scheme for a supernatural and organic ethic. It was also in part conditioned by new problems born of a growing commerce and the early stages of industrialism in England, problems of the family, class relationships, population, the role of the state in the economic realm, and war. The rising middle class generally disliked the traditional conception of a static and organic theory of politics and economics. Many entrepreneurs especially disliked the fettering restrictions imposed on business enterprise by English mercantilism. Adam Smith and other theorists explored the relations between land, industry, trade, wealth, and general well-being. With the appearance in 1776 of the *Wealth of Nations* the foundations of classical economics were laid and an intellectual defense for laissez faire was outlined.

American interest in economic problems was naturally stimulated by these developments in the motherland as well as by the increasing complexity of American social and economic life. The seventeenth-century theory that economic and social issues were tied to religion, which Puritans and Quakers had taken with special seriousness, was supplemented or even replaced by the new secular and rationalistic approach. The incidental attention given to economic and social theory in collegiate instruction in connection with the classics, theology, and philosophy was enlarged at William and Mary, where in 1724 Hugh Jones advocated the study of American history and the training of young men for colonial civil service through the social disciplines. In 1754 the College of Philadelphia announced instruction in "The Ends and Uses of Society," and King's College moved in the same direction. A larger proportion of students chose to wrestle with social, political, and economic theories in their disputations. The growing attention given to the study of law in the offices of practitioners was another indication of the increasing importance of a body of thought and knowledge directly related to the needs of an ever more complex economy. The classical curriculum was, to be sure, still regarded as the necessary preparation for the professions, but the increasing interest in the social disciplines was nevertheless well defined.

Economic conflicts within the colonies occasioned sharply pointed discussions in which the first American contributions to economic theory were made. Agriculture, trade, taxation, and, above all, currency provided the subject matter for a considerable body of writing in which every interest was supported and attacked by lawyers, newspaper editors, clergymen, planters, merchants, and public officials. Most of these ephemeral writings reflected heat rather than light, but they accustomed Americans to read and write on controversial economic issues. They also placed less emphasis than former discussions, especially those of the seventeenth-century Puritans, on the idea that God's plan and will, not man's, was the directing force in economic matters. The implication that can could control his earthly goods rationally was an evidence that the Enlightenment was operating in the field of American economic thought.

Franklin alone of the colonial writers on economic theory has continued to interest students of the subject, despite the fact that he developed no well-defined and systematic body of economic doctrine. He did not even master the greatest of the European theorists who dealt with the physiocratic dogma that all value inheres in the land, a doctrine he accepted in part. But his economic writing shows no trace of belief in the supernatural. He expresses unequivocally his conviction that economic relations should be and are by nature rational, and that man's mind can and should understand these relationships and guide him in advancing general well-being on this earth.

In their orientation to middle-class interests Franklin's economic ideas are further related to the Enlightenment. Within the middle-class framework of his economic thinking he generally weighted his ideas on the side of the less well-established artisans and indebted farmers. By insisting that gold and silver are commodities, he contributed to the development of the quantitative theory of monetary value. He followed Sir William Petty in selecting labor rather than precious metal as the measure of value. Franklin was generalizing from American experience when in his *Observations Concerning the Increase of Mankind* (1751) he argued that wages must be high in a country where free land is abundant. In subsequent years he developed the theory of the economics of high wages, and in the spirit of the economic freedom so dear to the Enlightenment attacked pleas for tariffs as "selfish arguments of a favored class." In discussing taxation in his later years the venerable philosopher emphasized the social in contradistinction to the individual origin of property; property, he maintained, is therefore all the more subject to the control of society in the interest of society.

These ideas were, to be sure, overshadowed in the minds of most Americans by Franklin's "Poor Richard" philosophy, which emphasized the so-called capitalistic virtues of hard work, thrift, saving, and expediency. The popularity of this philosophy no doubt lay in the appeal it made to men and women eager to get ahead in an economy in which, however scarce capital might be, opportunities for the enterprising were real.

Many of the older patterns of thought continued to endure and to retard the acceptance of the doctrine of progress, which European philosophers were developing into one of the favorite concepts of the Enlightenment. Many American intellectuals, including Franklin, believed in the so-called great-chain-of-being idea, a philosophical conception that conceived of an hierarchical order of creation in which each being imperceptibly merged with those above and below, filling the entire universe with a "plenitude" in which no further expansion or change could take place. The vogue of the classics in colonial culture must have inclined many who read of the conflict between the "ancients" and "moderns" to side with the "ancients." And, of course, the traditional Calvinistic doctrine of an unmalleable human nature ran counter to faith in unlimited progress.

Yet there was much in colonial life and thought that made the doctrine of progress acceptable. The rapid growth of everything in America encouraged its inhabitants to envision a limitless future development. The achievements of science and the Baconian conception of the social utopia that science might effect fed the springs of the faith in progress. A contributor to the *Virginia Gazette* in 1737 represented a fairly widely held faith in the glorious future of the human mind: "The world, but a few ages since, was in a very poor condition as to trade and navigation. Nor, indeed, were they much better in other matters of useful knowledge. All knowledge of mathematics, of nature, of the brightest part of human wisdom, had their admission among us within the last two centuries. The world is now daily increasing in experimental knowledge and let no man flatter the age with pretending we are arrived to a perfection in discoveries." The idea of progress, which was to enjoy a peculiarly American flowering in the Revolutionary era, was one of the most significant legacies of the eighteenth century to the America of the nineteenth.

## The Natural Rights Philosophy

No less characteristic of the Enlightenment or any less important in late eighteenth-century American thought than the idea of progress was the natural rights philosophy. According to this philosophy, to which ancient, medieval, and early modern writers had contributed, men originally lived in a state of nature without benefit of civil authority. Possessing the same natural rights and governed by the same natural laws—the rights to life, liberty, property, and the pursuit of happiness—each enforced these rights as best he could. Since the strong often took advantage of the weak, men surrendered, in accordance with the dictates of reason, the state of nature for the civil state. In doing so they merely surrendered the right to enforce their natural rights individually; the rights themselves were not surrendered, contrary to the view of Hobbes and other exponents of absolute monarchy. These rights, which were frequently identified with the law of God, no ruler could subvert. Implicit in the contract theory of the origin of civil authority were the corollary doctrines of the consent of the governed, popular sovereignty, and the right of revolution.

The seventeenth-century Puritans in Great Britain forged the natural rights philosophy into a powerful weapon in their contest with royal and ecclesiastical authority, and the Calvinists in New England and the Middle and Southern Colonies enjoyed as part of their inheritance this philosophy as elaborated in the writings of Harrington, Milton, Sydney, and, somewhat later, Locke. Not only were they acquainted with the natural rights philosophy; they actually put it into operation in covenanting with one another in the new communities established on the various frontiers of New England or in the backcountry of the Middle and Southern Colonies. In the realm of ecclesiastical organization too, this philosophy was frequently invoked. In 1648, for example, the Reverend Thomas Hooker, leader in establishing Hartford, supported the Congregational doctrine of the original ecclesiastical equality of all church members. Although men had mutually covenanted to subject themselves and thus had forged the sinews by which a religious society is "sustained and supported," they nevertheless reserved the right to proceed against any officer "that goes aside." At the beginning of the eighteenth century John Wise enlisted the natural rights philosophy in support of the traditional Congregational form of church polity, which was threatened by adherents of Presbyterianism.

While the natural rights philosophy was nourished chiefly by Calvinist clergymen and brought forth most often to serve the more democratic position in ecclesiastical controversies, it occasionally did service in the political sphere as well. The overthrow of the regime of Governor Andros in 1689 was justified by appeals to the right of revolution against tyranny. On the centennial anniversary of the execution of Charles I, the Reverend Jonathan Mayhew of Boston justified the action of the regicides by an appeal to the natural rights philosophy in general and to the right of revolution in particular. "When once magistrates act contrary to their office," Mayhew insisted, "when they rob and ruin the public, instead of being guardians of its peace and welfare, they immediately cease to be the *ordinance* and *ministers* of God; and no more deserve that glorious character than common *pirates* and *highwaymen*." In conclusion he declared that for a nation thus abused to resist their prince, even to dethrone him, was "but a reasonable way of vindicating their liberties and just rights"; it was merely "making use of the means, and the only means, which God has put into their power, for mutual and self-defense. And it would be highly criminal in them, not to make use of this means."[1] No wonder that this sermon by Mayhew was remembered and reprinted on the eve of the Revolution!

Lawyers as well as clergymen popularized the natural rights philosophy. In 1728 Daniel Dulany, attorney general of Maryland, quoted an array of great political philosophers to support the concept of a basic natural law which no human authority could subvert. The philosophy was still further popularized by the legal writings of Blackstone, which were read by plantation gentlemen as well as by candidates for the bar. James Otis, a Boston lawyer, cited the natural rights of self-taxation, personal liberty, and freedom in his opposition to the writs of assistance and the revenue act of 1764. "The colonists being men, have a right to be considered as equally entitled to all the rights of Nature with Europeans, and they are not to be restrained, in the exercise of any of these rights, but for the evident good of the whole country."

But it was only gradually that the colonists followed the precedent set by Otis and invoked the natural rights philosophy in their agitation against the policies of the mother country. They appealed rather to their rights as Englishmen, to their colonial charters, and finally to their conception of an imperial federation of self-governing dominions. When London brushed all these arguments aside, then the patriots resorted to the full implications of the natural rights philosophy. Erudite revolutionists like John Adams made good use of such authorities as Machiavelli, Bodin, and the still disputed author of *Vindiciae Contra Tyrannos*. But it was Burlamqui, Vattel, Grotius, and Pufendorf, together with the Puritan theorists of the seventeenth century, and above all Locke, who enjoyed the widest popularity. Hence when Jefferson put the doctrine of natural rights into the imperishable words of the Declaration of Independence, it was already familiar to Americans through the writings of well-known leaders and pamphleteers.

Although most colonial expositions of the natural rights philosophy showed little sympathy with its "leveling" implications, these played some part in the protests against special privileges. Judge Samuel Sewall

---

[1] Jonathan Mayhew, A *Discourse Concerning Unlimited Submission and Non-Resistance to the Higher Powers* (Boston, 1750), 24, 40.

of Boston, in his antislavery tract *The Selling of Joseph* (1700), not only appealed to Christian ethics but invoked the laws of nature and of Nature's God against slaveholding. As the Revolution approached, critics of slavery applauded the application of the natural rights theory to the slave, an early example being the declaration of the Rhode Island assembly in 1774: "Whereas . . . the inhabitants of America are generally engaged in the preservation of their own rights and liberties, among which that of personal freedom must be considered as the greatest, and as those who are desirous of enjoying all the advantages of liberty themselves should be willing to extend personal liberty to others," slaves were henceforth to be free. Advocates of social equality in other human relations were also to appeal to the equalitarian implications of the natural rights philosophy.

### The Growth of Humanitarianism

The growth of humanitarian thought and feeling—a major phase of the Enlightenment—can be understood only in terms of social and economic conditions in the Old World and the New. In Europe humanitarianism was largely, but by no means exclusively, a middle-class phenomenon; and this was inevitably true in America, where the middle classes dominated. The social sympathies of the middle classes with those less fortunate than themselves may have resulted in part from the fact that these social groups were dynamic, recruited from beneath and on the make, and thus somewhat better able to think in terms of social improvement than the traditionally static classes of long-established privilege. But this was not all. The very social evils against which humanitarians protested were the underpinnings on which middle-class prosperity rested—the slave trade; the rise of mines, mills, factories; the growth of grim cities and loathsome slums. Being sensitive in the way that all human beings are more or less sensitive and imbued with the Christian doctrine of brotherhood, middle-class men and women frequently inveighed against the injustice of the slave trade and slavery, against the suffering of the degraded poor. It has been argued that in so doing they were perhaps compensating for less praiseworthy traits, that their humanitarian activities may have been salve for troubled consciences. But whether this is true or not, one cannot deny the high-mindedness and obvious sincerity of the great humanitarian leaders of the middle class. Motivation in such matters varies with individuals and with groups. It is likely to be mixed, complex, impossible to analyze clearly. But the outcome of that motivation in word and deed the historian may trace.

In any case humanitarianism was a body of thought and feeling embracing many ideas and values. The doctrine of progress suggested the possibility, even the inevitability, of elevating the most unfortunate members of society. The natural rights philosophy could be interpreted to justify this elevation as right and just. The rising romantic sentiment, idealizing as it did primitive peoples and emphasizing the dignity of the individual and the beauty of God's creation, also encouraged sympathy for the Indian, the slave, or the wretch near at hand in jail or slum. The romantic poet James Thomson, whose *Seasons* (1726–1730) enjoyed some vogue in America, encouraged the organization of charity and prison reform; Edward Young, whose romantic *Night Thoughts* (1742–1745) rivaled *The Seasons,* also recommended kindness and benevolence as the duty of every living soul. Goldsmith and other romanticists showed their sympathies for the lowly. Carl Becker has suggested that romanticism, with its emphasis on sentiment, was the chief means by which the sons of the Enlightenment attempted to solve the problem of evil; in view of the actual existence of cruelty and brutality in both human nature and the institutions man had made, this problem was inexplicable by rationalism alone or by Locke's repudiation of innate ideas.

No constituent in humanitarianism was more important than Christian ethics and piety, especially as exemplified by Quakers and the evangelical sects. The Quaker doctrine that the golden rule should be put into daily practice led to concern for the unfortunate classes; and despite their preoccupation with eternal life, the evangelicals, because they ministered chiefly to the lowly, could not be blind to the actual miseries of the degraded and impoverished who flooded prisons and slums. Even before the Revolution Granville Sharp, a leading British adherent of evangelicism, was in close touch with colonial humanitarians.

Among other winds that filled the sails of humanitarianism was the deistic faith in the essential goodness and rationality of mankind. Indeed, the humanitarians translated into practice this rationalistic doctrine, which in the hands of so many of its philosophical exponents was largely divorced from action. Typical of the English deists who bridged the gap between theory and action in this respect was Lord Shaftesbury. In his *Characteristics* (1711) he maintained that human nature was not, as Hobbes insisted, egotistical, but was, on the contrary, imbued with moral sense and benevolence, and that this had nothing to do with any religious sanctions. Not only did Shaftesbury himself find admirers in the colonies, but Alexander Pope, whose heroic couplets reflected many of Shaftesbury's doctrines, was read from South Carolina to New Hampshire. Another exponent of natural religion known to colonial intellectuals, Wollaston, expressed the essential doctrine of humanitarianism with admirable incisiveness. "There is something in human nature, resulting from our very make and constitution, which renders us obnoxious to the pains of others, causes us to sympathize with them, and almost comprehend us in their case."

Also central to eighteenth-century humanitarianism was the conviction, not unrelated to deism, that physical and social environment is the dominant factor in shaping human institutions. Montesquieu among others had suggested that differing social environments account for differences in social institutions. As a result of the voyages of discovery which revealed strikingly varied cultures and of Locke's theory that human nature, being plastic at birth, is shaped by its surroundings, the environmentalist position in social thought became increasingly popular in the eighteenth century. The doctrine that physical and social environment determined institutions encouraged the belief that social evil resulted not from God's wrath and curse on mankind but from objective conditions which might be rationally attacked and bettered.

In Scotland Adam Ferguson did much to make environmentalism familiar, and his work was not unknown in the colonies. But Montesquieu was an even more effective popularizer. Among the youthful colonists who read Montesquieu were James Otis, Thomas Jefferson, John Adams, John Dickinson, and Richard Henry Lee. Colonial periodicals began as early as 1745 to include excerpts from Montesquieu's *The Persian Letters*. Before the close of the French and Indian War the *Boston Gazette* printed selections from the *Spirit of the Laws*, hoping that none might suppose that a "Frenchman may have juster Notions of Civil Liberty than some among ourselves." From 1770 to 1776 Montesquieu was not only cited but often quoted at length in the newspapers. Colonial intellectuals further familiarized themselves with the new climate of opinion when they read the *Encyclopedia* of Diderot, a great work which set forth the environmentalist conception of human nature and human institutions and plainly implied that man might control and shape both.

Although environmentalism has many earlier expressions, a classic one is that of the French-American literary husbandman Crèvecœur, who argued that laws, customs, and institutions are governed by the way of life imposed by physical resources. "Men are like plants; the goodness and flavor of the fruit proceeds from the particular soil and exposition in which they grow. We are nothing but what we derive from the air we breathe, the climate we inhabit, the government we obey, the system of religion we profess, and the mode of our employment."[2]

Among the specific humanitarian causes engendered by the doctrine of environmentalism prison reform stood near the top. Having investigated English prisons, James Oglethorpe, a high Tory, promoted the colonization of Georgia as a haven for England's disheartened debtors. Philanthropic persons supplemented the yearly grants of Parliament, which in 1732 made possible the Georgia experiment in humanitarianism and empire—for the new colony was also a pivotal outpost on the border of the Spanish domains. The haven which Georgia was intended to provide for victims of English social and legal anachronisms was also open to the persecuted Protestants of Germany and Switzerland. But despite Oglethorpe's devotion and the zeal of such evangelical leaders as John and Charles Wesley, the humanitarian aspects of the experiment fell by the board; American frontier conditions and individualistic ideology were not well adapted to the planned economy of small holdings and the paternalism on which the founders of the colony counted.

Humanitarian interest in the lot of criminals was also greatly stimulated by the teachings of Beccaria, the Italian philosopher, whose treatise *On Crimes and Punishments* interpreted crime in terms of environmental and utilitarian factors. Beccaria taught that punishments should reform the criminal and deter him from further crime. His devastating criticism of the common infliction of the death penalty for minor crimes found ready response in America, where human beings were more needed than in the overpopulated countries of the Old World. Beccaria was cited by John Adams in his defense of the British soldiers for their part in the Boston Massacre. Jefferson, too, made the acquaintance of Beccaria's book in the decade before independence. But Beccaria's philos-

---

[2] J. Hector St. John de Crèvecœur, *Letters from an American Farmer* (Philadelphia, 1793), 48.

ophy of crime, especially his theory that the penalty should be propor-
tionate to the antisocial character of the crime, was popularized chiefly
through Blackstone's *Commentaries*, the main fare of colonial students
of the law on the threshold of the Revolution.

The most single-minded spokesmen of humanitarianism in colonial
America were the followers of William Penn. It will be recalled that the
Quakers were virtually the conscience of the eighteenth century and
pioneers in almost all humanitarian endeavors. Their doctrine of human
benevolence found expression in their opposition to a harsh penal code.
As early as 1736 American Friends spoke out against excessive drinking,
which was held to be a major cause of poverty. The establishment in
Philadelphia in 1732 of a public almshouse maintained by public funds—
the first, probably, in the colonies—testified to the Quaker concern for
the well-being of the unfortunate immigrant paupers. At no time did the
Society of Friends forget its testimony against war as an institution both
inhuman and un-Christian. The importance of the Quakers was the
greater in that they influenced many outside their own ranks.

John Woolman's efforts in applying ceaseless pressure on his more
faint-hearted fellow Quakers by condemning the holding of slaves was
continued by his friend, Anthony Benezet, a French-English schoolmaster who settled in Philadelphia in 1731. Benezet's moving tracts on
slavery were circulated in England, where they influenced in all probability such consequential abolitionists as Granville Sharp, Robert
Shackleton, and John Wesley. Benezet mustered the bloodcurdling testimony of men who knew the slave trade at firsthand, and he provided
English and French abolitionists with arguments against the assumption
that the Negroes were after all an inferior people. His eloquent humanitarianism is illustrated by his insistence that slavery violated not only the
Gospel of Christ and the principles of natural justice but also "the common feelings of Humanity," and that it was moreover "productive of
infinite Calamities to many Thousand Families, nay to many Nations,
and consequently offensive to God the Father of all Mankind."[3] Benezet
also attacked the institution of war, not only writing stirring pamphlets
but pleading with members of the Continental Congress on the eve of
the Revolution to find some solution for the disturbing tension in order
that war, "the premeditated and determined destruction of human beings," might be avoided.

[3] Anthony Benezet. *Some Considerations on the Keeping of Negroes*, 2nd ed.
(Germantown, 1760). 4.

Representative of the more secular phases of humanitarianism was the versatile Franklin, Benezet's neighbor and friend. Franklin well exemplified the remark of Voltaire that "without humanity, the virtue which comprehends all virtues, the name of philosopher would be little deserved." Social responsibility bulked large in Franklin's thought. Thus the members of the Junto which he organized in 1727 promised to love mankind and took a stand against slavery and other inhumane customs. His growing dislike of slavery was expressed when in 1727 he printed Ralph Sandiford's *Practice of the Times,* an abolitionist tract. But the slave was not the only unfortunate who enlisted the attention of the busy statesman and philosopher. Those who somehow failed to achieve a due portion of man's worldly goods also aroused his sympathy. To lessen the likelihood of war, he spoke and worked for an imperial federation as the most promising method of solving the problem of colonial tensions with England; and when this failed he tried to delimit the scope of war by negotiating treaties for the young Republic providing that maritime civilians might be exempted from the relentless war machine. In still other ways Franklin, without thinking himself the less patriotic, fostered internationalism and cosmopolitanism.

In his insistence that women's intellectual inferiority was due to the limitations imposed on them by tradition Franklin was in yet another respect on the side of humanitarianism and enlightenment. Most Americans, holding that women are by nature inferior to men and at best diadems in their husbands' crowns, accepted without question the inferior legal status of women, a status which, while more advanced in many respects in America than in England, closely followed common law. In the position he took on the abilities and status of women Franklin was in advance of his American contemporaries. But a clarion call for the emancipation of women was sounded before the Declaration of Independence. Thomas Paine, editor of the *Pennsylvania Magazine* and protégé of Franklin, inserted in the issue of August, 1775, an essay on females which was perhaps the first general plea in America for the underprivileged sex.

Thus the colonial period saw the development of virtually every aspect of the Enlightenment. A sizeable minority of leaders of thought were attacking crude supernaturalism in religion, and more rational doctrines were preached from the pulpit with increasing frequency. The doctrine of progress and the natural rights philosophy took firm hold in the American colonies, and the latter was invoked in appeals to England for a more just colonial policy. Romanticism in literature and general thought helped feed the springs of humanitarianism. The ordinary man stood forth in new dignity. This quickening of American thought was to be regarded by later disciples of the Enlightenment as the brightest and most promising of the colonial legacies to the new nation.

# PART II

The
Growth
of
Americanism

# 6 The Revolutionary Shift in Emphasis

Here all religion rests, and soon thy race
Her purest lights, by wisdom's eye shall trace.
Here the last flights of science shall ascend,
To look thro' heaven, and sense with reason
    blend.
—JOEL BARLOW, The Vision of Columbus, 1787

The present may with propriety be styled the
age of philanthropy; and America, the empire
of reason.
                        —ENOS HITCHCOCK, 1799

In popularizing the natural rights philosophy and the humanitarian doctrines of the Enlightenment the American Revolution opened no new vistas in our intellectual life. But it did accelerate, if indeed it did not itself make possible, the realization of certain values in the Enlightenment that have come to be thought of as characteristically American. In affecting economic, social, and political life the American Revolution inevitably exerted an influence also on intellectual perspectives and cultural institutions. It dealt severe blows to the agencies of intellectual life, but it also did much to democratize American thought.

123

### Intellectual Losses

The Revolution did not put an end to all intellectual endeavor. The high level of Samuel Hopkins' theological writing indicates that even in the midst of the distractions of war and revolution New England theology was still vital and capable of growth. The *Literary Diary* of President Stiles of Yale shows that during the war he was able to deepen and broaden his scholarship by serious study and generous reading. Not far from Philadelphia William Bartram, whose father died in 1777, continued to maintain the botanical gardens that had brought fame to the family; in his spare moments he almost certainly worked on the manuscripts of his travels in preparation for the volume that in due time would be published. His cousin, Humphrey Marshall, labored during the Revolution on his forthcoming treatise on forest trees and shrubs in the United States, the first systematic book on botany to appear in the new country. Forced into rustication by the war, another Pennsylvanian, the Reverend Gothilf Mühlenburg, began the study of botany in the spring of 1778 and by the close of hostilities had well under way his work of collecting and classifying the flora in his vicinity in preparation for a notable botanical publication. Other scholars went on with their intellectual labor during the war.

Nevertheless, a larger number, including America's most distinguished intellectuals, put by their scholarly labors for public service. Despite the pleasure Franklin found in his diplomatic career, it was with a sense of pleasant expectancy that he sent Congress on December 26, 1783, a reminder of its promise to recall him at the end of the war. He frequently looked forward during the struggle to the leisure he finally found aboard ship, two years later, when he wrote out his ideas on "The Causes and Cures of Smoky Chimneys" and indulged his scientific curiosity by "making observations" of the temperature and character of sea water under varying circumstances. If Franklin was the young Republic's "first intellectual," Thomas Jefferson was a close second. Only in the last year of the war did Jefferson quit public life for a time to put in shape his observations on the topography, flora, fauna, and institutions of his native state. Other scientists who gave themselves to the patriot cause were similarly diverted from their inquiries and intellectual labors. David Rittenhouse, Pennsylvania's famous astronomer, supervised the manufacture of saltpeter and directed the new United States mint. Writing to him in 1778, Jefferson remarked half-reproachfully: "I doubt not there are in your country many persons equal to the task of conducting government; but you should consider that the world has but one Rittenhouse, and that it never had that before."[1]

In any period of action men's energies are largely absorbed in practical pursuits and speculative thought tends to go by the board. Years after the peace was won De Witt Clinton observed that "the convulsions, devastations, and horrors which attended the Revolution were ill calculated to cherish the interests of science. Our seminaries of education were broken up; and all our attention was occupied in resisting the calamities which pressed upon the country."[2] The vicissitudes of the Revolution led to the destruction of the two manuscript volumes which John Clayton of Virginia had written to supplement his great *Flora Virginica*, published under the auspices of Gronovius.

Clinton's gloomy remarks were borne out in the damage inflicted by the war on many agencies of intellectual life. In rural areas schools generally closed their doors, and even in the towns their work was hindered. From the time that the British occupied the city until the war ended, New York had no schools. The Anglican Society for the Propagation of the Gospel, an effective agency for elementary education in the Middle and Southern Colonies, abandoned its work during the conflict and did not resume it after England's final defeat. Many of the Latin grammar schools and other secondary institutions were crippled. Even in New England, where education was most deeply rooted, the schools often suffered because of the general preoccupation with the tasks of war. Illiteracy increased, as did indebtedness and poverty.

The colleges, when they continued their activities at all, did so with depleted ranks and under severe strains. Of the Yale staff a number were transferred to other locations. Tutor Dwight, for instance, took some of the students to Wethersfield; Professor Story centered his instruction at Glastonbury; and President Dagget visited "the different classes as often as he could with convenience." Harvard gave up its halls to the provincial troops, to reoccupy them after the British evacuated Boston.

[1] Julian P. Boyd (ed.), *The Papers of Thomas Jefferson* (Princeton University Press, 1950– ), II, 203.
[2] De Witt Clinton, *An Introductory Discourse delivered before the Literary and Philosophical Society of New-York* (New York, 1815), 13.

Financially it was in desperate straits, students fell off markedly, and the shortage of textbooks became so acute that Tory libraries were plundered with the consent of the authorities. The chief building of the College of Rhode Island was used as a barrack and hospital; at the end of the war President Manning reported that the 500 books which the college still possessed were "both very ancient and very useless, as well as very ragged and unsightly." Dartmouth's Indian students were dispersed, and the college was reduced to "nakedness and want." The College of Philadelphia quartered "hundreds of soldiers at one time, so that classes were discontinued." Worse, the college was abolished by an antiaristocratic legislature unable to stomach the Tory complexion of its governing board, and for some time the new University of Pennsylvania was a mere fledgling. King's College closed its doors.

In New Jersey and Virginia matters were not much brighter. At the College of New Jersey at Princeton the apparatus and library were scattered, and President Witherspoon devoted much of his time and energy to propagandizing for complete religious freedom and other public issues. So disturbed were conditions in the Old Dominion, especially during the last years of the war, that the College of William and Mary suffered considerably; the mother chapter of the Phi Beta Kappa Society, established after the beginning of hostilities, was obliged to discontinue its organization. But neither William and Mary nor the College of New Jersey nor, indeed, any of the colleges suffered complete ruin, and each in one way or another made some contribution to the patriot cause.

Book collections outside college halls also suffered. Although some libraries in Philadelphia escaped plunder, the rich Morrisania library was depleted. In Newport the famous Redwood library, which boasted 1500 books, many of great value, numbered little more than half that many at the conclusion of hostilities. "The pilfering hand of the British," observed a visitor to the empty library house that had stored the treasures, "in this, as well as in other instances, carried on war not only against men, but against learning."[3] It seems probable that the little libraries painfully assembled by the Society for the Promotion of Christian Knowledge and related organizations likewise came to an untimely end. At Charleston the Library Society, which on the eve of the Revolution possessed between five and six thousand books, was destroyed in 1778 by the conflagration

[3] John Drayton, *Letters written during a Tour through the Northern and Eastern States of America* (Charleston, 1794), 42.

that reduced half the city to ashes; only 185 volumes were saved, and these only in much-mutilated condition. Like other proprietary and subscription libraries, the Charleston Library Society suffered a great depletion of funds as a result of the chaos of revolutionary finance.

During the war it had been almost impossible to import imprints from England, and colonial presses were so poorly equipped that it was hard for their owners to supply substitutes. The first foundry for casting type had been established only in 1772, and it was almost impossible for American printers to maintain themselves without aid from abroad. Of the 43 newspapers published in 1783, not one, even of those in the leading towns, enjoyed an uninterrupted career throughout the war. Two of the three magazines being issued in British America on the eve of the Revolution were forced to abandon publication when hostilities began; another, inaugurated in the midst of the conflict, did not survive at all. Difficult as it was to maintain newspapers and magazines, it was even harder to publish books. Thus the war interfered with the composition and publication of the volumes of miscellaneous poems, inspired by the English lyricists as well as by Pope, which had appeared in the last two decades of the colonial period with increasing frequency and which gave growing evidence of literary skill.

For scientists the problems posed by war were also grave. The colonial man of science depended, perhaps even more than the poet or essayist, on contacts with Europeans. During the war many scientists on both sides of the Atlantic made strenuous efforts to keep the channels of communication and investigation open. Franklin, for example, overstepped his authority and directed American warships not to molest the exploring expedition of British Captain James Cook. Cook's men were not enemies, Franklin declared, but rather "common friends to mankind."[4] In general, however, American science suffered the same retarding effects of the war as did other intellectual pursuits. The closing of many of the colleges, the lack of books, the difficulties of correspondence, the interruption of the stream of young men to European centers of learning, all slowed the development of science in the new nation.

In disrupting the activities of the churches on which so much of the intellectual life of the colonial era centered, the Revolution dealt a severe blow to the life of the intellect. Much church property was de-

[4] Quoted in Brooke Hindle, *The Pursuit of Science in Revolutionary America* (University of North Carolina Press, 1956), 221.

stroyed and many schools sponsored by religious societies were abandoned. Preoccupation with political and military resistance permitted the older religious and moral sanctions to weaken, and there was widespread complaint of the prevalence of superficial worldliness and the consequent decline of the spiritual and intellectual virtues. The secularization of life that had characterized the later colonial era was greatly accelerated, and the separation of church and state advanced rapidly. Although in the long run intellectual life profited in many respects from this process, the immediate effect discouraged friends of learning.

The Revolution also deprived the country of the talents of many of the Tories whose claims to scholarship and culture few denied. "What the loss of the Huguenots was to commerce and manufactures in France," wrote a former English resident in the colonies, "that of the Loyalists was to religion, literature, and *amenity*, in America. The silken threads were drawn out of the mixed web of society, which has ever since been comparatively coarse and homely. The dawning light of elegant science was quenched in universal dullness."[5] Among the Tories who found refuge outside the land were Miles Cooper, witty and learned head of King's College in New York; Jonathan Boucher, classical scholar, teacher, and Anglican parson in Maryland and Virginia; Samuel Peters, talented clergyman who had done much to advance the interests of the Church of England in Connecticut; and Daniel Leonard, scholarly Boston lawyer and pamphleteer. American science lost Dr. Alexander Garden, Charleston's well-known naturalist, and Benjamin Thompson, subsequently Count Rumford. This picturesque figure went to England, where he made a notable contribution to theoretical physics, and subsequently to Bavaria, where, as the elector's chief minister, he gave further expression to his scientific talents.

## Advance in Intellectual Democracy

But if the Revolution dealt hard blows to intellectual life it also planted seeds that were destined, in the words of a contemporary observer, "to spring up and to bring forth fruit highly honorable to our country." Dr. David Ramsay of South Carolina declared in 1789 that "while Americans were guided by the leading-strings of the mother coun-

[5] Ann Grant, *Memoirs of an American Lady* (London, 1809), II, 317.

try they had no scope nor encouragement for exertion." It seemed, he went on, "as if the war not only required, but created talents." Men whose minds were "warmed with the love of liberty, and whose abilities were improved by daily exercise, and sharpened with a laudable ambition to serve their distressed country, spoke, wrote, and acted, with an energy far surpassing all expectations which could be reasonably founded on their previous acquirements."[6] Certainly many of the rank and file who participated in the Revolution enjoyed long afterward a dignified social and political status.

Intellectual democracy was also stimulated by the development of pamphleteering and the popularization of ideas that resulted from the mass circulation of literature. The natural rights philosophy with which Americans had become increasingly familiar during the rise of the Enlightenment was translated into stirring calls to action. Resistance to tyranny, the right of a people to determine its fate, the glories involved in a struggle for liberty—all these ideas found full expression. Such antimonarchical, prodemocratic, and militant pamphlets as *Common Sense* and *The Crisis*, written by a young and obscure recent arrival from England, Thomas Paine, were representative of a considerable body of popular literature. Republican pamphleteering helped to break the prop to conservative thought which the mystical, symbolical concept of monarchy had strengthened. Old ideas were further weakened by the publicity that was given to the uprooting of a variety of feudal vestiges of landholding. In examining the later history of the Enlightenment there will be occasion to consider this widespread political education in greater detail.

By accelerating the separation of church and state—a process that indeed had already started—the Revolution gave impetus to the concept of religious freedom. The new federal government was almost completely divorced from formal religion. Some of the new state constitutions followed Virginia's lead and completely separated church and state. Even the state constitutions that did not go all the way but retained civil disabilities on Catholics guaranteed them complete freedom of worship. In separating or in laying the foundations for separating church and state these revolutionary constitutions prepared the way for later developments in our intellectual life that were of far-reaching significance. The way

[6] David Ramsay, *The History of the American Revolution* (Philadelphia, 1789), II, 316.

was thus paved for the ultimate establishment of free tax-supported schools, a milestone in our intellectual history. Again, the separation of church and state removed a buttress of traditionalism and authoritarianism since in general, both in the American colonies and in Europe, established churches had supported the status quo.

In still other ways did the Revolution feed intellectual democracy. The more democratic enthusiasts insisted that intellectual life must be common to all the people. The great body of farmers, mechanics, and other plain folk who had hitherto taken only slight part in the intellectual life of the colonial period had to be provided, declared the intellectual democrats, with opportunities for education and culture, not only because an educated public was an indispensable condition for the success of a republican form of government, but because only through mass enlightenment could the fruit of the Revolution be reaped. In the words of Colonel David Humphreys, Washington's aide-de-camp,[7]

> No feudal ties the rising genius mar,
> Compel to servile toils, or drag to war;
> But, free, each youth his fav'rite course pursues,
> The plough paternal, or the sylvan muse.

To the argument of conservatives that republicanism was fraught with the dangers of anarchy, one champion of the people, speaking in Cambridge, Massachusetts, in 1783, insisted that the plain folk were as likely to make "a laudable and profitable use" of liberty as "the great men of the earth," and that if the masses were raised to wisdom they would improve their freedom "to the greatest and most happifying purposes."[8] A few months later the Universalist pioneer, the Reverend John Murray, declared that schools, academies, and colleges, as well as Olympic exercises to encourage the arts and the professions, should be put within the reach of every citizen. Tyranny and aristocracy, not democracy, endangered the destiny of the Republic, said this bold spokesman for cultural democracy; American culture, he insisted, must be as inclusive as possible.

Before the end of the century these ideas were developed at length by different minds. Of the cultural patriots who desired to see an inclusive,

[7] *The Miscellaneous Works of Colonel Humphreys* (New York, 1790), 45.
[8] Charles Turner, V.D.M., *Due Glory is to be Given to God. A Discourse* (Boston, 1783), 26–27.

democratic intellectual life, Dr. Benjamin Rush of Philadelphia was particularly outspoken. "The business of education," observed this distinguished physician, "has acquired a new complexion by the independence of our country. The form of government we have assumed, has created a new class of duties to every American."[9] If republicanism was to succeed, youth must be trained in public schools in the Christian religion, in patriotism, in civic understanding, in practical skills, and in physical culture. Thomas Jefferson was even more explicit. In 1779 he proposed a state plan of education which would have given every child in Virginia an elementary schooling in locally managed public schools. The most promising boys were to enjoy further training in academies and colleges, the poorer ones being provided with scholarships for that purpose. By such a selective process Jefferson hoped that the genuine talents of boys of the poorer class might be developed and utilized for public service. Washington, Hamilton, and Madison all approved the scheme for a national university that would enable talented young men, whatever their economic circumstances, to advance knowledge through research and to receive training for public service. Before the end of the century programs for a democratic education suited to American needs were developed in a series of essays submitted for a prize offered by the American Philosophical Society for the best educational plan for the Republic.

Most proponents of a democratic culture included within its scope the education of girls, whose opportunities for study had been so circumscribed in the colonial period and were still similarly circumscribed both in America and in Europe. In 1783 the Reverend Timothy Dwight, who trenchantly criticized the superficial character of the education meted out to girls of the more favored class, removed to Greenfield Hill, Connecticut, where he opened a school that trained girls as well as boys in college preparatory subjects. About the same time another pioneer in the education of girls, Caleb Bingham, opened a school for girls in Boston. The general feeling among cultural patriots and democrats was that mothers exerted a profound influence on their sons during the impressionable years, and that they should for that reason, if for no other, be sufficiently trained in history, civics, and related fields to enable them to mold the characters and minds of the future officeholders and voters of the nation. Even more truly democratic was the application of the

---

[9] Benjamin Rush, "Of the Mode of Education in a Republic," *Essays, Literary, Moral, and Philosophical* (Philadelphia, 1798), 6–7.

philosophy of the natural rights of man to the problem of women's participation in the life of the mind.

The most liberal of the cultural democrats thought that Negroes as well as women should be included in the scope of the new culture. Although in condemning the slave trade and slavery itself such men as the Reverend Samuel Hopkins of Newport and Anthony Benezet, the Philadelphia Quaker, rested their arguments largely on Christian grounds, they also pointed out the inconsistency between the Declaration of Independence and the institution of slavery. Hopkins, in addressing the Continental Congress, hoped that it would be sensible of "the equal unrighteousness and oppression as well as inconsistence with ourselves, in holding so many hundreds of blacks in slavery, who have an equal right to freedom with ourselves, while we are maintaining this struggle for our own and our children's liberty."[10] The Reverend Samuel Miller of New York City declared in a Fourth of July sermon in 1793 that the American patriot must shudder at the existence of slavery. "Alas," he lamented, "that we should so soon forget the principles, upon which our wonderful revolution was founded!"[11] Others took a similar point of view, and this note was struck not only during the Revolution itself but in the years following. Some, notably Anthony Benezet, demonstrated by actions as well as words the conviction that the Negro must be not only freed but educated as well.

Although inspired more by cultural nationalism than by democracy, a few of the new textbooks entertained some implementation of the idea of intellectual democracy. In the preface to the second part of his *Grammatical Institute* Noah Webster pleaded for a simplified spelling on the ground that it was appropriate to a republican society in which all must be literate in order to fulfill their political duties. Jedidiah Morse did not, it is true, identify a republican form of government with a democracy; yet his plea for the rejection of English "geographies" on the ground that American youth must not be molded by the monarchical and aristocratic ideas of England had democratic implications. The democratic idea is more apparent in Erasmus Root's preface to his *Introduction to Arithmetic* (1796). Root admonished his countrymen to be independent and anti-aristocratic even in their system of monetary reckoning.

---

[10] Samuel Hopkins, A *Dialogue Concerning the Slavery of the Africans* (Norwich, 1776), and A *Discourse upon the Slave Trade* . . . (Boston, 1854), 549.

[11] Samuel Miller, A *Sermon Preached in New-York, July 4, 1793* (New York, 1793), 27.

Let us, I beg of you, Fellow-Citizens, no longer meanly follow the British intricate mode of reckoning. Let them have their way, and us, ours. . . . Their mode is suited to the genius of their government, for it seems to be the policy of tyrants, to keep their accounts in as intricate and perplexing a method as possible; that the smaller number of their subjects may be able to estimate their enormous impositions and exactions. But Republican money ought to be simple and adapted to the meanest capacity.[12]

If the fine arts and esthetic values were to have a valid and vital place in the life of the Republic they had, it was widely believed, to be related to the common life. Washington, who dearly loved the theater, justified it not on the ground of sheer beauty of the drama or pure enjoyment but on the score that it would "advance the interest of private and public virtue . . . and have a tendency to polish the manners and habits of society." Franklin held that in the existing stage of American development a schoolmaster was worth a dozen poets and that a taste for the arts should not be generally cultivated until the means for its indulgence existed. "Nothing is good or beautiful," he wrote, "but in the measure that it is useful: yet all things have a utility under particular circumstances. Thus poetry, painting, music (and the stage as their embodiment) are all necessary and proper gratifications of a refined state of society but objectionable at an earlier period, since their cultivation would make a taste for the enjoyment precede its means." In commenting on the Declaration of Independence as a literary document Jefferson maintained that its chief merit lay in the fact that, while it drew upon difficult and subtle literary sources, it communicated commonly shared beliefs. This idea that the arts are intimately related to the society from which they spring and on which they rest was frequently to be shunted aside and overlooked; but it was characteristically American and continued to enjoy popular approval even when patricians and intellectuals denied or condemned it.

In the field of music the democratic conception of culture found expression in the establishment of popular singing schools and in the vogue of musical forms dear to simple rural folk. William Billings, the Boston tanner, was a leader in this movement, as was Oliver Holden, a Charleston carpenter. In Philadelphia Andrew Adgate, the son of simple people, projected in 1786 a great choral concert with singers from every social rank in which simple antique modes with gapped scales ("solfa"

[12] Erasmus Root, *An Introduction to Arithmetic for the Use of the Common Schools* (Norwich, Conn., 1796), Preface.

or "fasola") were to find their place along with such genteel pieces as Handel's *Messiah*. Adgate was attacked by another Philadelphia musician, Alexander Juhan, who belittled the practice of solfa as becoming only to artisans, mechanics, and farmers. But Adgate held the concert and went on to publicize his scheme for universal musical education. Even Juhan made a concession to the democratic cultural impulse by establishing the City Concerts, which, unlike the concerts of colonial days, were public functions. A Philadelphia newspaper in 1792 hailed this departure with the comment that "one bench supports you and one joy unites—there is no struggle for precedency or for place."

The idea of cultural democracy at no time, in fact, enjoyed unanimous approval among American patriots. Conservatives who thought of the Revolution as a revolt against English authority rather than a social movement had little taste for the democratic idea that caste and privilege could or should be eliminated from intellectual life. They agreed with John Adams that the natural aristocracy of talent should enjoy superior cultural privileges along with the direction of affairs. "The people of all nations," wrote Adams, "are naturally divided into two sorts, the gentlemen and the simple men . . . the poor are destined to labor, and the rich, by the advantages of education, independence and leisure, are qualified for superior stations."[13] Many members of the economically dominant group had no notion of sharing with the common people the intellectual and esthetic values of which they considered themselves the proper guardians and patrons. Nothing had happened to lessen their conviction that as individuals the common people were shiftless, unreliable, ignorant, and vulgar, and as a class were vicious and dangerous unless disciplined by an education emphasizing obedience, subordination to authority, and skill in the necessary routines of everyday work. Embittered at the pretensions of ordinary fellows to wisdom and learning, aristocrats made such jests as

> Down at night a bricklayer or carpenter lies,
> Next sun a Lycurgus, a Solon doth rise.

It is not easy to determine what the plain people themselves thought about the idea of an intellectual democracy, for few had the desire, equipment, or opportunity to express their views. Many of these people,

[13] Charles Francis Adams (ed.), *The Works of John Adams* (Boston, 1851), VI, 185.

it will be recalled, possessed and read almanacs, the Bible, and perhaps a book or two of sermons. But in general the great majority of farmers, mechanics, longshoremen, fishermen, and small shopkeepers had acquired only a very elementary introduction to book knowledge and on the whole felt little need of an acquaintance with more than the tool subjects of reading, writing, and figuring.

To such learning as the plain people possessed the Revolution itself made some contribution. Military service acquainted many with parts of the country other than their own. Even those who did not read the patriotic broadsides and pamphlets which were scattered everywhere listened at taverns to heated discussions of monarchy and of the right of the people to resist tyranny. In New England the Congregational clergy popularized such ideas in sermons and cited the authority and reasoning of Locke, Harrington, Milton, and Sidney. The Revolution enriched folk culture by occasioning and popularizing such marching songs as "Yankee Doodle" and ballads celebrating patriotic heroes and heroines. Altogether it is likely that the plain people merited the judgment of Johann David Schoepf, the German geologist and physician, that the great majority of ordinary Americans, despite their indifference to book learning, possessed a good natural understanding and manifested "a better expression of their understanding than people of the same rank in Europe."[14] There was a basis for this in colonial experience, but the Revolution accentuated it.

Occasionally a spokesman for the plain people expressed himself in print on the issue of intellectual democracy. In the preface to *Reason the Only Oracle of Man* (1784) Ethan Allen, a Vermont revolutionist and farmer, took it for granted that he had as good a "natural right to expose himself to public censure, by endeavoring to subserve mankind, as any of the species who have published their productions since the Creation." Completely confident of the right of an ordinary man to have his say in the realms of higher knowledge, Allen asked no favor at the hands of philosophers, divines, or orators.

Before the end of the century another New England farmer, William Manning, put his ideas on a shared culture into crude but vigorous idiom. "Larning is of the greatest importance to the report of a free government, and to prevent this the few are always crying up the advan-

[14] Johann D. Schoepf, *Travels in the Confederation* (W. J. Campbell, 1911), II, 212.

tages of costly collages, national acadimys & Grammer schools, in order to make places for men to live without work, & to strengthen their party. But are always opposed to cheep schools & woman schools, the ondly or prinsaple means by which larning is spred amongue the Many."[15] With keen insight this shrewd Massachusetts husbandman demanded not only education for the masses but also their control over newspapers and other agencies of cultural life in order that the common people might be able to protect their interests from the learned aristocracy. Let farmers and workers unite in societies to that end, Manning advised.

Many of the humble people may have yearned for a more democratic intellectual culture, but many more were neither equipped intellectually nor sufficiently free from the tasks of everyday labor to give much thought to such matters. Equally important, many were deeply suspicious of the so-called intellectual class and therefore of learning itself. Most intellectuals earned their living by the practice of law, medicine, or theology, or lived abundantly on the income from land or commercial property. In the hard times that became acute with the establishment of peace the intellectual group aroused the increasing hostility of ordinary men. The clergy by and large aligned themselves with the privileged merchants and well-to-do landowners, however much some of them berated the rich for the speculative tendencies of the times and for their worldliness. Physicians were suspected of robbing graveyards for corpses to dissect, and accused of otherwise exploiting the poor.

But it was the lawyers, the country's chief literary spokesmen, who were especially disliked by the plain people. Subservient to the creditor class, they could and did foreclose mortgages on farmers and imprison urban debtors who were unable to meet their obligations. So great was the hostility to the law that its practitioners were sometimes asked by irate citizens of humble status to leave town. In 1786 the citizens of Braintree, a town near Boston, requested in town meeting that "there may be such laws compiled as may crush or at least put a proper check or restraint on that order of Gentlemen denominated Lawyers, the completion of whose modern conduct appears to us to tend rather to the destruction than to the preservation of the town." The conviction was widespread that, as one man writing in 1783 put it, the courts might be purged and "voluminous laws curtailed into a plain command, which the

[15] William Manning, in Samuel E. Morison (ed.), *The Key of Libberty* (The Manning Association, Billerica, Mass., 1922), 20–21.

common people, of plain sense, may understand." In view of such prejudices it is probable that many of the plain folk paid little or no attention
to the demands for universal participation in the higher intellectual interests of the favored classes.

The plain people suspected those who demanded state support for the
theater on the ground that America should be less dependent on Europe
for "genius, wit, and refinement." Their spokesmen feared that a govern-
ment-supported theater, such as was proposed in Pennsylvania in 1785,
might become a dangerous tool in the hands of conservatives, and that in
any case the drama might blind the citizenry to its political responsibilities. That such fears were groundless subsequent events demonstrated.
Royall Tyler's *The Contrast* (1787) satirized aristocracy and glorified
the simplicity and virtue of the agrarian hero, our first stage Yankee. In
1789 New York City witnessed the first play by William Dunlap, a democrat who berated aristocratic patronage and viewed the drama as an effective instrument for the improvement of society.

## Nationalism in Intellectual Life

Although a sharp line separated social radicals from social conservatives on matters involving intellectual democracy, the two groups were
united in support of cultural nationalism. This idea was shared in greater
or less measure by all members of the learned class save those who regretted, openly or secretly, that the colonies had embarked upon and
won the struggle for independence from England—a large number, to be
sure. The self-consciousness that had become increasingly articulate in
the later decades of the colonial era not only had contributed to the
movement for independence but was in turn greatly heightened by the
Revolution.

In establishing a confederation and finally a federal capital the Revolution brought together periodically some of the best minds of all the
states, together with the representatives of foreign powers, and thus provided new facilities for the interchange of ideas and for the development
of the spirit of American nationalism. But nothing contributed as much
to the growth of cultural nationalism as the fact that Americans ceased
thinking of themselves as citizens of the British Empire. Learned colonists had participated in the cultural life of various countries on the

European continent, and the struggle for political independence and the alliance with France lessened the disposition to look to England as the chief intellectual center of the world. Indeed, the bitter anti-British propaganda that was circulated during the Revolution aroused ill feelings which persisted long after the close of the war and which help to explain why Americans resented any criticism emanating from Great Britain.

For the time being at least, French ideas and culture enjoyed popularity not only among intellectual leaders but among a certain number of ordinary townsfolk as well. The increased vogue of French etiquette, art, literature, and philosophy reflected the influence of French military officers and diplomats and the spokesmen of the French Enlightenment. Most likely the ideas of the Enlightenment would have become increasingly popular in America even without the revolution; but association with French liberals and the acceptance, at least for the time, of the doctrine of the rights of man certainly strengthened that great movement of ideas. It is noteworthy that the ideas of the French "philosophes" helped Americans to throw off the intellectual tutelage of England and to formulate the cultural character that they desired for an independent America.

Even during the conflict itself efforts were made to provide for many types of professional and cultural activities fitting to an independent country. In 1782 the Harvard Medical School began its work; and one of its instructors, himself a product of European schools, observed that before the war it had been thought necessary to go abroad to complete a medical education. "A country so completely independent in other respects as the United States, however ready to receive information in the higher grades of science, by the cultivation of literary correspondence abroad, should blush to be indebted to foreign seminaries for *first principles of professional instruction.*"[16] Dr. Benjamin Waterhouse in this reference to the establishment of the medical school at Harvard expressed a widely held idea.

This point of view explains in part, though only in part, why so many new institutions of learning were established by religious organizations in the last years of the war or in the years immediately after the conclusion of peace. At Andover in Massachusetts and at Exeter in New Hampshire

[16] Benjamin Waterhouse, *The Rise, Progress, and Present State of Medicine* (Boston, 1792), 28.

new academies bearing the family name of their donor, Phillips, were already attracting students from distant parts. Dickinson College was launched in Pennsylvania in 1783, and St. John's at Annapolis was reorganized as a college the next year. Within the decade the Episcopalians established Washington College in Maryland and the College of Charleston in South Carolina; the Presbyterians founded, in addition to Dickinson, Hampden-Sydney in Virginia (1782) and Transylvania Seminary in Lexington, Kentucky (1785). In 1784 Judge Tapping Reeve formally opened at Litchfield, Connecticut, a law school that was to become nationally celebrated for its method of instruction through moot courts, and for its distinguished pupils. New schools for girls marked by a more serious educational purpose were also founded with increasing frequency. National pride contributed to the rapid restoration of the older colleges that had suffered so much devastation during the war.

Perhaps the most striking evidence of the feeling that an independent nation should play a larger role in promoting knowledge was the establishment of the American Academy of Arts and Sciences at Boston in 1780. The membership included leading patriots. The object of the Academy was

to promote and encourage the knowledge of antiquities in America, and of the natural history of the country, and to determine the uses to which the various natural productions of the country may be applied; to promote and encourage medical discoveries, mathematical disquisitions, philosophical inquiries and experiments, astronomical, meteorological, and geographical observations, and improvements in agriculture, arts, manufacture, and commerce, and, in fine, to cultivate every art and science which may tend to advance the interest, honor, dignity, and happiness of a free, independent and virtuous people.[17]

The members of the Academy listened regularly to papers on mathematics, astronomy, electricity, geography, chemistry, agriculture, and the mechanical and medical arts; and after 1785, when the first volume of the Academy's memoirs was published, the general public was enabled to share these contributions.

Such enterprise was by no means confined to New England. Prominent Virginians lent material aid to Quesnay de Beaurepaire, who was promoting the Academy of Sciences and Fine Arts in this country and

[17] *Memoirs of the American Academy of Arts and Sciences* (Boston, 1785), I, 3–4.

in France. This institution, for which a building was begun in Richmond in 1786, was to have branches in the leading towns and affiliates in Europe. The ambitious plans fell through partly because of the outbreak of revolution in France. But in Philadelphia the American Philosophical Society renewed with vigor the work that the war had hampered. The exigencies of the struggle had compelled the Society to suspend the publication of its transactions, but with the return of peace plans were immediately made for the continuation of the series.

The determination to make not only the advancement of learning, but piety itself less dependent on Europe was another result of the increase in national self-consciousness. It was, for instance, considered improper for an independent nation to depend on the importation of Bibles from the Old World. Robert Aiken, the Philadelphia printer who in 1777 issued the first American version of the New Testament in English, brought out in 1782 the first complete English Bible in America. This chunky volume, almost cubic in shape, was so poorly printed and so expensive that it could not compete with the cheaper imported volumes, and it put Aiken in debt some three thousand pounds. Nevertheless, the event was one of national importance, for Congress by special resolution commended the Aiken Bible to good patriots. No doubt this American Bible helped stimulate a new feeling of cultural independence by providing tangible evidence that God's printed word could issue from Philadelphia as well as from Oxford. By the beginning of the new century at least twenty editions of the complete Bible, including the Catholic Rheims-Douai version, had appeared. In the preface to his first folio Bible Isaiah Thomas, the well-known Boston and Worcester printer, linked the patriotic life of America with the Bible. It must be the ardent and united wish of civil authorities, he remarked, to see their fellow citizens supplied, independently of foreign aid, with copies of the sacred Scriptures.

The Revolution stimulated the belief that America was destined not only to achieve intellectual independence from Europe but to win the cultural hegemony of the entire world. The time was at hand, the argument ran, for America to realize the prophecy that Bishop Berkeley had made in 1731, when he visioned the transfer from Europe to America of supremacy in the arts, letters, and sciences. Joel Barlow, in a commencement poem delivered at Yale in 1778, had spoken boldly on this point; in the new Republic the arts and sciences were to flourish as nowhere else. The young poet further refused to take too seriously the warning that in a small and poor country there was no likelihood that a man of letters could exist without a patron. Barlow pictured the role of the poet in the new America as one of importance.

Foreign observers confirmed the cultural nationalists in their conviction that America possessed the material and human resources for intellectual leadership. The German Johann Schoepf, who served King George during the Revolution, thought at its conclusion that in time geniuses in America would measure themselves with those of the Old World. On completing a three-year residence in the United States, the Marquis de Chastellux said in 1782: "Doubt not, Sir, that America will render herself illustrious by the sciences, as well as by her arms, and government. The extent of her empire submits to her observation a large portion of heaven and earth. What observations may not be made between Penobscot and Savannah? Between the lakes and the ocean?"[18]

The conviction that political freedom nourished intellectual genius contributed more to the optimism of the patriots who proclaimed the future triumph of culture in America than did European assurances. As early as 1771 Philip Freneau and H. H. Brackenridge, in their commencement ode at the College of New Jersey, prophesied of the Muses:[19]

> Hither they wing their way, the last, the best
> Of countries, where the arts shall rise and grow,
> And arms shall have their day—Even now we boast
> A *Franklin*, prince of all philosophy . . .
> This is a land of every joyous sound,
> Of liberty and life, sweet liberty!
> Without whose aid the noblest genius fails,
> And Science irretrievably must die.

This belief that a free republic was the chief nursery of genius, a belief which was in part based on the analogy of the classical cultures of Greece and Rome, overlooked the fact that contributions to knowledge had been and were being made in despotic Europe. Nevertheless, this view continued to be a favorite theme of commencement orators. In 1797 Joseph Perkins, in his Harvard "part," declared that native endowments best flourish where "the eagle genius is at full liberty to expand

---

[18] Marquis de Chastellux, *Travels in North-America* (Dublin, 1787), II, 376–377.
[19] Frederick L. Pattee (ed.), *The Poems of Philip Freneau*, 3 vols. (Princeton University Library, 1902), I, 74.

her vigorous wings, to build her nest among the stars." And many other orators, equally fervid, agreed with the young Harvardian that in the not distant future the United States would become "the seat of the Muses, the Athens of our age, the admiration of the world."[20]

But if the United States was to realize this promise of cultural supremacy, it was obvious to men of the time that the young Republic must not pattern its intellectual life on European models. In his *Literary Importations* (1786) Freneau thundered his denunciation of Europe:[21]

> Can we never be thought to have learning or grace
> Unless it be brought from that horrible place
> Where tyranny reigns with her impudent face?

At about the same time Noah Webster, a Connecticut schoolmaster, wrote that "this country must, at some future time, be as distinguished by the superiority of her literary improvements as she is already by the liberality of her civil and ecclesiastical institutions. Europe is grown old in folly, corruption, and tyranny—in that country laws are perverted, manners are licentious, literature is declining, and human nature is debased. For America in her infancy to adopt the present maxims of the old world would be to stamp the wrinkle of decrepit age upon the bloom of youth, and to plant the seed of decay in a vigorous constitution."[22]

It was realized, of course, that it would be no easy task to achieve an American culture. Simeon Baldwin of Connecticut said in his Fourth of July oration in 1788 that it had been found "more difficult to root out those unnatural prepossessions, which tend to idolize the persons and productions of foreigners, to the prejudice of humble merit among ourselves, than to break the chain of political oppression. A single blow of the decisive sword destroys the one—the slow progress of reason and mental development the other."[23] But though they were aware of the difficulty of building an American culture, patriots drew from the Revolution inspiration to proceed with the task.

Whatever their social attitudes, cultural nationalists agreed that

[20] Joseph Perkins, *An Oration upon Genius, Pronounced at the Anniversary Commencement of Harvard University in Cambridge, July 19, 1797* (Boston, 1797), 9.

[21] *The Poems of Philip Freneau*, II, 304.

[22] Noah Webster, *A Grammatical Institute of the English Language . . . Part I* (Hartford, 1784), 14.

[23] Simeon Baldwin, *An Oration, pronounced before the Citizens of New-Haven, July 4, 1788* (New Haven, 1788), 14.

scholarship in America had to concern itself with the American scene. American geography received increased attention. Decade by decade more and more light had been thrown on the great hinterland stretching west from the line of settlements along the tidewater of the Atlantic coast. Dr. John Mitchell, the Virginia naturalist, had made in 1746 what has been designated as the most important map in our history because of its role in many boundary and diplomatic controversies. Thanks to the hardy pioneers and the interest of land speculators in the trans-Allegheny country, explorers and map makers were adding to the knowledge of that vast domain. In 1755 the Pennsylvanian Lewis Evans published his geographical essays, which with their accompanying maps marked an important increase in the knowledge of a considerable part of British America. Valuable information was also made available as the result of the western explorations of Daniel Boone, Jonathan Carver, John Filson, Thomas Hutchins, and others.

One result of the pride that the Revolution stimulated among the citizens of the several states was the preparation of geographical surveys of the states. The best of these by far was Jefferson's *Notes on Virginia*, a comprehensive treatise on the topography, natural history, and natural resources of the largest state. Hearsay and fancy melted before the scientific procedure that Jefferson had employed in collecting his data. His book not only increased knowledge about the Old Dominion but induced others to make similar surveys for other states. Moreover, the *Notes on Virginia* assumed special significance in contemporary eyes because of Jefferson's able refutation of the claims of such distinguished European scientists as DePauw, Buffon, and others, who had held that a less favorable physical environment in America dwarfed the representatives of all species common to the Old World and the New. By the end of the eighteenth century virtually all states possessed maps and geographical surveys of considerable accuracy, although none enjoyed the distinction of *Notes on Virginia*.

In spite of the fact that Arrowsmith's map of the United States was a noteworthy contribution to cartography, the country was without a good general map when the nineteenth century began. Indeed, the status of map making was so low and the gaps in geographical knowledge so many at the end of the colonial era that existing maps of America were, by present-day standards, hardly worthy of the name. So scanty was the knowledge of the great domain west of the Mississippi that Imlay, an authority on the geography of the West, could write in 1792 that crossing to the western sea should be relatively easy "as it does not appear that the ridges of hills which divide the waters of the Pacific Ocean from the waters of the Mississippi, are either so high or so rugged as the Allegheny Mountains."[24]

However limited the knowledge of American geography was, cultural patriots insisted that citizens should depend on the country's own workers in that field rather than on foreigners. "To depend on foreigners partial to a proverb to their own country," wrote Jedidiah Morse in the preface of his *American Universal Geography*, "for an account of the divisions, rivers, productions, manufactures, navigation, commerce, literature, improvements, etc., of the American states, would certainly be a disgraceful blot upon our literary and national character."[25] Morse himself undertook the preparation of a geographical textbook to replace British gazetteers and books in this field. *Geography Made Easy* (1784) was followed by many other textbooks from Morse's study in the parsonage at Charlestown, Massachusetts. The early editions of his geographies contained inaccuracies resulting from scanty information or uncritical acceptance of material sent to him from the various localities he described, and his books suffered further from bias in favor of New England, of religious orthodoxy, and of extreme conservatism in morals. But all his geographical textbooks were staunchly American; all emphasized the superiority of America over other countries, and all provided far more comprehensive treatments of the country than could be found in the existing works of British authors. A compiler rather than an original scholar, Morse nevertheless greatly widened the extent of geographical knowledge among his countrymen by making available inexpensive as well as relatively comprehensive treatments of the subject.

Patriots not only insisted on the value of native studies of our terrain but taught that in our geography lay proof that providence had intended us to be a *united* nation. "Our lands are marked by the very hand of nature," declared an orator in 1794 before the New York Tammany Society. "On the east, the Atlantic washes a various and extensive coast; on the west, the broad and rapid Mississippi pours its stream along; and

[24] Gilbert Imlay, A *Topographical Description of the Western Territory*, 3rd ed. (London, 1793), 116.

[25] Jedidiah Morse, *American Universal Geography* (Boston, 1793), Preface.

on the north the river St. Lawrence, and a chain of august lakes, form a natural boundary. Within these limits marked by invariable lines, and abundantly extensive for the purposes of one empire, do we not find a variety of climate and of soil, and a rich diversity of productions, sufficient for all the conveniences and elegancies of life?"[26]

With the growing spell of the Romantic movement in the last decade of the century both foreign visitors and native Americans celebrated with new fervor the esthetic beauties of the American landscape and noted its unique character. The year after independence was won, the Reverend Jeremy Belknap called attention to the grandeur and dignity of the White Mountains; and President Dwight of Yale, who began his extensive tours of New England and New York in 1797, boasted that nowhere else could such variety of landscape be found. "Neither the poet nor the painter can here be ever at a loss for scenery to employ the pen or pencil." But celebrations of the American landscape were not confined to specific regions. William Bartram's *Travels* described unique features in the landscape of several states, and Joel Barlow's *Vision of Columbus* with its rhapsodic lines on America's magnificent rivers, stupendous mountains, broad savannahs, and picturesque woodlands was definitely nationalistic.

The interest that colonists had taken in the provincial past was greatly enhanced by patriotism released by the Revolution. Although Ebenezer Hazard's scheme for collecting and publishing a "Documentary History of the Revolution" was not carried to completion, the patriotism aroused by the struggle against England was vigorously reflected in the histories of the Revolution that came from the pen of Dr. David Ramsay of South Carolina. Before the end of the century John Marshall was culling the ever-increasing literature on the "father of his country" in preparation for his *Life of Washington*. In spite of its Federalist bias and lack of originality, it became a classic. Others who, like Gouverneur Morris, had been associated with the recent struggle wrote memoirs. In part as a result of his American experience the Reverend William Gordon prepared his history of the Revolution.

The most praiseworthy achievements in American historiography were the histories inspired by state pride and influenced by Jeremy Bel-

[26] John B. Johnson, *An Oration on Union, delivered in the New Dutch Church in the City of New-York on the Twelfth Day of May, 1794* (New York, 1794), 6.

knap's admirable *History of New Hampshire,* the first volume of which was issued in 1784. Written with concern not only for political but for cultural and institutional history and for the influence of geographical factors, Belknap's history also owed something to the new patriotic pride in America's past. The histories of Vermont by Samuel Williams and of Pennsylvania by Robert Proud, to be followed later by those of Virginia by John Burk, of North Carolina by Hugh Williamson, and of South Carolina by David Ramsay, introduced many relatively untutored folk to the reading of secular history, aroused an interest in the collection and preservation of local historical materials, and gave testimony to the generating influence of patriotism on scholarly achievement. The establishment of the Massachusetts Historical Society in 1791 is further evidence of the new interest in the preservation of the records of the past.

Cultural nationalism affected thought about language and literature no less than thought about geography and history. In 1781 President Witherspoon of the College of New Jersey pointed to the differences between the English language in America and in the mother country and coined the term "Americanism" to designate linguistic peculiarities of American English. The great champion of national self-consciousness in language was, of course, the New England teacher Noah Webster. The first edition of Webster's "blue-backed speller" declared that he had "too much pride to stand indebted to Great Britain for books to learn our children the letters of the alphabet." This speller was the product of American experience and was more appropriate to the needs of American schoolrooms than such British textbooks as Dilworth's. The phonetically simplified spelling and common American grammatical usages advocated by Webster went further than custom in America warranted; his scheme for artificially differentiating the American language from that of the mother land was too extreme to be generally acceptable. But the idea of an American language did not die.

Pride in American achievements also inspired Joel Barlow's *Vision of Columbus* (1787), the most notable literary product of the rising tide of cultural patriotism. In narrating the development of civilization in America, Barlow paid tribute to the accomplishments of artists, inventors, scientists, and literary men as well as statesmen and military heroes. His extravagant praise of American intellectual achievements was sophomoric, but it won wide acclaim. The most ardent cultural patriots charitably overlooked the fact that most of the intellectual achievements

Barlow celebrated in reality demonstrated the close ties between American and European culture.

The Revolution did not democratize American intellectual life or establish the uniquely American culture about which patriots boasted and dreamed. But it did focus attention on a cultural program. If pressed to admit the intellectual dependence of America on Europe, such patriots as Dr. Benjamin Rush would have replied that the Revolution had not ended. In an address delivered in 1787 this pioneer psychiatrist developed in some detail the idea of the unfinished Revolution. "It remains yet to establish and perfect our new forms of government; and to prepare the principles, morals, and manners of our citizens, for these forms of government, after they are established and brought to perfection."[27] Similar views were advanced by British and French disciples of the Enlightenment, who saw in the American Revolution a significant chapter in that pattern of thought. Richard Price, an English liberal, rejoiced that the American Revolution, in opening a new prospect in human affairs, would so leaven the world that the sacred blessings of liberty and humanity would spread until they became universal. Condorcet, in his *Influence of the American Revolution on Europe* (1786) praised as pioneer steps toward freedom the American separation of church and state, the republican form of government, and the devotion to antimilitarism. He saw in our enlightened citizenry a token of America's promise to accelerate progress both in America itself and throughout the whole world.

The development of American thought during the Revolution illustrated dramatically the manner in which political, economic, and social changes affect the life of the mind. On the most basic level, the disruption of the agencies of intellectual life—libraries, printing establishments, churches, colleges—discouraged many scholarly, literary, and scientific pursuits. Men of talent often had to turn from the laboratory or the classroom to tasks connected with the conduct of the war. Where the frontiers of knowledge did make rapid advances, as in the field of military medicine, it was usually as a result of some concrete aspect of the war. More indirectly, the Revolution and its political and social results worked a deep and significant change in the nature of American thought. The related ideas of intellectual democracy and cultural nation-

[27] Benjamin Rush, "An Address to the People of the United States," in Niles, *Principles and Acts of the Revolution* (Baltimore, 1822), 402.

alism received some of their strongest and clearest early statements during the Revolution and the years that followed. These two themes were to remain central to American thought for many decades to come. Indeed, American intellectual history can be largely understood in terms of the continual criticism, revision, and restatement of the two ideals of nationalism and democracy.

# 7 The Expanding Enlightenment

*The foundation of our Empire was not laid in a gloomy age of ignorance and superstition, but at an epoch when the rights of mankind were better understood and more clearly defined, than at any former period: Researches of the human mind after social happiness have been carried to a great extent; the treasures of knowledge acquired by the labours of philosophers, sages, and legislators, thro' a long succession of years, are laid open for use, and their collected wisdom may be happily applied in the establishment of our forms of government.*

—GEORGE WASHINGTON, 1783

Though challenged at every point, the ideas of the Enlightenment nevertheless gained ground during the war years and in the decades that followed. Not until the last years of the century, when Federalism dominated the political and in a large measure the intellectual life of the land, did the Enlightenment face a really serious threat. Only then was it doubtful whether the philosophy of natural rights, deism, humanitarianism, the idea of progress, and faith in natural science would survive the conservative onslaught. But even this conservative reaction, which continued to affect many aspects of American life after the triumph of political liberalism in 1800, did not strike the death knell of the Enlightenment itself.

The advance of the Enlightenment may be understood partly in terms of the favorable soil provided by the American Revolution. The natural rights philosophy was put to work not only to justify the revolt against England but also to give sanction to the efforts of shopkeepers, artisans, and small farmers to obtain political privileges from the dominant propertied groups. Hard pressed by the still ascendant commercial creditor class and irritated by the survival of undemocratic privileges in the new constitution of Massachusetts, small farmers rallied around Daniel Shays in 1786 and defied the ruling authorities. The rebellion itself was put down. The agrarians failed to defeat the adoption of the new federal Constitution, which they regarded as a potentially oppressive instrument likely to strengthen the hands of the substantial propertied classes. But these defeats, and that suffered a few years later by the Whiskey Boys in Pennsylvania, did not mean that the political liberalism of the Revolution and the Enlightenment had been smothered; Jefferson's election in 1800 proved otherwise.

Just as the American Revolution provided impetus for the popularization of the natural rights philosophy, deism, humanitarianism, and a democratic conception of culture, so the French Revolution clarified and sharpened political and social philosophies and invigorated American democratic thought. "Tom, Dick, and Harry" wore the revolutionary cockade and addressed each other as "Citizen" and their wives as "Citizeness" or "Citess" for short. They gave evidence in bold demonstrations and at civic feasts, as well as in the newly organized democratic societies, of their intention to translate the slogan "liberty, equality, and fraternity" into political and social realities. And the enthusiasm for the French Revolution, from which conservatives quickly shied away after momentary applause at the first events of that upheaval, naturally fed the springs of all the more advanced ideas of the Enlightenment.

## The Spread of Deism

The growth of deism and the militancy of its chief apostles resulted in part from the secularization which the struggle against England quickened. This secularization found expression in that worldliness against which devout men and women vehemently protested, in the growth of anticlericalism, and in the movement for separation of church and state. But the association of Americans with French rationalists who had come to help the colonies in the revolt against Britain or whose writings enjoyed vogue also fanned the fame of militant deism. The adamantine resistance of the clergy, in both France and America, to the ideals of the French Revolution confirmed its American sympathizers in their opposition to the supernatural doctrines on which the power of the clergy rested. But the spread of deism among the American masses, even under these favorable circumstances, would scarcely have made such headway as it did without the appearance of new leaders and new methods for spreading the doctrine.

In the early period of the American Enlightenment many deists had hesitated to espouse the cause openly lest they forfeit the approval of those more conservative than themselves. They feared that deism might open the gates to social unrest and equalitarianism by undermining the social control of the masses provided by orthodox religion. But because of the new democratic spirit released by the revolution at home and further stimulated by that in France, deists appeared who took positive joy in spreading their ideas among the masses. Since periodicals and newspapers did not reach the rank and file, new organs appeared which were popular in appeal and specifically dedicated to the cause of winning the people. Enthusiastic deists inaugurated popular societies for spreading the cult and undertook missionary journeys up and down the land. Readable tracts also proved a promising method for taking deism to the people.

The first militantly deistic work from the pen of an American appeared in 1784 under the title *Reason the Only Oracle of Man*. Although the book was nominally the work of the notorious Green Mountain rebel, Ethan Allen, probably a considerable part of this lively if somewhat crudely executed polemic was actually written by Dr. Thomas Young, a patriotic physician whom Allen had known in Connecticut. The book found few readers; perhaps this was because a fire destroyed all but thirty copies of the first and only edition (an act of God, the orthodox piously held). Yet the revolutionary prestige of its author made it well known, and the diatribes of the orthodox, typical of which are the lines from Timothy Dwight's *Triumph of Infidelity*, familiarized many with its existence:

In vain thro realms of nonsense ran
The great clodhopping oracle of man.
Yet faithful were his toils; What could he more?
In Satan's cause he bustled, bruised and swore;
And what the due reward, from me shall know,
For gentlemen of equal worth below.

Yet in spite of the scoffing of Timothy Dwight, *Reason the Only
Oracle of Man* was important because it was symptomatic of the new
militant mood of deism. It unmincingly rejected the doctrine of revelation on the ground that natural religion, based on reason alone, was
entirely sufficient, and it repudiated miracles on the score that they
implied that the machine the Deity had created was imperfect in its
functioning. The Old Testament account of creation was subjected
both to satirical jibes and to a rigorous criticism in which inconsistencies
were thoroughly aired. Ethan Allen's treatise was not original. Nor was
it free from serious philosophical defects. It failed adequately to identify
or relate creator and creation or to attack the problem of evil and of
moral freedom. But Ethan Allen expounded the deistic position without
hedging. Moreover, he identified deism with Americanism. Let feudal
and corrupt Europe, with its kingcraft and its aristocracy, worship an
absolute, arbitrary sovereign before whom men kowtowed like serfs!
According to the Green Mountain leader, deism would provide America
with a republican religion based on law rather than on whims, and on
the dignity and freedom of man rather than on his depravity and
servility.

Far more influential than Ethan Allen's homespun book was *The Age
of Reason* by Thomas Paine, pioneer champion of American independence. The first part of this sincere if somewhat bumptious attack on
what Paine regarded as fiction and fable in religion appeared in Paris
in 1794; the second part, written by its imprisoned author in the shadow
of the Paris guillotine, reached America two years later. The cosmopolitan humanitarian wrote his fiery deistic tract because, in his judgment,
the reactionary clergy in France made use of Scriptures to strengthen
their authority and thus to block human progress. The former Quaker
incidentally desired to check the tide of atheistic materialism by strip-
ping orthodox Christianity of the "claptrap" that discredited it in the
eyes of rationally minded men. For the thesis of *The Age of Reason* was
that Christian theological doctrines are irreconcilable not only with

man's divine gift of reason but also with the knowledge that man gains about the power and wisdom of God through the scientific study of the universe. In advancing his arguments against Christian cosmology, theology, and ethics, Paine popularized the long line of English anticlerical and rationalistic thinkers. Holding the account in Genesis to be merely an Israelite myth, he insisted that it was possible to know through reason that the universe was created by God, not as a showman whimsically performing his tricks but as a First Cause working through the laws of nature. Only if religion were purified by eliminating its myths, only if it completely dissociated itself from political systems, could it render its truly ennobling functions; only then could it aid rather than fetter man in his struggle for freedom and fraternity.

*The Age of Reason* was scattered the length and breadth of the land. Newspapers advertised it, together with the counterblasts that conservatives wrote to overthrow it. Bishop Mead of Virginia found even Parson Weems selling the heretical tract at the tavern in Fairfax County Courthouse. The democratic clubs and the deistical societies used it as a textbook. College students swallowed it whole, to the great alarm of their preceptors; and humble men in villages from New Hampshire to Georgia and beyond the Alleghenies discussed it by tavern candlelight. The storm of criticism which the book brought forth for the time only seemed to feed the fire, nor did the epithets cast on Paine slow down the conflagration. He was abused as a filthy atheist, a dissolute drunkard, a malignant blasphemer, a superficial reasoner. Believing him guilty of spreading a damnable heresy among the people, the orthodox overlooked his earlier services to American freedom and vilified him without stint. When he returned to America in 1802, he was well received by those who had come under his spell, but the tide had turned in favor of conservatism. His last years were impoverished, lonely, and wretched.

Another example of the more brilliant type of deism was the book by the French savant Volney entitled *Ruins: Or A Survey Of The Revolution Of Empires* (1791). This was an oversimplified examination of comparative religions that rejected all supernatural accounts on the ground that it was impossible to know which religion possessed the truth. It was anticlerical in tone and critical of most of the theological and certain ethical doctrines of the New Testament. The *Ruins* was translated by Jefferson and Joel Barlow, and enjoyed a popularity that was promoted even further by Volney's sojourn in the United States.

But the propagation of deism among the people owed more to a former Baptist clergyman trained at Dartmouth than to any other single person. Elihu Palmer, the blind deist who devoted all his energy to the attack on orthodox supernaturalism, was, like Paine, largely motivated by a devotion to republicanism, which in his view was jeopardized by the alliance of aristocracy, despotism, and revealed religion. In his *Principles of Nature* (1802) Palmer elaborated a system of naturalistic ethics divorced from theology, attacked as absurd and immoral the orthodox tenets of revealed Christianity, and ridiculed the story of the flood as a mere superstition which in effect destroyed the order, beauty, and harmony of the universe.

Palmer's contributions lay less in his written exposition of deism, which after all rethreshed old straw, than in the force that he gave to the organization of a bold and, in its appeals to the masses, engaging movement. Palmer became the center of a group of militant deists that included such men as John Fitch of steamboat fame, Colonel John Fellows, a revolutionary patriot and democrat, Dennis Driscoll, an ex-Irish priest, and the eccentric Scotsman "Walking John Stewart," a quasi-materialist who lectured and wrote during his American sojourn in 1796. These men, with Palmer the chief dynamo, organized deistic clubs such as the Society of Ancient Druids and the theophilanthropist societies and established ties with the pro-Jacobin democratic societies that had sprung up in 1794. Popular organs, including *The Beacon, The Temple of Reason,* and *The Philanthropist,* testified to the open and proselyting character of the newly organized movement. Elihu Palmer's efforts did not cease until his death in 1806. Though no one person formally took his mantle, the deistic gospel was carried on by British residents in the United States, among them George Houston, Robert Owen, and Frances Wright. The *rapprochement* of free thought and some elements of the organized labor movement in New York and other cities in the late 1820s owed much to the labors of Robert Owen, his son Robert Dale Owen, and Frances Wright. But Palmer's work marked the high tide of the movement.

Although it is impossible to know how many persons held to the main tenets of deism, it is plain that deists were confined to no single area and to no one class. It seems clear that the spread of heterodoxy among the masses, or the fear that it might spread among them, was the chief occasion for the anxiety displayed by men and women of conservative religious faith.

Since deism was associated with equalitarianism, above all with the "infidel" and "materialistic" doctrines and practices of the French revolutionists, any support that it found in high places in the young Republic provoked the wrath and bitterness of the standpatters. Thus Federalists welcomed the diatribes of the orthodox New England clergy in the presidential campaign of 1800. Hostile clergy declared that Jefferson had so thoroughly subscribed to French infidelity that his election to the Presidency would result in the confiscation of every Bible in New England! Jefferson had, in fact, been influenced by deistic thought, but he had never lent open aid to militant deism. He had come to feel that the teachings of Jesus were superior to those of any other leader and that the church, if purified of corruptions of dogma and of its tie-up with politics, might serve useful ends. His position, in short, was closer to Unitarianism than to the extreme doctrines of infidelity with which the conservative clergy charged him.

### Universalism and Unitarianism

If in general the substantial groups in society did not openly favor deism, especially after men in humble walks of life responded to its appeal or seemed to be on the point of doing so, rationalistic and humane versions of Christianity did make headway among well-to-do people, especially in New England.

Spokesmen in New England for the new liberal theology were a group of ministers known in the eighteenth century as "Arminians," led by Charles Chauncy and Jonathan Mayhew. Chauncy was a Lockean in his conception of human nature, and he was firmly committed to the idea of progress. Intelligent beings, he wrote, "are continually going on, while they suitably employ and improve their original faculties, from one degree of attainment to another; and, hereupon, from one degree of happiness to another, without end." The liberal theologians did not hold man in contempt, as did the older Calvinists, but exalted him, chiefly because of his reason. "It is by our reason that we are exalted above the beasts of the field," Mayhew preached. "It is by this that we are allied to the angels, and all the glorious intelligences of the heavenly world: yea, by this we resemble God himself."[1] As they praised reason and

---

[1] Quoted in Conrad Wright, *The Beginnings of Unitarianism in America* (Starr King Press, 1955), 138.

affirmed the idea of progress, Chauncy, Mayhew, and their followers also rejected the harsh conception of God that was central to the old Calvinism. God was not for them an incomprehensible tyrant, meting out stern justice to contemptible creatures, but rather the wisest and best of fathers. Such concepts of God and man were congenial to the spirit of the Enlightenment, and they bore institutional fruit in Universalism and Unitarianism.

Universalism owed its inception to the Englishman John Murray, who organized a congregation in Gloucester, Massachusetts, in 1779. But Chauncy had anticipated the central doctrine of Universalism when he declared that God, being infinitely good, could only have decreed that all men were to be saved. In 1794 a Universalist convention in Philadelphia formally organized the sect; but only with the promotional work of its great leader, Hosea Ballou, did its doctrine proclaiming the Fatherhood of God and the Brotherhood of Man and rejecting the idea of eternal punishment win a substantial following.

Similar to Universalism in some respects, Unitarianism was both more comprehensive in its theology and more influential. When James Freeman and his congregation at King's Chapel in Boston formally took the Unitarian position in 1783–1784, the note most prominent in their new prayerbook was the emphasis on the subordinate nature of Christ in the Trinity. Even before King's Chapel broke with Anglicanism on this point, such liberals in the Congregational churches as Thomas Barnard and John Prince had subscribed to the related Arian conception, which denied the consubstantial nature of the persons of the Trinity. In 1786 the Reverend William Bentley of Salem read with approval the objections to Trinitarianism in the writings of the well-known English scientist and Unitarian, Joseph Priestley. Priestley himself came to Pennsylvania, but his efforts to popularize Unitarianism there met with slight success. In New England itself, on the other hand, the visit of the English Unitarian, William Hazlitt (1783–1785), crystallized much that was already under way. Boston theologians of a rationalistic bent had begun in 1783 to correspond with such English Unitarians as Dr. Theophilus Lindsey. The subsequent publication of their letters revealed how rapid was the movement toward Unitarianism in the postrevolutionary years, and also brought into the open the cleavage within the Congregational churches that had hitherto existed more or less covertly. With the establishment of Unitarian parishes in Portland, Worcester, and other towns, and with the appointment of Henry Ware as Hollis professor of divinity at Harvard (1805), Unitarianism became a force with which orthodoxy had to reckon.

In the place that Unitarians made for revelation and even for miracles they were at odds with the deists and indeed with the leading exponents of the Enlightenment. But in emphasizing the importance of reason as an instrument for discovering the true meanings of God, in setting great store on conscience as authority and on freedom of inquiry, the early Unitarians were children of the Age of Reason. The spell of the Enlightenment was also evident in their conviction that human nature is divine and that man is therefore too good to be damned. These attitudes, together with their rejection of authoritarianism and terrorism in religion, were exemplified in the opening hymn of Jeremy Belknap's collection (1795), so popular in Unitarian circles:

> Absurd and vain attempt to bind
> With iron chains, the freeborn mind!
> To force conviction, and reclaim
> The wandering, by destructive flame!

The tendency of the early Unitarians to separate theory from social action, their emphasis on thought rather than on feeling, and their somewhat mechanical, logical habit of weighing texts suggested some of the limitations of the Enlightenment. But the moral and ethical teachings of the Scotch philosophers and the intuitional inspirationalism of Coleridge and the Kantian idealists were ultimately, through the agency of William Ellery Channing, to lead to new revolts within the Unitarian ranks. That, however, is a later story. Meantime the new faith satisfied the upper classes who were its principal but by no means only adherents.

## Materialism

More characteristic of the full-blown European Enlightenment than the mild rationalism of Unitarianism was the general materialistic philosophy. This assumed that the universe could be adequately explained in terms of the existence and nature of matter. Although Cadwallader Colden, who combined an interest in medicine, science, and philosophy with high office in colonial New York, had approached the materialistic position, the general climate of opinion in America was too much ingrained with religious orthodoxy to nourish its growth. Yet it was not unknown. Members of the American Philosophical Society in Philadelphia kept abreast with the materialistic theories of d'Holbach, Buffon, Condorcet, Condillac, and La Mettrie. Without accepting French materialism, the eclectic Jefferson enjoyed a firsthand acquaintance with much of its literature, and if the Scotch common-sense school seemed on the whole more satisfying to him, he did not dismiss offhand the doctrine of Cabanis that explained thought as a secretion of the brain.

When Dr. Joseph Priestley came to Philadelphia in 1794 as a refugee from reactionary thought and persecution in England, he familiarized a small circle of Americans with the British materialistic philosophy rooted in the thought of Hume and Hartley. In religious matters Priestley was, it will be recalled, a Unitarian, but this did not interfere with his philosophical materialism, to which he won even fewer converts than to Unitarianism. It is possible that his more outspoken son-in-law, Dr. Thomas Cooper, similarly an exile from the reactionary mood of England, reached a larger number, since his career included the teaching of college youth. Yet even Cooper failed to found a genuine school of materialistic thought. Only a few men and women listened receptively to his doctrine that the soul did not exist previous to the body and ceased to exist with the destruction of the body.

Native-born Americans did contribute something to materialistic doctrine. In 1776 and 1784 publications appeared with a materialistic explanation of the cosmos and of body-and-mind relationships. These treatises were in truth unimpressive, and the pontifical theologians who deigned to notice them at all dismissed them as a wrestler might a featherweight dummy. Far more consequential was the careful and learned address that Dr. Benjamin Rush delivered before the Philosophical Society. *An Inquiry into the Physical Causes upon the Moral Faculty* (1786) demonstrated the influence of disease and the particular physical condition of the brain upon memory, imagination, and moral faculty, dreams, and insanity. The year that Rush published his paper before the American Philosophical Society, the question whether the construction of the organs of the body "made all the difference between an idiot and a wise man" was decided in the affirmative at a Harvard disputation. The theory of the physical causation of many types of insanity had to wait for a full exposition until 1812, when Rush published his *Medical Inquiries and Observations Upon the Diseases of the Mind.*

A far greater number of Americans glimpsed some small part of the materialistic outlook in the *Thanatopsis* (1811) of William Cullen Bryant. Only three years before writing this famous poem Bryant had shared the orthodox Calvinism dominant in his community at Cummington, Massachusetts; but he had come under the influence of Unitarianism, deism, and the pantheism and stoicism of the classics. In *Thanatopsis* the grave is not the road to immortality but the means by which man is united with the vast, timeless, and insensate universe:

> Yet a few days, and thee
> The all-beholding sun shall see no more
> In all his course; nor yet in the cold ground,
> Where thy pale form was laid, with many tears,
> Nor in the embrace of ocean, shall exist
> Thy image. Earth, that nourished thee, shall claim
> Thy growth, to be resolved to earth again,
> And, lost each human trace, surrendering up
> Thine individual being, shall thou go
> To mix forever with the elements,
> To be a brother to the insensible rock
> And to the sluggish clod, which the rude swain
> Turns with his share, and treads upon. The oak
> Shall send his roots abroad, and pierce thy mould.

True, shortly after writing the poem, Bryant emphasized in his subsequent verse the Unitarian conception of an all-powerful, all-knowing Nature identifiable with God, which guided not only the waterfowl from zone to zone in the boundless sky but man's own steps no less.

## Environmentalism and Its Implications

Less offensive to faith than materialism, dispensing as it did with the First Cause in the explanation of the cosmos and of body-mind relationships, was the doctrine that the natural and social environment profoundly influences human nature. The older Calvinistic idea of the essential vileness of human nature was repudiated, it will be recalled, by such liberal theologians as Charles Chauncy, who insisted on the divine nature of mankind. It was also attacked by the Universalists and Unitarians who tended to accept the environmentalist theory, which attributed man's wretched characteristics to irrational surroundings, institutions, and training. Those who did not derive this idea of the essential goodness of human nature from liberal theologians might read the same lesson in the teachings of such thoroughgoing environmentalists as Helvetius, La Mettrie, D'Holbach, and Rousseau.

The environmentalist theory of human nature was in general as distasteful to conservatives as it was acceptable to radicals. In speculating on the causes of mental differences radical and conservative thinkers of that day alike assumed that "reason" dictated the particular view dear to them. Actually, of course, important determinants of such beliefs operated outside the realm of logical and conscious reflection. Preexisting social philosophies shaped attitudes and determined to an appreciable extent the selection of, and weight given to, evidence. Such an hypothesis is strongly supported by the alignment of leading thinkers of the day on the subject of heredity. In disparaging the influence of environment in conditioning mediocrity and talent Alexander Hamilton and John Adams spoke for the majority of their social group. Jefferson, on the other hand, believed that a favorable environment, such as the American countryside, nourished virtuous characteristics in humankind, whereas cities bred or brought out man's lowest and weakest traits.

Influenced by the environmentalist theory of human nature in general and by Condorcet, Godwin, and Mary Wollstonecraft in particular, many liberal Americans, though not Jefferson himself, accepted the idea that the differences in mental ability between the sexes were attributable to the more favorable opportunities provided the male portion of the race. This explanation of the inferior mental accomplishments of women became generally familiar to intellectuals with the publication in Philadelphia in 1794 of Mary Wollstonecraft's A *Vindication of the Rights of Women*. With harsh words she took her sex to task for its complacent acceptance of its degradation, and she chided men for their selfishness in making women inferior by refusing them the educational opportunities that would establish their equality with males. A *Vindication of the Rights of Women* was known to some of the young ladies at Mrs. Susanna Rowson's school in Medford, Massachusetts. In the same vicinity the wife of the leading Universalist minister, Judith Sargent Murray, contributed to the *Massachusetts Magazine* essays suggesting the influence of Mary Wollstonecraft; the "old-fashioned" notion that women were incapable of great achievement was dismissed as a chimera of darkness and prejudice. After having read A *Vindication of the Rights of Women* in the English edition, Aaron Burr remarked in a letter to his wife that woman was capable of the greatest genius and that her deficiencies were to be laid at the door of inadequate education. He straightway embarked on the task of applying these ideas to the education of his daughter Theodosia. At ten she was introduced to Greek; and soon she was reading Terence and Lucian. Enos Hitchcock, a Rhode Island clergyman and educator, refused to accept Rousseau's view that women are an inferior species, and Hannah Adams, the Massachusetts historian, implied that environment had much to do with the inferior achievements of women in many areas of life; woman, she contended, was made not out of man's heel to be trampled upon but out of his side to be equal to him. If this trampling ceased she would rise to the level that nature had intended her to enjoy.

Even wider publicity was given to the new feministic ideas by Charles Brockden Brown. This pioneer American novelist declared that since circumstances molded human beings, who were inherently or innately all of a piece, "the differences that flow from the sexual distinction are as nothing in the balance." In *Alcuin* (1797) this exponent of democracy and of enlightenment pleaded for the legal, political, economic, and cultural freedom of women, and in *Clara Howard* the new independent-minded woman appeared to advantage.

Soil favorable to the growth of these relatively new ideas was present in these postrevolutionary days. Liberal ideas in general were abroad, but special conditions favored a growing appreciation of women's ability. The economic importance of women in a new society where labor was scarce and large families were necessary helped to raise them in the esteem of society. Further there was a growing conviction that women as molders of youth needed to be educated in citizenship, if the republican experiment were to succeed. This position was advanced by Dr. Benjamin Rush in his *Thoughts on Female Education* (1787); it anticipated similar arguments expounded during the following decade in plans for a national system of education suited to a democratic republic. And in real life at least a few women proved that their sex was capable of intellectual achievement. Such women as Abigail Adams, Mercy Warren, Margaret Winthrop, and Martha Ramsay were familiar with many of the great works in theology, religion, and philosophy, with the classics, contemporary literature, and science, and even with politics. The capacity of women to contribute to knowledge had been demonstrated by Jane Colden, who won the approval of eminent botanists for her drawings of unclassified specimens, and by Mercy Warren, who in the revolutionary period wrote plays and made preparations for writing her realistic history of the struggle for independence. However sentimental and imitative of European models their tales and poems were, Elizabeth Ferguson, Sarah Wentworth Morton, Judith Sargent Murray, Susanna Rowson, and Ann Eliza Bleeker were making contributions to the struggling American literature for which high hopes were entertained. These were promising beginnings. Nevertheless, the conservative view of women's ability and function generally held the field.

Many apostles of the Enlightenment applied the doctrine of environmentalism to racial differences. The psychology of Locke and Hartley emphasized the importance of sensory stimuli in developing character, and the environmentalist theories of Montesquieu and his more doctrinaire successors paved the way for the idea that race differences result from environmental inequalities. The rising humanitarian and democratic impulses further nourished the environmentalist theory that race differences are acquired rather than innately stamped by God as a blessing or a curse. In writing to Condorcet, Franklin implied that the poor state of free Negroes resulted from the fact that they had been deprived of an education rather than from any deficiency in natural understanding. Governor James Bowdoin took a similar position in 1785 in addressing the American Academy of Arts and Sciences.

One of the most outspoken champions of this view was Samuel Stanhope Smith, of the College of New Jersey. In 1787 Smith completed his *Essay on the Causes of the Variety of Complexion and Figure in the Human Species*, in which he explained racial differences, including mental traits, on the basis of such natural forces as varied climates and different social modes of living. "The body and mind have such mutual influences," wrote Smith, "that whatever contributes to change the human constitution in its form or aspect, has an equal influence on its powers of reason and genius. . . . The minutest differences, existing constantly, and long continued, will necessarily create great and conspicuous differences among mankind."[2] Such an interpretation of the racial

[2] Samuel Stanhope Smith, *An Essay on the Causes of the Variety of Complexion and Figure in the Human Species* (Philadelphia, 1787), 117–118.

characteristics of the Negro furnished philanthropic slaveowners ideological grounds for emancipating slaves, who in many cases, to be sure, had become a burden rather than an asset.

The vogue of such an environmentalist theory of Negro nature must not be overemphasized. In observing the superiority of the children of mixed unions, Jefferson himself, who was an excellent representative of the Enlightenment, favored the doctrine of the original mental inferiority, perhaps even the separate origin, of the blacks.

Striking an environmentalist note similar to that of Samuel Stanhope Smith, a Philadelphia physician, Dr. Benjamin Smith Barton, argued on the ground of his pioneer studies of Indian languages that the peoples of America and those of Asia had a common origin. He also contended that the physical differences between red and white men are in fact inconsiderable, and that varying environments account for the superiority in the arts and crafts displayed at different times by different peoples. The implication of such an environmentalist doctrine, which many of its exponents held explicitly, was that the white man who had despoiled the Indian should teach him the ways of civilization so that he might enjoy with white men "the desired inheritance." Thus the older missionary ideal of Christianizing the Indian was consciously enlarged to include the bestowal of all the virtues of an enlightened culture. In contrast to this position was the romantic idealization of the red man as a noble savage who in his natural primitive state exemplified dignity, innocence, and bliss. Most Americans, to be sure, were little influenced in their views on the aborigines either by the environmentalist theory so dear to the Age of Reason or by that of the rising Romantic school which engaged many literary men.

## Humanitarianism

The humanitarianism which arose in the later colonial period, and to which the environmentalists' tenets contributed, advanced notably during the Revolution and the succeeding years. In part this was related to the natural rights philosophy of the Revolution, which implied the impropriety of holding slaves, imprisoning honest debtors, and meting out cruel punishments to unfortunate criminals. It reflected the even more comprehensive spirit of the Enlightenment—the belief that human institutions should be tested by reason, that the dignity of man should be recognized and elevated, that steps should be taken to realize the idea of progress. Antislavery sentiment was strengthened by the reading of such writers as Voltaire, Rousseau, and Brissot de Warville, all of whom condemned slavery, and by the abolition of slavery in the French colonial possessions. This sentiment expressed itself in measures for the gradual emancipation of slaves in the northern states and in the manumission of many bondsmen in the South.

The fact that slavery no longer appeared to be profitable made this easier to do. But there was also a widespread conviction that slavery was uncongenial if not contradictory to republican principles, that it stood in the way of realizing the rights of man. William Pinckney, in discussing the proposals for emancipation in the Maryland legislature in 1789, took sharply to task men who talked like philosophers in regard to liberty and at the same time held human beings in bondage. Slavery, he concluded, could only undermine that reverence for liberty which sustained democratic institutions. George Mason of Virginia declared before his death in 1792 that slavery was a slow poison contaminating the minds and morals of slave owners and that it was no less an infernal school of tyranny for future legislators. St. George Tucker, professor of law at William and Mary, wrote in a pamphlet published in 1796 that slavery was completely at variance with the Bill of Rights; he advocated gradual emancipation. Jefferson also favored it, and Washington actually freed his own slaves. In the young commonwealth of Kentucky transplanted Virginians, including Henry Clay, foretold the evil effects of an institution inimical to both justice and good policy. Southerners in Congress approved the section in the Ordinance of 1787 which forbade slavery in the Northwest Territory. If such sentiments could be proclaimed in the South by men who owned slaves, they were even more at home in the North where none could pretend that emancipation would create a race problem or seriously threaten property rights.

Such Enlightenment values, together with the sentiments of humanity so congenial to Quakerism and evangelicism, also suggested the wisdom of acting on the precepts of Beccaria and the example of English prison reformers like John Howard. Pennsylvania in 1794 and Virginia in 1796 revolutionized their criminal codes by greatly decreasing the number of crimes punishable by death. Thanks to the efforts of such Pennsylvanians as Tench Coxe, Benjamin Rush, and William Howard, working through the Society for Alleviating the Miseries of the Public Prisons, the legislature of Pennsylvania in 1790 took important steps toward the reform of prison conditions. The new laws required the classification of criminals, private cells, adequate clothing, religious teaching, and protection from thievery and extortion at the hands of their keepers. At least four states, prompted by the distress induced by the unsettled currency and the misfortune that the tide of speculation had caused many respectable people, ameliorated their laws respecting imprisonment for debt.

## The Idea of Progress

The idea of progress, inherent in the environmentalist theory, found congenial soil in the colonies. Freneau and Raynal spoke for many Americans and Europeans who saw in the uncontaminated wilderness beyond the frontier the ideal setting for a new type of society in which both the poverty and the artificialities and inequalities of a settled society should be abolished. The final blow which the Revolution struck to such feudal relics as primogeniture, entail, union of church and state, and monarchism, as well as the humbling of the aristocracy, invited faith in Utopianism, as did the idealized versions of the Revolution which emanated from such European radicals as Richard Price, Condorcet, and Brissot de Warville. These men saw in our struggle for independence, and later in the French Revolution, an immense impetus to the universal abolition of war, poverty, priestcraft, absolutism, feudalism, and all the special privileges that violate the dignity and equality of mankind. And the prophecies by Godwin and Condorcet of a future Eden rising through science and technology awakened response in the new Republic.

The belief in the perfectibility of human nature and of social institutions found concrete expression in Thomas Paine's *Rights of Man* (1791) and his *Agrarian Justice* (1796). These argued for a continuous reaffirmation by each generation of the original compact by which men established government. In this way government could be kept pure and responsive to the sovereign will of an enlightened people expressed through its majority. Within our grasp, Paine further contended, lay a political economy that could abolish poverty and provide security for the aged through graduated inheritance taxes and ground rents; thus society would receive back what it had created. The security of all would be augmented by the reduction of armaments and the abolition of war itself, an ideal close to the heart of this former Quaker, and, indeed, dear to all apostles of the Age of Reason.

The idea that progress could be accelerated by the agency of the democratic state had other champions. Philip Freneau was hopeful that poverty and war might be uprooted, that the ideal of the perfectibility of human nature and institutions might be realized:

> How can we call those systems just
> Which bid the few, the proud, the first,
> Possess all earthly good;
> While millions robbed of all that's dear
> In silence shed the ceaseless tear
> And leeches suck their blood. . . .
>
> Let laws revive, by heaven designed,
> To tame the tiger in the mind;
> And drive from human hearts
> That love of wealth, that love of sway,
> Which leads the world too much astray,
> Which points envenomed darts:
>
> And men will rise from what they are;
> Sublimer, and superior, far,
> Than Solon guessed, or Plato saw;
> All will be just, all will be good—
> That harmony, "not understood,"
> Will reign the general law.

The doctrine of progress incorporated the Baconian belief in the possibility of the amelioration of society through inductive science. Freneau, in spite of his melancholy primitivism, was reasonably sure than an enlightened science operating on America's vast physical resources would ultimately insure the triumph of equality and freedom. Dr. Benjamin Rush, although less sympathetic than Freneau to the ideal of democracy, nevertheless believed that America might achieve progress by shunning the luxury and sophistication of Europe, promoting Christian piety, and cultivating the utilitarian virtues with the aid of natural science. Franklin, too, saw in science a means to progress. In writing to Priestley he remarked that "it is impossible to imagine the Height to which may be carried, in a thousand years, the Power of Man over Matter. We may perhaps learn to deprive large Masses of their Gravity and give them absolute Levity, for the sake of easy Transport. Agriculture may diminish its Labour and double its produce; all Diseases may by sure means be prevented if not cured, not excepting Old Age, and our Lives lengthened at pleasure even beyond the antediluvian Standard."[3]

No other American expressed so unqualified a faith in the idea of progress and in this country's relation to it as did Joel Barlow. He began his literary career as an associate of the Hartford Wits, whose verse showered satire on all leveling tendencies, but he became a convert to militant democracy during his residence abroad. The development of Barlow's rationalism, humanitarianism, and utilitarianism and the closely related doctrine of progress is revealed by contrasting *The Vision of Columbus* (1787) with the revised and elaborated *Columbiad* (1809). In the former he delineated human history in orthodox fashion, subscribed to the Scottish common-sense distrust of abstract reason, and viewed progress in theological, passive terms. In *The Columbiad*, on the other hand, Barlow now argued that progress could be realized only through effort, and that democracy, science, and a rationalistic, humane education provided the key to that realization. Highly republican and nationalistic in tone and completely in tune with the ideas of the Enlightenment, *The Columbiad* indicted the feudal remnants in civilization, glorified the perfectibility of human nature and institutions, and argued for the application of scientific method in morals and government as the most certain means of opening the door to unlimited good. America was set apart by Providence itself for this world mission:[4]

> For here great nature with a bolder hand,
> Roll'd the broad stream and heaved the lifted hand;
> And here, from finisht earth, triumphant trod,
> The last ascending steps of her creating God.

The decadence of ancient nations, largely the result of war, poverty, and the privileged status of the arts, would find no parallel in America, which was to end war by bringing the nations together in a league of peace and to inaugurate a democratic humanism by elevating everyone to enjoy the highest level of comfort, beauty, and knowledge.

[3] Albert H. Smythe (ed.), *The Writings of Benjamin Franklin* (Philadelphia, 1905–1907), VIII, 10.
[4] Joel Barlow, *The Columbiad* (Philadelphia, 1809), I, 39.

Barlow's devotion to the idea of progress was unqualified, but many of its exponents had certain reservations. Few of them, indeed, had even glimmerings of the possibility that science, instead of enlightening and emancipating mankind, might become the instrument of a competitive economic order that would foster inequality and materialistic values and, by providing new and deadly weapons, further war itself. But many did have their doubts about the essential goodness and potential altruism and wisdom of human nature. Franklin, after prophesying his mechanical utopia, regretfully added, "O that moral science were in a fair way of improvement, that men would cease to be wolves to one another, and that beings would at length learn what they now improperly call humanity!" Franklin in particular feared that our progress, intimately related as it was to our abundant resources, might one day be halted when those resources were exhausted. Nor was he the only one who had his misgivings about human nature. Jefferson, whose conception of progress was also bound up with his faith in an agrarian society of small freeholders, gloomily distrusted the nonlandowning proletariat born of the cities.

While some of the exponents of the idea of progress entertained such qualifications, they believed that the chief dangers to the realization of the idea might be neutralized. To his dying day Franklin hoped that mutual cooperation between men and nations might remedy many of the shortcomings of human nature. Rush believed that the inculcation of Christian piety and discipline and the utilitarian virtues which science fostered would serve the same end. The enlightened use of science, he thought, might even result in new resources to replace those that became exhausted.

Others suggested even more definite measures for insuring the triumph of progress. The authors of plans for a national system of education suitable for a republic, including Rush himself, advocated greater emphasis on the social and natural sciences and all the values inherent in a democratic humanism. Nathaniel Chipman, a Vermont legislator and judge, argued (1795) the value of a new type of history. In his judgment historians should pay less attention to the cyclical theories of history that engaged Polybius, Machiavelli, and Vico; make less of battles, the intrigues of statesmen, and the "revolutions of empire," and select for emphasis the forces that had advanced social progress and the improvement of the human mind. By promoting a better understanding of psychological and social forces the historian might enable Americans to direct their future course more certainly along the path of progress.[5]

Political measures appealed to others as the best way to overcome threats to progress. Convinced that progress was merely a chimera if Federalist policies were unchecked, John Taylor of Caroline, Virginia, called on agrarian America to mobilize against the menace of chartered banks, protective tariffs, and moneyed corporations. In his *Enquiry into the Principles and Tendency of Certain Public Measures* (1794) Taylor attacked these rising institutions as instruments of the moneyed aristocracy for exploiting other classes. In subsequent writings this economic realist warned his fellow citizens that unless corporations were checked they would erect a new moneyed aristocracy that would sink America to the level of former aristocracies.

### The Vogue of the Modern Languages and Literatures

While it would be too much to say that the classics were disparaged by all the disciples of the idea of progress and the Enlightenment, they unquestionably did hold a less important place in the liberal climate of opinion of the late eighteenth century than they had once held. Jefferson, who so well exemplified the Enlightenment, continued to find inspiration in the classics, and Franklin himself looked with greater favor on them in later life; but Dr. Benjamin Rush was more representative of the American exponents of the Enlightenment. Writing in 1791, Rush declared that the emphasis the classics had received explained in large measure the prejudice which the masses felt for institutions of learning. So long as Latin and Greek remained the only avenues to education, universal diffusion of knowledge beyond the bare rudiments was impossible. In a new country where the chief task was to explore and develop natural resources, education should be functional to the main concern. "Under these circumstances, to spend four or five years in learning two dead languages, is to turn our backs upon a gold mine, in order to amuse ourselves catching butterflies." If the time spent on Latin and Greek were devoted to science, continued this champion of

[5] Nathaniel Chipman, *Sketches of the Principles of Government* (Rutland, Vermont, 1793), 31–33.

utilitarianism, we might expect within a short time a revolution not only in science but in human affairs. For in Rush's eyes science was the chief instrument of social progress.

Though the time had not come for uprooting the classics in American education, Rush's attack was nevertheless prophetic. That they were declining even then was suggested a few years later by the Reverend Samuel Miller's lament that much college instruction in the classics was superficial, a state of affairs which he attributed not only to the appeal of natural science but to the increasing vogue of the modern tongues.

French and German were known to many cultured colonists in the seventeenth century, and with the development of commercial interests in the mid-eighteenth century private schools began to offer instruction in French, Spanish, Portuguese, and Italian. But a marked increase of interest in French is traceable after 1770. Thanks to the subsequent alliance with Louis XVI, enthusiasm for French science, philosophy, and culture ran high. Private tutors were much in demand, and both academies and girls' schools offered instruction in the language. At Jefferson's suggestion, the College of William and Mary appointed a professor of modern languages in 1780, and about the same time Harvard provided for the study of French, even going so far presently as to permit students to substitute it for Hebrew. Columbia appointed a French professor in 1794, and Rhode Island College sought the aid of Louis XVI to that end. So great was the importance attached to French that in 1792, when Williams College was launched, it was accepted in lieu of the classics for entrance. A few years later the University of North Carolina did likewise. Although this enthusiasm for the language and culture waned among conservative groups after the execution of Louis XVI and the more radical turn of the French Revolution, it increased among the democrats, who nonchalantly tripped off phrases to show their political and social sympathies. Not until the close of the century did the great reaction against French set in.

The interest in modern languages and literature extended to English itself. Jefferson endeavored to facilitate the study of Anglo-Saxon by the preparation of a simplified grammar. General acclaim was accorded to Noah Webster's studies in orthography and linguistics. Having mulled over in his mind his bold theory that language should be phonetically simplified to render it more suitable to the untutored people using it, Webster in 1800 took up seriously his long-contemplated task of compiling *The Compendious Dictionary of the English Language* (1806).

Colonial Americans had always taken pride in the fact that they could participate in the glories of English letters, and the favored classes even in the seventeenth century read more widely than has been supposed. But the rise of literary circles in the postrevolutionary years was indicative of a new type of interest in letters. These groups gossiped about living English writers, read their works as they appeared, went back and familiarized themselves with earlier authors, and tried their own hand at imitating the prevalent literary forms. In fact, to judge from the space devoted to belles-lettres in newspapers and from book inventories, advertisements, and library lists, the vogue for literary works was considerable. Even the colleges responded by paying greater attention to rhetoric and belles-lettres; the esthetic principles of such British authorities as Blair and Kames aroused attention in academic circles. At Yale the interest in English literature that was apparent on the eve of the Revolution continued; and in 1794 William Ellery Channing, on entering Harvard, found that undergraduates were passionately fond of Shakespeare who, it is true, was not yet recognized in the curriculum.

While the interest in modern English letters was largely fed by the importation of books from the British Isles, in Boston in the early 1790s two of Shakespeare's plays were printed for the first time in America; in 1795 the first complete American edition of Shakespeare, with an apology for the dramatist's morals and some textual criticism, began to issue from a Philadelphia press. Before the end of the century, a "speaker" included oratorical passages from Shakespeare. Thus with the decline of interest in the classics the body of humanistic English letters won increasing favor.

At least one voice pleaded for the elevation of everyday tasks to an esthetic level, for the eradication of the old aristicratic separation between beauty and use. Thomas Odiorne, in *The Progress of Refinement* (1792), set forth a conception of a democratic esthetics characteristic of the American Enlightenment:

> Let not America's aspiring sons,
> To independent greatness born, to arts
> Refined, and virtue eminent, deserve
> The imputation low of idle clowns.
> To make the towering forest to the axe
> Submit, to pile the enormous log, apply
> The fire, subdue and cultivate the land,
> In no mean labor of the ambitious swain . . .

And all, performing their allotted part,
Become shrewd artists at their work, expert,
Exact; and, by the mutual task of all,
Society, just like an instrument,
With various unisons, which harmonize
In concord sweet, and breathe the general song,
Is to perfection reared, to wealth and fame,
Obtains utensils for convenient life,
Heaps high emolument, and in the tide
Of honour riots, while kind fortune smiles.

## Science

The advances in natural science testified even more markedly than
the interest in modern literature to the hold of the Enlightenment on
the young Republic. Certain conservatives who associated the vogue for
science with the subversive Jacobinism of the French Revolution satirized the passion for the investigation of natural phenomena. Followers
of the Enlightenment, on the other hand, were devoted to science. In
their view science, more than any other single force, challenged supernaturalism and the weight of the past and promised the acceleration of
the era of peace, progress, and plenty.

Captain Cook's voyages in the South Seas, on one of which he was
accompanied by John Ledyard, a Connecticut roamer of fearless courage, greatly extended geographical knowledge. Subsequent expeditions
enlarged man's knowledge of all the continents and seas. America's sense
of isolation was lessened by anticipation of commercial intercourse with
the newly discovered parts of the world; in 1784 the first American ship
reached Canton, paving the way for cultural contacts, albeit limited.
Pride was taken in the increase of comforts and elegancies which the
enlarged world had made or promised to make. In addition, every department of science profited from the eighteenth-century discoveries;
new light was thrown on meteorology, mineralogy, biology, and what
would now be termed anthropology.

Although the young Republic played no direct part in the overseas
undertakings that enlarged men's horizons and stimulated their imaginations, the Lewis and Clark expedition to the Pacific northwest, befriended by President Jefferson and undertaken under government

auspices in 1804, greatly enlarged knowledge of the geography, geology, botany, zoology, and ethnography of the vast regions lately acquired from Napoleon.

American naturalists followed the investigations of European geologists. They were stimulated by the controversy over the origin of the surface of the earth waged by the Vulcanists, who contended that subterranean heat was responsible for the superficial structure of the earth, and the Neptunists, who maintained that the earth's surface had been built by successive deposits of rocks, the precipitates of a great primeval ocean. Both the Wernian or Neptunist and the Huttonian or Vulcanist theories assumed a catastrophic rather than an evolutionary origin of the earth's surface; nevertheless, as naturalistic explanations they reinforced the rationalists' insistence on the inadequacy of the Mosaic account of creation.

Americans in general contributed little to the Neptunist-Vulcanist controversy, but two men threw some light on the problem and in so doing strengthened a naturalistic interpretation of geological formations. In 1793 Benjamin De Witt, recognizing perhaps for the first time the phenomenon known as glacial drift, tried to explain the presence of various minerals on the shore of Lake Ontario by "some mighty convulsion of nature." He further remarked that perhaps "this vast lake may be considered as one of those great fountains of the deep which were broken up when our earth was deluged with water, thereby producing that confusion and disorder in the composition of its surface which evidently seems to exist." Jefferson, unable to explain in terms of Mosaic cosmogony the existence of marine fossils on the highest mountains of the American continents, preferred to follow the evidence of sense experience, measurement, and accurate calculation rather than to rely on Biblical authority. With other naturalists he also devoted much effort to the classification of elephant-like fossils discovered in several parts of the country—baffling witnesses of a prehistoric past which suggested that the earth was of greater antiquity than students who made their deductions from Biblical chronology thought.

In a less spectacular way the supernaturalistic conception of the earth was weakened by the accretions to the geological knowledge of America made by such investigators as Schopf and Volney, and by a company of American amateurs who sent to the learned societies specimens and descriptions of newly discovered oilstones, yellow and red pigments, and a variety of minerals. Especially noteworthy was the appearance in 1798 of a work from the hands of a New York physician, Dr. Samuel L. Mitchill, in which he accurately described the granite, schistic, limestone, and sandstone tracts of eastern New York.

Other investigators, impelled by curiosity, patriotism, or the love of rational truth so characteristic of the Age of Reason, helped to rub off the dust from the murky lamp of hearsay by providing more accurate descriptions and classifications of American flora and fauna. William Peck, a Harvard graduate who had settled on a Maine farm, studied insects and aquatic life and in 1794 contributed a description of a new species of fish in what has been called the first American paper on systematic zoology.

To the descriptions of American flora made by André Michaux and his son, native citizens of the Republic added their contributions. In Pennsylvania Humphrey Marshall, a farmer, Gothilf Mühlenburg, a pastor, and Benjamin Smith Barton, a college professor, surveyed the natural history of their state. In Massachusetts Manasseh Cutler, the parson who helped organize the Ohio territory, collected and classified the flora of his neighborhood. Even when investigators saw in the natural world evidences of the unfolding of a divine purpose, as did the gentle Quaker William Bartram in his admirable *Travels through North and South Carolina, Georgia, East and West Florida* (1791), the accurate knowledge that was contributed paved the way for a naturalistic understanding of the universe. Bartram, in making man merely one of God's creatures, still further undermined the orthodox Biblical conception of man as the center of the universe and ruler of all living things.

Although American naturalists were chiefly concerned with the problem of collecting and classifying data, they were not entirely indifferent to the larger theoretical problems that, even in a period of description and taxonomical emphasis, concerned European scientists. In the controversy between Linnaeus, who advocated classification according to the stamens and pistils of flowering plants, and Buffon and the de Jussieus, whose superior system was based on natural resemblances, American botanists, including Jefferson, sided with the great Swede. Not until 1815, when Jefferson's Portuguese friend, the Abbè Correa, reduced the genera of Mühlenburg's catalogue to "the natural system," did it begin to come into its own.

If the pioneer genetic theory of Charles Bonnet, who died in 1793, seems to have aroused little interest in America, some of our naturalists, familiar as they were with the quasi-evolutionary conceptions of Leibnitz, Maupertuis, Diderot, and Buffon, must have had glimmerings of the developmental hypothesis. Jefferson, with his fossils strewn over a room of the American Philosophical Society and later over the White House, recognized that all beings had not been created to continue for all time. The origins of physical life occupied the specific attention of Dr. Benjamin Waterhouse of Harvard, who explained the beginnings of life in terms of "the principle of vitality" or "animation" (which in turn was related to the First Cause). The majority of American students no doubt accepted this a priori explanation; but in its studies of the phenomenon of drowning, the Massachusetts Humane Society, established in 1795, utilized the scientific method for investigating the nature of life and death.

In chemistry the eighteenth century witnessed a virtual revolution. Tables of chemical affinities, the first isolation of a gas, the discovery of new metals and acids, and the invention of instruments for precise measurement laid the foundations for the incalculably important contributions made toward the end of the century by French chemists, particularly Lavoisier. Rejecting the widely held phlogiston theory, which assumed that but one element, phlogiston, existing in combination with metals, was capable of combustion, the French chemists set down the metals as simple substances rather than combinations of substances and phlogiston. This capital contribution, together with the new nomenclature and the new table of chemical symbols, greatly accelerated chemical advance.

The coming of Joseph Priestley to Pennsylvania in 1794 on the one hand greatly stimulated the rising group of American chemists but on the other tended to retard the reception of the new French theories. Dr. Priestley, famous not only for his espousal of Unitarianism and of materialistic philosophy but for his discovery of oxygen and for other notable chemical contributions, endeared himself all the more to liberal Americans by virtue of the fact that he had been driven out of his own country by the wave of reactionary persecution. His experiments in his little laboratory at Northumberland, Pennsylvania, led to the discovery of carbon monoxide, the liberation of air from water, and increased knowledge about spontaneous combustion and the action of caustic alkalies on flint glass. Priestley, who proved to be a vigorous stimulus to other chemists, increased the scientific prestige of Philadelphia, which had long been the scientific center of America. But his efforts to rehabilitate the phlogiston theory which the French chemists had made obsolete occasioned sharp controversies with American chemists who either accepted or leaned toward the new school.

At Columbia Dr. Samuel L. Mitchill, the distinguished naturalist whose work included pioneer investigations in both geology and biology, introduced in 1792 the system of Lavoisier and attempted to reconcile it to the phlogiston theory. Three years later John MacLean, a Scottish surgeon, expounded the French theory at the College of New Jersey with less deference to Priestley. But the most redoubtable foe of the phlogiston theory was Dr. James Woodhouse, of the medical school in Philadelphia, who in 1792 established what was one of the first chemical societies in the world. In the society's ill-equipped little laboratory Woodhouse conducted experiments that established the basaltic character of certain rock formations, demonstrated the action of nitric acid on metals, and laid the foundations for subsequent contributions to the chemistry of white starch, camphor, and anthracite coal. His *Young Chemist's Pocket Companion* (1797) has been regarded as the first published guide for American students of experimental chemistry. A true son of the Enlightenment, Woodhouse gave lectures that were distinguished for their want of reference to the dominantly held idea that the character of the Creator was reflected in the chemical kingdom. The practicability of Lavoisier's theories was also demonstrated when Eleuthère Irénée du Pont de Nemours, physiocratic philosopher and friend of Jefferson, started the powder business in Delaware.

American scientists were zealous in putting their specialized knowledge to the service of mankind. Mitchill advanced (1795–1797) his theory of "satanic septon," according to which the chemical union of oxygen and azote (or septon) emitted from putrefying matter acted as an acidic febrile poison in producing many diseases. Although he was incorrect in assuming that the organic decay which emitted "satanic septon" was itself the cause of disease, his teaching on the value of alkalies for neutralizing acidified matter was well founded as was his insistence on sanitation.

Science was also drawn upon to promote the improvement of agriculture. The work of Jared Eliot of Connecticut and Arthur Young in England was continued by David Humphreys, who experimented with livestock breeding. While in Paris Jefferson sent to Americans for experimental purposes many seeds and plants, including the olive, the cork oak, and an improved variety of rice. This versatile gentleman farmer's design in 1798 for "the first scientific basis for the curve of the mold-board" in the plow was notable because it symbolized the transition from trial-and-error invention to invention by scientific law. The growing interest in scientific farming also found expression in agricultural socie-ties, which were established from 1785 on by merchants, professional men, and large landowners. These pioneer societies, in offering premiums for discoveries in plant and animal economy, were more akin to the learned academies of the eighteenth century than to popular farmers' organizations.

Americans of the early Republic also displayed ingenuity in applying scientific principles to inventions designed to control nature, promote human comfort, and make a profit. Shortly after independence was won, facilities for carding cotton and wool were improved by Oliver Evans' invention of a machine which in performing three functions broke a new path. Other pioneers were experimenting with the steamboat. On August 22, 1787, John Fitch sailed a twelve-side-paddle steamboat up the Delaware. John Stevens, whose attention was called to this boat, invented an improved vertical steam boiler and savery type of steam engine which, with other experiments in steam engineering, were to make him a pioneer in the development of a steam engine for railways. An equally significant invention was, of course, the cotton gin. By 1793 Eli Whitney, a guest on the Georgia plantation of General Nathanael Greene's widow, had produced a model of a cotton gin which, with the rivals it suggested, was presently enabling short-fiber cotton to be pro-duced profitably on a large scale. This process was destined to rehabili-tate the institution of slavery and to make possible the immense development of cotton textiles. Before the end of the century Whitney had formulated the principle of interchangeable parts of machinery in the manufacture of muskets at his factory near New Haven. This prin-ciple, which Samuel Colt, of arms-making fame, was later to develop, finally came to be one of the important reasons for the superiority of American technology. To what extent all these and other inventions would promote the ideals of the Enlightenment no contemporary could be sure; but its optimistic exponents felt that these advances in science and in its application augured well for their values. Meantime interests and ideas hostile to the Enlightenment were being asserted.

# 8 The Conservative Reaction

> We have had too many French philosophers
> already, and I really begin to think, or rather
> to suspect, that learned academies, not under
> the immediate inspection and control of gov-
> ernment, have disorganized the world, and
> are incompatible with social order.
>
> —JOHN ADAMS, 1798

The exuberance with which many plain people and their leaders hailed the French Revolution, accepted deism, celebrated the idea of progress, and proclaimed the dawn of a new day was met by the counter-defense of those who saw little but evil in the claims of democracy at home and in the Revolution abroad. The conflict was not formal or sharply defined. Many substantial merchants and planters repudiated the political, social, and economic philosophy of the Enlightenment and the French Revolution without rejecting deistic and rationalistic ideas. Some clergymen and a great number of plain people accepted democratic ideas but rejected skepticism and rationalism in the religious realm. Yet a conservative defense did emerge and, among different groups, became well formulated by the 1790s. The American Enlightenment, strong in the first flush of the revolutionary enthusiasm that created the new nation, was now under sharp attack. The conservative attack was both negative and positive, and the two aspects overlapped at many points. Negatively the defense of the established pattern of

178

economic, social, and political arrangements centered in an attack on the French Revolution and alleged Jacobinism at home; positively a case was made for institutionalism, aristocracy, the continued restriction of suffrage to substantial property owners, and revealed religion.

Given ideas, whether liberal or conservative, were not sharply and precisely identified with particular social and economic groups. Some of the leaders of the people were, like Jefferson, large slaveowners and landowners. Some humble people in the cities and a great many in the villages and on the farms did not share democratic ideas at all. Professional men were divided, some siding with the champions of democracy or the Enlightenment or the French Revolution, some taking a conservative position in political and economic matters or in religion, or in both.

It is still true, however, that it was the substantial merchants and planters and the professional men most closely associated with them who were the chief critics of the Enlightenment and the French Revolution, of Daniel Shays and Thomas Jefferson. The critics of many of the ideas associated with the Enlightenment enjoyed a large measure of political power in the years between the framing of the Constitution in 1787 and the election of Jefferson in 1800. The Jay Treaty of 1794 and the quasi-war against France represented political victories for conservative interest and ideas. The cause of democracy and the Enlightenment suffered even more from the Alien Act, which enabled the government to deport noisy agitators who had sought asylum from European reaction in America, and the Sedition Act, intended to silence the fulminations that American "Jacobins" directed against their Federalist foes. The victory of political liberalism in 1800 did not end the conservative criticism. Conservatives drew support from England, where the great Edmund Burke had forged a brilliant defense of the authority of the past, of institutionalism and legalism, of property rights, and of the rule of the substantial classes, and where Hannah More was representative of a great evangelical and pietistic pattern of thought.

The intellectual bulwarks erected by the conservatives to hold off the democrats were too strong to be taken even with Jefferson's entrance into the White House in 1801. Despite the political victory of the liberals and the encouragement President Jefferson gave to many values of the Enlightenment, the intellectual life of the nation remained in large measure in the hands of the conservatives and their sympathizers. True, forces were at work that slowly, imperceptibly, weakened the aristocratic control of intellectual life; but the great victories for the democratization of knowledge had to await the rise of an urban labor movement, technological advances, and the political upheavals associated with Andrew Jackson. Even then many of the ideas that took form during the conservative reaction against the Age of Reason continued to exert a stubborn sway. It is thus all the more important to understand their formulation and the role they played in the conflict of interests, in the battle between champions of the common people and the privileged members of society.

### The Denunciation of Violence and the Defense of Property

The first task the intellectual champions of the larger property interests set themselves was to attack the whole tribe of "Jacobins," domestic and European, and the philosophers of the Enlightenment who were held responsible for the tumult in France and at home. Sometimes the diatribes against Tom Paine, William Godwin, Mary Wollstonecraft, and their fellow revolutionists in France and America were bitingly sarcastic; sometimes they were marked by ribaldry, ridicule, racy audacity. Sometimes they fell like the thunderbolts of John Adams. The insulting calumny, scurrilous gusto, and abusive virulence of William Cobbett, the transplanted English journalist who wrote under the name "Peter Porcupine," and of John Fenno of the *United States Gazette* equaled or exceeded that of such vitriolic democrats as William Duane and Philip Freneau. Promising poets like William Cliffton of Philadelphia and gifted essayists like Joseph Dennie of the Philadelphia *Port Folio* were only somewhat less savage dispensers of reactionary invective. The Hartford Wits achieved greater fame. The patriotic and didactic gentlemen of this school sometimes stood abreast or even ahead of their times in their psychological and esthetic ideas; but their pretentious burlesque of "levelers" and their celebrations, in the florid couplets of Queen Anne's age, of the idyllic charms of the uncontaminated New England village in general expressed religious orthodoxy and political conservatism.

In denouncing the violence of the French Revolution its American critics idealized stability and order and at the same time appealed to the humanitarian horror of bloodshed. "When will these savages be satiated with blood?" asked John Adams, who viewed the turmoil and upheaval in France with an understandable fear. A Harvard commencement orator of 1798, in referring to the French Revolution, declared that "it has in a manner annihilated society" by its subversive and violent temper. Even those favorably disposed toward its ideals were impressed by the incessant diatribes against the lust for blood displayed by its leaders. Lest America be sucked into the gory maelstrom, Thomas Green Fessenden, New England lawyer, journalist, and versifier, warned his readers in *Democracy Unveiled* (1805) to beware of all the French Revolution stood for:

> Such principles, alas, will flood
> Columbia's "happy land" with blood,
> Unless kind Providence restrain
> These demons of the hurricane.

Richard Alsop, millionaire Connecticut merchant, a genial fellow among the Hartford Wits, wrote a mordant satire on the guillotine, and William Cliffton delighted a Philadelphia literary club with his vivid descriptions in prose and verse of the French bloodletters' torment in hell while the beheaded Louis XVI basked in Elysium. The riotous factionalism which the Revolution engendered in France especially dismayed the conservatives, to whom order was as much a virtue as chaos and violence were evils. And the factionalism promoted in their very midst by the conduct of Genêt, the French emissary who appealed to the people over the government to enlist aid for France, only increased their dismay. In sharp contrast the conservatives painted a picture of the peace and order that had prevailed when the authority of the past prevented such violent overturns.

When violence was directed against property, American conservatives were stirred to wrath. The Federalists, protectors of commerce, were disgusted with agrarian attacks on "sound currency." For some of them were beginning to look forward with Hamilton to the glorious development of manufactures, so dependent on accumulated capital and peaceful markets. Fisher Ames spoke for the financial class when he lamented the waste and desolation that followed in the wake of revolution. "Capital, which used to be food for manufactures," he remarked, "is become their fuel. What once nourished industry, now lights the fires of civil war, and quickens the progress of destruction."[1] When the confiscatory policies of the French Revolution were inaugurated, John Adams insisted

---

[1] Seth Ames (ed.), *The Works of Fisher Ames* (Boston, 1854), II, 33.

that "property must be secure or liberty cannot exist." If the French revolutionary attacks on landed estates should be imitated, chaos, despotism, and horror would rule the day.

## Aristocracy and Democracy in Conflict

The equalitarian ideas of the French Revolutionists and their American votaries were no less distasteful to conservatives than the violence and disorder of the struggle. Their attack on equalitarianism was based on a conservative doctrine of human nature. In contrast to the radical insistence that men are by nature equal and potentially good, the conservative picture stressed the idea of innate differences in the abilities of individuals and assumed human nature to be inherently depraved, passionate, and motivated by self-interest rather than by altruism. In some respects this view of human nature corresponded to that of Calvinism; in others, particularly in its emphasis on self-interest as the basic human motive, it strongly suggested Mandeville. Whatever its intellectual precedents, it found considerable support in the postrevolutionary years. Tired of upheaval and fearful of new violence, some grew lukewarm toward revolutionary ideas who had once been stirred by them. Many had never really believed the high-sounding words in the preamble of the Declaration of Independence. The extreme form in which the doctrines of equality were often stated seemed to many, at least on sober second thought, to make them plain contradictions of common knowledge—obviously some men were not and never had been equal to others.

Even before the levelism of the French Revolution provoked conservative onslaughts against the conception of human nature as innately altruistic and equalitarian, Shays' rebellion and the debate over the federal Constitution had occasioned clear-cut pronouncements from spokesmen of substance and standing. General Henry Knox, writing to Washington in 1786 in regard to the "faction and licentiousness" which Shays' revolt had occasioned, declared that men actually possess all the turbulent passions belonging to the animal and that only a government of force can exercise the restraint necessary for the protection of life and property. During the discussions over the ratification of the federal Constitution *The Federalist* advanced similar arguments. Only a strong central government, the argument ran, could suffice, since the passions of men do not and will not "conform to the dictates of reason and justice, without restraint." Madison, one of the authors of *The Federalist*, further emphasized "innate diversities in the faculties of men," from which, he argued, spring inequality of property and the consequent selfish strife of the less well-to-do for the possessions of those whom superior talents have blessed with greater wealth. Hamilton, in defending the thesis that government must be both strong and sensitive to the interests of the great property holders, emphasized even more baldly the theory of the innately unequal and selfish nature of man.

These arguments received classic expression in *The Defence of the Constitutions* and *Essays on Davila*. In these erudite and closely reasoned writings, John Adams attacked the equalitarianism of both American and French levelers as unrealistic and based on a false and untenable conception of human nature. In his eyes, "by the law of nature all men are men and not angels—men and not lions—men and not whales—men and not eagles, that is, they are all of the same species. But man differs by nature from man almost as man from beast. . . . A physical inequality, an intellectual inequality of the most serious kind is established unchangeably by the Author of nature; and society has a right to establish any other inequalities it may judge necessary and good." Far from being kindly and rational as the Utopian democrats assumed, man by nature is "so corrupt, so indolent, so selfish and jealous, that he is never good but through necessity."[2]

According to Adams, men are impelled not primarily by ideals, reason, and altruism but by a desire for goods; on one occasion he added sex expression. Democracy was therefore to his mind utterly unworkable and in fact the first step toward anarchy. Property had to be represented in government with due weight if the masses were to be restrained from controlling government and using that control to strip the well-to-do of their property—the chief insurance of liberty. The people had to be curbed, through this and other checks, from expressing their naturally selfish and turbulent passions of aggrandizement. On the other hand, Adams was both too logical and too realistic in his conception of human nature to assume that the well-to-do, if left to themselves to control government, could be depended on to act with justice toward the people. Governmental checks were needed to hold them in proper restraint.

[2] Charles Francis Adams (ed.), *The Works of John Adams* (Boston, 1856), I, 462.

Unlike Hamilton, who frankly urged that government be strengthened in order to enable it the better to serve the class interests of promoters, bankers, and industrialists, Adams feared the rise of an unprincipled oligarchy if the rich were allowed full rein. He also emphasized the important role of the natural aristocrat, well-born, educated, disciplined, and sufficiently well off to be free from the crudest temptations for self-advancement. Such views prompted Adams, during the early sessions of Congress, to try to establish such titles for the President as "His Elective Majesty" and to surround the high dignitaries of government with ceremonials fitting to their distinction.

But the emphasis on the unequal abilities of men and on the essential selfishness of human nature was not the only accent in the defense of aristocracy. John Adams shared with many others of similar temperament and class affiliations or sympathies the veneration bestowed on institutionalism and legalism by Burke in his *Reflections on the French Revolution*. This respect for established institutions, for the authority of the past, for law, found its most important expression, perhaps, in the judicial thought of John Marshall. As chief justice of the Supreme Court, which continued long after the election of Jefferson to be largely Federalist in its makeup, Marshall lent powerful support to the defense of property interests. In the Yazoo fraud case he ruled that even though a legislature steeped in corruption had bestowed public lands on private investors, such a bestowal was a sacred contract. Thus judicial authority upheld the irrevocable nature of contract in spite of fraud against the public interest. The sanctity of the contract as a defense of property rights long remained as a testimony of the victory of private over public interest.

The well-reasoned and philosophical arguments of a John Adams or a John Marshall excited less public attention, to be sure, than the more uninhibited and cruder diatribes against democracy. Thus Fisher Ames, a dyed-in-the-wool New England aristocrat, cast off all restraint in expressing his conviction that the "barbarous, infuriated, loathsome mobs" of revolutionary France would be duplicated in America, that any democracy was foreordained to end in a military despotism. George Cabot, another New England Federalist, frankly regarded democracy as the government of the worst and would have agreed heartily with the remark imputed to Alexander Hamilton, "Your people, Sir, is a great beast." William Cobbett, the raucous Englishman who edited Federalist newspapers and conducted a bitter pamphlet warfare on such democrats as Bache, Duane, and Freneau, exclaimed on one occasion, "O base democracy! Why, it is absolutely worse than street-sweepings, or the filth of the common sewers." One of his Philadelphia fellow apologists for aristocracy, Joseph Dennie, declared in 1803 in his periodical *The Port Folio* that a democracy, scarcely tolerable in any period, would in America issue in civil war, anarchy, desolation. "The institution of a scheme of policy so radically contemptible and vicious is a memorable example of what the villainy of some men can devise, the folly of others receive, and both establish in spite of reason, reflection, and sensation."[3] As an esteemed arbiter of taste Dennie bestowed praise on Irving and Paulding when, in 1807, their *Salmagundi* exposed "Jacobinical shortcomings."

Verse makers, among whom Thomas Green Fessenden was typical, called on the Muse to aid in the fight against such allies of equalitarianism as faith in reason and the idea of the perfectibility of human nature:

> . . . democrats, Illuminees,
> Are birds obscene, and of a feather,
> Should therefore all be class'd together.
>
> They all object to the propriety
> Of law and order in society,
> Think *reason* will supply restraints,
> And make mankind a set of saints.
>
> Now it appears from what I state here,
> My plans for mending human nature
> Entitle men to take the chair
> From Rousseau, Godwin, or Voltaire.
>
> They are of immense *utility*
> And tend to man's perfectibility;
> And if pursu'd, I dare to venture ye,
> He'll be an angel in a century!
>
> And I'll unmask the Democrat,
> Your sometimes this thing, sometimes that,
> Whose life is one dishonest shuffle,
> Lest he perchance the *mob* should ruffle.

[3] *The Port Folio*, III (April 23, 1803), 135.

On another occasion Fessenden turned from satire and vilification to present the conservative prescription:

> Next, every man throughout the nation
> Must be contented with his station,
> Nor think to cut a figure greater
> Than was design'd for him by Nature.
>
> No tinker bold with *brazen* plate,
> Should set himself to *patch* the State,
> No cobbler leave, at Faction's call,
> His *last*, and thereby lose his *all*.
>
> The greatest number's greatest good
> Should, doubtless, ever be pursu'd;
> But that consists, *sans* disputation,
> In order and subordination.

The devotion of many literary men to the aristocratic cause was deepened by their conviction that culture could not flourish in a democracy. Joseph Dennie was certain that under the patronage of a royal government his talents would have won the recognition and honors that a churlish democracy refused. "Had not the *Revolution* happened," he wrote in 1800 from Philadelphia, where he enjoyed a post in the Department of State,

had I continued to be a subject to the King, had I been born in *England* or resided in the City of London for the last 7 years, my fame would have been enhanced; and as to fortune I feel a moral certainty that I should have acquired by my writings 3 or 4 thousand pounds. But, in this *Republic*, this region covered with the Jewish and canting and cheating descendants of those men, who during the reign of a *Stuart*, *fled away* from the claims of the Creditor, from the tythes of the Church, from their allegiance to their Sovereign and from their duty to their God, what can men of liberality and letters expect but such polar icy treatment, as I have experienced?[4]

In Philadelphia, the literary as well as the political capital, William Cliffton lamented the indifference of a democratic republic to literary genius and took severely to task the demogogical crowd for dictating to the fancy of a poet as the price for appreciation:

[4] Laura G. M. Pedder (ed.), *The Letters of Joseph Dennie* (*University of Maine Studies*, 2nd series, No. 36, Orono, 1936), 182.

> In these cold shades, beneath these shifting skies,
> Where Fancy sickens, and where Genius dies;
> Where few and feeble are the Muse's strains,
> And no fine frenzy riots in the veins,
> There still are found a few to whom belong
> The fire of virtue and the soul of song.
>
> .     .     .     .     .
>
> Then, if some thoughtless Bavius dared appear,
> Short was his date, and limited his sphere;
> He could but please the changeling mob a day,
> Then, like his noxious labors, pass away;
> So, near a forest tall, some worthless flower
> Enjoys the triumph of its gaudy hour,
> Scatters its little poison thro' the skies,
> Then droops its empty, hated head, and dies.[5]

The same sentiment prevailed in Boston, where in 1807 a contributor to the *Anthology* declared "that in this land, where the spirit of democracy is everywhere diffused, we are exposed, as it were, to a poisonous atmosphere, which blasts everything beautiful in nature and corrodes everything elegant in art; we know that with us the 'rose-leaves fall ungathered'; and we believe, that there is little to praise, and nothing to admire in most of the objects, which would first present themselves to the view of a stranger."[6]

There was some justification for the complaint that there was a dearth of intellectual and cultural achievements in the American Republic; but the conservative aristocrat's view that this was the result of such democracy as prevailed was not accepted by all men of letters. The conservative view stood in striking contrast to Freneau's and Barlow's apostrophes to the genius-nourishing qualities of a democracy.

## The Attack on the New Ideas of Sex and Race Equality

The counterattack on the values of the Enlightenment and the fervid expression given them by the French Revolution did not stop with the attack on democracy. The idea, dear to the Enlightenment, that women

[5] William Cliffton, *Poems, Chiefly Occasional* (New York, 1800), 53.
[6] *The Monthly Anthology and Boston Review*, IV (January, 1807), 44.

are potentially capable of high intellectual achievements and worthy
as human beings of equality in legal, political, and social matters was
fought with vigor and invective. No doubt many cultured and well-to-do
men and women did not sympathize with this assault; and no doubt
many plain people, if the attack had come to their attention, would have
approved. Nevertheless, the attack on the idea of sex equality enlisted
the support of many of the critics of democracy and of many orthodox
religious leaders who associated feminism with religious skepticism.

Joseph Dennie inveighed against the newfangled ideas about women,
including the latest mode of women's dress, which he associated with
other French innovations. Scandalized representatives of the conventional proprieties made capital of the bold way in which Talleyrand,
a representative of the French Revolution, sported about on Philadelphia's streets with his mulatto mistress. Scurrilous verses insulting
Jefferson for his alleged intimacies with slave women issued from the
workshops of rhyme makers who shared the conservative views of sex
and race. Clergymen scathingly denounced what they described as the
profligacy, voluptuousness, and uncleanness of "infidels." Deists were
berated as libertines abandoning themselves to the sexual passions that
religion alone could restrain. Jedidiah Morse cursed the "lust and de-
bauchery" to which, he argued, the new ideas generally led, and Timothy
Dwight attributed to the Illuminati, whom he regarded as the engineers
of the French Revolution, the uprooting of marriage, chastity, and
decency from the world. "In the societies of Illuminati," Dwight
declared,

doctrines were taught, which strike at the root of all human happiness and
virtue; and every such doctrine was either expressly or implicitly involved
in their system. The being of God was denied or ridiculed. Government was
asserted to be a curse, and authority a mere usurpation. Civil society was declared to be the only apostasy of man. The possession of property was
pronounced to be robbery. Chastity and natural affection were declared to
be nothing more than groundless prejudices. . . . For what end shall we be
connected with men, of whom this is the character and conduct? . . . Is it
that we may see our wives and daughters the victims of legal prostitution;
soberly dishonoured; speciously polluted; the outcasts of delicacy and virtue;
and the loathing of God and man?[7]

[7] Timothy Dwight, *The Duty of Americans, at the Present Crisis, July 4, 1798*
(New York, 1798), 20–21.

While womanhood was thus being idealized, women and even girls found employment in the rising factories and mills with the approval not only of humble men who needed the help of wives and daughters to support their families but of such champions of the manufacturing interests as Alexander Hamilton. The hours of labor were from sunup to sundown; the shops and mills were often dark and damp, even according to the standards of the time. It was these mills and factories that Hamilton, foe of equalitarian doctrines, regarded as nurseries of virtue for lower-class children and women. "It is worthy of particular remark that, in general, women and children are rendered more useful, and the latter more early useful, by manufacturing establishments, than they would otherwise be."[8] Colonel Humphreys, one of the minor Hartford Wits, a patriot and a gentleman, a bitter critic of the French Revolution, a factory owner and a guardian of public morals, believed with Hamilton that American men of wealth might elevate morals and promote general well-being by providing children of both sexes with opportunities to work in factories. The ideas which Hamilton and Humphreys held regarding women and children of the poor did not, of course, meet with the approval of all men of substantial wealth. But these ideas found comfortable support, and they ran counter to the notion that children of all classes and both sexes might achieve approximate equality if given equal opportunities.

Progressive thinkers, it is true, continued to cherish the doctrines laid down by Mary Wollstonecraft in her *Vindication of the Rights of Women*. But another Englishwoman, Hannah More, exerted far more influence in shaping American views as to the proper role of the female sex. Emphasizing the domestic virtues and the happiness to be derived from subordination, Hannah More became a general favorite and had many American imitators. It is also interesting to recall that Susanna Rowson, whose feministic sympathies have been noted, achieved her greatest literary success in *Charlotte Temple, A Tale of Truth*—a tale that had a moral, namely, that tragedy follows any violation of the conventional code of behavior for young women. Charles Brockden Brown's novels, which actually incorporated the feministic theories which he accepted, did not fare nearly so well. Nor did the proposals for the education of the future mothers of the Republic, that their sons

[8] John C. Hamilton (ed.), *The Works of Alexander Hamilton*, 7 vols. (New York, 1850–1851), III, 207–208.

might become better citizens, meet with approval sufficient to stir up any very noteworthy action.

Many spokesmen of the established order, such a Timothy Dwight, roundly denounced slavery. The Act of Congress of 1807 which forbade the further importation of slaves also marked some limitation of slavery. But there are many indications that the application of humanitarianism and of the rights of man philosophy to the Negro enjoyed less favor than in the years immediately following the struggle for independence. The prohibition of slavery in the Old Northwest by the Northwest Ordinance was challenged by many who had migrated into the region from slaveowning states. The existence of slavery in the growing states and territories south of the Ohio and the acquisition of Louisiana in 1803 extended its reach. In 1793 Congress made the escape of slaves more difficult by passing a fugitive slave act. After 1798 the promising American Convention of Delegates from Abolition Societies lost the buoyancy of its early years, and some of its important constituents as well. Antislavery pamphlets and petitions to the legislature dwindled, and by 1814 Jefferson was apologizing for his reluctance to lead a crusade for emancipation.

Discriminations against the free Negro in the North led to the establishment of separate churches in some places. Moreover, it became increasingly difficult for free Negroes to obtain an education. The growth of sentiment against miscegenation and in favor of the colonization of freedmen in Africa or elsewhere was testimony to the conviction which many Northerners as well as Southerners held regarding the capacities of the Negroes. The colonization movement, in other words, reflected the belief that even a free environment could not elevate young Negroes to a position of equality with the whites.

The invention of the cotton gin and the growth of cotton textile factories in the Northeast during the years preceding the War of 1812 no doubt began to set in motion an undercurrent against the doctrines of race equality and freedom. But the change was aided by the general reaction against the Enlightenment. An article in Joseph Dennie's *Port Folio*, for example, declared that the Negroes had become less industrious "since their heads had been turned by the modern jargon of liberty, and the rights of man." John Randolph of Roanoke objected to the restriction of the slave trade on the score that it would curtail property rights and the right to acquire property. More important than any other considerations was the fear that Negro emigrants from the French West Indies, where slavery had been abolished and a Negro republic established, might foster revolts such as that which Gabriel, a Virginia Negro, plotted in 1800. Rumor had it that Negro emissaries from Santo Domingo proselyted among American slaves and if unchecked might win them over to the equalitarian doctrines of the French Revolution. Fear of slave insurrections, and actual revolts in Camden, South Carolina, in 1816, and in North Carolina somewhat later, kept nerves taut and minds hostile to the doctrines of humanitarianism and equalitarianism. Slaveowners had not yet begun a systematic defense of the bondage of the Negro—that was to come. But it was clear that a change was underway both in the South and in the North, and that a waning of zeal for emancipation was part of the general conservative reaction against the Enlightenment.

## The Attack on Infidelity

In the minds of many champions of wealth the French attacks on religion were closely associated with the confiscation of church lands and the estates of French nobles. "I know not what to make of a nation of thirty million atheists," exclaimed John Adams, who had himself once flirted with deistic ideas. In his attacks on Jacobinism Hamilton argued that it had annihilated the church and imposed a profane gospel. "A league has at length been cemented between the apostles and disciples of irreligion and anarchy," he charged. "Religion and government have both been stigmatized as abuses; as unwarrantable restraints upon the freedom of man; as causes of the corruption of his nature, intrinsically good."[9] To crush such heresy Hamilton proposed the organization of a Christian Constitutional Society devoted to upholding the Christian religion and the Constitution by checking the influence of "Jacobins" in the populous American towns.

Conservative clergymen took the lead in fastening on the French Revolution the "triumph of infidelity" not only in France but in America itself. As early as 1794 the Reverend Joseph Lathrop of Massachusetts was denouncing the "infamous combination of Jacobinism

[9] Henry Cabot Lodge (ed.), The Works of Alexander Hamilton, 9 vols. (G. P. Putnam's Sons, 1885–1886), VIII, 598.

and atheism." Even William Ellery Channing, hospitable as he was to new and liberal ideas, felt that the "French Revolution had diseased the imaginations and unsettled the understanding of man everywhere." At Harvard students were presented with Bishop Watson's *Apology for the Bible* in the hope that it would wean them from the subversive doctrines of French revolutionary "atheism." At Yale, where "the college was in a most ungodly state," according to Lyman Beecher, where the undergraduates went so far as to nickname each other Volney, Voltaire, and the like, Timothy Dwight mustered all his talents to lead his straying lambs back to God. At other colleges similar efforts were made to break the spell of the "irreligion."

The general conviction that the spread of infidelity was to be laid at the door of French philosophy was given a melodramatic emphasis when the Reverend Jedidiah Morse of Charlestown, Massachusetts, chanced to read John Robinson's *Proofs of a Conspiracy against all the Religions and Governments of Europe.* This somewhat unbalanced professor at Edinburgh charged that the Bavarian Illuminati, a free-thinking offshoot of the Masonic order, had deliberately plotted and engineered the French Revolution in order to spread its nefarious and antireligious doctrines. With even less care than he displayed in checking reports for his geographical textbooks, Morse rushed into his pulpit on the morning of May 9, 1798, and shared his momentous discovery with the world. The appearance of the Abbé Barruel's "confirmation" of Robinson's charge led Morse to forego his prejudices against Catholicism for the moment and welcome this Jesuit ally. William Cobbett of Philadelphia printed Morse's sermon in *Porcupine's Gazette;* Dr. David Tappan of the Harvard Divinity School and President Timothy Dwight of Yale, with other prominent clergymen, were easily converted. The radicals, with the aid of well-balanced clergymen, exposed the ridiculousness of the conspiracy charge, but its memory continued to serve as a warning against the pernicious union of Jacobinism and atheism. Orthodox upholders of the faith were strengthened in their determination to make the true religion prevail.

Revivalism was at the heart of the reassertion of religious faith and piety. As early as 1792 there had been some indications in New England that the revivalism which had so shaken the country in the time of Jonathan Edwards might again become a vital force. This reassertion of emotional religion was probably inevitable in a period of marked intellectual confusion and sharp ideological conflicts. Many who had lent an ear to deistical ideas no doubt reacted against them when their most enthusiastic champions seemed to carry adulation of skepticism and radicalism to extremes. Hard times may have facilitated the evangelical outburst, although there are few references to economic difficulties in the evangelical sermons of the day. It is certain that the New England revivals were welcomed by such opponents of revolutionary deism and radicalism as Timothy Dwight and Jedidiah Morse. The chief support for the revivals came from villagers and farmers; the substantial merchants who were moving toward Unitarianism were, of course, indifferent or hostile. A considerable number of merchants, however, some of whom had been indifferent or hostile toward orthodox Christianity, were attracted to the evangelical movement; Benjamin Tallmadge, staunch conservative Federalist, land speculator, and well-to-do merchant of Litchfield, Connecticut, is representative of this group.

The middle and southern states also felt the new religious impulse. Many planters who had been more or less avowed skeptics accepted some form of orthodox Christianity or, like John Randolph of Roanoke, made religious affirmations. The chief strength of the revival movement in the South was, however, the small farmers whose political affiliations were democratic and Jeffersonian. Throughout the southern seaboard states, Baptists, Methodists, and the evangelical wing of Presbyterianism gained much strength in the opening decades of the nineteenth century.

By the year 1800 itinerant preachers had begun to attract great throngs in the frontier country beyond the Appalachians. At camp-meeting revivals these new Savonarolas preached a muscular, shirt-sleeves religion of fear and hope that attracted roughhewn frontiersmen and their women folk. Hankering for emotional release, lonely in soul and starved for companionship, they welcomed, sometimes hysterically with shrieks, groans, and bodily contortions, the huge get-togethers where tense nerves and repressed feelings found satisfaction in emotional debauches in the name of God. The revivals also brought genuine religious inspiration to countless thousands and were an important factor in checking the religious indifference and skepticism that had begun to spread among the common people of the West as well as among those of older regions.

The orthodox attack on irreligion did not depend solely on revivalism. In fact, champions of the faith planned and executed what Dixon Ryan Fox called the "Protestant Counter-Reformation." New agencies for the inculcation of orthodoxy sprang up under the fostering care of devoted leaders. This movement owed much to the example of pious evangelicals in England, where the skepticism of the French Revolution was the object of a frontal attack. Hannah More began in 1795 to prepare a series of tracts for inculcating piety and Christian faith in the hearts of everyone, children as well as adults, the humble as well as the more fortunate. These tracts proved acceptable in America and soon were being imitated. In 1807 the Connecticut Tract Society was launched, and in 1814 the half dozen local organizations of a similar nature multiplied their power by forming a national body, the American Tract Society.

Efforts were made to familiarize Americans more thoroughly with the Bible. Dr. Benjamin Rush, without abandoning his faith in science, progress, and other ideas associated with the Enlightenment, became a leader in the movement for renewed emphasis on Christian faith and Bible reading. In 1791 in his vigorous *Defense of the Use of the Bible as a Schoolbook* he urged the importance of the school as an agency for advancing Christian faith and morals through the Bible. Before long, Bible societies took their place with the tract societies. To promote the work of putting a Bible in every home, the American Bible Society in 1816 began its long career.

Other agencies for advancing Christian piety and morals were the societies that were founded to check Sabbath breaking, profanity, and sports, such as racing, that could not be justified as useful. But no cause promised more for the future than the crusade against intemperance. Although an occasional voice had denounced drinking even in the seventheenth century, and although attempts had been made to regulate the liquor traffic in the interest of decency and morality, it was not until the late eighteenth century that there was systematic opposition to the use of spirits. To the earlier condemnation of inebriation by such zealous souls as the Puritan Mathers and Jonathan Edwards, the Quakers Anthony Benezet and Thomas Chalkey, and the Methodist Thomas Coke, Dr. Benjamin Rush added his influential testimony. His *Inquiry into the Effects of Spirituous Liquors on the Human Body and Mind* (1784) contended that an excessive amount of alcohol had deleterious physical and mental effects. Through correspondence with leading men and through his promotion of a petition from Philadelphia physicians to Congress in 1790 urging the restriction of the liquor traffic, he helped prepare the stage for a definite temperance movement. As early as 1789 a partial abstinence society appeared at Litchfield, Connecticut, but a general movement did not get under way until the years preceding the War of 1812, when several temperance societies were organized. In 1812 the Presbyterian General Assembly in Philadelphia appointed a committee to inquire into methods for restricting indulgence. The new crusade was closely allied to the evangelical movement. It also reflected the growing humanitarian sentiment. At the same time many advocates of temperance believed that it would help check the secularism and radicalism associated with the relaxation of orthodox faith and Christian piety.

The Sunday school, which had been established in England to provide elementary secular instruction to children who toiled by day in coal mines or factories, was apparently introduced in America for the same purpose. But it soon became an accepted means for advancing Christian faith and morals among all children.

Early in the nineteenth century missionary societies were organized in the several New England States. These were designed to spread the gospel in the West and Southwest, where indifference to religion was believed to be especially widespread. By 1816 a Board of Home Missions was systematically cultivating the field beyond the Alleghenies. Foreign missions likewise enlisted support. To aid the work of the missionary activities new periodicals were begun, of which the most widely read was *The Panoplist and Missionary Magazine*. By 1809 it boasted 7000 readers. It was strictly orthodox, as were a number of the other periodicals that campaigned against deism and skepticism. The missionary movement, like revivalism, relied heavily upon the plain people in villages and on farms, although men of substantial property also contributed.

The Protestant Counter-Reformation was concerned chiefly with winning people to the Christian faith through evangelical methods, but it did not neglect scholarship and education. Hebrew, which had virtually disappeared from the college curriculum, again had its defenders. Systematic theology, represented by the writings of such men as Samuel Hopkins, Joseph Bellamy, Timothy Dwight, and others, had a surprising vogue. To counteract the religious liberalism of the Unitarian variety which had invaded Harvard, the Andover Theological Seminary was established by orthodox Congregationalists, and before long other denominations were founding theological schools to train a clergy to combat more effectively the intellectualism of skeptics.

Within the ranks of organized Christianity itself the new militant evangelical and missionary movement met with some opposition. Certain old-fashioned predestinarians still believed it useless to try to alter what God had decreed, and some High Church Episcopalians showed disdain for the movement. But it nevertheless marched forward as with seven-league boots.

Of the decline of deism and "infidelity" in this period there can be little doubt. Newspapers and periodicals gave less space to these ideas, and when they gave any, it was chiefly to scoff and condemn. The evangelical sects greatly increased their membership and strength. So powerful were they in Virginia, for example, that Jefferson was forced to revoke an invitation he had issued to Dr. Thomas Cooper, the well-known English philosophical materialist, to become a member of the faculty of the university. True, Dr. Cooper was called to South Carolina College, but his plain-spoken language and his insistence that the new geology failed to confirm the Mosaic account of creation aroused orthodox Presbyterians, who charged him with heresy. At Transylvania University, once the seat of the Enlightenment in the West, Dr. Horace Holley was forced to retire because of his sympathy for liberal religious ideas. So general, indeed, was the aversion to infidelity that James Fenimore Cooper in his early novel *Precaution* presented religious faith and piety as the prime virtue in a prospective husband.

## The Delimitation of Natural Science

Although many social and political conservatives befriended natural science and many devoutly religious men continued to add to the store of scientific knowledge, the general reaction against the Enlightenment engendered efforts to belittle the claims of natural science. This was especially true when these claims appeared to challenge orthodox religion or the established social order, or when they were intimately associated with radical Utopianism.

Dr. Richard Alsop, a conservative in politics and in social views, poked fun at the Newtonian theory, which had long enjoyed almost universal approval among learned men. In 1793 this Connecticut wit and millionaire merchant ridiculed the doctrine of the attraction of matter as contrary to common sense and revelation:

> That Matter's chain'd to *Matter*, seems to be
> The underpinning of philosophy
> By Newton taught—the wonder-working sage,
> With this idea blotted many a page.
>
> .  .  .  .  .
>
> If Matter is by Matter still attracted,
> This only proves that *Matter* is distracted.
> Long has the world been lur'd by Newton's schemes
> His systems strange, and philosophic dreams,
> And long his fashion bid all ranks proclaim,
> In terms of loud applause his hallow'd name.
>
> .  .  .  .
>
> But hence Newtonians vain no longer dare
> With heaven-taught truths your sophistry compare,
> Nor with your brittle arguments essay
> To prove that Matter's legs, and runs away.[10]

Other spokesmen for the conservative reaction took occasion to ridicule their opponents' enthusiastic devotion to science. In *Terrible Tractoration* (1803) Thomas Green Fessenden not only satirized pseudo-scientific quack remedies but heaped scorn on such naturalists as the English botanist Dr. Erasmus Darwin, on Buffon, and on political and literary liberals who dabbled in science. Vivisection and the breeding of animals for experimental purposes also evoked his jibes. In a period in which naturalism was being subjected to criticism this satire, which went through several editions, was particularly acceptable because it seemed to demolish the chief argument of the radicals. David Daggett, a New Haven lawyer and high Federalist who shared the pessimism of his fellow conservatives regarding the future of America, delivered a Fourth of July oration in 1799 with the fetching title, *Sun-Beams may be extracted from Cucumbers, but the Process is Tedious*. In pungent English somewhat reminiscent of Swift he derided scientific projects to grow lambs without wool, to devise automatic machines capable of navigating beneath water as well as in the air (as if God would have neglected to provide man with wings had he been intended to fly!), and, ridiculous of the ridiculous, to extract sunbeams from cucumbers.

---

[10] Richard Alsop, *The Echo, with other Poems* (New York, 1807), 23 ff.

Daggett laid bare the association of all such preposterous scientific notions with deism and democracy. In a work of greater literary merit Hugh Henry Brackenridge, a democratic lawyer of Pittsburgh with conservative leanings, poked fun at the members of the American Philosophical Society for mistaking a tarred-and-feathered culprit for a rare type of bird!

The more serious criticism of science and naturalism took the form of attributing the yellow fever epidemic that devastated Philadelphia in the 1790s to divine wrath over the vogue for infidelity. Some even held that only the removal of certain Philadelphians by the scourge had saved President Washington from being dragged out of his house by a mob and the United States from "a  fatal revolution of government."

The common opinion that the medical profession was heavily tainted with skepticism and materialism occasioned more than one attack on its members. Incensed at the practice of grave robbing by medical students and the dissection of the bodies of the poor on the score that they were poor and that the human body, made in the image of God, was sacred, a mob attacked the house of a Baltimore physician in 1788 while he was dissecting a cadaver for his pupils. About the same time the famous "doctors' mob" in New York City, occasioned by a similar circumstance, showed even greater venom on the part of plain people with religious feeling.

At the very time when some conservative spokesmen were ridiculing natural science as a central idea in radical Utopianism and a contradiction to orthodox Christianity, others were assimilating it to religion and to socially conservative doctrine. Properly interpreted, some argued, science might confirm orthodox faith. Naturalists had long been accustomed to the idea that the marvelous intricacies of nature, together with the obvious usefulness of the animal and vegetable kingdoms to man, proved beyond doubt that the world was ruled by the divine conscience of its Creator. This point of view, which had never been obscured, was now advanced with renewed zeal. In 1793 Charles Christopher Reich endeavored to combat heresy among youth by demonstrating to them in his *Fifteen Discourses on the Marvellous Works of Nature* that divine purpose, not fate or chance, governs the natural world. This worshipful attitude toward nature fed the springs of the Romantic movement, which was to enjoy much favor throughout the period in which the conservatives gave the tone to the nation's intellectual life.

In addition to the testimony offered by the world of plants and animals to supernatural claims, champions of the orthodox account of the creation found support for their position in the voyages of Captain James Cook. Prior to his demonstration of the proximity of Asia and America, pious men had been perplexed by the Scriptural story of the deluge; for if the entire world had been covered by water and if only Noah and his immediate companions had been saved, how could the American continent, seemingly at such a great distance, ever have become peopled? Now, however, it was apparent that the Asiatic descendants of Noah's tribe could have crossed easily to America on the ice or in canoes; and thus faith in Scripture was reinforced and skepticism dealt a blow by the hand of science.

The necessity of recognizing science and of making certain that it was used to confirm rather than to undermine orthodox faith no doubt was in part responsible for President Timothy Dwight's decision to establish a chair of science at Yale in 1803. Benjamin Silliman, the incumbent, having been converted to orthodox Christianity in the Yale revival and having properly prepared himself for his duties by studies in Philadelphia and in Europe, began a long and distinguished career which fully justified the hope that science might lend support to Christianity.

The religious sanction for scientific inquiry was reinforced by the feeling that science might be useful to the commercial interests so dominant in conservative social and political thought. It is true that it was Jefferson rather than a representative of commercial New England who was responsible in 1807 for the first steps which ultimately resulted in the execution of a coast survey, so helpful to commerce. It is also true that the physiocratic President enlarged scientific knowledge through the Lewis and Clark expedition to the far Northwest. But the fur trade occasioned the expedition sponsored by John Jacob Astor into the Oregon country, an expedition which enabled two naturalists, John Bradbury and Thomas Nuttall, to advance botanical and ornithological knowledge. The voice of commerce also spoke in *The New American Practical Navigator* (1801), an important manual which Nathaniel Bowditch, an anti-Jeffersonian New England mariner, prepared. This classic in its field made use of the method of lunar observation originated by Theophilus Parsons, the conservative lawyer, who is generally remembered for his restatement of English common law in terms of American and, particularly, mercantile needs. Industry as well as commerce attracted the talents of scientists; Robert Hare, a Philadelphia brewer and subsequently a noted chemist, invented the compound blowpipe.

To point out that scientific advance sometimes resulted from the stimulus of economic interest is in no sense to maintain that disinterested scientific curiosity and love of investigation did not often provide the chief if not the sole incentive to scientists. Alexander Wilson, the distinguished ornithologist, is probably a case in point. His *American Ornithology*, the first volume of which appeared in 1808, was followed by others no less distinguished for accurate observations than for the human analogies which lent so much fascination to the beautifully illustrated work. Another Scottish immigrant, William Maclure, was beginning his important geological surveys; and the work of such physicians as Samuel Bard in obstetrics, David Hosack and Philip Syng Physick in surgery, and Caspar Wistar in anatomy, brought added prestige to the medical profession.

However favorable conservatives might be toward science when it advanced their interest, the period of reaction against the Enlightenment saw some modification of the zeal for applying science to inventions for the increased well-being of man. Henry Adams has called attention to the popular inertia, skepticism, and conservatism which greeted the pioneer efforts of such inventors of steam locomotion as "poor John Fitch" and Oliver Evans, the "American Watts." Faith in the efficacy and social benefits of invention had so waned that only after repeated demonstrations, sometimes involving the ruin of inventors, did men of substance risk their capital in support of the later projects of Livingston and Fulton. However much leaders in Jefferson's camp might favor the application of science in the interest of human well-being, they shared the general failure of the Enlightenment to foresee the subordination of science and invention to profits, a subordination the more likely by reason of the Jeffersonian enthusiasm for laissez faire, which made government support of science and invention difficult if not all but impossible.

Thus the political victory of Jefferson in 1800, a victory won with the aid of humble farmers whose religious conservatism was marked, did relatively little to promote the realization of many of the ideals of the Enlightenment to which the author of the Declaration of Independence still subscribed. But if conservative interests so largely won the day in Chief Justice Marshall's decisions, in the decline of deism and the advance of orthodoxy, and in the delimitation of reason, equalitarianism, and science, it would be wrong to assume that the triumph of reaction was complete.

The all-important fact remained that the victory of the Jeffersonians was a rebuke to the aristocratic condemnation of democracy. This was of greater moment in the realm of facts than all the verbal denunciations of democracy. Moreover, the Alien and Sedition Acts, instruments for the limitation of freedom of discussion and the right of asylum, were allowed to lapse after the Jeffersonian victory. The mere memory of them reacted to the discredit of their conservative authors. If Jefferson and his successor seemed to do disappointingly little to promote the values of the Enlightenment, it must be remembered that they did make a sincere effort to preserve the country's peace through an embargo on exports and other devices resembling economic planning. These efforts failed, it is true. In spite of the growing conviction that America ought to remain aloof from Europe's strife, the youthful country plunged into the titanic conflict between Napoleon and Britain. But here and there a few men stood out against even this last resort to war, on grounds other than mere political and economic interest. No sooner was peace declared in 1815 than two Unitarian ministers, Noah Worcester and William Ellery Channing, took steps to launch a permanent protest against war and an unceasing campaign to build peace. The Enlightenment was not dead.

Nevertheless, the time had not come as yet for any sustained efforts to popularize knowledge through widespread education. Nor had the industrialization which had begun to transform the northeastern seaboard advanced sufficiently to call forth a labor movement and a series of humanitarian causes. But although the gulf separating the intellectual experiences of the professional and other privileged groups from those of the great body of plain people remained wide, genuine advances in the life of the mind were made under patrician direction.

# PART III

## Patrician Leadership

# 9 : Patrician Direction of Thought

> The learning of the country was almost entirely
> on the side of that party which began the ad-
> ministration of national affairs, and which soon
> became the minority.
>
> —WILLIAM TUDOR,
> Letters on the Eastern States, 1820

When Washington declared in his Farewell Address that the diffusion
of knowledge was of prime importance in a republic, he was voicing a
conviction with which most of the leading men of his time would have
agreed. Educational architects provided plenty of plans to this end, but
unfortunately circumstances stood in the way of their realization.

Pressing problems of state and economy absorbed most of the energy
and talents of those at the helm: rivalries among the several states and
antagonisms between merchants and planters, debtors and creditors; the
unruly Indians on the frontier, who had to be pacified or removed into
the further hinterland if settlement was to advance; the War of 1812,
fought in large part to secure advantages for commerce and to expand
the western boundaries; turnpikes and canals, which ultimately served as
bonds of union but which for the time being were the cause of bickering
and strife; governmental favors demanded by men of substance in the
Northeast who were busily diverting capital from ships to factories and
mills; the changing order in the South, where planters were being called

on to cultivate cotton in a big way; the rapid dispersion of the people into the trans-Appalachian country and the renewal of foreign immigration after the downfall of Napoleon. These wide-ranging problems of a new and inexperienced government help to explain why such slight headway was made in the systematic diffusion of knowledge on which the fathers of the Republic had pinned so much faith.

But they are not the entire explanation. Governors and other officials appealed in and out of season for public support of common schools and literary institutions, and the well-to-do paid tribute to the importance of an informed public; but there was little support of these measures, especially when the taxation of property was involved. New York permitted the promising beginnings of state subsidies for education to languish, and Virginia refused to carry out Jefferson's proposal for a state-wide system of graduated schools. Planters, merchants, and professional men everywhere preferred to manage the education of their own children in their own way and to leave that of the less fortunate to church and charity.

There were other factors too. The period following the War of 1812, marked as it was by hard times, was scarcely an auspicious time for instituting a program of taxation for public education. Many though by no means all conservative religious leaders preferred to keep education in the hands of the churches in order that it might inculcate piety, faith, and morals; public education might well become godless and promote the spread of deism and skepticism. Above all, the rapid dispersal of the population hampered the execution of the paper plans that were duly formulated from time to time in behalf of public education.

An equally effective check on the democratization of knowledge was the status of class and political relationships during the years following the conclusion of peace with England in 1815. On the one hand, the small farmers and working people of the cities were not yet fully aroused to a realization of their political power and their needs. Though they won certain concessions, such as an extension of the suffrage and the relaxation of imprisonment for debt, they were not yet in a position to demand universal free schools and other cultural privileges. On the other hand, the collapse of the French Revolution and the conservative reaction abroad heralded by the Age of Metternich, together with the moderate tone of the administrations of James Monroe and John Quincy Adams, softened the bitterness with which the favored classes had regarded democracy during the high Enlightenment and Jacobin furor. A democracy led by gentlemen might after all be made palatable.

Just as gentlemen continued to keep affairs of state in their own hands until the triumph of Jackson's long-threatening forces in 1828, so too did they continue to dominate cultural matters. The specialization and the pressure of competition which characterize a highly technical, industrial society were not yet present to discourage the business or professional man from taking an active interest in the cultural aspects of life. Men of affairs not only entered actively into cultural life themselves but associated on intimate terms with the professional group. This was relatively small. According to an estimate of 1823, the country contained some 6000 lawyers, 10,000 physicians, and 5000 clergymen. These favored classes differed in intellectual equipment and attitudes from the plain people. Thus while other interests were at work beneath the surface, the values of the patrician class largely shaped the intellectual life of the new nation in the decades just before Jackson's election.

To the patrician himself it was clear that his function was to lead, to maintain standards, to refuse to truckle to the vulgar whims of the lower class either in ideas or in taste. He not only was to preserve the knowledge and culture of the past, he was also to increase the store. And if, as some seriously maintained, the absence of such well-defined classes as existed in the Old World might prevent the rise of a school of fiction, there were other spheres in which the writer and artist might preserve and extend the great traditions of the past.

## Books, Magazines, and Newspapers

Under the guidance of the favored classes the new nation's intellectual life made vigorous growth during the first quarter of the nineteenth century, at least by quantitative standards. The 375 printing offices of 1810 almost tripled, and the quality of the books issuing from them was greatly improved. According to the estimate of an enterprising book-jobber, these presses supplied Americans with 20 percent of the current books in 1820, and with 30 percent in 1830. The rest were imported from the British Isles. Despite this relative dependence on the mother country, it has been estimated that some 50,000 titles (books, pamphlets, and magazines) bearing an American imprint appeared in the first three decades of the century. During the decade 1820–1830 the annual value of this output increased from something like two and one-half to three and one-half million dollars.

Naturally the reading public grew with the population, but books still reached only a relatively small proportion of the people. In 1830 the sale of few books, even those regarded as successful, exceeded a thousand copies. Nor did the quasi-public proprietary libraries reach very far down into the social structure. The 50 libraries of 1800 with their 80,000 books were matched in 1825 by as many libraries and twenty times as many books in the four largest cities alone, but the era of the free public library for all the people was still a long way off.

Periodicals, many with high-sounding names and short lives, showed comparable growth within the same limited social framework. The forty-odd magazines of 1810 enjoyed no more than local support; and even in 1825, when cultural patriots took pride in the fact that the country had almost a hundred periodicals, only a few served more than a numerically limited local clientele. This is borne out not only by the constant pleas of the editors for contributions to fill their columns and for unpaid back subscriptions to pay the bills of clamoring printers but by the circulation records themselves. Such specialized periodicals as the *Medical Repository* took satisfaction in a subscription list of 300, and Silliman's *American Journal of Science* "never reached one thousand paying subscriptions." *The Port Folio*, the only general literary magazine in the first quarter of the century which could claim anything like substantial success, had no more than 2000 subscribers in its palmiest days. In 1820 the *North American Review*, which evoked praise even from the Scottish and English critics who were disposed to belittle all American literary efforts, had fewer than 600 subscribers. True, this number had increased to 3000 by 1826. It was regarded as remarkable when a circulation of 25,000 was reached by the *Christian Journal and Advocate*, a Methodist weekly.

The limited appeal of periodicals was partly owing to exorbitantly high postal rates, which sometimes added as much as 40 percent to the cost of a subscription, and partly to the status of printing (hand presses and "balls" still prevailed, making large issues all but impossible). For these reasons most periodicals were designed for the well educated, whose number was few; the pontifical discussions of weighty problems in the manner of the English and Scottish periodicals could not make even the most eclectic of the magazines palatable to any but the smallest circles. Still another factor helps to explain the limited appeal of certain periodicals. As intellectual interests became more specialized in this period—an important evidence of advance—periodicals devoted to such subjects as medicine, law, the theater, and natural science were launched, with the result that general magazines devoted less space to specialized material and became less indispensable to specialists.

Although the masses were not yet reading newspapers, the newspaper-reading public was expanding with the growth of population and commercial interests. By 1815 the United States produced annually 3 million more copies than did Great Britain. Whereas in 1810 only 376 newspapers were published, almost 900 appeared in 1828. In 1810 the annual issue was 22,321,000 copies; by 1828 the 852 journals boasted an annual issue of 68,117,971. This is to say that whereas in 1810 there were 3.81 copies per person annually, in 1828 there were 13.8 copies. Moreover, the newspapers were improved both in plan and in execution.

Despite this expansion newspapers were still for the most part organs of the mercantile and professional classes. The metropolitan journals cost from five to eight dollars per year, but all papers, both urban and rural, were too costly for most people in the humble walks of life. Not until new mechanical devices made mass production possible, a development that coincided with the political and educational awakening of the people, did "penny newspapers" purchasable on street corners become generally available.


## The Support of Intellectuals


In the first quarter of the nineteenth century conditions did not permit even the most gifted man of letters to embark on a professional literary career if he had to earn his livelihood thereby. Few aspirants to literary fame followed the courageous example of Charles Brockden Brown, the first American to support himself solely by his pen. His death in 1810, and the quiescence of Freneau after his patriotic outburst during the second war with England, left the scene largely to more conservative-minded men. Fortunately most of them enjoyed sources of support other than writing. Indeed, many refused to accept payment for contributions to the first periodicals that inaugurated the policy of honorariums—that would have been too sordid a business for a gentleman.

Publishing as a separate commercial enterprise hardly existed. In 1820 over 70 percent of the books sold to the public were bought abroad. In any case none but schoolbooks, Bibles, and devotional works could be counted on to reach many purchasers. Books by native writers fared badly for two reasons. Most of the demand for polite letters could be supplied by reprinting English authors to whom royalties did not need to be paid because no international copyright existed. In the second place, the number of readers they attracted was small; hence the editions were limited, the unit cost high, and profits, if there were any at all, very meager.

The result was that printers and bookdealers thought twice before embarking on the costly task of printing a manuscript. Usually an author had to pay the cost himself or guarantee in advance a suitable number of subscribers, whose names were sometimes listed in the volume when it appeared. Unless a writer was well-to-do or enjoyed patronage, or unless he was willing to shoulder what might prove to be a ruinous debt, he found it very difficult to procure a publisher. Hence those who wrote at all wrote for the small class that could purchase books. And they did not write if they hoped to make money. Bryant, our best poet of the 1820s regarded two dollars as a reasonable compensation for a poem. The popular songwriter George Pope Morris, author of "Woodman, Spare that Tree," was exceptional in being able to count on $50 "for a song unread" and $3500 for *Briar Cliff*, a drama of the American Revolution. Such rewards were rare indeed. Noah Webster's experience was unique; in 1818 he was able to sell for $50,000 the copyright of his *Spelling Book*, 5 million copies of which had already found their way into cities, hamlets, and homesteads.

In all the large and many of the smaller towns much of the activity which found expression in the publication of books and periodicals centered in the literary groups of young lawyers, physicians, and journalists, and a sprinkling of ministers and men of affairs. Such bookstores as Charles Wiley's in New York were a natural rendezvous for the members of these literary coteries. Some circles in New York, notably the quasi-secret Calliopean Society, maintained a library and with some formality encouraged literary and oratorial endeavors. More commonly such groups met at one another's homes for conviviality, talk, and praise of the writings of their fellows. Frequently these groups fostered a periodical. The Anthology Club in Boston maintained *The Monthly Anthology and Boston Review;* the Literary Confederacy of New York supported various ventures, as did the Ugly Club, the Bread and Cheese Club, and others similarly famed for wit and revelry. In Philadelphia the Tuesday Club was a pillar of strength to *The Port Folio;* and at the famous "parties" of Dr. Caspar Wistar and the celebrated soirees of Robert Walsh, Catholic journalist and critic, literary gossip and brilliant talk flourished. The *Portico* was launched by a literary circle in Baltimore; at Charleston the Literary and Philosophical Club became known for the high intellectual tone of its gatherings.

Most of the men of letters and science in whose hands lay the advancement of culture came from substantial families able to indulge their sons' interest in literature or learning. Wealth ultimately derived from land enabled scions of well-to-do families to promote cultural values as patrons or scholars. De Witt Clinton, governor of New York, sponsored educational and scientific enterprises; Edward Livingston, who also followed politics, was the author of a scholarly legal code for Louisiana. James Fenimore Cooper was endowed from the landed estates of his family in central New York. In South Carolina plantation wealth enabled John Izard Middleton to study archeology abroad and to win praise for the excellence of his drawings in his *Grecian Remains in Italy* (1812), a pioneer work in its field; Stephen Elliott, an authority on the natural history of South Carolina, for a time managed the family plantation. Virginia's brilliant social philosopher, John Taylor of Caroline, supported his family from his plantations while he wrote tracts on agricultural reform and systematic treatises blasting the centralizing and capitalistic developments in American government and economic life.

Directly or indirectly commerce also enabled many men to enjoy the luxury of letters and scholarship. Sometimes men of affairs became patrons of literature and science. Thus in 1818 the rich Boston merchant Israel Thorndike purchased for Harvard the treasury of books that Ebeling, the great German authority on America, had collected. After helping to build a fortune by marketing ice in the tropics, William Tudor of Boston devoted himself to critical and descriptive writing and to the editorship of the *North American Review,* which he founded in

1815. Nathaniel Bowditch, during the years of his service as an actuary to insurance companies, contributed mathematical papers to learned societies and translated with sagacious and clarifying annotations Laplace's classic *Mécanique Céleste*. He was able to shoulder the printing cost of $12,000 and thus to put the great work within the reach of serious American students. Boston also took pride in Charles Sprague, who combined banking with the writing of poetry. James Hillhouse, whose artificially Miltonic dramas were correct but dismal, for a time engaged in hardware merchandising in New York. Scholarship profited richly from the labors of John Pickering of the famous maritime family of Salem. Pickering enjoyed prestige as an authority on Roman law, a master of many American Indian dialects, and a scholar in the languages of China and India, which the recently opened commerce with the Orient had brought nearer to New England's interests. But no commercial fortune did more for science than that of the liberal-minded William Maclure, a wealthy Scotch-American who completed in 1817 a geological survey of a vast area, the first such undertaking in the history of the science. His *Observations on the Geology of the United States* not only sketched in masterly fashion the grand features of the geology of the eastern half of the country, but presented new data which supported neither of the two leading European schools in the field.

Sometimes the fortunes of established families permitted an exceptional son to enjoy a competency while pursuing literature. Richard Henry Dana, the elder, was able to abandon all thought of any profession save letters; to this he devoted himself with complete pecuniary failure. Well-established merchants were often able to give at least a running start to sons with literary inclinations. William Crafts, the South Carolina wit and orator whose frothy pieces won him a considerable local reputation, was a merchant's son. So too was George Ticknor of Boston, who brought back from an extended European sojourn much learning and a great library in modern literature. Robert Sands, author of metrical romances in the manner of Scott, and Washington Irving were both sons of successful merchants. So too was Fitz-Greene Halleck, whose countinghouse clerkship ultimately won an annuity from John Jacob Astor. Henry Schoolcraft, to cite yet another example, was the studious son of the director of the great Van Rensselaer glassworks. Schoolcraft's desire to discover mineral deposits that might serve the interests of his father's business played some part in his decision to explore the West in 1817. This exploration led to pioneer studies not only in geology but in ethnology as well.

While the professional class in general enjoyed less wealth than the merchants and landed proprietors, many practitioners of law and medicine were among the richest men of their community. Among the men whose fathers were prominent and substantial physicians, able to give many advantages to their sons, were Joel Poinsett, public figure of South Carolina and patron of many worthy cultural enterprises; Joseph Story, the distinguished scholar in jurisprudence; James Gates Percival, author of the Spenserian *Prometheus* (1821), which struck a melancholy note; and Thomas Say, "father of American zoology." Bryant's father, while not wealthy, was a country doctor of standing. As in former times, medical men themselves often made contributions to knowledge. The Danas in their *Outlines of Mineralogy and Geology of Boston*, Horace Hayden in his *Geological Essays* (1820), and especially Dr. Archibald Bruce, founder of the first geological journal, enriched science through studies ranging from the discovery and classification of minerals and ores to the promulgation of novel theories.

Success in law enabled many men to play important roles in the cultural life of the period. Chancellor James Kent was in a position to pay out over $1000 for the publication of the first of the eight volumes of his great *Commentaries on American Law*. In this instance the investment was profitable, for according to good authority Kent subsequently reaped $5000 annually from this venture. Charles J. Ingersoll, literary critic and stout defender of Americanism in the life of the mind; Joseph Hopkinson, versifier and littérateur; and Peter Stephen Duponceau, a naturalized Frenchman celebrated for his work in Indian philology, enjoyed lucrative law practices. The list of lawyers with an active interest in letters also includes William Wirt, author of the much-admired *Letters of a British Spy* and a life of Patrick Henry; William Austin, writer of Hawthornesque tales; and the rising orator Daniel Webster. The list could be extended almost indefinitely.

The ministry, on the other hand, included few well-to-do men, but it did enable a goodly number to follow a scholarly or literary bent and to give their sons the advantages of a scholarly home, association with leaders in the community, and a college education. Indeed, ministers' families far exceeded their quota of sons destined to win laurels in letters, science, and scholarship.

But not all the contributions came from families of wealth and prestige. In the decades after the War of 1812 at least a few men of humble origin achieved places of distinction in cultural life. A blacksmith, Charles Brayton, acted as judge in Rhode Island's highest court. Thomas Nuttall, a botanist who had risen from printer's apprentice in Liverpool, somehow managed without patronage to meet his frugal needs while exploring the continent and classifying specimens for his magnificent *Genera of North American Plants*. Respite from the pressure of poverty came at length in 1822, when Harvard appointed him curator of its gardens. College instructors too are represented among the pioneers of scholarship. Though they were engaged chiefly in the transmission of knowledge, some found even in poorly equipped and inadequately financed institutions a security that enabled them to make original contributions to knowledge. Rutgers, Columbia, and Pennsylvania at different times harbored Robert Adrian, a mathematician who suggested the *cateraria volvens* curve and preceded by a year the German mathematician Gauss in demonstrating the exponential law of error generally associated with the European's name. Bowdoin and Amherst, through the geological work of Parker Cleaveland and Edward Hitchcock, showed that even the smaller and poorer institutions might support original endeavors.

In spite of the generally held laissez-faire philosophy which at least in theory reduced the government to the role of a policeman, the ideals of the founding fathers regarding the duty of government to promote knowledge were not entirely forgotten. Expeditions primarily military in character generally took along scientists, whose contributions to knowledge were often considerable. The expedition of Zebulon M. Pike, dispatched by the War Department in 1806 to explore the headwaters of the Arkansas and Red Rivers, would no doubt have augmented geographical knowledge considerably had not Pike's papers been seized by Mexican authorities. Schoolcraft investigated the Missouri lead mines and in 1820 joined the Cass expedition, which provided opportunity for exploring the lead mines in the Lake Superior area. There he obtained much valuable geological information and gathered material for his ingenious speculations on the Indians.

The most important governmental expedition in this period was that on which Stephen Long embarked in 1820 at the instance of the Secretary of War, John C. Calhoun. Accompanied by able geologists and naturalists, Long's expedition resulted not only in an impressive extension of geographical knowledge about the Rocky Mountain area but in the discovery of sixty new or rare animals, several hundred insects, and many interesting new plants. In 1824 Long led another expedition that quarried geological knowledge from the region bounded by the Mississippi, the Missouri, and the Canadian boundary.

Government support of intellectual interests was frequently urged with vigor and broad vision but without marked success. Among those who attacked the problem of government subsidy most courageously was John Quincy Adams, whose scholarly report on weights and measures was published in 1821 at the expense of the federal government. In his inaugural address he asked for public support of the arts and sciences, and especially for a government observatory and exploring expedition so that the United States, like other countries, might contribute to the advancement of knowledge and the improvement of the lot of mankind. But his plea fell on deaf ears. Other reverses retarded the program of government encouragement to culture. In 1825 fire damaged the Library of Congress, which had been reestablished in 1815 by the purchase of Jefferson's enviable collection of rare and important volumes. But a new beginning was made in what ultimately was to become a great national monument to learning. In the field of state enterprise the commonwealths began to follow the example of New York and New Hampshire, which in 1820 established state libraries.

In the arts the situation was much the same. The federal government was not utterly indifferent, but most artists were dependent on their own resources. Under public auspices the work of planning the national capitol, which had been so ably undertaken by Major l'Enfant, a French officer in the American war for independence, was continued by Benjamin Latrobe, who took charge of the construction of the south wing of the building. English by birth and German by training, Latrobe was largely dependent on foreign artists for the decorative work. At length two American artists, Rembrandt Peale and John Trumbull, were subsidized for their contributions to the beautification of the capitol. In general, however, artists, like men of letters, were self-dependent. Even the patronage of the well-to-do failed to relieve Samuel F. B. Morse, John Trumbull, and many of their fellow artists of grave financial worries.

Most of the few young men who succeeded without family support as scientists, men of letters, and painters shared the views of the favored classes. There were exceptions, of course. One was John Neal, son of a Quaker schoolmaster, whose liberal and democratic ideas owed much to Jeremy Bentham, with whom he had enjoyed an intimate association during a residence in England. In his writings Neal championed women's rights and other reforms. More typical was Hezekiah Niles, once a printer's apprentice, who aligned himself with men of substance and position in championing the manufacturing and commercial interests in his famous *Register*. And Jared Sparks, after working his way from poverty to eminence as a biographer and historian and president of Harvard, absorbed with little difficulty most of the values and ideas of the patrician class.

### Crosscurrents in the Colleges

In some ways the colleges responded to the undercurrent of democracy but on the whole they retained their aristocratic tone. The paternalistic despotism that marked the supervision of colonial students still prevailed. Nor did democratic values and ideals profit from the unending preoccupation with emulation, with the desire for rank, which all too often killed the love of knowledge for its own sake. The traditional curriculum, in which the classics, mathematics, and logic were heavily weighted, continued to dominate all the colleges. There was already much opposition to this policy from those who saw that it tended to exclude some youths ambitious to succeed in business and engineering. In any case, it symbolized a venerable and aristocratic culture that seemed to have little immediate value to a utilitarian middle-class democracy.

Thus the patrician concept of higher education prevailed. Most of the academic profession probably agreed with the head of Dickinson College in Pennsylvania that while a few fine minds were sometimes lost for want of formal culture, "persons with uncouth and rugged minds" would be far better employed at a plow than in making themselves ridiculous by trying to obtain a liberal education. When the University of Virginia got under way in 1819, it was virtually restricted to the well-to-do. As late as 1830 the yearly fees for attendance at American colleges, though they seem very low today, were large in terms of the cash income of the great majority of American families: from $180 to $201 at the University of Pennsylvania, $170 at Harvard, $140 at Yale, and a minimum of $120 at Brown and Williams. Naturally registrations were low. In 1820 James Fenimore Cooper estimated that less than 8000 graduates of the twelve oldest colleges were then living. These, together with the 3000 undergraduates, constituted a small fraction of the total population of approximately 10 million.

Yet the road to a collegiate education was by no means entirely closed to bright and energetic sons of the poor. The rapid spread of private academies enabled many boys from families of limited means to prepare for college; the lads "boarded themselves" in the dormitory on food largely produced on their fathers' farms. Young men intending to enter the ministry could obtain help from various societies that existed for this purpose; and in the northeastern states college youths might still earn their way by teaching school during the long holidays. New colleges, moreover, were constantly being founded to increase educational opportunities in the rapidly growing country. To the thirty colleges existing in 1810 seven permanent institutions were added during the following decade. During the years from 1820 to 1830 twelve more took root.

Certain educational leaders were also aware that the classical curriculum might not be well suited to the needs of every youth. At Vermont President Marsh tried to democratize the university so that any Green Mountain boy might profit from the offerings according to his abilities and needs. The curriculum was liberalized at Brown, Amherst, and above all at Jefferson's University of Virginia and Eliphalet Nott's Union College in New York, where the elective system struck roots. The establishment of Norwich University in Vermont in 1820 and of Rensselaer Polytechnic Institution four years later at Troy, New York, supplemented the opportunities for technical training hitherto available chiefly at West Point. Even with these new facilities only a small proportion of college youth could obtain engineering and technical training at academic institutions. Colleges were by no means caste institutions, but in comparison with the larger facilities of the mid-nineteenth-century decades, opportunities for college education were still limited.

One idea widely cherished during the postrevolutionary years was greatly modified in the decades following the War of 1812. Most liberals had favored the state direction of colleges because they felt that the state could safeguard the schools from the influence of religious sects and the aristocratic classes and, on the assumption that the future would be molded by the colleges, best promulgate democratic ideals. But actually the educational system developed quite differently. The so-called state universities in North Carolina and Vermont received little public support and in most respects resembled private institutions; this was also true of the University of Virginia. The efforts to convert William and Mary, Pennsylvania, Harvard, and other colleges into state universities were resisted by patricians, imbued with the older values and traditions, who feared that state direction might transform the institutions into political footballs and open the gates to all manner of objectionable democratic invaders. When in 1816 the New Hampshire legislature tried to transform Dartmouth into a state university, the effort was blocked by a decision of the United States Supreme Court in which Chief Justice Marshall held that a college charter was an inviolable contract which a legislature might not impair. This significant decision guaranteed the perpetuity of private colleges and encouraged philanthropists and religious sects to found new institutions. And since it was clear that private colleges could not easily be transformed into public- or state-controlled institutions, there was a clear call for the newer states to embark on the establishment of truly public universities.

## Museums, Libraries, and Galleries

Among the lasting contributions of the patrician class during the period of its more or less unchallenged direction of American intellectual life was the foundation of libraries, historical societies, galleries, and museums. The Massachusetts Historical Society, established in 1791, was supported by the Boston aristocracy; in 1822 local gentry fostered similar organizations in Rhode Island and Maine and in the following year in New Hampshire and Connecticut. In 1807 another institution, stemming from the Anthology Society and destined to become a repository of rich treasures, was launched. This institution, the Boston Athenaeum, was a private subscription library which the business and professional classes of Boston used as a social center as well as a useful reference library and a museum of natural history. Its founders, men of substance and leadership, observed that Boston's commerce was highly productive and that "the class of persons enjoying easy circumstances, and possessing surplus wealth, is comparatively numerous. As we are not called upon for large contributions to national purposes, we shall do well to take advantage of the exemption, by taxing ourselves for those institutions, which will be attended with lasting and extensive benefit, amidst all changes of our public fortunes and political affairs."[1] Thanks to the benefactions of such public-spirited men of affairs as John Quincy Adams, John Lowell, James Perkins, and William Shaw, the Athenaeum absorbed many special collections and in a relatively short time became a popular literary center for its restricted shareholding membership, and a model for other athenaeums.

Other cities saw the rise of similar institutions. Not to be outdone by Boston, a group of prominent Worcester men, including Isaiah Thomas, the far-famed publisher of almanacs, Bibles, and other books, incorporated the American Antiquarian Society in 1812. This organization was to assist the future historians of the country by preserving materials that would serve as landmarks in the progress of civilization. It was not long before it had a notable collection of materials that became the pride of Worcester's first families: Indian and other American antiquities, maps, newspapers, manuscripts, and books. It issued annually a volume of proceedings to which friends of the society contributed. In New York, John Pintard, a merchant prince of scholarly tastes, took the lead in establishing the New York Historical Society in 1804; on its rosters were the names of many men prominent in the professional and business life of the metropolis.

In other cities also leading citizens established museums and academies of natural history. In 1812 such an institution was organized in Philadelphia, and five years later the Lyceum of Natural History in New York began its useful career when prominent citizens assembled collections of specimens, contributed original papers, and published memoirs. About the same time museums of natural history were founded in Richmond, Raleigh, and Charleston, and within a few years in Baltimore, Cincinnati, New Orleans, and at least a dozen small places. All these agencies enriched American intellectual life by encouraging a spirit of

[1] Josiah Quincy, *The History of the Boston Athenaeum* (Cambridge, 1851), 39–40.

accurate observation and rational inquiry. To them subsequent developments in science owed much.

These institutions for the promotion of natural science did not monopolize the interest of the patrician class. The American Academy of Arts in New York (1802–1808), organized by the sale of shares of stock, broke new ground; and in 1805 seventy-one gentlemen of Philadelphia, chiefly merchants and lawyers, organized the Pennsylvania Academy of Fine Arts. Although a plan formulated in 1820 for the promotion of an American Academy of Letters did not materialize, the roster of its proposed members shows that the cultural leadership was in the hands of the well-to-do. In the words of Edward Everett, the list comprised "no small proportion of the respectability of our country"; and he added that great value would be attached to their opinions on any subject.

## Progress in the Popularization of Knowledge

Aristocratic leadership in cultural life did not, of course, prevent the gradual advance of the popularization of knowledge. In fact, a period that experienced the stirrings of industrialism, the breakdown of the old apprenticeship system, the rise of a labor movement, the beginnings of the application of steam to printing presses, and the political unrest associated with Jacksonism was in the nature of things almost bound to see important steps taken for the popularization of knowledge. Such treatises as Smith's and Meases' *The Wonders of Nature and Art* (1806–1807) and William Duane's *An Epitome of the Arts and Sciences,* the second edition of which appeared in 1811, played their part in breaking the traditional monopoly of knowledge by the well educated and well-to-do. That the idea of free public libraries was in the air is clear from the address of Dr. Jesse Torrey, at Ballston Spa, New York, in 1817. Torrey insisted that most of the evils distracting mankind might be laid at the door of ignorance and that therefore in the interest of prosperity, security, and happiness legislatures must not stop with the endowment of universities for the few but must "diffuse knowledge among the many who supply their legislators with power as well as with money."[2]

---

[2] Dr. Jesse Torrey, Jr., *The Intellectual Torch; developing an original, economical, and expeditious plan for the universal dissemination of knowledge and virtue; by means of free public libraries* (Ballston Spa, 1817), 3–4.

The proposal for the establishment of publicly supported free libraries did not take root at once. But the middle classes in the cities, longing for more reading matter, took things in hand by forming their own libraries. In 1820 two new institutions, the Mercantile Library Association and the Apprentices' Library Association, were organized in New York; and presently Boston and Philadelphia announced the establishment of similar libraries. Even in rural districts reading opportunities gradually broadened. Thanks to the promoting genius of Mathew Carey, the Philadelphia publisher, book agents such as Parson Weems traveled up and down the land peddling in quantities biographies, histories, and manuals designed for the use and moral uplift of people in the ordinary walks of life. Moralistic and anecdotal chapbooks found a place in the wagons of the 200 peddlers that by 1823 were canvassing the country.

As a result of the evangelical movement the old staples of the Bible and the almanac were now supplemented by tracts designed to inculcate piety, temperance, and Christian zeal. Appealing to human interests as these tracts often did, they must have encouraged the reading habit among the common people. More solid matter—theology, biography, and history—found its way into the parish libraries that multiplied in New England. It was in such "social libraries" that boys like Elihu Burritt, the "learned blacksmith," laid the foundations for their later learning.

Significant in the popularization of knowledge were the museums established by the artist Charles Willson Peale and his sons in Philadelphia and Baltimore. From a modest beginning in 1794 in Peale's studio, the museum in Philadelphia developed until in 1808 it was self-supporting and had become not only one of the recreational showplaces of the city but an agency of definite educational value. For a moderate charge one might see in its rooms an electrical machine and exhibits of wampum, scalps, tomahawks, historical curiosities, stuffed birds, preserved reptiles, and strange animals standing lifelike in front of painted skies and woods. Or one might contemplate the reconstructed skeleton of a mastadon, one of Peale's great achievements, or scrutinize a minute insect under a microscope. Brief readable descriptions and provision for oral explanations of the exhibits added to the educational value of the institution. But it deteriorated into the sensationalistic type of "dime museum" when the municipality and the federal government refused Peale's offer to hand over the exhibits and he himself became too old to supervise his cherished specimens. As an early experiment in the popularization of scientific knowledge Peale's museum deserves an important place in our intellectual history.

Although little was done in this period to improve the condition of rural common schools, Noah Webster estimated that by 1818 over 5 million copies of his *Spelling Book* had introduced the art of reading to a large portion of the population. The private academies, which sometimes enjoyed public subsidies, spread rapidly not only in the northeastern but in the southern and western states as well. To these people's seminaries many a poor country lad owed his start in the classics, in science, and in modern literature, fields in which some later achieved distinction.

The cities, growing rapidly with the advance of manufacturing, trade, and immigration, were unable to expand the private charity schools sufficiently to meet the new demands. But in 1805 the New York Free School Society relieved the situation somewhat by supplying the charity schools maintained by various religious groups with private subscriptions and public funds, and comparable steps were taken in other cities.

Another boon came the following year when the first Lancasterian school opened in New York. "Youthful corporals of the teachers' regiments," as the pupil-teachers were called, instructed the less advanced children in what they had just learned from the monitor above them or from the master himself. The methods of instruction were mechanical, but the Lancasterian schools enabled a great many children to learn at least something in a single room directed by one teacher. Congenial as it was to a society in which laissez faire was rapidly gaining popularity and in which the well-to-do opposed state taxation for public education, the Lancasterian system spread over the entire country. Its English founder, Joseph Lancaster, came to America in 1818 to carry on the work; and the prestige which it gained from the sponsorship of De Witt Clinton served it well. Under way by the end of the War of 1812, the Lancasterian system was given a new lease on life by the hard times that dampened the enthusiasm of the few who contended for more widespread public support of the schools. Until the great educational revival in the later 1820s and 1830s, this system did good service in popularizing the idea of mass instruction.

It would be easy to overemphasize the distance between the favored classes and the rank and file of Americans with respect to intellectual equipment and perspectives. For the unlearned had at least entered the outer portal even before the patrician monopoly of learning began to be broken during the Jacksonian period. The learned and the ignorant, as Judge James Hall observed in his *Letters from the West* (1828), came into contact with one another more frequently and more intimately than in societies with well-defined castes. This was somewhat less true in the East than in the West; but even in the older rural communities common association in church societies, town meetings, and similar institutions presented a striking contrast with Europe. Seeing this, and the general literacy of the ordinary man, Hall prophesied, somewhat optimistically, that the gulf between the ignorant and the learned could not persist forever.

A stronger case might be made for Timothy Dwight's contention that if the common man in America knew less about his particular task than the European peasant or artisan, he knew a great deal more about other matters. This view was frequently advanced even in the writings of the English travelers whose antipathy toward America was patent. Henry Bradshaw Fearon, for example, admitted that because of his mobility the American agricultural laborer surpassed the English yeoman in intelligence and information. A transplanted Englishman, John Bristed, wrote in 1818 that the mass of Americans excelled every other people in the world in shrewdness of intellect, general intelligence, versatility, and readiness to experiment with untried things.

Still others confirmed the observation made by William Cobbett on his return to America in 1817 that every farmer, unlike the European peasant, was more or less a reader. At about the same time Lieutenant Francis Hall of His Majesty's Light Brigade was impressed, like other travelers, by finding mathematical manuals and other useful books of knowledge in houses that made no pretense whatever to luxury or learning. He also noted that the common people in America were better informed and had a greater aptitude for agricultural and mechanical innovations than their European counterparts. Jefferson, whom Hall visited at Monticello, ascribed these characteristics to the fact that Americans of all ranks and conditions, in greater degree than in Europe, found time to cultivate their minds after the cultivation of acres less hard to work than those of Europe. The great Virginian added that in town, court, and county meetings plain people found an opportunity for thinking and discussing common problems in a way closed to humble men in the Old World. Surely, in this period of generally conservative orientation, there were powerful forces working toward the development of a people's culture. Before tracing the growth of that culture, it will be well to examine in some detail the nature of the intellectual activity of the patrician leadership.

# 10 Nationalism Challenges Cosmopolitanism

> Dependence, whether literary or political, is a state of degradation, fraught with disgrace; and to be dependent on a foreign mind, for what we can ourselves produce, is to add to the crime of indolence, the weakness of stupidity.
>
> —*The Port Folio*, 1816

> We are the Romans of the modern world,—the great assimilating people.
>
> —OLIVER WENDELL HOLMES, 1858

> You are very energetic in America; and in all matters regarding Education you are likely to outstrip Europe. You have undoubtedly suggested many improvements, and we are very willing to have the benefit of your wisdom and experience. . . . America has long since taken the highest place in Jurisprudence, and all Europe must confess its obligations to the distinguished Jurists of that country. We have no such writers in Jurisprudence as Kent, Story & Greenleaf. . . . In Theology, too, America stands very high, and some of her writers in that department are esteemed throughout Europe.
>
> —J. S. MORE TO HENRY BARNARD, 1856

No simple formula epitomizes the complex pattern of ideas that characterizes the thought of the better-established classes in the first three decades of the nineteenth century. Broadly speaking, the desire for a distinctive American culture, which conservative intellectuals often shared with the radicals, conflicted with the continuing cosmopolitan and eclectic tone of intellectual life. To explain precisely what interests or motives led some patricians to favor one or another of the currents of thought, feeling, and taste obviously European, and others to uphold a programmatic cultural nationalism, would be impossible. Indeed, the same person frequently displayed both a fondness for classicism or Romanticism and an enthusiasm for what appeared to be a uniquely American idea or value. Certain factors may be kept in mind for the light each throws on this conflict.

However much cultural patriots desired to have America stand on its own feet in intellectual matters, the young Republic did not yet have the intellectual resources to do so. The stream of young aristocrats who had gone to Europe in colonial times to study medicine, law, and theology had dwindled, but this did not mean that America now supplied all the specialized training and knowledge of which it stood in need. Individual students who had formerly sought European centers of learning each with his own cup to fill were now largely but not entirely replaced by college teachers who, in the words of Robert Spiller, made the trip with gallon jugs to be brought back full of the priceless liquor for home distribution. The list of Americans who went to Europe to purchase apparatus for the scientific laboratories established in the older as well as in the newer colleges, or to equip themselves with specialized knowledge in the sciences or the modern languages they were to teach on returning, is too long to enumerate even in part. The odyssey of Benjamin Silliman at the turn of the century and of Henry Wadsworth Longfellow twenty-five years later must represent the long line of scientists and students of modern languages who lighted their torches at European hearths.

Nor was the development of greater facilities for higher education at home, a cause dear to the hearts of such cultured patriots as Jefferson, achieved without the aid of European scholars. If Jefferson clung adamantly to his early conviction that young Americans were in danger of being hopelessly corrupted by the antirepublican manners and principles of a European education, he was nevertheless unable to build the University of Virginia without the help of European scholars; having considered with equanimity the transfer of the entire faculty of the

University of Geneva, he finally borrowed heavily from British universities.

The force of habit also helps to explain the continuing eclectic and cosmopolitan character of the cultural life of American patricians. Noah Webster, an early conservative advocate of a distinctive intellectual life, had been no more able than Jefferson to realize his ambitions without compromises—compromises dictated by habit. It is true that certain of his reforms in orthography, such as the characteristically American spelling of wagon, plow, mold, ax, labor, honor, center, and theater, were taking root, and it is also true that John Pickering, in his dictionary of words and phrases presumably peculiar to the United States, issued in 1816, listed some 500 specimens. But Webster, in subsequent revisions of his ubiquitous *Spelling Book,* had yielded to the pull of deep-rooted habits by omitting many of his extreme innovations. So, too, in his *Compendious Dictionary of the English Language* (1806) he had, without entirely abandoning his role as a reformer, relinquished many innovations of his earlier linguistic chauvinism. The demand for the further Americanization of the language was still heard, but the hope of early patriots that American English would become as differentiated from the mother tongue as Dutch was from the German was not to be realized. Habit and tradition were too strong.

Having always been the recipients of ideas and culture from abroad, educated Americans naturally continued to be. However strongly American patriots may have desired a distinctive cultural life, they could not, as men and women of ideas, taste, and learning, turn their backs on the wealth of traditional European culture or on the rising currents of thought in the Old World. Side by side on their shelves with the great treasures of Greece and Rome stood the eighteenth-century classics that inspired such imitations as Washington Irving's Addisonian sketches. Old-fashioned southern gentlemen surprised James K. Paulding in 1817 not only in stubbornly standing by English writers but in preferring older English writers. They refused to give up Milton for Byron, Newton for Herschel, or Locke for Stewart.

The continued appeal of European currents of thought and the paradoxical appeal of cultural nationalism can be explained in terms of the congeniality of the one or the other to the particular needs of the cultivated classes or the particular situation in which they found themselves. In disdaining the newfangled notions and standing faithfully by their

Addison, Pope, and Johnson, the conservative southern planters with whom Paulding talked in 1817 were acting, consciously or otherwise, in accordance with their own best interests. For the great classical tradition, emphasizing as it did the judgment of convention and the group rather than the individual, venerating discipline rather than self-expression, was congenial to the spirit of keeping things as they stood. Other time-tested props of the established order were not forgotten; Paley, with his justifi- cation in terms of a divine expediency of whatever existed, and Burke, with his reverence for the institutionalism of the past, remained favorites.

No group of writers using the English language was more esteemed in cultivated circles than the Scottish common-sense school of philosophers. From prerevolutionary years when President Witherspoon of the College of New Jersey had introduced the Scottish realistic or common-sense philosophers down to the time when Jefferson found so much to admire in their thought, Reid, Brown, and Stewart gradually pushed Locke into a less favored place. By 1823 eight American editions of Stewart's *Philosophy* had appeared. The Scotch rhetoricians and critics, particu- larly Lord Kames, Hugh Blair, and Archibald Alison, invaded American colleges to shape the oratorical and literary tastes of the rising generation. They were assisted by the *Edinburgh Review, Blackwood's,* the *Quarterly Review,* and the *New Monthly Magazine;* not only were these journals generally read by the mansion people but they provided a congenial pat- tern for American editors. The Scottish common-sense realism, pervading literary and esthetic criticism as it did, thus became familiar to the well read. The appeal of the Scottish philosophy lies in the fact that for the baffling subtleties of the philosophic idealism of Berkeley, the negations of Hume, and the quasi-materialism of Locke, it substituted a common- sense assurance of the validity of Christian morals and Christian prin- ciples generally. It was, in short, admirably suited to the needs of conservative-minded intellectuals recovering from the hysteria that deism and Jacobinism had aroused and primarily concerned in their everyday life with the hardheaded tasks of consolidating the existing order and promoting commercial and industrial enterprises.

Finally, to understand the conflict between the continuing influence of European currents of thought and the ideal of cultural nationalism one must keep in mind the ever-changing conditions of life in the first decades of the nineteenth century. These changing conditions, closely associated with the growth of commerce and industry in an agricultural frontier country and with the recession westward of the frontier itself, continued to require the accommodation of European ideas to American needs. The ideal of cultural nationalism frequently facilitated this process of accommodation or modification.

The status of legal thought in the first three decades of the century illustrates these tendencies. It will be recalled that in general social and political liberals objected to the common law on the ground that it was British and therefore aristocratic and un-American, and that it was likewise an instrument for the protection of creditors rather than debtors and of property rights rather than human rights. These radicals, influenced by the eighteenth-century concept of rationally made legal codes, favored the rejection of common law and the establishment of an American law based on natural rights. Edward Livingston, who framed a legal code for Louisiana, represented this faith in a conscious juristic effort to construct a rational and humane law. But most trained lawyers and virtually all conservatives had no use for artificially made laws; they revered the common law for its organic nature, its time-tested precepts, and its provisions for personal rights and the sanctity of property rights.

Many trained lawyers figured in the accommodation of English common law to American conditions, but two figures, Joseph Story of Massachusetts and James Kent of New York, stood head and shoulders above the others. Both shaped much law by their notable court decisions. Story in his *Commentaries on the Constitution* and Kent in his *Commentaries on American Law* supplemented and systematized their court decisions, thus further contributing to the acceptance of English law. This they did by identifying it with the generally accepted law of nature, supplementing it through comparative law, and translating many of the social and political ideas and practices of the New World into legal concepts in harmony with common-law traditions.

What made this law especially congenial to conservatives was that it met so well the needs of the directors of an expanding commercial and industrial society. The doctrine so dear to many radicals, that liberty rested on economic equality, was rejected; the extent to which government might regulate property rights was carefully restricted; barriers were thrown around individual rights, especially property rights; and the primacy of the federal government as the most effective means of protecting propertied interests against assaults by the states was upheld. No wonder that Jackson, agrarian and champion of popular rights, regarded

Story as the most dangerous man in the land! He might well have coupled Kent with him.

An organic law which could not easily be changed and which protected property rights appealed to conservative interests. But this alone does not explain the reception of English law. The great jurists recognized American departures from English practices, especially in the sphere of landownership. With an American law derived basically from common law was amalgamated the simpler American methods of conveying real property, the less exalted status of land among other property categories which resulted from its abundance in a new country, and the elimination of the English preference for male stocks in the law of descent.

## The Romantic Mood

The eclectic and cosmopolitan character of patrician thought was also exemplified by the growth of Romanticism in this country. The complex pattern of ideas and feelings commonly termed Romanticism owed much to America. Into this generous catchall had gone enthusiasm for the noble savage, the mysteries of the American wilderness, the primitive in general. The cult of simplicity and the state of equality which the Americans, particularly frontiersmen and Quakers, presumably exemplified were other quarries from which the imagination and sentiment could secure foundation stones for the Romantic structure. Thus the picturesque, strange, and fantastic phenomena of the terrestrial paradise beyond the Atlantic gave to Romanticists the very stuff of dreams. Herder, Goethe, Chateaubriand, Byron, Wordsworth, Blake, and Coleridge, among many others, were deeply in debt to America.

Among the earliest of the Romantic types of literature to excite enthusiasm in America was the so-called Gothic romance. The fondness for these widely read and widely imitated thrillers has been attributed to the general reaction against naturalism; in a time when reason was being sharply delimited, the incredible plots, bewildering spectacles of goblins, giants, ghosts, and damsels in distress stalking or stumbling through somber dungeons and dilapidated castles was in truth a tribute to the spell of the supernatural. Or perhaps all the exciting unreality of these funereal and demoniac debauches provided that notoriously satisfying emotional escape which is always welcome and doubly so in a tumultuous world in which the old order breaks down through economic and social revolutions.

The desire to escape from the unpleasant requirements of grim reality may also explain the lure of the picturesque and the remote, whether in time or place (another ingredient of Romanticism). Irving, always detached from the most acute realities of his own time, shifted from the rollicking wit of the *Salmagundi Papers* to his graceful and shadowy illusions of olden times on the banks of the Hudson, in the leisurely towns of Spain, and among the picturesque byways of England—not the England of factories and coal mines. All this may reflect Irving's lack of ease in the bustling, gross, and practical America, which he so little understood. Cooper too, devoted as he was to America in so many ways, was unable to accept the "crude levelism" that violated his idealized picture of a decorous eighteenth-century landed aristocracy, and so may have found solace in an exciting wilderness and a romantic sea. Paulding's fondness for the ways of the lowly, so evident in his homespun pictures of old Dutch New York, also reflects Romanticism; if his angle of vision was somewhat different, it was no less remote from existing actualities. And, finally, Scott's great popularity—during the decade 1813–1823, 5 million volumes of the Waverley Novels issued from American presses—may have sprung from the half-felt need for compensatory escape. Or it may have been that his stirring tales of border warfare struck a responsive chord in the hearts of Americans because they themselves knew something of the strife and adventure of the frontier, both from experience and from the alluring tales of their own Cooper. Or perhaps the mansion people were fascinated by Scott's glowing accounts of the lords and ladies of feudal castles who lived on an even more pretentious and glamorous plane than any to which they themselves could aspire.

Byronic melancholy and gloom also had its charms in a world that was still stormy and tumultuous, and it enticed Americans with facile pens into imitative efforts. But to those in comfortable circumstances the mood of optimism that was unmistakably present in the new currents of Romanticism was even more congenial as the old Federalist pessimism, which assumed that calamity was just around the corner, that the Republic could not endure, was giving way. The collapse of radicalism abroad, the relaxation of political rivalries, the security of property, and economic expansion at home—all contributed to the reassertion of belief in a roseate future. Confidence in personality which the popular Byron glorified, in the power and destiny of the individual to set up judgments and values even in defiance of those established by authority and convention, took possession of people who saw about them tremendous human power constructing incredible canals and turnpikes, impressive factories, and magic cities. As one of the editors of the *North American Review* observed, "practical, satisfied men cannot do justice to a gloomy poetic mood which is critical of the world."

The worshipful attitude toward nature, another powerful element in the Romantic structure, inspired lyrics to solitude and melancholy, but it also confirmed the mood of optimism. No disciple of Romanticism felt so animated, so buoyant, so confident of the scheme of things, as when he reverently contemplated the beauties and mysteries of nature, when he gave himself up to flowers, birds, streams, and forests. Audubon, who made the wilderness his studio, felt that he had been commissioned by divine ordinance to observe and paint the Creator's feathered creatures; he reveled in his intimate comradeship with them; he felt their delicious murmurs and melodious songs to be his own. Noteworthy as his unforgettable paintings of birds are for their scientific value, they are no less significant evidence of the rhapsodic admiration that possessed Audubon. They show how the music of the forest reechoed in his soul and how respectfully he bowed "before that vast and thousand-chorded instrument formed by the eternal author of all." Hundreds of other nature lovers who lacked Audubon's genius glowed with optimism as they contemplated in the works of nature the inscrutable hand of the Creator, the promise of immortality, and divine immanence itself. At a moment when the standing social order sought the reaffirmation of religious values as a final blow to atheism and nihilism, the light and life fostered by the mysteries and beauties of nature were as useful to religion as they were congenial to tastes surfeited with eighteenth-century formalism.

In the sphere of architecture the Romantic revolt against classicism did not get under way until after 1830. But the great exponents of the neo-Greek style—Benjamin Latrobe, Robert Mills, and William Strickland—were not unfamiliar with the Gothic vogue. The Gilmor house which Alexander Jackson Davis constructed in Baltimore in 1832 pointed in the new direction.

In the field of painting the full tide of Romanticism did not set in until the period of Jacksonian individualism. Shortly after 1823, however, Thomas Cole began to paint romantic landscapes of the Hudson valley and the Catskills. At about the same time Asher B. Durand, the engraver of "Musidora" (a nude figure in rustic surroundings which owed its inspiration to Thomson's "Seasons") virtually launched the Hudson River school of landscape painting. Rapturous in its celebration of romantic scenery, this school was to enjoy splendid triumphs.

Closely allied to the reverential regard for nature was the vogue for the "falsely feminine" sentiment and moral didacticism that stamped so much of the drearily genteel writing of the Romantic school. Joseph Story spoke for many of his class when at the Harvard Phi Beta Kappa exercises in 1826 he bestowed high praise on American literature for the distinctive quality flowing from its moral earnestness.

Sometimes dimly, sometimes quite consciously, the conservatives sensed danger in the implications of a Romanticism which after all did sacrifice discipline and all the checks of a more or less objective conventionalism to subjective fancies and judgments. Such an alluringly romantic poem as Byron's "Childe Harold's Pilgrimage," for instance, offended the respectable by what appeared to be its licentiousness; his new work was received with doubt and hesitation. Social no less than spiritual well-being was likely to suffer if abandonment to natural impulses became the order of the day. Writing in the *North American Review* for 1823, Samuel Gilman, the Unitarian minister at Charleston, gave some praise to the poetry of James Gates Percival but went on to point out the dangers inherent in a break with tradition and a reliance on mere personal experience. Not until the period of Jacksonian democracy and the rampant individualism of the social reformers did the full implications of the radicalism inherent in Romanticism become apparent.

## The Growing Interest in Non-British Culture

The cosmopolitan and eclectic nature of patrician thought was reflected in a growing interest in the culture of non-British lands, especially Germany. For a long time, as a matter of fact, learned men had had some acquaintance with German thought, so that the enthusiasm for

German culture expressed in the years following the War of 1812 was not a sudden discovery but the culmination of a growing interest. The Reverend William Bentley of Salem was a leading figure in the development of this interest in the postrevolutionary years, when commercial contacts with Hamburg and the Baltic ports were increasing. His *Impartial Register* (1800–1819) summarized the scientific, literary, and artistic advances in Germany. The circle of Americans who shared Bentley's knowledge of Germany was broadened still further by the interest which the Hamburg geographer, Professor Ebeling, aroused and by the translations of German tales, plays, and poems which became available in America.

Nevertheless, certain circumstances in the years immediately after the War of 1812 promoted this long-growing interest in German culture. In the general reaction against Great Britain incident to the war, it was natural to look for intellectual sustenance elsewhere. Moreover, British Romanticists too were celebrating the glories of German thought and poetry. German culture did not embody the radicalism and materialism that had long been associated with the French, nor the reactionary monarchism and, what was worse, the Catholicism, of postrevolutionary France. The North German states were reputed to be, if not conservatively republican in politics, at least idealistic in thought and Protestant in faith.

These circumstances and the long-developing interest in German culture provide the setting for a new chapter in the cultural relations of America and Germany. In 1814 an English translation of Madame de Staël's *De l'Allemagne* appeared in New York. This famous book was full of enthusiasm for German thought. About the same time the first of a long line of young Americans went to the German universities for study. In 1816 Edward Everett went to Göttingen, and somewhat later George Ticknor, George Bancroft, and Joseph Cogswell. All came back enthusiastic about German scholarship and determined to elevate the intellectual life of America by shaping its universities and schools according to the German pattern. Everett failed to effect the transformation of Harvard, but Bancroft and Cogswell had better success at the Round Hill School, which they opened in Northampton, Massachusetts. Modeled on a *gymnasium* of the more liberal type, this celebrated school during its first eight years attracted 293 students from nineteen states. Knowledge of German culture was increased also by Edward Everett's brilliant review of Goethe's *Dichtung und Wahrheit,* which appeared in the *North American Review* in 1817. American periodicals, which had hitherto paid little attention to German letters, save for Goethe's *Sorrows of Werther* and the plays of Schiller and Kotzebue, now began to find a place for a whole series of essays on German literature, philosophy, scholarship, and education. Goethe gave a set of his works to Harvard in 1819, and other German imprints flowed into the country.

The arrival of a small group of refugees also had its effect. In 1825 Charles Follen, a fugitive student leader, introduced German gymnastics in Boston and began instruction in his mother tongue at Harvard. In the same year the University of Virginia introduced the study of German. Those who were not among the small but enthusiastic group of pupils of German masters or did not study the language in their own libraries could become acquainted with German idealistic philosophy indirectly through Coleridge's *Aids to Reflection,* which President James Marsh of the University of Vermont, himself a student of German philosophy, published with an illuminating introduction in 1829. Through still other channels German influence was felt; Francis Lieber, a refugee, undertook shortly after his arrival in 1827 the preparation of the *Encyclopaedia Americana.* This followed German principles of scholarship and organization.

But northern Germany, which in the 1830s and 1840s was to play so important a role in both American philosophy and education, was not the only source of the new fare. William Maclure, the Scottish geologist, introduced into America Pestalozzi's educational theories, which in their emphasis on individual development and nature study were closely related to Romantic ideas. Although the time had not yet come for Pestalozzianism to soften the harsh, disciplined, book-centered, and mechanical pedagogy of the traditional schools, it did nevertheless arouse interest. It inspired Warren Colburn, a Massachusetts teacher, to reorganize the presentation of elementary arithmetic, and at such liberal centers as Robert Owen's New Harmony it came into its own. The theories of another Swiss educator, Fellenberg, also aroused interest in limited circles and stimulated efforts to combine the training of the mind with physical labor.

Patrician interest in the culture of Italy and Spain also increased. Philadelphia and New York profited from the presence of that extraordinary adventurer, Lorenzo Da Ponte, importer of books from the Latin countries, littérateur, dramatist, and librettist for some of Mozart's best-known operas. As a teacher of Italian this gifted if erratic south European shared with the patrician class his knowledge of Dante and of Italian culture in general. At Washington an occasional representative of the diplomatic corps, such as the Portuguese minister Correa Da Serra, reminded limited circles of upper-class Americans of the glories of southern European culture. George Ticknor, returning in 1819 from a *Wanderjahr* during which he visited Spain, became a distinguished expositor of the literature of that land.

Most citizens of the United States knew little or nothing of Latin America, but a few intellectuals, such as the members of the American Philosophical Society, the New York Historical Society, and similar organizations, stimulated by growing trade relations and by the conviction that South Americans were copartners in throwing off Europe's yoke, acquired considerable knowledge about this region. Dr. Samuel Latham Mitchill of New York, who acquainted himself with the leading writings on Spanish and Portuguese America, pleaded for closer cultural relations and as a member of the House of Representatives drew up in 1811 a significant report on Latin America. The Venezuelan agent in the United States, Manuel Rorres, and David Porter, an American naval officer, also contributed appreciably to the Americans' knowledge of their southern neighbors. The great diversity that prevailed among the Latin Americans was seldom appreciated, and the common factors in the struggles for liberty on the two continents were overemphasized. Yet, despite the lack of perspective and the confusion of ideas and sentiments, American leaders of thought were not only developing an interest in and a knowledge of Latin America but were coming to regard the upheavals there as a great opportunity for serving both the United States and humanity itself.

## The British Attack on American Culture

The peculiarities of the developing American economy and society led to vigorous reassertions of the well-established idea of cultural nationalism—an idea, it will be recalled, shared with varying interpretations by both liberals and conservatives. But the new crop of British criticisms of America and the chauvinistic self-consciousness these criticisms engendered in the United States were also factors of considerable weight. The patronizing or condemnatory evaluations of American life and culture expressed in travelers' accounts and reviews published in the British literary magazines were no new thing. But after 1815 these attacks increased both in volume and in bitterness. No doubt the long-standing disdain and resentment over the growth of America were greatly replenished by the American declaration of war at the very height of the struggle against Napoleon. No doubt the enhanced rancor of the British owed something to the irritating patriotic conceit of an American public oblivious of its own shabby military record. In the United States the conviction deepened that these scurrilous attacks were inspired no less by a desire for revenge than by a determination to belittle everything American in a desperate attempt to stave off parliamentary reform and, above all, to check emigration and protect British markets against the competition of American enterprise.

Whatever the motives, English travelers returning from America joined with the literary critics of the great quarterly and monthly periodicals in patronizing or excoriating the Americans, or both. The retorts which the smarting Americans were quick to make, accompanied by attacks on the decadently feudal character of English culture, only goaded the British into making still more sweeping assaults. Americans were ridiculed for their execrable taste, their vulgar manners, their unlimited bigotry, their colossal ignorance and vanity. Or they were denounced as a slave-flogging, materialistic, gross, undisciplined people devoid of true religious feeling. In the United States, it was charged, democracy ran riot, political corruption fouled public life, demagoguery reigned supreme, and property was unsafe from the mob. Franklin, the only American who was conceded any claim to genius, had been nurtured under the British flag; subsequent inventors merely stole British ideas.

American men of letters were characterized as pale and utterly unworthy imitators of British writers. The words of the Reverend Sydney Smith, whose famous article in the *Edinburgh Review* was less unfriendly than many, have often been quoted:

During the thirty or forty years of their independence, they [the Americans] have done absolutely nothing for the Sciences, for the Arts, for Literature, or even for the statesman-like studies of Politics or Political Economy. . . . In the four quarters of the globe, who reads an American book? or goes to an American play? or looks at an American picture or statue? What does the world yet owe to American physicians or surgeons? What new substances have their chemists discovered? or what old ones have they analyzed? What new constellations have they discovered by the telescopes of Americans?— what have they done in mathematics? . . . Finally, under which of the tyrannical governments of Europe is every sixth man a Slave, whom his fellow-creatures may buy and sell and torture? When these questions are fairly and favourably answered, their laudatory epithets may be allowed. . . .[1]

To such exasperating indictments the most malicious added an even worse one: However pitiful the stature of America, it could probably never rise higher because it was totally lacking in all the elements that make for greatness. If some of the attacks were less biting, if the more moderate ones admitted some virtues and patronizingly prophesied future accomplishments, they were no less irritating for their condescension to a people aroused to a new sense of achievement, power, and destiny.

The effect of such diatribes was to promote American cultural self-consciousness in patrician circles. In the field of literary criticism the British attacks on American life led to spirited replies in which the shortcomings of the mother country were held up to scorn and the achievements of America in every field, including the cultural, were reiterated. And finally, in our intellectual history itself the British criticisms reinforced the conviction that America must shake off its cultural dependence on Europe, that it must achieve uniquely American glories in science, the arts, and letters. Of the effects of the new nationalism which the British onslaughts helped to nourish, some account must be taken.

### The Call for Cultural Nationalism Renewed

The bulk of the American replies to the British indictment forbids any thorough analysis; only their general character can be suggested. Before the full fire of the British onslaught, Charles J. Ingersoll, a Philadelphia lawyer, had come to the defense of American cultural achievements in his moderate *Inchiquin, the Jesuit's Letters* (1810), the

[1] *The Edinburgh Review, or Critical Journal,* XXXIII (January-May, 1820), 79-80.

fictitious account of a Jesuit touring the United States. The Jesuit rejected the charge that Americans were a degenerate species given over to materialism; he praised much in their culture, especially the bold, nervous, and beautiful tones of their eloquence. It was high time, he concluded, for Europe to be undeceived "respecting a people, in many respects the first, and in none the lowest in the scale of nations." James Kirke Paulding, who on four different occasions took up his pen in the defense of his country, inaugurated his efforts with *The Diverting History of John Bull and Brother Jonathan* (1813), a satire on the British caricatures of his native land. Neither the fictitious traveler's account nor the burlesque were forgotten in the subsequent crusade.

As the literary war became more heated, Robert Walsh, Alexander H. Everett, Christopher Gore, and others added a new note in the American defense by undertaking a counter analysis of England, which was significant as an evidence that Americans were now sufficiently self-conscious to describe the mother country in detail, just as any other foreign land might be described. Weak spots in the civilization of Great Britain were laid bare. Paulding in particular denounced what he insisted was the exploitation of the mass of the common people by an idle and vicious remnant of the feudal aristocracy. At least one American, Joshua E. White, a Savannah cotton merchant, warned his fellow countrymen to beware of the factory system which had cast such dark shadows over the liberty no less than the well-being of the English people.

The most characteristic note in the American defense was the effort to explain the cultural shortage in terms of the brief national history and the tasks imposed by the wilderness. Without any consciousness of paradox the positive defense glorified America's intellectual contributions. In this defense Timothy Dwight, William Tudor, and a long list of champions mustered their most redoubtable literary weapons. Nor did they give up the combat until American magazines were flooded with their outpourings. The truculent John Neal of Portland and Baltimore even carried the war into the enemy's camp by visiting England for the purpose of dispelling British illusions about America. To the surprise of many Americans he succeeded in persuading the editors of some of the leading journals to accept for publication his own evaluations of American letters, art, and affairs.

No defense was more impressive than that which Charles J. Ingersoll made before the American Philosophical Society in 1823 in his *Discourse*

*Concerning the Influence of America on the Mind.* Foregoing the opportunity to paint a brilliant picture of progress by contrasting the state of
the American mind in his day with that of an earlier period, Ingersoll
made so bold as to compare the cultural achievements of his country
with those of the most advanced nations of Europe. Overgenerous
though his evaluation of American education, law, science, invention,
medicine, art, literature, and drama was, he nevertheless argued plausibly
for the thesis that "the average of intellect, and of intellectual power in
the United States, surpasses that of any part of Europe," though he
admitted that "the range is not, in general, so great, either above or
below the horizontal line." Insisting that his efforts had not been inspired by hostility toward any other country, Ingersoll concluded with
a stirring peroration: "Let our intellectual motto be, that naught is done
while aught remains to be done: and our study to prove to the world,
that the best patronage of religion, science, literature, and the arts, of
whatever the mind can achieve, is SELF-GOVERNMENT."[2]

The note on which Ingersoll ended had already become a customary
part of the reply to the British critics. Cultural patriots insisted that
what America had done was only a beginning, that it needed to throw
off entirely the shackles of subservience to the European mind, that a
culture corresponding to the genius of American institutions had to be
created. To the conception of what should constitute a distinctively
American literature and culture many of this country's first minds
contributed.

In his review of Ingersoll's *A Discourse Concerning the Influence of
America on the Mind*, William Ellery Channing outlined a credo which
ranks high among the appeals for intellectual independence. In these
justly celebrated *Remarks on National Literature*, Channing, after
gently taking to task the cultural patriots who had exaggerated the
literary accomplishments which foreign critics seemed to undervalue,
contended that "we want those lights which make a country conspicuous
at a distance." Valuable as English and, even more markedly, Continental letters are for us, he continued, it were better to exclude them altogether if their acceptance will prevent us from creating our own
intellectual life. "A country, like an individual, has dignity and power
only in proportion as it is self-formed." And the literature and intellec-

[2] Charles J. Ingersoll, *A Discourse Concerning the Influence of America on the
Mind* (Philadelphia, 1823), 67.

tual glories of a people must not be divorced from its institutions and its life. It was fruitless to seek inspiration in themes which had distinguished other civilizations; veneration for the past, patriotism, even romantic love, had already spent themselves in literature.

But America, Channing went on, was destined to frame new social institutions, to release new human powers, to reap new spiritual harvests. Here man, unembarrassed by all the outworn disguises which in the Old World concealed those qualities which made him man, might, better than anywhere else, rise to communion with the Supreme Mind, receive and minister to the Infinite Spirit. And not a few gifted men alone; a better race of men could spring up only if the more talented freely shared their genius with the less gifted. Released from antiquated institutions, America could create an intellectual life truly expressive of itself—a life in which man could rise to his full stature through the release of all human potentialities, in which he might advance, in ways hitherto undreamed, science, the refinement of taste and imagination, moral and religious truth. The inspiration that Channing expressed so well lay back of many of the achievements of the American mind.

Meanwhile many who shared with Channing this heightened zeal for a distinctively American intellectual life looked to other formulas for its realization. Some, imbued with the romantic enthusiasm of Scott, advocated the utilization of the American past in literature and the arts. Professor Thomas C. Upham of Bowdoin expressed what was in the minds and on the pen of a vociferous group of contributors to periodicals: "Europeans may ridicule our name, our country, and our prospects," he wrote in 1819,

. . . but in the clime so grossly misrepresented and defamed, it is not possible for them to deny, that an ample and most interesting field is open for literary speculations and exertions. The character and civil habits, the piety and magnanimity of the first settlers, the sufferings and devotedness of the missionaries, who penetrated into dreary forests and abodes of savages; the societies of Christianized Indians; the character of celebrated chiefs; the adventures of the first explorers of the country; the seclusion, devotions, and sufferings of frontier villages, are enchanting topics as well for the pencil of the limner as the lyre of the bard; and are so remote and indistinct as to admit, where they require it, the inventions of fiction and the adornments of fancy.[3]

[3] Thomas C. Upham, *American Sketches* (New York, 1819), 15.

When certain skeptics began to insist that even these materials were too thin for a rich literature, they were promptly contradicted by others who claimed that American resources were inexhaustible. James Fenimore Cooper, who better than anyone else had shown in his *Leatherstocking Tales* the fertility of frontier romance, declared that American principles rather than local color could alone insure cultural nationalism. "The only peculiarity that can, or ought to be expected," he observed in *Notions of the Americans*, "is that which is connected with their [the Americans'] distinctive political opinions." In addition to the republican polity Cooper emphasized the common sense, the practicality, the sound morality in the American fabric. "I have seen," he remarked, "more beautiful, graceful, and convenient ploughs in positive use here, than are probably to be found in the whole of Europe united. In this single fact may be traced the history of the character of the people and the germ of their future greatness."[4] In calling attention to the particularly intimate connection between thought and action in a free society, Samuel L. Knapp likewise put his finger on a vein that ran deep in American experience, a vein, moreover, destined to become important in the cultural pattern of the future.

Not only in literary criticism but in other fields of endeavor the national spirit inspired assessments of past achievements and programs for distinctive contributions. Reference has already been made to the demand for Americanism in religion and for missionary activities independent of those in England. In the field of the fine arts the patrician domination of the rising galleries and schools connected with them led Samuel F. B. Morse and other like-minded democratic associates to brand subserviency to patronage as a mark of European aristocracy and to demand in the name of Americanism institutions controlled by artists with a sense of social obligation to the public. We shall hear more of this in the story of the crusade to break down the intellectual and artistic monopoly of the patrician period.

Even in the realm of science, which was relatively less responsive than literature to social currents, the impact of nationalism was felt. Naturalists who sought in foreign lands training for themselves and equipment for their laboratories swelled with patriotic pride at the thought that they were thus laying the foundations for an American science. In 1818 Benjamin Silliman, who established scientific studies at Yale on a new

[4] James Fenimore Cooper, *Notions of the Americans* (London, 1828), II, 152.

level, founded the *American Journal of Science*. This pioneer undertaking announced at the start that it would function as a depository for "original American communications." National pride should not, Silliman warned, cause American scientists to reject the rich treasures of European investigators, but it should stimulate them to make a return in kind. Frankly appealing for support from all sections of the country regardless of the rival claims of the larger cities and the local feelings nourished by state sovereignties, Silliman declared that the new venture was based on "permanent and momentous national interests" and designed to advance "both the science and reputation of our country." It did both. With justifiable pride he could note in 1829 that the character of the *Journal* was "strictly national" and that its files were indispensable to anyone who would examine the progress of American science.

In a remarkable survey of the achievements of natural science in America Dr. James E. De Kay of New York called attention to the effect of the War of 1812 in awakening the spirit of inquiry.

The forest, and the mountain, and the morass have been explored. The various forms and products of the animal, vegetable, and mineral kingdoms have been carefully, and in many instances, successfully investigated. A proper feeling of nationality has been widely diffused among our naturalists; a feeling which has impelled them to study and examine for themselves, instead of blindly using the eyes of foreign naturalists, or bowing implicitly to the decisions of a foreign bar of criticism. This, if restrained within due bounds, if it is not perverted into a narrow and bigoted sentiment, that has not infrequently been mistaken for national feeling, must be attended with beneficial consequences.[5]

De Kay took special pride in the fact that the knowledge of natural history and geology had advanced by leaps and bounds and that American phenomena had stimulated and challenged European scientists. He proudly described the publication of American textbooks based on indigenous materials in the spheres of botany, zoology, and geology. He took delight in the fact that Charles Lucien Bonaparte had completed the ornithology by Alexander Wilson and in the zoological contributions of Leseur, Say, Harland, and Godman. But in De Kay's view American conditions had affected the advance of scientific knowledge in even more significant ways. The simple yet grand features of American geology

[5] James E. De Kay, *Anniversary Address on the Progress of the Natural Sciences in the United States* (New York, 1826), 7.

excited and challenged the geologists of Europe who "not infrequently deduced principles on which depended the formation of a world" from "the phenomena of a molehill." It was moreover possible, De Kay contended, for American naturalists, removed from the rivalries and contentions of their European colleagues, to examine controverted points "with the same justice and impartiality as if we were removed from them by intervening centuries."[6]

In still other respects nationalism stirred the imagination of American scientists. In dedicating the Western Museum Society in Cincinnati, Dr. Daniel Drake attributed the greater respectability and dignity of character for which the middle and lower ranks of American society were noted to the cultivation and diffusion of scientific no less than literary knowledge. "Let the architects of our national greatness," he admonished, "conform to the dictates of science; and the monuments they construct will rise beautiful as our hills, imperishable as our mountains, and lofty as their summits, which tower sublimely above the clouds."[7]

## The Impact of Economic Nationalism

Nationalism, a general term for intertangled sentiments, ideas, and interests, was heightened by the War of 1812 and the naval victories that saved the conflict from appearing to be a colossal failure. But it was also fostered by frontiersmen, merchants, manufacturers, and farmers, who found that the federal government could meet their growing needs far better than municipalities, counties, or states. Only the national government, for example, could supply certain types of information on a national scale. Thus Dr. Adam Seybert proudly observed in his *Statistical Annals of the United States, 1789–1818* that "no other nation has hitherto furnished an equal body of authentic information." More and more the manufacturers of the seaboard thought in terms of national tariffs to protect home manufacturers against foreign competition; and manufacturers, merchants, and farmers clamored ever more frequently for internal improvements at federal expense in order that their products might reach an expanding national market.

[6] *Ibid.*, 16, 69.
[7] Daniel Drake, *An Anniversary Discourse on the State and Prospects of the Western Museum Society* (Cincinnati, 1820), 39–40.

The relation of economic interests to cultural patriotism was often subtle and intangible, but occasionally it was clear and measurable. In 1816 Congress enacted a duty on imported foreign books, much to the satisfaction of American paper manufacturers, printers, and book-makers who now felt themselves able to produce books in quantities for the American public. Thomas Jefferson, John Pickering, and other scholars, on the other hand, memorialized Congress to revoke this duty so that foreign books would enter the country freely and enrich the nation's intellectual life. Paper and book manufacturers replied that if the duties were withdrawn, British bookmakers would overwhelm the American market. "Our Government," declared the sympathetic chairman of the finance committee of the Senate,

. . . is peculiar to ourselves and our books of instruction should be adapted to the nature of the Government and the genius of the people. In the best of foreign books we are liable to meet with criticism and comparisons not very flattering to the American people. In American editions of these the offensive and illiberal parts are expunged or explained, and the work is adapted to the exigencies and tastes of the American reader. But withdraw the protection, our channels of instruction will be foreign; our youth will imbibe sentiments, form attachments and acquire habits of thinking adverse to our prosperity, unfriendly to our Government, and dangerous to our liberties.[8]

The duty on foreign books was not repealed in spite of the influence of the American Philosophical Society, the American Academy of Arts and Sciences, Harvard, Yale, and ex-President Jefferson himself. These years also marked the beginnings of agitation on the part of American writers for an international copyright. Without this American publishers could "pirate" or reissue the books of foreign authors, to whom no royalties had to be paid, at far less cost than it was possible to print the writings of Americans to whom some return was due.

The impact of economic nationalism on economic theory was more patent than its influence on belles-lettres. Not until the middle 1820s did the South, which had shared the national enthusiasm, including that for domestic manufactures, reject the theoretical justification for protective tariffs and insist on the validity of the laissez-faire doctrines of the classical British and French schools. This about-face, which was

[8] Harriet S. Tapley, *Salem Imprints, 1768–1825* (The Essex Institute, 1927), 259–260.

shared by all save two or three southern writers on economic theory, reflected the shift from an economy in which industry was expected to develop to one based on the export of cotton.

In response to the needs of a rising industry in the northeastern part of the country competent economic theorists undertook to modify the laissez-faire doctrines of the classical English school, which were proving so acceptable to the southern planters. With an eye on American conditions several writers on economic theory subjected to criticism the Ricardian theory of rent, which had been defined by the influential English economist as "that portion of the produce of the earth which is paid to the landlord for the use of the original and indestructible powers of the soil" and which assumed that the general economic condition of society rests entirely on the status of agricultural exploitation. Although the Americans who modified the prevalent classical theories were in effect meeting the needs of the rising industrial class, they assumed that these needs were identical with those of the entire nation and that they were therefore exemplifying the national interest.

Daniel Raymond, a New England lawyer who had migrated to Baltimore, declared in his *Thoughts on Political Economy* (1820) that classical economy was unsuited to American needs; that social principles, far from being absolute and universal, are always relative to time and place; and that America sorely needed a political economy of her own. Raymond's work did not exert wide influence, but he was praised for refusing to do "homage to the theories advanced in Europe under the name of political economy." In the same spirit in which Alexander Hamilton and Tench Coxe in the early days of the Republic pleaded for government support of industry, Raymond insisted that national prosperity required deliberate economic control in the interest of production. The support of this contention required modification of the laissez-faire theories of Smith, Ricardo, and Malthus. Economic control was, in Raymond's mind, to be so exercised as to promote the harmonious development of agriculture and manufacturing.

Others developed the argument. In his *Essays on Political Economy* (1822) Mathew Carey, the Philadelphia publisher, supported not only protective tariffs but the idea of internal improvements at government expense for the sake of a true harmony of interests. His son Henry became an even more enthusiastic and learned champion of this thesis. Philadelphia, the home of the Careys, had industrial ambitions. For the brief period of his American residence it was the home of the German economist Friedrich List, whose doctrines were to play a subsequent role in the movement for the customs union of the German states. In his *Outlines of American Political Economy* (1827) List developed the argument of Raymond and Carey by maintaining that a nation found its true wealth in the full, many-sided development of its productive power rather than in the quantity of exchange values it possessed. New England industrialists, sensitive to the increasing shift of capital from commerce to industry, appealed to the theoretical justifications of tariffs, which loomed large among their needs. Outstanding among these justifications were those of Daniel Webster, who himself shifted from a free trade position in response to the shift from commerce to manufacturing, and Willard Phillips, a Boston lawyer, editor, and business man who made a skillful use of statistics in A *Manual of Political Economy* (1828).

At the same time the abundance of natural resources in the United States and the relative sparsity of population bred an optimism that resulted almost inevitably in the rejection of the pessimistic doctrines of Malthus, especially his insistence that, in view of the tendency of the race to reproduce itself more rapidly than subsistence justified, continence must become widespread to supplement war and famine, nature's means of checking overpopulation. In America a high birth rate was regarded as an excellent means of increasing a labor supply inadequate for the exploitation of natural resources assumed to be inexhaustible. Alexander Hill Everett, a Massachusetts lawyer, orator, legislator, and diplomat, was unable to accept the Malthusian implications that progress was a chimera, that a beneficent God had ordered a universe in which the poor must either forego the joys of marriage or be subject to nature's curtailment through war, famine, vice, and misery. Such a gloomy and fatalistic doctrine might be valid in England, where the means of subsistence was inadequate to the population, but not in America where, even in times of unemployment, the community could provide relief. In the long run, according to Everett and such anti-Malthusians as Willard Phillips and Jacob Cardozo, population would adjust itself to the existing state of industrial development.

The more reflective among cultural patriots from time to time considered the obstacles to a distinctively American culture. On the one hand some regretted that cultural activities did not enjoy more generous support, whether governmental or private, without which America could not produce a culture worthy of its greatness and the genius of its institutions. But others, of whom Dr. De Kay and William Tudor were representative, contended that intellectual efforts benefited from the lack of liberal patronage. Men devoting themselves to literature and science, they argued, must be motivated not by the hope of financial reward but by a disinterested devotion or the hope of lasting fame—"natural and generous consequences of liberty" which were far more likely to produce the highest efforts and achievements. It was even well that conditions in this country did not permit the man of learning and science to withdraw from public employment and degrade himself in unworthy subserviency to private or public patron. The American way, Tudor insisted, "brings men of learning and men of the world more into contact; it blends the business of life and its instruction more intimately; it destroys pedantry, and enriches literature."[9]

Thus in the first quarter of the nineteenth century, during which the patricians largely directed American intellectual life, some of its most enduring problems were recognized and defined. It was a question of first importance whether American intellectual life should be frankly cosmopolitan and eclectic by design as well as circumstance, or whether cultural nationalism should dominate. Nor was it certain that cultural patriots themselves could be counted on to support native literature and art on the sole ground of its nationality and without reference to merit and price; it was one thing to shout for an American literature and another to buy American books even if they were dearer and poorer. But these were not the only questions. Whether Americanism was to be thought of in terms of a struggle for the realization of the full stature of all men, or whether it was to stop short with the cultivation of the minds of the gifted or the fortunate few; whether intellectual life was to advance, or could better advance, with little or no support from the government and wealthy patrons, or whether these were indispensable to the flowering of the spirit here as elsewhere; and finally, whether American culture was to fuse action and thought or to remain content with the traditional dichotomy between them—these too were problems in some measure to be explored.

The answers to be given to all these questions were, of course, wrapped

[9] William Tudor, Letters on the Eastern States (New York, 1820), 143.

up in the unfolding structure of American society. And among the stages of that unfolding none was more important than the struggle between aristocratic and democratic values. On the cultural no less than on the political level this struggle was presently to reach a climax in the Jacksonian period. But Jackson's triumph owed much to the exodus of people to the frontier, which in turn played a part in the intellectual life during the reign of the patricians. No less important, the march westward also prepared for the new assault on the monopoly of learning by the few.

# 11 The West Challenges Patrician Leadership

> No people ever did, in the first generation, fell the forest, and construct the roads, and rear the dwellings and public edifices, and provide the competent supply of schools and literary institutions.
> —LYMAN BEECHER, *A Plea for the West*, 1835

> My brother, will you meet me on that delightful shore?
> My brother, will you meet me where parting is no more?
> —"We'll March Around Jerusalem"

The increasing importance assumed by the West in the first three decades of the nineteenth century promoted the concept of a unique national culture and challenged the leadership of the patrician class in intellectual life. Despite occasional setbacks, the trans-Appalachian region grew rapidly in material and political stature. This development of actual power was coupled in the minds of many Americans with a vague but persistent picture of the American West as the seat of a young and vigorous empire that eventually would take its place as the last and best of the long succession of empires in western civilization. Americans continued to hold, in varying degrees and for different reasons, to a belief that the course of history and empire lay westward, and that in the West man would reach his destiny and his fullest development.

250

## The West in the Thought of Europe and the East

The vast forests, prairies, and rivers beyond the Alleghenies, home of the Noble Savage and of strange, fascinating beasts, had become the subject of romantic legend before the great migration of Atlantic sea-coast peoples began in the later years of the eighteenth century. Indeed, a whole literature had emerged in Europe which, with curious paradox, pictured the wilderness beyond the mountains as both the seat of idyllic peace and the scene of exciting adventure and golden opportunity. In this romantic legend much of reality was obscured: the bickerings of officials and clerics in the old French regime in the Mississippi valley, gruesome hardships, squalid, vindictive, suspicious Indians. The extravagant imaginations of the Rousseaus and Chateaubriands had drawn highly embroidered, sentimental, and glamorous pictures. Byron, who helped create the Daniel Boone legend, celebrated his heroic virtues along with the exotic and engaging life of the wilds. Poets like William Blake, identifying the western country with pristine purity, thought of it as a blank tablet on which was to be penned a new chapter in man's history even more glorious than that being written on the Atlantic seaboard. This picture of the West as a Utopia for dreamy idealists had little influence in the East, but the somewhat less overdrawn picture of glamorous adventure was not without effect; the vision of the wilderness as an ever-beckoning finger of opportunity lured many a man across the mountains.

The West of legend did not exert unbridled sway over the minds of men and women. As the *Jesuit Relations* testify, some of the *voyageurs* and Catholic missionaries had provided accurate information regarding the Mississippi country. Realistic notes had been struck by the Jesuit explorer Charlevoix and by such English colonial trail breakers as Daniel Coxe, Christopher Gist, and James Adair. Some of the narratives of captivity among the Indians were marked by a kind of stark realism. And an increasing number of travelers expressed disillusionment with the meanness of the frontier. The French scientist Volney had been one of the first to do so. In the early years of the nineteenth century Englishmen, drawn to the West by curiosity and lust for adventure or by hope of gain, painted it in their travel books in the blackest hue. They dwelt on its unhealthfulness, its infertility, its poverty; they condemned its inhabitants for their ignorance, crudeness, downright bestiality, and wickedness. More judicious English visitors who depicted the West in appreciative terms were quite overshadowed by fellow countrymen whose disillusionment and bitterness knew no bounds.

Easterners themselves often reinforced the English indictment of the West. Some believed with President Timothy Dwight of Yale that the new country was being settled by men impatient of the restraints of law, religion, and morality, together with down-and-out debtors and troublesome grumblers who resented the taxes so necessary for the support of school, church, and state. Dwight felt that Providence had provided the western wilderness as a retreat for those restless, innovating men who, had they stayed in the East, might well have brought about the downfall of the Republic, just as their kind had spelled the ruin of ancient Greece and Rome. The pristine beauty of the landscape might provoke a certain vision of grandeur and innocence in Dwight's mind. But, like so many other eastern men, he was shocked to dismay at the actual conditions that prevailed in the relatively settled areas behind the frontier.

When migration to the new country increased by leaps and bounds in the first two decades of the nineteenth century many Easterners did not hide their fear of the West. Such aristocratic admirers of eighteenth-century decorum as James Fenimore Cooper lamented the raw, muddy democracy born of the frontier. Others shuddered when the western states seemed to threaten conservative bulwarks by providing for the election, rather than executive appointment, of judges and, above all, by clamoring for cheap money, decentralized banking, and free lands. Many felt that if the movement of peoples westward continued unabated, the East would be depopulated, its property values lessened, its schools, colleges, churches, and other cultural agencies enfeebled.

Fear of the growth of the West found expression in a variety of ideas and proposals. Easterners who had been disillusioned or disappointed in the West often gave repelling accounts of the miseries of western settlers and frankly tried to discourage prospective pioneers from venturing into the new country. Many in the East opposed the acquisition of the Louisiana territory and did what they could to delay the admission of new states beyond the Appalachians. The alarm felt lest the older areas be depopulated expressed itself not only in political efforts to retard the disposition of the public domain to homeseekers, but also in efforts to promote public education and other social benefits in the older states in order that the East might become more attractive to the ambitious among her poorer sons.

Fear of the West sometimes gave rise to serious efforts to reclaim it by the spread of God's word. The movement to send missionaries from the East to the West, it will be recalled, was in one of its aspects part of the conservative reaction against the Enlightenment. Catherine Beecher in writing to Mary Lyon expressed a widely held view: "If we gain all we are aiming at in Foreign Missions & *the West* is lost all is lost!" The home missionary movement was to influence profoundly American intellectual development. Missionaries in the West advanced such all-important agencies of intellectual life as the school, college, and church, and did much to inculcate respect for law and property rights. At the same time their reports to the East helped discredit the older romantic legend of the West.

In the Great Revival of 1800 western evangelists had sung:

> Come hungry, come thirsty, come ragged, come bare,
> Come filthy, come lousy, come just as you are.

The response was striking, but religious indifference remained widespread. In 1812 two young eastern missionaries, Samuel Mills and John Schermerhorn, toured the West and reported that in spite of revivalism, in spite of the efforts to send Bibles and missionaries into the wilderness, lawlessness, sin, and skepticism prevailed in vast stretches of the western country. Even when allowances are made for the Presbyterian tendency to regard any deviation from orthodoxy as skepticism, it is plain that there must have been much irreligion. At the time it was regarded as evidence of growing irreligion that lawyers in their fear of sectarian domination sometimes persuaded legislators to make no mention of religion in educational charters. According to general report, rowdyism, swearing, drinking, gambling, fighting, Sabbath-breaking, and other impieties were the order of the day in many part of the West. "It is of high importance," wrote Samuel Mills of Indiana, "that the standard of truth should be immediately planted here. . . ."[1] The herculean Methodist missionary bishop, Francis Asbury, wrote from the West in 1797: "When I reflect that not one in a hundred came here to get religion; but rather to get plenty of good land, I think it will be well if some or

---

[1] Samuel J. Mills and Daniel Smith, *Report of a Missionary Tour.* . . . (Andover 1815), 16.

many do not eventually lose their souls."[2] A Connecticut missionary, Isaac Reed, was shocked to visit a cabin "without chairs, and, what is worse, without a Bible." He was even more shocked to find, in a 380-mile stretch of the Ohio country, that the people sat "in moral darkness, having little of the light of the preached gospel."[3]

This dark picture was relieved only by the belief that in the West itself friends of "good order and religion" prayed daily that God would incline the hearts of their brethren in the East to illuminate the darkness of the new country by flooding it with missionaries, pious tracts, and, above all, Bibles. "What will become of the West," demanded the Reverend Lyman Beecher in 1835, "if her prosperity rushes up to such a majesty of power, while those great institutions linger which are necessary to form the mind, and the conscience, and the heart of that vast world?"[4] Such reports as those of Mills and Reed and such pleas as that of Beecher stimulated much of the educational and religious missionary effort of the East in trans-Appalachia.

In the main those who still cherished the values of the Enlightenment did not regard the West as a menace. Its vast elbowroom, its relative freedom from the cramping restrictions of older regions, and its hospitality to "come-outers" permitted violent contrasts and attracted champions of free thought and social experimentation. Under the presidency of the Bostonian, Horace Holley (1818–1827), Transylvania University in Lexington, Kentucky, became a center of mildly liberal Unitarianism. Although religious orthodoxy overthrew Holley, it was still possible a few years later for James Freeman Clarke, a Boston Unitarian, to write from Louisville: "Everything here is free, open, active. To be useful one must lay aside all narrow tastes and exclusive feelings, and from a pure love to humanity, plunge into the life around him."[5] Even the critical Mrs. Trollope was impressed by the tolerance that prevailed in Cincinnati in the spring of 1829 when the orthodox Reverend Alexander Campbell and the freethinking Robert Owen publicly debated their respective convictions. Among the plain people, considering their heritage of generations of unquestioning Christianity, actual free thought must have been rare. But there was some, and certainly there was less formal religion than in the East.

[2] *The Journal of Bishop Asbury* (New York, 1821), II, 286.
[3] Isaac Reed, *The Christian Traveller* (New York, 1828), 34, 38.
[4] Lyman Beecher, *A Plea for the West* (Cincinnati, 1835), 30.
[5] James Freeman Clarke, *Autobiography, Diary, and Correspondence* (Boston and New York, 1891), 104.

The humanitarian ideals of the Enlightenment and of liberal Christianity found expression in the West. Elisha Bates, a Quaker of Mt. Pleasant, Ohio, made the *Moral Advocate* the mouthpiece of a crusade against intemperance, capital punishment, dueling, war, and slavery. In 1830 the periodical edited at Vandalia, Illinois, by the liberal-minded Judge James Hall included a remarkable sketch on social justice. In a dream the artisans of St. Louis were seen crying for bread and frantically plundering the demolished buildings of their exacting and pressing employers, to be at length shot down by troops. The moral was that only by ceasing to be reckless of each other's welfare could men prevent such dire calamities.

Community experiments designed to eliminate exploitation of human beings were by no means confined to the West, but its vast spaces seemed to be especially congenial to the promoters of Utopian enterprises. Frances Wright, a Scottish freethinker, feminist, and friend of humanity, established on the banks of the Mississippi near Memphis a community intended to demonstrate the feasibility of emancipating slaves through the accumulated profits of their labor. Although she failed to make her community, Nashoba, a success, she never lost faith in the ideal and program it exemplified. Robert Owen's community experiment on the banks of the Wabash met with only slightly greater success. Having experimented with profit sharing at New Lanark, Scotland, Owen came to the United States to elaborate his "new idea of society" under more favorable conditions. The communal society of the Rappites in Indiana was purchased in 1825 and within a few months a group of outstanding liberal thinkers, including eminent natural scientists, had been assembled. Though Owen's New Harmony community did not prove harmonious and soon collapsed, its enlightened educational program continued for some time to exert an influence.

In reviewing Owen's *A New View of Society* the editor of the *Cincinnati Literary Gazette* declared that "there are no people, probably, in the world, who are so ready to make experiments respecting social relations and domestic arrangements, as those of the western country, —none who are so little fettered by established habits, or who are less disposed to consider hereditary prejudices and heirlooms which cannot be parted with."[6] Timothy Flint, another literary figure in Cincinnati, expressed qualified sympathy with Owen's environmentalist views of human nature, and wished him well.

[6] *The Cincinnati Literary Gazette*, III (June 18, 1825), 193.

Thus the West meant different and frequently contradictory things to men in the older parts of the country. To those of a rationalistic and humanitarian frame of mind, the new land beyond the Alleghenies offered an opportunity for social experiment. To some it was, in the words of Judge Hall, the refuge from poverty, tyranny, and fanaticism. If the vision of the romantic West was increasingly replaced by a more realistic picture, there was enough romance left to provide material for creative efforts in the field of letters. In the East James Kirke Paulding, Robert Montgomery Bird, and Nathaniel Beverley Tucker—to single out only a few—exploited the romantic and mawkish legends of the West. and in the new country itself such leading writers as Timothy Flint and Judge Hall followed in the same path. The "godlessness" of the West presented the religiously orthodox in the East with the challenge of winning it for Christ. But to the common man, who left his eastern farm or shop and struck out on the new trails, the West was a promise and a hope for a better life for himself and for his children.

### Obstacles to the Growth of Intellectual Life

Perhaps the most important single fact affecting the transit of the white man's culture to the wilderness was the actual fighting which it involved. Earlier pioneers, notably the fur trader, had discovered the Indian trails into the interior, and land promoters had gained more or less knowledge of the wilderness itself. But these very land promoters had sown the seeds of the future conflict. During the Revolution and in the decade that followed, Kentucky was indeed "the dark and bloody ground" of tradition. In the Old Northwest the danger of Indian raids was real and present. Whether homeseeking pioneers migrated as individual families or in groups, they found the scattered military posts of limited help when Indian braves took to the warpath. By the 1830s the savages had been conquered throughout the region lying between the Alleghenies and the Mississippi. In the autobiography he dictated to a government interpreter in the summer of 1833 Black Hawk declared that the tomahawk was buried forever and expressed the hope that the Great Spirit might keep the children of the forests and the palefaces always at peace.

The Indian danger was not the only practical problem that preoccupied and sometimes gave a gloomy cast to the pioneer mind. Grinding labor never ceased from morn to night, from winter to summer. Forests had to be cleared. If surplus grain could by good fortune be harvested, it had to be marketed by perilous raft voyages down turbulent rivers. The picturesque boat songs the rivermen sang were useful in helping them over the rough places:

> Some rows up, but we rows down,
> All the way to Shawnee town,
> Pull away! pull away!

Pioneers also often suffered from hunger and cold, from malaria and other baffling ailments; and since danger came quickly and help was often far distant, they sometimes fell back on remedies first learned in the childhood of the race, remedies they may have heard of as children in their old homes. Sometimes there was failure. This necessitated turning back toward the East or striking off to new frontiers or sticking it out. The last decision sometimes involved frustration, mental conflict, nostalgia, bitterness, and gloom.

Under such conditions intellectual life of a formal kind had little place. Much that the pioneer had learned in the newspapers, schools, churches, and libraries of his old home, if he had come in close contact with these, was now useless and often forgotten. Even if it was not forgotten—and it often of course was not—conditions made it difficult if not impossible to establish agencies of cultural life. Many men and more women yearned for the amenities of the old life but found no satisfactory way of realizing them. As one pioneer preacher put it, "Men must have bread before books. Men must build barns before they establish colleges. Men must learn the language of the rifle, the axe and the plough, before they learn the lessons of Grecian and Roman philosophy and history; and to those pursuits was the early American intellect obliged to devote itself, by a sort of simple and hearty and constant consecration."[7] Since first things come first, the typical frontiersman in the earlier stages of his life in the new country opposed taxes for anything save absolute necessities, chiefly defense and roads. No sooner had these been in some measure secured than hard times came, when the pioneer found himself in debt to land promoters, the government, or perhaps eastern creditors. Thus until the hardest battles had been won, until the most pressing material wants had been met, there could be little thought of schools, of

[7] William H. Milburn, *The Pioneers, Preachers and People of the Mississippi Valley* (New York, 1860), 391–392.

books, of learning, of the amenities and refinements of a settled life.

To these difficulties in the way of an intellectual life must be added that of isolation. In the first stages of the struggle against the wilderness, communications with older regions were too meager to permit even the importation of books and newspapers. For instance, the arrival of the post in Cincinnati in 1794 was so important a happening that it elicited special comment from the editor of the struggling newspaper. Two or three months frequently intervened before a letter mailed in the East reached its destination. Only at camp meetings or at the crossroads tavern, which might serve as school, church, court, theater, and platform for the stump orator, was the dreary isolation of the early frontier partly broken.

Another obstacle to the development of intellectual life in the new country was the cardinal fact that so many of the men and women who pioneered in it were opposed to schools. One of Henry Barnard's Ohio correspondents, in writing to him in 1838 on the deplorable conditions of the schools, estimated that "a large minority, if not a majority" were "utterly opposed to any legislative action to support them." No figures of illiteracy before the census of 1840 are available; but from the rough estimates for that year and from a great many examples set out in travel literature, in the reports of missionaries, and in other records it is plain that the proportion of illiterate and semi-literate people must have been high everywhere in the West and especially high in the regions largely settled by southern upland stocks. "Many adults, especially females," wrote John Mason Peck, a Baptist missionary in Illinois, "are unable to read or write, and many more, who are able to read a little, cannot readily understand what they attempt to read, and therefore take no pleasure in books and study."[8] Circuit riders and missionaries learned that before parting with one of their precious Bibles or religious tracts it was well to find out whether the prospective recipient could read. Even when adults could read and were ambitious for learning, their training was often so inadequate that when they entered the backwoods "colleges" or academies they were compelled to devote themselves to the elementary branches.

In view of the large proportion of illiterate people on the frontier and in view of the fact that academic learning was not only useless but often considered a handicap in the work of clearing forests, fighting Indians, and the like, the widespread prejudice against intellectuals, against edu-

[8] John M. Peck, A Guide for Emigrants (Boston, 1831), 243.

cation, was natural enough. Self-reliant and versatile by necessity, the frontiersmen distrusted the claims of the expert. Ignorant of any way of life except his own, the pioneer was apt to ridicule the man of learning. Indeed, much of the learning represented by scholars on the frontier was, as it appeared to the untutored, dry, cold, and impractical. Furthermore, educated men frequently expected deference and respect. To the democratic frontiersman this was still further occasion for resentment, for, in the words of a keen observer, Judge James Hall, the pioneer would not be "patronized or high-hatted."

One consequence of this anti-intellectualism was to deepen still further the gulf between the "highbrow" and the "lowbrow." Another was to encourage some educated men to conceal their learning. As Timothy Flint, himself a scholar and at the same time a champion of the West, remarked, "An unwarrantable disdain keeps back the better informed and more powerful minds from displaying themselves."[9] John Reynolds, who in spite of the educational limitations of the West acquired some part of a classical training, concealed such culture as he had when he electioneered, feigning ignorance out of deference to popular prejudice against "book larnin'."

The anti-intellectualism of the common man was confirmed by unlettered preachers. The disparagement of learning by these men was partly based on the conviction that head-religion was inferior to, and in fact antagonistic toward, heart-religion. On its highest level this position was illustrated by the remarks of John Strange, one of the greatest of the circuit riders. His alma mater, he remarked, was "Brush College, more ancient, though less pretentious, than Yale, or Harvard, or Princeton. Here I graduated and I love her memory still . . . her curriculum is the philosophy of nature and the mysteries of redemption; her library is the word of God; the discipline and the hymn book, supplemented with trees and brooks and stones, all of which are full of wisdom and sermons and speeches; and her parchments of literary honors are the horse and saddle bags."[10]

James Hall, in *Legends of the West*, noted a different brand of anti-intellectualism. A certain "Father Bangs" wrote a tract to show that thirst for human knowledge drove our first parents from paradise, and that "through the whole course of succeeding time *school larning* had

[9] Timothy Flint, *Recollections of the Last Ten Years* (Boston, 1826), 49.
[10] J. C. Smith, *Reminiscences of Early Methodism in Indiana* (Indianapolis, 1879), 38–39.

been the most prolific source of human misery and mental degradation.
. . ." Even Bible Societies, he insisted, were among the instruments
Satan used to subjugate man to his power.[11] "Yes, bless the Lord,"
declared another preacher, "I are a poor, humble man—and I doesn't
know a single letter in the A B C's, and couldn't read a chapter in the
Bible no how you could fix it, bless the Lord!—I jist preach like Old
Peter and Poll, by the Sperit. Yes, we don't ax pay in cash nor trade
nither for the Gospel, and aren't no hirelins like them high-flow'd
college-larned sheepskins. . . ."[12]

In such words the rationalizations of ignorant or at least unlettered
men are clear. Their jealousy of trained preachers was frequently spoken
of by the missionaries of the Congregational and Presbyterian sects,
whose discipline required an educated clergy. The fact that the Baptists
and Methodists came to emphasize education as the frontier was pushed
further back suggests that the earlier indifference or antagonism toward
education on the part of many in those sects was related to the crying
need for preachers in the wilderness and the impossibility of supplying
the need if insistence on trained men was maintained.

Almost overwhelming obstacles thus stood in the way of the growth
of formal intellectual life in the early West. The inadequate communications, the sparseness of population, the lack of homogeneous backgrounds on the part of settlers in a given community, the great numbers
of illiterate or semiliterate people that sought the new country, the anti-
intellectualism of great numbers of plain folk and some preachers—all
these factors were of prime importance. The fact that formal intellectual
culture was not necessary and in some respects was even a handicap in
conquering the wilderness constituted an even greater obstacle to the
transit of intellectual culture to the frontier. Until the need for intellectual skills and values should be felt, even the courageous work of the
intellectual pioneers could meet with slight reward.

## Allies in the March of the Mind

Yet almost from the start some factors, such as the operation of man's
natural curiosity, promoted the growth of an intellectual life in the new

[11] James Hall, *Legends of the West* (Philadelphia, 1833), 43.
[12] Bayard R. Hall, *The New Purchase, or Early Years in the West* (New Albany,
Ind., 1855), 117.

country. Of great importance was the presence of a few men and women of education among the majority of simple, untutored pioneers. Like the rest, the men and women of refinement and mental training who did not return East had to subordinate these values to the exigencies of the new situation. But they could not entirely surrender all their past habits and tastes, and they clung to the few books they could bring with them as symbols of the world of learning. Thus the father of John Reynolds of Illinois, being a reading man, bent every effort to supplement the single book he possessed, the Bible, by other fare; Rollin's *Ancient History* was borrowed, and his son read and reread it. When at last an opportunity came for the son to attend a crude school, this pioneer succeeded in buying a geography and an astronomy textbook to the amazement of his son, who had never even imagined that such knowledge existed. Another example was the miner whom Charles Fenno Hoffman observed at Galena, Illinois. Unable to part with his books, he cherished an old Bible, a Shakespeare, a Pelham novel, and a *Western Songster*. In the Western Reserve Zerah Hawley admitted that most families from New England had three or four books. Cultured Southerners on the southwestern frontier sometimes succeeded in taking some books with them. One in the wilds of Mississippi, for example, owned volumes of Burns, Cowper, Sterne, Young, and other classics. To his surprise an English traveler found a farmer in Tennessee who owned several standard works in poetry, theology, history, philosophy, and science. Such cherishing of books under frontier conditions not only met certain psychological needs on the part of their possessors but preserved a continuity with the culture of the older areas of the country.

To meet the psychological need for continuity with the intellectual culture to which they had been accustomed, families of education, if remote from others of like mind and able to afford it, employed a teacher for their children. More frequently, especially in the country north of the Ohio, families banded together and employed a teacher who instructed the young, at first perhaps in one of their own houses. Just as the social life of house-raisings on the frontier was a by-product of the need for mutual help, so were the beginnings of organized intellectual life.

Certain families sometimes launched a subscription library equally unpretentious and similarly supported by voluntary contributions. Thus in 1804 the little community of New Englanders that had only sixteen years earlier founded Ames in Ohio commissioned one of their group, who had business in Boston, to purchase a collection of books with the coonskins they subscribed. When the books, which included Morse's *Geography*, Ramsay's *History of the American Revolution*, Burgh's *Dignity of Human Nature*, and a good many others appeared, one subscriber who had contributed his entire hoarded wealth of ten coonskins felt that the volumes were an "unbounded intellectual treasure."[13] As facilities permitted and means of communication improved, families such as these subscribed to newspapers from the nearest town that printed them. As frontier conditions gave way to a more settled type of rural life, as a little leisure appeared, and as the tussle with nature became less exacting, the need which scattered individuals or families felt for some intellectual culture became easier to satisfy. As towns and cities developed, moreover, the agencies of intellectual life that arose in them increasingly spread their influence into the surrounding rural areas.

In spite of the anti-intellectualism of many proponents of heart-religion, churches did reinforce the nuclei the more or less cultured families provided for the future development of intellectual life. Paradoxical though it seems, even the revivals which swept the West in 1800 and later years were not without indirect effects on intellectual life; in advocating temperance and morality, in opposing slavery, and in encouraging a philanthropic spirit, some of the revivalists helped prepare the soil for the intellectual values that they themselves often disparaged.

Even the sects which put the least emphasis on the need for a trained clergy and on education gave some encouragement to the life of the mind. Occasionally preachers who, like James Havens, could barely read became men of considerable culture. Untutored circuit riders often carried religious books in their saddlebags, such as Wesley's sermons, Fletcher's *Appeal*, and Baxter's *Call*. These they read under the most adverse circumstances. All of them knew the Bible; some of them incorporated into their preaching Milton's powerful descriptions of perdition.

In several important ways leaders in the sects least inclined to emphasize education made notable contributions to it. Rigidly dogmatic in sectarian and schismatic zeal, their minds worked vigorously in the polemics that characterized sermons, the pamphlets and the warfare in the periodicals. Furthermore, rivalry among Shakers, Campbellites and Baptists,

---

[13] S. J. Cutler, "The Coonskin Library," *Ohio State Archaeological and Historical Society Publications*, XXVI (1917), 58 ff.

Presbyterians and Methodists stimulated the promotion of institutions for theological training. Asbury's *Journal* shows that he was something of a scholar in his reading tastes and that he gave much aid to educational enterprises. After plowing through the wilderness for eight days to attend the first Methodist Conference in Kentucky in the spring of 1790, Asbury and six other preachers planned for a future college and obtained by subscription land and money for what eventually was to become Bethel College. One preacher knew "many a man who could not construct a half dozen sentences grammatically to bestow half of his yearly stipend to establish an institution of learning."[14] By 1824 the General Conference of the Methodist Church in the West was committed to an active educational program. No one could have been more self-sacrificing or more zealous than the Baptist missionary on the Illinois frontier, John M. Peck. Everywhere he gave himself to establishing elementary schools and to improving those that existed. He endured 4000 miles of travel to raise funds for Rock Spring Seminary, the forerunner of Shurtleff College.

Itinerant preachers in the new lands distributed Bibles, hymnbooks, and religious tracts. These were often provided by eastern missionary societies or by printing concerns under the control of the church itself. After 1817 the American Tract Society furnished much religious literature, which circuit riders scattered. In many cases such books were the only ones a family possessed, and children learned to read from them. No doubt some who later became scholars entered on the path of learning in just such a way. "It has often been a question that I shall never be able to answer on earth," observed Peter Cartwright, one of the best known of the circuit riders, "whether I have done the most good by preaching or distributing religious books. . . . For more than fifty years I have firmly believed, that it was a part and parcel of a Methodist preacher's most sacred duty to circulate good books wherever they go among the people."[15] Cartwright himself in a single year sometimes distributed a thousand dollars' worth of such books.

Johnny Appleseed (John Chapman, *ca.* 1775–1847) was no Baptist or Methodist, but like these itinerants he scattered religious tracts in pioneer cabins. Best known for planting appleseeds in advance of civilization in the Ohio country, Johnny Appleseed, companion of forest

[14] William H. Milburn, *op. cit.*, 267.
[15] *The Autobiography of Peter Cartwright* (New York, 1857), 279–280.

animals, a man tender by nature without any concern for worldly goods, traveled through the frontier country reading to families from his Swedenborgian book.

Thus wandering preachers spread some light and learning. But the activities of religious groups committed to a trained clergy were even more important. Except at St. Louis, where the Jesuits founded an institution for training priests, and at Detroit, where Father Richard published religious books and favored schools, Catholics were too few to achieve much. Congregationalists and Presbyterians, however, made great contributions. These denominations, like the Episcopalians, Lutherans, and Catholics, regarded a well-trained clergy as indispensable. If therefore they were to flourish in the West, it was necessary to spare no pains to advance learning. James B. Finley well expressed the position of these denominations when he wrote that man's happiness and usefulness depend on education, which raises him from the brutish level to the exalted dignity of a rational human being. Of the fourteen permanent collegiate institutions—quasi-academies, quasi-colleges—which were established west of the Alleghenies between 1780 and 1829, seven were founded by Presbyterians and one by Congregationalists and Presbyterians together. In addition, four state institutions were begun under Presbyterian influence. In general, these fledgling colleges were staffed by overworked if not ill-equipped ministers and attended by ill-prepared and self-supporting young men. The classical curriculum, taken over from Yale or the College of New Jersey, was followed so far as circumstances permitted—and often they did not permit. The libraries, inadequate and meager, limited the work of scholars. Nothwithstanding these facts, the backwoods colleges, serving chiefly the interest of certain religious groups, were of incalculable importance in the transfer of culture to the frontier; and a score of their leaders, including such able men as John McMillan, Robert Hamilton Bishop, and Philip Lindsley, planted well the seeds of learning in western soil.

## The Towns as Intellectual Centers

The towns and cities that sprang up in the western country—Pittsburgh, Cincinnati, Louisville, Lexington, St. Louis, Chicago, Milwaukee —offered along with churches and colleges special incentives and opportunities for the growth of intellectual life. The spokesmen for the new towns and cities—their newspaper editors, their professional men and promoters—tended to exaggerate both the quality and the quantity of the local culture. But within the rhetoric and the braggadocio lay an element of truth. The towns because of their relatively dense populations could support newspapers, libraries, and other agencies without which even the beginnings of a transit of culture would have been impossible.

By virtue of the fact that from the start towns had certain economic functions they attracted a larger proportion of men of some intellectual training than did the country districts. The business of the land offices required the services of surveyors; and the courts and territorial legislatures which frequently migrated from town to town necessitated the presence of printers and lawyers, the function of the latter becoming more important as inevitable squabbles over land titles filled the courts with litigation. Merchants functioning as the needed distributors of consumers' goods had to possess at least a limited knowledge of accounts and found it expedient to keep somewhat abreast of the conditions of trade. Printers were needed to supply information regarding the distribution of goods, the business of local courts and legislatures, and other matters of practical concern. As the community developed into a distributing center for the surrounding country, physicians also found larger opportunities and were less frequently compelled to eke out a living by conducting apothecary shops and by farming.

The growing towns also required the services of ministers and teachers. A considerable number of people were deeply religious and naturally wanted ministers and churches to help fulfill their spiritual needs. Some also valued the church as a stabilizing force, a symbol of respectability. Teachers were required to train a rising company of surveyors, clerks, lawyers, doctors, and ministers. Many also believed that education was necessary for the well-being of religion, of the state, and of society itself. By 1830 Louisville, Lexington, Cincinnati, and Detroit were well in advance of other western communities in public education. Towns quickly caught the enthusiastic promotional fever, developed a sense of civic pride, and, when means permitted, sought prestige by imitating the architectural vogue of the East in the schools, courthouses, and churches that replaced the early primitive structures.

The presence in every town of a certain number of men and women who represented the tradition of culture and education provided a basis for the growth of intellectual life. Such people often came from the East or from some other western city. They came primarily because of the economic opportunities they thought the new town offered; but many were in addition crusaders. This was especially true of printers and ministers. Frequently the printers were devoted to a political party and sought to promote its fortunes through their newspapers. Many physicians, lawyers, and clergymen also became genuine crusaders for the development of culture in the western towns and cities.

A few examples may serve to illustrate the early steps in the development of professional life in western towns. Printers and publishers played an important role in furthering the general intellectual growth of a community as well as the communication between pioneers. In 1786 in Pittsburgh John Scull and Joseph Hall of Philadelphia established the *Gazette* and, the year following, the Pittsburgh *Almanack*. A few years later Zadok Cramer, a printer in Washington, Pennsylvania, yielded to the persuasive arguments of Hugh Henry Brackenridge, a leading Pittsburgh lawyer, and established a press that became famous for *Cramer's Pittsburgh Almanack* and for *The Navigator*, a much-prized pioneer guide. Similarly John Bradford of Fauquier County, Virginia, set up at Lexington, Kentucky, in 1787 the press that became celebrated for the *Kentucky Gazette*, one of the principal newspapers in the West. Within a few years Bradford, like the Pittsburgh printers, was issuing both almanacs and books. The first newspapers in Cincinnati, Chillicothe, and most other western towns similarly owed their existence to enterprising printers who came from older settlements or from the East itself. In addition to publishing newspapers, almanacs, gazetteers, and guides, these printers also issued religious, educational, and other types of books, and in some cases magazines as well.

Doctrinaire though they tended to be in their political enthusiasms, these printers and editors were frequently men of good education and almost inevitably supported every movement for schools, colleges, libraries, and museums. In opening their columns to local bards and crackerbox philosophers they did much to encourage literary aspiration and salty wit—fertilizers, if not the roots, of intellectual culture. To such transplanted eastern printers as William Maxwell, William Gibbes Hunt, the Bradfords, and Charles Hammond, merely to cite representative examples, the West owed a great intellectual debt.

In the rising towns lawyers, physicians, ministers, and educators from the older parts of the country, in addition to their immediate tasks, sponsored the broader development of intellectual life. The Reverend Timothy Flint, a well-educated New Englander, went into the Ohio valley in 1815 in search of health. Besides carrying on his missionary activities he journeyed about the West before settling down in Cincinnati, where he wrote his famous *Recollections of the Last Ten Years* (1826), *A Condensed Geography and History of the Western States* (1828), and his novels, and where in 1827 he launched the *Western Monthly Review*. An equally important figure was Judge James Hall of Philadelphia, whose family had been connected with *The Port Folio* and other magazines. After service in the War of 1812, Hall migrated to the West, succeeded in law, and in 1830 established at Vandalia the *Illinois Monthly*. He had meantime published his *Letters from the West*, a remarkable account of the geography, people, manners, and life of the frontier country. A third representative of this large group of eastern migrants to whom the West owed so much of its intellectual development was Caleb Atwater, the versatile, eccentric, and somewhat visionary New Englander who, after graduating from Williams College and teaching for a time in New York City, became a Presbyterian minister and settled in Circleville, Ohio, in 1815. Atwater, in addition to his services to the church, practiced law, labored for the establishment of Ohio's school system, and did pioneer work in archeology and ethnology. These men, it must be remembered, are representative of many others who contributed to the growth of intellectual life in western towns and cities.

But soon intellectual activities in the new country were also furthered by some of its own sons. Apprenticing themselves to printers, doctors, and lawyers who had obtained their own training in the East, ambitious lads started out on their own to make their fortune and to supply the new country with the services it increasingly needed. Many of these men had no training other than that acquired in elementary schools and in the shops and offices of their masters. To supplement their training some managed to make the long journey to the seaboard, and a few the even longer one to Europe. Thus the second step in the transit of culture to the frontier was, as Dixon Ryan Fox has pointed out, the sojourn of natives of the new country in older seats of learning.

In this category of men none was so outstanding as Dr. Daniel Drake of Cincinnati, sometimes called "the Franklin of the West." His parents took him at the age of three from New Jersey to Kentucky, where he learned not only from his father's handful of books but from nature itself. His powers of observation and his curiosity were sharpened by nature's wealth in the Kentucky woods, above all by the curious fossils of extinct mammoths near Blue Licks. After irregular attendance at a very inadequate school where he learned to spell the words in Dilworth and "a good portion of those in Noah Webster," arithmetic as far as "the double rule of three," and a little surveying, young Drake became apprenticed at the age of fifteen to Dr. William Goforth, a Cincinnati physician who had introduced the use of cowpox into the West. In Dr. Goforth's office he read a few of the standard medical treatises and was strengthened in his interest in natural science, to which the doctor was devoted.

At the age of eighteen Drake became his preceptor's partner, and in two years had saved enough to go to Philadelphia for further study. His means were so limited that he was not able to buy even a ticket admitting him to the hospital library and could not obtain his degree until a subsequent visit to Philadelphia. In Cincinnati he not only practiced his profession but spared no pains to promote medical education in the Ohio valley. He was chiefly instrumental in establishing a circulating library, a school of literature and arts at which lectures on various subjects were given, a Lancasterian school, and a museum of natural history. In addition Dr. Drake wrote many descriptive accounts of the geography, natural resources, flora, fauna, and economic development of Ohio. In and out of season he encouraged the intellectual life to which he was so devoted.

Benjamin Winslow Dudley, another man who enriched the life of the mind in the West as a result of experiences in older centers, had been brought to Lexington at the age of one. Not satisfied with the medical training he obtained in Philadelphia, he took a flatboat down the river to New Orleans and sailed to Europe, where he disposed of his flour at Lisbon and at Gibraltar at so handsome a profit that he was enabled to continue his medical studies in Paris and London. On his return to Lexington he enjoyed great prestige and gave a good account of himself.

The third step in the transit of culture to the frontier was the effort to establish a kind of intellectual independence of the older regions. This involved the upbuilding of libraries, hospitals, professional training schools, and professional journalism. The West did not make great progress in any of these respects before 1830, and yet, in view of the difficulties involved, the beginnings were remarkable. In 1817 Dudley organized a medical faculty at Transylvania University in Lexington. This faculty included such well-known men as Charles Caldwell, who had been trained in Philadelphia and in Paris and who introduced phrenology into the West; Dr. Joseph Buchanan, a thinker of vigor and of some independence; and, for a time, Daniel Drake. In spite of the great difficulty of importing books and apparatus from the East and from Europe, and notwithstanding the personal quarrels of its staff during the 1820s, the Transylvania Medical School became nationally famous. With less success Dr. Drake tried to establish medical schools in Cincinnati. He achieved somewhat happier results as a pioneer of medical journalism in the Ohio valley.

At Transylvania a law faculty was also established, and theological instruction was offered at virtually all of the rising colleges. In 1831 Cincinnati saw the beginning of the professional education of teachers, when the Western Literary Institute began its notable work. Thus by that year the West had begun to establish agencies of professional training which made it less dependent on an imported supply of doctors, teachers, ministers, lawyers, and educators.

In still other ways towns became intellectual focal centers. The mere presence of groups of men with a background of education and culture, together with the costliness of books for individual purchase, accounted for the rise of various types of libraries. In general these followed the pattern of the proprietary, subscription, and "social" libraries of the East. Often printers and bookdealers launched these libraries; sometimes public-spirited citizens took the first steps; and in other instances the characteristically American method of voluntary association by like-minded people was followed. In 1814 the several circulating libraries in Pittsburgh, chiefly of a joint-stock type, united to form the Pittsburgh Permanent Library; and in 1823 the free Apprentice Library got under way to meet the interests and needs of a growing social-economic group. Libraries appeared in Lexington in 1795, in Cincinnati in 1802, and in Athens and Dayton, Ohio, in the years immediately following.

The first generally accessible library in Cincinnati was the Apprentice's Library, which was established by private subscription in 1824. Libraries also existed at Vincennes (1808), Detroit (1817), Louisville (1816), the English settlements at Albion, Illinois (1818), and St. Louis (1824). While of course these libraries were all small, they provided opportunities for keeping abreast with new books as well as for reading more standard works. James Flint, to cite an example, found in 1822 that the Athenaeum or Reading Room in Lexington was equipped with the standard periodicals of England and the East, with Rees's encyclopedias, and with other books. If a town was fortunate enough to possess a college, that constituted another treasure house. In 1830 Transylvania University, with its 2000 books, had the largest library in the whole western country.

The country crossroads tavern provided an opportunity for political harangues and occasional debates, and the towns early saw the appearance of organized debating societies and discussion clubs. At Danville, Kentucky, the Political Club, founded in 1786, met Saturday evenings for discussing problems of the day. In addition to the literary societies which centered in the colleges, literary and scientific clubs appeared (and disappeared) in all the larger towns. These were especially vigorous at such intellectual centers as New Harmony and Lexington. At the Kentucky Institute in Lexington one might have heard, in the spring of 1824, weekly papers dealing with subjects as varied as the theories of language, yellow fever, Indian antiquities, geology, the atomic theory, morning and evening dews, and the importance to western development of roads, education, and the manufacture of whiskey and gin. Cincinnati had its Society for Investigation (1824), and the other towns followed suit.

The western towns also boasted museums of natural history modeled on those of Philadelphia, New York, and Baltimore. As early as 1810 professional men in Pittsburgh undertook to establish such a museum, and travelers referred to the crude but brave effort to display natural phenomena in New Orleans. The outstanding museum, however, was that which Dr. Daniel Drake promoted in Cincinnati. To some European visitors the collections of waxworks, Indian weapons, pipes, scalps, and other objects, the birds, quadrupeds, minerals, and ancient and modern coins, seemed well arranged and altogether commendable; to others, the museum was "little worthy of notice" with its "mean" contents and "miserably deficient" arrangement. Even these critics admitted that the fossil mammoth bones were notable and that the microscopic drawings of the curator, M. Joseph d'Orfeuil, were executed with skill. Although commercialism led the proprietors of this museum to establish in connection with it a "chamber of horrors" executed by the future sculptor, Hiram Powers, it was nevertheless a notable agency for scientific education. Before 1830 a rival museum of natural history appeared in Cincinnati. Notable collections also existed at Transylvania and especially at the University of Nashville, for which the Dutch naturalist, Dr. Gerard Troost, was responsible.

Even in a frontier society the esthetic side of life was not completely ignored. In the vast rural districts the popular musical expressions were the melancholy, mystical, and militant gospel hymns of the revival and the Psalms of David, along with the traditional ballads and the indigenous boatman's songs, and such ballads as "The Michigan Emigrant's Song," "Western Trappers' Camp Song," and "The Gallant Old Backwoodsman." In towns and cities professional concert artists appeared on tours as early as 1812. In Bardstown, Kentucky, a German immigrant, Anthony P. Heinrich, in 1818 began his career as a composer; *The Dawning of Music in Kentucky* (1820) was a collection of compositions for the piano, violin, and voice which had taken shape in a region where hardly a day before, as it were, the first pioneers were struggling with the Indians for their lives.

While esthetic interests, like zeal for religion and education, sometimes reflected the persistence of old tastes and habits on the frontier, their career in the new country was furthered by their utilitarian functions. Thus at the shop of David Guion, a Cincinnati stonecutter, young Shobal Vail Clevenger, in learning how to carve allegorical reliefs for gravestones, laid the foundation for the achievements that by 1836 were to make him well known as a sculptor. In some instances the arts received patronage because they lent prestige to the families that were, or aspired to be, superior in status to their neighbors. In the larger towns foreign gentlemen taught painting to the daughters of the merchants and professional leaders, and did portraits of the local gentry.

Chester Harding, an American who had taken up sign painting in Pittsburgh after the close of the War of 1812, found many clients in Paris, Kentucky, who were quite ready to pay him $25 per portrait; only the appearance of hard times cut short his career in Cincinnati. Although he did not fare too well in St. Louis, he added to his fame by seeking out the venerable Daniel Boone in his faraway cabin and startled the weather-beaten pioneer and his progeny by producing a likeness such as their untutored minds had never even imagined. In 1829 another artist, George Catlin of Philadelphia and Washington, started on his western tours to paint portraits of the Indians and their way of life—pictures which demonstrated that the West had a body of native material awaiting the hand of creative artists.

The theater was primarily an agency for the recreation of town dwellers. Local Thespian clubs in colleges and in the towns themselves now and again experimented with plays of some literary pretensions. Notwithstanding heavy taxes and religious opposition to the theater, traveling troupes opened the first professional season in the West at Lexington in 1810, and thereafter regularly performed plays in that city, Louisville, Cincinnati, St. Louis, and New Orleans. The farces and melodramas of the day prevailed, but Shakespeare, admired for the gusto of many of his scenes, was frequently on the boards. Far from being passive spectators, western audiences often identified themselves with the action and in their own boisterous way took vigorous sides in the dramatic conflict on the stage.

Thus the towns, regardless of whether they were dominated by New Englanders, by men from the middle states, or by Southerners, became centers of intellectual life. As early as 1816, one Cincinnatian even thought his town offered too much in the way of culture. He counted "Twenty sermons a week, Sunday evening Discourses on Theology— Private assemblies—State Cotillion Parties—Saturday Night Clubs, and chemical lectures" which "like the ague, return every day with distressing regularity."[16] In the main this intellectual life was directed by the better-established political and social leaders, and it resembled in many respects that of the East. But the differences will become clear from a consideration of western contributions to knowledge and letters, and of the ways in which the environment affected the ideas of the plain people.

## Contributions to Knowledge

"Who shall say," asked a contributor to the *Western Monthly Review*, "that when decay shall have laid his finger on the pride of American greatness, who shall say that the glories of the American name may not beam with unabated lustre over the waters of these inland seas? Here may science and the arts take refuge, and the spirit of liberty intrench itself, secure from the taint of foreign influence." Such enthusiasm for the future culture of the West was strengthened by substantial beginnings to which the champions of learning could point. Naturally the most distinctive and significant contributions made to the intellectual

[16] Quoted in Richard C. Wade, *The Urban Frontier: The Rise of Western Cities, 1790–1830* (Harvard University Press, 1959), 157.

culture of the West dealt with the peculiar characteristics of the new country. While the government-sponsored expeditions to the Far West enabled Lewis and Clark, Pike, Schoolcraft, and Long to add much information to the existing knowledge of that vast hinterland, the broad outlines of knowledge of the Ohio country were being filled in and sharpened. Sometimes local pride was largely responsible for these undertakings. Dr. Daniel Drake, for instance, was inspired by a desire to publicize his beloved Ohio valley—witness his *Natural and Statistical View, or Picture of Cincinnati and the Miami Country* (1815). Gazetteers of the more pretentious and valuable sort, such as Dana's *Geographical Sketches of the Western Country* (1819), were designed to aid prospective immigrants in selecting intelligently the kinds of land best suited to their purposes. Sheer love of increasing the fund of knowledge also moved the scientist in the new country. This in large part explains the heroic sacrifices of William Maclure, who crossed and recrossed the Alleghenies dozens of times to prepare the final version of *Observations on the Geology of the United States* (1817).

No less noteworthy were the contributions to the knowledge of the West's natural history. Thanks to Maclure, New Harmony became for a time the center of scientific work in this field. Gerard Troost, the Dutch naturalist who in the course of twenty years of world-wide travels had gathered a rich collection of specimens, did not, it is true, stay very long at Owen's community. In 1828 he accepted the professorship of the scientific branches at the University of Nashville and inaugurated his significant geological investigations of Tennessee. But Thomas Say, a Philadelphian, remained at New Harmony until his death in 1834. The discoverer of more new insects than any other American naturalist, Say also called attention to the chronological value of fossils. His contributions to the learned publications of the Philadelphia Academy of Natural Science and to the Linnaean Society in London made him a major figure in the fields of conchology and entomology. The third and last volume of his *American Entomology* was published at New Harmony in 1828, and his *American Conchology* was issued from the School Press of New Harmony two years later. Some of its drawings were from the hand of Charles Lesueur, a French naturalist who cooperated with Maclure, Troost, and Say in making scientific surveys in Indiana and the surrounding states.

Natural history owed much to the work of other pioneers. Constantine

Rafinesque, born in Constantinople of foreign parentage, in 1819 accepted a professorship at Transylvania, where he carried on investigations in a half dozen scientific fields. Brilliant, credulous, eccentric, Rafinesque nevertheless broadened the fields of conchology, ichthyology, and anthropology. He was given to vagaries, but in 1833 he anticipated Darwin in declaring that plants and animals had developed from remote predecessors through gradual deviations and mutations which exemplified "the great universal law of perpetual mutability in everything." His picturesque associate, Audubon, who took delight in amusing himself by titillating Rafinesque's credulous imagination, gave lavishly of his time to the study of rare birds in the Kentucky and Ohio forests. An expert huntsman, a skillful observer, and a gifted sketcher, Audubon acted for a time as taxidermist in the Western Museum at Cincinnati, and finally determined to bring his work to the attention of the scientific world. In 1828 the first volumes in his magnificent *Birds of America* series appeared in London, where he had gone to promote his venture. Cuvier hailed his work as the greatest contribution to ornithology, and Darwin was to cite it forty times.

Physicians, who did much to promote an interest in natural science, made contributions to their special field in spite of all the handicaps under which they worked. Dr. Daniel Drake, in his *Notices Concerning Cincinnati, its Topography, Climate and Diseases,* described some of the diseases seemingly peculiar to the Ohio country. Other physicians took up the discussion, some maintaining that western diseases were peculiarly malignant, and others, with fiery local patriotism, denying such allegations. Convinced that many ordinary physicians could add to medical knowledge as a result of their experiences, observations, and experiments, John Esten Cooke, editor of the *Transylvania Journal of Medicine and the Associate Sciences,* urged doctors to share their acquired knowledge with their fellows. The fact that frontier physicians frequently were impelled to take risks less readily taken in closely settled communities may explain, in part, the occasional notable surgical achievements of the West in this period. In any case, in 1809 Dr. Ephraim McDowell of Danville, Kentucky, performed the first recorded ovariotomy. In 1819, when he had four more such operations to his credit, the skeptical professional world began to pay attention to the backwoods innovator. And in 1822, William Beaumont, an army surgeon at Fort Mackinac, began to make scientific studies of digestion, using as his subject a French-

Canadian named St. Martin, whose stomach had been punctured by a gunshot wound. These investigations, first reported in the *Medical Recorder* in 1824, overthrew some prevalent theories of digestion and remain one of the notable contributions of nineteenth-century American medicine.

The prehistoric past of the West also fascinated men with a bent for scientific inquiry. Drake described the mounds in the Cincinnati region, but Caleb Atwater's work in this unique field was of greater significance. Atwater personally examined the mounds and made drawings and accurate descriptions—an invaluable contribution in view of the hasty destruction of many of them by settlers. He took care to check his findings by referring to Roman accounts of backward peoples and travelers' descriptions of existing primitive tribes in various parts of the world. His contributions to the proceedings of the American Antiquarian Society, beginning in 1820, were subsequently collected as *A Description of the Antiquities Discovered in the State of Ohio and other Western States.* At least one independent mind challenged his theories of racial origin. Writing in the *Illinois Monthly Magazine*, this critic disputed Atwater's contention that the Ohio country was once the seat of an advanced culture related to that of the Aztecs and ultimately to that of the Tartars. The theory that this culture had vanished with the invading and conquering ancestors of the Indians was also challenged. Atwater's work was outstanding, and his theory regarding the uses of the various earthworks was in a general way confirmed by later archeologists.

Others turned their attention to the existing primitive peoples. Joseph Doddridge, an Episcopal missionary, provided an enlightening description of Indian character. Henry Schoolcraft's account of Indian customs and folklore, however faulty, opened a new source of materials for American literature; and John Heckewelder's descriptions of the Indians of the upper Ohio, where he had labored many years as a Moravian missionary, likewise presented the Indian in terms more sympathetic than was customary in frontiersmen's thoughts. Dictionaries of the Indian tongues, such as that by Atwater on the Sioux languages, proved to be contributions of lasting value.

New though the West was, its more intellectually minded residents spared no effort to preserve the memories and traditions of the first settlers and all documentary accounts on which they could lay hands. Humphry Marshall's *The History of Kentucky* (1812), though biased by the personal views of its author, in making use of public documents and conversations with early settlers added something to the works of Imlay and Filson on the Kentucky legend. Daniel Drake, Timothy Flint, and James Hall also collected and preserved the traditions and memories of pioneers and river boatmen; Amos Stoddard, the first civil and military commander of Upper Louisiana, had a keen eye for archival material which he safeguarded and put to account in his *Sketches, Historical and Descriptive, of Louisiana* (1812).

To further historical consciousness societies were organized. The one founded in Nashville in 1820 was probably the first; but that founded at Vandalia (1827) was the most active in the period before 1830. James Stuart was much impressed by the fact that in a town where no house had stood in 1821, there was, within six years, an Antiquarian and Historical Society. "The whole of their published proceedings," he continued with some exaggeration, "are as regular, as well conducted, and as well printed from the Blackwell press of Vandalia, as if the seat of the society had been at Oxford or Cambridge."[17] The effort to establish an historical society in Ohio in 1822 failed, but one was successfully launched nine years later. Thanks to Lewis Cass, such a society was also started in Detroit in 1828.

## Western Literature and Western Characteristics

Western intellectuals were quite as keenly interested in promoting a western literature as they were in sponsoring the writing of western history. Convinced that eastern periodicals failed in their notices of books by Westerners to do adequate justice to them, Flint, Hall, and other pioneer editors of periodicals looked on these as necessary instruments for nourishing frontier letters. In their eyes no one save a Westerner or a thoroughly transplanted Easterner could deal adequately with frontier history and contemporary values and themes in western life.

In view of the rapid progress in material civilization, these western literary pioneers believed that the time had come for the creation of a western literature differing from that of the East in much the way that life in the West differed. The traditions and legends, the humor and racy hyperboles of frontiersmen were, in the first instance, material of

---

[17] James Stuart, *Three Years in North America* (Edinburgh, 1833), II, 227.

unique significance, for, it was held, life in the West had brought out new moral characteristics, such as individuality, heroism, independence, vigor, perseverance, generosity, and enthusiasm for liberty. A homespun democracy, in short, had been realized on the frontier and must now be reflected in a distinctive literature. Hitherto, insisted Caleb Atwater, poets, orators, historians, and novelists had done little for the great mass of the people. They had "employed themselves in placing on the very front of the stage, the warriors, the kings, the nobles, the rich, the proud, the haughty, standing on stilts or in buckskins, while the common people were seated, out of our sight, behind them."[18]

In addition to celebrating such allegedly frontier traits, western literary enthusiasts of course favored proper attention to the unique natural scenery of the new country—the majestic rhythm of the Mississippi, the mysterious forests, the prairie sun. And in spite of the tendency of many aspiring western writers to imitate classical forms the value of purely utilitarian books was not overlooked. In reviewing the *Western Agriculturist* James Hall declared that "in a country like ours, where every thing should be measured by its usefulness, the exertions of those who point out new paths of industry to the people, and explain the means of rendering labour more productive than it has been, are entitled to great respect."[19]

With such values in mind, western literary enthusiasts believed with Timothy Flint that "amidst the freshness of our unspoiled nature, beneath the shade of the huge sycamores of the Miami, or cooling the forehead in the breeze of the beautiful Ohio, and under the canopy of our Italian sky, other circumstances being equal, a man might write as well as in the dark dens of the city."[20] "The time is at hand," he continued, "when the political and moral claims of this great region, will be as well understood, and as promptly admitted, as its physical extent and resources are at present."[21]

It proved to be extremely hard to find sufficient patronage for the literary reviews that appeared, and there was a wide gulf between the aspirations for a uniquely western literature and the actual achievements. Even Flint could not muster enough western patriotism to praise such

[18] *The Writings of Caleb Atwater* (Columbus, 1833), 381–382.
[19] *Illinois Monthly Magazine*, I (March, 1831), 288.
[20] *Western Monthly and Review*, I (May, 1827), 10.
[21] *Ibid.*, iv.

tedious and pedantic epics as Dr. Richard Emmons's *The Fredoniad* (1827), which cumbersomely celebrated frontier exploits. Much of the singsong verse that filled "poets' corners" and the pretentious magazines was even more florid, overblown, stilted and artificial than eastern verse was at that time. Imitative of Pope, Young, Byron, Scott, and Hemans, western verse derived little from the western soil. Nor were Westerners more successful in fiction. Flint and Hall, together with a few others, did succeed in achieving some of the values toward which they aspired, but even their tales and novels fell far short of their ideals. In its vigorous yet florid political oratory alone, perhaps, did the West of the first decades of the nineteenth century make a distinctive contribution to literature.

Yet on the other side of the scales, the foundations of an intellectual life had been laid. Publishing houses in the larger cities issued large numbers of school textbooks, religious writings, and historical and agricultural books. The clause in the Ordinance of 1785 setting aside public lands for educational purposes had, it is true, failed to result in well-maintained public school systems and state universities; pioneers had been too eager to realize immediate returns from these lands, too impatient to wait until their value was sufficient to make larger returns possible. Nevertheless, the beginnings of state-supported colleges and public school systems, especially in the cities, had been made. In the following period, genuine state systems of common schools were to take shape. However small the libraries and however crude the so-called colleges, they were at least tangible realities. The wonder is not that intellectual development was checked or limited, not that all these agencies of intellectual life were so meager, but that they were relatively so ample. In many respects they had developed at a more rapid rate than the importance of their functions in the new society warranted. As society itself became more complex, it was certain that the intellectual culture that had been carried to the new country and had begun to develop there would become broader, deeper, and richer.

The rapid spread of agencies of intellectual life on the frontier was a reflection of the fact that on the whole Westerners were merely Easterners who had emigrated, bringing with them the basic assumptions of eastern thought and feeling and thus the need for the same kind of institutions. In some ways the thought of the West undoubtedly differed from that in the East, owing partly to selective forces determining who should emigrate, but largely to the very different conditions prevailing in the West. We have seen what leading Easterners thought of the intellectual life of the new lands; we have considered what the West's actual contributions were in the building of institutions and of ideas; and we have asked what leading Westerners thought of themselves. What of the plain people of the West? How if at all did their ideas differ from those of their fellows in the East?

In seeking to answer our question we must remember that the thought of the period might be expected to differ according to the stage of immigration represented (whether the early pioneer stage or the later stages in the transit of ideas), according to social, religious, and economic groupings, and according to residence in the wilderness itself or in a growing town. Yet it is possible that certain broader aspects of western thought, more or less transcending such differences, may usefully be distinguished.

The thought of ordinary western pioneers can be inferred only from indirect sources—from their songs and proverbs, their jokes and stories, the letters some of them were able to write back home, from almanacs and the like, and from those newspapers and magazines that soon sprang up in the cities and were read by some portion of the literate. Their mode of thought can also be inferred, to a certain extent, from their ways of daily living. The scantiness and unreliability of such materials and the uncertainty of oral tradition make it impossible for the historian to say with any great confidence what the common people of those days in the West thought about the world in which they lived.

The background of their thought was the same as that of Easterners and Europeans, for they were all immigrants from older regions—they were the heirs of western European thought, the inheritors of a Christian tradition, and, in the main, the descendants of Englishmen. As such there was, of course, implicit in their thought the acceptance of a life of action and hard work; the life of contemplation played no part in popular thought. Although the dualism of mind and body was a part of their Christian heritage, otherworldliness was not unduly emphasized—the early Puritanism of the blue-law type had been modified even in the colonial period, and in the eastern states it had become considerably altered.

In the new West the forms of religious life of course greatly changed. Where churches were at first absent, then few in number, religious observances could naturally not be maintained; where a population was so scattered, the strength of sectarian ties and veneration for certain usages had to lessen; where there was so much work to be done, the Sabbath had to be "desecrated." It seems highly probable that the godlessness decried by eastern churchmen was in large part only superficial lack of ceremony; a whole people could hardly cast away its basic Christianity overnight, however much its forms might alter.

Yet the conditions of the frontier did undoubtedly favor an increase of informality in religious thought, and some of the pioneers no doubt actually drifted into "freethinking" habits without in any sense giving up the basic assumptions of the Christian thought of western Europe. There were village atheists in the East—and on the frontier these may well have been more numerous. In the wilderness too there was very likely a larger number of careless, adventurous, and daring spirits than "at home," for these would naturally be the sort who would first emigrate. James Hall reported that from the time of the first settlements in the colonies there was always a fringe of these bold adventurers on the frontier, pushing ever westward as older settlements became "crowded," they and their descendants never becoming a really settled, conservative community.

There was also, it seems quite clear, a definitely lawless and even criminal element made up of some men who had actually fled from the more settled communities to escape the clutches of the law, and others who felt they could carry on shady trades with less chance of detection or punishment than in the East. Thus there were the horse thieves, the gamblers, the roving bandits. Although notorious, this element was very small. Early observers expressed the belief that many frontier communities were unjustly called lawless and wicked because of the noisy activities of a few characters whose exploits were spread abroad, such as, for example, the canal men, the Erie men, and the river boatmen of the Ohio. Of course frontier conditions, where courts and the law were weak, did tend to accentuate in all men the human tendency that loathes being wronged, the tendency independently to take into one's own hands the protection of one's rights. The western country as a whole, however, seems to have had a wholesome respect for order and in reality established it quickly.

Certain other qualities of mind present in Easterners were also accentuated and brought to the fore by pioneer life. The consideration that among the earliest newcomers to the western lands were crude fighting men used to blood and violence helps us to realize that the cruelty and injustice toward the Indian on which some early travelers comment was indeed a reality in the West and a factor in the bitter enmity that persisted. Cruelty begets cruelty. There is no doubt that the Indian was not the only one who cherished unreasoning hatred and executed deeds of revenge. Mere physical prowess was glorified in pioneer times. The tall tales of the early 1800s, illustrated by the deeds of Mike Fink the riverman, lay special emphasis on the tremendous strength of the hero. Mike Fink was only one of the giants of those days, one of a line of American folk heroes of great strength.

Another trait much developed in the West was pride in place and country. The western settlers, perhaps feeling deep down a little inferior to the cultured Easterners who traveled among them, but undoubtedly genuinely rejoicing in the fertility and promise of the new country, were apt to be loud in its praises and resentful of criticisms. Thus a critical visitor, whether an Easterner or a European, might provoke boastfulness or abuse of the East from the same people who would receive an appreciative traveler with generous welcome. This consideration helps explain discrepancies in accounts of early travelers. The British, for example, often found the natives uncouth and surly and impertinent. That there was uncouthness is unquestioned; and there must have been some surliness, but that it was highly characteristic of the pioneer is doubtful.

In fact the friendliness and the natural curiosity of these dwellers in the wilderness may well have occasioned criticisms of their impertinence by English and other "foreign" travelers. Actually the common enterprise, the hospitality and neighborliness that were inseparable from life in the new country gave rise to a friendliness of which many American observers of the time were proud. Pioneer conditions were inevitably levelers of rank and station; and a great pride in democracy, in being able to speak one's mind, to dress as one liked, to think one's own thoughts could flourish more readily on western than on eastern soil. The West undoubtedly had all the virtues and all the vices of the parent East, but as some of the vices flourished more luxuriantly in open spaces, so did some of the democratic virtues; American democracy was growing.

# PART IV

# Democratic Upheaval

# 12 New Currents of Equalitarianism

*The age of philosophy has passed, and left few memorials of its existence. That of glory has vanished, and nothing but a painful tradition of human suffering remains. That of utility has commenced, and it requires little warmth of imagination to anticipate for it a reign lasting as time, and radiant with the wonders of unveiled nature.*

—WILLIS HALL, 1844

*Our religion has been Judaized; it has been Romanized; it has been orientalized, it has been Anglicized, and the time is at hand when it must be Americanized. Every age has to shape the Divine image it worships over again—the present age and all our own country are busily engaged in the task at the time.*

—OLIVER WENDELL HOLMES, 1859

In the 1830s and 1840s the plain people took a more active role than ever before in intellectual life and were the object of greater interest on the part of scholars and writers. This development accompanied the advance of political and social democracy which in turn owed much to the continued growth of the West, the advance of industries and cities, the coming of immigrants on a striking scale, and the general democratic ferment in western Europe.

European revolts against privilege gave many shopkeepers, artisans, small business people, and farmers a feeling of being part of a great onward movement. The struggles in Europe encouraged the common man in America in his efforts to complete the battle for universal manhood suffrage, to abolish imprisonment for debt, to oppose moneyed and landed monopolies, to experiment with labor unions and with even more drastic economic programs. Emissaries of Chartism came from England, and such social radicals as George Henry Evans and Frances Wright did much to augment the class consciousness of American urban workers. Orestes Brownson, in an article that created a sensation in New England, identified the interests of the "working classes" in America with European reform and revolutionary movements, past and present. The "middle class" of owners and employers "was strong enough to defeat nearly all the practical benefit of the French Revolution," Brownson complained. Currently, the middle class "is the natural enemy of Chartism. . . . Our despair for the poor Chartists arises from the number and power of the middle classes."[1] After the collapse of the revolutionary movements of 1830 and 1848, American liberalism was reinforced by the migration of political exiles, some of whom stirred the waters with the ideas of Proudhon and Marx. The American lower middle and working classes could see in the European democratic movements, in the struggles of the Greeks, the Belgians, the French, the Italians, the Germans, the Irish, and the Poles, both the influence of American ideas and a further challenge to efforts in behalf of a democracy conceived of as a world struggle against privilege. Large numbers did see what was going on in Europe in this light. Enthusiastic mass meetings and processions greeted the victories of European liberal nationalists and democrats, and expressions of faith in the ultimate triumph of the cause cushioned the shock of reverses abroad.

Leaders of American democracy warned their comrades against overlooking the faults in the American system in their enthusiastic denunciations of the aristocracy and priestcraft against which their brethren across the seas were fighting. At a meeting in Faneuil Hall on May 8, 1849, resolutions of sympathy were accompanied by the admonition: "While we rejoice in the organization of free institutions in the Old World, we

---

[1] "The Laboring Classes." *Boston Quarterly Review*, III (July, 1840), 364.

are not indifferent to their support at home, and we regret the despotic attitude of the Slave Power at the South, and the domineering ascendancy of the Monied Oligarchy in the North as equally hostile to the interests of labor, and incompatible with the preservation of popular rights."[2]

## The Impact of Industrialism

Of the forces that were transforming western Europe none was more important than the advance of industrialism, an historical experience which the northeastern states in America shared. The progress of industrial development in New England and the middle states, affecting as it did all parts of the land, enhanced the power of the common man in many respects; it promoted both his comfort and his chances for acquiring knowledge and culture.

The increased facilities provided by the new and more rapid means of communication for moving to places in which opportunities promised to be more abundant greatly increased the average person's sense of power. The common man was no longer anchored as he had been in earlier times; he could more readily try his fortune in the rising cities or the growing West. He often met reverses, but he often succeeded too.

In addition to improvements in steamboats and the successful advance of the steam railroad, a series of inventions similarly enhanced the power and comfort of the common man. The electric telegraph (1844) brought him news from distant places in an incredibly short time and greatly widened his horizons. In 1847 the Hoe rotary press facilitated the cheap production of newspapers on a mass scale; in consequence virtually for the first time, he could buy newspapers as a matter of course. In 1828 the annual circulation of newspapers was about six for each individual in the country; in 1850 it was approximately twenty-two. In 1840 Dr. John Draper of New York University took what was apparently the first complete photograph ever made by sunlight; the way was open for familiarizing the common man with far places and peoples. The new lithograph process, commercialized and dramatized by Currier and Ives, brought into his own home realistic records of actual events—fires, races, wrecks,

[2] Cited in George E. McNeill, *The Labor Movement* (Boston and New York, 1887), 115.

and mobs—a folk art of sorts. The enjoyment of all these satisfactions was facilitated by the invention of the reaper and the sewing machine, which provided greater amounts of leisure for farmers and housewives. Most promising of all, sons of farmers and of the city's poor could occasionally acquire mastery over the ever more important machine in such schools as Rensselaer, the Franklin Institute, and the technical institutions at Harvard and Yale. Thus many avenues to a more thoughtful life were opening to the great majority of the population.

The fact that the swift advance of the Industrial Revolution concentrated population in cities also affected the cultural life of the common man. In 1830, 6.7 percent of the population lived in towns over 8000; in 1850, 12.5 percent inhabited such centers. Obviously the poorer people in the rapidly growing cities did not share directly or immediately many of the cultural advantages which they afforded. Yet some at least were affected by these opportunities. And in the long run urban growth was fraught with momentous consequences for the plain people. For the new aggregation of population compelled public authority to assume certain responsibilities that in smaller communities were left to individuals. Thus in 1830 New York City felt impelled to introduce gas lighting on the streets as a municipal function. The transfer from private to public auspices of the supply of water and of such services as sanitation and fire and police protection began the long modification of laissez faire and the substitution of public responsibility and control. This substitution was full of significant implications for the common man in a society destined to become increasingly interdependent and insecure.

In some respects, of course, the advance of industrialism made the lot of the urban worker less eligible; the new lords of the loom controlled the destiny of the toiler in ways unknown in the older America of handicrafts, self-sufficient agriculture, commercial patricians, and local gentry. But the growth of slums, poverty, and insecurity, the long hours, the low pay, the execrable conditions in the mills, factories, and shops aroused many workers to make new demands and to struggle for their realization.

Poor conditions in cities and factories prompted halting efforts at organizing workingmen into craft unions and even political parties. Especially during times of inflation such as the years 1834–1836, urban craftsmen organized into societies for their own protection and advancement. The first city central union was formed in Philadelphia in 1827. In 1834 there was founded the National Trades' Union, and in the two following years five other national craft unions were organized.

The ranks of the laborers often included journalists, professional men, and even merchants and bankers, men who were interested in opposing monopoly in order to open the way for their own economic advancement. Nevertheless, the demands included in the programs of the labor organizations were aimed at creating a greater equality of opportunity for all members of society. Two demands received the heaviest emphasis: the abolition of imprisonment for debt and the creation of a system of free public education. The workingmen's societies also promoted libraries and other devices for self-improvement. Thus they helped open the way for the diffusion of knowledge among the plain people.

### The Development of Equalitarian Thought

Alongside increased participation by the common man in the nation's social, political, and intellectual life, there grew up a rhetorical rationale for democracy. This rationale owed much to older "republican" formulations, and it did not receive a definitive statement at the hands of any single American thinker of the 1830s and 1840s. Rather, it was a congeries of assumptions, attitudes, and opinions meant to explain and promote the rise of the common man. Democratic ideas formed a platform for those who wished to alter the political system received from the founding fathers.

Jeffersonian and Federalist political theories had agreed in one important respect. They both distinguished between citizenship and suffrage. All men born into the community might be citizens and share the rights of citizens. But suffrage was a privilege, and should be restricted to those with a proper stake—usually an economic stake—in society. The innovation of democratic theory in the 1830s and 1840s was the idea that suffrage, no less than citizenship, belonged to every man. The democratically oriented intellectuals were ready at hand with theoretical rationalizations for this development. James Fenimore Cooper, despite his Jeffersonian and aristocratic fear of "demagoguery," wrote that America had "come to the conclusion, that it is scarcely worth while to do so much violence to natural justice, without sufficient reason, as to disfranchise a man merely because he is poor." Attacking a favorite conservative comparison of governments and private corporations, Cooper continued: "A man may be a voluntary associate in a joint-stock company, and justly have a right to a participation in its management . . .

but life is not a chartered institution. . . . Now, though government is, beyond a doubt, a sort of compact, it would seem that those who prescribe its conditions are under a normal obligation to consult the rights of the whole."[3]

George Bancroft, a less hesitating advocate of democracy than Cooper, put the issue more plainly. "If reason is a universal faculty"—a favorite notion of New England intellectuals—"the universal decision is the nearest criterion of truth. The common mind winnows opinions; it is the sieve which separates error from certainty. . . . The public happiness is the true object of legislation, and can be secured only by the masses of mankind themselves awakening to the knowledge and the care of their own interests."[4] Bancroft was a determined Jacksonian in politics, and his monumental *History of the United States* was an account of how the common, collective mind of the American people had come into maturity and control of its own destiny. Erastus Root, a New York Democrat, summed up the more radical democratic thinking in the New York constitutional convention of 1821: "We are all of the same estate," he asserted, "—all commoners."[5]

The widening of suffrage, the formation of workingmen's societies and political parties, the heightened sense of conflict promoted by such men as Brownson, all these developments prompted some of the cultured well-to-do to turn their eyes inward, to examine their own social ethics and activities. One result of this was the growth of an ethic of philanthropic humanitarianism. Touched by the misery of tenement dwellers, clergymen in Boston and New York inaugurated the beginnings of religious missionary work in the poorer quarters. The victory of the crusaders for free public schools, a victory which was to mean much to the poor, owed something to the support of humanitarians among the better-established ranks of society. Private philanthropy opened limited opportunities for the unfortunate. Stephen Girard of Philadelphia left the fortune he gleaned from overseas commerce to establish a training school for boys. The Dwights gave of their wealth to establish a training school for teachers in the old Bay State. Thomas Perkins of Boston be-

[3] James Fenimore Cooper, *Notions of the Americans*, 2nd ed., (Philadelphia, 1839), I, 264–265.

[4] George Bancroft, *Literary and Historical Miscellanies* (New York, 1857), 415, 422.

[5] Quoted in Marvin Meyers, *The Jacksonian Persuasion: Politics and Belief* (Stanford University Press, 1957), 189.

came the generous benefactor of a school for the blind. Such men as the Lawrences, the Lowells, the Lennoxes, and the Stuarts endowed many an educational cause and numberless worthy charities. According to Francis Bowen, professor at Harvard and an exponent of a conservative social philosophy, "the sums which are contributed here [in the United States] by individuals for the support of schools, colleges, churches, missions, hospitals, and institutions of science and beneficence, put to shame the official liberality of the oldest and wealthiest governments in Europe."[6]

Several factors explain the growth of philanthropy as a response to urban and industrial ills. The Christian doctrine of the stewardship of great riches, which taught the responsibility of the rich for the poor, can hardly be overemphasized. The desire for prestige also counted. As Francis Bowen put it, "The most natural and sensible way of deriving personal gratification from newly acquired wealth, and of making a show of it in the eyes of the world, is to give largely to public charities."[7] The use of philanthropy as a part of the defense of business against the criticisms of radical theorists and class-conscious urban workers was less general in this period than in the post-Civil War era, but it was not absent. George Hillard, an able legal representative of the conservative interests of Boston, declared in the Massachusetts Convention of 1853 that he had often felt, and sometimes said, that

in our great cities, the aggregation of immense wealth at one end of the scale, and the increasing amount of hopeless poverty at the other, did involve an element of peril to wealth itself, and that the moment the rich men forget the duties of property, the moment that they cease to bridge this interval between themselves and the poor by the perpetual exercise of sympathy, and by the constant recognition of a common humanity and a common brotherhood, then their wealth would be in danger of falling upon the mercy of the merciless. And it is only in this—it is only in the moral element, flowing from Christianity and humanity, that a corrective is to be found to the danger which always threatens a country in which, while the rich are growing richer, the poor are growing poorer.[8]

If it was exceptional for anyone in high position to admit such pronounced extremes of wealth, it was by no means unusual for the apolo-

[6] Francis Bowen, The Principles of Political Economy (Boston, 1859), 545.
[7] Ibid.
[8] Massachusetts Official Report of the Debates and Proceedings in the State Convention of 1853 (Boston, 1854), 11, 131.

gists of industrialism to cite philanthropy in reply to attacks upon them.

The rise of industrialism also promoted the enunciation of a social philosophy that identified economic individualism with democracy. This philosophy was formulated in response to the critics of commerce and industry—the more doctrinaire and radical reformers, the Romanticists, the Transcendentalists, many of whom condemned capitalism as unjust, undemocratic, or excessively materialistic. The defense of commerce and industrial capitalism came to have a direct bearing on the aspirations and struggles of the common man and woman.

The existence of vast natural resources and the absence of fixed classes in the United States figured in many of the efforts to demonstrate the essentially democratic character of the new industrial order. It was only necessary to argue that the system of free competition for natural resources was in accord with the doctrines of liberty and equality. The industrial organization of society, wrote Professor Bowen, had broken down and removed the fixed and arbitrary divisions and barriers that had hitherto closed the doors to the skillful, industrious, and economical man in the lower ranks. "Neither theoretically nor practically, in this country, is there any obstacle to any individual's becoming rich, if he will, and almost to any amount that he will. . . . How is it possible, indeed, that the poor should be arrayed in hostility against the rich, when . . . the son of an Irish coachman becomes the governor of a State, and the grandson of a *millionaire* dies a pauper?"[9] Henry C. Carey, the Philadelphia economist, went so far as to suggest that the ideals of the Declaration of Independence were being fulfilled in the economic sphere by the essential justice with which wealth was distributed in a system of free economic enterprise. He even saw the possibility in some future time of economic equality.

The justification of industrial capitalism on democratic grounds included the argument that in his efforts to better his condition the individual was free of paternalism and of the unfair favors which government interference with God's natural economic order involved. If laws were impartial and prohibitive only of crime against persons and property, then each man, working his own way for his own gain, could enjoy the full fruits of economic democracy. When, Bowen claimed, man meddled in the handiwork of God, he only marred it and brought down on his fellows the curse of panics and hard times. However complex, intricate,

[9] Francis Bowen, *op. cit.*, 122–123.

and far reaching the devices by which private gain and public advantage were to be ultimately harmonized, the reconciliation was certain, in Bowen's mind. Only in the relations of one nation with another was the principle of laissez faire inoperable and undemocratic; each nation, the argument ran, was the natural economic unit the inner harmony of which was never to be disturbed by governmental regulations. But since economic life followed national lines, the citizens of each nation must be protected through tariffs against those living in lands with lower living standards. Bowen was certain that perfectly free competition would "tend slowly but irresistibly to the equalization of wealth. . . ."[10]

In identifying the principles of laissez faire with an ultimate tendency toward equality, Bowen was following in a long tradition of nineteenth-century moral philosophy. The clergymen who taught moral philosophy —a pot pourri of philosophy, sociology, political science, economics, and family life—in American colleges during the first half of the nineteenth century were almost unanimous in their support of the principles of property rights and economic liberty. One of the earliest of the moral philosophers, Samuel Stanhope Smith, taught a generation of Princeton students that the function of government was to protect property. The law of supply and demand was an inviolable law of nature, which no early "law or authority of the state could alter without violence to liberty and manifest injury to the interests of trade." Francis Wayland, president of Brown University and author of the most popular text on "moral science," also supported a strict laissez faire position. State aid for the poor was perhaps the most contemptible of all kinds of legislation, Wayland argued: "Where poor rates [direct government aid] are highest, the poor will be found the most discontented and lawless and the most inveterate against the rich." Thus academic philosophers laid in the first half of the nineteenth century the basis for the business rationale of the latter half. They identified liberty almost exclusively with the right to hold and use property. The only practicable kind of equality they would admit was that equality which competition might tend to produce. And they equated these conceptions of liberty and equality with democracy by arguing that the best interests of the common man, even of the poor, would be served by a policy of laissez faire.

When urban workers and proslavery critics of industrialism maintained that the factory system was autocratic, apologists for business

[10] *Ibid.*, 505.

brushed aside this contention. They insisted that humble folk could pool their little hoardings in the corporation, the legal basis of the factory system, with no less benefit than that derived by the established capitalist. Nor was any factory worker bound to stay behind his loom like some dumb creature. The *Lowell Offering* proved that factory girls could write literary pieces of distinction. Industrial workers could and did leave the factory—to become managers or even capitalists! "The steps from the foot to the summit are not many," declared a successful Boston merchant, "but each has its name which must be distinctly known by all who would seek to climb. The first step is faith, and without this none can safely rise; the second, industry; the third, perseverance; the fourth, temperance; the fifth, probity; and the sixth, independence."[11] Poor Richard's philosophy was obviously still flourishing.

On the political front no less than on the economic, the values of democracy were associated with commerce and industry. That some rose to the top in the free competition in which every man was equal to every other was a sign that the best man had won. Francis Bowen spoke for many in declaring that the wealthy, as nature's demonstrated aristocrats, should rightly have "the command or the leading influence in the State."[12] Athough Daniel Webster and those of like mind had argued that property must be duly represented in legislative bodies, others with an eye on democratic dogma saw that wealth might rule through prestige and influence as well as through direct methods. "Our New York merchant," declared one writer, "can map out his own political future. He has only to say he will accept political advancement, and he will get it." In any case, "not an ambassador or foreign consul to any nation or part of the world can be appointed without the consent of the merchants of New York."[13]

Champions of business declared that the influence of men of wealth was no contradiction to the Declaration of Independence. Equality, interpreted as equality of opportunity, and liberty, interpreted as freedom from restraint, could be enjoyed only if the individual were fully protected in his property rights. American democracy, in the minds of champions of industry, implied not only freedom and equality but

[11] Freeman Hunt, *Worth and Wealth* (New York, 1856), 63.
[12] Bowen, *op. cit.*, 505–506.
[13] Joseph M. Scoville (Walter Barrett, *pseud.*), *The Merchants of New York City* (New York, 1885), II, 17.

security against the power of a majority which might, in its lust for power and gold, destroy the whole fabric. The American political system, declared Rufus Choate in the Massachusetts Constitutional Convention of 1853, while "purely and intensely republican," was designed to achieve two ends above all others, liberty and security. To accomplish this twofold object, two sets of institutions were created by the fathers in the fullness of their wisdom. The one set was intended to bring out

the popular will in its utmost intensity of utterance; . . . In this great mansion of liberty resided free elections, a majority voice in the popularly chosen legislatures, a free press, and liberty of worship. The other set was designed to secure the life, liberty, character, and property of each against majority will and power; in another quiet, smaller chamber, far from the torchlight processions, the emotional tugs of the polls and the legislative halls, sat the judiciary, devoted to restraint, reason, and security, the guarantee, in the last analysis, of democracy against itself.

Thus, instead of repudiating democracy as the southern proslavery apologists were to do, the champions of the rising industrialism interpreted it in such a way as to make it sanction the influence of the wealth that in the eyes of slaveowners and economic radicals alike threatened the very basis of democracy.

## Romanticism and Transcendentalism

The Romantic philosophy shared the individualism and optimism of business enterprise, but there the kinship was apt to end. The Romantic concern with nature and primitivism, with the remote in time and place, was a far cry from machines, shops, and offices. The fascination of the South Seas made it possible for Melville to forget foundries and factories. *Walden Pond* was Thoreau's antidote to railways and cities. Longfellow's recapture in *The Golden Legend* of the soul of the medieval monk and his embroidered pictures of the primitive red men were assertions of values remote from those of the new industrialism that was transforming America. The Romantic protest against urbanism and industrialism was shown in the rising vogue for Gothic cottages, for landscape gardens, for the picturesque and the monumental in natural scenery. Nathaniel P. Willis wrote his paean to the nation's natural beauty in *American*

*Scenery* (1840), but this was only one of many ecstatic appreciations. Donald G. Mitchell's appealing idylls of the countryside and the "pipe dreams" of its devotee, "Ik Marvel," enjoyed astounding popularity. In painting, idealizations of the landscape issuing from the brushes of Cole, Kensett, Church, Bierstadt, and others similarly testified to the spell of a nature unspoiled by mines, factories, railroads, and cities.

Although many Romanticists agreed with Emerson in seeing a danger to individualism in the mass values which glorified the common man or with Melville in distrusting democracy, many others idealized humble folk. Such an idealization obviously had democratic implications. English and French Romanticists, particularly Cowper, Wordsworth, Blake, Dickens, and Béranger, expressed sympathy with the common man or advocated some reform for his relief; but Burns and von Chamisso were apparently almost alone in Europe in sentimentalizing, idealizing, and even glorifying the poor, humble, obscure figure. Whittier's rural pieces, "The Barefoot Boy" and "Snow-Bound," and Longfellow's "The Village Blacksmith" have few European counterparts. Whittier's "Skipper Ireson's Ride," Holmes's ballads, and Thompson's *The Green Mountain Boys* celebrated the homely virtues of the plain people. Other writers, such as Maria Cummins and George Lippard, graphically depicted the miseries of the slums, the wickedness of the capitalists, and the sterling qualities of a simple rural folk caught in the industrial maelstrom.

Transcendentalism was in a sense part of the larger Romantic movement. It was a revolt against the rationalism of the eighteenth century. It emphasized those aspects of man's nature that were said to transcend or be independent of experience. Derived partly from Coleridge and the English intuitionalists, partly from Kant, Schelling, Fichte, Jacobi, and the other German philosophical idealists, partly from the French eclectic philosophers, and partly from Oriental sources, American Transcendentalism was spiritual and practical rather than metaphysical. The Transcendentalists, who began to meet informally in Boston in 1836 and established *The Dial* as their leading organ, sought the springs of inspiration and action in the mind rather than in authority, in nature rather than in man-made institutions.

Transcendentalism did not appeal in its philosophical form to the masses, yet there was much that was democratic in it. The exaltation of man, of all men; the doctrine that all power, all wisdom, comes from nature, with which man must establish an original and firsthand relationship; the relegation of books to a secondary place in the hierarchy of values; the insistence that instinct is good and must be obeyed rather than curbed in accordance with conventions and authority—all these ideas were closely related to the democratic impulse. "Let man stand erect, go alone, and possess the universe," declared Emerson. The endless seeking, the glorification of the individual, and the social sympathies that characterized the thought of most of the Transcendentalists correponded to the democratic doctrine that all men possess a sacred, irrevocable right to govern themselves and to reach for the stars. As Emerson put it, democracy has its root "in the sacred truth that every man hath in him the divine Reason." The plain corollary was that every man is capable of making this "divine reason" his guide in life.

Transcendentalists in the main opposed the idea that industrialism is democratic and desirable. Melville's criticisms of the factory and Thoreau's satires on the machine and on human exploitation for profit are less well known than their glorification of the primitive, but they are intrinsically a part of their thought. The whole Transcendentalist group, with Emerson in the lead, had much fault to find with the way in which industrialism glorified the "old Yankee trait of materialism." The Reverend Frederic Hedge spoke for his fellows in commenting on the dichotomy between scholarship and creative genius on the one hand and an industrial society on the other. The latter rewarded "none but those who will do its work, which if the scholar undertake, he must straightway neglect his own. . . . [In] an endless multiplication of physical conveniences—an infinite economy has become the *cultus*, the worship of the age. Religion itself has been forced to minister in this service."[14]

It remained for Theodore Parker to indict the materialistic and undemocratic aspects of industrialism in the most sweeping terms. He was aroused by the lot of the industrial laboring class. He had only scorn for "the institution of money—the master of all the rest." For the temporizing expediency, the inhumane and selfish principles and behavior of the moneyed class, he had only condemnation. Such a society in his eyes ran counter to the basic tenets of Christian Transcendentalism—the daily rebirth of God in each individual soul, the dictate that the divinity in man must rule the world, the truth that each man and woman, by virtue of being identical with nature, must enjoy equal rights and privileges. Parker developed the social implications of Transcendentalism further

[14] *The Dial*, I (October, 1840), 177–178.

than most of his fellows, but each one in the circle determined to do all he could to rescue spirit and mind from human exploitation and inequality, from subservience to physical comfort and materialism, and above all to resist the emphasis of an industrial society on preparation for living by bringing living itself to the foreground.

There was a certain ambiguity in the social attitudes of the Transcendentalists. Some of their doctrines might imply democratic assumptions, but in other respects, Transcendentalism was out of tune with the democratic temper of the times. Emerson gloried in his own contradictions, and he was governed more by moods and sympathy than by a developed and consistent social philosophy. At one time he might counsel that "The philosopher, the poet, or the religious man will of course wish to cast his vote with the democrat . . . for wide suffrage." At other times, however, he feared the political power of "The hordes of ignorant and deceivable natives and the armies of foreign voters." Emerson was, above all, an individualist, and he condemned majority opinion as "the argument of fools, the strength of the weak." To Thoreau, politics was not really relevant to man's deepest problems. He disdained "To turn from the voices and deeds of earnest men to the *cackling* of political conventions." Bronson Alcott, though a zealous reformer and antislavery man, rejected the fundamental premise of majoritarian democracy: "The number of those who advocate . . . any particular doctrine," he wrote, "is an indication of its incorrectness."[15]

### The Democratization of Religion

The democracy and individualism represented by the Transcendentalists' insistence on the identity of every human being with the Over-Soul or the sum total of universal truth and reality made its impact on the very Protestantism against which the Transcendentalists reacted. The rapid development of the West, with the opportunities it provided the common man to get ahead and express himself, and his general advance in political, social, and economic matters all tended toward the demo-

---

[15] Edward Waldo Emerson and Waldo Emerson Forbes (eds.), *Journals of Ralph Waldo Emerson* (Houghton Mifflin Company, 1909–1914, 10 vols.), VII, 12; Thoreau, "A Plea for Captain John Brown," *The Writings of Henry David Thoreau* (Houghton Mifflin Company, 1893), X, 213; Odell Shepard (ed.), *The Journals of Bronson Alcott* (Little, Brown and Company, 1938), 7.

cratization of religion. In the field of ecclesiastical organization many denominations reflected the democratic tendencies of the age by admitting the laity to a larger share in church government. Even within the Catholic church a group of laymen defied canon law by insisting on sharing with the clergy the control of church property. In still other respects ordinary people enjoyed greater freedom in religious matters. In 1818 Connecticut completed the process of separation of church and state; Massachusetts similarly terminated the traditional connection in 1833. This did not mean that the individual was free from the influence of community opinion, which was still largely dominant, especially in rural areas. But it did mean that the relationship between the individual and religion was less determined by the state or by a particular favored sect. The increasing secularization of life was also reflected in the relaxation of the traditionally strict observance of the Sabbath. It would be easy to overemphasize the extent of this relaxation, for strict Sabbaths were still kept in a great many places. Nevertheless, the tendency was clear. Religious practice was, in brief, becoming more largely a private matter, less markedly a public one. In view of the fact that secularism was making great advances and in view of the additional fact that Americans everywhere worshiped in a variety of ways, a voluntary relationship between the individual and religion was more democratic than the official or public relationship implied in established churches and legal regulations regarding conduct on the Sabbath.

The spirit of democracy was even more evident in matters of belief. Although free thought enjoyed relatively little influence in the 1830s and 1840s, its champions tried to identify it with the cause of the common man. Such leaders of the industrial workers as Robert Dale Owen, Frances Wright, and Thomas Skidmore espoused deism or agnosticism. *The Beacon*, a periodical launched in New York in 1840, coupled the cause of labor with the rejection of all religious theories. However strongly entrenched religious theories were under antiquated formulas and "pretended divine revelation," these theories, according to *The Beacon*, all failed when subjected to "open and fair investigation." In Boston orthodoxy was defied by Abner Kneeland, who actually declared in print that God is a chimera of the imagination, that the story of Christ is a fable, and that immortality is an impossibility. Though such blasphemy was gall and wormwood to many religious men and women of position, Kneeland could not be muffled.

Certain religious bodies themselves reflected democratic conceptions of theology. Unitarianism, it will be recalled, was characterized by a democratic insistence on salvation by character rather than by autocratic fiat of the Deity. Although it gained little support among the working classes and made slight headway generally outside New England, there it succeeded in tempering the beliefs of the traditionally Calvinistic Congregationalism. The Reverend Horace Bushnell of the Congregational church in Hartford refused in the face of charges of heresy to abandon his emphasis on mysticism, free will, and Christian nurture, rather than election, as the road to salvation. His insistence that theology is not intellectual but intuitive, and his "comprehensivism," the doctrine that all sects possess portions of the truth, opened the way to democratic "come-outism" in matters of faith and creed. The rapid progress among the common people of the Methodist and Baptist faiths, which emphasized free will at the expense of predestination, was another evidence of the interrelations of democracy and religion.

The impact of the rise of the common man on religion was reflected in the growing social consciousness of religious leaders. William Ellery Channing, whose Boston constituency included men of position and wealth, was genuinely concerned over the social and moral effects of the prevailingly unequal distribution of wealth. Joseph Tuckerman, a Unitarian colleague, made serious efforts to apply Christ's teaching of brotherhood in the bleak and revolting slums of Boston, and Edwin Chapin and others followed his example in New York. A growing number of ministers shared the feeling of the Reverend Elias Magoon, a Baptist minister, who declared that the church must "work for the millions rather than for aristocratic cliques." In his *Republican Christianity* Magoon maintained that the time had come when Christianity must forego its historic connection with tyranny, aristocracy, and priestcraft, and instead play the part of "patron of the aspiring, the fortifier of the weak, the deliverer of the oppressed."[16] Warnings were sounded against the "alliance offensive and defensive actually formed between the *pretended religion and the real wealth* of the country, the hierarchy and oligarchy combined . . . [that] compass dominion over the people. . . ."[17]

Nothing reflected more clearly the democratization of religion and the emancipation of the common man from conventional and authori

[16] Elias L. Magoon, *Republican Christianity* (Boston, 1849), 312–313.
[17] *New England Galaxy*, VII (June 11, 1824), 1.

tative ecclesiastical organizations than the phenomenon known as "come-outism." This tendency for men and women believing themselves inspired to set up new cults was partly the result of the doctrine of self-expression and partly a reflection of equalitarianism. To repressed and obscure souls with flaming ambitions the launching of a new gospel of salvation was a way out of their obscurity. Those who followed the new leaders similarly asserted their individuality and freedom in religious matters by defying established sects, authorities, and traditions. Largely but by no means solely a phenomenon of rural New England and the West, "come-outism" in religion was one of the striking evidences that the common man was in revolt.

The Shaker sect or United Society of Believers in Christ's Second Appearing was an early illustration of democratic "come-outism." The foundress of the movement was an extremely humble, neurotic, and magnetic Englishwoman, Mother Ann Lee, who was given to religious prophecies and ecstasies. Her condemnation of marriage and her advocacy of celibacy, related no doubt to her own unhappy marital experiences, occasioned suspicion and enmity in the various neighborhoods in which she found herself after her arrival in America in 1774. The opposition to her and her followers was deepened by reason of her denunciation of all war and private property and her advocacy of the communal way of life. Mother Ann Lee also rejected many accepted religious beliefs, including the Atonement, the resurrection of the body, election, and the authority of the Bible. Each individual in the Shaker communities contributed in the course of everyday living to "new religious truths" which in turn were shared by others. Women were regarded as equal with men not only in their capacity to contribute to religious revelation but in all other matters.

The communal life of the dozen or more Shaker communities established by the end of the eighteenth century in New England, New York, Ohio, and Kentucky was also essentially democratic. All shared and shared joyously in the common tasks of the community; both Mother Ann and her competent successor, Lucy Wright, advocated the entire fusion of religion and work. All shared in the creation of the "gifts" or religious-esthetic worship through songs and dances. Although these dances and songs followed a general pattern, they were nevertheless always regarded as new living expressions designed to effect a progress from one spiritual level to another and higher one. In the same way the "testimony" or spiritual autobiography was a living expression, both individual and communal in nature and function. The Shaker crafts, marked by an economy and symmetry of line and mass, were group products designed for use, and were a thoroughly integrated part of the common life. "What they created was all of a piece," Constance Rourke has written in her appreciative essay on the Shakers in *The Roots of American Culture*: "it was all social, all functional, all for use, chairs, tables, labor-saving devices, seeds, herbs. Perhaps their philosophy of change gave the Shakers still further creative strength, permitting flexible adaptations and a free flow of inherent creative powers." Thus a simple people, proud of its humble lineage and status, created in a democratic way arts, crafts, dances, songs, customs, even a language, which were truly communal, a folk expression. At the same time the Shakers defied the authority of churches and religions, institutions, and the state.

Far less significant but also representative of the "come-outism" of the time was the community which Jemima Wilkinson of Rhode Island established at Seneca Lake in upstate New York. Imbued with the idea of imitating Mother Ann Lee, Jemima Wilkinson also advocated celibacy and the community life. Although she attracted followers who were dissatisfied with other religions, her disciples became restive because of the imperial majesty that she feigned and because of her lust for power and property.

Jemima Wilkinson was quickly forgotten, but other leaders of religious revolt appeared. Those common folk who had no heart for Calvinism with its low view of human nature and its aristocratic implications or for the intellectualism of the Unitarians turned to new cults. Christian Perfectionism promised to fulfill the need. This doctrine, which had a long history in Christian thought, was rediscovered by Charles G. Finney, who in the 1820s began an amazingly successful career as an evangelist. To the common people who flocked to barns, schoolhouses, and open-air meetings to hear him, Finney preached the doctrine that every human being, by exercise of the will and by cultivation of "right intention," might achieve a high state of spiritual stability (sanctification). Since sin and holiness could not exist in the same person, Finney's theology was attacked by conservatives as tending toward Perfectionism. It is easy to see how such preaching, with its high estimate of human ability and power, appealed to the common man in a period when he was emerging to a new consciousness of his actual and potential significance.

As the years passed, other leaders emerged with varying interpretations of the basic Perfectionist tenet that sin cannot exist in a state of sanctification. Oberlin in Ohio became a center of one interpretation, Oneida in New York the focus of another. The Oberlin group made a point of Scriptural orthodoxy; the Oneida group, led by John Humphrey Noyes, frankly held that divine guidance superseded Scripture and theology. "Our business," wrote Noyes, "is to be coworkers with God in ushering in the last period of man's education—the second Reformation —*the victory and reign of spiritual wisdom and power.*"[18] Noyes achieved notoriety by joining with Perfectionism the idea of community living and the doctrines of eugenics and free love. These innovations implied the power of ordinary men and women to become free of sin and to conduct themselves as colleagues of God Himself in the business of everyday living.

Perfectionism by no means marked the limit of inventiveness on the part of religious leaders in this age of "come-outism." In 1831 William Miller, a simple farmer, began to preach in the churches in his vicinity in Massachusetts, New York, and Vermont the doctrine of the immediate second coming of Christ. By ingenious interpretations of the time periods mentioned in Daniel and Revelation, Miller concluded that in or about the year 1843 the Lord Jesus Christ would return to earth in visible form, gather His faithful, raise the dead, reward the saints, and establish the literal Kingdom of God under the whole heavens. Through preaching and published tracts, Miller and his disciple, the Reverend Joshua V. Himes, gripped the imagination of great numbers in the city and the country. In spite of, perhaps because of, the opposition of evangelicals, Calvinists, and Unitarians, the cult developed so rapidly that by 1843 it numbered 1,000,000 followers, many of whom assembled on housetops in special ascension robes on the day appointed for the second coming. In part the popularity of Millerism was the result of the hard times of the later 1830s. Life was so harsh for many that the gospel of the Second Coming was grasped in an effort to solve what seemed to be insoluble difficulties. But Millerism spread not only because it promised the troubled and hard-pressed common man an immediate Utopia, but

[18] *The Perfectionist,* III (February 15, 1843), 1.

because its defiance of established authoritarian religions and its insistence on the wiping out of all earthly distinctions on Judgment Day expressed democratic yearnings.

Puritan mysticism, let loose on new soil without the conventional restraints, found expression in the visions of emotionally unstable sons of the people. No vision was destined to have more far-reaching results than the appearance of an angelic visitor to young Joseph Smith in upstate New York on a memorable evening in 1827. By the help of two curious transparent stones, this restless, semiliterate but shrewd youth of Vermont origin was enabled, he claimed, to read the hieroglyphic characters engraved on two golden plates. What he read and had transcribed was the story of one of the lost tribes, the ancestors of the American Indians, and the prophecies of Mormon, who revealed God's special and latest Word for the particular benefit of His people in America. The *Book of Mormon* and the cult which grew up around it purported to be a distinctively American religion and as such appealed to the rising nationalistic fervor which sought independence from the Old World in every sphere of thought.

The appeal of Mormonism to the common people also resulted from certain features which promised to elevate their lot and to provide satisfactions to them on many levels. The Mormon emphasis on highly moral conduct revivified among people of Puritan background the old Puritan virtues, which were given new religious sanctions. Polygamy appealed to unmarried women as an economic solution for the difficulties imposed by the frontier on women without husbands. Although Mormonism in its social and economic as well as its religious aspects was based on a dictatorial paternalism, this involved group cooperation for the well-being of the group. In the course of its migrations westward and its persecutions at the hands of "Gentiles," Mormonism developed the "United Order," an experiment in economic planning designed to redistribute property in the interest of greater equality. Influenced no doubt by the religious communism of such groups as the Rappites and Shakers, Smith "revealed" God's will that surplus property and surplus production beyond family needs be turned over to the Bishop's Storehouse for the use of the needy and the upbuilding of the community. This plan, which did not survive in its totality, greatly influenced Mormon conceptions of group responsibility, particularly after the great trek to Utah. Mormon followers at least experienced the blessings of a sense of social responsibility for all members of the group. The conviction, spread by proselyters among the masses of the Old World as well as in the East, that Mormonism promised a social Utopia accounted for much of its success in recruiting disciples.

The multiplication of sects did not proceed without efforts for church unity in the interest of popular understanding of confusing religious dogmas. When Alexander and Thomas Campbell, Scotsmen and Presbyterians, found themselves the leaders of a new sect, the Disciples of Christ, they did what they could to promote unity between their followers and another group called Christians. The Christians had stemmed from the Methodists, Baptists, and Presbyterians under the leadership of James O'Kelley, Abner Jones, and Barton Stone. The name "Christian" reflected the effort to bring an end to denominationalism; the plea to return to the Scriptures reflected a hope that all subsequent denominational quarrels might be prevented. This position was in part a reaction against excessively bitter sectarianism. But its support among ordinary people was also an expression of their conviction that untutored minds could grasp the essentials of Christian faith. To that degree at least, the Campbellite and Christian movements were democratic protests on the part of people weary with denominational wrangling over the fine issues of abstruse theology.

The essentially democratic developments in the religious expression of the period did not sweep away all traces of undemocratic thought within the Christian fold. The churches only hesitantly faced some of the great issues involving the democratic principle. Clergymen frequently blessed that which was least democratic in the rising industrial capitalism; the doctrine that poverty and the ills of this world are inconsequential, for instance, found eloquent exponents in the pulpit. This doctrine was acceptable to many among the poor because it helped them endure their lot. By reason of their divided constituencies many religious leaders hesitated to take a definite stand on slavery. In 1844, however, the majority of the Methodists, one of the most democratic sects, condemned it; the result was a cleavage within the church along sectional lines. Similar cleavages followed in other denominations. Still other denominations succeeded in evading the issue, and the southern churches blessed slavery. Yet in spite of these limitations to the democratic impulse in religion, impressive gains in the democratization of the churches could not be denied.

## Immigrant Contributions

Driven to America by economic hardships, religious dissatisfaction, political persecution, and ambition for a fuller life, at least 2,500,000 immigrants sought, during the 1840s and 1850s, the opportunities offered by railway construction, rising factories and mills, and the rich farm lands of the advancing frontier. In 1850 the foreign-born constituted one-tenth of the population.

The great majority of the newcomers were simple, uneducated folk, but men of cultivation and learning also sought our shores. The latter's contributions to American intellectual development did not always have a direct bearing on democratic ideas. Yet in a sense the presence of newcomers of intellectual and artistic stature helped break down the traditional association of arts, letters, and the sciences with patrician leadership.

Students of American immigration have emphasized the contributions that music-loving Germans made to a broader appreciation of music by native-born Americans, many of whom rationalized their ignorance of the art by belittling it as useless and effeminate. Often a single immigrant broke down the prejudice toward music and inculcated a love of it among his neighbors; thus Johann Heinrich Weber, to cite but one example, put to good use the scores of Bach, Beethoven, Handel, Haydn, and Mozart which he brought with him to St. Louis in 1834. Amateur singing societies held music festivals that educated many Americans to an appreciation of the value of music in everyday living. The great German migration of the 1830s and 1840s included talented professional musicians who organized numerous orchestras, the most famous of which was the "Germania." This orchestra introduced Beethoven's Ninth Symphony to Bostonians and in the six years of its existence performed over 800 concerts in several cities. The rise of many conservatories and the improvement of musical instruments also resulted from the presence of the Germans. Nor was music the only art that the newcomers enriched. In painting, the stimulus given and the contributions made by Bierstadt, Leutze, and others constituted a chapter in the growth of esthetic appreciation among Americans.

Science, too, gained much from the activities of immigrants. To Ferdinand Rudolph Hassler and Claude Crozet Americans owed the introduction of analytical and descriptive geometry, and Hassler established the work of the geological survey on firm foundations. In 1845–1846 a scientifically designed suspension bridge—it spanned the Monongahela River—introduced to the American public the name of John A. Roebling; but he was only one among many immigrant engineers in whom American railways, bridges, and urban waterworks systems found master designers. Other immigrants virtually established the manufacture of scientific instruments. Medicine profited from the arrival of excellently trained men, who frequently established the first specialized practices in hitherto slightly known fields. Homeopathy and pharmacy—each important in view of the crude and excessive use of drugs in those days —were launched on their American careers by Germans. One immigrant, Louis Agassiz, a Swiss by birth, opened a new chapter in the history of American geology and biology.

Newcomers also enriched the humanistic disciplines. Charles Follen introduced the study of German at Harvard. Francis Lieber, in editing his *Encyclopaedia Americana*, persuaded specialists to share their knowledge with a wider public and popularized the German idea of bibliographical references and documentation. From his chair at South Carolina College Lieber also produced the first works in political science by an American private scholar. Along with Beck and other Germans, he helped popularize the idea of physical education as a requisite basis for the well-rounded cultivation of the mind.

In certain areas of thought immigrants definitely reinforced or broadened the concept of liberalism and democracy. When they reached American shores many of them felt as did Hans Barlien, a disciple of Voltaire and a leader of the small farmers in Norway in their long struggle with the aristocrats, when he wrote, "Now for the first time am I able to breathe freely." The introduction of Fourierism into the United States owed much to American proponents, but the presence of many immigrants imbued with these ideas was also a telling factor in the social experimentation of the Jacksonian era. Victor Considérant founded a Fourieristic phalanx in Texas, and the Icarian settlements of French immigrants also aroused interest. Other Utopian experiments flourished for a time at Dr. Wilhelm Keil's Bethel community in Missouri and at the settlement of Bishop Hill in Illinois founded by the Swede, Eric Janson. German immigrants later founded in Iowa the renowned cooperative community, Amana. Carl Heinzen, a disciple of

Proudhon, promoted the anarchistic ideas of his master, and Wilhelm Weitling, a friend of Marx and Engels, gave direction to the German socialist workers in the large cities. The opposition of many German immigrants—members of the rank and file as well as such leaders as Carl Schurz—to slavery was another evidence of the support which the newcomers gave to democratic thought in American life.

The presence of great numbers of recent immigrants aroused the opposition of many who for various reasons were prejudiced against them. Southerners were inclined to look with disfavor on them partly on the ground that they tended to oppose slavery. The radical ideologies of the relatively small number of immigrants subscribing to some form of Utopian socialism aroused the opposition of property-conscious and individualistic Americans. American workers resented the fact that the newcomers were willing to accept lower wages than the prevailing ones. But the hostility toward them, which found expression in the 1830s in the Native American or Nativist movement, seems to have rested largely on other grounds.

The deep-dyed Protestant suspicion of Catholicism, the religion of considerable numbers of Germans and of the bulk of the Irish, was expressed in violent attacks on Catholic churches and institutions and in a vehement crusade in the press and on the lecture platform. Catholicism was regarded by militant Protestants as undemocratic and therefore un-American. The failure of a movement on the part of Catholic laymen in Philadelphia and Buffalo to wrest the control of church property from the clergy confirmed many Protestant Americans in their conviction regarding the undemocratic character of Catholic ecclesiasticism. Samuel F. B. Morse, portrait painter and inventor of the telegraph, led in the onslaught against the Catholics. "The question of Popery and Protestantism, or Absolutism and Republicanism, which in these two opposite categories are convertible terms," he wrote, "is fast becoming and will shortly be the great absorbing question, not only of this country, but of the whole civilized world."[19]

Nativism, however, aroused opposition. Even though we admit the prejudice, the credulous bigotry, the violence, and the political repercussions incident to the Nativist movement, it seems probable that the great majority of old-stock Americans welcomed the immigrants. Na-

---

[19] *Samuel F.B. Morse; His Life and Letters* (Houghton Mifflin Company, 1914), II, 36.

tivism was regarded as antithetical to the traditional idea that America was an asylum for the oppressed of all the world. The essence of Americanism, in the minds of men like Emerson and Whitman, was the opportunity that the United States provided to one and all alike, whatever their background. Robert Dale Owen contended that Nativism was itself un-American by reason of the basic suspicion of democracy which it implied.

The presence of a mass of immigrants indirectly promoted the democratic ideal of free public schools. Owing largely to the increase of the foreign-born in the population, illiteracy among the whites jumped from 3.77 percent in 1830 to 5.03 percent in 1850. Concerned lest this illiteracy of the foreign-born, together with their unfamiliarity with American institutions, might jeopardize the national experiment, educational reformers appealed for larger support for public schools in order that the immigrant might be Americanized. His presence was a weighty factor in the growing conviction that public schools were indispensable to the well-being of the Republic. This conviction was confirmed in 1841 when Archbishop Hughes, the Catholic bishop of New York, seemed about to win a victory in a heated campaign for state support of parochial schools.

Democratic theory and practice, then, were greatly affected by and in turn affected immigrants, new religious sects, the revolutionary impulse in the Old World, and the rise of an industrial culture. But this was not all. Equalitarian thought and practice interpenetrated many other areas of American life. Science and technology, the popularization of knowledge, social relationships, and patriotic sentiment—all these were related to the new currents of equalitarianism.

# 13 The Advance of Science and Technology

*To one great lesson the world is beginning to listen: Faith in human power. The truth it enforces is all potent for good. Before it, every obstacle must eventually give way, and to it every element and influence in nature will be subject. Not till mechanical as well as ethical science is fully explored and universally applied can man attain his destiny and evil be swept from the earth.*

*—THOMAS EWBANK, 1855*

*How many fine inventions are there which do not clutter the ground? We think that those only succeed which minister to our sensible and animal wants, which bake or brew, wash or warm, or the like. But are those of no account which are patented by fancy and imagination, and succeed so admirably in our dreams that they give the tone still to our waking thoughts?*

*—HENRY THOREAU, 1843*

Closely connected with the equalitarian currents of the second quarter of the nineteenth century was the continued progress of natural science. It was no longer the concern merely of learned men and the cultivated few; the life of the common people increasingly provided science with new problems, and common people even helped to solve them. The rapid progress in science was thus partly the result of the awakening of

310

the people in the ordinary walks of life, and it was also one of the causes of this awakening.

## The Continued Stimulus of Patriotism, Religion, and Utilitarianism

The advance of democracy as a factor in scientific thought and activity did not exclude the continued operation of traditional forces. The early patriotic zeal for initiative and achievement sufficient to free America from the charge of thralldom to Europe still motivated friends of science and scientists themselves. In the minds of such men as John Quincy Adams patriotic pride in the contributions America might make to learning was enough to justify any modest outlay of funds from the public treasury. Especially dear to the heart of the learned President from maritime New England was a government observatory. He pleaded for it in his first annual message in 1825: "While scarcely a year passes over our heads without bringing some new astronomical discovery to light, which we must fain receive at second hand from Europe, are we not cutting ourselves off from the means of returning light for light while we have neither observatory nor observer upon our half of the globe and the earth revolves in perpetual darkness to our unsearching eyes?"[1] Patriotic intellectuals felt humiliated seven years later when the English astronomer Airy, in writing on the state of astronomy in the world, reported he could say nothing of American astronomy inasmuch as there were no public observatories in that country. That situation was remedied, to the great satisfaction of patriotic intellectuals, when observatories were established in the 1840s at Harvard and in Cincinnati and Washington.

In 1847 Benjamin Silliman of Yale, who had founded the *American Journal of Science* in 1818 to advance science to "the elevation of our national character," proudly reported that science had progressed by leaps and bounds in the United States. Its devotees, he pointed out no less proudly, had even awakened European interest in American research by the treasure of facts they had provided.

Yet the debt of American science to Europe gave no sign of ending. It was no longer indispensable for every young aspirant to go abroad,

[1] James D. Richardson (ed.), A Compilation of the Messages and Papers of the Presidents, 1789–1902 (Government Printing Office, 1896–1897), II, 314.

but travel in the Old World was still thought highly desirable. John Torrey, when appointed to the faculty of New York University, went to Europe to buy apparatus for a laboratory much as Silliman himself had done a quarter of a century earlier. Henry D. Rogers of Dickinson College, like dozens of fellow Americans, studied with the great scientists of the Old World. Seven years after Dr. Joseph Henry had anticipated Faraday in the discovery of self-induction in electromagnetism, he felt impelled to seek the stimulus of Europe's masters of specialized knowledge. Asa Gray, in Darwin's eyes destined to become one of the great botanists of his time, crossed the Atlantic in 1838 to equip himself in the Old World herbaria for his projected description of American flora. Gray also purchased on this trip a basic library for the University of Michigan, and observed European higher education, both scientific and general. Gray's journey illustrates early American respect for European science, and the dependence of the young American universities on Europe as a scientific guide. In the field of medicine the great French clinician, Pierre Louis, inspired Dr. Oliver Wendell Holmes and other eminent American students of medicine—particularly William Gerhardt, C. W. Pennock, and George Shattuck—to abandon the traditional preoccupation with general theories and to turn to clinical observations and quantitative case histories—methods that enabled them to make notable contributions to the pathology of cholera, typhus, tubercular meningitis, and general medicine.

Immigration, it will be recalled, was continually enriching American science in every field. But the coming of Louis Agassiz in 1846 was of almost incalculable importance. His robust, animated spirit generated contagious enthusiasm for science irrespective of its practical applications and implications. Introducing the laboratory method in zoology, Agassiz encouraged American naturalists to break away from concern with classification and to explore the internal functioning of animals. Of great moment in the field of geology was his bold glacial theory, which explained curious land formations and the chaotic distribution of great boulders in terms of vast retreating ice sheets. Here was testimony to the value of the hypothetical, philosophical approach, to the search for the larger meaning of things.

European scientists, as Silliman proudly observed in 1847, continued to learn from America as they had done from the time of Linnaeus. Lyell, the greatest among the geologists of his time, paid this country two scientific visits. In Berlin Humboldt followed with appetite the researches of American scientists, taking pride in the great advances in knowledge made in the Republic that he had visited at the beginning of the century. Darwin himself eagerly sought data from the New World. Thus American science continued to be closely related to that of England, Germany, and France.

Still other inherited patterns guided American scientists in the Jacksonian era. The traditional conflict between naturalism and supernaturalism had not been resolved. For instance, Dr. Thomas Cooper of South Carolina in 1833 published a pamphlet, *On the Connection between Geology and the Pentateuch,* in which he deplored the efforts to square irreconcilables. More important than the survivals of the earlier assumption that science contradicted Revelation were the continued and ever more prominent efforts on the part of religious-minded scientists to reconcile naturalism and supernaturalism.

Virtually all the leading scientists in the 1830s and 1840s accepted in one or another form the basic doctrine of Christian theology and explicitly tried to show that no contradiction existed between science and religion. In his college edition of Bakewell's *Geology* Silliman tried to make the facts of that science accord with Genesis. Despite the fact that this effort aroused the wrath of Dr. Thomas Cooper, Silliman continued to maintain that all the findings of field study and the laboratory confirmed Scripture. His gifted pupil, James Dwight Dana, was of one mind on this point with his master. So, too, was the Swiss-American, Arnold Guyot, who, like Dana, tried to see in the Bible's misty, poetical account of creation a more or less exact statement of natural phenomena. In the same spirit Lieutenant Maury, the Virginian who won world fame for creating oceanography, clung to the literal interpretation of the Bible. "If the two cannot be reconciled," he declared in speaking of science and Revelation, "the fault is ours, and it is ours because, in our blindness and weakness, we have not been able to interpret aright either the one or the other."[2]

Some scientists, however, did not insist on the literal truth of the Scriptural account of creation and the deluge. The Reverend Edward Hitchcock, director of the geographical survey of Masachusetts and president of Amherst College, making no efforts at literal reconciliation,

[2] Diana Fontaine Maury Corbin, A *Life of Matthew Fontaine Maury* (London, 1888), 106.

argued in *The Religion of Geology and its Connected Sciences* (1852) that the principles of science are a transcript of Divine Character. Furthermore, Hitchcock continued, the main use of science is its confirmation of religion. In somewhat the same vein Agassiz wrote that natural history is a means for analyzing the thoughts of the Creator of the Universe, for discovering and thinking God's ideas after Him.

Geologists did not monopolize the efforts to prove that science confirmed religion. In his popular *Letters on Astronomy* (1840) Dennison Olmstead, a leading astronomer, declared that the structure and arrangement of, as well as the laws prevailing among, heavenly bodies proved the existence of God and His unity, wisdom, and power. If the heart were already under the spell of religion, Olmstead concluded, the frequent and habitual contemplation of the heavenly bodies must promote the religious virtues of humility, devotion, and grateful adoration.

Outside the ranks of scientists proper scholars such as John Quincy Adams and the liberal Congregational minister of Hartford, Horace Bushnell, likewise declared that the lessons of field and laboratory confirmed those of religion. Indeed, the assimilation of science by the more progressive religious thinkers began long before the appearance of new conflicts aroused by Darwinism.

In this period, as in other times, sheer curiosity and a disinterested love of truth exerted a powerful sway over scientific investigators. Such motives undoubtedly explain why young Dr. Joseph Leidy of Philadelphia undertook his researches in vertebrate paleontology, researches which proved that long before Columbus discovered America the horse, the camel, and the rhinocerous had roamed the western plains. Scientific curiosity was very likely the motivation for Ephraim George Squier's archeological studies of ancient monuments in the Mississippi valley.

But definitely utilitarian needs claimed increasing attention from scientists. In the older parts of the country soil exhaustion, already a problem in the earlier decades of the century, continued to challenge agricultural chemists to experiments in which they profited from the pioneer work of the great German, Liebig. The studies of the Virginia planter, Edmund Ruffin, were especially notable in this field. The West no less than the seaboard states posed practical problems which stimulated scientific advances. With the expansion of the frontier, new demands arose for engineers trained in surveying lands and minerals beneath the earth, and for charts of rivers and lakes for a rising inland commerce. The formidable and important task of exploring and evaluating the vast reaches of land beyond the Mississippi was one of the most important factors in making the federal government a powerful and often effective patron of science.

Maritime commerce also set concrete problems for scientists. Dr. Joseph Henry, whose work in electromagnetism was of prime significance, spent much time in the laboratories of the College of New Jersey and the Smithsonian Institution experimenting with acoustics in order to perfect a foghorn for mariners. Commercial interests obviously stood to benefit from the work of the Coast Survey, which added materially to topographical and geological knowledge. Maritime America also supported far-reaching plans for charting leading sea lanes under government auspices in the interest of greater speed and safety. While it would be too much to say that the monumental achievements of Lieutenant Maury in this field were the direct result of the behests of merchantmen and whalers, these shrewd and adventuresome Americans were quick to see the bearing of his work.

In the discussions arising in the late 1820s and 1830s over the projected naval exploring expedition, the patriotic argument that such a project would bring America the prestige European governments had won by similar ventures was coupled with a utilitarian justification. The expedition, it was argued, would chart better ocean highways by discovering shoals and reefs and dangerous currents; it would detect superior whaling waters; and it would insure respect for American merchantmen when they touched savage-inhabited islands in the southern seas. "Should it be said," asked one enthusiast in Congress, "that we, who are the second if not the first commercial nation in the world, must continue to navigate the ocean with the defective charts furnished us by foreigners?" Before Congress finally committed itself to the project, considerable pressure had been exerted not only by the indefatigably patriotic and sea-minded Ohio lawyer, John N. Reynolds, but also by the East India Marine Society and the legislatures of eight interested states.

The rising mines and factories also stimulated scientists to pursue problems closely related to industrial needs. In his *Report to the Corporation of Brown University* (1850) President Francis Wayland declared that, in view of the imperative industrial demands of the country, colleges must respond by equipping young men for useful careers in foundries, shops, and mills. Instructors in chemistry at Brown inaugurated lectures on metals and on calico printing, lectures that were designed to promote Rhode Island's industries. The experiments with crude oil made by an instructor at Dartmouth sank into the memory of a student, George H. Bissell, who leased land in western Pennsylvania and sent a specimen of the oil which seeped up to the surface to Benjamin Silliman, Jr., professor of chemistry at Yale. In a remarkable report drawn up in 1855, Silliman advanced the opinion that a first-rate illuminant might be made from petroleum at slight cost, and on the basis of this report Bissell became a promoter of a great new industry. Academicians made other contributions to the development of industrial wealth. Amos Eaton, itinerant lecturer on science, promoter of the first geological survey of New York, and virtual founder of Rensselaer Institute, was a pioneer in the use of the laboratory to prepare boys to become "operative chemists" and builders of many of the bridges and other engineering projects so indispensable to the development of industry. A discussion of the advances made in applied science or technology will demonstrate that on the whole, however, the needs of industry were met by inventors rather than by academic scientists. Nevertheless, Louis Agassiz, European-trained but devoted to his adopted land, deplored the prevailing tendency of American scientists to concentrate on problems of utilitarian significance. Indeed, many agreed with Tocqueville in believing that the failure of American scientists in this period to contribute substantially to general theory was to be laid at the door of utilitarian pressure.

## Professionalism and Organization

In many respects the years between 1830 and 1850 formed, in spite of the survival of older influences and problems, a new chapter in the history of American science and technology. Most of the earlier leaders passed from the scene. The death of Dr. Samuel Latham Mitchill in 1831, of Thomas Say in 1834, and, before 1840, of Nathaniel Bowditch, Constantine Rafinesque, William Maclure, and Dr. Thomas Cooper, marked a turning point. The men that took their places were in large measure professional scientists. Devoting their entire time to the laboratory and field work, they also drew their chief means of livelihood from science; the increasing support given it by the colleges and government made this possible. This is by no means to say that interest in science as an avocation on the part of physicians, merchants, planters, and ministers disappeared. On the contrary, scientific interest became more widely diffused than ever before. But the leadership was now provided not by busy statesmen like Jefferson or versatile physicians like Dr. Mitchill or planters, merchants, or parsons, but by college professors and the civil, naval, and military servants of the government. In addition, the rapid growth of popular interest in science made lecturing and the writing of textbooks such profitable supplementary sources of revenue for scientists.

One mark of professionalism was the specialization that tended to replace the former concern with the whole field of science. The breaking down of science into its particular fields was necessitated by the vast developments in science that had taken and were taking place. But such specialization was made possible only by virtue of the fact that American society was now becoming more complex, more populous, and more wealthy. Equally important was the growing awareness on the part of farmers, merchants, and industrialists that science promised to provide solutions for problems and instruments for further efficiency and expansion.

Thus the United States Exploring Expedition, as it set out on its voyage to the antipodes in 1838, carried with it not only all-round scientists devoted to many fields, but also a mineralogist, a conchologist, a horticulturist, a botanist, and a philologist, in addition to two distinguished naturalists and two navy officers competent in hydrography, geography, astronomy, meteorology, and physics. When Benjamin Silliman retired from the faculty of Yale in 1853, no one dreamed of replacing him by a scientist competent to teach geology as well as chemistry and the other branches for which he had been responsible when he began his work in 1806. The classical curriculum might continue to dominate the colleges, but the particularized sciences made many inroads. Moreover, new institutions such as Rensselaer, the Franklin Institute, and the Lawrence and Sheffield foundations at Harvard and Yale devoted themselves solely to research and training in the scientific fields.

The degree of specialization can be further appreciated by a study of scientific publications. The *American Journal of Science* did, it is true, devote itself to the field of general science. But periodicals for the particular disciplines, which in earlier years had proved to be of short endurance, now came to be accepted as if in the nature of things. Another reflection of this specialization was the fact that Noah Webster had to add some thousand scientific terms to his revised *Dictionary* of 1840. Perhaps the best way to appreciate the growing division of labor is to turn through the pages of Max Meisel's monumental *Bibliography of American Natural History*, which lists the titles of scientific publications in the century spanned by the years 1765 and 1865.

Science entered into a new era not only by reason of its growing specialization but also by virtue of the greater attention given to its organization and promotion. In the late eighteenth century and the first quarter of the nineteenth, many scientists had indeed belonged to one of the learned societies, such as the American Philosophical Society, the American Academy of Arts and Sciences, or the natural history societies in New York, Philadelphia, and Charleston. But these were local groups so far as attendance and participation went, and there was no central organization that included all scientists, with provisions for the constant association of specialists within the larger framework. Nor was there any central clearing house which regularly received and distributed the publications of foreign societies. Such investigations as individuals carried on were pursued largely in isolation; there was little planned coordination of efforts. In the 1830s and 1840s this general situation underwent marked changes.

If any name must be singled out among those who contributed to the promotion and organization of science, it would have to be that of Benjamin Silliman. The *American Journal of Science* became one of the great scientific journals of the world. The notices it gave to scientific publications created an *esprit de corps* among scientists, and in providing a regular vehicle for original researches it encouraged investigators throughout the land. Through the training he gave to his assistants at Yale, Silliman was also largely responsible for the brilliant group of young scientists who took such active roles in all the scientific enterprises of the period. And finally, by his extremely successful popular lectures delivered from Boston to New Orleans, he did much to stimulate a nation-wide enthusiasm for science.

Silliman was not alone, of course. Joseph Henry and his associates at the Smithsonian encouraged a wide variety of scientific inquiries and explorations. Alexander Dallas Bache, an adept politician as well as a trained scientist, worked to make government participation in science more purposeful and fruitful. Asa Gray and Benjamin Peirce used their rising reputations and their energies to promote closer cooperation among scientists, and between science and the federal government.

But the tendency toward organization was broader and more significant than any one leader could account for or provide. The traditionally American way of effecting through mutual and voluntary association larger purposes than individuals alone could achieve found expression in 1848 in the organization of the American Association for the Advancement of Science. The stimulus was given by the Association of American Geologists and Naturalists, but the statement of purposes and rules indicated that the new group was patterned after the British Association established in 1831. Meeting annually or even semiannually in widely scattered cities, the American Association, through its subsections devoted to the discussion of papers in particular fields and through its publications, not only brought scientists together but stimulated investigation and cooperation. By 1854 the original 471 members had increased to over a thousand, including two women. One of these, Maria Mitchell, was known throughout the western civilized world by reason of her independent discovery of a comet.

## Government Participation

During the years between the election of Jackson and the Civil War, the state and federal governments became perhaps the most important agencies for the promotion of science. Stimulated by the hope of discovering unknown minerals, state after state embarked on geological surveys. The North Carolina survey (1824–1828) was a pioneer undertaking. The Massachusetts survey, begun in 1830 under the direction of Edward Hitchcock of Amherst, published its findings in 1833. Before the opening of the Civil War almost every state had carried out one or more such surveys. That of New York was of particular significance because it included the stratographic record for which the great paleontologist, James Hall, was responsible. Beginning about 1840, many states also surveyed their flora and especially their fauna; the natural history surveys of Massachusetts and New York were outstanding examples of cooperative investigation. All these state surveys involved systematic investigation which no isolated individual could perform.

Gradually, and against opposition, the federal government itself took an enlarged share in the promotion of scientific research. The overland expeditions into the frontier country, which had become well established in the public mind as a result of the work of Lewis and Clark, continued to yield, under army leadership, valuable knowledge of the geography, geology, and natural history of the remoter areas of the West. Notwithstanding these precedents, it was no easy task to break down the barriers standing in the way of an enlargement of the functions of the federal government in the field of scientific investigation.

A variety of interests and arguments emerged to thwart exponents of federal support of research. Advocates of laissez faire, a philosophy which in theory enjoyed growing popularity, would have none of it. Advocates of states' rights looked with profound distrust on any measures tending to expand the powers of the central government. If a projected undertaking, such as the Coast Survey, redounded chiefly to the benefit of the maritime East, inlanders raised protesting cries of favoritism.

Many laymen found it hard to grasp the importance of scientific research. The people's money, they contended, had better be spent on practical needs at home rather than in remote regions. Thus one congressman declared that the United States Exploring Expedition might as well try to explore the bizarre cylindrical world of the crack-brained Symmes as to pursue the journey that it proposed; another compared the venture to a voyage to the moon! In addition to all these obstacles, jealousy and bureaucratic vices in the armed services sometimes hindered the scientific enterprises that the government did undertake. This was notably true in regard to the naming of a commander for the United States Exploring Expedition, which got under way only after disgraceful bickering and delay.

Nevertheless, in response to the urgings of commercial and maritime interests and in recognition of the military and naval need for scientific knowledge, the area of federal activity in scientific investigation was steadily enlarged. After Ferdinand Hassler had twice undertaken and twice been relieved of the responsibility for a coast survey, Jackson reinstated him in 1832. In the decade left to him, the Swiss engineer set such high standards for an exact geodetic survey of the coasts that the pattern he outlined was followed in subsequent extensions of the enterprise. His successor, Alexander Dallas Bache, a great-grandson of Franklin, extended the work into the hydrographic and magnetic fields. In the seventeen years between 1843 and 1860 Bache was permitted to spend $4 million on the Coast Survey and related activities. To parallel the work of this survey Congress in 1841 provided for an up-to-date survey of the Great Lakes.

These admirable beginnings in the field of marine geography were greatly forwarded by Lieutenant Matthew Fontaine Maury, the Virginia naval officer to whom reference has already been made. Before Maury became director of the National Observatory and Hydrographical Department he was known chiefly as the author of *A New Theoretical and Practical Treatise on Navigation* (1836), for many years a standard treatise. In his new office he studied the old logs of vessels to determine relationships between winds, currents, and temperature in various seasons, in the hope that existing charts of routes on the high seas might be tested and ultimately replaced by superior ones. Maury obtained permission to present blank forms or abstract logs to every master of an American vessel, to be filled in during the course of a given voyage. As one of his admirers put it, the sea was asked "to grant a continuous interview and thus to have its autobiography written." From the data thus obtained he established definite relationships between winds, tides, waves, currents, and storms. In fact, when he published *The Physical Geography of the Sea* (1855), he was hailed by no less an authority than Humboldt as the creator and master of a new science, oceanography. The maritime world proclaimed its gratitude to the man whose charts enabled mariners to cut down lengthy voyages by many days, to avoid hitherto unknown drifts and unforeseen storms, and to insure the safer delivery of goods at lower insurance rates. The obvious advantages to commerce led in 1853 to an international conference at Brussels which Maury dominated and which recommended to the maritime nations cooperation with the American's project.

Closely related to Maury's work and that of the coast and geodetic survey were the investigations which centered in the Naval Observatory at Washington. Long desired by Jefferson, John Quincy Adams, and other leaders, this observatory grew out of the astronomical work of the depot of charts and instruments. With the dispatch of the United States Exploring Expedition in 1838, daily observations and calculations were made in order that the expedition's longitudinal observations might subsequently be evaluated. This work, accomplished with a high degree of accuracy by Lieutenant James M. Gilliss, was published in the official documents of the Senate as *Astronomical Observations*. It constituted the first notable contribution to research in celestial mechanics sponsored by the federal government.

After purchasing in Europe a library and instruments for the new government observatory which was completed in 1844, Gilliss was authorized by Congress to conduct observations in Chile. In addition to meteorological and magnetic observations, he and his two assistants made 33,000 observations of 23,000 stars at Santiago. Though the results fell short of what might have been accomplished with adequate complementary work at home, the volume of government documents which incorporated the findings gave one more evidence of federal support of scientific research.

The federal government's crowning achievement in scientific research during the 1830s and 1840s grew out of the celebrated United States Exploring Expedition. Commanded by Lieutenant Charles Wilkes, the expedition, after wearing delays and much controversy, set out in 1838. In the four subsequent years it surveyed, in addition to 800 miles of coasts and streams in western North and South America, some 280 islands in the South Atlantic and South Pacific. Moreover, by tracing a 1600-mile shore line, Wilkes demonstrated for the first time the existence of an antarctic continent. He and his naval colleagues also made astronomical observations in the South Seas and assembled a vast amount of data in the fields of navigation, geography, meteorology, terrestrial magnetism, and hydrography.

The civilian scientists, the best known of whom were Dr. Charles Pickering, Titian Peale, and James Dwight Dana, acquitted themselves admirably. In addition to the help they gave Wilkes in the preparation of his five folio volumes, their labors resulted in the gradual appearance of some twenty volumes on mineralogy, geology, biology, and ethnology. Dr. Pickering's *The Chronological History of Plants* was a monument of learning and industry; and the related volumes prepared by Asa Gray, who had been originally designated as botanist, added to the importance of this part of the work. In the field of ethnology the expedition yielded studies of the Polynesian dialects, the geographical distribution of races, and the physical history of man. Perhaps the most significant contributions were those of Dana. By demonstrating that the valleys of the Pacific islands owed their origin, position, and form not to the sea or to structural factors but to existing streams which had eaten their way headward, Dana confirmed the Huttonian theory of the importance of the drowned mouths of river-made valleys. His reports on Crustacea described hundreds of new species and included the first comprehensive studies of coral-forming zoophytes.

In addition to enriching knowledge and making possible the comparative study of science in America, the expedition, through the specimens it brought back, provided the nuclei for the United States National Museum and the United States Botanical Garden.

Although none of the explorations that followed that of Wilkes approached it in scientific importance, the federal government continued to add to the world's knowledge of remote places in a series of expeditions undertaken primarily for commercial purposes. Most of these resulted in the publication of official reports with new data on geography, hydrography, terrestrial magnetism, and other sciences allied to navigation. In South America Lieutenant Thomas Jefferson Page investigated La Plata River and its tributaries, and Lieutenant Isaac Strain explored the Isthmus of Darien. More rewarding was the remarkable expedition of Lieutenant William Herndon, who in 1851 crossed the Andes from the Pacific to the headwaters of the Amazon, which he then followed to its mouth. Even the Dead Sea was surveyed in an expedition led by Lieutenant William Lynch.

In the zest for explorations the arctic was not neglected. Important scientific discoveries resulted from the search which Lieutenant Edwin J. De Haven made in 1850 for the lost English explorer, Sir John Franklin; a similar expedition headed by Dr. Elisha Kane extended knowledge of the Greenland seas. The expeditions of Commander Cadwallader Ringgold and Commander John Rodgers in the early 1850s explored and surveyed the Bering Strait, the North Pacific, and the China Seas. Thanks to the zoological labors of William Stimpson, much new information concerning the marine life of the coasts of Alaska and Japan was gathered. Finally, the three impressive volumes which resulted from Commodore Perry's famous visit to Japan enlightened the world regarding that remote kingdom.

In one additional area the federal government assumed responsibility for the advancement of science. On the seventeenth of December, 1835, President Jackson informed Congress of the bequest of $500,000 to the federal government by one James Smithson, a scion of the English aristocracy and a scientist of some note. John C. Calhoun advocated the rejection of the legacy on the grounds that the government had no power to receive and administer such a sum and that it was beneath the dignity of the United States to accept such a gift from a private individual. But the majority of Congress favored acceptance of the windfall.

It soon became clear that there was no common mind in regard to the proper disposition of the legacy. Smithson's will, indicating as it did that the fund was to be used for the advancement and diffusion of knowledge, occasioned endless discussion. One group preferred to emphasize the diffusion of knowledge. Jefferson Davis, for example, believed that a perpetual series of popular lectures could best effect that end. Andrew Johnson pleaded for the establishment of a normal school to train teachers for the nation's common schools. Rufus Choate, dismissing the objection that the really important thoughts of the world could all be found in a few thousand books, favored the creation of a great library. Others emphasized the importance of the advancement of knowledge and favored the establishment of either a great university, or an observatory, or laboratories for scientific research.

The appeals made for the utilitarian value of science, which was thoroughly discussed, finally prevailed. Thus it was that Congress, in 1846, at length accepted the general outlines of Rufus King's proposal for an institution named for Smithson and administered by the federal government. In its final form the Act specified that the new institution was to further investigation and to disseminate information through a library and museum. The terms were sufficiently general to permit the director, Dr. Joseph Henry, to put the main emphasis on original research. Under his able leadership the Smithsonian Institution became a center for original scientific research especially in physics, archeology, and ethnology. It also functioned as a clearinghouse by making available for the scientists not only of America, but of the entire world, researches in virtually every field of scientific endeavor.

## Technology, Democracy, and Profits

The promotion and organization of science that resulted from the growing spirit of professionalism, from patriotic zeal for achievements, and from the needs of commerce and industry would alone have constituted a new chapter in the history of American science. But the increasingly close collaboration between scientists and mechanics and the quickened tempo of the application of scientific principles to the practical arts still further differentiated scientific activities in the Jacksonian era. The day of the machine was dawning and predictions were forthcoming regarding the lights and shadows of that day.

One of the earliest scientists of repute to use the term technology and to defend what it represented was Dr. Jacob Bigelow of Harvard. In his *Elements of Technology*, published in the year that Jackson entered the White House, Bigelow maintained that the application of science to the arts constituted the chief superiority of modern civilization over that of the ancients. It had transformed not only the physical but the moral and political condition of society. Technology had enabled modern man to "ascend above the clouds and penetrate into the abysses of the ocean"—things the ancients had dreamed of in their fables. It had created the printing press and thus dispersed the darkness of the Middle Ages. It had also revolutionized the art of war by giving the mind great advantages over brute force. Above all, technology had effected profound changes in ways of living in amazingly short periods of time.

The relationships, or assumed relationships, between technology and democracy provided champions of the machine with justifications and arguments in their tussles with classicists, traditionalists, and realistic critics of technology. In the Jacksonian era science and thought about science were profoundly influenced by the idea that investigations in the laboratory and the field might, within the framework of private enterprise and profit, promote the comfort and well-being of the common man. Those who profited by machine industry promoted it, of course, even where benefits to the plain people were not strikingly in evidence. And one could not expect the lords of industry to work for scientific advances that might interfere with their profits. But they as well as ordinary people saw that science and invention could greatly enrich the lives of the masses. This was no new concept, to be sure. At least since the time of Francis Bacon it had found advocates, and, as we have seen, exponents of the Enlightenment cherished it with special tenderness. But many signs indicated that in the 1830s and 1840s this idea enjoyed increasing prestige and found exemplification in practice on a scale more impressive than ever before.

One sign of this was the frequency of references in orations and addresses to Francis Bacon himself. His writings, to be sure, had been known to cultivated men in the colonial period. But in the 1820s and 1830s his defense of the inductive method and especially of the union of natural science and the practical arts exerted wide appeal. Exponents of the application of science to the problems of everyday life could find no authority more venerable. As one writer would have it, Bacon had shown the common man how to defy the authority of church, state, sect, and class by discovering for himself the secrets of nature and using them for his own well-being. He had further taught the artisan, long despised as the drudge of the few, how to elevate himself to comfort and undreamed-of mental heights; he had, in short, foretold how the machine might bring about a true Utopia.

What Bacon had faintly seen and heralded was now in the immediate offing. Modern democracy, holding as it did that man was born to enjoy physical and mental well-being, gave powerful impetus to technology just as, in turn, technology furthered the ideal of democracy, the elevation of the common man. Such a philosophy of action, of utilitarianism, of Utopianism, justified as nothing else could the efforts to harness science for man's well-being. It was no accident that Francis Bacon's ideas were rediscovered and put to work in an era characterized by the rise of the common man.

Of all the writers on technology in the middle period none can excel Thomas Ewbank in interest. Apprenticed at the age of thirteen to a tin and coppersmith in Durham, England, Ewbank subsequently devoted his spare moments in London to scientific study. No doubt he came under the influence of Godwin's thought regarding the relations of science to Utopianism. Convinced that America offered a more congenial soil for proving what applied science could do for mankind, Ewbank migrated to the United States in 1820. His success in the manufacture of lead, tin, and copper tubing in New York was sufficient to enable him to devote much of his leisure, and finally his entire time, to study and to the invention of a variety of useful and important devices. His treatise, A *Descriptive and Historical Account of Hydraulic and other Machines for Raising Water* (1842), was favorably received at home and abroad and long remained a classic; it went through fourteen editions before 1856. In 1849 President Taylor made him Commissioner of Patents. His *Reports*, which as a result of the publicity given them by the abolitionist Horace Greeley were attacked by proslavery members of Congress, seem to have been responsible for his retirement from office. But they were widely read and, together with *The World a Workshop*, they systematized his philosophy of invention.

The machine, Ewbank thought, might enable man, for the first time in his long history, to be master of his fortunes. Already, he insisted in his *Report* for 1852, it had given the entire body of mankind something like equal opportunities in the race for happiness and power. By reducing the cost of the comforts of life and the tools of knowledge, by freeing the common man from the necessity of toiling from dawn to dark, and by increasing the wages of intelligent and skilled labor, the machine had done much to enable him to share advantages previously monopolized by the privileged.

Ewbank did not rest his case for technology merely on the advantages which he felt it had brought the common man, and was to bring him in increasing measure. In his *Annual Report* (1849) as Commissioner of Patents he implored society to weigh more adequately the claims of the inventor:

It is a singular vagary that men to whose genius and industry the world is indebted for what is most valuable in it, should have always been held in low esteem. A habit of moderns, it was a passion in former times, to look askance at those who use the hammer or spade, under the fond delusion that the less wise men have to do with gross matter the nearer they resemble the Great Spirit; whereas God is the greatest of workers—the chief of artificers. So far from locking up his wisdom in abstractions, he is incessantly embodying it in tangible things, and in them it is that his intelligence, ingenuity and resources are made manifest. What is this world but one of workshops, and the universe but a collection of inventions?

In this identification of the Deity with the mechanic, in this rubbing out of the ancient line separating the worker from the thinker, the doer from the contemplator, Ewbank elevated technology to new heights and provided a philosophical basis for a democracy in which all should work with their hands as well as think with their minds.

Ewbank maintained that invention could not function freely and beneficently in a world in which a ruling class or an interest group smothered inventive genius and throttled inventions. But he was certain that the engineers and mechanicians held the future in their hands.

Some day they would work together in a bond of union and, faithful to their mission, they would defy the warmakers and the exploiters. Sooner or later, he argued, the technicians would make themselves dominant in the management of the society they were revolutionizing.

To such analyses of the potential social use of technology strenuous objections emanated from a variety of critics. Southerners who based their system of values on human slavery and who cared neither for machine civilization nor for socialism ridiculed all that Ewbank stood for. A writer in *De Bow's Review*, the leading organ of the commercial South, feared that the mechanical arts might oversharpen the appetite for material benefits at the expense of esthetic values and prove to be a boomerang by enslaving the masses to the poverty, vice, and despair of manufacturing centers. In the North the Reverend Edwin H. Chapin, prominent Universalist minister in New York City, pointed out the tendency of machinery to enrich the few and injure the many. With others he warned of the danger of technological unemployment. "Machinery and pauperism are marching hand in hand," declared Senator Isaac P. Walker of Wisconsin. Would a prison here and a workshop there, he queried, be any solution for the poverty and depression which the machine is thrusting on the masses?

It remained for a New England Trancendentalist to make one of the most witty and penetrating critiques of the machine. In reviewing *The Paradise within the Reach of All Men*, a tract by J. A. Etzler, a German who resided for a time in Pennsylvania, Henry David Thoreau objected on several counts to the Utopian's vision of a society in which the machine would free man from arduous toil and enable him to live in affluence. With homespun shrewdness the Yankee primitivist insisted that machines required, in the last analysis, three very stubborn and very real elements: men, time, and money. To his way of thinking, Etzler had not even come near solving the relationships between these factors and the machine. But Thoreau's basic quarrel with the German dreamer was that the machine insulted a nature that already served man on a higher and grander scale. The price paid for science was too high for Thoreau, the romantic idealist. He preferred no Mahometan's castle, bound to fall to earth because it was not secured to Heaven's roof, but Heaven itself.

While such arguments raged regarding the role of technology in society, actual inventions continued to affect the lot of the common man. If he were thrown out of work when new machines were installed, he also found new work as a result of machines. If he tasted the bitter dregs of insecurity and degradation in the mill towns and city slums created by the machine, he also enjoyed opportunities and comforts his fathers had not even entertained in their dreams. Reference has already been made to some of the new inventions. Now Charles Goodyear, after many vicissitudes, at length succeeded in discovering the process for making India rubber commercially useful; as a result, the common man could henceforth enjoy an almost endless series of comfort-promoting devices. Samuel Colt's improved repeating revolver proved a boon to the plain man in his struggles on the frontier. No less important than the inventions themselves was the further development of the principle of interchangeable parts, which Eli Whitney and Samuel Colt had first used on a large scale.

Commendable though the record was in technological invention and in the filling in of details in the various scientific fields, Americans could hardly boast the discovery of important general laws of mechanics and science. Only two European-Americans approached the great generalizers and theoreticians of the Old World: Agassiz in geology and Adrian in mathematics. It is true that Joseph Henry's name was often coupled with that of Faraday for having independently discovered the principle of self-induction, but Henry laid down no far-reaching theory or principle. James Dwight Dana did important work in geology, and Asa Gray was highly regarded abroad for his contributions to botany; but neither was of the same stature as Lyell and Darwin.

The Americans' fertility in technology and their sterility in abstract theoretical laws during this period occasioned some comment. Their inventiveness was attributed to the Yankee's moral flair for improving not only his mind and character but the tools he used; to the fact that a continent was to be civilized by inadequate manpower, with the result that a premium was put on the invention of time-saving devices; and to the probability that the creative impulse which in some societies expressed itself in the fine arts found outlet in America rather in mechanical invention. Perhaps the theory advanced by Tocqueville was as satisfactory as any. He suggested that in Europe, where a "permanent inequality" of condition prevailed, men confined themselves to "the arrogant and sterile researches of abstract truths, whilst the social condition and institutions of democracy prepare them to seek immediate and useful practical results of the sciences."[3] Certain it was, in any case, that the aid of science was enlisted for the well-being of the masses.

### The Common Man in Sickness

The plain man, often too poor to take advantage of the best practices in medical science, had long resorted to homemade nostrums. During the 1830s and 1840s a variety of new schools of medicine, each with extravagant claims, demanded freedom to propagate their creeds. Dietary panaceas and water cures were urged upon the people. The Thompsonians and homeopaths, among others, preached a hygienic millennium while they attacked the orthodox medical profession. The common people listened—and believed. Out-and-out commercial quacks with their elixirs, syrups, and magical pills succeeded even better in winning disciples. So marked was the spirit of lay "come-outism" in medicine that a reaction set in against a principle that had only slowly been established—that of state supervision of medical practice through licensing. State after state in the Jacksonian period revoked legislation which, in accordance with European precedent, had restricted dubious practice.

This reaction was explained in various ways. State Senator Scott of New York, in supporting his repeal bill in 1844, declared: "A people accustomed to govern themselves, and boasting of their intelligence, are impatient of restraint. They want no protection but freedom of inquiry and freedom of action."[4] Francis Lieber, in an effort to throw light on the American tendency toward excessive indulgence in quack remedies, similarly expressed the belief that the versatile and independent spirit which so often led the American to act for himself with good results frequently also led him to act for himself in situations in which he had inadequate knowledge and experience.

Although the common man opposed public regulation of his own health, in these years of his rise he saw the beginnings of the public health movement. The mounting mortality rates in the growing cities, the need for sanitary reforms, the devastating cholera epidemics all testi-

[3] Alexis de Tocqueville, *Democracy in America*, 4 vols. (London, 1835–1840), III, 89.
[4] Richard H. Shryock, "Public Relations of the Medical Profession in Great Britain and the United States: 1600–1870," *Annals of Medical History*, II (1930), 322–323.

fied to the fact that laissez faire in public health, however democratic it might appear, militated against the common good. In 1851 Dr. Wilson Jewell of the Philadelphia Board of Health planned a national public health association; six years later he led in its establishment. Formed in 1847 in the interest of professional progress, the American Medical Association recommended sanitary reforms and the collection of vital statistics in the interest of good health. Massachusetts in 1843 had set the example of recording vital statistics and despite the influence of laissez faire, popular individualism, and ignorance, the practice grew.

The plain man was in more than one respect a beneficiary of the advance of medical science. No doubt he or his wife pored over the fugitive copies of Dr. Charles Knowlton's *Fruits of Philosophy* (1832), the first American treatise on birth control, which went through many editions in spite of the strong religious and moral opposition it aroused. In 1843, several years prior to the epoch-making discovery in Vienna that childbed fever was the result of infection through lack of complete cleanliness at childbirth, Dr. Oliver Wendell Holmes advanced the same theory, but medical opposition delayed the time of its general acceptance.

On the other hand, the discovery of anesthesia, which revolutionized surgery and brought "the death of pain," was quickly adopted. Dr. Crawford Long of Georgia, as a result of his observation that ether deadened pain, performed eight operations with its aid between 1842 and 1846, but his failure to publish his results deprived him of the title of discoverer. Unaware of these events in Georgia, Dr. William Morton, a Boston dentist, acting on the suggestion of the well-known physician, Dr. Charles Jackson, that sulphuric ether deadened pain, successfully demonstrated its effectiveness as an anesthetic in extractions. In 1846 Dr. John C. Warren was persuaded to use it in a major surgical operation at the Massachusetts General Hospital. After the operation had been quietly performed in the presence of skeptical but tense onlookers, Dr. Warren said to them, "Gentlemen, this is no humbug."

### Growing Interest in Mental Phenomena

Although modern psychology was then in the womb of the future, this era saw some effort to introduce inductive methods into the study of mental life. It is true that credulousness, superstition, and faith in supernaturalism played a large role in the popular cult of mesmerism and "animal magnetism." Its sponsors, chief among whom was Andrew Jackson Davis, claimed occult powers for mesmerists. Some even claimed that mesmerism could not only heal the body but regenerate society! But in spite of the common tendency to combine and confuse religion, therapeutics, and materialism, the best man in the cult, Dr. James Stanley Grimes, did through experimental methods come close to the conclusion that mesmerism was the result of mental suggestion rather than of some subtle electromagnetic fluid.

In 1850, when the fake rappings of Margaret and Kate Fox were attracting national attention, at least some Americans were asking for scientific evidence before accepting the phenomena as genuine. Scientific principles governed the examinations that a committee of physicians made on the famous sisters from upstate New York. If the common man failed to appreciate fully the inductive methods so necessary in such investigations, nevertheless for the first time curiosity and interest in such matters were advanced somewhat beyond the realm of mere superstition.

Phrenology enjoyed an even more widespread popularity than animal magnetism and spiritualism. The work of Gall and Spurzheim, the founders of phrenology, had been introduced into America in the 1820s by physicians and others who had studied abroad, above all by Dr. Charles Caldwell, a well-known member of the medical staff of Transylvania University. But it was not until 1832, when Spurzheim himself visited America and demonstrated to medical men his technique of dissecting the brain, that phrenology received much of a hearing. Spurzheim's charm and idealistic insight into human nature, as well as his technical skill, aroused the admiration of such men as Benjamin Silliman, Dr. Samuel Gridley Howe, Horace Mann, President Quincy of Harvard, Poe, Bowditch, and Emerson. After his untimely death the gospel which he expounded was engagingly preached by the Scotch visitor, George Combe. Before long, phrenological societies, a phrenological magazine, and practicing phrenologists testified to the popularity of the new cult.

Before the popularization and oversimplification of phrenology by dollar-minded quacks brought discredit, the doctrine seemed to exemplify the new scientific spirit of the times. Repudiating the traditional mental philosophy of the highly academic and metaphysical type which dominated American colleges and intellectual life generally, phrenology taught, in the words of Combe, that "the mind, as it exists by itself, can never be an object of philosophical investigation." For mind, to the phrenologist, was not independent of matter. "The operations of the mind are the mind itself." These operations were said to be rooted in the complex and multiple organs making up the brain and the nervous system, the seat of Philoprogenitiveness, Amativeness, Idealty, Eventuality, and all the other faculties or propensities of behavior. The locale of the organs in which the propensities were centered had, according to phrenology, been determined by Gall's and Spurzheim's dissection of brains; and since these various organs of the brain affected the size and contour of the skull (as it was supposed) it was possible, with the aid of the famous phrenological "charts" and "heads," to make character analyses.

The vogue for phrenological "readings" among the common people can be in part explained by the prevailing social atmosphere. In a period when the common man began to feel within him the stir of power and ambition, phrenology had much to offer him. It was not merely that he could have, from a wandering "practicing phrenologist" or at the "parlors" of Fowler and Wells on Broadway, a reading which would set him right regarding the kind of mate that he, with his propensities, should choose; nor was it even that he might be told the vocation or business for which he was best adapted. These things, of course, were important. But as one of the critics of phrenology remarked, the common man seeks for something which will solve all his difficulties, something which will reveal nature's secrets and savor of a mystery or miracle. What the more esoteric mental philosophies were supposed to do for the college-bred man, phrenology claimed to do for any man.

Nor was that all. As James Freeman Clarke, a prominent and liberal Unitarian clergyman remarked, phrenology inspired hope and courage in those depressed by the consciousness of some inability. For, at least as interpreted by Combe and his disciples, it taught that man was in a state of transition between bondage to the animal propensities and governance by the moral ones. Phrenology could tell one in which of the desirable propensities he was weak, in which of the undesirable he was overendowed; and by the deliberate cultivation of the one and the inhibition of the other he might in fact alter his endowments. That, in brief, was the meaning of the motto of the eminently successful phrenologist, Orson Squire Fowler, "Self-made, or never made." Obviously phrenology's implications for social reform through mass education were enormous.

The learned quickly came to be critical of the claims of phrenology and even of the essential doctrine itself. But in making the common man more interesting to himself and more powerful, at least potentially, phrenology was a boon to him. Tom, Dick, and Harry may not have read Combe's opinion that the American citizen might so conduct himself in private and in public that each of his powers could play gracefully and happily within the sphere of its legitimate action. But some of the conditions which explained the rapid popularization of phrenology among the masses also explained the impressive movement for the general popularization of knowledge.

Science, which enjoyed so many triumphs in the era of the rise of the common man, could do much to control nature for the benefit of the plain people; it could even do much, as the auspicious beginnings of better institutional care for the insane were proving, to aid in the salvaging of human beings hitherto deemed beyond hope. Indeed, in this period of religious faith in abstract thought and in will power, the possibilities of control over the mind were greatly overemphasized. But to that age the possibilities of scientific control over physical and human nature seemed to promise realization of all the brightest dreams of the Enlightenment.

# 14 The Popularization of Knowledge

Let us diffuse knowledge throughout the length
and breadth of this great country; multiply the
means of information,—send the schoolmaster
into every hovel,—dot every hill with the school-
house and college,—let the press, without inter-
mission, night and day, pour forth its steady
streams of light,—foster science and the Arts,
—let the civilizing and Godlike influences of
machinery uninterruptedly extend. Then will
the future of our country open, boundless and
great, beyond all example, beyond all compare,
and countless ages bless its mission and acknowledge its glorious dominion.

—DE BOW'S REVIEW, 1854

The decades between Jackson and Lincoln witnessed an extraordinary
development in the spread of ideas and knowledge among the people.
This was largely accomplished through the improvement of existing cultural institutions and the rise of new agencies. The three decades preceding the Civil War saw the appearance of the penny newspaper and
the inexpensive magazine and book, the lyceum platform, and the public
library. It was the age of the common school awakening, the development
of the academy, the emergence of the high school, and the multiplication
of colleges.

The flourishing growth of these agencies for the diffusion of knowledge was an expression of deeper forces. Some, like evangelical religion with its zeal for spreading piety among the people, were of long standing. Others were more recent: the concentration of population in cities, the growth of a wealthy class with philanthropic inclinations, the technological developments which facilitated the mass communication of ideas. The movement was also an expression of the growing power of the people in all walks of life. Their desire to "know," to share more fully in the life of the mind, reflected an awareness of their growing power, their potentialities. The movement for popularizing knowledge was also stimulated by their own leaders, by democratically minded intellectuals who deprecated the separation of theory and practice, knowledge and action, and, finally, by enthusiastic reformers who believed that the truth, if widely disseminated, would set man free.

### Business Enterprise and the Diffusion of Knowledge

The expanding population and the rise of literacy which followed from the common school awakening resulted in a vast potential reading market. Business enterprise was quick to take advantage of this by providing the people with inexpensive reading matter designed to appeal to popular taste. New mechanical processes cheapened the cost of paper and of printing, and these improvements, the result in part of emerging needs, in turn facilitated the diffusion of knowledge.

Among the new literary fashions which proved a boon to publishers and authors no less than to the culturally ambitious among the middle class with money to spend, was the literary annual or gift book. In 1826, three years after the *Forget-me-not* saw the light of day in England, the *Atlantic Souvenir* appeared in Philadelphia. A plethora of gift books followed this venture—from 1846 to 1852 an average of sixty titles appeared each year. Made up of highly moral and sentimental verses, tales, proverbs, and admonitions to virtue, the gift book was embellished with engravings and color tints and bound ornately in embossed and decorated silk or gilded leather. It both met and created a demand for "better literature and art" among the rising middle classes. It provided such unknown writers as Hawthorne with their first tangible encouragement. It also familiarized a wide public with the names and at least fragments of the work of such writers as Byron, Southey, Scott, Wordsworth,

Coleridge, Lamb, Ruskin, Dickens, Thackeray, Poe, Nathaniel P. Willis, Longfellow, Whittier, Emerson, Holmes, and a long list of others. Tokens of affection, of refinement, even of luxury, "these luscious gifts," in the words of one of their publishers, "stole alike into the palace and the cottage, the library, the parlor, and the boudoir" to create an ever-widening taste for purchasable culture, ornate, exquisite, sentimental, and uplifting.

For those who could not afford the expensive gift books, enterprising publishers found cheaper but no less profitable disseminators of knowledge and culture. The multiplication of lyceums, debating societies, and district school libraries created a wide market for new books. No sooner had the New York legislature enacted a law encouraging the establishment of district school libraries than an agent of Harper's obtained at Albany a contract to supply books for the new venture. Harper's District School Library was by no means the only uniformly bound and cheaply priced series which this enterprising firm sponsored. Harper's Boys' and Girls' Library, Harper's Family Library, which ran up to 187 volumes, and Harper's Library of Select Novels, reaching at length the six hundred and fifteenth title, all bore witness to the way in which an alert and profit-conscious publisher might take advantage of, and contribute to, the zeal for popularizing knowledge and culture.

What Harper's did others were quick to imitate. Publishers catered to the more serious intellectual aspirations of a public untrained in the foreign languages by bringing out an impressive range of translations of the writings of European philosophers, publicists, and men of letters. On a more popular level cheaply priced books of useful information, travel, history, biography, and religion appeared. Encyclopedias and popular "books of knowledge," ponderous or of pocket size, enjoyed an ever-growing vogue.

Pious folk distrusted the novel, but it had no real rival. Anxious to put perspective "best sellers" on the market as speedily as possible, publishers sometimes dispatched messengers to incoming European packetboats and within a single day set up, printed, and bound in paper covers the most recent novel of Bulwer or Dickens. Newspaper boys sold for a half-quarter or a dime these "pirated" novels, the cheap cost of which was due to the fact that no international copyright existed. Thanks to new promotion methods, these inexpensive books quickly became available to travelers on canals and railroads and to dwellers in remote byways. Even more profitable than respectable novels was the sensational adventure story, frankly designed to appeal to the masses by exciting democratic prejudices, patriotic fervor, and sex interest (sugarcoated by highly moral sentiments). These paperback predecessors of the later Beadle dime novels enjoyed increasing popularity in the 1840s and 1850s.

In consequence of such factors the domestic manufacture of books increased by leaps and bounds. Valued at three and a half million in 1830, it had by 1840 increased 60 percent; in 1850 it was 125 percent greater than it had been in 1840.

The older highbrow magazines did not enjoy all to themselves the field of periodical literature. New ventures, such as the *Magazine of Useful and Entertaining Knowledge, Graham's, Peterson's, Godey's Lady's Book, Parley's Magazine* and dozens of others sought and won through popular appeal a wider audience than the *North American* or *The Port Folio* had ever known.

No discussion of the role of the publisher in meeting and further stimulating the demand for the diffusion of information can properly neglect the rise of the penny newspaper, which, like so many American agencies of cultural life, was influenced by English example. Mass production and mass distribution in journalism resulted from the introduction of the steam rotary press and from the discovery that a new type of newspaper, frankly designed to appeal to the less well educated, was a profitable enterprise. While the discussion of party politics and political principles by no means disappeared, it was overshadowed by a different conception of news interest. Publishers and editors were increasingly willing to cater to the common man and his wife by filling the pages of their newspapers with the sensational doings of those in high or lowly walks of life—with the records of court trials, with stories of phenomenal successes and grim failures, with human interest stories of any and every type. Together with new methods for the rapid collection of news, this emphasis on sensationalism and on everyday matters virtually revolutionized journalism.

Since the common man could ill afford to buy the older and dearer papers, even if he could have relished their elevated if acrimonious discussion of politics, it was obviously necessary to lower the price of the new type of paper. The *New York Sun* appeared in 1833 as the first penny newspaper, and within a short time James Gordon Bennett of the *New York Herald* carried the penny paper further on its unique road than anyone had deemed possible. Frankly bent on tapping as wide a market as possible, Bennett offered, instead of the old type of serious, dull paper tied to a political faction, an organ which capitalized sensational news, vivacious gossip and prattle, and dramatic human interest stories. On a higher political and moral level and yet partaking of many of the features of the new journalism was Horace Greeley's *New York Tribune*. Its advocacy of reforms promising to elevate the common man to vast heights appealed to the self-interest and idealism of the plain people who subscribed to it in mounting numbers.

The agricultural press also developed rapidly in this period. The dirt farmer often complained that the contents of the agricultural journal were useless. Yet, in addition to hortatory and inspirational articles on the evils of the city and the glories of agriculture and on the need for temperance and schooling, it contained many pieces of an informational character. These included articles on soil, on state and federal aid to agriculture, on travel, politics, laws, and catastrophic events and accidents. The farm paper also contained household hints, rural poetry, and suggestions for the improvement of farm architecture.

All these ventures in the popularization of information, related as they were to an expanding business enterprise, both exemplified the widespread enthusiasm for the diffusion of knowledge and contributed to it.

At least one other development in the social and economic life of the period—improvement in communication and reduction of the cost of postage—was indirectly related to the rise of the common man. The law of 1825 lowered the postal charges that in the interest of additional revenues had been fixed at the close of the War of 1812. But even with these reductions the rates remained burdensome to the ordinary man who in his migration to the West and to cities found it costly to communicate with his homefolk. Following the example of Rowland Hill in England, American reformers inaugurated a campaign to induce Congress, in face of the general opposition of the postal authorities, to eliminate the complex and burdensome practice by which the initial high cost of letters increased with the distance. The preservation of family affections, so the petitions ran, required cheaper postage; so too did the spread of the light reflected by the various crusades for moral reform. Business enterprises, especially the publishers of newspapers and magazines, added their voices to the hue and cry for cheaper rates. At length, in 1851, Congress responded by virtually adopting the principle of cheap and uniform postage rates; and the leader of the reform, Barnabas Bates, could maintain, as he had done at the beginning of the agitation, that the people had been aroused to demand revision in order that every avenue might be opened for the diffusion of useful knowledge. Nor did the movement stop here, for Elihu Burritt, the learned blacksmith, determined to extend the idea to the international area. Although his motives were largely to enable immigrants to keep in touch with their people in the old home and to promote international good will, the argument was also advanced that "ocean penny postage" would diffuse more widely the knowledge of our free political institutions among "the misruled multitudes of the Old World."[1]

## The Established Classes and the Diffusion of Knowledge

The movement for the diffusion of knowledge was paralleled by similar phenomena abroad. These frequently provided America with patterns. The common man in England did not achieve full political power during these years, but he at least emerged as a problem for statesmanship. Philanthropically minded members of the privileged class attempted to meet the problems posed by the emergence of the masses through the diffusion of knowledge. In 1824 Lord Brougham described in the *Edinburgh Review* the beginnings of education for the working classes at Glasgow. This piece, reprinted as *Practical Observations on the Education of the People,* quickly ran through twenty editions and stimulated the establishment of mechanics' institutes throughout the kingdom. The new movement had its chief focus in the Society for the Diffusion of Useful Knowledge, which not only promoted evening classes for mechanics but sponsored "A Library of Useful Knowledge." The sixpence pamphlets of the Society made available much information in the fields of natural history, mechanics, and the useful arts; and presently the even cheaper "penny pamphlets" like the *Penny Magazine* and the *Penny Encyclopedia* further extended the spread of information. Much of this literature was republished in America by the Society for the Diffusion of Useful Knowledge founded in Boston in 1829, and by the more inclusive American Society for the Diffusion of Useful Knowledge that was established seven years later.

[1] *De Bow's Review,* XVI (June, 1854), 563.

In justification of the new movement Brougham urged in his *Practical Observations*—much read and admired in the United States—that the diffusion of knowledge promised to prevent a crisis in class relationships. Such a crisis, he warned, must result if ignorance regarding the "true causes" of the steady decrease in wages and prosperity blinded the masses. The education of adults in mechanical skills might well further result in new discoveries of inestimable benefit for all concerned. In addition Brougham urged that the practical education of the masses would greatly reduce expenditures for charity; a well-trained populace would be less prone to idleness and crime, improvident marriages, and an unseemly increase in the number of paupers. Finally, so the argument ran, the diffusion of knowledge would undermine skepticism, superstition, and intolerance.

Many American men of property generously responded to the movement for the popularization of knowledge through voluntary organizations of mechanics and apprentices. The fast-disintegrating apprenticeship system no longer provided adequate surveillance for young employees in the larger cities, and mercantile and mechanics' libraries and institutes seemed all the more necessary if young men in countinghouses and other business establishments were to be kept off the streets and away from taverns of evenings and encouraged to acquire practical tools for more effective work, the road to business success and the formula for becoming self-made men.

Nor did the diffusion of knowledge among women fail to win support from entrepreneurs. The Lowell millowners encouraged female operatives, many of whom came from farms, to improve their minds in off hours by attending lyceum lectures. Working girls were encouraged to write skits for the factory magazines that brought pleasant publicity to the mills and kept minds off such matters as hours, wages, and strikes. In other social circles rising men in commerce and industry looked with favor on the movement for the better education of their daughters, both for the sake of the daughters themselves and for the social prestige incident thereto.

The part of businessmen in supporting institutions for the diffusion of knowledge and in founding new ones has already been mentioned. In addition to the philanthropies to which attention has been drawn, there are many other examples: the institutions for scientific training endowed by Rensselaer, Bussey, Sheffield, and Lawrence, the benefactions of

George Peabody to town libraries, the bequests of Joshua Bates and John Jacob Astor to the libraries of Boston and New York, and the far-flung educational gifts of the Tappans. To them might be added the Lowell Institute, founded in 1836 by John Lowell to bring distinguished lecturers annually to his fellow Bostonians, and the Cooper Institute, set up in New York in 1857–1859 by the philanthropic industrialist Peter Cooper as a practical school for adult sons of toil.

The most important single plank in the platform for the diffusion of knowledge was the tax-supported public school, but to it many substantial men expressed indifference or opposition. In the first place, men of power and substance frequently argued that education had been, and properly so, a family matter; they themselves were quite satisfied with the training their children received in private schools; if the poor did not or could not provide schooling for their offspring, the fault must be laid at the door of their own shiftlessness and incompetency. Free school laws, it was argued, merely filled the bellies and covered the backs of the indigent at the expense of the taxpayer; what could be more patent than the certainty that if free schools were granted, the concessions would not end short of socialism itself? To provide free schooling for the less well-to-do would result in the loss of their self-respect and initiative; it would, in brief, pauperize them. Some argued that free public schools must be opposed on the ground that they would provide education to those "who were better suited to their station without it." Educated workmen were not, it was argued, a necessity. On the contrary, so the contention was, prosperity depended rather on an abundant supply of labor "comparatively uneducated."

Such arguments did not convince all the men and women of position and property. Many assumed with Lord Brougham that popular education was both desirable and necessary in the interest of prosperity and social stability. Edward Everett, spokesman of the powerful New England industrialists, could indeed reject the doctrine that every man has a natural right to education at public expense; one might as well argue, he went on, that the state must pay his tailor. But, he continued, the duty of educating the people rested on great public grounds, on moral and political foundations. What he had in mind was trenchantly expressed by Catharine Beecher, daughter of the distinguished clergyman Lyman Beecher, when she wrote that "the education of the common people, then, who are to be our legislators, jurymen, and judges, and to whom all our dearest interests are to be entrusted, this is the point around which the wisest heads, the warmest hearts, the most powerful energies should gather, for conservation, for planning, for unity of action, and for persevering enterprise."[2] When further argument was necessary educators endeavoring to win the support of commerce and industry declared that a workman imbued as a child in the common schools with thrift, honesty, and obedience could always be counted on to work "more steadily and cheerfully, and, therefore, more productively, than one who, when a child, was left to grovel in ignorance and idleness."[3]

## Scholars and the Diffusion of Knowledge

The division of merchants, industrialists, property owners, and people of substance generally on the issue of the diffusion of knowledge was also reflected in scholarly circles. Some scholars, like John Pickering, a wealthy Boston lawyer and eminent philologist, lamented the fact that so few of their countrymen read Newton's *Principia* and Kant's *Critique*. Pickering attributed this sad circumstance to the general diffusion of knowledge; this bane, he feared, equipped people with just enough knowledge to read children's books and to belittle profound learning as useless pedantry. Such sentiments were echoed by other scholars. The Reverend Caleb S. Henry, an Episcopal clergyman and academic philosopher, buttressed his pleas for a highly specialized learned class with telling disparagements of the cult of diffusion. A priesthood of creative scholars, he argued, might in part offset the superficial knowledge encompassed in such epitomes for the people as "Familiar Elements" of this, that, and the other; such a group of erudites might even counterbalance the predominantly gross material tendencies inherent in the rise to prominence of the degraded, the idle, and the ignorant.

But many scholars more or less identified with the mansion people took an opposite stand. George Ticknor, scholar of scholars and patrician of patricians, worked hard to establish a public library in Boston in order to put culture within the reach of those who were grasping for it. At the

---

[2] Catharine Beecher to Mary Lyon, Walnut Hills, Ohio, in Monroe Collection of Henry Barnard Papers (New York University).

[3] George B. Emerson and Alonzo Potter, *The School and Schoolmaster* (Boston, 1843), 113.

same time he insisted on every concession to the handicaps and slower rate of cultural growth which conditions had imposed on the people.

Other scholars of social position looked with favor on the movement for popularization for different reasons. Thus the eminent German-American publicist, Francis Lieber, in the early 1840s was exhorting men of means to club together and with an ample fund employ competent scholars to prepare inexpensive tracts for the people designed "truly to instruct" them on such topics as industry, property, and "public faith and repudiation," subjects on which they were being led astray by unwarranted attacks on basic institutions. Less clearly serviceable to the interests of the substantial classes was the argument of Edward Everett, president of Harvard. Everett believed that the time had come to end the traditional divorce between science and the useful arts, a divorce that had led theorists into such chimerical pursuits as the quest for the philosopher's stone and at the same time had blunted the inventive aptitudes of practical craftsmen.

Scholars more warmly democratic in sympathy than Everett favored efforts to break down the age-old barrier between a small learned class engaged in the disinterested search for knowledge on the one hand and practicians and a more or less ill-informed populace on the other. In democratic Vermont the Reverend James Marsh, disciple of Coleridge and president of the university, declared that American civilization was chiefly distinguished from that of Europe by reason of the fact that Americans had not limited thought to the few only, but had begun its extension to all members of the body politic. "Here alone, among civilized nations," declared Marsh, "is political aristocracy entirely abolished, and the aristocracy of nature permitted and assisted to grow up unrestrained by artificial relations and forms of society."[4] If no class could render its condition more secure and happy by repressing the aspiring efforts of others, then it followed that in the interest of general well-being knowledge should be shared. Marsh inaugurated an educational reform designed to make available the resources of the University of Vermont to all Vermonters who, regardless of general deficiencies in preparation, might advantageously profit from the pursuit of any branch of learning of which they were capable.

[4] James Marsh, *An Address . . . in Burlington, . . . Nov. 26, 1826* (Burlington, Vt., 1826), 11.

Years later another democratic scholar, the Reverend A. D. Mayo, declared in words reminiscent of those of Marsh that the whole experience of European society argued against the division of men into a learned fraternity and an ignorant populace. Intellectual culture in America, Mayo maintained, would be less given to pedantry if scholars isolated themselves less from society and broadened the circle of their mental operations into the whole field of actual life, if they sneered less at the superficiality of popular oratory, fugitive literature, and other evidences of the people's cultural strivings. Let them rather, he expostulated, as older brothers encourage the people to eschew an overemphasis on the merely practical and to value abstract principles for themselves.

Nor did the fine arts fail to enlist champions of cultural democracy. On his return from Europe Samuel F. B. Morse parted company with the conservatism of his father, Jedidiah Morse, by leading a revolt in 1828 against the undemocratic American Academy of Fine Arts in New York. The patronage of wealthy laymen, Morse declared, degraded artists, undermined the integrity of art, and was a disgrace to the human spirit. Native artists, he went on, had to cease cringing before moneyed men who, at best, for reasons of prestige preferred to import the works of European painters rather than risk encouraging unknown American artists. The National Academy of Design, which Morse founded, both repudiated control by lay patrons and frankly undertook to enlist the support of the people by promoting an art congenial to the morality and republicanism so dear to them.

In much the same vein the flamboyantly democratic George Bancroft declared that "genius will not create, to flatter patrons or decorate salons. It yearns for larger influences; it feeds on wider sympathies; and its perfect display can never exist, except in an appeal to the general sentiment for the beautiful." Bancroft went on to say that Americans would do well to recall that Homer and Shakespeare wrote for the people, not for an aristocracy. In any case, concluded the patriotic historian, the chief thing to be kept in mind was that "the universality of the intellectual and moral powers, and the necessity of their development for the progress of the race, proclaim the great doctrine of the natural right of every human being to moral and intellectual culture."[5]

[5] George Bancroft, "The Office of the People," *Literary and Historical Miscellanies* (New York, 1855), 419, 428.

### The Cult of Self-Improvement

The tradition of self-improvement so well exemplified by Benjamin Franklin continued to develop. The rising tide of democracy reinforced the conviction that every human being possesses both a natural right to knowledge and the potentiality for achieving it. The deeply rooted Christian concept of moral self-improvement was popularized by Dr. Thomas Dick, a Scotsman celebrated for his "reconciliation" of science and religion. Harper's Family Library in 1833 published Dick's *On the Improvement of Society by the Diffusion of Knowledge*, in which the argument was advanced that the dissemination of knowledge, together with the moral renovation always accompanying such diffusion, would at length overcome man's natural depravity. The publication of other writings by Dr. Dick in "the Christian Library" still further contributed to making his name a household word in the United States.

On a different intellectual level a group of Unitarians and Transcendentalists popularized the philosophical concepts of self-culture developed in Europe by Rousseau, Hutcheson, Ferguson, and Degérando. American soil in the 1830s and 1840s was congenial to the leading ideas advanced by these moral philosophers—the concept that man is a free agent designed to achieve moral and spiritual progress on his way toward perfection. In 1830 the Reverend George Ripley, a Unitarian minister in Boston, reviewed at length in the *Christian Examiner* Degérando's *Concerning Moral Perfection, or Self-Education*. This eclectic treatise was a synthesis of the optimistic faith in the perfectibility of human nature associated with the Enlightenment, the cult of individualism dear to disciples of the Romantic revolt, and the moral struggle implicit in Christian doctrine. Ripley's essay on Degérando's book became the subject of considerable discussion.

Eight years later, in 1838, William Ellery Channing, foremost figure in the Unitarian church, published *Self-Culture*. This widely known essay is a characteristic expression of the fully developed American philosophical version of the doctrine of self-improvement. The great Unitarian defined man not as a machine designed to be governed by a foreign force, to do a fixed amount of work, and finally to break down altogether, but rather as a being of free spiritual powers. "The common notion," wrote Channing, "has been that the mass of the people need no other culture than is necessary to fit them for their various trades;

and, though this error is passing away, it is far from being exploded."[6]

In and out of season Channing and his fellow Unitarians, and the Transcendentalists in an even more romantic and intense way, declared that the ground of man's culture lay not in his calling or station but in his nature. He was to be educated, as Channing put it, not because he is to make shoes, nails, or pins, but because he is a man. To achieve self-culture, man's destiny, it was first of all necessary to fasten onto the ideal with all deliberateness, to spare nothing to make the most and the best of the powers bestowed by God. Intercourse with superior minds through books and lectures, the curbing of the animal spirits, participation in the political duties of a free republic, and manual labor performed in such a way as to be a high impulse to the mind and to fellow men—all these, Channing said, were among the practicable ways to self-culture.

This gospel, spread wide and far through sermons, tracts, lectures, and schoolbooks, inspired imitators of Franklin to self-improvement. It was at the root of young Margaret Fuller's daily routine set down in her diary:

Rose at 5. Walked for an hour. Practiced the piano till 7. Breakfast. Read French till 8. Attended 2–3 lectures in Brown's phil. 9.30 went to Mr. Perkins school. Gk. till 12. Home—piano until 2. If the conversation were agreeable sometimes lounged ½ hour at desert—tho' rarely so lavish of time. 2 hours Italian. At 6 walked or drove—sang for half an hour—wrote in journal—retired.

And the appeal of self-culture led another young New Englander, Elihu Burritt, blacksmith, to learn over the forge the Latin and Greek he would have mastered had his poverty-stricken father been able to send him to school. He was further impelled, having acquired these languages, to study after working hours some thirty languages, both European and Asiatic, one after another.

No brief account can convey any adequate impression of the hold of the cult of self-improvement. In Boston twenty-six courses of lectures, not including those that numbered less than eight lectures, attracted over 13,000 people during the winter of 1837–1838. So great was the zeal to obtain admission to Silliman's lectures on chemistry at the newly established Lowell Institute that the crowd filling the streets adjacent to the hall crushed in the windows of the Old Corner Book Store, the place where the tickets were distributed.

If Boston was more given to lectures for self-improvement than many

[6] *The Works of William Ellery Channing*, 6 vols. (Boston, 1853), II, 368.

other cities, the others were not far behind. In Cincinnati Ormsby Mitchel's lectures on astronomy were so popular that in 1846 the citizens provided him with a telescope second only to that in Greenwich, England; the next year the *Sidereal Messenger*, the first popular expository magazine of astronomy in the world, quickly found favor among the disciples of self-improvement. In every city and in thousands of towns and villages lectures, lyceum discussions and debates, evening schools, libraries, manuals on self-culture all testified to the popularity of the idea. Except in the Old South the cult of self-improvement took the country by storm.

A number of circumstances were responsible for this cult's tremendous popularity. Public schools on the secondary level were still opposed by taxpayers and by the dominant idea of laissez faire. Self-culture, on the other hand, was inexpensive and ready almost at hand. In a highly individualistic society which could spare little for formal agencies of education and which, in view of the vast work to be done in factory and on the frontier, put a premium on physical labor, long terms of schooling served little purpose. Yet the rise of the common man did call for some onslaught against the traditional barriers to his share in the life of the mind. The cult of self-improvement was an answer.

Farmers, artisans, small shopkeepers, and their wives were by no means passive as philanthropists, businessmen, educators, and scholars discussed the diffusion of knowledge. Many humble people firmly believed that in the unequal struggle between the "haves" and the "have-nots" the possession of knowledge was an advantage of momentous weight. The conviction that every man has a natural right to knowledge, that its attainment would elevate its possessor both socially and economically, was widely and enthusiastically held. The labor press and the speeches of labor leaders repeat these ideas again and again. One of the spokesmen for the common man, Robert Dale Owen, phrased this widely held idea in picturesque words: "We must reach the minds and hearts of the masses; we must diffuse knowledge *among men*; we must not deal it out to scholars and students alone, but even to Tom, Dick, and Harry, and then, as a witty female writer of the day expressed it, 'they will become Mr. Thomas, and Mr. Richard, and Mr. Henry.' "[7]

Paul Brown, a New York Locofoco, expressed the ideas and prejudices of many of the more militant plain people when he excoriated priestcraft, masoncraft, and lawcraft for building their projects on the igno-

[7] *Congressional Globe*, Appendix, 29th Congress, 1st session (April 22, 1846), 471.

rance of the people which they had taken pains to perpetuate. "It advances the common interests of these crafts, to distribute knowledge *partially*, and circumscribe the benefits of what is called a 'liberal education' to a few favorites of fortune, who happen to be born of those who are rich; also, to make a gloss of Latin and Greek the popular model of literary accomplishments. . . . We want a COMMON and EQUAL education—also PUBLIC because it is of general concern. It belongs to the public interest. As rational beings, it is in the INTEREST OF ALL, that ALL should be equally well educated."[8] Such pronouncements might be multiplied until they became wearisome.

The common man not only spoke unequivocally for the popularization of knowledge but, like those nearer the top of the ladder, worked for it as well. This was especially true of the mechanic class in the cities. Timothy Claxton, an English immigrant who had become familiar with the stirrings of adult education for workers in his own land, stimulated much of the activity in the early days of mechanics' institutes in Boston. In addition to establishing the first Boston Mechanics' Institution in 1826, he launched the *Young Mechanic,* a periodical which did much to promote zeal for self-improvement among the members of his class. While employers fostered and sometimes assumed the initiative in founding mechanics' institutes, the mechanics themselves not infrequently took the first steps. They quite generally assumed responsibility for the maintenance of evening classes in natural and applied sciences, in public speaking, and in other practical branches, together with the reading room and library.

Among lecturers that the mechanics' institutes welcomed none was in greater demand than Elihu Burritt, whose glorification of the union of physical toil and mental exercise was so well exemplified in his own accomplishments. Nor was Burritt the only workingman who spoke in these institutes on various branches of knowledge and on the issues of the day. The zeal for knowledge among working people impressed Louis Agassiz, who with amazement saw 3000 laborers, assembled to form a library, listen in perfect quiet to a two-hour discourse on self-culture. The testimony of a woman book peddler that blacksmiths, coopers, and mechanics "almost universally take books" supports the impression of others.

In rural districts, it is true, farmers showed far less militant zeal for

[8] *The Radical: An Advocate of Equality . . . Addressed to the People of the United States* (Albany, 1835), 79.

improved educational facilities than did urban workers. In the farmers' eyes the demand of educational reformers for taxes to improve the common schools often seemed a request for a needless, newfangled frill. Yet in joining with the villagers in supporting debating societies and lyceums, farmers proved that they were not altogether indifferent to the popularization of knowledge. The growth of the agricultural press was another witness to the genuine interest in knowledge deemed useful.

By 1850 the achievements in extending educational opportunities to young and old, however short they fell of the goal set by cultural democrats, exceeded those in any other country. What had been accomplished was a mere beginning, but even this was an impressive tribute to the impact the rise of the common man had made on the intellectual life of the nation.

## The Public School

The battle for the extension of educational opportunities to the children of common men was not entirely won by 1850. But at least in the North and West the half-century year marked the triumph of the principle of state-supported and -supervised schools for all children, regardless of social rank. Twenty years earlier only New England and New York had gone so far as to provide for the education at public expense of children whose parents could not themselves afford it. Even as late as 1840, only one-half of New England's children were given free education, only one-seventh of those in the middle states, and only one-sixth of those in the West. In 1850 many children of the well-to-do could still be found in private institutions; but the tax-supported free public school no longer bore the stigma of a pauper's school; it was well on the road to becoming a school for the great majority of children of all classes.

One factor in this change was the propaganda by which educational reformers convinced a large part of American society that the public school was an institution worthy of more generous and enthusiastic support. But even the arguments of educational leaders would have counted for little had the public schools themselves stood still. State after state followed the example which Massachusetts set in 1837 in creating a board of education headed by an official responsible for improving and enforcing school laws, raising the qualifications for teaching, and bettering the physical equipment of schoolhouses. Thanks to such men as Horace Mann, Henry Barnard, Calvin Stowe, Caleb Mills, Calvin Wiley, and others, many of the best features of the well-established state schools of Prussia were grafted onto the American educational plant without marked protest on the part of cultural patriots.

These men and their colleagues, in creating public sentiment for better schools, actually brought organization, supervision, standards, teacher training, and the beginnings of a professional attitude into American public education. Nor was this all. The Massachusetts Act of 1842 set a new precedent in extending the traditional compulsory principle which required each town to maintain a school in which any child could obtain schooling. The requirement was now made that every child attend some school for a minimum number of months during each year and for a minimum number of years.

The 1830s and 1840s also saw the beginnings of the extension of the principle of public responsibility for education from the elementary to the secondary level. Massachusetts led the way in 1827 by requiring every large town to maintain a free high school, an example which other states followed. By 1850 an auspicious start had been made in this field, though it was no more than a beginning.

In rural districts the academy offered opportunities to the offspring of the common man. From 1820 to 1840 the academy spread rapidly over the land, until by 1850 one out of every eighty-eight persons was listed by the census as a pupil in one of the 6000 academies the country boasted. In addition to the classical course the academy offered to those unable to attend college an introduction to the modern languages and literatures, the natural sciences, logic, and mental philosophy. Aiming as he did to present material in such a way as to make it meaningful and useful, the academy instructor had a definite idea of preparing his pupils for a richer life. Even when it owed its existence to the initiative of an individual or a religious sect, the academy nevertheless deserved its name, the people's college. Its low-cost tuition and the custom of "boarding oneself" on a goodly stock of provisions from the farm meant that for the first time the sons and even the daughters of farmers and village tradesmen might receive an education that was more enriching than that offered by the district school. In some cases the state itself increasingly tended to subsidize the academies and, especially in New York, to exercise some supervision over them. This custom paved the way for the transformation of many academies into high schools when the principle of public responsibility for secondary education gained momentum, as it was to do in the 1860s and 1870s.

## The Higher Learning

Even the college was touched by the democratic currents of the time. It is true that the traditional classical curriculum and the concept of mental discipline continued to prevail in spite of grudging concessions made to the sciences everywhere and in spite of experiments with something like the elective system at Amherst, Harvard, and Brown. Leaders like Eliphalet Nott of Union, Philip Lindsley of Nashville, and Francis Wayland of Brown formulated a more democratic philosophy of the function of the college. These men believed that the college owed a major responsibility to a democratic society and to democratic ideals. It should prepare young men, they contended, not merely for the learned professions but for every walk of life. Wayland, in his *Thoughts on the Present Collegiate System in the United States* (1842), pointed out the respects in which the existing pattern contradicted the democratic goal. The colleges, he insisted, not only trained the few rather than the many, but they trained the few superficially and inadequately. In addition to favoring a more widely selected student body, the president of Brown urged the enrichment of the curriculum by such free electives as economics, history, applied science, agriculture, and the art of teaching. Before his reforms took root they were undone. The period closed with no utilitarian or democratic reshaping of college objectives.

In certain respects, nevertheless, the rise of the common man and the concept of popularizing knowledge did affect higher education. For a few brief years the manual labor college, based on the institutions that Fellenberg established in Switzerland, promised to provide poor youths an opportunity to earn their way through college. The plan involved combining study with systematic manual toil sufficiently remunerative to bear the costs of higher education. The argument was also advanced that such a regimen promised to conserve and promote physical health. But the institutions that tested the plan found it unsatisfactory. Its devoted apostle, Theodore Weld, reluctantly turned to other causes. The failure of the manual labor college was in part offset by the fact that a large number of new colleges brought higher education within the reach of many boys who could not have afforded to go to institutions remote from their homes. Thanks not only to the feeling that college opportunities should be extended but also to denominational rivalry, the number of colleges increased from 173 in 1840 to 239 in 1850.

Of even greater significance was the wedge opened to women when, in 1837, Oberlin admitted four girls to candidacy for the A.B. degree. This precedent, which was to be imitated at Antioch and elsewhere before many years, meant that the barriers to the higher education of the daughters of the common man had begun to break down. Thus notwithstanding the setback which the Dartmouth College decision gave to the principle of public control of colleges and the faltering progress made by the so-called state universities in the South and West, higher learning was somewhat shaken by democratic impulses.

## Libraries for the People

Much more striking was the progress made in extending to the lower ranks of the rising middle class opportunities for self-improvement through libraries. It will be recalled that the original proprietary library had been somewhat democratized by admitting nonshareholders on payment of an annual fee. In periods of hard times this arrangement often broke down. Now, thanks to the general popularity of the philosophy of the diffusion of knowledge and also to important changes in the traditional apprenticeship system, new institutions for mechanics were established. With the gradual transformation of craftsmanship into factory production and the expansion of mercantile business, it was no longer possible for employers to exercise the close supervision over apprentices than had been their wont. Nor was it possible, as a result of the virtual breakdown of the old apprenticeship system, for trade secrets to be handed on in the traditional manner. All these factors, together with the enthusiasm of such a liberal merchant as William Wood and such an alert mechanic as the English immigrant Timothy Claxton, accounted for the rise of mechanics' libraries and institutes. In 1820 Wood, whom Lord Brougham hailed as the originator of the mechanics' and apprentices' libraries, established the Apprentices' Library in Boston. At about the same time similar institutions appeared in Portland, New York, and Philadelphia, and before long almost every city boasted one.

What these agencies accomplished may be suggested by the fact that in 1829 the New York Apprentices' Library housed 10,000 volumes of which 1600 apprentices made use; by 1857 this library served three-quarters of a million people, of whom "the working class forms a large majority."[9] Frequently these libraries also sponsored lectures, debates, and discussions, and in some instances evening classes and even museums became a feature.

In addition to the mechanics' libraries, mercantile libraries sponsored by clerks and young merchants also made their appearance in the 1820s and spread to every trade center of any consequence. Like the mechanics and apprentices, the mercantile aspirants added lecture courses and classes to their ventures. But utilitarianism did not exclude the conviction that merchants must be men of culture, as the emphasis on books of literature, philosophy, and science testifies.

Important though these agencies were in extending cultural opportunities to skilled workers and what might now be called the white-collar class, they were, of course, quasi-private institutions supported not by public funds but by fees and benefactions. This traditional concept of mutual association and private responsibility for the popularization of knowledge did not, however, exclusively hold the field. As early as 1817 Dr. Jesse Torrey of Ballston Spa, New York, in a striking brochure urged the support of public libraries by government moneys. Other voices echoed the sentiment.

The first steps were modestly taken when New York provided in 1838 for the encouragement of district school libraries by public funds. Statistics for these libraries are somewhat contradictory, but it appears that by 1850 over 12,000 such libraries, chiefly in New York and New England, stored more than 1,500,000 books. Even though these meager libraries, inefficiently administered in obviously too small units, failed to meet the popular need, they helped prepare the way for the idea of public responsibility for libraries.

Meantime, here and there a New England town actually assumed such an obligation. In 1827 Castine, on the Maine coast, acquired the shares of the Social Library, one of the typical proprietary institutions which almost every town possessed. Six years later Peterborough, New Hampshire, voted to use money acquired from the state for the maintenance of a free town library, and in 1846 Orange, in Massachusetts, voted $100

[9] Sidney Ditzion, "Mechanics and Mercantile Libraries," *The Library Quarterly,* X (April, 1940), 199–200.

to establish a town library. Two years later the Massachusetts legislature permitted Boston to use public funds for the support of the projected Boston Public Library, the first important institution to establish the pattern of the public library as we know it. But to New Hampshire went the honor of enacting the first state-wide law permitting towns to establish tax-supported libraries. Massachusetts and Maine followed her example. With such a beginning, the way was paved, when social, economic, and cultural conditions became ripe, for the widespread adoption of the principle of public responsibility for libraries. Had the period contributed nothing else in the library field, this would have been sufficient glory. But in fact the years between 1825 and 1850 saw the establishment of 550 libraries of all sorts—more than twice the number founded in the preceding quarter of a century.

### The Lyceum

What the mechanics' and merchants' libraries and institutes did for the urban lower middle classes, the lyceum accomplished for the population as a whole in towns and cities and, of particular importance, for the plain men and women in villages and farming communities. These mutual improvement associations assembled books, conducted forums on a wide variety of noncontroversial subjects, and supported the movement for improved common schools. Gradually they came to import well-known lecturers who found in the lyceum not only profitable revenue but an opportunity for popularizing knowledge and moral values. Although, in view of the important function it fulfilled, something like the lyceum would have emerged, the form it took and the rapidity with which it caught on owed much to Josiah Holbrook. Holbrook, a New England farmer, had acquired from Silliman at Yale an enthusiasm for natural science. He conceived the idea of popularizing this utilitarian branch through voluntary organizations formed in every town in accordance with the time-honored principle of mutual association for common benefit. But Holbrook, being a promoter and thinking of the larger aspect of things, proposed the formation not only of town but of county and state lyceums, with a national federation tying the innumerable units together.

Only by taking into account the fact that the time was ripe for such an idea can one explain the fire-like spread of Holbrook's proposal. The little lyceum organized in 1826 in Millbury, Massachusetts, was the start. Before a year was over ten neighboring villages had set up lyceums and joined hands in a county organization. Devoting his entire time to this project, Holbrook publicized it through lectures, articles in magazines and newspapers, and correspondence. Within two years he had helped create over a hundred lyceums; and in 1831 delegates representing 1000 town lyceums organized the National American Lyceum in New York City. By 1835 the movement had spread to at least fifteen states. Although the majority of the 3000 lyceums were to be found east of the Alleghenies, within the succeeding years the lyceum marched rapidly westward until it reached the fringe of settlement in Iowa and Minnesota.

Designed to promote the diffusion of knowledge through the encouragement of the common school revival, the rehabilitation and establishment of libraries, and the holding of debates and weekly lectures, the lyceum especially in its early years also did much to familiarize Americans with natural science. It stimulated the collection of geological specimens and the installation in schoolhouses and town halls of the scientific apparatus manufactured by Holbrook himself. At its meetings the more articulate members discussed a wide variety of topics, varying from the merits of manual labor colleges and female seminaries to the uses of science, internal improvements, tariffs, and other issues of domestic economy. Such controversial subjects as war and slavery were discouraged until popular interest in them was too keen to brook any censorship.

When home talent no longer satisfied, the custom developed of inviting well-known figures from neighboring cities. Nationally celebrated men traveled over the country meeting the insatiable demand of the lyceums for knowledge and moral inspiration. Silliman, Agassiz, Mann, Phillips, Lowell, Holmes, Webster, Beecher, Sumner, and others hardly less notable found in the lyceum not only a welcome source of revenue but an opportunity to popularize ideas and causes dear to them. Emerson, whose fee was $50, was especially popular. His audiences heard him deliver most of the material subsequently shaped into the *Essays*, and his *Journals* threw much light on the communities in which he lectured. Although audiences came to demand superficial and even sensational lectures as the phenomenal success of the temperance reformer, John B. Gough, demonstrates, the lyceum was a remarkable liberalizing force in our intellectual history. In spite of its opposition to many of the radicalisms of the day, it was in a genuine sense a free forum serving to broaden the minds of the people and to make them more ready to entertain new ideas. Thomas Wyse, M.P., exaggerated of course, when on his return to England he wrote that as a result of the establishment of lyceums "thousands of children of not more than 8 or 10 years old, know more geology, mineralogy, botany, statistical facts etc., of what concerns their daily and national interests and occupations, than was probably known 30 years ago by any five individuals in the United States."[10] Another visitor, P. A. Siljeström, who came from Sweden to study such intellectual institutions as the lyceum, warned the Old World that if it was to escape both despotism and revolution it must imitate the American example of diffusion of knowledge. He made the remark, amazing for a European of that day, that popular culture in America was so important that Europe would be outstripped even in the higher learning unless she caught up with the young giant across the Atlantic.

The gap between the knowledge of the people and that of the classes whose means and position enabled them to enjoy a share in the world's culture remained wide. Thanks to the democratization of knowledge in the 1830s and 1840s, however, it was less broad and less deep than in any other country. The common man might still disparage the specialized knowledge of the scholar and the culture of the well-to-do, and they in turn might still deplore the anti-intellectualism, the prejudices, the ignorance of the masses, or the superficiality of the knowledge that was diffused among them. But a new era had begun.

[10] *Publications of the Central Society of Education*, II (1839), 216.

# 15 New Goals for Democracy

The triumph of reform is sounding through the world for a revolution of all human affairs. . . . Already is the ax laid at the root of that spreading tree, whose trunk is idolatry, whose branches are covetousness, war, and slavery, whose blossom is concupiscence, whose fruit is hate. Planted by Beelzebub, it shall be rooted up. Reformers are metallic; they are sharpest steel; they pierce whatsoever of evil or abuse they touch.

—The Dial, 1841

And yet we have reformers—yea, they swarm
Like bees in summer, pleased with the hum
Of their own insignificance, tho' no harm
Come from their stings, for they are silent, dumb;
Where they should cry loudest, their snarling word,
Save in their own praise, is weak, and therefore unheard.

—SAMUEL BENJAMIN JUDAH, 1823

"What is a man born for," asked Emerson, "but to be a Reformer, a Remaker of what man has made . . . imitating that great Nature which embosoms us all, and which sleeps no moment on an old past, but every hour repairs herself, yielding us every morning a new day, and with every pulsation a new life?"[1] In these words the popular lyceum lecturer from Concord expressed a central tenet in the reform philosophy which inspired men and women in their efforts to reform dress and diet in the interest of universal health, to uproot capital punishment and imprisonment for debt, slavery, intemperance, war, and prostitution, and to agitate for the full rights of women, the humane treatment of the insane and the criminal, and even for the overthrow of such venerable institutions as the family, private property, and the state itself. In another mood, to be sure, Emerson half-whimsically, half-seriously, laid at the door of the reformers many an idiosyncrasy; and in no mood did he ever, like the whole-hearted reformer, surrender his very self to any cause; he was too much an individualist for that, as his criticism of Brook Farm implied. "Spoons and skimmers," he remarked in connection with that idealistic effort to build a better society in microcosm, "you can lay indiscriminately together, but vases and statues require each a pedestal for itself."

Nevertheless, Emerson put his finger on the essential faith of the reformer when he assumed that institutions exist to be improved, that man can improve them along with himself, that the law of human society, like that of physical nature, is one of change. It was this faith that gave a sense of fellowship to reformers even when they vied with each other in celebrating the merits of the particular cause to which they had given the largest place in their hearts. It was this faith in reform as a law of nature that preserved some bond between the most doctrinaire reformers and those of milder temperaments and more pragmatic attitudes. The essential faith Emerson expressed remained even after reformers were bitterly separated on the basic issue of "immediatism" (faith in the possibility of realizing the desired objective in the near future) and "gradualism" (doubt concerning such optimism). Not even the condemnation of powerful and respectable voices or the general indifference of the plain people discouraged the zeal of the true reformer.

[1] "Man the Reformer," *The Complete Works of Ralph Waldo Emerson* (Houghton Mifflin Company, 1892), I, 236.

## The Roots of Reform: The Enlightenment

Back of this cardinal faith of the reformer was a heritage of European ideas. These found fertile soil in the northern and middle states and inspired men and women of certain temperaments to devote themselves to one or another of the specific reform causes of the mid-century.

Checked by antithetical ideas and interests, the Enlightenment nevertheless inspired some of the movements that replaced its reign. It has already been pointed out that this was true in the case of Unitarianism. On the ideological level humanitarianism itself sprang from the Enlightenment and from Christian ethics. In the fertile ground that a rising industrial and urban society provided, it struck deep roots, shot up many branches, and flowered luxuriantly in the mid-nineteenth century reform movements. Nor, in spite of the blight of critical realists and proslavery apologists, did the natural rights philosophy of the Enlightenment wither completely away. No reform movement failed to support its program by appeals to the inherent and inalienable rights of man to life, liberty, and the pursuit of happiness. Advocates of the abolition of capital punishment pointed out that the gallows destroyed the most basic of all the natural rights; temperance enthusiasts declared that unless society restricted the right of inebriates to frequent the dramshop their offspring would all be deprived of their natural rights; labor reformers decried moneyed monopolies and corporations on the score that they violated all the natural rights of men; and the abolitionists, in the use they made of the doctrine of "the higher law," were merely putting to work the venerable eighteenth-century concept of natural rights and natural laws.

Reformers also drew much strength from the revivification of the idea of progress. This doctrine, it will be recalled, owed much of its popularity to the amazing growth of the West and the startling achievements of science and technology. By the 1840s it interpenetrated every aspect of American thought and feeling. Without faith in the inevitable improvement of man and society it is at least questionable whether reformers would have continued their fight against evil when the odds mounted, as they did, and when victories dearly won seemed lost by backslidings. The literature of every movement for moral and social reform gives abundant evidence, both implicit and explicit, of the important role which the unquestioned faith in ultimate progress played. Wars might break out today, but, contradictory as they were to the law of improvement, they would one day cease plaguing mankind. The battle for temperance legislation was a hard one, but without it the law of progress could not be fulfilled; it was necessary for man's foreordained moral, religious, material, and political advance. The power of slavocracy and its northern allies was indeed formidable, but even it must at length give way to the justice and brotherhood the law of progress decreed. Thus ran the arguments.

But progress in all these spheres was not merely something supinely to be waited for. "Nature . . . ," wrote Albert Brisbane, one of the most thoroughgoing of reformers, "has implanted in man an instinct of social progress, which, it is true, will lead him through a series of transformations, to the attainment of his Destiny; but she has also reserved for his intelligence the noble prerogative of hastening this progress, and of anticipating results, which, if left to the gradual movement of society would require centuries to effect."[2]

The role of the doctrine of progress in reform movements may be illustrated by specific reference to the labor cause. Some friends of the working class, for whom Frances Wright spoke, held that progress might be realized through a just system of universal education and a fearless spirit of inquiry. Others believed that if government assumed control of machinery in the interest of the people, the machines would no longer throw the worker out of mills and shops penniless but would clear the way for increasing comfort and well-being. Still others, such as Orestes A. Brownson, Albert Brisbane, Parke Godwin, and George Ripley thought that the competitive principle in production had to be replaced by the cooperative before true progress could be achieved. Man had developed, Brisbane said, the industry, art, and science which had replaced savagery by civilization; he was now, through cooperation or association, to transform the earth which had flowered for some into a heaven for all.

Even such philosophical anarchists as Josiah Warren and Stephen Pearl Andrews predicated their Utopias on a law of progress which had gradually borne the sovereign individual on his way from complete subordination to the tyranny of the group to that ultimate realization of perfection—untrammeled freedom. Such an interpretation of progress, however, was even at the time contradicted by cold facts: the emergence

[2] Albert Brisbane, *The Social Destiny of Man* (Philadelphia, 1840), 331–332.

of the corporation and the challenges to laissez faire offered by the cry for subsidies for canals and railroads on the one hand and for conditions of well-being and regulation of hours of labor on the other.

## The Roots of Reform: Romanticism and Utilitarianism

Of the rising bodies of doctrine imported from abroad and taking root because they were related to the problems America shared with Europe, two, Romanticism and Utilitarianism, transcended all other patterns of thought by which reformers guided their way. The catch-all character of the term Romanticism may perhaps be the only thing about it that is entirely clear. But its enthusiasm for the idea of man as man, irrespective of any status acquired by inheritance or education, did blow heat into the Enlightenment's formula of natural rights. Concerned as it was with all living things, all spontaneous human feelings, Romanticism further assumed that all men were born with the same nature and that beneath superficial and outward differences lay "natural men."

One of most characteristically American outgrowths of Romanticism was the idea that here in the New World, and especially in the American West, this "natural man" might at last come into his own. The old civilization of Europe, encrusted with centuries of sin and corruption, might be sloughed off like an old skin, and man in America could stand forth once more an innocent and happy creature. For some, this hope was translated into a rejection of the past. The *Democratic Review* in 1839 boasted that "Our national birth was the beginning of a new history . . . which separates us from the past and connects us with the future only."[3] In the writings of a few intellectuals the concept of the innocent American, freed of corruption and of history, emerged as a full-blown literary metaphor, in which this new man was identified with Adam before the Fall. But many held to a less codified and extreme form of the idea that man in America was—or could, at least, become—less sinful, selfish, and corrupt than he had been in Europe.

This idea was typical of the optimistic view of human nature that characterized both Romanticism and the Enlightenment. In a certain sense, it was only a modification of the idea of progress. The idea also

[3] Quoted in R. W. B. Lewis, *The American Adam: Innocence, Tragedy and Tradition in the Nineteenth Century* (University of Chicago Press, 1955), 5.

had, in some contexts, strong patriotic overtones. It was, in short, an idea that could and did have wide circulation. Probably very few believed that a thorough regeneration of man was taking place in America. But many shared the belief that things would at least improve for man more rapidly in the New World than in the Old.

Such doctrines often inspired or reinforced generous efforts to redeem womankind from a thralldom to law and custom that stifled her human qualities, her individuality; to fetter the Demon Rum; to relax the hardened grip of the keeper of the insane and the criminal; to dispense altogether with the hangman; and to throttle once and for all the tyranny of the slave dealer and overseer. For however brutalized and degraded, every human being, according to the Romanticists, possessed a spark of the divine. No matter how dimmed this might be, it could never be entirely extinguished. Human love might fan it into a bright flame. In Emerson's words, "an acceptance of the sentiment of love throughout Christendom for a season would bring the felon and outcast to our side in tears." And Whitman's preachment of the solidarity of all animate things, his identification of body and soul, was but an extension of the Romantic gospel of universal brotherhood to a democratic pantheism. If all who shared such Romantic enthusiasm did not become reformers, the ideas themselves kindled the hearts of those who did give their all to elevate the oppressed and lowly, to usher in an order governed by the precepts of human fellowship.

To reformers with little taste for the abstractions of natural rights and the soft sentiments of Romanticism another doctrine of European origin, Utilitarianism, proved more congenial. We have already had cause to note the influence of one of the leading Utilitarians, Lord Brougham, on the American movement for the diffusion of knowledge. The teachings of Jeremy Bentham, who described himself to Andrew Jackson as "more of a United-States-man than an Englishman" and who further professed sympathy with what the hero of the people stood for, also played a part in the ideology of reform.

It would indeed be easy to overemphasize this influence in view of the fact that America had already realized so many reforms dear to Bentham's heart—the abolition of remnants of feudal custom, the amelioration of the penal code, the apparent elimination of war through a federal union, universal suffrage, and a sufficiently wide diffusion of knowledge to give practical weight to public opinion.

In addition to the blessing Benthamism bestowed on such reforms, it also established as the criterion for human laws, institutions, and customs the formula expressed in the memorable phrase, "the greatest good of the greatest number." Bentham's insistence that both morals and law arose because of their supposed utility and without any a priori assumptions, and that they were constantly to be tested and revised in the light of changing needs invited and reinforced reform activity quite as effectively as the antithetical assumption that all human laws and institutions had to be brought into conformity with an eternal, absolute, inexorable higher law, the law of nature and of God.

It is known that in varying degrees Dr. Thomas Cooper, Albert Gallatin, and even John Quincy Adams all came under Bentham's influence. In 1817 Adams, at Bentham's request, brought back to America twenty-five copies of each of his principal writings for distribution to strategic repositories. It is also clear that such legal reformers as William Beach Lawrence, champion of the abolition of imprisonment for debt, and Edward Livingston, author of the Louisiana legal code, owed much to Bentham. But less conspicuous figures also publicized his writings, notably David Hoffman, a New York lawyer, and Gilbert Vale, a New York publisher. In 1840 Vale launched a periodical frankly devoted to the ideals of Bentham. *The Diamond*, which enjoyed two years of life, weighed laws in the balance of reason "to abate the evils which the worst part of them inflict on society" and in advocating political, administrative, and social reforms through the reordering of legal provisions proved itself true to Bentham's creed. But the chief impetus to Bentham's doctrines was given by John Neal of Portland, who for two years resided in Bentham's London house and on his return to America propagated the ideas of his distinguished English friend in his novels and in the periodicals he edited. Neal also brought out an American edition of Bentham's writings and presented to the public his diary notes on Bentham's table talk.

The inspiration Benthamism provided reformers frequently expressed itself in specific terms. John Neal himself, foe of the death penalty, of imprisonment for debt, of women's wrongs, and of war, frequently showed in good Benthamite form that these hoary evils no longer served any useful function and, worse, positively interfered with the happiness of the greatest number. His friend, the Reverend John Pierpont, champion of the slave and of the untutored common man, likewise mustered Utilitarian arguments in his onslaught against outworn evils. Nor should the virile antislavery historian and critic of common law, Richard Hildreth, be overlooked in this connection.

Indeed, virtually all the propaganda for reform shows Utilitarian influence. Utilitarians insisted that capital punishment, the withered and rotted fruit of a bygone era, failed to check crime and prevented more realistic attacks from being made on this important social problem. Temperance advocates contended that the closing of the dramshops and distilleries would save the masses from squandering their wages, raise the standard of living, increase the efficiency of labor, and by checking crime limit society's expenditures for prisons. Pacifist propaganda likewise made much of the idea that anachronous war wasted vast sums that might otherwise be channeled into welfare and educational undertakings; that, equally bad or even worse, it solved no problems permanently and conferred no good even on the victor. Above all, proponents of the abolition of imprisonment for debt and the harshest features of the criminal code drew heavily from Bentham's armory of arguments.

But the general spirit of Utilitarianism also played a part in the thought of reformers. Edwin Chapin, Universalist minister, crusader against the vices of the city, and advocate of leading reforms of the day, expressed what was in the minds of many of his colleagues when he declared that true greatness was not indicated by splendid achievements, hollow adulation, and groveling fear, but rather by usefulness, the only true test of distinction. "He who has wrought out some thing for the benefit of his fellowmen, who has labored in some truly good cause, is essentially a far greater man than many a wealthy millionaire, successful politician, robed conqueror, or laurel-crowned poet," Chapin declared.[4] It is obvious that such insistence on the supreme value of contributions to human well-being must have both inspired reformers and provided them with sanctions for their activities.

The opposition which Utilitarianism provoked testified no less than its support to the popularity it enjoyed as a bulwark of reform. Interests that feared the cutting edge of change denounced a philosophy that repudiated "fundamental principles" by frankly proposing an annual canvassing of constitutions and laws in the name of the greatest good to the greatest number. To some critics Utilitarianism was a pernicious casuistry which, reduced to practice, merely awakened the mind to the consciousness of self-love and provided as a rule of conduct the calcula-

[4] Edwin H. Chapin, *An Address on True Greatness* . . . (Richmond, Va., 1840), 5, 9.

tion of interests with arithmetical precision. To others knowledge, education, and truth were great ends in themselves, not merely the means to some "petty, external good."[5] Thus such critics gave themselves exercise in exposing what to them was "the folly and foul spirit" which put man's worldly comfort and well-being above natural law and divine truth.

Some of the critics of Benthamism stressed most of all the fact that Utilitarianism was not built on a Christian base, and no doubt many Americans rejected Bentham's brand of Utilitarianism for this reason. For these, however, another Englishman, Bishop William Paley, could provide a similar social philosophy. Paley's Christian Utilitarianism was consistent both with reform on the basis of utility, and with the dominant Protestantism of the young Republic. His textbook of moral philosophy was the most popular source of ethical teachings in the American colleges during the early part of the century. Paley was too much a gradualist to retain favor with the more radical reformers, especially among the abolitionists, but his writings did exert a strong influence on others, particularly in the contests over prison reform.

But all these bodies of traditional and rising systems of thought imported from Europe, effective though they were in providing reformers with argument and support, do not entirely explain the intensity and spread of the social crusades in the Jacksonian era. Many persons read the literature of Romanticism, especially in the South but elsewhere too, and utterly failed to be guided by it into any humanitarian crusades; indeed, they found in that gospel reasons for some of the very conditions, such as the pedestal status of women, so repulsive to reformers. And many, even in the North and West where reform had its chief innings, must have read Benthamism or reread the natural rights philosophy only to set themselves the more adamantly against them. It is thus clear that there must have been in operation more basic forces which in larger measure explain why, in a given time and place, reforms enjoyed so much favor.

### The Roots of Reform: Social and Economic Tension

Many years ago, the economist and historian Frank Tracy Carlton suggested that the bulk of the reformers came from what had tradi-

[5] Le Roy J. Halsey, *Address to the Alumni Society of Nashville* . . . (Nashville, 1841), 9–10.

tionally been the dominant classes, the merchants and clergy, rather than from the rising industrial and lower middle classes on farm and in shop. More recently, other historians have taken up this thesis, and have attempted to work it out in detail, not only for the Jacksonian period but for other periods of reform agitation as well. It is true that many of the sons and daughters of older professional and mercantile families did condemn the new moneyed aristocracy of industrial entrepreneurs, and the slums, poverty and degradation of industrialism. Leaders of reform movements recruited from classes of waning power might be inclined to denounce, as many did, the rising "lords of the loom," as Charles Sumner called the owners of cotton textile mills who in general tacitly supported the chattel slavery on which their own profits seemed to depend. So too might reformers recruited from the once-powerful classes be the more likely to excoriate—and many did—the industrial system which was associated with depressions, slums, poverty, crime, and prostitution. That many reformers did come from the formerly dominant ministerial and commercial classes is borne out by a study of the backgrounds of the men and women judged sufficiently distinguished in humanitarian crusades to be included in the *Dictionary of American Biography.* But enough also sprang from the families of plain farmers and from the craftsman-mechanic class, and even from the ranks of the entrepreneurs themselves, to suggest that other factors in the motivation of reformers were at least as important as changes for the worse in their economic status.

While no clear relationship seems to exist between the periods of political revolt and the business cycle, much evidence could be mustered to support the thesis that the hard times following the panic of 1837 played a part in the expanding interest in social reform. Complacency toward the existing equilibrium naturally suffered a severe shock when whalers and other sailing ships were tied up lifeless at their moorings; when blast furnaces, shoe factories, and textile mills closed down; when in the great cities tens of thousands, penniless, ragged, and hungry, knew not which way to turn; when even professional men, shopkeepers, and farmers felt the pinch. When all these vicissitudes "drowned hope and created misery," it was natural for certain people from every social group to turn toward one or another of the reform causes.

In the name of democracy the special privileges of business were attacked and the rights of the working class vigorously asserted. Leaders of the trade unions, which revived in the early 1850s, protested against the exploitation of workers by powerful employers. The *Democratic Review* warned that if new machines continued to throw men out of work and if the rich western lands became exhausted as they one day would, the American industrial worker would be in the same desperate condition as his fellow in England. The autocratic relationship between capital and labor, the wretched conditions of work, and the physical as well as the moral deterioration of workers were all thoroughly aired by a Massachusetts investigating commission. Others pointed out that the vast accumulation of wealth in the hands of a few while the masses remained insecure and poverty-stricken had no place under professedly democratic institutions. Still others deplored the vast power of the corporation, a "new moneyed feudalism" which, it was said, bribed legislators, drove the small business man to the wall, and sucked the very lifeblood of democracy. Workmen in the mills of Lowell and Lawrence avowed that they had been forced or bribed by their employers to vote as they would have them.

Such testimonials led Emerson to declare that the northern industrial employer, no less than the southern planter, bought his slaves. In pleading for the Homestead Bill one of the followers of George Henry Evans warned that it was a measure necessary to aid the weak against the strong in an unequal struggle "between the bones and sinews of men and dollars and cents. . . ."[6] All these evidences of fear that democracy might not survive if existing evil conditions continued were reechoed by European commentators on the American scene.

It remained for a thoroughly democratic reformer, Lydia Maria Child, to anathematize the new spirit of trade and industry in words that no critic could rival:

In Wall-Street, and elsewhere, Mammon, as usual, cooly calculates his chance of extracting a penny from war, pestilence, and famine; and Commerce, with her loaded drays, and jaded skeletons of horses, is busy as ever fulfilling the "World's contract with the Devil." . . . I have often anathematized the spirit of Trade, which reigns triumphant, not only on 'Change, but in our halls of legislation, and even in our churches. Thought is sold under the hammer, and sentiment, in its holiest forms, stands labelled for the market. Love is offered to the highest bidder, and sixpences are given to purchase religion for starving souls. In view of these things, I sometimes ask whether the Age of Commerce is better than the Age of War? Whether

[6] *Cong Globe*, 32d Cong., 1 Sess., 1852, Append., 427.

our "merchant princes" are a great advance upon feudal chieftains? Whether it is better for the many to be prostrated by force, or devoured by cunning?[7]

Spokesmen for the less fortunate classes promoted programs for reform. The more extreme leaders who preached religious agnosticism or favored the distribution of landed property equally among the people won few recruits. Nevertheless, the agrarian proposals augmented the growing conviction that the problems of the urban laborer might be solved if the lands of the West were given away freely to any prospective settler. Other leaders of the urban worker favored the organization of trade unions capable of striking for better wages and working conditions. An even larger number emphasized political action and looked forward to the development of sufficient strength at the polls to enable the workers to obtain ten-hour-day laws, the ideal of those times, the abolition of imprisonment for debt, lien laws protecting the wages of the earner from unscrupulous exploitation by the employer, the abolition of privileged monopolies, and free compulsory education.

The appeal for free compulsory education aroused great interest among the industrial working class, which pinned its faith in the power of universal schooling to solve economic and social problems. The masses of urban poor were either illiterate or semiliterate, and few of their children could attend the handful of charity and church schools designed for them. The proud poor refused to take advantage of schools that stigmatized as paupers the children attending them. Some demanded day schools, but others advocated boarding institutions in which the state was to bear the entire expense of the upbringing of its wards. This extreme position was abandoned. Labor leaders and labor organizations, however, continued to demand free public schools at government expense and their demands carried weight in the crusade for universal free education.

A few labor leaders, chief among whom was Thomas Skidmore of New York, believed that any effort to redress the grievances of the working class through education alone was bound to prove both ineffective and detrimental. The system of production and distribution had to be reorganized, Skidmore held, before economic grievances could be redressed; and any effort to *"hold back* the people from their rights of property . . . until *education,* as they call it, can first be communicated

---

[7] Lydia M. Child, *Letters from New-York* (New York, 1843), I, 40.

. . . either do not understand themselves, or pursue the course they *are* pursuing, for the purpose of diverting the people from the possession of these rights."[8]

The collectivistic communities stood for a thoroughgoing type of economic transformation. By 1840 all of the communities inspired by Owen's experiment at New Harmony had petered out, but the hard times of the late 1830s and early 1840s and the general reform currents prepared the ground for Fourierism. In 1840 Albert Brisbane, scion of a well-to-do New York family and a convert to the Utopian socialism of Fourier, published his *Social Destiny of Man*. This popularization of Fourier's psychological, economic, and social creed at once took hold of the imagination of Americans. Brisbane's subsequent writings and tireless zeal in lecturing and promoting his scheme, together with the friendly sympathy bestowed on the movement by Horace Greeley in the *Tribune*, Parke Godwin in the *Post*, and George Ripley in the *Harbinger*, had their results. Within three years between forty and fifty phalanxes, as the joint-stock communities were called, had been established throughout the country. This marked a revolt against the competitive profit system and expressed the economic equalitarianism which colored an important segment of reform thought. Conservatives were alarmed. For a time Fourierism threatened to make even greater inroads. But the weaknesses of the phalanxes, which included inept recruiting, bad management, and inadequate financing, together with the difficulties of rowing against the mainstream, accounted for the collapse of many of them with the first signs of the return of better times.

### The Roots of Reform: The Example of Christ

Organized religion, although it sanctioned many of the social inequalities against which reformers protested, at the same time provided an important element in reform philosophy. Even essentially conservative Christians, like Bishop Hopkins of Vermont, sometimes spoke out against the privileges and practices of business enterprise and championed the cause of the working class. The son of a merchant and himself a superintendent of a Pittsburgh iron works before his entrance into the Episcopal ministry, Bishop Hopkins declared that society owed a

[8] Thomas Skidmore, *The Rights of Man to Property!* (New York, 1829), 369.

reasonable subsistence to every indivdual able and willing to work for it and that in so far as industrialism failed to provide it, industrialism failed. Moreover, he continued, the economic tyrant who drew blood-stained income from the lives and hearts of the miserable victims forced to provide unrighteous profits to employers or landlords could be neither a Christian nor a true citizen. "Their money is accursed, because it is coined out of the tears and sorrows of humanity." The bishop went on to condemn the perjury of merchants at the customhouses, speculation at the risk of others, the defrauding of creditors by concealments, and the making of profits by acts of insolvency. In New York the Unitarian leader, Orville Dewey, denounced "the insane and insatiable passion for accumulation," the concentration of immense fortunes in a few hands while the rest of the world, in comparative poverty, enjoyed neither the fair rewards of industry nor an equal share in its advantages.

Religion played a large part in the inspiration of reformers themselves. Even those who, like William Lloyd Garrison, bitterly denounced the churches for their approval of slavery or their silence regarding it were essentially religious men. Indeed, most of the reformers eminent in the pre-Civil War decades were influenced greatly by ideas that grew out of the Puritan, Quaker, and evangelical traditions.

No one can read widely in the reform literature without being profoundly impressed by the religious character of the arguments that filled the tracts, periodicals, lectures, and private correspondence of the crusaders. The temperance reformers, most of whom were devoutly pious, not only insisted that Scriptures gave no warrant for alcoholic beverages; they opposed them on the score that they interfered with the progress of revivals and the spread of Christ's word, that in the tavern and dram-shop men and women most frequently began their downward course to sorrow and ruin. Peace advocates cited the Sermon on the Mount and other texts in proof of their contention that Christianity condemned war. But war was anathema to them not only because of their belief that the Bible forbade it, but also because it seemed to promote worldliness, the corruption of morals, and the stagnation of churches. Critics of capital punishment likewise found Scriptural texts to support their crusade; at the same time they pointed out that the irrevocable sentence to death sometimes cut the condemned off from a possible later repentance and always prevented his true moral reformation. No crusade was more directly inspired by Christ's doctrine of love and brotherhood than that waged by the abolitionists. Western evangelism furnished many leaders with tactics, ideologies, and inspiration. One need only to examine a fair sample of the plethora of abolitionist literature to be reconfirmed in the belief that the Welds and the Tappans, the Childs and the Garrisons and the Motts condemned slavery because in their eyes it plainly contradicted both the literal word and, above all, the spirit of Christ's teachings.

These crusaders were probably influenced not only by the Christian doctrine of human brotherhood and love but also by the traditionally Puritan and Quaker sense of community responsibility for sin. Attention has already been drawn to the humanitarian crusades against the slums and poverty of Boston and New York that were led by Joseph Tuckerman and Edwin Chapin. If these men, the one a Unitarian clergyman and the other a Universalist, were largely inspired by the emphasis those faiths put on salvation by character and the divinity of all mankind, they were also inspired by somewhat the same spirit that inspired Cotton Mather when he took on his shoulders responsibility for the moral well-being of all Boston.

The activities of the Reverend John R. McDowall, trained in the Presbyterian faith, were more sensational than those of Tuckerman and Chapin, but they reflect the same conception of community responsibility for sin. In 1832 McDowall, horrified at the moral vice in New York City, frantically called on Christians to face the evil and aid in its suppression. Moral reform societies, Magdalen Houses, and a special organ, *McDowall's Journal*, carried on a melodramatic crusade to rescue "female profligates" from the dens of iniquity that held them, willingly or unwillingly. When the young enthusiast exposed the responsibility of prominent citizens for the existence of commercialized immorality, a halt was called.

Account must, of course, be taken of the fact that many Friends, many offspring of the Puritans, and indeed many evangelicals, North and West as well as South, were either indifferent or actually hostile toward every reform. We shall find proslavery champions buttressing their defense by appeals to the Scriptures; the opponents of the crusaders for peace, temperance, and the abolition of capital punishment spared no pains to prove that Holy Writ supported their own contentions rather than those of the crusaders. If, then, Christian ethics and religious drive must be given rank among the causes generating and propelling the currents of reform, it is clear that still other basic factors were at work.

## Democracy: Women's Rights

The wave of reforms which enlisted so much enthusiasm and so much condemnation in part reflected the advancing force of democracy and in part extended this force into the field of social relationships. Although American democracy in many ways was related to comparable patterns of thought in the Old World, especially to humanitarianism and Romanticism, in some ways it was a unique creed and program of action.

With much plausibility Ralph Gabriel has argued that the American democratic faith which had emerged by the mid-century included both a naturalistic and a supernaturalistic base. On the one hand it rested on the eighteenth-century faith in an orderly, law-governed universe in which both man and his institutions, the more these were harmonized with natural law, improved. On the other hand American democracy merged these concepts with a religiously fervent, transcendental faith in the dignity and potentiality and power of the individual, including the common man. The thoroughly consistent exponents of democracy widened the circle to include women and emphasized the individual not only as a final end but as a means of achieving that end. That end was the full growth and power of the individual, of every individual; the means by which this was to be achieved was individual effort, combined with that of others, to break down all the barriers, be they tradition, law, or interest, that stood in the way of elevating every individual in the most depressed ranks to full power and glory.

It was the merging of the rational doctrine of perfectibility and progress on the one hand with the religious emotion of individualism on the other that came to be identified with America both as a symbol and as an actuality. This complex of democracy and Americanism, as we shall discover in discussing nationalism and patriotism, further implied an inexorable faith in the eternal and universal superiority of America's republican and democratic institutions, of their fitness for all people, at all times, in all places, and of the duty of furthering their final triumph.

The relation of the democratic philosophy to the reform movements could easily be illustrated by an analysis of almost any one of them. Yet for several reasons the agitation against "women's wrongs" is an especially appropriate movement for detailed consideration. For one thing, this crusade was aimed to elevate one-half of the entire population rather than a mere minority of unfortunates. Again, the increasing participation of women in the larger world of ideas, itself of course the result of complex economic and social changes, has so affected the character of American intellectual life in the past three-quarters of a century that the early feminist agitation becomes, in an intellectual history, an obvious illustration to choose for bringing out the democratic implications of the whole humanitarian movement.

The revolt of the feminists—it must never be forgotten that they represented a small fragment of their sex—was in large part a protest in the name of democracy against the subordinate role of females, to use the word most common to the mid-century. Every argument that men had ever employed for their rights as citizens and human beings women crusaders now used. Henceforth, they insisted, the relations between the sexes must be governed by the doctrine of equality, of democracy. And the equality and democracy they had in mind and made explicit in stirring manifestoes was that of mid-century America; its foundation was the natural rights philosophy, its framework was the religious faith that God had created all human beings equal, that He intended each individual to achieve the full realization of every potentiality.

To appreciate the vigor of the demand for the redress of women's wrongs the inferior status of women at that time must be visualized as concretely as possible. In spite of the early interest in Mary Wollstonecraft's *Vindication of the Rights of Women* (1792) on the part of a handful of democratic idealists, and in spite of the example of sex equality among the Shakers, opinion almost universally continued to regard women as unfitted by nature for exercise of the higher mental processes. In consequence they were barred from opportunities for any education beyond the elementary or, at best, the secondary branches. The more usual course was for girls of the farming and lower middle classes to acquire practical skills at home, and for those of better-off families to be polished at boarding schools in the social amenities and the esthetic arts of fancy embroidery and painting on velvet. In general, women did not discuss politics or the larger social issues. According to common law, husbands and fathers not only controlled the property of their wives and daughters but were entitled to complete submissiveness. Even the churches—the Quakers alone excepted—subordinated women by excluding them not only from the ministry but from any public participation in church affairs. Even in what presumably was woman's own sphere, the home, she was bound to be submissive to her husband's will in theory if not in practice. Catharine Beecher expressed in characteristic phraseology the prevailing ideas of sex relations in 1840: "Heaven has appointed to one sex the superior, and to the other the subordinate station," she observed, "and this without any reference to the character or conduct of either. It is therefore as much for the dignity as it is for the interest of females, in all respects to conform to the duties of this relation."[9] The prose articles and fiction in the popular women's magazines of the time faithfully reflect this point of view—the view of the plain people as well as of most intellectuals.

The first clear-cut and dramatic protest against such ideas came when Frances Wright, a Scottish friend of Lafayette, took up residence in the United States in 1824. Her championship of labor, of public education, and of gradual emancipation of the slave was no less ardent than her devotion to woman's rights. Undeterred by ridicule and venomous threats of physical violence for daring to support greater freedom in marriage relationships, birth control, and what was almost as shocking, the appearance of the delicate sex on the public platform, Frances Wright continued her agitation. Except in Quaker circles, where women had traditionally taken part in "meeting" and in ministration, her campaign met only with rebuffs. Nevertheless, the subsequent feminist campaign owed much to the clear, logical, and forceful arguments by which this courageous crusader denounced the subjection of women by law and custom and pleaded for their emancipation on every level—economic, social, and cultural.

What really launched the feminist crusade was the desire on the part of a small group of women to participate in the movement for the abolition of slaves. The refusal to admit women to the existing antislavery societies or even to permit them to speak in public for the cause led to defiance on the part of such women as Lucretia Mott, the Philadelphia

[9] Quoted in Arthur W. Calhoun, *The Social History of the American Family* (Arthur C. Clark Co., 1917–1919), II, 83–84.

Quakeress, and Angelina and Sarah Grimké, South Carolina aristocrats who had become converted to Quakerism and abolitionism. Barred from existing organizations, women abolitionists formed a national organization of their own in 1834. So great was the opposition that in 1838 a Philadelphia mob burned the hall in which they were meeting. The next year the issue of admitting women to the existing national antislavery society of men broke up the organization into two movements, one composed of men alone, and one in which women cooperated with men on equal terms.

The refusal of the World's Antislavery Convention in London in 1841 to admit the American women delegates led two of them, Lucretia Mott and Elizabeth Cady Stanton, to launch a formal women's rights movement on their return to America. Their program was set forth in the Declaration of Sentiments issued in 1848 at the Seneca Falls Convention. This declaration paraphrased the Declaration of Independence in indicting men for their tyrannies over women. Notwithstanding great opposition, the advocates of women's rights continued to hold conventions, to agitate for the revision of state laws affecting their rights over property, and, in addition, to demand full political, economic, and cultural rights.

It was necessary for the champions of women's rights to shift the arguments that both religion and the natural rights philosophy provided. In spite of Garrison's firm statement, "We *know* that man and woman are equal in the sight of God," the Bible could be and was used with much effectiveness by the conservatives. The Bible apparently made God a male and woman responsible for man's woes. Besides, many specific texts seemed clearly to consign women to a role of inferiority. Gradually the most logical among the crusaders were forced to put greater relative emphasis on natural rights. Women, the argument went, were human beings; all human beings possessed the same inalienable rights to life, liberty, property, and the pursuit of happiness. But able conservative foes were quick to point out that nature meant that which had always existed; women had been eternal inferiors, *ergo* they were so by nature's dictate. Thus it became necessary for feminists to insist that nature included not alone what had been but that which might come. However inferior and degraded women might be as a result of their immemorial thralldom, God and nature alike ordained the necessity of growth.

But the foes of women's wrongs did not stop with reinterpretations of Christianity and of natural law in the interest of an all-inclusive democracy. In the course of time more and more emphasis was put on the argument of utility. The full emancipation of women would, in the words of Elizabeth Oakes Smith, not only enable women to achieve that individuality which was their due; it would also make "the world the better for it." Once free women from the slavery that welded them, regardless of their true individuality, into one stereotype, and they would raise to new heights every cause dear to the best of men: justice, religion, freedom, democracy. The subordination of women, concluded Mrs. Smith, had made them a retarding force in civilization; their emancipation would convert them into a dynamic agent for its progress.

The most profound treatise on women's rights was Margaret Fuller's *Woman in the Nineteenth Century*. In this remarkable book the New England Transcendentalist critic brought together virtually all the arguments in behalf of the full development of women as individuals, and to these she added certain psychological insights and social visions of her own. Sex, she contended, is a relative, not an absolute, matter: "There is no wholly masculine man, no purely feminine woman." Thus all nature cried out against the hard and fast barrier society had drawn between the two. Once this truth was recognized, women would cease living so entirely for men and begin to live for themselves as well. And in so doing they would, in truth, help men to become what had been promised, the sons of God. For men's interests were not contrary to those of women; they were identical by the law of their common being, a law which, if observed, would make them the pillars of one porch, the priests of one worship, the bass and contralto of one song. Man had educated woman more as a servant than as a daughter and had found himself a king without a queen. Stripped of its occasionally vague mysticism and its Transcendentalist verbiage, *Woman in the Nineteenth Century* is seen to demand, on the score of reason, religion, and beauty, the elevation of sex relationships to a new and thoroughly democratic level.

Nor did the feminism of the mid-century decades operate merely on the plane of ideas. Thanks to the courage and energy of the pioneers and the encouragement of such sympathetic men as Channing, Emerson, Garrison, Greeley, and Phillips, a few women created careers that not only enabled them to support themselves and in some cases the less effective members of their families also, but at the same time afforded them deep satisfaction. Elizabeth Oakes Smith seems to have been the first of her sex to lecture on the lyceum platform. In journalism and writing Margaret Fuller, Sarah J. Hale, Jane Swisshelm, Lydia Maria Child, Harriet Beecher Stowe, Catharine Sedgwick, Alice and Phoebe Cary all achieved distinction. If the law remained closed, medicine became a possible profession for at least a few after Elizabeth Blackwell, the first woman physician of modern times, opened an infirmary for women in New York in 1854, six years after she obtained her M.D. degree. In 1852 the Congregational church ordained Mrs. Antoinette Louisa Brown Blackwell as a minister.

The time had not yet come when more than a very few young women could take advantage of college training in such institutions as Oberlin and Antioch; but in the normal schools they were finding opportunities to acquire professional training for the lower schools which increasingly came under female direction. Tocqueville probably summarized the situation fairly when he observed (1835) that while Americans "have allowed the social inferiority of women to subsist, they have done all they could to raise her morally and intellectually to the level of man; and in this respect they appear to me to have excellently understood the true principle of democratic improvement."[10]

## Reform and Democracy Criticized

If in general reformers were too greatly blinded by their zeal for the cause to which they gave unstinted labor, a few at least did occasionally analyze both the motives of many of their colleagues and the shortcomings of the group as a whole. No conservative critic, for example, ever wrote a more witty and penetrating account of "the lunatic fringe" than Thomas Wentworth Higginson, a devoted abolitionist and advocate of other "causes." William Ellery Channing, friend of peace and of the slave, on more than one occasion warned fellow reformers to let their genius have full play, to avoid too narrow modes of action, to give a wide range to thought, imagination, taste, and the affections. In much the same spirit Lydia M. Child, an intense abolitionist, warned her coworkers against permitting "the din of the noisy Present to drown the Music

[10] Alexis de Tocqueville, *Democracy in America*, II, 224.

of the Past."[11] Horace Greeley approached some of the conservative critics in analyzing reformers' motives in terms of personal factors. In his essay, "Reforms and Reformers," the crusading editor of the New York Tribune wrote that a great number of persons in a democratic society, believing themselves to be underrated in the world's opinion, promoted some reform not because of any genuine quarrel with the actual structure of society but solely because of their own place in it. According to this reformer the desire to be someone, the frustration of being unable to do with impunity much that desires promoted, led many a restless soul into the reform camp. "This class sees the Social World," Greeley declared, "so covered, fettered, interpenetrated by laws, customs, beliefs, which plant themselves firmly across the path whereon its members are severally pressing forward to gratification of every impulse, that it is plain that either Society is or they are sadly in the wrong; and imperious Appetite forbids the conclusion that *they* are."[12]

It remained for conservative intellectuals to criticize the reformer for what they termed his "dyspeptic zeal," inflexible commitment to an oversimplified formula, and indifference to the niceties of social convention. In a bright but mordant essay James Russell Lowell, once of the breed himself, declared that every reformer had a mission (with a capital M) to attend to everybody else's business and to reform, at a moment's notice, everything but himself. Other critics, pushing to an extreme the idea that Greeley expressed, charged that reformers were reformers by reason of mental dyspepsia. One of New York City's four hundred, a scion of the Astor family, facetiously had it that Mr. So-and-So took up with Fourieristic socialism because, being the most henpecked of men, he hoped that in the general distribution of women and goods incident to the triumph of the Cause someone else might get his wife!

That personal motives, psychological maladjustments, the unconscious drive to compensate for feelings of inadequacy and frustration did motivate many a reformer to take up the cudgels for the still more unfortunate Negro or inebriate or criminal is probably as true as it is undemonstrable. In any case the suspicion is at least present, to cite one or two from a score of possible examples, that Joshua Giddings found it

[11] The Letters of Lydia Maria Child (Houghton Mifflin Company, 1883), 46–47, 72.
[12] Horace Greeley, Recollections of a Busy Life (New York, 1868), pp. 515–516.

easier to turn his back on orthodox Whiggery and take up with reforms after he had lost heavily in land speculations and been generally defeated by hard times. Nor can anyone read of the sorrows and frustrations of such a high-strung child and young girl as Dorothea Dix without sensing some connection between them and her subsequent devotion to the cause of the ill-treated, even tortured victims of insanity.

On the other hand, certain considerations suggest the need of caution in attributing zeal for reform to personal maladjustment. It is open to question whether any one geographical area, such as the northeastern states, was marked by a disproportionate number of psychologically maladjusted persons. Nor is there available evidence to prove that social and economic conservatives included a higher proportion of well-adjusted men and women.

However much conservatives belittled reformers for their personal idiosyncrasies, the wisest admitted, at least in times of crisis when reform views became popular, as abolitionism did after the Emancipation Proclamation, that these men and women were not without a social function. Oliver Wendell Holmes observed that reformers, interfering as they did with vested rights and time-hallowed interests, must needs perform an office comparable to that of nature's sanitary commission for the removal of material nuisances. "It is not the butterfly, but the beetle, which she employs for this duty, . . . not the bird of paradise and the nightingale, but the fowl of dark plumage and unmelodious voice."[13]

The jibes against the reformer on the score that he was a fanatic, a misfit, or a scavenger did not exhaust the onslaughts of the opposition. If Lydia Maria Child may be taken as an authority on the antiabolitionists, the major contingent among the critics of reform, the root of the trouble lay not with the farmers and mechanics. "Manufacturers who supply the South, . . . ministers settled at the South, and editors patronized by the South, are the ones who really promote the mobs," declared this able lady in 1835. "Withdraw the aristocratic influence, and I should be perfectly ready to trust the cause to the good feeling of the people."[14] Mrs. Child no doubt oversimplified the relationship between the opposition to abolitionism on the one hand and personal interest and the aristocratic spirit on the other. Yet an analysis of the arguments of

[13] Oliver Wendell Holmes, *Oration delivered before the Authorities of the City of Boston* . . . (Boston, 1863), 20.
[14] *The Letters of Lydia Maria Child*, 18.

critics of reform and of the democracy to which it was related suggests that much truth lies in the words of this penetrating crusader for the black man's freedom.

The southern tendency to identify all reforms with abolitionism—an understandable tendency—gives the Southerners an outstanding place among the critics of reform. The southern critique of reform, however, will be considered later in the discussion of the intellectual life of the Old South.

To those to whom the present seemed best to the degree that it preserved the past in customs and institutions, reform was a ruthless scythe. In urging the female graduates of an Alabama seminary to cling to the old, the ministerial orator declared that the Amazons of the age who raised a hurricane over such harebrained notions and speculations as women's rights and abolitionism were "no co-laborers with the mighty spirits of the past, who have bequeathed to us this good land, and the glorious institutions that we inherit." They were rather, he went on, "the disorganizers of civilization, the foes of liberty, the vampires of high-toned morals and chivalrous deeds."[15] In the words of a critic of the movement for the abolition of capital punishment, reformers had better "recollect that all movement is not progress, and that 'to innovate is not to reform.' "[16]

But reverence for the past was no more important a sentiment in the antireform literature than patriotism. Again and again feminism, abolitionism, and Utopian socialism were condemned as imported European vagaries that had no place at all in America. Even the British-born and British-trained scholar, George Frederick Holmes of the University of Virginia, himself a friendly correspondent of Auguste Comte, Europe's great philosophical innovator, began a critical review of Greeley's *Hints Toward Reforms* by stigmatizing the proposals under discussion as European importations and therefore un-American. More logical was the deeply felt fear that reform might disturb the traditional love of laissez faire, that it might augment the powers of centralized government and "the seductive embrace of power." Equally frequent was the argument in discussions of Utopian socialism that least of all countries should America permit it, inasmuch as here men of wealth had generally earned

---

[15] Joseph J. Nicholson, *The Influence of Literature, Art and Science, in Forming, Refining and Elevating Character* (Mobile, 1856), 14.

[16] *Southern Literary Messenger*, XVIII (November, 1852), 654.

their fortunes and treated the industrious poor with as much courtesy as a rich neighbor. In attacks on the peace crusade patriotism was appealed to in support of war and in criticism of the men who would abolish the institution by which our independence had been won and our liberty preserved and extended. Even the temperance cause aroused patriotic denunciation. In opposing it Alexander S. Davis of Hanover, Pennsylvania, declared that the temperance agitation repudiated the principles of 1776—the right to life, liberty, property, and happiness!

Recognizing the importance of a small but active group of the clergy in almost every reform cause, certain critics tried to mobilize anticlerical and free thought sentiment in their denunciations of reform. Thus Alexander Davis, to whom temperance was an un-American crusade, went on, in his *A Loud Call to the Citizens of this Nation*, to defend the constitutional right of manufacturing and selling spiritous liquor without consulting any "bastardly priest in existence . . . and without worshiping, kneeling, cringing to the army of wicked, aristocratic, kingly, haughty, lounging and dissipated priests who are ever engaging in seducing, gulling and blind-folding the people, that the people can be more easily wheedled to support their humbuggery, blackguardism, scoundrelism and beelzibubism."[17]

On the whole the religious interest was more frequently regarded as an anchor to the past than a propeller to the future. If the reformers relied on Scripture, the antireformers did so no less. Indeed, Biblical texts were hurled like David's stones in the counterattacks against the movements for the abolition of capital punishment, Negro slavery, and the alleged wrongs of women. In his criticism of Utopian socialism George Frederick Holmes did not, to be sure, quote Scripture, but he did remind his readers that God, not man, had decreed the curse of labor. He spoke for many gentlemen of the cloth in attributing "the lust for equality in material goods" to a want of earnest religious faith.

Nor did these arguments exhaust the weapons of those who spoke against reform in the name of religion. The old Calvinistic theory of human nature continued to be urged as an impassable barrier in the way of the most philanthropic reforms. Moved by tender sympathy for the sufferings of mankind, the reformer, according to the Reverend James W. Massie, forgot that "men are incurably fallible, that absolution from

[17] Alexander Davis, *A Loud Call to the Citizens of this Nation* (Hanover, Pa., 1842), 104.

pain and woe is impossible."[18] But no churchman represented this position so engagingly as the layman Nathaniel Hawthorne. It is true that
this faithful follower of the Jackson men in politics had no illusions
about American aristocrats, and that his sympathy with the exploited,
whether on the plantation or in the mill, found expression. At the same
time he was unable to pin his faith to mere reform. "Earth's Holocaust"
allegorically pictured the reformers relentlessly heaping into a huge bon-
fire all that stood in the way of their object, only to find in the end that
by neglecting to throw the human heart into the flames they had burned
all but the earth itself to a cinder in vain! "The heart, the heart!—There
was the little, yet boundless sphere wherein existed the original wrong
of which the crime and misery of this outward world were merely types.
Purify that inward sphere, and the many shapes of evil that haunt the
outward, and which now seem almost our only realities, will turn to
shadowy phantoms and vanish of their own accord."[19]

It was such an attitude, no less than the actual record of the churches
on the reforms of the day, that led Greeley to indict professing Christians as obstacles to reform: "To the Conservative, Religion would seem
often a part of the subordinate machinery of Police, having for its main
object the instilling of proper humility into the abject, of contentment
into the breasts of the down-trodden, and of enduring with a sacred
reverence for Property those who have no personal reason to think well
of the sharp distinction between Mine and Thine."[20]

All these sources of special interest, patriotism, and religion bulked
large in the pressure of public opinion against reform. This despotic and
intolerable restraint of conventional forms, Lydia Maria Child urged, led
men and women to check their best impulses, suppress their noblest
feelings, conceal their highest thoughts. "Each longs," she commented,
"for full communion with other souls, but dares not give utterance to
such yearnings." What hindered chiefly was the fear of what Mrs. Smith
or Mrs. Clark would say, "or the frown of some sect; or the anathema of
some synod; or the fashion of some clique; or the laugh of some club; or
the misrepresentation of some political party. Oh, thou foolish soul!
Thou art afraid of thy neighbor, and knowest not that he is equally

[18] James W. Massie, *An Address delivered before the Society of Alumni of the
Virginia Military Institute* (Richmond, 1857), 11–13.
[19] Nathaniel Hawthorne, *Mosses from an Old Manse* (Houghton Mifflin Company, 1882), 445.
[20] Horace Greeley, "Reforms and Reformers" in *op. cit.*, 524–525.

afraid of thee. He has bound thy hands, and thou hast fettered his feet. It were wise for both to snap the imaginary bonds, and walk onward unshackled."[21]

Reformers never lost faith in their ability sooner or later to make the common man see eye to eye with them on all the matters which to the active humanitarians so vitally affected the well-being of the masses. Humble folk did, to be sure, take active parts in the reforms immediately affecting their own status, such as the movement for the abolition of imprisonment for debt, manhood suffrage, and the onslaught against monopolies. Temperance also enlisted fairly widespread support. But in general it seems clear, from present knowledge of the reform causes, that the majority of the people in the ordinary walks of life were either indifferent or hostile to the reform movements that did not seem to touch their own interests in some fairly immediate or obvious way. The industrial workers for the most part were apparently indifferent to the anti-slavery argument that linked the advance of the wage earner with the freedom of the slave. Artisans and farmers were represented in the Fourierist communities, but in many instances at least they were outnumbered by the small business and professional men and their wives who provided the leadership. By and large, neither the plain man nor the plain woman had much except contempt for the democratic doctrines of the feminists.

The doctrine of democracy, which did indeed arouse the enthusiasm of the common man, also felt the sting of critics. The sympathetic account of America by Tocqueville, perhaps the most profound and original of the European commentators on American institutions in this period, was nevertheless qualified by a basic reservation. Equalitarianism, according to this French aristocrat, on the whole tended to promote despotism, the despotism of the masses. Once the leveling of individuals had progressed far enough, the historical and conventional barriers which protected individuals from invasions of state power by the masses no longer held. This position was probably publicized in greater measure by Francis Lieber, the German-American scholar whose writings in political science were widely read among scholars. Lieber never tired of denouncing the tendency of democracy to jeopardize individual liberties, especially property rights. His attacks on the social contract theory, similar to those of Story and other legal conservatives, were as vigorous as his de-

[21] Lydia M. Child, *Letters from New-York*, 202–203.

mands for the restraint of the people by fundamental laws, the best buttresses, he thought, for individual liberties.

Among the literary critics of democracy James Fenimore Cooper and Herman Melville may be taken as representative. Cooper, it will be recalled, quarreled with democracy not from any theoretical concern —he approved of democratic theory—but because of the everyday churlishness of ordinary people with their disrespect for the aristocratic values of decorum and dignity. As a large landowner he found additional reason to vent his spleen when the New York antirent agitation demanded the abolition of tenantry; equalitarian agrarianism was in his jaundiced eyes the worst possible of the evils born of democracy. Herman Melville's distrust of democracy was both more theoretical and more profound. He observed in one of his allegorical novels, *Mardi* (1849), that, after all, political freedom was not a prime and chief blessing; it was good only as a means to personal freedom, uprightness, justice, and felicity. These, continued the adventuresome and mystical sailor of the Southern Seas, were qualities not to be shared or to be won by sharing. On the contrary, they were virtues either born with the individual, civilized or barbarian, flesh of his flesh, blood of his blood, or to be won and held by him and by him alone. However loudly the thrall yelled out his liberty, he still remained a slave. In a universe in which chronic malady was a fact, the individual was more likely to be free, upright, just, and happy under a single monarch than if he were exposed to the violence and whims of twenty million monarchs, though he be one of them. "That all men should govern themselves as nations, needs that all men be better, and wiser, than the wisest of one-man rulers." Moreover, "That saying about *levelling upward, and not downward,* may seem very fine to those who cannot see its self-involved absurdity. But the truth is, that, to gain the true level, in some things, we *must* cut downward; for how can you make every sailor a commodore? or raise the valleys, without filling them up with the superfluous tops of the hills?"[22]

Cooper with his whining thrusts at men in shirtsleeves and Melville with his dislike of mankind in the mass spoke largely for themselves, though in a sense they also voiced the misgivings of the older Calvinist and Episcopalian mercantile and landed classes toward democracy. The most systematic attacks, however, came not from these quarters in the

[22] *The Works of Herman Melville* (Constable and Co., London, 1922–1923), VI, 206.

North or, certainly, from the rising industrialists, but from the southern planting aristocracy. These attacks will be considered later. Meantime it may be well to turn to the varied and often paradoxical interpretations which democrats and reformers as well as aristocrats and their intellectual sympathizers attached to the words patriotism and Americanism, words appealing to a sentiment more deeply rooted in the heart of the common man than reform.

# 16 The Rising Tide of Patriotism and Nationalism

While the republics of North America are new, the ideas of the people are old. While these republics were colonies, they contained an old people, living under old institutions, in a new country. Now they are a mixed people, infant as a nation, with a constant accession of minds from old countries, living in a new country, under institutions newly combined out of old elements. It is a case so singular, that the old world may well have patience for some time, to see what will arise. . . . The Americans have no national character as yet.

—HARRIET MARTINEAU, 1834–1836

By some, patriotism or love of country is regarded as an airy bubble, raised by cunning statesmen to dazzle and bewilder the multitude. . . . Our country, if we truly love it, evokes our feelings, our judgment, our imagination, and solicits these, by an unforeseen persuasion, to employ themselves in adorning and exalting the object of their regard.

—CORNELIUS MATTHEWS, 1839, 1845

387

The goodly company of foreign visitors who came to the United States during the mid-century era differed with each other on the basic point of what constituted the unique features of American culture. Many agreed with Charles Latrobe, who, after surveying the differences in the origin, blood, style of life, and habits of the American people, declared that they could hardly be said to possess any nationality at all. Their only distinctive marks, he concluded, were a hearty dislike for the monarchical form of government, a boundless admiration for republicanism, and an abnormal sensitiveness to foreign criticism.

Francis Grund, a many-sided Austrian who was to throw in his lot with the Americans, represented the views of a different group of visitors from Europe. The American people, he observed, were not united by a unique language, an ancient past, nor homogeneity; but in spite of the absence of these ties, ties which made European countries true nations, the Americans nevertheless did constitute a nation. American nationality rested on powerful material and moral bases, Grund believed. In the universally shared hope of acquiring property and consideration that American institutions held out to all persons, regardless of birth, he saw the most powerful of the ties holding this people together. It was this hope that in his eyes explained what constituted "the characteristically American habit" of making a pleasure and an amusement out of business. Grund's economic interpretation went deeper than this. In his view the progress of the West was "the greatest safeguard of the Union." For the West, he observed, was indispensable to the prosperity of both South and North, and in case of a quarrel between these two the alliance of the West with the one or the other would force the isolated section to yield in the interest of its economic well-being.

But Grund did not think that material interests were the only ones uniting Americas and making them a true nation. Religious sentiment also played a great role. Related to this religious bond, he argued, was the deep conviction that America was the physical means and instrument for realizing moral power. This moral power involved a transcendent faith not merely in the America of the fathers but in the America of tomorrow's children, an America that coupled prosperity for all with harmony, righteousness, and light. Such an idealistic analysis was in keeping with the moral and religious spirit of the age.

Americans themselves indulged in much speculation on what constituted the American feeling of nationality which with some exceptions they cherished, and what best promised to deepen and strengthen American patriotism. From a multitude of Fourth of July orations and academic addresses before the literary societies of the colleges, as well as from less ephemeral and out-of-the-way literature, it is possible to reconstruct a native diagnosis of American nationalism and patriotism in the period between South Carolina's nullification act in 1832 and the great Compromise of 1850. Few of these writings, it is true, were either systematic or philosophical. But some gave evidence of comprehensiveness and pentration. This was true of the writings of George Perkins Marsh, the Vermont philologist and diplomat who discussed the roles played in the development of national character by hereditary opinions, foreign relations, religious beliefs, climate and soil, and habitual modes of American life and institutional arrangements. Not everyone then saw so clearly as Marsh that a long period must elapse before what were at first impulses or passions of individuals or groups became the characteristics of a united people, and that ages might be required to change Old World habits of thought which ages had been employed to create.

## States' Rights, Sectionalism, and Cosmopolitanism

The fact that a marked development of nationalism and patriotism in thought and feeling is apparent during the years between 1830 and 1850 should not obscure the countertendencies of the period. We have seen that in the West a good deal of sectional self-consciousness was developing and that cultural regionalism was beginning to strike roots. And we shall see that the striking growth of sectional self-consciousness in the South was already paving the way for the experiment to be launched in 1861 in the name of southern nationalism. New England, too, thought in sectional terms even when her representatives, such as Daniel Webster, best succeeded in identifying her own interests with the interest of the nation itself. All this sectional self-consciousness was, of course, affected by such things as material conflicts over tariffs, internal improvements, and public lands.

In addition to sectionalism, state pride, especially on the Atlantic seaboard, continued to be a vigorous sentiment, and states' rights were jealously guarded. However much a variety of interests besieged the central government for favors, the theory of laissez faire won lip service in almost every quarter. Always suspicious of the powers of the central government, states' rights men everywhere, together with the most powerful spokesmen of the South, rejoiced at the whittling down of federal authority when the movement for the recharter of the national bank failed and when in 1846 a period of low tariffs began.

The existence of cosmopolitanism and internationalism in American intellectual life was another deterrent to the development of a strong sense of nationality in Americans. The cooperation of humanitarians with their European colleagues—feminists, abolitionists, prison reformers, and pacifists—proved that the intellectual and emotional interests of many Americans transcended purely national boundaries and values. Reformers not only attended, but in the case of Elihu Burritt actually organized on European soil, popular congresses for the promotion of humanitarian crusades. In fact, the closest cooperation existed between the British and American movements against war and against slavery. And notwithstanding the predominant conviction that America should remain aloof from European turmoils, a small but vociferous group calling itself "Young America" demanded and even plotted for official intervention in behalf of the European liberals who, after the crushing defeats of 1848–1849, refused to abandon all hope for the downfall of imperialistic tyranny.

The stridently chauvinistic demands for self-sufficiency and a unique culture, which gave no signs of ending, did not blind any but the most obtuse patriot's eye to the fact that in every sphere of mental and artistic endeavor America continued to derive much from Europe. The increasingly close physical connection with the Old World, marked by the inauguration in 1838 of steamship ties, made for even more intimate relations. "Farewell nationality!" wrote Nathaniel P. Willis when the *Great Western* was welcomed to American shores. "In literature we are no longer a distinct nation. We have shrunk from the stranger to the suburban or provincial."

No nation was showing greater eagerness to learn from others. The Reverend Ezra Gannett of Boston, in speaking of foreign countries in 1840, declared that "the arrival of a steamship every fortnight at our doors, freighted with the influences which the Old World is no less eager to send than we to receive, must increase the danger of our losing independence, as well as our neglecting to cultivate originality of character. . . . All that we can do," he continued, "is to form a national character *with the help of these influences.* . . . We must exercise discrimination, and reject what is bad while we accept that which is good."[1] The treaty Caleb Cushing negotiated with China in 1844 departed from English precedent in providing for the free intercourse of Americans with the learned men of China, for facilities for the study of the Chinese language and literature and the purchase of books, manuscripts, and other aids for gathering wisdom in all the arts and sciences from Chinese storehouses. It will be recalled that European and American scientists exchanged visits and publications and that, in spite of the patriotic pride of naturalists in descriptions of American geological formations, flora, fauna, and ethnological remains, American science was part and parcel of that of Europe. In a general sense this was true in other fields of learning. One evidence was that in 1835 four Americans were studying in German universities and that in 1860 twenty-seven could be found in those institutions.

Cosmopolitanism and eclecticism had votaries in literary circles. The proof of this may be found in the first instance in the indictments of American literature by patriots who resented its imitativeness. "Why cannot our literati comprehend the matchless sublimity of our position among the nations of the world—our high destiny—and cease bending the knee to foreign idolatry, false tastes, false doctrines, false principles? When," continued this patriot, "will they be inspired by the magnificent scenery of our own world, imbibe the fresh enthusiasm of a new heaven and a new earth, and soar upon the expanded wings of truth and liberty?"[2] But the fact that such enthusiasm for cultural nationalism also provoked criticism is additional evidence of the eclecticism of American letters in this period. Thus, for example, a writer in the *Whig Review* in 1845 took cultural patriots to task: "Amidst uncertain institutions and a heterogeneous population, we have mainly but a feeble and imitative literature, that servilely copies everything from abroad, and then seriously pretends to call its secondary inanities 'an American literature.' "

Others were impatient with the doctrine that America must turn its back on the glories of traditional literature. Lowell claimed Shakespeare and Milton as our own and deprecated a nationality that was "only a less narrow form of provincialism, a sublimer sort of clownishness and ill-

---

[1] Ezra S. Gannett, *A Sermon delivered in the Federal Street Meeting House in Boston, July 19, 1840* (Boston, 1840), 17.
[2] *Democratic Review*, VI (November, 1839), 428–429.

manners."[3] At the same time his friend Henry Wadsworth Longfellow brought to his fellow Americans in his simple poems of pathos much of the ballad literature of the Old World. "Vast forests, lakes, and prairies cannot make great poets," observed the author of *Hiawatha*. "They are but the scenery of the play, and have much less to do with the poetic character than has been imagined. . . . We have, or shall have a composite [literature], embracing French, Spanish, Irish, English, Scotch and German peculiarities. Whoever has within himself most of these is our truly national writer."[4] Oliver Wendell Holmes, picking up the argument and meeting it on a somewhat different level, wittily declared that those who entered the Temple of the Muses, even when they hailed from a Republic, must not outrage propriety by ostentatiously flaunting their working-day dress.

Such sentiment was not confined to verbal proclamations. These writers, together with the great majority of their associates, exemplified their cosmopolitan creed in their own writings. Less gifted amateurs even more patently imitated English models in the "falsely feminine" and mawkish pieces they wrote. Literary dependence and cosmopolitanism were also reflected in the reissue of British periodicals in America. British novels gave no sign of wearying American readers. What was true in literature was even more true in the other arts.

But in spite of its cosmopolitan and eclectic elements, the intellectual and esthetic life of America was thought by some Americans whose main concern was the pursuit of culture to be too slender and too much marred by democratic vulgarity and material crassness. Hence some went to Italy to find in its classical and Renaissance treasures inspiration for trying mythological and grandiose themes with their own hands. For others the ateliers of Florence, Rome, Düsseldorf, and Barbizon provided the technical training lacking in America. Some lingered on in Europe, true expatriates. Others, having bitten the European apple, sensed a sharp privation when, on their return, "the fruit was snatched from their lips" and that of America put in its place; for, as Henry James remarked, the American apple, however firm and ruddy, was not to be negotiated by the same set of teeth.

[3] *North American Review*, LXIX (July, 1849), 207–208.
[4] Samuel L. Longfellow, *The Life of Henry Wadsworth Longfellow* (Houghton Mifflin Company, 1893), II, 19–20, 73.

## Geographic and Economic Foundations

Evidences of cosmopolitanism in the new country were greatly overshadowed by a heightening of traditional patriotism and by the rise of newer elements, both materialistic and emotional, in American nationalism. In the discussions of nationalism during this period race played little part, though Gobineau, a French champion of Nordicism, was translated and published in Philadelphia. The Nordic concept of race was further expounded by George Perkins Marsh in *The Goths in New-England* (1843), by George Bancroft in his *History of the United States,* by such advocates of native Americanism as Frederick Saunders, and by occasional exponents of Manifest Destiny.

Geography figured more frequently than race in the ideology of American nationalism during this period. The time-honored conviction that God and nature had designed a unique geographical arena for the American experiment found continuous expression. "God designs that each country should wear a peculiar ideal physiognomy," wrote Thomas Starr King in 1851. The breakup of the Union into two or more confederacies would degrade God's handiwork—this was the moral King and his fellow nationalists did not hesitate to draw. The doctrine that God and nature had prescribed a fixed stage for the American experiment implied that the country was so blessed by isolation from Europe's quarrels that it might enjoy a kind of irresponsibility in international affairs. It is in large part this conviction that helps explain the quick collapse of the feeble movement for intervention in behalf of the crushed liberal revolutionists in 1848. The growing conviction that geography had provided material barriers for the antithetical political and social systems of the Old World and the New was related to the revival of the Monroe Doctrine in the 1830s and its growth in the following decades in popular sentiment and public policy.

If God had given the American people a unique physiognomy in the national terrain, expediency sometimes required the temporary modification of the presumably fixed and final lines. Albert K. Weinberg has shown, with a wealth of proof, that each time any section or group within the nation cast jealous eyes on some appendage, such as the Floridas, or Louisiana, or Oregon, or California, it was easy to declare that the natural boundaries in actuality lay thither, beyond the desideratum. When the impulse for expansion known as Manifest Destiny got well under way in the later 1840s and 1850s, Canada and the Caribbean, Mexico and Central America, and even the islands of the Pacific were conveniently declared to be the limits nature and geography had imposed on the nation's boundaries.

Within the national confines the hand of nature had here and there omitted to render the national terrain entirely functional to the nation's needs. The Union would find its greatest safeguard, declared many an orator and promoter, in public improvement of communication and transportation. The rapid annihilation of distance between Connecticut and Carolina through railways, insisted Asa Child, would make enmity between these two states an impossibility. "Our prejudices will recede, as our proximity to each other shall increase. New bonds will be thrown around the Union, which will grow stronger as we pursue our onward march."[5] Other voices declared that one of the most powerful means of producing harmony and good fellowship among the different states was the system of internal improvements, which permitted even the humble and plain people to broaden the narrow circle of their village acquaintances by personal observation of the ways of life of their fellow citizens in more remote parts of the land. Thus in the minds of enthusiasts for roads, canals, and railways these devices were to cement together the states and sections into one national whole.

The physical basis of nationalism and patriotism was supplemented, so the belief went, by the economic ties of the country. Joseph P. Bradley, corporation lawyer and justice in the supreme court of New Jersey, spoke for many others in declaring that agriculture, commerce, and manufactures constituted "an indissoluble bond which unites and keeps us together as one nation, one people." Interlocking and weaving together into one mutuality of interests, the industrial productions of the land and the commerce to which they gave rise constituted, so it seemed to men of practical bent, an inescapable bond of national unity. Even the "clouds of commercial embarrassment" which hung darkly over the country in 1837 and the years following could not, in the eyes of the editor of the *Charleston Courier*, darken the bright picture of a land "possessed of all the elements of national wealth, power, and greatness"

[5] Asa Child, *An Oration, delivered before the citizens of Norwich, on the anniversary of National Independence, July 4, 1838* (Norwich, 1838), 18.

and a people that, from oppressed and dependent colonists, had become "a mighty nation, blessed beyond all others in social, civil, and religious privileges."[6]

The needs and values of business enterprise were intimately associated with patriotic and nationalistic ideas and sentiments. The Constitution was increasingly regarded as an incarnation of that law and order so essential to the countinghouse, the factory, and the mercantile establishment. Choate, Hillard, Webster, and other legal spokesmen for business regarded the Constitution as a sacred document on which the entire economic, political, and social fabric rested. It was the instrument that tied the states together into the national whole so essential to a national market and to the foreign and domestic policies through which business alone could expand. Protecting property rights as the Constitution clearly did, its provisions, once clarified by the Supreme Court, had to be obeyed even if, as in the Dred Scott decision, humanitarian sentiments were outraged. Thus the Constitution became a symbol of an order secure against revolutionary change and congenial to all the values dear to business enterprise.

Commerce and industry in demanding a strong national government furthered nationalism in another way. Only through a strong central government could many of the basic needs of business be met. Only a strong, respected central government could compel Chinese pirates, for example, to respect the Stars and Stripes; such a government alone could protect expanding commerce and win privileges for it through favorable commercial treaties. Moreover, a national government was of great use in the improvement of harbors, the maintenance of lighthouses, and the subsidizing of shipping. Nor was a strong government less indispensable to industry than to commerce. In addition to securing law, order, and property rights, to curbing reckless changes emanating from any one of the states, a national government could control finances in such a way as to eliminate the state issues of worthless paper; it could bear the expense or at least part of it for transcontinental railways and other internal improvements, and safeguard the protective tariff system. Friends of the tariff pointed out that besides benefiting industry a tariff would promote the self-sufficiency of the country, an inestimable boon in time of war.

In the exposition of the nationalism which was so congenial to the interests of commerce and industry the spokesmen of the new business

[6] *Charleston Courier*, July 4, 1840.

order no doubt firmly and honestly believed that the policies of business were bound to benefit all sections and all classes alike. Southerners might oppose internal improvements, tariffs, and centralized banking, but in reality—so the champions of economic nationalism insisted—southern planters would profit from this program no less than industrialists. Only through tariff protection, the argument ran, could the planter be assured of an ever-expanding market for his staple, and behind the walls of protection he too might build mills close to the source of supply of raw material. To the West the champions of tariffs and internal improvements pointed out manifold values inherent in these policies. The growth of home industry promised the farmer steady and ever-widening markets for the surpluses he must otherwise export under conditions beyond his control. The value of internal improvements to the West was of course apparent. And finally to the urban worker the champions of economic nationalism urged that tariffs, by building up home industry, would eliminate unemployment and end crises and hard times once and for all.

Spokesmen for commerce and industry claimed that these interests promoted nationalism in still other respects. Granting that sectional cleavages and class tensions did exist, commerce and industry would provide an effective cement for unity. Just as the commercial interest had led in the movement for that separation from England which had resulted in independence, so now, with industry, it was knitting together the various constituents of the Union into an ever firmer and tighter entity. It is true that the merchants and entrepreneurs, with their investments in the South and with their business associates and sources of raw cotton below the Mason and Dixon line, did forge a powerful bond.

The economic nationalists failed, however, to reckon adequately with a dissident note sounded by Tocqueville. A nationalism and patriotism founded on interest, he declared, could not be relied on in times of rapid change of economy and high tension; a shift of interests might obliterate such an equilibrium. However much merchants and industrialists favored the preservation of the Union through concession and compromise, a union they could not sufficiently control for their own interests was of little worth. The refusal of the plantation aristocracy to surrender its grip on national policy was bearable in the short run. The reduction of tariffs in 1857, the veto exercised by the plantation spokesmen on projects for binding the North with the Pacific coast through a transcontinental railroad—these embarrassing obstructions to national unity might disappear in the course of time. But the militant demand of the slavocracy to win over to itself the potentially powerful West through implanting slavery in the new country was something else; farmers and other humble people were involved in any such plan no less than business itself, which had increasingly important ties with the West. What choice business would make, what role patriotism and nationalism would play in this choice were to be revealed only in the critical year of 1861.

### Emotional Factors in Patriotism and Nationalism

Material considerations such as geography and economic ties by no means dominated the nationalistic and patriotic thought and feeling of the mid-century. Many would have applauded Thomas Starr King for brushing aside mere material factors and reminding the less well-off that even "the poor man should not feel poor when he thinks that his humble roof and circumstances are sheltered by a canopy of ideas and sentiments, such as never before arched over any palace in the world."[7]

Of these ideas and sentiments one was intimately connected with the physical features of the terrain itself. American writers in prose and verse gave no hint of becoming weary of their paeans to the American landscape. Artists of the Hudson River School with their romantic canvases, Currier and Ives with their popular prints of American scenes, and John Rawson Smith and John Banvard with their vast and much admired panoramas of the Mississippi valley endeared to American hearts the characteristic features of the country's landscapes. In the hope of still further developing the growing appreciation of America's unique landscape—its "physique, morale, its historic tradition, its poetic legend, its incident, adventure and suggestion," cultural patriots prepared illustrated volumes celebrating American scenery.

The sanctions of physical science were also invoked in behalf of patriotism and nationalism. The proneness of idealistic technologists to regard science as the means by which the promise of America was to be fulfilled has already been noted. This was not all, however. Thomas Starr King, who had some acquaintance with the ideas of both Newton and Galvani, declared in a popular lyceum lecture that the law of love

[7] Thomas Starr King, *Patriotism and Other Papers* (Boston, 1864), 40.

in the spiritual universe operates much like that of gravitation in the physical; it binds each particle to every other, but in attracting inversely as the square of the distance, love, like gravitation, permits man to have intense local affections without in any way militating against his accentuated devotion to the larger national body. If further analogy were wanted—and the Reverend Mr. King was apt at this—it need only be pointed out that "the oneness of the nation is the unity of the galvanic current that is generated from the many layers of metal and acid," which layers in turn might be compared with the individuals who similarly contributed their energy to make the larger whole or nation.

Religion, like science, reinforced patriotism. The religious faith of the fathers was explicitly related to their heroic sacrifices for the country; children's literature, sermons, and orations all emphasized this association of Christian faith and patriotism. The voice of the pulpit was not silent when national laws and policy seemed to run counter to God's "higher law," but at the same time the sermons of the period were intended to inculcate love of country. "The prime instructions of the Old Testament," declared Thomas Starr King, "are Patriotism and the fear of God." This sentiment was reechoed in scores of sermons. In identifying religion and patriotism some clergymen reminded their flocks that Scripture commanded the faithful to render unto Caesar that which was Caesar's. Others insisted that all man's experience has proved that the religious spirit is necessary for the purification and elevation of the life of the nation. The Reverend Edwin H. Chapin, in a discourse delivered in Boston in 1841 on the responsibilities of a republican government, expressed a common idea when he declared that republicanism and Christianity are intimately associated, that Americans have a duty to make Christianity practical.

The religious argument for patriotism and nationalism reached still further. To the argument of certain moralists of an internationalist bent that patriotism is a kind of sectionalism of the heart, the patriotic parson replied that the divine method in evoking man's noble affections is always from the particular to the general, from the family to the community, the community to the nation, the nation to the world. Finally, the venerable idea that from the start the hand of God had guided American development continued to be heard, not only in New England, where in the early days of the Republic hardly a sermon failed to mention it, but in the capital of the nation itself. In 1850 Henry Reed, editor of the texts of classical English authors and professor of literature at the University of Pennsylvania, declared at the Smithsonian Institution in his lectures on the history of the American Union that the hand of Providence had welded together the diverse materials of the colonies into one federal nation. In the generally religious climate of opinion this view of the national mission, with its implications of international irresponsibility, laissez faire, and individualism, somewhat overshadowed the rationalistic idea that here, in America, enlightened man was to conduct a great experiment in accord with the blueprints of the equalitarian philosophers.

Among the sentimental elements in the pattern of nationalism and patriotism the reverence for and idealization of the nation's past was of much moment. If the fiftieth anniversary of the adoption of the Constitution passed virtually unnoticed, the ubiquitous annual celebration of the Fourth of July kept alive the memory of the birth of the nation. The interest of the early Republic in the foundations of its history also broadened as a result of the movement for the diffusion of knowledge. Between 1830 and 1850 at least 35 historical societies were launched. Apart from focusing interest on the local history of the state or community, these societies did much to collect and preserve historical materials. Beginning with the Bunker Hill Monument near Boston, a series of monuments to the heroes and events of the Revolution served to perpetuate its memories and traditions in the eyes of the people. In 1833 the Washington National Monument Society began its work of issuing addresses to the American people, collecting funds, and organizing the sentiment of patriotism in various ways.

History textbooks were a supplementary means of presenting the American past in patriotic and nationalistic terms. Weems' biographies of national heroes were augmented by those of other no less patriotic authors and compilers, among whom Samuel Goodrich and William McGuffey take high rank. Other writers of schoolbooks in this field spared no pains to create in the minds of the growing generation of Americans dislike of England and a conviction that the Revolution was a heaven-sent revolt against intolerable tyranny, that the American people had been essentially united, not divided, in the struggle for independence, and that in subsequent historical events the nation and its leaders had right on their side. Some writers, it is true, did occasionally criticize the treatment of the Indians or suggest some of the grays in the all but universally bright picture of the American past. But the general impression conveyed in the texts would have been approved by Gideon Hawley, who in 1835 declared:

In the character of the men, who stood foremost in the contest for independence, the measures of provocation, by which they were roused to resistance, the trials through which they passed, the reverses which they sustained, the triumphs which they achieved, and the great political principles which were vindicated by them, there are lessons of instruction not inferior in value, to any which can be drawn from the history of any age or people; and if the mind of every youth can be made familiar with them, and his feelings imbued with the moral they contain, no better security can be provided against the degeneracy of that unconquerable spirit, in which the foundations of our freedom were laid.[8]

While, to be sure, many children did not imbibe patriotism through American history in school texts or the classroom, the Massachusetts act of 1827 requiring the introduction of United States history in the curriculum—an example followed by Vermont, New Hampshire, and Virginia—suggested that the compulsory teaching of patriotism through history was already in the offing.

A study of addresses dealing with the functions of historical study reveals that nationalistic and patriotic motives ranked high among the alleged values of which Clio was the guardian. The republican statesman and ordinary citizen, according to George Perkins Marsh, required knowledge of a set of facts totally different from those appropriate to the rulers and subjects in aristocracies and autocracies. Conditions which promoted the health and happiness of the people were far more important to the American than war, diplomacy, and court intrigues. He must be acquainted with "the fortunes of the mass, their opinions, their characters, their leading impulses, their ruling hopes and fears, their arts and industry and commerce" as well as their religious ceremonies, festivities, and domestic morals. Indeed, all other forms of history—constitutional, political, diplomatic, economic, legislative, and judicial—must be subordinated, according to Marsh, to the grand theme of "popular history," or the account of the moral and physical prosperity of the people. This able New Englander appreciated the full import of the frontier in mold-

[8] *Annual Report of the Regents of the University of the State of New York to the Senate* (Albany, 1835), 95.

ing American institutions and outlooks. He also pleaded for the importance, in a republic, of rigid respect for the principles of historical criticism.

The difficulties confronting the historian in this respect were fully elaborated by an orator who pointed out that every speculative man possessed his own "peculiar notions of human nature, its whence and its whither, its progress and tendency," and that almost without exception these notions formed "the mould into which his generalizations were apt to run, and the bend of his mind will be, to discover a wonderful harmony, between his own preconceived opinions and the facts which history may have evolved."[9]

The inspiration of the past was coupled with that of the future as a source of patriotic pride and nationalistic feeling. Reference has already been made to the American doctrine of progress and its complex and pervasive penetration of American thought. It may be well briefly to indicate here the chief ideas in the doctrine of America's future. One was expressed in the slogan "Manifest Destiny." This assumed that fate had decreed the inevitable physical expansion of the United States to the Pacific. Extreme adherents of this doctrine believed that the entire continent of North America was destined to come under the jurisdiction or at least the sway of the United States. One toastmaster expressed this doctrine in characteristically fervid words: "The Eagle of the United States—may she extend her wings from the Atlantic to the Pacific; and fixing her talons on the Isthmus of Darien, stretch with her beak to the Northern Pole." During the Mexican War many a patriot similarly subscribed to the words of Senator H. V. Johnson, who, admitting in one breath the evils of war, in the next declared that it had been made by "the All-wise Dispenser of events, the instrumentality of accomplishing the great end of human elevation and human happiness" implicit in the extension of the sway of the Stars and Stripes over the Mexican provinces.

Others insisted that the true mission of America was not to inaugurate mere material prosperity and expanding power but rather to advance the moral elevation of the entire world. Robert J. Breckinridge of Kentucky declared that if the great principle that man is capable of self-government, the principle on which the fathers built the fabric, be true,

[9] S. Teackle Wallis, *Lecture on the Philosophy of History, delivered before the Calvert Institute, January 24, 1844* (Baltimore, 1844), 9.

then "no mortal power can estimate the height of grandeur waiting to receive us—nor compute the depth and thoroughness of that tremendous change which the influence of our spirit must operate throughout the world." The destiny of America, Breckinridge continued, was to spread

. . . the great ideas of a new dispensation, to elevate and improve the individual, to establish in the highest degree on the scale of human progress the standard of national greatness—to teach man to govern himself, to love his fellow, to love his God; to teach the nations that all are equal . . . to teach them to kindle on all their altars the light of religion, to reverence human rights and bestow human privileges, to raise up the down trodden, to sheathe the sword and furl the banner and live in peace. . . .[10]

Americans regarded themselves as true and ardent patriots, whether they subscribed to the concept of the expansion of American territory and material power or to that of the mission to effect the moral regeneration of the world through the expansion of American ideals and influence.

National symbols played an unmeasurable part in the growth of patriotic sentiment. It is true that the custom of hoisting the flag over schoolhouses, begun in the War of 1812, did not become general until the Civil War; but it is also true that poems about the national emblem, especially Joseph Rodman Drake's "The American Flag," were at one time or another on almost every schoolchild's lips. To the older national anthems that had been born in earlier days was added, in 1832, Samuel Francis Smith's "My Country 'Tis of Thee." The song, notwithstanding its provincially New England words, quickly became nationally popular as a result of its promotion by Lowell Mason, a genius in the cultivation of musical taste among both children and adults.

No less important as symbols of national sentiments were such graphic sobriquets as "Brother Jonathan" and "Uncle Sam." Brother Jonathan, a symbol for the American people, was pictured as a tall, stout, double-jointed, large-for-his-age youth, awkward and simple in appearance, but not without a certain lively shrewdness and promise of great strength; and Uncle Sam, the symbol for the federal government that emerged during the War of 1812, was a plain man obviously goodhearted and kindly in his benevolence who, in spite of the troubles his somewhat

[10] Robert J. Breckinridge, *Formation and Development of the American Mind* (Baltimore, 1837), 4, 21.

pinched shoulders had to carry, was undoubtedly equal to the task. These symbols became familiar to the people through popular songs, sketches, and cartoons and by their engaging concreteness figured materially in the growth of patriotic and nationalistic feeling.

Allied to the national symbols were the national festivals. Of these the most important, of course, was the Fourth of July. Celebrated throughout the land with conviviality and the high-blown oratory of the time, the nation's birthday was an occasion for at least a temporary unity of sentiment that quite obliterated party and sectional cleavages. A thorough sampling of the addresses delivered on Independence Day clearly suggests that it played a significant role in reminding people of their national traditions, struggles, hopes, and aspirations. Less important than the Fourth with its pompous oratory and gay funmaking was Thanksgiving, a festival observed at first chiefly in New England and with considerable variation of date. But beginning in 1846 Mrs. Sarah Josepha Hale, poetess and editor of the nationally read *Godey's Ladies' Book,* pursued a campaign for nationalizing the custom. "There is a deep moral influence in these periodical seasons of rejoicing," she wrote, "in which whole communities participate. They bring out . . . the best sympathies in our nation." As a result of her campaign, which involved the writing of thousands of letters to presidents, congressmen, and governors, as well as editorials in her magazine, the last Thursday of November came to be observed in a growing number of states. By 1858 all but six states celebrated the Pilgrims' feast on that day.

No doubt such symbols as the flag, "Brother Jonathan," and "Uncle Sam," the flowery oratory of the Fourth of July, and the idealization of national heroes, including the thanks-giving and courageous Pilgrims, did more to kindle sentiments of patriotism and nationalism among the plain people than did the discussion in which intellectuals indulged regarding race, geography, federal economic control, and a uniquely American literature and art. For although it is impossible to prove or disprove, there is probably much truth in Emerson's remark regarding the function of patriotic sentiment in the life of plain people:

. . . the dusty artisan who needs some consolation for the insignificant figure his sordid habits and feelings make in comparison with the great, and in comparison with his own conscience and conceptions, is fain to remember how large and honourable is the confederacy of which he is a member and, that, however low his lot, his resources are yet reckoned an integral part of that awful front which the nation presents to the world. Hence the unaffected, boisterous enthusiasm with which any spirited allusion to the idea of Country is always received by a mixed assembly.[11]

## Patriotism, Nationalism, and Cultural Achievements

The spirit of patriotism and nationalism is assuredly too complex and subtle to trace with any high degree of certainty in the cultural achievements of a given period. The sentiment of country probably affected the work even of those men of letters and the arts who repudiated cultural chauvinism and tried to walk along the road of cosmopolitanism and eclecticism. It unquestionably influenced the work of those who frankly espoused and gloried in the idea of a national culture.

The fine arts reflected nationalism less than any other aspect of esthetic and intellectual endeavor. As late as 1853 a commentator expressed the consensus in lamenting that, owing in part to the deference paid to foreign as opposed to native artists, the decorations of the Capitol at Washington betrayed the imitative nature of the arts in America. Arabesques and mythological figures, even when relieved by an occasional eagle, were a far cry from the representation of actual American birds, trees, and flowers, of American heroes and American experiences. The American people's valor, fortitude, genius, and patriotism were yet to be commemorated in American art. Other critics and artists deplored with Samuel F. B. Morse the tendency in American art to imitate the sensualistic "stench of decay" that marred the galleries of Europe; American art must buttress Truth and Virtue. To all these indictments the majority of Americans, if they thought of the matter at all, would probably have subscribed.

It is less likely that either the plain people, or the gentry, or artists themselves would have subscribed to the novel conception of Americanism advanced by Horatio Greenough. This sculptor, of whom Emerson once remarked that he would, if he could, bottle up commerce with Europe in order to insulate the American from the foreign influence that denationalizes him, took his fellow countrymen to task for borrowing architectural forms for purposes utterly alien to those of their first uses and then, by way of adaptation, spoiling the original beauty which con-

[11] Emerson and Forbes (eds.), *Journals of Ralph Waldo Emerson*, II, 174–175.

sisted in the harmony of materials and lines to use or function. We had built Gothic temples of wood and omitted all ornament for economy, forgetful of the fact that material and ornament were essentials of the Gothic style. We had sought to bring the Parthenon to our streets by shearing the Greek temple, designed for worship, of its lateral colonnades, piercing its walls for light, and setting a chimney on its top! If Americans would create beauty in building, Greenough went on, let them learn from the animals, proportioned as they were for the type of activity that characterized them. Or let them learn from the majestic clipper ships, whose every line, spar, rigging, and sail was beautiful because proportioned to speed and safety.

American architecture, save in the clipper ship itself and in the traditional story-and-a-half house rooted in New England's hills, failed to develop as Greenough would have had it. Even his own colossal statue of Washington was garbed in a Roman toga! Nor were the comparable classic-inspired statues of Jefferson and Patrick Henry which Thomas Patrick carved, and those that Hiram Powers made of Adams, Jackson, and Webster, any more American than Greenough's. Even in painting there was little that could be called truly American. The Hudson River School did indeed capture some of the romantic loveliness of the Catskills, but in both technique and spirit these paintings by Cole, Durand, Kensett, and Doughty were derivative. Emanuel Leutze's "Washington Crossing the Delaware" was American and patriotic in theme to be sure, and so too were Bierstadt's panoramas of American scenery and Catlin's paintings of the Indians. But the American art that probably best exemplified American needs and American ideas consisted of the figureheads of sailing ships, utensils hewn of wood, and homemade furniture, rugs, and quilts and similar objects of folk craft. The rapid disintegration of craftsmanship, however, was a blow to any hope that a people's art might provide background and inspiration for a truly national school.

Cultural nationalists dared to hope that music, no less than art, might find inspiration in the American spirit. But however patriotic the words of "America" were, the air, of course, belonged to Germany. The music of the Italian and French opera in New York and New Orleans, the adaptations which Lowell Mason made of Handel, Haydn, and Beethoven for church services, and the impressive festivals of German immigrants all bore witness to the derivative character of music in America.

Nor was this any less true of the earliest operas by native composers. One, indeed, *Rip Van Winkle* by George Bristow, did take a native legend for its theme.

In rural regions, especially in the Allegheny highlands, the plain people continued to sing the traditional ballads of their European ancestors and on occasion to weave into them, or even into a new song, dramatic episodes of frontier life. Something like a native American music could also be found in the modifications that seafaring men made of British and Irish chanties and in the amusing ditties of the boatmen on the canals, lakes, and rivers of the West. The melancholy or at times gay work songs and touching religious spirituals of the Negroes possessed distinctive qualities, whatever their borrowings; and when Stephen C. Foster was inspired by them to write his haunting, tuneful melodies with sweet and touching sentiments of home and loved ones, America at last possessed a body of admirable folk songs known and sung by everyone everywhere in the country. The time had not yet come when other native materials, such as the plaintive rhythms of the forest red men, would enter into the consciousness of the music-loving among the cultivated classes and into the work of nationally self-conscious composers. However disappointing the achievements of this period were to cultural patriots, the songs of the American people were neither meager nor inauspicious.

Historiography reflected the patriotic and nationalistic spirit in larger measure than the arts. Theodore Parker was not alone in feeling that historical writing in any field should promote the values of liberty and democracy cherished by the American people, and he held up to scorn the histories that in his judgment failed to fulfill this purpose. In his eyes Motley was too aristocratic to be a good American, and Prescott was the subject of one of his most bitter indictments of American scholarship on the score that the historian of the Mexican conquest was insufficiently critical of the arrogance of the aristocracy, the iniquity of slavery, the inhumanity of the Spanish governing class. But even Motley's history of the struggle of the Dutch against Spain and Prescott's history of the Spanish triumphs over the Aztec and Inca revealed some part of the nationalistic sentiment; the glories of freedom and liberty, the shadows of tyranny and despotism color their pages. George Bancroft, however, reached the peak of nationalism in historiography. Neither the admirable respect which he showed for accuracy in factual statements nor his zeal for discovering and exploiting archive material could conceal his ringing enthusiasm for political freedom and individualism and his faith in the Providence that from the start had guided America on its path toward unknown future glories. Nor, as the work of Richard Hildreth indicates, were Federalist historians, however lacking in Bancroft's worship of democracy, wanting in devotion to the nationalistic ideals that governed Federalist-Whig thought.

Editors and compilers rivaled historians in their display of patriotic ardor. Only intense national pride could have sustained Peter Force in his labors to persuade Congress to sponsor the publication of a massive collection of documents of the revolutionary era. However reluctant the national legislature was to go the full way toward meeting Force's ideal, it did purchase the papers of some of the fathers of the country for preservation in the Library of Congress. The records of the birth of independence which Jared Sparks collected in his *Diplomatic Correspondence of the Revolution* supplemented the work of Force and other archivists. Sparks also presented his fellow citizens with editions of the writings of Benjamin Franklin and George Washington, marked by editorial liberties designed to cover up any evidence of shortcomings in these revolutionary fathers—even misspellings! Nor were the patriotic efforts of collectors of records confined to the Atlantic seaboard. Lyman C. Draper won support from the youthful state of Wisconsin for his admirable work in collecting from the cabins of pioneers not only account books and other records but life histories as well. Thus in large measure patriotism inspired the collection of materials which ultimately would make possible the critical and scientific evaluation of patriotic myths.

Other types of literature proved to be less sensitive to the tugs and pulls of nationalistic sentiment than historical writing. In a minor degree this was the result, no doubt, of the failure of the plans for the full achievement of a distinctively American language. In some part the imperviousness of American belles-lettres to the nationalism of the critics was also to be ascribed to the failure of the cultural patriots to achieve the international copyright, which in their eyes would have encouraged a native literary product by excluding the cheap reprints of competing English authors. But the relative failure of American writers to discover new forms of expression suitable to the American spirit was also the result of the fact that American nationalism itself was only in the making. However much immigrants enriched American intellectual and esthetic life and however much Americans disliked England, book culture, at least, was still largely English both in root and in branch.

The task of pointing out the essentially nationalistic elements in the writing of Cooper, Simms, Irving, Melville, Hawthorne, and John Pendleton Kennedy in fiction and of Poe, Bryant, Emerson, Longfellow, Whittier, and Holmes in poetry, vastly exceeds the limits of this discussion. In varying degrees all these writers displayed both in the selection of materials and in the manner of treating them evidences of nationalistic and patriotic sentiment, along with many evidences of indebtedness to the great literary traditions of the Old World. The most nationalistic of all, Walt Whitman, remained obscure throughout this period.

Among the evidences that American literary expression was coming into its own was the fact that at least 386 American books were reprinted in England during the years 1841 to 1846—striking testimony of the attention paid by British publishers and the reading public to the products of the American mind. Leading English writers found much in American books that seemed to them characteristic of the rugged individualism, the social and political freedom, the buoyancy and the optimism thought to be our national characteristics. Carlyle, Tyndall, Ruskin, and Matthew Arnold, among others, acknowledged indebtedness to Emerson's thought. American scholarship and American ideals of democracy, as reflected in American writings, played some part, at least, in the thought of such varied figures as Frederick Schlegel, Auguste Comte, Edward Wakefield, Richard Cobden, John Stuart Mill, Karl Marx, and, in distant Russia, the youthful Kropotkin and Tolstoy.

America, if the testimony of a traveler who took pains to question peasants and workers is to be credited, supplied these classes with hope. "Even to those who never go there," he wrote, "it is a blessing, in giving them the hope of improving their condition. It is the Eldorado, the land of golden plenty, where every man can have a home of his own, and leave his children comfortable when he dies."[12]

American literature achieved its own marks of national distinctiveness in the writings closest to the common man. This was natural in view of the fact that the plain people differed from their European counterparts in greater measure than did the intellectuals. Plays written for the theater—still, of course, in disrepute among many respectable citizens— have numerous earmarks of patriotism and nationalism. It is true that

[12] James Freeman Clarke, *Eleven Weeks in Europe* (Boston, 1852), 50.

many pieces obviously patriotic in material and inspiration followed in form the melodramas of Kotzebue and the Gothic school; this was clear in such plays as Bannister's *Putnam, the Iron Son of '76*, Conrad's pro-democratic *Jack Cade*, and Stone's *Metamora*, which exploited the Indian theme. The dialect plays featuring the "tarnally cute" Yankee, such as *The Vermont Wooldealer* and *The People's Lawyer*, were more original in form as well as in substance. The hairbreadth adventures, the bustle, the lawlessness, and the tall tales of the "gamecocks of the wilderness" made such pieces as *The Lion of the West* and *The Kentuckian* redolent of the backwoods.

Much material that is both close to the plain people and authentically American was tucked into country newspapers, popular organs of sports and humor, especially in *The Spirit of the Times*, jest books, and almanacs. The improvisations and homespun wit of the "crackerbox philosophers," the understatements of the Yankee peddler or stay-at-home "down-Easterner," the racy dialect and mimicry of the backwoodsman yarning his vivid, incongruous, and feverish incidents and caricatures —in these above all else is to be found the expression of regionalisms which easily merged into the distinctive elements of a national culture. And to them must be added the humor of the black man, a humor which, beneath its fun and pathos, good-naturedly criticized the white man's shortcomings. With the rise of commercial minstrelsy, blackfaced white comedians interpreted the indigenous songs and fun of the Negro to ordinary people everywhere. Thus he who searches for what was distinctively American in the literature of the 1830s and 1840s will turn to Longstreet's *Georgia Scenes*, Hooper's *Some Adventures of Captain Simon Suggs*, Thompson's *Major Jones' Courtship*, Baldwin's *Flush Times in Alabama and Mississippi*, the "autobiography" of Davy Crockett, and the inimitable Yankee sketches in which Seba Smith, Charles A. Davis, and Thomas Chandler Haliburton made "Major Jack Downing" and "Sam Slick" household characters.

School education was a basic force in the development of American nationalism. During this period American educational thought and practice were subjected to foreign influence. Lancaster, Pestalozzi, and Fellenberg were important figures in this country's educational thought. Above all, from the reports which Bache, Barnard, Mann, Smith, and Stowe brought of Prussian education, Americans gleaned much that served to raise professional standards. Yet American education, which cultural patriots continued to criticize for its failure to conform to the genius of American institutions, did in fact display many characteristic features.

By 1850 the inherited English idea of education as chiefly a private or religious concern had given way in all but the southern states to the doctrine that, on the primary and even the secondary levels, provision for education was a civic function to which no stigma of charity could be attached. Nor did American public education possess the centralization, standardization, and caste distinctions that characterized the Prussian system. On the contrary, initiative was still largely local, and control still largely resided in lay hands. It is true that a feeling prevailed in the minds of many educators that popular education could never really become perfect until it had become a national concern, and that only a national system of education could inculcate "the same tones and manner of thinking and acting . . . which, whilst it would render us more emphatically one people, would give us increased respectability in the eyes of the whole world, as well as in those of each other."[13]

### The Critique of Nationalism and Patriotism

The sentiments of nationalism and patriotism, congenial though they were both to many intellectuals and probably to the great majority of people, did not hold the field without opposition. Many literary and artistic circles approved of cosmopolitanism and eclecticism in cultural and intellectual life. In addition, certain concepts of nationalism and patriotism were subjected to the direct criticisms of both pacifists and socialists. These groups were unimportant from a numerical point of view, but no discussion of nationalism and patriotism in the thought and feeling of the American people should be dismissed without some reference to them.

Pacifists in general insisted that loyalty to righteousness, to God's command of neighborly love, exceeded any contradictory obligation that the state might impose in the name of patriotism. Consistent opponents of war did not hesitate to condemn the American Revolution which had resulted in the birth of the nation. In their eyes resort to the sword even for independence contradicted God's Word, and besides failed to justify

[13] B. F. Foster, *Education Reform* (New York, 1837), iv.

the losses involved in the impiety and immorality incident to war. That the colonies might ultimately have won their freedom, or at least the kind of freedom enjoyed by Scotland, seemed in the minds of consistent pacifists an additional reason for daring to oppose even the struggle so thoroughly enshrined in the hearts of all patriots. The Mexican War, even more than the Revolution, was condemned by pacifistically minded men as an unjust crusade in the interest of power, slaves, and lands. The *Advocate of Peace* published documents illustrating the Mexican position and exposed the patriotism evoked by the war as a mere coverage for profiteering, army corruption, and the taxation of the working classes.

Similar views of the Mexican War were also widely held outside the ranks of the peace movement, especially in New England. James Russell Lowell's celebrated *Biglow Papers* pulled no punches in calling war plain murder. The venerable Albert Gallatin of Pennsylvania regarded the conflict as an excellent example of the perversion of patriotism. If, during the War, some condemned what passed for patriotism, other critics went even further. Gerrit Smith, a New York reformer and member of Congress, ridiculed as an exceedingly fanciful and pernicious doctrine the idea that a nation is a being apart from its people, morally responsible and punishable. Under the influence of the venerable tradition of natural law, many moral doctrinaires insisted that when government defies Higher Law, man must resist or separate himself from the offending hand. Still more pronounced extremists, like William Lloyd Garrison with "Our Country is the world—Our Countrymen are mankind" as his motto, embraced the whole creed of nonresistance and for a time refused to cooperate with a government based in their eyes on force. Uncompromising individualists who pushed the nonresistance position to philosophical anarchism believed with Stephen Pearl Andrews that ultimately nations, representing as they did the modern form of tribalism, would dissolve into the individuals composing them; that patriotism would expand into philanthropy; that piece by piece the clumsy fabric of government would be disposed of.

The classic statement of this kind of thinking is, of course, Henry David Thoreau's *Essay on Civil Disobedience* (1849). In part a protest against the Mexican War, which he took to be unjustified aggression in behalf of materialistic values, and in part an explanation of his refusal to pay a tax that he assumed was being used in support of the War,

Thoreau developed the thesis that the state is potentially or actually an evil institution inimical to the freedom of the individual. It has no moral right to compel an individual to act contrary to his own sense of right, and when it tries to do so, the individual must resist. He would, to be sure, pay the consequences, but the fact of resistance to evil could become a powerful, if not a compelling, moral force. In simple, eloquent prose Thoreau probed more comprehensively and more deeply into the whole spectrum of relations between individual and state than any of his contemporaries, and his essay had more influence than any of its counterparts. Years later Tolstoy read it and was stirred by it. In 1907 Mahatma Ghandi drew inspiration from it and found in it useful suggestions for his later campaign of nonviolence in India. And in our own day Martin Luther King found in the *Essay on Civil Disobedience* an American precedent for the campaign of nonviolent resistance to racial discrimination and segregation.

To the pacifist indictment of nationalism and war the Utopian socialists added their own onslaught. The indictment which *The Harbinger* made during the Mexican War of patriotism and its "buttress," religion, must be quoted to do it justice:

You talk about the connection of religion and patriotism, vainglorious Pharisee; yet, when the homes of the defenceless and innocent are dripping with the warm blood of those who have bared their breasts to the sword of the invader, when the gaunt and haggard emigrant, fleeing from the intolerable agonies of famine in an oppressed land, finds no cheerful welcome in this abode of the free, when the cry of unrequited labor is ringing in the ear of Christian benevolence, from the cotton fields of Carolina and cotton mills of New England, when the Gold calf is enshrined as the supreme object of worship in the seats of our money-changers and the halls of our merchants—no thrill of indignation convulses your heart, no words of fiery rebuke fall from your lips, no hope of the victory of the true God over the demons of hell kindles your eye. Your love of country and your love of religion are both equally a pretense.[14]

But the rank and file of Americans, cherishing the Union as an increasingly precious symbol of a revered past and a bright future, identifying it as they did with abundance, opportunity, and ultimate peace, were deaf to such shrill indictments of a widely cherished type of patriotism and nationalism. So too were all the intellectuals for whom

[14] *The Harbinger*, V (June 19, 1847), 31.

Henry Wheaton, the distinguished authority on international law, spoke when he wrote: "May our happy union not be torn asunder, even before we have gathered its best fruits in the successful cultivation of science and letters, under the shadow of its protecting wings; and before we have produced any works of art or genius to command the admiration and envy of posterity, and worthy of that glorious liberty, the choicest of the many blessings which Providence has showered upon us!"[15] In spite of the Compromise of 1850, disunion remained a dark and threatening shadow. Nationalism, in the sense of both confidence in the strength of the federal government and devotion to the nation as a whole, remained a partial reality, a hope, and an aspiration.

[15] Henry Wheaton, *An Address pronounced at the opening of the New York Athenaeum* (New York, 1824), 22.

# PART V

Triumph of Nationalism

# 17 Cultural Nationalism in the Old South

*Because the brood-sow's left side pigs were black,*
*Whose sable tincture was by nature struck,*
*Were you by justice bound to pull them back,*
*And leave the sandy colored pigs to suck?*
    —GEORGE MOSES HORTON, *The Slave,* 1829

*Of the masses of the South, black and white, it is*
*more difficult for one to obtain information, than of*
*those of any country in Europe.*
    —FREDERICK LAW OLMSTED, 1856

*Many in the South once believed that it [slavery]*
*was a moral and political evil. That folly and delu-*
*sion are gone. We see it now in its true light, and*
*regard it as the most safe and stable basis for free*
*institutions in the world.*
    —JOHN C. CALHOUN, 1838

"We were all of us Americans—intense, self-satisfied, self-glorifying Americans," wrote George Cary Eggleston in looking back on the 1840s, "but we had little else in common. . . . We had different ideals, . . . different traditions, and different aspirations."[1] This was true of rural in contrast with city dwellers. It was true of old Americans in contrast with

[1] George C. Eggleston, *Recollections of a Varied Life* (Holt, Rinehart and Winston, Inc., 1910), 6.

417

more recent comers. The well-differentiated colonies of the various eastern states that had sprung up in the West differed from each other and from the older regions. In spite of the great differences between the topographical and cultural areas below the Mason and Dixon line, the South differed in a quite special sense from the rest of the country.

By 1840 and increasingly from 1850 to 1860 many Southerners were coming to be ever more conscious of the fact they were Southerners, to have definite conceptions of a particular past, a geographical, economic, and social unity, and a future all their own. The chief economic and political problems of southern leaders were to promote the well-being of plantation economy and to safeguard southern power in federal councils; the leading intellectual problem was to deepen the sense of southern solidarity. This was no easy task. Class cleavages separated the small group of great planting slaveowners from the lesser sort, and these from the large class of yeoman farmers, and all of these from the poor whites and the blacks, slave and free. State pride was nowhere more marked. Striking regional variations set off each from the other—tidewater and pine barrens, the Piedmont and the Appalachian country, the black belt of the deep South, the bluegrass of Kentucky, Louisiana with its Creole and Catholic culture, and the woods and prairies of frontier Arkansas and Texas. In this vast and complex South visitors found immense differences between an appreciative if not brilliantly creative intellectual culture on the one hand and ignorance and superstition on the other, between harmonious relations founded on *noblesse oblige* and bitter class tensions, between a disparagement of the pushing materialism of the Yankee and a movement to further the commercial and industrial resources in the South itself. It is important to keep in mind the striking contrasts in the South in seeking to understand the intellectual life of that region and the challenge of a rising southern nationalism to northern industrialism and northern nationalism and patriotism.

### The Mind of the Negro

Climatic contrasts and the existence of such staples as cotton, rice, and tobacco differentiated the South from the North in a very general sense; but what made the South, or essential parts of it, unique in relation to the rest of the country was the existence in 1860 of more than 4,000,000

Negroes in a population of 12,000,000. Of these 3,838,765 were enslaved. In contrast with this situation slavery had disappeared in all the northern states except Delaware. The free Negro in the North was an obscure minority. Since the Negro constituted a third of the population of the southern states and in a special sense differentiated them from the predominately rural states in the North, it may be well to begin an examination of the intellectual life and problems of the South by considering the mind of the Negro.

This is no easy task. The underlying assumptions of everyone who has interpreted the evidence or tries to interpret it greatly influence what is made of the evidence. Nor is there much firsthand evidence. The Negro was for the most part illiterate and left no written records. Those who escaped to the North and wrote their memoirs were, in one sense at least, exceptional. Furthermore, many of the ex-slave autobiographies were edited by abolitionist friends. Long after emancipation some were questioned regarding their happiness or unhappiness in bondage, but these limited and random interrogations, 70 or 80 years after Appomattox, obviously have limited value.

The Negroes, it is true, did sing, and it might be supposed that these songs reflect their views regarding cosmology, God, human nature, the whites, the South, and slavery. Yet it is all but impossible to determine when particular songs began to be commonly sung. It is also true that many of the religious songs or spirituals were either taken over from or greatly influenced by the camp-meeting gospel hymns. The words of many of these, common to both whites and blacks, contrasted worldly sufferings with heavenly bliss; thus it is not easy to say whether originally and in the minds of the Negroes the references to Egyptland meant merely the bondage of sin, or physical slavery; nor is it easy to say whether the references and symbols in the spirituals symbolize in some peculiar way the fears, hopes, and dreams of the blacks. Though perhaps the work songs were less affected by the music of the dominant race, the field hands were nevertheless definitely encouraged to sing these gay rhythms in order that they might work more efficiently.

In addition to the songs, the Negroes also told stories in their cabins which no doubt reflected their African cultural heritage and their views on many matters. But this folklore again has come to us largely through the whites and long after the days of slavery; it was, in fact, only when Joel Chandler Harris began in postbellum years to set down the dialect lore of Uncle Remus that these folk myths became generally accessible.

The whites also wrote about the Negro's thoughts and feelings, but what was thus written is, naturally, biased. On the one hand there are the accounts of northern abolitionists who visited the South or fraternized with fugitives. However honest in their intentions, these idealists naturally were convinced in advance that the slave was utterly wretched and discontented with his lot. On the other hand southern whites who interpreted the Negro mind in novels, stories, essays, and memoirs were no less biased. This was true of those who wrote while slavery existed and even more true of those who, after the crushing defeat of the South and the hardships of reconstruction, idealized the good old days.

From the materials available and from the actions of the Negroes themselves it is possible only to suggest very tentatively the broad and rough outlines of the mental and emotional equipment of the Negroes, slave and free. To begin with, only an extremely small minority of slaves possessed the bare rudiments of reading. The promising beginnings of literary instruction sponsored by the Society for the Propagation of the Gospel were not systematically continued, but the natural rights philos⸱ ophy and the growing idea that slavery was neither a permanent nor a profitable system provided a favorable atmosphere for further educational efforts on the part of the whites. With the decline of the Enlightenment religious evangelicals sought chiefly to bring the Negro to God by way of religion of the heart rather than of the head.

More important, when the cotton gin and the textile factory made the cultivation of cotton by slave labor profitable, owners on the whole discouraged efforts to teach their slaves the art of reading. This tendency was reinforced by the fact that in the 1820s and 1830s book-reading Negroes led insurrections in South Carolina and Virginia. Indeed, the majority of the slave states forbade the instruction of slaves in book learning. Indulgent masters and mistresses, of particular religious zeal, did permit their slaves to learn their letters for the sake of reading the Bible. It is also true that ambitious slaves sometimes persuaded or bribed white children to teach them the forbidden art or learned it while hired out to others. There are records of self-taught slaves who made heroic sacrifices to learn reading.

With such extremely meager opportunities it is remarkable that even a few slaves learned the rudiments, that a Georgia slave wrote a manuscript of the Bible in Arabic characters and a book of hymns in the same script, and that George Horton, a pure African who remained in bondage until Appomattox, published two volumes of poems on religion, death, nature, love, play, slavery—and freedom:

> Alas! and am I born for this,
> To wear this slavish chain,
> Deprived of all created bliss
> Through hardship, toil, and pain?

But the most impressive contributions of the Negroes to literature in this period are, of course, to be found among the hundred-odd autobiographies written or dictated after escape to the North. In these, even when allowances are made for the editing by abolitionists and in some cases for invention, are evidences of ability to tell a dramatic story effectively, of poetic imagination, of the power of indignation and bitterness, and occasionally of an amazing objectivity. Sojourner Truth's *Narrative* (1850) and Frederick Douglass' *My Bondage and My Freedom* (1855) are writings of simple beauty and power.

Educational opportunities for the free Negro were extremely limited in the South. Free Negroes in such cities as Charleston, Savannah, and New Orleans now and then maintained schools for their children or sent them to institutions supported by charity and in a few instances by public funds. As late as 1833 John Chavis, an able Negro scholar in Latin and Greek, trained unofficially at Princeton, was still teaching the sons of North Carolina's gentry. But in the main free Negroes possessed no more than the rudimentary branches. Nor did the southern free Negro, even if he was lucky enough to be able to take advantage of the relatively superior educational opportunities in the North, always fare well. Opposition to coracial education led to mob violence against schools in Connecticut and New Hampshire. Notwithstanding race prejudice, however, it was still possible for a few Negroes to obtain academic degrees at Bowdoin, Dartmouth, and Oberlin, and even to practice professions for which they had been trained abroad.

The testimony of ex-slaves and travelers as well as that of certain songs suggests, if common sense does not, that many slaves yearned for freedom. A study of the Negroes' conception of God shows that the black folk tended to select from many variants of the Christian God values which answered in part their need for freedom—the values that made Him the Creator of all mankind from one blood and clay, that pictured

Him as no respecter of persons, and, as the friend of the oppressed, certain at length to bring justice to the righteous and punishment to the wicked who disobeyed His law of love. Even if the plaintiveness and the Egypt-bondage imagery of the spirituals be discarded as evidence of the yearning for freedom, the increasing number of fugitives in the decades preceding the Civil War shows that not all the slaves were as happy with their lot as southern whites insisted in their descriptions of the blessings slavery conferred on the slaves. No doubt the whites' fear of slave insurrections, exaggerated though it was, had some basis in fact. Notwithstanding the loyalty of great numbers of slaves during the Civil War, many field hands quickly sought freedom within northern lines.

The daydreams and yearnings of slaves for freedom were not the only ways by which they made adjustments to their surroundings. The Negro's songs and folklore show that, by reason of his way of life, the slave neither said all he meant nor meant all he said; secretiveness was one way of getting along in a troubled world. Humor was another way of doing the same thing. The poetic imagination that enabled the Negro allegorically to identify various kinds of human beings with animals and to select the rabbit, the weakest and most harmless of creatures, to come out victorious in competition with the fox, bear, and wolf was another compensatory device. The folklore of Uncle Remus displays, in addition to these values, a fondness for getting even with the stronger by a kind of craft or trickery which does no real harm, and shows, withal, a certain lack of sympathy with the white man's ways.

These common characteristics, the result of the survival from the African cultural background as well as of "selection" from their culture surroundings, express the ideas and attitudes that best helped them over the rough places. But this must not hide the fact that the Negroes as a group cannot definitely be said to have possessed any one set of attitudes. Despite the stereotypes of the abolitionist and the southern apologist, the Negro did not conform to a single type. He was neither the saintly Uncle Tom nor the irresponsible, whimsical Topsy of Mrs. Stowe, nor was he necessarily endowed with all the elevated feelings and noble sentiments of the northern humanitarians. Nor was he merely the childish, docile, loyal, and at times rascally creature southern whites were prone to make him. He was probably all these things, since individual and class differences are present in Negroes as in whites. He was also snobbish in his disregard for Negroes less privileged than himself, and religious with an emotional tenseness heightened by his need for an outlet. Supernaturalist and realist at the same time, he was finally an artist, as the great beauty of the songs he sang will always testify.


## The Poor Whites and the Yeomanry

The so-called poor white is not to be confused with the much larger and far more important yeoman class. The poor white's environment— the sand barrens or the sterile soils abandoned by the planter, or the mountains and hills—fashioned his outlook on life just as the slave's environment molded his. If he was as ignorant of book learning as the Negro, he differed from the black man in disparaging it. This was in part the result of a "sour-grapes mechanism" and in part an expression of his deep-seated suspicion and hatred of the cultured planting class. Like the Negro a frequent victim of hookworm, he was sapped of vitality and ambition. His color, which almost alone differentiated him from the free Negro, became in his mind a fetish, and this accounts not only for his hatred of the Negro but also for his willingness to accept and support the institution of slavery. He may have dimly suspected or even in some cases have been conscious of some of the arguments against slavery which Hinton Rowan Helper, a North Carolinian of yeoman background, expressed in *The Impending Crisis* (1857), a book which the planting aristocracy largely succeeded in suppressing. Helper maintained that slavery degraded the poor white by forcing him to compete unequally with slave labor and by crowding him from the richer lands, which the planter could always buy, into the poorer and exhausted soils of abandoned plantations or steep, eroded hillsides. Often proud, bellicose in his clannishness but wanting in ambition, superstitious and at times given to an indulgence in a primitive sort of revivalism, the poor white really possessed but one esthetically satisfying way of expressing himself, his songs. He was apt to know both gospel hymns and the ballads inherited from his Scotch-Irish or English ancestors, and his creative instinct found some outlet in the new versions he occasionally gave to a ballad.

The yeoman, a more or less substantial farmer who might own no slaves at all or might have a few with whom he himself worked in the fields, merged on the one side into the small planter class and on the other into the mass of poor whites. With the poor whites he cherished the balladry of olden times, was proud, and looked down on the Negro. But there the similarity was apt to end. For the yeoman, even when modestly content with his respectable if humble position, in some measure shared the values of the planting class. It is true that in religion he was likely to prefer the Baptist or Methodist faith to the Presbyterianism and Episcopalianism of the substantial planter, and that he was apt to be more God-fearing and pious. But he had much in common with his richer neighbors in the great houses. Like them he was also hospitable, he too held women "in high esteem," and he often tried to emulate, on a small scale, the merry and carefree ways of the planting class. It might therefore be expected that the yeoman would push his children along the educational path as a means to that end. He might indeed occasionally send his sons to a neighboring private academy or even to one of the smaller nearby colleges. In the eyes of one southern writer these lads all too frequently swelled with self-importance and a pretentiousness that did not conceal their meager intellectual achievements after they entered law, politics, or medicine.

On the whole the yeomanry was apt to see less value in book learning as a means for advancement than did the ambitious farmer youths in the North who set their eyes on college, the countinghouse, or the law courts. The most certain means by which the ambitious yeoman could rise was to acquire slaves, or more slaves. The refinement of the upper planting class would then, presumably, come of itself. Meantime almanacs, country newspapers, or farm journals containing useful information such as that which the pioneers of scientific agriculture were trying to disseminate were likely to be the only things, beyond the Bible, that the yeoman read. But very likely he enjoyed the flowery oratory at the hustings and on court day at the county seat. The ambitious politician increasingly learned to exploit the yeoman's feeling of superiority to the Negro and his dislike of the planting aristocracy, however ambitious he was to rise into it. The political leader also nourished in the yeoman the consciousness that he too was a Southerner who could have little liking for an alien and hostile North. Yet in spite of the support given by this numerous class to slavery, many cherished a deep love for the Union. At all events, the yeoman, together with the smaller planter, the skilled mechanic, and the storekeeper in village, town, and city, constituted a middle class with intellectual attitudes that in many respects resembled those of the middle class in the North.

## The Planting Class

In 1860 only a small proportion of the white population in the South approximated the gentry class in status and culture. According to the census of that year, only 383,637 were slaveholders in a total white population of over 8 million; thus not more than one-fourth of the whites were identified with slavery by ownership or family ties. Less than 50,000 slaveowners held twenty or more chattels; probably no more than 250,000 whites were closely associated with this large planter group. Nevertheless, the values of this group increasingly became the ideal of small planters and even of the more ambitious yeoman. In addition, the professional classes in the cities of this overwhelmingly rural section generally thought in terms of the planting aristocracy and aspired to become owners of plantations. Thus the intellectual values and achievements of the planting aristocracy were of much greater importance than the number of this class would suggest.

The typical large planter, especially if of seasoned family, was a man of intellectual culture. As a boy he had enjoyed the instruction of a tutor more than likely the product of a northern seminary or college. He might well have attended one of the large number of private academies in which he continued the studies he had begun at home in preparation for college. Thence he was likely to have gone to West Point, Annapolis, Princeton, Yale, Harvard, or some other northern college, or to one of the state universities or denominational institutions in his own section—institutions that approximated in curriculum and instruction all but the two or three most exceptional colleges of the North. An occasional young planting aristocrat tasted the culture of Europe on a grand tour or studied at one of the British or Continental universities.

The culture of the large planter continued to reflect the old-time ideal of versatility. He was likely to have received training in the humanistic classics and in law. His library contained the ancient classics, Shakespeare, some of the eighteenth-century writers—especially Addison, Steele, Johnson, and Goldsmith—and a sprinkling of legal, religious, philosophical, and scientific books. The shelves not infrequently housed a handsomely bound file of one of the British or northern quarterly reviews as well as the debates of Congress and perhaps a file of a leading southern newspaper. The planter's library also reflected the interest of his household in current belles-lettres, especially in Bulwer, Byron, Campbell, and, above all, Scott. Wherever natural science touched agriculture specifically, the planter was likely to have a partly professional interest in it.

Often the wife of a great planter possessed both practical knowledge and an interest in literature and the polite arts. As the responsible head of several departments of a large estate she was something of a factory manager, nurse, physician, and stewardess. She obtained many practical hints from the northern and southern ladies' magazines. From her childhood governess and in one of the private female academies she acquired such accomplishments as drawing, painting, embroidery, dancing, music, and French. Nor was it unusual for the southern lady to have some familiarity with the classics. Visitors to the South also commented on the ability of an exceptional matron to share in her husband's most serious intellectual interests.

Both sexes believed in what two southern historians have well called the half-chivalric, half-Puritan moral code of the planting aristocracy. The church was respected and supported. Gallantry in gentlemen, charm and purity in ladies—these values were much written about and frequently achieved. Notwithstanding the cares of estate management, the plantation aristocracy cherished a carefree and merry love of sports and of social life, of joy in the moment rather than of consideration for the future, whether worldly or heavenly. The chivalrous ideals of womanhood and of personal honor, the *code duello*, family pride and fondness for the tradition that the planting aristocracy had sprung from Cavalier England—these values stood high in the minds of the plantation aristocracy.

At the same time the great planter possessed a certain sense of *noblesse oblige*, manifested in kindly consideration for his less well-to-do neighbors. And if he were not an absentee planter, the southern aristocrat's attitude toward his slaves was often marked by concern for their physical well-being and a kindly sympathy with many of their problems. Relatively few achieved either the best intellectual culture or the chivalrous ideal of the planting aristocracy, but this ideal exerted great influence on the antebellum South as well as on the subsequent generations who have overidealized, at least quantitatively, the glamour of tournaments, magnolias, moonlight, happy "darkies," gallantry, and humanistic culture in the great porticoed mansions. At the same time it is important not to overlook the fact that the southern planter, however much he disparaged "Yankee" materialism and acquisitiveness, yearned for ever larger estates and an ever larger number of slaves—the basis of plantation economy and prestige.

## Contributions to Natural Science and Belles-Lettres

No discussion of the original contributions made in the Old South to intellectual development can be very illuminating without reference to the relation of the small professional class in the towns and cities to the plantation aristocracy. The professional group, recruited from the North, the yeomanry, and the plantation class itself, was in the main thoroughly sympathetic to the plantation philosophy which came to dominate increasingly the intellectual life of the Old South. The planter himself was for the most part appreciative and receptive, rather than original and creative, in his attitude toward learning and the arts. Occasionally, however, a planter did contribute with his pen to southern scholarship and literature; this he did, of course, without ceasing to be a planter.

Contrary to a long-prevailing impression, natural science figured in the intellectual life of the Old South as well as law, oratory, and letters. The Smithsonian Institution owed much in its inception to Joel Poinsett of South Carolina, a generous patron of the fine arts and of natural history. It will be recalled that Gerald Troost, of Dutch birth and training, promoted geological knowledge during his long residence in Nashville. It will also be remembered that Matthew Fontaine Maury was southern by birth and sympathy. His exploration of the seas was complemented by the investigations which Joseph Le Conte of Franklin College in Georgia carried on in connection with a study of the reefs of the Florida coast. Le Conte not only showed the importance of the affinities of gymnosperms in the formation of barrier reefs; in a paper read before the American Association for the Advancement of Science he aroused discussion in European circles by his effort to correlate physical, chemical, and vital forces.

Though the vast mineral resources of the South were all but unknown, important beginnings were made by the studies in the chemistry of minerals which won for J. Lawrence Smith of South Carolina a leading reputation among American chemists. And the geological survey of Virginia, directed by William B. Rogers, pointed in an original fashion to the peculiar structure of the Appalachian chain. Even the frontier South aroused the interest of naturalists. If the labors of Benjamin L. C. Wailes, collector of peculiar specimens in the fields of geology and zoology and principal agent in the survey of the geology and natural history of Mississippi were limited by their pioneer character, they did much to awaken scientific consciousness and to mark out broad outlines for future investigations.

As was natural in an agricultural society, the branch of science that aroused the greatest interest was that bearing on the chemistry of soils. Many Southerners contributed to this field, but the leaders were J. Lawrence Smith and William B. Rogers, who experimented with the marls of South Carolina and Virginia, Joel Poinsett, and, above all, Edmund Ruffin. Ruffin's *Essay on Calcareous Manures* (1832) reported the experiments proving that marls corrected the acidity of overcultivated soils sufficiently to permit the assimilation of fertilizers which, with drainage, crop rotation, the proper plowing, were of immense restorative value.

However receptive many planters were to the progress of scientific agriculture, the intellectual aristocracy of the Old South frequently deplored the premium set by the modern age on useful knowledge and upheld the classical concept of culture as the one most becoming to a true aristocracy. Hugh Swinton Legaré of Charleston, one of America's most widely read linguists and a profound legal scholar, wrote erudite essays on the classics and diatribes against science and Bentham's Utilitarianism. Such perspectives were shared by many of his class.

A great deal of the literature of the Old South mirrored the sentimentality, piety, and glamorous romance of the most generally admired English authors. But a great deal also reflected various aspects of southern life. Partisan prejudices and political sympathies figured in many southern romances. The more liberal Jeffersonian thought of the early 1800s was reflected in the novels of the genial and witty Virginian physician, William Alexander Caruthers. His tale, *The Kentuckian in New York,* was written in defense of sectional good will and bore little of the narrow parochialism that marked other romantic writers in the South. In his *Cavaliers of Virginia* Caruthers showed considerable sympathy with Nathaniel Bacon's rebellion against the aristocratic regime of Governor Berkeley. On the other hand, John Pendleton Kennedy, who in *Swallow Barn* painted a nonpolitical idyll of plantation life, in *The Annals of Quodlibet* satirized the crudities and foibles of the democratic Jacksonianism, which was anathema to him as a Whig lawyer rooted in the traditions of Virginia's aristocratic tidewater and Baltimore's patrician society. It remained for Nathaniel Beverley Tucker to do full justice to the rising southern impatience with Yankee "domination." His prostates' rights and prosouthern *The Partisan Leader* (1836) predicted secession and was no doubt intended to promote a war psychology in defense of plantation interests.

If the plantation ideal was reflected in much that was written, the frontier stage through which the trans-Appalachian South passed in the early decades of the century also found its way into letters. Among the humorists already mentioned in connection with the achievement of a distinctive Americanism in literature, many wrote of the southern frontier. Augustus Baldwin Longstreet, William Tappan Thompson, Johnson J. Hooper, and others realistically depicted the racy, swashbuckling life of the back country in its earlier stages. The amusing rascals and saucy fellows with their practical jokes, vulgar pranks, and fighting, their picturesque dialect and curious epigrams, all served to give distinction to the humorous writings inspired by the southern frontier.

In general, the southern aristocracy found it more congenial and fitting to express the creative intellectual impulse in oratory than in historical novels, plantation romances, and humorous sketches. Aristocratic politicians appreciated oratory as a weapon for winning the support of, or at least rendering politically impotent, the semiliterate masses. Some of the great orations of John Randolph and John C. Calhoun, rich in classical allusions and true to the Aristotelian pattern of an oratorical composition, survived, but most of the embroidered oratorical rhetoric was as ephemeral as it was florid.


## Social and Economic Thought

Economic and political essays and treatises were often as serviceable to the plantation interest as oratory, and more enduring. Even before Jefferson's death in 1826 the liberal thought for which he stood had already begun to be pushed into the background as patterns of thought emerged more congenial to the changing character of the population.

The new philosophy, it is true, owed a good deal to that aspect of Jeffersonianism which had elaborated defenses of agrarianism and at the same time indicted commercial and industrial capitalism. But for the most part it put less emphasis on natural rights, on public education for a republican society, on intellectualism, and on humanitarianism than had the philosophy of Jefferson. It tended to attach importance to historic institutions rather than to natural law; it questioned and finally denounced humanitarianism; and, as the appointment of William McGuffey, author of the famous "readers," to a post in the University of Virginia in 1845 bore witness, it substituted for the older rationalism of the plantation aristocracy the middle-class doctrine of morality, piety, and orthodox religious faith.

All of this was congenial to a changing South. Thanks to the fact that the cotton gin made slavery economically profitable, at least to the great planters, it was less and less regarded as a necessary evil to be gradually eliminated by emancipation. More and more it came to be looked on as a positive good. The profitable growing of cotton for an expanding world market thus tended to deflect the interest of southern leaders from a diversified economy to a staple-producing plantation regime based on slavery. Free trade in consequence became an ever more popular doctrine, since it would enable the agrarian South to purchase manufactures in the cheapest world markets in which it traded and to avoid taxation for subsidies to internal improvements and public education. Furthermore, states' rights, regarded as a necessary defense of free trade, slavery, and other regional interests, became not merely an instrument for the protection of Jeffersonian local democracy and individualism against Federalist and capitalistic nationalism, but a means for insuring full scope to plantation economy, an instrument for protecting it against tariffs and centralized banking. Finally, as the amazing growth of industry in the North and the equally amazing expansion of a free-labor society in the West threatened permanently to reduce the slave-plantation South to a minority section, a movement for southern nationalism arose. This was, in the first place, a protest against the northern type of nationalism based on an expanding "national" market, on free enterprise and free labor, and on the doctrine of an all-embracing unique past and future and a distinctive people within the total geographical boundaries of the country. In the second place the movement for southern nationalism was designed to strengthen the plantation interest in federal councils by checking the traditional southern emphasis on states' rights, an emphasis that promised to be less and less effective in Washington in curbing policies deemed hostile to southern interests and values. All these changing interests and ideas evoked champions among social thinkers.

In many respects George Tucker of the University of Virginia was a transitional figure in the changing social thought of the South. His sympathies were more largely with the intellectualism of Jefferson than with the piety and morality of Professor McGuffey. He had scant respect for a scholarship that made intellectual values secondary to piety, morality, or Utilitarianism. He followed the older Jeffersonian liberalism, too, in his belief that slavery was an economic and social evil of which the South, if left to her own devices, would somehow rid herself. But in reacting against the rising Jacksonianism Tucker tended to identify himself with the more conservative Whigs who, in a sense, were the descendants of the Federalists rather than of the Jeffersonians. Yet Tucker, although he espoused the Whig tenet of government control over money and banks in the interest of property, parted company with northern Whigs in opposing protective tariffs. In addition to writing essays on money, banking, statistics, and other aspects of political economy, he prepared *The History of the United States*, which was intended to correct the penchant of northern nationalistic historians by emphasizing the great importance of localism and states' rights in the country's past.

Southern political and social thought reached its greatest height in the writing of a practical political leader, John C. Calhoun. Puritan in his asceticism, morality, and even his Episcopalianism, Calhoun was, for all his quasi-romantic talk about the resemblance between southern and Greek democracy, a profound realist. In the interest of the planting aristocracy and, as he thought, in the interest of the whole South, the South Carolinian tore to pieces Jefferson's castle built on the ideas of humanitarianism, natural rights, and an educated democracy of small landholders. In its place he reared a structure designed to do two things: to justify slavery and the aristocratic domination in the South on the one hand, and, on the other, to insure the protection of the southern minority in the federal scheme. In one sense, but only in one sense, did Calhoun shift from the highly nationalistic position which, at the time of the War of 1812, promised to serve the South well. He remained a true lover of the Union, a nationalist at heart, but he came to believe that the

Union, the nation, could be preserved only if a political philosophy and a political machinery could be elaborated and accepted which might balance the majority and minority interests in the federal framework.

Calhoun's political thought, which represents a high level of analysis, reflection, and synthesis, borrowed from Jefferson the doctrine of states' rights and from the Federalists the concept of a balance of interests, rights, and powers. These he put together, along with a Hobbesian conception of human nature and, as he understood it, the Greek idea of a democracy of free citizens in which the degree of liberty any citizen enjoyed was related to his competence. That the free citizens might devote themselves to the public well-being, they, like the ancient Athenians, were freed from physical toil by the slaves who in turn profited from the intelligent guardianship of masters stronger and wiser than they.

Implicit in this philosophy and closely related to one purpose at hand —the justification of the plantation and slavery interest—was the idea that any economic and political system based on the mistaken concept of the equality of human nature could not succeed. Man was born neither free nor equal, and it was this "inequality of condition between the front and rear ranks, in the march of progress, which gives so strong an impulse to the former to maintain their position, and to the latter to press forward into their files. This gives to progress its greatest impulse."[2] But the weaker and less competent, both for their own welfare and for the good of the whole, must, while moving forward, submit to the leadership of those endowed by nature with greater wisdom and competence. In any society, Calhoun insisted, some such arrangement had to be made; in the industrial society of the North the wage slave served the function of the chattel slave in the South. But chattel slavery, the argument continued, was a wiser and more beneficent institution than wage slavery. It must therefore be not only protected but actually extended; the North must come to recognize its superiority. Only if this took place could the naturally endowed, free, and ruling citizenry enjoy leisure and facilities for successful self-government and for the wardship of nature's inferior and incompetent.

Moreover, anticipating some of Karl Marx's theory of history, Calhoun regarded the exploitation of the poor and the subsequent class struggle between capitalists and laborers as an ever-present element in civiliza-

[2] *The Works of John C. Calhoun* (New York, 1851–1856), I, 56–57.

tion. Eventually, as power and ownership became more and more concentrated in the hands of the rich, and as the resources of the laboring class neared the subsistence level, a revolution would destroy the economic and social structure. In order to ward off this eventuality, Calhoun proposed an alliance between northern capitalists and southern planters in the interest of preserving the status quo. The South's more stable social system, including the "necessary" institution of slavery, would act as a conservative force, delaying the revolution. In return the northern capitalists would attempt to stifle abolitionist agitation.

In the absence of such a league of capitalists and planters, Calhoun devised a system to preserve both the Union and slavery against the rapidly growing industrial North and the free-labor West. This system at the same time appeared to be the only possible means of achieving what Calhoun called justice. The majority, he would have it, always and inevitably tyrannizes over the minority, which must in consequence have ways and means for protecting itself; this, he insisted, was the great unsolved problem in government, a problem that became particularly acute in a democratic confederation. The South, being the minority, must through states' rights, nullification, and a kind of sectional referendum be able to set aside any federal law or arrangement deemed contrary to its interest. And if these protective mechanisms broke down, the southern states could always withdraw from the Union—a mere confederacy of limited powers. However unfortunate this eventuality would be to all who like Calhoun loved the confederacy and hoped to see it perpetuated, it would be far preferable to the tyranny imposed by a majority. All these ideas Calhoun worked out in his political speeches and in the *Disquisition on Government* with a calm logic and a persuasive abstraction about justice and freedom. If democracy be regarded as multiple leadership, multiple participation, and the sharing of values deemed good, Calhoun's conception was indeed limited. But this limitation should not obscure the fact that he did make a bold and original effort to come to grips with one of the great problems of democracy—the protection of minorities.

The broad basis which Calhoun thus laid down was elaborated in great detail by the school of thought he represented. His contention that liberty would prove a curse rather than a blessing when forced on a people unfit for it was specifically applied to the North in the writings of a Virginia planter, George Fitzhugh. Like Calhoun, Fitzhugh argued that when liberty became perverted by its extension to those unfit for it, protection and security, even greater values, suffered in the resulting anarchy. Thus the South, Fitzhugh argued, was free from that turbulence characteristic of the North and, indeed, all other free societies. In the South, unlike the North, the interest of the governing class was conservative. This prevented those violent fluctuations between conservatism and radicalism, fluctuations inherent in the fact that no society had ever existed, or could exist, in which the immediate interests of the majority of its constituents did not conflict with all existing institutions, including the family, property rights, and established order. In slavery northern property owners and capitalists would find a staunch ally against the subversive radicalisms—feminism, abolitionism, socialism, communism. Such was the burden of the arguments in Fitzhugh's *Sociology for the South* and *Cannibals All!*

It remained for the moderate-tempered and genial South Carolinian customs collector and planter, William J. Grayson, to elaborate these arguments still further in *The Hireling and the Slave* (1854), a long poem in heroic couplets. Labor exploitation, according to the poet, was in every age and society an inevitable result of the primeval curse God had laid on the children of Adam; the hireling in the factory and the slave on the plantation alike were exploited and alike received as compensation the reward of subsistence. But the slave, Grayson maintained, enjoyed a larger return from his labor than did the hireling in factory and mill, for the slave, unlike the mill hand, could not be thrown onto the streets to suffer from hunger and cold once his labor power had been exhausted. On the contrary, the aged "Uncles," "Aunties," and "Mammies" on the plantation enjoyed a security unknown to the northern proletariat. And even during the period of active labor the slave had no worries about his maintenance, about unemployment; he worked hard, but he enjoyed hunting possums and coons, merriment and song and dance, and the consolations of religion. For the abolitionist who with ignorance and sentimentality closed his eyes to the cruel fate of the wage earner at his door and wasted his tears on the Negro slave, Grayson had only bitter contempt.

The full implications of the apology for slavery developed by a score or more writers can be appreciated fully only by perusing such volumes as *The Pro-Slavery Argument* (1852), a collection of essays written by the chief protagonists of the South's "peculiar institution." The argument from Scripture was regarded as an especially important buttress. The Tenth Commandment and innumerable references in the Bible proved beyond doubt that slavery was a divine institution; St. Peter, St. Paul, and Christ Himself had urged slaves to obey their masters. Moreover, just as slave labor had erected the magnificent Temple of Solomon, so now in the South slave labor was erecting a civilization of dignity and beauty and splendor. All this could come to a terrible end if abolition triumphed, for that, alas, would mean the triumph of barbarism, the Africanization of the South.

The fear that with abolition the South would cease to be a "white man's country" encouraged speculation regarding the innate inferiority of the Negro and the obscure problem of the origin of the races. In 1854 Dr. Josiah C. Nott of Mobile, with the aid of George R. Gliddon, a former consul in Cairo, published *Types of Mankind*, an impressive volume in which the ethnological argument for slavery was elaborated. These writers cited as an authority for the doctrine of the diverse as opposed to the unitary origin of races, Dr. Samuel Morton, a Philadelphian who, on the basis of his comparative study of 1655 skulls, had inferred that environmental differences could not explain the differences in crania, and therefore the various races must have originated separately. Though, as the Reverend John Bachman, a Lutheran minister in Charleston and a scientist in his own right, pointed out, this contradicted Scripture, the argument fitted in too well with the need of proving the Negro to be innately a race debased and inferior in both body and mind, to be lightly cast aside.

Through the pulpit, the newspaper, and the oration, as well as through formal treatises, all these aspects of the proslavery argument became familiar to Southerners in the two or three decades preceding secession. The apology for slavery and the indictment of northern industrial capitalism and of the abolitionists also found their way into fiction. At least fourteen proslavery novels appeared shortly after *Uncle Tom's Cabin*, and each made use of one or more of the arguments from the Bible, from expediency, from ethnology, and from example. At the same time the South, by a vigorous system of censorship, closed its mind to the efforts of critics of slavery to refute the most distinctive and original results of southern scholarship in the field of social thought.

### Reasons for the South's Limited Contributions to Intellectual Life

When full allowance is made for the fact that in science, belles-lettres, and social thought the Old South made larger contributions to the nation's intellectual life than many critics have assumed, it is still true that these contributions do not compare favorably either with those of eighteenth-century Virginia or with the New England and the middle states of the pre-Civil War decades. Contemporary critics of slavery, especially Frederick Law Olmsted, who reported his tours in the South in the 1850s, and Hinton Rowan Helper, the North Carolinian who wrote *The Impending Crisis,* attributed the South's poor showing in the field of creative intellectual endeavor to the institution of slavery itself. Both northern abolitionists and many subsequent historical students have likewise assumed that slavery was the root of the intellectual sluggishness of the plantation aristocracy.

Impressive evidence has been summoned to support this thesis. In the first place, the necessity which the most creative minds felt of defending slavery, especially after it had become obviously profitable to plantation owners and was being attacked by abolitionists, channeled ability into political and sociological polemics. The defensive psychology of southern intellectuals must indeed have been an inhibiting force in the life of the mind.

The older freedom of thought which had marked the intellectual life of the seaboard South during the Enlightenment gave way, particularly after 1830, to marked repression. Postmasters seized abolitionist literature to destroy it. A price was set on the head of any northern abolitionist who dared enter Dixie; many of those who did were brutally harried out of the land. Even liberal or humane Southerners who could not accept the proslavery argument found it increasingly hard to express their ideas. The Grimké sisters of Charleston, who had preached their antislavery views in the North, were warned that they could not return to visit their family in their native city. Helper's book was virtually suppressed. Daniel Reaves Goodloe of North Carolina, a "home-bred" abolitionist, found his native state uncongenial if not impossible soil on which to express his views. Benjamin S. Hedrick, professor of chemistry at the University of North Carolina, was forced out of that institution in 1856 because of his announced intention to vote for the Republican candidate, John C. Fremont. Francis Lieber of South Carolina College disliked slavery but by the exercise of great tact was able to keep his position until he was called to Columbia. His correspondence testifies to his conviction that slavery cramped scholarship by suppressing freedom of discussion. Quakers, some Germans, an unknown number of yeomen and mechanics, and even a few planters continued to cherish antislavery views; but the forum, the press, the church, the school, and the college became so restricted that it was all but impossible for them to make their views known. If they did, opprobrium, or worse, was likely to be their lot.

Thus a relatively free mind, an ingredient in any vigorous and creative intellectual life, was difficult to achieve in the antebellum South. At the same time it must not be assumed that the South was unique in this respect—the repression of abolitionists during the 1830s in the North must not be forgotten. College students were occasionally forbidden to form abolitionist societies, three professors were dismissed from Western Reserve College because of their antislavery views, and the abolitionism of Professor Charles Follen at Harvard seems to have accounted in part for his having to discontinue his instruction there. But certainly more freedom of thought prevailed in the North than in the South.

In so far as slavery was responsible for limiting the economy of the South to the plantation system and for checking the growth of commerce, industry, and urbanism, its indirect effects in retarding a creative intellectual life were considerable. Several considerations, however, suggest that it was only one factor in explaining the predominantly rural character of the Old South. Another great section of the country which did not have slaves, the West, was also predominantly rural. The Tredegar iron works in Richmond and other industrial enterprises proved that slave labor could be profitably employed in shops and factories. Although slavery did militate against the development of commercial and industrial capital by turning back profits into slaves, the general lack of fluid capital and the prevailing extractive character of American economy also help explain the rural basis of life in the Old South.

The prevalence of a rural economy had much to do with the fact that the South was far behind the North in many of the agencies of intellectual life. In spite of the hopeful beginnings of public school education in a few states, especially in North Carolina, the South provided less opportunity to the mass of white population for schooling than the other sections. According to the census of 1850, the South Central States sent but one white pupil out of ten to school, while the North Central States sent one out of five. Illiteracy among the whites of the South Atlantic States, who were roughly equal in number to New England's population, was in 1850 five times as great as among the people in the northeastern section. In 1850 in the South Central States illiteracy was nearly twice as great as it was in the comparable new and likewise rural North Central States, nearly three times as great as in the Middle Atlantic States, and four times as great as in New England. Whether the backwardness of the South in public education and literacy was more largely the result of its more rigid class society, maintained and strengthened by slavery, or of the scattered character of the rural population, the fact remains that with so much illiteracy there was neither the audience for a southern literature nor the opportunity for potential talent to develop that there would have been in a more urbanized region. On the level of the colleges, which were largely attended by upper-class Southerners, the South made a good showing; a larger proportion of the white population was in college on the eve of the Civil War in the South than in the North.

The predominantly rural economy, for which slavery was in part but only in part responsible, also explained the relative shortcomings of the South in other agencies of intellectual life. Cities, the natural center for exchange of ideas and for such agencies as libraries and publishing houses, were few in number and small in size. New Orleans alone, if Baltimore and Louisville, border cities, are excepted, had more than 50,000 people on the eve of secession. Five other cities—Richmond, Charleston, Memphis, Mobile, and Savannah—numbered each between 20,000 and 50,000. The leading newspapers of three or four southern cities ranked high in the journalism of the country, and a certain number of printing establishments brought out a limited number of religious, legal, and political writings. But almost no publishing facilities existed south of Baltimore for the encouragement of southern authorship; the leading writers had to depend on northern publishers. While these houses did not neglect the southern market for their books, they were not advantageously situated to supply mass publications to the South, even had there been a demand for them. The rueful regrets of regional patriots that the South lacked publishing houses to stimulate a native literature were no doubt a rationalization. But there was some justification for the feeling that this lack was a factor in the habitual reluctance of many cultured men who might occasionally have something worth saying in print to do so. In library facilities too the South was lamentably behind the North.

The rural character of southern life was further responsible for its failure to make as good a showing on a creative intellectual level as New England and the middle states. More than one ambitious young physician, lawyer, or college teacher confessed that the difficulties of sustained creative study and writing were enhanced by the tendency of the southern aristocracy to attach great value to out-of-doors sports, to the demands of hospitality, to "gracious living" and the social amenities that distinguished the plantation way of life. Moreover, the leisure which the lord and lady of the great white-columned house had in theory was pared down in fact by a multitude of tasks and responsibilities.

The planting aristocracy, however proud of its polite learning, looked with condescension on any of its sons who might be ambitious to make a career of literature; this attitude had a discouraging effect on youth who were ambitious for a life of letters or had the scholar's temperament. Richard Henry Wilde, famed for his romantic lyric "My Life is Like the Summer Rose," was regarded as a derelict for spending seven years in Italy on his two-volume work on Tasso. Save for Poe and William Gilmore Simms, all the men who achieved any distinction in letters were primarily concerned with professional interests other than writing. The fate of Poe is well known. Simms, in spite of his defense of slavery and his celebration of South Carolina's heroic past during the Revolution, felt that he was unappreciated by the aristocracy. His second marriage brought him somewhat within its social nexus. But he always felt alienated because his work failed to be appreciated by the southern blue bloods. This may, of course, have been partly the result of the technical shortcomings in his novels; it may also have been the result of the paradoxical distaste of the vigorous, sports-loving aristocracy for what Parrington has called the Elizabethan qualities of Simms—his gusto, virility, robust poetical feeling, and picaresqueness. But Simms was not entirely wrong in his conviction that to the ruling class the making of literature was of relatively little consequence in the hierarchy of values of plantation society.

Further evidence of indifference toward professional letters was the failure to support southern literary periodicals—Legaré's *Southern Re-*

*view* lived for only four yours. The *Southern Literary Messenger*, less heavy and dull and more versatile in its offerings, did survive the years; but its editors chronically complained that, in spite of all their efforts to encourage a distinctively southern literature, the most meager support from the culture of the South was forthcoming.

If all these factors are added together and if in addition it is remembered that a considerable portion of Dixie was essentially frontier country until 1850, even later in the case of Arkansas and Texas, it is apparent that the failure of the Old South to contribute more significantly and enduringly to the life of the mind was rooted in the rural basis of her civilization as well as in slavery and the plantation ideal it inspired.

## The Ideal of Southern Nationalism

The official declaration in 1861 that the South constituted a separate nation and that Southerners were ready to die for the recognition of its distinctive institutions and way of life, which they regarded as superior to all others, embodied views that had been heralded for years by southern patriots. The argument was advanced that in geography, in climate, in common traditions, in its pure "Anglo-Saxon" and "Cavalier" stock, in its economic life and its glorious future the South constituted a nation, and that this nation had a Manifest Destiny to dominate the western plains and the shores and islands of the Caribbean. But even the staunchest southern nationalists recognized that Dixie was dependent on Yankee mills and Yankee colleges, Yankee commercial houses and Yankee publishing houses, Yankee ships and Yankee textbooks. However much southern leaders disliked Helper's *Impending Crisis*, they themselves, with examples that might have come from this classic indictment, deplored the thralldom of the South to the North. Before true southern nationalism could be achieved, it was clear that Dixie would have to develop her resources to the point of something like self-sufficiency, develop direct shipping connections with Europe, and free herself intellectually from her dependence on the North.

Cultural ties between the two sections were subjected to increasing strain. The division of the northern and southern Baptists and the Methodists over the issue of slavery indicated that one of the traditional bonds between the sections was breaking. Other denominations, especially the Presbyterians, were threatened by a similar cleavage. Northern literature was attacked in the South on sectional grounds, and demands for a distinctively southern literature became more frequent and more extreme. As early as 1835 the editor of the *Southern Literary Journal* declared that the periodical would, "at all times, breathe a Southern spirit, and sustain a strictly Southern character." *The Southern Literary Messenger* deplored the literary vassalage of the South to the North and urged southern writers "to press onward to the zenith of distinction, with unswerving purpose."[3] Years later another editor of the same periodical urged southern writers to cease trying to imitate Shakespeare and Tennyson, to give up straining at the false historical, and in coming down to the soil that gave them birth to achieve true southern distinction. Other cultural patriots had fewer doubts in regard to southern talent and achievements. The reluctance of Southerners to patronize southern authors was bitterly attacked by the *Richmond Whig*, which insisted that the South had numberless men of ripe scholarship, profound acquirements, and elegant and forcible style, richly deserving of the support and applause given to inferior authors in the North. In the same vein the editor of the *Southern Field and Fireside* wrote that the southern people had too long been content to look to northern periodicals for instruction in agriculture and to northern literary papers for mental recreation. But, he continued, "our people are awakening to the conviction that we have the elements of success in the experience, knowledge, and scientific investigation of the dwellers in our Southern homes. The truth is gleaming upon us that we have literary resources of our own worthy to be fostered—that among Southern writers should be divided some portion of that vast stream of Southern money that flows perpetually Northward to sustain Northern literature."[4]

The educational dependence of Dixie on Yankeedom was deplored in much the same terms. Southern youth, declared speakers at the Southern Commercial Conventions and writers in *De Bow's Review*, should not be sent North to be corrupted by "free" institutions; they should be kept at home for proper training in their own academies and colleges. This plea seems to have had effect, for during the heated 1850s South-

---

[3] *Southern Literary Journal*, I (September, 1835), 58; *Southern Literary Messenger*, III (September, 1836), 72 ff., 77.

[4] Cited by John D. Wade, *Augustus Baldwin Longstreet, a Study of the Development of Culture in the South* (The Macmillan Company, 1924), 330.

erners withdrew in impressive numbers from northern educational institutions to swell the enrollments of their own colleges. Cultural patriots
were also much aroused by the fact that the textbooks used in the South
were published and written by Northerners. These books, exclaimed the
orators at the Commercial Conventions, not only ignored or slighted
southern claims to greatness in resources but perverted southern youth
by hostile or apologetic references to slavery. A definite effort was
launched to encourage the able literary men of the South to write the
textbooks for their sons and daughters.

The social philosophy which thus became crystallized in the South
differed materially from that which was coming to have increasing influence in the North—a philosophy emphasizing industry and commerce,
glorifying the democracy of both capitalism and northern agriculture,
and, above all, identifying these values with nationalism and patriotism.
In our intellectual history the Civil War was a conflict between these
antagonistic social philosophies.

# 18  The Civil War and Intellectual Life

> Weeping, sad and lonely,
> Hopes and fears, how vain;
> Yet praying
> When this cruel war is over,
> Praying that we meet again.
> —When this Cruel War is Over, 1863

> And let the hands that ply the pen
> Quit the light task, and learn to wield
> The horseman's crooked brand, and rein
> The charger on the battle field.
> —BRYANT, Our Country's Call, 1861

Every aspect of life, including that of the mind, felt the impact of the war which few people, North or South, had believed would be the outcome of the growing tension between the two sections. The issue of bloodshed was accepted dubiously in many quarters on both sides of the Mason and Dixon line, enthusiastically in others. A small minority of the members of the peace societies in the North refused to compromise with their principle of absolute opposition to all war, and a growing number of men and women in both sections, distrustful of their leaders, sympathetic with the enemy, or merely war-weary, preferred compromise or even defeat to the continuation of the struggle. The fact of war affected the thinking not only of these dissidents but of the great majority of people who accepted it as inevitable and hoped that good would come from it.

In spite of the influence of the war on all aspects of life, ordinary routine, cherished ideas, and long-term historical tendencies were not entirely thrust aside. Many Northerners and Westerners carried out well-laid plans for joining the great migration to the unsettled lands of the frontier or made up their minds to trek to the ever-growing cities. Schemes to make fortunes played their parts in the minds of men, North and South, as in times past. On both sides devotion to family ties, love of knowledge, faith in the ultimate triumph of progress and right, religious zeal—all these values continued to temper the lives of men and women even in the midst of war. All the ordinary values seemed to prevail just as before.

Actually they were changed in various ways. The war sharpened many ideas and brought others to the fore. The impressive opportunities for gain did much to advance the business class and to publicize its values —a factor of moment in the nation's intellectual life. Costly display and luxurious amusements testified to material success and material values in many quarters. The social philosophy of business, especially the idea of the self-made man, the equality of opportunities provided by business, and the general beneficence of business, was now contrasted even more strikingly than ever before with the ideas symbolized by the plantation system and even more insistently identified with nationalism and democracy. Spokesmen for the Confederacy denounced Yankee commercialism and materialism even more vehemently than in antebellum days. They glorified the values of the great plantation, of the agrarian way of life, of slavery, and they boasted of the unique and superior past of the South, its distinctive geography and ethnic character, its glorious future.

In the North itself many patriotic intellectuals saw in the outburst of national feeling released by the firing on Fort Sumter a much-needed check on the prevalent emphasis on material success. The editor of The Independent was convinced that the war would uproot and put an end to the luxurious life and the insidious tyranny that had marked the late era of peace; "the nation is electrified into a new consciousness of its life, its duty, its destiny."[1] According to the editor of Harper's Weekly the mad clamor for gold and the crass weight of materialism were giving way to moral and spiritual values. At least part of the nation's intellect,

[1] The Independent, XIII (April 18, 1861), 4.

continued the editor of this popular periodical, must inevitably be diverted from the scramble for dollars into nobler and higher aims, and the rising military class itself would be a healthy counterbalance to the dominant and selfish commercial aristocracy.

Almost all the intellectuals of the North shared the view that the war was touching and would increasingly touch the soul of the nation. At Concord the ailing Henry Thoreau felt uplifted at the moral regeneration the upheaval had already brought in its wake. His neighbor, Ralph Waldo Emerson, saw war come "as a frosty October, which shall restore intellectual and moral power to these languid and dissipated populations."[2] Across the Atlantic young Henry Adams, secretary to his father the minister to England, was certain in the summer of 1863 that this generation had been stirred up from the lowest layers. "We cannot be commonplace;" of this, at least, the future skeptic was certain.

By and large, scholars did not fear that the war held any threat to the values dear to them. "If the presence of a free, quickened national existence can elevate the scholarly mind and ennoble its pursuits," remarked a writer in the North American Review, "that presence is with us, and its fruits will surely appear." The young scholar, continued this contributor to the venerable Boston review, might be fighting in the trenches of Virginia, or penning words of fire for the press, or speaking in churches and assembly halls; but even in the quiet of his own study he could not be blind or deaf to the surging life of his countrymen. Scholarship had long enough been sterile by reason of its divorce from actuality; and it might well be, concluded this observer, that the war would further the American penchant for allying scholarship and life, thought and action.

Nor was sight lost of the unforgotten ideal of an American literature and science and art. The fact that conservative Europe affected to see in the war the breakdown of republican institutions stirred Henry Wilson, the self-educated cobbler who represented Massachusetts in the Senate, to sponsor the organization of a national academy of science. "I wanted the *savants* of the Old World, as they turn their eyes thitherward," Wilson told the first meeting of the Academy, "to see that amid the fire and blood of the most gigantic civil war in the annals of nations, the statesmen and people of the United States, in the calm confidence of assured power, are fostering the elevating, purifying, and consolidating

[2] Emerson and Forbes (eds.), *Journals of Ralph Waldo Emerson*, IX, 494.

institutions of religion and benevolence, literature, art, and science."[3] The new National Academy of Science set itself to the task of aiding the federal government, of breaking down further the chasm between thought and action.

Southern intellectuals were equally certain that the life of the mind would flower once the war was over, once the independence of the Confederacy had been recognized. But the dominant mood was expressed by the Confederate official who, according to his wife, Mary Chesnut, told some theological students who had requested exemption from military service: "Wait until you have saved your country before you make preachers and scholars. When you have a country, there will be no lack of divines, students, scholars to adorn and purify it."

What actually did happen to the intellectual life during the four years of combat? What happened to the agencies of intellectual life, North and South? What of religion? How did such ideas as democracy, aristocracy, humanitarianism, and nationalism fare? What was done to bring reading matter and inspiration to the common soldier in field and camp? Was the newly freed slave provided with a chance to acquire the knowledge without which real freedom was impossible? Were American life and thought indeed lifted to new heights?

### The Disruption of Older Intellectual Patterns

Although intellectual life in the North was affected by the war, the dislocation amounted to little in comparison with what took place in the South. No social group in the entire land was so much affected in its attitude toward life as the slaves. The Negroes in general did not, of course, appreciate the causes of the war or the forces at work during its progress. But after the Emancipation Proclamation great numbers gradually became aware that their freedom was at stake. In *Up from Slavery* Booker T. Washington describes the thanksgiving, the scenes of ecstasy, the wild rejoicing on the part of the slaves when they heard this proclamation read to them. He tells of the tearful joy of his own mother, who had been praying for years for the event she feared she would never live to see. Wherever Union troops controlled parts of the South, slaves deserted to their lines in appreciable, sometimes overwhelming, numbers.

[3] *National Academy of Science Annual 1863–1864* (Cambridge, 1865), 12–13.

When the government at Washington somewhat reluctantly enlisted Negro troops, the former slaves demonstrated their capacity to perform acts of great courage.

Fearing insurrection and sabotage, slaveowners tightened the patrol system and in order to check desertion to the Union lines spread rumors regarding the cruelty of the Yankees. One story graphically described the northern soldiers as devilish beasts capable of throwing women and children into a river or even of roasting their enemies alive. It is impossible, of course, to determine the effect of such propaganda in keeping the slaves on the plantations. In any case the majority of house servants and a large number of field hands did remain loyal to their masters—some with genuine personal devotion, others in the mood of just waiting to see what would happen.

The beginnings of education for the freedman in areas occupied by the Federal armies inaugurated a new era in the intellectual history of the Negro. Philanthropic organizations in the North, such as the American Missionary Association, the Boston Educational Commission, and the United States Commission for the Relief of National Freedmen, established schools for Negroes, equipped classrooms, and sent out teachers. Of the some fifty schools thus set up in Virginia in 1863, many used Negro assistant teachers; one, in fact, employed fifteen in that capacity. Nor was the training of teachers neglected, for in 1863 Congress incorporated in Washington the Institution for the Education of Colored Youth, an outgrowth of a pioneer Negro teacher-training institution founded a decade earlier by Myrtilla Miner. More substantial aid came from Congress in the last weeks of the war with the establishment of the Bureau of Freedmen, a federal agency authorized, among other things, to supplement the private and voluntary educational enterprises for freedmen.

If southern whites saw in the beginnings of Negro education under Yankee auspices a threat to their own ideas of cultural hegemony, some were impelled by war needs to bestir themselves intellectually and even to imagine in the exhilaration of activity that a new chapter in their own intellectual life was under way. The South's most gifted scientist, Matthew Fontaine Maury, returned from his long residence in Washington and undertook experiments in Richmond designed to perfect the submarine electrical torpedo. Wits were sharpened and all available ingenuity was brought to the fore by the necessity of providing substitutes for a wide variety of products hitherto imported from the North or from Europe. The inspiration that the war provided southern poets seemed to promise a glorious southern literature. The opportunity was seized to promote the antebellum dream of a thoroughly southern type of elementary education. Confederate textbooks appeared with no trace of "subversive" northern doctrines; one taught its little readers that the United States had once been a great and prosperous country, that its people were noted for their skill in driving a bargain, and that the Confederacy was a great country with a people noted for high-mindedness and courtesy.

But the war did not bring an intellectual renaissance to the white South. Before the struggle was half over almost all the agencies of intellectual life had either suffered materially or broken down completely. The blockade prevented the importation of any considerable number of books. The South, unlike the North, was the actual scene of fighting. This meant that ordinary life was so thoroughly disorganized that it was possible to maintain little more than a faint outline of the older pattern of intellectual life. Invading armies sometimes destroyed fine old plantation libraries, like that of Jacob Thompson, whose scattered books found their way to various parts of the Union. At least one spirited patriot preferred to burn her library rather than have Yankee officers make use of it.

The war struck a severe blow to the promising beginnings of public education and undermined or destroyed many private institutions. Except in a few places like Charleston and Mobile, and in North Carolina, public school systems, feeble at best, collapsed. School funds, invested chiefly in bank and railway stocks, were either diverted to war chests or rendered worthless as finances broke down, and times were too hard to collect even meager school taxes. Many private academies maintained hand-to-mouth existence throughout the war; many others closed their doors altogether.

The picture in the field of higher education was even darker. College buildings put to military uses were frequently destroyed. In the early months of the war most students hurried to enlist. In many cases professors abandoned their classrooms. Of these Basil Gildersleeve, the gifted classicist at the University of Virginia, was representative. Others gave up their established intellectual interests for war work. Joseph Le Conte, the nationally known geologist who had taught at the College of

South Carolina and the University of Georgia, undertook to provide powder and drugs for the army. Although several colleges remained open in the first years of the war, almost all ceased even to ring the bell long before Appomattox. The slender resources of endowed institutions were quickly dried up, and state universities, with the exception of Virginia, were left without support. Jefferson's foundation remained nominally open, though with little life. In Professor Maximilian Schele de Vere Virginia possessed an exceptional scholar; in spite of everything he found time, between drilling the handful of his colleagues and students, to continue his pioneer studies in comparative philology.

Newspapers and periodicals suffered as well as educational institutions. The scarcity of paper, ink, and type, the difficulties of communication, and the high costs of postage all militated against the maintenance of a periodical press. Issues of once prosperous newspapers appeared on half-sheets, on mere slips of paper, and increasingly on wallpaper. A few of the well-established periodicals, such as the *Southern Presbyterian Review* and the *Southern Cultivator*, survived the war in depleted form. But *De Bow's Review* was suspended in 1862, and the leading magazine of antebellum days, *The Southern Literary Messenger*, closed its office in 1864. A few new enterprises were launched only to fail. Of these the *Magnolia* and the *Southern Illustrated News* published verse and stories by the South's leading writers; the latter was distinguished for the wood-cuts by W. L. Sheppard and the portraits and sketches of Confederate generals. *Southern Punch*, with its army jokes and bitter satires on Richmond profiteers, was less successful than another new venture, the *Record*. Ably edited and neatly printed, it was valued for the competent weekly editorials by John R. Thompson and the admirable summaries of the news of the world.

Depleted though the newspapers and magazines were in many respects, they carried on with little interference from government authorities and with the loyal support of men and women of literary inclinations. The mass of narrative and lyric verse, much of which was in crude vernacular, included some pieces of merit and distinction. Dr. Francis O. Ticknor's "Little Giffen of Tennessee" is a memorable and moving tribute to the heroism of a son of the soil; Father Ryan's "The Conquered Banner" and Albert Pike's version of "Dixie" are patriotic verses of much merit; and such humorous verses as John R. Thompson's "On to Richmond" rank high among their kind. But all these were transcended by the war poems of Paul Hamilton Hayne and Henry Timrod. Timrod's "The Cotton Boll," "A Cry of Arms!" and "Ode to the Confederate Dead" must always remain powerful and beautiful expressions of a gifted poet in a time of crisis and hope.

In view of the obstacles confronting publishers, few books were issued. Sunday school pamphlets, sermons, religious songbooks, and "The Soldier's Pocket Bible" were published to provide the armies with spiritual comfort. Almanacs were frequently held back for lack of paper, and E. A. Pollard's popular *Second Year of the War* in its second edition was delayed for similar reasons. *Macaria* by Augusta J. Evans, the Mobile author whose *Beulah* had been a best seller, was one of the few novels from southern pens that found a publisher; it appeared on coarse brown paper. George Cary Eggleston bought in Charleston for seven dollars a wallpaper edition of *Tannhäuser*. New translations of *Les Misérables* (known as Lee's Miserables among the soldiers of the Army of Northern Virginia), of *The Last Moments of Murat*, and of Mulbach's *Joseph II* appeared. It was also possible to buy southern editions of Dickens' *Great Expectations*, Thackeray's *Adventures of Philip*, and Bulwer's *Strange Story*.

Yet these imprints fell far short of the need. The reminiscences of officers relate the dearth of reading matter, the joy provided by such old standbys as Byron's *Don Juan*, Thomson's *Seasons*, Dick's *The Christian Philosopher*, and such volumes by Carlyle, Macaulay, and Thackeray as might be turned up. At least one officer read several chapters of the Bible every morning before breakfast, and others, deprived of modern books, turned to their Greek and Roman classics. The federal government permitted northern Episcopalians to send prayer books to men in the field, and blockade runners sometimes brought in Bibles from England.

Although the war absorbed much of the energy of the Northerners, public education in the North went on in almost normal fashion. It is true that the movement for free high schools was retarded and that for two years the National Teachers' Association failed to assemble. It is also true that male teachers everywhere volunteered in numbers; in Ohio alone, for example, 5000, or one-half the state's entire number, had enlisted before the war was half over. But schools were not in general suspended. Women, who had been increasingly entering the field of schoolteaching, took the places of the men who left for the front. By and large, public education did not greatly suffer as a result of the war.

Nor were colleges destroyed and depleted as they were in the South. It is true that attendance declined in some measure on almost every campus and that in many smaller institutions in the West the great majority of undergraduates deserted Minerva for Mars. But buildings were not destroyed, and classes everywhere continued to be held. College histories record only an occasional faculty member who, like Joshua L. Chamberlain of Bowdoin, entered the army. Memorials for fallen classmates and patriotic celebrations, together with military drill, were in evidence, but college life was in no sense materially altered. Indeed, higher education expanded during the war years in an impressive manner.

Periodicals felt the war currents, and some suffered. *Harper's* and *Godey's Lady's Book* forfeited their large southern constituency. The *Princeton Review*, one of the leading religious quarterlies, lost a considerable portion of its subscribers. But in spite of the rising cost of paper and the tax on advertising, the ability of most magazine readers to buy periodicals was not seriously or widely impaired. In contrast with the southern press, newspapers enjoyed an immense boom.

In some respects scientific studies went by the board. Not only did the geological surveys in the seceding states come to an abrupt end; even in the North several legislatures failed to make the necessary appropriations. Professional science was the loser from the suspension of the annual meetings of the American Association for the Advancement of Science. The membership of this organization, which had run upwards of a thousand at the outbreak of the war, was considerably under half that number in 1865. At least some scientists of talent curtailed basic researches to meet the exigencies of the war situation. Oliver Wolcott Gibbs, who had introduced into America the German method of laboratory research in chemical instruction, did not, it is true, drop his important researches on platinum metals; these contributed to his clarification of vaguely held notions about atomicities or valences. But this eminent scientist gave generously of his time to the government, now advising on matters of tariff and scientific instruments and on other occasions putting his vast knowledge at the service of the Sanitary Commission. Dr. Joseph Leidy, the foremost paleontologist and anatomist of his time, put by his researches to become surgeon in an army hospital, but even there he put to good account the autopsies he performed. Still others, such as Ferdinand D. Hayden, explorer of the Bad Lands and the Yellowstone River, also interrupted researches to become war surgeons.

In the humanities, no less than in natural science, gifted scholars withdrew from investigation and threw themselves into war work. Charles Eliot Norton of Cambridge put aside his Dante studies to cull patriotic editorials from the press for distribution in quantities to country newspapers. Henry C. Lea, the Philadelphia scholar and publisher, diverted time from his study of medieval superstition and religious persecution to prepare pamphlets for the Union League, a propagandist agency. Francis Lieber, the political scientist at Columbia, was happy to write propaganda for the Loyalist Publication Society. Yet if scientific research and scholarship were hampered by the war, the disruption of intellectual life in the North was not comparable to that in the South.

In certain respects the life of the mind in the North was seared by the titanic struggle. Freedom of the press, a cherished ideal of American democracy, was set aside by government authority when newspaper editors betrayed evidences of disloyalty. Such encroachments, it is true, were neither general nor permanent. In rare instances academic freedom was hampered. Thus the case of President Lord of Dartmouth, who was unable to support the Lincoln administration on emancipation and as a result was virtually forced to sever his connection with the college, was exceptional. More important than these infringements on traditional freedoms in a great emergency was the impetus given by the war to emotional and even hysterical propaganda. In the North as in the South, fear and hatred of the enemy were deliberately promoted by the circulation of atrocity stories, such as that which pictured General Lee flogging a slave girl with his own hands and pouring brine on her bleeding wounds, or those charging southern ladies with drinking out of Yankee skulls, butchering children of Unionist sympathies, and poisoning wells and streams. Southerners told and believed similar stories about Northerners. The cultivation of exaggeration, hypocrisy, and hysteria did not augur well for the realization of the ideals of intellectual life to which so many Americans had long subscribed.

The war evoked impressive manifestations of charity but at the same time diverted energy from, and even shunted aside, all the reform crusades except abolition. The peace movement collapsed. Condemned as cowards, only a few ardent souls continued to support pacifism, and they could hardly make themselves heard. The temperance organizations continued to publish literature and to hold forth on the lecture platform, but the gains they had made in obtaining state prohibition were lost as a result of the clamor for revenues from the taxation of liquors. Woman's rights conventions were suspended so that leaders of the movement might give all their time to war pursuits. They circulated petitions for the emancipation of the slave, they threw their strength into relief work, they supported Lincoln in the critical campaign of 1864. They assumed that, once the war was over, such services would be rewarded by the concession of the suffrage. Moreover, they found an additional reason for expecting this long-desired boon in the declaration that the war was waged for the fulfillment of the traditional ideal of government of the people, by the people, and for the people.

But if the movement for woman's rights was temporarily suspended by the war, the general position of women greatly improved. Everywhere —on farms, in shops, in schoolrooms, in hospitals, in industry—their services were called for and their competency demonstrated. "Listless young girls and fancied invalids rose from their sofas, at first to wind bandages and pack supplies," wrote a chronicler, ". . . later to do the household work, which there were no servants to perform, or to earn their living in unaccustomed occupations that there were no men to undertake."[4]

### Continued Growth of the Agencies of Intellectual Life

The war did have some immediate adverse effects on the life of the mind. Whether it had any direct favorable effect in stimulating intellectual activity is a question impossible to answer with any confidence. Striking developments, especially in the expansion of equipment and facilities for intellectual activity, took place in the North during the actual struggle, but these were for the most part already under way and might have occurred, or been even more striking, had there been no war. Indirectly the war was one factor in the expansion of facilities, in that it brought great profits to some men who supported education and thus stimulated philanthropy in the field of intellectual endeavors. It is possible that the patriotism and idealism aroused by it may well have had

[4] Amy L. Reed, "Female Delicacy in the Sixties," *Century Magazine*, LXVIII (October, 1916), 863.

something to do with the new evidences of sustained American faith in education and in broadening the opportunities of intellectual life.

On the civilian front all the older agencies for the diffusion of special skills and information continued to flourish. In six cities business colleges with evening courses appeared for the first time. Almost every mercantile and mechanics' library reported marked increases in the loans of books. This was also true of the Boston Public Library. Lynn and Worcester in Massachusetts and Detroit in Michigan established new public libraries. Almost every town continued to support a lecture course graced by the old favorites who discussed, in addition to the customary cultural subjects, the issues of the war. Thanks to the attention given the war by such weekly magazines at *Leslie's* and *Harper's*, the number of their readers grew apace. New periodical ventures, such as *The Continental Monthly* and the *United States Service Magazine*, provided much military and naval news, war stories and verse, and discussions of the larger issues involved in the struggle. The demand for war news was so insistent that the reading of daily newspapers increased enormously. This led to the use of new technological processes for mass production, such as stereotyping and papier-mâché, to improvements in the presentation of news, and to more comprehensive and accurate military correspondence. Eagerness for the latest news also led to the appearance of the Sunday issue of papers.

To combat lukewarmness for the cause, patriots undertook to supply the public with special pamphlets on the issues of the struggle. The New England Loyal Publication Society, supported by the well-to-do business man John Murray Forbes, and by Charles Eliot Norton, distributed broadsides reprinting patriotic editorials, reports of progress on the production of cotton by free labor, and other material designed to clarify war issues and instill patriotism. These broadsides were sent to country newspapers and to various organizations. In New York the Loyal Publication Society, with Francis Lieber at the head, issued specially prepared pamphlets to particular groups, racial, national, and regional. Peace-at-any-price men were exposed and denounced; emancipation was urged as a military necessity; the theory of secession and of nationalism was expounded; and the position of prominent Europeans on the war was popularized. In 1864 this organization distributed 470,000 copies of documents.

The soldier in the field was not neglected. While few commanding officers took so broad an educational view of his needs as did General John M. Palmer, who believed that it was possible and desirable to associate military service with intellectual, moral, and religious growth, many recognized that proper reading matter promoted discipline and morale. The Christian Commission, which sprang from a meeting of YMCA. delegates early in the war, established reading rooms and libraries in camps and hospitals. It appealed for "good reading matter" as a "valuable hygienic appliance." The books and reading materials distributed by the Commission were on the whole of a religious and moral character. In 1864, for instance, it put into the hands of soldiers and sailors almost 6 million "knapsack books" like Newman Hall's *Come to Jesus*, almost one million hymnbooks and psalmbooks, over a million Bibles and Testaments, and 11 million tracts with more than 36 million pages. Yet an appeal for gifts urged the importance of lively, interesting books, pictorial weekly and monthly periodicals, and works on art, science, and literature. One of the printed catalogues of 125 books included *Bryant's Selections from American Poets, Halleck's Selections from British Poets*, Lamb's *Tales from Shakespeare*, the *Lady of the Lake* and *Ivanhoe, Paradise Lost*, Irving's *Sketch Book* and *Columbus*, Creasy's *Decisive Battles*, and well-known titles on geography, travel, and science. Manuals of drill and tactics were eagerly desired by men ambitious for promotion; and newspapers were specially sought for. There is even evidence that *Godey's Lady's Book* found many readers in the army!

According to the testimony of the "delegates" or workers in the Christian Commission, the soldiers repeatedly asked for reading material, and chaplains frequently spoke of the same desire. "Go into a tent," wrote one delegate, "and almost the first question is, 'Chaplain, can you give us anything to read?' And the Christian Commission's slices and crumbs from the bread of life," concluded this pious soul, "seem sweeter to them than any luxuries or delicacies."[5] In any case, soldiers not only eagerly sought for reading material, but sometimes edited newspapers of their own, wrote verse, and conducted debates.

The extension of facilities for adult education was accompanied by continued support for elementary public education. The frontier states of Minnesota and Nevada set up school systems during the war. In spite

[5] The Reverend Horatio Q. Butterfield, *United States Christian Commission, A Delegate's Story* (n.p., 1863), 4–5.

of the pressing demand for public funds, the teachers' scandalously low salaries slowly increased as the cost of living mounted. The immense importance of developing a teaching profession was not overlooked. Teachers' institutes continued to assemble and state teachers' associations seldom abandoned their meetings; in Chicago, in the midst of the war, 1600 enthusiastic teachers, summoned by the National Teachers Association, held the largest educational gathering America had yet seen. Six states hitherto without normal schools established at least one each. Schoolbooks continued to be published in ever greater numbers.

In the field of higher education $5 million from private sources were diverted to college purposes. New buildings went up and new professorships were established as a result of this beneficence, but a large part of it went into the founding of a dozen new colleges. Of these the most important were Vassar and the Massachusetts Institute of Technology, which dedicated their first buildings before Appomattox; but Swarthmore, Lehigh, and Cornell were also planned for and in part provided for. In addition several established theological schools received important gifts; Daniel Drew, railway promoter, determined to endow a theological seminary. Columbia established its School of Mines. Law schools and medical schools at a number of universities reported both larger enrollments and more substantial support.

But this was not all. For the first time in the nation's history the federal government embarked on a policy of aiding education not only in the newer states but in the older ones as well. An Act sponsored by a self-educated Vermonter, Senator Justin Morrill, conferred on every state 30,000 acres of public land for each senator and representative in its congressional delegation. This land was to endow colleges designed to teach, in addition to scientific and military subjects, the branches of learning especially related to agriculture and the mechanic arts.

The agitation for this epoch-making Act had a long and controversial history. While it had important friends in the West, its chief support came not from that allegedly utilitarian section but from the East itself. It seems clear that the Morrill Act was designed in part to provide compensation to the older states for the free homesteads which the West had long clamored for and at length obtained, and that it was further designed to aid the East by promoting more efficient agricultural methods, thus to enable farmers to compete with those on the richer lands of the West, and to provide industry with trained technicians. But the

Morrill Act also reflected the democratic and nationalistic principles for which the armies of the North and West were contending. The type of education visioned in it promised not only to be useful to the economic life on which the Union was based, but to help cement East and West in the common interests now uniting them. The agricultural and industrial education thus to be supported by the federal government also offered poorer boys greater opportunities, helped to equalize educational advantages in disparate regions of the country, and narrowed the gulf between academic and practical pursuits, in other words, between thought and action. The grant to the loyal states of an endowment of $10 million thus laid the foundation for a momentous expansion of a new type of higher education at government expense.

## Scholarship in War Time

If the agencies of intellectual life were little hampered in their growth by the war exigency, the crisis, directly or indirectly, did militate in some respects against the intellectual life. Zeal for obtaining revenue and general enthusiasm for the principle of protective tariffs accounted for the failure of Charles Sumner's efforts to defeat the proposal for a tax on books; his colleagues in Congress turned deaf ears toward his plea that such a tax was a tax on knowledge comparable to a tax on the light of day, and that by refusing to embark on such a course at such a crisis the nation might do itself great honor. Nor was Sumner any more successful in his effort to capitalize on the national enthusiasm evoked by the war by obtaining national academies for the promotion of art, literature, and moral and political science to take their places alongside of the newly established National Academy of Science. Too many strict constructionists and devotees of local rights feared that national power was already, in consequence of the war, expanding overrapidly. Some also suspected that such national academies might prove to be exclusive, aristocratic, and dictatorial; many plain people had no desire to set up institutions that might attempt in some fashion to tell the ordinary man what pictures to prefer, what books to venerate, what ideas to entertain.

Almost all the leading men of light and learning exemplified ardent patriotism. It was an exceptional figure in the intellectual world who, like Samuel F. B. Morse or President Lord of Dartmouth, distrusted the war aims of the Washington government. Although some hastened to leave their libraries and laboratories for war service, the great majority felt with Agassiz that in such a national crisis scholars could do no better than to fortify the strongholds of learning and keep their particular armories bright.

Thus many eminent figures in natural science kept at their appointed tasks. Agassiz himself continued to spread knowledge of natural history through public lectures, to arrange the exhibits of the new museum at Harvard, to make his own investigations in zoology and geology. At Yale James Dwight Dana published his monumental *Manual of Geology* (1862), a classic in the field. Geologists continued field investigations; Joseph Dwight Whitney, author of the important *Metallic Wealth of the United States*, directed the newly established geological survey of California and fathered its Academy of Science. Other geologists found opportunities to advance knowledge in the surveys set up during the war by Kansas, New Jersey, and Maine. In other fields, Charles Francis Hall, who from 1860 to 1862 was engaged in his explorations of the northern seas, set forth again in 1864 in search of the Pole; his *Arctic Researches* (1865) established him as one of the great arctic explorers of his time. At St. Louis Chancellor William Chauvenet of the university of that city completed in 1863 his *Manual of Spherical and Practical Astronomy*, which the great European astronomer, Herman Struve, regarded as the best existing work on practical astronomy.

Organizational work in scientific inquiry kept its course. The Sheffield Scientific School dispatched its promising young apprentice Othniel Charles Marsh, to Europe, where during the war years he laid the foundation of a scholarship that made him one of the great paleontologists of his day. From the Smithsonian Institution young Edward Cope, on the threshold of becoming America's leading zoologist, went abroad to continue his studies. Joseph Henry, ever ready to put his knowledge at the service of the government, found no special reason to deviate from the tasks at hand; and his colleague, Spencer F. Baird, continued his important ornithological studies. The Coast Survey similarly kept at its work. It offered an opportunity for astronomical study to F. A. P. Barnard, the northern president of the University of Mississippi. The duties of service in the Coast Survey left sufficient time to C. S. Peirce to germinate ideas which, published shortly after the war, established him as a great logician by reason of his pioneer conception that even the most abstract logic rests on ethical and social theories.

What was true of the Smithsonian and the Coast Survey was true also of such scientific foundations as the American Philosophical Society, the American Academy of Sciences, and the museums of natural history; their publications during the war years show that the interests of the prewar period continued to yield new fruits in ethnology, mathematics, and the physical sciences. Similarly a survey of the *Annual of Scientific Discovery* reveals that European advances in the various fields were duly received in America and that publications at home maintained the level of those that preceded the crisis.

This does not mean that the war had no effect at all in presenting scientists with problems. On the contrary, the *American Journal of Science* published papers on explosive forces in gunpowders; the National Academy of Sciences investigated for the Surgeon General methods of testing the purity of whiskey, of medical importance in the war, and pursued ad hoc researches in the fields of counterfeit coins, weights and measures, and ballistics. The list of patent inventions suggests that impetus was given by the war to work in magnetoelectric lights for signaling as well as in ballistics. The American Medical Association devoted in its annual meetings sections to military hygiene. Surgeon General William Hammond, before a crisis in his relations with the Secretary of War removed him from office by court-martial, published a pioneer treatise on military hygiene. But by and large the war did little to divert scientific investigation from paths already marked. It may possibly have postponed the discussion of Darwinism, but it was merely a postponement.

The publications issued during the war years indicate that scholars in linguistics went about their work much as usual. Classical studies were augmented by the publication of Greek and Latin texts and grammars. Of these, one of the most important was William Goodwin's second edition of his *Syntax of the Moods and Tenses of the Greek Verb*. Even more than in the first edition (1860) Goodwin, Eliot professor of Greek at Harvard, rejected metaphysical German concepts of Greek syntax and advanced knowledge of the field through his own power of classification and insight into meanings. The last year of the war also saw the publication of Francis A. March's *Method of Philological Study of the English*

*Language.* Our first scholar to apply exegesis in its full scientific rigor to the classics of English literature, March was a true pioneer in the American study of comparative philology. The appearance in 1864 of a new edition of Webster's *American Dictionary,* revised by Noah Porter and Chauncey Goodrich, was also a noteworthy event.

The furor of war did not blot out interest in the humanities. George Ticknor in 1863 published a thoroughly revised edition of his great *History of Spanish Literature.* In addition to writing a mordant satire on the Copperheads, the much-read *New Gospel of Peace,* Richard G. White, a New York lawyer, music critic, and journalist, brought out the first important American edition of Shakespeare. This edition called attention to the fabricated emendations in a second folio of Shakespeare which the English Shakespearean scholar, John P. Collier, had declared to be those of a seventeenth-century corrector who had access to better authorities than did the earliest editors. In Boston Dr. Thomas Parsons, a dentist, continued throughout the war his translations of Dante which had begun to appear in 1843; in 1865 and 1867 he published his sensitive and felicitous translations of the *Inferno.* In the latter year Longfellow's *Divine Comedy* also appeared, the fruit of long labor, now appropriately released as if in tribute to the nation's dead. An outstanding event in the field of the humanities was the publication in 1863 of Francis J. Child's *Observations on the Language of Chaucer,* a book which, through the contributions it made to the knowledge of the poet's language and versification, marked a new era in Chaucerian studies. Professor Child, from his home near the Harvard Yard, wrote occasional war ballads for soldiers and also continued work on his great collection of English and Scotch ballads, eight volumes of which had appeared before the struggle broke out.

Achievements in the field of history and the social sciences were no less rich. This harvest was in some part touched by the storms of war. George Bancroft's already highly pitched patriotism could hardly reach any point higher in the scale than that achieved in the first eight volumes of his monumental *History of the United States;* but the ninth volume, appearing in 1866 and dealing with the Revolution, brought to the foreground the heroic nature of the birth of the country now struggling for life. The Revolution provided other historians with themes and inspiration. In 1864 Lorenzo Sabine completed his revised study of the Loyalists. George Washington Greene wrote a useful *His-*

*torical View of the American Revolution;* Parton brought out his *Life and Times of Benjamin Franklin;* Henry B. Dawson's edition of *The Federalist* and a reprinting of Elliot's debates on the Constitution also reflected a heightened interest in the nation's birth. Nor was the Civil War itself neglected. Frank Moore and Edward McPherson compiled, during the struggle and the years thereafter, important collections of documentary material relating to the war.

Interest in the past, well launched before Appomattox, transcended concern with the nation's great crises. New historical societies were founded at Dover, Brooklyn, New Haven, and Buffalo. There were scholars who had begun long-term investigations who did not falter in their labors; Parkman's *Pioneers of France in the New World* appeared in 1865. John G. Palfrey brought out a new volume of the *History of New England,* characterized by general accuracy of details but also by a pronounced bias for Massachusetts and the clergy. In the parsonage at Albany William B. Sprague completed the seventh volume of his useful *Annals of the American Pulpit.* Even in the midst of a great contest of arms there could appear a notable study of the role of ideas in the development of civilization. Professor John W. Draper, the distinguished chemist of New York University, published in 1863 his frequently inaccurate and uncritical but much-translated and highly influential *History of the Intellectual Development of Europe.* The *North American Review* praised this volume as one of the "most truly original, profound and instructive contributions of the age." No doubt it did blaze a trail for many essentially modern ideas of the interrelations between climate and social institutions. Draper subscribed to the Lamarckian doctrine of the inheritance of acquired characteristics and to the Comtean idea of history as an exact science. His entire book was marked by faith in science as opposed to supernaturalism, in ideas and laws in contradistinction to mere chance and physical force.

In the related field of the social sciences the war years saw the appearance of several studies of note. Professor Draper did not confine his attention to physical science and to the intellectual history of Europe. Convinced that the Republic had reached "one of those epochs at which it must experience important transformations," he undertook, in lectures given at the New York Historical Society in 1864 and in the book which grew out of them, *Thoughts on the Future Civil Policy of the United States* (1865), to apply specifically to the United States his theory that physical agents and laws influence national development and human history. Draper's emphasis on the role of climate, immigration, and political ideas in America opened new vistas for social control.

Many of the books that appeared during the war bore little or no direct relation, of course, to the struggle itself. But it is significant that scholars produced such books and that they were published and read in the midst of the fierce and bloody effort to insure the very life of the nation.

More directly related to the issues raised by the war was Francis Lieber's *Instructions for the Government of Armies of the United States in the Field.* This code was to become the basis of much future work, both in Europe and in America, in this field of international law, and its humane provisions and attitudes aroused much comment. Less influential for America's future development, John C. Hurd's *Law of Freedom and Bondage,* the second volume of which appeared in the middle of the war, was a work of careful erudition.

The impact of the war on social thought brought forth a wide variety of interpretations of the great struggle. Orestes A. Brownson, at last anchored firmly to Catholicism, speculated with no less feeling than learning on the meaning of the war. His *American Republic* (1865), indebted as it was to Augustine, St. Thomas, Suarez, and other Catholic lights, rejected the doctrine of the state of nature, natural rights, undiluted individualism, and democratic theory. But if Brownson seemed to be out of line with the majority of his fellow citizens in these particulars, he was with the incoming tide in his attribution of national sovereignty not to the several states, but to the states united as integral and organic parts of the nation.

In a strikingly different fashion Josiah Warren, a bizarre extremist of the philosophical anarchist school, analyzed events in *True Civilization an Immediate Necessity* (1863). In the new wave of nationalism Warren saw a tragic reaction toward "barbaric clan-ism," a repudiation of the doctrine of the free, sovereign individual. But his voice spoke in a wilderness. So did that of Lysander Spooner, a Massachusetts lawyer whose devotion to laissez faire had once led him to combat singlehanded the United States post office, for which he tried to substitute private service. Spooner regarded the war as the result of the breakdown of the alliance between northern capitalists and southern slaveholders. In his mind this breakdown resulted from southern distrust of her allies' fidelity and from the determination of industrial and financial capitalists to enforce their monopoly of southern markets. Spooner argued that the capitalists meant "to plunder and enslave" laborers in the North as well as in the South.

Charles Loring Brace's significant study in ethnology, *The Races of the Old World* (1863), was in some sense a war product. Brace, a pioneer in the development of social service in New York City, had been a close student of racial theories long before Sumter. But he was led to prepare a synthesis of the best available works in this field as a result of his distress at the evidences of prejudice against the Negro which the draft riots in New York displayed, and in order to redeem American scholarship in European eyes by offsetting the "perverted argument for the oppression of the Negro" which southern racialists had publicized. Brace spared no pains in striking a scholarly blow at the "narrow prejudices and false theories in regard to Race ideas which have been at the base of ancient abuses and long-established institutions of oppression."[6] In refuting the prosouthern ethnological doctrine of the separate origin of races he depended in considerable part on linguistic evidence. Under the influence of Darwin's theory of natural selection he maintained that biology also pointed in the direction of unified origin. Disregarding the scruples of religious orthodoxy Brace insisted that the human race had existed "hundreds of thousands of years before any of the received dates of the Creation" and cited archeological evidence, including specimens of fossilized man, in support of his thesis. Thus in the midst of war an American scholar and humanitarian presented a pioneer study of races.

### The War and Belles-Lettres

The time-honored conviction that there could be no great literature until there was a nation aroused hopes in the breasts of intellectuals that with the triumph of nationality a glorious and immortal literature would emerge. Intellectual patriots admitted that the trials of the war were great, the evil that accompanied it considerable. But they maintained that "a great believing people" would rise above the demoralized conduct exemplified by tainted traffic with the enemy and corrupt profiteering. "When," prophesied the author of a striking essay entitled "War and Literature," the varieties of the "popular life begin to coalesce, as all

[6] Charles L. Brace, *The Races of the Old World: A Manual of Ethnology* (New York, 1863).

sections are drawn closer together towards the center of great political ideas which the people themselves establish, there will be such a rich development of intellectual action as the Old World has not seen." The war, in making a people great by reason of its sufferings, its sacrifices, its new sense of comradeship, was also making a land correspondingly great, a land where souls might have "their chances to work, with the largest freedom and under the fewest disabilities, . . . to strike poverty and misery out of those glorious traces, and to chisel deep and fresh the handwriting where God says, This is a Man."[7]

The performance fell considerably short of the promise. Emerson's "Boston Hymn," in honor of the Emancipation Proclamation, and Whittier's "Laus Deo," in celebration of the adoption of the Thirteenth Amendment by Congress, were sincere and noble but hardly great, and "Barbara Frietchie" is not forgotten. Lowell wrote, at the close of the war, his great "Ode Recited at the Harvard Commemoration," but his second series of Biglow Papers lacked the merit of the first. Other New England writers of established repute failed to add much to their stature. Hawthorne, already near the end of his road, was numbed by the national catastrophe. New names appeared, it is true, but of these only Henry Howard Brownell, teacher, lawyer, sailor, and journalist, achieved distinction; his Lyrics of a Day and War Lyrics, marked as they are by a vivid detail and lyric exultation, by passionate recital of heroic action, are indeed memorable. Melville's Battle Pieces, however formless, reveal spirit and at the same time a poignant humanity. Above all, Whitman's Drum Taps and subsequent Civil War poems greatly enriched the nation's literature. Haunting lyrics of suffering and comradeship and spiritual triumph, of the great leader, Abraham Lincoln, and of the nobler destiny of the nation, Whitman's war poetry reflected his humanity and democracy, his mysticism and skill in the use of symbols. No mere denouncer of the Confederates, Whitman himself believed that it was the experiences of the war, the emotional depths it sounded and aroused, "the strong flare and provocation of that war's sights and scenes and final reasons-for-being" that alone consummated his poetic growth which, of course, had already begun before the conflict.

The conviction that the great struggle had profoundly affected and must continue to influence intellectual life found expression after Appomattox. In 1866 the newly established Nation, observing that wars

[7] Atlantic Monthly, IX (June, 1862), 680, 682.

generally exerted cataclysmic effects on the mind, found evidences that the recent contest would be no exception. Speaking to a Yale audience on the nation's obligation to its dead, the Reverend Horace Bushnell declared that the huge flood tide that had lifted American nationality had, in a little more than a short day, released and stimulated loftier ranges of thought. He even foresaw a new and mighty literature, not English in spirit but American, a literature comparable to that which had followed the wars of Elizabeth, Anne, and Napoleon. Walt Whitman, dismissed from a minor federal office for the alleged immorality of his poems, expressed in *Democratic Vistas* in movingly beautiful language the profound conviction that the war, by welding together the nation and lifting it to new spiritual heights, had set the stage for the long-hoped-for glories in American art, letters, and thought. But Whitman's realistic insight also enabled him to detect signs that it had heightened materialism and corruption, that democracy was on trial, that the promise of American life was yet to be fought for and won. Carl Schurz, the "forty-eighter" who had done much to save the Union through both political and military means, more than a quarter of a century after the war asked the question: "Is it really true that our war turned the ambitions of our people into the channels of lofty enthusiasm and aspirations and devotion to high ideals? Has it not rather left behind it an era of absorbing greed of wealth, a marked decline of ideal aspirations . . . ?"[8]

On a more popular literary level the songs of the people reveal not only the feelings of the common man but crystallized sentiments of home and loved ones which transcend the immediacy of the battle itself. "Maryland, My Maryland," has become a permanent song of Americans, and Julia Ward Howe's "Battle Hymn of the Republic," with its rich Biblical imagery and spirited measures, has endured and no doubt will continue to endure. Such songs as "Dixie," "Tenting Tonight on the Old Camp Ground," "Just before the Battle, Mother," "Tramp, Tramp, Tramp, the Boys Are Marching," and "John Brown's Body" achieved the status of folk songs. The most widely sung song north and south, "When This Cruel War Is Over," expressed the love of home and peace among the soldiers of both sides.

Humorous stories as well as songs helped relieve the tension and hardships which the war thrust on civilians as well as on the men in the field.

[8] Carl Schurz, *The Reminiscences of Carl Schurz* (The McClure Co., 1908), III, 135–136.

It is no accident that the troubled crisis saw the ripening or the appearance of some of America's great humorists. Henry Wheeler Shaw, "Josh Billings," helped northern people through weary weeks and dark months with his witty aphorisms and kindly, bucolic satires; and David Ross Locke, "Petroleum V. Nasby," was especially popular with the soldiers by reason of his takeoffs on the office-seeking, whiskey-drinking, illiterate parson of backwoods Kentucky who symbolized the Copperheads and much else that all good Yankees despised. Two of these "gloom-lifters" delighted President Lincoln, who in so many respects stood close to the common people. Robert Henry Newell, "Orpheus C. Kerr," poured out impudent, even fantastic burlesques on avid office seekers and inept military leaders; and Charles Farrar Browne, "Artemus Ward," gifted in the use of verbal quips and plaintive puns, enjoyed the distinction of having his "High Handed Outrage in Utica" read by the President to the Cabinet on the occasion of its acceptance of Lincoln's Emancipation Proclamation. On the far fringes of the frontier Samuel Clemens was coming into his own as the greatest of all America's humorists. Soldiers and home folk were diverted from grim realities by the flood of Beadle dime novels which taught patriotism through recounting the thrilling adventures and romance of the American Revolution.

But the tribulations and terror of war also required sustained faith in great principles. The South no less than the North possessed such faith in high degree. Most Southerners began the war, and many ended it, with supreme faith in their cause; to them the Stars and Bars symbolized a contest for their homes, their way of life, their dearest values. Among the people of the Confederacy were some who suspected that slavery was neither the glorious nor holy institution it was supposed to be; that, on the contrary, it was a wasteful, an outworn, a vicious system. An even larger number of simple folk suspected that the whole contest in arms was "a rich man's war and a poor man's fight." War weariness, defeatism, disloyalty to the Richmond regime became widespread in many areas. Appomattox was a blessed release to these men and women. But to a great many it was a stinging, bitter defeat. It was also a defeat for much in the social philosophy of the Old South; for how much, only the years ahead could disclose.

The North, too, had its high ideals and its doubts and suspicions. Opposition to the war by the Copperheads was fairly widespread, especially in the Old Northwest, with its severed but unforgotten ties, commercial and cultural, with the South. The draft was resisted, even to the point of bloody riot in New York City, and the Knights of the Golden Circle did much to increase opposition to the war and the demand for an immediate armistice on any terms. But the majority of the plain people, together with virtually all the intellectual leaders, remained steadfast in their loyalty to the Union. To them it symbolized democracy, that is, a good life for everybody, one destined to become ever richer, ever more completely realized. This faith fed the fires of patriotism, and they burned brightly in spite of the damp chill of defeatism. Associated with this democratic faith and patriotism was the social philosophy of business enterprise. The victory at Appomattox was a victory for all these related but not entirely consistent articles in the northern creed. No one knew, when Lincoln's death hushed the nation, how these conflicts would be resolved, or even whether they would be resolved at all. But for the moment other things ruled men's minds.

The war did not disrupt the basic economic life of the North, as it did that of the South. The armed contest even quickened the pace of development in the North. Thus many intellectual agencies, such as schools and colleges, expanded with an expanding economic life.

But the war, which in some respects was merely an incident in the development of the nation's life, did affect intellectual perspectives in vital ways. It put to rest, once and for all, the ghost of states' rights and secession which had haunted Hamilton and Webster and Clay. It testified to the success of the principle of national unity. It cleared the way for an extension of democracy—the black man at least was no longer a chattel slave, and the path was opened for his participation in the life of the mind on a level higher than superstition. The war also pushed aside the hindrances—notably a plantation aristocracy—that had checked the free flow of business enterprise, and thus the stage was set for new triumphs of capitalism and of the ideas and cultural agencies functional to it, South as well as North. At the same time the war posed new problems for democracy, problems of the status and role of the common man in a society that was more homogeneous and yet, paradoxically, more stratified. All this meant that in spite of the continuity with the past a *nation* had emerged, with new problems, new issues, new ideas; these were to influence profoundly the growth of the American mind.

# 19 The Nature of the New Nationalism

*If we have not hitherto had that conscious feeling of nationality, the ideal abstract of history and tradition, which belongs to older countries, compacted by frequent war and united by memories of common danger and common triumph, it has been simply because our national existence has never been in such peril as to force upon us the conviction that it was both the title-deed of our greatness and its only safeguard. But what splendid possibilities has not our trial revealed even to ourselves! What costly stuff whereof to make a nation! Here at last is a state whose life is not narrowly concentered in a despot or a class, but feels itself in every limb; a government which is not a mere application of force from without, but dwells as a vital principle in the will of every citizen.*

—JAMES RUSSELL LOWELL, 1865

*It is the free American who needs to be instructed by the benighted races in the uplifting word that America speaks to all the world. Only from the humble immigrant, it appears to me, can he learn just what America stands for in the family of nations.*

—M. E. RAVAGE, 1917

The first five decades of the nineteenth century had witnessed heated debates on the nature of the union established by the Constitution; that authority had been appealed to again and again by competing interests in search of legal justifications for desired courses of action. The appeal to arms and the victory of the North did not end the discussions concerning the nature of the American nation. It is true that even the most ardent apologists for the Lost Cause did not deny that, regardless of the past, the nation was henceforth superior to the states. But the persistent question of the boundary between federal and state powers continued to occasion much debate. So did the relation of the sections and of minority peoples to the nation.

The highest authority on such matters spoke in the case *Texas* v. *White* (1869). In this important decision the Supreme Court maintained that the acts constituting the Rebellion had been unlawful deeds of usurpers and not the acts of states, inasmuch as the political system of the United States was an "indestructible union of indestructible states." According to the Court, the "union of the States was never a purely artificial and arbitrary relation. . . . It began among the Colonies and grew out of a common origin, mutual sympathies, kindred principles, similar interests, and geographical relations."[1]

This general conception of the nature of the nation was now elaborated in a series of philosophical formulations. Most of the writers paid relatively little attention to the legalistic arguments which had characterized the writings of such early nationalists as Webster, Kent, and Story. The prewar idea that the nation was the result of a contract by which the states had ceded their sovereignty to the new Union was largely replaced by the doctrine that the nation was the product of a gradual, evolutionary growth. In consequence it was a true organism with sovereignty resting in the nation at large. One of these writers, Elisha Mulford, an Episcopal minister, interpreted American national theory in terms of Hegelian philosophy. All emphasized the doctrine of the historic mission of the American nation in modern civilization.

Of all the theoretical writers on nationalistic doctrine none was more original or more influential than Francis Lieber whose writings, which had begun to appear before the Civil War, marked the transition from the earlier contract theory to the newer one of organic growth. His interest in nationalism as an historic phenomenon made his work especially

[1] 7 Wall 700 (1869).

significant. In his mind "nation" implied a homogeneous population living in a coherent territory, a population possessing a common language and literature, common institutions and traditions. The nation was an organic unity. Lieber also preached the doctrine of the world mission of the national state in general and of the American nation in particular; the latter had largely succeeded in solving such age-old and universal problems as those involved in the relation of sovereignty to liberty, of local to central government, of commonwealth to the family of nations.

Lieber did not, however, foresee that the most significant discussions of the nature of the relations between the federal government and the states were those that the conflicts between corporate wealth and the interests of farmers, laborers, and other plain folk were to occasion. When, under pressure from these groups, the states began to regulate railroads and other types of industrial enterprise, the corporate interests denied the authority of the states and in appeals to the courts insisted that only the federal government had jurisdiction in such matters. When corporations were at length subjected to federal regulation in the public interest, business enterprise often tried to protect its interests by appealing to the old states' rights theory and insisting that the powers of the government at Washington should be limited. This shift tended to enhance in the minds of the plain people the belief that the federal government was the most effective instrument for controlling private interests for the benefit of the people.

The nature of the American nation involved other issues, too. The triumph of the North at Appomattox insured the political but not the intellectual and emotional unity of the nation. Bitter feelings and a wide gulf in thought separated the people of the North and South. The vituperative war propaganda in each section continued to bear fruit after the defeat of the South. Reconciliation was made doubly hard by the "radical" Reconstruction policy; the rule of carpetbaggers and Negroes rankled long in the memory of the planting class. In an almost unending stream the writings of "unreconstructed" Southerners offered compensatory defenses of the Old South and the Lost Cause. In part, of course, these nostalgic daydreams were designed to justify what had been done in secession and in the war; in part they were a response of men and women unable to adjust themselves to the new order of nationalism and industrialism that invaded the South; and in part they served to reinforce the southern white theory of Negro inferiority. In any case the legend of the Lost Cause nourished thoughts and feelings that did not square with the new doctrine of an organic nation.

Nor did Easterners and Westerners see eye to eye with each other. The West was hardly less self-conscious than it had been during the early decades of the century. Western leaders insisted that the West had been chiefly responsible for winning the war and that henceforth, instead of being treated as a stepchild, it must take the principal place at the family board. The common assumption on the part of many eastern intellectuals that the seaboard was the fountain of intelligence and genius, of all that was really significant in American thought, was indignantly repudiated by western editors, clergymen, physicians, and politicians. Western partisans insisted that their section not only possessed great cultural possibilities but even at the moment enjoyed the only distinctively American culture. Easterners with a missionary bent continued to send teachers and preachers to "civilize" that land of reputed darkness, but at least some Westerners resented such activities; western religion, western morals, even western education, it was argued, excelled eastern counterparts in all the really essential things. But even these regional patriots had to admit that the remaining frontiers had to be won from the Indians and integrated into national life and thought.

Whatever the strength of sectional pride, the bonds of union were growing stronger. New social and economic ties did much to soften antagonisms between East and West and between North and South. The expansion of industrial and finance capitalism from the East into both South and West forged a new and tightly knit web of interests. Both business and labor tended to assume the pattern of national organization. Machine-made products continued with increasing tempo to create similar tastes and habits all over the land. The problems arising from the expansion and integration of business inevitably became issues for discussion on a nationwide scale. Economic developments occasioned the expansion of the activities of the Departments of Interior, Agriculture, and Commerce; federal administrative agencies multiplied the contacts between citizens of the several states and sections. By the 1860s the transcontinental railroad was a visible band of steel across the country, and railways uniting South and North provided a material basis for reconciliation. Added to all this was the fact that the railroads facilitated the dissolution of prejudices and the growth of common ideas by enabling people to go to and fro on a scale that never before had been possible. The multiplication of telegraph lines and the organization of the Western Union, the consolidation of news services in the Associated Press, and the appearance of the telephone in the late 1870s promised to break down isolation and sectionalism by reducing both time and space within the national domain. All these agencies of communication extended in some measure to all sections the more rapid tempo of life that had come to be characteristic of the urban Northeast.

Such material ties were naturally accompanied by intellectual ties. The growing tendency of professional men to organize along national lines helped to break down sectional isolation and to provide more effective channels for these groups to interpret and publicize the forces that were unifying the sections. The editors of such periodicals as *Hunt's Merchants' Magazine* and the *Commercial and Financial Chronicle* appealed frankly for a relaxation of the drastic Reconstruction policy to enable capitalists to invest in the South with some feeling of security. Here and there southern voices began to plead for burying the dead ghosts of the past in order that the industrial resources of the South might be developed. Only in that way, Henry Grady of the *Atlanta Constitution* later argued, could the South take her rightful place in the nation. Southern writers of history and fiction discovered in the North a profitable market for their quaint interpretations of the Negro and their nostalgic idealizations of the Old South, and their books, articles, and stories contributed to the reconciliation of the two peoples. Northern novelists discovered in "Dixie" a fascinating field, and romances of reconciliation in which northern soldiers and beautiful southern belles found happiness in romantic love enjoyed mounting popularity.

Voices in both East and West began to interpret these two regions to each other. During the war itself such nationalistic spokesmen as Edward Everett and Theodore Tilton had sung the praises of the West in eastern periodicals and before eastern audiences. E. L. Godkin, brilliant editor of *The Nation*, might and did disparage monetary ideas popular in the agrarian West; but he also rebuked politicians for trying to magnify the differences between East and West into an antagonism which could break, as had almost happened in the case of North and South, and all but destroy the Union. Gradually a cult of the West emerged in American literature; whatever its purpose, in effect it did much to soften antagonisms.

Hundreds of thousands from all sections visited the Centennial Exposition in Philadelphia in 1876 and took pride in the nation's past and in the prospects for an even more glorious national future. It took such concrete demonstrations as the Exposition to awaken in the minds of the plain people a heightened sense of national pride. Some Americans who visited it were startled to find their country far behind European lands in artistic achievement, but their hearts swelled with satisfaction at the evidences of material prosperity and mechanical genius that none could deny. The vast crowds from all parts of the land experienced at Philadelphia a new and nobler comprehension of the American past and of the purpose and design of the government which had endured in spite of stupendous obstacles, and they caught a vision of even vaster future triumphs in invention, industry, labor, science, and the arts.

## The Negro in the Intellectual Life of the Nation

Ethnic as well as regional differences testified to the fact that in spite of all the theories of American nationalism, the general recognition that everyone was as much an American as anyone else could not be said to exist. For one thing, emancipation pushed to the fore the old and stubborn problem of the Negro's place in the national life. That the great majority of Northerners looked on the colored people as inferior and incapable of ever becoming the equal of whites may be fairly inferred from the fact that Negroes continued during the postwar years to suffer from legal, political, and educational disabilities in almost every northern community in which any sizable number of them were congregated. No doubt the views of Samuel F. B. Morse, who took it for granted that the Negro was innately inferior both physically and mentally, more or less expressed the ideas of most plain people and most conservative leaders.

Only the radical abolitionists who followed Stevens, Sumner, and Wade believed that Negro inferiority could be explained by the ignorance and docility to which slavery had condemned the colored race. These men and women argued for political and civil rights for the freedmen. These rights were deemed necessary both to insure them from being reduced by their former masters to serfdom and to provide them with a political education to supplement the schooling which humanitarian organizations and the Freedmen's Bureau had already begun to provide. If any large section of Congress or of public opinion in the North had seriously entertained such equalitarian racial ideas, the radical Reconstruction policy would not have been given up and the freedmen would not have been turned over to the control of their former masters. As it was, the Civil Rights case (1883) stamped the authority of the nation's highest court on the policy of relegating the race problem to the local communities. The provision in the Fifteenth Amendment that no state was to deprive any person of the right to vote by reason of his race or previous condition of servitude virtually became a dead letter.

Northern liberals and humanitarians increasingly came to accept the southern white position. Godkin in *The Nation* and Gilder in *The Century* took elaborate pains to explain the conditions in the South which, in their eyes, justified the white race in disciplining and keeping the black man in his place. In 1878 even Thomas Wentworth Higginson, who as a radical abolitionist had subscribed to the idea of potential race equality, praised the southern whites for their treatment of the blacks in the educational sphere. Whether such humanitarians were influenced by the propaganda of Northerners and Southerners for reconciliation or whether they were affected by misrepresentations of the positive achievements of the Negro during the Reconstruction period one can only surmise. Nor did American urban workers differ materially from the general view in their attitude toward the Negro; William Sylvis was exceptional in insisting that white and black workers must stand shoulder to shoulder against a common exploiter. Thus northern opinion came increasingly to accept Godkin's judgment that the Negro could never be worked into the American system of self-government and in doing so frankly confessed to the fact that America lacked a true national unity of all its people.

Hating the fallen planter class as they did, many southern poor whites cooperated with the Negro during Reconstruction and gave slight evidence of racial chauvinism. But the great number no doubt shared the views of Hinton Rowan Helper. This sometime critic of slavery, who in *The Impending Crisis* had attributed the South's backwardness to its "peculiar institution," now confessed his conviction that the Negro was the most degraded race of man, that he approached the brute animals in physical form, and that he was incapable of arriving at anything beyond a fourteen-year-old child's imagination, judgment, and ability to invent and organize knowledge. When President Johnson in 1866 told a delegation of colored people that any further concessions to the race in the South would merely increase the poor white's antagonism, Frederick Douglass, the leader of his race, observed that the master class had won its supremacy over both poor whites and blacks by planting enmity between them, by dividing to conquer.

The plantation class tempered its attitude toward docile and faithful Negroes by a kindly paternalism, but it still regarded the black people as innately inferior. So bitter was the old aristocracy in its determination to keep the blacks in subjection, to check their "uppity" behavior and their zeal for education, that Yankee teachers and other humanitarians who devoted themselves to improving the lot of the freedmen found themselves socially ostracized, if indeed they were lucky enough to escape a worse fate at the hands of the Ku Klux Klan. The vicissitudes of the northern friend of the Negro in the post-Civil War South are memorably pictured in the dramatic if somewhat overdrawn novel by Albion Tourgée, A Fool's Errand. The Southerners themselves continued to justify white supremacy with the old arguments they had used to defend slavery. Thus it was not strange that the Negro, once federal troops were withdrawn from the South in 1877, was permitted to vote only when his vote could be skillfully used by one group of whites in political contests; when he threatened to become a political force he was disenfranchised. Even during the period of radical Reconstruction Negro officials frequently accepted social inferiority, and gradually segregation or "Jim Crowism" became the accepted practice. The sharecropper system, which had begun even before the Civil War, increasingly became the means by which the Negro was held in economic control. Southern writers of the local-color school—Thomas Nelson Page, Joel Chandler Harris, and others—subscribed to the concept of white superiority; George Cable was the notable exception.

It is not mere guesswork to infer what the Negro thought about himself and his relations to other social groups during Reconstruction itself. Many loyal and devoted servants avoided any overt behavior that could be interpreted as a desire for equality, and many more from force of habit probably never seriously thought of themselves as equal in ability to the whites. But a good many sang with at least half-serious intent

> De bottom rail's on de top
> An we's gwine to keep it dar.

Many Negroes were bitterly disappointed by the failure of their northern friends to provide them with the economic independence symbolized by "forty acres and a mule"—of this there can be little doubt. Where he was able to seize and hold land, as in the Sea Islands, the Negro's progress was impressive. The confiscation of plantations was too radical a measure for the property-conscious class in the North to sanction, but political and educational privileges were extended to colored folk and eagerly seized. With the cooperation of the carpetbaggers the Negroes in constitutional convention and legislature provided for the first time in the South for mandatory, free, tax-supported schools open alike to the children of both races. The task of giving the Negro even an elementary education was colossal. Of the 4 million living in the southern states in 1870, almost 90 percent were illiterate. The desire to read the Bible and to explore the unknown but intriguing world of the white man's books proved an important incentive. Many Negroes disappointed their teachers, but others did well and even clamored for a classical education as a symbol of equality. These conned Latin and Greek verbs at Atlanta University, Straight University, Shaw University, and other institutions, and caught glimpses of the world of learning.

With the restoration of white rule in 1877 the promising beginnings of public school education suffered serious setbacks. There was financial retrenchment at once, and race consciousness dictated the policy of separate school systems for the two races. Had Senator Henry Blair of New Hampshire succeeded in allocating funds from land sales, patent receipts, and other public moneys for the support of southern education, the educational backwardness of the South would have been far less marked. The benefactions of two northern capitalists, George Peabody and John Slater, did, however, do much for southern education. The Peabody fund, amounting to three and a half millions, was chiefly used to encourage the southern states to provide taxation for the maintenance of the feeble school systems frequently existing only on paper. The Slater Fund was earmarked for Negro institutions dedicated chiefly to the training of young men for the manual trades and the study of medicine. In spite of these funds and notwithstanding the sacrifices of Negro educational leaders, illiteracy remained amazingly high among the Negroes.

Although the social philosophy that prevailed among southern whites militated against any serious and widespread efforts to elevate the Negro race through education, the more progressive southern whites were gradually won over to the cause of vocational schooling for the colored people. At Hampton Roads in Virginia northern philanthropic effort had developed a pattern of Negro vocational education. In 1881 a small group of Negroes in Tuskegee, Alabama, invited General Armstrong of Hampton Institute to send a graduate to begin a vocational school in their community. The young man chosen was Booker T. Washington, who not only built up a highly successful institution but became the leader of his race. Washington urged the colored people to abandon, at least for the time, any claims to equal treatment with the whites; to look up to the substantial southern whites as friends; and through the cultivation of practical skills in trade and agriculture to make themselves economically self-sufficient and indispensable to the prosperity of the white South.

While the Negroes tended to accept Washington's leadership and philosophy, outward deference to the ruling race did not keep them from entertaining privately their own ideas about white superiority:

> Niggers plant de cotton,
> Niggers pick it out
> White man pocket money,
> Nigger goes without.

> Missus in de big manse
> Mammy in de yard
> Missus holding her white hands
> Mammy workin' hard.
> White man in starched shirt setten in de shade
> Laziest man God ever made.

Such songs no doubt expressed the real feelings of many who sang them. In contacts with the white world, however, most Negroes found it expedient to appear to accept the idea of the superiority of the white race.


## The Immigrant in the Intellectual Life of the Nation

The immediate problems of the Civil War for the time laid to rest the nativist ideology. Indeed, the immigrant, being needed in factory and field during the conflict between the states, had actually been encouraged to come to America. The Fenian troubles in Ireland, hard times in England, and wars on the Continent, together with the solicitations of American railways and steamship companies and the organized encouragement given to immigration by the western states, resulted in a greatly increased inflow of immigrants in the postwar years. In 1873, for example, more than 400,000 newcomers entered the country. In 1875, of the 40 million people in the States, almost 8 were foreign-born. For the time British, Irish, and German immigration ranked highest in proportion to the whole. But new signs pointed to a growing tendency for southern and eastern Europeans to flood in. By 1882 the so-called "new immigration" promised to exceed that from northern Europe.

This immense immigration, together with its changing character, was in the nature of things bound to affect the intellectual life of the nation. Ever since Crèvecœur had speculated on the contributions of non-English stocks to American life and thought, writers had from time to time returned to the question. Many agreed with Walt Whitman—and with Herbert Spencer—in believing that the eventual mixture of stocks making up the population would in time produce a finer type of man than had hitherto existed, a type of man in Spencer's words "more plastic, more adaptable, more capable of undergoing the modifications needful for complete social life."[2] At last the scientists began seriously to concern themselves with the problem of measuring the effects of immigration on the American population. Dr. B. A. Gould's *Investigations in the Military and Anthropological Statistics of American Soldiers* (1869) was based on materials collected by the Sanitary Corps and by the Provost Marshal General. Gould's analysis indicated that the physical measurements of native-born American soldiers were on the whole larger than those of the immigrant. Whether this meant that a natively superior American race had developed, or whether it indicated that more favorable conditions of life in the United States increased physical stature, or whether both deductions were valid, was not clear.

Whatever their limitations, such studies were, in any case, the first large-scale efforts to determine by scientific method the physical characteristics of the American people as a people. Other scientists speculated on the influence of immigration on American nationalism and the American way of life. Dr. John Draper, inclined as he was toward an

[2] Herbert Spencer, *Essays, Scientific, Political and Speculative* (Appleton–Century–Crofts, Inc., 1891), III, 471–492.

environmentalist position, concluded that, while the incoming stream brought mental as well as physical peculiarities, the general conditions of life and the historic principles of the Republic would serve as a powerful amalgam. Nevertheless, he thought it quite probable that the presence of so many immigrants affected the whole community by making its ideas less settled, its intentions less precise.

The growing recognition that America lacked ethnic unity paved the way for the growth of a compensatory doctrine of an intense integral "psychological" nationalism, differing markedly from the traditionally humanitarian nationalism of the Enlightenment. Moreover, disturbances within American society played an important role in the conversion of "Anglo-Saxonism," originally a liberal faith in English parliamentary and democratic institutions, into the powerful racist philosophy it became in the 1890s and early 1900s. Partly searching for a new nationalistic faith in America's ability to rise above her new problems, and partly expressing a nostalgic longing for bygone days of aristocratic cultural superiority, such figures as Henry Cabot Lodge, Francis A. Walker, John W. Burgess, Nathanial S. Shaler, and to a lesser extent Theodore Roosevelt spread a doctrine of Anglo-Saxon racial superiority and shouted warnings of "race mongrelization" from immigration. Clothing their racial theories with the new-found authority of science, the proponents of Anglo-Saxon superiority alleged that southern European "races" were biologically inferior. They argued that the influx of these peoples would ruin institutional stability and lower the rate of cultural achievement. Besides directing itself against further immigration, the doctrine of Anglo-Saxon or Teutonic superiority also contributed to the frantic extension of the Jim Crow system in the South in the 1890s and to the popularity of the notion of the "white man's burden" as a rationale for imperialist expansion.

The effect of immigration on the American mind was the subject of much speculation. That the great mass of newcomers represented the less-educated European social strata led men like E. L. Godkin of *The Nation* to see in immigration a challenge to education. Godkin believed that only energetic and wise educational measures on a mass scale could keep the immigrants from becoming tools with which unscrupulous politicians might undermine the foundations of the Republic.

It was apparent that the rapid growth of Catholicism through immigration was introducing a new and strange element into American

culture. The strenuous efforts of Father Hecker, a convert from Transcendentalism, and of other Catholic leaders to convince the public that
the Roman church was neither undemocratic nor un-American met with
little success. American nationalism and democracy had in fact been
traditionally identified with Protestantism. The general reluctance of
foreign-born priests to throw themselves into the main channels of
American life confirmed this widely held idea. In addition, the growth
of Catholic parochial schools seemed to threaten the traditionally
American concept of public schools. The Catholics were bending every
effort to augment parochial schools by obtaining state support for them.
To many Americans this seemed a threat to the American principle of
separation of church and state. Anti-Catholicism found some support, of
course, among rationalists who saw in the Roman church an authoritative supernaturalism even more effective among the masses than the
Protestant variety of supernatural faith. But the chief source of opposition to Catholicism came from evangelical Protestants. This rising opposition found expression in the Reverend Josiah Strong's widely read
book, *Our Country* (1885), and in the formation, about the same time,
of the American Protective Association. This organization, primarily
anti-Catholic, combined propaganda with efforts to check the influence
of the church on political life.

The Protestant dislike of Catholicism and the fear that the ignorance
of the immigrants endangered American principles of self-government
were not the only causes of the anti-immigrant feeling. American society
had reached a crisis when old economic and social relations seemed to be
breaking down before the attack of industrialization and urbanization.
The resulting social dislocation and conflicts between labor and capital
tended to aggravate anti-Catholic and anti-immigrant emotions. Events
such as the Haymarket Riot of 1886 seemed to prove to nativists that the
unrest in society was a result of foreign "pollution" rather than of basic
weaknesses or new problems within American life. The depression of the
1890s increased the number of economically discontented people, thereby
adding to the number who were susceptible to the hysterical nativist
ideologies.

Many immigrant groups, especially when led by able editors, teachers,
and clergymen, maintained the integrity of their own culture and in so
doing remained set off from old-stock Americans. The latter naturally
regarded the immigrant groups with suspicion.

The vigorous cultural life maintained by various immigrant groups is well exemplified by the Norwegian-Americans. Strongly nationalistic and Lutheran, many Norwegian communities maintained their own parochial schools and established denominational colleges. They welcomed leaders from the motherland unless they were, like Björnson, religiously unorthodox. The Norwegian press published newspapers, magazines, religious books, and the fiction that Norwegian-Americans began to write. An interest in Norwegian-American history also developed.

Prejudice against immigrants was natural during the slow process of acculturation. But the fact that the interests of many old-time Americans were jeopardized or seemed to be jeopardized by the presence of the newcomers heightened prejudice. In the minds of both the leaders of organized labor and the rank and file the ever-increasing immigrant hordes checked the advance of the trade union movement, glutted the labor market, and depressed the living standards of the native worker. The mind of business was divided on the immigrant. The traditional position favored unrestricted immigration in the interest of cheap labor and the open shop. Once the vast railroad net was substantially completed and the main industrial plants were established, the cry for cheap labor was less frequently heard; the advance of the machine diminished the need for hands. An important factor in the growing distaste that certain business leaders felt for immigration was the fear that the immigrants were the main source of socialistic and anarchistic doctrines. "The ranks of anarchy and riots," declared Chauncey Depew in 1892, "number no Americans. The leaders boldly proclaim that they come here not to enjoy the blessings of our liberty and to sustain our institutions but to destroy our government, cut our throats, and divide our property."[3] This sentiment, though resting on flimsy foundations, was widely held. The increase of crime in the swiftly growing cities was also commonly attributed to the presence of the immigrants.

If the great bulk of the newcomers were ignorant of book learning, the knowledge of many among them enriched American intellectual life. Perhaps no immigrant group contained so high a proportion of scholars as the Jews. American Biblical scholarship and exegesis are deeply indebted to erudite Jewish masters of obscure tongues. Egyptology owed much to Goetzel Selikovitsch; Semitic studies profited vastly from the

[3] John D. Champlin (ed.), *Orations, Addresses and Speeches of Chauncey Depew*, 10 vols. (Austin and Lipscomb, 1910), III. 264–273.

contributions of Max Margolis; and the whole range of Hebraic scholarship was admirably covered in Abraham Rosenberg's *Hebrew Cyclopedia*, the first two volumes of which he set up in type with his own hands in his humble quarters in the ghetto of New York. None of these scholars, however, equaled Arnold Ehrlich in learning. Although he was armed with an incredible linguistic equipment he was forced, on arriving in New York in 1878, to earn his bread by rolling barrels. His contributions to Old Testament scholarship were both comprehensive and erudite.

The learning of immigrant scholars was not confined to linguistics. Charles David Spivak, who in 1882 was loading and unloading freight in railway yards and working in woolen and cotton mills, achieved a national reputation as an authority in the field of gastroenterology. Within a few decades after his arrival in 1883 Samuel Meltzer had written 250 scientific papers on such subjects as excitation and inhibition, theory of shock, the action of adrenalin, and artificial respiration, thereby deepening the world's knowledge of physiology and medicine. Boris Sidis, who was without funds when he landed in the United States in 1887, had before the end of the century broken virgin ground in his studies of the unconscious and of the psychology of personality. Jacques Loeb's basic studies in tropisms supported his thesis that a mechanistic theory could explain some of the most baffling mysteries of life. Other fields of learning also profited from the presence of such immigrants as Luigi Cesnola, an archeologist whose collections from Cyprus stirred up much controversy before their authenticity was at last established.

Immigrant Catholic priests also made contributions to knowledge and scholarship. The long-established Catholic interest in the Indian languages was maintained by Father Gregory Mengarini, whose *Dictionary of the Kalispil or Flathead Indian Language* appeared in 1877. Father Lawrence Palladino's *Indians and Whites of the Northwest* (1894) has remained one of the important sources of knowledge in its field. In other disciplines, especially in higher mathematics, astronomy, and philosophy, such Italian-born priests as Joseph Bayma and Benedict Sistini carried on original studies amid all their other duties.

Immigrant poets and playwrights were agents in strengthening the traditional idealizations regarding America's place and future in the world. Jacob Rombro, for example, interpreted American science, literature, and sociology to immigrants in such a way as to deepen their appreciation of their new home. Morris Winchevsky, a Lithuanian, sang of oppression's yoke and of the blessings of freedom, and still others instilled loyalty to a somewhat idealized America. Native-born Americans by long familiarity with the rich blessings of their own land tended to grow forgetful of their high blessings and of America's meaning to the world's oppressed and underprivileged, but immigrants revitalized American social idealism for many "old Americans." Not only articulate foreigners, such as the Rumanian Jew, M. E. Ravage, but countless sweaty, smelly, and bundle-carrying immigrants did their part in confirming the American faith in the common man, in the right of equality of opportunity for everyone, in the toleration of creeds and opinions, and in the ideal of a cosmopolitan sympathy for weaker nations and peoples.

## The Indian in American Thought

No one Indian, certainly none among the small minority able to express their ideas to the white men, represented the thought of the Indian peoples adequately; the scattered tribes of the western plains and mountains and deserts presented a wide variety of cultures. But the message which Chief Joseph of the Nez Percé sent to his conqueror when he was forced to surrender after a desperate flight over 1300 miles of incredibly mountainous terrain represented an idea that was coming to be increasingly held by the Indians of the last West. Chief Joseph realized that the fight against the invading white man was a hopeless one:

I am tired of fighting. Our chiefs are all killed. Looking Glass is dead. Too-hul-hul-sote is dead. The old men are all dead. It is the young men who say yes or no. He who has led on the young men is dead. It is cold and we have no blankets, no food. The little children are freezing to death. I want to have time to look for my children and see how many of them I can find. Maybe I shall find them among the dead. Hear me! My chiefs, I am tired; my heart is sick and sad. From where the sun now stands, I will fight no more, forever.

When the Indians at last surrendered and the buffalo were gone, the hearts of the Indian people, in the words of another chief, Plenty-Coups, fell to the ground, and they could not lift them again. Without the bison on his hunting ground the strange emptiness of the plains mocked the Indian's hope—a hope that turned into sullen resentment when corrupt government agents on the reservations to which the conquered Indians were confined doled out worthless blankets and rotten rations. Chief Joseph said:

The earth is the mother of all people, and all people should have equal rights upon it. You might as well expect the rivers to run backward as that any man who was born a free man should be contented when penned up and denied liberty to go where he pleases. If you tie a horse to a stake, do you expect he will grow fat? If you pen an Indian upon a small spot of the earth, and compel him to stay there, he will not be contented, nor will he grow and prosper. When I think of our condition my heart is heavy.[4]

The great majority of the whites who built the transcontinental railroad across the Nebraska plains and the Wyoming mountains, who rushed into the Black Hills to mine gold, or who brought great herds of cattle to fatten on the vast prairies had little appreciation—indeed, almost no awareness—of the Indian's heroism or of the pathos and the tragedy in such words as those of Chief Joseph and Chief Plenty-Coups. Nor did most whites show more than a commercial or strictly practical interest in the gaily painted buffalo hides with their geometrical designs recounting time-rhythms, personal exploits, and poetic visions. The last vanguard of the invading whites viewed the Indian in much the same way that earlier generations had done. An old scout expressed the dominant view:

> We fought the red-skin rascals,
> Over valley, hill, and plain;
> We fought him to the mountain top,
> And fought him down again.

Even while the fighting continued, the authorities in Washington early in the Grant administration officially abandoned the idea that the Indian had to be fought to extermination. He came rather to be regarded not as an enemy, not as a member of a semisovereign "nation," but as a ward of the federal government.

The great Indian fighter, General Custer, declared that the Indian was capable of "recognizing no controlling influence but that of stern arbi-

---

[4] Chief Joseph's message of surrender is in the *Report of the Secretary of War, 1877* (Washington, 1878), I, 630; his comments on reservation life in an article he contributed to the *North American Review*, CXXVIII (April, 1879).

trary power." But a group of humanitarians—Bishop Whipple of Minnesota, the Quaker Smiley brothers of Lake Mohonk, New York, Herbert Welsh of Philadelphia, and above all Helen Hunt Jackson—turned their attention toward improving the lot of the red man. As a result of much publicity and pressure the government took steps toward providing individual Indians on the reservations to which tribes had been assigned with separate pieces of land, in order to develop a sense of responsibility and to prepare them for citizenship through education in day and boarding schools. The Indian Rights Association exposed abuses in Indian administration and tried to teach the public to regard the Indian not as a cruel savage but as a mistreated primitive capable of taking on the attributes of the white man's civilization. After 1873, when the government assumed the primary responsibility for the education of the Indian, considerable progress was made in teaching him the ways of white civilization. Only as his way of life altered did the Indian begin gradually, in certain tribes, to become acclimated to the white man's ideas.

Meanwhile white scholars patiently studied Indian folklore, myths, arts, and religious rites. Pioneer ethnologists, such as Bandelier, gradually revealed the main outlines and many of the details of primitive American cultures. Students of the American Indian thus acquired a new understanding of the fatalism of the red man, of his passivity before physical nature, of his devotion to communal rather than to individual values, and of his imaginative poetry and richly symbolical decorative arts. Although some of this knowledge found expression in popular literature, the mass of Americans continued to think of the Indian as the demon of the dime novels and the depraved creature of frontier tradition.

## The Impact of the Last Frontiers on Thought and Feeling

On the vast prairies, mountains, and deserts that stretched from the frontier states of Wisconsin, Iowa, and Kansas to the Pacific coast, the years between the firing on Fort Sumter and the celebration of the Centennial saw feverish activity. This period also saw the development of another chapter in the history of the scientist's interest in the West, together with the appearance of a new type of glamorous western literature. There were also, in a subordinate place to be sure, interesting intellectual developments.

Along the eastern rim of the last West, in the states of Wisconsin, Minnesota, Iowa, Kansas, and Nebraska, frontier conditions were slowly giving way to those of a settled society. From the older parts of the country Civil War veterans came to take up homestead farms, and Scandinavian, German, and Czech settlers flooded into the raw country. The prairie soil was unbelievably rich, but droughts and grasshoppers and hard times sorely tried the spirits of even the most resolute pioneer farmers. Sometimes bodies and minds were broken by unendurable hardships. In these heartbreaking times many found comfort in the pronouncements of the preachers who declared that these misfortunes were God's scourge, His way of making His people see how weak and helpless man was in the face of his Creator. The more imaginative and idealistic men and women kept before them, even in the darkest times, a faith in what the new country might become. Even those more prosaic by nature frequently possessed enough practical idealism during the years of great hardship to keep faith in the future of the country.

However much men and women on the last frontiers lived in and for the future, the great majority were eager to transplant old and tried ideas and values to the fascinating but exacting new homeland. This was true no less in the realm of family ideas and morals than in the field of religious thought and faith. In the sphere of political ideas the last frontiersmen were generally democratic. In economic ideas they were, with important exceptions, individualists. Land hunger, quarrels between homesteaders and cattlemen, bounty-jumping, and get-rich-quick promotion schemes often accentuated American reliance on individual strength.

Paradoxically the very conditions which in some respects enhanced individualism also modified it. Voluntary cooperative associations to discipline bounty-jumpers and violent lawbreakers emerged in accordance with the established frontier pattern of joining hands for common ends when individual brawn was ineffective. When railways exacted high freight rates—rates all the harder to pay in view of the country's shrinking monetary supply and the indebtedness of the western farmer—the individualists of the agricultural frontier bethought themselves of various devices to improve their lot. They insisted that government possessed the power to fix railway rates and services through such regulatory commissions as that with which Massachusetts had earlier experimented. But this limitation of corporate power broke no new ground and, operating as it did within the framework of the existing economic order, implied no fundamental change. Nor, for that matter, did the demand of Greenbackers and Grangers for an expansion of the currency; debtor classes in the older sections had traditionally clamored for similar relief from their burdens. Nevertheless, conditions in the prairie West gave old ideas wide publicity. Thus new legislation limiting the private enterprise and profits of railways extended the area of state concern with general well-being.

The ideas of immigrant prairie farmers were similarly akin to those common in the old countries. The Scandinavian communities clung to most of the pietistic, paternalistic, tight attitudes that characterized farmer and parson alike in the homelands. If these people yearned for the beautiful fjords of Norway and for the pleasant rural communities of Sweden and Denmark, they also took pride in the soil and in the promise of the new land. The conflict between those who longed for the old home and those who doggedly clung to their hopes for the new land was not the only one springing up in the immigrant communities; cleavages in outlook often developed between first and second generation immigrants.

In the farmhouses of the older American stock the struggle to make a living often precluded much attention to intellectual life even when there was some precedent for it in a particular family. Yet when there was such a precedent, or when some member of the household had leanings toward the life of books, a boy or girl with zeal and talent was frequently encouraged to take advantage of the opportunities offered in the academies or high schools of towns nearby, or even those offered by the young state universities in Minneapolis, Iowa City, Lincoln, and Lawrence. And if most farm households had no reading matter beyond the Bible, the local newspaper, and the patent-medicine almanac with its medley of fact and fancy, some possessed miscellaneous volumes brought in the covered wagon from the old home. Perhaps it might be a Waverly Novel, or Porter's *Scottish Chiefs*, or Headley's *Lives of the Presidents*, or merely two or three McGuffey readers with their excerpts from the accepted writers. Some farmsteads cherished a goodly shelf of books that included many of the classics of English and American literature. An exceptional farmer pored over some lawbooks and used to advantage what he gleaned from them in the farmers' fight against railroad or cattlemen's encroachments. Another exceptional farmer, like Old Jules, the Swiss immigrant in northwestern Nebraska, might carry on, with the help of the embryonic state college of agriculture, experiments in the development of new and better grains, plants, and animals.

Even before settlers in sodhouses could make permanent homes it was not unusual for them to provide for the elementary education of their children. If the territory or state had not yet acted to aid schools, volunteer movements in the shape of subscription schools carried on the pattern of earlier frontier communities. After schoolhouses had been built by cooperative neighborhood action and a teacher found, efforts were made to secure aid from the territorial or state school fund. If the early laws requiring school attendance were poorly enforced, if standards were lamentably low, the foundations in any case were laid, and the struggle for improvement began almost from the start. Teachers' institutes, such as that held at Lone Tree, Nebraska, in 1873, provided pedagogues with the opportunity to review the fundamentals of the "three R's," to imbibe maxims on school government, and to listen to inspirational talks on moral training and the spiritual values in teaching. Everywhere, as in the older areas of the country at an earlier time, educational advance owed much to outstanding leaders. Typical of these was Ignatius Donnelly, Minnesota champion of popular rights who fought to break the commercial monopoly of publishers of schoolbooks and to provide these free to the people's children.

The Grange and the Farmers' Alliance worked for the extension and improvement of schools and especially for the introduction into the curriculum of such practical subjects as agriculture. The Grange meetings themselves were important agencies in the development of intellectual interests on the prairie frontier. In addition to offering social recreation and release from the grim toil and dreary isolation of the remote farm, these meetings, frequently held in schoolhouses, initiated many a farmer and farmer's boy into the intricacies of parliamentary law—sometimes to stand him in good stead in future tussles in the state legislature. What was more, the Granges debated social, political, and economic subjects. The complex problems of cheap or dear money and the regulation of railroads, for example, were threshed over. They also circulated tracts, leaflets, and agricultural periodicals, and in some instances encouraged members to read by establishing circulating libraries.

Westward, beyond the distant rim of the prairie states, lay the barren plateaus, the formidable Rockies, the cattle and mineral frontiers. The mining camps, given over as they were to material ends, direct action, and boisterous recreations, exhibited in most respects the very antithesis of the conventional moral and intellectual values of the older regions. At the start there was no law, and subsequently lawlessness persisted because the laws imported from the settled areas were ill designed for the peculiar conditions of high plains and mountains. And here, as on the prairie frontier of Minnesota, Iowa, Nebraska, and Kansas, the life of action bred suspicion of contemplativeness and critical-mindedness. The ideal was a society of strong individuals, glorying in physical courage, but all more or less conforming to a single type and intolerant of any other. If a man had book learning, he did well as a rule to conceal it.

But even mining camps that sprang up like lush weeds maintained, before fading into ghost towns, a certain interest in ideas. Miners liked theatrical entertainments, and for their gold these were forthcoming. Ephemeral and struggling newspapers purveyed, as Mark Twain's *Roughing It* narrates, the doings of the vigilantes, the school committee, and the territorial legislature, as well as the homespun humor and philosophy of the camp. The showy dissipation, the reckless excitement, the brutality and animal spirits of the mining camp were tempered by the occasional recrudescence of the good even in the blackest souls and by a kind of picturesque camraderie which Bret Harte began to exploit in a new genre of literature. There were at first few women and fewer children, but it was not long before some educational Moses—in Arizona, for example, it was Governor Anson P. K. Safford—laid the crude foundations of public schools. Bold men of the cloth brought Christ's words to barrooms and shanty settlements.

Like the miner, the cattlemen and cowboys followed a way of life that put a premium on action and adventure. Yet out of that way of life sprang folk songs which, imitative though they were of older ballads, reveal some of the yearnings and feelings of the men of the cattle frontier; they remain, furthermore, one of the characteristically American contributions to song. From these rhythmical and reckless songs, quasi-pathetic and quasi-gay, one gathers that the cowboy idealized the home he had turned his back on, his mother and her God, his lost sweetheart. On the other hand, he disparaged the crowded cities and their lawyers, doctors, and merchants. His songs also show that he found compensations in his hand-to-mouth existence and in the lonely freedom that was his lot. For all his admiration of physical courage, even that of the bad men whose antisocial action he condemned, he knew the value of cooperation and comradeship:

> Did you ever go to a cowboy when hungry and dry,
> Asking for a dollar, and have him you deny?
> He'll just pull out his pocket book and hand you a note,
> They are the fellows to help you whenever you are broke.

Beyond the western edge of the prairie frontier virtually no sizable towns could be found in these decades. Occasionally a mining or distributing center like Denver struck root and provided a nucleus for the development of the agencies of cultural life. Santa Fe lingered on as a relic of earlier missionary activities and Catholic culture, and of trading enterprise.

Salt Lake City was the center of Brigham Young's flourishing Mormon empire—the intellectual as well as the political capital of an extraordinary structure built out of the desert through cooperative enterprise, paternalistic industry, and religious zeal. The Mormons approved of merrymaking, if religiously oriented, and the theater was a flourishing institution in Salt Lake City. They also supported a vocational type of education well suited to their needs, an education that emphasized the cultivation of strong bodies and vigorous minds and the preservation of the distinctively Mormon institutions and values. Of these the most publicized was that of "celestial marriage," a means of enhancing individual glory and immortality through the family; polygamy linked man's earthly existence to the eternities and gave the family a continuity from the very beginning to the very end of time. In the eyes of the Gentiles who visited the impressive Temple, the Mormon capital conjured up a variety of polygamous orgies. To the respectable East, polygamy was the symbol of all that was immoral, anti-Christian, and generally infamous.

In the decade before the Civil War the Oregon pioneers had begun to transplant the ways of life to which they were accustomed in their older homes in the central West, the South, and the Northeast. But it was only in California that the west coast boasted anything like an intellectual life sufficiently rooted to bear flowers. Save in the sphere of outdoor recreation the old Mexican culture seems to have exerted little direct influence. Ideas and values that Josiah Royce, a native son of California destined to become a distinguished philosopher, regarded as truly American did emerge—thanks in part to the fact that Northerners and Southerners alike rubbed elbows and occupied themselves chiefly with a new set of problems bearing little relation to the bitter contests in their home sections.

In the bonanza days when everyone bent his energies to get gold, when lawlessness and dissipation and recklessness were little restrained by family, church or state men sang such songs as:

> Oh, what was your name in the States?
> Was it Thompson or Johnson or Bates?
> Did you murder your wife
> And fly for your life?
> Say, what was your name in the States?

But even in these days of turmoil San Francisco and Sacramento had some papers, magazines, books, and theaters. Such journals as *The Golden Era* and the *News Letter* compared well with their eastern prototypes. When the *Overland Monthly* was begun in 1868, California possessed in Charles Warren Stoddard, John Muir, Mark Twain, Bret Harte, and presently Joaquin Miller and Henry George, a group of vigorous literary men sensitive to the peculiarities of life in the Far West.

Moreover, there was even some tradition of an intellectual culture in the theater, which from the early days had presented Shakespeare, along with a great variety of less admirable entertainment. The first literary institute was started in San Francisco in 1851, and about the same time mercantile libraries in Sacramento and San Francisco appeared. Thanks to the heroic labors of John Swett, a New Hampshire schoolmaster known as the Horace Mann of California, a public school system was well under way. Other New Englanders, notably Thomas Starr King, the Unitarian minister of San Francisco who had done much during the war to keep California in the Union, had familiarized many of their fellow citizens with the doctrines of Unitarianism and at least the elements of a rich literary culture. The University of California, projected as early as 1850, did not open its doors until 1869, but it then attracted, among other notables, Joseph Le Conte, well known in eastern academic circles for his work in geology. The Catholics boasted several centers of higher studies. Thus the pattern of older eastern culture was transmitted to the western empire.

But the West figured in other ways in the intellectual life of the nation during the two decades from 1860 to 1880. As L. P. Brockett made clear in an influential description of the new country, it provided opportunities for professional men, especially for lawyers whose talents in mining litigation were much in demand, and for artists and musicians whose services rich patrons eagerly sought.

More significant, perhaps, was the discovery of the West by a group of scientists who revealed it to the rest of the country. Raphael Pumpelly, a mining engineer who operated in the Southwest and whose gifts were admired at Harvard, published in 1870 his engaging *Across America and Asia*. This pulled back the curtains and displayed the physical beauty and natural resources, as well as the social disorganization, of the Southwest. Henry Adams' friend, Clarence King, whose gift for literary description won the admiration of a notable circle, did important work in revealing to the scientist the nature and significance of many hitherto unknown regions in the mountainous West. In California John Muir, Scotch-born and Wisconsin-reared naturalist, began in 1868 his explorations of the Yosemite which were to demonstrate the origin of the valley in glacial erosion.

None of the students of the West, however, equaled in understanding and in vision John Wesley Powell, an ethnologist and geologist who explored the Colorado River, the Grand Canyon, and the homeland of Indian tribes of the Southwest, and promoted extremely important surveys in the West for the Federal government. Powell's *Report on the Lands of the Arid Region of the United States* (1878) documented his conviction that the future of the West depended on reform of land usage and on storage and diversion of water to small irrigated farms and to the hayfields of ranches. The *Report* also challenged the prevailing ill-adapted transfer of land settlement familiar in the wet areas of the older sections of the country. Powell's plan, in putting public interest and planning for the future ahead of the current ruinous exploitation of the arid west by settlers, land, cattle, and timber men, aroused the antagonism of these groups. Despite his ardent and sustained battle with these interests and their spokesmen in Washington, Powell's *Report* was not, for the time, implemented. But as shrewd analysis of what was taking place, as prediction of the droughts, floods, and crop failures current practice was making inevitable, and as wise planning for future general interest, the *Report* was in time to become regarded as one of the most notable intellectual documents of the period.

The fellow Catholic missionaries of Father De Smet in the Northwest continued to study the red man's language and lore. But in this field the highly significant researches of the Swiss-born Adolph Bandelier towered above all others. Having completed his study of the ancient Mexicans in the late 1870s, Bandelier turned his attention to the Pueblo Indians of Arizona and New Mexico. Making critical use of original sources, both archeological and historical, he raised the standards of ethnological work and overthrew many accepted myths regarding the Indians of the Southwest. Scientific appreciation of the uniqueness of the West led such men as Bandelier, Muir, Cornelius Hedges, and F. V. Hayden of the Geological Survey to persuade the federal government to set aside the Yosemite and the Yellowstone as national parks. These treasures were thus secured in all their scenic grandeur and scientific significance from ruinous exploitation by private enterprise. On another level Hubert H. Bancroft began his cooperative venture of collecting historical sources for a history of the Far West. He produced his impressive work on the *Native Races of the Pacific States* (1874–1876) in five volumes and his *History of the Pacific States of North America* (1882–1890) in twenty-one volumes.

The scenic beauty and scientific significance of the Far West probably meant little or nothing to the average Easterner. But thanks to the majestic canvases of Bierstadt and the highly colored and vividly realistic sketches of Frederic Remington some part of the grandeur of the West began to capture the imagination of the artistically untrained men and women in towns and villages throughout the land. A still larger number, of course, became conscious of the last frontiers through the legends of Kit Carson and Jesse James and through the Beadle dime novels and their like. These tales, highly melodramatic, highly moral, made glamorous folk figures of bad men and banditti, of vigilantes and rangers, and celebrated with breathless tempo and in high blacks and whites the romance and adventure and enterprise of the last frontier. This picture of the departing West took firm hold of popular consciousness and only gradually began to wane decades after the frontiers had been closed. Before then the concept of the frontier and of its disappearance had become a major factor in American social thought.

The frontier was going. As it went it left distinctive traces on the American mind through its cult of action, rough individualism, physical freedom, and adventurous romance. But these peculiarities yielded to the pull of national unity, to the undertow that was creating, in spite of the Indian, Negro, and foreign-born minorities, in spite of particularistic regions, a new sense of national unity, a new nation.

# 20 Business and the Life of the Mind

> You can't keep such men down. They are very shrewd
> men. I don't believe that by any legislative enact-
> ment or anything else, through any of the States or
> all the States, you can keep such men down. You
> can't do it! They will be on top all the time. You see
> if they are not.
>
> —WILLIAM H. VANDERBILT, 1879

> If liberty, science, property, and labor are to continue
> to work together in the future as in the past for the
> advancement of civilization, the institutions of higher
> learning must be extended to the limits of their
> possibilities.
>
> —ABRAM S. HEWITT, 1896

Of the forces creating a new nation in the years between the Compromise of 1850 and the last decades of the century, the rapid advance
of the business class was unquestionably one of the most important for
American intellectual life. The advance of business was, to be sure,
inextricably associated with the more basic transition from a society
mainly rural and decentralized to one largely urbanized, mechanized,
and centralized. The men of big business, the organizers of the new
integrated economy, did not effect this transition, but in the sphere of
intellectual history they were dramatic symbols of it. Even before the
Civil War business itself or its spokesmen had begun to develop a

494

rationale or justification for capitalistic enterprise, but intellectual leadership in the country had lain with professional men, with cultured representatives of old and established mercantile families, and with educated interpreters of the agricultural way of life. This leadership and the values associated with it were now challenged by a new type of entrepreneur who came to wield great economic and political power in the third quarter of the century. The triumph of business enterprise raised many new questions about the future development of American intellectual life.

Perhaps the most important question was what the fate of the American dream, as James Truslow Adams has called it, would be. This dream, it will be recalled, was born of the Enlightenment and of Christian humanitarianism and was nourished by the ample opportunities afforded by a new country thinly peopled but rich in natural resources. Especially after 1870 did the rapidly increasing power of large-scale business rest on and give focus to materialistic and acquisitive values that differed appreciably from those that had been characteristic of the older America. In earlier times materialistic acquisition had in general been looked on not as an end in itself, not as something for the few, but as the means by which everyone in every walk of life might achieve comfort, security, education, the enrichment of personality—in short, the good life. Now the ruthlessness of the few great titans of industry and finance, who piled up huge fortunes through manufacturing or land and railway manipulation, threatened to block the progress of the plain people in their quest for the means to secure comforts and to fulfill modest cultural aspirations. In addition, the new order of business monopoly or near-monopoly seemed to emphasize the acquisition of material fortunes as ends in themselves rather than as a means to security, comfort, and personal development. The morning promises were no longer so bright and fresh as in the "golden day" when everyone took for granted an open road to moderate success.

A second important question posed by the rapid growth in importance of the business element was what its attitude toward esthetic and intellectual values and achievements would be. Conceivably the great figures in railway and land promotion and speculation and in industrial and banking enterprise might ignore or deprecate the values of scholarship, the creative arts, the humane tradition generally. Or they might consciously or unconsciously put so high a premium on the type of training and skills useful in an age of business enterprise that the older humane values would be overshadowed. Or they might become patrons of the arts and of education, influencing the whole current of intellectual and artistic life.

The third important question raised by the triumph of business enterprise was what reaction of scholars, journalists, men of letters, the clergy, and related groups that had enjoyed intellectual leadership would be. Would spokesmen of the intellectual life identify themselves with the new order of monopoly and enterprise, of get-rich-in-any-way-you-can, singing its praises, lending their pens to an elaboration and popularization of the business rationale that had already been formulated in broad outline? Or would the professional classes challenge the new order of acquisitive materialism directed by the few great leaders and reassert and reinterpret the older American dream of democratic opportunities for everyone, opportunities designed to promote universal well-being, to provide rounded and rich personalities in every walk of life and an esthetic and intellectual culture shared by all? Might the new dominance of business and the accompanying tendency toward the integration of society blight the creative esthetic life and the intellectual endeavors of scholars?

## Masters of Capital and Intellectual Life

In the pre-Civil War decades an effort was made by writers to broaden the concept of culture to include business. Freeman Hunt, editor of the leading business periodical, did his best to convince business men and the general public that business was both a science and an art. He wrote in *Wealth and Worth* (1856) that trade had already penetrated the world and given the keynote to civilization. Before long, he continued, someone would construct a rationale of business management which might be studied by the merchant's clerk just as students of law and medicine equipped themselves for their profession by becoming familiar not only with the techniques but with the underlying as well as the auxiliary disciplines.

The argument was also heard in the 1850s that the merchant and industrialist was showing an inclination to elevate his mind by familiarizing himself with the classics, the modern poets, the philosophers and scientists, the authorities on public affairs. Addresses at the mercantile societies and the books listed in mercantile libraries suggest that in addition to these practical or utilitarian motives for self-culture, merchants felt that a familiarity with humanistic culture might elevate their rank in the eyes of society, enable them to pursue wealth with a higher and nobler purpose, and serve as protection against possible misfortunes by enabling them to acquire values and interests unconnected with their main concern. Spokesmen of business reminded the American public that the acquisition of wealth had always been the chief index of civilization and that without it no cultural refinement, no great intellectual achievement, had ever been or ever could be realized.

Other considerations, however, are important in explaining the culture and knowledge of certain business leaders and their sons. Sheer love of art and zeal for collecting account for James Jackson Jarves of Boston, who spent a fortune in acquiring Italian masterpieces that rivaled the great Bryan collection which had come to America in 1853. J. Pierpont Morgan, who had acquired a passion for rare books and pictures during his student days at Göttingen, believed that the love of finer things was of practical utility in leavening life's trials. Henry Lee Higginson, the Boston financier, was governed by a less purely personal consideration. When he founded the Boston Symphony Orchestra in 1881 he was carrying out a youthful dream of his Viennese student days, a dream of enriching American life by enabling his fellow countrymen to enjoy permanently the symphonies of the great masters. It is also true that Higginson was not without class interest in the attitude he took toward philanthropy on occasion. In urging a wealthy kinsman to endow Harvard liberally, he bluntly declared that democracy had got fast hold of the world and that we must educate "to save ourselves and our families and our money from the mobs!"[1]

The rise of obscure and uncultivated men to great wealth was even more significant for the intellectual character of the period than the role of the cultured rich. It has been common to emphasize the narrow social outlook of the titans who through shrewdness and strength made immense fortunes. No one can well deny that their social philosophy often crudely identified exploitation of natural resources with progress, that it was frequently marked by a kind of law of the jungle, and that from a social standpoint it was irresponsible. Lust for speculation and preemption, huge wastefulness of natural wealth, bustling materialism, splendid audacity—these were all, to some extent, characteristic of the new busi-

[1] Bliss Perry, *Life and Letters of Henry Lee Higginson* (Little, Brown, and Co., 1921), 329.

ness class. Nor is it easy to overemphasize their identification of private gain getting with public good. In Parrington's picturesque words, this expressed itself in a grand paternalistic barbecue in which booms and land promotion and land stealing went hand in hand with a free and easy way of giving and taking bribes and with even more sensational scandals which hardly marred the crude and greedy enjoyment of the feast. It has been equally common to emphasize the Gargantuan vulgarity of the new business class. Its tawdry and grandiose buildings, its conspicuous waste and display, its generally meretricious splendor have more than once been celebrated in song and story.

From such a group not much could be expected in the way of individual pursuit of intellectual culture. The titans were self-made men, and in general self-culture was not a part of the self-making. In commenting on the proper steps to a business career, Henry Clews, the successful Wall Street broker, advised an early practical training, "even to the partial neglect of school and college." Practical business, he continued, was the best school and college from which young men could possibly graduate. The well-informed publisher, George Haven Putnam, had the products of such a training in mind when he regretted that the new wealthy class was too little interested in literature to buy and read books. "I didn't get very much schooling—somehow never took to it," remarked Daniel Drew. "I always got spelled down the very first time around. But I never minded that very much."[2] Men of action did not mind being spelled down and were not ashamed of their lack of formal schooling. But even if they had desired book knowledge, they were for the most part too busy on the exchange, too immersed in building gaudy palaces and buying swift race horses and cutting a figure. Nor were their women folk inclined to cultivate their minds.

Nevertheless, some did confess to a yearning for book knowledge. "I'd give a million dollars today, Doctor," declared Commodore Vanderbilt to a clergyman, "if I had your education. Folks may say that I don't care about education; but it ain't true; I do. I've been to England, and seen them lords, and other fellows, and knew that I had twice as much brains as they had maybe, and yet I had to keep still, and couldn't say anything through fear of exposing myself."[3] Andrew Carnegie, with

[2] Bouck White, The Book of Daniel Drew (Doubleday & Co., 1918), 8.
[3] William A. Croffut, The Vanderbilts and the Story of their Fortune (Bedford, Clark and Co., 1886), 137.

an income of $50,000 a year and only on the threshold of his career as a great steelmaker, turned over in his mind the appeal of a three-year sojourn at Oxford "to get a thorough education" and "to make the acquaintance of literary men." He at least brought Matthew Arnold to America as his guest and began to cultivate such scholars as Lord Bryce, John Morley, and Frederic Harrison. He did more; he avidly read Herbert Spencer, "the man to whom I owe most," as he put it. But businessmen were seldom scholars themselves. A woolen manufacturer, Rowland Gibson Hazard of Rhode Island, stands out because both before and after his retirement in 1866 he wrote on philosophical, political, and economic questions. He corresponded and even conversed with John Stuart Mill, who wrote that Hazard's *Letters on Causation and Freedom in Willing* (1869), like his previous books, did honor to American thought. Indeed, Mill quite naturally approved Hazard's thesis that the moral government of human beings rested largely on their expectation of consequences from their acts. The great English philosopher wrote that he wished Hazard "had nothing to do but philosophize . . . for I see in everything that you write a well-marked natural capacity for philosophy."

Only a few of the self-made industrialists went in for the cultivation of literary men or for writing, but many patronized the other arts. It is true that when thirst for praise led newly rich men to dig into their pockets for the rising Metropolitan Museum in New York, they were cold-shouldered by some of the older aristocracy because they were not gentlemen. Nevertheless, it became increasingly customary for promoters of such ventures to enlist the support of the new business titans and for these in turn to shower gifts on established institutions or preferably to endow new ones bearing their names.

The conception of art as a relic of past grandeur and as something to be acquired as an evidence of success and "culture" dominated the thought of the new men of wealth. William H. Vanderbilt became a great collector of the art of the past. Stillman, a New York banker, went in for Rembrandts and Titians, with which he embellished his house. William A. Clark filled the art gallery in his palatial New York residence with Titians, Rembrandts, Van Dycks, Hals, with Reynolds and Gainsboroughs, and with Gobelin and Beauvais tapestries. William Corcoran, who had begun to collect art in 1859, opened his gallery in Washington in 1872. Baker collected jades. Gates collected Corots. By the early 1880s James J. Hill, railway promoter and empire builder, was collecting French paintings. On the Pacific coast Adolph Sutro, mining engineer and tunnelmaker, built up a rich collection of incunabula by ransacking European repositories; the portion saved from destruction in the San Francisco fire in 1906 found its way into the public library of that city. Frick, the great steel magnate, was later remembered as sitting on a Renaissance throne under a baldacchino holding a copy of the *Saturday Evening Post!*

A few of the new men of wealth did have some faint concept of art as a living thing, but they were the exceptions. William Ralston, whose huge fortune rested on railroads, steamship lines, and factories, patronized the drama and other arts in San Francisco. Harriman insisted that nothing except American art decorate his estate, Arden. The great rich sometimes threw open their palaces to creative artists. Thus at the Fifth Avenue mansion of Alexander T. Stewart, the fabulously wealthy retail and wholesale merchant, struggling musicians and artists mixed with diplomats and millionaires. By and large, however, the men who had made gigantic fortunes and who had no background in taste did not think of art as a continuous means of enlarging the realm of beauty; for them art consisted of relics of older times.

Sometimes magnates spent part of their surplus accumulations in endowing existing universities or founding new ones. George Peabody, who accumulated an immense fortune through marketing American securities in London, not only generously endowed public education in the South but founded great museums of natural history at the oldest American colleges. Cyrus McCormick of reaper fame gave liberally to Presbyterian seminaries and colleges. The University of Wisconsin owed its observatory to the great milling magnate of the Twin Cities, Cadwallader Washburn; the University of California owed its great telescope, the most powerful in the world, to James Lick, who had made his fortune largely in real estate speculation. Armour Institute in Chicago trained young men for the technical world and perpetuated the name of the great meat-packing family. Jonas Clark, a successful New England industrialist, had decided by 1880 to establish some sort of technical school at Worcester, Massachusetts. The million dollars he gave for the purpose enabled G. Stanley Hall to build a remarkable center for graduate study. In Baltimore the Quaker bachelor, Johns Hopkins, whose mercantile and financial pursuits won him a sizable fortune, handsomely endowed a university which became an even greater center of research. Under Daniel Coit Gilman the new Johns Hopkins University, the first true graduate school in America, lived up to the hope of its founder in avoiding ecclesiasticism and partisanship and in widening many fields of knowledge. Ezra Cornell, carpenter and mechanic, having piled up a fortune in the telegraph business and public lands, was persuaded by Andrew D. White to enlarge his original idea for advancing agricultural education. The institution bearing the founder's name became a living tribute to his conviction that the "industrial and productive classes" deserved the best facilities for mental culture and practical knowledge. While Cornell was to be an institution where any person whatever could find instruction in any study, Vassar, Wellesley and Smith, similarly founded by the newly rich, concentrated on establishing opportunities for women to achieve the highest standards in collegiate education. From the fortune which Leland Stanford harvested in railroading emerged the university which he and his wife lovingly built in memory of their son.

The most important of the newly established universities was that which John D. Rockefeller endowed at Chicago. In 1896 the fabulously wealthy oil king could declare that the great secular university he had founded was the best investment he had ever made in all his life. "The good Lord gave me the money, and how could I withhold it from Chicago?" he asked. The philanthropies which he increasingly supported not only greatly advanced the cause of original research but gradually tended to lessen popular hostility against the man who had driven so many little fellows to the wall in building his great oil empire.

It remained for Andrew Carnegie to develop the best-articulated philosophy of philanthropy. In 1889 there appeared in the *North American Review* an article entitled "The Gospel of Wealth." It bore the name of the steel magnate and was introduced with high praise by the editor. In this essay Carnegie, after justifying the free enterprise system on the ground that it accorded with natural law, democracy, and human nature, went on to speak of the obligation of men of wealth to pour large parts of their means into socially useful causes. By so doing, Carnegie concluded, profits were socialized with the least possible harm to the free enterprise system, and any shortcomings in the workings of that system were compensated for with interest. The Scottish immigrant who had so miraculously succeeded in Pittsburgh had already established a public library. Believing that libraries were the most democratic form of educational enterprise, he began on a grand scale to encourage that type of philanthropy. By insisting that provision be made for the upkeep of the libraries he built, Carnegie gave more than an initial impulse to the movement. In 1896 he founded the Carnegie Institute at Pittsburgh—the first of a number of Carnegie foundations devoted to scientific and historical research, the advancement of the teaching profession on the university level, and education for international peace.

## The Reorientation of Education

Education and the life of the mind in general were affected by the expanding forces of business under the leadership of educators as well as businessmen themselves. With the inauguration of Charles W. Eliot at Harvard in 1869, a new type of college president appeared. Eliot was primarily neither a teacher nor a research scholar. He had not come from a business family, nor were his associations in his formative years principally with businessmen; but he was above all else an administrator, and with the skill and foresight and persistence of a man in business he guided the transformation of Harvard from a small undergraduate institution with a few loosely affiliated schools into a great modern university. What Eliot did with such notable success was likewise done by William R. Harper at Chicago, by James B. Angell at Michigan, and by Andrew D. White at Cornell. At the same time businessmen came increasingly to dominate boards of trustees and regents, and almost imperceptibly and unconsciously university administration took on many of the attributes of business organizations.

The needs of an expanding industrial and business civilization were reflected in the discussions of educational objectives. Long before the Civil War, of course, the issue of practical versus classical offerings in the college curriculum had been debated. Radical innovations in the direction of scientific and nonclassical subjects generally fell by the board, but gradually the so-called modern disciplines made their way into the curriculum. The new demands for professional training, for technical pursuits, and for business education became increasingly acute in the Civil War decade. The old debate was resumed with great intensity. In some respects this debate, which gave no sign of ending, reflected a parallel one in England arising from similar problems. Herbert Spencer and Thomas Huxley were arguing that education had to serve the needs of an industrial and democratic order. In his famous essay, *What Knowledge is of Most Worth* (1859), Spencer held that science needed to be accorded a much larger place in education inasmuch as it was more valuable than the classics for the chief functions of living; these, according to Spencer, included self-preservation, health, earning a livelihood, parenthood and citizenship, and the enjoyment of art and leisure. On the other hand Matthew Arnold upheld the primary value of the classical languages and literature in forming mind, character, and taste, in acquainting man with the best that had been said and thought throughout the ages. In the United States the arguments advanced by Spencer and Huxley were received with applause by such champions of scientific education as Edward L. Youmans, who spread the word through lectures, manuals, and the *Popular Science Monthly*. The exponents of the classical tradition received the arguments of Matthew Arnold with enthusiasm.

Step by step concessions were made to the modernists, who spoke principally for the needs of an expanding civilization in which the natural and social sciences were foundation stones. The first great step was the elective system which President Eliot inaugurated at Harvard. It is true that this reflected not only the needs of the new industrial civilization but the good old Emersonian doctrine that the individual knows what is best for him and can be trusted to rely on himself. In any case the elective system dealt a blow to the classics and opened the way to collegiate training more directly suited to the needs of a business and technical civilization.

In 1871 the authorities of Yale published a brochure entitled *The Needs of the University*. This was very different in spirit from the famous Yale report of 1828, which had upheld the classical curriculum without concession to anything else. The Yale authorities still emphasized the value of mental discipline and liberal education, but they conceded that the study of the laws and forces of material nature by so-called laboratory or object lessons was of great importance. The claims of the Sheffield Scientific School were not overlooked. The appointment of Josiah Willard Gibbs to a new chair of mathematical physics at Yale in 1871 was, it is true, hardly a recognition of the needs of a new class of industrial capitalists concerned with steam and machines. But in time industry would handsomely profit from Gibbs's labors in thermodynamics.

In the ever more unrestrained acquisitive order the individual's desire to acquire money and property seemed to necessitate some educational reorganization. On every side demands were heard that education must become more practical, that it must train more specifically for industrial and business pursuits. In 1867 Professor Jacob Bigelow of Harvard put the argument on high ground. It is the duty of educational institutions, he insisted, to "adapt themselves to the wants of the place and time in which they exist. It needs no uncommon penetration to see that we are now living in a great transition period."[4] The dead languages, Professor Bigelow went on, were dead, but modern sciences and studies were full of vitality, expansion, progress. Nor were the utilitarian subjects without their beauty. What was more beautiful than a railroad train shooting by with a swiftness that made its occupants invisible—sinuously winding through forests, cleaving hills and mountains asunder, steady, smooth, unerring, like a migratory bird!

This pioneer champion of technology was not without support in some esthetic quarters. James Jackson Jarves, author of a whole series of books on the Italian masters and collector without peer, praised fire engines, locomotives, and other machines for their equilibrium of lines, proportions, masses. "Their success [that of machines] in producing broad general effects out of a few simple elements," he observed, "and of admirable adaptations of means to ends, as nature evolves beauty out of the common and practical, covers these things with a certain atmosphere of poetry." Such a generous view of the industrial machine, however, was far from typical in academic circles.

The requirements of a technical and business world were too great for traditional institutions to meet, in spite of their concessions. The land-grant colleges and private technical and business schools arose in answer to the needs. The Civil War decade alone witnessed the foundation of twenty-five scientific institutions designed, like the new Massachusetts Institute of Technology, to train engineers and technicians for the new age of business enterprise. These technical schools provided industry with new secrets for utilizing materials formerly wasted and thus added appreciable sums to the budgets of corporations. On the level

---

[4] Jacob Bigelow, M.D., *Modern Inquiries: Classical, Professional, and Miscellaneous* (Boston, 1867), 30–31.

of business itself the Wharton School of Finance broke precedents when in 1884 it decided to give men the new degree of Bachelor of Finance as proof of special competence in this field.

Even the public schools felt the new impulses. The great international exhibitions brought home to American industrialists the importance of drawing and design in certain types of competitive production. By 1870 Massachusetts, the leading textile state, required instruction in drawing in the schools of the larger towns and cities, and in the same year Walter Smith was brought from South Kensington Art School in England to become state supervisor of drawing and art. Three years later the Massachusetts Normal Art School was opened. Although other factors entered into the picture, the need of industry was a major consideration in all this development. Powerful impetus was given to a similar movement when William T. Harris, the outstanding superintendent of the St. Louis schools, pioneered in introducing scientific instruction into the curriculum. This he justified in part on the ground that an industrial civilization required skills and training in the sciences.

But these were by no means the only influences of business on schools. In the appeals for enlarged support of secondary public education much was made of the training that high schools would give to future clerical workers. Even more was said of the value of a high school education in giving the voters of tomorrow sound economic knowledge and fortifying them against the lure of false panaceas.

## The Intellectuals and the Triumph of Business

The aid that school men consciously or unconsciously gave the new industrialism was paralleled in other intellectual circles. A leading historian of the period has maintained that journalism degraded itself in the post-Civil War years in an unprecedented degree. Never before, according to Oberholtzer, "had newspaper owners been such creatures of the corporation financier and the politicians who were being fed from the rich man's hands."[5] That a similar generalization could be made concerning a considerable segment of the legal profession is beyond reasonable doubt. In the eyes of some of his colleagues David

[5] Ellis P. Oberholtzer, A History of the United States Since the Civil War (The Macmillan Company, 1917–1937), II, 541.

Dudley Field, a leading New York lawyer, was guilty of chicanery in promoting the interests of such "criminals" as Fisk and Gould. Field came uncomfortably close to being expelled from the bar association. Other lawyers found fortune if not fame in devising legal formulas by which monopolists rode to power and escaped the penalty of statutes.

Literary men, educators, and publicists also lent support to the men of new fortunes in the post-Appomattox decades. Older arguments for the sanctity of property rights were applied as well as they could be to the activities of the new type of entrepreneur, manipulator, and monopolist. Mark Hopkins, president of Williams College, declared in his *Lectures on Moral Science* (1862) that men with a strong desire for property had done the most for public institutions. "As men now are," he observed, "it is far better that they should be employed in accumulating property honestly, to be spent reasonably, if not nobly, than that there should be encouraged any sentimentalism about the worthlessness of property, or any tendency to a merely contemplative and quietistic life, which has so often been either the result or the cause of inefficiency or idleness."[6] On one occasion J. G. Holland, popular novelist, moralist, and journalist, wrote that wealth, being "a legitimate spur to endeavor," is a natural good. "There always will be rich men and there always ought to be rich men," he concluded.[7] According to the Reverend Jonathan Harrison, the superficial character of the culture of the more fortunate classes should be the main concern of intellectuals. "It will not do to confine our interest or efforts to the lower strata."[8] In a somewhat similar vein the Reverend Samuel Henry Lee, an influential figure in the Congregational Church, declared that education could provide the means for the increase and the stability of property; "the way to get a market that shall be stable is to promote the higher civilization of the people." Nor was it less important, Lee declared, to keep in mind that business might become "sanctified and transfigured" through "a hearty alliance with learning."[9]

Property-conscious intellectuals did not stop with assertions of the real value of acquisition and philanthropy, and the possibility of elevating the men of great wealth. Critics of the new industrial order and

[6] Mark Hopkins, *Lectures on Moral Science* (Boston, 1862), 104.
[7] Josiah G. Holland, *Every-Day Topics* (Charles Scribner's Sons, 1876), I, 320.
[8] Jonathan Harrison, *Certain Dangerous Tendencies in American Life* (Boston, 1880), 40.
[9] *New Englander and Yale Review*, XLVIII (June, 1888), 404.

advocates of the rights of labor or of some control of business or of outright socialism were roundly denounced. Oliver Wendell Holmes used his bright wit to excoriate labor leaders as blindly selfish; Thomas Bailey Aldrich in *The Stillwater Tragedy* (1880) described the walking delegate as "a ghoul that lives upon subscriptions and sucks the senses out of innocent human beings"; and John Hay, in *The Breadwinners* (1884), pictured labor as violent, lawless, and overambitious. President Theodore Woolsey of Yale summoned much erudition to attack socialism and communism and to defend the rights of property. In brief, the main arguments outlined in the pre-Civil War defense of commerce and industry were asserted and applied, with some qualifications and hesitancy, to the rising business titans and the consolidation of corporate wealth under their auspices. Only after big business became the object of drastic and far-reaching criticism in the late 1880s and early 1890s was the conservative defense thoroughly elaborated and widely publicized.

But this is only a small part of the story of the reaction of intellectuals to the triumph of business enterprise in the third quarter of the century. Many, perhaps a majority, refused to have any more traffic than necessary with the giants of industry, and some did not hesitate to express disdain for them. "I have known, and known tolerably well," remarked Charles Francis Adams, "a good many 'successful' men—'big' financially —men famous during the last half-century; and a less interesting crowd I do not care to encounter. Not one that I have ever known would I care to meet again, either in this world or the next; nor is one of them associated in my mind with the ideas of humor, thought or refinement."[10] His brother, Henry Adams, was no less severe. "America contained scores of men worth five millions or upwards, whose lives were no more worth living that those of their cooks," he observed.[11] The Adamses spared neither their scholarship nor their spleen in damning "caesarism in business." Their withering indictment of the Fisks, Goulds, Drews, and Vanderbilts remains a classic in the literature of railroad high finance.

The Adamses were not alone. In certain circles in Boston wealth counted for little unless it was accompanied by some degree of intellectual distinction. This at least was the fond belief of wealthy and cultured

[10] *Autobiography of Charles Francis Adams* (Houghton Mifflin Company, 1916), 190.
[11] *The Education of Henry Adams* (Houghton Mifflin Company, 1918), 348.

Bostonians such as Henry Cabot Lodge. Charles Eliot Norton bemoaned the fact that art and letters "led a difficult existence in the midst of the barbaric wealth of the richest millions of people in the world." Bayard Taylor similarly regretted that money and leisure were in the power of a people who had little or no intellectual training. The heartlessness of trade, its injustice, and its antipathy to the immaterial values of chivalric love, the beauties of nature, the satisfactions of art, and the kindliness of Christianity formed the theme of Sidney Lanier's novel *Tiger-Lilies* (1867) and his poem, "The Symphony." Even Walt Whitman's ebullient faith in the power of his beloved states to create a great and distinctive culture suffered some strain as he contemplated the ruthlessness, the injustice, the inhumanity, the crass materialistic barbarism displayed by titans of wealth.

Intellectuals thus disillusioned with the new business class and the cheap and dishonest temper of the times could follow one of several paths. The easiest, and the one that was largely taken in Boston, was the revival of the old colonial feeling toward Europe—the old feeling of deference. As Van Wyck Brooks has observed, intellectuals of the older families that had not adjusted themselves to the new order found themselves rootless, adrift in a world beyond their ability to understand. Commerce and business, absorbing as they did the lion's share of prestige, left those of taste and ideas doubtful about the country of their birth, the country that in an earlier time of cultural nationalism had aroused their proud enthusiasm. Thus they turned to Europe. If they could not live there, they could at least bring as much of Europe as possible into their midst. "Boston is very well up in all things European," wrote Henry Adams in 1873, "but it is no place for American news." Indeed, the intellectuals in the "hub of the universe" for the most part turned their backs on the traditional reform causes and went in for esthetics in a big way. Arnold, Ruskin, Browning, and Tennyson were on everyone's lips; Siennese architecture and Roman inscriptions and primitive paintings were the order of the day. Henry Cabot Lodge wrote of the dominance of English habits among his class in the post-Appomattox years: "Our literary standards, our standards of statesmanship, our modes of thought . . . were as English as the trivial customs of the dinner table and the ballroom."

Henry James is, of course, the classic example of escapism. In 1870 he wrote to his friend Charles Eliot Norton: "It behooves me, as a luckless American, diabolically tempted of the shallow and superficial, really to catch the flavour of an old civilization (it hardly matters which) and to strive to raise myself, for one brief moment at least, in the attitude of observation."[12] In somewhat the same vein the future novelist of the cosmopolitan American and the American who tried unsuccessfully to be cosmopolitan wrote complainingly of the vulgar, ignorant, crude self-complacency of his bad-speaking and bad-mannered countrymen. It was therefore appropriate for James to take as his main theme the plight of Americans in the sophisticated society of Europe. *Roderick Hudson* (1876) portrayed the collapse of the integrity of a New England sculptor when he abandoned Puritan discipline for the rich culture of the Old World. In *The American* (1877) a retired gentleman who could neither cast off his Americanism nor understand the subtle ways of the French family of Claire, his fiancée, came to grief. Similarly *Daisy Miller* (1879) was the tragedy of an American girl whose American manners gave a Europeanized fellow countryman an erroneous impression of her true character.

Henry James set an example. In varying degrees others sought the same escape from what they regarded as a culture devoid of beauty, antiquity, and interest. They did not need to be told by Matthew Arnold, who visited the United States in the 1880s, that their country was without an interesting civilization because it lacked roots, the discipline of awe and respect—everything, in short, that made for distinction. In Europe it was easier for them to close their eyes to the self-made businessmen, many of whom shared with their American fellows crude materialistic values. It is true that Mark Twain, in his witty and satirical *The Innocents Abroad* (1869), refused to look with awe on the "museum of magnificence and misery" he saw in Italy, and refrained from adulation of overrated landscapes, dingy ruins, desolation, and decay. William Dean Howells could appreciate the charms of the Old World, but he was a leader of those who chose to write about common actualities in his own country. Nevertheless, a large number of American men of letters, artists, and other intellectuals preferred with Henry James and F. Marion Crawford to become virtual expatriates or to live and think, so far as it was possible, like Europeans.

An impressive number of gifted American writers did not turn their

[12] Percy Lubbock (ed.), *The Letters of Henry James* (The Macmillan Company, 1920), I, 12.

backs on the American scene, but responded to the new currents of the machine, industrialism, and big business by depicting in literary form the impact of these forces on American life. By and large, these writers vigorously criticized the new business order and reasserted the older values of a democratic society in which everyone might seek a moderate well-being with reasonable expectation of success. Some sixty novels dealing with the American businessman were written before the end of the century, and of these at least fifty were critical of the activities and values of this group.

The most outstanding writers dealing with this theme—Mark Twain, Hamlin Garland, William Dean Howells, and Edward Bellamy, all agreed in presenting a generally critical picture of big business. Mark Twain, in collaboration with Charles Dudley Warner, depicted in *The Gilded Age* (1871) the itch for speculation that had captured the country and portrayed vividly many of the corrupt political figures of the day together with land promoters, lobbyists, and others of that ilk. Far from having thwarted Twain's natural genius, industrial capitalism seems to have stimulated him both to criticism and satire on the one hand and to the proclamation of humane, democratic values on the other. If, in focusing attention on the spoils-loving West as the source of political corruption, Mark Twain and Charles Dudley Warner failed to do justice to the rapacious capitalists of the East and to the relations between the desire for profits and corruption, the authors of *The Gilded Age*, by implication at least, excoriated economic exploitation. *The Connecticut Yankee*, a defense of industry and the machine and a satire on romantic feudalism, did not fail to reveal the withering blight that an exaggerated property-consciousness cast over civilization. Hamlin Garland's stories portraying the evil effects of monopoly on rural and especially midwestern America expressed the older faith in economic equalitarianism. Howells' *Annie Kilburn*, *A Hazard of New Fortunes*, and *A Traveler from Altruria* displayed the sterility of the lives of many of the new rich, the corrupting effect of materialistic acquisitiveness on mind and heart, and the social and human injustice of an economics of exploitation. All this he depicted with the new technique of literary realism.

These major writers did not stand alone. Henry F. Keenan's *The Money-Makers* delineated the character of a pitiable tool of unscrupulous capitalists and revealed the blighting effect of the thirst for big money on law, morals, and all decent human values. Joaquin Miller, fresh from California, asked Jay Gould at a New York dinner party for a "tip" on the market. The man who "knew" stated the exact opposite of the truth, namely, that he was buying Vandalia Railroad and selling Western Union. Joaquin Miller, taking the tip, had his fingers burned; in fact, by following Gould's tricky lead, he lost most of his fortune. *The Destruction of Gotham* was Miller's reply. In this novel the poet of the Sierras excoriated the iniquities of the stock exchange and the class identified with it. Such examples could be multiplied.

While many writers spent their talents in ridiculing and condemning the moneyed class, in emphasizing the withering effects of unrestrained competition for gold, others took the part of the laborers. The *Atlantic Monthly* published Rebecca Harding Davis's "Life in the Iron Mills," an early portrait, fierce and stark, of the lot of the industrial worker. Seven years later the same periodical brought to the public a story in which the brutalizing insecurity of labor was dramatically depicted when a factory collapsed, with its inevitable havoc to lives already twisted by deprivation and toil. The author, Elizabeth Stuart Phelps, again pleaded for Christian justice to the mill worker in a subsequent piece of fiction, *The Silent Partner* (1871). Less unctuous than this Puritan idyll was Edward Bellamy's *The Duke of Stockbridge* (1879). Far from flawless as a piece of literature, this historical novel of Shays' rebellion nonetheless revealed a fairly acute understanding of exploitation, injustice, and revolt. These works showing humane sympathy for the underdog and criticizing sharply the ways of the rich were merely the beginnings of a crop of novels, stories, and essays which in the 1880s and 1890s testified to the sympathies of a great company of American writers.

If some intellectuals contented themselves with literary onslaughts against the new business class and with sympathetic portraits of industrial workers, others went further. In California in 1871, Henry George, who had known the sting of poverty in that land of fabulous wealth, published a little tract that contained the germ of the single-tax idea and of the movement subsequently launched in its behalf. About the same time the veteran abolitionist, Wendell Phillips, was striking out boldly on new paths. Refusing to share the contentment displayed by most of his fellow workers in the antislavery crusade, Phillips continued to condemn intellectuals for their indifference toward new social evils. He himself bestowed sympathy on the movement for the eight-hour day, spoke and labored for a cooperative system of production, and demanded heavy taxation of a profit economy. For the most part, however, intellectuals who ventured into the sphere of action shrank from anything that betokened genuine struggle over class relationships.

## The Call for Civic Responsibility

E. L. Godkin, a brilliant Protestant emigrant from Ireland, a journalist of great talent, and a disciple of Mill and the English Utilitarians, was a leader in emphasizing the idea that American intellectuals should assume a greater measure of civic responsibility. This, rather than government control of industry, seemed to Godkin the most promising way of combating corrupt political machines, public dishonesty, and the undue influence of the shoddy aristocracy and the venal henchmen. Through *The Nation* he contended for civil service reform and for honesty, decency, and competency in political life.

In reply to the contention that a cultivated man had no chance for a political career this vigorous champion of the duty of intellectuals to cleanse the Augean stables cited the work of Edward Everett, George Bancroft, Andrew D. White, George W. Curtis, Dorman Eaton, and James Russell Lowell. If the man of culture would but drop his own sense of superiority over the people, Godkin argued, he had, other things being equal, a great advantage in the competition for public office over a man devoid of polish and education. But Godkin failed to understand why the standard of honesty in public life was so flagrantly violated by the captains of industry under the banner of the very economic individualism upheld by the high-minded intellectual himself.

The growing civic consciousness on the part of intellectuals and educated citizens generally was greatly deepened and broadened by the interest aroused by James Bryce's *The American Commonwealth* (1888). Bryce admired much in America and went so far as to write that the United States had reached "the highest level, not only of material well-being, but of intelligence and happiness which the race has yet attained." Hence this friendly visitor, so well and favorably known as a distinguished British scholar, man of letters, barrister, and parliamentarian, could make far-reaching criticisms the effect of which was to challenge rather than antagonize Americans. His reports were furthermore largely based on what American themselves told him. His great book was a fairly accurate picture of the corruption and timidity of legislators before business pressure, of the boss and the spoils system, of the contempt that most cultured Americans felt toward politics. *The American Commonwealth* did much to prepare the ground for the growing interest in reform.

The protests and actions of the intellectuals who refused to apologize for and serve the new business giants or to escape into the culture of the Old World merely heralded the more drastic and widespread criticism of the last decade of the nineteenth century and the first years of the twentieth. Meantime other currents of thought were dividing both the leaders of intellectual life and even the plain people themselves.

# PART
# VI

## Individualism
## in a
## Corporate
## Age

# 21　The Delimitation of Supernaturalism

> You are more than anyone else the master of your
> subject. I declare that you know my book as well as
> I do myself; and bring to the question new lines of
> illustration and argument . . . which excite my
> astonishment and almost my envy! Every single
> word seems weighed carefully, and tells like 32-
> pound shot.
>
> —CHARLES DARWIN TO ASA GRAY, 1860

The most striking event in the intellectual history of the last third of
the nineteenth century was the blow dealt the historic doctrine of supernaturalism—the doctrine that a divine Creator stands above the laws of
nature and intervenes directly in natural events and the affairs of men
through miracles and the granting of grace—by new developments in the
biological and physical sciences.

From early colonial times, to be sure, the area dominated by supernaturalism had been slowly shrinking. Each scientific advance imperceptibly reduced the range of the unknown and, as men had supposed,
unknowable mysteries. The Newtonian system, at first a challenge to
orthodoxy, was gradually assimilated to Calvinism and Anglicanism
alike. This assimilation had implanted in the minds of intellectuals, and
to some degree in those of ordinary people, a growing appreciation of
the ideas of natural law, of cause and effect, and even of a somewhat
greater degree of human control through knowledge of nature's appar-

ently whimsical and baffling ways. Under the spell of the growing scientific spirit and of rationalism, many accepted the full implications of Newton's concept of a mechanistic universe and became deists. Deism, as well as "free thought" and other movements derived from it, never had a large popular following. But a considerable number of men and women did accept a watered-down version of deism, Unitarianism. Without rejecting supernaturalism altogether, the Unitarians, it will be recalled, limited its role. In the pulpit of Theodore Parker, the most thoroughgoing rationalistic Unitarian of the mid-century, supernaturalism had no place at all. Even within the folds of the theologically more conservative sects the impact of rationalistic and deistic ideas and of scientific advances slowly modified the idea of an absolute, arbitrary, unpredictable God, who could and did defy what appeared to be the regular workings of natural phenomena.

Newtonianism, which had once seemed to be the last word in science, was itself slowly undergoing modifications. The nebular hypothesis relaxed the fixed and absolute doctrine of mechanically moving orbs. In biology the teachings of Erasmus Darwin and above all of Lamarck introduced into the fixed classifications of Linnaeus a developmental conception. Most important of all, the work of Sir Charles Lyell in the second third of the nineteenth century postulated the gradual evolution, over immense periods of time, of the earth itself. These newer scientific developments had all tended to be upsetting both to the Newtonian conception of a universe created by the fiat of the Divine Architect and to its allied Christian doctrine of a fixed creation.

After some resistance on the part of the orthodox leaders the newer scientific doctrines and supernaturalistic theism were more or less reconciled. This was done partly through the convenient doctrine of "design," which saw in every new scientific fact or relationship or theory evidence of God's all-wise purpose. The accommodation of Christian theism to the newer scientific concepts was also accomplished through the doctrine of "secondary causes." This doctrine, so to speak, divided the fiat functions of the Creator in the first instance from the detailed and subsequent working out, by scientific law, of His ultimate intentions. Lyell's doctrine that the earth, instead of having been created in seven days, was the result of a long glacial development could thus be hailed as a new proof of God's design and of His use of "secondary causes." Similarly the growing knowledge of the complexity and all but miraculous processes of life in the plant and animal world were accommodated to theism by the doctrine that God was immanent in all His creatures. In other words, by the end of the century the march of science had been on the whole, and certainly on the surface, adjusted by theologians to fit Christian doctrine. Yet the process by which this was accomplished inevitably delimited the area of supernaturalistic faith and increased that of naturalism.

## Theology, Systematic and Popular

If supernaturalism was losing ground among intellectuals, it was by no means, in the post-Civil War period, on the road to extinction among the masses. One evidence of this is the fact that in proportion to the growth of population church membership more than held its own. It is true that mere adherence to a church was not in itself proof that the churchgoer was a full-fledged supernaturalist. But within most of the traditional sects a large part of the laity and a considerable portion of the clergy themselves clung to traditionally supernaturalistic views. Moreover, a large portion of the increase in church membership resulted from the new wave of Catholic immigration; and Catholicism, which brooked few compromises with science or anything else that weakened the supernaturalistic foundation of the church, reinforced supernaturalistic doctrines.

The days in which the theologians wrote great systematic treatises such as those of Jonathan Edwards, Joseph Bellamy, and Samuel Hopkins were almost over. Post-Civil War scholars still remembered and respected the quasi-Kantian *Rational Psychology* (1848) of Laurens Hickok, president of Union College and America's most competent technical philosopher between Edwards and the rising pragmatists. The learned devout welcomed Hickok's *Humanity Immortal* (1872) and *The Logic of Reason* (1875) as able defenses of theism. In 1873 a voice from an even older past spoke in the ponderous, wooden, and yet in a sense sublime *Systematic Theology* by Charles Hodge, a sustained defense of the infallibility of the Word of God. In accordance with that Word, it was not for men, whom Hodge likened to worms of the dust, to grapple with the problem of the duration of future punishment. In the mind of this Princeton theologian "it should constrain us to humility, and to silence on this subject, that the most solemn and explicit declarations of the everlasting misery of the wicked recorded in the Scriptures, fell from the lips of Him, who, though equal to God, was found in fashion as a man, and humbled Himself unto death, even the death of the cross, for us men and for our salvation."[1] Hodge's plea was reechoed by William G. T. Shedd in his *Dogmatic Theology* (1888), a no less closely reasoned defense of Calvinism. Although parsons may have let the dust collect on these impressive theological treatises, they nevertheless held them in deep reverence and from their pulpits preached doctrines that squared with their teachings.

Evangelical Christianity reached incalculably wide audiences through the preachments of the great revivalist, Dwight L. Moody. Insisting that the "Bible was not made to understand," this powerful "moulder of souls" brought stragglers from the fold back to Jesus and upheld in their pristine and dogmatic glory the fundamental Christian tenets. If Moody reached chiefly the middle classes, the lower depths did not remain in utter darkness. In the city's "dens of iniquity" the down-and-out heard exciting invitations to repent and join General Booth's Salvation Army. This quasi-military and thoroughly evangelical organization, which was introduced into the United States about 1880, appealed to the lowest fringes of city life because of its colorful uniforms, intriguing trombones and bass drums, and gospel hymns. To these it began in 1880 to add more material inducements in the form of cheap shelter for the fallen and coffee and doughnuts for the hungry. But shelter and manna were meant to enhance rather than to diminish dependence on the super-natural—for whatever was done, was done in His name and for His ends.

Allied to evangelicism was the widespread and emphatic insistence on divine sanction for traditional Christian piety and morals. In response to the growing secularization of life fanatical Christians demanded the incorporation into the federal Constitution of an amendment declaring Christ to be the Ruler and the Bible the controlling law in national life. Old-time Puritanism, revivified by Victorian prudishness, supported the activities of Anthony Comstock, a moral crusader who, in Christ's name, fought alike pornography and all that he regarded as immoral in the classics. A federal Act of 1873 and supporting legislation in some states testified to the popular support of his efforts to legislate into the law of

---

[1] Charles Hodge, *Systematic Theology*, 4 vols. (Charles Scribner's Sons, 1872–1873), III, 880.

the land a narrow concept of Christian morals based on supernatural revelations and sanctions.

The popularity of certain books revealed, no less than evangelical revivals and moral crusades, the appeal of supernaturalistic ideas and ethical values. When, in 1868, Elizabeth Stuart Phelps published *The Gates Ajar*, she tapped a vast reservoir of need; people still mourning for sons and husbands lost on the battlefields craved reassurance that life really is eternal, that Heaven really is just within reach. The subsequent psychic novels of Mrs. Phelps elaborated with much detail the actualities of the Other World and of daily life within the golden portals. At the same time the highly pious novels of E. P. Roe and J. G. Holland enjoyed immense popularity. But no book swept the land with such force as General Lew Wallace's *Ben Hur* (1880). This volume succeeded in dramatizing Christ as a hero without in the least lessening reverence for Him as a supernatural force.

On the young people's level supernatural doctrines appeared to be equally well rooted. In the early 1890s the child psychologist, Earl Barnes, revealed by the popular questionnaire technique that a great majority of a thousand California school children pictured God as a tall white-haired old man, generally benevolent but quite capable of provoking an earthquake at will; Heaven as a place of golden streets with angels strumming on golden harps; and the devil as the horned and tailed creature of ancient lore. Less anthropomorphic but no less supernatural ideas found their way into school textbooks. "Every tiny atom," declared Steele's *Fourteen Weeks of Chemistry* (1873) "is watched by the Eternal Eye and guided by the Eternal Hand." Variation of climate and other environmental influences failed to explain the peculiarities of animals; these were the result, according to Colton's *Geography*, of God's superior wisdom and beneficence. In terms similar to those that had been employed a hundred years earlier children learned in Cruikshank's *Primary Geography* that "God made the world for man to live in and has fitted it for man's convenience and comfort." Rules of good conduct in consequence rested directly on divine sanctions. This was the burden of much of the reading designed for the instruction of children in science. And what was true of the scientific literature for children was true of much of the popular science that reached adults and, indeed, of a vast body of widely read fiction and other secular literature.

The prewar interest in spiritualism was upheld after the war by the

mesmerist and social reformer, Andrew Jackson Davis, and other oc-
cultists. A new wave of spirit rappings enlisted the support or at least
the interest of serious intellectuals and scientists as well as untutored
plain people. The once rationalistic freethinker, Robert Dale Owen,
succumbed to the appeal of spiritualism. Hardly less significant was the
fact that Simon Newcomb, America's leading astronomer, accepted the
presidency of the Association for Psychical Research, which an English
visitor had persuaded a group in the American Association for the
Advancement of Science to launch in 1874. Newcomb perused the
English publications and observed the exhibitions of a variety of
mediums, including the performances of Lulu Hurst, "the Georgia
magnetic girl." Although after all this he was convinced that the entire
cult was a mixture of coincidences, supposed facts, tricks, exaggerations,
and illusions, other scientists, including William James himself, were
favorably impressed or at least sympathetically inclined. The spiritualistic
cult was, in short, by no means smothered by the advance of naturalism.

In 1875, theosophy was added to the native varieties and the English
importations of supernaturalism. In that year Madame Helena P.
Blavatsky, immensely corpulent, slovenly and reckless, romantically hysterical, founded the Theosophy Society. Its platform fused spiritualism
with the Brahmanic and Vedaic teachings of India. Relatively few
Americans took up the new cult, but it managed to survive and, especially
during the World's Fair in 1893, to enlist a certain amount of publicity
and favor. Ella Wheeler Wilcox's poems, which enjoyed great popularity both in the women's magazines and in book form, also disseminated
spiritualistic and theosophical ideas.

Far more important as evidence of readiness to accept innovation was
the astonishing success of Christian Science. Originating in the post-Civil
War decade among lower middle-class groups in Lynn and Boston,
Christian Science had become, before the end of the century, a religion
that found considerable support among the comfortable, respectable
urban dwellers. Its founder, Mary Baker G. Eddy, like most young
women of her day, did not have the advantage of a formal education.
Chronically nervous and ill, she nevertheless possessed great personal
power, superb organizing gifts, and a magnetic hold over her followers.
What she did in *Science and Health* (1875) was to synthesize, in her
own way, a variety of ideas and values. Students who have not accepted
the divine inspiration of Mrs. Eddy have claimed that she was indebted

to P. P. Quimby, a Maine mental healer, to Shakerism, to the "orphic sayings" of the Transcendentalist Bronson Alcott, and possibly to a diluted Hegelianism. Whether or not she was divinely inspired, as her followers maintained, she was certainly profoundly influenced by the Bible. The central doctrine of her teaching was that matter has no real existence and that therefore sin, poverty, sickness, and death are all alike illusions or "errors" of mortal mind. In consequence of this cardinal truth all these "errors" disappear just as soon as mortal mind puts itself in true harmony with Eternal Mind. "Healing the sick," wrote Mrs. Eddy, "through mind instead of matter, enables us to heal the absent as well as the present." But vindictive persons might, through evil thought or "malicious animal magnetism," produce misfortune and disease in their victims. Although Mrs. Eddy made no distinction between the physical and the mental and, indeed, denied the very existence of the physical, she nevertheless freely used such analogies from natural science as "mental chemicalization" and "gravitation downward." The cryptic passages in *Science and Health* seemed rather to impress than to discourage many seekers after light.

The appeal of the new cult has been in part explained by the American love for novelty in religions and in part by the repressed but nonetheless authentic yearning for mysticism in the American as in all forms of civilization. It took hold mainly, but by no means exclusively, in cities where, in common belief, the pace, the stress, the strain of life produced more nervous disorders than in the country. It appealed to the restless and the aspiring, but it also appealed to the comfortable and the prosperous—possibly because it provided a psychological compensation for their actual overemphasis on material values in daily living; it was people of this latter type that Edward Eggleston satirized in his novel, *The Faith Doctor*.

In a general sense, no doubt, the continued vogue of supernaturalism in the more traditional as well as in the more heterodox forms answered the emotional needs of large numbers of Americans. It provided assurances in a period of change and dislocation incident to industrialization and urbanization and to the challenge of the new science with all its uncertainties. If the earthly road was hard—and he who stumbled in depressions or in droughts or in the visitation of locusts knew that it was hard—supernaturalism as of old provided explanations for misfortune and faith for the future. Thus special emotional needs reinforced mere tradition and habit in maintaining the hold of the supernatural in the intellectual lives of the American people.

## The Challenge of New Ways of Life and Knowledge

However useful supernaturalism was to the American life of the last quarter of the nineteenth century, it was in actuality being challenged as never before. Once the smoke of the Civil War lifted sufficiently, it became clear that new developments were arousing fear in the hearts of both thoroughgoing and more moderate supernaturalists. The quickening pace of the inroads of naturalism in the still considerable area dominated by supernaturalism was in the first instance the result of the rising doctrines of organic evolution and, in a lesser degree, of the theory known as the correlation of forces. It was more difficult to reconcile these doctrines with supernaturalism than it had been to accommodate earlier ones. The greater difficulty lay partly in the implications of the new scientific doctrines themselves and partly in the accelerated breakdown of old ways of life and the values associated with them.

Of these changes in ways of life and thought none was so significant as the advance of urbanism. In rural areas the church was the most important social tie in the lives of men and women, a tie which provided occasion for friendly intercourse. But in great cities it could not serve that function so well. In metropolitan areas it was only one of many competing social interests. It had to operate not in a small homogeneous community but in a highly mobile and heterogeneous one. The Catholic church alone possessed the organization, the authority, and the dramatic appeal adequate to hold within its fold a substantial portion of the urban working class. The Protestant pulpit, generally supported by the well-to-do, largely ignored the squalor and misery of the dwellers in tenements and preached a gospel with little meaning to sweatshop workers. The rise of the social gospel among Protestants was a definite response to the growing realization that the church was failing to maintain its influence among the urban poor.

Urban life also contributed to the steady decline of the traditionally strict observance of the Sabbath. It is true that the incoming of immigrants from the Continent, to whom the seventh day was one of recreation as well as worship, did much to undermine the Puritan Sabbath. It is also true that the decline of the old-fashioned Sunday was already marked even before the Civil War, and that the war itself, while accelerating the decline, was only a minor factor in it. What was chiefly responsible was the plain fact that the ordinary industrial and business worker after a week of routine and grinding toil craved excitement and amusement on Sunday. To provide this, commercial recreations became organized on an ever-larger scale. In response to these new patterns of life state laws enforcing strict Sabbath-day observances were gradually relaxed, especially in the urbanized parts of the country. The orthodox made impressive efforts to keep the old, straightlaced Lord's Day. But, as Arthur M. Schlesinger has pointed out, even these efforts came increasingly to be governed by the argument that the Sabbath should be respected not merely because it was man's duty to consecrate the day to God, but rather because man himself stood in need of a rational day of rest after a week of work and strain.

Urbanization also indirectly worked against supernaturalism inasmuch as it was the focal point of the general advance in science. For example, the city, with its crowded slums and invitation to the spread of contagious diseases, offered a fresh stimulus to scientists to meet the threat to life itself imposed by urban conditions. At the same time it provided both the wealth and the specialization necessary to advance research in medicine and to put into operation the new discoveries of Pasteur, Lister, Koch, and other European pioneers in bacteriology. The knowledge that bacteria caused many ailments which could be controlled through neutralization of the germs served in the popular mind to steady if not to control God's hand in disease and death. In 1896 a Yale scientist tried out Roentgen's epoch-making discovery of the X ray, and before the end of the century the no less important discovery of radium by the Curies inaugurated a new period in therapeutics. Thanks to all these and other innovations, in the decade of the 1890s the average mortality rate in the country fell nearly 10 percent and the expectancy of life rose from 31 to 35 years.

The countryside, hardly less than the city, experienced acute needs which stimulated scientific inquiry and control. The introduction in 1889 of the Australian ladybird beetle saved California's citrus crop from the devastating white scale. Experimentation sponsored by the the land-grant colleges and the Department of Agriculture in Washington provided new methods for the elimination of plant and animal diseases that had baffled farmers and encouraged them to fall back in despair on supernatural explanations. Each advance which knowledge of bacteria made in animal husbandry—the isolation and control of the germ causing Texas fever among cattle was but one—made it easier for country folk to put less stock in supernatural agencies. If the laboratory could not provide a formula to prevent the droughts that plagued the farmers on the parched western prairies, it could at least predict what might be expected. Such predictions of weather by means of scientific methods must likewise have helped to delimit the role of the supernatural in the minds of men and women on farms and in villages.

The foundations of orthodox belief in supernatural powers were being shaken by other things as well as by new ways of life and the knowledge which these evoked. In England, France, and Germany comparative philologists and scholars trained in the criticism of documents had long been applying themselves to a rigid examination of the texts of the Bible and to the whole problem of the relation of these texts to tested knowledge in various disciplines. These studies made it increasingly clear that Holy Writ had not originated in the way in which Christians who accepted it as literal truth had long believed. On the contrary, it was shown that the Bible was a compilation of a great variety of writings during a period of over a thousand years. The confusion and error in its pages simply did not square with the doctrine that it was the product of divine knowledge. Philologists demonstrated that language originated not in the babble of tongues created by the wrathful fiat of Jehovah but rather by a gradual process; the Hebrew tongue itself was clearly not a special creation but the product of the mingling of Semitic and non-Semitic tribes.

Scholars in the fields of anthropology and comparative religion demolished the Biblical account of the peculiar origin of the Hebraic-Christian faith. Their painstaking labors demonstrated that accounts of deluges, virgin births, crucifixions, and atonements were present in the religious writings of many peoples other than the Hebrews. In particular the scholarly exploration of the ancient religions of India which followed the British conquest, and the excavations of archeologists in Egypt, Babylonia, and elsewhere convinced many thoughtful scholars that what had been regarded as the unique features of Christianity were common to many other religions. That all these faiths had naturalistic rather than supernaturalistic origins seemed no less clear.

In considerable degree American theologians limited themselves to translating the findings of Continental scholars in the field of higher criticism and to synthesizing, interpreting, and popularizing the work of Old World colleagues. In this field no one did such distinguished service as Philip Schaff of the Union Theological Seminary. A *Commentary on the Holy Scriptures* (1865–1880), a twenty-five-volume work based on the studies of John P. Lange, and the *Religious Encyclopedia* (1882–1884), which rested on the scholarship of Herzog, Plitt, and Hauck, were important agencies for the transmission of the higher criticism. It will also be recalled that other immigrants, especially Jews, enriched American Old Testament scholarship. The revised version of the King James Bible which appeared in the 1880s was the result of the cooperative labors of American and English scholars. The Hebrew and the New Testament lexicons of Francis Brown and J. Henry Thayer were creditable achievements. In 1891 Professor Orello Cone, of the theological school at St. Lawrence University, published *Gospel-Criticism and Historical Christianity*, an original study that did honor to American scholarship. In the eyes of some of Europe's greatest authorities on higher criticism Cone's *Paul, the Man, the Missionary, and the Teacher* (1898) was the ablest monograph on its subject in any language. And in the field of comparative religion James Freeman Clarke's *Ten Great Religions* (1871) and the works of Arthur H. Smith and James S. Dennis found many readers.

These European and American contributions to the higher criticism and to comparative religion served to limit the area of supernaturalism, at first among the leaders, then among the masses. Professor William N. Clarke of Colgate University no doubt spoke for many when he wrote:

I may describe my forward step by saying that hitherto I had been using the Bible in the light of its statements, but that now I found myself using it in the light of its principles. . . . At first I said: "The Scriptures limit me to this"; later I said, "The Scriptures open my way to this." . . . As for the Bible, I am not bound to work all its statements into my system: nay, I am bound not to work them all in; for some of them are not congenial to the spirit of Jesus and some express truth in forms that cannot be of permanent validity.[2]

This general position of regarding the Bible as a source not of re-

[2] William N. Clarke, *Sixty Years with the Bible* (Charles Scribner's Sons, 1909), 97–98, 210–211, 120, 121.

vealed truth but rather as a literature rich in wisdom, a source of beauty, ethical guidance, and inspiration, won increasing acceptance. It is true that within the Presbyterian fold alone, during the years from 1883 to 1900, five liberal theologians were brought to trial for heresy by reason of the favor they showed toward the results of the higher criticism. Similar heresy trials and threatened trials likewise marked the annals of other denominations. But the tide was definitely turning by 1892. In that year Charles A. Briggs, a leading Presbyterian clergyman, was acquitted by the New York Presbytery for holding that "all *a priori* definition of inspiration is not only unscientific but irreverent, presumptuous, lacking in the humility with which we should approach a divine, supernatural fact." His critics appealed the decision of acquittal to a higher ecclesiastical body which in turn condemned him. But the victory was a hollow one; Briggs had found a welcome in the Episcopal Church, and the die-hards knew they were on the road to defeat.

Although millions of American Christians, especially among the poorer folk of villages and countryside, refused to abandon their faith in the literal meaning of Scripture, a growing number of laity as well as clergy came to doubt its infallibility. Within no less than a week after the publication of the revised New Testament over 200,000 copies were sold in New York City alone, and two of the principal newspapers of Chicago gave their readers the entire text. The popular reception of books like Washington Gladden's *Who Wrote the Bible?* (1891) further suggests that a great many were accepting the new position that the Bible was neither in origin nor in nature what had been traditionally believed. Still further evidence of the crumbling of the old dogmatism was provided by the vogue of such liberal religious novels as Margaret Deland's *John Ward, Preacher* and Mrs. Humphrey Ward's *Robert Elsmere,* both of which were best sellers in 1888. Hundreds of thousands even read or listened with sympathy to the great agnostic orator, Robert Ingersoll, who, more than any single person, disseminated in his own way the results of the higher criticism.

Another blow to supernaturalism in its specifically Christian form was the influx of a large group of professionally trained philosophers into the universities. Philosophy—which usually included such areas of study as psychology and even economics—was taught in most of the antebellum colleges by a minister and theologian who was normally a Scottish realist. The newer generation of philosophers, men like Josiah Royce,

George S. Morris, and George Trumbull Ladd, were idealists, strongly influenced by Hegelian and post-Hegelian German philosophy. Idealism always involves a kind of supernaturalism—in the broadest sense of the word—but the new philosophy was not so precisely Christian as the Scottish common-sense philosophy of James McCosh or Francis Wayland. The idealists defended "the Absolute," not the God of Protestant Christianity. When the German-trained thinkers replaced the more orthodox theologians in American colleges and universities, the league of Christianity and higher education was severely shaken.

### The Physical Universe

In 1851, just twenty years before publishing the *Linear Associative Algebra* which had much to do with Benjamin Peirce's reputation as the greatest of nineteenth-century American mathematicians, the Harvard scholar declared:

. . . in approaching the forbidden limits of human knowledge, it is becoming to tread with caution and circumspection. Man's speculations should be subdued from all rashness and extravagance in the immediate presence of the Creator. And a wise philosophy will beware lest it strengthen the arms of atheism, by venturing too boldly into so remote and obscure a field of speculation as that of the mode of Creation which was adopted by the Divine Geometer.[3]

The explorers of the secrets of the universe were indeed sufficiently awed by its mysteries to preserve circumspect reverence, and many maintained their own personal faith in theism. Nevertheless, the developments abroad in astronomy and in physics, developments to which Americans added some contributions of importance, did tend in several respects to delimit the area of supernaturalism.

In astronomy the researches of Herschel and Struve broke down the older belief that stars form stable systems in the sense in which the solar system is stable. It was clear, in other words, that the traditional Newtonian conception of a permanent scheme of movement of heavenly bodies in accord with fixed laws of gravitation no longer explained much

[3] Benjamin Peirce, "On the Constitution of Saturn's Ring," *The Astronomical Journal*, II (June 16, 1851), 19.

that astronomers had learned about the remoter heavens. The star clusters and the nebulae appeared to be fixed only in comparison with the brief years of man; in relation to their own long existence they too were as changing as human beings themselves. As astronomers tended to emphasize less the "old" astronomy of positions and to explore with new instruments and new mathematical formulas the physical structure of planets and stars, what had been pure speculation came to be precise knowledge. At the same time the Biblical conception of a fixed and final creation of the firmaments gave way to the evolutionary view.

In one way or another American astronomers contributed to the growing knowledge of the universe, to the newer views of the heavens. Edward C. Pickering, who took charge of the Harvard Observatory in 1877, recognized that physics held the key to the "new" astronomy of stellar structure and evolution; by his scale for fixing magnitude or the brightness of stars he was able to catalogue 40,000 stars. With John C. Draper and others, Pickering also did pioneer work in applying photography to the exploration and study of the heavens. In 1885 the Harvard Observatory began to chart the skies by making permanent photographic records, which, accumulated over the decades, provided rich data for studying not only the position but the composition, temperature, and physical conditions of thousands of suns. At the new Lick Observatory in California Edward E. Barnard began in 1889 to reveal through photography the intricate structure of the hitherto hazy and little-known Milky Way. Samuel P. Langley, of the Allegheny Observatory, used his bolometer (1878) to make spectral measurements of solar and lunar radiation; it was thus possible to calculate the distribution of heat in the spectrum of the sun and to determine the transparency of the atmosphere to the various solar rays. Simon Newcomb of the Smithsonian Institution, in addition to his famous studies of the moon's motion, explored the records of over 100,000 observations made in the principal observatories of the world since the year 1850. These and other data gave rise to new insights about the skies.

Astronomy was as never before affected by new developments in physics. In Europe the work of Helmholtz, Joule, and Lord Kelvin clarified hitherto vague ideas regarding the indestructibility of energy and the mutual convertibility of the forces of nature. In 1851 Lord Kelvin's statement of the principle of the conservation of energy was so plausibly argued that its general acceptance was foreordained. In the same paper he advanced the so-called second law of thermodynamics. According to this, the inevitable result of the fact that no new energy could be created was the ultimate dissipation, so far as the earth was concerned, of the sun's heat as it spread farther and farther into remote space.

The implications of these theories for supernaturalism were momentous. It appeared that physical force was indestructible and that matter was no less permanent. If neither force nor matter underwent change save in accord with definite laws, what became of the supernaturalistic faith in the priority of spirit and mind over matter? If in the infinitude of time and space natural laws governed both force and matter, there was little room for supernatural explanations of the origin and course of the universe. Moreover, the second law of thermodynamics seemed irreconcilable with Christian ethic. If total and endless eclipse set in when the sun's candle at length burned down to its socket, it was difficult to believe in an all-wise, all-provident Creator whose work was designed with man in mind and for His own perpetual glory. Samuel P. Langley, as if to answer such misgivings, did suggest in *The New Astronomy* (1888) that there might be something "more enduring than frail humanity," something higher than man with his limited sensations, limited experience, limited power of conceiving anything for which his experience had not prepared him. But any such suggested accommodation of Christian doctrine to the new physics could at best hardly fail to unsettle in men's minds the traditional faith in progress and providence, a faith for which Newton's tightly mechanistic system in its unmodified form provided.

Physicists not only advanced doctrines that increased faith in natural forces and in scientific law. They also continued to point to new ways in which man could control forces their fathers had regarded as beyond human reach. At Yale Willard Gibbs virtually laid the foundations for the science of chemical energetics or physical chemistry. His pioneer and unusually creative work in vector analysis, in statistical mechanics, and above all in the measurement of energy involved in the shifting variables and the achievement of a given equilibrium in homogeneous and heterogeneous substances canceled many mysteries of nature. In a great paper written in 1876 Gibbs advanced his famous Rule of Phase, a principle which provided a key for classifying the innumerable details in the behavior of "coexistent phases of matter," especially the relationships within a given equilibrium in a system. The discovery of the "chemical potential" and "the thermodynamic potential" or "the free energies" in the behavior of a system or portion of the material universe selected for considering the various changes taking place within it had momentous implications. Gibbs, who taught only a handful of advanced students and lived much apart from the main currents of American life, felt no sense of responsibility for putting his findings at the service of industrial enterprise or mankind in general. Nevertheless, his work ultimately made possible the more efficient management of mixed substances and a reduction in costs through the determination of the amount of necessary energy consumed in each stage of a process. On the basis of his work also rest significant developments in radioactivity, the theory of relativity, electrochemistry, colloid chemistry, and modern synthetics generally. Eminent European scientists hailed Gibbs as one of the leading creative scientists of the nineteenth century and much modern opinion supports that view.

If Gibbs, the little-known but most brilliant synthetic physicist in the America of his day, assumed little or no responsibility for applying his theories to human needs, one of his contemporaries at Johns Hopkins, Henry A. Rowland, was less indifferent. Having advanced the modern theory of electrons while experimenting in Helmholtz's laboratory in 1876, Rowland explored in Baltimore the relation of terrestrial magnetism to the rotation of the earth. His measurements for the mechanical equivalent of heat and his designs for dynamos and transformers showed that physicists no less than other scientists might work with conscious reference to a definite economic and technological milieu. In 1896, Samuel Langley flew a power-driven heavier-than-air model for a distance of some three thousand feet. Before long—in 1903—the Wright brothers demonstrated at Kitty Hawk, North Carolina, the entire practicability of man's control over the air. By replacing the eagle as king of the air man again triumphed over what had long been regarded as a fixed and final obstacle.

The most startling revelations in physics were to come in the twentieth century. Nevertheless, Albert A. Michelson's direct optical proof of the existence of molecules, his new theory of light, and the measurement of its velocity heralded much that was to come. In 1878 Michelson published the first of his epoch-making researches. With the aid of his newly invented interferometer he measured vast distances by means of the length of light waves without reference to the source or the observer. In 1881 this wizard measurer of hitherto incalculable distances determined cosmic motions to the extent of reporting on the absolute motion of the earth as it followed the sun's course through space. This was to enable scientists to measure accurately the diameter of incredibly remote stars. All this, more fully developed by Einstein's fertile mind, was a point of departure for the theory of relativity.

These ideas, together with the findings of Darwin, affected geological studies. The fact-finding geologists, working under the auspices of the states and the United States Geological Survey (1879), continued to fill in the larger outlines of knowledge. The work of Thomas C. Chamberlin and others modified the older theory of glaciation by establishing the high probability that not one but at least five great glacial periods had formed the earth's surface. But this was less startling to traditionalists than the "planetesimal hypothesis" which Chamberlin, a professor at the University of Chicago, advanced in germ form in 1897. According to this theory the earth owed its birth to the disruption of the sun on the approach of some other star, with the consequent expulsion of an amorphous mass out of which ultimately the earth was formed as an incalculable number of minute particles swirled about in the sun's orbit until final coalescence. Even if not fully accepted, this theory, together with Chamberlin's investigation of the evolution of geological climates and of the atmosphere, threw into an entirely new and startling perspective much about which the ignorant had been dogmatic or indifferent and the learned vague and mystical.

### Darwinism

If the higher criticism, the study of comparative religions, and the new astronomy, physics, and geology were slowly undermining the fortress of supernaturalism, the doctrine of organic evolution was an even more devastating force. By the time Darwin's *Origin of Species* appeared in 1859, the more intelligent and well trained among the theologically minded, together with most natural scientists, had accepted the implications of Lyell's geological studies: the earth had not been made in seven days but had developed over eons of time. (Henry Adams remarked that Lyell had completely wrecked the Garden of Eden!) Lyell had indeed been useful in preparing for the doctrine of organic evolution. Neverthe-less Darwin's theories, the culmination of a trend of thought long in motion, proved far more upsetting to traditional supernaturalism than Lyell's conclusions regarding the age of the earth.

By marshaling overwhelming evidence against the reality of fixed species Darwin and his school took the props from under the super-natural belief that man was especially created by God in His image. If Darwinism was true, the wall between the animal kingdom and the human realm broke down altogether. If organic evolution was accepted, the Bible was wrong in holding that man had fallen from an elevated state; rather he had slowly, almost imperceptibly ascended from simple animal origins. If man evolved through natural selection, if survival and adaptation, variation and struggle governed the course of development, it was hard to believe that an all-wise and all-beneficent Creator had presided over a single act of creation. Since in the theological argument from design plants and animals were the strongest adaptive links in the chain of design, the concepts of mutation of species, struggle, adaptation, and survival seemed to annihilate the whole conception of design.

But the conflict between evolution and supernaturalism was even more profound. The whole a priori method of arriving at truth which men had long cherished must, it was felt, go by the board if Darwinism were accepted. Moreover, Darwinism threatened to take from the faith-ful all sense of security just when security was desperately needed in a civilization rapidly shifting from a rural to an industrial and urban basis. The foundations of life seemed to be crumbling. If Darwinism repre-sented a new cornerstone, it was a cornerstone that seemed to make life a mere variant of matter without mystery or spiritual meaning.

In view of the hold of religious values on almost all Americans, in-cluding naturalists and scientists, it is little wonder that Darwinism at first met with general rebuff. It is true that the sturdiest and most authoritative opponent, Louis Agassiz, did muster scientific arguments against the doctrine of organic evolution. He pointed out, for instance, that not all primitive organs are simple or explicable in terms of gradual development. But underlying his opposition to Darwinism was his earlier rejection—partly on philosophical grounds—of Lamarckianism, a pre-Darwinian theory of evolution that emphasized the inheritance of acquired characteristics. In his *Essay on Classification* (1857) Agassiz had insisted that the great diversity of species resulted from the repeated creations of God after succeeding cataclysms which set off one geological age from another, and that the species, being the thoughts of God, were immutable. To his death in 1873 he refused to accept the new teachings of Darwin.

Loyalty to religion partly explained the opposition of James Dwight Dana, holder of the British Royal Society's Copley Prize and America's leading geologist. A deeply religious man who reverenced the sublime mysteries in nature, Dana found the best evidences of an all-comprehending Creator in the doctrine that God had planned and evolved the organic kingdom step by step in accordance with a prearranged design. Only gradually did he modify this position. In fact, it was not until the final edition of his famous *Manual of Geology* (1895) that he accepted Darwinism without reservation. Other religious-minded scientists were deterred from avowing the new doctrine by reason of predilection for the supernatural. President Barnard of Columbia College, a distinguished scientist, wrote in 1873 that the existence of God and the immortality of the soul could not be maintained if organic evolution were true.

The influence of religious faith and values explains the tendency of the first scientists who accepted Darwinism to insist that it was not at all incompatible with the divine creation and governance of the universe. Asa Gray, the distinguished Harvard botanist with whom Darwin had corresponded before the *Origin of Species* appeared, quickly brushed aside his first doubts and qualifications and became the outstanding scientific champion of the new doctrine. But Gray was a devout Christian, and always maintained that Darwinism did no substantial harm to Christianity. In his first essays on the subject, which appeared in the *Atlantic Monthly* in 1860, Gray made a great point of the argument that natural selection was not inconsistent with natural theology. In contending that natural selection did not exclude the doctrine of design, in arguing that in consequence the new position was not identical with skepticism and materialism, Gray did enormous service to Darwinism. More than anything else the weight of his authority made it possible for scientists with religious views to accept the doctrine. Among other scientists who took up Gray's idea that Omnipotent fiat did not exclude the development theory and secondary causes, George Frederick Wright, a geologist at Oberlin, was especially important. Wright, who was a minister as well as a geologist, popularized Gray's interpretation of Darwinism far and wide among orthodox believers. So too did Alexander Winchell at Ann Arbor and Joseph Le Conte at Berkeley.

One by one liberal theological leaders accepted the position that evolution was in harmony with the essentials of Christian faith. Henry Ward Beecher's espousal of this point of view was of incalculable importance, for no minister commanded so wide a hearing. In *Evolution and Religion* (1885) the great Brooklyn preacher declared that evolution was merely "the deciphering of God's thought as revealed in the structure of the world."[4] What Beecher preached in metropolitan New York, Washington Gladden preached in Ohio. In Boston Phillips Brooks, the revered and popular rector of Trinity Church, spoke less of evolution; but in serenely refusing to be upset by it, in teaching that even if it were true it in no way militated against Christ's message, he did his part in making it possible for the faithful to accept it.

But it was not only the liberal or Protestant leaders of religion who came to terms with evolutionary theory. James McCosh, the crusty old leader of Presbyterianism at Princeton, found in evolution certain elements that were congenial to his neo-Calvinist conception of God and nature. He accepted the general notion of natural selection, interpreting each minute variation within species as "special providences" of God. As McCosh summed it up, "Supernatural design produces natural selection." McCosh also picked up the element of struggle and tragedy in Darwinism and identified it with the similar aspects of the Christian moral struggle. " 'The whole creation groaneth and travaileth in pain together until now,' " McCosh quoted his Bible. "Our academic theists were refusing to look at our world under this aspect. Even some of our sentimental Christians were turning away from it. It is a curious circumstance that it is science that has recalled our attention to it."[5] Within the Catholic Church, Father John Zahm, vice-president of Notre Dame University and author of several volumes on science and religion, urged American Catholics to follow the lead of their European brethren by denying that the evolutionary hypothesis was necessarily opposed to revealed Christianity.

In 1887 Henry Drummond, a British scientist and evangelical Christian, well known for his *Natural Law in the Spiritual World*, lectured at Chautauqua as well as in the principal colleges and universities. Drummond preached the essential identity of evolution and Christianity.

---

[4] Henry Ward Beecher, *Evolution and Religion* (Fords, Howard and Hulbert, 1885), 45–46.

[5] Quoted in Herbert W. Schneider, *A History of American Philosophy* (Columbia University Press, 1946), 371.

Both, he insisted, had the same Author, the same spirit, the same end; Christianity adopted man's body, mind, and soul at the exact point at which organic evolution had brought them, and then carried on the building by the gradual spiritual process which was putting the finishing touches on the ascent of man.

The chief credit for reconciling theism and evolution and for popularizing the results belongs to John Fiske. From the time when this young philosopher delivered his Harvard lectures on evolution in 1869, until his death, he spared no pains in trying to convince his countrymen that evolution was immanent in the plan of the universe, that it was God's way of achieving His divine purposes. Fiske's *Outlines of Cosmic Philosophy* (1874), in which he advanced these views, went through sixteen editions. His even more pointed and popular later books put him in the front rank of the reconcilers of faith and science. In these he made natural law clearly purposive, man's spiritual evolution the unquestioned goal of all development past and present, and the cosmos itself theistic. The Reverend Lyman Abbott, Beecher's successor, rendered Fiske's somewhat roseate interpretation of evolution even more fashionable.

In their own ways other scholars helped to accommodate Christian thought to the doctrine of evolution. By showing that Christianity's stubborn opposition throughout history to every scientific innovation had on the whole been futile, John William Draper and Andrew D. White took much ground from under the feet of those who fought Darwinism. The Cornell president's *History of the Warfare of Science with Theology in Christendom* (1896) was widely read and no doubt convinced many critics of evolution that continued opposition would be not only useless in the long run but actually harmful to organized Christianity. Yet in spite of the growing acceptance among liberal Christians of the Darwinian teachings, many, especially in rural areas, resolutely refused to have any traffic with the new doctrines. Even in the twentieth century four or five states tried by law to prohibit the teaching of evolution as established truth in public schools and colleges. As late as 1925 William Jennings Bryan attracted world-wide attention in a trial of a teacher at Dayton, Tennessee, by upholding the Scriptural account of creation. But this was a back eddy in the mainstream.

The reconciliation of evolution and religion was not, of course, the only factor in the victory of Darwinism. Certain able champions of evolution defended it without any reference at all to the necessity or desirability of harmonizing it with Christian thought. Chauncey Wright, of Cambridge, Massachusetts, in an article in the *North American Review* in 1865 clearly distinguished between the nature of scientific and of religious ideas and gave priority to the former. In 1870 this remarkable scholar published the first of a series of highly important papers on natural selection, its applications and implications. Darwin expressed high appreciation of the originality and significance of Wright's studies.

Many scientists, with little or no reference to the battle between naturalism and supernaturalism, modestly pursued researches which provided new evidence for the Darwinian hypothesis. At Yale Professor O. C. Marsh arranged a collection of fossils in such a way that few who saw the exhibit would doubt that the horse, at least, had evolved from simpler forms. Indeed, Marsh's impressive specimens of dinosaurs, toothless birds, reptiles, and mammoths won enthusiastic praise from Darwin for their contribution toward taking evolution from the hypothetical realm and establishing it as a scientific truth. Marsh's great rival, Edward Cope of Philadelphia, deviated from Darwinism by supporting a Lamarckian brand of evolutionary theory, but his indefatigable labors in collecting fossils in the West and his amazing study of the evolution of the camel in reality supported the Darwinian theory. Dozens of other scientists made their contribution to Darwinism by patiently reexamining the traditional classifications in the plant and animal kingdoms and re-arranging them to accord with the theory of descent and selection. In the field of applied botany as well as in laboratory studies of embryology, morphology, and physiology, and in studies of the geographical distribution of plants and animals, American scientists provided fresh evidences for the Darwinian theory. None of them gave so dramatic a demonstration of the theory as Luther Burbank. In 1875 he began at his nursery in California to develop new forms of plant life and to improve well-known varieties by selecting superior strains and using cross-fertilizing and grafting techniques.

In still other ways the doctrine of evolution was spread without special reference to its compatibility with religion. The lectures of the visiting English scientist, Thomas Huxley, did much to familiarize Americans with purely naturalistic arguments. So too did the teachings of Herbert Spencer. Long before Spencer's visit in 1882, John Fiske, William Graham Sumner, and Edward Livingston Youmans had been acquainting Americans with the great exponent of evolutionary philosophy. The crusade did much, in spite of certain metaphysical implications in Spencer's thought, to weaken faith in supernaturalism. Youmans especially popularized the evolutionary position. He made available to American readers the great scientific classics of contemporary Europe, he wrote useful and popular scientific textbooks, he lectured hither and yon, and he founded and for many years edited the *Popular Science Monthly*, a periodical which carried the message of evolution into many corners.

The doctrine of organic evolution spread fairly rapidly among the well-educated members of the well-to-do and middle classes. No doubt Darwinism found acceptance in part at least because it provided a rationale for a rapidly changing way of life. To thoughtful men it became increasingly clear that the doctrine had in fact long been heralded, that it was a part of a long naturalistic tradition. By these men and their followers Darwin was accepted with a sense of high excitement; he was another guide to the bright world of reason which they and their forebears had long been seeking. Darwinism reduced the irrational, absolutistic, and transcendental elements in philosophy, in life itself. If some lamented the loss of faith in supernaturalism which it brought, others rejoiced in their sense of new-found power as human beings.

Thus when man began to account for his own origins in naturalistic terms; when he began to describe the chemical and physical composition of the planets, the sun, and the Milky Way; when he devised instruments to measure the velocity of light and the distances of heavenly bodies; when he probed into the mysteries of the earth's origin and that of solar systems remote from his own, then indeed he had proceeded far on his way toward solving the mystery of the universe. He had not, he knew, grasped the ultimate mysteries, but he had vastly reduced the scope of supernaturalism and enlarged the horizons of knowledge. Even more important, he had achieved new perspectives, invented instruments of incalculable potentialities, and even formulated new conceptions of the nature of knowledge and of reality itself.

# 22  Impact of Evolutionary Thought on Society

*I must deem any man very shallow in his observation of the facts of life and utterly lacking in the biological sense, who fails to discern in competition the force to which it is mainly due that mankind has risen from stage to stage, in intellectual, moral, and physical power.*

—FRANCIS A. WALKER, 1890

The impact of science and above all of the new biology of Darwin and his disciples profoundly altered ideas about man's mind and society in the last quarter of the nineteenth century and the first decades of the twentieth. It would be too much to say that the basic conceptions of life were transformed by the influence of natural science; the vast intellectual shifts were at first of course merely suggested by pioneer scholars, European and American, and only gradually penetrated the world of learning. But thanks to the agencies for popularizing knowledge, the new ideas had begun, by the opening of the First World War, to make some impression even on the minds of the plain people.

In spite of traditional supernaturalism the American environment provided congenial soil for the growth of the scientific and evolutionary point of view. On the whole the United States lacked the rigidly fixed system of ancient traditions and institutions which in older societies directed thinking toward the past rather than toward a future which men might themselves shape. American life, largely mobile because of the frontier experience, the shift of population to urban centers, and the incoming of throngs of immigrants, suggested that there was little indeed

540

that was fixed and final. The rapidly growing technological character of the culture, like the traditional frontier experience, further suggested that ordinary affairs and everyday life were in constant process of remaking. Moreover, the fact that men had visibly and within the memory of two or three generations actually created so much of the physical culture of the country suggested the unfinished character of the experiment. All these reasons, then, help explain why the scientific and especially the evolutionary position, emphasizing as it did the long-favored doctrine of progress, the power of man to reconstruct society, and a generally optimistic faith in the future, found congenial soil in America.

## The Science of the Mind

Nowhere was the impact of the new science more revolutionary than in the field of psychology. In 1870 learned men regarded the human mind much as it had been viewed for centuries. Individual minds were all presumably patterned after a universal type; mind was specially created to set human kind off from the other creatures; it existed separately from the body, "parallel" to corresponding bodily activities but made of different stuff; and it was in the main considered from a static rather than an evolutionary standpoint. It could be studied with success and profit by "armchair" introspective methods. These were leading doctrines of the times.

While these traditional views of mind prevailed in the United States the objective technique for studying mental life was making great headway in Wundt's laboratory in Leipzig. It had begun to dawn on Wundt and a few other pioneers that mental activity must be studied not as mind but as minds, and that sensations could be measured and understood in scientific terms. The influence of physics and physiology on the study of mental phenomena was transforming psychology into a natural science.

While no one can dispute the contribution of Wundt's American disciples in establishing objective techniques for the study of mind and divorcing mental phenomena from teleological and supernatural characteristics, the same end was even more strikingly promoted by the gifted pioneers working within the Darwinian scheme of things. In both the

*Origin of Species* and the *Descent of Man* Darwin himself had provided striking evidence for viewing the behavior or mind of the animal as the product of long growth. He pointed to considerations suggesting that the esthetic and moral no less than the intellectual capacities have in man a natural not a miraculous history; that they are subject to variation and natural selection in much the same way as man's bodily structure, to which, indeed, these mental phenomena are closely related. By showing the resemblance of infant behavior to that of animals and by correlating emotions with bodily expressions, Darwin made the study of man's mind a part of the study of nature. He had a far-reaching influence on the founders of a new biological psychology. Spencer also contributed to the evolutionary point of view in the study of mental phenomena, and his influence in the United States was to be widespread.

Under the general Darwinian influence the pioneers of the new psychological orientation in the United States viewed the mind as part of nature, to be studied and understood in relation to other phenomena and to man's own evolutionary past just as the stars, atoms, tissues, and cells were studied and understood. These students of the mind showed that, as in other areas, so in the mental, the same cause produces the same effect.

The direction of this biological evolutionary tendency was clear in the contribution that Chauncey Wright made to a naturalistic explanation of self-consciousness, a trait commonly held to be the feature distinguishing the human from the animal mind. Wright, a Cambridge disciple of Darwin, a pioneer in developing a tychistic conception of nature and a pragmatic theory of experience, undertook in an article published in the *North American Review* in 1873 to explain the appearance of self-consciousness. Self-consciousness, according to him, may have been involved potentially in preexisting powers; in the evolutionary process it could have arisen as an adaptation of existing powers to new uses. The development of this naturalistic explanation of the genesis of self-consciousness was achieved in the spirit of Wright's conception of a philosophy of science which enabled him to use scientific facts and laws as instruments for the discovery of new truths.

Although G. Stanley Hall, George Trumbull Ladd, James M. Baldwin, and E. L. Thorndike were to contribute materially to developing the evolutionary conception of the human mind, the real pioneers were William James and John Dewey. In the psychological field James's work, the monumental *Principles of Psychology* (1890), was far more systematic and extensive than Dewey's. Each, moreover, approached psychology from different backgrounds and by different roads. James was a student of medicine and biology, as well as of the British empiricists; Dewey had been a close student of the post-Kantians, and especially of Hegel. James, while not a thoroughgoing experimentalist, did make some firsthand investigations and approached the problem of personality from the modern clinical point of view. Dewey was not, in the technical sense, an experimenter, though he closely observed children in learning situations. Although the psychological theories of the two differed in various respects, they may nevertheless be conveniently treated together.

The traditional conception of the mind as something only indirectly and remotely connected with the body was rejected. The whole conscious field was regarded as a function of the nervous system. Both emotional and problem-solving factors in so-called thinking were given a new and highly significant role. Mind, in other words, became a function of living. The conception of mind as an instrument that enabled the organism to adjust to its environment or even to transform it was novel and far-reaching in its implications; the ability of any organism, including man, to survive rested on its capacity to maintain an ever-shifting equilibrium or adjustment with its environment. To maintain this equilibrium, either the organism or the environment had to be "adjusted"; both organism and environment might be adjusted or readjusted at the same time. The selection of blind or random impulses that worked most effectively in achieving the equilibrium became the basis of learning. Mind was, so to speak, a function of the adjustment of the organism to its environment. The impulses or movements by which the organism adjusted itself to its shifting environment became fixed in habit systems, of which James wrote in the *Principles of Psychology* in a characteristically spirited and engaging way. Meantime his pupil, Edward L. Thorndike, was carrying out experiments in animal learning which provided telling evidence for the new conception of mind.

The influence of Darwin on the concept of ideas was also plain. Ralph Barton Perry has clearly demonstrated that James's conception of the a priori factors in human knowledge was an application of the Darwinian concept of a spontaneous or accidental variation; whether individual variations are great or small, they survive or disappear as their environment, roughly speaking, determines. In Dewey the emphasis was different, but the essential relationship was the same. Thoughts, which Dewey roughly defined as plans of action or as imaginative projections of possible lines of action derived from previous experience in achieving an equilibrium or adjustment, came to be regarded not as something "separate and self-sufficing" but as an essential part of the process by which life is evolved and sustained. This conception of ideas was basic to the new philosophy largely associated with James and Dewey. It not only basically altered conceptions of child training and education, it revolutionized the conception of the mind itself. As Thorndike put it graphically: "Among the minds of animals that of man is the chief, but also kinsman; ruler, but also brother. . . . Among the minds of animals that of man leads, not as a demigod from another planet, but as a king from the same race."[1]

The religiously orthodox, of course, objected to the "materialistic" implications of such a conception of the human mind. It shocked Catholics and orthodox Protestants alike. Exponents of the evolutionary position tried to show that the biological conception of mind was not incompatible with religious and spiritual values. Fiske, in extending the doctrine of evolution to all psychical phenomena, at the same time took care to make the psychic activities stand outside, rather than within, the circuit of the nervous system. A more successful reconciliation, even if unacceptable to the most devout, was proposed by Octavius B. Frothingham, the historian of Transcendentalism and, with Francis Abbot, the promoter of a new humanistic, naturalistic concept of religious and ethical values. In his *Religion of Humanity* (1872) Frothingham maintained that the doctrine of the evolution of the mind compressed all power within the compass of human attributes. It made the race its own provider, its own reformer, its own savior. The source of moral power no longer stood outside the race like the traditional providence, sending down inspiration into it; standing within actual human beings, moral power grew by the use and development of its own human faculties. Thus limits were set to the disappointment felt in the inadequate achievements of a human nature allegedly divine. In fact, the biological origin of mind actually in some cases confirmed rather than lessened optimism and faith in man's power to effect progress; after all, had not great headway on the long journey from the world of the lower animals already been made?

[1] Edward L. Thorndike, "The Evolution of the Human Intellect," *Popular Science Monthly*, LX (November, 1901), 65.

## Pragmatism and Instrumentalism

The new spirit of natural science, especially Darwinian biology, re-shaped fundamental philosophical conceptions at the same time that traditional notions about the mind were being replaced by naturalistic ones. John Dewey, in calling attention to the influence of Darwin on philosophy, wrote that for 2000 years the familiar furniture of the mind assumed the superiority of the fixed and the final, the unreality and defectiveness of all conceptions of origin and change. But once the full implications of evolution were grasped, all ideas and values were to be thought of in terms of origin and process; it then became natural to view life itself as an experiment, the physical order as the result of a natural selection that had given no signs of ending.

Perhaps the point of departure for this development, which was characteristically but not uniquely American and which came to be known as pragmatism, instrumentalism, and experimentalism, was a general position implicit in Darwinism and made explicit by Chauncey Wright. According to this disciple of the great naturalist, most of the philosophical puzzles if not all of them might be reduced to unseen ambiguities of terms, since all the ends of life are within, rather than without, the actual sphere of life itself. Wright also remarked at a discussion group in Cambridge, which included William James and Charles S. Peirce, that the Newtonian experimental philosopher always translates general propositions into prescriptions for obtaining new experimental facts. This remark was a clue for Peirce, who, as he put it, had already developed the "laboratory habit of mind."

Peirce developed the suggestions of the Cambridge discussion group, his practical experience as a scientist, and his gleanings from Kant and from medieval thought into a complex and even systematic philosophy. In many respects, Peirce was not a Pragmatist at all—at least in the sense in which James and Dewey were Pragmatists. He began his career as a philosopher with prolonged daily study of Kant's critical idealism. He was also influenced profoundly by the medieval realist, Duns Scotus. And Peirce always tried to dissociate himself from the British empirical tradition of Locke and John Stuart Mill. His concepts of truth and reality, viewed within the context of his philosophy as a whole, have a distinctly un-Pragmatic cast. They look forward always to the presumed existence of an abstract "community" of intelligent beings in an indefinite future. In the short run, and strictly speaking, there is no truth and no reality. James and Dewey, by contrast, were temperamentally bound up in the immediate. Philosophy and science were not for them, as they were for Peirce, oriented toward a community indefinitely distant in time, but toward the more pressing problems of men here and now. It was these profound differences which led Peirce to discountenance James's formulation of Pragmatism and to try to reassert his own under the title "Pragmaticism."

In spite of their differences, Peirce had a strong effect on James's thought, and he formulated concepts that helped shape the development of Pragmatism as a body of thought. To begin with, Peirce rejected any sort of mechanistic and deterministic analysis of nature. Chance, for Peirce, was one of the essential characteristics of the universe. Thus evolution could be creative, and no state of affairs, no so-called eternal laws, could finally define the world or limit the possibilities of further change. He also developed the conception of the love of parents for their children and of thinkers for their ideas as creative causes of evolution. Thus Peirce forecast James's conception of the "open universe." What held true of the universe must also be true of men's knowledge of it. If there was validity in Wright's remark that general propositions are to be translated into prescriptions for attaining new experimental facts, then there could never be a "last analysis," nor any conclusion above criticism and revision.

In addition to this general attitude toward nature and knowledge, Peirce contributed specific maxims to Pragmatism. The most important of these was probably his concept of meaning, first spelled out at length in a paper in the *Popular Science Monthly* of 1878, "How to Make Our Ideas Clear." Peirce rejected traditional tests for the clarity and meaning of ideas, and substituted this famous definition of meaning: "Consider what effects, which might conceivably have practical bearings, we conceive the object of our conception to have. Then our conception of these effects is the whole of our conception of the object." Thus no idea could have any a priori or transcendental meaning independently of activity. In a spirit that became characteristic of Pragmatism, Peirce maintained that "the whole function of thought is to produce habits of action . . . and there is no distinction of meaning so fine as to consist in anything but a possible difference of practice." For him a pragmatic definition must be in terms of social communication; logic was a theory of signs, but a social-biological as well as a purely mathematical theory of signs. Even without an understanding of Peirce's efforts to reconcile free will and fate, the general and the particular, metaphysics and empiricism, it is possible to grasp the essence of his method, which is of fundamental importance to the logic of pragmatic philosophy. To the traditional classes of logic, deduction and inference, he added the concept of the hypothesis as basic in logic. In enlarging logic to include the traditional faculties of "imagination" and "originality" he extended the boundaries of its essentially static field.

While Peirce rejected any method of making ideas clear that tested their consequences in terms of particular or personal ends, William James, who was much influenced by him, emphasized the personal or emotional satisfaction which an idea provided. The influence of his Swedenborgian father and his own emotional dissatisfaction with "materialism" accentuated in his mind the limitations of the traditional empiricism which rested on sense experience alone. In the spirit of the pragmatist and experimentalist James tried to push empiricism to more radical lengths by giving the *connections* between sense experience a psychological status on a par with whatever was actually connected. Thus people's thoughts about things were important, were data, in themselves. This, together with James's emphasis on the emotional or personal satisfactions that any idea gave any person confronted by problems in life's endless and risky struggle, led him to regard religious experience as "true" if and when it "worked," if and when its consequences to the individual conformed to what the individual expected. But in thinking of any idea, even of any supernatural idea, as true if it enabled the individual to deal satisfactorily with concrete experiences, James did not at all go back on the scientific and evolutionary character of his philosophy; any idea "true" at any given time for a given person might not be true for others, or even for that person under different circumstances.

Thus even so-called supernatural ideas which were "true" by virtue of their effects were merely ideas on trial, instruments subject to constant retesting in the hazardous experiment which all life in essence really was. And James's conception of "the open universe," his emphasis on "the unfinished experiment," his opposition to any and all dogmatisms, including scientific dogmatisms, and his view of all life, of the whole universe, as an effect of progressive selection, all these meant that he operated within the evolutionary, naturalistic framework. As Morris

Cohen has remarked, he restored "the fluidity and connectedness of our world without admitting the necessity for the idealists' transcendental glue to keep together the discrete elements of experience."[2]

John Dewey was influenced by the Cambridge psychologist and philosopher and in turn influenced him. Dewey developed in precise yet comprehensive logical terms the pragmatic theory of knowledge. Conceiving of ideas not merely in terms of biological function, he also emphasized their instrumental character as applied in society. In Dewey's thought the philosopher must assume the serious responsibility of clarifying public rather than personal incongruities, conflicts, and issues. The rule of logical method which pragmatism originally was, and the personal and emotional emphasis which James gave it, were now expanded into a fundamental law of social practice and growth. Both James and Dewey emphasized, in the evolutionary spirit, the unfinished character of society and the universe. James viewed these, in Santayana's phrase, as "wild and young." But Dewey also laid stress on the potentiality of remaking for the better both man and society through the planned application of the experimental method of testing ideas on the larger stage of social issues.

While James makes room for the truth of the supernatural if it provides personal emotional satisfactions, Dewey regards the naturalistic account of the origin of ideas (plans for solving problems) as incompatible with the supernaturalism latent in traditional philosophic idealism and in conventional religion. James is certainly American in his emphasis on individualism, on risk, freedom, and progress through insuring opportunity for the ideas of the minority to have their chance. Dewey is no less American in his emphasis on the public and democratic test of the validity of programs, and his view of physical nature and social environment as material to be molded by intelligence to man's will. Above all, he is American in the central relationship between his democratic ideas and the American democratic tradition, in his vision of America as a way of life in which opportunities for participation in common tasks and the enjoyment of the fruits of common labor are shared.

In some respects Dewey stems from the eighteenth-century philosophers of the Enlightenment; like some of them he conceives of human

---

[2] William Peterfield Trent, et al. (eds.), The Cambridge History of American Literature (G. P. Putnam's Sons, 1917–1921), III, 251.

nature as plastic in character and capable of improvement through improved social environment. But through his conceptions of the individual and the group, and of the role of education in promoting social change, he amplified the eighteenth-century view and concretely related it to the new science of the later nineteenth century. For Dewey neither animals nor man face their environment and their struggle alone; most go down or survive in groups. In a constitutive way the group influences the individual. To put it differently, the individual is the microcosm of which the enveloping group is the macrocosm. The individual and the group of the future might be reciprocally changed by intelligently selecting from the group values those likely to achieve the results desired, the selection to be constantly tested by results.

This was the psychological and philosophical basis for Dewey's educational program. By the middle of the 1890s he was demonstrating, in his experimental school at the University of Chicago, how a new type of education far removed from traditional schoolroom practice might promote two interdependent values—the growth of full individuality in all and a more democratic society. These goals were to be promoted by selecting for emphasis methods designed to develop multiple leadership, the full flowering of each personality, and cooperative habits through group attacks on common problems.

The progressive education movement reflected more, indeed, than the application of pragmatism and instrumentalism to education. It reflected the direct impact of the doctrine of evolution itself. This doctrine undermined the traditional conception of human nature as something "bad," the "will" of the child as something to be "broken" by harsh discipline. Evolutionary doctrine did not view the youthful mind as an adult mind in miniature, subject to the same drives and discipline as the minds of mature men and women. In addition to the doctrine of evolution, other philosophical concepts fed the stream of the philosophy of progressive education. Felix Adler, pioneer in the Ethical Culture movement, Colonel Francis Parker of Quincy, Massachusetts, and Chicago, and Ella Flagg Young, also of Chicago, contributed ethical, social, and pedagogical ideas to progressive education. Yet Dewey, who specifically applied the instrumentalist philosophy to education, was the real father of the movement. Above all, education was always for him a more comprehensive process than that implied in his concept of school and society; it was in reality instrumentalist philosophy clarifying ideas by pointing out how the conflicts involved in them might be resolved through the experimental attack.

Nor did the pragmatic and instrumentalist position leave untouched traditional concepts of fixity and absolute law in the realm of esthetics. Just as the mind and philosophic ideas were reconsidered from a relativistic and experimental point of view, so too was the esoteric realm of esthetics. Some of Darwin's English followers had emphasized the relation of esthetic principles to sex competition. Spencer had sought an explanation for esthetic ideas in a compound of nature and society in which art was associated not only with utilitarianism but with a useless yet pleasurable exercise of energy known commonly as play. All this paved the way for such experimentalists as Fechner, who introduced the laboratory study of esthetic principles, and for the instrumentalists in the United States, who looked on beauty from a functional point of view. Until the period of World War I, esthetics for the most part remained under the spell of the older philosophic idealism and the conception of art for art's sake, but the new point of view had been slowly gaining strength.

Although Dewey's precursors in the functional or instrumental conception of esthetics did not in all instances owe to the new science their approach to the problem of beauty, they were influenced or at least strengthened by it. Walt Whitman found in Darwin support for his theory that no part of life can be separated from any other part or from the whole, and that new substructures of society demand corresponding new decorative effects functional to the total structure. In *Democratic Vistas* he urged that American letters and art must express and advance the values that constituted the essence of American democracy—youth, bold adventure, "a healthy rudeness," cosmic breadth, and faith in the average man.

Influenced both by Whitman and by Darwin and Spencer, Louis H. Sullivan fairly early in his career as an architect formulated the creed that art, in addition to being founded on the scientific method, must liberate man's creative powers from the spell of tradition and authority that he may live more truly, more abundantly, more in accord with the natural order of which he is a part. What Sullivan felt and partly realized, Frank Lloyd Wright carried much further. His conception of organic architecture functional to the needs of a changing culture, his conviction that a building must be part of its surroundings and that everything in it must be appropriate to its functions definitely reflected the influence of the evolutionary outlook.

Artists increasingly deserted traditional forms, left their cloisters, worked in the laboratories of scientists to learn through experiment the true functions of light and color, and attempted to find a living, organic, functional art in new relationships of angles, surfaces, forms, and lines.

A quarter of a century after the first modernistic exhibition in New York in 1913, John Dewey at last systematized the esthetic principles of the instrumentalist philosophy. He showed how and why exponents and practitioners of the fine arts had come to deprecate the practical arts, to reject any positive and intimate association of the fine arts with the normal processes of living. In Dewey's mind this was a pathetic and tragic commentary both on artists and on the life actually lived day by day by ordinary men and women. The tendency of traditional esthetics to elevate ideal above and beyond sense had made art pallid and bloodless; art, true art, proves the realized and therefore "realizable union of material and ideal."

It is true that older views of esthetics as well as of the nature of ideas and of education continued to be maintained not only in the smaller Christian colleges but in the great universities. Authorities on esthetics did not share the views of Dewey, Sullivan, and Wright in any large measure. It is certainly true that the vast majority of people in the cities and towns and on the farms continued to look on art and literature as mere decoration rather than essential elements in their lives; the way of life of these people of course conditioned such an outlook far more than traditional esthetic ideas. The men and women who directed American schools were, until the World War I, far more influenced by the Hegelian idealism of William T. Harris and the Herbartianism of the McMurry brothers than they were by William James's *Talks to Teachers* and John Dewey's *School and Society*.

Nevertheless, Darwinism and modern science had exposed traditional conceptions of esthetics, ethics, ideas, and mind itself to profound change. The absolute in every field of philosophy tended little by little to give way to the relative, the supernatural to the natural. The ancient conflict between mind and matter, the real and the ideal, between particulars and generals, was resolved in the writings of the pragmatists and instrumentalists by making "function the essential problem and emergence the norm." The old walls were beginning to crumble.

## Social Studies

The newer concept of evolution, adaptation, function, and survival made itself felt in the disciplines concerned with social relationships no less than in psychological and philosophical fields. As late as 1880, when Bancroft was putting the finishing touches on his great *History of the United States*, the role of providence as a causal factor did not seem incongruous to American scholars. Economics, law, and political science were still largely governed by concepts of absolute law and a priori reasoning. But these disciplines, together with history, sociology, and anthropology, came to be affected more and more by the evolutionary outlook and by pragmatic philosophy. Legal, political, and social ideas came to be thought of in terms of the evolution of their subject matter and the function they played in society. The scientific technique of going to original data and critically testing it for the establishment of facts on which all generalizations were presumably to rest was becoming the order of the day in the social disciplines. It would be easy to overemphasize these changes. The older ideas continued to find their champions. Even those who sympathized with the newer perspectives often failed to achieve them in their own work. Nevertheless, a profound change set in during the last quarter of the nineteenth century, the larger fruits of which are only gradually being realized in our own day.

While various figures abroad and at home contributed to this change, the influence of Spencer was paramount. In 1894 Oliver Wendell Holmes, Jr., already a distinguished jurist, wrote to Sir Frederick Pollock that no writer in English save Darwin had done so much as Spencer to affect our whole way of thinking. It will be recalled that before the end of the Civil War John Fiske and Edward L. Youmans had become ardent disciples of the synthetic philosopher of evolution; by 1866 there were enough American admirers to enable Youmans to collect several thousand dollars for the continuation of Spencer's studies and publications. On his visit to the United States in 1882 the Englishman was hailed with high enthusiasm.

American faith in the doctrine of progress and American optimism found support in his teachings; and in an era of rapid change the application of the evolutionary concept of politics, economics, and institutions generally aroused wide response. Spencer's theory of social evolution seemed to fit the needs of American development. And if the doctrine of mutability of customs, beliefs, and institutions was disconcerting to the champions of "permanent institutions," it was by the same token congenial to the growing number who frankly advocated change and adjustments to new needs and conditions. Moreover, as the discussion of "Social Darwinism" will make clear, Spencer's emphasis on laissez faire could be cited against reformers, and his emphasis on the survival of the fittest admirably suited the needs of the great captains of industry, who were crushing the little fellows when these vainly tried to compete with them.

The influence of the idea of evolution on the study of history was, in the nature of the case, bound to be quickly felt, for history dealt with the past, with origins, and with development. Before Darwin and Spencer, men like Bancroft, Parkman, and Motley had seen an orderly progress in the development of modern civilization and had ascribed this largely to the superiority of certain peoples and institutions in the competition with inferior ones. Fiske, whom Huxley advised to make historical writing the vehicle for promoting the doctrine of evolution, carried this conception even further. He traced the evolutionary development not only of language but of the Anglo-Saxon people from earlier stocks, and he likewise taught that the political superiority of this people explained its contributions to such institutions as the town meeting and the federal type of organization. Convinced that historical changes, like physical ones, conformed to fixed and ascertainable laws, Fiske continued to relate American institutions to a process of political development that had been going on from the earliest phases. What he did on a popular level, Herbert Baxter Adams and his students at Johns Hopkins did in learned monographs that traced certain American institutions back to their "beginnings" in the German primeval forests. The work of John W. Burgess at Columbia illustrated the same tendency, and also showed how evolutionary ideas could be combined with the Hegelianism so influential among American thinkers.

In a more philosophic vein Henry Adams opened his course on medieval history at Harvard with primitive man and sought to find in evolution the law of history which Fiske and the Johns Hopkins group supposed they had discovered. Although one of his students, J. Lawrence Laughlin, believed that Henry Adams throughout his career actually insisted that human history must be treated as an evolution, this was not precisely the case. Adams, a pessimist by temperament, reacted against the chaos of modern science, took seriously the second law of thermodynamics, which postulated the eventual disappearance of energy from the universe, and pondered over what seemed to him retrogression in human affairs.

If Henry Adams failed to find the key to historical law in the doctrine of evolution, other historians worked, consciously or unconsciously, within the Darwinian-Spencerian framework. Theodore Roosevelt felt that the historian must know Darwinian biology, and wrote the *Winning of the West* in terms of natural selection and the survival of the fittest. Frederick Jackson Turner, while refusing to accept the idea that American institutions all originated in Europe, nevertheless conceived of the development of civilization on the American continent in terms of process, development, evolution. Insisting on the influence of environment in selecting and adapting forms, on the process of interaction among topography and people and culture, Turner was a true social evolutionist. Indeed, his whole emphasis on continuity, on adaptation, and on improvement in terms of environment formed the underlying presuppositions of most Americans who worked in the new and so-called scientific or objective school of history. Charles Francis Adams hardly exaggerated when he declared that the *Origin of Species* marked the opening of a new epoch in the study of history.

The new era was not fully heralded until James Harvey Robinson conceived of all history in terms of evolutionary development. Robinson thought of the writing of history in terms of the struggle between the privileged groups and the common man; history, he declared, had been traditionally written by men sharing the point of view of the elite and it reflected their outlook, but it might be made an instrument for radicals in their struggle for a greater measure of justice. This relativist or working conception of truth was subsequently further developed by Carl Becker, who noted that the writing of history by any generation largely made the history of the group palatable. Charles A. Beard, in developing the philosophic implications of the relativist and instrumentalist conception of historical studies, was to deal a severe blow to the older assumption that the writing of history is merely an objective matter.

Meanwhile Thorstein Veblen, middle-western son of Norwegian immigrants, published the first of his notable critiques of orthodox economics from the standpoint of the evolutionist and modern psychologist.

Pointing out that the conception of human behavior tacitly or implicitly held by economic theorists was sadly outdated, Veblen contended that men are primarily creatures of instinct and habit, rather than hedonistic calculation, and that instincts have remained an almost constant factor whereas habits have undergone a cumulative development. If modern economic life was to be understood, he went on, its evolution in terms of the cumulative development of habits and institutions, economic and otherwise, must be investigated. Veblen showed how the daily discipline of tending machines, competing for prestige, and making money had produced changes in the inherited habit patterns of earlier generations, and how these interacted with the more nearly constant instincts. The Darwinian conception of causation—the process of cumulative change —was taken over by Veblen after he pointed out that existing academic economics, retaining antiquated anthropological and psychological pre-conceptions, were largely rationalizations of myths no longer functional to a machine and a pecuniary culture. As an evolutionary social philosopher, he saw throughout the history of civilization a conflict between the predatory and the industrious, a conflict that shifted its forms from the naked force and fraud of the pirate chieftain, the robber baron, the captain of industry, to the ingenuity with which the financial magnate clothed his interest with ethics by identifying it with the general interest.

In more orthodox economic quarters the Spencerian conceptions of laissez faire, progress, and the survival of the fittest were frankly appealed to as a rationale for the operations of the titans of industry. In the *Popular Science Monthly*, the organ in which Edward Youmans popularized Spencerianism, appeared articles condemning socialism and trade unionism on the score that such aberrations clasped rigid fetters on the natural process of economic life. Abram Hewitt, an industrialist of power, observed that "the industrial world has been steadily moving during the present century in the right direction for the welfare of mankind, and the disturbances which have occurred have been necessary incidents of a beneficent evolution in the steady advance in the wages of labor and in the distribution of the proceeds of industry upon the basis of equality and justice."[3]

Andrew Carnegie, who was convinced that "all is well since all grows better," at the same time welcomed the conditions imposed by nature

[3] Allan Nevins, *Abram S. Hewitt: with Some Account of Peter Cooper* (Harper & Row, 1935), 133.

herself, great inequality of environment, "the concentration of business, industrial and commercial, in the hands of the few, and the law of competition between these, as being not only beneficial, but essential to the progress of the race." However hard competition might be for the individual, it was necessary, continued the great steel magnate, because it is "best for the race, because it insures the survival of the fittest in every department."[4] While those engaged in the struggles of the market place invoked evolutionary doctrines to justify their activities, scholars often did the same thing. "It would be strange if the 'captain of industry' did not sometimes manifest a militant spirit," wrote a professor in the great university founded by John D. Rockefeller, "for he has risen from the ranks largely because he was a better fighter than most of us. Competitive commercial life is not a flowery bed of ease, but a battle where 'the struggle for existence' is defining the industrially 'fittest to survive.' "[5]

In the field of law the same evolutionary and pragmatic influences were at work. In *The Common Law* (1881) Oliver Wendell Holmes, Jr., declared that "the life of the law has not been logic: it has been experience. The felt necessities of the time, the prevalent moral and political theories, intuitions of public policy, avowed or unconscious, even the prejudices which judges share with their fellowmen, have had a good deal more to do than the syllogism in determining the rules by which men should be governed."[6] He went on to say that "the law embodies the story of a nation's development through many centuries and that in order to know what it is, we must know what it has been, and what it tends to become. Much that was taken for granted as natural, has been laboriously fought for in past times: the substance of law at any time corresponded fairly well to what was regarded as convenient by those making or interpreting it, but the form and machinery and the degree to which it is able to work out desired results, depended much upon its past." In his own decisions Holmes seemed, in the words of Max Lerner, to believe in the law of the economic jungle in which, however, he wanted the beasts to behave like gentlemen, to observe the rules of the game.

The realism and pragmatism operating in Mr. Justice Holmes's legal

[4] *North American Review*, CXLVIII (June, 1889), 654–655.
[5] C. A. Henderson, "Business Men and Social Theorists," *American Journal of Sociology*, I (January, 1896), 385 ff.
[6] Oliver W. Holmes, Jr., *The Common Law* (Boston, 1881), 1–2.

thought also began to affect criminology. Concepts of heredity and environment were introduced in the study of "the Jukes," a family to which was attached a notorious record of crime, pauperism, and disease. The conclusion in this study was that heredity depends on the permanence of the environment, that a change in environment may produce an entire change in the career and in the actual character of the individual. The administration of criminal justice was, then, to be governed by these concepts; this was the implication.

Political science also came within the evolutionary orbit. The older view of a static state and of eternal verities in politics gave way to organic and relativist ideas. The conception of the state as an artificial and deliberate creation, of something which could be made and unmade at will, was now contrasted with the idea that the state, being a slow accumulation, could be altered only slightly and very gradually. We shall see, in discussing the defense of existing arrangements by conservatives, that this doctrine was a comfortable one, useful in opposing radical demands for an abrupt departure from state noninterference in economic activities. But radicals also delighted in pointing out what they regarded as inconsistency on the part of conservatives who, having admitted that political forms had evolved, set themselves against any further evolution.

The conception of the slow growth of political institutions was reinforced by the doctrine of evolution through struggle and adaptation. It was probably the brilliant English conservative, Walter Bagehot, who first clearly and thoroughly applied to the state the doctrine of evolution by group struggle. *Physics and Politics* (1873) pictured an early age of conflict (the state-making age) in which various groups with different "cakes of custom" struggled to make dominant a preferred procedure. The contests and wars that marked this state-making age at length gave way to the age of discussion, in which the "cakes of custom" were broken and further progress made possible. Woodrow Wilson, who wrote two essays on Bagehot, was greatly influenced by him. Indeed, Wilson's conviction that the parliamentary and democratic political types, involving discussion as they did, must not be obliterated by the retrogressive type of force states, was to bear practical consequences.

Theodore Roosevelt, Wilson's rival, apologist that he was for the use of force, opposed such a position. In *The Strenuous Life*, written shortly after the Spanish-American War, he declared that "in this world a nation that has trained itself to a career of unwarlike and isolated ease is bound, in the end, to go down before other nations which have not lost the manly and adventurous qualities."[7] Mahan's arguments for navalism and for imperialism were strongly colored by such considerations. After tracing the development of commercial and imperial rivalries, a Yale economist declared that Darwin "gave scientific and philosophic basis to nationalistic and commercial struggles."[8]

On the more formal level professional writers gave support to the application of evolutionary conceptions to political thought. In 1908 Arthur F. Bentley in *The Process of Government* analyzed political action and found that most of it could be resolved into the conflict of groups. Bentley, moreover, pointed out the relation between group interest and group thinking. "What a man states to himself as his arguments or reasoning or thinking about a national issue, is, from the more exact point of view, just the conflict of the crossed groups to which he belongs."[9] Others, too, showed specifically that arguments followed interests, and that these were all in conflict. J. Allen Smith and Charles A. Beard even dared to argue that the Constitution, far from being a political abstraction or a disembodied structure of sheer political wisdom, grew out of definite group conflicts.

It was in anthropology and sociology, even more than in history, economics, political science, and law, that the impact of the evolutionary doctrines was most widely felt. In the orderly pattern dictated by the evolutionary hypothesis Lewis H. Morgan, a student of the American Indian, found a complete scheme of institutional progress. Paying special attention to marriage, kinship, government, and property, he popularized his evolutionary scheme of institutional development in *Ancient Society* (1877). According to this, culture the world over developed through the successive stages of savagery, barbarism, and civilization. Morgan, together with European ethnologists, virtually overthrew previously existing conceptions of primitive origins. According to the cultural evolutionists, human institutions developed gradually and cumulatively with adaptation and survival as operating factors. Cultural changes were thought to be progressive on the whole, leading to higher forms. The optimistic implications of this position accorded not only with Spencerianism but also with the expanding patterns of western civilization.

---

[7] Theodore Roosevelt, *The Strenuous Life* (The Century Company, 1901), 6.

[8] Henry C. Emery, *Some Economic Aspects of War* (Government Printing Office, 1914), 7.

[9] Arthur F. Bentley, *The Process of Government* (University of Chicago Press, 1908), 204.

In due time the concept of cultural evolution was subjected to serious criticism, which resulted in the modification of the earlier position. Anthropologists, using the scientific fact-finding technique of the field survey, showed that even in primitive societies sudden change, or even a religious or social cataclysm, was not unknown. The newly acquired facts simply did not square with the concept of uniformity and of progressive stages of development. Regression was common, and culture seldom advanced in all respects. The evolutionists' conception of separate cultures developing in a void was answered in part by the so-called diffusionists and more persuasively by the advocates of convergence. Boas and his school found that cultural similarities developed or converged in two or more places out of conditions or features at one time dissimilar. Even though cultural evolution was thus refined, modified, and in many cases overthrown altogether, anthropologists continued, under the impetus of evolutionary influence, to search for causes and effects in the historic process, and to see that among past events only those carrying over into the future may truly be regarded as significantly historical.

The sociologists were concerned with many of the same problems as the anthropologists and like them were greatly influenced by evolutionary thought. Both Darwin and Spencer carried great weight, however different were the interpretations of their work. William Graham Sumner at Yale, accepting Spencer's basic position, taught persuasively that social evolution is a more or less automatic process, virtually unamenable to social control and direction. Moreover, he held to the Darwinian idea that, like organic evolution, social evolution is a blind struggle in which even the most skillfully planned arrangements are crushed ruthlessly if they fail to meet the inscrutable requirements of the struggle for survival. In 1907 he published *Folkways*, a notable study in which man was pictured as being guided in the selection or rejection of certain types of conduct by instincts inherited from his animal ancestors which had proved to be useful in the struggle for survival. Sumner went on to show that folkways or group habits were gradually transformed into mores when they reached the level of conscious reflection and were viewed as well suited, if not necessary, for the security of the group. It was this general doctrine which he used to oppose reform measures, socialism, and, indeed, any serious modification of laissez faire.

Lester Frank Ward, although far from approving the laissez-faire implications of the type of social evolution Sumner stood for, was like his rival profoundly influenced by the doctrine of evolution. A self-taught paleobotanist and a government clerk, Ward approached the problems of society in an essentially new way, from a functional as well as a structural point of view. In the evolutionary process, he argued, social structures improved first by a spontaneous development, the key to which was a "struggle for structure" rather than a mere struggle for survival. By a conscious improvement of society the process of evolution could be still further continued. Ward believed that, thanks to the development of scientific method, it had become increasingly possible for man consciously to improve evolving society. Thus education, which has always bulked large in the thought of Americans bent on improvement, whether of individuals or society or both, received special attention in what Ward called "applied" sociology, which he contrasted with "pure sociology," or the study of the evolution of social structures. He set great store on the scientific participation of government in the advancement of human welfare. Thus the sociology of Ward, like the philosophy of Dewey, favored social reform just as the folkways and mores of Sumner lent support to the laissez faire on which social conservatives so frequently relied.

If space permitted, it would be possible to demonstrate the influence of Darwin and Spencer on other American sociologists. Albion W. Small of the University of Chicago was influenced by them and by Ratzenhofer, who emphasized the interest-struggle theory of development. At Columbia Franklin Giddings, who succeeded Ward and Sumner as the leader of the field, made Spencerian evolutionism the core of his theories. "Every social group, animal or human, since time began," he wrote, "has been in ceaseless struggle with its material environment and with other social groups." It is true that in his later works Giddings softened this crude evolutionism by putting much more emphasis on psychic factors and on "the consciousness of kind," a concept which Kropotkin had found in Darwinism and which had been used to develop a sociology of cooperation in opposition to the prevailing one of struggle.

## The Refutation of Social Darwinism

Social Darwinism is the name loosely given to the application to society of the doctrine of the struggle for existence and the survival of the fittest. It is clear that this doctrine permeated much of the thought of those who applied evolution to social problems. Social Darwinists cited not only the alleged approval of Darwin himself but, somewhat more appropriately, that of Spencer. An imposing company of other authorities was unequivocally cited in support of the concept of social struggle. Sir Henry Maine's *Popular Government* referred to the struggle for existence as "that beneficent private war which makes one man strive to climb on the shoulders of another and remain there through the law of the survival of the fittest." Gumplowicz, a Polish sociologist, influenced Ward, Small, and other Americans by his conception of a "war of races." Ruskin, Kingsley, and Carlyle, with their sentimental but attractive romanticizing of the "will to power" and "the cult of force," were appealed to in support of the doctrine, as were the English hereditarians, Galton and Pearson. Haeckel and Nietzsche were great names to the Social Darwinists. Even William James regarded war or its "equivalent" as a biological or sociological necessity since "our ancestors have bred pugnacity into our bone and marrow and thousands of years of peace won't breed it out of us." A subsequent discussion of war and imperialism will reveal the extent to which Social Darwinism figured in the defense of these institutions.

Although Darwin was influenced by Malthus, who had seen in war and famine nature's means for eliminating some in the competition for limited resources, it appears that he himself never lent much countenance to the sweeping applications of his theories to social problems. At least he expressed hearty sympathy for the sustained efforts of Charles Loring Brace, an American disciple, to relieve human suffering through beneficent social action. Even Spencer, while insisting that war had played a major role in social evolution in the past, believed that in the present industrial society war was an ineffective instrument for accomplishing further evolution.

The first criticisms of Social Darwinism in the name of Darwin's own teachings seem to have been made in 1880 by a Russian zoologist, Kessler, and to have been developed somewhat later by Kropotkin, who saw in organic evolution an even more important factor than struggle, that of mutual aid. If mutual aid had enabled individuals and species in the animal and human worlds to survive in a measure greater than struggle had, the whole basis of Social Darwinism fell to the ground. Kropotkin visited the United States in 1897 and again in 1901 and did much to popularize his refutation of the teachings of the Social Darwinists.

Meanwhile American sociologists themselves had ventured to question their teachings. In 1894 Professor E. A. Ross of Stanford University wrote to his sociological friend Ward that he was about to lock horns with the Social Darwinists in a lecture entitled "Dollars and Darwinism." He could not, he continued, see eye to eye with President David Starr Jordan, who in his lectures on evolution seemed to link up the "repulsive dog-eat-dog practices of current business and politics with that 'struggle for existence' which evoked the higher forms of life."[10] Ross began to teach that the ruthless and wasteful "fight for the spoil" was not helping the abler strains to multiply faster than others, and that it is the systems of social control rather than the social natures of their members that are tested when groups struggle. President Jordan himself, who at first seems to have believed no artificial control necessary, inasmuch as the altruistic survive and the selfish peter out, modified his own views in his crusade against war. In a series of arresting little books he contended that war, far from having promoted the survival of the fittest, had played a devastating role by causing the less heroic, the less physically fit, to stay at home and breed while the abler went down to death in battle.

To the criticisms of Social Darwinism which Kropotkin, Ross, and Jordan made, others were presently added. In *Human Nature and the Social Order* (1902) Professor Charles H. Cooley of the University of Michigan rejected the widespread social applications of Darwinism. Emphasizing sympathy and cooperation as dynamic factors, he also insisted that the self could be understood only in social terms, that society and the individual were aspects of the same process, and that therefore Social Darwinism, so far as the relations of individuals went, was full of fallacies. At the Wharton School of Finance at the University of Pennsylvania the economist Simon N. Patten carried the refutation still further in a significant book published in 1907, *The New Basis of Civilization*. The world's food supply, according to Patten, could be doubled by scientific and engineering processes; for the first time in history the means of satisfying needs exceeded the needs themselves. There were, moreover, no basic or inherent differences between the poor

[10] "Ward-Ross Correspondence," *American Sociological Review*, III (June, 1939), 387, 391.

and the rich. "Abolish poverty, transform deficit into surplus, fill depletion with energy, and the ascribed heredity of the poor will vanish with its causes." Since struggle breeds emotion not strength, since it lowers man's tone and throws him back to primitive conditions, it cannot, he urged, be regarded as a cause of the improvements attributed to natural conditions or natural selection. Patten insisted that "nature will care for progress if men will care for reform." He contended that there can be no progress without an acquired equality, and that the proper utilization of resources through scientific knowledge makes this acquired equality a possibility. All this pointed to the welfare economics which was at length to become the basis of daring thought and experimentation.

While Patten was criticizing Social Darwinism in terms of economic theory, the American disciples of Kropotkin and Tolstoy, men like Ernest Crosby, were showing not only its unscientific but its un-Christian and unethical character. Before the outbreak of World War I Margaret Sanger was turning from muckraking and socialist activities to the European pioneers of birth control in her search for a realistic method of combating not only the doctrine of Social Darwinism but unhappiness and a desperate fatalism in millions of families among the poor.

Thus the speculative souls who in the name of science diagnosed the nature of the mind, of thought, of ideas, and of society varied considerably in the particular implications of science which they chose to emphasize. But in spite of these variations, no one on the eve of World War I could doubt that the advancing spirit and technique of science had brought great changes in the older concepts of the nature of things. Some of this awareness of change was beginning to reach into the popular consciousness. The road was at last open to new vistas of the mind and of society, vistas that suggested that they were far less secure, far less absolute, far less static than men and women had long assumed. These vistas also suggested that men and women could make society and indeed nature itself more congenial to their taste and their needs, that they could mold them in ways that even the Utopians had not conjured up in their fondest dreams. Of course, even the idealists knew that science could not alone banish all that stood in the way of realizing these dreams. But the time was one of optimism.

# 23 Scholarship and Popularization of Learning

*When the historian of a later day comes to search out the intellectual antecedents of his modern society, he will devote an interesting chapter to the rise and progress of ideas as illustrated in the institution of the public lecture. He will record that at one time Emerson, Alcott, Phillips, Beecher, Garrison, and a great many other awakeners of American intelligence, were lecturers; that philosophers and scientists were persuaded out of their studies and laboratories to take a stand on the platform; in short, that Plato's Academe and Archimedes' workshop were turned into the lecture room.*
—New York Tribune, December 18, 1869

*There is a new spirit of research abroad—a spirit which emulates the laboratory work of the naturalist.*
—JUSTIN WINSOR, 1886

In the last quarter of the nineteenth century and the first decade of the twentieth intellectual life became ever more specialized and professionalized. This was apparent in the rapid shift from the older apprenticeship system of training doctors and lawyers to reliance on the professional school, in the new type of foundation for the promotion of learning, in the graduate faculties with well-equipped laboratories and libraries, fellowships, and research seminars, and in the swiftly growing number of professional organizations.

A number of factors were responsible for these changes. Some of them have already been taken into account: for example, the presence of scholarly immigrants with highly specialized intellectual skills. The growing custom of organizing interests and activities on a national scale also partly explains the appearance of many new national organizations of experts, organizations which could function tellingly by reason of much-improved means of communication. The tendency toward professionalization and specialization in the intellectual sphere also reflected the feeling that in a society that was becoming ever more interdependent and complex the efforts of individual scholars had to be coordinated and reinforced.

But scholars would not have organized and zealously attended the annual meetings of their learned societies or published their technical monographs had not the new urban and industrial civilization made all this specialization and professionalization possible. Money would not have poured into institutions for the advancement of knowledge had not the economy of the nation developed to the point which permitted it and made it seem necessary and good. Expanding industry, commerce, and finance needed the help of technical experts in chemistry, physics, engineering, biology, and economics. In the cities, problems of transportation, housing, charity, utilities, and finance, to name only a few, called for the specialized services of economists, political scientists, and sociologists. The problems of rural life, many of which were related to the growth of industry and of cities, required attention from specialists in plant bacteriology and soil chemistry, rural economics and sociology. All of these needs functioned in a culture marked by a great faith in the power of knowledge to provide answers and solve problems.

## The Impact of German Scholarship

In his baccalaureate address at the University of Michigan in 1905, President James B. Angell called attention to an important change which had taken place during the last fifty years in the intellectual ideals American scholars and university students were taught to hold dear. A half century before, Angell observed, the prevalent ideal was the acquisition of the largest possible amount of knowledge and familiarity with the ideas of great scholars, and the achievement of the culture such acquisition presumably brought about. But the ideal had come increasingly to be the power and passion for discovering new truth. This change had not been as complete, probably, as President Angell suggested; but that it was a reality there can be no doubt. Of the many factors contributing to it, none was so important as the influence of the German university on American intellectual life.

The little stream of students that sought the German universities in the second decade of the nineteenth century had broadened until, by the sixth decade, it numbered 300; by the seventh it had reached 1000; and by the ninth, more than 2000. In that decade the tide began to turn, inasmuch as American graduate faculties had now become sufficiently well established to provide admirable training at home. The stream nevertheless continued; in all, some 10,000 Americans matriculated in German universities between the War of 1812 and World War I. In addition, a vast body of American-trained scholars imbibed from their German-trained mentors the university ideals of scholarship.

The prestige of the German university rested only in part on the fact that it provided excellent professional training. What caught the imagination and aroused the devotion of American students in German universities was their emphasis on the disinterested pursuit of truth through original investigation. The German ideal of scholarship assumed that truth is not final, that therefore habitual premises are susceptible of revision. In order that truth might be sought and found, narrowly limited areas had to be plowed deeply. Freedom of teaching and freedom of learning within certain limits of fact had to prevail; only thus could man become freed from superstitions held in veneration as final "truth." German scholarship utilized the specialized library, the laboratory, the seminar, the monograph, and the learned periodical in the quest for objective and disinterested truth. Thousands of American students must have felt as Nicholas Murray Butler did: ". . . Each great scholar whose lecture-room was entered, if it were only for a single visit, left an ineffaceable impression of what scholarship meant, of what a university was, and of what a long road higher education in America had to travel before it could hope to reach a plane of equal elevation."[1]

[1] Nicholas Murray Butler, *Across the Busy Years* (Charles Scribner's Sons, 1939), I, 122, 127.

In every field scholarship was influenced by the German university ideal. Long before the great migration of American students German theological scholarship, based on the conviction that through textual criticism and auxiliary disciplines man might come to the true meaning of the sacred texts, had begun to affect theological circles in the United States. Professor Moses Stuart at Andover first opened to his fellow American scholars the rich treasures of German Biblical scholarship. He was supported by Henry Boynton Smith of Amherst, by Theodore Parker, and by a later generation of scholars trained in German centers of learning. Now, with the increasing drift of young men to that country's universities, every field of intellectual endeavor felt the impact of German scholarship. George Herbert Palmer, Josiah Royce, George Sylvester Morris, and George H. Howison brought back zeal for German idealistic philosophy and the technique for its study. The growing autonomy of psychology, for which German scholars—above all Wundt —were responsible, similarly resulted in the launching of that new discipline in America; men like William James, G. Stanley Hall, Joseph Jastrow, William L. Bryan, James McKeen Cattell, and E. L. Titchener set up psychological laboratories in which the study of the mind was pursued with relatively objective techniques. In philological studies the German influence was likewise far reaching. The minute preoccupation with textual criticism and the use of the methods and findings of the archeologist and comparative ethnologist brought in a new era in that field. To the older German-trained classicists—Gildersleeve, Lane, Woolsey, and Whitney—was added a new group, trained in the latest and most refined techniques of classical archeology and philology. Minton Warren of Johns Hopkins was typical of these scholars.

Americans also discovered new techniques in German scientific laboratories which put an indelible stamp on American biology and physics. Germany was the scene of much of the most precise demonstration of basic aspects of the Darwinian theory. The work of Koch in developing Pasteur's discovery of disease-producing bacteria was hardly less significant. To the authoritative work in physics associated with the names of Hertz and Helmholtz, German scholarship added, in 1900, the revolutionary quantum theory of Planck; by 1905 Einstein had advanced the theory of relativity which, with the quantum theory, materially modified Newtonian physics.

Again, fields of knowledge which had little of the scientific spirit, such as education, were in Germany discovered to be susceptible to some of the same scientific techniques as other disciplines. In the social studies that country exerted a profound spell on American scholarship. The ideal of investigating objectively the phenomena of social existence and the methods for doing so were largely responsible for establishing such fields as economics, political science, sociology, and history on their modern basis in America. The collection of documents, the testing and criticism of data, these opened new doors to young Americans. The ideal of objectivity and faith in the objectivity of the results of scholarship in the social field held sway. Inspired by these ideals, Americans began to investigate actual social conditions in their own country, endeavoring as they did so to apply the concept of disinterested search for truth.

The idea of the relativity of what had been regarded as "laws' was also expounded in German universities. Rudolph Jhering, who lectured in jurisprudence at Giessen, Kiel, and Göttingen, taught that the validity of legal rules was determined by results; thus he constructed a social theory of law. Schmoller's historical approach to economics did much to undermine the classical view of absolute laws.

German-trained social scientists have frequently testified to the impact of German scholarship on another aspect of the social disciplines in America: the obligation of the scholar to promote the general well-being of the community. Richard T. Ely has written of the effect of the "warm humanitarianism" and the "ethical view" of economics of such scholars as Conrad, Wagner, and Knies. Certainly these Germans and others did much to quicken in their American students a sense of the priority of public to private interests; this was in good Prussian tradition. No doubt, the preoccupation with welfare economics of Ely, Ross, E. J. James, and the younger Americans who came under their spell—Bemis, Commons, and others—owed much to the German concept of the role of the trained expert in civil service and welfare activities. To say this is not, of course, to imply that the concept of the scholar as a public servant was entirely a German importation. In England the rise of Fabian scholarship and the influence of Christian Socialism on American scholars operated in much the same way. America itself was not without this tradition. In 1884, when Wendell Phillips was delivering his famous indictment of American scholars for their indifference to great public issues, the state universities in the West were already well on the way toward developing the conception of the public responsibility of university faculties. But in the growth of this ideal, as in so many aspects of American university life, German influence was direct and important.

## The Organization of Research and Scholarship

The zeal for organization and systematization of intellectual life made itself felt in America in the establishment of graduate study in the arts and sciences, in the beginnings of research at a few of the professional schools of law and medicine, and in the multiplication of agencies for the promotion of original research. Advanced study in a few fields had been begun at Yale, and perhaps in other institutions, before 1870. But this did not amount to much. About that year Yale reorganized graduate study, and Harvard began systematically to provide facilities for advanced work. The seminar method, which Henry Adams introduced at Harvard and Charles K. Adams began at Michigan, was readily adopted as the logical means for advanced instruction in research methods. Candidates for the Ph.D. degree, which Yale had first granted in 1861, began to appear. A quarter of a century after the degree was first granted, requirements for it became more or less standardized.

Meanwhile the greatest impetus to graduate study came from the Johns Hopkins University which Daniel Coit Gilman launched at Baltimore in 1876. From the start this was a center for research and advanced study. Both in the academic fields and in medicine the spirit of original investigation prevailed, for everything was arranged to promote that end. The success of Johns Hopkins greatly stimulated Harvard to give more thought and larger resources to graduate study, and the influence of the institution at Baltimore profoundly affected advanced work in all other American institutions. By 1880 Columbia has established the Faculty of Political Science. Eight years later G. Stanley Hall opened Clark University which, like Johns Hopkins, was devoted to training for research. Thanks to the administrative genius and imagination of President Harper, the University of Chicago, richly endowed by John D. Rockefeller, was able from the start to give much attention to graduate study. Even the larger and better-established state universities convinced their legislatures of the importance of research; before the end of the century Michigan, Wisconsin, and California had entered on their careers as graduate centers.

Advanced studies assumed an ever more important place in American universities, and larger funds for libraries, laboratories, and fellowships had to be found. By 1890 twenty-five universities had established in all 170 fellowships, and the number grew rapidly. In 1910, when graduate instruction was little more than three decades old, some 6000 young men and women were enrolled as candidates for advanced degrees. This whole development involved not only a considerable reorganization of the curriculum and the use of resources, but a basic change in educational philosophy; the universities assumed the responsibility for preparing specialized scholars and increasing man's knowledge as well as for preparing cultured men and disseminating what was already known.

Professional training in law and medicine still suffered from lax standards even at leading universities and from the alarming practice of diploma-selling in chartered institutions. Yet great progress was being made in these branches of training at Johns Hopkins, Harvard, Chicago, Pennsylvania, and elsewhere.

In the twentieth century the foundations established by titans of wealth brought new strength to organized research. The Rockefeller Institute for Medical Research and the Rockefeller Foundation, the Carnegie Institution of Washington, the Carnegie Corporation of New York, and the Mayo Foundation at Rochester, Minnesota, were by 1915 generously endowing investigation and research. In 1907 the Russell Sage Foundation began researches designed to improve social conditions. Immense funds were given to the universities for research purposes.

The last quarter of the nineteenth century saw changes in the prevailing type of professional organizations. Until well after the Civil War the professional organizations were in general either local in character or comprehensive in aim. The Massachusetts Historical Society, the American Academy of Arts and Sciences, the American Antiquarian Society and the natural history societies in the larger cities were essentially local institutions. The American Association for the Advancement of Science (1848) embraced all science in its scope. The American Social Science Association, with general or comprehensive programs, was also characteristic of the learned societies; its annual meetings and its *Journal* during the post-Civil War years were given over to discussion of quasi-scientific and quasi-humanitarian subjects varying from Texas cattle disease to the protection of the ballot, civil service reform, and criminal law, the education of defectives, currency and finance, prison discipline, the treatment of the insane, boards of health, and statistical techniques for census-taking. By the 1870s the need for more specialized professional organizations was keenly felt.

The precedent set by the statisticians in 1839, the ethnologists and orientalists in 1842, the geographers in 1852, and the etymologists in 1859 was rapidly acted on in the 1870s and 1880s by an increasing number of specialists who formed their own learned organizations. In 1869 the American Philological Association met for the first time; ten years later the Archaeological Institute of America was established; and two years later the American School of Classical Studies at Athens opened. The Modern Language Association, organized in 1883, testified to the advance of special interest in its field. In 1884 the American Historical Association began its activities, and the following year the American Economic Association took shape. So marked was the specialization in the social studies field that early in the twentieth century the political scientists and sociologists formed their own organizations, and so did specialists in international law.

Even in the more precisely defined fields the rise of specialists led to the subdivision of labors; thus in 1888 the American Society for Church History was organized, to be followed in 1897 by the American Irish Historical Association, and by a dozen or more similar interest groups. The American Psychological Association was established in 1892, nine years before the American Philosophical Association was founded.

The organization, professionalization, and specialization of scholarship through learned societies went on apace. At least 79 local and national learned societies were formed in the 1870s, 121 in the 1880s, and 45 in the 1890s. In 1908 the *Handbook of Learned Societies* listed 120 national and some 550 local societies (including, it is true, such unusual ones as the American Mosquito Extermination Society). The tendency toward further breakdowns in specialized organization went on unabated. In 1915, however, the more general interests of scholars in higher education found expression in the newly formed American Association of University Professors, which was designed to promote higher standards of teaching, scholarship, and research, and to protect academic freedom.

Learned societies broke down the isolation of scholars by bringing them together for annual meetings. But they promoted investigation in many other ways. They stimulated the preparation and publication of specialized monographs and papers in transactions, proceedings, and journals. The *Journal of Speculative Philosophy*, founded in 1867 by William T. Harris, the Hegelian superintendent of schools in St. Louis, was a pioneer. It was followed by the journals of the American Chemical Society (1879), the American Mathematics Society (1888), and a long list of others. Some of the learned societies further promoted research by offering prizes for outstanding monographs in given fields, and others undertook labors basic to research. Thus the American Historical Association, which did so much to direct historical endeavor away from the general treatise to the specialized study, facilitated research through the preparation of bibliographies, guides to archives, and the publication of important collections of documents. Closer association on the part of scholars was also indicated by the appearance of such cooperative works as Justin Winsor's *Critical and Narrative History* and Hubert Howe Bancroft's *History of the Pacific States*.

The organization of research in the nonacademic professions was stimulated by the establishment of such specialized organizations as those of the mining engineers (1871), the mechanical engineers (1881), and the electrical engineers (1884). The American Bar Association was established in 1878; the older American Medical Association (1847) continued to flourish along with more specialized groups in the field.

Both government and private business encouraged research. The geological surveys, and the important ethnological work of the federal government in collaboration with the Smithsonian Institution, have already been spoken of. The Department of Agriculture was in a sense the outstanding pioneer among government agencies in the organization and subdivision of research; its work involved an ever-growing number of fields. Other governmental bureaus, commissions, and agencies also arose to meet the need for research in such fields as transportation, finance, and labor. Although the iron and steel as well as other industries had long supported a certain amount of research, a new era was marked when, shortly after its organization in 1892, the General Electric Company retained the brilliant immigrant engineer, Charles P. Steinmetz, whose researches in alternating electric current phenomena and related fields were to be almost revolutionary. The literature of industrial research in applied chemistry and other fields became increasingly significant in the early years of the twentieth century.

## Accomplishments and Criticisms

At the turn of the century certain scholars and scientists were moved to appraise American contributions to knowledge, and the character of American research and learning. In a much-discussed article in the *North American Review* in 1902 Carl Snyder pointed to the fact that anesthesia had been discovered in America; that Joseph Henry was with Faraday the codiscoverer of electrical induction; that Draper had first photographed stars; that Newton, Pickering, Burnham, and Keeler had put American astronomy in the front rank; that Hill, Rowland, and Michelson had become world authorities in mathematics and physics; and that Cope, Leidy, and Marsh had helped to establish the truth of evolution. He pointed with some pride to the fact that, except for Lord Kelvin, Simon Newcomb was the only English-speaking associate of the French Academy and that Josiah Willard Gibbs had helped lay the foundations of the new field of thermodynamics and physical chemistry.

Snyder nevertheless concluded that in the scientific world America's position was an inferior one; Americans had made no discoveries comparable to those of Helmholtz, Clerk-Maxwell, Hertz, Pasteur, Lister, Koch, Behring, Sir William Crookes, J. J. Thomson, and Berthelot. American scholarship, in the estimation of another observer, Charles S. Slichter of the University of Wisconsin, had chiefly contented itself with filling in details within the larger framework made by European masters. None of the great scientific achievements of the century—the theory of evolution, the atomic structure of matter, the existence of ether and the undulatory theory of light and electricity, the principles of electromagnetic induction and electrolytic action, the discovery of microorganisms and the concept of conservation of energy—none of these was the work of Americans. In the humanities American scholarship, it was said, was matter-of-fact, statistical, archeological, hard, thin, and dry. According to Paul Shorey, a University of Chicago classicist, American scholarship in this field never rose to the comprehensiveness and the generous *élan* of the German; it lacked the grace and charm of the French, the restrained emotion and finished eloquence of the English.

These evaluations underestimated the value and originality of American contributions to knowledge. Yet in a broad sense they contained a considerable degree of truth. In any case, they were generally held not only in Europe but at home. They occasioned much speculation concerning the causes for the inferiority of American scholarship and science.

Those who maintained that neither the state nor rich Americans had been niggardly, that the United States lacked neither the means nor the material for original work, did not represent majority opinion. A larger number of commentators held that American institutions, in comparison with those of Europe, lacked resources and equipment. Many deplored the overburdened schedules of American college teachers. It was frequently observed that in the fields in which America did enjoy front rank—astronomy, geology, and meteorology—the American teaching system was least influential. The scholars in these fields, who were frequently directors of private observatories and experiment stations and organizers of the government geological surveys, had little or nothing to do with actual instruction. In the eyes of these writers, therefore, the remedy lay in the development of research institutions free from the burdens of routine instruction. The low salaries of American college faculties also figured in the discussion. President Harper of the University of Chicago pointed out that the salaries of university professors could be honestly compared with those of skilled workmen—the general average in a hundred institutions in 1893 was $1470. He thus lent support to the thesis that American scholars were too burdened and too limited in leisure and means to compete with their European colleagues.

But these explanations did not stop the never-ending discussion. In 1886 James Russell Lowell deplored "the new dry rot of learning," the alienation of scholarship from culture and criticism, the narrow pursuit of those facts which are to truth "as a plaster-cast to the marble." Lowell, one of the most learned and at the same time one of the most cultivated of American scholars, went on to express his great debt to German scholarship. Yet this poet felt, as did many who followed him, that a great danger lurked in the pedantry of German erudition. The endless, meticulous absorption in method and textual criticism, Lowell felt, obscured the wisdom, the beauty, and the civilizing qualities in literature.

Others declared that just as craftsmen lost the values of their craft by subdivision, so scholars ceased, through the subdivision of research, to be true scholars and men. Among these critics one of the most effective was Lowell's kinsman, A. Lawrence Lowell of Harvard. There could be no doubt, Lowell remarked in 1903, that the division of labor and specialization had been important elements in the world's progress. Yet these things might be carried too far, and if specialized learning was permitted to become an isolated, narrow eddy in the great stream of human thought and culture, it would defeat its own purposes.

A few years later Professor Paul Shorey similarly suggested that we might have paid too high a price for German scholarship (or, for that matter, he continued, for that of France and England). Until American scholarship ceased trying merely to imitate that of Europe, until our scholars were trained at home "in an environment and by methods that shall subject the form and relate the content of their knowledge to the high tradition of their own language, literature, and inherited culture," they could not correct the shortcomings of American scholarship or grow to full stature. Thus cultural nationalism, which had been invoked throughout the nineteenth century to explain the shortcomings in the life of the mind and to stimulate Americans to greater literary and scientific achievements, continued to figure in the evaluations of the products of our scholarship.

If the lack of self-reliance explained, in the minds of some, the deficiencies in American intellectual life, the existence of democracy here seemed to others a more basic factor. Simon Newcomb, for example, believed that if there were an aristocracy of scholars, if men of letters and science were honored as they were in Europe, their achievements would be far more important than in fact they were.

In response to such criticisms democratic scholars maintained that our entire history proved the contrary; democracy, they insisted, admits of sufficient refinement, and the evils noted by aristocratic critics of American intellectual life were merely incidental to certain phases of our development and by no means essential. Some went so far as to say that the enrichment of American intellectual achievements required not less but more democracy. American scholars, it was held, must be less neutral than they had traditionally been in the great struggles of the common man for a larger measure of justice and well-being. If research were employed consciously in the solution of social, economic, and political problems, if it were explicitly put to work for the common good, American science and scholarship would be able to boast more originality and significance on the intellectual level itself.

The obligation of the scholar to the commonweal was ably argued by educational democrats. The inaugural address of President Van Hise of the University of Wisconsin was a brilliant plea that the university must be a watchtower, a fortress in which research was used in the interest of all the people. This conception was further developed in 1913 in a clear-cut paper written by Professor T. Atkinson Jenkins of the University of Chicago. Tribute was paid to the civic ideas of such great intellectual leaders as Gilman, Angell, Eliot, Hadley, and Van Hise. Professor Jenkins cited with approval the doctrine, fervently held by such European thinkers as Fechner, Eucken, Paulsen, and Bergson, and by our own pragmatist William James, that scholars who cut themselves off from social instincts doomed themselves to become cranks. "It rests with each of us, as with all men, to help or not to help in making this world more inhabitable, a better place to live in. A real neutrality is unattainable: he who is not for the commonwealth, is against it."[2]

Such philosophy came to exercise more and more influence. The democratic conception of the scholar's role lay back of the researches of John R. Commons into sweatshop conditions, the regulation and public ownership of utilities, and the effects of immigration on American standards of living. Walter Weyl was responding to similar currents when he investigated conditions of work in the anthracite coal industry. Edward A. Ross examined the causes of social discontent in the same spirit. Such a philosophy explained the zeal of Richard T. Ely and Edmund J. James in their researches in the field of railway transportation, cooperation, and public control. Governed by a similar ideal, Fernow and others brought research techniques to bear on the problem of the conservation of natural resources. In short, American social and natural science was increasingly identifying itself with the problems of American life.

## Popularization: The Motives

The gulf between the knowledge of the intellectual and that of the common people has always been wide, everywhere, but it has been less wide and deep in America than elsewhere. In this fact, perhaps, lies the unique characteristic of American intellectual history. In the last hundred

[2] T. Atkinson Jenkins, "Scholarship and Public Spirit," Modern Language Association Proceedings, XIX (1914), lxxxvii–cxvi.

years steady progress has been made toward bridging the gap, toward extending to the people a larger measure of opportunity for taking part on some level in the life of the mind. Progress was particularly marked in the final quarter of the nineteenth century and the early decades of the twentieth; the gains made in this era rivaled those of the pre-Civil War period when the penny newspaper, cheap magazines and books for the untutored, the common school awakening, the expansion of academies and colleges, and the lyceum movement did so much to democratize intellectual life.

Many factors explain the headway made. Among them was the zeal of such men as Edward Youmans for popularizing the rapidly developing fields of natural science. It will be recalled that Youmans was responsible for the appearance of the great scientific classics of Europe in an inexpensive form, that he prepared a series of scientific textbooks which popularized great bodies of material, and that the *Popular Science Monthly* became under his editorship an important channel for disseminating knowledge of new scientific achievements. Gifted lecturers like John Fiske helped to popularize the theory of evolution.

The movement for popularizing knowledge also owed something to English example. British precedents led in the 1880s to the beginning of university extension. Herbert Baxter Adams of Johns Hopkins, whose contacts with English scholars were close, began a crusade to bring university learning to noncollege people through lectures and correspondence courses. In this leaders in the public library movement provided much support. Within a few years President Harper of the University of Chicago, who had acquired a rich background at Chautauqua Lake for this sort of adult education, organized university extension on a sound basis. Soon afterward state universities, eager to democratize higher education, took up the work. In 1914 the University of Wisconsin, a leader in this crusade of service, boasted an extension enrollment of over seven thousand men and women.

An indigenous American faith in the desirability and necessity of applying the democratic principle to the intellectual life continued to bulk large among the forces back of all the emphasis on popularizing knowledge. The lyrical faith in education as the best means of promoting equality of opportunity was a main cause for the increasing public responsibility for schools and for the vast expansion of other agencies for popularizing knowledge. The traditional argument that mass education was necessary for intelligent participation in political democracy and that it must extend beyond the common school was heard in discussions regarding high schools, libraries, and Chautauquas. The growing complexity of American life and the recognition that this imposed new burdens on democratic political machinery were additional arguments for spreading knowledge through every possible channel.

The democratic zeal for the popularization of knowledge was strongly tinged with religious conviction. This religious-democratic idealism largely explains the pioneer work in adult education which Henry Leipziger inaugurated in 1874 at the New York City Men's Hebrew Association, and which he later extended by persuading the board of education to sponsor popular lectures in the less privileged areas of the metropolis. In 1871 the evangelically-minded YMCA took the significant ground that Christian associations should try to comprehend the science and literature of the time in the interest of elevating taste, promoting self-culture, and advancing the growth of the individual and the social and secular progress so necessary to Christian well-being. During the 1880s evening classes, in both the practical and the cultural branches, became a generally recognized part of the activities of the YMCA. In the course of time the YWCA followed this example.

The beginnings of the famous adult education movement at Chautauqua Lake in western New York also reflect the religious-democratic faith in the popularization of knowledge. Lewis Miller, an Ohio manufacturer and Sunday school teacher, and Bishop Vincent of the Methodist church, initiated a camp meeting for the training of religious workers; this grew into the highly organized and successful Chautauqua Assembly (1874). Miller believed that all knowledge, secular and religious, is of God and therefore the natural and necessary right of each of His children. Men of all ranks—trade, factory, and field—Miller thought, need association with the professional man and the theorist, who in turn require contacts with the artisan and the merchant so that knowledge in all forms and on all levels may be shared to the enrichment of everyone. In times past knowledge was the privilege of the few. But, said Miller, in a democracy in which men follow God, knowledge becomes the valued possession of the many. Thus the neglect of the intellectual capacity of any single person is no less than criminal. To say this, Miller remarked, is not to say that there is or must be equality of privileges and rights. In other words, the whole of life must be regarded as a school, with educating agencies and influences at work from the earliest moment to the day of death, agencies and influences applied by and in behalf of each individual, through life, according to capacities and conditions.

The recognition of the obvious inequalities of opportunity for obtaining book knowledge stimulated efforts to bring light and learning to rural folk. This in part explains the enthusiasm for the traveling circuit lyceums and Chautauquas. Commercial though these agencies were, many of the promoters and "entertainers" regarded themselves as missionaries of culture among country people. The phenomenal success of these organizations testified to the yearning of rural dwellers for inspiration, glimmerings of the remote world of ideas, and, of course, diversion and entertainment.

The literature for the promotion of the public library movement likewise made much of the duty of bringing sound knowledge to the toiling masses. Thus the Chicago Public Library urged public support on the ground that it provided the city's workers with "the opportunity of that mental improvement denied them by a hard fortune, or extreme penury" and salvaged them from "the haunts of vice and folly." In the depths of the depression of 1893 the argument was heard that "if society cannot provide work for all, the idle, chronic or temporary, are much safer with a book in the library than elsewhere." The public library, it was urged, would help the wage earner regain some of the ground lost in the battle of life when necessity compelled him to leave the schoolroom for the factory. In arguments for the support of both the public library and the high school it was frequently maintained that democratic institutions and ideas could be preserved from demagoguery, communism, and other subversive doctrines only through larger facilities for a sound understanding of the true principles of economics and the American way of life.

The movement for the popularization of culture also profited from the time-honored devotion to self-improvement. Self-culture continued to be esteemed as a means of personal growth. It was this concept which led many farmers' wives to make endless sacrifices in order to "take in" all the "culture" offered in the humid tents of the traveling Chautauquas. It was this which led the Scottish errant-philosopher, the gifted Thomas Davidson, in 1898 to begin his pioneer experiment in teaching the literary and philosophical classics and the theory of evolution to workers on the lower East Side of New York City. It was a similar consideration that accounted for the amazing spread of the woman's club movement and the arduous toil of many an untutored lady over a "paper" on Browning or some other literary theme often beyond her depth. And it was the same faith in the value of knowledge for personal self-culture that explained the popularity of the Chautauqua Literary and Scientific Circle. Beginning in 1878 this agency of Bishop Vincent offered a four-year reading course in the humanities, sciences, theology, and social studies. In 1908 somewhat the same impulse led President Eliot to make available in the Harvard Classics the great writings of ancient and modern literature to enrich, refine, and fertilize the observant readers' mind.

On its highest level the desire for self-culture was often associated with a somewhat vague feeling that the acquisition of culture was in itself a satisfaction and that it further enhanced the value of living by opening the doors to better associations and to vistas, at least, into the intriguing world of the elite. Thus one of the thousands of members of the Literary and Scientific Reading Circle of Bishop Vincent's Chautauqua wrote to headquarters:

I have always felt that there were people in the world somewhere, if I could only find them, who would understand that poverty-stricken people may have aspirations, and yet be honest and true, and that we may wish for wealth in order to make progress, and not to enable us to live idle and vicious lives. I presume you will say, "of course"; but I have so often been exhorted to "be content in the station in life in which it has pleased God to call you." But I do hunger and thirst after knowledge, whether right or wrong; and I cannot subdue that hunger unless I crush out all that is purest.[3]

Such a combination of motives was also exemplified in the life story of a book-loving farm woman whose none too prosperous, penurious and anti-intellectual husband would not permit her to indulge her fancy for "culture." The indefatigable lady finally succeeded in taking a commercial correspondence course. This opened a new world of culture and even enabled her to make a bit of pin money by marketing an article from her own pen.

But many who succumbed to the sensationally alluring advertisements of commercial correspondence schools aspired only to getting ahead in the world of material things. It would, indeed, be impossible to explain the great advances in the popularization of knowledge in this period

[3] John H. Vincent, *The Chautauqua Movement* (Chautauqua Press, 1886), 130.

without taking economic factors into account. The steady advance in the income of a large segment of the middle classes, accompanied as this was by added leisure, made possible the pursuit of learning for its own sake or for advancement in the sharply competitive world of business and the professions. Thus a market existed for the great variety of commercial ventures with educational and pseudo-educational appeals.

In 1868 James Redpath, a Scottish immigrant with a long journalistic career on the *New York Tribune*, reorganized the enfeebled old lyceums into a highly commercialized lecture bureau. Redpath paid as much as $250 or $500 for a single appearance of any figure who could bring in the gate receipts. On this circuit Gough, the temperance advocate, Nast, the cartoonist, Russell Conwell, the evangelist of self-help, and John L. Stoddard, the travel lecturer, appeared for the edification and amusement of Redpath's patrons. In general, this commercialized series, and those succeeding it, emphasized less the informative lecture of the old-time lyceum and went in more for the humorous, the dramatic, and the recreational type of program. Redpath insisted that entertainment must always be clean, free from anything that might endanger public welfare, and congenial to the basic American devotion to religious observance, the sanctity of the home, the spirit of neighborliness, and the Constitution.

What was true of the post-Civil War commercial "lyceums" was no less true of the circuit Chautauquas which, it must be remembered, had no official connection with the philanthropic Chautauqua Assembly and Literary and Scientific Reading Circle centering at Chautauqua Lake, New York. The commercially organized traveling Chautauqua was a combination of the Redpath Lyceum Bureau and Bishop Vincent's summer lectures and study courses. In 1903 Keith Vawter, an agent of the Redpath Lyceum Bureau, organized a traveling "Chautauqua" which took inspirational lecturers and musical and dramatic talent to towns all over the land. Other Chautauqua circuits quickly appeared. Until the movies, radio, and the automobile ruined this venture in the years after World War I it brought information, inspiration, and amusement to villagers and farm people hungry for culture and diversion.

The commercial motive was more blatantly operative in the correspondence schools, which catered to the desire for specialized training in the trades, industries, and professions as well as to the yearning for culture for its own sake and for the advantages it presumably offered in the hard ascent of the ladder of success. In the late 1880s Thomas J.

Foster, editor of the *Mining Herald* at Shenandoah, began the preparation of a correspondence course on mining and surveying. The International Correspondence Schools of Scranton grew out of this venture. By the end of World War I at least 300 private correspondence schools, varying from fairly reliable institutions to outright frauds, were in operation and boasted millions of enrolled students, past and present. What characterized all of these schools was the amazing breadth of the curriculum—the cultural arts, courses on personal efficiency, business, technical, and vocational subjects were all to be had. No less characteristic were the high-pressure salesmanship methods used to enroll the discouraged, the ambitious, or the pliable prospect.

One of the most striking exemplifications of the commercial motive in the popularization of reading matter was the appearance of such series of cheaply priced books as the Standard Library, Franklin Square Library, Seaside Library, Leisure Hour Series, Lakeside Series, New Handy Volumes, Town and Country Library, Munro Library, Acme Library of Standard Biography, and Lovell's Popular Library. These series contained both fiction and nonfiction, good books and bad. Until the passage of the International Copyright Act in 1891 the series were weighted with foreign titles. The prices of each volume in some of the series ran as low as ten or twenty cents.

New methods for distributing cheap—and costly—books on a mass scale were also perfected. The most spectacular of these was the practice of "book butchering." Department stores, having purchased huge lots of books, sold them "dirt cheap"—often at an actual loss—in order to entice customers for other goods. The mail-order houses like Sears, Roebuck also became agencies for the mass circulation of inexpensive titles. The technique of subscription-selling of books by house-to-house canvassing was carefully cultivated. The book agent, with a glib sales talk designed to appeal to every human instinct and prejudice, waylaid the poor plowman at the end of the furrow and intrigued the housewife on the farm and in the village. Millions of volumes, some pretentiously bound in half leather and on the subscription plan bringing vastly more than they were worth, thus found their way into farmhouses and small-town cottages. Bibles, sermons, and other religious writings; encyclopedias, dictionaries, and books of knowledge; memoirs of Presidents and Civil War generals; popular histories and other miscellanies thus entered into the life of the common people.

The commercial motive, tempered though it might be by other factors, was of inestimable importance in the vast expansion of the newspaper and periodical press. Magazines designed to cater to average and below-average tastes and newspapers edited for the masses multiplied and their circulation increased by almost incredible leaps and bounds. It would be impossible to list all the new ventures or to indicate the volume of their circulation. But a word must be said of the *Ladies' Home Journal*, which Cyrus Curtis began in 1883, and of which Edward W. Bok took the editorial helm six years later. Selling for only ten cents a copy, the *Ladies' Home Journal* dealt with household concerns, with advice to the lovelorn, and with the growing civic interests of women— interests which Bok, indeed, did something to stimulate.

The popular muckraking magazines were fathered by Samuel S. McClure when, in 1893, he launched *McClure's*. Talented writers and illustrators found lucrative employment on these magazines, which became tremendously popular in the first decade of the twentieth century when they went in for "the literature of exposure"; corruption in city governments, in state and federal affairs, and in business was mercilessly revealed to the delight and enlightenment of the vast constituency which eagerly devoured their *McClure's, Cosmopolitans, Forums, Americans, Everybody's, Pearson's*.

The man in the shop, the woman in the kitchen, and the girl and boy in the office, the store, the factory, and the street read newspapers as well as magazines. Joseph Pulitzer and William Randolph Hearst achieved enormous success with newspapers for the masses. This success rested in part on the fact that popular reforms were championed but even more on the emotional appeal of sensational events and human interest stories. Pulitzer and Hearst had their imitators, and from the vast increase both in the number of newspapers and in their circulation it was clear that the plain people were reading in an unprecedented fashion. What they read and how it affected them, as well as the general tone of American intellectual life, is another story.

## Popularization: Its Effects

It is not easy to assess the influence of the movement to extend some part of the intellectual life to the great masses of Americans. Some things, however, are clear. Although literacy is not learning and although a sanity of judgment is often found among completely unlettered men, still the ability to read is indispensable for any full participation in the world of ideas. In the nation at large, illiteracy declined approximately from 17 percent in 1880 to 13 percent in 1890 and to 11 percent in 1900. The gains that were made resulted in part from the work of evening classes in public schools but more largely from the multiplication and better enforcement of state laws requiring a minimum of school attendance. These laws explain the fact that whereas in 1880 the entire schooling of the average American was less than four years, it had reached the five-year mark in 1900 and the six-year mark in 1914.

The qualitative improvement of schooling during this period of vast expansion occasioned pride in educational circles. It is true that in most of the rural areas of the country, especially in the South, schooling was still woefully defective from the point of view of the best practices in our own day. Nevertheless, the offerings in the city schools were constantly being enriched; methods of instruction improved from the point of view of both individual learning and social effectiveness; and the training of teachers was gradually becoming better as a result of the expansion of the normal schools and the growth of summer sessions in colleges and universities. The work of G. Stanley Hall, father of the child study movement, of E. L. Thorndike, founder of an objective educational psychology, and of William James and John Dewey, all of whom contributed to the undermining of the sterile scholasticism of the schools, was having telling effects.

The amazing expansion of the high school movement meant that popularization of knowledge was not limited to the elementary level. Between 1878 and 1898 the number of high schools increased from somewhat less than 800 to 5500, and in the next fifteen years it more than doubled. Between 1890 and 1918 a new high school was opened for every calendar day in every year. Many of these schools were deficient in equipment and were taught by men and women of inferior ability and training. Still, they opened hitherto unknown fields and provided a large proportion of the rising generation with at least a vision of knowledge.

Several agencies offered the generation that had finished its formal schooling opportunities to keep abreast of new knowledge. The lecture platforms of the large cities provided the middle class with lectures on almost every conceivable subject. A study of the New York lecture platform shows that New York audiences in the post-Civil War decades were more sophisticated in their tastes than in the mid-century and that scientific lectures were more specialized and exact in character than elementary discourses on scientific subjects in the 1850s had been. Free public libraries reached many who could not afford lecture fees. It would be hard to overemphasize the significance of such men as Enoch Pratt of Baltimore, Samuel J. Tilden of New York, and above all, of course, Andrew Carnegie. In 1876 the American Library Association was organized; as a result, library techniques and services were presently much improved.

The Chautauqua Assembly and Literary and Scientific Reading Circles introduced their disciples, in the words of George Herbert Palmer of Harvard, to "Round Tables upon Milton, Temperance, Geology, the American Constitution, the Relations of Science and Religion, and the Doctrine of Rent." The Chautauqua reading courses brought into the homes of their constituency literary and philosophical classics, together with standard works on the social and physical sciences. Newer points of view and findings in the world of knowledge were also surprisingly well represented on the required and recommended reading lists. Distinguished scholars lectured at the Chautauqua Assembly during the summer season. Among them were Professor Mahaffy, the well-known Greek scholar of Trinity College, Dublin; Herbert Baxter Adams, the Johns Hopkins historian; and Richard T. Ely, fresh from his economic studies at the German universities.

William James, who also participated at one of the summer assemblies, was amused, it is true, by the many "earnest and helpless minds" he encountered, by the lack of any epicureanism or sense of humor, and by the dull if high tone of morality. He was likewise somewhat shocked at the premium which Chautauqua necessarily put on a certain shallowness and glibness. But like his colleague at Harvard, Josiah Royce, he saw great value in such popularized learning. Royce properly realized that even though enthusiasm and memory were emphasized at the expense of rational intelligence, nevertheless Chautauqua set in motion minds that had been dull and lifeless, that it gave hundreds of thousands a glimpse of the intellectual world beyond their petty personal and domestic affairs.

The intellectual tone of the traveling commercial Chautauquas was on a lower level than that of Bishop Vincent's philanthropic and high-minded organization. Yet even in the tents that went up in countless towns and villages, illuminating political discussions by minor leaders and, more rarely, by such men as Lincoln Steffens, James Bryce, Robert M. La Follette, Charles Evans Hughes, William Jennings Bryan, and Theodore Roosevelt had a definite educational value. Jane Addams made Hull House live in the minds of rural folk, Judge Lindsey told the story of the Children's Court, and Samuel Gompers publicized the aims of the "organized toilers."

Although the four-hundred-odd local organizations of women which in 1889 formed the General Federation of Women's Clubs did not include the wives of men who labored in mines, in factories, and on farms, the women's club movement was an important factor in the popularization of knowledge among women of the middle class. The "literary" clubs, the dominant type of organization in the 1880s and 1890s, were shallow, but they tended to become increasingly specialized and less superficial. Through these organizations women studied not only literature, science, and art, but such social questions as feminism, peace and war, temperance, crime, imperialism, and even capitalism. In 1904 the newly elected president of the General Federation urged the membership to give up studying Dante's *Inferno* and "proceed in earnest to contemplate our own social order." American civic consciousness owes a great debt to the women's club movement. American women of the middle class in turn, together with their children, owe an equally large debt to the much-ridiculed clubs.

Country women much more gradually became identified with village women's clubs, but this was exceptional in many areas of the country. Apart from the summer circuit Chautauqua, these women, if they had any yearning for "culture," were compelled to depend largely on what they could get from the catalogues of Sears, Roebuck and other mail-order houses. In the general catalogue of 1906 Sears, Roebuck devoted sixteen pages to books; these included seventy-five kinds of Bibles, ten books about the Bible (none of which revealed any of the teachings or discoveries of the evolutionists, philologists, or astrophysicists), and a goodly list of novels which the descriptions guaranteed to be pure, inspiring, and wholesome. Of the older authors, Irving, Shakespeare, Grote, Gibbon, Browning, Scott, and Hugo were represented; of the newer, Augusta J. Evans, Kipling, and the authors of the Rollo books, the Elsie books, and a vast miscellany dealing with the secrets of acquiring popularity. Although discussions of sex could be found under a few well-veiled titles, such as Fowler's *Science of Life*, sex, which was still generally identified with sin, was largely absent from the volumes obtainable from Sears, Roebuck.

If one leaves aside the unmeasurable but obviously important effects which all the popularization of knowledge had on individual lives and asks what impact it had on American intellectual life as a whole, he can do little more than speculate. It is possible that, as George Herbert Palmer feared, the university extension movement, in putting new burdens on already overburdened professors, lowered the level of scholarship in certain universities and decreased the amount and quality of research. But this does not seem to have been generally true. It is clear that American writers for the first time found a sufficiently large audience to make literature a really profitable profession. It is also clear that much writing, whether in books, magazines, or newspapers, was geared to the taste or training of the masses; this meant that "standards" in the traditional sense were lowered or ignored.

On the other hand, the gains were impressive. Of these none was more important than the effect which all this popularization had on the attitude of the plain people toward learning and culture. Traditionally suspicious of it, perhaps because they did not understand it and knew they could not partake of it, the common men and women now tended to become less hostile toward the scholar and the specialist. For all who subscribed to the democratic faith, the narrowing of the gulf separating the plain folk from the scholars was a rich and significant gain. In any case, the sober judgment of an English scholar who knew America well possessed a large measure of truth: "The average of knowledge is higher, the habit of reading and thinking more generally diffused, than in any other country."[4]

[4] James Bryce, *The American Commonwealth* (The Macmillan Company, 1888), II, 2.

# 24 Formulas of Protest and Reform

*Thanks to St. Matthew, who had been*
*To mass meetings in Palestine,*
*We know whose side was spoken for*
*When Comrade Jesus had the floor.*
*Ah, let no local Him refuse!*
*Comrade Jesus has paid His dues.*
*Whatever other be debarred,*
*Comrade Jesus has His red card.*
—SARAH CLEGHORN, 1914

*America was created in order that every man should have the same chance as every other man to exercise mastery over his own fortunes.*
—WOODROW WILSON, 1912

After Appomattox social idealists sometimes wondered whether reform would ever again enlist as much intellectual and emotional enthusiasm as in the old days. Many former abolitionists rested on their oars with the feeling that the greatest evil, slavery, had been abolished. No reform tract now took the place of *Uncle Tom's Cabin* or *Ten Nights in a Barroom;* only a few communities replaced the two score that had borne witness to the vogue of Utopian socialism. Yet contrary to the gloomy forebodings of the veteran reformers, the reservoir of social protest was by no means exhausted. All the old ideas of social betterment were again vigorously championed—women's right, temperance and prohibition, international peace, the equality of Negroes, the well-being of farmers and factory workers. These ideas found expression not only in lobbying activities and at the polls but in books, pamphlets, magazines, newspapers, lectures, and speeches.

In the decades between the Civil War and World War I the ideology of protest and reform became broader in scope and increasingly important in influence. Even in the earlier decades large numbers of country people heatedly discussed ideas of reform in the widening circles of Granges and Farmers' Alliances and in the conventions of the Greenback and Populist parties. Judged by their participation in union activity, only a small minority of factory workers, miners, and railway operatives joined in the movement of protest. Yet the rapid growth of the Knights of Labor, and subsequently of the American Federation of Labor and the Industrial Workers of the World, indicated that laborers were thinking more and more about the distribution of industrial profits and even about the nature of capitalist economy. After the turn of the century no other intellectual interest excited more general enthusiasm than protest against political, social, and economic ailments and grievances.

One evidence of the growing interest in protest and reform was the appearance of an ever larger number of novelists, poets, publicists, ministers, journalists, and social workers devoted to the idea of improving the social order. Small in numbers in the 1870s and 1880s, this group of intellectuals was considerably augmented in the last decades of the century. Before the outbreak of World War I liberal intellectuals constituted an impressive company in American letters and scholarship. The concept of social justice and of revolt against the practices of corporate wealth found able champions in social workers like Robert A. Woods, Jane Addams, and Florence Kelley; in journalists like Henry George, John Swinton, Benjamin O. Flower, Jacob Riis, and Lincoln Steffens; and in literary men such as William Dean Howells, Hamlin Garland, Edwin Markham, and Robert Herrick. Ministers—Josiah Strong, W. D. P. Bliss, Washington Gladden, and George D. Herron, to cite only a few names—and scholars like Edward Bemis, Richard T. Ely, and President Van Hise played leading roles in formulating protest and reform thought. The wide vogue of the muckraking magazines in the first decade of the twentieth century and the influence of such figures as Tom Johnson, Robert M. La Follette, William J. Bryan, Theodore Roosevelt, and Woodrow Wilson also testified to the popularity of revolt and social justice in the minds of the American people.

This growing interest of men and women in social amelioration reflected changing social and economic conditions. At the very time when American industries were pouring out swelling streams of commodities and great fortunes were becoming greater, the fair pictures presented in conservative journals of opinion were marred by many grim realities. Peter Cooper, a man with a social conscience and the temperament of a reformer, called attention to these realities in a letter to President Hayes in 1877. "For four years past," he wrote, "millions of men and women, in this hitherto rich and prosperous country, have been thrown out of employment, or living on precarious and inadequate wages, have felt embittered with a lot, in which neither economy nor industry, nor a cheerful willingness to work hard, can bring an alleviation."[1] These and similar matters troubled the minds and tried the hearts of the plain people. In Henry George, father of the single-tax program, they found a spokesman. George wrote passionately of "complaints of industrial depression; of labor condemned to involuntary idleness; of capital massed and wasting; of pecuniary distress among business men; of want and suffering and anxiety among the working classes."[2]

Still other widely felt grievances were voiced by Hamlin Garland, a son of pioneer farmers. The souls of the characters in *Main-Travelled Roads*, his first notable literary achievement, were seared by foreclosures of bank-held mortgages, the high cost of manufactured goods in comparison with the prices of farm produce, and the dreary isolation and cultural bleakness of western farm life. In the preface which he wrote for this book, William Dean Howells expressed the dominant mood of Hamlin Garland's characters. Howells spoke of "the life of the men who hopelessly and cheerlessly make the wealth that enriches the alien and the idler, and impoverishes the producers. . . . The stories are full of those gaunt, grim sordid, pathetic, ferocious figures, whom our satirists find so easy to caricature as Hayseeds, and whose blind groping for fairer conditions is so grotesque to the newspapers and so menacing to the politicians. They feel that something is wrong, and they know that the wrong is not theirs."

Other intellectual allies of the farmers and industrial workers wrote more exactly of the conditions and actions deemed responsible for unemployment, low wages, insecurity, poverty, mortgages, and hard times generally. A contributor to the *Methodist Review* in 1888, in analyzing

[1] Peter Cooper, *Ideas for a Science of Good Government* (New York, 1883), 118.
[2] Henry George, *Progress and Poverty* (Robert Schakenbach Foundation, 1940), 5.

the causes of social ailments, summarized views widely held in protest and reform circles: in the "unhallowed temple of Mammon men are taught how to frame plausible theories in defense of gambling, speculation, 'corners,' 'trusts,' 'combinations,' 'pools,' briberies, railway wrecking, betrayals of official obligations, adulterations of food, fraudulent manufacturing, dealing in things injurious to health and public morals, and similar methods of gaining wealth by wronging other men."[3] Frank Norris in his novels, *The Octopus* and *The Pit*, told stories of small business men driven to the wall by the tactics of great industrial and railway corporations, stories in part documented by Henry Demarest Lloyd and Ida Tarbell, pioneers in the journalistic literature of "exposure."

## The Theory of Individual Rights Underlying the Protests

A common theory underlay the ideas of reform, even the most extreme. This was the old theory of human rights—the idea that the individual has a natural right to an existence worthy of a human being, that institutions and social arrangements are but means to the realization of this right. After quoting the Declaration of Independence on the natural rights of men to life, liberty, and the pursuit of happiness, Henry George declared that "these rights are denied when the equal right to land—on which and by which men alone can live—is denied. Equality of political rights will not compensate for the denial of the equal right to the bounty of nature."[4] In much the same way General James Baird Weaver, a leading exponent of Populist philosophy, identified the fight against monopolies with the crusade the fathers had fought in 1776 for their natural rights. "Throughout all history we have had ample evidence that the new world is the theater upon which the great struggle for the rights of man is to be made, and the righteous movement now in progress should again forcibly remind us of our enviable mission, under Providence, among the nations of the earth."[5]

Even the minority among critics and reformers who looked forward to the reign of socialism justified their position on the basis of human rights.

[3] *The Methodist Review*, LXVIII (May, 1888), 453.
[4] Henry George, *Progress and Poverty* (San Francisco, 1879), 545.
[5] James B. Weaver, *A Call to Action* (Iowa Printing Co., Des Moines, 1892), 445.

Only socialism, they argued, could recapture natural rights and individuality for the great mass of the people. Edward Bellamy, author of the widely read novel of Utopian socialism, Looking Backward (1887), explained how natural rights had been achieved in 2000 A.D. through collectivism: "Our ethics of wealth is extremely simple. It consists merely in the law of self-preservation, asserted in the name of all against the encroachments of any. It rests upon a principle which a child can understand as well as a philosopher, and which no philosopher ever attempted to refute, namely, the supreme right of all to live, and consequently to insist that society shall be so organized as to secure that right."[6] In Bellamy's Utopia the supreme and natural right to live which socialism made possible did not mean that the individual was to be regimented and thus lose his individuality. The main business of existence in the socialist society of the year 2000 was to be "the higher and larger activities which the performance of our task will leave us free to enter upon. . . . A government, or a majority, which should undertake to tell the people, or a minority, what they were to eat, drink, or wear, as I believe governments in America did in your day [i.e., 1887], would be regarded as a curious anachronism."[7]

The right to life, liberty, and the pursuit of happiness was the cornerstone of the ideology of protest and reform, but it was not the only foundation stone. The doctrine of natural rights had been discredited by the rise of a body of political and social theory commonly termed the historical school. According to this position, men had not, at some remote time, entered into contracts to form society and the state; these institutions had rather been the result of a very gradual growth. Many conservatives had already rejected the natural rights theory and were erecting a social theory more nearly in accord with the historical conception of institutions. This may have led certain radicals to search for some intellectual support other than the much-impugned natural rights doctrine. In any case, Edmond Kelly, a thoughtful exponent of reform philosophy, accepted the doctrine that nature supported inequalities, including a radical inequality of men. But he insisted that man, the product of nature, had come to be what he was through his efforts to control nature for his own ideal ends: "Justice may, then, be described as the effort to eliminate from our social conditions the effects of the inequalities of

---

[6] Edward Bellamy, Looking Backward, 2000–1887 (Houghton Mifflin Company, 1926), 74.
[7] Ibid., 26, 184.

Nature upon the happiness and advancement of man, particularly to create an artificial environment which shall serve the individual as well as the race, and tend to perpetuate noble types rather than those which are base."[8]

Faith in man's dignity and in his natural rights was a heritage of the Enlightenment. It was also a heritage of actual experience on American soil. The *philosophes* had emphasized man's power through reason to tear down dungeons and build mansions. The conquest of the American physical environment by individuals, families, and groups seemed in the minds of American men and women to be living evidence of human ability to do this very thing. The old American society of relatively equal opportunity was changing, but belief in the individual continued. In the words of the Populist spokesman, General Weaver, monopolies and corporate wealth might control "the articles which the plain people consume in their daily life" and cut off their accumulations, thus depriving them of "the staff upon which they fain would lean in their old age." But the people could "rise up and overturn the despoilers though they shake the earth by the displacement."[9]

The most commonly held theories of protest and reform accepted as a part of man's natural rights the main body of existing laws relative to the ownership, transmission, and distribution of property. These theories assumed that if no unfair or objectionable practices intervened, under these laws individuals would attain a state of well-being representing a high degree of social justice. Thus the individualism on which conservatives largely based their defense of the economic and social status quo served equally well the protestants against monopolies and corporate wealth. Populists and their intellectual heirs, the Progressives and the Wilsonian Democrats, alike assumed that the dissolution or public control of monopolies would restore the individual's opportunity to compete fairly for a decent living. Property rights of the individual were not under attack; the only thing under attack was the alleged unfair behavior of corporations that had hounded the little man and kept him from acquiring the livelihood and property to which he was entitled by natural right. The doctrine of protest was, in brief, essentially middle class in character.

Reformers believed that the desired social order of equal opportunity

[8] Edmond Kelly, *Government or Human Evolution* (Longmans (David McKay Co.), 1900), I, 360.

[9] James B. Weaver, *op. cit.*, 393–394.

for all might be built within the existing framework of political democracy. They placed their trust in free discussion and the reasonable decision of issues by the majority, although they increasingly demanded that political machinery "be salvaged from the hands of spoilsmen and politicians."[10] Government was to be recaptured from "the interests" and made to serve the well-being of every individual man, woman, and child.

A few radicals rejected this idea. A tradition of extreme individualism utterly distrustful of the state survived among the intellectual heirs of Thoreau and found a rationale in the thought of the American philosophical anarchists, Stephen Pearl Andrews and Benjamin Tucker. European anarchists, particularly Bakúnin, Tolstoy, and Kropotkin, also found disciples both among immigrant groups and among a small section of American workers and intellectuals who disliked the discipline and regimentation they believed to be inherent in socialism. Johann Most and his colleagues who repudiated political action and advocated "the propaganda of the deed," or violence, made few converts. Yet the tradition they represented, together with the related syndicalism of the French thinker Sorel, was fundamental in the ideology of the Industrial Workers of the World. This organization of class-conscious workers became a factor of consequence in the labor movement of the early twentieth century. The songs and banners of these "Wobblies," as they were called, and the poems of Giovannitti, one of their number, reflect their conviction that government could in no case be made into an instrument for achieving economic justice and true individual freedom. But with the exception of the IWW and the anarchists, reformers and radicals put their faith in the political machinery of democracy as the instrumentality through which freedom and opportunity for all individuals were to be restored or achieved.

### Theories of Reform Through Currency and Taxation

The determination of small businessmen, farmers, and urban workers to curb monopoly occasioned a variety of programs. None enjoyed more general popularity in reform thought than those based upon unorthodox monetary theory. The prevailing or intrinsic-value theory assumed that

[10] Frederic C. Howe, *The Confessions of a Reformer* (Charles Scribner's Sons, 1925), 5.

money possesses an intrinsic value which government cannot alter without injustice. According to this theory, the law of supply and demand answers all the needs of money regulation. As a result the government should never issue paper or coin irredeemable in gold, the necessary standard of exchange. This theory enjoyed the support of classical economists, of the financial and industrial groups whose interests it served, and of national law.

The debtor groups—farmers, workers, small business people, and many professional families—became convinced in the post-Civil War years that public policy based on the prevailing monetary theory was the major cause of their ills. In ever larger numbers they subscribed to an antithetical theory of money, the quantitative theory. This concept, which had a long history, had traditionally found favor among the debtor classes. In pre-Civil War years a group of obscure writers developed what had hitherto been a vague popular concept into a fairly elaborate monetary theory. The quantitative or legal-tender theory held that the value of money depends on the amount in circulation. Since gold and silver are commodities that fluctuate in value in relation to the amount in circulation, the government must regulate the per capita circulation in accordance with economic and social needs. In the opinion of legal-tender advocates, it must take from the bankers and their industrial allies the control of the currency and regulate it in the interest of the great mass of people. Then the grip of the nonproducing classes on the producing classes would be destroyed; land speculation would be impossible, pressure on debtors would be reduced, the small businessman would again enjoy a fair chance in the world of enterprise, and the income of the farmer and laborer would increase.

In the words of one of its earliest systematic advocates, Edward Kellogg, such a monetary theory would effect a social revolution. "Wealth, instead of being accumulated in a few hands, would be distributed among producers. Products would be owned by those who performed the labor, because the standard of distribution would nearly conform to the rights of man." This program for the abolition of poverty would not interfere with private property in production and business, or, indeed, with private enterprise itself. Its individualistic character was especially attractive to small entrepreneurs, who yearned for the freedom of opportunity of which they claimed the lords of wealth had robbed them in the name of free enterprise.

The legal-tender theory enjoyed its widest support among the indebted farmers in the West, but labor leaders like William Sylvis and such humanitarians as Wendell Phillips and Peter Cooper also espoused the program. Surfeited with unmarketable silver, western miners allied themselves with indebted groups in the hope that the government would purchase their commodity for coinage. Even when the more technical aspects of the theory were not fully grasped, the idea of free silver appealed to all who felt bitterly toward corporate wealth and longed for what they deemed the good old days when industrial and financial monopolies did not exist to crush honest individual enterprise. The doctrine that the grievances of the common man might be resolved by free silver was widely publicized by the picturesque "Coin" Harvey, by Populist leaders such as Colonel S. F. Norton of the *Chicago Sentinel*, and by William Jennings Bryan in his presidential campaign of 1896. Bryan's defeat, despite his popular following, was a crushing blow to the doctrine of free silver.

The idea that a greater measure of opportunity might be restored to the individual through the revival of the discarded Civil War income tax on wealth also enjoyed wide acclaim. The well-to-do denounced a tax on income as "rank class legislation." "In a republic like ours, where all men are equal," declared Senator John Sherman of Ohio, "this attempt to array the rich against the poor or the poor against the rich is socialism, communism, devilism." Opponents of the income tax rejoiced when the Supreme Court by a five-to-four decision in 1895 declared unconstitutional the income tax provision of the Wilson Tariff Act. But the forces that rallied behind Bryan, convinced that they were without an adequate voice in the government and that government machinery had to be democratized, called for an amendment to the Constitution legalizing the income tax. This tax became a symbol of justice to the farmers and workers, who believed that it would help equalize wealth and restore individual opportunity by shifting some of their tax burden to the well-to-do.

The attractive philosophy of the income tax was overshadowed by the dramatic and Utopian claims advanced in behalf of the single tax. The father of this doctrine, Henry George, developed his analysis of existing social ailments and advanced his remedy in *Progress and Poverty*. Only with great difficulty could a publisher be found for the book, which finally appeared in 1879. But it went through more than a hundred editions and by 1906 had probably been read by 6 million men and women. Its appeal lay partly in Henry George's passionate indictment of the "monopolization of the opportunities which nature freely offers to all," in the stirring pictures contrasting "The House of Have" with "The House of Want." Readers often knew from their own experience what George meant when he wrote of "all the dull, deadening pain, all the keen, maddening anguish" involved in the words "hard times." The appeal of *Progress and Poverty* lay also in the simplicity of the author's proposed remedy. In brief, a new system of land taxation promised to abolish large fortunes and to provide a decent and secure living for the plain people.

Through his own observations and experiences in California in the 1860s, rather than through the perusal of the writings of his many predecessors, Henry George came to the conclusion that as civilization advanced, poverty increased. "Where population is densest, wealth greatest, and the machinery of production and exchange most highly developed—we find the deepest poverty, the sharpest struggle for existence, and the most of enforced idleness."[11] The contrast between the destitution and the affluence of neighboring areas in New York City confirmed him in this belief; he had visited the eastern metropolis in 1869. The peculiar paradox of the advance of progress and poverty he attributed to two facts. In the first place, the high wages incident to a labor shortage in a new country were forced down as the region became settled and the labor supply abundant. In the second place, land monopolists, including railroad and speculative absentee owners, had seized upon the better, more accessible land in advance of settlement, land that was ultimately sold or rented to actual users at exorbitant profits. As the value of this land increased with "progress," or the incoming of people and the upbuilding of a civilization, poverty grew because the land monopolists kept the entire gain or rent for themselves. Thus the laborer and businessman alike, instead of enjoying their due share in the enlarged wealth of the community created by the community, were deprived of that share with resulting distress.

In place of the existing system of taxation George proposed a single tax on all increments in the value of land. This would merely allocate to the public, to all individuals, that part of the value of a given piece of land that the public, or all individuals, had created. George urged that

[11] Henry George, *op. cit.*, 6.

such action would prevent speculation in land and the depressions which inevitably followed such speculation, that it would put an end to the impoverishment of the small businessman, the wage earner, and the farmer.

The appeal of the proposal was enhanced by the argument that the receipts from the social acquisition of the unearned increment of land monopolists would be sufficient for all government purposes; hence the magic phrase, the single tax. In other words, the single tax promised to relieve the public of all other forms of taxation, whether on improvements, on productive labor, or on the imported goods bought by consumers.

The program assumed the possibility of restoring and permanently preserving the individualistic society of George's great hero, Thomas Jefferson. According to George, taxation on socially created land values would wipe out the evil results of unfettered individualism and special privilege that had permitted monopolists to seize the wealth of the people. Thus his basic idea postulated the return of an era in which the true individualism of equal opportunity would enable everyone to live moderately well. Even the concept of the state outlined in *Progress and Poverty* was essentially Jeffersonian; the state was a mere police and tax-collecting agency. Hamlin Garland, one of George's early converts, explained the individualistic character of the single-tax philosophy. "We are individualists mainly; let that be understood," he wrote. "We stand unalterably opposed to the paternal idea of government."

The doctrine of the single tax attracted intellectuals, a few businessmen, and large numbers of industrial workers. The intellectuals were represented by Hamlin Garland, Louis Post, a lawyer and journalist, Brand Whitlock, a Toledo writer, and Father McGlynn, a Catholic priest who was excommunicated for his devotion to George and his defiance of ecclesiastical authority. Tom Johnson, a transportation monopolist who befriended the people of Cleveland by fighting their enemies in business and politics; "Golden Rule" Jones, a beneficent Toledo manufacturer; and Joseph Fels, a Philadelphia soapmaker whose magnanimity helped finance the cause, were the best-known business disciples of the single-tax doctrine. According to a well-informed student of the working class, Professor Richard Ely, "tens of thousands of laborers have read *Progress and Poverty* who never before looked between the covers of an economic book, and its conclusions are widely accepted in the workingmen's creed." In his New York mayoralty campaign in 1886 Henry George enjoyed the support of both the trade unions and the socialists.

Although the ideas of Henry George aroused many plain people to passionate indignation against economic inequality, the single-tax doctrine did not win general acceptance and exerted little practical influence on land taxation. The interests of the small propertied class generally ran counter to his proposal to confiscate the unearned increment on land. Most farmers were cold toward the single-tax idea because farm profits and potential profits were dependent upon increasing land values. Moreover, the unearned increments of mines, real estate, and other landed properties were distributed in widely held insurance policies, stocks, bonds, and mortgages. Henry George in reality never understood the pervasive nature of capitalistic society. Consequently he provided for no adequate political means for effecting his program. Nor did he understand the obstacles in the way of mobilizing power behind a program that in effect would have entailed a virtual revolution against capitalism. His failure, like the failure of many other reformers in this period, arose from an overconfidence in the power and altruism of the individual and from an underestimate of the momentum and pervasiveness of corporate wealth.

## Proposals for Public Control

Among the proposals for the restoration of individual opportunity to the mass of the people the doctrine of breaking down or controlling monopolies enjoyed general popularity. Opposition to monopoly was rooted in English thought and law and had been reflected in the program of the Locofoco Democrats in Andrew Jackson's day. The rapid advance of monopolies during and immediately after the Civil War aroused bitter resentment in the minds of small businessmen, urban workers, and especially farmers. Throughout the western states farmers met on July 4, 1873, to listen to the reading of "The Farmers' Declaration of Independence." This stirring document condemned the "tyranny of monopoly" and demanded the dissolution or control of trusts by government action. Farmers also believed that the cooperative creameries, elevators, and general stores they were promoting might break the grip of monopolies.

The antimonopolist philosophy found full amplification in the speeches of the Populist leader, James Baird Weaver, and in the social views of William Jennings Bryan and his followers in the Democratic party. "The absorption of wealth by the few, the consolidation of our leading railroad systems and the formation of trusts and pools require a stricter control by the Federal government of those arteries of commerce," declared the Democratic party in its platform of 1896. Bryan himself spoke for millions of his followers when he declared that democracy could not endure if the livelihood of the vast mass of people continued to be controlled by "the moneyed element of the country in the interest of predatory wealth."[12]

Even before it became evident that laws and court action could not effect the permanent breakup of trusts, many Americans had urged government control of business monopolies. The Granges, which spread rapidly in the agricultural states during the 1870s, were especially active in promoting the idea of public control. "We are opposed to such spirit and management of any corporation or enterprise as tends to oppress the people and rob them of their just profits," declared the Illinois Grange in 1873. Illinois farmers "in mass meeting assembled" therefore resolved that the railroad "despotism" which "defies our laws, plunders our shippers, impoverishes our people, and corrupts our government, shall be subdued and made to subserve the public interest at whatever cost."[13] Beginning in 1869, several states, including Massachusetts, Illinois, Wisconsin, and Iowa, responded to this frame of thought by enacting laws designed in some degree to regulate railroads and grain elevators. In spite of opposition from the railroads and the courts, the idea that private corporations vested with a public interest should be subject to government control made headway. This idea found expression in the Interstate Commerce Act of 1887.

Populist thought went even further. "We believe that the time has come when railroad corporations will either own the people or the people must own the railroads," declared the Populist platform of 1892. Public ownership of the telegraph and telephone and the postal savings banks

[12] *The Speeches of William Jennings Bryan* (Funk & Wagnalls Co., 1913), II, 59.
[13] Jonathan Periam, *The Groundswell* (Chicago, 1874), 286 ff.

also met with Populist approval. In short, a vast body of men and women in villages and on farms had come to believe that the modification of individual enterprise was the surest way to restore the freedom of opportunity associated with the past.

Many wage earners also sympathized with the idea of public control of business. Under the leadership of Samuel Gompers the American Federation of Labor was, it is true, shying away from the doctrinaire reform philosophies and the political action that earlier American labor leaders had espoused. But even the concentration of this body on building strong unions in order that these might control the labor market did not entirely blind it to the importance of government control over business, especially in matters directly affecting labor. Thus the labor movement supported the regulation of railway rates, an eight-hour day, and factory inspection by government authority. Urban labor by and large was to vote for Theodore Roosevelt and Woodrow Wilson in return for their promise to subject business to a larger degree of public control through social legislation and the recognition of collective bargaining.

Intellectuals and philanthropists supported the growing idea of public control over business. In the 1880s a group of men and women, inspired by the example of Toynbee Hall in London and the rise of the Social Gospel, began to devote their talents and their lives to the improvement of living conditions and social relations in the slums of great cities. Such women as Maude Nathan, Josephine Shaw Lowell, and Florence Kelley not only supported the settlement-house idea but founded the Consumers' Leagues to persuade the public to purchase goods from factories and shops whose fair labor policies were not open to question. These leaders became increasingly convinced that there was need for more thoroughgoing measures. Thus they supported the idea of government control over labor policies, housing conditions, and municipal services as an effective program to improve the lot of the less well housed and the less well fed. In Cleveland and Toledo idealistic young lawyers and journalists like Frederic C. Howe, Brand Whitlock, and Newton D. Baker not only rallied to the support of reform mayors but insisted on the importance of municipal control or even ownership of basic services and utilities. In calling attention to the tie-up between business and corrupt politics, muckraking journalists also contributed to the conviction that democratized municipal governments needed to tighten their control over all business affecting the public interest.

The promotion by intellectuals of the ever more widely held idea of public control over private enterprise was not confined to the municipal scene. Chemists in government service—Dr. Harvey W. Wiley in the Department of Agriculture was the outstanding pioneer—began to expose the prevalent use of poisonous preservatives in processed foods and of dangerous narcotics in patent medicines. Wiley's work in arousing consumers to demand restrictive legislation was reinforced in 1906 when Upton Sinclair, in his sensational novel, *The Jungle*, exposed the filth and poison in canned meats and the generally deplorable conditions in packing houses. The control to which corporate enterprise was subjected in the Pure Food and Drugs Act and the Meat Inspection Act was not the only victory for the idea of government curbs on business. The idea that private enterprise must no longer be allowed ruthlessly to exploit the remaining natural resources of the people was promoted by literary men and women, university professors, and scientists in government service.

Among the intellectuals who helped advance the idea that laissez faire must be modified in the interest of individual dignity, freedom, and opportunity, Henry Demarest Lloyd is of special significance. In 1880 Lloyd's analysis of the anatomy of the Standard Oil Company revealed to readers of the *Atlantic Monthly* some of the ruthlessness in the practices of big business. Fourteen years later this crusader for human rights returned to the same theme in his notable book, *Wealth Against Commonwealth*. The picture he revealed of the rise of Standard Oil to power through chicanery was documented by overlooked court decisions, buried government commission reports, and the forgotten findings of legislative hearings. Although Lloyd's selection and interpretation of data were open to criticism, his basic thesis was advanced with much persuasiveness. In pleading for the necessity of government control over monopolies, he tried to show that free competition among individuals no longer existed and that therefore public control could not destroy an idea which had no validity in fact.

The man for himself destroys himself and all men; only society can foster him and them. We can become individual only by submitting to be bound by others. We extend our freedom only by finding new laws to obey. . . . The locomotive off its track is not free. The isolated man is the mere rudiment of an individual. But he who has become citizen, neighbor, friend, brother, son, husband, father, fellow-member in one, is just by so many times individualized.[14]

Lloyd was not the first to expose corruption. Thomas Nast in his famous cartoons had opened to view the guilty Tweed Ring in New York City a full decade before Lloyd began his work. In California "Philosopher Pickett," known as a "crackpot" pamphleteer, had protested almost alone against the ruthless and corrupt exploitation of the state. Such publicists as Lord Bryce, E. L. Godkin, and Andrew D. White had spoken at length on public corruption. But Lloyd traced corruption to the doors of respectable businessmen, named names, cited authorities, and refused to pull his punches. Gradually he found that he was not alone. Enterprising publishers of widely read newspapers, Pulitzer, Hearst, and Scripps, were increasing the circulation of their journals by sensationally exposing the corrupt methods through which big business won favors from governments. In so doing these men were the successors of McClure, Walker, and Munsey, the greatest of the muckraking publishers in the first decade of the twentieth century.

Excesses and abuses were laid mercilessly bare by journalists employed to investigate the object of exposure: the Standard Oil Company, the insurance firms, the meat trust, the drug and food combinations, "the money trust," and government itself. The popularity of the literature of exposure was reflected in the geometrical increase in the circulation of the muckraking magazines. The graphic and sensational exposure of scandals in business and the high moral tone of most of the muckrakers had much to do with their vogue. So too did the long-mounting rage of the middle class at the malpractices of corporations in putting individuals, whether petty rivals or workers or consumers, at the mercy of the titans of industry and finance.

Muckraking popularized as nothing else had done the awareness of the power of corporations, their ruthlessness and antisocial practices, their corrupt relations with government. Not all the muckrakers explicitly demanded the extension of government control over corporations, but such extension was implicit in almost every muckraking article in *Collier's*, *McClure's*, *Cosmopolitan*, the *American Magazine*, and *La Follette's Weekly*, to name only the best known. The fervor and sweep of the Progressivism of the older La Follette and the first Roosevelt can

[14] Henry Demarest Lloyd, *Wealth Against Commonwealth* (Harper & Row, 1894), 527, 534.

be understood only by taking into account the moral indignation aroused by the muckrakers in the minds of the plain people.

Between the election of Wilson in 1912 and the outbreak of World War I the decline of muckraking, which had already set in, proceeded rapidly. This resulted in part from the fact that the public became weary of sensational exposure, in part from the boycott imposed on the muckraking magazines by bankers and advertisers, and in part from the actual extension of government control over business. This extension appeared to have remedied the most flagrant abuses.

In the later stages of government control over business Louis D. Brandeis played a leading role. A Louisville attorney of German-Jewish background, Brandeis, after moving to Boston, became known as "the people's lawyer" by virtue of his championship of the popular interest against the encroachments of big business. More than that, in his work for state insurance and other social benefits he showed how through the government the little fellows might conduct their own business to their own great advantage. Brandeis, both in his writings and in his participation in lawsuits, attempted to strike an effective balance between the traditional values of voluntary action and individual initiative and the new imperatives of social control of the power inherent in great aggregations of wealth. Convinced that the traditional individualistic philosophy of unrestricted property rights was both anachronistic and detrimental to genuine individualism, he mustered facts and figures in his briefs and showed how law might become an instrument for social improvement as well as for individual justice. Above all, he pointed to ways for the restoration of some measure of free competition among business units. Brandeis came increasingly to influence Woodrow Wilson, whose political conservatism was in part abandoned when he served as governor of New Jersey in 1910 and 1911. In the spirit of Brandeis, Wilson insisted in *The New Freedom* that the economically strong had crushed the economically weak. He demanded effective antitrust laws and the restoration of freedom for the little fellow. Like other antimonopolists he also believed that protective tariffs had helped build up the great trusts and that a reduction of tariffs would promote the restoration of competition among smaller industrial units. The antimonopolist idea found legislative expression in the revision of the Sherman Anti-Trust Act of 1890 by the new Clayton Act of 1914. When, in 1916, President Wilson appointed Brandeis to the Supreme Court in the face of much opposition on the score that he was both a Jew and a radical, the Democratic leader extended the influence of "the people's lawyer" by enabling him officially to help interpret the law of the land.

## The Purification and Extension of Democracy

In a restricted political sense the Progressive movement emerged in the Republican party, but the pattern of thought exemplified in Roosevelt and La Follette also governed in considerable measure the thought of Bryan and, ultimately, of Wilson. Progressivism, as a body of loosely-tied-together and not always consistent ideas, appealed to an ever larger number of middle-class men and women, who felt that corporate wealth had come to control the government and that it threatened the whole scheme of values they cherished. From the Populists Progressive thought inherited the idea that monopolies must be dissolved or regulated and that the natural resources of the country in the remaining public lands must be conserved for the use of the people in future generations. The belief in social legislation also figured in Progressive philosophy. At least a few intellectuals, particularly Herbert Croly in *The Promise of American Life* (1909), argued strongly for enhancing the power of the national government through social planning for the general good.

One of the leading ideas shared by all Progressives was that the extension of political democracy could restore popular rights and general well-being. Virtually all Progressives assumed that corporate wealth had come to control the government—local, state, and federal—and that this control must be regained by the people. To insure the popular control of the government, they advocated various programs, some old, some native, some imported. The extension of the civil service, a measure which earlier liberals like George William Curtis, Carl Schurz, David A. Wells, Dorman Eaton, and E. L. Godkin had publicized, still found favor. The secret ballot and the short ballot, devices which Australians had promoted, and the initiative, referendum, and recall, practices well known in certain of the Swiss cantons, found their enthusiasts. The direct election of senators, the abolition of the electoral college, the restriction of a powerful and conservative judiciary by the recall of judges, the direct primary, and direct legislation had all been advanced in the days of the Populists. But it was not until the era of La Follette, Roosevelt, and Wilson that these formulas came to enjoy wide acclaim.

The general conviction that private interests corruptly controlled many

American cities was sharpened in the minds of intellectuals when, in 1888, Bryce's *American Commonwealth* pointed to the scandalously low political morals in municipalities. "With very few exceptions," wrote Andrew D. White, "the city governments of the United States are the worst in Christendom—the most expensive, the most inefficient, and the most corrupt;" there were few to contradict him. Recurrent reform efforts, beginning in New York City, Cleveland, and Toledo, enlisted the support of professional men and women, small shopkeepers, housewives, and other members of the middle class. In some instances, businessmen like "Golden Rule" Jones and Tom Johnson took a leading role in the agitation for municipal reform. Good Government Clubs, Civic Federations, champions of the commission form of government and the city-manager plan all expressed the view that the city was the nursery of democracy, that municipal reform would lead the way to the restoration of the good life of an older time and bridge the way to an even better life for the plain people in time to come. William T. Stead's *If Christ Came to Chicago* (1894) and Lincoln Steffens' *Shame of the Cities* (1905) publicized the corruption in municipal governments, and Frederic C. Howe's *The City the Hope of Democracy* became the creed of the municipal reformers.

Reformers committed to the doctrine of advancing social justice and equality of opportunity through extending popular control over government devoted little attention to an important limitation on political democracy—the denial of suffrage to Negroes in the South. In the South itself conservatives used race prejudice to prevent any permanent union of the agrarian radicals and the Negroes. In the North, race prejudice and the trade-conscious character of the American Federation of Labor prevented organized workers from enlisting the support of Negroes, a part of the vast mass of unskilled laborers. An occasional humanitarian like Moorfield Storey, a Boston lawyer, did champion the cause of political and social justice for the Negro, and in the muckraking period the general disenfranchisement of the southern Negro was aired. In 1910 a group of militant Negroes and vigorously humane whites organized the National Association for the Advancement of the Colored People in an effort to realize the democratic implications of American life for Negroes. The Progressive party of Theodore Roosevelt was able to advocate Negro suffrage since it could not in any case count on much support from the "solid" Democratic South. But the necessity of keeping the good will of

Southerners prevented Bryan and Wilson from demanding the extension of political democracy through the enfranchisement of southern Negroes.

The remaining limitation on political democracy—the general denial of suffrage to women—met with more widespread criticism in reform circles. Convinced that the vote of women workers would promote social legislation, the American Federation of Labor favored woman suffrage as early as 1886. The democratically minded Populists, desiring the support of the wives and daughters of farmers, also advocated it. The renewed campaign of the women suffragists themselves was testimony to the interrelated nature of reform ideology. Women identified their campaign with the movement to restore natural rights to all individuals, to provide equality of opportunity, to abolish political corruption, and to defeat "the interests." The woman suffrage idea gained momentum as the movement made headway in Europe and individual states bestowed the vote on women. Theodore Roosevelt's reform program in 1912 included a woman suffrage amendment to the Constitution. But it took World War I with its need for the fully mobilized support of women to achieve victory.

Closely connected with the movement for the extension of political democracy through the enfranchisement of women was the antisaloon crusade. Largely but by no means exclusively supported by women, this crusade identified the liquor interests with political corruption. The ratification of the prohibition amendment was acclaimed as a great victory for purer politics and for the truly public control of political life.

## The Theory of Collectivist Protest

In the very years when moderate reformers were attempting to restore some part of the older individual dignity and opportunity within the existing political-economic structure, more radical reformers called for socialism. Although the doctrines of Marx and Engels had been in some small part introduced into American thought through the letters they contributed to the *New York Tribune* in the 1850s, the *Communist Manifesto* had been first published in English in the United States in the scandalous feminist and ultra-crusading magazine known as *Woodhull's and Claflin's Weekly*. In view of the questionable reputation of the two ladies for whom the *Weekly* was named and quixotic character of their sponsor, Stephen Pearl Andrews, a philosophical anarchist, the cause of Marx and Engels hardly benefited by this association. The real fathers of Marxism in the United States were a few devoted German immigrants, chief among whom was Frederick Sorge, a friend and correspondent of both Marx and Engels. This tiny band had little understanding of the American worker. Even the effort of the Danish immigrant lawyer and journalist, Laurence Gronlund, to link Marxism with tradtional values by emphasizing the evolutionary rather than the revolutionary character of the transition to socialism failed to win many converts.

Florence Kelley, a pioneer in promoting factory inspection legislation and consumers' education in the interest of fair labor practice, translated Engels' *The Condition of the Working Class in England in 1844,* and corresponded with its author. But the most important intellectual exponent of Marxism was Daniel de Leon. Born in Curaçao and a graduate of Columbia, where he lectured for a time, de Leon became the leader of the feeble Socialist Labor party in the 1890s. His numerous tracts and editorials in *The People* presented to his readers not only clear and vigorous expositions of the labor theory of value, the theory of surplus value, the class struggle, and the Marxist interpretation of reform, nationalism, and internationalism, but his own outline of a tactic by which the workers might take over the machinery of the state when the revolutionary crisis became acute. Lenin saw in this plan the theoretical basis of the soviets and declared that de Leon made important additions to the doctrines laid down by Marx.

Already weakened by internecine strife with the adherents of Bakúnin's brand of anarchism and the revisionist socialists, the Marxist Socialist Labor party was still further torn by the tactics of de Leon. His policy of dual unionism split the ranks of his followers who at best represented a very small fraction of American wage earners. These factors, together with the possibility, or belief in the possibility, of climbing the social and economic ladder, throw light on the slow progress of Marxism in this country. The existence of free political institutions and faith in them, the absence of a feudal tradition, and the power of religion also help to explain why Marxism made so little headway in popular thought.

Early in the century, as a result of the split in the ranks of the Socialist Labor party, a new group emerged more largely under the auspices of

American leaders. Of these Eugene Debs, a railway union organizer and the dominant figure in the Pullman strike, was outstanding because of his "Americanism" and his attractive personality. The new movement, which took the name Socialist party, made phenomenal headway in spite of the vitriolic denunciations of de Leon and the persisting obstacles to the spread of socialist doctrine. The *Appeal to Reason*, edited at Girard, Kansas, reached many thousands of people in country and city alike, and the *Internationalist Socialist Review* provided a vehicle for the writings of a group of literary men and women who had become or were to become converts. Brilliant writers expounded socialist theory and practice. A. M. Simons interpreted American history from a Marxist point of view. Others publicized the socialist platitudes. Upton Sinclair and Jack London, in essays and novels, gave the cause additional prestige. By 1912 the party had learned to combine its revolutionary ideology with many of the traditional and idealistic values of American individualism. In that year it mustered almost a million votes in a presidential election in which two of the three major candidates bid impressively for radical support.

Although destined to make no such political showing as Marxian socialism did in the United States, the varieties of socialism stigmatized by the Marxists as Utopian nevertheless were far more to the taste of middle-class American professional men and women. The Utopian impulse in socialism expressed itself not as it had done in the 1840s in the advocacy of Fourieristic communities, but rather through literary mediums and religious channels. Virtually all of the forty-odd Utopian novels appearing between 1885 and 1900 and all of the writings of the Christian socialists repudiated the doctrine of class struggle and maintained that collectivism could be realized through education and political and religious appeals. Utopian and Christian socialists assumed that human nature is essentially good and reasonable and that the achievement of socialism through love is in full accord with God's law.

By far the most impressive and influential of the literary expressions of non-Marxist socialism was Edward Bellamy's *Looking Backward* (1887). The social ideas in this Utopian romance and in its sequel, *Equality* (1897), were simple enough. Competition as it existed in the American economic system was assumed to be merely the application of "the brutal law of the survival of the strongest and most cunning." But competition did not rule alone; coexistent with it was the law of the

Brotherhood of Humanity, an eternal truth governing the world's progress "on lines which distinguish human from brute force." This principle
explained the transformation of what was called the inefficient, brutal,
stupid, wasteful, and undemocratic capitalism in the America of 1887
into the efficient and humane collectivism of the year 2000.

In Bellamy's scheme there was much planning, much regimentation,
much efficiency based on machines, but there was also scope for every
individual's fancy. After his term of service in the state industrial army
each faithful servant of society retired at the age of 45 to follow his own
whims with security and comfort. The collectivistic state, the argument
ran, guarding as it did the welfare of all, served each individual's prefer-
ences. Abilities were given due consideration and, in the full power of
manhood and womanhood, full range.

No book since *Uncle Tom's Cabin* had appealed so widely to American idealism as Bellamy's romance. Within three years of the publication
of *Looking Backward* 162 Nationalist Clubs were operating in twenty-
seven states with the avowed purpose of spreading Bellamy's message.
Within a decade more than half a million copies of the book had been
sold. In the political arena the Nationalist movement, as Bellamy called
it, was captured by the Populists, who accepted some of the milder items
of the Nationalist program. On the technological level, many of Bellamy's
predictions were to be realized under the auspices of capitalism. For the
rest, the Bellamy ideal of a humanized collectivistic society was destined
to live in the realm of the Utopian ideals of the middle class, for it did
not take hold either in the grass roots or at factory benches. But in those
segments of the middle class that *Looking Backward* did reach, the vivid
and graphic argument helped to break down the older conception of an
individualism that operated within a framework of laissez faire, competition, and production for profits. Bellamy's work also helped to advance
the idea that only under collectivism could true individuality flourish.

## The Theoretical Grounds of Christian Socialism

Bellamy's criticism of industrial capitalism, including his proposal
for collectivism, was couched in secular terms. His underlying philosophy, however, which looked on the interdependency of all individuals
as "a striving to absorb or be absorbed in or united with other lives or

life," resembled one of the basic assumptions of social Christianity. The idea that Christian duty requires the application of the law of love to everyday relationships was, of course, of long standing. So too was the related idea that the Kingdom of God is not merely in Heaven, but that it is to be realized, under God's will through sustained human effort, on earth itself. The note of social crisis, which was so often to be found in the thought of Christian Socialists, likewise had a long history. These general ideas seem first to have been comprehensively applied to the problems of modern industrial capitalism by Saint-Simon, who, early in the nineteenth century, insisted on the Christian duty of transforming competitive industrialism into a cooperative society. It will be recalled that many Americans in the 1840s greeted with enthusiasm the doctrines of the Utopian socialists and shared this general position.

It was not until the issues of industrialism became sharpened in the post-Civil War years that a well-formulated body of ideas emerged to stir the souls of Christians and to guide their actions. For it was not until the 1870s and 1880s that the actualities of industrial capitalism contradicted Christian ethics on such a scale as to awaken a strong protest against it among the clergy. Nor was it until these decades that the strength of Protestant Christianity in the large cities was seriously challenged by the growing indifference of the working masses for whom Protestantism, whether in its evangelical form or in its more modern scientific guise, offered little help in meeting the harsh conditions of life in the sweatshops and slums. Once the Christian Protestant interest was thus jeopardized and challenged, a positive and constructive response to the evils of industrialism and the ills of workers was almost inevitable.

Two influences, both largely English, guided the attempt of Protestant Christianity to meet the challenge. One influence was Toynbee Hall, London's pioneer social settlement house, which provided Americans with a model. The first report of the American College Settlement Association expressed a vision of "brotherhood wherein no man lives unto himself, of a neighborhood where no man may fall among thieves; of a house wherein are many mansions and no dark rooms; of a freedom that is perfect service." But the writings of William Morris, John R. Seeley, Frederick D. Maurice, and John Ruskin, English pioneers in the social gospel and in Christian Socialism, were hardly less influential than the British social settlement movement and related programs of meliorism. In 1872 the Reverend Jesse H. Jones, a Massachusetts Congregationalist clergyman who owed his chief inspiration to Ruskin, founded the Christian Labor Union, promoted the eight-hour day, labored for cooperative factories and stores, and called for public ownership of the means of production. Vida D. Scudder, who took an active part in the labor movement and through her teaching at Wellesley and her writing attempted to apply the Franciscan spirit to concrete economic issues, owed much at the start of her career to the lectures she heard Ruskin give at Oxford in 1884. William Dwight Porter Bliss, an Episcopal clergyman who founded the Church of the Carpenter in Boston in the working district, joined the Knights of Labor, and enlisted influential figures in his church to battle for justice to the wage earners, was consciously influenced by Maurice and other English writers when he launched the Society of Christian Socialists in 1889.

Another intellectual force which profoundly affected the emerging doctrines of social Christianity was the theology of Horace Bushnell and his disciple, Theodore Munger. According to them, salvation is a matter not of individual conversion and atonement but of Christian nurture from infancy itself. But Christian nurture involves a Christian environment in the larger as well as in the more intimate sense. Salvation cannot be achieved without reference to the community of which the individual is a member and by which he is so largely molded. The sacredness of every individual life can have little meaning in a society that fails to respect the most elementary prerequisites for the nurture of the divine spark through Christian social relationships and all-permeating fellowship. The implication was that Christian duty involves the Christianization of the total environment.

Neither Bushnell nor Munger saw, or at least acted as if they saw, the full implications of this conception, but men who were influenced by them did. Thus Washington Gladden, a Congregational minister at Springfield, Massachusetts, and later at Columbus, Ohio, rejected in the 1870s and early 1880s the practice of unregulated competition, the prevalent business ethics, and the doctrine of survival of the fittest in economic life. Gladden also sought to promote the interests of labor by insisting on its right to organize and to strike. He himself adjudicated conflicts between employers and wage earners. He called on the Christian church to reform itself by thoroughly committing itself to promote justice in social relations. The Reverend Charles Sheldon of Topeka, Kansas, stirred the hearts of millions and millions of readers who found the message of the Social Gospel in his fictionalized piece, *In His Steps* (1897). This famous book pictured daily life in an American community in which every church member pledged himself to be guided in all his actions for an entire year by the constant consideration of what Jesus would have done in the identical situation. Thus was born "a church of Jesus without spot or wrinkle or any such thing, following him all the way, walking obediently in His Steps."[15]

Others went much further than these advocates of the Social Gospel and advocated full-fledged Christian Socialism. Among them were W. D. P. Bliss, the Episcopal minister who had been so responsive to the Social Gospel; George D. Herron, a middle-western Congregational minister, writer, orator, and professor at Grinnell College; and Walter Rauschenbusch, professor at the Rochester Theological Seminary and founder of an intimate fellowship of Christian Socialists known as the Brotherhood of the Kingdom. Christian Socialism differed from Marxism not in its objective, a collectivist society, but in its conception of the methods of achieving the goal and in its philosophy of life. The doctrine of the class struggle and the materialist philosophy of life and of history were rejected outright, although some of the Christian Socialists were influenced by these ideas. Christian Socialism took the ground that collectivism could be realized only through the power of human love and the inspiration of God. Man, being the son of God and the brother of all his fellow men, must be guided by God's law of love. In the eyes of the Christian Socialists the materialistic emphases of the Marxists ignored the most important elements of all: the spiritual nature of man and his spiritual destiny, the divine process of social redemption, and the poetic beauties of faith, ultimate reality, the eternal life. The Marxists, in turn, regarded the theological basis of Christian Socialism as mere supernaturalism and the rejection of the class struggle as a source of fatal weakness.

It is impossible to determine, even roughly, the extent of the appeal made by Christian Socialism. It failed to capture any large part of the clergy and laity even in the denominations in which it exerted its greatest influence. Nevertheless, in some measure it touched the emotions of great numbers of men and women. The less radical Social Gospel, which found an institutional exemplification in the Protestant denominations and even in the Catholic church, must be regarded as one of the domi-

---

[15] Charles M. Sheldon, *In His Steps* (Thompson and Thomas, n.d.), 301.

nant ideas in the patterns of protest evoked by the advance of industrial capitalism. Indeed, no arguments against laissez faire, private enterprise, and corporate wealth caused more concern to the champions of the existing order than those advanced in the name of Christ.

Thus the triumph of big business and the worship of wealth did not set the whole tone for American thought. The end of the century was the mid-point for new currents of protest and reform.

# 25 The Conservative Defense

*The idler gets what is coming to him—and that is nothing. The United States stands for individual effort and self-reliance. . . . It would be an unfortunate thing for us if we all became merged into one mammoth society with individualism suppressed and personal initiative suppressed and discouraged.*
—JAMES O. FAGAN,
The Autobiography of an Individualist, 1912

*And just as the petty gambler's faith is fostered by runners and "cappers" for faro, policy, roulette, and keno, so the faith of the industrial underling is fostered by a tremendous trumpeting of the ways and means to worldly "success." The preaching of "success" has become, in these last five years, a distinct profession, honored and well recompensed.*
—WILLIAM GHENT,
Our Benevolent Feudalism, 1902

On the threshold of the century William Graham Sumner, the distinguished economist and sociologist at Yale, observed that "an air of contentment and enthusiastic cheerfulness characterizes the thought and temper of the American people." The growing strength of socialism and of reform ideology had not materially shaken the traditionally individualistic and optimistic faith of the great mass of the American people.

One reason for this was sensed by Professor Edward A. Ross of the University of Wisconsin. "Those who have the sunny rooms in the social edifice have . . . a powerful ally in the suggestion of Things-as-they-are," he wrote. "With the aid of a little narcotizing teaching and preaching, the denizens of the cellar may be brought to find their lot proper and right."[1] The conscious and articulated defense of the existing order by conservatives could hardly have succeeded had not the great body of plain people naturally clung to the ideas that had served them or their fathers in the past, ideas made dear and familiar by a thousand associations, memories, and aspirations. In spite of failures and disappointments, men and women kept an ingrained belief that anyone might still follow in the footsteps of the few who had achieved great fortunes. The rainbow lay somewhere within the grasp of any man who persisted in reaching for it. In this faith the ordinary American was supported by long-standing and deep-seated folk beliefs arising from early actualities in American life.

So general was this individualistic faith during the expansive period of the 1870s and 1880s that leaders in industrial enterprise found little need to elaborate intellectual defenses of the prevailing system. Simple assertions or actions bereft of theoretical justification were the characteristic defense of business interests. George Baer of the Philadelphia and Reading Railway stated, as if it were a self-evident truth, that "the rights and interests of the laboring man will be protected and cared for not by the labor agitators, but by the Christian men to whom God in his infinite wisdom has given the control of the property interests of the country." An attitude of indifference to popular protests was generally prevalent. When the militant action of the Knights of Labor or other unions challenged businessmen in a manner they could not ignore, they often answered with armed private detectives or the militia. When opposition to business proposals arose in legislatures, spokesmen for industry and finance were accustomed to turn for defense not to arguments but to bribes, favors, and retainers.

As prolonged periods of depression began to cast doubt upon the

[1] Cited by W. J. Ghent, *Our Benevolent Feudalism* (The Macmillan Company, 1902), 156.

popular faith and as the strength of reform groups mounted, industrial leaders and their defenders began to elaborate theoretical defenses. Gradually they came to use the slogans, symbols, and ideas in the general cultural heritage which promised to be most suitable to their needs. The conservative ideology was not invented out of whole cloth; neither was its formulation the result of entirely conscious and purposeful effort to meet new situations. The set of assumptions, slogans, values, and ideas which may be called the conservative defense was organized and publicized in part by the more articulate business leaders themselves and in part by ministers, educators, literary men, and social scientists. The conservative defense was identified by its exponents with the general good, with universal and immutable values. It was adopted, consciously or unconsciously, by practically the entire business class, save for such exceptional men as N. O. Nelson, "Golden Rule" Jones, Tom Johnson, and Joseph Fels, who themselves joined the vanguard of protest and reform. Many only loosely associated with business, and many others who stood outside its ranks, accepted the assumptions and arguments of the conservative defense.

The defense varied in accordance with the social and philosophical assumptions of the individuals who developed its arguments. It was affected by definite situations and by the specific audience to whom the arguments were addressed. As the economic structure of the country changed and as the radical and reform ideologies underwent development and gained strength, the character of the conservative defense was in turn modified. In general, during the period of rapid expansion of the economic system in the last decades of the nineteenth century, American conservatives, unlike their fellows in England and Germany who accepted certain measures of social legislation, were willing to make few or no concessions. Only in the twentieth century did they reluctantly begin to admit the need for some modification of the doctrines they had so staunchly defended.

On the negative side conservative spokesmen belittled as mistaken or mischievous the inflationary doctrines of the Greenbackers and Populists. David A. Wells, who enjoyed a great reputation as an authority in economics, declared that anyone who stood out against contracting the currency was in effect a repudiator and disloyal to the national honor and to the government itself. If Greenbackers persisted in their follies, Wells continued, they were more stupid than the donkeys which, observing the death of their green-goggled comrade who was fed on shavings, demanded grass for themselves. In *Robinson Crusoe's Money* (1876), a pamphlet illustrated vividly by Thomas Nast and widely used as a campaign document against Greenbackers and Populists, Wells portrayed the gropings and mistakes of Robinson Crusoe and his man Friday until they at last passed beyond the paper money stage and found in gold the only workable and sensible standard of monetary exchange.

Others indicted radicals in more general terms. E. L. Godkin, editor of *The Nation,* declared that he knew of "no more mischievous person than the man who, in free America, seeks to spread . . . the idea that they [the workers] are wronged and kept down by somebody; that somebody is to blame because they are not better lodged, better dressed, better educated, and have no easier access to balls, concerts, or dinner parties."[2] In similar vein Elbert Hubbard, whose fortune rested on his promotion of new techniques in pressure salesmanship, was certain that socialism attracted men who needed to get attention and were unable to obtain it in any other way. One of the most common indictments was to label as un-American, as a foreign importation, any idea that challenged the doctrines of laissez faire, the efficiency of the profit system, and the sanctity of private property.

### The Divine and the Natural Order

Appeals to religious authority, while not absent in the negative denunciations of radicalism, figured even more markedly in the positive aspects of the conservative defense. The Christian concept of the individual as a free moral agent and the not altogether consistent doctrine that God has determined the success or failure of His children were again and again cited to justify the inequality of riches prevailing under the competitive order of private and corporate enterprise. Supernatural sanction for inequality in the economic sphere was more frequently invoked in the later decades of the nineteenth century than it was in the twentieth, but it did not disappear after the turn of the century. Christians who did not respond to the Social Gospel continued to believe the sentiment expounded in 1877 by Henry Ward Beecher. In that year of unemploy-

[2] Edwin L. Godkin, "Social Classes in the Republic," *Atlantic Monthly,* LXXVIII (December, 1896), 725.

ment, hard times, and profound suffering, the popular Brooklyn preacher, who enjoyed an income of perhaps twenty thousand a year, declared that "God has intended the great to be great and the little to be little. . . . I do not say that a dollar a day is enough to support a working man. But it is enough to support a man! Not enough to support a man and five children if a man insists on smoking and drinking beer. . . . But the man who cannot live on bread and water is not fit to live."[3]

Such stark asceticism was not the only argument in the support which Christian leaders gave to unequal riches. Mark Hopkins contended that God had implanted in man the natural desire to acquire property in order to impel him to labor, to make tools, garments, shelter, on which the well-being and progress of society depend. In the long run, wrote another leader, William Lawrence, the Episcopal bishop of Massachusetts, it is only to the man of morality that wealth comes, for "only by working along the lines of right thinking and right living can the secrets and wealth of Nature be revealed."[4] James McCosh, the president of Princeton, went further than many in defending private property as a divine right. He argued that "God has bestowed upon us certain powers and gifts which no one is at liberty to take from us or to interfere with. All attempts to deprive us of them is theft."[5]

The more common contention was that of Daniel S. Gregory, who emphasized the Pauline doctrine of the stewardship of great riches. "The Moral Governor," wrote Gregory in his popular textbook, *Christian Ethics* (1875), "has placed the power of acquisitiveness in man for good and noble purposes,"[6] the chief of which were that man might use the money God had given him to relieve the poor and to advance God's word. No single preacher of the Gospel did so much to popularize this idea as the Baptist clergyman of Philadelphia, Russell Conwell. In his popular address, *Acres of Diamonds*, Conwell declared that while there were indeed things higher, grander, and more sublime than money, any one of them could be greatly enhanced by the use of money. For money is power, he argued, and for a man to say "I do not want money" is to say "I do not wish to do any good to my fellowmen." To try to get rich

---

[3] Henry Ward Beecher in the *New York Times*, July 30, 1877; cited in Paxton Hibben's *Henry Ward Beecher, an American Portrait* (Doubleday & Co., 1927), 326.

[4] The Right Reverend William Lawrence, "The Relation of Wealth to Morals," *World's Work*, I (January, 1901), 289–290.

[5] James McCosh, *Our Moral Nature* (Charles Scribner's Sons, 1892), 40.

[6] David S. Gregory, *Christian Ethics* (Philadelphia, 1875), 244.

by honorable methods was a duty to one's fellow men that no Christian could properly avoid.

The inequality of riches in American society was justified by the argument that riches rested on natural laws no less than on God's revelation. In the earlier part of the period the law of nature was often interpreted in terms of the eighteenth-century doctrine that every man had, among the other natural rights, that of acquiring and keeping property. This being so, no government could deprive him of that natural property right without due process of law. As a dissenter in *Munn* v. *Illinois* and in the slaughterhouse cases, Mr. Justice Field pioneered in developing the substantive interpretation of due process. In his famous minority opinion in the slaughterhouse cases he maintained that the right to profit from butchering livestock in Louisiana was an inalienable right which the state could not annihilate. "I cannot believe," he wrote, "that what is termed in the Declaration of Independence a God-given and an inalienable right can be thus ruthlessly taken from the citizen, or that there can be any abridgement of that right except by regulations alike affecting all persons of the same age, sex, and condition." Although the majority of the Supreme Court did not take Field's extreme position on the Fourteenth Amendment, the Court later adopted the principle that no state, in regulating corporations, could fix their rate at a point so low as to deprive them of a fair return on their capital.

The legal interpretations of a "law of nature" in a manner beneficial to corporate wealth were reinforced by the doctrines of the classical economists and by those of Herbert Spencer. Both held free competition to be a natural law of economics, the great regulator of economic life and the most certain guarantor of community well-being. Any interference with the natural law of competition, any concession to paternalism or socialism, not only curtailed an otherwise inevitable progress but brought depressions, unemployment, falling prices, and other artificially induced ills.

William Graham Sumner of Yale, a disciple of Spencer, deplored any extension of state activity in economic matters as a betrayal of the individualism nutured by the United States and embodied in the laws of economy. "The truth is," he wrote, "that the social order is fixed by laws of nature precisely analogous to those of the physical order. The most that man can do is by his ignorance and conceit to mar the operation of the social laws." In Sumner's eyes all political contests were struggles of interests for larger shares in the produce of industry. The decision of these contests might better be left to the natural economic laws of the free contract than to any type of legislative or administrative interference. Any fiat currency, any social legislation, any influence of trade unions resting on state support was, in effect, an effort to cure poverty "by making those who have share with those who have not."[7]

The note of individualism was the dominant one in other defenses of laissez faire. "In point of natural resources," wrote David A. Wells,

Providence has given us all that we desire. And that these resources may be made productive of abundance, great and overflowing, to all sorts and conditions of men, there must be, *first*, industry and economy on the part of the individual, *second*, on the part of society, a guaranty that every man shall have an opportunity to exert his industry, and exchange his products, with the utmost freedom and the greatest intelligence; and, when society has done this, we will have solved the problem involved in the relations of capital and labor, so far as the solution is within the control of human agency; for in giving to each man his opportunity, conjoined with freedom and intelligence, we invest him, as it were, "with crown and mitre," and make him sovereign over himself.[8]

In other refutations of socialism and communism a great variety of arguments and authorities was brought into service. After surveying Utopian and Marxist socialism, Theodore Woolsey concluded that these would fetter individuality, corrupt the morality of the family, destroy religion, and negate basic economic laws as well. He devoted considerable attention to John Stuart Mill's opposition to socialism on the ground of its incompatibility with economic law. Four years later, Professor J. Laurence Laughlin of Harvard University, in preparing a college text edition of John Stuart Mill's *Political Economy*, deleted chapters and passages in which the great English thinker attacked laissez faire on the score of its incompatibility with high productivity and good social morals, deplored existing economic inequalities for women, and spoke of "the total absence of regard for justice or fairness in the relations between capital and labor." In thus misrepresenting Mill by throwing out portions the author regarded as necessary to his system of thought, Laughlin may have been acting deliberately or he may merely have been

---

[7] William Graham Sumner, "Reply to a Socialist," in *The Challenge of Facts and Other Essays* (Yale University Press, 1914), 55–62.

[8] David A. Wells, *Practical Economics* (G. P. Putnam's Sons, 1885), 259.

rationalizing his own predilections. In his preface he stated that he was omitting that which might properly be classed as sociology or social philosophy.

No opponent of socialism reached more people than did William T. Harris, a leading educator of St. Louis who became United States Commissioner of Education. Harris wrote and spoke tirelessly in behalf of the principles of self-help, a competitive economic system, and the sanctity of private property. An Hegelian, he believed that the whole process of history had been a steady advance toward the emancipation of the individual from the authority of the group, and that American institutions represented the culmination of the world spirit. Hegel had taught in effect that whatever is, is right; Harris glorified laissez faire not only because it was the existing creed and, as he supposed, the existing practice, but also because to him it represented the greatest imaginable measure of individual self-realization. Socialism on the contrary he saw as a primitive economic form which had flourished in early medieval economy and had greatly restricted the individual. Harris believed that socialism not only would destroy that precious gain, the idea of the sacredness of personality, which private property had brought; it would throw civilization back to the primitive and Oriental stages in which the individual was completely subordinated to the group.

In and out of season, before meetings of educators, in the press, and at public gatherings of every kind, Harris sought to refute not only Marxism but the doctrines of Henry George, Edward Bellamy, and the Bryanites. He argued that education might be used to combat all these subversive ideologies by training Americans to detect the fallacies in them and to take their places as disciplined, competent, and respectful participants in the process by which the country's historic mission was to be fulfilled. That mission was, in brief, to advance prevailing institutions—the family, the church, the state, and private enterprise—in order that in and through these institutions Americans might achieve true individuality.

The appeal to the authority of philosophy and classical economy in support of laissez faire came increasingly to be overshadowed by the doctrine of Social Darwinism. Although the natural law of competition is sometimes hard on the individual, wrote Andrew Carnegie in 1889, it is best for the race, since it insures the survival of the fittest in every department. The laws of economic individualism and of competition, he argued, bring wealth to those with the superior energy and ability to produce it, and keep it from the drones, the weak, the incompetent. If the swiftest win in the race, the rest may be consoled by recalling the sage advice:

> The fault, dear Brutus, is not in our stars,
> But in ourselves, that we are underlings.

William Graham Sumner declared that inequality is rooted in human nature and in the very order of the universe itself; no one is responsible for this inequality and no one can change it. It is fortunate, he continued, that this is so, for the competition resulting from inequality develops whatever powers the individual possesses. The more intense men's struggle for the limited resources of nature, the more thoroughly the individual's talents are developed. To lessen the inequalities by artificial methods merely favors the survival of the unfittest and penalizes the hard-working, the thrifty, and the upright in behalf of the lazy and incompetent. Sumner argued on another occasion that human nature, being selfish and the result of development through eons of time, could not be reshaped by a law here and an act of misguided philanthropy there.

These general ideas, especially that which attributed individual success and failure in material efforts to heredity, were given support by the writings of two eminent psychologists, G. Stanley Hall and E. L. Thorndike. Although no adequate scientific techniques existed for measuring precisely the relative importance of heredity and environment in determining human traits, sweeping generalizations were made in the name of science. Hall and Thorndike maintained that inherited intelligence is the predominant factor in success or failure. Thus natural science was made to reinforce the individualistic ideology of the conservative defense.

## The Cult of the Elite

The psychological justification of social and economic inequality on the score of inherited differences in the mental ability of individuals easily lent itself to the development of the doctrine of the elite. This doctrine was phrased in less crude terms than those employed by many

Social Darwinists. Nevertheless, the idea of the elite was antithetical to the democratic doctrine of a fellowship of equal individuals, and thoroughly in accord with one important aspect of individualistic thought—that which assumed the right of superior persons to have, to hold, and to rule.

An outstanding advocate of the cult of the elite was Elbert Hubbard, of East Aurora, New York. Hubbard edited popular magazines, developed the Roycroft craftsmanship, and promoted "soulful esthetics" with methods resembling those that had won him success in multiplying the sales of a mail-order house in Buffalo. In *The Message to Garcia*, a brochure widely adopted for mass circulation by business firms, Hubbard contrasted the natural aristocracy with the mass of incompetents. The natural aristocracy is made up of men like Rowan, who, without asking idiotic questions, without complaining or demanding privileges, endure hardship, prove their ability to take responsibility, to undergo discipline, to do the necessary job. Such men in the great world of industry never go on strike, never have to demand higher wages, never are laid off. On the contrary, civilization is "one long search for just such individuals," and they inevitably find themselves climbing the ladder into the realm of success.

It is this elite, Hubbard argued, that make up the business class, the class which, rather than preachers and professional reformers, is to redeem the world from sickness, want, and distress if it is ever to be so redeemed. On the other hand, the mass of incompetents, the underlings, the "morally deformed" are incapable of taking any independent action. They are stupid; they are unwilling "to cheerfully catch hold and lift"; and they include among their number "firebrands of discontent" who, "impervious to reason, are to be impressed only by the sole of a thick-soled No. 9 boot."[9] These men are failures because they deserve to be; they stand in marked contrast to the elite, the men who know what discipline means, who put duty and service to employer above mere rights and privileges, and who find their reward in so doing.

On a far more sophisticated level Paul Elmer More at Princeton and Irving Babbitt at Harvard also preached a doctrine of the elite. Primarily literary critics, these men nevertheless expounded a conservative social philosophy, which emphasized both the doctrine of the elite and a certain kind of individualism and severely criticized radical and reform

---

[9] "The Message to Garcia," *The Philistine*, VIII, 109–116.

ideologies. According to the new humanism, as More and Babbitt termed their body of thought, men are by nature unequal and justice consists in a fair division of rewards according to the intrinsic importance of the task and the excellence with which it is performed. The proper function of education is not to prepare one and all alike to compete in the race for an impossible and false equality, but rather to serve as a sifting discipline by which individuals find their proper level and learn best how to do that for which nature has fitted them. Essentially a savage, man becomes humanized only in so far as he discovers his inward self, only in so far as he wages on the inner and spiritual level the battle against primitive instincts and the false values of society—particularly its emphasis on extensiveness at the expense of intensiveness, its vulgar worship of material success, its false equalitarianism, its sentimental humanitarianism.

Although in humanist eyes the real conflict of life takes place on the inner level, exteriors are nevertheless of consequence. In fact, the humanists elevated property rights to a position of paramount importance despite their dislike of the grasping materialism of the plutocracy. Since civilization has advanced, More argued, in relation to the security that property has enjoyed, to the civilized man "the rights of property are more important than the right to life." Property rights are in actuality superior to so-called human rights, to dubious ideals of liberty, equality, and fraternity. Indeed, the new humanism discredited emphasis on rights and on the elevation of sympathy as a social value and insisted on the greater importance of discipline, duty, restraint, and responsibility.

Radicals and reformers, especially those with upper-class backgrounds, appeared to the new humanists as sentimental traitors who sought repentance in milk-and-waterish humanitarianism. The experience of the past, they argued, proved that the radical and the democrat were wrong in supposing that society is perfectible. Only the individual can be saved, and salvation lies in subordination to the tested standards evolved by the long past. These values—respect for property rights, the classical canons of the golden mean in literature, art, and philosophy, the disciplined restraint of the outgoing, expansive, and sentimental individual urges—leave no place at all for enthusiasm for the new, for change, for revolution. Half a loaf is better than none, the argument ran; an imperfect freedom is preferable to a regimented and slaving equalitarianism; quality excels quantity; selection of superior individuals capable of relative perfection transcends sympathy for mankind in the lump. Such, in essence, was the doctrine of the new humanists.

Outside academic circles Agnes Repplier popularized Matthew Arnold's idea of "culture and anarchy," together with many of the basic ideas of the new humanism. Her gracious, witty, and urbane essays, which began to appear in the 1890s, continued to decorate the polite periodicals of taste and culture. With a charming irony she poked fun at the zeal for change which radicals cherished. She endowed the past with mellow appeal and with the virtues of restraint, dignity, and proportion. "The conservative's inheritance from the radical's lightly rejected yesterdays gives him ground to stand on." The dignity of the individual, irrespective of his outward conditions; the eternity and the universality of honor; the solace of religion and of the memories of a great past—these Miss Repplier wove into so delicate a defense of the status quo that it could hardly be recognized as such and probably was never consciously and explicitly so regarded by that charming Philadelphia lady.

Agnes Repplier's graceful pen and wit spoke only for a small intellectual aristocracy. The deep-seated general respect for the more democratic type of individualism cherished by the great bulk of the American people was expressed in very different terms by the common people themselves and by those who wrote for them. Thus a "defense" was developed that identified the conservative values and interests not with the theory of an elite but with the doctrine that success is open to all alike.

### The Self-Made Man and the Cult of Success

The cult of the self-made man had emerged long before the 1880s and 1890s. Freeman Hunt, Charles C. B. Seymour, and others had compiled popular biographies of self-made men, and innumerable writers had put out guides to self-help and success. All these writings emphasized the possibility of fame and fortune for any persevering, hard-working, frugal, virtuous, and intelligent boy, no matter how obscure, how poor or otherwise handicapped he might be. In the development of the cult of the American hero no theme played so great a part as that of victory over obstacles, the rise to eminence in the face of poverty and hardships. Faith in the possibility of getting ahead through individual effort, which had been so well expressed in *Poor Richard's Almanac*, was reflected in

Emerson's "Hitch your wagon to a star," in Margaret Fuller's "Genius will thrive without training," in J. G. Holland's "We build the ladder by which we rise," and in the various versions given these aphorisms in ordinary speech. The cult of getting ahead through one's own efforts was both reflected in and still further popularized by the McGuffey readers and other schoolbooks, by tales, essays, and verses in popular magazines and newspapers, and by commencement addresses in academies and high schools which frequently began and ended on the theme "Beyond the Alps lies Italy!"

In the post-Civil War decades the idea of success through self-effort as a possibility for everyone became vastly more popular and widespread than ever before. The men and women responsible for this never-ceasing popularization did not consciously write their stories and their books in order to defend the existing order of private property, competitive enterprise, and corporate wealth. They did so largely because they believed in the reality of what they wrote; and there was certainly a reality behind it. While the cult of the self-made man was being elaborated in the 1870s, 1880s, and 1890s, there was truth in Carnegie's insistence that many of the millionaires in active control had started out as poor boys. While the literature of success was being written and read in the same decade, Darwin P. Kingsley was on his way from his job as chore boy on a Vermont farm to the presidency of the world's largest insurance company. John D. Rockefeller was tasting the bitterness of relative poverty and then the sweets of incredible material success. Thomas A. Edison was growing from newsboy to world-famous inventor. James Farrell was forging ahead from humble labor in a wire mill to the presidency of United States Steel, and Charles Schwab was pushing on from driving a coach into leadership in the same industry. Henry Ford was emerging from a job at two and a half dollars a week polishing steam engines; and Julius Rosenwald, a peddler of chromos, was on his way to the captaincy of a great mail-order business.

But such actualities only in part explain the growth of the cult of the self-made man. The demand for this type of literature was related to the fact that in the years following the Civil War the plain people felt keenly the effects of the contraction of credit, of the recurring periods of depression and unemployment, and of the prevailing downward trend in farm prices. As it became ever more difficult for the small enterpriser to compete with the growing corporation, there was need for a reaffirmation of the traditional faith that however hard the times, however great the obstacles, America provided opportunity to reach high places. The cult of the self-made man synthesized respect for the older moral values with the dream of personal success and belief in the power of the individual to rise above his environment.

Thus the cult served not only to buoy up the discouraged but to confirm faith in the prevailing order. The psychological uses of the idea were well exemplified in the continued popularity of such older proverbs as "Genius thrives on adversity" and "Every man has a goose that lays golden eggs, if he only knew it," and such characteristically American vernacular gems as "There's always room at the top," "Sweat and be saved," and "You can't keep a good man down."

A further explanation for the vogue of the success literature lay in the returns it afforded to the author. One biography of Lincoln, *The Pioneer Boy and How he Became President*, went through thirty-six editions. Horatio Alger, the most successful of all the writers of success stories for boys, wrote 119 books and still did not exhaust the demand for such stories.

Although many writers enjoyed great popularity, William Makepeace Thayer and Horatio Alger were the two best-known figures in the literature of success. Both men were college graduates, the one a Brown man, the other the holder of two Harvard degrees. Both were trained for the ministry, and both preached. Thayer's personal life was reasonably happy, Alger's was tragic. Alger's idealization and sentimentalization of city street boys who took bold risks and succeeded in worldly affairs undoubtedly represented in part a compensation for his own sense of inadequacy and personal frustration. Thayer merely reflected prevailing beliefs and sensed the popular need for encouragement. The two men also differed in the mediums in which they worked. Alger chose the fictionalized story, while Thayer for the most part confined himself to writing biographies of actual self-made men—Franklin, Lincoln, Grant, Garfield. But the basic idea in the writings of the two was the same.

In his preface to *The Poor Boy and the Merchant Prince*, the life story of Amos Lawrence, Thayer raised the question of how any boy might attain success in any pursuit of life. He declared that the purpose of his volume was to show how it might be done by showing how it had been done. Taking Lawrence as his model—a captain of industry who differed in his deference to conventional moralities, piety, and religion from some of the buccaneers of the 1860s and 1870s—Thayer indicated that the same elements explaining the success of his hero explained that of other self-made men in a variety of fields. The rules were neither complex nor long. First of all, the youth must find out his talents (for God had endowed each person differently) and then choose the proper pursuit. Equally important was the adoption of a moral code early in life, and the rigorous adherence to it ever after. The upshot of the code was expressed in the admonition, "Be true to yourselves and your God, and success will crown your efforts."

Thayer realized the importance of being specific. In his life of James A. Garfield, *From the Log-Cabin to the White-House*, he reminded his readers that Garfield, like Lincoln, had worked hard and improved every moment of leisure by reading, and that he had become known for his industry, tact, perseverance, integrity, courage, economy, thoroughness, punctuality, decision, benevolence, and geniality. Such traits were indispensable for the success which, Thayer never forgot to remind his readers, could be won only through strict regard for morality and religion. In addition to his biographies, this writer popularized his doctrine of success through self-help in *Tact, Push, and Principle, A Guide to Young Men*, in *Aim High: Hints and Helps for Young Men*, and in a series of school readers, *Turning Points in Successful Careers, The Ethics of Success*, and *Men Who Win*.

Alger subscribed to the same virtues. His titles pithily expressed his basic ideas. In one of the autographs he wrote for an admirer, he collected some of the representative names of his 119 books:

> *Strive and Succeed*, the world's temptations flee—
> Be *Brave and Bold*, and *Strong and Steady* be.
> Go *Slow and Sure*, and prosper then you must—
> With *Fame and Fortune*, while you *Try and Trust*.

In the *Ragged Dick* series, which was launched in 1867, and its successors, which included *Luck and Pluck* and *Tattered Tom*, the heroes were depicted in white, the villains in black; the heroes inevitably came out on top after many desperate tussels. The heroes were poor, obscure boys to whom fate had been unkind, but who, through their willingness to risk, to be bold, to adventure, above all through their steadfast loyalty to the pious and moral virtues, triumphed in the end. The triumph was always one of worldly success. The city—to which Alger heroes frequently came from the village or countryside—was depicted as a vast stage of opportunity, the equivalent of the old frontier. Alger wrote his stories in a simple and utterly undistinguished style, with little imagination, less originality, and almost no thought. Yet his sentimental but masculine stories were read and reread by youngsters on farms, in villages, and in cities, by poor youth who were to remain obscure and by those later to achieve distinction.

Alger did not stand alone as the creator of the fictionalized success story. Not only on the juvenile level but in the adult sphere, writers turned out thousands of tons of books based on the very acceptable theme of the individual rising above his surroundings to a triumphant material success. Even the writers of the dime novel, long concerned with the romantic adventures of historic wars, with detective mysteries, and with physical adventure on the frontier—even these authors frequently turned to the subject of material success through pluck and luck.

So deep-seated and widespread was the hankering for the literature of individual success that the moralistic biographies of self-made men and the juvenile and adult romances of achievement could not supply the need. In spite of the advance of naturalism and secularism, many preferred to have their success stories crowned by God's sanction. To such men and women Russell Conwell was the last word. Conwell, a self-made man, had achieved success as a lawyer and editor. In 1879 he finally turned against the "atheism" he had long entertained and became a Baptist minister. He made the Baptist Temple in Philadelphia the largest Protestant church in America, and he created a college for lower-middle-class and working people which, before his death, had given 100,000 young people a start in life.

The great significance of Conwell lay in the message he preached to the some thirteen million American men and women who listened to his magnetically resonant voice and imbibed inspiration from his teachings. Able to recall thousands of individual success stories, Conwell distilled their essence in the famous *Acres of Diamonds*, a lecture which he delivered over the entire country some six thousand times. Its message was that "opportunity is in your own backyard." Conwell believed that material riches were a mark of God's approval if honestly earned and generously spent; they were to be won not in far-off places, not by chasing the rainbow, but "right at home." It is impossible to estimate the effect of this message upon the millions of middle-class Americans who heard it, but it undoubtedly encouraged many to strive for success by the old-fashioned and "divinely sanctioned" methods of personal effort, and bolstered their support of the prevailing economic and social order in which such individual success was possible "right where you are."

Even Russell Conwell did not exhaust the market for nonfictionalized success stories. Many with whom theological sanctions no longer carried weight preferred a version which, while thoroughly inspirational and idealistic, was strengthened by the authority of science. Those who thus yearned for an "intellectual" and "scientific" reaffirmation of the power of the individual to triumph over any and all odds found fare to their liking in the writings of Orison Swett Marden. Marden was an orphan who read and took to heart the famous *Self-Help* of the Englishman Samuel Smiles—for England too had its cult of personal success through self-effort. He not only earned his way through Boston University by catering but graduated with $20,000 in his pocket. After making the grand tour on the Continent, Marden pioneered in resort, hotel, and advertising enterprises, only to meet with financial ruin in Chicago in 1893.

Undaunted, Marden returned to Boston to begin all over again. His first book, *Pushing to the Front* (1894), went through 250 editions. In 1897 he founded a new magazine, *Success*, which flourished until 1912, when it failed. But Marden did not fail. Three millions of his fellow countrymen had purchased his books and thirty of his volumes had been translated into German. He never doubted the truth of his basic idea, the idea that the will to success is the only thing that is vital to success. The law of prosperity and success, he insisted in his pseudo-psychological terminology, is a mental law as certain as the law of gravitation, as fixed as the movements of the planets and the tides of the sea, as unerring as the fundamentals of mathematics.

Marden's doctrines were either hit upon or borrowed by many other writers; some, like Elizabeth Townsend, developed them into the cult of New Thought; others, like Frank Crane, popularized them in much-read columns of the newspaper press. Thus many who were veering away from the orthodox theology and found the success ideology of Christian Science unpalatable discovered in the more secular but equally inspirational writings of Marden and the New Thought exponents, and in the homely banalities of newspaper columnists, that doctrine of personal success through sustained will power which was music to their individualistic ears.

## The Beneficence of Capitalism

As the nineteenth century gave way to the twentieth the conservative defense tended increasingly to emphasize not only the doctrine of self-help and the possibility of personal success but also the natural and inherent beneficence of capitalism as it actually functioned and would presumably continue to function in the future. This aspect of the defense was expressed in theoretical expositions, in high-powered publicity, and in practical philanthropic works.

Being complex and dynamic, capitalism required a variety of intellectual defenses. In *The Philosophy of Wealth* (1886) John Bates Clark, a leading economist, insisted that if the principle of the open market and free competition could be maintained by state action against the trust and the trade union alike, the prevailing capitalistic system would function effectively in distributing economic goods in ever larger measure to the mass of the consuming public. This assumption rested on Clark's conviction that society is dynamic, not static, as the classical economists had supposed; that human nature is good even in economic relationships, not bad, as opinion had often held; and that wealth must be thought of in broader terms than mere dollars. In consequence, continued this exponent of distributive economics, the mere application of the principle of free competition would enable the rich to become richer and the poor to become ever more capable of enjoying comforts and even luxuries. If, Clark continued, the worker, the manager, and the capitalist all received their fair proportion from industrial profits, the wage earner might enjoy a mountain vacation on the earnings of a single day or a European trip on the savings of a hundred days' labor.

The concept of the beneficent potentialities of capitalistic distribution was carried still further by a group of economists whose ideas were by no means congenial to the older type of economic individualist or the rising type of monopoly capitalist. Indeed, from the point of view of their own time, these economists were often regarded as unorthodox critics of capitalism or even as radical reformers. Yet in suggesting certain modifications of capitalism they were in a genuine sense defending it against the more drastic onslaughts of socialists and laying the foundations for a new line of defense which many capitalists themselves were ultimately to accept.

When Richard T. Ely suggested that the evils of capitalism could be remedied by the public ownership of natural monopolies, he was virtually in the camp of the Christian Socialists. But his advocacy of legislation in the interest of the worker and the consumer, which was frowned on and on occasion bitterly fought by many capitalists, nevertheless was a foundation stone in the structure known as "welfare capitalism." This was carried still further by another German-trained economist, the eccentric and original Simon N. Patten of the Wharton School at the University of Pennsylvania. As early as 1885 Patten insisted on the inadequacy of Mill's principle of laissez faire for American economy. Like Henry C. Carey before him, he advocated a harmony of economic interests to be achieved by the promotion of industry through government subsidies and the enhancement of the consuming power of the masses through comparable measures of social control. Society, Patten thought, had passed from the older deficit economy to a new economy of abundance. Cooperation and planning, especially in the field of distributive economics, would raise the living standard of the common people and thus achieve more effectively a larger measure of economic equality than any direct or socialistic redistribution could possibly do. This was the main import of *The Theory of Prosperity* (1902) and *The New Basis of Civilization* (1907).

The socialist criticism of capitalistic production as wasteful was countered by the development of a new body of theory and practice called scientific management. The pioneer in this field of endeavor was Frederick W. Taylor, an engineer of imagination and talent who, after wide experience, entered the service of the Bethlehem Steel Company in 1898. Taylor maintained that the efficiency of the men and machines in any given plant might be greatly increased by the scientific study of every minute step in the productive processes of the plant. On the basis of such studies wasteful motions could be eliminated and maximum efficiency achieved. The theories and actual achievements of Taylor and his associates convinced the more progressive managers and owners that the efficiency engineer was a tower of strength to capitalistic production. Although workers frequently resented the pressure involved in the plans of many efficiency engineers, the exponents of the idea argued that the savings it made possible would in part filter down to the wage earner through larger pay checks and to the consumer in lower prices. Before the outbreak of World War I Taylorism was beginning to be used publicly as a defense of capitalistic production.

The emergence of techniques for developing favorable public opinion toward big business was even more significant in the conservative defense. Corporations gradually began to realize the importance of combating hostility and courting public favor. The expert in the field of public relations was an inevitable phenomenon in view of the need for the services he could provide. As early as the 1890s George Harvey, a news-paper man and publisher, was engaging in public relations activities for Thomas Fortune Ryan and Harry Payne Whitney, well-known promoters and financiers.

The first great figure in the field was Ivy L. Lee, the prototype of subsequent public relations counsels. The son of a Georgia Methodist preacher and a graduate of Princeton, Lee followed journalism in New York City before hitting on the idea of counteracting muckraking by selling American business to the American people. Retained by the Pennsylvania Railroad, Bethlehem Steel, and Armour and Company, he came really into his own as an adviser of the Rockefellers. During the strike of the employees in one of their subsidiaries, the Colorado Fuel and Iron Company, Lee was rewarded for his valuable public relations services to the Rockefellers by a directorship in the firm. When asked to divulge the secret of his effectiveness in weaning the public away from its hostility to big business he replied: "I try to translate dollars and cents and stocks and dividends into terms of humanity." In any case, what this "physician to corporate bodies" did was rapidly being accepted in business as the first bulwark in a planned conservative defense.

When the public relations counsels began to emphasize the impor-tance of philanthropy in breaking down hostility toward big business, Andrew Carnegie had already developed his philosophy and practice of philanthropy. Carnegie, it will be recalled, had himself applied the theory of Social Darwinism in the economic field. Nevertheless, he softened that grim doctrine by supplementing it with a curious mixture of ideas regarding the accumulation and distribution of great wealth. On one occasion he declared that nearly all wealth is social in its origin. On other occasions he developed an Americanized version of the ancient theory of the stewardship of great riches. According to the great steel titan, the man of wealth, if he would fulfill his duty, must live modestly and divert all his revenue, beyond that necessary for the legitimate needs of his family, to trust funds calculated to advance community well-being. Since this method would not interfere with the development of character inherent in pushing ahead in business and since it would provide succor to the man who for the time had fallen behind in the race, it was the best means of equalizing riches. In addition, Carnegie pointed out, the man of wealth would allocate his funds more justly and efficiently than the government could.

As capitalists began increasingly to follow Carnegie's example in establishing philanthropies, sections of the public reflected on the motives of the men of great wealth in endowing foundations for the advancement and popularization of knowledge and the arts. According to one fairly popular view, capitalists found in philanthropy a means of perpetuating their name and heightening their prestige. Others believed that they saw in philanthropy a method for strengthening capitalism and weakening its enemies by proving the beneficence of production for profit.

What was the effect on public opinion of the great gifts bestowed on universities, research, libraries, public education, and the arts? The fact that public relations counsels so frequently urged on men of great fortunes the beneficent effect of philanthropy in breaking down popular opposition to wealth is significant. On the other hand, much evidence suggests that large sections of the public were not easily won over to big business as a result of philanthropic endowments. The attitude of many people found official articulation in the report of the Congressional Commission on Industrial Relations, which declared in 1915 that the Carnegie and Rockefeller benefactions constituted a public menace. These benefactions were said to be based on the exploitation of the laborer and the consumer; they were criticized on the score that the public exerted no control over them and the uses to which they were put; and they were declared to constitute a liability in so far as they benumbed the responsibility of the state in fields proper for state activity. Not only radical intellectuals but many readers of such periodicals as the widely circulated *Appeal to Reason* believed that philanthropies and foundations rested on "tainted money" and tended to blind the public to the evils of the capitalistic system.

Such suspicions did not, however, deter wealthy men from establishing

new foundations and philanthropies; in fact, the practice greatly increased. Gradually, as it became clear that the foundations were administered efficiently and, in many cases at least, with no explicit
reference to the maintenance of capitalistic ideology, suspicion became
less pronounced and widespread.

## Confession and Concession

Among the rich themselves in the first decade of the new century
there came to be an increasing sensitiveness to public criticism and a
growing awareness of the need for assuming public responsibilities apart
from mere generous giving. In 1911 Frederick Townsend Martin, a New
York "society" leader, published his startling book, *The Passing of the
Idle Rich*. Page after page of graphic irony described the feverish search
of the wealthy for some new sensation to be had only at tremendous cost
and only by the most fantastic "conspicuous waste." Parties at which
guests sat between monkeys, and lighted cigarettes wrapped in new
dollar bills, revealed pathetic efforts to escape from boredom and to
outdo friends in the bizarre lavishing of gold on entertainment. But,
Martin went on, this belonged to a past era. In view of the alarming
increase of tenant farming, the consolidation of wealth in corporate
form, and the failure of hundreds who had owned small factories; in
view of the "fearful price in human blood and suffering" that has been
paid for industrial triumphs; in view above all else of the misery and
discontent of men and women on farms, of children in sweatshops, of
human beasts in mines, the idle rich must reform or be annihilated by
social revolution.

Martin insisted that charity was not enough, beautiful though it was
in many individual instances. The American people were not plebs or
slaves, but free men, shrewd, strong, and literate. "The grim truth is that
we as a class are condemned to death. We have outlived our time. . . .
In fact, today we stand indicted before the court of civilization. We are
charged openly with being parasites and the mass of evidence against us
is so overwhelming that there is no doubt whatever about the verdict of
history, if indeed it must come to a verdict."[10] Martin concluded by in-

[10] Frederick Townsend Martin, *The Passing of the Idle Rich* (Doubleday & Co.,
1911), 220.

sisting that reform and adjustment long overdue must be forthcoming immediately in business no less than in government if cataclysmic revolution was to be prevented.

Although few among "the idle rich" accepted any such blanket indictments or such forthright demands for concessions, it became more and more common for spokesmen of the middle classes to admit the necessity of reform. Theodore Roosevelt, himself a member of the established class, led the way in the movement of concession by opportunistically adopting one after another of the measures hitherto pushed by progressives and radicals. In 1900 the National Civic Federation was formed, at the instance of a group of businessmen, to minimize conflicts between capital and labor through the cultivation of a spirit of mutual concession.

In the earlier decades the champions of conservatism had generally refused to admit the desirability of any modification of laissez faire; but in 1916 Elihu Root could declare that "democracy turns again to government to furnish by law the protection which the individual can no longer secure through his freedom of contract, and to compel the vast multitude on whose cooperation all of us are dependent, to do their necessary part in the life of the community."[11] On the eve of World War I Root was joined by other outstanding representatives of conservative America who conceded that the doctrines of Herbert Spencer had to be modified in the direction of public control. Other conservatives admitted the need both for broader social and industrial welfare legislation and for reforms in governmental machinery in the interest of efficiency. The point was always made, however, that if catastrophe was to be avoided, all changes and reforms should be gradual and under conservative auspices.

Thus in the midst of an advancing order of corporate business, an ideology congenial to it gradually emerged. This ideology was derived in part from deep-rooted folk ideas, in part from the sanctions of religion, in part from concepts of natural science. But whatever the source, its arguments rested upon the concepts of individualism, equality of opportunity, and the promise of well-being under a profit economy. The conservative defense, crystallized by business leaders and by allied members of the legal, educational, and literary professions, was popularized in sermons, speeches, novels, slogans, and essays. It became part and

[11] Elihu Root, *Addresses on Citizenship and Government* (Harvard University Press, 1916), 519.

parcel of American popular thought. Between this body of thought and the pole of protest and reform were those who remained more or less indifferent and the moderates who shifted from the right to the left according to temperament and the pressures of the particular situation. One of the great needs in the study of intellectual history is the further exploration of the role played in ideological conflicts by those who took the middle of the road.

# PART VII

# Diversion, Criticism, and Contraction

# 26 America Recrosses the Oceans

*With how much more glory and advantage to itself does a nation act when it exerts its powers to rescue the world from bondage and to create to itself friends than when it employs these powers to increase ruin and misery!*
                                        —THOMAS PAINE, 1791

*Expansion and imperialism are at war with the the best traditions, principles, and interests of the American people, and . . . they will plunge us into a network of difficult problems and political perils, which we might have avoided, while they offer us no corresponding advantage in return.*
                        —WILLIAM GRAHAM SUMNER, 1899

*This is a war of high principle, debased by no selfish ambition of conquest or spoliation. . . . We know, and all the world knows, that we have been forced into it to save the very institutions we live under from corruption and destruction. . . . From the first the thought of the people of the United States turned toward something more than winning this war. It turned to the establishment of the eternal principles of right and justice.*
                        —WOODROW WILSON, 1917, 1919

Once the young United States had set its course independently of England there was little reason for the great majority of Americans to be concerned about foreign matters. Living in a vast and expanding country far from Europe's border quarrels and rivalries, they had less reason than their European cousins for thinking and talking about their "neighbors." Throughout the great part of the nation's history a majority of Americans entertained no well-formulated set of ideas regarding their country's destiny in the larger world. But there was a general assumption that the United States was superior to all other lands and was to enjoy a glorious future. And this belief gradually became explicitly crystallized on the Fourth of July, during acute upheavals and dramatic happenings in the Old World, and during the wars that engaged this country.

From the beginning of the nation's history to the end of the nineteenth century groups of intellectuals and public men cherished more or less well-defined ideas regarding America's destiny in the world. One conception, emerging early in the career of the Republic and enjoying widespread support throughout the nineteenth century, pictured the mission of America as building at home, on the ever-expanding continental domain, a civilization of plain folk secure in the enjoyment of political freedom and economic opportunity. This was to be preserved and extended by steering a well-defined course away from the turmoils of the rest of the world. A second pattern of thought emphasized the American mission of championing movements in the Old World designed to achieve national freedom and republican institutions. Such movements were readily associated with the American faith in an individualistic democracy. A third idea was that of an American mission to promote commerce based on a well-developed agriculture and industry and to secure commercial advantages by a vigorous foreign policy and a strong Navy. By and large, the exponents of both the second and third programs assumed that force would not be a necessary instrument in the pursuit of the desired ends; neither, however, entirely excluded it as an ultimate necessity.

## The Mission of America to Advance World Liberty

The outbreak of the French Revolution occasioned the demand on the part of certain militant American democrats that the government aid the struggling champions of freedom in France. Their argument stated that the struggle for liberty was worldwide and that American democracy and Old World autocracy were incompatible. The Proclamation of Neutrality in 1793 and Washington's Farewell Address dealt a mighty blow to eighteenth-century interventionism. Yet in later struggles of the Greeks, Irish, Germans, Hungarians, French, Poles, and Italians for national freedom or republican institutions, American sympathy was widespread and the unofficial and voluntary aid of Americans was considerable.

On only one occasion, however, did the idea that America should intervene in the European upheavals win any appreciable support among officials or the general public. In the years immediately following 1848 foreign-born patriots in the United States, militantly self-conscious American nationalists, international idealists, and a few political leaders who saw advantage in fanning the enthusiasm of these groups, argued with much persuasiveness that American freedom and American interests were jeopardized by the reactionary triumph abroad and that America had a moral obligation to aid the defeated revolutionists. Senator Isaac P. Walker of Wisconsin announced in Congress on December 16, 1851, that the country should "interpose both *her moral and physical* power" against the interference of one nation (Russia) in the affairs of another (Austria-Hungary) in violation of public law and morality. The Wisconsin Democrat argued that the country ought to be ready, if necessary, to fight for Hungarian freedom. Others, including Senator Cass of Michigan, indulged in similar talk. The world must know, declared Cass, that there are "twenty-five millions of people looking across the ocean at Europe, strong in power, acquainted with their rights, and determined to enforce them."[1] In 1852 the Democratic candidate for the Presidency reminded his countrymen that "in the weakness of our infancy . . . not only words of cheer were sent across the ocean to greet us, but upon its bosom were borne to our shores, hearts to sympathize and arms to strike."[2] The argument for intervention rested by and large on moral obligation but also on the doctrine that American democracy was threatened by the existence of European autocracy. A New York Whig, Senator Seward, and a Louisiana Democrat, Senator Soulé, pointed to the commercial advantages that would result from the favor-

---

[1] *Congressional Globe*, 32 Cong., 1 sess., 310.

[2] W. J. Stillman, *Autobiography of a Journalist*, 2 vols. (Houghton, Mifflin Company, 1901), I, 142.

able trade agreements the European republics would extend to their American sister.

The prevailing belief, however, held that America could best promote the struggles for freedom which its example had inspired by insuring the success of the American experiment. This country could make its best contribution to the freedom of the Old World, as Clay put it, by keeping its "lamp burning brightly on this western shore as a light to all nations" rather than hazarding its "utter extinction among the ruins of fallen and falling republics in Europe."[3] Our policy, declared President Fillmore, "is wisely to govern ourselves, and thereby to set such an example of natural justice, prosperity, and true glory as shall teach to all nations the blessings of self-government and the unparalleled enterprise and success of a free people."[4] Thus American official policy reflected the pattern of thought that deemed it best merely to express our sympathy for the Old World struggles for freedom by quickly recognizing newly launched republican regimes and welcoming conquered heroes and other refugees from Old World oppression.

This conception dominated our policy until the end of the nineteenth century. At that time Americans embarked on their first crusade to promote freedom overseas through war and power politics. Less than two decades later the long-felt, generally shared sympathy for European liberalism and the equally widespread moral condemnation of tyranny played a large part in the decision to launch a second and much grander effort to promote liberty abroad.

## The Idea of Commercial Destiny Overseas

Another conception of American destiny in the world involved the promotion by the federal government of overseas commerce and the maintenance of a substantial Navy. This was clearly outlined by Alexander Hamilton. Writing in *The Federalist*, he declared that even a small navy would enable the new federal government "to become the arbiter of Europe in America; and to be able to incline the balance of

---

[3] Clavin Colton (ed.), *The Works of Henry Clay*, 10 vols., (G. P. Putnam's Sons, 1904), III, 224.

[4] James D. Richardson, *Messages and Papers of the Presidents* (Government Printing Office, 1898), V, 180.

European competitions in this part of the world, as our interests may dictate; . . . to dictate the terms of connection between the Old and the New World." In the prevailing and future contests in the West Indies, "a few ships of line, sent opportunely to the re-inforcement of either side, would often be sufficient to decide the fate of a campaign, on the event of which interests of great magnitude were suspended."[5] This program was adopted and promoted by such Whig leaders as Daniel Webster and William E. Seward. In consequence American interests in the Sandwich Islands were extended; Japan was opened up to American commerce; a naval base in the Bonin Islands was seized; and in 1863 and 1864 American war vessels fired on the base of a stubborn Japanese prince at Shimonoseki.

Commercial spokesmen developed a rationale justifying the idea that American destiny involved the promotion of trade in the Pacific and the expansion of trade overseas generally through diplomacy and naval strength. In so elaborating this conception of our destiny, merchants were obviously promoting interests to which they were committed. In 1840 Abbott Lawrence, a leading Massachusetts textile industrialist, presented to the House of Representatives a memorial from American merchants in Canton asking for trade agreements with China and for naval protection. In 1851 *Hunt's Merchants' Magazine* published an article in which the author, after commenting on the actual and potential resources of America, favored overseas commercial expansion on the ground that "we cannot if we would live up to our means of support, and the accumulations of industry furnish us with a constantly augmenting capital that must seek for new channels of employment." The inevitable contest with Great Britain for commercial empire, continued the writer, could end only in American supremacy over "the whole Oriental trade."[6]

Another contributor to *Hunt's Merchants' Magazine* not only predicted the triumph of American enterprise overseas but assumed that expansion would result either in the Americanization of remote peoples or in their extermination. "As in modern society the capitalist has the pauper in his power, so among nations the rich ones will require the service of the poor ones, or cause their destruction. Nor is the universal and irresistible operation of this law to be regretted. . . . It is better that

[5] Paul L. Ford (ed.), *The Federalist* (Holt, Rinehart and Winston, 1898), No. 11.
[6] *Hunt's Merchants' Magazine*, XXIV (June, 1851), 779.

an inferior race should thus become extinct, than that the development of a superior race should be prevented."[7] *De Bow's Review*, an influential organ designed to promote southern commercial interests, frequently spoke in similar vein. In 1846 Senator Benton of Missouri went so far as to declare that the Celtic-Anglo-Saxon division of the Caucasian race, which was then advancing to the shores of the Pacific, was destined to penetrate Asia. Thanks to its moral and intellectual superiority, he went on, the youngest branch of the white race, which, it would seem, had "alone received the divine command, to subdue and replenish the earth," would become "the reviver and the regenerator" of the inferior and torpid yellow peoples.

Naval officers were no less alert than spokesmen of commercial interests in the development of arguments for overseas enterprises. In 1851 Commander James Glynn recommended to the President the negotiation of a commercial treaty with Japan and the securing of a port "if not peaceably, then by force," in the interest of shipwrecked sailors and the proposed steamship line to the Orient. Commodore Perry, who succeeded in obtaining advantages for American trade in Japan, declared that "the duty of protecting our vast and growing commerce" required the acquisition of trading settlements in the Far East, and that we could no longer escape from "the responsibilities which our growing wealth and power must inevitably fasten on us." Perry made it clear that, should a display of force be necessary to carry out American purposes, he would not shrink from such an eventuality. In his outspoken ardor for a reorganization of the Navy along modern lines and for a vigorous foreign policy in behalf of American commercial interests, Lieutenant Matthew Fontaine Maury, a contributor to the *Southern Literary Messenger*, outdid even Perry. The navalists of the mid-century regarded the Navy not only as an instrument for the defense of American business abroad but also as a means for dealing with a possible enemy in the remoter seas as well as in those near our shores.

## The Argument for Expansion into Contiguous Areas

Despite the growing strength of commerce, finance, and industry, agrarian interests in the main dominated federal policy until the Civil

[7] *Ibid.*, XXXII (June, 1855), 708.

War. Hence the third concept of American destiny—that of building a civilization at home with an abundant and good life for all within the expanding continental domain—dominated thought and action on the whole from the 1790s until the 1890s. This idea was not only well suited, in the narrower and more material sense, to the interests of the agrarians whom the Jeffersonians, Jacksonians, and early Republicans represented. The program of consolidating the national domain and expanding it into areas contiguous to the boundaries at any given moment in order to provide fertile soils for exploitation and enjoyment was virtually inescapable by reason of the compulsion of geography and interest.

This idea of Manifest Destiny also happened to blend fairly well with prevalent world economics. Such a program fitted in with a political pattern that dominated the politics of continental Europe; on that seething stage national boundaries were also being rounded out and political nationalism promoted.

Among the more or less materialistic arguments advanced in the first two-thirds of the nineteenth century to justify the incorporation of contiguous agricultural territory, the doctrine of self-interest bulked large. At the time of the acquisition of Louisiana, the Floridas, Texas, and California, the argument was again and again advanced that these territories were necessary to provide security against savage Indians, crafty Mexicans and Spaniards, and potential British interlopers.

The doctrine that the superior use of the soil entitled the superior user to seize the land of others similarly did good service. Frontier expansionists repeatedly justified the incorporation of Indian territory and vast expanses of Mexico north of the Rio Grande on the grounds that the actual owners failed to make good use of these dominions.

Without repudiating the doctrine of self-interest, exponents of contiguous geographical expansion frequently cloaked their arguments in high-sounding analogies. As early as the 1820s John Quincy Adams, seeking to apply a physical law to the political sphere, expressed the belief that Cuba, a "natural appendage," would inevitably be attracted to the United States as a bit of iron is to a magnet. Such humanitarians as Ralph Waldo Emerson similarly found in the law of gravitation the formula explaining the inevitable pull without war which this country exerted on territories contiguous to it. As the dynamic view of nature tended to overshadow the static Newtonian conception of the universe, the idea of natural growth figured increasingly in the argument for expansion. In the middle of the century expansionists contended that just as any living organism must grow until decline sets in, so the body politic must expand unless the process of ultimate extinction has already begun. In spite of American devotion to the doctrine of free will (in all save theological matters, and increasingly even in that area), the theory that continuous expansion of territory, institutions, and influence was our inevitable or manifest destiny enjoyed wide favor.

The argument that America had a mission to extend the blessings of freedom and civilization through expansion and, if need be, through conquest was both less laissez faire in its theoretical basis than the doctrine of inevitable destiny and less frankly based on self-interest. The expansionists of 1803 had insisted that the acquisition of Louisiana was justified not only on the grounds of self-defense but on the score of an American obligation to extend American liberties to a backward people. The War Hawks of 1812 had advanced the same thesis in justification of their determination to conquer and annex the Canadas. Advocates of the incorporation of "all Mexico" in 1848 likewise insisted that such a course would fulfill the American mission to regenerate backward and, according to prevailing ideas, "racially inferior" neighbors by conferring on them the blessings of American institutions—political, religious, and educational. Filibusterers who sought to seize Canada and Central America indulged in similar talk. All these and many related arguments were devised in support of the triumphant movement for agrarian expansion into neighboring domains. These arguments and ideas were not forgotten.

### Shifting Currents

The long-prevalent justifications of American territorial expansion into contiguous territories continued to enjoy some vogue—chiefly in connection with Canada—in the later decades of the nineteenth century and even the first decade of the twentieth. During the upheavals in Mexico in the years following the overthrow of Díaz in 1911 chauvinistic imperialists sometimes insisted that conquest and annexation were the only possible solutions of our troubled relations with our southern neighbor. But in general this pattern of thought had become dim in the decades following the purchase of Alaska in 1867. At the turn of the century the hitherto competing and subordinate concepts of American destiny in the world came into their own.

The triumph of the idea that national destiny lay beyond the seas, whether on the ground of alleged national interest and necessity or on the score of a moral obligation to advance liberty by force, can be explained only in terms of the new conditions prevailing in the country and the world at large at the end of the nineteenth century.

In the later decades of the century the struggle for world empire which France, England, Spain, and Holland had inaugurated 300 years earlier seemed to be entering its final stage. The achievement of national unity in Italy and Germany and the general advance of industrialism in Europe stimulated new adventures in colonialism. Italy and Germany both desired to obtain colonies, and the competition resulting from a growing industrial economy heightened the value of colonies in the eyes of political and business leaders in the older imperial states. American leaders observed the sharpened thrust of the European powers for the remaining unoccupied regions of the earth. Senator Henry Cabot Lodge declared in *The Forum* in 1896 that "The great nations are rapidly absorbing for their future expansion and their present defense all the waste places of the earth" and that in consequence the United States must not "fall out of the line of march."

Changing interests within the United States itself also help explain the shifting emphases regarding national destiny. It is difficult to believe that the program of overseas colonial expansion could have triumphed before the victory of political unity at home or prior to the shift in the balance of power from an agrarian economy to one in which industry and finance enjoyed primacy. A sectionally contentious confederacy in which the agrarian interest held the balance of power was no adequate instrument for pursuing vigorously and consistently the "large policy" of overseas expansion. So long as expansion into contiguous territories provided economic opportunities not only for farmers but for merchants and entrepreneurs, there was no pressing need for a powerful Navy, for an aggressive foreign policy in the interest of markets, or for colonialism.

Only in the last two decades of the old century and the first decades of the new did the development of industry, trade, and banking reach the point at which trading posts and naval bases, colonialism and financial imperialism appeared to be necessary. Only toward the end of the century did the rate of expansion of the domestic economy begin to slow down as the west that had provided such great opportunities for railroad building disappeared and as industrial plants capable of producing in excess of domestic purchasing power were constructed. Actualities now gave some point to the declaration of Senator Beveridge of Indiana in 1898 that "American factories are making more than the American people can use; American soil is producing more than they can consume. Fate has written our policy for us; the trade of the world must and shall be ours. . . . And we will get it as our mother England has told us how."[8]

If the Guggenheims, the Stillmans, the Morgans, the Bakers, the Ryans, the Harrimans, the Sinclairs, and the Doheneys did not formulate and express in public statements their ideas on such matters, they did seize opportunities to advance their interests in remote lands, and they naturally expected the government to aid them in obtaining concessions and, if need be, defending their property interests. Just prior to the decision for war in 1898, the melodramatic prelude to colonialism, owners of the great sensationalistic New York City newspapers competed with each other to enlarge their circulations and their profits by publicizing both true and false accounts of Spanish atrocities in Cuba.

At least one public figure believed that, by arousing patriotic idealism, a foreign war of an imperialist variety would deflect popular opinion from internal tensions and reform causes. A Texas congressman urged on Secretary of State Olney militant action in the Venezuela-British Guiana boundary controversy.

It is, moreover, when you come to diagnose the country's internal ills that the possibilities of "blood and iron" loom up immediately. Why, Mr. Secretary, just think of how angry the Anarchistic, socialistic and populist boil appears on our political surface, and who knows how deep its roots extend or ramify? One cannon shot across the bow of a British boat in defense of this principle [the Monroe Doctrine] will knock more pus out of it than would suffice to inoculate and corrupt our people for the next two centuries.[9]

This was extravagant talk, but what was explicitly expressed by the Texan may have been implicit in the thought of other economic conservatives. There is little doubt that the desire on the part of leading

[8] Albert J. Beveridge, "The March of the Flag," *Indianapolis Journal*, September 17, 1898.
[9] Charles A. Beard, *The Open Door at Home* (The Macmillan Company, 1934), 101.

Republicans to maintain the power of their party did affect the decision to embark on a war for the liberation of Cuba—a war which also resulted in overseas colonialism.

The relationship between the consciousness that the frontier era was at an end and the movement for overseas expansion is a fascinating subject for speculation. Certain religious leaders saw, as early as the mid-1880s, a relationship between the new urbanism that was replacing the older frontier era and the need for a militant Protestant missionary movement both at home and abroad. During the debate over the issue of retaining the Philippines Senator Beveridge argued that the country needed colonies far more than it had earlier needed the contiguous frontier territories it had acquired. It is also possible that more subtle relationships existed, but these would be difficult to document. Perhaps the fact that the West was disappearing made some men more ready to favor overseas opportunities for romance and adventure, for manly prowess, for the fighting and disorder toward which, in the eyes of some students of human nature, man is consciously or unconsciously inclined. At any rate, it was at the time when economic, political, and psychological conditions were favorable that Americans for the first time turned from the task of rounding off the national domain and trying through domestic reform movements to put their own house in order. It was then that they embarked on the task of promoting abroad both American economic and political interests and American morals and ideals.

The political leaders, naval officers, missionaries, businessmen, journalists, and others who promoted this program in some instances did so because of personal commitments. In other cases the position taken by proponents of the new policy provided psychological satisfactions the nature of which they themselves did not try to analyze. We cannot assign specific motives to particular people, but we do know that, in the organic whole which a society is, ever integral yet ever subject to cleavage and change, intellectuals like others are bound to respond to shifting conditions which influence their judgments about public matters.

## The Rationale of the New Departure

The rationale for the new policy of promoting freedom overseas and acquiring colonies, naval bases, and a great fleet resembled in many striking ways the arguments that the early philanthropic internationalists and the exponents of rounding out the national boundaries had developed. Indeed, champions of a war on Spain to free Cuba, advocates of the retention of Puerto Rico, Guam, and the Philippines, and enthusiasts for a great Navy which might be used both for moral righteousness and for national interest, elaborated arguments that paralleled almost exactly those employed earlier to justify the annexation of northern Mexico and to extend aid to the struggling liberals and nationalists in Europe. The last two decades of the century saw two significant syntheses of all the old arguments pointedly directed toward future policy.

The first of these syntheses was Josiah Strong's *Our Country* (1885). Strong was a minister in the service of the Congregationalist home missionary society. In his little book he spoke of the dangers of Roman Catholicism in the world and urged the importance of Protestant missionary efforts to counterbalance it; he emphasized the perils involved in the exhaustion of free lands and the dominance of an urban civilization; and he put much stress on the threat to the older American values implicit in the new waves of immigration from southern and eastern Europe. Strong then developed an idea which had a long history—the idea of the innate superiority of the Anglo-Saxon race. This idea, it will be recalled, had been used to justify the conquest of northern Mexico and the spread of American institutions and commerce over the Far East. The idea of Anglo-Saxon superiority, only a little more than a decade before Strong wrote *Our Country*, had been reinforced by the historical teachings of the English scholar, E. A. Freeman, and the writings of the Social Darwinists. Freeman, who visited the United States in 1881, expounded the idea that the Anglo-Saxons, including the Americans, possessed natively superior governing talents and in consequence were destined to extend their empires over those less fortunately endowed. As we have seen, the Social Darwinists seemed to give scientific sanction to the idea that in the contest between peoples the superior must always triumph.

Strong now adopted these ideas and elaborated them in a notable chapter in *Our Country*. The idealism of his message, which emphasized the historic mission of the Anglo-Saxon American people to implant in all the remote areas of the earth the great values of civil liberty and "spiritual Christianity," was bound to appeal to the moral sentiments of many fellow countrymen. "This race of unequalled energy, with all the majesty of numbers and wealth behind it—the representative, let us hope, of the largest liberty, the purest Christianity, the highest civilization—having developed peculiarly aggressive traits calculated to impress its institutions upon mankind, will spread itself over the earth." At times, to be sure, Strong spoke of the needed harmony of races for the unity of mankind and of the ways in which the differences between the races supplemented and served one another. But his main emphasis was on the idea that the inferior races, in being destined to give way before the Americans, "were only the precursors of a superior race, voices in the wilderness crying: 'Prepare ye the way of the Lord!' "[10] Strong's book went through many editions and reached hundreds of thousands of readers.

The other synthesis was even more remarkable, for it included not only the concept of a superior race and a moral mission, but the traditional realistic arguments laid down by the early Hamiltonians in their program for overseas power. Captain Alfred Mahan's theories, rooted in American experience and in centuries of British naval policy, were advanced in *The Influence of Sea Power on History* (1890) and in subsequent popular articles and books. Mahan first of all advanced an interpretation of history which gave seapower pivotal importance in the destiny of nations. He further outlined in his early writings a philosophy of self-interest, force, and power politics. In his eyes no nation could enjoy true prosperity unless it successfully based its policy on mercantilistic imperialism—unless, in competition with other countries for world markets, it possessed a powerful navy, a strong merchant marine, naval bases, and colonial possessions. Mahan hoped that the United States would embark on a colonial policy and did what he could to promote that end. In the meantime he insisted that the Navy should be sufficiently strengthened to enable it to keep our ports open in case the United States became involved in war.

In addition to espousing a philosophy and policy of self-interest and relating imperialism to it, Mahan also accepted the doctrine of America's Christian and racial mission to spread its ideas over backward regions and even among such highly developed but "inferior" peoples as those of India, China, and Japan. At the same time he came increasingly to link war and imperialism on the one hand, with moral righteousness and idealism on the other. Evil being inherent in the world, the righteous

[10] Josiah Strong, *Our Country* (The Baker and Taylor Co., 1885), 222.

nation, which could never submit questions of national honor and interest to arbitration, must use force to curb evil and to promote well-being in the commonwealth of the world. The moral nation, the powerful nation, must, in short, be responsible for the triumph of morality on the earth. Every nation, even the evil nation, must follow its conscience and use force to defend its judgment and its course; but Mahan, whose faith in God and His righteousness was deep, believed that if adequate preparations had been made by the nation espousing the good, if sufficient sacrifices were undergone, if inner discipline and morals were what they should be, God would never permit a just cause to go down in defeat.

Mahan's doctrines were popularized by his friend and admirer, Theodore Roosevelt. Like Mahan, Roosevelt had little faith in arbitration as a means of protecting a nation's vital interests and honor. The Rough Rider had only disdainful wrath and contempt for the "whole flapdoodle pacifist and mollycoddle outfit," so lacking in manly athleticism and moral fiber. On one occasion he wrote that "the man who fears death more than dishonor, more than failure to perform duty, is a poor citizen; and the nation that regards war as the worst of all evils and the avoidance of war as the highest good is a wretched and contemptible nation, and it is well that it should vanish from the face of the earth." If the nation must be God's instrument for righteousness and not hesitate to use the sword to promote it, it must keep itself in a state of military preparedness for still other reasons as well. War and military preparedness, Roosevelt claimed, kept modern industrialized and urbanized peoples from growing soft and purposeless.

Such doctrines stood in marked contrast to those that the fathers of the country had entertained, and to those that had prevailed after them, at least in theory. The fathers of the Republic believed that war was an evil to be avoided if possible. If necessary it was to be waged heroically. But they never glorified war as a good in itself. If now and again a romantic soul had found in war a means of personal catharsis of the emotions or some other means for promoting public good, war had not been generally glorified in this country save, perhaps, among the ruling class of the Old South. The organized peace movement had found crusading against war uphill business, but it had met with indifference rather than with outright hostility. The arguments of Mahan and Roosevelt in regard to war marked a new emphasis in American thought.

This philosophy met with opposition in the United States, but it also enjoyed considerable vogue, thanks to the Social Darwinists, the preachments of such Romanticists as Ruskin and Nietzsche, the scrambles of the European powers for colonies, and the realization that our frontier no longer existed to nourish the more "manly" virtues.

The exponents of war against Spain and the champions of colonialism during the aftermath also made bold and frequent use of arguments forged when the Floridas, Louisiana, Oregon, and northern Mexico were the bone of contention. The time-honored doctrines of utilitarianism and self-interest continued to be serviceable. Quite as frontier expansionists had argued, Professor Burgess of Columbia maintained in 1890 that a few thousand savages in the Polynesian islands had no moral right to reserve for their own purposes lands capable of sustaining millions of civilized men. This was also the thesis advanced by Lyman Abbott, editor of *The Outlook* and a leading Congregational clergyman, in an effort to justify retention of the Philippines in 1900. Expansionists also now urged, as they had done in other situations a half century before, that the acquisition of the Philippines was imperative for defense and security. Naval bases in the Caribbean and control of Puerto Rico, the Isthmus of Panama, and Hawaii were urged as a necessity to prevent a menacing foreign power from occupying them.

The theory of organic evolution and the doctrine of Social Darwinism seemed to provide new scientific support for the earlier argument based on the idea of natural growth. This argument was frequently heard in the 1890s and was applied specifically to the desired acquisition of Hawaii, Puerto Rico, and even the Philippines. Whitelaw Reid of the *New York Tribune*, Professor H. H. Powers of Stanford and Cornell, and Homer Lea, hunchback Californian who preached the Japanese peril and became a military adviser to the Chinese, all appealed to the doctrine of biological growth in their pleas for the inevitability of expansion.

The doctrine of inevitability, like that of natural growth, was broad enough to enable its champions to make use of it in different ways as their temperaments and perspectives suggested. For pious and evangelical men, it was possible to see God's will in the doctrine of the inevitability of overseas expansion. Thus the wavering McKinley went down on his knees in the White House to ask for divine guidance, and God's answer resolved his doubts in regard to the wisdom of retaining the Philippines. But those of a more secular frame of mind emphasized naturalistic rather than supernaturalistic elements in the doctrine of inevitable destiny—racial determinism and the imperatives of naval strategy, commercial interests, and humanitarian obligations.

The doctrine of inevitable destiny left open the question whether it was to be realized through passive, acquiescent policy or through acts of will dictated by the course of events. "Whether they will or no," wrote Mahan, "Americans must now begin to look outward."[11] But neither Mahan nor those who thought with him were content with mere outward looks. Mahan's fellow expansionists included Assistant Secretary of Navy Theodore Roosevelt, Senator Henry Cabot Lodge of Massachusetts, and Brooks Adams, an exponent of geo-politics who mixed promises of national glory and threats of national disaster. Mahan, like his associates, realized that in practice events are not automatically determined without acts of human will. These men and others, such as the editors of the "yellow" journals, the Hearsts and the Pulitzers, created situations and events which in turn were interpreted to the American people as the automatic course of events foreordained by our inevitable destiny. It should be pointed out, of course, that in so thinking and acting these men were probably only dimly aware, if indeed they were aware at all, of any inconsistency between the theory of inevitable destiny and their own behavior, unless they regarded themselves as automatons.

Finally, the idea that America was destined to act as the regenerator of backward or decadent peoples was used to justify the decision to suppress the insurrection in the Philippines and to extend American influence over the Cubans. The argument which Senator Benton had used in 1848 to rationalize westward extension to the Pacific and beyond into Asia was now given new prestige and further elaboration. Some frankly accepted Kipling's concept of the White Man's Burden. In a poem of that title which appeared in *McClure's Magazine* in 1900 the British imperialist displayed a disdainful hostility to the brown peoples who, he thought, could never overcome their inferiority, could never develop the capacity for self-government. If the white man, in taking up the burden of governing the darker peoples, could hardly hope to do the subject races much good, he was nevertheless obligated to assume the task as a token of his manly athleticism.

Senator Beveridge of Indiana assented to this doctrine:

[11] Alfred T. Mahan, *The Interest of America in Sea Power* (Little, Brown and Co., 1897), 21.

God has not been preparing the English-speaking and Teutonic peoples for a thousand years for nothing but vain and idle self-contemplation and self-admiration. No! He has made us master organizers of the world to establish system where chaos reigns. He has given us the spirit of progress to overwhelm the forces of reaction throughout the earth. He has made us adept in government that we may administer government among savage and senile peoples. Were it not for such a force as this the world would relapse into barbarism and night. And of all our race He has marked the American people as His chosen nation to finally lead in the regeneration of the world.[12]

Anti-imperialists objected that the conquest and retention of the Philippines were a repudiation of our traditional tenet of the right of self-determination of peoples. But Senator Henry Cabot Lodge met this by the argument that the Malays were incapable of learning democracy.

Others, to be sure, regarded the subject peoples as merely undeveloped and entirely capable of achieving, under American guardianship, an ultimate ability to govern themselves. Thus President McKinley, Senator Foraker, and others declared that our rule over the Filipinos was solely a trusteeship during which they might learn to rule themselves. This idea, championed by Woodrow Wilson, found official expression in 1916 in the Jones Act.

### Anti-imperialism and Pacificism

The growing enthusiasm for colonialism and the cult of force met with opposition. The feeble peace movement of the 1880s and 1890s grew in strength with the growth of the opposition. In addition to the religious, ethical, and humanitarian arguments against war, navalism, and imperialism, advocates of peace emphasized what they regarded as the wastefulness, the inexpediency, the futility of such policies and more strenuously than ever demanded arbitration and international organization as alternatives. The waxing movement for intervention in behalf of Cuban liberty was opposed on the grounds that the desired goal could be achieved through peaceful methods and that the doctrine of means justifying ends was a highly dangerous one.

Organized pacifists saw insurance of inevitable wars in the policies pursued by the leaders of the world, in international rivalries and balances of power. In general they talked as if such measures as curtailment

[12] *Congressional Record*, 56 Cong., 1 sess. (January 9, 1900), 711.

of imperial policies and limitation of armaments would in themselves prevent war. Few of them saw the compelling importance of trade, investments, and the economic exploitation which gave rise to the imperial policies and the demand for armed protection. They failed for the most part to realize the strength of the economic forces favoring "the larger policy." But in the midst of the crusade of 1898 they foresaw other struggles, and they stood by their principles then and during the imperialistic aftermath. Through such channels of publicity as were available to them, they sought to convince the government and the people that war led to imperialism and imperialism to war in a never-ending circle, and that both alike ran counter to the principles of Christianity and humanitarianism, to the dictates of common sense, economic interest, and moral well-being.

In its struggle against the imperialism that followed the first crusade of 1898 the peace movement enjoyed the support of new allies. Well-known and able publicists and social scientists, such as Edward Atkinson, a Boston statistician and economist, William Graham Sumner, William James, and David Starr Jordan, vigorously opposed imperialism. They were joined by such social workers as Jane Addams and by almost all of the leaders in the various humanitarian causes. A small number of well-known journalists, especially E. L. Godkin of *The Nation* and Samuel Bowles of the *Springfield Republican*, cast in their lot with the anti-imperialists. Gertrude Atherton, Thomas Nelson Page, Richard Hovey, and Bliss Carman took the side of the expansionists, but the majority of literary figures, including Hamlin Garland, William Dean Howells, Mark Twain, Henry Blake Fuller, Thomas Wentworth Higginson, and William Vaughn Moody, expressed sympathy for the anti-imperialists. More important to the cause was the support of such well-known political leaders as Carl Schurz, George F. Hoar, George S. Boutwell, ex-President Cleveland, and William Jennings Bryan.

The anti-imperialist argument included the chief tenets that the pacifists advanced: the imperialist venture would not profit the nation as a whole, it would involve heavier taxes, it would promote navalism, militarism, and war, and it would bring in its train all manner of horrors such as the atrocities laid at the door of the American Army in the suppression of the Filipinos. The leading idea of the anti-imperialists was that colonialism and world power violated the basic traditional philosophy of the natural right of all peoples to self-determination. The Declaration of Independence, Washington's Farewell Address, and Lincoln's Gettysburg speech had stated or implied that no government should rule peoples without their consent, that the American government had been created of, by, and for the American people as an instrument for the advancement of its own well-being. It could not be made successfully into one for the advancement of the well-being of remote, alien, and reluctant or bitterly opposed peoples. Any attempt, on whatever pretext, to imitate foreign powers in their policy, or to interfere in the affairs of other nations was inimical to everything that had made America a great and unique land. If it was to continue so, it must keep to a course wisely charted and amply vindicated by experience. These ideas were repeated again and again in the addresses and the pamphlets, poems, and other writings of the anti-imperialists.

The vigorous campaign of this group, together with the support of the Democratic party under Bryan's leadership in the presidential campaign of 1900, aroused the hope in many breasts that America might return once and for all to its older conception of its destiny. This was not to be the case. The election of 1900 involved other issues than imperialism and anti-imperialism, but the decision favored the new course. The great mass of the people, however, probably supposed that by this course we had merely wet our feet rather than plunged into midstream.

## Preparation for the Second Crusade

Although the colonies were retained, although the Navy was expanded, although participation in world politics reached new levels in the administration of Theodore Roosevelt, neither the movement for domestic reform nor that for international peace was shunted aside. On the contrary, the Progressive movement and the New Freedom alike enjoyed signal support and reaped material victories. The growing strength of imperialism and navalism was accompanied by an extraordinary development of the peace movement. Leading educators, clergymen, writers, labor spokesmen, and businessmen joined peace societies and testified to their opposition to war and to their conviction that America must lead the world in establishing peace. There is also evidence that peace propaganda reached down among the people as it never had done before. Thus Wilson's gradually developing internationalism was to strike responsive chords.

The growth of this peace sentiment did not mean the growth of sentiment for isolation from the affairs of the world. On the contrary, the organized peace movement, at least an ever-growing section of it, emphasized the idea that peace could not be achieved through isolation. American leadership in the calling of the Second Hague Conference, in the movement for the codification of international law, and in the negotiation of more thoroughgoing arbitration treaties indicated consciousness of a need for American cooperation with other nations for the delimitation of war. It is true that the idea of the use of an international police force did not appeal to the majority of peace leaders. Yet even this idea gained headway, especially in the year and a half following the outbreak of World War I in 1914.

Meanwhile another pattern of thought, corresponding not to the humanitarian interest which the peace movement represented but to more material forces, made headway. This was the concept of America's duty to police the disorderly areas of the world and to take the lead in world power politics. It must be said that the majority of plain people doubtless had little concern with such talk beyond feeling a certain patriotic pride in an ever-grander Navy and their nation's ever-expanding influence in the world. There is evidence that some, but certainly not all, American businessmen used their influence to push the government into an extension of its police power in the Latin American sphere and the Far East. But the most articulate spokesmen for this pattern of thought were journalists, publicists, navalists, and political leaders—above all, Theodore Roosevelt, whose love of power and influence led him ever further into world power politics. It is important to keep in mind that Roosevelt identified power politics, in the case of America, with moral righteousness.

The conviction had been growing that, in consequence of the breakdown of distance through intercommunication, the various parts of the world were largely interdependent. In view of this, it was logical to argue that the welfare of any one portion was affected by whatever happened elsewhere. "Disorganization and disorder," declared Professor Talcott Williams in 1900, "will not be long permitted in a world grown as small as ours."[13] The Outlook's similar declaration that "either we must take our share of the responsibilities of keeping the modern world in order, or we must cease to profit by what other nations are doing in this direction"

[13] Annals of the American Academy of Political and Social Science, XVI (September, 1900), 240.

was another way of phrasing an idea increasingly dear to intellectuals. About the same time Woodrow Wilson wrote that "the day of our isolation is past." In the new age before us, he continued, "America must lead the world."[14] Though he had moral influence and leadership in mind, he was on the point of visioning a leadership that also involved the use of power for the promotion of international order.

Wilson's anti-imperialistic sentiments did not keep him from resorting, during his first administration, to the doctrine of international police power in his efforts to make Mexico and the Caribbean republics orderly, peaceable, and moral. In this he clearly followed in Roosevelt's steps. Thus the doctrine of international police power, which had traditionally been countenanced only when it had seemed necessary to ward off the encroachment of "contaminating" European powers in our immediate neighborhood, was now operating as a definite policy.

In view of the idea of the interdependence of the world and the fear for American institutions when threatened by encroaching autocracies, it was only a relatively short step to the new position finally taken in 1917. This position was expounded in memorable words in Wilson's war message:

> Our object . . . is to vindicate the principles of peace and justice in the life of the world as against selfish and autocratic power. The right is more precious than peace, and we shall fight for the things we have always carried nearest our hearts—for democracy, for the right of those who submit to authority to have a voice in their own governments, for the rights and liberties of small nations, for a universal dominion of right by such a concert of free peoples as shall bring peace and safety to all nations and make the world itself at last free. . . . The world must be made safe for democracy.

Shortly after, Wilson said: "We are saying to all mankind, 'We did not set this Government up in order that we might have a selfish and separate liberty for we are now ready to come to your assistance and fight out upon the field of the world the cause of human liberty.' "[15]

The step, though short, was not taken easily, either by President Wilson or by the American people. The change of mind involved in this momentous decision was made possible only because of a juxtaposition

[14] *Atlantic Monthly*, XC (December, 1902), 734.
[15] Ray Stannard Baker and William E. Dodd (eds.), *The Public Papers of Woodrow Wilson: War and Peace* (Harper & Row, 1927), I, 11, 53, 66.

of many interests, ideas, and personalities. From regarding the maelstrom in Europe as an imperialistic conflict, Wilson himself came to regard it as a struggle between good and evil. From regarding the great upheaval as an anachronism and a remote and alien contest, a larger and larger number of Americans came to look on it as a struggle between darkness and light, barbarism and civilization.

The concept of an American obligation to save humanity from Kaiserism and Prussianism became more widely accepted as Allied propaganda sharpened the ideological aspects of the conflict. This result was facilitated by long-accumulating efforts to establish an Anglo-American entente. Political and economic considerations were partly responsible for this movement which had been gaining impetus since the turn of the century; but in addition it was promoted by an imposing company of British and American intellectuals who believed that Anglo-American kinship, friendship, and cooperation in world affairs was necessary for the salvation of a common, precious heritage. The bonds thus created now helped provide a favorable reception of the British interpretation of the war and of the all but incredible German atrocity stories which reached America via England.

German submarine attacks involving the loss of American lives as well as property increased the already mounting indignation. The German refusal to accept President Wilson as a mediator, as the world leader in reconstruction, made the final decision—on his part—less difficult.

All these changes in mental outlook took place within a framework of tangible realities. That Colonel House, Wilson's intimate adviser, believed it desirable to turn to foreign affairs when the domestic New Freedom program had gone about as far as circumstances seemed to permit, no doubt had some influence on the President. However much industrialists and bankers denied that the loans made to the Allies led them to favor intervention when it appeared that Great Britain and France might collapse without American military aid, there was undoubtedly some truth for them in the Biblical injunction: "For where your treasure is, there will your heart be also." That many, including Senator Norris of Nebraska, Senator La Follette of Wisconsin, and Congressman Lindbergh of Minnesota, maintained that financial interests were largely responsible for the decision to fight, made little difference in the final turn of events in the spring of 1917.

Thus American minds became ready for the acceptance of Wilson's international idealism. The pattern of thought that had enjoyed the support only of minorities throughout the nineteenth century was now extended from the Pacific and the Caribbean area, where it had been in operation since 1898, to Europe itself. America was to recross the Atlantic not only in defense of what was regarded as vital American interests. She was "to show the world that she was born to serve mankind," to lead in "a People's War, a war for freedom and justice and self-government amongst all the nations of the world, a war to make the world safe for the peoples who live upon it and have made it their own, the German people themselves included."

### The Scholar in the Second Crusade

Before the scholar in the White House had made the final decision for war in April, 1917, academicians in general had taken the lead in mobilizing opinion for intervention in the European maelstrom. Because the effort to defeat the Central Powers involved as no previous war had done the entire mobilization of civilian life, intellectual activity was more profoundly affected than in any earlier military crisis. As never before, American scholars left their ivory towers.

For some time scholarship had been becoming more and more a matter of cooperative planning and organization, and the war greatly accelerated this tendency. The National Research Council, formed to coordinate research in the scientific field, facilitated the task of the government in innumerable ways. Committees of economists, political scientists, historians, and other scholars were summoned to Washington where they enlisted the help of their colleagues in planning war activities in which specialized knowledge was of importance. Historians publicized the official aims of the Allies, ourselves included, and discredited the foe. Other specialists aided Colonel House in preparing data to guide the delegates at the peace conference once the Germans were crushed. The close association of scholars in related social disciplines promoted the development of the idea of "the social sciences" and paved the way for the subsequent organization of the Social Science Research Council. The organization of the American Council of Learned Societies after the war similarly illustrated the growing tendency toward cooperative scholarship which the struggle promoted.

During the war itself, few important discoveries were made in the natural sciences, few theoretical contributions were recorded in the social disciplines or the humanities. This resulted in part from the readiness of scholars to turn aside from their own research projects and to apply their specialized knowledge and techniques to war problems and situations. It was also in part the effect of the dislocation of ordinary academic routine in colleges and universities, most of which were quasi-militarized. But if the war failed to stimulate important new theoretical contributions to knowledge, in certain fields nevertheless it advanced knowledge as a result of the application of known facts and techniques to new situations. Thus surgery and military medicine in general made important gains, as did psychiatry. Psychological testing, which had advanced only slightly beyond the theoretical stage, was given new impetus. Aeronautics similarly leaped ahead. The impetus given to the practical application of existing knowledge for utilitarian purposes even swept through levels of intellectual life below the laboratories and libraries; both in colleges and in public schools vocational subjects, useful or thought to be useful for the war effort, made marked headway.

Another characteristic tendency in American intellectual life—the narrowing of the gulf between the scholar and specialist on the one hand and the general public on the other—was likewise reinforced. It is true that the soldiers in their free time generally preferred revelry to self-improvement; yet the facilities offered in reading, in vocational and general instruction, especially during demobilization, greatly exceeded the somewhat feeble efforts of the Christian Commission during the Civil War. Moreover, the war quickened curiosity and widened knowledge of geography.

The movement for the popularization of knowledge among civilian as well as military sections of the nation owed a good deal to the renewed and expanded efforts to reduce illiteracy and to push forward the program of the Americanization of immigrant groups. Specialists in various fields engaged in feverish efforts to popularize bodies of knowledge hitherto largely closed to the public. Historians used their talents—sometimes not too wisely or in entire accord with the canons of their profession—to popularize history for the promotion of morale. One result of all this emphasis on organized "drives" to promote public information was to open the road to new developments in the field of propaganda—the effects of which were to become apparent only in the postwar decades.

The Revolution and the Civil War had both promoted the idea of cultural nationalism, and although American intellectual life by 1917 had come to be far less dependent on that of Europe than in any earlier crisis, the second crusade also heightened cultural nationalism in considerable measure. Scholars no longer deferred to German learning and science. But if there was some tendency to substitute French leadership and thought for German, there was an even more marked tendency to rely on our own resources.

The war spirit frequently exacted a tax on freedom of expression. Eugene Debs, the popular socialist leader, was sentenced to a ten-year imprisonment for having denounced the administration's prosecution of men charged with sedition. Randolph Bourne, a gifted young literary critic, trenchantly expressed the opposition of the "suppressed minority" to the war—but no one would publish his denunciation of the compulsive power of the state in war time.

Academic freedom also suffered considerable restriction. Columbia University demanded the resignation of two professors who criticized America's entrance into the war. The trial of a dozen professors at the University of Nebraska was a lamentable example of hysteria. In the public schools, too, professional patriots frequently sought and obtained the dismissal of teachers judged to be lukewarm in their war enthusiasm or tinged with socialism or even old-fashioned American liberalism. This was, indeed, a repercussion of the hysteria that had been stimulated by professional patriots throughout the land, an hysteria marked by a passionate and unreasoning hatred of everything German—including German literature and music—a wild and fearful hatred of the Hun, the German beast, the murderous Kaiser.

When soldiers were not seeking release in fun from the regimentation of Army life, when home folk were not torn too much by the absence of sons and lovers or vexed unduly by the inconveniences of the war, when fierce hatred did not poison souls, the popular mind experienced considerable genuine idealism. The concept of the American mission of promoting an international order of peace and righteousness seemed, for a time, to enlist much general support. A good deal of the moral idealism previously channeled into movements for social justice at home was now diverted into the channels cut by President Wilson in his historic war messages.

That the second crusade checked the program for reform in our economic and social life occasioned regret in some circles. Randolph Bourne declared that "there is work to be done to prevent this war of ours from passing into popular mythology as a holy crusade. . . . There is work to be done in still shouting that all the revolutionary by-products will not justify the war, or make war anything else than the most noxious complex of all the evils that afflict man."[16] But the peace movement, for the time at least, was thoroughly disrupted. Most of its adherents were supporting the war, and those who refused were paying a heavy price. Socialism, having been split wide open on the issue of the war, was enfeebled; the great majority of the party maintained its loyalty to its international proletarian ideals and in consequence suffered great opprobrium. Most important of all, enthusiastic champions of the New Freedom program lost their zeal for it in the heat and distraction of the second crusade for justice across the seas.

Two reform movements alone seemed to suffer only temporarily. All signs indicated that, as a result of the necessity for food conservation, advocates of the prohibition of alcoholic beverages would realize their Utopia. It was also clear that, thanks to their war efforts, women would be rewarded by the suffrage. Whether in the postwar decade the reform spirit in other areas would be channeled into constructive achievements, whether the international idealism kindled by President Wilson would be applied in the postwar world were leading questions that perplexed the minds of many thoughtful men and women when the armistice was finally signed.

[16] Randolph S. Bourne, *Untimely Papers* (B. W. Huebsch, 1919), 45.

# 27  Prosperity, Disillusionment, Criticism

*The vast repetitive operations are dulling the human mind.*
—HERBERT HOOVER, 1920

*Never was our heritage of civilization and culture so secure, and never was it half so rich.*
—WILL DURANT, 1926

The ideal of internationalism did not disappear from American thought in the 1920s but it figured less in the intellectual life of the nation than it had during the War. Nor was domestic reform as deeply eclipsed as many at the time, and since, supposed: but it occupied a less prominent place in the minds of most Americans than it had in the first decade and a half of the century. In the discussions of public affairs great emphasis was put on the idea that capitalism in its big-business form had brought a new and permanent era of widespread and ever-increasing prosperity. Much publicity was also given to the idea that the United States, being immensely superior to the rest of the world, might well let Europe and Asia work out their own salvation.

Many who did not share in the new prosperity had doubts about the beneficence of large-scale business organization. Others, especially the so-called intelligentsia, expressed cynical disillusionment with the whole

American way of life, middle-class respectability, acquisitiveness, commercialism, the genteel tradition in letters, and the assumption of national superiority. Many among the younger generation tended to share the intellectuals' revolt against Victorian manners and morals and noisily insisted on the right to defy conventions and enjoy life. Thus the 1920s, in spite of the prevailing complacency, were not without contradiction and confusion.

Writers of the 1920s frequently ascribed to the war many of the tendencies which, on the surface at least, characterized the whole decade. If the general prosperity was not laid directly at the door of the war, everyone knew that the struggle had made thousands of new millionaires and put all Europe deeply in debt to Uncle Sam. Prohibition was frequently spoken of as if it had resulted solely from the necessity of wartime economy and wartime psychology. The relaxation of conventional morals incident to war was often cited as an explanation of the antics of the younger generation. antics which often shocked their elders. The note of cynicism and disillusionment on the one hand, and on the other the dizzy gaiety that looked on life as a "meaningless accident," were frequently attributed to the war and its aftermath. So too was the "wave of gangsterism" and defiance of law which troubled so many decent people in America's greatest cities.

The war, and especially the collapse of moral and international idealism that followed the armistice, no doubt did accentuate, bring to the surface, and give publicity to many of the ideas that had begun to find expression before 1917. It would be impossible to say how much influence the war itself had in conditioning many of the attitudes commonly assumed to be new in the 1920s. Many had appeared before the war the movement for greater opportunities for women, the self-consciousness of youth, the waxing prohibition crusade, the revolt against middle-class respectability and the genteel tradition, the activities of the underworld—none of these was new. The trends that seemed to give a distinctive flavor to the postwar decade thus reflected underlying and far-reaching changes in American life that had already begun to provoke dislocations on every level and were to continue to do so in the 1930s.

## The Reaction Against Idealistic Internationalism

The war was not forgotten, but it was never taken to heart and idealized by the American people as earlier wars had been. A common attitude was to regard it as a mistake, an attitude that was strengthened by the revisionist historians. In 1926 Harry Elmer Barnes, professor of historical sociology at Smith College, published his *Genesis of the World War*, an attack on the widely accepted idea of unique German responsibility for the conflict. Two years later *Origins of the World War*, a two-volume study by one of his colleagues, Sidney B. Fay, left little doubt that the official Allied propaganda did not square at many points with a critical analysis of archival and other material.

Virtually all American literary men and women who wrote about the War expressed either a mellow but sad disappointment, as Willa Cather did in *One of Ours*, or the downright disillusionment of *Three Soldiers* by John Dos Passos, *What Price Glory* by Stallings and Anderson, and *Farewell to Arms* by Ernest Hemingway. The prevailing antipathy toward any idealizing of the war also found expression in the popularity of Remarque's *All Quiet on the Western Front* and the movie based on it which brought to an even larger public the horror, grimness, and spiritual annihilation of the struggle.

Popular sentiment reacted not only against the war itself but against the idea of international idealism and the related idea of American responsibility for some measure of planned control of international forces. Just as there was a popular reaction against the idea of public planning, responsibility, and control in the domestic area, so there was one in the international. In spite of the warnings of ex-President Wilson, whose physical collapse contributed to the failure of his international program, Americans by and large were more convinced of their country's self-sufficiency than ever before. The League of Nations was rejected. Affiliation with the much-circumscribed World Court was considered in official quarters and among large sections of the public as too risky an international commitment. The pronounced noninterventionism that dominated American thought was expressed not only in official policy but in such popular slogans as "Let Europe stew in her own juice."

Far from assuming any responsibility for her well-being, the predominant mood was expressed by the member of Congress who declared, "Right now the United States wants to see Europe do some housecleaning without delay." Or, as someone else put it, Europe in debt and demoralized must "clean up and pay up." For the most part, Americans looked down on the "backwardness, the decadence, the political chaos" of Europe. They scorned her failure to resolve age-old difficulties. They did not see that profound dislocations almost inevitably resulted from the rise of a revolutionary technological interdependence that was at odds with inherited convictions and habits. An amazing number of middle-class American tourists invaded Europe and admired the picturesque villages and quaint countryside. But many, if not most, returned thanking God that this government had washed its hands of the "whole European mess."

The repudiation of international duties and responsibilities did not mean a complete victory for isolationism. Many liberal intellectuals continued to advocate American affiliation with the League of Nations and the World Court. More important, leaders in the business community, led by Secretary of Commerce Herbert Hoover, militantly promoted markets for American surpluses and the establishment of branches of American corporations not only in the less industrially developed parts of the world but in Europe itself. The neo-mercantilistic justification of this policy found effective spokesmen in the business community and the public arena.

Americans more confidently than ever before gloried in the superiorities of America. The *Ladies' Home Journal* declared editorially that "there is only one first-class civilization in the world today. It is right here in the United States. . . ." Canada was also graciously included. Some attributed the superiority of the United States to the predominance of the so-called "Nordic" stock; they did not take into account the fact that the American people was in truth a conglomerate folk, and they overlooked England's claim to be regarded as a better representative of "Nordic" strains. In any case, Lothrop Stoddard and William McDougall publicized the doctrine of the supremacy of the "Nordic race" and sought to justify their arguments with an impressive array of biological and psychological "evidence." The widespread acceptance of this belief helps to explain the considerable degree of tolerance and even support of the revived Ku Klux Klan, a secret anti-Negro, anti-Jewish, anti-immigrant, anti-Catholic order that flourished in the 1920s among the lower-middle-class groups. The faith in Nordic superiority also contributed to the decision to restrict immigration and to discriminate among the limited number of future newcomers in favor of northern Europeans.

Others attributed the superiority of America to the superior morals of its people. Thomas Nixon Carver, a professor of economics at Harvard, wrote that the good fortune of America was the result of American good behavior, of the fact that Americans sought, and continued to seek, "the Kingdom of Heaven and righteousness."[1] The same theme was developed by Dr. Frank Crane, the beloved columnist. This clerical mentor of the people believed that the only trouble with Europe was that, unlike America, it had never learned to work and to love work. Many thought that America, in exporting factories, techniques, and efficient industrial organizations to Europe, would confer a blessing that might yet rescue the Old World from an almost hopeless decadence.

The harsh rejoinders from Europe to all such talk about American superiority and the Americanization of Europe aroused little response in the United States. In any case, whatever patriots hoped the export of American goods might accomplish in Europe, most Americans agreed with Calvin Coolidge when in effect he called for no importations —industrial, intellectual, or political.

Yet, in the eyes of many patriots, the obvious superiority of the United States was inadequately appreciated at home and required high-pressure methods to sustain it. Many found much emotional outlet in organizing patriotism along professional lines. Superpatriotism was, of course, in part an idealistic expression of an emotion rooted in early training and in the whole culture of the country. "One hundred percentism" also reflected property-consciousness, for patriotism was often associated with the security of property.

But now there were special reasons for a renewal of professional patriotism. During the struggle unity had been artificially imposed by the exigencies of war. Once the crisis was over, the disunity of American society was evident. The IWW reappeared, and strikes began again. The possibility that the old program of reform might be resumed alarmed many men and women of position and substance. Such signs of disunity led to legal efforts to compel Americans to be patriotic and above all to identify patriotism with the security and sanctity of private property. There followed the Lusk Laws requiring New York teachers to take oaths of loyalty and, in effect, of conformity, attacks on social studies textbooks deemed either too internationalistic or too socialistic, and the circulation of black lists stigmatizing even the mildest liberals as "sub-.ersive" and "un-American." In addition, Constitution worship became an almost religious cult in certain quarters. Thus the effort was made, in

[1] Thomas Nixon Carver, *The Present Economic Revolution in the United States* (Little, Brown and Co., 1925), 65.

the name of patriotism, to conceal divisions within American life and to maintain the social and economic status quo.

The prevailing mood of "one hundred percent Americanism" and anti-internationalism did not, of course, go unchallenged. The fact that dissenters spoke out against it reflected the confusion and conflict of the period. Sensitive—and sometimes disappointed—men of letters and artists rebelled against the smug implications of the American assumption of complete superiority to the rest of the world. Sometimes these men and women expatriated themselves to the more mellow lands of Europe, where they could live well if modestly on incomes derived from the prosperity of their families at home. But many of America's most gifted writers who did not thus turn their backs on their country nevertheless refused to bow to the creed of "one hundred percentism" and even satirized it with stinging pens.

Nor were novelists and critics alone in rejecting the concept of American self-sufficiency and superiority. Scholarly men at home in the cosmopolitan republic of letters and ideas, and social scientists sensitive to the actual interdependence of the modern technological world deplored the prevalent anti-internationalism and pointed out the necessity of American cooperation with other lands if war and the breakdown of civilization were to be avoided. Religious leaders mobilized church sentiment for international cooperation in a more far-reaching and realistic way than ever before. Indeed, the peace movement not only revived but became more extensive than at any other period, and prevailing opinion in it was definitely internationalist.

More influential than many of the internationalist persuasion were the spokesmen for one group of America's economic leaders. Ivy Lee, well-known public relations counsel, bluntly demanded:

Shall we so fear entanglement with other nations and consequent subservience of our policies to theirs that we shall in turn become slaves to events we shall have refused to help shape before they become critical? What do we propose to do when complications grow out of our economic penetration in various parts of the world? Shall we bring political pressure or attempt political intervention when our investments abroad are endangered or when foreign countries default on their debts to Americans? Shall we leave our protection in such matters to other nations, or shall we join in advance in responsible and cooperative efforts so to shape events that independent or selfishly protective action by any nation will be unnecessary?[2]

[2] Ivy Lee, "The Black Legend," *Atlantic Monthly*, CXLIII (May, 1929), 588.

Thus a voice for business spoke out against isolationism. Moreover, business in general looked with favor on any reduction of taxes through the limitation of competitive armaments.

In response to such felt needs as well as to the demands of pacifists and internationalists that the government do something to reduce armaments and make war less likely, the Harding administration cautiously turned its attention toward the financial stabilization of Europe and the problem of limiting armaments. But only in the Pacific, where the maintenance of the existing equilibrium seemed imperative, was constructive action recorded; the Washington Disarmament Conference performed useful if limited functions. Apart from these evidences of internationalism, the most striking contradiction to the prevalent sense of self-sufficiency was the continuation and refinement of imperialism in Latin America. But Latin America, of course, was regarded as within our own sphere of interest.

### "Farewell to Reform"

International cooperation and leadership for world peace were not the only value of the preceding period to be largely overshadowed in the postwar decade. From the time of the Populist uprising to the second election of President Wilson in 1916, political, economic, and social reform had been an impressive element in American thought. At the end of the 1920s, however, John Chamberlain, surveying the preceding decades, could entitle his survey *Farewell to Reform*. Frederic C. Howe, a veteran champion of municipal improvement, struck a note of defeat in his autobiographical *Confessions of a Reformer*. Lincoln Steffens, whose muckraking had been so spectacular, expressed a disillusionment with reform and muckraking and even suggested that America would achieve socialist goals under the auspices of beneficent capitalism.

The prevailing mood in American literature thus did not represent a development of the school of Upton Sinclair's *The Jungle*, Jack London's *Martin Eden*, Ernest Poole's *The Harbor*, the proletarian poems of Giovannitti, or the critical essays of Randolph Bourne, Max Eastman, and Van Wyck Brooks. The doctrine of the Social Gospel did not disappear from Protestant thought, but no book in this tradition enjoyed the vogue that Charles Sheldon's *In His Steps* had enjoyed. Indeed, no other book on a religious subject could touch the popularity of Bruce

Barton's *The Man Nobody Knows*, a book which, identifying Jesus as the prototype of the modern businessman, remained a best seller for two years.

Instead of regarding big business as an evil colossus to be controlled by the public for the public good if it could not be broken up, prevailing opinion in the 1920s accepted the view that the government should leave business alone. The dominant idea, in short, came to be that of "prosperity, mass production, high wages, high-pressure selling, installments, service, bigger and betterism." Advertisers, public relations experts, and columnists did much to make big business corporations acceptable. The lingering doubts of some were resolved when President Harding sold the country the idea symbolized by the slogan "Back to normalcy" and when President Coolidge declared that "the business of America is business." Even President Hoover, who in 1920 had pointed out to the Federated Engineering Societies grave flaws in the economic and social fabric, now, in the late 1920s, announced with conviction that there would be a chicken in every pot, a garage and car for every house.

The new acceptance of the philosophy of mass consumption and mass prosperity had overshadowed the older reform ideology. When the public utilities were proved guilty of scandalous behavior and blatant corruption of public officials and school textbook writers, even when promoters in high office were convicted of stealing the nation's oil reserves, popular sentiment on the whole was indulgent. The 4,800,000 men and women who voted for La Follette in 1924 did constitute a considerable body of protest; but in view of the fact that women now cast ballots, this vote was hardly comparable to that of the dissenters and Progressives who in 1912 supported Wilson and Roosevelt. Socialism, supported by almost a million voters in 1912, was now reduced to a feeble fragment. Communism was virtually driven underground. The government was vigorously supported by the American Federation of Labor in its refusal to recognize the Soviet Union years after the Revolution of 1917. Criminal syndicalist laws in numerous states virtually made it a treasonable offense to advocate the right of revolution. Yet that right had been cherished by the fathers of the Republic, and leading nineteenth-century Americans had included it in their political philosophy.

Reform sentiment and thought did not entirely disappear. Many liberal intellectuals supported the fight of Senator George Norris of

Nebraska for public ownership of electric power and for the removal of legal barriers against the use of injunctions in labor disputes. However lush the new prosperity was in certain quarters and however extensive it was reputed to be, real wages of unskilled labor, and in some degree of skilled also, remained more or less stationary from 1923 to 1929, the high tide of the new prosperity. The income of the lowest tenth, largely the poorest of the marginal farmers, actually decreased. It was, in fact, only the upper 10 percent of the population that enjoyed a marked increase in real income. But the protests which such facts might normally have evoked could not make themselves widely or effectively felt. This was in part the result of the grand strategy of the major political parties. In part it was the result of the fact that almost all the chief avenues to mass opinion were now controlled by large-scale publishing industries. These seldom featured the shadows in the picture.

Yet even if relatively few heard the articulated protest, its survival indicated that beneath the surface all was not well. Vigorous articles exposing ailments in the social, political, and economic areas filled the pages of *The Freeman, The Nation, The New Republic,* and other organs with slender constituencies. Revelations of shamefully inadequate housing and of lack of basic decencies among the urban masses found their way into the *Survey Graphic.* The same grim squalor was revealed in *Jews Without Money,* the autobiography of Mike Gold, one of the few men of letters to maintain the old radical literary position of the *Masses* group with which John Reed had been associated. The conflict in ideas was also reflected in the never-ending stream of novels from the pen of the veteran reformer, Upton Sinclair. In addition to his novels, those of Sinclair Lewis, Theodore Dreiser, and others, if they did not represent an out-and-out reform ideology, did, as we shall see, reveal a scheme of values utterly different from that of the dominant social and economic conservatism.

Competent authorities on another level declared that the existing prosperity rested on inflated credit and the wildest promotion and speculation. Income was too unevenly distributed to enable the masses really to purchase consumers' goods and services on a scale sufficiently vast to maintain the overexpanded system of production; the matter was made worse, these critics continued, by the fact that much of the spending was spending not of savings but of future earnings (installment buying). John Dewey, among others, pointed to the primary need of enlarged social control over an economy rapidly becoming more collecti-vistic. But few heeded these critics. Indeed, they were commonly re-garded as "Bolsheviki" or called befuddled cranks. Little attention was paid to protests against inadequate housing, technological unemploy-ment, depressed mining districts, down-at-the-heel factory towns, or the insecurity and squalor that hung heavily over farmers and tenants on marginal lands. The decline of the labor movement also reflected a waning of the protest psychology.

Only when some event dramatically personalized the injustice incident to the dominant conservatism did protest enjoy a wide hearing. Thus liberals succeeded in enlisting much support for their vigorous protests when Sacco and Vanzetti, two Italian laborers of anarchist persuasion, were charged with murder by the Commonwealth of Massachusetts and on dubious evidence sentenced to the electric chair. Similarly liberals won a general hearing for Mooney and Billings, two San Francisco labor leaders sentenced to life imprisonment on the charge of having planted a bomb during a preparedness parade in 1916. Sacco and Vanzetti went to the chair; Mooney and Billings remained in prison throughout the 1920s. But in spite of the fact that reform and protest exerted little apparent influence on public thought, the mere existence of this ideology was symptomatic of cleavages in American thought and life.

The traditionally American democratic faith in the free and more or less equal individual, in multiple leadership and multiple decision, was subjected to less widespread attack than the reform movement, but even democracy did not escape. In part the much-vaunted criticism of democracy heard in certain quarters of the intellectual and pseudo-intellectual world was an after-war reaction. It was part of the general disillusionment with World War I, fought presumably to make the world safe for democracy. Students of political science wondered whether democracy could survive the onslaught of highly organized pressure-group minorities. The war, moreover, had occasioned the first extensive use of intelligence tests, and the results of these, widely publicized in the years after the armistice, did much to convince the "elite" that the average intelligence was so low that the democratic ideal could never be achieved. Subsequent explanations indicating that the tests had been inadequately standardized and hence were no exact measure of the national "mental age" were accepted only slowly even among knowl-edgeable laymen.

Opponents of democracy also ridiculed the idea of free choice—a concept basic to democracy—and cited the authority of scientists who held that the whole universe including man was governed deterministically. Although many scientists were already criticizing the concept of scientific determinism, these criticisms were in general not related specifically to the deterministic criticisms of democracy. Henry L. Mencken's *American Mercury* witheringly jibed at the foibles and stupidity of the masses. This periodical owed much of its popularity to the fact that it appealed to city slickers and to good old raucous Yankee laughers. Yet many of its readers considered themselves a sophisticated elite or "civilized minority." On other grounds the "new humanists," led by Paul Elmer More and Irving Babbitt, deplored the debasing of standards by democracy.

The onslaught against democracy cut more deeply into the popular mind than the writings of Mencken, Babbitt, and More suggest. Many a popular novel belittled the values and symbols associated with democracy. In official and semi-official circles the lawlessness identified with gangsterism and flagrant violations of prohibition was sometimes laid at the door of democracy in terms hardly complimentary to that form of government and way of life. An Army *Training Manual* used by the War Department defined democracy as "a government of the masses. Authority derived through mass meeting or any other forms of 'direct' expression. Results in mobocracy. Attitude toward property is communistic—negating property rights. Attitude toward law is that the will of the majority shall regulate, whether it be based upon deliberation or governed by passion, prejudice, and impulse, without restraint or regard to consequences. Results in demagogism, license, agitation, discontent, anarchy."[3]

These criticisms of democracy did not go unchallenged. Charles and Mary Beard's *Rise of American Civilization* and Vernon L. Parrington's *Main Currents in American Thought* testified to the vitality of democratic scholarship. John Dewey redefined democracy in terms of the increasingly collectivistic trends in the culture. Such periodicals as *The Survey, The New Republic,* and *The Nation,* and such groups as the Civil Liberties Union represented democratic thought and feeling. The plain people themselves were probably little affected by the criticisms

[3] United States Army *Training Manual,* No. 2000–25 (Government Printing Office, 1928), 91.

of democracy. The American democratic tradition had by no means been laid on the shelf!

## The Cult of Prosperity

The decline of reform, the criticism of democracy, and the generally favorable attitude toward business reflected profound changes in the economic and financial structure. The rate of capitalistic expansion had begun to slow down even before World War I. While the effects of it had been felt in Europe even before 1914, it was not until the 1920s that America experienced the results of this slowing-down process. The effects were chiefly felt in the shift from an economy *short* of capital, i.e., savings for investment in production goods expansion, to one with a surplus of capital (savings) for any kind of expansion, in either producers' or consumers' goods. So basic a shift in economy could hardly take place without influencing ideas of what constituted economic and social virtues.

The old virtues of thrift and saving now largely gave way to the idea that spending is a virtue, even the highest of all economic virtues. One writer expressed the new philosophy when he declared that "one reason for America's prosperity and one reason why . . . that prosperity will continue, is that we have committed ourselves to a standard of living far beyond our wildest pre-war dreams. . . . It is impossible to call Americans back to a petty thrift, and I personally am glad of it. . . . We have ceased to count our pennies in America, and I certainly hope we never return to the days of the most graceless of all virtues, a niggardly and penny-pinching thrift."[4] In spending, so the argument ran, one not only enjoyed the comforts and luxuries now available through the magic of mass machine production; one also fed the springs of prosperity by insuring the indefinite expansion of producers' goods industries. As Bruce Barton put it in an article in the *Woman's Home Companion:* "I say, 'Encourage the Interests. Let them go ahead and make more products at lower prices. Let them make profits, because that will enable them to pay high wages and high taxes. Let the government stand as an umpire and insist that the game be played fairly.' "[5]

[4] Quoted in James T. Adams, *Our Business Civilization* (Albert and Charles Boni, 1929), 44–45.
[5] *Woman's Home Companion,* LI (November, 1924), 12.

Public relations counsels, high-pressure advertisers, and salesmen, story writers, columnists, and economists popularized the doctrine that prosperity had come to stay through this new economic policy of high wages, mass consumption, and mass spending. It was an engaging and plausible idea. It appealed to the natural desire of men and women to enjoy comforts and luxuries. It thrived on competition for prestige and the desire to be in the swim expressed by the popular expression, "Keeping up with the Joneses." The amazing spread of the new cult was facilitated by the emphasis advertising and salesmanship put on the ideal of service. "The man who does me most good," wrote the author of *The Blessing of Business*, "is the one who sells me necessary supplies and conveniences at a low price, because of economies of production."[6] Rotarians and Kiwanians put an extra sugarcoating on the ideal of service by insisting that business was the only real democracy, the only true brotherhood of man.

The cult of prosperity was publicized in the most widely circulating dailies by popular columnists, among whom Arthur Brisbane took high rank. But the new philosophy of mass consumption was also popularized by bigger and better advertisements that appealed as never before to the desire for prestige and success. *System*, to cite a single example, carried an ad of the American Laundry Company which announced that 90 percent of American bankers wore starched collars "because it's good business."

With the possible exception of the movies, nothing better exemplified and popularized the cult of prosperity than a new type of folk literature —the human interest and human problem sketches of "actual" men and women that appeared in *True Stories*, a Bernarr MacFadden publication boasting millions of readers. The editors declared in 1930 that the character of the "true stories" contributed by readers had so changed during the decade that the magazine could hardly be recognized by the editors themselves. "From tales of misery and privation and struggle ten years ago, the stories that now pour into us from all quarters of America are tales of ultimate success and happiness."[7] Even the vocabulary, continued the editors, had changed—"just jumped into the car"—"didn't know me in my new suit"—"got tickets for the show"—"went down to the store and bought it on the installment plan." People who had been too weary to want fine clothes, amusements, and thrills; people who had

[6] E. W. Howe, *The Blessing of Business* (Crane and Co., 1918), 39–40.
[7] *The American Economic Evolution* (True Story Magazine, 1930), 8.

begun their stories with such sentences as "We were very poor" or "We had no time to enjoy each other," now spoke with their chins up, their eyes on the level, knew how to select the right things at the store, knew how to do the "right things." "You Business Executives, sitting at your desks," wrote a *True Stories* editor, "thinking ever in terms of factories and output and financial setup, *you have been making a fairy tale come true!*"

It would be easy to illustrate the cult of prosperity from hundreds of tales in *True Stories* or *The Saturday Evening Post* or from the synopses of scores of the most popular stories. The mere listing of characteristic titles of articles in the *American Magazine*, "Middletown's" most popular periodical, provides striking evidence of the cult. The faith in buying goods and services was reflected in such titles as "Clothes Don't Make the Woman—But They Help a Lot"; "There's Not Much Use to Grind Unless You Advertise Your Grist"; "A Man's Debts Are Sometimes the Measure of His Courage"; "Don't Fear to Attempt Things Just Because They Look Big"; "The Girl Who Was Tired of Being Poor"; "Courage to Dive Off the Dock"; "Are You Discouraged About Your Business?" and "How to Play Your Game, Whatever It Is." Optimism, the ability to take failure and to start over again with confidence in ultimate success, and the conviction that the big businessmen are where they are because they deserve to be, found expression in such articles as "Do You Think That Luck Is Against You?" "How Charlie Taught Me to Laugh at Failure"; "The Bookkeeper Who Refused to Stay Put"; "I Was a Failure for More Than Fifty Years"; "How an 'Ordinarily Stupid Boy' Became a Great Merchant"; "The Story of a Man Who Gets Things Done"; "The Man Who was 'Made' by Being Fired"; "You Needn't Pity *This* Orphan"; "A Blunt Boss Taught Me a Good Lesson Thirty Years Ago"; "You Do Not Have to Like a Job to Succeed in It"; "A Man Who Never Lost Sight of His One Big Idea"; "It Is up to You"; "No Big Men Hit the Nail on the Head"; "The World's Most Tragic Man Is the One Who Never Starts"; "What a Whale of a Difference an Incentive Makes"; "How Did You Put It Over?" and "S. Kresge, a Story That Makes You Take a New Grip on Yourself." The impression gained from a listing of the entire contents of the *American Magazine* throughout the 1920s would not be essentially different from this sample from 1922 and 1927.

Closely identified with the cult of prosperity was faith in efficiency.

Business was heralded for its skill in doing things well with a minimum of effort, time, and expense. Earnest Elmo Calkins, writing in the *Atlantic Monthly* in 1928, the year before the great collapse, declared that "the work that religion, government, and war have failed in must be done by business. . . . That eternal job of administering this planet must be turned over to the despised business man."[8] The ideal of efficiency even invaded the home as it had never done before—if we can judge by writers on and for the home. Homemaking, a traditional American concern of the great mass of women, was becoming, at least in many middle-class homes, a profession in which efficiency was given dominant emphasis. The women's magazines featured efficiency in success stories bearing such captions as "Great Men Have Had Great Mothers" and "Being a Great Mother is a Life Work." But the advertisements, stories, and feature articles in the *Woman's Home Companion*, the *Ladies' Home Journal*, and the *Delineator* reiterated the theme of efficiency as the keynote to success in buying food and clothing, mastering etiquette, preserving good looks, beautifying the home, looking out for the health of children, and making marriage happy. Plain efficiency, these magazines would have it, leads to success in promoting moral cleanliness and civic spirit, in using leisure, in dulling heartaches, and in promoting hope and happiness. If the women's magazines gave some attention to ways and means for succeeding in careers in the big world outside the home, they naturally gave more to illustrate the conviction that "they also serve who do the small things well."

Professional perspectives as well as general patterns of thought reflected business mores and especially the new belief in permanent prosperity based on mass consumption. Every profession, whether education, medicine, nursing, law, engineering, or journalism, emphasized the ideals of efficiency and of service to the public. The older professions, after the example of business, endeavored to impose higher professional standards on their own conduct through their own associations in the interest of reducing competition and providing better service to the public; the newer professions, and the multitude of vocations that aspired to be regarded as professions, similarly endeavored to convince the public of their high and efficient standards and their public-mindedness and devotion to the ideal of service. Indeed, public relations became

[8] Earnest Elmo Calkins, "Business the Civilizer," *Atlantic Monthly*, CXLI (February, 1928), 157.

an impressive area within the professions. This, of course, reflected the new economy of mass consumption, efficiency, and prosperity. It is to be noted, moreover, that average annual professional incomes also reflected the new well-being; during the 1920s they were on the average greater than ever before. According to a study by Harold F. Clark, only nursing and public school teaching averaged less than the skilled trades —$1310 and $1350 respectively.

In spite of the fact that public education ranked so low among the professions in the scale of average yearly income, no profession prided itself more on its efficiency and public service. School administration tended to become business administration. Even classroom procedure did not escape the impact of the ideology of business and the new prosperity. Moreover, public school enrollment expanded vastly. This was the result not only of larger incomes on the part of many industrial workers, but of the fact that funds for the expansion of school plant and staff were available as a result of the higher tax revenues garnered from increasing assessments on urban business property. In 1920 about two and a half million boys and girls were attending high school, whereas in 1930 the number had almost reached the five million mark. Never in its history had public education functioned on so impressive a budget—a budget of nearly three billion dollars annually.

Nor did higher education fail to respond to the new orientation. Like education at the lower levels, it felt the impact of business in the administration of its affairs no less than it did in the increasing emphasis put on the more vocational or so-called practical subjects. As on the lower levels, higher education responded to the demand of the middle class for whatever promised to promote comfort, economic success, and social prestige. Colleges and universities expanded like balloons as youth from families now enjoying prosperity inflated them to unheard-of dimensions. In 1920 the colleges and normal schools together enrolled about half a million students; in 1930 the number was appreciably above a million. The funds available for scholarly research and creative endeavor in the arts exceeded similar funds not only in prewar America but in any other civilization at any earlier time. The foundations, like the colleges, multiplied in numbers and resources.

The increased prosperity and spending power, together with the additional leisure released by shorter working hours and the application of the machine to so many departments of living, accounted for the phenomenal expansion of newspapers, books, and magazines. The amount of material published continued to increase, as it had done during the forty years before the war, more rapidly than the rate of population. In 1929, about 95 percent of the literate adult population read newspapers, three-fourths read magazines, and about half read books. The total annual output of books was 60 percent larger at the end of the decade than it was at the beginning. The literary and intellectual level of reading materials varied enormously, of course. Careful students of reading interests called attention to the fact that the annual output of fiction doubled during this period. On the basis of an analysis of this reading, students concluded that more people read to forget than to learn. But if much that was read reflected a desire to escape reality, a great deal reflected the desire to "keep up" with current events, and above all to succeed and to improve oneself. Suburban women, despite their interest in golf and bridge and mah-jongg, read more books concerned with the contemporary world of affairs and self-culture than ever before. The plain people who bought the hundred million five-cent booklets sold by Haldeman-Julius included among their favorites the titles on his list that dealt with success, self-help, and self-improvement.

The all but overwhelming emphasis on prosperity and the values attached to it met with sufficient criticism to prove that the intellectual climate of the 1920s was marked by more contrasts than surface appearances indicated. Even on the level of the popularization of culture among the masses or the middle classes, the soft-toned *Ladies' Home Journal* made some caustic remarks on the superficiality of a quest for culture based on commercially motivated "outlines," "quizzes," radio "universities," choose-your-book clubs, and choose-your-art clubs. While the clever commercial folk squeezed profits out of this birth of "Thought for the Many" who did not know what to do with their leisure, the multitude actually supposed, according to the *Ladies' Home Journal*, that they were "getting something out of" working crossword puzzles, reading an outline of something or other, spending an hour with a quiz book that had all the answers in the back pages.

Others criticized the so-called lock step in public schools which resulted from the problems of mass education itself and the emulation of business efficiency. These critics promoted a type of progressive education designed to release the potentialities of the individual child. In response to the scorching criticisms of the ad hoc or vocational inroads on higher education emanating from such authorities as Dr. Abraham Flexner, colleges and universities began to take some stock of the need for the more effective development of the varied talents of the undergraduate population and assessed anew the meaning of the cultural tradition. Aware of the criticisms heaped on the rising foundations in the muckraking period, the directors of these agencies tried to administer them in such a way as to avoid any charge of interfering with freedom of research.

Nor were American writers of one mind in their attitude toward the cult of prosperity. Authors of innumerable stories in *The Saturday Evening Post* glorified the values of mass consumption, success, comfort, and prosperity for all and forever, but some of the most gifted writers, including Ellen Glasgow, Eugene O'Neill, Sherwood Anderson, and Edmund Wilson, depicted what they regarded as the blighting effects of these values. John Dos Passos in *Manhattan Transfer* and Theodore Dreiser in *An American Tragedy* attributed the "disintegration of human character" to a competitive, ruthless, materialistic urban environment. Sinclair Lewis, choosing the village and the town, revealed the disrupting effects on the lives of his characters of the very values so much celebrated by the prosperity cultists. Indeed, Lewis' telling satires on the middle-class philistinism of Main Street and on the American businessman as its chief exemplary created a literary sensation and won him the Nobel Prize. The work of all these figures was a protest against the overemphasis on prosperity, mass production, mass consumption, competition, and personal success in material matters. But it was more than a protest. These men, in depicting the American scene as they saw it, proved once more that American life and thought during the 1920s were marked by less smoothness and uniformity than many surface indications suggested.

## Science Further Challenges Traditional Ideas

Concern over the "conflict between religion and science" was no longer widespread. As science had made its remarkable gains, more and more Christian leaders and more and more among the educated religious class accommodated Christian doctrine to its findings. Without ceasing to offer much spiritual comfort to many thousands of earnest Christians, the Protestant church had become, especially in the great cities and even in the smaller ones, an institution increasingly concerned with social and civic improvement. This may account for the fact that in a predominantly secular period church membership and church wealth were maintained on a high level in comparison with the preceding decades.

The general serenity in the more theologically liberal Protestant churches did not prevail in many rural sections in the South and West, where leaders and people often continued to see in science a menace to Christian truth. The religiously conservative, or fundamentalists, who accepted a more or less literal interpretation of the Bible, were sufficiently powerful in certain southern states to achieve the passage of laws forbidding the teaching of the theory of evolution in public educational institutions. In 1925 John T. Scopes, a high school science teacher at Dayton, Tennessee, was publicly tried for teaching Darwinism. Defended by the greatest freethinking lawyer, Clarence Darrow, Scopes was defeated, legally though not intellectually, by William Jennings Bryan, who had espoused the cause of fundamentalism with all the intensity he had earlier shown in championing free silver and anti-imperialism. The battle between fundamentalism and modernism had reached its high point. Nevertheless, the controversy, which had shaken a considerable section of the religious world, was an evidence of residual intellectual conflict.

As life became more secularized and science overshadowed religion in many localities and among many groups, the traditional religious sanctions for morals were greatly weakened. Youth, especially among the expanding and prosperous middle classes, not infrequently defied inherited patterns of behavior toward the older generation and the opposite sex. Often attributed to the relaxation of morals during the war and less frequently ascribed to the impact of the new philosophy of mass consumption of luxury goods in the interest of happy and full living, the new concern with breaking the bonds of restraint was probably in part a reflection of the waning influence of traditional religious sanctions and the rising vogue of what was regarded as the scientific conception of human nature and human behavior.

While largely concerned with pushing the boundaries of scientific knowledge into new areas and applying results in the field of technology, many scientists, especially biologists with a bent for popularization, interpreted human nature and behavior in biological terms. In rejecting traditional religious and moral sanctions these scientists could only substitute pragmatic sanctions—and pragmatic sanctions allowed enormous scope for trial and error. The more extreme exponents of the biological, naturalistic, and even mechanistic views of human behavior frequently failed to take this sufficiently into account. The result appeared to many to be moral anarchy.

Even before the war, new movements heralded a more realistic and more consistently biological view of human nature. From the time of William James's *Principles of Psychology* (1890), psychologists had increasingly thought of mind as a function of the physical organism in time and place. From the point of view of the development of psychology as a scientific discipline a further gain was made when the behavioristic school associated with John B. Watson still further delimited the area of subjectivism and dealt a blow at the still dominant dualistic views of mind and body. But the behavioristic interpretation of human nature in terms of reflexes or inherited responses and acquired and "determined" responses to internal bodily stimuli and external stimuli created new conflicts. Many who cherished a quasi-religious or spiritual view of human nature were shocked at Watson's materialistic and mechanistic conception of mind. On the other hand, these views, popularized and oversimplified by the facile pen of Watson and some of his followers, won acclaim among the more sophisticated partly by virtue of the fact that behaviorism was often associated with the general reaction against older moral standards.

The theories of Freud, which had begun to attract the attention of physicians, scientists, and even the intelligentsia before World War I, now vied with behaviorism in popular esteem. Whatever their weaknesses, the Freudian theories contributed to an understanding of the roles played in human conduct by such unconscious factors as infantile experiences, sex drives, and inhibition. Popular interpretations of Freudianism seemed, like those of behaviorism, to provide scientific sanctions for defiance of conventional standards and morals. Freudianism also seemed to carry still further the long process by which science had whittled away the traditional belief in man's intrinsic dignity and importance in the universe. New developments in astronomy had already made man and his earth of infinitesimal significance. New developments in biology had put him in the animal kingdom. The new doctrines in the psychological field now seemed to make him a creature of blind impulses and automatic responses to stimuli and to rob him of the last remnants of free will and human dignity. So, at least, it seemed to many who cherished the older religious and humanistic values.

Of the exponents of the new views of human behavior and social relations no one was more hard-hitting and controversial than Harry Elmer Barnes, whose wide-ranging scholarship embraced diplomatic and cultural history, criminology, and the development of social thought. In lectures, books, and articles Barnes dramatized, in what seemed to some critics an oversimplified manner, the new findings of the social and psychological sciences. In a sense Barnes, by showing some of the implications of modern science and social science for traditional concepts of religion and morality, played a role not unlike that of Thomas Paine, who aroused much antagonism in the late eighteenth century when he popularized the views of the Enlightenment.

While the popularizers of the more or less deterministic and allegedly scientific theories of human nature were winning ever larger audiences, the absolutistic character of science was being subjected to criticism by scientists themselves. It is true that these criticisms had begun to be heard long before the 1920s—De Vries and others had raised doubts in regard to determinism in biology; Rutherford had broken down the simple concept of the atom and his work with radioactivity had upset concepts of matter long cherished as final and absolute; and Planck had demonstrated inadequacies in the hallowed faith in the differential calculus. The work of Einstein, Millikan, Compton, and others had also been undermining certain features of the much-venerated Newtonian physics. Now, in the 1920s, the new theories of all these and other scientists made it clear that many of the long-accepted views of the universe were in reality not universal and final law; that the scientists were less convinced of absolutes and certainties within the realm of science; that there existed a universe of relationships as well as one of matter and motion, and that possibly the former was more significant than the latter. Some eminent physicists with a bent for religious and mystical values declared in public statements designed to reach the laymen that the new findings and theories opened the way for the reassertion of spiritual values and truths. The man in the street may not have paid much attention to these pronouncements, but the new uncertainties which seemed to be shaking the foundations of science added to the confusion that many intellectuals felt.

## The Machine

Probably the mass of ordinary people paid little attention to these uncertainties, but almost every American was affected by the application of scientific principles to the production, distribution, and communication of commodities and ideas. On every level of intellectual life the machine had long created conflicts. Thoreau and his fellow Romantic naturalists deplored it as the enemy of craftsmanship, of man's reliance on his own primitive strength and skills, and as the creator of false values of time, place, and destiny. Henry Adams, rootless and disillusioned in part by the impact of the machine and of the science on which it rested, admired its immense energy and deplored the apparently unpassable gulf between it and its human creator. Folk songs had long portrayed the workingman's fear of the machine and his defeat by it. Mike Fink, king of the keel-boat men, was at last driven off the western waters by the stern-wheeler; Maine sailors and boatbuilders went down before steam and steel; and John Henry, the Herculean laborer, broke his heart as a result of a devastating competition with the steam crane or, in the railroad version, the steam drill.

But now in spite of the worker's deep-seated fear of the machine and for the job it jeopardized, the American, whether an intellectual or a plain man or woman, had at least come to accept the machine—on one level. By the 1920s the "miracles" incident to new inventions no longer amazed the American people as they had once been amazed; they now accepted what their fathers and mothers would have regarded as impossible a score of years before World War I. By the 1920s, no matter how ignorant the people were of the sciences on which the machine rested, they were in general no longer startled by the appearance or prophecy of new mechanical wonders.

The machines that had been invented before World War I were now perfected and, thanks to mass production and mass consumption, influenced almost every American locality save such pockets as those inhabited by the "Hollow Folk" in the Blue Ridge and Appalachians or the

Ozarks. These machines seemed greatly to release and enhance the power of individuals. Machine operations, by shortening the working day, provided leisure never before regarded as possible. The apologists for the machine insisted that it did not make a robot of the average worker; they maintained that no more than five percent of the population was actually engaged in routine machine labor in which dull and monotonous movements were endlessly repeated. The never-ending multiplication of automobiles broke down barriers of space and gave even the common man an exhilarating control over distance, and the increasing familiarity of almost everyone with airplanes still further symbolized man's new power over time and space. Lindbergh's successful transatlantic flight in 1927 dramatically brought home to the nation man's new power over the seas and the heavens. Moreover, the machine actually increased the power of his senses; the movie in effect gave him a magically far-seeing eye, the talkie and the radio multiplied the powers of his ears and thereby opened up worlds hitherto unknown. The machine age improved decoration and design in mass-made products for common use and promised to give more leisure, more comforts, more amusements, more pleasures to one and all. No wonder that the machine became celebrated as the eighth wonder of the world, destined to set man free!

But there was another side to the story. Those to whom the old craftsmanship tradition was still a genuine value—and these included a diminishing but unknown number of workers as well as sensitive artists—felt that the machine was robbing the worker of the sense of creating a product in its entirety. According to Sherwood Anderson, the machine, in destroying the cunning of the average man's hands, decreased rather than increased his power, his sense of individual responsibility, of effectiveness, of completeness. The machine, declared Ralph Borsodi, made us live to consume, not to live; until we learned again to live for values other than the mere consumption of material machine-made goods, we could not truly live. Still others believed that the machine age, in supplying ordinary people with autos, radios, and dozens of gadgets for comfort and pleasure, had increased the feverish activity and accelerated the pace of living. Another group of thoughtful men agreed with Irwin Edman in deploring the effect of the machine in making leisure and recreation standardized rather than spontaneous.

Serious students of the machine age pointed to still other troublesome problems created by dynamos, motors, the assembly line, and mass consumption. Accumulating evidence in such studies as the Lynds' *Middletown, Recent Social Trends,* and scholarly essays in the *Encyclopaedia of the Social Sciences* clearly indicated that while men and women accustomed themselves to the use of new machines fairly readily, they generally failed to modify the premises of their thinking in directions that a machine economy made almost imperative. Guy Stanton Ford of the University of Minnesota contrasted the traditional individualism, localism, group interest, social inertia, and national isolation which had characterized American civilization with the new world and the new civilization which science had created—a world and a civilization that required "some conscious social purpose transcending the interests of the individual, of the locality, and at times even of the nation itself."

Others emphasized the idea that the multiplicity of machines required coordination, planning, and collective control if technological unemployment was to be avoided. Stuart Chase insisted that one technical improvement or even a whole system of developments could not always heedlessly be piled on one another with no awareness that a halt here, a failure there, might dislocate the entire structure. In the existing planless state of affairs in which the machine was used so largely for profits, Chase concluded, the balance of benefits and evils swung definitely toward the evil side. Only if the machine economy could become assimilated with human purposes and subordinated to them, only then, was the conclusion of not only Chase but Edman, Mumford, and other exponents of a new synthesis between the machine and humanism, could men and civilization bless the machine. Added to all these criticisms was the dark warning of technicians, pacifists, and even militarists that mechanized warfare might destroy civilization itself.

## The Revolt Against the Genteel Tradition

The genteel tradition in American letters found some spokesmen in the 1920s; the warmth and quiet heroism of the characters in Willa Cather's mellow *Death Comes for the Archbishop,* Thornton Wilder's *The Bridge of San Luis Rey,* and the critical essays of Stuart Sherman in the first years of the decade represented this tradition at its best. But the dominant note was one of protest against it.

The cult of self-expression and pleasure, especially in the realm of sex, and the corresponding reaction against so-called Puritanism and Victorianism constituted one of the most obvious patterns among both intellectuals and "the flaming youth" of the middle classes. Floyd Dell in his *Intellectual Vagabondage* tells how, even before the war, the rising generation of intellectuals had begun to rebel against the genteel tradition and the Victorian code. In the writings of Oscar Wilde, Frank Harris, George Moore, George Bernard Shaw, Havelock Ellis, and Ibsen, and of Baudelaire and other French primitivists, this group learned to regard sex not as a mystery, not as a hallowed, sentimentalized, idealized experience never to be indulged in except after marriage, but rather as a natural enjoyable bodily function common alike to women and to men, and not inherently sinful.

Even before America's entrance into World War I the novels and verse of Theodore Dreiser and Edgar Lee Masters reflected the rising revolt against the conventional treatment of sex by the writers of the genteel tradition. The breakdown of many inhibitions during the war, the popularization of Freudian and behavioristic psychology, and the growing economic independence of women on all levels explain in part the widespread defiance of traditional sex morals during the 1920s. The general reaction against conventional moral idealism contributed, of course, to this revolt. The sophisticated treatment of sexual freedom in the writings of James Branch Cabell, Edna St. Vincent Millay, Carl Van Vechten, and Scott Fitzgerald; the more whimsical and poetic treatment of the same theme by Sherwood Anderson and Floyd Dell; and the naturalistic, behavioristic, hard-boiled treatment by Ernest Hemingway and John Dos Passos and Theodore Dreiser, the pioneer in the movement, did not exhaust the nuances characterizing the new concern with sex. D. H. Lawrence and Mable Dodge Luhan, with their disciples, preached the mystically romantic gospel of "the wisdom of the flesh" and of salvation through indulgence in "the wise vices of the body."

Nor was the new cult of sex freedom and indulgence limited to the literati or to the gin-drinking, carousing, living-for-the-moment college youth pictured in Scott Fitzgerald's *This Side of Paradise* and *Tales of the Jazz Age*. One-fourth of the entire radio space in 1928 was given to passionate jazz tunes that bore such titles as "Baby Face, I Need Lovin'," "Hot Mama," "Burning Kisses," "I Gotta Have You," and "Hot Lips." Haldeman-Julius reported that sex ranked first in popularity among the many titles making up the first hundred million five-cent booklets reaching the masses. Sex themes, hard-boiled or glamorous as the case might be, explained the immense popularity of such lowbrow magazines as *Snappy Stories* and *True Confessions*. The sensational daily tabloid newspapers waxed fat on the exploitation of sex. Interest in sex themes had increased even among rural folk if the long list of books on sex in the Sears, Roebuck catalogues was any evidence.

At least the discussion of sex had come into the open. The appearance of many books on sex hygiene was also symptomatic of a new attitude. So too was the popularity of sex themes in the movies. Edgar Dale, after surveying 1500 moving pictures for the years 1920, 1925, and 1930, concluded that the love theme led in all years, that crime came second, and that sex in the biological sense came third. Sex experimentation found a well-known advocate when Judge Ben Lindsay frankly upheld the idea of companionate marriage. The *Ladies' Home Journal*, having in mind these and other evidences of the new tendency to deal with sex in an open, even public, fashion, declared that virtue, instead of being its own reward, was in the minds of the exponents of the new cult merely "the reward of dullness and the punishment of the drab." This magazine deplored the growing assumption that there are "no impulses save sex impulses, no innocence save in babies, no innocence anywhere, save perhaps in protoplasm, no excitement save in the tragedies of perversion and the dissolution of all decencies and inhibitions."[9]

The truth was that great numbers of Americans felt much as the *Ladies' Home Journal* did. Although that magazine undoubtedly overemphasized the tendencies it deplored, such ideas were finding some support among sophisticated groups. Moreover, the prewar disillusion that had made Edgar Lee Masters' *Spoon River Anthology* stand out in such stark contrast with the optimism and complacency of the genteel tradition was only the herald of what was now at hand. In a whole series of novels and plays, typical of which was Noel Coward's stage piece, *Cavalcade*, the Victorian tradition of optimism, complacency, and propriety was ridiculed. In plays and books alike the whole American emphasis on standardization, conformity, moral idealism, utilitarianism, service, keeping-up-with-the-Joneses, and bigger-and-betterism was satirized. Nor were the Puritan and utilitarian folk heroes of the American people spared. Not only the *American Mercury* and the much-talked-

[9] *Ladies' Home Journal*, XLIV (January, 1927), 26.

about novels of Theodore Dreiser and John Dos Passos, but such best sellers as Sinclair Lewis' *Main Street, Babbitt, Dodsworth*, and *Elmer Gantry*, held up to ironical scorn city boosting, small-town snooping, and the philistinism, optimism, and materialistic complacency of the cultists of prosperity.

No one dealt more realistically and at the same time more wistfully with the American cut of success than Ring Lardner. His popular stories and quips depicted with a kind of poignant satire the over-inflated ambitions of baseball players, golf caddies, shop girls, and other commonplace simple souls to be somebody. In his stories these ambitions almost inevitably turned out to be ridiculous, ending in pathetic frustration; the society of the 1920s, which paid so much lip service to "success" and to opportunities for everyone to get big money and be somebody, in reality had chiefly rebuffs for the naïve, simple-minded, expansive little men and women who fell prey to shibboleths of success. In so far as the 1920s were mirrored in the stories of Ring Lardner, and some critics believe they were, the stories show that the outward complacency and optimism and the affirmations of the plain people were only part of their lives. If in that decade intellectuals alone made explicit the limitations of an acquisitive culture, the events of the next decade were to make explicit the latent confusion and frustration of the plain people.

The literary deflation of optimism was not the only indication of revolt against the genteel tradition. Some read and agreed with Spengler's *Decline of Western Civilization*, with its inevitable gloom, defeatism, and anti-intellectualism. Others enjoyed Santayana's beautifully written philosophical essays on skepticism and animal faith. American prosperity provided sufficient income to a considerable group of intelligentsia to enable them in Greenwich Village or on the Left Bank to turn away from the American scene and concern themselves with esoteric abstractions of Dadaism or the profound psychological insights of Marcel Proust or James Joyce's exciting use of the stream-of-consciousness technique in *Ulysses*. Others, in their own serious works of art, reflected the boredom, the languor, the meaningless sophistication of the "lost generation" who, like the characters in Hemingway's novels, lost themselves in drink, sex, and the acceptance of the tragic dissociation of force and intelligence.

The preoccupation with subjects other than the larger economic and cultural issues in American society was condemned by a small group of leftist critics, who insisted that all that was not concerned with social content according to the canons of socialist realism was "escapist." The writing thus condemned out of hand was indeed a part of the strategy of escape. But the Marxist critics failed to take into account the eternal values of "escape" literature and art; they ignored the need of human beings at times for such "escape" as that provided by "art for art's sake," and those elements in human life that have seemed to poets and novelists to transcend time and place.

The cynicism which was so articulate in the 1920s did not, of course, meet with approval in all intellectual quarters. Some who could find no satisfaction in it sought the tradition and authority of the past. Thus Ezra Pound delighted in Provençal poetry and Japanese prints. T. S. Eliot, after writing his erudite and obscure lyric of despair, *The Waste Land*, found solace in Anglo-Catholicism, monarchism, and the authority of the classics. Thornton Wilder recreated an incident involving religious faith and set this incident in the mellow antiquity of Spanish Peru. For those who did not find escape into the past congenial, it was possible to celebrate the moral and psychological disintegration of primitive characters and scientific nihilism as the poetry of Robinson Jeffers did. Some writers who did concern themselves with the American scene painted pictures of mellow if haunting decay, like Robert Frost's *New Hampshire*.

Apparently even the best artists in the 1920s were unable to accept as a successful working formula Stuart Sherman's admonition that beauty has a heart full of service from which art cannot be separated, that the nonconformity and moral earnestness of Puritanism and the democracy of the American tradition challenge the creative artist to achieve new levels of integration. The loneliness of the gifted writers who tried to express America in other terms than those of ironic satire or nostalgic escape no doubt reflected the difficulties of personal and artistic integration in a period of affirmations of prosperity and half-commercial, half-sentimental emphases on service.

Although, in brief, the predominant mood of intellectuals was one of revolt against the genteel tradition and against much that seemed to characterize the contemporary American scene, the decade saw the beginnings of a new and realistic interest in American regions and American folk. If many young critics, influenced by the early Van Wyck Brooks, deplored the sterility of the American past and its emphasis on acquisitiveness, a small group was exploring the rich body of American folklore and folk art which writers and painters had so largely neglected. This interest, which Ruth Suckow, Bernard de Voto, and Constance Rourke represented, was to come to flower in the 1930s.

## The Quest for Certainties

In his defense of the Puritan and democratic traditions as he understood them, Stuart Sherman led the way in the quest for certainties. But the seeds he scattered fell on barren ground. Even the scholarly evaluations of the American past which pointed to so much that was not only admirable but significant—the evaluations of Turner, Parrington, the Beards, and Arthur M. Schlesinger, Sr., to name only a few—failed for the time to provide the assurance that was so needed or to answer the yearning for more certain values which so many felt in the midst of their confusion. Neither did the example of T. S. Eliot in affirming the value of the Catholic and classic traditions satisfy any considerable number among the intellectuals. The plain people, of course, never heard of the author of *The Waste Land*.

A gifted group of writers, essentially humanistic and modern in spirit, believed that nothing was so futile as the effort to escape the existing realities and conflicts so poignantly phrased by Joseph Wood Krutch in *The Modern Temper*. Krutch himself did not overstate the difficulties involved in finding satisfactory solutions—new roots, new codes, new certainties. We have seen that such students of technology as Stuart Chase and Lewis Mumford and such philosophers as Irwin Edman tried to assimilate human values to those of the machine. Walter Lippmann in his *Preface to Morals* sought for some certainty, at once scientific, naturalistic, and pragmatic, and yet with a core of permanence; but in the eyes of his most sympathetic critics he did not entirely succeed. Taking account of the reaction in many scientific circles against the older and cruder determinism that was exemplified in the work of the theoreticians of relativity, Alexis Carrel, Harry Emerson Fosdick, and others searched for a reconciliation of science with spiritual values. But all these quests for certainty reflected the difficulty of making new syntheses.

America's most eminent and original philosopher, John Dewey, had long taught that conflict is a condition of thinking and of progress, that science is essentially a method, that values and standards exist for man, that man does not exist for standards. Dewey pointed out, in his penetrating little volume, *Individualism Old and New*, that most Americans were still trying to think in patterns that no longer squared with realities; that conflicts and confusion would continue as long as men and women clung to, and tried to find solutions in, the old individualism; that a recognition of the basically collective character of our culture was indispensable to the solution of conflicts; and that the growth of all individuals, the realization of the democratic ideal, might be achieved through intelligence. If truth at any moment is relative, he continued, if the only certainty is change and the power of intelligence to direct change for desired human ends, if the only certainty, in short, lies in method or rather in human ends utilizing that method, then it is not necessary to feel lost, helpless, and utterly at sea. In his conception of the universe in temporal and natural rather than in absolute and spiritual terms, Dewey gave one answer to the quest for certainty.

But the difficulty of finding emotional satisfaction in the faith in intelligence, in man's ability to enter the green pastures he could clearly see just beyond the wasteland, was largely unresolved when the great debacle of 1929 struck the United States. That debacle brought to the surface the new contradictions in the economy and thought of the cultists of prosperity, with calamitous effects on all who reflected, on whatever level. The prosperity and contentment of the 1920s had not entirely concealed inner conflict in the American culture. But that prosperity and contentment had, after all, merely been jostled by disillusionment and criticism—a disillusionment and criticism that were now to lead to the most profound pessimism and the most heroic efforts to convert the American dream into a lasting reality that the American people had ever experienced.

# 28 Crisis and New Searches

*Blight—not on the grain!*
*Drought—not in the springs!*
*Rot—not from the rain!*
*What shadow hidden or*
*Unseen hand in our midst*
*Ceaselessly touches our faces?*
—ARCHIBALD MACLEISH, 1935

*I would ask no one to defend a democ-*
*racy which in turn would not defend*
*every one in the nation against want*
*and privation.*
—FRANKLIN D. ROOSEVELT,
*Fireside Chat, December 29, 1940*

Even in the midst of the first shocked bewilderment following the crash of 1929 our indomitable American optimism still held firm. Those who had lost everything blamed themselves, or a banker or a broker or a political party, but did not think of questioning the basic soundness of our social and economic structure. There was much talk about this being just one more depression, similar to the many that had characterized our economic history and from which the country had always recovered. The only thing to fear is fear, editorial writers repeated, one after another. President Hoover assured the American people that "the fundamental business of the country, that is, production and distribution of commodities, is on a sound and prosperous basis."

697

## The Cult of Optimism Questioned

As the crisis deepened month after month and as the months ran into years, pep talks, reassurances, the pull of established habits of confidence failed to absorb all the doubts incident to wage cuts, unemployment, shanty towns, bread lines, hunger. On the lowest economic level, where the depression struck its cruelest blows, inarticulate unorganized men and women seemed dazed. The great majority had no thought of joining the demonstrations and hunger marches organized by radical leaders or by evangelistic missionaries of socialism and communism. But enough did so to suggest that faith in the beneficence and justice of the capitalistic order had suffered a severe blow.

In previous depressions the middle classes had suffered inconveniences and even hardships, but these jolts had never undermined their essential feeling of security. Now, however, the appalling shrinkage in their incomes and, worse, the complete collapse of many, shook confidence to the very foundation. The long-cherished belief that real estate, urban or rural, meant security received a major jolt. The deflation of farm values in 1920 and 1921 had been attributed to an overinflation incident to wartime expansion; but now so many who had felt secure in bonanza farms and city properties saw the bottom drop out of their holdings that they were compelled to wonder whether something more fundamental than "just another depression" had not descended on the land. Many professional people—artists, writers, physicians, teachers, architects, and research workers—as well as people living on income from small investments now found themselves without jobs or funds. Some were compelled to seek public relief along with millions of less tutored but nonetheless respectable members of the middle classes and an even greater number of men and women who even before the depression had ranked among the ill housed, the ill clothed, the ill fed.

Such events forced some readjustment of values. The successful businessmen and the substantial bankers who had stood on pedestals not only during the Harding-Coolidge era but through a much longer period of time were no longer heroes. Conservative politicians who had been associated with them or had been blind to the disruptive forces in the national economy were in large measure discredited. It did not help much when President Hoover began to attribute the depression to the backwash of the World War and to point out that the collapse was world-wide in character.

Writers, scholars, and thinkers had occasionally been shocked by earlier economic dislocations into making fundamental inquiries into the nature of capitalistic economy, but they had always been a small minority and they won only slight hearing. Now, as public libraries ceased purchasing books, as public schools shortened their terms, found it impossible to pay teachers, and in many instances closed their doors altogether, the implications of the depression for cultural life became starkly apparent. Sixteen small colleges closed. Hundreds of others reduced salaries as student enrollment decreased. Foundations were compelled to cut by nearly three-fourths their annual grants for scientific research. "The climate in which the foundations lived and flourished," wrote Frederick Keppel, president of the Carnegie Corporation, "changed from one of optimism to one of acute pessimism."[1]

It was natural for a growing company of intellectuals to express the general sense of emergency and to question the capacity of the existing economic system to weather the crisis. Such doubts found a wide expression in novels, plays, and critical reviews, in a revival of pamphleteering, in discussion groups, and on the public platform. The literary figures of the 1920s who had protested that business enterprise "could not provide for the needs of the spirit" now maintained, in the words of one of their spokesmen, that it could not even provide men with food and clothing. "We are facing a new era," wrote Louis Adamic. "This is a time of transition and profound frustration, of agony and decay."[2]

Even more impressive than the doubts of men of letters were those of economic and legal authorities. Thurman Arnold, a Yale professor of law, saw in the capitalism that had been hailed as an absolute good a mere complex of myths, slogans, and rationalizations. When economists traced a sharply rising curve of "prosperity" from 1934 to 1937 and when this so-called "statistical prosperity" failed to result in widespread reemployment and general prosperity, many found additional reasons for believing that the depression differed fundamentally from earlier depressions. Dean Donham of the Harvard Graduate School of Business Administration, viewing the economic plight with grave concern, ob-

---

[1] *Report of the President and Treasurer of the Carnegie Corporation for the Year Ended September 30, 1941* (New York, 1941), 40.
[2] *Harper's Magazine*, CLXIV (January, 1932), 178.

served that "capitalism is on trial and on the issue of this trial may depend the whole future of western civilization."[3] Still others declared that the end of a great economic cycle had come; that there would be no recovery in the older sense of the word; that capitalism as it had been known was dead.

The doctrine of inevitable progress—a central idea in American thought to which few save die-hard Federalists, doctrinaire proslavery apologists, and such disillusioned intellectuals as Brooks Adams had ever taken exception—was now thrust into the realm of doubt. Americans, many with eyes opened, saw in Chicago the spectacular Century of Progress exposition in a city ringed with idle factories. They heard the stupendous achievements of technology and of human endeavor in every sphere proclaimed, but they knew that millions of Americans were actually facing want.

Such penetrating scholars as Carl L. Becker and Charles A. Beard pondered on the idea of progress, discussed its wider implications, and analyzed it in terms of the scientific developments that men had failed to control for social and rational ends. Reinhold Niebuhr, a religious leader influenced by the theology of crisis expounded in central Europe by Karl Barth, wrote in 1932 that "the middle-class paradise which we built on this continent, and which reached its zenith no later than 1929, will be in decay before the half-century mark is rounded."[4] The house, said Niebuhr, has been built on sand. An article written by the English archeologist, Stanley Casson, occasioned much comment and reflection. Casson saw a tendency on the part of man to retrograde, if a long view were taken. "We are hovering on the brink of a precipice, winding round that dizzy path up which we may ultimately reach the peaks of wisdom, but off which we may so easily topple to destruction."[5]

The situation thus gave rise to fundamental fears. It was seriously argued in many circles that impending world war, of which there were increasingly numerous omens, might result in the destruction of civilization. In short, faith in progress and in the prevailing economic order was overshadowed by doubts in the minds of sensitive students, doubts

---

[3] Wallace B. Donham, *Business Looks at the Unforeseen* (McGraw-Hill Book Co., 1932), 207.

[4] *Harper's Magazine*, CLXV (June, 1932), 118.

[5] *Atlantic Monthly*, CLVI (July, 1934), 78.

shared by many millions of unemployed, by millions whose shrunken income now called the piper's tune.

The national cult of optimism was still further limited by the effects of the depression on the status of women. The expanding economic opportunities from which so many ambitious women had profited in the 1920s now shrank and in shrinking dealt blow after blow at women in the professions, in the arts, and in business. Feminists regretted that the new turn of events undermined the progress women had been making in attaining self-realization apart from biological functions. Outspoken veterans in the feminist movement took women to task for supinely accepting their lot in the home, for resigning themselves to a "retrogressive" step. The revelation that women's magazines contained little discussion of great public issues and that millions of women read only these magazines still further depressed those who had foreseen the advance of women as voters and citizens. They might not have been so depressed, of course, had they been able to study parallel analyses of the reading habits of American men.

In one matter, to be sure, freedom for women did make gains. About 1930, partly no doubt as a result of the depression, the stubborn opposition to birth control rapidly weakened, and despite the firm stand of the Catholic church, court action permitted the dissemination of contraceptive information under medical direction. In the prevailing mood of pessimism some intellectuals, at least, agreed with Dorothy Thompson in regarding this long-sought achievement as a symptom not of progress but of dissolution. "There is something basically wrong," she wrote, "with a society in which the affirmation of life itself, the will to live and to create life, becomes atrophied. No amount of civilization, culture and technical achievement will save such a society in the end. The barbarians, with healthier instincts, will eventually inherit it."[6] Probably only a small number of men and women deliberately refrained from becoming parents because they were imbued with despair regarding the future destiny of offspring. But it was nevertheless true that whereas the generation that was passing had taken large families as a matter of course without ever questioning the possibility of a good future for all their children, a growing number in the rising generation at least discussed the question.

[6] *Ladies' Home Journal*, LIV (May, 1937), 12.

Uncertainty in Scientific Thought

In the search for formulas for reconstruction science was called on to provide reassurance. A few decades earlier faith in science might have been a rock of certainty for intellectuals in the midst of growing national confusion. But there was more than one reason why that faith was not sufficient now. In the first place the belief in science as an automatic key to happiness had long been weakening. James Harvey Robinson had not been alone in urging the necessity of intelligent application of science to human affairs, and it had been increasingly evident that our scientific knowledge far outstripped our accomplishments. By this time thinking people knew that science could provide enough food, shelter, and comforts to permit everyone to live in ease or at least in decency. Yet malnourished children fainted at school while fruit rotted unpicked and grain was plowed under. Plainly science was not enough. "In any event," wrote one scientist, "it would be well if we got rid of the quaint notion that all we need to do is to wait until our scientists have discovered enough formulas and our laboratories developed enough processes to give the World of Tomorrow—Today."[7]

There was, of course, a more important reason why science brought only cold comfort to thinkers of the 1930s. Science itself was now permeated by basic uncertainties. For many years after the post-Darwinian controversy had died down and science and religion had become more or less comfortably reconciled, students of science had derived peace of soul from their faith in the orderly processes of nature and above all in the possibility of explaining any natural phenomenon. By this time, however, functionalism in biology and studies of relativity in the physical sciences had slowly changed the face of science. And now its very basis, the theory of determinism, was subject to attack.

Not only were there questions within the fold of science itself, but popular writers on science spread the news of confusion. If phenomena were always relative to time and place, they asked, did not the old concept of causality break down? As one writer put it, "We cannot say what *must* be, but only what the chances are that any one thing must happen

[7] Harold Ward (ed.), *New Worlds in Science* (Robert M. McBride Co., 1941), 15.

rather than any other shall happen."[8] In many circles it became less common to assume that all processes are strictly determined. Some even questioned the venerable scientific doctrine that the future is an inevitable outcome of the present. In the words of an interpreter of the new tendencies,

The General Theory of Relativity brings us to a picture of the cosmos in which space by itself and time by itself have ceased to exist, and the blend of the two has become a supple theater for events. The theater continually changes with the events which it stages. Not only is space-time moulded and transformed at every point by the matter and motions which it contains, but the very rules of the geometry by which its manifold is measured are shown to be relative, and the relations are expressed in purely physical terms.[9]

The universe, in short, was in the expositions of one school of scientific thought conceived to be without "hitching posts." The principle of indeterminism, of uncertainty—at least as popularly interpreted in the "quality" magazines—appeared to be the only principle anyone could be certain of, if indeed he could be certain even of that.

It is true that many eminent scientists continued their investigations and their interpretations of these new conceptions, greatly interested in them but not disturbed by them. That the plain people were unaffected by the uncertainties raised by the indeterminacy principle was no less true. Yet at the same time the expositions given to the more or less thoughtful lay public in the more popular highbrow periodicals added another note to the confusion and the general feeling that all the old props were disappearing.

Reasons for the vogue of indeterminism become apparent when one tries to picture scientific activity in the 1930s. New and highly significant experimental findings portrayed a physical universe in which macrocosm and microcosm were in process of incessant transformation and flux. Biological developments were spectacular and unsettling. Theories of nutrition were revolutionized by the newly discovered vitamins. Concepts of the origin, nature, and conditions of life itself were

[8] J. W. N. Sullivan, "The Mystery of Matter," *Atlantic Monthly*, CLVII (May, 1936), 363.

[9] George W. Gray, "No Hitching Posts," *Atlantic Monthly*, CLVII (February, 1932), 252.

undergoing substantial revision. Richard B. Goldschmidt, a refugee from Nazi Germany, cited evidence for his contention that in the course of evolution the mutations of De Vries might involve very great changes, so that there might be "macroevolution" in the course of which the final transition from one species to another might take place in one decisive leap. More striking was the work on the cell, once thought of as a stable, simple anatomical unit. Now plant and animal cells were clearly seen as greatly influenced by surrounding cells, and as themselves dynamic centers of growth, the growth processes of the whole organism being regulated in complex ways just beginning to be understood. "Cells," one writer said, "are subtle mechanisms of chemical balance, pulled now one way, now another, in endless trial and error relationships."

Such developments profoundly affected theories of heredity. Confidence in the earlier theories was weakened and experimental work went on apace. It would be years, of course, before scientists in various related fields, let alone the educated public, would fully catch up with the new theories and then discard mistaken social applications of the old. But biologists were excited and the readers of newspaper science interested and perplexed.

Psychiatry and psychology shared in the biological advances of the time. In psychiatry such pioneers as Adolf Meyer and his associates discovered that serious mental disorders might yield to treatment involving the introduction of malarial organisms into the blood stream, but could not explain how the "miracles" were effected. American psychiatrists confirmed the European discovery that dementia praecox, till lately believed incurable, could in many cases be cured by insulin or other shock treatments, and this opened up new vistas of experiment and speculation, upsetting hoary theories. The precise mechanisms by which thyroid deficiency affects mental life remained in some doubt, as did the problem of the relationship between the newly discovered electric waves in the brain and various aspects of mental life.

Much solid work in psychology advanced the frontiers of knowledge in that discipline. Painstaking experimental work enlarged psychological knowledge, and new theories reflected the impact of the newer physiology and the newer physics. American functional and organismic psychology and the imported Gestalt psychology emphasized the importance of relationships in physical-mental processes, of totality of experience, and of the effect of the totality on the individual factors in experience. Psychology now appeared far less simple, and to many far less useful, than it once had seemed. In cultivated circles there was a decided reaction against the oversimplifications of John B. Watson which once had captured popular fancy, just as the psychologists themselves were reacting against previous oversimplifications. Thus both the psychologists and their followers were ready for new complexities—and this readiness left open a door for mysticism.

Mystical implications in the work of some of the newer physicists doubtless influenced the psychologist, J. B. Rhine of Duke University, who maintained that experiments in extrasensory perception refuted the prevailing theory that sensation and perception have a purely biological and mechanistic basis. Both the experiments and the interpretations were received with great skepticism by members of the American Psychological Association, who, however, advocated careful research on the problem. Less informed and more credulous general readers, groping for religious-scientific reaffirmations, were heartened indeed by Professor Rhine's new proof of "spiritual powers."

One might suppose that training in physics, one of the most exact of the "natural sciences," would produce in its followers resistance to mystical explanations in scientific fields, an insistence on suspended judgment until adequate data are at hand. But it seems that this is not the case. The physicist is as likely, apparently, to be led beyond the facts by his emotions as any scientist—perhaps more likely. One recalls the case of Sir Oliver Lodge, who was perfectly willing to be convinced by evidence no competent psychologist would accept.

When one considers the experimentation on the nature of matter and energy with its ceaseless revelation of new mysteries, one can understand how in those so inclined such study might encourage mysticism. During the first quarter of the century the doctrine of relativity not only permeated the scientific world but gave great aid and comfort to the tender-minded laymen who needed evidence in support of "spiritual values." In the postwar decades, years of trouble throughout the western world, certain physicists brought spiritual comfort to the scientific or scientifically inclined who needed it. The English physicist John Dunn impressed American readers with his effort to show how the future could sometimes be foreseen. Later his countrymen Eddington and Jeans, with their abstruse discussion of the limitations of science, had a considerable vogue among scientists and the intelligentsia in this country. Through his writings for educated laymen, the American physicist Millikan also lent strength to the idea that modern science, no longer "mechanistic," must call upon the supernatural, that, as the Beards have put it, scientific indeterminism means free will.

Within the inner circle of science itself the 1930s saw some waning of interest in such interpretations; probably most research scientists never had seen in the new physics evidence for "spiritual" in the sense of supernatural control. But the intelligentsia had been infected by a new contagion; and its force was far from spent. Thus physics contributed its bit to the current general weakening of faith in human reason.

Undoubtedly the most dramatic and perhaps the most significant development that shook the older certainties was the isolation and partial control of hitherto unsuspected primary units of energy. The breathtaking experiments of Lawrence at Berkeley, of Anderson at the California Institute of Technology, of Fermi of Columbia, and of other scientists in smashing atoms removed merely the outer veils surrounding the mystery of energy. The work of probing the depths of an atom undergoing radioactive disintegration was enormously difficult and created many new uncertainties. The discovery of techniques by which the transmutation of elements takes place removed props from theories long regarded in many quarters as certainties. The possibility of isolating uranium [235] posed the problem of how its incredible stores of energy might be used. It was apparent that if the technique could be refined, the colossal energy might be used, as one writer put it, to transform the earth into a physical Eden or a psychological hell.

The decade also saw light thrown on the cosmic rays with which scientists had been concerned for several decades and which were first described about 1935 as superlative energy carriers. At the Carnegie Institution in Washington Merle Tuve discovered a super-powerful cosmic force, sealed, apparently, in the very "hearts" of atoms. Although it was not proved, some supposed that this force, which held the tiny particles in the "heart" of the atom, was in a sense the cement that kept the universe together. In any case, the cosmic ray was surveyed both at sea level the world over and at distances twenty and more thousand feet above the earth. No wonder the scientist began to feel even more humble about his work.

The essential nature and extent of the universe were widely debated. Ingenious new techniques of measurement revealed new and startling indications of the infinitesimal size of the earth in relation to the universe; the earth apparently bears the same relation to the whole universe that a grain of pollen bears to our own solar system. While Ellsworth and Byrd were discovering hitherto unknown mountain ranges in the frozen Antarctic, aerial and radio explorers were probing the heavens and revealing the existence of even vaster mountain ranges and plateaus in the ionosphere. Edwin Hubble of the Mount Wilson Observatory, a modern Ulysses, was penetrating the secrets of regions the very existence of which had never been suspected. He even photographed "outside" systems or Milky Ways—at a distance estimated to be 5 million light-years. Scientists debated the question whether the universe was, as Einstein had supposed, a more or less fixed universe in equilibrium, or whether it was expanding. Recordings of measurements of it at given times would throw light on the problem. In 1934 Hubble cautiously stated that if what was seen through the largest telescopes was a fair sample and if the density of space was uniform throughout, the universe in that year had a radius of curvature of the order of 3000 million light-years.

As authorities speculated on the inner recesses of the sun, the older fear that its energy might become exhausted was allayed by the calculation that it would shine for at least another twelve billion years. However, scientists discussed the possibility that in the course of terrifying cosmic processes an explosion might occur within the sun which would release such a cyclone of energy that every trace of life on the earth would be obliterated in a second.

These were the uncertainties presented to the searching layman who hoped for reassurance from scientific experiment, calculation, and speculation. In a period of profound economic dislocation and of widespread doubt of the inevitability of progress, the startling discoveries in science provided no new or thoroughly satisfying assurances. At best, a universe vastly more complex, inconceivably more baffling than had hitherto been supposed, challenged further scientific endeavors.

Uncertainties about the physical universe were paralleled in the field of communication and knowledge. The pragmatists and instrumentalists, especially F. C. S. Schiller, an English philosopher residing in America, and John Dewey, had for many years been virtually undermining formal logic, and now their followers were no longer considered radical. Absolutism in philosophy was now cherished only by a minority group.

The impact of the doctrine of relativity on students of language provided the background for the work of the semanticists. Their findings and speculations called the attention of scholars, and finally of a considerable part of the reading public, to the limitations of language as an accurate channel of communication. Much intellectual confusion was ascribed to the tendency to identify words with general principles, when actually there was only a more or less general correspondence between them. Richards, Korzybski, Malinowski, Ogden, and Burke examined the whole problem of the meaning of meanings. They pointed out that, as in the world of physical nature the concept of relativity, of time-space relationships, affects the whole meaning of reality, so in language meanings result from and are affected by the interplay of one word with another. The linguistic and psychological context of a word colors its meanings. True meaning is to be found, they argued, not in the face value of a verbalization but in the whole contextual situation—above all, in the action associated with the word. Being essentially metaphorical, words convey more or less than they seem to convey; being living and organic, language, in so far as it is conventionalized, does violence to the ever-shifting, contextual, psychological, and anthropological setting of which it is an expression.

In point of fact this conception was not altogether new. Critical scientists, recognizing words as mere symbols, had always been beset by the difficulties of definition. But now this old idea, given a high-sounding new name, was dressed up and publicized as it had never been before. The relation of words to symbolic action, to rituals and faiths, to adjustment mechanisms was philosophically analyzed in the brilliant writings of Kenneth Burke, who emphasized the idea that words, works of art, and philosophy can create and communicate meanings only in a society where symbols and their emotional connotations are fairly homogeneous and stable. On the more popular level Stuart Chase in *The Tyranny of Words* and Thurman Arnold in *The Symbols of Government* and *The Folklore of Capitalism* discussed the decoy character of words, the significance of emotionally weighted words in social action, the use of symbol words as means of social control, the unconscious function of words in the self-training of men for the struggle with their environment. Although the sharp, hard indictment of language as an inexact instrument of communication promised to pave the way for a more precise understanding, at the same time the semanticists added to the sense of baffling contradictions, uncertainties, and confusions of which the 1930s were so full. In the words of Stuart Chase, "A community of semantic illiterates, of persons unable to perceive the meaning of what they read and hear, is one of perilous equilibrium."[10]

The popular mind was less impressed by the implications of semantics than by the growing role of propaganda in modern life. In such articles as "The Poisoned Springs of World News" and "The Pull of the Printed Word" and in such books as *100,000,000 Guinea Pigs* and *The Popular Practice of Fraud,* popular credulity and the manipulation of the people by profit-bent and interested groups were widely publicized. The more carefully refined techniques for measuring public opinion, especially those employed by *Fortune,* the Institute of Propaganda Analysis, and the Institute of Public Opinion, extended knowledge of the psychology of propaganda and public opinion; but the doubt cast upon the efficacy of long-accepted concepts of public opinion helped to add to the general sense of skepticism, uncertainty, and disillusion.

The doctrine of relativity, it will be recalled, had already affected the social sciences in the decade after World War I. The general confusion of the 1930s, the vogue of the semanticists, and the influence of the German sociologists of knowledge, especially Karl Mannheim, provided a more receptive atmosphere for the considerations which Becker, Beard, and other scholars had already brought to the attention of their colleagues. In a witty and penetrating little book, *The Discussion of Human Affairs* (1936), Beard urged those concerned with social matters to distinguish between the little they *knew* and could *prove* and the much that they approved, longed for, and loved. Like Mannheim, Beard emphasized the importance of the sustained search for facts, for knowledge, for as much objectivity as possible. But he pointed out that values are subject to constant change and are affected by realities often regarded as extraneous to them; that facts, meanings, and interpretations are defiantly elusive; that all social knowledge is contingent, that there are no absolute norms. Such ideas were upsetting to those who had thought objectivity possible and presumed that their own work was really objective.

[10] Stuart Chase, "The Tyranny of Words," *Harper's Magazine,* CLXXV (November, 1937), 569.

### New Formulas for Recovery and Reconstruction

New problems, persisting, give rise to new ideas. Hence the uncertainty experienced by the mass of plain people caught in the depression inclined them to listen to new leaders. And intellectuals and reformers, though beset in many instances by uncertainty, endeavored to provide formulas for recovery and reconstruction. The 1930s not only were thus characterized by the great achievements of natural scientists and the challenging implications of scientific speculation, but they were primarily a decade of rich and varied social thought, questioning, and searching. All these inquiries and proposals were part of a search for security amid dislocation and the dissolution of old values.

On every level and in every area of intellectual life formulas for recovery and reconstruction were matters of the utmost importance. Such formulas filled the pages of periodicals and provided the subject matter of innumerable books, of endless lectures and private discussions. They were the occasion for clashes among educators, publicists, and other intellectuals, and the subject of contention before legislative committees and in the halls of Congress. Many of the formulas were old. But they were advanced in the context of what appeared to be a new situation, for never before had depression been so widespread or so acute. The old formulas were publicized with new emphasis and were seen to have new bearings on the life and thought of the time.

Among intellectual circles and to some small extent among the working class, Marxist analyses of the depression and Marxist proposals for reconstruction occasioned serious discussion. The Marxists argued with confident dogmatism that capitalism was in its final stage of collapse, that the middle class as such had virtually disappeared, that the proletariat was at length aroused and would presently be ready for revolutionary action, and that in any case compromise proposals, such as the New Deal, would not work. The Soviet Union, they argued, pointed the way; the forces of fascism, both at home and abroad, had to be broken by the organization of workers and the mobilization of intellectuals. In the discussion of Marxist theory its economic, social, and historical aspects were explored. Its literary and artistic implications were expounded at length in magazines read by the intelligentsia.

Long kept alive in the United States by struggling and factious minority parties, Marxism was acclaimed in widening circles as the new gospel. The success of the Five-Year Plan in Russia, in contrast to the economic breakdown at home, seemed to prove the inability of the middle-of-the-road liberals to accomplish reconstruction. Students of economics, sociology, history, and philosophy, including Lewis Corey, Max Lerner, Louis Hacker, Dr. Henry Sigerist, and Sidney Hook, related Marxism both to historical developments and to the current American scene. Such literary critics as Vernon Calverton, Granville Hicks, Newton Arvin, Edmund Wilson, and Malcolm Cowley, and such creative writers as Theodore Dreiser, Genevieve Taggard, Clifford Odets, John Dos Passos, and James T. Farrell were in greater or less degree impressed by Marxism. In spite of over-mechanical structures and faulty conceptions of human nature, such novels as *Call Home the Heart*, *The Disinherited*, *To Make My Bread*, and *Native Son* were heralded as Marxist literary triumphs. The communists among the intellectuals succeeded in enlisting the support of so-called "fellow travelers" in opposing fascism, in supporting strikes and the militant demands of left-wing labor leaders, and in publicizing violations of civil liberties.

The influence of Marxism was less widespread and deep than most radicals believed and most conservatives feared. Despite setbacks, the New Deal proved itself to be a going concern. It thus provided an effective argument against the Marxist contention that reform was impossible, or, if possible, destined to be of little consequence.

The trials of the "Old Bolsheviks" in the Soviet Union and the later pact between Stalin and Hitler discredited the Russian Revolution in the eyes of many of its supporters. In spite of the subsequent tendency to justify the trials and the Russian invasion of Finland and Poland, Marxism did not recover from these successive blows. Intellectuals who had been attracted by it came to question whether it was an adequate instrument for understanding the American scene or for resolving American problems, whether it was not too mechanical, doctrinaire, and unrealistic to achieve the ends it promised. Yet the impact of Marxism cannot be dismissed as of no consequence. It forced many Americans to consider thoughtfully class relationships and the nature of capitalist economy, of dictatorship, and of revolution. It compelled consideration of historical materialism, of Marxist conceptions of philosophy, science, and esthetics.

Without adopting all the Marxist doctrine, one group of educational leaders felt its challenge for the times and tried to act as well as think in the interest of a better future society. Led by George S. Counts, this group stressed the increasingly collectivistic character of American society. The emphasis which conventional schools and even many "progressive" schools put on the child as an individual, with little or no reference to the impending cooperative collectivistic society in which, it was argued, he would eventually take his place, was subjected to trenchant criticism. The group especially attacked the prevailing tendency of the schools to inculcate in children the ideas and values of an individualistic capitalism and culture that in their opinion was breaking down.

These educational reformers thought the school should align itself with the broad democratic tendencies in American life; it should select for emphasis those values of the American cultural heritage that would aid in the task of insuring democratic control of the new technology, the new interdependence of life. These educators defined education far more broadly than mere school training. They sought an alliance between education, organized labor, and other progressive forces in the community in order to lay the basis for recovery and reconstruction along collectivist democratic lines. The influence of this outlook was reflected in a plan drawn up by educators and social scientists, commissioned by the American Historical Association and generously supported by the Carnegie Corporation. This plan called for far more governmental responsibility than had been customary for the economic and social security and well-being of young children, youth, and adults. It advocated a program of social studies in the schools designed to emphasize the need for developing collective responsibility for American well-being.

At the same time that this group was attacked by the Hearst press and other conservative groups as subversive and un-American, it also met with criticisms from the left. Education, declared those who saw eye to eye with the Marxists, cannot rise above the dominant controls in the society of which it is a part. Others pointed out that democratic collectivism implies certain contradictions. Democracy, they argued, implies free men with free choices; it posits a property arrangement such as the simple one Jefferson admired and designed, with no complications like absentee ownership, widespread tenantry, division of ownership and management, division of financial control and production control, and the whole complex of qualities of corporate institutions and factory production.

Among the critics of the educators who espoused reform and democratic collectivism was President Robert Hutchins of the University of Chicago. The neo-Thomism of Hutchins and his associates, including Adler, Barr, and Buchanan, was not indifferent to the depression and the quest for security. But it looked not to some golden age in the future in which security would reign, but to a golden age in the past. Without embracing Catholicism, this group advanced an essentially Aristotelian, neoscholastic program, which was based on the assumption that American life had vastly overemphasized material values, individual self-interest, and a soft form of democratic humanitarianism. In consequence the arts and learning had been corrupted by false utilitarianism, and religion had been enslaved as a pampering "social gospel."

According to the exponents of neo-Thomism, man's nature is an admixture of the selfish and base with the rational and moral; it is the job of education to develop the latter. Since these elements are unequally distributed in human kind, since in fact only a small minority are highly endowed with the rational, education must be so planned that the mass receive a training that will fit them for vocations and citizenship. This can be accomplished through emphasis on the "essentials" in the elementary schools and on subjects of general significance at the high school and junior college level. The universities should be restricted to the education of the intellectual elite. These young men and women should be trained in what the neo-Thomists regarded as the great principles derived from historical experience, the concepts of morality, truth, and beauty; they should be taught not to subordinate these principles to pragmatic uses and values. Through such a reformation of education the neo-Thomists hoped that "intellectual verities" would triumph over what they described as excess materialism, loose and out-of-hand individualism, and false democracy. These, they seemed to think, had brought about a condition of impending economic, social, and moral collapse. In their eyes the cure lay in a return to the great classics of the past, to first principles.

Critics of neo-Thomism saw fascist implications in its indictment of democracy and humanitarianism and its doctrine of the elite. But they realized that fascism drew its chief strength from other sources, both foreign and native. Many tourists, students, and even professors returning from visits to Germany expressed their admiration of the efficient methods in use there, and felt that America had much to learn from Hitler. This opinion was echoed in the press and on the street. Units of the Bund waxed strong and numerous and toward the end of the 1930s began to arouse open resentment. How many paid and secret agents of the Axis powers were operating can only be guessed.

The ability of such a demagogue as Huey Long, Senator from Louisiana, to win a great following and to wield vast power in his home state and neighboring areas still further alarmed the foes of fascism. Liberals and radicals regarded as ominous the activities of Father Coughlin, the Detroit priest who used the radio as well as the press to preach anti-Semitism and other fascist ideas. Alarm was similarly felt at the appearance of the fascist-like secret societies, such as the Khaki Shirts, the Silver Shirts, the Crusaders, and the National Watchmen. The motion picture, *The Black Legion*, was a striking though exceptional attack on organized American fascism. The antiradicalism, especially the antilabor bias, and the "pseudo-Americanism" of certain patriotic societies and of such influential organizations as the National Association of Manufacturers seemed to many liberals even more dangerous signs of fascist potentialities in American life. When Sinclair Lewis published his own personal alarm call to the nation, *It Can't Happen Here*, there was widespread discussion of the book, and few leaders of American thought stood up to call it foolish. On the whole, however, formal fascist or totalitarian organizations aroused litttle enthusiasm. Their promise to provide security to the American masses fell, for the most part, on indifferent ears.

Nevertheless, a few intellectuals openly avowed fascism and others expressed ideas closely related to it. Lawrence Dennis did his best in his writings to adapt European fascist ideologies to the American scene. Some agreed with Thurman Arnold, who wrote that democracies always lead to dictatorship and that the best to be hoped for was a benevolent dictator who, like an enlightened keeper of the insane, would make the patients as comfortable as possible. But many others expressed less generous views of human nature. Ralph Adams Cram maintained that the overwhelming majority of people were mere raw material out of which an occasional human being was produced, and others celebrated the doctrine of the elite in similar terms. The Secretary of War published in *Liberty* an article in which he likened the National Guard to "storm troops" that might preserve order by putting down labor unrest. Although many refugees arrived from Europe and found genuine sanctuary, anti-Semitism was certainly not decreasing as the decade drew near its close.

Above all, there was much talk about the need for national regeneration, leadership, discipline. Some insisted that the American character had become "flabby" and overfeminized. Decrying the influence of humanitarian zeal for the weak and jobless, Raymond Pearl declared that the relief of the inept was virtually contrary to biological law inasmuch as no living organism unable to fend for itself had long survived.

Of the many formulas for recovery, none was so widely accepted and so well implemented in legislation as the body of thought that came to be known as the New Deal. Its point of departure was the belief, long prevalent in this country, that scientific techniques were well enough developed and that sufficient natural resources were available to make possible an economy of abundance in which everyone could live an eligible life. The basic idea was one of a balanced economy in which government sought to maintain within the framework of capitalism an equilibrium between the producer and the consumer, the manufacturer, merchant, and worker. In a general way this idea had been suggested by Henry C. Carey in the second quarter of the nineteenth century, and it had been elaborated in the early decades of the twentieth by such writers as Simon N. Patten, Herbert Croly, and Walter Weyl.

The concept of a balanced economy in which neither private property nor production for profit was relinquished involved many related ideas. The gradual advance in both the United States and Europe of collectivism, that is, the theory of a centralized and socialized state in which political and economic institutions are closely integrated, had familiarized many with the idea of enlarged state functions in the interest of public well-being. Nor was the extended use of public credit for public benefits, economic, social, and cultural, entirely unprecedented. In many areas of American life the use of the expert in public affairs had paved the way for the so-called "Brain Trust," for the vast expansion of trained personnel incident to the advance of a public service state. In private industry and in municipalities economic and social planning had made impressive strides. Technical experts had maintained that, despite the lavish squandering of the nation's resources, American economy was capable of producing an abundance for everyone. Through balanced production and consumption, through increased purchasing power for the masses, through an extension of public credit for public works and public services, the existing economy of sparsity might bring into being a true and lasting economy of abundance.

By means of these and related agencies the New Dealers hoped to effect not only recovery but reconstruction, hoped to preserve the maximum of personal liberty and individual opportunity under new and effective public controls which would guarantee at least some security. The idea of economic Darwinism, the doctrine that anyone who failed to obtain work deserved to fail and must suffer the consequences, was repudiated. The idea of a good life for all was acclaimed far and wide.

One of the most interesting applications of New Deal ideology was a change in federal policy toward the Indians. The government had long assumed that the Indians could adopt the white man's ways and become Americanized citizens and individual landowners. But no adequate account had been taken of the difficulties involved in the transformation of a primitive tribal culture into the prevailing one of the white men. Above all, the policy of Americanizing the Indian had been pursued without adequate recognition of the economic shortcomings of reservation life. Now, in line with the general New Deal policy of promoting the well-being and happiness of the less privileged groups, the government modified its traditional policy by stimulating the economic rehabilitation of tribal economy through federal assistance. Indian tribal government and the tribal arts were also encouraged. Thus cultural pluralism found recognition in the New Deal for the Indian. At last those in power recognized an obligation to help the Indian live a more satisfying and successful life, not merely in terms of the white man's culture but in terms of his own traditions and his own needs.

Although vigorously challenged from many quarters, New Deal ideology became widely accepted. In 1936 sixty percent and in 1940 fifty-five percent of the voters of the nation cast their ballots for the sponsor of the New Deal. Even when allowances are made for habitual voting, for the commitment of the South to the Democratic party, and for the immediate personal interest of New Deal beneficiaries, these figures are impressive. A study of the various polls on specific measures and principles associated with the New Deal indicates that a similarly large percentage of the population favored the concept of public responsibility for individual well-being. Support of the new ideas was even more general among youth. Existing student organizations in colleges and a new type of student forum concerned themselves increasingly with liberal political and economic ideas. The rapid development of the American Student Union suggested a growing interest in leftist tactics and objectives.

Outside the college campus, if the Maryland survey of 1937 was a fair sampling, youth showed general sympathy toward the basic purposes of the New Deal. According to the findings of this study, three-fourths of the young people interviewed felt that the government should fix minimum wages and maximum hours of labor, and ninety percent believed that the federal government was obligated to provide relief to the unemployed at a health and decency level. There are long-established and deep-rooted precedents in American thought for these ideas, but the widespread favor they now enjoyed marked a new chapter in the intellectual history of the nation.

The new chapter becomes the more significant when account is taken of the direct impact of the New Deal on the agencies of intellectual life and on the creative spirit. Before 1929 the federal and state governments had confined their cultural activities to restricted fields. But in the 1930s the federal government undertook such vast projects for the advancement and spread of knowledge and culture that, for the time at least, the foundations seemed to be quite overshadowed. School leaders, long opposed in principle to federal aid lest it jeopardize local control, now accepted federal grants for school buildings and equipment and for educational services. Thanks in some measure to the financial aid administered through the National Youth Administration, enrollment in the colleges, which had been drastically curtailed in the early stages of the depression, recovered. By the autumn of 1933 more than a hundred thousand undergraduates were being assisted in their studies at a cost to the federal Treasury of $1,500,000 monthly.

Confronted by a vast unemployment problem, the federal government decided to provide relief to intellectuals through work projects. Thus some forty thousand intellectuals, no longer able to earn their living, became affiliated with the Federal Arts Projects of the Works Progress Administration. For more than six years the Federal Arts Projects provided artists, actors, musicians, writers, and scholars with opportunities for creative expression and for research in cultural fields.

The nature of the situation required these newly sponsored federal projects to follow the cooperative rather than the old individualistic pattern. For some time, it will be recalled, American intellectual life had in many respects emphasized planned cooperative activities. Thus the American Council of Learned Societies had sponsored such cooperative enterprises as the *Dictionary of American Biography* and the *Linguistic Atlas of the United States and Canada*. It had also assisted individual scholars, societies, and institutions to undertake similar large-scale enterprises, including the *Middle English Dictionary*, the *Dictionary of American English*, the *Census of Incunabula in American Libraries*, and many similar activities. The Social Science Research Council and the National Research Council likewise had promoted large-scale cooperative researches. In all these activities the individual scholar in considerable measure depended for support and direction on organized committees sponsored by the councils and the foundations. Now when the federal government entered the field of cultural activities in a large way it was both natural and necessary to follow this pattern.

Federal support of cultural activities under the new program was both extensive and comprehensive. The Historical Records Survey collected, inventoried, and indexed vast and frequently unknown or deteriorating documentary records, prepared guides to archival collections, and sponsored the American Imprint Series—a catalogue of all the printed materials that had ever appeared in the several states. The Art Project, in addition to its support of painters and sculptors in their artistic work, prepared an historical Index of American Design. The Music Project did more than compile an Index of American Musicians and collect American folk songs. On many evenings in cities all the way from Portland, Oregon, to Atlanta, Georgia, one might have heard WPA orchestras and even seen people dancing on the pavements to their spirited music. The Writers' Project surveyed American folklore, undertook ethnic studies, and prepared the American Guide series for the various states. The Theater Project, in addition to producing plays and supporting the creative writing of plays, engaged in research and documentation. These were only a few of the cultural and scholarly projects on which millions of dollars were expended by the government.

Authorities differed regarding the competence with which much of the federally sponsored work of this character was executed. Commentators also differed in their evaluations of the significance of what was accomplished. To some all the codifying, indexing, arranging, and classifying suggested the end of an era, an effort to summarize the past, now that all the returns were in, before moving on to a new chapter.

In any case, knowledge and appreciation of the American past were greatly enlarged, especially in the field of folk culture. Many American writers had assumed that their country, unlike the older, more mellow lands of Europe, possessed no folk arts. Thanks to the activities of the Federal Arts Projects, it was now abundantly clear that the facts did not bear out such assumptions. It is true that the migratory habits of the American people and their tendency to build houses of wood rather than of fireproof brick and stone, together with the rapid spread of machine-made materials, had dealt severe blows to the remains of American folk culture. But in spite of the havoc thus wrought, enough remained and now came into the consciousness of writers, artists, musicians, and the general public to demonstrate the richness of the heritage. The growing tendency to rediscover and cherish the American past was in one sense a part of the search for security in an age of dissolution and world crisis; and to this tendency the Federal Arts Projects made a substantial contribution.

Thus within as short a time as a decade after the crash striking changes in ideas about, and procedures in, our cultural and intellectual life had taken place. Research projects involving the work of many people had yielded significant materials for further evaluation by trained scholars. New conceptions of the role of the intellectual and artist in a democratic society had emerged and become realities. Although conceived as an emergency relief measure, the policy of federal support of intellectuals, artists, and actors actually revived on a mass scale ideas cherished by the fathers of the Republic who had visioned cultural enrichment under government auspices. The era of laissez faire in the sphere of mental and esthetic activity apparently had passed. The official indifference of government toward the well-being of men and women devoted to ideas and to cultural values had been replaced by a new conception. The common people were gaining a new respect for the artist and the scholar. The general indifference of intellectuals and artists to social issues and public well-being, to the common man and woman, likewise seemed to be ending.

According to Robert Cantwell, the autobiographies of some fifty creative spirits of the pre-depression decades revealed that although their lives had been closely interwoven with public issues their works had largely been concerned with subjective values. In the depression years men and women of letters, painters, photographers, sculptors, theatrical folk, and even dancers expressed a new and vigorous sensitiveness to social issues, to insecurity and suffering, and to possible salvation through the growth of public responsibility. The realities of the Depression, more than any theory, were responsible for this new direction. Less emphasis was put on the idea of art for art's sake, on the esoteric, on the stream of consciousness, on the irrational, on sex. Plays (*Waiting for Lefty, They Shall Not Die, Of Mice and Men, One Third of a Nation, Pins and Needles*); novels (*Call Home the Heart, The Big Money, The Trouble I've Seen, The Foundry, Union Square, Nobody Starves, Christ in Concrete, The Grapes of Wrath*); documentary photography and art (*You Have Seen Their Faces, We Too are the People, Say, Is this the U.S.A.?, An American Exodus, Land of the Free*, the panels in the Department of Justice and the Treasury Department and in hundreds of public buildings from one end of the land to the other)—all these and dozens of other expressions of the mind and imagination testified to a new social consciousness, to a new interest in the lot of the common man. The documentary film (*The River, The Plough That Broke the Plains*) and the personal document revealing ordinary experiences of ordinary men and women and ordinary boys and girls brought American people themselves to the foreground of the stage of American life.

The depression and the enlarged role of public support for learning and culture also affected millions of Americans hitherto little touched by any save the simplest ideas and the crudest, most commercial forms of art and music. It is true that new technical developments, such as the radio and the movie, a new sort of folk art in a new machine age, had already paved the way for an esthetic awakening. But now, under government encouragement, millions of Americans who had never attended a dramatic performance or heard the best classical music were introduced to the esthetic and intellectual values of such experiences.

Adult education classes and public forums under WPA auspices attacked the problem of illiteracy and the general ignorance of public issues. That such an attack was needed was borne home to the American people when, after the outbreak of World War II, it was revealed that 20 percent of the men of military age possessed less than a fourth-grade education, that 433,000 men of draft age were without sufficient education to serve in the Army, and that some 13,000,000 adults could not read a newspaper or write a simple letter.

The achievements of the depression campaign against illiteracy and ignorance obviously left much to be desired. It was significant, however, that whereas in 1930 approximately 6,000,000 adults could not read, in 1940, when the population was larger by some 8,000,000, only 3,000,000 were without some reading ability. The WPA projects could not claim to have been the sole contributor to this progress, but they were undoubtedly a factor. Although no measuring rod, save perhaps the public opinion polls, exists for determining the effect of the public forums on social intelligence, many students of the problem believed that the American masses displayed increasing competence in this area. All in all, then, the New Deal, in addition to providing a formula which stimulated recovery in some degree and effected many overdue reforms, materially narrowed the gulf between the more and the less privileged.

### Reassertion of Old Values

The vigorous spokesmen for the New Deal were quickly answered back—and in the answering, values dear to the hearts of Americans were reasserted. The criticism was led by men and women of property and position, but millions of others shared their general philosophy and saw serious dangers in the new formulas of economic and social planning. They did not talk much about the danger to their own pocketbooks but dwelt instead upon the harm that would come to poor people through made-work and "general pampering." Their moral fiber would be weakened, their initiative seriously impaired. Private charity could be relied upon as always for the worst cases; the rest should help themselves as Americans always had. After the inauguration of the New Deal there was deep pessimism among men and women who had insisted that the depression was only temporary. Hundreds of articles, essays, brochures, columns, and addresses at meetings of Rotary Clubs, the Chamber of Commerce, and the National Association of Manufacturers talked darkly of the impending ruin the New Deal was bringing to the American way of life.

There was opposition on similar grounds even among liberal and semi-liberal groups. Writing in 1937, the popular columnist Dorothy

Thompson concluded that the New Deal "has offered us no compre-hensible picture of a future in which we can believe. We cannot believe that this vague eleemosynary humanitarianism, coupled with ruthless aggrandizement by politicians, is a picture of a new heaven and a new earth."[11] The New Deal was also criticized by such writers as Albert J. Nock, who favored a decentralized, highly individualistic culture and feared that the new formula of recovery and reform meant "the absorp-tion of all spontaneous efforts by the state," and consequent degradation. Newton D. Baker deplored the decay of self-reliance which the old pioneer order had bred and which the trend toward state responsibility for individual well-being presumably undermined; the decay of moral virtue, he thought, spelled catastrophe. Others saw in the growing bureaucracy at Washington the beginning of the end of the Republic.

These liberals did not realize that the old values associated with that individualism, such as personal "freedom," self-reliance, and individual initiative, no longer flourished as they once had, and had been losing their old meanings long before the New Deal. Thus these liberals and the conservatives like Westbrook Pegler who publicized the same senti-ments added to the intellectual confusion of the decade.

Naturally the New Deal was attacked as being socialistic. *The Saturday Evening Post* denounced the program as class legislation, as the first step toward dictatorship. "It is a very fair question," it remarked editorially, "whether our difficulties are not less economic at bottom than they are moral."[12] The prevalent idea that the federal government had an implied obligation to relieve individual losses was, in the eyes of the editor of this weekly, "one of the strangest delusions which have ever seized large numbers of people in any country."[13] Professing to see in the New Deal a government by amateurs, by college boys who had taken hearty swigs of Russian vodka, *The Saturday Evening Post* cried out against the spending program, the unbalanced budgets, the whole effort to regulate economy, the variety of theoretical and experimental projects for the "hazy purpose of bringing about a new or different social and economic order."[14]

*Liberty* declared that if "we must slug business by soaking the rich, let

---

[11] *Ladies' Home Journal,* LIV (September, 1937), 13.
[12] *The Saturday Evening Post,* CCVI (March 3, 1934), 22.
[13] *Ibid.* (May 19, 1934), 22.
[14] *Ibid.* (April 7, 1934), 25.

us not be deceived. We are aiming sledge-hammer blows at the very men upon whom we must depend to get us out of the slough of Despond into which we have sunk in this present emergency."[15] Besides, observed *Liberty* on another occasion, "the poorest man is often the richest in happiness."[16] Our government should leave business absolutely alone; the creator, the true builder, should not be handicapped by taxation. In the *Atlantic Monthly* and *Harper's Magazine* occasional articles expressing the same ideas in more elegant form reached other strata of the population. Thus rugged individualism braced itself against the new order.

One prominent way of meeting the depression consisted in trying to argue it away as being largely "psychological." Good old American optimism was invoked, KEEP SMILING signs were hung up in offices, and popular publications radiated cheer. "There is nothing to fear except fear," wrote the editor of the *Ladies' Home Journal*. "The silver lining of this present cloud is already beginning to show. Right now we need courage to buy the future instead of selling the present. But first of all we must have confidence in America and its great institutions." Then normalcy would return.[17] The same periodical urged its readers to stop spreading calamity. "It's up to the women to help restore prosperity by maintaining normal living standards, eliminating fear and hoarding, returning currency to circulation, demanding peace and disarmament, tax economy, balanced budgets, economical administration."[18]

Although somewhat less strident than in the golden 1920s, the *American Magazine* continued to spread warmth and confidence. The personal self-help theme found ample illustration. "Strange Ways to Make a Living," "What Worries You Most," "Youth at the Wheel," "Out of Thirty Years' Experience a Broker Tells You What Your Chances Are in the Stock Market," "Business Where It Wasn't," "How to Go After a Job," "He Could Take It," "Times Are Getting Better," "That's Where the Tall Corn Grows," "What Is a Safe Investment?" "A Stone That Rolled Up Hill," "Go to It, Kid, Show 'Em What You Can Do," "It must be the Climate," "She's Doing Her Own Work"—these are fair samples of leading articles in the *American Magazine* for 1933. A

[15] *Liberty*, IX (June 4, 1932), 4.
[16] *Ibid.* (June 18, 1932), 4.
[17] *Ladies' Home Journal*, XLIX (January, 1932).
[18] *Ibid.* (April, 1932), 3.

St. Louis manufacturer writing in that periodical somewhat later dared youth "to push out into the deep, to shoulder more responsibility, to build magnificently . . . to share the fruits of your daring . . . to be the 'Bigger You' which is the full measure of your talents."[19]

President Dodds of Princeton evidently approved of the spirit of such articles. "When we begin," he wrote for the *American Magazine*, "to place our hope in measures of security rather than in ventures toward larger growth, decay will set in. . . . True security is a byproduct of life spent in a more constructive purpose. . . . If we are to make anything of ourselves we must be willing to face the risks of insecurity. In life as in golf, the best rule is to play straight for the pin, scornful of hazards."[20]

The time-honored ways of thinking and feeling which were now asserted in lieu of new formulas for security included personal religion. The swing toward religion as a response to the depression did not, it is true, materialize on the scale that was expected in many quarters. But religious spokesmen interpreted the depression in terms of an emphasis on materialism and saw the way out in a return to faith. "It is the Christian's confident faith in God's care for His world that will be the starting point of our recovery," declared a writer in the *Ladies' Home Journal*. "It is the Christian's cheerfulness and bravery that will help others to carry on."[21] Henry C. Link's *Return to Religion*, a best-seller, insisted on the utilitarian value of Christian faith in times of trouble. Thousands of middle-class men and women found strength and satisfaction in the Oxford Group, a movement led by Frank Buchman. In the intimate week-end parties sponsored by the Group, weary spirits confessed their sins and shortcomings and thus, emotionally rehabilitated, faced the confusion in the world around them.

Some Negroes of Harlem found escape from their troubles in the movement led by Father Divine. This messianic leader persuaded his followers to surrender their worldly possessions and find emotional exhilaration and security from starvation at the Banquet Tables in his "Kingdoms." Regarded by many disciples as an incarnation of God, as God himself, Father Divine spoke and wrote in a way to inspire optimism and confidence. "Wishing you all success, and that as I AM, so might you be, this leaves ME well, healthy, joyful, peaceful, lively,

[19] *American Magazine*, CXXVI (July, 1938), 62.
[20] *Ibid.*, CXXV (January, 1938), 166.
[21] *Ladies' Home Journal*, XLIX (September, 1932), 20.

loving, successful, prosperous, and Happy in Spirit, Body, and Mind, and in every organ, muscle, sinew, vein and bone and in every atom, fiber and cell of My Bodily Form."[22]

During depression days the movies continued, as they had from the first, to provide escape and release. It has been noted that some few dealt with great social issues; but for every *Cabin in the Cotton, Dealers in Death, All Quiet on the Western Front, The River,* and *The Plow That Broke the Plains,* there were thousands of films concerned, as always, with romance, physical passion, humor, adventure, and mystery. The movies of escape included some of the decade's finest art, such as Walt Disney's fairy tales of the machine age. Few would have thought, in the 1920s, that *Snow White* might soon become the nation's favorite heroine.

Reading continued to provide solace and excitement for the masses. Many thousands of people who were above reading *True Confessions* took pride in their enjoyment of such writers as Faith Baldwin. For these people *Collier's,* with its veneer of culture, was a godsend. This magazine, revamped completely, was now challenging *The Saturday Evening Post's* long leadership in the field of mass-circulation magazines. It sold almost three million copies and in 1937 netted gross revenues of $13 million. The few articles in *Collier's* which were generally favorable to the New Deal were sprinkled among a vastly greater number on "Hollywood fluffies," heavyweight champions, war lords, ski-jumpers, and glittering personalities, with sketches of action, sports, mystery, murder, and "tingling young love." As Hickman Powell pointed out in an article on this magazine, all these pieces minimized psychological conflicts and all were brightly, even flashily illustrated with young men's and young women's "vibrant bodies and gay faces." *Collier's* "bits of information in small capsules," sugar-coated, represented the intellectual level, no doubt, of far more than its three million weekly purchasers.

Some ten million Americans each month paid tribute to the pulps and near-pulps, which made no pretense of featuring even "bits of information in small capsules, sugar-coated." The unimaginative readers who found escape from their humdrum troubled lives in the romantic stories of "infallible heroes" and "yearning feminine arms" relished a

[22] Quoted in George E. Sokolsky, "Giants in These Days," *Atlantic Monthly,* CCLVII (June, 1938), 699.

considerable variety of emphases: "girly-girly" sheets, the "he-men" magazines, the near-naughty books, the out-and-out sexy ones: *True Romances*, *True Story Magazine*, *Hot Dog*, *Whiz Bang*, *Wild Cherries*,
*Paris Nights*, *Passion Stories*, *Astounding Stories*, *Medical Horrors*,
*G Men Stories*, *Thrilling Love*, *Miracle Science* and *Superman*. The last
two magazines represented a tangle of ideas—power, mysticism, overblown mechanical grandeur—and featured a new type of folk hero who
might be, some feared, an ominous forerunner of future fascist heroes.
These titles represent only a few of the publications relished by factory
girls, bellhops, shop girls, taxi drivers, mechanics; and they were read, no
doubt, by many others in so-called higher walks of life.

Unlike the old dime novels, these pulps made little pretense of holding out hopes for great worldly success. On the contrary, they suggested
that action, mystery, and sex are the exciting and interesting things. The
pulp stories never suggested any possible satisfaction in ideas, in intellectual curiosity, in esthetic pleasures; their dominant note was one of
escape from personal worry and humdrum into a world of romance
and excitement.

Radio offered similar satisfactions. The get-rich-quick motif was inconspicuous here as in sub-literature, and from coast to coast, all day
long, vast radio audiences suffered vicariously with heroes and heroines
who escaped one tragic situation only to encounter another. This presumably harmless vicarious suffering could be mitigated by listening to
*Amos 'n Andy*, *Eno Crime Clues*, and *Rudy Vallee's Varieties*. Thus,
while some received constructive counsel from the radio and were heartened by splendid music, vast hordes preferred a different type of entertainment.

For the educated and the intellectual, peace was to be found as always
in distant lands and in the past. It is significant that in the early 1930s
when the values of thrift and industry were becoming less valid in American life, the writings of Lin Yutang should have had a great vogue in
this country. Lin Yutang contrasted the American hustler with the
Chinese loafer, questioned the effects of a mechanical, profit-bent culture, and glorified leisure, grace, courtesy, and dignity. It was easy to
overlook the fact that these values in Chinese civilization were values
shared chiefly by the gentle classes.

In a time of questioning and doubt about American institutions many
found reassurance in stories, movies, and other re-creations of the Ameri-

can past—in Mae West's colorful screen pictures of the gay 1890s or in the sentimental movie dramatization of Louisa May Alcott's *Little Women*. The amazing vogue of *Anthony Adverse, Gone with the Wind,* and *Oliver Wiswell* likewise testified to the charm that an unrecoverable past held for many people.

As the threat of totalitarianism abroad enhanced the feeling of insecurity, more and more writers called upon American traditions to provide both security and strength. Van Wyck Brooks, Howard Mumford Jones, John Dos Passos, Archibald MacLeish, and others either became critical of much of the "international" and "modern" accent of the literature of the 1920s or sought in the American past a credo and a fortress. Almost insensibly people who had turned to our past for entertainment alone found themselves viewing it with pride and affection. Those who had taken democracy for granted began to think about its meaning as they read books like *The Wave of the Future*. Before the 1930s were over, more absorbing problems even than those of the depression were forcing Americans to reexamine their heritage, to take stock of themselves as never before.

Thus the response of Americans to the economic dislocation took a variety of forms, old and new. From an early point in the depression occasional prophets had sounded the warning that yet another escape might be forced on the American world—the escape of war. Such an escape was not sought; it came, feared, unwanted, unprepared for.

### The Challenge of Totalitarianism and War

By a curious turn of affairs one of the first noticeable effects of the growth of the various forms of fascism in Europe was the enrichment of American intellectual and cultural life. The expulsion of some of the most gifted scientists, artists, and literary men from Italy and Germany meant an enhancement of the cosmopolitan tone and the distinction of cultural life all over America. The University in Exile, established in 1932 by Alvin Johnson and ultimately organized into the graduate faculty of the New School of Social Research, harbored great minds and personalities. Every leading American university and many colleges profited from the presence of refugee scholars. As the life of the mind and spirit in European countries was subjected to regimentation, propa-

ganda, persecution, preparation for war, and war itself, Americans came
to think of their land as the center and sanctuary of light and learning.
The old dream of American intellectual supremacy had come true at last!

Even the presence of refugees did not at once awaken all American
intellectuals to the implications of the fascist advance for the life of
the mind. Though the Nazis burned the books of some of the great
writers of all lands, though they perverted science and scholarship to
party purposes, though they persecuted all critics of the regime and
all people "tainted" by Jewish blood, many American intellectuals continued to remain indifferent or even to apologize. In 1936 Harvard, Yale,
Columbia, and Stanford took part in the 550th anniversary of Heidel-
berg. Sharp protests in the liberal journals and among academicians
did not prevent other universities from participating in the bicentennial
celebration at Göttingen the following year. The indifference and the
apologies evidenced blindness to the plain fact that Nazism threatened
all the ideals of scholars and intellectuals—sustained search for truth,
freedom of inquiry and expression, the supremacy of the mind, the
dignity of all men.

This indifference can be partly explained in terms of the confusion
regarding the nature and significance of the totalitarian onslaught. The
"left" generally maintained that fascism was in essence a desperate effort
to preserve the capitalistic system by subjecting it to rigid state controls,
and that Jew-baiting, the repression of minority criticism, the steam-
roller propaganda, the nationalistic and racial pageantry were to be
interpreted in this light. Others insisted that there was little essentially
new in the movements holding Italy and Germany in their grip, that
the emphasis on discipline, militarism, violence, regimentation, and
racialism had deep roots in the soil on which they now flourished. Still
others argued that the passionate and hysterical but dangerous proselyting zeal of the exponents of totalitarianism, including its Russian form,
could be understood only in terms of a revolutionary pattern, a revolution against the nationalism and capitalism that had dominated the
nineteenth and twentieth centuries.

Nor was there any agreement regarding the proper attitude of the
United States toward the fascist aggressions. Some few insisted that
totalitarianism was "the wave of the future" and that Americans could
only effect inner adaptations to it and protect themselves by building
up outer defenses. Even thoroughgoing democrats were divided between

those who held that the only security for democracy was to reinvigorate and expand it at home and those who maintained that the only defense in a shrunken world was to give aid to all those still resisting the overwhelming menace with their lifeblood.

Although the noninterventionists triumphed in the Neutrality Acts of 1935, 1936, and 1937, other signs indicated that the tide was turning toward interventionism. When France collapsed in the early summer of 1940 a group of intellectuals led by Van Wyck Brooks, Lewis Mumford, and Archibald MacLeish charged American scholars and writers with having been indifferent toward the totalitarian advance, and pictured them as working on in their own ivory towers unaware of the danger to all the values of the mind involved in the Nazi onslaught. The indictment occasioned much discussion in which it was pointed out that many intellectuals had in fact long been awake to the danger. Some had repeatedly warned the world that catastrophe could not be avoided unless great sacrifices were made and by deed as well as by word had indicated their own willingness to bear their share of these sacrifices.

As war crept closer, always against the wish of the great majority of the American people, as step by step aid was given to the democracies resisting the totalitarian onslaught, a larger number of men and women, both among the intellectual leadership and the rank and file, realized that fascism menaced much that Americans had long held precious. The traditional American love of individual freedom, opposition to regimentation, devotion to fair play and the doctrine of live and let live, and above all, loyalty to the ideal of a moral law—these values seemed clearly jeopardized. As intellectuals wondered whether democracy and the life of the mind could survive the totalitarian menace abroad and the ominous fascist-like patterns of thought at home, and as more and more plain folk sensed that what was at stake was their way of life, the Japanese struck at Pearl Harbor.

# 29   American Assertions in a World of Upheaval

*In our time great revolutions and world wars and world crises have rolled over the continents. The bankruptcy of reason and manners increases. The old specters rise up from the graves of history. . . . Irrationalism is triumphant; nationalism excels.*
— HERMANN KESTEN, 1946

In the intellectual sphere, as in every other, the years between Pearl Harbor and the sharpening of conflict with the Soviet Union in 1947–1948 were dominated by World War II. Internationalism seemed to be the theme and to infuse the purposes of that war. "One world" was a slogan heard almost everywhere. And after the fighting stopped, the United States was committed to the manifold international activities of the United Nations and of the administrators of the Marshall Plan, as well as to its own cultural relations programs.

But these activities, whatever their implications for international cooperation, carried strong overtones of nationalism. This was clear, not only in the conquered countries where military government was established, but elsewhere as well. In fact, American policies overseas were reflections of a determined effort to encourage political and economic systems—and loyalties—congenial to the American faith. Nationalism

730

as an active force became dominant in the United States, and indeed throughout the world.

This militant nationalism was supported by the articulate at all levels —by the men on the street and in the country store, by city and rural editors, by magazine writers, preachers, and poets, by college professors and scientists, by officials and diplomats. There was not much analysis of the concept of nationalism itself, except by a few intellectuals. But the renewed vigor and influence of the idea were clear, even though largely implicit and to be inferred from attitudes taken and policies advocated.

Besides this overarching concept of the war decade, other more or less related concepts and doctrines were involved in, and were in various ways affected by, the war. The meanings of individualism, communism, humanism, progress, and democracy were pondered. Esthetic and religious doctrines received new emphases, as did the nature of man and of the universe itself. In the first half of the 1940s the war seemed to give at least a surface unity to almost every aspect of intellectual life.

The resurgence of militant nationalism explains, at least in part, the official nature of much of the intellectual life of the time. The role and weight of government was seen in directed propaganda and information, in the intercultural relations programs, the national monopoly of atomic power, and the federal subsidies to scientific investigation. It was seen in the influence of the military on research and on educational programs and personnel. Official views were reflected in the group reports on schools, universities, the press, and civil liberties. The individual wellsprings of intellectual endeavor and expression did not dry up, as the names of Niebuhr, Eliot, Beard, Hutchins, Lilienthal, Conant, and Einstein testify. But individual leadership in intellectual life tended to retreat before an expanding officialdom and the mass media of communication. Individual expression became increasingly sensitive to government policy, at least in the discussion of foreign relations. Here, where criticism appeared at all, it was likely to be interpreted as communistic, however far from communist belief the critics might be. In this situation may be found a leading feature of the intellectual history of the later years of the decade and of much of the 1950s—the retreat of the critical attitude toward American life and values which had marked the 1920s and the 1930s. Thus the official aspects of intellectual life take an important place in any survey of the war years and of those that immediately followed.

## National Loyalty and National Faith

It seems fair to say that no war had been fought with as much unanimity as World War II. Most of those who, as isolationists or pacifists, had opposed entering the war quietly accepted the situation, whatever their reservations may have been. There were, to be sure, conscientious objectors, officially more than 9000 of them, with an undetermined number who were not put in a position to declare themselves publicly. Of the 9000, some 4000 chose to contribute to the larger ends of society by toiling at peacetime tasks in the civilian camps set up for that purpose. Approximately 5000 refused to register or accept any sort of alternative to military service. Two-thirds of these were Jehovah's Witnesses. Many of them went to prison.

But American patriotism on the whole stood up well under pressure. Only a very small number of Americans could be labeled traitors. In the summer of 1943 a federal court indicted eight persons on the charge of broadcasting for the enemy. The group included Ezra Pound, distinguished innovator of strange stanza forms, who, a rootless expatriate in foreign lands, had long denounced what he called the "degeneracy" of democracy. Subsequently other men and women were indicted, but the number was small. In short, the American public accepted the imperatives of the war effort. To say this is not to say, of course, that business, labor, and ordinary individuals did not often put their own interest above that of country. American patriotism, unlike that of the totalitarian enemies, was undisciplined, something more or less apart from day-by-day life, somewhat sentimental. But it met the test of adversity.

The lack of a clear general understanding of the larger meaning of the struggle did not make this the less true. The Atlantic Charter, for all its idealism, was after all vague, more vague than Wilson's Fourteen Points; the doctrine of unconditional surrender was negative, not positive. There was among the rank and file a wholesome absence of romanticism—to them the war was a job to be done, not a shining crusade. Few faced the underlying issues squarely. Nor was a penetrating light shed on the ideology of the war by business advertisements in the press and on the radio, which implied that the country was fighting in order to get back to bigger and better bathtubs, radios, and automobiles. It was enough for most to understand that America had been attacked, that it was necessary to fight back.

There was still less flag-waving or sentimentalism about patriotic duty within the ranks of the fighting men. Much evidence—personal testimony, letters, and the results of questionnaires—suggests that the great majority neither gave much thought to the larger social and political problems nor basically changed their pre-Army pattern of thought. To be sure, the new environment wrought certain changes. But there was little broadly based patriotic understanding of the larger meaning of the struggle. While the War Department's Information and Education Department dramatized the war for the Four Freedoms, the average fighting man reconciled himself to performing the undesirable but obviously necessary job of overpowering the enemy. Some critics insisted that the timidity of the War and Navy Departments in neutralizing the teaching materials used during training and the failure generally to adopt the British practice of free give-and-take discussion of the issues of the war and the peace, accounted for this state of affairs. But it is possible that the soldier's lack of perspective and his failure to take seriously the official thesis of the nature and objectives of the war reflected rather the fact that "the country had never made up its mind about its relationships to other peoples, but had merely essayed the impossible feat of being in the world but not of it."[1] The indictment by Karl Shapiro, the best-known war poet, was hardly true of the average GI:

> He hated other races, south or east,
> And shoved them to the margin of his mind.
> To him the red flag marked the sewer main.

Rather, the GI, like other citizens, tended to ignore, or to hold in mild contempt, peoples other than his own.

Neither the popular war cartoons by Bill Mauldin nor the novels written by veterans cast the conflict in heroic mold. The Mauldin cartoons with good-natured edge featured the prevailing distaste for the big brass, the military routine and protocol, and what appeared to be the senselessness of much that took place. In fiction the war of waiting was best captured in Thomas Heggen's *Mister Roberts*. To some critics it seemed that in many of the novels, dealing as they did with whole divisions and armies, the individual, seldom a hero, was lost in vast, impersonal organization. Norman Mailer's *The Naked and the Dead*

---

[1] David L. Cohn, "Should Fighting Men Think?" *Saturday Review of Literature*, XXX (January 18, 1947), 7. See also Cohn's *This is My Story* (Houghton Mifflin Company, 1947).

labored the thesis that the war merely revealed the worst that was in men in their earlier civilian life. In *From Here to Eternity* James Jones dramatized the problems of a man whose violence was needed by society but who was penalized by the Army when his violence, enmeshed in powerful and chaotic feelings, got him into trouble. The slogan, "One war is enough," made sense to fighting men who spoke or wrote of the war and its dull aftermath in the armies of occupation, an aftermath marked by loneliness, thirst for sex and adventure, and indulgence in black-marketeering. Sometimes the message that one war was enough was phrased in the brutal idiom of Mailer. On other occasions it was reflected in the sensitive stories of Irwin Shaw, or in Major Joppolo's moving struggle to maintain the dignity of man in John Hersey's *A Bell for Adano*. All this helps explain why, once the fighting stopped, the most articulate ex-fighters worked, not as professional veterans, but as civilians. At least some were consciously intent upon building an America in which all might enjoy jobs, freedom, and peace, and where there would be no lost generation.

## Intellectuals and the War Effort

Although, as we shall see, intellectuals took an important part in the war effort, some stood apart from the swift canalizing of intellectual activity into national service. Sensitive to the peculiar long-time responsibilities of those entrusted with maintaining the life of the mind and the arts, these men and women determined to sustain the broader cultural foundations so far as circumstances permitted. Many artists, for example, quietly kept at their work, experimenting with the increasingly favored non-representational rhythmic distortions, multiple or "split" images, heightened colors, and sensational depictions of speed, movement, and kaleidoscopic change. Some writers, sticking to tasks already assumed, were only indirectly affected by the war. Some responded only half consciously to the war temper by turning to historical themes with, to be sure, strong sex overtones but also with nationalistic implications. Certainly much commendable artistic work was done during the war and the years that followed. But many critics felt that in comparison with preceding decades the 1940s were less fruitful in original and significant achievements. To the ranks of intellectuals only indirectly affected by the war must be added an unknown but probably small number of scholars who unobtrusively kept on with long-range investigations.

Certainly the great majority of intellectual workers were directly drawn into the vortex of the struggle, which used intellectual and artistic talents as no previous war had done. Scholars, writers, artists, and teachers fought in the armed forces or became enmeshed in the drudgery of army requisitions. Others joined in the great mobilization of intellectual talents consciously sponsored by the government—a mobilization that included social scientists, philologists, and even philosophers, as well as the scientists and engineers who dramatically discovered the key to the release of nuclear energy. Under the leadership of Francis Biddle forty-two artists went to twelve overseas fronts to record their impressions of the war. Actors from Broadway and Hollywood and musicians from everywhere contributed their talents to the recreational programs in the Army and Navy centers. Some scholars did their war work unpretentiously in their classrooms as colleges and universities opened their doors to give special training to more than one million members of the armed forces.

No agencies of intellectual life made such drastic readjustments as institutions of higher learning. With the major brunt of our military demands falling on youth, colleges and universities shifted as rapidly as possible to a wartime basis. In the men's colleges the depletion of the student body cut the liberal arts program to the bone. Liberal education would have been virtually suspended for the duration except for the presence of women in the academic ranks. Even for them the traditional pattern was accelerated and altered that they might also prepare for special wartime service. The overwhelming majority of colleges and universities accepted short-time contracts with the War and Navy Departments for the accelerated training of personnel in the applied sciences, especially in radio, aviation, engineering, medicine, and nursing. Some institutions set up a course in military government.

By the early months of 1944 more than 1,200,000 men and women had received technical training in these specialized programs. Never before had the United States given opportunities for higher education to such a large proportion of young people. Although administrators and teachers did their best, confusion in directives and even in objectives worked against entire satisfaction in all quarters. In January, 1944, the Army slashed the program despite the outcry from educators that many institutions would have to close their doors. But just as the last trainees left the campuses in the spring of 1944, the first returning veterans enrolled in classes.

In addition to providing training for the armed forces personnel on college campuses, educators cooperated with military authorities in extending educational opportunities to soldiers and sailors in camps and even on the fighting fronts. Several hundred colleges organized instruction and discussion groups at nearby military centers. For soldiers isolated from centers of learning the United States Armed Forces Institute was organized, with the technical assistance of the University of Wisconsin Extension Division, which had pioneered in college correspondence courses. Before the year 1944 was over, USAFI offered 275 courses in addition to the 7000 courses which affiliated colleges and universities made available. By the early part of 1946 some 800,000 servicemen had enrolled in the correspondence self-teaching courses, and one million had taken classes conducted at Army installations.

Correspondence courses were not the only outlet for the intellectually or vocationally ambitious. After VE Day thousands of officers and GIs enrolled in improvised colleges in England, France, and Italy, and later in the Far Eastern theater, as well as in some of the established universities. Hundreds of American scholars crossed the seas to take part in these educational programs.

Formal classwork comprised but one aspect of the armed forces educational program. Reading was undoubtedly one of the fighting man's greatest time killers, and informed estimates held that the men in this war read far more widely than the doughboys in World War I. Publishers, editors, and educators prepared special armed forces issues of classics and best sellers for distribution among the Army and Navy. In addition, academicians responded to the War Department's request for specially prepared pamphlets on a wide variety of subjects of public import. News maps and films aided Orientation and Special Services officers, drawn largely from the educational profession, in conducting discussion groups. Despite the recognition by the military of the importance of such activity in the armed forces and the generous cooperation of intellectuals in preparing and administering educational programs, it would be easy to overstress the extent of learning in the services. Mysteries, detective stories, and above all, the ubiquitous comic book provided, when all was said and done, the great bulk of the actually used reading material.

The revelation that 676,000 men failed to qualify for selective service on the ground of having received less than four years of schooling shocked the intellectual leadership of the nation. The number rejected for physical deficiencies suggested further that the schools and society in general had paid too little attention to health and physical well-being. Critics within the ranks of professional educators had, to be sure, known something of the educational deficiencies of the country, but the war experience served as a nation-wide survey of these shortcomings. The situation was worsened when thousands of teachers, attracted by the higher pay in industry and in various types of war work, left the profession.

It appeared increasingly clear that if the ideals and aims of American education were to be approximated, the educational enterprise needed a larger share of the nation's wealth. The war further revealed shortcomings in the actual quality of the available education. The widespread deficiencies of young Americans in foreign languages led to an experiment in accelerated instruction in the oral use of language. In creating a demand for personnel trained in specialized knowledge of many areas of the world, the war also stimulated a new type of area study. This combined the development of competence in the relevant language with knowledge of the history, geography, government, economy, and culture of the area. On the assumption that this country was certain to play a more important part on the world stage than it had done in the past, the war encouraged educational authorities to give more attention to international problems.

The special educational obligation to veterans whose training had in many cases been interrupted by the war was a principal factor in the decision to subsidize the vocational rehabilitation of servicemen and to enable those who were qualified, and so chose, to obtain college and professional training. Thanks to the GI Bill of Rights (Public Law 346) which Congress passed in 1944, the trickle of veterans into the colleges swelled to large proportions as the war ended.

Before the war, educational objectives and programs, especially in the liberal arts, had occasioned much discussion. For many years those preoccupied with the humanities had confessed their concern for the status and prospects of the liberal arts. But the war, breaking down—at least for the time—traditional modes of thought and action, transformed this concern into a bubbling ferment. In countless institutions postwar planning committees pondered the objectives and procedures of liberal education. National committees designated by the American Philosophical

Association, the American Council on Education, and the Association of American Colleges—to name only a few—prepared and issued soul-searching statements, and dozens of educational leaders wrote books on liberal education. Perhaps at no time in the history of the Republic had education in its broadest aspects evoked such searching consideration.

In general the exponents of liberal education held with one of their spokesmen that unless "we Americans can get some pattern of belief and understanding which will give us a moral and intellectual equivalent for the principles which have become a religion to a generation of National Socialists, we shall be the victims of a cultural dimout no matter how glorious our military victories."[2] It was not enough, the argument ran, to oppose the fascist disparagement of the individual; liberal education must positively assert the dignity of man and faith in humanity. Some argued that the humanities had taken too narrow a view of their subjects, that they had underestimated the value of the classics in translation and the potentialities of the humanistic approach to all fields of knowledge, including the sciences themselves. Many more agreed that the influential German nineteenth-century scheme of precise textual criticism had robbed the humanities of their inner meaning and spiritual significance, had left a worm's-eye view of the great cultural heritage. The humanities, the argument went, needed to be taught in terms of their universal meaning so that their full moral wisdom and beauty might be thoroughly appreciated.

A growing number of educational leaders reacted against the elective system which had enabled students to neglect the cultural for the "practical" subjects. They contended that every undergraduate should at least stand on the threshold of all branches of knowledge, including the humanities. General education won increasing favor in the reaction against overspecialization, the compartmentalization of knowledge, and the prevailing vogue for vocational training in the natural sciences and their applications. Only by a militant reassertion of the common core of the liberal arts could man again, it was argued, come to speak the same idiom and accept a universal standard of values. Nor were the broadening potentialities of the humanities and the social studies overlooked in the discussions of education in the postwar era of anticipated internationalism.

[2] John W. Dodds, "Should We Lift the Cultural Dimout?" *Saturday Review of Literature*, XXVII (January 29, 1944), 5.

In 1945 Harvard put the stamp of approval on some of these modes of thinking in its much-discussed report, *General Education in a Free Society*. There was little in it that was new; in fact several institutions had long been doing what Harvard now recommended. But the prestige of the oldest and wealthiest institution of learning in the land gave the report a special importance. Like many educational documents, this one represented a compromise between the traditional departmentalization and specialization and the values of general liberal training. Nevertheless, the report broke with the German tradition of higher education imported in the 1880s, carried further President Lowell's reaction against the free elective system, and argued for the value of a common core of knowledge of which no educated man, no responsible man, should be ignorant. This included not only the great humanistic tradition of the past; it also embraced the newer fields of knowledge. Moreover, this core of knowledge was to be treasured not merely for the personal values it carried. It was to be fully geared to the needs of a changing society. Finally, the report emphasized not only the importance of training the gifted but the necessity of educating the masses for good citizenship and for life.

While the war and the prospective problems of the postwar world precipitated these discussions, scholars and scientists contributed their part to the actual winning of the war. In view of the traditional American suspicion of learned specialists, the prestige intellectuals enjoyed as the important nature of their contributions became known was significant. In the most relevant fields investigation was "accelerated," and fresh impetus was given to spot research for immediate needs, the application of existing information to new situations and problems, and emphasis on planning and cooperation. Even before Pearl Harbor the National Roster of Scientific and Specialized Personnel listed almost half a million specialists to be called on when occasion required. Now professors and experts flocked to Washington to give a hand in war work. The "man who knows" found himself sought after as never before. Secrecy about much of the work of these scholars was of course imperative, but in time the informed public came to know some part of their contributions.

The Office of Strategic Services coordinated and directed much of this intellectual activity. Historians, political scientists, and economists, as well as scholars in other fields, studied all manner of things—the transportation systems of countries to be invaded; the psychological and cultural characteristics of people in occupied countries, including some remote Pacific islands so necessary to be won and held as springboards in the encirclement of Japan; the weather and currency and the costumes and the family life in far-away countries. Even scholars in some fields hitherto regarded as esoteric, such as Iranian and African linguistics, now found their specialties of immediate use as plans for military operations in the far stretches of the globe took form. Some made movies of war crimes for the benefit of the Joint Chiefs of Staff, and others as secret agents gleaned all sorts of pertinent information. The intelligence reports thus gathered enabled the military to consider and reconsider strategy and tactics. Other scholars found their place in the Office of War Information, along with advertising experts and newspapermen. The OWI not only publicized the objective and course of the war, but also developed techniques of psychological warfare.

In order to keep the record straight and to record accurately information of possible future importance, the history of the fighting forces and the related services was in large part written on the spot, or at the time the reports were assembled in Washington. In no previous war had there been such systematic observation. Professional historians wrote a great number of "on the scene" case histories. If these failed to reveal struggles for prestige and power, slumps in morale, and the workings of Army bureaucracy, they were often notable for their clarity and their unvarnished reflection of the initiative and responsibility that combat thrust on countless individuals and outfits. Each branch of the service prepared histories of its activities, with the result that a vast body of material, a tribute to cooperative and largely anonymous research, was available to the high military command, to curious participants in the struggle, and to the interested public.

The far-extending ad hoc investigations in the historical, economic, geographical, sociological, and anthropological disciplines did not prevent the examination of basic and theoretical issues in the social sciences both during the War and in the years immediately afterwards. The Social Science Research Council stated that man's knowledge of the basic problems in social relations was woefully deficient. Yet social scientists often expressed a reluctance to make use of available results and techniques. This may in part be ascribed to the liberal's revulsion against the uses of the social sciences made by the Nazis in order to achieve their ends, and to the fear of the possible consequences if social science provided causal controls over human behavior. George H. Sabine argued that this conflict in liberal thought reflected "a deficiency in liberal social philosophy itself, or rather a neglect on its part of conditions necessary to realizing its own liberal ideals."[3]

The equivocal status of the social sciences also resulted from the uncertainty within and without the profession concerning the possibility of achieving objectivity by the known techniques. Some maintained that the methods of the natural sciences were only in minor degree applicable to social data. But even if they were, the argument ran, no one, in view of the contingencies and imponderables in man's social relationships, could be sure of his classifications and measurements, or, if he ventured to make them, of his predictions. Thus no one could offer much valid counsel on the most feasible means of achieving the desired ends. Indeed, some even argued that those concerned with social relationships could at best merely study fragments, whether in the past or present, of man's activities and relationships, and reminded readers that even these fragments could be viewed only within a frame of underlying assumptions and values.

Some writers in the field were more optimistic, insisting that the social disciplines had already achieved in many respects the status enjoyed by the natural sciences. Stuart Chase in his popular book, *The Proper Study of Mankind*, called attention to such reliable instruments as the statistical series used in the analysis of economic behavior, the culture concept, and the methods for measuring and predicting the rate of production in industry, for anticipating the reactions of various civilian populations to bombing, for foretelling the behavior of prisoners on parole, and for accurately prophesying the future of the airplane from the curves of the past. Whatever the revelations of inadequacies in polling public opinion, no one could deny that advances had been made in refining this instrument of measurement and prediction.

On the basis of all these and other achievements it was possible to argue that if society or the controlling powers in it were ready to give social scientists support comparable to that given the natural scientists, especially during the war and in the postwar years, the sociologists, cultural anthropologists, economists, social psychologists, and political

[3] George H. Sabine, "Beyond Ideology," *Philosophical Review*, LVII (January, 1948). 4.

scientists could provide blueprints and techniques for coming to grips with man's most pressing social problems, many of which the war and its aftermath accentuated. The refusal of Congress to include the social sciences within the frame of the proposed National Science Foundation no doubt reflected the lay view that these sciences dealt primarily with controversial issues in controversial ways.

The debate within the social sciences did not preclude efforts to use available knowledge in dealing with several specific problems. According to those responsible for reporting and evaluating the efforts to apply social science techniques in the armed forces, "For the first time on such a scale the attempt to direct human behavior was, in part at least, based on scientific evidence."[4] Using the methods and knowledge gleaned by private industry in its efforts to gauge both audience reaction to radio programs and movies and consumers' interests and potential interests, social scientists studied the motivation and adjustments of men differing in background, susceptibilities, and length of military service. They tried to find out why men fought, what explained their differences in battle fear, which men sought promotion and why, and how valid rating procedures and standards were. Never in peacetime had the knowledge social scientists made available been used in attacking the problems of group association and morale in so direct and constructive a way.

During the war some social scientists also sought to clarify thought on public questions and to contribute to decisions deemed desirable. Carl L. Becker in his wise and witty book, *How New Will the Better World Be?*, injected a wholesome note of caution into the roseate expectations that somehow, with the defeat of the enemy, democratic and humane ideals would become actualities. In two books another historian, Thomas A. Bailey, indicated some of the reasons for the rejection of the Wilsonian ideal of international peace at the end of World War I, and suggested how such mistakes might be avoided and American acceptance of world responsibility for promoting peace and order insured, once the Nazis and Japanese met with defeat.

In contrast to these inquiries, undertaken by individual scholars, was the growing tendency toward cooperative research. This approach was exemplified by the study of a Massachusetts community directed by William Lloyd Warner, the purpose of which was to find out what

---

[4] Samuel Stouffer, in the preface to *The American Soldier: Adjustment During Army Life* (Princeton University Press, 1949).

the basic structure of the community had been and was and to explain the dynamics of its behavior; and by the well-financed investigation of the Negro problem made by Gunnar Myrdal and his associates, which was published in 1944 under the title *An American Dilemma*.

## The Atomic Era

The many contributions of the natural scientists to the war effort pale before the dramatic dominance of their chief creation, the atomic bomb. Yet even apart from this final fruit of scientific enterprise, the unparalleled mobilization of scientific talent proved its military worth. The need for marshalling scientific resources for total war was evident from the start. So too was the imperative necessity for saving time, for the Axis powers enjoyed at least a two-year start in the development of instruments of warfare. Thus in June, 1940, even before the first conscription, the Office of Scientific Research and Development, headed by Dr. Vannevar Bush, began to mobilize and consolidate science for the war effort.

The war only slightly advanced scientific knowledge on the theoretical level. Research in such problems as the nature of growth and development and the source of cosmic rays remained at almost a standstill. The great emphasis was on the speedy and effective application of existing knowledge. Secrecy surrounded the application and perfection of discoveries even in the field of medicine, lest the enemy profit. Scientific and technological work during the war, however, helped tie theory and practice more intimately together. Competent authorities believed that in time the new instruments developed in the war might be useful in advancing general theory.

Chemistry played a leading role, especially in the development of techniques for rapid and enormous production of synthetic rubber, fibers, and plastics, and the use of DDT, penicillin, and blood plasma. Medicine experienced important advances in malarial control, in surgery and psychiatry. In aviation, and subsequently in naval science, the most dazzling and important advance was the development of radar. The radar wave became man's super eye. It enabled him to observe the outline of terrain despite darkness, clouds, mists, or fog. It lengthened the range of the human eye to a hundred miles, and in thus extending man's senses and powers proved of incalculable advantage in combat. Only less startling were the advances in submarine warfare, the development of new explosives and propellants such as incendiaries and flame throwers, and the improvements in the rocket and the magnetic mine. In commenting on the Office of Scientific Research and Development the Appropriations Committee of the House of Representatives justly remarked that "the contribution it has made to the winning of the war is inestimable."

The splendidly organized work of applying scientific theory and knowledge to modern war reached its high point in the development and application of nuclear energy. The idea that energy might be produced from atoms was not new. Albert Einstein had suggested it as early as 1905. A group of brilliant physicists, including Lord Rutherford, Nagaoka, Fermi, Bohr, Hann, and Meitner, had shown that the atom possesses a nucleus at the center of concentrated matter and energy; that the atoms of one element can be converted into atoms of other elements by the bombardment of radium rays; that the neutron, or tiny atomic fragment, is highly effective in such conversions; and that these neutrons can be used to bring about fission in the uranium atom with the consequent release of tremendous energy. At the Universities of California, Columbia, and Chicago, American and European physicists in their atom-splitting investigations had confirmed and in some respects carried further the basic work in the field that had come to be known as nuclear energy.

Despite all this it took foresight and courage on the part of President Roosevelt and his advisers to channel almost $2 billion into the effort to use atomic energy in explosive form. In highly secret experiments American and European scientists set to work on the immense and formidable technological project of finding means to release nuclear energy on a gigantic scale, to make uranium in its unstable form available in quantity, and to discover how a bomb might be created in which the explosion of one uranium atom would release titanic energy simultaneously in all the rest.

On July 16, 1945, the dramatic test of the new weapon took place in great secrecy on the deserts of New Mexico.[5] The expensive gamble succeeded. In the words of Henry De Wolf Smyth, a weapon was developed "potentially destructive beyond the wildest nightmares of the imagina-

[5] James Phinney Baxter, *Scientists Against Time* (Atlantic Monthly Press, 1946), 447.

tion."[6] So well had the experiment succeeded that many of the scientists expressed horror at the prospect of utilizing the bomb in the war against Japan, which continued after the fall of Hitler and his regime in Europe before Allied power. Nevertheless, on the morning of August 6 a plane flew over Hiroshima and the city became a flaming ruin. The world was stunned a few hours later when President Truman in matter-of-fact fashion announced the era of atomic warfare.

Even the Japanese surrender nine days later after another bomb had blasted Nagasaki seemed anticlimactic to the American public, which was still grappling with the significance of Hiroshima. True, there was relief and some celebration that the war was finally over, but there was little of the hysterical joy that had marked the end of World War I. Instead there was, at least in thoughtful circles, a sense of fear and distressing urgency as the nation ended a victorious war and embarked upon the problems of peace in an atomic era. Immediately following Hiroshima Norman Cousins wrote an editorial, "Modern Man Is Obsolete," which struck close to the thoughts of thousands who feared that peace was but the prelude to extinction. "The beginning of the Atomic Age has brought less hope than fear," Cousins wrote. "It is a primitive fear, the fear of the unknown, the fear of forces man can neither channel nor comprehend. . . . It has burst out of the subconscious and into the conscious, filling the mind with primordial apprehensions. It is thus that man stumbles fitfully into a new era of atomic energy for which he is as ill equipped to accept its potential blessings as he is to control its present dangers."[7] Nor was there comfort to be gained in later months when the power and significance of the bomb could be weighed in the measure of sober reason. John Hersey's *Hiroshima*, for example, told in unembellished reporter's style the story of those fateful days and left no doubt as to the effects of the holocaust on human beings.

Those chiefly responsible for the making of the bomb and for the decision to use it fully appreciated the grim and far-reaching implications of atomic warfare. Secretary of War Stimson voiced a common feeling when he wrote that the bombs, which carried to a new level the increasingly barbarous and destructive methods of war, demonstrated

[6] Henry De Wolf Smyth, *Atomic Energy for Military Purposes* (Princeton University Press, 1947), 223.

[7] Norman Cousins, "Modern Man Is Obsolete," *Saturday Review of Literature*, XXVIII (August, 1945), 6–7.

that man's ability to destroy himself was almost complete. Atomic warfare made it "wholly clear that we must never have another war. This is the lesson men and leaders everywhere must learn, and I believe that when they learn it they will find a way to lasting peace. There is no other way."[8]

Leading nuclear physicists expressed far more social consciousness and responsibility than had been customary among scientists. They substantially agreed that there could be no adequate defense against the atomic bomb, that the means of producing it could not be kept a secret, and that other countries might be expected to develop it within a few years. In view of these considerations one leading physicist wrote: "We realized that, should atomic weapons be developed, no two nations would be able to live in peace with each other unless their military forces were controlled by a common authority. We expected that these controls, if they were effective enough to abolish atomic warfare, would be effective enough to abolish all other forms of war."[9] Another declared: "It was apparent to all of us who participated in that test at Jornada del Muerto that this new power which we had unleashed could not become the plaything of so-called power-politics. . . . A new revolutionary force demands a revolution in methods of dealing with the problem of peace. It is a problem which cannot be solved in the framework of existing sovereign nations."[10] Still another, warning against the growing tendency to pooh-pooh the dangers of the atomic bomb, insisted that atomic energy was to be either the great hope or the doom of civilization; that only the radical step of internationalizing the atomic bomb held any hope for a practical solution.[11] Albert Einstein predicted that a new atomic war might be expected to wipe out two-thirds of mankind. The great scientist urged that world government was the only alternative.[12] It is true that on earlier occasions when deadly weapons were introduced, men had predicted that warfare was thus made too horrible ever to be undertaken again, but the urgency with which such suggestions were now made had never before been equaled.

[8] Henry L. Stimson, "The Decision to Use the Atomic Bomb," *Harper's Magazine*, CXCIV (January, 1947), 107.

[9] Eugene Wigner, "Are We Making the Transition Wisely?" *Saturday Review of Literature*, XXVIII (November 17, 1945).

[10] Robert R. Wilson, "Cooperation or Annihilation," *ibid.*, XXVIII (December 22, 1945), 15.

[11] J. Robert Oppenheimer, *ibid.*, XXVIII (November 24, 1945).

[12] "Einstein and the Atomic Bomb," *Atlantic Monthly*, CLXXVI (November, 1945), 43–45.

The serious discussions of scientists were carried on in all quarters of the intellectual world. These discussions in general revealed an uncertainty, a fear of the implications of science unless technology could be socially and ethically controlled. Again and again the question was asked whether men might learn any lessons from the methods that had introduced the atomic age, whether before it was too late men might learn to think in new ways to meet the new age. It was pointed out that the prevailing gaps between revolutionary science and evolutionary anthropology, between intellect and conscience, between power and wisdom, hardly augured well for the possibility of rational control. For some social scientists the answer was to be sought in the expenditure of as much money, thought, and effort in effecting social controls by advancing social knowledge as had been spent in subduing the forces of physical nature.

The prediction of President James B. Conant of Harvard that the shock of atomic warfare might lead to a reassertion of religious sanctions was apparently realized. Einstein himself, a scientific humanist, testified to the impossibility of dealing wisely with the atomic era by logic alone, maintaining that only "the deep power of emotion which is a basic ingredient of religion" could point home the lesson. But few religious leaders asked for a moratorium on scientific research and its applications. In a notable report a special committee of the Federal Council of Churches refused to condemn science; it merely insisted on a change in the human heart. How the forces of ethics and religion were to bring about the moral control of technology for human purposes was a question to which no easy and satisfactory answer was at hand. Yet in sharply and insistently posing the question, religious leaders made a significant contribution.

In the midst of the early discussions Congress passed in 1946 the Atomic Energy Act, a highly significant event in the intellectual history of our time. The Act, despite misgivings on the part of influential groups in both the Congress and the military, broke with precedents in creating a government monopoly of atomic power hedged about with many prohibitions on private action; in refusing to hand over control to the armed forces; and in providing that as soon as national security permitted, knowledge of atomic energy for industrial and medical purposes would be shared reciprocally with other nations. The law also established an Atomic Energy Commission which, within these limitations, was to operate in a spacious frame. The counselor of the Senate committee that drafted the law declared that the Congress, in voting for the Atomic Energy Act, "in effect announced the end of the institution of the sovereign national state based on capitalistic free enterprise."[13] Never before in peacetime, continued this authority, had Congress vested any agency with "such sweeping authority and awesome responsibility." Whatever else was true, the Atomic Energy Act accepted the idea of planning the future use of a great undeveloped natural resource under government direction.

The Atomic Energy Commission, headed by David Lilienthal, whose appointment conservative senators fought bitterly, proceeded to organize and direct basic researches through contracts with universities, research institutions, and industry. The application of atomic energy to industry and the use of radioactive isotopes in medicine led one of its members to write that "only those of myopic vision today believe that the long-range developments of atomic energy will not in time contribute very greatly to man's general well-being and cultural advancement if he can but stir up the wisdom needed to handle the tremendous forces which have been unleashed."[14] The implications of the last clause in this statement might have been borne home by the much publicized tests of improved atomic bombs dropped on Bikini, a remote islet in the Pacific, for the military aspects of the Commission's work was in most circles regarded as paramount, in view of the tension between the United States and the Soviet Union which became acute after 1947.[15] The various proposals for international safeguards against the use of atomic energy for destructive purposes met with stubborn opposition in Moscow; and Russian proposals in turn found no favor in Washington.

Thus the Commission guarded closely its knowledge and its operations. This involved controls over the scientific workers on the various projects that the Commission sponsored and directed, which led some to protest that scientific work could not be carried on properly under hamstringing restrictions. These scientists emphasized the incalculable importance of freedom of communication in research as it had historically developed.

Before the Cold War, as the conflict between the United States and

[13] James R. Newman, "America's Most Radical Law," Harper's Magazine, CXCIV (May, 1947), 444.

[14] Richard F. Bache, "Research and the Development of Atomic Energy," Science, CIX (Jan. 7, 1949), 7.

[15] See Chapter 30.

the Soviet Union was called, became acute in the years after 1947, the Atomic Energy Commission pointed to the great public importance of having the citizenry acquainted with the basic facts of atomic energy and with some of its social, economic, and international implications. According to the press and to public opinion polls, this hope was not realized. A group of Nieman Fellows in Journalism at Harvard declared that the press was in large part responsible for this state of affairs: it had failed to do its part in educating the American people. That the public was not well informed was suggested by a series of polls. These seemed to indicate that "public indifference, widespread ignorance, inconsistent thinking, a failure on the part of the masses to understand what their leaders were doing, and blindness to the social and political implications of the atomic bomb" marked the mind of the "average" American.[16] A month after Hiroshima 70 percent of those responding to a poll thought the development of the atomic bomb was "a good thing"; seventeen percent took a pessimistic outlook. By 1947 two independent polls indicated that 38 percent of the respondents now felt that the world was worse off because somebody had learned to split the atom.

There may well have been a relationship between the Cold War with Russia and the growing uneasiness with which the American public eyed nuclear power. In August of 1945 public opinion was split practically even on the question, "Will the United States fight another war within the next 25 years?" By 1947 nearly three-fourths of the persons polled registered a pessimistic belief that the United States would have to fight another war within 25 years. The explosion at Hiroshima had created a psychological and moral crisis. There was widespread hope that this weapon of destruction would make war impossible. But events of the following months showed that even such an awesome weapon could not automatically insure a peaceful world or provide answers to social and moral problems.

Deeply impressed, even before the achievement of the atomic bomb, by the tremendous contributions of science and technology to the war effort, President Roosevelt in the autumn of 1944 addressed a now famous letter to American scientists asking advice on a series of far-reaching questions. How soon and how fully should the story of developments in science during the war be told? What was the responsibility

[16] *Annals of the American Academy of Political and Social Science*, CCLX (November, 1948), 209.

of the government for discovering and encouraging new scientific talent and for maintaining and advancing the remarkable achievements in science, medicine, and engineering? Dr. Vannevar Bush, to whom the letter was in reality addressed, after requesting replies from fifty scientists, consolidated their replies in a remarkable report, *Science, the Endless Frontier*. It outlined in engaging fashion the thesis that scientific and technological horizons appeared to be endless and that these could be most advantageously conquered if the federal government supported the natural sciences. Insisting that a political democracy was the type of government most conducive to original and significant work and that freedom of investigation must be assured, Dr. Bush proposed the establishment of a federally supported National Science Foundation.

In the debates in Congress over the bill that the Bush recommendations inspired, arguments pro and con indicated the controversial and precedent-breaking aspects of the proposal. Some pointed out that the United States had long excelled in the practical application of scientific theories, but that it had leaned heavily on Europe for the theories themselves. In view of the seeming bankruptcy of the Old World the time had come to dig deeply into basic problems. Moreover, some indicated that burdensome taxation had depleted the resources of many private foundations which in the past had liberally supported research. The importance of scientific work in the national defense was not overlooked; some noted that Russia, for example, was spending not only a higher proportion of its national income on research but dollar for dollar more than was the United States. On the other side some argued that government had no business to support scientific investigation, that such support would fetter research and increase bureaucracy, and that it marked too dangerous a departure from American tradition. Nevertheless, in 1947, Congress passed a bill establishing a National Science Foundation. President Truman vetoed it, not because he opposed the principle, but because he believed that the bill was deficient in several regards. Finally, in 1950, a modified bill became law. The National Science Foundation, with a director and a board of twenty-four members appointed by the President with the approval of the Senate, stimulated a rapid increase in federal support of research and education in the mathematical, physical, engineering, biological, and medical sciences.

Thus World War II and the problems asociated with its aftermath occasioned, for the first time in American intellectual history, sustained concern for the development of a national scientific policy. Science was explicitly recognized as a great national resource to be supported by government, and scientists played roles of importance in advising government agencies and in making decisions that influenced the national life and its future.

# 30 ✻ Dialogues in Our Time

> *The worldwide clash of communism and capitalism under-*
> *lies every major conflict between the nations and within*
> *them.*
>
> —CARL DREHER, 1947

> *We are passing through momentous times where no debate*
> *takes place even on crucial issues.*
>
> —WILLIAM O. DOUGLAS, 1962

In the years after World War II the intellectual and cultural life of the nation continued to be influenced, as it always had been, by movements of thought and by economic and political conditions across the seas. But now, from 1947 through the 1950s, world revolution and spectacular developments in military technology exerted an influence on American thought that was without precedent. To be sure, developments at home also influenced the intellectual and cultural life of the American Republic. Overarching in importance was the cult of widespread prosperity, the substantial basis for it, and the related consciousness of abundance. Most Americans, assuming affluence and prosperity to be continuing realities, paid little attention to Marxist and non-Marxist warnings that such might not be the case.

In a notable but little publicized address in the midsummer of 1962 Mr. Justice William O. Douglas of the United States Supreme Court, argued that the American public was no longer an active party to genuine debate on crucial issues, domestic and international. The apathy of "the submerged American" was in striking contrast, Douglas continued, to the widespread and sustained interest in national policy and destiny that Americans had shown both before and after the Civil War and in the first decades of the twentieth century. While Mr. Justice Douglas regarded the lack of debate as ominous for democracy and indeed for the whole American future, others took satisfaction in what they regarded as a fundamental agreement or American consensus. In their eyes this consensus united the Americans in the struggle with the Communist world.

A good deal of evidence supports the thesis that in the postwar world Americans had, to a considerable extent, foregone fundamental debate, especially in the field of foreign policy. Yet on this and on other matters dialogues, if not debates, did take place among intellectuals. Public opinion polls also indicated a wide spectrum of views on many issues.

## The Problem of Communication

If postwar America lacked the kind of debate that marked the discussion of slavery in pre-Civil War years, the difficulties of communication provide a partial explanation. The problem of communication existed on many levels. The most obvious involved the relation between the experts on the one side and the rank and file of the people on the other. The rapid development of knowledge and its increasing complexity made it ever more difficult for lay intellectuals, popularizers, and interpreters to keep up with and to understand what was taking place in the sciences, the social studies, and even the humanities. The transmission of information and understanding to the people through commercially dominated mass media—TV, radio, and the press—offered additional difficulties. Moreover, the continued and accelerated fracturing of the intellectual community itself into more and more complex and narrow specialties posed sharp problems of communication among scholars and investigators. All these difficulties were reflected in the fact that no intellectual leaders seemed able to systematize ideas and values in such a way as to command a widespread following. The years after World War II did not produce a representative group of thinkers or a commanding "school" of thought.

In no field of intellectual endeavor was the problem of communication so marked as in the natural sciences. In astronomy and the earth sciences, in the life sciences (especially genetics), and in the physical sciences revolutionary developments of extraordinary complexity continued to take place with breathtaking rapidity. Many scientists confessed that they were unable to keep abreast of new findings. The increasing complexity of science was further complicated by the bureaucratic context of research, whether it was sponsored by corporations, universities, or government. Official "security" regulations made international communication in many fields even more difficult, although the earth scientists of many nations succeeded in cooperating in such projects as the Geophysical Year and in Antarctic research.

Long before the British scientist and novelist C. P. Snow divided modern intellectuals into two "cultures," the scientific and the humanistic, Americans had pointed to the same phenomenon. In fact, Snow's theme was somewhat belied by the number of intellectuals who expressed concern over the chasm dividing the sciences and the more traditionally conceived culture at large. There was disagreement over how wide the chasm actually was, and over which side should make the greater effort to bridge it, but there was wide agreement that the problem was real and serious.

In view of the difficulties scientists themselves experienced in trying to communicate with one another, it is little wonder that laymen felt at sea when confronted even by "popularizations" of highly technical theories and findings. J. Robert Oppenheimer, a leading atomic physicist, after musing on the "mystique" of scientific discovery, doubted whether laymen could ever share the experience, or even approach a crude understanding of it. On the other hand, James B. Conant, a distinguished chemist who had sponsored general education during his presidency of Harvard, insisted that laymen could grasp the essentials of scientific method and discovery and showed in his writings on the history and the "strategy and tactics" of science that this could be done, at least in some cases.

Because of the ever more specialized nature of science, politicians and lay intellectuals who tried to influence public opinion had to depend on the statements of the scientific experts. Hence meaningful dissent over scientific policy could occur only when scientists themselves disagreed. When there was debate among scientists, as between Edward Teller and Linus Pauling over atomic testing and fall-out, this was mirrored by debate among other intellectuals and policy-makers. But when the experts seemed to be in substantial agreement, as on the subject of the exploration of space, there was little public disagreement. The lines of dissent, as well as its possibility, were determined by or among the scientific specialists.

The difficulties of communication and of more and more narrow specialization were also a matter of concern in the social sciences, which made increasing use of complex mathematical tools and psychoanalytical concepts. Even philosophy, which had always at least pretended to provide a viable kind of "summing up" of knowledge, seemed intent on specializing. Unlike John Dewey, who died in 1952, most philosophers seemed content to ignore the discussion of large, complex issues that were close to the center of public concern, and to concentrate instead on the technical problems of epistemology in the field of symbolic logic.

Intensive specialization and burgeoning bureaucracy in science and scholarship reflected what seemed to be the most complex and impossible problem of communication: the difficulty of arriving at any sort of understanding between the United States and the Communist world. There was a solid basis for the conflict between the two power blocs, but this was so continually clouded and confused by scientific and ideological considerations that it seemed no language could provide an efficient and unambiguous method of communication. The increasing complexity of life at home and the apparent impossibility of ending the Cold War created related anxieties in the minds of many Americans and helped give rise to strenuous campaigns to preserve in pristine simplicity the supposed virtues and ideals of "Americanism."

### Fear and National Loyalty

The Cold War stimulated a great deal of anxiety over the internal and external security of the nation. This anxiety was enhanced by the realization that in the hydrogen bomb first detonated in 1952, and in the new missiles and space satellites, man possessed for the first time in his long career weapons capable of destroying civilization and even organic life itself. When the Soviet Union's remarkable progress in military technology indicated that the United States no longer enjoyed its initial monopoly and in some ways lagged behind its foe, anxieties and fear reached an intensity that contrasted markedly with traditional American self-confidence.

In addition to the Cold War itself, several related factors explain the intensified emphasis on loyalty to Americanism and the increased fear of conspiratorial subversion on the part of Communists and their sympathizers. As Archibald MacLeish had noted, the country's mind had been divided as it fought World War II. Officially and in public statements the war was waged for a new and better world, but "privately and in our domestic reassurances, we fought to return to the world we had."[1] But neither of these contradictory worlds had issued from the struggle. Americans saw victory as the triumph of capitalistic democracy; but in Europe, Asia, and Africa the war released powerful revolutionary forces that threatened both the means by which victory over the enemy had been won and every fruit of that victory. In view of such disappointment and confusion, the drive against disloyalty, in the larger context of the Cold War, was understandable enough. Americans increasingly understood the challenge of the Soviet Union, aggressively imperialistic, uncompromising, bombastic, and baffling. But relatively few sensed the fact that in many foreign eyes the United States had come to stand for the continuation of an established way of life not entirely acceptable to that part of the world gripped by revolutionary dislocations and aspirations.

In part, the fear of, and concern over, subversion and disloyalty, pronounced after 1947, was a reflection of internal tensions about foreign policies. The isolationists—the term itself was seldom used—criticized what the Truman administration's leadership of the non-Communist world involved: recognition of interdependency; financial aid to rehabilitate broken economies; military aid to friendly governments to check internal Communist movements; and an active role in the United Nations. The Truman administration was also attacked from the left. The loose entente of liberals and radicals under the leadership of Henry Wallace bitterly denounced the administration for fomenting the Cold War and demanded cooperation with the Soviet Union on the ground that modern technology and common sense alike called for peace between the interdependent parts of the whole world, however marked the conflict of ideologies and interests might be.

In domestic politics Truman's stand on civil rights and his welfare policies associated with the New Deal did not go far enough to win

[1] Archibald MacLeish, "Victory Without Peace," *Saturday Review of Literature,* XXIX (February, 1947), 199.

the approval of the Wallace liberals and radicals, even had Congress more fully implemented them. On the other hand, Truman's domestic policies met with opposition from conservatives in his own party and with bitter denunciation from Republican critics of the New Deal. Disappointed at their failure to capture the presidency in 1948 and to nominate an old-guard leader in 1952, these Americans saw in the New Deal and in Truman's Fair Deal frightening steps towards socialism and communism at home; at the same time they regarded the administration as too "soft" toward communism abroad. To these critics, the Truman security measures adopted in 1947 to discover Communists or "Communist sympathizers" within the government, seemed far too mild. Such a conviction seemed to them confirmed with the disclosure of espionage (Julius and Ethel Rosenberg) and of perjury in regard to alleged espionage (Alger Hiss). If there were some rotten apples in the barrel, might there not be more? Such questions were insistently asked in an atmosphere of frustration, fear, and anxiety.

As the Cold War became intensified, the nation witnessed on both the official and unofficial levels a crusade against men and women deemed "un-American." The criteria for this stigma were far ranging and ill defined. In general, they included membership, past or present, in the Communist party or association with Communists or fellow-travelers; and commitment to measures that the Communists also favored—federal housing, socialized medicine, an end to racial discrimination.

On the federal level the State Department removed from overseas information libraries books by controversial authors. It refused passports to citizens whose views were suspect. Special loyalty boards investigated officials whose records did not square with current conceptions of loyalty and patriotism. In loyalty proceedings questions were sometimes asked which seemed, at best, irrelevant or foolish: "Do you believe in God?" "Do you read a good many books?" "What newspapers do you buy or subscribe to?" "How do you explain the fact that you have an album of Paul Robeson records in your home?" "Do you ever entertain Negroes in your home?"[2] Professor Chafee of Harvard, a leading authority on civil liberties, noted that a Negro bootblack in the Pentagon who had once given $10 to the defense of the Scottsboro boys was interviewed seventy times by the FBI before he was found worthy of shining the

[2] A. Powell Davies, "Loyalty Needs Better Friends," New Republic, CXXIV (February 4, 1952), 11.

shoes of Army officers. Investigating committees in both houses of Congress, in an effort to probe the dimensions of espionage, subversion, and loyalty, summoned not only government officials but also teachers, professors, ministers, authors, Hollywood producers, and actors. Some, out of a sense of guilt or a craving for regeneration or from satisfaction with the publicity thus won, confessed past affiliations. Others, unwilling to expose former associates now leading quiet lives, refused to answer questions about these men and women or about their own views, claiming either the rights of private conscience or the immunity guaranteed by the Fifth Amendment. Many citizens noted with alarm what they regarded as failure on the part of the investigating committees to observe due process. The seeming refusal of the FBI and officials with access to its files to evaluate the reliability of witnesses and the fact that those accused were sometimes not permitted to know the identity of their accusers and the precise nature of the charges against them suggested to some the beginnings of a police state.

Several states followed the federal example in setting up their own un-American investigating committees. Others required teachers to take special oaths indicating that they were members neither of the Communist Party nor of organizations regarded as subversive or questionable by the House Committee on Un-American Activities, the Senate Internal Security Committee, or the Department of Justice. With some dissent the Supreme Court upheld New York's Fineberg law which, broadly speaking, took such a position. At the University of California the refusal of twenty-two faculty members to take a special loyalty oath led to their dismissal; an action which they contested in the courts with ultimate victory, reinstatement, and compensation. As a result of either state or federal action or pressure from patriotic organizations or the decision of the governing authorities of the institutions, members of faculties in several colleges and universities were dismissed; the number cannot easily be determined.

In such a climate of fear and suspicion, it was easy for demagogues to make political capital. One of these, Joseph McCarthy, junior Republican Senator from Wisconsin, attracted world-wide attention, thanks to television, radio, and the press. McCarthy made most of his reckless charges on the floor of the Senate, where he was exempt from legal proceedings for libel. His tactics included reading from documents purporting to prove the disloyalty of men in public office or those who had once served as advisers to them, innuendo, attacks on highly placed and respected Army personnel and on the Democratic Party itself, whose record was stigmatized as "twenty years of treason." Adlai Stevenson, a man of learning with a serious interest in ideas and the hero of many American intellectuals, was a special object of attack, both before and after the presidential campaign of 1952 when McCarthyites dubbed intellectuals "eggheads." Especially persuasive to many of McCarthy's followers was the thesis of guilt by association. In speaking of those who had in some way at some time been associated with Communists, McCarthy declared that "the fact that these people have not been convicted of treason or of violating some of our espionage laws is no more a valid argument that they are fit to represent this country in its fight against communism than the argument that a person who has a reputation of consorting with criminals, hoodlums, gamblers, and kidnappers is fit to act as your baby-sitter, because he has never been convicted of crime."[3] If McCarthyism lacked a grassroots and a top-level organization and a genuine ideology, it was nevertheless a central fact in American life until 1954, when a Senate committee censured McCarthy for procedural improprieties and discourtesies.

In view of McCarthyite attacks on intellectuals—the most intense and far-reaching in American history—it is appropriate to consider some of the explanations scholars have advanced for the rise and power of McCarthyism. No one of the explanations of the phenomenon seems in itself adequate; in fact, most of them lack sufficient sustaining evidence to lift them above the level of hypotheses, but all of the explanations represent ideas and analyses advanced by serious students of American life.

Some thought McCarthyism was a belated example of the old Populist grassroots concern with "conspiracy" against the general welfare; the movement reflected the American penchant for sensational exposure of misdeeds and sin, for prying and indifference to privacy. Others, contending that in times of economic hardship the pursuit of clear-cut economic interests predominates, whereas in periods of prosperity like the 1950s the contest is one for vaguely defined social position, thought McCarthy personified the aspirations and frustrations of several groups: newly rich people who sought to achieve a sense of belonging by becom-

---

[3] Joseph McCarthy, *McCarthyism: The Fight for America* (The Devin-Adair Co., 1952), 79.

ing super-patriots; rural people who saw themselves being pushed ever further from the center of American life; and offspring of immigrants who needed assurance of their Americanism.

To still others McCarthyism was a neoisolationist phenomenon tied up with the Cold War. Support for this interpretation was found in the fierce hostility toward the "internationalism" of the Truman regime. Active membership in the world community led many to fear that the values and morals they had supposed to be uniquely American were threatened by contamination. It is indeed certain that the "one-worlders" bore a large part of McCarthyite criticism. This so-called neoisolationism became acute when President Truman involved the United Nations in a war to halt Communist aggression in Korea, a war, however, fought chiefly by American troops. (That a few GIs, captured by Communists, succumbed to "brainwashing tactics" was regarded as "proof" by Mc-Carthyites that American schools, under liberal-radical domination, had failed to inculcate an understanding of, and dedication to, true American principles.)

These explanations did not exhaust the hypotheses advanced. Some commentators, imbued with psychoanalytical doctrine, saw in the whole affair evidence that the American people were psychologically disturbed; the people, naïvely convinced that every problem could be solved speedily, felt that the Roosevelt and Truman administrations and the intellectuals associated with them were to blame for the failure to safeguard the nation's security. According to the psychological interpretation, rank and file McCarthyites, like many disturbed people, did not know what they wanted or why they acted as they did. They thought they were fighting communism, but all along were actually fighting the Eastern, genteel, aristocratic, intellectual Ivy League "Establishment." Such an explanation of McCarthyism illustrates the mid-century preoccupation of intellectuals with unconscious, nonmaterial drives and aspirations.

The position in the McCarthy episode of Americans who might be called conservatives is easier to describe than to explain. Broadly speaking, three attitudes can be noted. A few conservative intellectuals defended McCarthy publicly. Many others, though shocked at McCarthy's tactics, did not speak out. Perhaps their silence sprang from loyalty to the Republican party. Perhaps it reflected a feeling that McCarthy was after all publicizing a genuine and neglected danger. Perhaps their silence was related to fear: Any criticism invited the Senator's indictment that his critics were themselves obviously disloyal. A third group of conservatives joined with liberals in attacking McCarthyism as a violation of decency, constitutionalism, and American traditions of freedom of expression and association.

Liberal critics defended with vigor their claim that to dissent was essential to American traditions and well-being. They insisted on the basic difference between criticism and dissent on the one hand and communism on the other. In making this distinction no national spokesman played as important a role as Adlai Stevenson, who did much to make intellectualism politically feasible. In addition to individual protests in the anti-McCarthy movement, the American Civil Liberties Union and the American Association of University Professors valiantly defended the civil liberties.

In the discussion of loyalty which McCarthyism occasioned, few new ideas were developed. Among the exceptions was the theme that Professor Morton Grodzins of the University of Chicago worked out in his book *The Loyal and the Disloyal*. Grodzins brought to bear on the issue of loyalty and disloyalty much new knowledge about the nature of groups. He advanced the idea that disloyalty and treason are not primarily ideological in character but rather grow out of men's social circumstances. Disloyalty, for the most part, is the means by which one seeks, in the frustrations of loneliness, dissatisfaction, and alienation, more advantageous group affiliations. The argument was also made, with some supporting evidence, that the methods in vogue to detect traitors more often created new traitors than uncovered existing ones.

Some liberals took severely to task not only particular liberals but "liberalism" in general for having failed, from the 1930s on, to expose the true nature and dangers of communism at home and abroad and for having defended the civil liberties of Communists and conspirators. Such a failure, these critics argued, made it easy for McCarthy and his associates to identify liberals and Communists. There was some point, no doubt, to the charge. But it overlooked two considerations. One was the fact that McCarthyism attacked liberals for supporting social welfare measures and programs for peace, not merely because Communists also supported them but because, generally speaking, these ideas were anathema, if not to McCarthy himself, then to many of his followers. The second point was that a great many liberals had in fact vigorously opposed communism, at home and abroad, long before McCarthy was accepting support from Wisconsin "Reds" in his senatorial campaign against Robert M. La Follette, Jr.

The breaking of McCarthy's power represented a victory for fair play and for the freedom of dissent. Yet McCarthyism was not without serious effects. In many parts of the world it damaged the image of America as a champion of freedom. *McCarthyism* became, like *Quisling*, a term of derogation in some foreign vocabularies. The movement further diverted attention from important issues, both by pushing them into the background and by linking them with the whole matter of loyalty. Many believed that McCarthyism left scars on the reputation of innocent Americans, that it substituted suspicion for the American trust in human nature and in the other fellow, and that it discouraged discussion of controversial issues and participation in liberal organizations. Facts which would back up these contentions were hard if not impossible to come by. One empirical study maintained that McCarthyism intimidated students and teachers, another that it had little effect on academic readiness to speak and write on controversial issues. It is probable that for a time there was a relative reluctance to take open stands that might later prove embarrassing. But before the end of the decade American intellectuals and a minority of students were actively participating in controversial matters. American dissent was not dead.

What came in the late 1950s and early 1960s to be called the Radical Right was related to, and in a way a continuation of, McCarthyism. It accepted the same conspiratorial thesis: Liberals and radicals were promoting socialism and communism and betraying American institutions and values, especially free enterprise, individualism, patriotism, and Christianity. Like McCarthyism, the Radical Right was convinced that American foreign policy, linked as it was to the United Nations, put the interests of others before those of America, spent taxpayers' money on useless and even harmful foreign aid and cultural relations programs, and failed to provide enough military strength for an all-out war on potential Communist aggressors. In favoring the censorship of school books allegedly short on American patriotism and old-fashioned individualism and in denouncing or belittling scholars and social critics whose views were unacceptable, the Radical Right was anti-intellectual.

Hardly a movement (for it included many organizations, positions, and leaders), the Radical Right embraced the older "hate groups"—the fanatical anti-Semitic and anti-Negro organizations whose prejudices were being challenged as never before by countercurrents; well-established patriotic societies; some Texas oil millionaires who had supported Mc-Carthy; and members of the National Association of Manufacturers who were extreme champions of laissez-faire individualism. Ardent religious fundamentalists also identified themselves with the Radical Right. Some Army, Navy, and Air Force officers, until challenged, indoctrinated rank and file military personnel with ideas that were very similar to the tenets of the Radical Right. The military also lent a hand in the showing of such films as "Communism on the Map" and "Operation Abolition," films which many Americans regarded as distorted propaganda.

Three leaders symbolized varying nuances of the Radical Right. Senator Barry Goldwater of Arizona insisted that the government disengage itself from subsidizing agriculture and welfare, abandon the progressive income tax, give up cultural relations programs, and end foreign aid to countries not actively resisting communism. A second leader, William F. Buckley, Jr., agreed essentially with Goldwater but directed his efforts primarily to college undergraduates. Buckley, an able and sophisticated writer and speaker, became a nationally known figure through his book *God and Man at Yale*, an attack on the alleged atheism and socialism of the New Haven institution's faculty. In an early issue of *The National Review*, founded in 1956, he declared that "the liberals control just about everything" and that the time had come to restore American traditions and values. Buckley was a spirited and popular speaker on college campuses, where conservative clubs blossomed, many with their own subsidized periodicals. He also encouraged the Young Americans for Freedom, the national focus of the student Radical Right. Neither Goldwater nor Buckley approved of a third leader of the Radical Right—Robert Welch, a Massachusetts candy manufacturer and founder of the much publicized John Birch Society. Welch wanted to go further than Goldwater and Buckley by undoing everything that had happened in the field of social legislation since 1929. He actualized the idea of a secret, authoritarian organization, which McCarthyism had lacked, but which had forerunners in the Know-Nothing party and in the Ku Klux Klan. His book, *The Politician*, dubbed President Eisenhower, his brother Milton, Allen Dulles, head of the Central Intelligence Agency, and Chief Justice Earl Warren as parties to the Communist conspiracy. The John Birch Society, which included a few Congressmen, several columnists and publishers, and an unknown number of rank and file McCarthyites, assigned its members specific tasks in their communities, such as writing to congressmen, ferreting out "dangerous" liberals and textbooks and supporting the anticommunist "schools" which Fred Schwartz, an Australian physician-evangelist, organized. Other spokesmen for the extreme wing of the Radical Right included Dr. Billy James Hargis, a fundamentalist from Oklahoma, the veteran columnists Westbrook Pegler and Fulton Lewis, Jr., and the former dean of the Notre Dame law school, Clarence Manion.

## Military Security and Foreign Policy

In a period marked by fear, anxiety, and concern with communism, foreign policy and military security were inevitably major intellectual interests. While the McCarthyites and the Radical Right focused on the danger within the nation from the "Reds" and their liberal "allies," other groups concentrated on how best to meet the threat of an aggressive and doctrinaire Communist power bloc on the world stage. Even after World War II the world was divided into two contestants, each, due to the revolution in the weapons of destruction, with power to destroy the other. The central problem was that put by Albert Einstein: "The unleashed power of the atom has changed everything except our way of thinking. Thus we are drifting toward a catastrophe beyond comparison. We shall require a substantially new manner of thinking if man is to survive."[4]

Save for a small minority, Americans, like men and women elsewhere in the world were, however, unwilling to abandon the idea of national sovereignty and ultimate reliance on military force. Despite partial demobilization immediately after World War II, despite the dislike of most veterans for military caste and the benevolent authoritarianism of the armed forces, there were many indications that the military continued to influence thought and policy. The fear that another war might come only to find the country again unprepared, and the realization that only limited reliance could be placed on the United Nations for security explain the maintenance of peacetime conscription and the influence of

[4] Quoted by John H. Herz in *Nuclear Weapons and the Conflict of Conscience*, John C. Bennett, ed., (Charles Scribner's Sons, 1962), 16.

the military on scientific research, education, labor relations, industry, and foreign policy. It was not that ordinary citizens or intellectuals, even those most concerned with preparing America for another possible war, had any liking for military power in itself. It was rather that reliance on force seemed to most Americans the inevitable response to fear and insecurity and to the responsibilities of protecting freedom in the western world.

Intellectuals debated the basic assumptions underlying American foreign policy and whether this policy should be implemented by power or moral persuasion. Some insisted that foreign policy should rest on national interests while others insisted on a normative or ideal criterion.

Military policy from 1947 through the 1950s rested on a few basic ideas. One was the "containment" of communism within its existing territorial domain, an idea fathered by George Kennan, a foreign policy expert. "Containment" involved military strength and the willingness to use it, if Communist aggression could not be otherwise halted. Containment also involved building alliances in Europe, the Middle East, and Asia, with military and economic support to the governments of these countries. In addition to containment, official policy rested on the idea that economic and technical aid to the less industrialized but as yet noncommitted neutral nations was necessary to prevent these lands from succumbing to Communist aggression, intrigue, or high promises. Point 4, with successive but related programs, including President Kennedy's Peace Corps, implemented this basic idea.

In order to counteract Communist misrepresentation of American aims and policies as aggressive, warmongering, and selfishly capitalistic, and American civilization as too decadent to offer effective aid in the modernization of the newer countries, a program of cultural relations was made a part of official policy. This rested on the idea that minds could be won if it was demonstrated that Communist propaganda about America was untruthful. The idea was implemented by the establishment of the United States Information Agency and by the maintenance of information libraries in foreign capitals stocked with books and periodicals designed to give factual information about America and to further understanding of every phase of American life. The staffs of American embassies were also enlarged to include experts in various cultural and scientific fields. The government also supported the presentation abroad of American cultural achievements in theater, music, art, ballet, and technology. Under various programs foreign government officials, labor leaders, engineers, technicians, professional people, and students were invited to spend longer or shorter periods in America to observe at first hand American achievements and problems. At the same time American Fulbright scholars were chosen for overseas teaching and research with reference not only to their standing in their field but also their potential competence as cultural ambassadors.

These programs and the ideas on which they rested met with challenges from several quarters. The Radical Right, while denouncing the government for being "soft" on communism, opposed the policy of checking it abroad through foreign aid and cultural relations programs. It rejected the idea that Americans should view themselves as instruments for winning the world-wide war against poverty and disorder while at the same time arguing that not enough was being done by way of military preparation. The Radical Right, however, was not alone in criticizing the ideas and programs of the Truman, Eisenhower, and Kennedy administrations. Some felt it was hazardous thus to spend so large a part of the national income, both because of the difficulties of supervising foreign aid to reactionary and corrupt indigenous regimes, and because of the danger of taking on tasks larger and more complex than the economy could shoulder or than American leaders could profitably and effectively direct. Others questioned whether foreign aid and technical assistance might not speed the already too rapid adoption of new techniques and values. On a different level was a residue of the old and somewhat outworn idea of an "innocent" America becoming enveloped by craftier and unscrupulous villains (the "Bad Guy *v.* the Good Guy" theme).

The Soviet Union's detonation of hydrogen bombs and increasing evidence of competence if not superiority in missiles and satellites (Sputnik, 1957) shook Americans as nothing else in the arms race had done. Prominent political and military leaders began to talk more frequently about the impossibility of victory in modern war. Survival itself seemed a matter of grave uncertainty. "There are no alternatives to peace," President Eisenhower declared. If the sustained effort at negotiation for limitation of the new weapons failed, as it did again and again, and if no one could win a modern war, then some theory of deterrence was in order. How, in other words, might the enemy be restrained from beginning an atomic attack? Several theories were put forth. These ranged from a simple statement of limited war and disengagement from commitments to sophisticated formulae involving game theory and admitted imponderables. The "fiasco" of civil defense gave added relevance to the discussion but did not promote a consensus.

Deterrence had its critics. So did the whole atomic arms race, continued atomic testing, and the thorny business of international inspection. As might be expected the Quaker voice was heard both at home and abroad. In 1956 Clarence Pickett led a delegation of Friends to Moscow to try to open a way to understanding and common sense. The National Committee for a Sane Nuclear Policy sponsored by leading intellectuals, local Peace Walks, and the Women for Peace movement were all organized to protest official policy. The militancy of these and other organizations indicated new vitality in the argument against war. But, except for the increased sense of urgency, for the vision of total annihilation, and for the idea of passive resistance, there were few new developments in the peace movement. Absolute pacifism, an ideal long held by uncompromising foes of war, seemed to some a possible answer to an otherwise insoluble issue. In a world of uncertainty this was one example of many efforts in the continuing search for absolute answers.

## The Continuing Search for Absolute Values

In the later 1940s and throughout the 1950s the age-old quest for absolutes was pursued with fresh zest. Men perennially have longed for absolute answers and assurances, but several unsettling developments in the postwar years prompted intellectuals to intensify the search and expand its scope. On every side, man's world seemed more and more contingent, shifting, and elusive. The physical sciences almost daily revealed the uncertain character of what was once taken for granted as physical reality. In human affairs the perilous and increasingly complex quality of life in the age of the atomic bomb and the Cold War seemed to threaten every vestige of what men in other times had been able to count on as sure and dependable. Even the continued existence of human civilization was open to realistic doubt. It appeared obvious, in short, that something had gone seriously awry in the human career.

To many intellectuals the villain of the piece clearly seemed to be the relativism and liberalism dominant in American thought during preceding decades. Some Americans believed, for example, that the liberal concept of human nature as something plastic and changing was ultimately related to Nazi and Communist attempts to manipulate behavior. Closer to home, the concept of a plastic human nature was associated with attempts to control mankind, whether by well-meaning utopian psychologists such as B. F. Skinner of Harvard, or by mere "servants of power" on Madison Avenue. Intellectuals, shocked by such efforts at manipulation and by the vast amount of actual irrational behavior in the world, searched for a concept of human nature that was more realistic than the concept inherited from the Enlightenment and nourished in the Progressive period. They sought a view of man that would be true for all seasons and all places, and that would set limits, as did the Christian doctrine of original sin, to man's presumptions about his perfectibility and rationality.

To find the permanent beneath the flux, to seek out the true man, to discover some kind of enduring justice that might limit man's inhumanity to man, many intellectuals turned—as so often in the past—to religion. Literally interpreted Christian theology did not return to vogue; it had been too much discountenanced in the late nineteenth and early twentieth centuries. Instead, literary historians, critics, and other scholars often identified religious symbols and myths as the highest truths. The great religious myths, sharing common themes and associations, could assure men of the objective validity of their moral, political, and esthetic values, and could harmonize such diverse needs as those for freedom and order, religious satisfactions and rational thought. As Henry B. Parkes put it, the great religions, as sources of enduring social myths, sustained civilizations by revealing the outlines of an ideal justice inherent in the cosmos. Edmond Taylor in *Richer by Asia* (1947) attempted to delineate lasting values of the Orient which should be assimilated into a new world order. In a similar vein Vincent Sheean's *Lead Kindly Light* (1949) found a universal standard in Hindu philosophy as exemplified by Gandhi's teachings and actions.

Another indication of the search for absolute values was the favorable reception given to Arnold Toynbee's *A Study of History,* the twelfth volume of which appeared in 1961. Toynbee's slanted essays sought to prove that the growth of civilizations was a spiritual process and that historical decline was the result of spiritual failure. Toynbee found in a creative elite the key to the rise and prosperity of civilizations; the disappearance of such an elite could result only in decay and decline. The implication plainly was that the challenge to present-day civilization could be met only by a creative minority thoroughly committed to Christian values, faith, and ideals. These doctrinal overtones of Toynbee's work made it an instrument in the ideological warfare of the late 1940s and the 1950s—the conflict, broadly, between those who subscribed to reason, science, democracy, and the process of trial and error, and, on the other side, those who sought guidance and salvation in a return to philosophical or religious absolutes.

The essentially religious emphasis of the reaction against relativism and pragmatism was illustrated in a collection of essays which appeared in 1947 under the title *Our Emergent Civilization*. The contributors— among others Brand Blanshard, George P. Adams, F. S. C. Northrop, and George E. G. Catlin—rejected determinism, opportunism, and materialism. The ills of contemporary life, the fragmentation of the individual and the confusions and tensions, were, the essays argued, the result of the materialistic and irrational postulates of modern psychology and psychoanalysis, the "anchorless inconsistencies" of instrumentalism, the confusions of relativism, the worship of power implied in the mere acceptance of science. As a cure the group of essayists called for a morality that would do more than merely rationalize individual or group interest. They insisted that men abandon uncritical faith in science and material power, which in no case could save mankind from death and destruction. And they urged a renewed faith in the possibility of discovering and cleaving to absolute values and truths that could satisfy man's deepest emotional and spiritual needs. The best clues in the search for a better life for man lay in what religion at its best had always taught.

Direct and indirect support for this revival of supposedly enduring religious values came from many quarters. T. S. Eliot's erudite arguments for Christian tradition and authority continued to appeal to intellectuals. So did the insistence of the followers of Robert M. Hutchins on the "eternal verities" to be found in religion as well as in Aristotelian and Thomistic philosophy. Under the leadership of President Nathan Pusey, the Harvard Divinity School developed from a traditional home of Unitarianism into a distinguished nondenominational center for theological study. Its faculty included Catholic and Jewish scholars, as well as such leading Protestant theologians as Paul

Tillich. Reinhold Niebuhr, sometimes called the "Protestant Pope," gained a large following for his neoorthodoxy. Niebuhr criticized modern liberal Christianity for its sentimentalism, fundamentalism for its rejection of science, and Catholicism for turning to St. Thomas instead of to St. Augustine. He led a widening group of intellectuals in rejecting liberal, optimistic conceptions of human nature and history as entirely too innocent and unrealistic. Only a more realistic Christianity, he insisted, could have honest relevance to contemporary ethical and political problems. An interest in the Christian existentialism of Soren Kierkegaard, a nineteenth-century Danish theologian, reflected a related emphasis on commitment and a fear of moral drift and moral neutrality.

In Catholic circles spokesmen of influence included Thomas Merton, Cardinal Spellman, Bishop Sheen, the Jesuit Gustave Weigel, and the neo-Thomist scholar Jacques Maritain, who visited and taught in America and whose writings were thoughtfully received. Man had too long assumed, Maritain contended, that salvation could be found without religion. He argued that the old world order had collapsed largely as a result of materialism and the selfish competition inherent in secularism. A new world order must revivify "the power of Christianity in its temporal existence."[5] Much in the same spirit, the Catholic magazine *Commonweal* warned that "economic dogmas of liberalism . . . have so deeply permeated all our lives that we accept them unthinkingly as though they were moral or natural laws. . . . Yet this is a profoundly un-Christian nation."[6]

Jewish scholars and theologians also attracted attention in Gentile circles. Will Herberg's *Protestant, Catholic and Jew* (1955), essentially a sociological study, found common ground in all three religions within the frame of American culture. Speaking primarily to Jews, Mordecai Kaplan called for a strengthening of the elements of Hebraic faith that were meaningfully functional in an American environment. And long before Martin Buber of the Hebrew University in Israel visited the United States, his revival of Hasidic mystical enthusiasm found some response among both Jewish and non-Jewish intellectuals.

On the popular level interest in religion seemed to be expanding. An opinion poll in 1948 indicated that 95 percent of those sampled believed in God. In the same inquiry, 90 percent stated that they prayed, and

---

[5] Jacques Maritain, *Christianity and Democracy* (Charles Scribner's Sons, 1945).
[6] *Commonweal.* XLI (November, 1944), 55.

three-fifths expected to go to heaven. Whereas in Lincoln's day, only one out of five Americans belonged to a church, in the 1948 poll three out of five claimed membership in a church or synagogue.[7] Church membership grew with particular rapidity in the millennial and pentecostal sects. As rural folk migrated, especially from "poor white" Southern areas, to cities and to the Southwest Evangelist Billy Graham, though he did not achieve the following of some earlier revivalists, drew huge crowds. Books on religion, especially those which struck the inspirational and therapeutic note reached by Norman Vincent Peale, made the best-seller lists. At the first Eisenhower inauguration, "God's Float" headed the parade. Congress did its part by setting up a special room in the Capitol for prayer, by inserting the words "under God" into the pledge of allegiance, and by making the inscription "In God We Trust" mandatory on all coins. In 1962 the Supreme Court seemed out of step when it outlawed a simple, nondenominational prayer used in New York schools. But President Kennedy assured the nation that this decision merely provided new reasons to pray more in the home. Several congressmen responded by proposing to amend the Constitution to permit such religious practices in the schools.

Whether all this indicated more than a desire in a highly mobile society to be identified with a church for social advantage or for some other sociological reason, no one could say for certain. But many religious leaders took no satisfaction in outward evidences of piety and faith, and even deplored the frequent association of religion with personal success, prosperity, and health.

The issue of church-state relations continued to be so ambiguous as to throw little light on the question of how seriously Americans took their religious commitments. Actually, separation of church and state had never been a really consistent constitutional policy. In 1947 the Supreme Court seemed to press for a more absolute separation when it ruled that the Constitution prohibits not only any law that gives one religion advantage over others, but also any law that seeks to aid all religions equally. But in 1952 the court sanctioned the New York policy of releasing pupils during the school day for religious instruction. Still later, however, the court disapproved the New York school prayer. The whole issue was further complicated by the Catholic demand for public support of parochial schools, a demand that President Kennedy opposed

[7] *Time*, LII (November 1, 1948), 64–65.

as a violation of the separation of church and state. Americans in the 1940s and 1950s thus failed to resolve the old issues surrounding church-state relations, church-supported education, and religious observances in public schools.

In addition to the revival of interest in religion, both among intellectuals and plain people, there were secular expressions of the quest for absolutes. The movement that came to be known as the New Conservatism was the most sophisticated and, for a time at least, the most fashionable example. The movement was not unique to the United States. It was paralleled by similar currents in Europe, including the resurgence of political conservatism in England and the rise of Christian democratic parties on the Continent. The American New Conservatives, whose spokesmen included Francis Wilson, Russell Kirk, Clinton Rossiter, Peter Viereck, and John Hallowell, derived their thought frankly from Aristotle, St. Thomas, Burke, and such later thinkers as Brooks Adams, George Santayana, Paul Elmer More, Irving Babbitt, and T. S. Eliot. Rossiter and Kirk claimed to discover a continuous conservative tradition in the American past in Hamilton, John Adams, Calhoun, and a variety of thinkers from the later nineteenth and twentieth centuries. Peter Viereck modeled his conservatism in part on an interpretation of Metternich.

The spokesmen of the New Conservatism may have viewed Marxism as the principal enemy on the world horizon. But in the United States Marxism seemed to have lost its appeal, so the New Conservatives focused their attack on liberal democracy, relativism, and instrumentalism. While there were individual differences among them, their beliefs were summed up adequately in Viereck's definition of conservatism: "The conservative principles *par excellence* are proportion and measure; self-expression through self-restraint; preservation through reform; humanism and classical balance; a fruitful nostalgia for the permanent beneath the flux; and a fruitful obsession for unbroken historical continuity."[8] Thus, in human affairs, social growth should be organic and slow, institutions ought not be lightly cast aside or modified, and proper social change should preserve traditional morality.

John Hallowell's *The Moral Foundation of Democracy* (1954) was perhaps the most intellectually sophisticated expression of the New Conservatism. Hallowell went back to the classical realism of Aristotle:

[8] Peter Viereck, *Conservatism Revisited* (Charles Scribner's Sons, 1949), 6.

Beneath all apparent flux and change is order and permanence. This is true in political ethics as well as in nature. Therefore, the only true basis for society is a set of absolute standards of behavior. True democracy cannot be a mere art of compromise in a context of majority rule, Hallowell argued. Such a conception of government leaves out the "spirit" and "morality" which must pervade a really good society. Modern liberal and "positivist" governments deny the absolute standards and values which alone can provide the foundations of society. The only protection against despotism from such governments, Hallowell claimed, lies in a reassertion of a transcendent moral order, best expressed in Platonic and Aristotelian humanism.

Several prominent intellectuals, while not identifying themselves explicitly with the New Conservatives, shared many of their views. Walter Lippmann, for example, became a spokesman for the idea of natural law and the necessity of consensus among the members of a society, at least on controversial public issues. In *The Public Philosophy* (1955) Lippmann criticized the radical individualism implicit in some liberal concepts of society, and held up as a model citizen the Socrates who had been willing to sacrifice his life to what he believed to be the good of the state. In the historical guild Samuel Eliot Morison called for a conservative interpretation of American history; several of his younger colleagues were ready at hand. The result of their effort—what one historian called "homogenized history"—played down conflict and emphasized continuity and consensus in the American past. This version of the national story was a sharp revision of the liberal interpretations of Beard, Parrington, and others, who had taught that such democracy as America had achieved was sometimes the fruit of bitter conflict.

The writings of the New Conservatives, and the many other products of the quest for absolutes, did not go unchallenged. An occasional critic like Horace Kallen pointed out that in periods of Western history when "spiritual" and "rational" philosophies had been dominant, cruelty and intolerance had also been common. Or a scientific humanist from time to time insisted that human knowledge was the only knowledge, and that the only true "religion" for man lay in his own creative efforts to express "his highest insights into the meaning of the evolution of life on earth and the development of mind and society."[9] It may even be that the

---

[9] Oliver L. Reiser and Blowden Davies, "Religion and Science in Conflict," *Annals of the American Academy of Political and Social Science*, CCLVI (March, 1948), 138.

proponents of relativism, science, and trial-and-error democracy were in a majority all through the postwar years. But it is nonetheless apparent, from the vantage point of the early 1960s, that a growing preoccupation with absolutes was one of the most significant intellectual developments of the preceding decade and a half.

### Democracy and Power

A concern with the problems of power in the economy and the political and social structure, with implications for democracy, also figured in the intellectual dialogues of the 1950s. The discussion of both power and democracy took place within a context of what was generally regarded as an age of prosperity and even affluence.

Corporation executives, public relations spokesmen, and academic intellectuals defended large-scale business by arguing that it was both democratic and beneficent. Big business was democratic because management no longer commanded but, in the interest of morale and the efficient functioning of the machine, allowed labor to participate in decisions. Motivation research revealed what complaints the workers had, what they wanted, while management went far (according to the argument) in meeting these demands. Corporate business was also democratic because of wide participation in stock ownership and because competition was maintained through diversification. The incorporation of many socialist aims in the mixed capitalist-government economy was also cited as an evidence of democracy. Professor John Galbraith in *American Capitalism* was aware of the vast power of the new corporate organization, but he maintained that this power was checked by countervailing forces—labor unions, government, and voluntary associations. The association of corporations with democracy was also implied in the argument that business was no longer a separate entity in the totality of America, but an integral part of it. The alleged democratic character of the great corporation did not, moreover, militate against its high-level efficiency: It was better suited than small enterprise to serve the public through sustained research in ways of improving and marketing the product. Inflation and depression were no longer inevitable: Free enterprise under corporate auspices provided the necessary base for a continuing diffusion of well-being, prosperity, and democratic freedom. So it was claimed.

Yet there was dissent. Able scholars in a volume edited by E. S. Mason of Harvard pictured the modern corporation as dominating not only the whole of the economy but virtually all of society and culture as well. Studies by Gardner Means likewise presented a picture of great corporate power which seemed to support the traditional democratic tenet that big business was incompatible with individual freedom.

Nor was dissent confined to scholarly books. On a popular level Vance Packard's best seller, *The Hidden Persuaders* (1957), piled up sensational examples of the ways in which corporation motivation research manipulated people's images and opinions not only about their dollars but about their adjustment to working and general living conditions.

The stress on organization, teamwork, on taking one's cue from the group provided William H. Whyte, Jr., with a theme widely publicized in *The Organization Man* (1956). Whyte argued, somewhat in the manner of David Riesman in *The Lonely Crowd*, that Americans were giving up their traditional belief in self-reliance, in individual salvation through work, thrift, competitive struggle, entrepreneurship (the Protestant ethic with its "inner-directed personality") and accepting in its place the cult of "belongingness," the doctrine, so congenial to corporate structure, that the group is the source of creativity (the "other-directed personality"). In Whyte's view the new tendency or cult exalted bureaucratic mediocrity and discouraged creativity in every aspect of daily life, in and out of business circles. To be sure, Whyte's focus on the young executive limited his indictment to a small segment of American society. Moreover, Whyte was indicting not so much a sharp change in American ideology as an ad hoc way of dealing with the problems of big organizations (business, labor, education, government). Still his book raised important questions about power and democracy. Insofar as the individual was absorbed into the organization, insofar as power in decision-making was surrounded by the make-believe of general participation, then the "free individual," so central in the democratic faith, was considerably shrunken.

As if to refute these indictments, big business executives and their spokesmen went further in indicating the essential democracy and humanism of great corporations in the age of prosperity and affluence for which they were in so large a part presumably responsible. The Bell Telephone Company and other corporations sent a group of their young executives to universities where they studied, not business administration, but Joyce's *Ulysses*, the *Bhagavad-Gita*, and the *Tales of Genji*. Other great corporations took similar steps. Also indicative of the social-mindedness (if not the democracy) of great corporations was the striking development of philanthropy. Sometimes candidly admitting to stockholders the tax advantage of large contributions to welfare, the arts, and higher education, corporation spokesmen also publicized these gifts as proofs of their good citizenship and their concern for raising the cultural as well as the economic level of the population. Nor was this all. In response, perhaps to John Chamberlain's call on novelists to present the businessman more sympathetically than had been done in the past, Sloan Wilson's *The Man in the Gray Flannel Suit* and Cameron Hawley's *Executive Suite* and *Cash McCall* humanized corporation executives, identified them with suburban living, and gave inside views of how big money was made and spent. Nor did historians lag much behind novelists. Allan Nevins defended John D. Rockefeller as a great, constructive statesman. Other historians also presented favorable views of the titans of industry. Thus the reaction against the Populist outlook was evident.

In the sphere of political inquiry scholars studied voting behavior with new techniques and noted how traditional ideas about democracy were challenged by shifts of population to urban areas and to the Far West as well as by the growing importance of the Negro vote. Samuel Lubell in *The Revolt of the Moderates* (1956) argued that in view of the expanding middle class much of the conventional political terminology (liberalism, conservatism) was meaningless. Although apparently not destined to capture the party, the Modern Republicanism formula of President Eisenhower likewise represented a reaction against the conflicts of "extremes," which many old-fashioned historians thought had aided the development of American democracy. Daniel Bell, a former socialist, maintained that the great drive for equality which had informed or inspired a good deal of political behavior in the past had, in the new age of abundance and affluence, lost much of its force. Widely read political novels also suggested that traditional ideas of democracy were no longer valid. Edwin O'Connor's *The Last Hurrah*, for example, revealed how and why the tricks of the old-time political boss did not work in the welfare state. Or again, Allen Drury's *Advise and Consent* offered an "inside view of manipulation, pressure, and chicanery in high places" in the making of an important decision while idealizing procedural integrity on the part of certain Senate leaders.

The implications for democracy of the corporate mass media were also debated. Particularly disturbing was the ability of Madison Avenue and the radio and TV networks to create a favorable public image of a candidate for office. In the 1956 presidential campaign Adlai Stevenson observed the inappropriateness of a candidate for the country's highest office being "built up" in the way advertisers publicized a breakfast cereal. To many observers and students the whole apparatus of public relations and mass media might be characterized as "the engineering of public consent" and "the Invisible Sell." Also, the cult of personality, which the mass media facilitated, tended both in the case of Eisenhower and of Kennedy to detract from the serious consideration of political issues.

The mass character of communication together with the complexity of the "big issues" explained in part what appeared to some to be the apathetic political attitude of many Americans. The implications for a democratic sharing of decision-making were obvious. On the other hand, there was a feeling that, if it was impossible to influence decisions in the national arena, the individual might still make his voice heard and his actions count in the local community, especially in the ever-expanding suburbia.

In the discussion of democracy as in that of the economy a major focus of attention was the problem of power. Social scientists analyzed institutions (labor unions, corporations, government) and communities in terms of power structure. C. Wright Mills's controversial and stimulating book, *The Power Elite*, argued that, particularly since World War II, an interlocking directorate of war lords, corporation chieftains, and big politicians dominated the country, in part by skill in using the rhetoric of liberalism when it no longer corresponded to reality, and in the main by exploiting the actualities of the power structure itself. Since, Mills further argued, such concepts as honor, integrity, and ability have only such content as someone chooses to give them, modern America was morally a primitive jungle. The picture in Mills's view was even darker: neither the middle classes nor what passed for pluralism counted as any real check on the power of the new elite. Many critics thought that the book proved too little and too much. It offered too "pat" an analysis, it underplayed the influence of the voting public and the realities of the democracy Mills regarded as defunct. But others thought that his argument made sense. Some years later Richard H. Rovere, *The New Yorker's* witty and clever Washington correspondent, lent some support to the Mills's thesis in a satire and parody. *The Establishment* was defined as "those people in finance, business, and professions who hold the principal measure of power and influence in this country, irrespective of what administration occupies the White House."[10] If there was even some truth in such a position, the implications for democratic theory were serious.

## Assertions of Democracy

Yet liberalism and democratic faith were by no means dead. Of the many reassertions and reorientations of the liberal position, two may be regarded as representative.

Arthur M. Schlesinger Jr.'s *The Vital Center* (1949) was acclaimed by reviewers for its brilliance, lucidity, sophistication, and vigor. Schlesinger saw liberty threatened by several dangers: by the conviction that the world's new problems could be solved only through such extreme measures as fascism or communism; by the drift toward the omnipotent state; by idealistic but bigoted abstractions; and, somewhat paradoxically, by the tendency in many conservative circles to deny the reality and the importance of the sort of conflict, which, historically, had generated freedom. But both the Right and the Left, Schlesinger contended, had failed to articulate the economic and social values they had promised. *The Vital Center*'s program for reinvigorating democratic liberalism called for a shift in alignments, not Left against Right, but the center against the extremes. If, as some maintained, the critique of the extremes was more persuasive than the program for present and future, *The Vital Center* was nevertheless an eloquent plea for freedom as a fighting faith, a call for democracy to recharge its moral batteries.

Like *The Vital Center*, Charles Frankel's *The Case for Modern Man* (1956) was a tract for the times. It was also more than that. It called on liberals to stop giving ground to their critics who blamed all the woes of mankind on liberalism and democracy. But the Columbia philosopher went further. He examined the intellectual factors in the erosion of liberal and democratic thought, selecting, for this purpose, the work of Mannheim, Toynbee, Maritain, and Niebuhr. In different ways these thinkers had denied the validity of the ideas and assumptions of liberal-

[10] Richard H. Rovere, *The Establishment* (Harcourt, Brace and World, 1962).

ism and democracy; had denied the sufficiency of secular morality, the "unlimited perfectibility of man," the possibility of an objective truth and of impartial judgment in the social studies, and the feasibility of reconstructing society through piecemeal reform. Frankel made clear the historical distortions underlying these critics' ridicule of the idea of "the unlimited perfectibility of man" (which no liberal maintained), and took note of the blindspots in their assessments of man's failures and limitations.

On the positive side Frankel emphasized the dignity of man, the reality of human freedom and of man's rational capability. He called for a revival of Emerson's open-minded conception of human potentialities. Abundant evidence demonstrated the capacity of man to take risks, to make choices, to learn from experience, and to apply what he learned in the quest for social justice and order. True, no one person can learn or experience everything: There must thus be some tentativeness in what one believes, some tolerance, some compromise. But the individual cannot look to the state to fulfill his highest needs: The state, which can only provide a framework inside of which these can be pursued, must always be scrutinized in terms of how well it performs this function. Social inventiveness, sorely lacking and desperately needed, was the essence of the liberal and democratic approach to problems. Inventiveness was preferable, at least in America, to reliance on tradition, to affirmations of inevitable and continuous frustration, and to anguish over sin. Frankel did not present a precise program, and did not in fact advance any ideas really new, but he pointed up the limitations of liberalism's critics and outlined what, in the revolution of modernity, the human imagination must envisage, demand, and seek.

The most vigorous and telling reassertions of democracy, however, fell within the sphere of race relations. The stimulus which World War II gave to democratizing race relations was intensified during the Cold War, for the Communists found it easy to publicize sensationally every incident of racial injustice and thus to further among the non-white peoples of the world the image of America as hypocritically professing democracy and behaving in flagrantly undemocratic ways. During the Truman administration desegregation in the armed forces and in government exemplified the growing feeling that at least on the official national level racial segregation must give way to the equality that the Constitution required. More dramatic was the unanimous decision by which the Supreme Court in 1954 held that segregation in local public schools on the basis of race alone denied the equality of the laws as guarteed by the 14th amendment. In taking this position the Court reversed its decision of 1896 that the requirements of the Constitution were met if states and communities provided for the Negroes "separate but equal" facilities and services. This momentous decision did not, to be sure, bring an immediate end to segregated schools. According to the *Southern School News* four years after the decision only 15 out of 1354 biracial school districts in the South (excluding the border states) had begun or completed desegregation. Tension, turmoil, violence, and what was termed massive resistance to the Court's decrees indicated a stubborn, determined will on the part of governing white elites in many parts of the South to maintain what they were pleased to call "the Southern way of life."

Such resistance rested on deep-seated prejudices, traditions, and convictions. Thomas R. Waring, expounding the position held by many of his fellow white Southerners, made much of putative differences between the races in home environment, marital habits, intellectual development, health, and tendency to crime. While most Southern whites, according to Waring, favored the improvement of the Negro and actually lived for the most part in friendly contact with them, few parents were "willing to sacrifice their own offspring in order to level off intellectual differences in this fashion." Such an attitude, Waring rightly noted, was not unknown in the North. The segregationists also pointed out that, at least in the early stages of the turmoil stirred up by the Supreme Court decision, the leadership in the South for desegregation came from the National Association for the Advancement of Colored People, an organization that white Southerners commonly regarded as an "outside" affair. The NAACP, Waring added, seemed more interested "in forcing the Negro into the white man's company than in equipping him to qualify for such association."[11] Such ideas, however, were far more temperate than the extreme racism expressed by the "hate" groups of the Radical Right and the White Citizens Councils or by the Louisiana Catholic woman who, in holding that the Bible sanctioned racial inequality, defied her Church.

On the other hand many Southern whites dissented from all such

[11] Thomas R. Waring, "The Southern Case Against Desegregation," *Harper's Magazine*, CCXII (January, 1956), 42.

ideas. To some, the significant thing was what segregation did to human relations and personality. Lillian Smith's passionate novels continued to reflect this view. Guilt feelings, conscious or unconscious, on the part of the whites was a note often present in the work of William Faulkner, while Robert Penn Warren retreated from early views that savored of racism. To still others segregation was doomed no less than the whole heritage with which it was enmeshed—the one-crop share system, the dominance of the Democratic party, the political exploitation of prejudice and, above all, the depressing poverty of many whites as well as of the mass of Negroes. Such a position was developed by Harry S. Ashmore, editor of the *Arkansas Gazette*, who opposed Governor Faubus' reliance on state troops to keep a handful of Negro children from attending a Little Rock high school. Still another view was brilliantly defended by C. Vann Woodward. This distinguished Arkansas-born historian documented the thesis that, contrary to a wide belief, Jim Crowism was a late phenomenon. It was, actually, foisted on the South only in the late 1880s and early 1890s and, Woodward argued, behavior that law spawned or nurtured, could be changed by law.

The torrent of words that flowed in the now bitter, now reasonable dialogue over race relations expressed deeply felt emotions and firmly held ideas. The Black Muslim movement reacted to racial injustice by preaching, especially to the impoverished urban Negroes, a doctrine of complete segregation, hatred of the dominant whites, and black superiority. In his Kafka-like novel *The Invisible Man*, Ralph Ellison indelibly set forth the bewilderment, the self-torture, the violence, the rape, and the riot which make it impossible for a Negro, by virtue of his race and rearing, to belong to any level of existence at all. Another gifted writer, James Baldwin, revealed to many readers, in novels and essays, the psychological complexity of race relations: the suspicion and hatred Negroes feel for whites; the impossibility of achieving any true rapport between the races as all whites, even those honestly professing equality, are bound by unconscious prejudice; the helplessness of the alienated, rebellious Negro in the face of the irrational white power under which he has to exist; and the necessity of trying to break through binding stereotypes and sociological abstractions.

The new fight in the South for racial justice can be understood only in terms of the social base on which it rested and of the ideas associated with it. For the first time large numbers of rank and file Negroes, including college students, challenged the wealthy, class conscious, and white-oriented older leadership that had paid little attention to poverty as a legitimate grievance and that believed legal victories would ultimately solve the problem of discrimination. Invoking the Declaration of Independence and the Christian message that the disinherited should also live, the new movement, largely spontaneous and strengthened by the support of courageous Southern whites, developed techniques hitherto unknown or seldom used in the fight to make the Negro a first-class citizen. The economic boycott of buses and of stores refusing to serve Negroes at lunch counters, the sit-in technique by which Negroes refused to leave even though they were, according to custom, refused service, and the defiance of other barriers to dignity and freedom rapidly caught on. Those taking part in these new militant and direct nonviolent tactics risked insult, imprisonment, and violent attack.

The Reverend Martin Luther King, Jr., became the first national spokesman for the new revolt. His personalist philosophy, developed during his theological studies at Boston University, was reenforced by his admiration for Gandhi's doctrine of massive and passive resistance to oppression, injustice, and evil. The idea of nonviolent resistance, King believed, could lift the power of love above the interactions of individuals and abstractions and turn it into a powerful social force. This remarkable Negro leader advocated passive resistance and noncooperation through boycotts, picket lines, and protest prayer meetings with militant singing based on traditional hymns and spirituals. Such action, King claimed, was not designed to widen the gulf between the two races, but to build mutual respect, trust, and friendship through appeals to conscience and demonstrations of spiritual strength. Many understood the philosophical aspects of King's message only vaguely. But there could be no mistake about the persistence, self-sacrifice, and courage of the freedom-riders and the boycotters who fought for equal rights in transportation facilities, at lunch counters, in schools, and at booths for registering voters.

The bombing of the houses and churches of Negroes, including those of King, the continued resistance on the part of White Citizens Councils in the Deep South, and the official resistance of governor Barnett and a considerable part of the population of Mississippi to a court order in 1962 requiring admission of a Negro student to the state university suggested the intensity of opposition to integration by decree. Yet in the early summer of 1962 Gunnar Myrdal believed that the swift progress made recently by the Negro was astonishing when measured against the preceding sixty years of stagnation. The tragic yet in some ways heartening events in Little Rock, New Orleans, Knoxville, Greensboro, and Montgomery served, Myrdal went on, to stir the conscience of the American people, to help make it impossible, morally and politically, to defend much longer a fixed position of inferiority for the Negro citizen. The author of *An American Dilemma* predicted that "with the rising levels of education the hold of [the Constitutional ideal of equality] will be continuously strengthened."[12] If Myrdal was right, then democratic ideas and values of enormous dynamic force were at work in a period of reputed complacency and conservatism.

## The Examination of American Civilization

Although by no means a new phenomenon, probing the nature of civilization in the United States formed a major part of the cultural dialogues of the 1950s. The intensity with which the subject was pursued can be understood only when the prevailing sense of prosperity of the time and the tensions of the Cold War are kept in mind. The self-consciousness of the search for so-called "national purpose" was reflected in discussions by *Life* and the *New York Times* and by the President's Commission on National Goals. The ambiguities and complexities of the inquiry were admitted, but the discussion did not come adequately to terms with the fact that Americans had never agreed on national goals and that, despite the current vogue of the consensus theory, the disagreements were not yet resolved. What the Luce publications and others liked to call the "American Century" was not, so far, a time in which assumptions were shared by the whole society.

The evaluations of American civilization ranged over a wide scale. At one extreme a small group maintained that American civilization had become soft and sick. Bernard Cannon Bell, indicting *Crowd Culture* (1954) was sure that it had. John Steinbeck was of like mind. Writing to Adlai Stevenson, Steinbeck declared that if he wanted to destroy a nation he "would give it too much and . . . would have it on its knees, miserable, greedy, and sick." One commentator felt that it was all but

[12] *New York Times*, June 9, 1962.

impossible to test Steinbeck's charge, for no sound judgments could be made on the basis of mass media reports of sensational crime, payola, labor racketeering, and instances of lack of morale among GIs in the Korean War. Not too much importance was to be attached to the campus popularity of Ayn Rand's message of cynical egotism. Nor was the night club and TV vogue for the "sick humor" dispensed by Tom Lehrer, Mort Sahl and dozens of others to be taken too literally: the genre's gruesome and neurotic morbidity might be merely a shock tactic, and there was no evidence that it represented the actual values of the audience which applauded it.

Yet there was much to indicate that a great deal was wrong. The alarming evidence of juvenile delinquency, expressing itself in drug addiction, sex crimes, and gang murder, could not be brushed aside. In the discussion of this alarming phenomenon (by no means confined to the United States) J. Edgar Hoover, head of the FBI, advocated getting tough as the best remedy, and many agreed. Others, influenced by Freudian theory and by psychiatric training, pointed to the brutality, alienation, and rejection which many of the delinquents had experienced. Others emphasized conflicts in American culture. Children were taught to be cooperative, honest, law-abiding: this, the lesson ran, was the way to success and happiness. But when they looked they saw ruthless competition, moral obtuseness, and defiance of the law as in fact contributing to "success." Related to this position was Paul Goodman's thesis that a society failing to provide useful and creative work for teenagers must expect them to grow up as absurd as the society itself was in fact.

Interest in sex was of course nothing new. But preoccupation with its physical aspects, the divorce of sex from love and from the larger meaning it could have for life and human destiny seemed to indicate a sick society. Nor was the exploitation of sex in commercial advertising and in sensational paperbacks (with admixtures of sadism and violence), the only evidence for believing that sex had pushed other values into the background. Gifted writers—Norman Mailer, John O'Hara, James Gould Cozzens, John Updike, James Baldwin, Nelson Algren and the renowned William Faulkner, to name but a few—either displayed distortions of what had seemed to many a wholesome role for sex or suggested that the exceptional was the universal. "The fact is," observed one critic, "that our novelists, floundering in their freedom, are all too liable to become bogged down in a mess of anatomical and physiological detail."[13] Hollywood, formerly bound to artificial romanticism by its own censorship, ventured to make films that dealt with types of sex behavior long taboo.

Yet it is by no means certain that these developments indicated any sickness in the American mind. The much discussed report of Professor Alfred C. Kinsey of Indiana University claimed, on the basis of an investigation of 5300 white males, that male sex behavior had in fact been relatively stable for at least two generations. The report was followed by another dealing with the sex life of a sample of women which suggested an increase in premarital intercourse but concluded that in the incidence, frequency, and type of sexual outlet, biological factors, along with age, social status, and educational background, played a major role. That many prevailing legal and moral contentions were not geared to the actualities of sex behavior was apparent. The implication seemed to be that the individual's sex needs were immutable and constant, and that society had best revamp conventions to give them ample outlet. Some 250,000 copies of the first Kinsey report, and a half a dozen books about it, became best sellers. (Possibly the reports were more widely talked about than read.) They were criticized on the ground that the samples were not adequately chosen, and that the statistical treatment of the data left much to be desired.

Nor were these the only counts of the indictment that American civilization was "sick." The figures on mental illness seemed alarming. The assumptions of most psychiatrists that mental disturbances had greatly increased and that the increase was the result of dislocations and tensions in modern civilization needed to be further tested, if possible, by statistical measurements and controls; but the fact that the assumption was made and so widely and uncritically accepted was itself significant. The growing concern with mental illness was also reflected in the theater, films, radio programs, and church counseling services. Dr. William C. Menninger called on society to take greater responsibility for mental health. He pleaded not only for better-supported institutions for the mentally ill, but for the inclusion in public health programs of preventive as well as remedial psychotherapy. Recognizing that relation-

[13] Ben Ray Redman, "Sex and Literary Art," *American Mercury*, LIII (October, 1946), 412–447.

ships exist between mental disturbance and social and economic conditions, Menninger called for intensive research on the nature of these relationships.

The examples used to establish the sickness of American society needed to be seen in perspective. As Arthur M. Schlesinger noted, there have been several periods of moral slump in American history each of which was followed by a rebound. Such a rebound, he noted, seemed already to be setting in, in the late 1950s. This was at least a hopeful judgment.

Other dialogues about American civilization, while serious and critical, yielded more limited conclusions than the indictment of American society as soft and sick. Those using the language of traditional economic democracy and social justice noted that despite prosperity, 14 percent of consumer units had an annual income of less than $2000 and that educational opportunity, facilities for health and recreation, housing, and many services associated with the American standard of living were still inadequately distributed. Data at hand indicated that the rate of economic growth in the United States was considerably less than in certain European countries only recently regarded as dependent on American bounty to avoid collapse. Evidences that the Soviet Union had passed America in space exploration were not easy to accept in a country that had long boasted of its superiority in all aspects of technology. That America really had a built-in capacity for innovation and for meeting new problems creatively, was both proclaimed and questioned. Few who aired their ideas seemed to be moved when George Kennan asked why it was necessary for a qualitative civilization to be so deeply concerned with the rate of economic growth. A larger number seemed to be impressed by John Galbraith's contention that the trouble lay in an overemphasis on the production of consumer goods and that the solution was to be found in vast and accelerated expenditures for education, health, public housing, recreation, and the arts. But Congress seemed more concerned with the smooth operation of the economic status quo, with balanced budgets, and with appropriations for military defense. These and related discussions, together with a growing awareness of the poor image of the United States entertained in many foreign circles, made it clear to thoughtful Americans that affluence and modernization created their own problems.

Another debate concerned the sticky issue of conformity versus individualism. The prevailing European image was of an America dominated by conformism, an America of the mass man and the mass media, of standardized and interchangeable parts in every segment of the national machine. Many American intellectuals shared this image and lamented.

The explanations offered for the putative mass conformity varied considerably. To some, the anonymity of urban life corroded true individuality. To others, the rapid development of automation not only promised to relieve human beings of routine but to depersonalize the individual worker by replacing much of his initiative and judgment with machines that operated machines. When educators hailed the invention of machines for teaching school, the principle of automation seemed to threaten the personal relations of teacher and pupil—a surviving stronghold of individuality. Still others felt that the manipulation of human behavior by public relations experts on Madison Avenue through the mass media was the root of the evil. It was also common to lament the prevalence on TV of Westerns, standardized to enable the otherwise zestless onlooker to identify himself with the hero and an America of individual initiative and strength that was now but a memory. The structured exploitation in the mass media of sex, the endless programs of horror and violence, occasioned criticism both on grounds of morality and conformity to stereotype. Science fiction paperbacks, which glorified gadgets without exemplifying a truly scientific conception of causation and of the universe, likewise seemed to some observers to conform to a pattern. So, also, did "canned music" whether on radio, TV or the jukebox, and the widely circulated so-called comic strips. Some social critics saw in all these products of mass conformity the desire of a business-dominated culture to profit from catering to the lowest common denominator of interest and taste.

On a more precise and scholarly level the widely circulated and popularized *The Lonely Crowd* of Professor David Riesman of Harvard offered another key to the alleged mass uniformity. In Riesman's view, a profound change in American personality types had gradually taken place with corresponding changes in the culture, the net effect being that the prevailing personality type had come to be the team-man, the "other directed" fellow who took his cue from standards established by his peer groups and perceived through his social contacts, in contrast with an earlier dominant "inner-directed" American whose behavior conformed to a set of internalized standards inculcated by society through parents and teachers. This thesis was not sufficiently documented to satisfy many social scientists. But there was some point to what Riesman said.

An even larger number of Americans saw in mass education the key to uniformity and conformity. According to this view, professional educators, misguided by John Dewey and his disciples, had abandoned traditional disciplines and the development of an individualized capacity to discriminate and to think independently, and had substituted life-adjustment programs, teaching how to get along with one's peers and play the game as a member of the team, how to fit in. The result, allegedly, was mass behavior. Too much was made of this argument. It idealized the old-time intellectual discipline of the schools. It failed to take into account the fact that with the vast expansion of the school population to include hitherto unschooled segments of the nation, it was neither feasible nor possible to hew to a course of education that had been appropriate in a very different situation. But few could question the fact that, wherever the responsibility lay, a good deal that took place in the class room reflected the American conviction that education was the surest road to personal success and an improved social status. Insofar as this was true, it meant, if not antiintellectualism, at least the retreat of the idea that the chief value of education is to cultivate independent thinking and richly individualized personalities. Concern over this issue, heightened by awareness of Soviet technological achievements, strengthened the movement to improve the quality of instruction, especially in the high schools, to search for talent and to enable it to achieve a large measure of its potentiality at every age level.

From this indictment of American civilization as conformity-ridden, there was considerable dissent. An English observer, Joyce Cary, insisted that the idea of American conformity was an expression of a romantic nostalgia for an earlier feudal society in which differentiation and spontaneity were limited to an upper crust. Real uniformity and conformity, as it existed, for example, in African tribal life, was not to be found in America. In the same key, American cultural pluralists continued to emphasize the reality of ethnic and regional differences. American fluidity, change and emphasis on unfinished process also seemed to many observers to refute the indictment that ours was a standardized and conformist civilization. Look, they suggested, at the great variety of consumers' goods, recreational and educational opportunities, and religious and voluntary organizations. The do-it-yourself cult, which included playing musical instruments as well as plumbing, was, as a 6 billion dollar-a-year business, testimony to American inventiveness and self-reliance. So was the mechanical ingenuity of boys in towns and small cities who built ham radios and assembled hot-rod automobiles from indiscriminate and cast-off parts garnered often from junk yards.

Several other trends, the argument ran, proved the continuing vitality of experimentalism and variety in American life. One was the growing concern for the preservation of what was left of the American wilderness, important not only for recreation but for ecological balance. Another was the beginning of a revolt against standardized city planning of "development" and "redevelopment." Dissatisfaction with convention was also evident in the increasing tendency to retreat to country life, to fish and hunt, to camp in the national parks, to visit historical sites and monuments, and to retire "early" to enjoy these and other diversions. But the most dramatic example of protest against a patterned life was the appearance of the beatniks. In one sense these rebellious youth expressed a neoromantic, bohemian protest against middle class prosperity and the "rat race" for place and success. In another sense the beatniks professed to find in uprootedness, in the adventures of narcotics and sex (which Riesman called the last American frontier to be explored) a means to personal assertion, social irresponsibility, and "individuality."

It was seemingly impossible to evaluate in any satisfactory way either the indictment of conformity or the dissent from it. That there was some truth in both positions was obvious. And the debate underscored at least the complexity of American life.

A related colloquy asked whether mid-century America was a land of cultural mediocrity or of a new renaissance. A central question was, whether the common man was too common. The debate of course involved the familiar claim that the mass media were geared to a lower common denominator than was actually necessary even when the business-orientation of the industry was taken into account. Those who believed American civilization had lowered its cultural standards pointed, for example, to the virtual disappearance of the hero and to the cult of "the common fellow" (as exemplified in the vogue of Paddy Chayefsky in the entertainment world). Some critics noted with alarm the fascination which the highbrow found in lowbrow culture (a phenomenon by no means new, as students of France's fifteenth-century writer Francois

Villon knew). Leo Gurko, in his provocative study, *Heroes, Highbrows and the Popular Mind* (1953) argued for the possibility and desirability of a synthesis between the cultural values and interests of the lowbrow and the highbrow. The dimensions of the issue were enlarged with the "discovery" of the so-called middlebrow, inhabiting suburbia and superficially delving into "culture" for its status value as well as for the release it offered from the dull conformity of middle-class life.

Two responses to this phenomenon suggested the liveliness of the whole dialogue. Richard Chase, a thoughtful literary historian and critic, developed the thesis that the highbrow was in danger of succumbing to the middlebrow, but he could offer as a remedy only the traditional plea for greater individual diversity. Sharper and more dogmatic was *The House of Intellect* by Jacques Barzun, a well-known historian and dean of the graduate school of Columbia. Barzun took issue with what he regarded as America's unfortunate overemphasis on science, which too often degenerated into a cult of "scientism"; on art, which stressed feeling at the expense of intellect and tended too frequently to become "artiness"; and on what he designated as philanthropy or the tendency to "do-goodism." This tendency, he thought, debased intellectual standards by an uncritical offering of cultural opportunities and encouragement without regard for talent or achievement.

On the other hand, it can be justly claimed that the 1950s witnessed an extraordinary cultural vitality. For one thing, there seemed to be a change of attitude on the part of American intellectuals. During the height of McCarthyism intellectuals indulged in considerable self-pity. There was much talk about the lack of public esteem for scholars, men of letters, and the arts (despite the fact that a public opinion poll rated intellectuals relatively high on the scale of prestige). It was common to fret over the lack of an intellectual elite and to look nostalgically toward Europe. Some, pointing to the opprobrium that the term "egghead" evoked from the public and to the harassing of intellectuals by Congressional committees of investigation, concluded that anti-intellectualism was a basic and permanent American prejudice.

By the mid-1950s the tide seemed to be changing. One heard and read much more about America's cultural achievement, which was now seen as a source of strength to this country and of inspiration to others. More writers, artists, musicians, and scholars seemed to respond to the urgent plea of Raymond-Leopold Bruckberger, a visiting French soldier-priest, that they begin to take a more active role in explaining America to the rest of the world, rather than leaving the job to professional advertisers and routine bureaucrats. The support the federal government gave to cultural presentations abroad continued to be entirely inadequate. Yet, increasingly, American music, theater, ballet, art, and books attracted interest and admiration not only in friendly and neutral countries but in Moscow itself.

In the midst of an era generally thought to be amazingly prosperous writers, poets, musicians, and artists continued to find the economic struggle a rough one. Yet culture received greater support than in any preceding period. An increasing number of colleges and universities appointed writers-in-residence and artists-in-residence, thus offering a measure of economic security along with a chance for creative work. Few claimed that there were enough fellowships, prizes, and awards for achievements in the cultural field. But no one could question the fact their number was rapidly growing. Summer festivals all over the country gave opportunities to actors, musicians, and dancers. Both the foundations and the business community supported the performing arts and higher education with unprecedented largesse.

Nor was interest in the arts confined to a single place. Although New York, with its new Lincoln Center for the Performing Arts and its great cultural institutions, continued to dominate the scene, Washington began to give increased support to art, theater, and music. Moreover, scores of cities all over the country strengthened their art galleries and symphony orchestras. Louisville found in the presentation of new musical scores and in other cultural innovations a means of invigorating a somewhat regressive economic and cultural life, while the larger cities of Texas and southern California supported outstanding ventures in architecture, music, theater, and art.

What appeared to be, in short, a blossoming of culture was hailed when a place was found at the inauguration of Pulitzer Prize winner John F. Kennedy not only for politicians and clergymen but for Marian Anderson and Robert Frost. In an unprecedented administrative action President Kennedy gave August Heckscher of the Twentieth Century Fund the job of coordinating cultural activities among governmental and private agencies, a notable recognition of the importance of the arts and scholarship. A White House dinner for Nobel Prize winners expressed esteem for this intellectual elite and, as the *New York Times* remarked, underscored the recognition that brilliance often goes hand in hand with nonconformity. Writers, musicians, dancers, and artists were also invited to the White House. Pablo Casals gave a memorable recital. If, as Thomas Hart Benton believed, there was something showy and dilettantish about all this, it is still true that never since the days of Jefferson had cultural achievement been so fully recognized at the Executive Mansion.

It was apparent that qualitative as well as quantitative criteria marked the interest in cultural achievements. Stimulated in part by fresh experiments in France and England the American theater, on and off Broadway and in repertories in many cities, demonstrated extraordinary vitality and versatility. Eugene O'Neill's later and hitherto unproduced plays won acclaim he had seldom enjoyed when he was alive. Older and newer playwrights, including Lillian Hellman, William Inge, Arthur Miller, and Tennessee Williams, to name only the best known, provided the stage with serious drama which, despite formidable producing costs, opened a new chapter in the history of the American theater. While European and Japanese art films enjoyed special prestige, Hollywood now and then produced a memorable picture. In literature the range of writing reflected variety as well as technical craftsmanship. In fiction, for example, no one style or theme excluded others. A boldly experimental use of the vernacular marked the writing not only of Jack Kerouac but of many other new novelists and poets: the casual style as well as the "precious" writing of Truman Capote found admirers. The major concerns were loneliness, tension, ambivalence, strange psychological labyrinths, and action, violence, and sex. Yet Hemingway stressed moral as well as physical courage. Faulkner's vast and prestigious output reflected not only regional decadence, guilt, and violence, but humor and, some said, a moral message. Several of the newer writers, such as J. D. Salinger, John Cheever, and Saul Bellow, were also concerned with values as well as with the seamy side of American life. Also in evidence was compassion: Carson McCuller's *The Member of the Wedding,* James Agee's *A Death in the Family,* and Harper Lee's *To Kill a Mockingbird.*

Making allowance for diplomatic protocol it was still of some point that André Malraux, distinguished French novelist and scholar, leader in the Republican air force in Spain's civil war and hero in the French Resistance, could offer on his visit in 1962 a toast to America as a champion of culture as well as freedom.

Evidence about the extent to which the so-called cultural boom affected the rank and file is contradictory. In 1953, for example, a Gallup poll indicated that only 17 percent of those questioned were at the time reading a book. There were, according to estimate, fewer book readers than in any major democracy. On the other hand, in 1939 only $3,000,-000 were spent on paperbacks, whereas $63,000,000 were spent on this ever proliferating inexpensive medium, which included reprints of the world's best literature as well as much that was cheap and vulgar. Quality magazines such as *Horizon, American Heritage* and *Art in America* proved to have more appeal than most people in the publishing world would have guessed. Hi-fi records of classical as well as of the now respectable and "smart" jazz music became incredibly popular. President Kennedy was mistaken in saying that in the summer of 1962 as many Americans attended symphony concerts as went to baseball games; actually, it seemed that only a third as many did so. But if concerts of all kinds were included, the White House announced that the figure originally given was correct. The other side of the coin, the prevailing jukebox, TV, and radio programs of "country music" (hackneyed jingles, rock and roll, and hill-billy songs), was something else again. But it seems fair to say that, except during the lyceum era of the mid-nineteenth century and, briefly, during the best days of Chautauqua, the popularization of culture had never met with as much success in terms of standards as was true in the 1950s.

If true, this suggested avenues of hope. If an American was able to keep even somewhat abreast of his cataclysmic times, he was likely to recognize the unlimited possibilities for the expansion of knowledge of the universe and of man's creative efforts within it. If men could meet contingencies at home and in the larger world, with resourcefulness and common sense, if men could check their proneness toward destruction and keep their marvelous capacities for creativity to the fore, they might, despite predictions of doom, realize in increasing part an American faith in human ability to overcome even the most threatening obstacles and realize potentialities long cherished.

# *Bibliography*

This book rests both on monographic studies and on primary sources. In some chapters my own researches have been drawn upon extensively. Primary sources in the field of intellectual history which have been used in one or another section of this synthesis and interpretation include files of periodicals and newspapers, government documents, reminiscences and memoirs, letters both published and unpublished, academic addresses, Fourth of July orations, belles-lettres, and such "sub-literature" as almanacs and dime novels.

Footnotes have been included only in the case of direct quotations, for the most part. I shall be glad to furnish any inquirer with references to the material on which the treatment of any topic is based.

The following bibliographical notes deal chiefly with the monographic literature to which I am especially indebted and which seems particularly useful for the further study of a given topic. These titles are representative and selective rather than exhaustive and are intended primarily for the inquiring student rather than for the scholar.

### General Works

The first sustained attempt to survey in a comprehensive fashion the entire history of American intellectual life was Vernon Louis Parrington's *Main Currents in American Thought: An Interpretation of American Literature from the Beginnings to 1920* (2 vols., Harcourt, Brace & World, 1927, and a third, uncompleted volume published in 1930; the first two volumes are available in an inexpensive paper edition, Harvest Book, Harcourt, Brace & World, 1954). Charles and Mary Beard prepared *The American Spirit: A Study of the Idea of Civilization in the United States* (Macmillan, 1942), as a part of their *Rise of American Civilization* (Macmillan, 1942). This work is so distinctive in character, however, that it stands independently of the other volumes as an intellectual history in its own right. Morris R. Cohen's *American Thought: A Critical Sketch* (Free Press, 1954), edited by Felix Cohen, is on the whole compact and incisive, especially on philosophy and scientific thought. Ralph H. Gabriel, *The Course of American Democratic Thought* (2nd ed., Ronald, 1956), is a keen and stimulating survey, beginning with the early nineteenth century and stressing the centrality of democratic ideas. Stow Persons' *American Minds: A History of Ideas* (Holt, 1958), discusses American thought as manifested in five "social minds." Harvey Wish's *Society and Thought in America* (2 vols., 2nd ed., Longmans (David McKay Co.), 1952) is characterized by broad coverage and a great volume of descriptive detail. Several essays by different scholars comprise *Paths of American Thought*, edited by Arthur M. Schlesinger, Jr. and Morton White (Houghton, Mifflin, 1963).

A number of studies, most of them completed in recent years, suggest interpretations of the general course of intellectual history in America by examining the role of a particular idea or cluster of ideas. A pioneer effort was Albert K. Weinberg's *Manifest Destiny* (Johns Hopkins, 1935); and a later work, Frederick Merk's *Manifest Destiny and Mission in American History* (Knopf, 1963). World War II helped stimulate attempts to discover the essence of American faith and belief. A notable product of this effort was Ralph Barton Perry's *Puritanism and Democracy* (Vanguard, 1944), which traces the career of these ideas in the American past. In *Virgin Land: The American West as Symbol and Myth* (Harvard, 1950), a work that has stimulated many scholars in the past decade, Henry Nash Smith discussed the profound influence that concepts of the West have exerted over Americans. In a brief essay which shares some of the characteristics of Smith's *Virgin Land*, Reinhold Niebuhr has stressed the extent to which "innocence," derived from Puritanism and the Enlightenment, has contributed to the modern American predicament in *The Irony of American History* (Scribner, 1952). In a different vein Howard Mumford Jones perceptively and wittily discusses American ideals of happiness in *The Pursuit of Happiness* (Harvard, 1953).

Daniel J. Boorstin's *The Genius of American Politics* (University of Chicago Press, 1953) presses the argument that Americans have been essentially empirical and legalistic. David Potter, *People of Plenty: Economic Abundance and the American Character* (University of Chicago Press, 1954), examines the effect of economic abundance and the idea of material plenty on the American character. For a markedly different interpretation, see Henry B. Parkes, *The American Experience: An Interpretation of the History and Civilization of the American People* (Knopf, 1955). Louis Hartz, *The Liberal Tradition in America: An Interpretation of American Political Thought Since the Revolution* (Harcourt, Brace & World, 1955), discusses the effect of the absence of a feudal tradition on American thought. A historical examination of conservatism, characterized by an explicit sympathy with the conservative tradition, is Clinton Rossiter's *Conservatism in America: The Thankless Persuasion* (2nd ed., Knopf, 1962). From a different point of view, Arthur Ekirch, Jr., has traced the decline of classical liberalism since the American Revolution in *The Decline of American Liberalism* (Longmans (David McKay Co.), 1955). Louis B. Wright's *Culture on the Moving Frontier* (Indiana, 1955) is a stimulating discussion of the life of the mind and the westward movement. Merle Curti, *American Paradox: The Conflict of Thought and Action* (Rutgers, 1956), briefly examines the roots of anti-intellectualism in American thought. Richard Hofstadter deals at length with the same theme in *Anti-Intellectualism in American Life* (Knopf, 1963).

A penetrating essay on a subject that needs a great deal more investigation is Hans Kohn's *American Nationalism: An Interpretative Essay* (Macmillan, 1957). A more detailed study, similar in many respects to Albert Weinberg's earlier *Manifest Destiny*, is Edward McNall Burns, *The American Idea of Mission: Concepts of National Purpose and Destiny* (Rutgers, 1957). Don M. Wolfe has attempted to open an important area of research in *The Image of Man in America* (Southern Methodist, University Press, 1957). Hans Huth has pioneered in a relatively neglected area in his *Nature and the American: Three Centuries of Changing Attitudes* (University of California Press, 1957). Arthur M. Ekirch's *Man and Nature in America* (Columbia, 1963) is a useful synthesis. Merrill D. Peterson, *The Jeffersonian Image in the American Mind* (Oxford, 1960), is a careful and original study of the varying reputation of Thomas Jefferson in American thought. William Appleman Williams, *The Contours of American History*

(World, 1961), is a provocative attempt to attain a synthesis of economic, political, social, and even esthetic ideas under three dominant outlooks, mercantilism, laissez-faire capitalism and corporate capitalism. Charles L. Sanford, *The Quest for Paradise: Europe and the American Moral Imagination* (University of Illinois Press, 1961), treats the role of the "Edenic myth" in American culture.

The best treatment of philosophical thought in America is Herbert Schneider, *A History of American Philosophy* (Columbia, 1963), which should be used in conjunction with the documents in Joseph L. Blau (ed.), *American Philosophic Addresses, 1700–1900* (Columbia, 1946). I. Woodbridge Riley, *American Thought from Puritanism to Pragmatism and Beyond* (Holt, 1932), still is quite valuable. Harvey Gates Townsend, *Philosophical Ideas in the United States* (American Book, 1934), emphasizes foreign influences. The introductions to the selections in Paul Russell Anderson and Max Harold Fisch (eds.), *Philosophy in America from the Puritans to James* (Appleton-Century-Crofts, 1939), are preceptive and informative.

Probably the best single introduction to American literature is Robert E. Spiller, *et al.*, *Literary History of the United States* (3 vols., Macmillan, 1948; rev. ed., 1 vol., Macmillan, 1953). The bibliography in the revised edition is greatly abridged. William Peterfield Trent, John Erskine, Stuart P. Sherman, and Carl Van Doren (eds.), *The Cambridge History of American Literature* (4 vols., Macmillan, 1931), is thorough. The essays in Arthur Hobson Quinn (ed.), *The Literature of the American People: An Historical and Critical Survey* (Appleton-Century-Crofts, 1951), and in Harry Hayden Clark (ed.), *Transitions in American Literary History* (Duke, 1954), are informative. The most exhaustive attempts to provide biographical studies of American literary figures are Charles Dudley Warner (ed.), *American Men of Letters* (22 vols., Houghton Mifflin, 1881–1909), and Mark Van Doren (ed.), *American Men of Letters* (Sloane, 1948–    ). The introductions to the selections in the volumes of Harry Hayden Clark (ed.), *American Writers Series* (American Book, 1934–    ), are intensive and scholarly. Useful surveys of American literature, concentrating on various topics and written from various points of view are Lucy Lockwood Hazard, *The Frontier in American Literature* (Crowell, 1927); Van Wyck Brooks, *Makers and Finders: A History of the Writer in America* (5 vols., Dutton, 1955); Carl Van Doren, *The American Novel, 1789–1939* (rev. ed., Macmillan, 1940); Edwin H. Cady, *The Gentleman in America: A Literary Study in American Culture* (Syracuse University Press, 1949); Edward Wagenknecht, *Cavalcade of the American Novel* (Holt, 1952); Robert E. Spiller, *The Cycle of American Literature: An Essay in Historical Criticism* (Macmillan, 1955); and Leon Howard, *Literature and the Amer-*

*ican Tradition* (Doubleday, 1960). Arthur Hobson Quinn's *A History of the American Drama from the Civil War to the Present Day* (2 vols., Appleton-Century-Crofts, 1936) is an impressive and scholarly study. Glenn Hughes, *A History of the American Theater, 1700–1950* (French, 1951), concentrates on the theater rather than on the dramas as literary texts. John Paul Pritchard's *Criticism in America* (University of Oklahoma Press, 1956) is a useful survey. The essays in Floyd Stoval (ed.), *The Development of American Literary Criticism* (University of North Carolina Press, 1955), are excellent. A neglected area is treated in Ernest E. Leisy, *The American Historical Novel* (University of Oklahoma Press, 1950).

The volumes of *Religion in American Life*, edited by James Ward Smith and A. Leland Jamison (4 vols., Princeton, 1961–   ), are a magnificent contribution to the history of religion in American history. The bibliography in the fourth volume is particularly useful. A valuable collection of source materials is the work in progress under the editorship of H. Shelton Smith, Robert T. Handy, and Lefferts A. Loetscher, *American Christianity: An Historical Interpretation with Representative Documents* (Scribner, 1960–   ). William Warren Sweet, *The Story of Religion in America* (2nd ed., Harper & Row, 1950), is a comprehensive and readable survey. H. Richard Niebuhr, *The Kingdom of God in America* (Harper & Row, 1937), suggests a stimulating interpretation, as do the essays in William Warren Sweet, *American Culture and Religion: Six Essays* (Southern Methodist University Press, 1951).

Winthrop S. Hudson, *American Protestantism* (University of Chicago Press, 1961), is a good, brief survey. Denominational histories, varying in quality and scope, include Gaius G. Atkins and Frederick L. Fagley, *History of American Congregationalism* (Pilgrim Press, 1942); Earl Morse Wilbur, *A History of Unitarianism* (2 vols., Harvard, 1945–1952), II; William W. Mancross, *A History of the American Episcopal Church* (2nd ed., Morehouse-Gorham, 1950); Robert G. Torbet, *A History of the Baptists* (Judson Press, 1950); William Warren Sweet, *Methodism in American History* (rev. ed., Abingdon, 1954); Gaius J. Slosser (ed.), *They Seek a Country: The American Presbyterian* (Macmillan, 1955), a collection of essays; Maurice W. Armstrong, Lefferts A. Loetscher, and Charles A. Anderson (eds.), *The Presbyterian Enterprise* (Westminster Press, 1956), a collection of source material; Abdel R. Wentz, *A Basic History of Lutheranism in America* (Muhlenberg Press, 1955); and Norman Allen Baxter, *History of the Freewill Baptists: A Study in New England Separatism* (American Baptist Historical Society, 1957).

John Tracy Ellis, *American Catholicism* (University of Chicago Press, 1956), is brief and balanced. It may be supplemented by John Tracy Ellis (ed.), *Documents of American Catholic History* (Bruce, 1956). Nathan Glazer's *American Judaism* (University of Chicago Press, 1957), raises many questions that deserve further exploration. For a more detailed treatment, see Rufus Learsi, *The Jews in America: A History* (Harcourt, Brace & World, 1954). Oscar Handlin's *Adventures in Freedom: Three Hundred Years of Jewish Life in America* (McGraw-Hill, 1954), is very readable.

H. Shelton Smith's *Changing Conceptions of Original Sin: A Study in American Theology Since 1750* (Scribner, 1955) is a fine study. Other topical studies of importance are Henry Wilder Foote, *Three Centuries of American Hymnody* (Harvard, 1940); George Huntston Williams (ed.), *The Harvard Divinity School, its Place in Harvard University and in American Culture* (Beacon Press, 1954); Roland H. Bainton, *Yale and the Ministry: A History of Education for the Ministry at Yale from the Founding in 1701* (Harper & Row, 1957); and Ralph H. Gabriel, *Religion and Learning at Yale: The Church of Christ in the College and University, 1757–1957* (Yale, 1958).

There is as yet no general history of science in America. A. Hunter Dupree, *Science in the Federal Government; A History of Policies and Activities to 1940* (Harvard, 1957), is based on extensive and thorough research. Another detailed and valuable study is Ralph S. Bates's *Scientific Societies in the United States* (2nd ed., Columbia, 1958). Biographical data on scientists is conveniently available in Jaques Cattell (ed.), *American Men of Science: A Biographical Directory* (3 vols., 9th ed., Science Press, 1955–1956). More exhaustive are the *Biographical Memoirs of the National Academy of Sciences* (The Academy, 1877–    ). Bernard Jaffe discusses twenty representative scientists in his *Men of Science in America* (rev. ed., Simon and Schuster, 1958). Florian Cajori, *The Teaching and History of Mathematics in the United States* (Government Printing Office, 1890); David Eugene Smith and Jekuthiel Ginsberg, *A History of Mathematics in America before 1900* (Mathematics Association of America, 1934); Edgar Fahs Smith, *Chemistry in America* (Appleton-Century-Crofts, 1914); R. T. Young, *Biology in America* (R. G. Badger, 1923); Francis R. Packard, *History of Medicine in the United States* (2nd ed., Hoeber-Harper, 1931); and Richard H. Shryock, *American Medical Research, Past and Present* (Commonwealth Fund, New York, 1947), are useful studies of particular fields of science. John W. Oliver, *History of American Technology* (Ronald, 1956) is the only comprehensive survey.

The role of immigrants and minority groups in America's intellectual life has received attention from a number of scholars. Maldwyn Allen Jones, *American Immigration* (University of Chicago Press, 1960), is a concise and readable survey. A pioneer work in the field, Marcus L. Hansen's *The Immi-*

*grant in American History* (Harvard, 1940), is still indispensable for the serious student. Carl Wittke details the contributions of immigrants to American culture in *We Who Built America* (Prentice-Hall, 1939). The essays in Oscar Handlin's *Race and Nationality in American Life* (Little, Brown, 1957) examine various aspects of the subject. The volumes of the *Peoples of America* series (Lippincott, 1947–    ), are uneven in quality, but some are of significant interest. Among the many discussions of particular ethnic and national groups, the most useful are Theodore C. Blegen, *Norwegian Immigration to America* (Norwegian-American Historical Association, 1931); Rowland Tappan Berthoff, *British Immigrants in Industrial America, 1770–1950* (Harvard, 1953); Henry S. Lucas, *Netherlanders in America: Dutch Immigration to the United States and Canada, 1789–1950* (University of Michigan Press, 1955); and William Hoglund, *Finnish Immigrants in America* (University of Wisconsin Press, 1960).

The most ambitious history of Negro intellectual life is Earl E. Thorpe, *The Mind of the Negro: An Intellectual History of Afro-Americans* (Ortlieb Press, 1961). The best survey, however, still is John Hope Franklin's *From Slavery to Freedom: A History of American Negroes* (rev. ed., Knopf, 1956). Richard Bardolph, *The Negro Vanguard* (Rinehart, 1959), is a useful collection of biographical sketches of notable Negroes. The documents in Herbert Aptheker (ed.), *A Documentary History of the Negro People in the United States* (Citadel, 1951), are almost entirely political in nature.

The ways in which Europe has influenced American intellectual history, apart from the effects of immigration, have never been discussed comprehensively in a single study. The essays in David F. Bowers (ed.), *Foreign Influences in American Life* (Princeton, 1944), are suggestive. Another collection of essays, Margaret Denny and William H. Gilman (eds.), *The American Writer and the European Tradition* (University of Rochester, 1950), concentrates on literary influences. A pioneer work is William Cunningham's *English Influence on the United States* (Putnam, 1916). Howard Mumford Jones's *America and French Culture, 1750–1848* (University of North Carolina Press, 1927), is excellent. Two somewhat dated studies, Albert B. Faust's *The German Element in the United States* (2 vols., Houghton Mifflin, 1909), and John A. Walz's *German Influence in American Education and Culture* (Carl Schurz Memorial Foundation, 1936), have been largely, if not entirely, replaced by Henry A. Pochmann's thorough and exact *German Culture in America: Philosophical and Literary Influences, 1600–1900* (University of Wisconsin Press, 1957).

The American influence on Europeans is analyzed in Halvdan Koht, *The American Spirit in Europe: A Survey of Transatlantic Influences* (University of Pennsylvania Press, 1949), which suggests many new avenues of investigation. A useful summary of the academic study of American life in Europe is

Sigmund Skard's *The American Myth and the European Mind: American Studies in Europe* (University of Pennsylvania Press, 1961). Other important studies of a general nature include Clarence Gohdes, *American Literature in Nineteenth-Century England* (Columbia, 1944); David Hecht, *Russian Radicals Look to America, 1825–1894* (Harvard, 1947); and Max M. Laserson, *The American Impact on Russia, Diplomatic and Ideological, 1784–1917* (Macmillan, 1950).

The long tradition of reform in American life can best be approached through Arthur M. Schlesinger, Sr.'s incisive *The American as Reformer* (Harvard, 1950). Merle Curti, *Peace or War: The American Struggle, 1636–1936* (Norton, 1936), and Eleanor Flexner, *Century of Struggle: The Woman's Rights Movement in the United States* (Harvard, 1959), and Robert E. Riegel's *American Feminists* (University of Kansas Press, 1963) are useful surveys of particular reform movements. Robert H. Bremner's *American Philanthropy* (University of Chicago Press, 1960), details efforts to reform society by voluntary giving.

The problem of freedom is discussed perceptively in Oscar and Mary Handlin, *The Dimensions of Liberty* (Harvard, 1961). Other important studies of various aspects of freedom and liberty include Merle Curti, *The Roots of American Loyalty* (Columbia, 1946); Anson Phelps Stokes, *Church and State in the United States: Historical Development and Contemporary Problems of Religious Freedom under the Constitution* (3 vols., Harper & Row, 1950); Robert Freeman Butts, *The American Tradition in Religion and Education* (Beacon Press, 1950); James J. Martin, *Men Against the State: The Expositers of Individualist Anarchism in the United States, 1827–1908* (Adrian Allen Associates, De Kalb, Illinois, 1953); James Willard Hurst, *Law and the Conditions of Freedom in the Nineteenth Century United States* (University of Wisconsin Press, 1956); Samuel P. Huntington, *The Soldier and the State: The Theory and Politics of Civil Military Relations* (Harvard, 1957); Loren P. Beth, *The American Theory of Church and State* (University of Florida Press, 1958); and Harold M. Hyman, *To Try Men's Souls: Loyalty in American History* (University of California Press, 1959).

Several scholars have prepared broad, general surveys of the history of education in America, varying in quality and emphases. Among the more useful are Ellwood P. Cubberly, *Public Education in the United States* (Houghton Mifflin, 1934); R. Freeman Butts and Lawrence A. Cremin, *A History of Education in American Culture* (Holt, 1953); Stuart G. Noble, *History of American Education* (rev. ed., Rinehart, 1954); H. G. Good, *A History of American Education* (Macmillan, 1956); and Adolphe E. Meyer, *An Educational History of the American People* (McGraw-Hill, 1957). Edgar W. Knight and Clifton L. Hall have assembled a useful selection of documents,

*Readings in American Educational History* (Appleton-Century-Crofts, 1951).

The essays in Richard Hofstadter and C. DeWitt Hardy, *The Development and Scope of Higher Education in the United States* (Columbia, 1952) are significant. Other useful discussions are Ernest Earnest, *Academic Procession: An Informal History of the American College, 1636 to 1953* (Bobbs–Merrill, 1953), George P. Schmidt, *The Liberal Arts College: A Chapter in American Cultural History* (Rutgers, 1957), and Frederick Rudolph, *The American College and University. A History* (Knopf, 1962). Richard Hofstadter and Wilson Smith (eds.), *American Higher Education: A Documentary History* (2 vols., University of Chicago Press, 1961), is a fine collection. Various aspects of American education are discussed in Thomas Woody, *A History of Women's Education in the United States* (2 vols., Science Press, 1929); Merle Curti, *The Social Ideas of American Educators* (rev. ed., Littlefield-Adams, 1959); Sidney Jackson, *America's Struggle for Free Schools* (American Council on Public Affairs, 1941); Howard K. Beale, *A History of Freedom of Teaching in American Schools* (Scribner, 1941); Richard Hofstadter and Walter P. Metzger, *The Development of Academic Freedom in the United States* (Columbia, 1955); Neil Gerard McCluskey, *Public Schools and Moral Education: The Influence of Horace Mann, William Torrey Harris and John Dewey* (Columbia, 1958); and Rush Welter, *Education and Democracy* (Columbia, 1962).

Richard M. Dorson's *American Folklore* (University of Chicago Press, 1959), is an excellent introduction to this aspect of popular culture. A model collection of folklore, among the many recent published collections, is Newman Ivey White (ed.), *The Frank C. Brown Collection of North Carolina Folklore* (5 vols. projected, Duke, 1952–      ). Holger Cahill's brief *American Folk Art: The Art of the Common Man* (Museum of Modern Art, 1933), is a seminal book. John Greenway's *American Folksongs of Protest* (University of Pennsylvania Press, 1953), is useful. Constance M. Rourke, *American Humor: A Study of the National Character* (Harcourt, Brace & World, 1931), examines comic stereotypes with an eye on the national character. Stephen Becker, *Comic Art in America* (Simon and Schuster, 1959), contains useful material. Sigmund Spaeth, *A History of Popular Music in America* (Random House, 1948), is most effective on the modern period. Frank Luther Mott's *Golden Multitudes: The Story of Best Sellers in the United States* (Macmillan, 1946), and James D. Hart, *The Popular Book: A History of America's Literary Taste* (Oxford, 1950), are very informative. Valuable insights and information are available in Arthur W. Calhoun, *The Social History of the American Family* (3 vols., Arthur H. Clark, 1917–1919); Arthur M. Schlesinger, Sr., *Learning How to Behave:*

A *Historical Study of American Etiquette Books* (Macmillan, 1946); and Sidney Ditzion, *Marriage, Morals and Sex in America: A History of Ideas* (Bookman Associates, 1953). Frank Luther Mott's studies, *American Journalism: A History, 1690–1960* (3rd ed., Macmillan, 1962), and A *History of American Magazines* (4 vols. to date, Appleton-Century-Crofts, Harvard, 1930–1957), are invaluable. Sidney Kobre's *Foundations of American Journalism* (Florida State University Press, 1958), is a useful survey.

Oliver W. Larkin, in *Art and Life in America* (Holt, Rinehart and Winston, 1962), relates the arts to other developments. John A. Kouwenhoven, *Made in America: The Arts in Modern Civilization* (Doubleday, 1948), is a provocative analysis, emphasizing the role of technology and democratic ideas. James T. Flexner has completed two volumes of his massive history of American painting: *American Painting: The First Flowers of Our Wilderness* (Houghton Mifflin, 1947), and *American Painting: The Light of Distant Skies, 1760–1835* (Harcourt, Brace & World, 1954). Convenient one-volume treatments are James T. Flexner, A *Short History of American Painting* (Houghton Mifflin, 1950); Virgil Barker, *American Painting: History and Interpretation* (Macmillan, 1950); and Edgar P. Richardson, *Painting in America: The Story of 450 Years* (Crowell, 1956). For architecture, see Lewis Mumford, *Sticks and Stones: A Study of American Architecture and Civilization* (2nd ed., Dover, 1955), and Wayne Andrews, *Architecture, Ambition and Americans* (Harper & Row, 1955). John Tasker Howard, *Our American Music: Three Hundred Years of It* (3rd ed., with chapters by James Lyons, McGraw-Hill, 1954), and Gilbert Chase, *America's Music, from the Pilgrims to the Present* (McGraw-Hill, 1955), are thorough histories of American music.

## 1. The Christian Heritage

Most of the studies of the colonial religious heritage have concentrated on particular religious groups or on geographical areas. William Warren Sweet, however, has provided an extended general treatment in his *Religion in Colonial America* (Scribner, 1942). Of all the various religious groups, the New England Puritans have received the most exhaustive attention. Perry Miller's volumes constitute the most nearly complete account of Puritan theology: *Orthodoxy in Massachusetts* (2nd ed., Beacon Press, 1959), *The New England Mind: The Seventeenth Century* (Harvard, 1954), *The New England Mind: From Colony to Province* (Harvard, 1953), and *Errand into the Wilderness* (Harvard, 1956). Somewhat less technical is Herbert W. Schneider, *The Puritan Mind* (Holt, 1930). Alan Simpson, in *Puritanism in Old and*

*New England* (University of Chicago Press, 1955), discusses divergences between colonial and English Puritanism. The internal development of New England religious thought can be traced in Frank H. Foster, *A Genetic History of New England Theology* (University of Chicago Press, 1907), and in the somewhat more up-to-date volume by Joseph Haroutunian, *Piety versus Moralism: The Passing of the New England Theology* (Holt, 1932). Samuel Eliot Morison, *The Intellectual Life of Colonial New England* (New York University Press, 1956, originally published as *The Puritan Pronaos*), is sympathetic but scholarly. Edmund S. Morgan, in *The Puritan Dilemma: The Story of John Winthrop* (Little, Brown, 1958), sums up a great deal of the religious history of colonial New England. For a different treatment, see the third volume of Thomas J. Wertenbaker's trilogy on the colonial period, *The Founding of American Civilization: The Puritan Oligarchy* (Scribner, 1947), and the pioneer study, still highly readable and informative, by Edward Eggleston, *The Transit of Civilization from England to America in the Seventeenth Century* (Beacon Press, 1959), with a perceptive modern introduction by Arthur M. Schlesinger, Sr.

In comparison with the Puritans, other religious groups in the colonies have received little attention. Three scholarly studies provide needed information on Anglicanism: Carl Bridenbaugh, *The Mitre and the Scepter* (Oxford, 1962), George MacLaren Brydon, *Virginia's Mother Church* (Vol. 1, Virginia Historical Society, 1947; Vol. 2, Church Historical Society, 1952), and Nelson R. Burr, *The Anglican Church in New Jersey* (Church Historical Society, 1954). A still useful study of the Quakers is Rufus M. Jones, *The Quakers in the American Colonies* (Macmillan, 1911). The essays of Frederick B. Tolles in *Quakers and the Atlantic Culture* (Macmillan, 1960) discuss various aspects of Quaker life. Tolles's *Meetinghouse and Countinghouse* (University of North Carolina Press, 1948) is an illuminating treatment of Philadelphia Quaker merchants. Other special studies that shed light on the colonial Quakers are John E. Pomfret, *The Province of West New Jersey, 1609–1702* (Princeton, 1956), and Ethyn Williams Kirby, *George Keith (1638–1716)* (Appleton-Century-Crofts, 1942). A chief authority on Presbyterianism is Leonard J. Trinterud, *The Forming of an American Tradition: A Re-examination of Colonial Presbyterianism* (Westminster Press, 1949). Scholars have been active in recent years in delineating the colonial origins of the American Jewish community. The principal and definitive work in this area is Jacob Rader Marcus' *Early American Jewry* (2 vols., Jewish Publication Society of America, 1951–1953). For a briefer introduction, see Lee M. Friedman, *Early American Jews* (Harvard, 1934). A valuable collection of source material is Jacob Rader Marcus (ed.), *American Jewry: Documents, Eighteenth Century* (Hebrew Union College Press,

1959). Some information on Lutheranism in the colonies can be found in Paul A. Wallace's somewhat popular study *The Mühlenbergs of Pennsylvania* (University of Pennsylvania Press, 1950). *The Road to Salem* (University of North Carolina Press, 1944), by Adelaide L. Fries, is an intensely human autobiographical account of the Moravians in Pennsylvania and North Carolina.

The influence of the clergy on higher education in the colonies may be studied in Samuel E. Morison, *Harvard College in the Seventeenth Century* (2 vols., Harvard, 1936), and in the histories of other colonial colleges. Of particular interest is Louis Leonard Tucker's *Puritan Protagonist: President Thomas Clap of Yale College* (Yale, 1962). Other valuable special studies of this subject include Allen G. Umbreit, "Education in the Southern Colonies, 1607–1773," *Iowa Abstracts in History* (1927–1934); William H. Kilpatrick, *Dutch Schools of New Netherland and Colonial New York* (Government Printing Office, 1912); and the proscholastic *Education of the Founding Fathers: Scholasticism in the Colonial Colleges* (Fordham, 1935), by James J. Walsh. Mary L. Gambrell has studied the education of New England clergy in her useful *Ministerial Training in Eighteenth Century New England* (Columbia, 1937). The influence of the colonial clergy on other aspects of culture and intellectual life has been discussed in a number of specialized works. William Haller, Jr., in *The Puritan Frontier* (Columbia, 1951), discusses the formation of new towns in seventeenth-century New England. Ola Elizabeth Winslow, in *Meetinghouse Hill, 1630–1783* (Macmillan, 1952), attempts to resuscitate the Puritan meetinghouse as an important cultural agency. Emil Oberholzer's *Delinquent Saints* (Columbia, 1956) is a thorough and accurate account of disciplinary action in the Puritan churches. The relation of law to Puritan religious and social ethics is treated in George Lee Haskins' solid monograph *Law and Authority in Early Massachusetts* (Macmillan, 1960). Daniel J. Boorstin in his provocative study, *The Americans: The Colonial Experience* (Random House, 1958), speculates on the social and political consequences of Puritan, Quaker, and Anglican religious belief and practice. William Kellaway, in a highly informative monograph, *The New England Company, 1649–1776* (Longmans (David McKay Co.), 1961), traces the history of the Company for the Propagation of the Gospel in New England. Although it is somewhat fictional in form, Marion L. Starkey's *The Devil in Massachusetts: A Modern Inquiry into the Salem Witch Trials* (Knopf, 1949) is a penetrating psychological study of one unfortunate form of religious influence in early American culture. Edmund S. Morgan presents the religious and domestic ideas of the New England Puritans sympathetically in *The Puritan Family* (Boston Public Library, 1944). Other aspects of the cultural influence of the clergy are dealt with in Lindsay Swift, "The Massachusetts Election Sermons," *Publications of the Colonial Society of Massachusetts*, I (Boston, 1895); in W. DeLoss Love, *The Fast and Thanksgiving Days of New England* (Houghton Mifflin, 1895); and in Philip D. Jordan, "The Funeral Sermon," *American Book Collector*, IV (September–October, 1933). The influence of religion on economic thought and practice is treated in E. A. J. Johnson, *American Economic Thought in the Seventeenth Century* (Russell and Russell, 1961), a scholarly study. Leonard W. Labaree has discussed the colonial clergy as a conservative force in his *Conservatism in Early American History* (New York University Press, 1948), ch. 3. Alice M. Baldwin's admirable monograph, *The New England Clergy and the American Revolution* (Duke, 1928), demonstrates clearly the influence of the New England clergy in popularizing the natural rights philosophy.

There is still an inadequate number of good biographies of leading colonial theologians. Janet Whitney's *John Woolman, American Quaker* (Little, Brown, 1942) is sympathetic and readable, though inadequately documented. John Woolman's journal is easily available in a paper edition edited by Frederick B. Tolles (Corinth Books, 1961), and Amelia M. Gummere (ed.), *Journals and Essays of John Woolman* (Macmillan, 1922), contains some of Woolman's other writings. An appreciative and sympathetic estimate of Woolman is included in Reginald Reynolds' introduction to *The Wisdom of John Woolman* (G. Allen, 1948). Of special importance and significance is Perry Miller's study of Edwards' thought in his *Jonathan Edwards* (Sloane, 1949). Still very valuable on Edwards is Ola Elizabeth Winslow's *Jonathan Edwards, 1703–1758* (Macmillan, 1940). Under Perry Miller's general editorship, a complete modern edition of *The Works of Jonathan Edwards* is under way (Yale, 1957–    ). Roger Williams has received contrasting treatments in two studies, *Master Roger Williams, A Biography* (Macmillan, 1957), by Ola Elizabeth Winslow, and *Roger Williams: His Contribution to the American Tradition* (Bobbs–Merrill, 1953), by Perry Miller. Ralph and Louise Boas provide a readable introduction to the character and thought of Cotton Mather in their *Cotton Mather, Keeper of the Puritan Conscience* (Harper & Row, 1928). Kenneth Murdock's *Increase Mather, The Foremost American Puritan* (Harvard, 1925) is a thoroughly documented and sympathetic biography. The first full-length study of John Wise is George Allan Cook, *John Wise, Early American Democrat* (King's Crown, 1952). Other colonial religious leaders may be studied with profit in collections of their writings: *The Winthrop Papers* (5 vols., Massachusetts Historical Society, 1929–1947); Frederick B. Tolles and E. Gordon Alderfer (eds.), *The Witness of William Penn* (Macmillan, 1957); *The Journals of Henry Melchior Mühlenberg* (3 vols., Muhlenberg Press, 1942–1958), edited and translated by Theodore G. Tappert and John W. Doberstein; William Bradford's *Of Plymouth Plantation* (Knopf, 1952), edited by Samuel Eliot Morison; and, for a somewhat later period, Elmer T. Clark, J. Manning Potts, and Jacob S. Payton (eds.), *The Journal and Letters of Francis Asbury* (3 vols., Abingdon, 1958).

Sister Mary Augustina Ray has amassed much evidence on the prejudice of colonial American Protestants against Catholicism in her *American Opinion of Roman Catholicism in the Eighteenth Century* (Columbia, 1936). Valuable on the subject of toleration is Abram V. Goodman's *American Overture: Jewish Rights in Colonial Times* (Jewish Publication Society of America, 1947). The relationship of Catholic thought to the development of toleration in seventeenth-century Maryland is discussed in Thomas O'Brien Hanley, *Their Rights and Liberties: The Beginnings of Religious and Political Freedom in Maryland* (Newman, 1959).

Christian attitudes toward esthetics are illustrated in Edward S. Ninde, *The Story of the American Hymn* (Abingdon, 1921); Percy Scholes, *The Puritans and Music in England and New England* (Oxford, 1934); William A. Haussmann, *German-American Hymnology, 1683–1800* (Philadelphia, 1899); Harold D. Eberlein, *The Architecture of Colonial America* (Little, Brown, 1915); Joseph Jackson, *American Colonial Architecture* (Longmans (David McKay Co.), 1924); Anthony B. Garvan, *Architecture and Town Planning in Colonial Connecticut* (Yale, 1951); Kenneth B. Murdock, *Literature and Theology in Colonial New England* (Harvard, 1949). Examples of colonial religious prose and verse are readily available in *The Bay Psalm Book: A Facsimile Reprint of the First Edition of 1640*, with a companion volume, *The Enigma of the Bay Psalm Book*, by Zoltan Haraszti (University of Chicago Press, 1956), and in Perry Miller and Thomas H. Johnson (eds.), *The Puritans* (American Book, 1938). The latter work has been somewhat revised in Perry Miller, ed., *The American Puritans, Their Prose and Poetry* (Doubleday, 1961).

In addition to such contemporary accounts of the Great Revival as Jonathan Edwards *A Faithful Narrative of the Surprising Work of God in Conversion of Many Hundred Souls in Northampton* (Boston, 1737); Charles Chauncey *Seasonable Thoughts on the State of Religion in New England* (Boston, 1743); and Devereaux Jarratt, *A Brief Narrative of the Revival of Religion in Virginia* (London, 1779), several sound monographs are available: Charles M. Maxson, *The Great Awakening in the Middle Colonies* (University of Chicago Press, 1920); Wesley M. Gewehr, *The Great Awakening in Virginia, 1740–1790* (Duke, 1930); and Edwin Scott Gaustad, *The Great Awakening in New England* (Harper & Row, 1957). An interesting attempt to trace out some of the social and political consequences of the Great Awakening in one colony is Dietmar Rothermund, *The Layman's Progress: Religious and Political Behavior in Colonial Pennsylvania* (University of Pennsylvania Press, 1962).

### 2. Legacies to the New Nation

The contribution of English-speaking colonists to the intellectual life of the nation is discussed in a great variety of general and specialized monographs. Many of these are cited, for convenience, elsewhere in the Bibliographical Note. For a general introduction to English culture during the colonial period, the student may profitably consult several distinguished studies: Louis B. Wright's richly documented *Middle Class Culture in Elizabethan England* (University of North Carolina Press, 1935); Wallace Notestein's volume in the New American Nation series, *The English People on the Eve of Colonization* (Harper & Row, 1954); A. L. Rowse's graceful study, *The Elizabethans and America* (Harper & Row, 1959). On the Scottish colonists, two recent monographs are quite informative: Duane Meyer, *The Highland Scots of North Carolina, 1732–1776* (University of North Carolina Press, 1961), and, more generally Ian Charles Graham, *Colonists from Scotland: Emigration to North America* (Cornell, 1956).

The third chapter of Louis B. Wright's volume in the New American Nation series, *The Cultural Life of the American Colonies* (Harper & Row, 1957), is a useful summary of the cultural influences of non-English-speaking groups. Also quite valuable are two volumes of Thomas J. Wertenbaker's trilogy: *The Founding of American Civilization: The Middle Colonies* (Scribner, 1938), and *The Old South* (Scribner, 1942). Thomas Tileston Waterman, *The Dwellings of Colonial America* (University of North Carolina Press, 1950), is especially informative on cross-cultural influences among different national groups. A fascinating contemporary glimpse into the rich variety of colonial culture is available in *Letters from an American Farmer* by J. Hector St. John de Crèvecoeur, published in 1793 in Philadelphia and available in several modern editions. See also Arthur H. Quinn, *The Soul of America: Yesterday and Today* (University of Pennsylvania Press, 1932), for a suggestive treatment.

A balanced account of Dutch contributions to colonial intellectual life may be found in Herbert I. Priestley's *The Coming of the White Man, 1492–1848* (Macmillan, 1929). Interesting information on the political role of the Dutch settlement in New York is available in Jerome R. Reich's *Leisler's Rebellion: A Study of Democracy in New York* (University of Chicago Press, 1953). Ralph Wood (ed.), *The Pennsylvania Germans* (Princeton, 1942), is an excellent collection of essays on various aspects of German life. An interesting contemporary glimpse of German life in Pennsylvania in the 1750s is contained in Gottlieb Mittelberger's *Journey to Pennsylvania* (Harvard, 1960), translated and edited by Oscar Handlin and John Clive. Henry Kauffman, *Pennsylvania Dutch American Folk Art* (American Studio Books, 1946), is an informative study. Monographs on Germans in colonial America may be supplemented by the abundant materials in the *Pennsylvania Magazine of History and Biography* and the publications of the Pennsylvania German Society, the *German-American Annals* and *Americana-Germanica*. A brief account of Swedish contributions may be found in Adolph B. Benson's "Cultural Relations Between Sweden and America to 1830," *Germanic Review* XII (April, 1938).

The subject of Huguenot influence in one colony is discussed in Arthur E. Hirsch's *The Huguenots of Colonial South Carolina* (Duke, 1928). An older study, Charles W. Baird, *The Huguenot Emigration to America* (2 vols., New York, 1885), is still useful. Readable and illuminating accounts of the French cultural legacy in the Mississippi Valley are to be found in Rufus Babcock (ed.), *Memoir of John Mason Peck, D.D.* (Philadelphia, 1864), and Hugh H. Brackenridge, *Views of Louisiana* (Pittsburgh, 1814). The Illinois and Wisconsin state historical societies have published many of the records of the French in the Mississippi Valley, in which may be found scattered material on intellectual and cultural history. See also Charles Gayarré, *History of Louisiana* (Hansell, 1903), and the useful account by Lewis W. Newton, "Creoles and Anglo-Saxons in Old Louisiana," *Southwest Social Science Quarterly*, XIV (June, 1933). For the Missouri area, there are several valuable studies: Edward L. Tinker, *Private Libraries in Creole St. Louis* (Johns Hopkins, 1938); Harvey Wish, "The French of Old Missouri, 1804–1821: A Study in Assimilation," *Mid-America*, XXIII (July, 1941); and John F. McDermott, "Voltaire and the Free Thinkers in Early St. Louis," *Revue de littérature comparée*, XVI (1936). A particularly interesting study of French attitudes toward the Indian is J. H. Kennedy's *Jesuit and Savage in New France* (Yale, 1950).

The literature of the Spanish impact on the Southwest and on California is voluminous. For the serious reader the work of Herbert Bolton is indispensable. In addition to the primary materials he made available, Professor Bolton contributed many excellent studies, including "The Mission as a Frontier Institution in the Spanish American Colonies," *American Historical Review*, XXIII (October, 1917), *Texas in the Middle of the Eighteenth Century* (University of California Press, 1916), and *Rim of Christendom: A Biography of Eusebio Francisco Kino, Pacific Coast Explorer* (Macmillan, 1936). Carlos E. Casteñeda, *Our Catholic Heritage in Texas* (7 vols., Von

Boeckmann-Jones Co., 1936) and Father Zephrian Engelhardt, *The Missions and the Missionaries of California* (4 vols., James H. Barry Co., 1908) are standard Catholic accounts. Herbert I. Priestley, *The Coming of the White Man, 1492–1848*, is useful. J. Manuel Espinosa, *Crusaders of the Rio Grande* (Institute of Jesuit History, 1942), is based on extensive research. Interesting primary accounts that have been recently made available by the University of New Mexico Press include *The Missions of New Mexico, 1776: A Description by Frey Francisco Atanasio Dominguez* (1956), translated and edited by Eleanor B. Adams and Frey Angelico Chavez, and *Don Juan de Oñate, Colonizer of New Mexico, 1595–1628* (2 vols., 1953), translated and edited by George P. Hammond and Agapito Rey.

No single satisfactory study of Indian contributions to American ideas and attitudes exists. James A. James, *English Institutions and the American Indians* (Johns Hopkins Studies, XXI, 1894), was a pioneer study but is now out of date. William E. Stafford makes some interesting observations on the problems involved in this field in "Our Heritage from the Indians," *Smithsonian Report for 1926* (Government Printing Office, 1927). Constance Rourke's discussion of Indian contributions to the white man's culture in *The Roots of American Culture* (Harcourt, Brace, & World, 1942) is suggestive and brilliant, but her generalizations need further probing. The essays in Part Two of James Morton Smith (ed.), *Seventeenth Century America: Essays in Colonial History* (University of North Carolina Press. 1959), are especially enlightening. Many of the numerous volumes of the series *The Civilization of the American Indian* (University of Oklahoma Press, 1932–    ), contain information on intellectual history. Le Roy Appleton's *Indian Art of the Americas* (Scribners, 1950) is a beautifully illustrated study. A. Hyatt Verrill, in *The Real Americans* (Putnam, 1954), stresses Indian contributions to white culture. Many primary accounts give glimpses of the relations between whites and Indians. The cult of the Indian in literature and thought has been the subject of a number of studies, in particular Gilbert Chinard's *L'Amérique et la rêve exotique* (Paris, 1913), Hoxie N. Fairchild's *The Noble Savage: A Study in Romantic Naturalism* (Columbia, 1928), and Roy Harvey Pearce's *The Savages of America: A Study of the Indian and the Idea of Civilization* (Johns Hopkins, 1953).

Melville J. Herskovits, in *The Myth of the Negro Past* (Harper & Row, 1941), overemphasizes the thesis that the Negroes did not come to America "culturally naked," and that much of their culture survived. Yet his point of view is a healthy corrective to widely held antithetical views. Frank J. Klingberg's *Anglican Humanitarianism in Colonial New York* (Church Historical Society, 1940) and *An Appraisal of the Negro in Colonial South Carolina: A Story in Americanization* (Associated Publishers, 1941) are well-documented studies. Carter Woodson, *The Education of the Negro Prior to 1861* (Putnam, 1915) and Marcus W. Jernegan, *Laboring and Dependent Classes in Colonial America, 1607–1783* (University of Chicago Press, 1931) contain much valuable material.

### 3. The Old World Heritage Modified

Judicious general treatments of the modification of the Old World heritage by American conditions are contained in several distinguished monographs. Curtis P. Nettels, *The Roots of American Civilization* (Appleton-Century-Crofts, 1963), though it is not primarily concerned with intellectual history, has a judicious discussion of the influence of the American environment on cultural life. Thomas J. Wertenbaker sums up a great deal of research into this field in his brief *The Golden Age of Colonial Culture* (New York University Press, 1942). Louis B. Wright's *The Atlantic Frontier: Colonial American Civilization* (Knopf, 1947) is also an excellent study. On the subject of the influence of the purely physical environment of colonial America, Archer Butler Hulbert has some suggestive ideas in *Soil, Its Influence on the History of the United States* (Yale, 1930). Although neither study is focused primarily on the colonial period or on intellectual life, J. Russell Smith's *North America and Its Geographic Conditions* (Houghton Mifflin, 1933) and Howard W. Odum and Henry E. Moore's *American Regionalism* (Holt, 1938) present useful material.

Louis B. Wright's *The First Gentlemen of Virginia* (The Huntington Library, 1940) sets a high standard for research and interpretation in the field of the adaptation of English ideas and values to colonial conditions. A contrasting view is available in Carl Bridenbaugh's lectures on the colonial South: *Myths and Realities* (Louisiana State University Press, 1952). The experiences of tutors in plantation Virginia are described with lively detail in John Harrower's diary, *American Historical Review*, VI (October, 1900), and in the *Journals and Letters of Philip Vickers Fithean* (Princeton, 1900). Edmund S. Morgan in *Virginians at Home: Family Life in the Eighteenth Century* (Colonial Williamsburg, 1952) discusses planter life with wit and charm. Thomas T. Waterman, *The Mansions of Virginia, 1706–1776* (University of North Carolina Press, 1946) is interesting and informative. Charles S. Sydnor, *Gentlemen Freeholders: Political Practices in Washington's Virginia* (University of North Carolina Press, 1952), is a brief, sympathetic discussion of the social life of the gentry as it affected politics. For the intellectual interests of the planters see, in addition to Wright's *First Gentlemen of Virginia*, George K. Smart, "Private Libraries in Colonial

Virginia," *American Literature*, X (March, 1938); William D. Houlette, "Plantation Libraries in the Old South," *University of Iowa Abstracts in History, 1927–1934*; and Louis B. Wright and Marion Tinling (eds.), *The Secret Diary of William Byrd of Westover, 1709–1712* (Dietz Press, 1941), Marion Tinling and Maude H. Woodfin (eds.), *Another Secret Diary of William Byrd of Westover, 1739–1741* (Dietz Press, 1942), and Louis B. Wright and Marion Tinling (eds.), *William Byrd of Virginia: The London Diary (1717–1721) and Other Writings* (Oxford, 1958).

The materials for an understanding of the intellectual interests of the plain people in rural areas are scattered. George Lyman Kittredge's witty and scholarly book, *The Old Farmer and His Almanack* (Ware, 1904) and Samuel Briggs's *The Essays, Humor, and Poems of Nathaniel Ames, Father and Son, of Dedham, Massachusetts, from their Almanacks, 1726–1775* (Short and Forman, 1891) provide a good introduction. Ola E. Winslow has collected fugitive specimens of colonial "mass literature" in her *American Broadside Verse from Imprints of the Seventeenth and Eighteenth Centuries* (Yale, 1930). A valuable account of white servitude and convict labor is Abbott Emerson Smith, *Colonists in Bondage* (University of North Carolina Press, 1947). Educational facilities are discussed in Jernegan, *Laboring and Dependent Classes in Colonial America*. For a more modern treatment, see Bernard Bailyn's suggestive essay in *Education in the Forming of American Society: Needs and Opportunities for Study* (University of North Carolina Press, 1960). There is some literature on folk culture in colonial times. W. W. Newell has discussed "Early American Ballads" in the *Journal of American Folklore*, XII (October–December, 1899), but Louis Pound's discriminating essay in *American Ballads and Folk Songs* (Scribner, 1922) is a better brief introduction. See also Frances Lichten, *Folk Art of Rural Pennsylvania* (Scribner, 1946), and John J. Stoudt, *Pennsylvania Folk Art* (Schlecter's, Allentown, 1948). In addition, there are a number of collections of published primary materials on folk culture. There is some information on the lives of the plain farmers in Stevenson Whitcomb Fletcher, *Pennsylvania Agriculture and Country Life, 1640–1840* (Pennsylvania Historical and Museum Commission, 1950). The lives of Georgia's settlers are treated in detail in Sarah B. Gober Temple and Kenneth Coleman, *Georgia Journeys* (University of Georgia Press, 1961). An interesting contemporary account from the Carolina frontier area is Richard J. Hooker (ed.), *The Carolina Backcountry on the Eve of the Revolution: The Journal and Other Writings of Charles Woodmason, Anglican Itinerant* (University of North Carolina Press, 1953).

Intellectual life in colonial towns has been most comprehensively dealt with by Carl Bridenbaugh, *Cities in the Wilderness: The First Century of*

*Urban Life in America, 1625–1742* (Ronald, 1938), and *Cities in Revolt: Urban Life in America, 1743–1776* (Knopf, 1955). Wertenbaker, in *The Golden Age of Colonial Culture*, has delightful essays on Boston, New York, Philadelphia, Annapolis, Williamsburg, and Charlestown. Michael Kraus's *Intercolonial Aspects of American Culture on the Eve of the Revolution* (Columbia, 1928) is a very informative study. On particular cities, see Carl and Jessica Bridenbaugh, *Rebels and Gentlemen: Philadelphia in the Age of Franklin* (Harcourt, Brace & World, 1942), and Frederick P. Bowes, *The Culture of Early Charleston* (University of North Carolina Press, 1942). The lives of colonial craftsmen and "mechanicks" are discussed in Carl Bridenbaugh, *The Colonial Craftsman* (New York University Press, 1950). Though they are not focused on intellectual history, several scholarly studies offer useful material on the lives of colonial merchants: Bernard Bailyn, *The New England Merchants in the Seventeenth Century* (Harvard, 1955); James B. Hedges, *The Browns of Providence Plantations: Colonial Years* (Harvard, 1952); and Byron Fairchild, *Messrs. William Pepperrell: Merchants at Piscataqua* (Cornell, 1954).

On books and libraries there is a useful summary in chapter 7 of Louis B. Wright's *The Cultural Life of the American Colonies, 1607–1763.* On printing and books in particular, see John T. Winterich, *Early American Books and Printing* (Houghton, Mifflin, 1935); Lawrence C. Worth, *The Colonial Printer* (Southworth-Anthoesen Press, 1928); Hellmut Lehmann-Haupt, *The Book in America* (Bowker, 1938); P. L. Ford (ed.), *The Journals of Hugh Gaine, Printer* (2 vols., Dodd, Mead, 1902); and Henry W. Boynton, *Annals of American Bookselling, 1638–1850* (Wiley, 1932). Library facilities in towns are discussed in Austin B. Keep, *History of the New York Library Society* (Library de Vinne Press, 1908); George W. Cole, *Early Library Development in New York State* (New York Public Library Publications, 1927); Stephen B. Weeks, "Libraries and Literature in North Carolina in the Eighteenth Century," *Annual Report of American Historical Association for 1895;* Charles K. Bolton, "Proprietary and Subscription Libraries," *Manual of Library Economy* (Chicago, 1912); Chester T. Hallenbeck (ed.), "A Colonial Reading List from the Union Library of Hatboro, Pennsylvania," *Pennsylvania Magazine of History and Biography,* LVI (1932); and Austin K. Gray, *Benjamin Franklin's Library: A Short Account of the Library Company of Philadelphia* (Macmillan, 1937).

The several histories of American journalism contains sections on the colonial newspaper. For a sociological approach see Sidney Kobre, *The Development of the Colonial Newspaper* (Colonial Press, 1944). Livingston Rutherford has an old but still useful life of *John Peter Zenger* (Dodd, Mead, 1904), and Clyde M. Duniway's *The Development of Freedom of the Press in Massachusetts* (Longmans (David McKay Co.), 1906) is still worth consulting. Lyon N. Richardson's *A History of American Magazines, 1741–1789* (Nelson, 1931) is a detailed study of colonial periodicals.

For special town schools, see William W. Kemp, *The Support of Schools in Colonial New York by the Society for the Propagation of the Gospel in Foreign Parts* (Columbia, 1913); Robert E. Seybolt, *The Private Schools of Colonial Boston* (Harvard, 1935); and *The Evening Schools of New York City* (University of the State of New York, 1921).

### 4. Diffusion of the Arts and Sciences

Michael Kraus has presented in an orderly and attractive way a great deal of information about the interchange of thought and culture between Europe and America in his *The Atlantic Civilization: Eighteenth Century Origins* (Cornell, 1949). For some interesting sidelights on this discussion, see William L. Sachse, *The Colonial American in Britain* (University of Wisconsin Press, 1956). Louis B. Wright, in *The Cultural Life of the American Colonies*, chs. 5–11, sums up a lot of scholarship on books, schools, drama, architecture, science, etc., in the colonial period.

The interest of the planting classes in the classics is well illustrated in such materials as the various diaries of William Byrd, and abundantly demonstrated in Louis B. Wright's "The Classical Tradition in Colonial Virginia," *Papers of the Bibliographical Society of America*, XXXIII (1939), and in Charles A. Barker's *The Background of the Revolution in Maryland* (Yale, 1940), ch. 2. The standard account of the Latin grammar schools in the colonies is Elmer E. Brown, *The Making of Our Middle Schools* (Longmans (David McKay Co.), 1903). A less conventional view of the New England grammar schools is Clifton K. Shipton, "Secondary Education in the Puritan Colonies," *New England Quarterly*, VII (December, 1934). For the classical interests and training of college students the best introduction is Samuel E. Morison's monumental *Harvard College in the Seventeenth Century*. The impact of the classics on the thought of leaders is traced in Charles F. Mullett, "Classical Influences on the American Revolution," *Classical Journal*, XXXV (November, 1939). A summary of colonial contributions to classical scholarship may be found in John E. Sandys, *A History of Classical Scholarship* (Cambridge, 1908, III).

For the reception of modern literature, Samuel E. Morison, *The Intellectual Life of Colonial New England*; Thomas G. Wright, *Literary Culture in Early New England* (Yale, 1920); Perry Miller, *The New England Mind: The Seventeenth Century*; Louis B. Wright, *The First Gentlemen of Vir-*

ginia; and Carl and Jessica Bridenbaugh, *Rebels and Gentlemen,* may be profitably consulted.

Of special value for the history of science during the colonial period are Brooke Hindle, *The Pursuit of Science in Revolutionary America, 1735–1789* (University of North Carolina Press, 1956), and Theodore Hornberger, *Scientific Thought in the American Colleges, 1638–1800* (University of Texas Press, 1945). A valuable series of papers on early American science is contained in "The Early History of Science and Learning in America," *Proceedings of the American Philosophical Society,* LXXXVI (September, 1942). For a convenient summary, see chapter 1 of Dirk J. Struik, *Yankee Science in the Making* (Little, Brown, 1948). The achievements of a large number of colonial scientists are usefully summarized in Whitfield J. Bell, *Early American Science: Needs and Opportunities for Study* (Institute of Early American History and Culture, 1955). Michael Kraus's paper, "Scientific Relations Between Europe and America in the Eighteenth Century," *Scientific Monthly,* LV (September, 1942), is illuminating. Valuable information on the influence of British science in America is available in Frederick Brasch, "The Royal Society of London and Its Influence upon Scientific Thought in the American Colonies," *Scientific Monthly,* XXXIII (October and November, 1931). Harry Woolf, *The Transits of Venus: A Study of Eighteenth Century Science* (Princeton, 1959) is an excellent study of both scientific ideas and international cooperation. Treatments of colonial mathematics are available in the several histories of mathematics in America. On the colonial period in particular, see Leo G. Simons, *Introduction of Algebra into American Schools in the Eighteenth Century* (Government Printing Office, 1924), and Frederick B. Tolles, *James Logan and the Culture of Provincial America* (Little, Brown, 1957). William Martin Smallwood, *Natural History and the American Mind* (Columbia, 1941), is based on extensive research.

There is no adequate life of David Rittenhouse, though William Barton's *Memoirs of David Rittenhouse* (Philadelphia, 1813) still has some value. Maurice J. Babb's essay on Rittenhouse in the *Pennsylvania Magazine of History and Biography,* XVI (1932) is useful. G. Brown Goode, *The Beginnings of Natural History in America* (Biological Society of America, Washington, D.C., 1886), is a pioneer study. For a more modern treatment consult appropriate chapters of Brooke Hindle, *The Pursuit of Science in Revolutionary America.* William Darlington's *Memorials of John and William Bartram and Humphrey Marshall* (Philadelphia, 1849) is valuable chiefly for the charming letters by its subjects. Ernest Earnest's *John and William Bartram* (University of Pennsylvania Press, 1941) is a popular study. Francis Harper has produced a superb edition of the *Travels of Will-*

*iam Bartram: Naturalist's Edition* (Yale, 1958). On natural history, Martti Kerkkonen, *Peter Kalm's North American Journey: Its Ideological Background and Results* (Finnish Historical Society, Helsinki, 1959), and George Frederick Frick and Raymond Phineas Stearns, *Mark Catesby: The Colonial Audubon* (University of Illinois Press, 1961), are informative. E. S. Balch, "Arctic Expeditions Sent from the American Colonies," *Pennsylvania Magazine of History and Biography*, XXXI (1907), gives the main facts. On Franklin's scientific work see I. Bernard Cohen, *Franklin and Newton: An Inquiry into Speculative Newtonian Experimental Science and Franklin's Work in Electricity as an Example Thereof* (American Philosophical Society, 1956), and Cohen's earlier critical edition of *Benjamin Franklin's Experiments* (Harvard, 1940).

Every student of colonial intellectual history should read Jefferson's *Notes on Virginia*, available in the several editions of his writings and in a special edition by William Peden (University of North Carolina Press, 1955). Edward Eggleston gives many picturesque examples of folklore in *The Transit of Civilization from England to America in the Seventeenth Century* (Beacon Press, 1959).

The general histories of medicine give some attention to the colonial period. For discussions of medicine in the colonies, see especially Richard H. Shryock, "Eighteenth Century Medicine in America," *Proceedings of the American Antiquarian Society*, LIX (1950), the same author's *Medicine and Society in America, 1660–1860* (New York University Press, 1960), and the first chapter of Henry B. Shafer, *The American Medical Profession, 1733–1850* (Columbia, 1936). On particular problems, valuable information is available in Betsy Copping Corner, *William Shippen, Jr., Pioneer in American Medical Education* (American Philosophical Society, 1951); Otho T. Beall, Jr., and Richard H. Shryock, *Cotton Mather, First Significant Figure in American Medicine* (Johns Hopkins, 1954); John B. Blake, *Public Health in the Town of Boston, 1630–1822* (Harvard, 1959); and John Duffy, *Epidemics in Colonial America* (Louisiana State University Press, 1953).

### 5. The Rise of the Enlightenment

The European background of the American Enlightenment is discussed from various angles in Carl Becker, *The Heavenly City of the Eighteenth Century Philosophers* (Yale, 1932); Crane Brinton, *Ideas and Men: The Story of Western Thought* (Prentice-Hall, 1950), chs. 10–11; Ernst Cassirer, *The Philosophy of the Enlightenment* (Princeton, 1951); Katherine Collier,

The Cosmogonies of Our Fathers (Columbia, 1934); Harold J. Laski, The Rise of European Liberalism (G. Allen, 1936); John H. Randall, Jr., The Making of the Modern Mind (rev. ed., Houghton Mifflin, 1941); Philip Shorr, Science and Superstition in the Eighteenth Century (Columbia, 1940); and Preserved Smith, A History of Modern Culture (Holt, 1934).

The Works of Roger Williams, edited by members of the Narragansett Club (6 vols., Providence, 1866–1874), contain the chief writings of this champion of freedom of religious thought. In addition to the studies by Perry Miller and Ola Elizabeth Winslow, Samuel H. Brockunier's Irrepressible Democrat, Roger Williams (Ronald, 1940) stresses the democratic aspects of Williams' thought. Herbert W. Schneider has an incisive and stimulating essay on Samuel Johnson in his collected works: Samuel Johnson, President of King's College: His Career and Writings (4 vols., Columbia, 1929), II. A more recent discussion of Johnson is chapter 4 of Claude M. Newlin, Philosophy and Religion in Colonial America (Philosophical Library, 1962). Max Savelle, in his Seeds of Liberty: The Genesis of the American Mind (Knopf, 1948) has a readable discussion of Enlightenment science and philosophy. Frederick E. Brasch has an informative article on Newtonianism, "The Newtonian Epoch in the American Colonies," American Antiquarian Society Proceedings, n.s. XLIX (October, 1939). The spread of Newtonianism is traced in Chester E. Jorgenson's "The New Science in the Almanacs of Ames and Franklin," New England Quarterly, VIII (December, 1935). Benjamin Colman's sermon, God Deals With Us as Rational Creatures (Boston, 1723) is very readable. Serious students cannot neglect John Wise's The Churches Quarrel Espoused (Boston, 1710). For a general treatment of religious liberalism in New England, see Conrad Wright's excellent The Beginnings of Unitarianism in America (Starr King Press, 1955). George Allen Cook, John Wise, Early American Democrat (King's Crown, 1952) is an adequate biography. On Wise, Perry Miller, The New England Mind: From Colony to Province, is interesting and informative. Clinton Rossiter includes essays on Wise, Jonathan Mayhew, and Roger Williams in his Seedtime of the Republic: the Origin of the American Tradition of Political Liberty (Harcourt, Brace & World, 1953). There is no life of Charles Chauncy, or an edition of his writings, but Conrad Wright, The Beginnings of Unitarianism, offers valuable information. On other aspects of religious liberalism, Claude Newlin's Philosophy and Religion in Colonial America is valuable. Howard Mumford Jones has a brilliant essay, "The Drift to Liberalism in the American Eighteenth Century," in Authority and the Individual (Harvard, 1937). Herbert M. Morais has given the main outlines of the development of deism in Deism in Eighteenth Century America (Columbia, 1934). I. Woodbridge Riley's exhaustive *American Philosophy, the Early Schools* (Dodd, Mead, 1907) is a pioneer and indispensable work. Useful studies of various phases of the Enlightenment are Mary Margaret H. Barr, *Voltaire in America, 1744–1800, Johns Hopkins Studies in Literature and Languages* (XXXIX, 1941), and Paul H. Spurlin, *Montesquieu in America* (Louisiana State University Press, 1940).

For general discussions of colonial social thought, see Max Savelle's *Seeds of Liberty*, ch. 6, and Clinton Rossiter, *Seedtime of the Republic*. On particular phases of social ideas in the colonies, there are several good studies. E. A. J. Johnson, *American Economic Thought in the Seventeenth Century* (Russell and Russell, 1961) is good, as is the discussion of natural rights philosophy in Benjamin F. Wright, Jr., *American Interpretations of Natural Law* (Harvard, 1931), chs. 2–4. Carl Becker, in *The Declaration of Independence* (Harcourt, Brace & World, 1922, and Vintage Paperback, 1958), demonstrates with his usual cogency and brilliance the fact that the natural rights philosophy was familiar to Americans before the Declaration of Independence. Lewis J. Carey, *Franklin's Economic Views* (Doubleday, 1928), is the most satisfactory study of this particular aspect of Franklin. John B. Bury, *The Idea of Progress* (Macmillan, 1920, and Beacon Paperback, 1956), provides the European background for an understanding of this idea in American thought. Jonathan Mayhew's *A Discourse Concerning Unlimited Submission and Non-Resistance to the Higher Powers* (Boston, 1750) is a classic.

Frank J. Klingberg's scholarly and illuminating studies of eighteenth century humanitarianism have indebted all students of the question to him. See especially his *The Antislavery Movement in England* (Yale, 1926) and "The Evolution of the Humanitarian Spirit in Eighteenth-Century England," *Pennsylvania Magazine of History and Biography*, LXVI (July, 1942). Amos A. Ettinger, in his *James Oglethorpe, Imperial Idealist* (Clarendon Press, 1936), offers a general interpretation. E. C. D. Beatty's *William Penn as a Social Philosopher* (Columbia, 1939) and George S. Brookes's *Friend Anthony Benezet* (University of Pennsylvania Press, 1937) are excellent studies.

### 6. *The Revolutionary Shift in Emphasis*

An excellent discussion of the American Revolution as part of a broad, international movement is available in the first volume of R. R. Palmer, *The Age of the Democratic Revolution: A Political History of Europe and America, 1760–1800* (Princeton, 1959). The monographic literature on the revolution is vast, and almost all of it contains at least some passing notice of intellectual history.

For illuminating observations on the American colleges at the end of the Revolution, see Marquis de Chastellux, *Travels in North America* (Dublin, 1787), II, 209–279; Henry Wansey, *An Excursion to the United States in the Summer of 1794* (2nd ed., Salisbury, 1798), 50; LaRochefoucauld-Liancourt, *Travels Through the United States of North America* (London, 1799), II, 660–663; Brissot de Warville, *New Travels in the United States of America* (London, 1792), 107; Isaac Weld, *Travels Through the United States of North America in the Years 1795, 1796, and 1797* (London, 1799), I, 167–168; Johann Schoepf, *Travels in the Confederation* (W. J. Campbell, 1911), I, 86–87; and Ezra Stiles, *Literary Diary*, edited by F. B. Dexter (Scribner, 1901), III, 366. The impact of the Revolution on scholarship is treated in Merle Curti, "The American Scholar in Three Wars," *Journal of the History of Ideas*, III (June, 1942).

Observations and reflections on the influence of the Revolution on agencies of intellectual life are contained in John Drayton, *Letters Written During a Tour Through the Northern and Eastern States* (Charleston, 1794); Edgar W. Knight (ed.), *A Documentary History of Education in the South Before 1860* (5 vols., University of North Carolina Press, 1949–1953); and De Witt Clinton, *An Introductory Discourse Delivered before the Literary and Philosophical Society of New York* (New York, 1815). For further illustrations, see the rich storehouse, *The Diary of William Bentley* (Essex Institute, 1905–1907). Other primary materials of special significance are David Ramsay, *The History of the American Revolution* (2 vols., Philadelphia, 1789); *The Miscellaneous Works of Colonel Humphreys* (New York, 1790); William Manning, *The Key of Libberty*, edited by Samuel Eliot Morison (The Manning Association, 1922); William Dunlap, *History of the American Theater* (New York, 1832); and Frank Moore, *Songs and Ballads of the American Revolution* (New York, 1856).

Material for the study of some of the intellectual leaders of the revolutionary generation is voluminous. Jefferson has received most attention. A definitive edition of the Jefferson papers is being prepared under the general editorship of Julian P. Boyd (Princeton University Press, 1950–    ). Dumas Malone, meantime, has provided a good edition of the *Autobiography of Thomas Jefferson* (Putnam, 1959). Malone has also completed three volumes of a biography, *Jefferson and His Time* (Little, Brown, 1948–1962), and Marie Kimball three volumes of her *Jefferson* (Coward-McCann, 1943–1950). Nathan Schachner's *Thomas Jefferson: A Biography* (2 vols., Appleton-Century-Crofts, 1951), is more suitable for the general reader because of its factual emphasis on Jefferson as a human being. There are a very large number of monographs on special aspects of Jefferson's ideas. Adrienne Koch attempts to paint a rounded and consistent picture of Jefferson's mind in *The Philosophy of Thomas Jefferson* (Columbia, 1943); the same author's *Jefferson and Madison: The Great Collaboration* (Knopf, 1950) is also useful. Daniel J. Boorstin, *The Lost World of Thomas Jefferson* (Holt, 1948), is an interesting if not entirely successful effort to recreate the intellectual milieu of Jefferson and his circle. Jefferson's ideas on civil liberties are discussed in Arthur Bestor, David C. Mearns, Jonathan Daniels, *Three Presidents and their Books: The Reading of Jefferson, Lincoln, Franklin D. Roosevelt* (University of Illinois Press, 1955). Jefferson's nationalism is treated in depth by Gilbert Chinard in *Thomas Jefferson, the Apostle of Americanism* (Little, Brown 1929). Caleb Perry Patterson, *The Constitutional Principles of Thomas Jefferson* (University of Texas Press, 1953), is a good, solid piece of scholarship. E. Millicent Sowerby's *Catalogue of the Library of Thomas Jefferson* (5 vols., Library of Congress, 1952–1959) is careful and invaluable. Two other informative studies are Eleanor D. Berman, *Thomas Jefferson Among the Arts: An Essay in Early American Esthetics* (Philosophical Library, 1947), and Karl Lehmann-Hartleben, *Thomas Jefferson, American Humanist* (Macmillan, 1947).

Benjamin Franklin's papers are being published in a new and definitive edition under the direction of Leonard W. Labaree (Yale, 1959–   ). Franklin's *Autobiography* is available in several modern editions, and there are a number of collections of his letters to various people. Max Farrand has provided an excellent edition of *Benjamin Franklin's Memoirs* (University of California Press, 1949). The best biography of Franklin still is Carl Van Doren, *Benjamin Franklin* (Viking, 1938), but other useful studies have appeared in recent years: I. Bernard Cohen, *Benjamin Franklin: His Contribution to the American Tradition* (Bobbs-Merrill, 1953), and Verner W. Crane, *Benjamin Franklin and a Rising People* (Little, Brown, 1954). In addition to monographs previously cited, there are other studies of particular facets of Franklin's life and influence. Alfred Owen Aldridge concentrates on cultural history in *Franklin and His French Contemporaries* (New York University Press, 1957), and Antonio Pace, *Benjamin Franklin and Italy* (American Philosophical Society, 1958), is an exhaustive study of Franklin's influence in Italy.

Lyman H. Butterfield has made available a great deal of valuable information in *The Letters of Benjamin Rush* (2 vols., Princeton, 1951). Also quite useful on Rush is George W. Corner (ed.), *The Autobiography of Benjamin Rush* (Princeton, 1948). These should be read in conjunction with Benjamin Rush, *Essays, Literary, Moral, and Philosophical* (Philadelphia, 1798). No good biography of Rush exists. John Adams has recently received increased attention as an intellectual in politics. Lyman H. Butterfield is general editor of a project to publish the papers of the Adams family (Harvard University Press, 1961–). In the meantime, see Charles Francis Adams (ed.), *The Works of John Adams* (10 vols., Boston, 1851). Although most of the letters were written after the Revolutionary period, Lester J. Cappon (ed.), *The Adams-Jefferson Letters: The Complete Correspondence between Thomas Jefferson and Abigail and John Adams* (2 vols., University of North Carolina Press, 1959), is useful. Catherine Drinker Bowen, *John Adams and the American Revolution* (Little, Brown, 1950), is readable and vivid but nonetheless scholarly. Concentrating more on intellectual history are two interesting and informative monographs: Zoltan Haraszti, *John Adams and the Prophets of Progress* (Harvard, 1952), and Alfred Iacuzzi, *John Adams, Scholar* (S. F. Vanni, 1952). George A. Lipsky, *John Quincy Adams: His Theory and Ideas* (Crowell, 1950), is a systematic presentation. The major writings of Thomas Paine are available in a number of modern editions, and Harry Hayden Clark has given a brilliant interpretation of the thought of Paine in the introductory essay of *Thomas Paine: Representative Selections* (American Book, 1944). There has been a recent revival of interest in Alexander Hamilton. The Hamilton papers, under the direction of Harold Syrett, are being published by Columbia University Press (1961–      ). Broadus Mitchell has written the most thorough biography, *Alexander Hamilton* (2 vols., Macmillan, 1957–1962). The brief essays in Broadus Mitchell, *Heritage from Hamilton* (Columbia, 1957) stress Hamilton's positive contribution; John C. Miller, *Alexander Hamilton: Portrait in Paradox* (Harper & Row, 1959), and Louis M. Hacker, *Alexander Hamilton in the American Tradition* (McGraw-Hill, 1957), are also sympathetic treatments.

J. Franklin Jameson's seminal essay, *The American Revolution Considered as a Social Movement* (Princeton, 1940), is still valuable and stimulating, though it should be supplemented with Frederick B. Tolles, "The American Revolution Considered as a Social Movement: A Re-Evaluation," *American Historical Review*, LX (October, 1954). Discussions of the social ramifications of the Revolution are available in Allan Nevins, *The American States During and After the Revolution, 1775–1789* (Macmillan, 1924); Evarts B. Greene, *The Revolutionary Generation* (Macmillan, 1943); and Elisha P. Douglass, *Rebels and Democrats: The Struggle for Equal Political Rights and Majority Rule during the American Revolution* (University of North Carolina Press, 1955). Moses Coit Tyler's *Literary History of the American Revolution* (2 vols., Putnam, 1879), is justly renowned. The development of political thought is discussed in Carl Becker, *The Declaration of Independence*; Randolph G. Adams, *Political Ideas of the American*

*Revolution* (3rd ed., Barnes & Noble, 1958), with an introduction by Merrill Jensen; Charles F. Mullett, *Fundamental Law and the American Revolution, 1760–1776* (Columbia, 1933); some chapters of Richard B. Morris, *Studies in the History of American Law* (Columbia, 1930); Andrew C. McLaughlin, *The Foundations of American Constitutionalism* (Oxford, 1932); Robert Allen Rutland, *The Birth of the Bill of Rights, 1776–1791* (University of North Carolina Press, 1955); and Stuart Gerry Brown, *The First Republicans: Political Philosophy in the Party of Jefferson and Madison* (Syracuse University Press, 1954), among many others. On opposition to the Revolution, see William H. Nelson, *The American Tory* (Oxford, 1961), which has some information on intellectual history despite its mainly political focus.

Education is discussed in detail in Oscar A. Hansen's *Liberalism and American Education in the Eighteenth Century* (Columbia, 1926). Valuable treatments of various aspects of religion in the revolutionary period are available in William Warren Sweet, *Religion in the Development of American Culture, 1765–1840* (Scribners, 1952); Alice Baldwin, *The New England Clergy and the American Revolution;* Carl Bridenbaugh, *The Miter and the Scepter;* Edward F. Humphrey *Nationalism and Religion in America, 1774–1789* (Chipman Law Publishing Co., 1924); Evarts B. Greene, *Religion and the State: The Making and Testing of an American Tradition* (New York University Press, 1941); Annabelle M. Melville, *John Carroll of Baltimore, Founder of the American Catholic Hierarchy* (Scribners, 1955). The women's rights movement is treated by Mary Benson, *Women in Eighteenth Century America* (Columbia, 1935), and Julia Spruill, *Women's Life and Work in the Southern Colonies* (University of North Carolina Press, 1938). In a delightful and well-documented essay, "The Puritan and Fair Terpsichore," *Mississippi Valley Historical Review,* XXIX (June, 1942), Arthur C. Cole discusses changing attitudes toward recreation, especially dancing.

The beginnings of American nationalism are treated by Merrill Jensen in *The New Nation: A History of the United States During the Confederation, 1781–1789* (Knopf, 1950). Some of Noah Webster's letters have been collected by Harry R. Warfel in *Letters of Noah Webster* (Library Publishers, 1953). Warfel's biography, *Noah Webster, Schoolmaster to America* (Macmillan, 1936), remains the best treatment. The beginnings of the American apotheosis of the founding fathers is informatively discussed in a number of monographs: William Alfred Bryan, *George Washington in American Literature, 1775–1865* (Columbia, 1952); Wesley Frank Craven, *The Legend of the Founding Fathers* (New York University Press, 1956); and Bernard Mayo, *Myths and Men: Patrick Henry, George Washington and Thomas Jefferson* (University of Georgia Press, 1959). An interesting attempt to apply the methods of intellectual history to foreign policy is Felix Gilbert's *To the Farewell Address: Ideas of Early American Foreign Policy* (Princeton, 1961).

## 7. The Expanding Enlightenment

In a provocative essay, "The Myth of an American Enlightenment," *America and the Image of Europe* (Meridian Books, 1960), Daniel Boorstin has questioned the historical accuracy of the idea that the United States participated significantly in the Enlightenment. For a brief introduction to the subject, see the early chapters of Russel B. Nye, *The Cultural Life of the New Nation 1776–1830* (Harper & Row, 1960).

On the relation of American thought to the French Revolution, several works are of value: Charles D. Hazen, *Contemporary American Opinion of the French Revolution* (Johns Hopkins, 1897); Bernard Faÿ, *The Revolutionary Spirit in America and France at the End of the Eighteenth Century* (Harcourt, Brace & World, 1927); Howard Mumford Jones, *America and French Culture, 1750–1848* (University of North Carolina Press, 1927); and Eugene P. Link, *The Democratic-Republican Societies, 1790–1800* (Columbia, 1941). From the opposite point of view, Durand Echeverria has provided an excellent study of French opinion of American society in his *Mirage in the West: A History of the French Image of American Society to 1815* (Princeton, 1957).

General treatments of deism are available in Herbert Morais, *Deism in Eighteenth Century America* (Columbia, 1934) and G. Adolf Koch, *Republican Religion* (Holt, 1933). Other manifestations of religious unorthodoxy are treated in Albert Post, *Popular Freethought in America, 1825–1840* (Columbia, 1943). The discussion of Ethan Allen's *Oracle of Reason* in John Pell, *Ethan Allen* (Houghton Mifflin, 1929), may be supplemented by George P. Anderson, "Who Wrote 'Ethan Allen's Bible'?" *New England Quarterly*, X (December, 1937). The unsympathetic view of Paine's *Age of Reason* in I. Woodbridge Riley's *American Philosophy, the Early Schools*, ch. 7, should be checked against Harry Hayden Clark's introduction to *Thomas Paine: Representative Selections*. Also useful for study is Moncure D. Conway (ed.), *The Writings of Thomas Paine* (4 vols., Putnam, 1894–1896). Nathan Goodman, *Benjamin Rush, Physician and Citizen* (University of Pennsylvania Press, 1934), is only adequate and should be used in connection with material cited in the previous chapter. David Lee Clark, *Charles Brockden Brown, Pioneer Voice of America* (University of North Carolina Press, 1952), is informative. The first-rate study by Dumas Malone, *The Public Life of Thomas Cooper* (Yale, 1926), should be supplemented by Maurice Kelley, *Additional Chapters on Thomas Cooper* (University of Maine Studies, second series, no. 15, 1934).

Conrad Wright, *The Beginnings of Unitarianism in America,* is an excellent study. For a convenient summary, see George W. Cooke, *Unitarianism in America* (American Unitarian Association, 1902). Herbert W. Schneider's excellent essay, "The Intellectual Background of William Ellery Channing," *Church History,* VII (March, 1938), emphasizes the influence of the Scotch philosophers on Channing. An excellent study of the softening of Puritanism is available in Edmund S. Morgan, *The Gentle Puritan: A Life of Ezra Stiles, 1727–1795* (Yale, 1962).

For varying views of the Indian held by colonists, see Frank J. Klingberg, *Anglican Humanitarianism in Colonial New York;* Samuel Stanhope Smith, *An Essay on the Causes and Variety of Complexion and Figure in the Human Species* (Philadelphia, 1787); Benjamin Smith Barton, *New Views on the Origin of the Tribes and Nations of American Indians* (Philadelphia, 1797); Hoxie N. Fairchild, *The Noble Savage: A Study in Romantic Naturalism;* and Roy Harvey Pearce, *The Savages of America: A Study of the Indian and the Idea of Civilization.*

A convenient introduction to the idea of progress in early America is Russel B. Nye, *The Cultural Life of the New Nation,* ch. 2. Two useful essays are R. E. Delmage, "American Ideas of Progress, 1750–1760," *American Philosophical Society Proceedings,* XCI (1947), and Gilbert Chinard, "Progress and Perfectibility in Samuel Miller's Intellectual History," in *Studies in Intellectual History* (Johns Hopkins, 1953). I am considerably indebted to an excellent monograph, Macklin Thomas' "The Idea of Progress in the Writings of Franklin, Freneau, Barlow, and Rush" (Unpublished doctoral dissertation, University of Wisconsin, 1938). James Woodress, *A Yankee's Odyssey: The Life of Joel Barlow* (Lippincott, 1958) is well documented and balanced, but does not entirely replace two earlier studies, Theodore A. Zunder, *The Early Days of Joel Barlow* (Yale, 1934), and Victor C. Miller, *Joel Barlow, Revolutionist* (Hamburgh, 1932). Nathaniel Chipman's *Sketches of the Principles of Government* (Rutland, Vermont, 1793) is a neglected work of real importance. Nelson F. Adkins' *Philip Freneau and the Cosmic Enigma* (New York University Press, 1949) is a masterly study, and may be supplemented by Frederick L. Pattee (ed.), *The Poems of Philip Freneau* (3 vols., Princeton, 1902). For varying views of John Taylor of Caroline, see Charles A. Beard, *Economic Origins of Jeffersonian Democracy* (Macmillan, 1915), and Eugene T. Mudge, *The Social Philosophy of John Taylor of Caroline* (Columbia, 1939). Russell Kirk's *Randolph of Roanoke: A Study of Conservative Thought* (University of Chicago Press, 1951) is informative.

The growing interest in modern languages can be traced in Charles H. Handschin, *The Teaching of Modern Languages in the United States* (United States Bureau of Education, 1913); Howard Mumford Jones, *America and French Culture*, ch. 6; Henry W. Simon, *The Reading of Shakespeare in American Schools and Colleges, an Historical Study* (Simon and Schuster, 1932); and Jane Sherzer, *American Editions of Shakespeare, 1753–1866*, Publications of the Modern Language Association of America (22, n.s. 15, 1907).

Science during the Revolutionary period is discussed at some length in Brooke Hindle's *Pursuit of Science in Revolutionary America*. Useful chapters on the subject are also available in Russel B. Nye's *The Cultural Life of the New Nation* and Dirk Struik's *Yankee Science in the Making*. Harry Hayden Clark's "The Influence of Science on American Ideas," *Transactions of the Wisconsin Academy*, XXXV (1944), is useful. The scientific aspects of Jefferson's career are treated in Edwin T. Martin, *Thomas Jefferson, Scientist* (Abelard-Schuman, 1952). The standard history of early geology is George P. Merrill, *The First Hundred Years of American Geology* (Yale, 1924). Courtney R. Hall, *A Scientist in the Early Republic, Samuel Latham Mitchill, 1783–1850* (Columbia, 1937), is a good biography of a versatile scientist. For a sympathetic treatment of Bartram, see N. Bryllion Fagin, *William Bartram, Interpreter of the American Landscape* (Johns Hopkins, 1933). Philip M. Hicks, in *The Development of the Natural History Essay in American Literature* (University of Pennsylvania Press, 1924), also makes illuminating comments on Bartram. Edgar F. Smith has evaluated Priestley's influence in *Priestley in America, 1794–1804* (McGraw-Hill-Blakiston, 1920). The same author's study of *James Woodhouse, a Pioneer in American Chemistry* (Holt, 1918) is readable and appreciative. No student of the intellectual history of the eighteenth century should overlook Samuel Miller, *Brief Retrospect of the Eighteenth Century* (2 vols., New York, 1803). Another informative primary source is Benjamin Waterhouse, *The Rise, Progress, and Present State of Medicine* (Boston, 1792). Roger Burlingame, *March of the Iron Men* (Scribner, 1938), gives a popular treatment of the development of the principle of interchangeable parts.

## 8. The Conservative Reaction

Alfred Cobban, *Edmund Burke and the Revolt Against the Eighteenth Century* (G. Allen, 1929), provides useful background information on European conservative thinkers like Burke, Coleridge, Wordsworth, and others. Arthur O. Lovejoy, in his *Reflections on Human Nature* (Johns

Hopkins, 1961), discusses conservative conceptions of human nature; Professor Lovejoy's chapter on the framers of the Constitution is particularly relevant for students of American history. Charles Francis Adams (ed.), *The Works of John Adams*, contains *The Defense of the Constitutions* and *Essays on Davila*, two of the most important documents of American conservatism. Correa W. Walsh has discussed the social philosophy of Adams in *The Political Science of John Adams* (Putnam, 1915); also quite informative and suggestive is Zoltan Haraszti's *John Adams and the Prophets of Progress*. The classic source for the controversy over ceremonials and titles is *The Journal of William Maclay, United States Senator from Pennsylvania, 1788–1791* (Boni, 1927).

For William Cobbett see Mary Clark, *Peter Porcupine in America* [Philadelphia (Gettysburg, The Times and News Publishing Co.), 1939]. Leon Howard's *The Connecticut Wits* (University of Chicago Press, 1942) is a work of learning and originality, emphasizing the complex and occasionally progressive nature of the ideas of the Hartford circle. The files of *The Monthly Anthology and Boston Review* and *The Port Folio* are highly interesting. Porter G. Perrin has made a useful contribution to the knowledge of the conservative reaction in *The Life and Works of Thomas Green Fessenden* (University of Maine Studies, second series, no. 4, 1925). Laura G. M. Pedder has edited *The Letters of Joseph Dennie* (University of Maine Studies, second series, no. 36, 1936). Timothy Dwight, *The Duty of Americans at the Present Crisis, July 4, 1798* (New York, 1798), is a good sample of conservative thought at the end of the eighteenth century.

On the conservative reaction as it was manifested in religion, Dixon Ryan Fox has written a very suggestive essay, "The Protestant Counter-Reformation," *New York History*, XVI (January, 1935). James K. Mores, *Jedidiah Morse, a Champion of New England Orthodoxy* (Columbia, 1939); Vernon Stauffer, *New England and the Bavarian Illuminati* (Columbia, 1918); and Charles R. Keller, *The Second Great Awakening in Connecticut* (Yale, 1942), are readable monographs of sound workmanship. Very valuable as a general treatment are the pertinent sections of William Warren Sweet's *Religion in the Development of American Culture, 1765–1840* (Scribner, 1952). Clara O. Loveland, *The Critical Years: The Reconstitution of the Anglican Church in the United States of America, 1780–1789* (Seabury Press, 1956), is a model of scholarship but emphasizes the institutional rather than the intellectual aspects of Anglicanism. Catharine C. Cleveland, *The Great Awakening in the West* (University of Chicago Press, 1916), is still a very valuable study. It can be supplemented by Walter Brownlow Posey's studies of religion in the Southwest: *The Development of Methodism in the Old Southwest, 1783–1824* (Weatherford Printing Company,

Tuscaloosa, Ala., 1933); *The Presbyterian Church in the Old Southwest, 1778–1838* (John Knox Press, 1952); and *The Baptist Church in the Lower Mississippi Valley, 1776–1845* (University of Kentucky Press, 1957). Two other useful monographs are Charles I. Foster, *An Errand of Mercy: The Evangelical United Front, 1790–1837* (University of North Carolina Press, 1960), and Dwight Raymond Guthrie, *John McMillan, The Apostle of Presbyterianism in the West, 1752–1833* (University of Pittsburgh Press, 1952).

For an account of attitudes toward sports in the period, see Jennie Holliman, *American Sports, 1785–1835* (Duke, 1931). Treatments of the origins of the temperance and peace crusades are available in John A. Krout, *The Origins of Prohibition* (Knopf, 1925), and Merle Curti, *The American Peace Crusade, 1815–1861* (Duke, 1929). The reaction against deism is traced in G. Adolf Koch, *Republican Religion*. Niels H. Sonne, *Liberal Kentucky, 1780–1823* (Columbia, 1938), and Clement Eaton, *Freedom of Thought in the Old South* (Duke, 1940), show the reactions against liberalism in the South. Hugh Henry Brackenridge's *Modern Chivalry* is available in a modern edition (American Books, 1937). *The Life and Writings of Hugh Henry Brackenridge* (Princeton, 1932) by Claude M. Newlin is a comprehensive and critical study.

### 9. Patrician Direction of Thought

Two general discussions of the intellectual, social, and cultural life of the first decades of the nineteenth century are Russel B. Nye's *The Cultural Life of the New Nation, 1776–1830*, and Dixon Ryan Fox and John A. Krout's volume in the *History of American Life* series, *The Completion of Independence, 1790–1830* (Macmillan, 1944).

Valuable information on patrician literary and critical circles and conventions is available in several monographs. William Charvat, *American Critical Thought, 1810–1835* (University of Pennsylvania Press, 1936), is quite informative. *The Cambridge History of American Literature*, edited by William P. Trent, *et al.* (4 vols., Putnam, 1917-1921), has indispensable bibliographies and essays.

Leon Howard's *The Connecticut Wits* and Harold M. Ellis'; *Joseph Dennie and His Circle, 1792–1812* (University of Texas Bulletin, no. 40, 1915) continue to be useful for this period in American letters. The first chapter of Van Wyck Brooks, *The Flowering of New England, 1815–1865* (Dutton, 1938), is a charmingly impressionistic introduction. Herbert R. Brown, *The Sentimental Novel in America, 1789–1860* (Duke, 1940), is useful.

Reese Davis James, *Cradle of Culture: The Philadelphia Stage, 1800–1810* (University of Pennsylvania Press, 1957), is a competent and scholarly study.

The following biographies and autobiographical material deserve special attention: Minnie C. Yarborough (ed.), *The Reminiscences of William C. Preston, 1794–1860* (University of North Carolina Press, 1933); Richard B. Davis, *Francis Walker Gilmer: Life and Learning in Jefferson's Virginia* (Dietz Press, 1939); Robert Colin McLean, *George Tucker: Moral Philosopher and Man of Letters* (University of North Carolina Press, 1961); Talbot Hamlin, *Benjamin Henry Latrobe* (Oxford, 1955); Benjamin Latrobe, *Impressions Respecting New Orleans: Diary and Sketches, 1818–1820*, available in a modern format edited by Samuel Wilson, Jr. (Columbia, 1951). Charles E. Cunningham, *Timothy Dwight, 1752–1817, a Biography* (Macmillan, 1942); Amos L. Herold, *James Kirke Paulding* (Columbia, 1926); Sister M. Frederick Lochemes, *Robert Walsh: His Story* (American Irish Historical Society, 1942); John Trumbull, *Autobiography, Reminiscences, and Letters from 1756–1841* (New York and London, 1841). *Epitome of Some of the Chief Events in the Life of Joseph Lancaster . . . Written by Himself* (New Haven, 1833); and Samuel Goodrich, *Recollections of a Life Time* (2 vols., New York, 1857).

Jesse H. Shera, *Foundations of the Public Library: The Origins of the Public Library Movement in New England, 1629–1855* (University of Chicago Press, 1949), is a scholarly study. Histories of learned societies and libraries are available. Among them are Hampton L. Carson, *A History of the Historical Society of Pennsylvania* (The Society, 1940); Josiah Quincy, *The Boston Athenaeum* (Cambridge, 1851); "The Origin of the American Antiquarian Society," *Transactions and Collections, 1820*; James G. Wilson, *John Pintard, Founder of the New York Historical Society* (New York, 1902); and Herman LeRoy Fairchild, *A History of the New York Academy of Science* (New York, 1888).

Among the wealth of contemporary materials the following are characteristic: John Bristed, *The Resources of the United States of America* (New York, 1818; H. B. Fearon, *Sketches of America* (London, 1818); John Quincy Adams, *Report upon Weights and Measures* (Washington, 1821); H. M. Brackenridge, *Voyage to South America, performed by order of the American Government, in the years 1817 and 1818* (Baltimore, 1819); Samuel Miller, *Letters from a Father to his Sons in College* (Philadelphia, 1833); Willard Sidney, "The State of Learning in the United States," *North American Review*, LX (September, 1819).

The beginnings of the popularization of knowledge under more or less patrician auspices may be followed in Edward A. Fitzpatrick, *The Educational Views and Influence of De Witt Clinton* (Teachers College, Columbia University, 1911); Joseph J. McCadden, *Education in Pennsylvania, 1801–1835 and Its Debt to Roberts Vaux* (University of Pennsylvania Press, 1937); John F. Reigart, *The Lancasterian System of Instruction in the Schools of New York City* (Teachers College, Columbia University, 1916); Charles C. Sellers, *Charles Willson Peale* (2 vols., American Philosophical Society, 1947); Harold S. Colton, "Peale's Museum," *Popular Science Monthly*, LXXV (September, 1909); Emily E. Skeel (ed.), *Mason Locke Weems, His Works and Ways* (New York, 1929); Earl Bradsher, *Mathew Carey, Editor, Author, and Publisher* (Columbia, 1912); Dr. Jesse Torrey, Jr., *The Intellectual Torch* (Ballston Spa, 1817); and James Marsh, *An Address delivered in Burlington* (Burlington, Vermont, 1826). Monica Kiefer's *American Children Through Their Books, 1700–1835* (University of Pennsylvania Press, 1948) is richly anecdotal and illuminating. The popularization of agricultural reform may be studied with profit in Harry J. Carman (ed.), *Jesse Buel, Agricultural Reformer: Selections from His Writings* (Columbia, 1947).

R. Freeman Butts has discussed the classical curriculum of this period in *The College Charts Its Course* (McGraw-Hill, 1939), and Donald G. Tewksbury has traced the extension of college opportunities in *The Founding of American Colleges and Universities Before the Civil War* (Teachers College, Columbia University, 1932). L. H. Butterfield, *John Witherspoon Comes to America: A Documentary Account Based Largely on New Materials* (Princeton, 1953), illuminates the early beginnings of the vogue of the Scottish philosophy in America. John M. Daley's *Georgetown University: Origin and Early Years* (Georgetown University Press, 1957) is based on exhaustive research. The revolt of Samuel F. B. Morse against aristocratic patronage in the arts is well handled in F. Carlton Mabee, Jr., *American Leonardo: A Life of Samuel F. B. Morse* (Knopf, 1943). Milton W. Hamilton, *The Country Printer, New York State, 1785–1830* (Columbia, 1936), is a work of careful scholarship.

### 10. Nationalism Challenges Cosmopolitanism

The materials illustrating the continuing influence of European currents of thought are almost innumerable. Howard Mumford Jones, "The Influence of European Ideas in Nineteenth Century America," *American Literature*, VII (November, 1935), is a brilliant and original essay of special significance. For persistent influences of British thinkers, see William Charvat, *American Critical Thought*; Merle Curti, "The Great Mr. Locke, America's Philosopher, 1783–1861," in *Probing Our Past* (Harper & Row,

1955); William D. Cairns, *British Criticisms of American Writings, 1783-1815* (University of Wisconsin Studies in Language and Literature, 1918); Jane Mesick, *The English Traveller in America, 1785–1815* (Columbia, 1923); and Robert E. Spiller, *The American in England During the First Half Century of Independence* (Holt, 1926). Arthur P. Whitaker, *The United States and the Independence of Latin America* (Johns Hopkins, 1941), has an interesting discussion of cultural relations between the United States and Latin America. Various editions of the *Memoirs of Lorenzo Da Ponte*, including that by Elizabeth Abbott and Arthur Livingston (Columbia, 1929), are available. George H. Danton, *Cultural Contacts of the United States and China* (Columbia, 1931), traces the earliest Sino-American cultural relations. Harold S. Jantz emphasizes the continuity of German influence in "German Thought and Literature in New England, 1620–1820," *Journal of English and Germanic Philology*, LXI (January, 1942). An important primary source for the late eighteenth century is William C. Lane (ed.), *The Letters of Christopher Daniel to the Reverend William Bentley and to Other American Correspondents* (*American Antiquarian Society Proceedings*, second series, XXXV).

For English and French influences on law, consult William B. Hatcher, *Edward Livingston: Jeffersonian Republican and Jacksonian Democrat* (Louisiana State University Press, 1940); William W. Story (ed.), *Life and Letters of Joseph Story* (Boston, 1851); Roscoe Pound, *The Formative Era of American Law* (Little, Brown, 1938); and the admirable biography of John T. Horton, *James Kent: A Study in Conservatism, 1763–1847* (Appleton-Century-Crofts, 1939). Some of the selections in Perry Miller (ed.), *The Legal Mind in America, from Independence to the Civil War* (Anchor Books, 1962), are informative on this subject.

The literature illustrating the Romantic influence on American thought is voluminous. John Durand, *The Life and Times of Asher Brown Durand* (Scribner, 1894), and Louis L. Noble, *The Life and Works of Thomas Cole* (New York, 1856), may be supplemented by the illuminating essays in George Boas (ed.), *Romanticism in America* (Johns Hopkins, 1940). James T. Flexner, *That Wilder Image: the Painting of America's Native School from Thomas Cole to Winslow Homer* (Little, Brown, 1962), is also useful. William Dunlap gives an interesting account of the early career of Alexander Jackson Davis in his classic *History of the Rise and Progress of the Arts of Design in the United States* (2 vols., New York, 1843). For Romantic influences in literature, see William E. Leonard, *Byron and Byronism in America* (Boston, 1905); George H. Orians, *The Influence of Walter Scott on America and American Literature before 1860* (Urbana, 1929); Stanley T. Williams, *Life of Washington Irving* (2 vols., Oxford,

1935); *The Life, Letters, and Journals of George Ticknor* (2 vols., Boston, 1876); Richmond L. Hawkins, *Madame de Staël and the United States* (Harvard, 1930); Emma K. Armstrong, "Chateaubriand's America," *Publications of the Modern Language Association*, XXII (1907); Walter Wadepuhl, *Goethe's Interest in the New World* (Jena, 1934); James T. Hatfield, *New Light on Longfellow, with Special Reference to Germany* (Houghton Mifflin, 1933); Sister Mary Mauritia Redden, *The Gothic Tradition in the American Magazine, 1765–1801* (Catholic University of America Press, 1939); John Dewey, "James Marsh and American Philosophy," *Journal of the History of Ideas*, II (April, 1931); and the introductory essay in *Edgar Allen Poe, Representative Selections, with Introduction, Bibliography and Notes*, by Margaret Alterton and Hardin Craig (American Book, 1935).

No more spirited account of the "paper war" between British and American writers has been written than that by John Bach McMaster in *History of the People of the United States* (Appleton-Century-Crofts, 1904), V, ch. 48. Edward Tatum's *The United States and Europe, 1815–1823* (University of California Press, 1936) presents much evidence regarding the role of anti-British sentiments in the formulation of the Monroe Doctrine.

In addition to the writings mentioned in the text, the call for cultural nationalism and American achievements in the realm of the mind may be followed in John C. McCloskey, "Campaign of the Periodicals after the War of 1812 for National American Literature," *Publications of the Modern Language Association* (March, 1935); Robert W. Bolwell, "Concerning the Study of Nationalism in American Literature," *American Literature*, X (January, 1939); William Ellery Sedgwick, "The Materials for an American Literature: A Critical Problem of the Early Nineteenth Century," *Harvard Studies and Notes in Philology and Literature*, XVII (1935); Robert E. Spiller, *Fenimore Cooper: Critic of His Times* (Minton, 1931); James Franklin Beard (ed.), *The Letters and Journals of James Fenimore Cooper* (Harvard, 1960–   ); and Benjamin T. Spencer, *The Quest for Nationality: An American Literary Campaign* (Syracuse University Press, 1957). Gustavus Meyers has quoted liberally from contemporary documents in the struggle for a characteristically American support of the arts in his *The History of American Idealism* (Liveright, 1925). The American spirit in the missionary movement is reflected in Oliver W. Elsbree, *Rise of the Missionary Spirit in America, 1790–1815* (Lewisburg, Pa., 1928). William Alfred Bryan, *George Washington in American Literature, 1775–1865*, details the development of Washington as a symbol of national pride.

Contemporary expressions of cultural nationalism include, among many others, Thomas C. Upham, *American Sketches* (New York, 1815); William Ellery Channing, *Remarks on American Literature* (Boston, 1829); John

Neal, *Wandering Recollections of a Somewhat Busy Life* (Boston, 1869); Samuel L. Knapp, *Lectures on American Literature*, available in a modern reproduction prepared by Richard Beale Davis and Ben Harris McClary (Scholars' Facsimiles and Reprints, Gainesville, Fla., 1961); James E. De Kay, *Anniversary Address on the Progress of the Natural Sciences in the United States* (New York, 1826); and Charles Ingersoll, *Influence of America on the Mind* (Philadelphia, 1823).

The impact of economic nationalism is illustrated in such contemporary writings as Mathew Carey, *Autobiographical Sketches* (Philadelphia, 1829); Alexander H. Everett, *New Views on Population* (Boston, 1823); and Daniel Raymond, *Thoughts on Political Economy* (Baltimore, 1829). Modern commentaries include Hugh M. Fletcher, *History of Economic Theory in the United States, 1820 to 1866* (Urbana, 1926); John B. Turner, *The Ricardian Rent Theory in Early American Economics* (New York University Press, 1921); and the commendable essays by Joseph Dorfman in the *Political Science Quarterly* and elsewhere, the substance of which has now been included in his general study of American economic thought, *The Economic Mind in American Civilization* (5 vols., Viking, 1946-1959).

## 11. The West Challenges Patrician Leadership

Although its focus is not primarily on intellectual history, Frederick Jackson Turner, *The United States, 1830–1850: The Nation and Its Sections* (Holt, 1935), is still of special significance. The discussion of Turner's famous frontier hypothesis has created a very large body of historical literature, some of which adds dimension to the study of intellectual history. Some of the essays in Hans Galinski (ed.), *The Frontier in American History and Literature* (Verlag Mority Diesterweg, 1960), are particularly perceptive. Louis B. Wright's volume of lectures, *Culture on the Moving Frontier* (Indiana University Press, 1955), is a stimulating and suggestive study. Other valuable general materials are Dixon Ryan Fox (ed.), *Sources of Culture in the Middle West* (Appleton-Century-Crofts, 1934); Ralph L. Rusk, *The Literature of the Middle Western Frontier* (2 vols., Columbia, 1925); and Dorothy Dondore, *The Prairies in the Making of Middle America* (Torch Press, 1926). Regional studies of importance include J. E. Wright and D. S. Corbett, *Pioneer Life in Western Pennsylvania* (University of Pittsburgh Press, 1940); James M. Miller, *The Genesis of Western Culture* (Columbus, The Ohio State Archaeological and Historical Society, 1938); Niels H. Sonne, *Liberal Kentucky, 1780–1828*; and Bessie L. Pierce, *A History of Chicago* (Knopf, 1937).

The development of agencies for the support of cultural life in the West is the subject of several scholarly studies. Robert S. Fletcher set a high standard in his *History of Oberlin College from Its Foundation Through the Civil War* (Oberlin College, 1943). James J. Hopkins, *The University of Kentucky: Origins and Early Years* (University of Kentucky Press, 1951), is a well-told story of the disputes that surrounded the early years of that institution. Richard C. Wade discusses the development of agencies of cultural life in the western towns in *The Urban Frontier: The Rise of Western Cities, 1790–1830* (Harvard, 1959).

The contributions of the West to the cultural life of the nation have been treated in a number of specialized monographs. Arthur Deen, "Early Science in the Ohio Valley," *Indiana Magazine of History*, XXXIII (March, 1937) is informative, as is Otto Juettner, "Rise of Medical Colleges in the Ohio Valley," *Ohio Archaeological and Historical Quarterly*, XXII (October, 1913). William T. Lipton, *Anthony Philip Heinrich, a Nineteenth Century Composer of Music* (Columbia, 1939), is a useful biography. H. B. Weiss and C. M. Ziegler, *Thomas Say, Early American Naturalist* (Charles C. Thomas, 1931), is a sympathetic treatment. Loyd Haberly's *Pursuit of the Horizon: A Life of George Catlin, Painter and Recorder of the American Indian* (Macmillan, 1948) is based on patient and enthusiastic research. John T. Flanagan, *James Hall, Literary Pioneer of the Valley* (University of Minnesota Press, 1941), is a good study, and may be supplemented by Logan Esarey, "The Literary Spirit Among the Early Ohio Settlers," *Mississippi Valley Historical Review*, V (September, 1918), and R. Carlyle Buley, "Glimpses of Pioneer Mid-West Social and Cultural History," *Mississippi Valley Historical Review*, XXIII (March, 1937).

Many of the social histories of the West suggest valuable insights into intellectual life. Ray Allen Billington, *The American Frontiersman* (Clarendon Press, 1954), is a brief and provocative lecture on "reversion to the primitive" on the frontier. This theme is worked out in greater detail in Arthur K. Moore, *The Frontier Mind: A Cultural Analysis of the Kentucky Frontiersman* (University of Kentucky Press, 1957). Harriette Simpson Arnow, in *Seedtime on the Cumberland* (Macmillan, 1960), writes sympathetically of the social life of the settlers of that area. Richard Lyle Power emphasizes the blending of northern and southern culture patterns in *Planting Corn Belt Culture: The Impress of the Upland Southerner and Yankee in the Old Northwest* (Indiana Historical Society, 1953). Logan Esarey's *The Indiana Home* (R. E. Banta, 1943), should not be ignored by serious students of frontier values and mores. William Francis English, *The Pioneer Lawyer and Jurist in Missouri* (University of Missouri, 1947), casts some light on the law as a social and intellectual institution. Mody C. Boatright, *Folk Laughter on the American Frontier* (Macmillan, 1949), is valuable, and Constance Rourke's *American Humor* (Harcourt, Brace & World, 1931) is a charming discussion. Madge E. Pickard and R. Carlyle Buley have brought together much useful material in *The Midwest Pioneer: His Ills, Cures, & Doctors* (R. E. Banta, 1945).

Religion played an important role in the development of thought in the West. An excellent general treatment of this subject is William Warren Sweet's *Religion in the Development of American Culture, 1765–1840.* Professor Sweet's *Revivalism in America: Its Origin, Growth and Decline* (Scribner, 1944) may be supplemented by Catharine C. Cleveland, *The Great Awakening in the West.* There are a number of excellent regional and state studies: Walter Brownlow Posey's *The Development of Methodism in the Old Southwest, The Presbyterian Church in the Old Southwest,* and *The Baptist Church in the Lower Mississippi Valley,* are invaluable. Whitney R. Cross, *The Burned-Over District: The Social and Intellectual History of Enthusiastic Religion in Western New York, 1800–1850* (Cornell, 1950), is a superior study. Studies of Catholicism in two western states are: Thomas McEvoy, *Catholic Church in Indiana* (Columbia, 1941), and J. Herman Schauinger, *Cathedrals in the Wilderness* (Bruce, 1952), a study of Catholicism in Kentucky. Valuable information on evangelism is available in Colin B. Goodykoonz, *Home Missions on the American Frontier* (Caxton, 1939), and Charles I. Foster, *An Errand of Mercy: The Evangelical United Front, 1790–1837.* A stimulating interpretive essay is Ralph H. Gabriel's "Evangelical Religion and Popular Romanticism in the Early Nineteenth Century," *Church History,* XIX (1950), 34–47. Useful biographies include John E. Kirkpatrick, *Timothy Flint, Pioneer, Missionary, Author, Editor, 1780–1840* (A. H. Clark, 1911); William Garrett West, *Barton Warren Stone: Early American Advocate of Christian Unity* (Disciples of Christ Historical Society, 1954); and Dwight Raymond Guthrie, *John McMillan, the Apostle of Presbyterianism in the West.*

This chapter is based chiefly on firsthand materials, the wealth of which is vast. Only samples from different categories are given here. The travel literature, which is particularly useful, includes Thomas Ashe, *Travels in America* (Newburyport, 1806); Henry B. Fearon, *Sketches of America* (London, 1818); Thomas Hamilton, *Men and Manners in America* (Philadelphia, 1833); Frances Trollope, *Domestic Manners of the Americans* (Philadelphia, 1832); James Stuart, *Three Years in North America* (Edinburgh, 1833); William T. Harris, *Remarks Made during a Tour Through the United States and Canada* (London, 1821); William N. Blane, *An Excursion Through the United States and Canada* (London, 1824); Karl Bernhard, Duke of Saxe-Weimar Eisenach, *Travels through North America during the Years 1825 and 1826* (Philadelphia, 1826); Zerah Hawley, *A Journal of a Tour Through Connecticut, Massachusetts, New York and Ohio* (New Haven, 1822); and Adam Hodgson, *Letters from North America* (London, 1824). Reminiscences include William H. Milburn, *The Pioneers, Preachers and People of the Mississippi Valley* (New York, 1860); James Freeman Clarke, *Autobiography, Diary and Correspondence* (Houghton Mifflin, 1891); *Life of Black Hawk, Ma-ka Tai-Me-She-Kia-Kiak* (Boston, 1834); *Memoirs of Gustav Philipp Koerner, 1809–1896* (Torch Press, 1909); J. C. Smith, *Reminiscences of Early Methodism in Indiana*; Timothy Flint, *Recollections of the Last Ten Years* (Boston, 1826); Bayard R. Hall, *The New Purchase or Early Years in the West* (New Albany, Indiana, 1855); John Reynolds, *My Own Times* (Belleville, Illinois, 1855); Charles Hoffman, *Winter in the West* (New York, 1835); Wilnathan Gavitt, *Crumbs from My Saddle-Bag* (Toledo, 1884); Julian Sturtevant, *Autobiography* (New York, 1896); T. A. Goodwin (ed.), *Autobiography of Joseph Tarkington* (Cincinnati, 1899); Rufus Babcock (ed.), *Forty Years of Pioneer Life. Memoir of John Mason Peck* (Philadelphia, 1899); Charles Caldwell, *Autobiography* (Philadelphia, 1855); *The Autobiography of Peter Cartwright* (New York, 1857); and *Autobiography of Rev. James B. Finley, Pioneer in the West* (Cincinnati, 1854). Other categories are represented by James Hall, *Sketches, History, Life and Manners in the West* (Philadelphia, 1835); J. L. McConnell, *Western Characters* (Redfield, New York, 1853); J. M. Peck, *A Guide for Emigrants* (Boston, 1831); Isaac Reed, *The Christian Traveler* (New York, 1828); Washington Irving, *A Tour on the Prairies*, in a modern edition by John Francis McDermott (University of Oklahoma Press, 1956); *The Journal and Letters of Francis Asbury*, edited by Elmer T. Clark, J. Manning Potts, and Jacob S. Payton (Abingdon, 1958); and the indispensable documents on frontier religious history edited by W. W. Sweet under the general title of *Religion on the American Frontier: The Baptists, 1783–1830* (Holt, 1931), *The Presbyterians, 1783–1840* (Harper & Row, 1936), *The Congregationalists* (University of Chicago Press, 1939), and *The Methodists* (University of Chicago Press, 1946).

Miscellaneous materials often have great value, as for example *The Writings of Caleb Atwater* (Columbus, 1833); John James Audubon's *Ornithological Biography* (Philadelphia, 1832–1839); C. S. Rafinesque, *A Life of Travels and Researches in North America and South Europe* (Philadelphia, 1836); William Maclure, *Opinions on Various Subjects* (New Harmony, 1831); Daniel Drake, *An Inaugural Address on Medical Education* (Cincinnati, 1820); Lyman Beecher, *A Plea for the West* (Cincinnati, 1834); Edward Everett, "Education in the West," in *Importance of Practical Education and Useful Knowledge* (Boston, 1840); and Bishop Philander Chase, *A Plea for the West* (Philadelphia, 1826). Samuel J. Mills and Daniel Smith, *Report of a Missionary Tour* . . . (Andover, 1815), is revelatory but must be used cautiously, as must similar promotional and propaganda literature. A valuable account from the late eighteenth century is Harry Toulmin, *The Western Country in 1793: Reports on Kentucky and Virginia*, edited by Marion Tinling and Godfrey Davies (Huntington Library, 1948). The files of western periodicals, especially the *Illinois Monthly Magazine*, the *Western Monthly Review*, the *Cincinnati Literary Gazette*, and the *Western Literary Journal and Monthly Review*, are mines of information.

## 12. The New Currents of Equalitarianism

The contemporary literature created by the rise of commerce and industry is extremely voluminous. I have found several books particularly useful: Francis Bowen, *The Principles of Political Economy* (Boston, 1859); the *Massachusetts Official Report of the Debates and Proceedings in the State Convention of 1853* (Boston, 1854); Freeman Hunt, *Worth and Wealth* (New York, 1856); and W. Barrett, *The Merchants of New York City* (New York, 1885).

Two recent studies concentrate heavily on the intellectual aspects of the Jacksonian movement: Marvin Meyers, in *The Jacksonian Persuasion: Politics and Belief* (Stanford, 1957), argues that the core of Jacksonian political belief was a desire to restore an agrarian republic. John William Ward, in *Andrew Jackson, Symbol for an Age* (Oxford, 1955), attempts to show that Jackson provided a unifying symbol for key moral beliefs of the period. Arthur M. Schlesinger Jr., *The Age of Jackson* (Little, Brown, 1945), is a readable and controversial treatment that gives considerable attention to intellectual developments. Joseph L. Blau has edited *Social Theories of Jacksonian Democracy* (Hafner, 1947), a useful collection of documents. Some of the documents in Perry Miller (ed.), *The Legal Mind in America, from Independence to the Civil War*, are pertinent. The development of moral philosophy in the antebellum period is partially traced in Wilson Smith, *Professors and Public Ethics: Studies of Northern Moral Philosophers before the Civil War* (Cornell, 1956). Also informative is Frederick Rudolph's *Mark Hopkins and the Log: Williams College, 1836–1872* (Yale, 1956). Glyndon G. Van Deusen, "Some Aspects of Whig Thought and Theory in the Jacksonian Period," *American Historical Review*, LXII (January, 1958), sketches the main outlines. Arthur Ekirch, Jr., *The Idea of Progress in America, 1815–1860* (Columbia, 1944), establishes the point that the doctrine of progress was virtually a popular secular secular religion, and vitally connected with the development of democratic thought.

F. O. Mathiessen, *American Renaissance: Art and Expression in the Age of*

*Emerson and Whitman* (Oxford, 1941), broke new ground and continues to inspire scholars. Van Wyck Brooks, *The Flowering of New England, 1815–1865,* is impressionistic but very suggestive. Herbert R. Brown, *The Sentimental Novel in America, 1789–1860,* is useful. The studies of literature and literary figures during this period are very numerous, though many are of less use to the historian than to the literary critic. One of the more interesting attempts to locate a central theme for the developing American literature is R. W. B. Lewis, *American Adam: Innocence, Tragedy and Tradition in the Nineteenth Century* (University of Chicago Press, 1955). David B. Davis, *Homicide in American Fiction, 1798–1860: A Study in Social Values* (Cornell, 1957), attempts to discover social attitudes behind the fictional treatment of murder in American works. In recent years there has been a renewal of interest in the historians of the Romantic period in American letters. David Levin, *History as Romantic Art: Bancroft, Prescott, Motley, and Parkman* (Stanford, 1959), is the most general treatment. There are two studies of Parkman as a literary figure: Howard Doughty, *Francis Parkman* (Macmillan, 1962), and Otis A. Pease, *Parkman's History: The Historian as Literary Artist* (Yale, 1953). Parkman's works are long out of print, but Samuel Eliot Morison has provided a judicious selection, accompanied by a balanced introduction, in *The Parkman Reader: From the Works of Francis Parkman* (Little, Brown, 1955). Mason Wade has discovered and edited *The Journals of Francis Parkman* (Harper & Row, 1947). Also quite valuable is Wilbur R. Jacobs, *Letters of Francis Parkman* (2 vols., University of Oklahoma Press, 1960). Howard F. Cline, C. Harvey Gardiner, Charles Gibson (eds.), *William Hickling Prescott: A Memorial* (Duke, 1959), places Prescott in historiographical context. C. Harvey Gardiner, *The Literary Memoirs of William Hickling Prescott* (2 vols., University of Oklahoma Press, 1961), is a rich source. Russel Nye, *George Bancroft, Brahmin Rebel* (Knopf, 1944), is a scholarly study. Among the many useful sources of information on other figures and movements of the period are: James Franklin Beard (ed.), *The Letters and Journals of James Fenimore Cooper;* James Grossman, *James Fenimore Cooper* (William Sloane Associates, 1949); Randall Stewart, *Nathaniel Hawthorne* (Yale University Press, 1948); Mark Van Doren, *Nathaniel Hawthorne* (Sloane, 1949); Vernon Loggins, *The Hawthornes: The Story of Seven Generations of an American Family* (Columbia, 1951); Gay W. Allen, *The Solitary Singer: A Critical Biography of Walt Whitman* (Macmillan, 1955); William Ellery Sedgwick, *Herman Melville: The Tragedy of Mind* (Harvard, 1944); Eleanor Melville Metcalf, *Herman Melville: Cycle and Epicycle* (Harvard, 1953), a collection of letters; Newton Arvin's *Longfellow* (Little, Brown, 1963); Edgar P. Richardson, *Washington Allston: A Study of the Romantic Artist in America* (University of Chicago Press, 1948); John Francis McDermott,

*George Caleb Bingham, River Portraitist* (University of Oklahoma Press, 1959); and James Hastings Nichols, *Romanticism in American Theology: Nevin and Schaff at Mercersburg* (University of Chicago Press, 1961).

The best approach to the Transcendentalists is through their own works. Unfortunately, most of the full editions are incomplete or heavily purged. Thoreau's *Walden* is available in any number of cheap modern editions, as are many of the essays of Emerson. Perry Miller has edited an excellent selection, emphasizing the religious aspects of Transcendentalism, *The Transcendentalists: An Anthology* (Harvard, 1950). A new edition of Emerson's journals is in progress under the editorship of William H. Gilman, Alfred R. Ferguson, George P. Clark, and Merrell R. Davis (Harvard, 1960–). Ralph L. Rusk has edited Emerson's *Letters* (6 vols., Columbia, 1939). Octavius B. Frothingham, *Transcendentalism in New England* (Putnam, 1876), is an old but still useful study. Harold C. Goddard, *Studies in New England Transcendentalism* (Columbia, 1908); Clarence L. F. Gohdes, *Periodicals of American Transcendentalism* (Duke, 1931); Arthur Christy, *The Orient in American Transcendentalism* (Columbia, 1932), and William R. Hutchison, *The Transcendentalist Ministers: Church Reform in the New England Renaissance* (Yale, 1959), are useful studies. Valuable discussions of relatively minor figures associated with the Transcendentalist movement are: Ronald V. Wells, *Three Christian Transcendentalists: James Marsh, Caleb Sprague Henry, and Frederic Henry Hedge* (Columbia, 1943), and *James Freeman Clarke: Apostle of German Culture to America* (John W. Luce, 1949), by John Wesley Thomas. David P. Edgell, *William Ellery Channing: An Intellectual Portrait* (Beacon Press, 1955), and Robert Leet Patterson, *The Philosophy of William Ellery Channing* (Bookman Associates, 1952), provide indispensable background material. The *New England Quarterly* is a rich mine of of articles on Transcendentalism and related New England movements of thought.

Roy F. Nichols' *Religion and American Democracy* (Louisiana State University Press, 1959), contains a brief and suggestive discussion of the relationship between religion and equalitarian thought in the antebellum period. Timothy L. Smith, *Revivalism and Social Reform in Mid-Nineteenth Century America* (Abingdon, 1957), stresses the impulse to reform provided by evangelical religion. The same thesis is maintained in Charles C. Cole, Jr., *The Social Ideas of the Northern Evangelists, 1826–1860* (Columbia, 1954). John R. Bodo's *The Protestant Clergy and Public Issues, 1812–1848* (Princeton, 1954) is a sound and scholarly discussion of the social thought of the orthodox New England clergy. Three recent studies emphasize the methods of revivalists: Charles A. Johnson, *The Frontier Camp Meeting: Religious Harvest Time* (Southern Methodist University Press, 1955); Bernard Weisberger, *They Gathered at the River* (Little, Brown, 1958); and William G. Mc-

Loughlin, *Modern Revivalism: Charles Grandison Finney to Billy Graham* (Ronald, 1959). Henry Steele Commager, *Theodore Parker* (Little, Brown, 1936), is an excellent biography, and should be read in conjunction with John E. Dirks's *The Critical Theology of Theodore Parker* (Columbia, 1948). Barbara M. Cross's *Horace Bushnell: Minister to a Changing America* (University of Chicago Press, 1958) emphasises the extent of Bushnell's orthodoxy, and may be supplemented by two older biographies by Mary A. Cheyney (Harper & Rowe, 1880), and Theodore Munger (Houghton Mifflin, 1899). Robert D. Clark, in *The Life of Matthew Simpson* (Macmillan, 1956), details the development of Methodism into a powerful denomination. The survival of deistic thought has been competently investigated by Albert Post, *Popular Freethought in America, 1825–1840* (Columbia, 1943). Elias L. Magoon, *Republican Christianity* (Boston, 1849), is an important book. Excellent material on perfectionism is available in Asa Mahan, *Scripture Doctrine of Christian Perfection* (Oberlin, 1839); the *Memoirs of the Reverend Charles G. Finney* (New York, 1876); and the periodical, *The Perfectionist*. Arthur Bestor, *Backwoods Utopias* (University of Pennsylvania Press, 1950), is the most useful account of the communitarian movement in both its religious and secular phases. Also valuable are Everett Webber, *Escape to Utopia: The Communal Movement in America* (Hastings House, 1959), and Mark Holloway, *Heavens on Earth: Utopian Communities in America, 1680–1880* (Library Publishers, 1951). Edward Deming Andrews' *The People Called Shakers: A Search for the Perfect Society* (Oxford, 1953) is a competent study. G. N. Noyes (ed.), *The Religious Experiences of John Humphrey Noyes* (Macmillan, 1923), is a fascinating firsthand account by a leading perfectionist, Joshua V. Himes, *Views of the Prophesies and Prophetic Chronology* (Boston, 1841), is an intriguing narrative of the Millerite movement by one of its leaders. It may be supplemented by the file of the *Second Advent Library* (Boston, 1840–1843), and by Clara Sears's popular study, *Days of Delusion* (Houghton Mifflin, 1924). Fawn M. Brodie's *No Man Knows My History: The Life of Joseph Smith, the Mormon Prophet* (Knopf, 1945) emphasizes personal rather than doctrinal factors as the source of Smith's power. Joseph A. Geddes has described the movement for security within early Mormonism in *The United Order Among Mormons, Missouri Phase* (Columbia, 1922).

One of the best studies of culture contacts is Oscar Handlin, *Boston's Immigrants: A Study in Acculturation* (rev. ed., Harvard, 1959). Ray A. Billington, *The Protestant Crusade, 1800–1860* (Macmillan, 1938), is a well-documented study of the early phase of nativism in American thought. A more specialized study of the same phenomenon is Barbara Miller Solomon, *Ancestors and Immigrants: A Changing New England Tradition* (Harvard, 1956). Two valuable studies of German refugees are Carl Wittke's *Refugees* of Revolution: The German Forty-Eighters in America (University of Pennsylvania Press, 1952), and a group of essays edited by A. E. Zucker, The Forty-Eighters: Political Refugees of the German Revolution of 1848 (Columbia, 1950). Marcus L. Hansen, The Atlantic Migration, 1607–1860 (Harvard, 1940), is a richly documented study emphasizing the causes for emigration. There is a wealth of valuable primary material. Among the more useful are the British Mechanics and Labourer's Handbook and True Guide to the United States (London, 1841); Samuel F. B. Morse, Foreign Conspiracy Against the Liberties of the United States (New York, 1835); and Robert Dale Owen, Native Americanism (Louisville, 1844).

### 13. The Advance of Science and Technology

Part three of Dirk J. Struik's Yankee Science in the Making is a useful survey of science and technology during the Jacksonian period. Richard H. Shryock has proposed a stimulating interpretation in "American Indifference to Basic Science During the Nineteenth Century," Archives International d'Histoire des Sciences, V (October, 1948). Older but still suggestive broad interpretations are available in Benjamin Silliman, Jr., "American Contributions to Chemistry," The American Chemist, V (1874–1875), and George Brown Goode, "The Beginnings of American Science," Smithsonian Annual Report, 1897 (2 vols., Washington, 1901).

Charles Wilkes, A Narrative of the United States Exploring Expedition (18 vols., Philadelphia, 1845), is a monumental body of material, comparable only to the files of the American Journal of Science. Somewhat more accessible to modern students is Jessie Poesch, Titian Ramsay Peale, 1799–1885, and His Journals of the Wilkes Expedition (American Philosophical Society, 1961). William J. Rhees, The Smithsonian Institution, Documents Relative to its Origin and Destiny (2 vols., Washington, 1901), is another major source. David A. Wells, Annals of Scientific Discovery (1850–1871); Jacob Bigelow, Elements of Technology (Boston, 1829); Samuel Tyler, Baconian Philosophy (Baltimore, 1848); Thomas Ewbank, The World a Workshop (New York, 1855); Report of the Commissioner of the Patents for 1852, 32nd Congress, 2nd Session, Executive Document No. 65, House of Representatives (Washington, 1853); and the discussions of Ewbank's ideas by members of Congress have been drawn upon heavily.

Among autobiographies and biographies, some are particularly helpful. Esther M. McAllister has written appreciatively and with sound knowledge of Amos Eaton, Scientist and Educator (University of Pennsylvania Press, 1941). George R. Fisher, Life of Benjamin Silliman (New York, 1866), has much useful information, but has been replaced by John F. Fulton and Elizabeth H. Thomson, *Benjamin Silliman* (Abelard-Schuman, 1947). Andrew D. Rogers, *John Torrey: A Study of North American Botany* (Princeton, 1942), pays tribute to a great botanist. Florian Cajori, *The Chequered Career of Ferdinand Rudolph Hassler* (Boston, 1929), is a convenient study. There are biographies of Maury by Dianna Corbin (London, 1880), J. A. Caskie (Richmond Press, 1928), John W. Wayland (Garrett and Massie, Richmond, 1930), and Charles L. Lewis (United States Naval Academy, 1927). Patricia Jahns, *Matthew Fontaine Maury and Joseph Henry: Scientists of the Civil War* (Hastings House, 1961), reaches into the antebellum period for background. Thomas Coulson, *Joseph Henry, His Life and Work* (Princeton, 1950), is a scholarly biography. William J. Rhees, *James Smithson and His Bequest* (Washington, 1880), has the main facts. Elizabeth Cary Agassiz, *Louis Agassiz: His Life and Correspondence* (2 vols., Boston, 1885), contains some useful and interesting documents, but the best study of Agassiz is Edward Lurie, *Louis Agassiz: A Life in Science* (University of Chicago Press, 1960). Other valuable biographies are: Merle Oger, *Alexander Dallas Bache, Scientist and Educator, 1806–1867* (University of Pennsylvania Press, 1947); Helen Wright, *Sweeper in the Sky: The Life of Maria Mitchell* (Macmillan, 1949); David B. Steinman, *The Builders of the Bridge* (Harcourt, Brace & World, 1945), a biography of the Roeblings; and Victor Wolfgang Von Hagen, *Maya Explorer: John Lloyd Stephens and the Lost Cities of Central America and Yucatan* (University of Oklahoma Press, 1947).

The history of science is dealt with in Edward Dana, *A Century of Science in America* (Yale, 1918); George Merrill, *The First Hundred Years of American Geology* (Yale, 1924); Harry Weiss, *The Pioneer Century of American Entomology* (New Brunswick, N. J., 1936); Palmer Ricketts, *Rensselaer Polytechnic Institute* (Troy, 1933); Thomas C. Johnson, *Scientific Interests in the Old South* (Appleton-Century-Crofts, 1936); C. A. Webber, *The Coast and Geodetic Survey, Its History, Activities and Organizations* (Johns Hopkins, 1923); *The Naval Observatory, Its History, Activities, and Organization* (Johns Hopkins, 1926); Philip I. Mitterling, *America in the Antarctic to 1840* (University of Illinois Press, 1959); Daniel Hovey Calhoun, *The American Civil Engineer: Origins and Conflict* (Massachusetts Institute of Technology Press, 1960); Richard H. Shryock, *Medicine and Society in America, 1660–1860*; and William F. Norwood, *Medical Education in the United States Before the Civil War* (University of Pennsylvania Press, 1944).

For health fads, see Thomas L. Nichols, *Forty Years of American Life* (London, 1874). Dr. Martin Paine's *A Defense of the Medical Profession of the United States* (New York, 1846) represents a literary defense of American doctors. Richard H. Shryock has set a high standard in his studies of the public aspects of the history of medicine: "Public Relations of the Medical Profession in Great Britain and the United States, 1600–1870," *Annals of Medical History*, II (1930); "The Origins of the Public Health Movement in the United States," *Annals of Medical History*, I (1929); and "The Early American Public Health Movement," *American Journal of Public Health*, XXVII (1927). Robert E. Riegel has written a delightful account of Knowlton in *The New England Quarterly*, VI (1933). The story of the discovery of anesthesia is told in R. M. Hodges, *A Narrative of Events Connected with the Introduction of Sulphuric Ether into Surgical Use* (Boston, 1891).

For animal magnetism and related phenomena see Andrew Jackson Davis, *The Magic Staff* (New York, 1857) and *Principles of Nature* (New York, 1847), and the writings of Dr. James S. Grimes, especially the *Etherology* (New York, 1845). For a pleasant account, see E. Douglas Branch, *The Sentimental Years, 1836–1860* (Appleton-Century-Crofts, 1934), ch. 9. The best general account of the American reception of phrenology is John D. Davies, *Phrenology, Fad and Science: A Nineteenth Century American Crusade* (Yale, 1955). Still useful is the brief treatment by Robert E. Riegel in *Medical Life*, XXXVII (July, 1930). Nahum Capen, *Reminiscences of Dr. Spurzheim and George Combe* (Fowler and Wells, 1881); Nelson Sizer, *Forty Years in Phrenology* (Fowler and Wells, 1882); O. S. Fowler, *Phrenology* (New York, 1837); the *Annals of Phrenology* (1834–1840); and George Combe, *Notes on the United States of North America* (Philadelphia, 1841), are interesting and informative contemporary materials.

## 14. The Popularization of Knowledge

This chapter is based principally on firsthand investigation in a wide variety of materials. Samuel G. Goodrich, *Recollections of a Life Time* (2 vols., New York, 1857), abounds with information, more or less accurate. Collections of gift books and of paper-covered novels by such writers as George Lippard, Edward Z. C. Judson ("Ned Buntline"), Emerson Bennett, and Joseph Holt Ingraham, and periodicals of the time, have been explored. Academic addresses yield a good harvest. Representative are Caleb S. Henry, *The Importance of Exalting the Intellectual Spirit of the Nation and the Need of a Learned Class* (Burlington, Vt., 1836); Samuel F. B. Morse, *Academies of Art, a Discourse* (New York, 1827); William Dunlap, *Address to the Students of the National Academy of Design* (New York, 1831); and George Bancroft, "The Office of the People," *Literary and Historical Miscellanies* (New York, 1855). Timothy Claxton, *Memoir of a Mechanic* (Boston, 1839), deserves to be better known. Firsthand material on the manual labor college movement may be found in D. L. Dumond and G. H. Barnes (eds.), *Letters of Theodore Weld, Angelina Grimké Weld, and Sarah Grimké* (2 vols., Appleton-Century-Crofts, 1934). The M.S. Record Book of the Richmond, Virginia, Mercantile Library is a splendid source for the study of the problems involved in the maintenance of a mercantile library. Charles C. Jewett, *Notices of Public Libraries in the United States* (Washington, 1876) was a pioneer study. P. A. Siljestrom, *Educational Institutions of the United States* (London, 1853), should not be overlooked.

A very convenient summary of the mass culture of the period is available in Allan Nevins' chapter, "Culture of the Masses," in the first volume of *Ordeal of the Union* (2 vols., Scribner, 1947). An interesting interpretation is Carl Bode's *The Anatomy of American Popular Culture, 1840–1861* (University of California Press, 1959). The essays in William Charvat, *Literary Publishing in America, 1790–1850* (University of Pennsylvania Press, 1959), are very informative. Pertinent material may be found in J. Henry Harper, *The House of Harper* (Harper & Row, 1912), and George Haven Putnam, *George Palmer Putnam* (Putnam, 1912). Merle Curti, *The Learned Blacksmith* (Wilson-Erickson, 1937), tells of Elihu Burritt's crusade for self-culture in his own words. Sidney Ditzion has done pioneer work in the social history of the library movement. See especially his "Mechanics and Mercantile Libraries," *The Library Quarterly*, X (April, 1940). Joseph A. Borome's biography, *Charles Coffin Jewett* (American Library Association, 1951) is especially useful. Lawrence A. Cremin, *The American Common School: An Historic Conception* (Teachers College, Columbia University, 1951), is an excellent treatment. Paul Monroe, *The Founding of the American Public School System* (Macmillan, 1940), is informative. For the antebellum beginnings of graduate education, see Richard J. Storr, *The Beginnings of Graduate Education in America* (University of Chicago Press, 1953). Louise Hall Thorp has provided a vivid study of Mann in her *Until Victory: Horace Mann and Mary Peabody* (Little, Brown, 1953). A useful study of a particular state is Lloyd P. Jorgenson, *The Founding of Public Education In Wisconsin* (State Historical Society of Wisconsin, 1956). Richard D. Mosier, *Making the American Mind, Social and Moral Ideas in the McGuffey Readers* (King's Crown, 1944), attempts to assess the influence of McGuffey's widely used books.

Alan Macdonald, "Lowell: A Commercial Utopia," *New England Quarterly*, X (March, 1937), and Bertha-Monica Stearns, "Early Factory Magazines in New England," *Journal of Economic and Business History*, II (August, 1930), correct erroneous ideas regarding the culture of female mill workers. Arthur C. Cole, in *A Hundred Years of Mount Holyoke College* (Yale, 1940), provides much material for an understanding of the crusade to make higher education available to women. The first full-scale treatment of the lyceum is Carl Bode's *The American Lyceum: Town Meeting of the Mind* (Oxford, 1956). Cecil B. Hayes, *The American Lyceum* (Bulletin No. 12, U. S. Department of the Interior, Office of Education, Washington, 1932), is still useful. Eliot Clark, *History of the National Academy of Design, 1825–1953* (Columbia, 1954), is a good institutional history. The popularization of music is well handled in Arthur L. Rich, *Lowell Mason: The Father of Singing Among the Children* (University of North Carolina Press, 1946).

### 15. New Goals for Democracy

A sympathetic and comprehensive account of reform movements is available in Alice Felt Tyler, *Freedom's Ferment: Phases of American Social History to 1860* (University of Minnesota Press, 1944). For a brief summary, see the fourth chapter of the first volume of Allan Nevins' *Ordeal of the Union*. Robert E. Riegel, *Young America, 1830–1840* (University of Oklahoma Press, 1949); Arthur M. Schlesinger Jr., *The Age of Jackson*; and Joseph L. Blau (ed.), *Social Theories of Jacksonian Democracy*, are useful. For a contrasting treatment, see Clifford S. Griffin, *Their Brothers' Keepers: Moral Stewardship in the United States, 1800–1865* (Rutgers, 1960). Merle Curti, "Reformers Consider the Constitution," *American Journal of Sociology*, XLIII (May, 1938), suggested a new approach to the social philosophy of the reformers.

Two excellent studies cast light on the religious background of reform: Charles C. Cole, Jr., *The Social Ideas of the Northern Evangelists, 1826–1860*, and Timothy L. Smith, *Revivalism and Social Reform in Mid-Nineteenth Century America*. Utilitarianism is treated in two studies of Richard Hildreth, Donald E. Emerson, *Richard Hildreth* (Johns Hopkins, 1946), and Martha M. Pingel, *An American Utilitarian, Richard Hildreth as a Philosopher* (Columbia, 1948). Wilson Smith, *Professors and Public Ethics*, contains discussions of phases of utilitarianism. George D. Lillibridge, *Beacon of Freedom: The Impact of American Democracy Upon Great Britain, 1830–1870* (University of Pennsylvania, 1954), is scholarly and suggestive. Gilman Ostrander, *The Rights of Man in America, 1606–1861* (University of Missouri Press, 1960) is a useful survey.

There is such a considerable body of literature on particular reforms and reformers that only illustrations of the monographic studies can be given here. Merle Curti, *The American Peace Crusade, 1815–1861*, is a full-scale treatment of the peace movement. John A. Krout, *The Origins of Prohibition* (Knopf, 1925), is the best account of the early temperance and prohibition crusade. Much detailed information concerning the women's rights movement may be found in the *History of Woman Suffrage*, edited by Elizabeth

Cady Stanton, Susan B. Anthony, and Matilda Joslyn Gage (Fowler and Wells, 1881). T. V. Smith, *The American Philosophy of Equality* (University of Chicago Press, 1927), ch. 3, provides a thoughtful discussion of the early feminist ideology. The older accounts of Utopian socialism by John H. Noyes, Charles Nordhoff, and William A. Hinds, have been in considerable part replaced by Arthur Bestor's *Backwoods Utopia*. Also quite useful on this subject are Mark Holloway, *Heavens on Earth*, and Everett Webber, *Escape to Utopia*.

No reform movement has received so much attention as the antislavery crusade. Gilbert H. Barnes broke new ground in emphasizing the contributions of western evangelists in *The Antislavery Impulse, 1830–1844* (Appleton-Century-Crofts, 1933). A contrasting treatment is available in Louis Filler, *The Crusade Against Slavery, 1830–1860* (Harper & Row, 1960). Dwight L. Dumond, *Antislavery: The Crusade for Freedom in America* (University of Michigan Press, 1961), is sympathetic and comprehensive. Special aspects of the antislavery movement are discussed in: Robert S. Fletcher, *History of Oberlin College from its Foundation Through the Civil War* (Oberlin College, 1943); Philip D. Jordan, *Singin' Yankees* (University of Minnesota Press, 1946), a biography of the Hutchinson family; Russel B. Nye, *Fettered Freedom: Civil Liberties and the Slavery Controversy, 1830–1860* (Michigan State College Press, 1949); Thomas E. Drake, *Quakers and Slavery in America* (Yale, 1950); Hazel C. Wolf, *On Freedom's Altar: The Martyr Complex in the Abolition Movement* (University of Wisconsin Press, 1952); Henry H. Simms, *Emotion at High Tide: Abolition as a Controversial Factor, 1830–1845* (William Byrd Press, 1960); Larry Gara, *The Liberty Line: The Legend of the Underground Railroad* (University of Kentucky Press, 1961); and P. J. Staudenraus, *The African Colonization Movement, 1816–1865* (Columbia, 1961).

Among the large number of biographies of individual reformers, the more useful are: Helen E. Marshall, *Dorothea Dix, Forgotten Samaritan* (University of North Carolina Press, 1937); Arthur M. Schlesinger, Jr., *Orestes A. Brownson, a Pilgrim's Progress* (Little, Brown, 1939); Ralph V. Harlow, *Gerrit Smith, Philanthropist and Reformer* (Holt, 1939); A. J. G. Perkins and Theresa Woolfson, *Frances Wright, Free Inquirer* (Harper & Row, 1939); Mason Wade, *Margaret Fuller, Whetstone of Genius* (Viking, 1940); Benjamin P. Thomas, *Theodore Weld, Crusader for Freedom* (Rutgers, 1950); Carl Wittke, *The Utopian Communist: A Biography of Wilhelm Weitling, Nineteenth Century Reformer* (Louisiana State University Press, 1950); Margaret Cole, *Robert Owen of New Lanark* (Oxford, 1953); Glyndon G. Van Deusen, *Horace Greeley: Nineteenth-Century Crusader* (University of Pennsylvania Press, 1953;) Charles H. Foster, *The Rungless Ladder: Harriet Beecher*

*Stowe and New England Puritanism* (Duke, 1954); Russel B. Nye, *William Lloyd Garrison and the Humanitarian Reformers* (Little, Brown, 1955); Betty Fladeland, *James Gillespie Birney, Slaveholder to Abolitionist* (Cornell, 1955); Harold Schwartz, *Samuel Gridley Howe, Social Reformer, 1801–1876* (Harvard, 1956); Jean Holloway, *Edward Everett Hale: A Biography* (University of Texas Press, 1956); Otelia Cromwell, *Lucretia Mott* (Harvard, 1958); Richard Hofstadter's brilliant essay on Wendell Phillips in *The American Political Tradition and the Men Who Made It* (Knopf, 1948); Oscar Sherwin, *Prophet of Liberty: The Life and Times of Wendell Phillips* (Bookman Associates, 1958); Irving H. Bartlett, *Wendell Phillips: Brahmin Rebel* (Beacon Press, 1961); Alma Lutz, *Susan B. Anthony: Rebel, Crusader, Humanitarian* (Beacon Press, 1959); Clyde S. Kilby, *Minority of One: The Biography of Jonathan Blanchard* (William B. Eerdmans Publishing Company, 1959); Merton L. Dillon, *Elijah P. Lovejoy: Abolitionist Editor* (University of Illinois Press, 1961).

This chapter is based on extensive research in the primary sources. These include the writings of Elihu Burritt, Lydia Maria Child, Sarah and Angelina Grimké, William Lloyd Garrison, Wendell Phillips, William Goodell, Horace Greeley, Theodore Parker, Orestes A. Brownson, George Ripley, Samuel J. May, Robert Rantoul, Jr., Joshua Giddings, Mrs. Elizabeth Oakes Smith, Frances Wright, Albert Brisbane, John R. McDowell, and many others. Byllesby's *Observations on the Sources and Effects of Equal Wealth* (New York, 1826); Stephen Simpson, *The Workingman's Manual* (Philadelphia, 1831); F. Byrdsall, *The History of the Locofocos* (New York, 1842); and Thomas Skidmore, *The Rights of Man to Property* (New York, 1829), may be supplemented by the materials in John R. Commons and others, *Documentary History of American Industrial Society* (11 vols., A. H. Clark, 1910-1911).

## 16. The Rising Tide of Patriotism and Nationalism

This chapter is based largely on investigations in contemporary materials. The most useful include travel accounts by European visitors, such as Francis J. Grund, *The Americans in their Moral, Social, and Political Relations* (2 vols., Boston, 1837), and Alexis de Tocqueville, *Democracy in America* (New York, 1838), which is available in several modern editions. Also quite revealing are academic addresses and Fourth of July orations, such as George Perkins Marsh, *The American Historical School* (Troy, 1847); Asa Child, *An Oration, delivered before the Citizens of Norwich, on the anniversary of National Independence* (Norwich, Conn., 1838); Joseph P. Bradley, *Progress —Its Grounds and Possibilities* (New Brunswick, 1849); and Robert J. Breckenridge, *Formation and Development of the American Mind* (Baltimore, 1837). Thomas Starr King, *Patriotism and Other Papers* (Boston, 1864), deserves special attention. T. Addison Richards, *American Scenery Illustrated* (New York, 1854), illustrates a large category of materials.

For nationalism and patriotism in the arts, see Samuel F. B. Morse, *Academies of Art, a Discourse* (New York, 1827), and Horatio Greenough, *Form and Function: Remarks on Art* (University of California Press, 1947). American influence on European thought in this period is illustrated in Frederick Grimké, *Considerations upon the Nature and Tendency of Free Institutions* (New York, 1856); Michael Chevalier, *Society, Manners and Politics in the United States* (Boston, 1839); E. O. Haven, *Increased Mental Activity of the Age, Its Cause and Demands* (Ann Arbor, 1854), and Samuel Perkins, *The World as it is in 1841* (5th ed., Hartford, 1841).

There are several general histories of various aspects of American nationalism, such as Hans Kohn's *American Nationalism* and Albert K. Weinberg's *Manifest Destiny*, which are cited among the "General Works" at the beginning of this Bibliographical Note. Unfortunately, the history of nationalism and patriotism is a relatively neglected field, and monographs on the antebellum period are scarce. For a general introduction, see Merle Curti, "Wanted: a History of American Patriotism," *Proceedings of the Middle States Association of History and Social Science Teachers*, XXXVI (1938), and "Young America," *American Historical Review*, XXXII (October, 1926), and *The Roots of American Loyalty* (Columbia Univ., 1946). Frank Freidel, *Francis Lieber, Nineteenth-Century Liberal* (Louisiana State University Press, 1947), is an interestingly told story. See also Merle Curti, "Francis Lieber and Nationalism," *Huntington Library Quarterly*, IV (April, 1941). Agnew O. Roorbach, *Development of the Social Studies in American Secondary Education before 1861* (University of Pennsylvania Press, 1937), offers some useful insights, as does Bessie L. Pierce, *Public Opinion and the Teaching of History* (Appleton-Century-Crofts, 1926). Other helpful monographs are Albert Matthews, "Brother Jonathan," *Colonial Society of Massachusetts Publications* (January, 1901); "Uncle Sam," *Proceedings of the American Antiquarian Society*, n.s., XIX (April, 1908); Ruth Finley, *The Lady of Godey's, Sarah Josepha Hale* (Lippincott, 1931); Arthur M. Schlesinger, "Patriotism Names the Baby," *New England Quarterly*, XIV (December, 1941); and Milo M. Quaife, *The Flag of the United States* (Grosset & Dunlap, 1942).

Oliver W. Larkin has emphasized nationalism and democracy in his *Samuel F. B. Morse and American Democratic Art* (Little, Brown, 1954). For other studies of nationalism and patriotism in literature and the arts, see Gustavus Meyers, *The History of American Idealism*; William Alfred Bryan, *George Washington in American Literature, 1775–1865*; John Stafford, *The*

*Literary Criticism of "Young America"* (University of California Press, 1952); Roger Cahill, *The Art of the Common Man in America, 1750–1900* (Museum of Modern Art, 1942); John T. Howard, *Stephen Foster, America's Troubadour* (Crowell, 1934); R. Walters, *Stephen Foster: Youth's Golden Dream* (Princeton, 1936); and Perley I. Reed, *The Realistic Presentation of American Character in Native American Plays prior to 1870* (Columbus, 1915). Three excellent studies of American characteristics in humor are Walter Blair, *Native American Humor* (American Book, 1935); Jeanette R. Tandy, *Crackerbox Philosophers in American Humor and Satire* (Columbia, 1925); and Constance Rourke, *American Humor* (Harcourt, Brace & World, 1931). Carl Wittke's *Tambo and Bones: A History of the American Minstrel Stage* (University of North Carolina Press, 1930) is a delightful account. For opposition to nationalism and patriotism, see Merle Curti, "Non-Resistance in New England," *New England Quarterly*, I (January, 1929), and Eunice Schuster, *Native American Anarchism, Smith College Studies in History*, XVII (October–July, 1932).

## 17. Cultural Nationalism in the Old South

Avery O. Craven, in *The Growth of Southern Nationalism, 1848–1861* (Louisiana State University Press, 1959), sums up a great deal of recent scholarship, and concentrates on opinions and attitudes of Southerners. There are many insights in pertinent chapters of Clement Eaton's, *A History of the Old South* (Macmillan, 1949), which stresses the emergence of a regional culture. William Robert Taylor, *Cavalier and Yankee: The Old South and American National Character* (George Braziller, 1961), is an excellent study from a fresh angle. Other suggestive general discussions are available in the relevant chapters of Frederick Jackson Turner, *The United States, 1830–1850* (Holt, 1935); the first section of W. J. Cash, *The Mind of the South* (Knopf, 1941); Benjamin B. Kendrick and Alex M. Arnet, *The South Looks at its Past* (University of North Carolina Press, 1935); Richard L. Shryock, "Cultural Factors in the History of the South," *Journal of Southern History*, V (August, 1939); chs. 2 and 3 of Arthur C. Cole's *The Irrepressible Conflict, 1850–1865* (Macmillan, 1934); William B. Hesseltine and David L. Smiley, *The South in American History* (rev. ed., Prentice-Hall, 1960); and Francis Butler Simkins, *The South Old and New* (Knopf, 1947). A competent and detailed state study is Harold L. Schultz, *Nationalism and Sectionalism in South Carolina, 1852–1860: A Study of the Movement for Southern Independence* (Duke, 1940).

Various facets of the intellectual and cultural life of the Old South have received monographic treatment, but a great deal remains to be investigated. Grace C. Landrum, "Notes on the Reading of the Old South," *American Literature*, III (March, 1931), and "Sir Walter Scott and His Literary Rivals in the Old South," *American Literature* II (November, 1930), were pioneer essays. Rollin G. Osterweis, *Romanticism and Nationalism in the Old South* (Yale, 1949) explores a fertile field, although it overemphasizes the importance of the romantic movement. Many of the essays in David K. Jackson (ed.), *American Studies in Honor of William Kenneth Boyd* (Duke, 1940), are concerned with southern antebellum intellectual history. On scientific interests see Thomas C. Johnson, *Scientific Interests in the Old South* (Appleton-Century-Crofts, 1936). Garvin Davenport's *Cultural Life in Nashville on the Eve of the Civil War* (University of North Carolina Press, 1941) is an interesting local study. Henry C. Forman's *The Architecture of the Old South: The Medieval Style, 1585–1850* (Harvard, 1948) is a welcome addition to cultural history, and may be compared with John P. Coolidge, *Mill and Mansion, A Study of Architecture and Society in Lowell, Massachusetts, 1820–1865* (Columbia, 1942). E. Merton Coulter, *College Life in the Old South* (Macmillan, 1928), may be supplemented by Albea Godbold's *The Church College of the Old South* (Duke, 1944). J. H. Easterby, *A History of the College of Charleston* (Charleston, 1935), is a competent monograph. Edgar W. Knight, *Public Education in the South* (Houghton Mifflin, 1932), is useful in spite of an overreliance on educational programs and expressions of aspiration. Edgar W. Knight (ed.), *A Documentary History of Education in the South Before 1860* (5 vols., University of North Carolina Press, 1949-1953) is revealing. For the response to intersectional controversy see William S. Jenkins, *Proslavery Thought in the Old South* (University of North Carolina Press, 1935); Virginius Dabney, *Liberalism in the South* (University of North Carolina Press, 1932); and Clement Eaton, *Freedom of Thought in the Old South* (Duke, 1940). Stanley M. Elkins, *Slavery: A Problem in American Institutional and Intellectual Life* (University of Chicago Press, 1959), casts new light on the subject from several angles. Though it does not concentrate on the South, William Stanton's *The Leopard's Spots: Scientific Attitudes Toward Race, 1815–1859* (University of Chicago Press, 1960) is useful.

The social life of the Old South is discussed at some length in Clement Eaton's *A History of the Old South*. The lives of the plain people are illuminated by Frank L. Owsley's *Plain Folk of the Old South* (Louisiana State University Press, 1949). Also quite useful are Paul H. Buck, "The Poor White in the Ante-Bellum South," *American Historical Review*, XXXI (October, 1925); Shields McIlwain, *The Southern Poor-White from Lubberland to Tobacco Road* (University of Oklahoma Press, 1939); E. Merton Coulter, *The*

*Other Half of Old New Orleans* (Louisiana State University Press, 1939); and
A. N. J. Hollander, "The Tradition of 'Poor Whites.'" in W. E. Couch
(ed.), *Culture in the South* (University of North Carolina Press, 1934). On
plantation life, see Francis P. Gaines, *The Southern Plantation: A Study of
the Development and Accuracy of a Tradition* (Columbia, 1924). An unusual
approach to social history is Jack Kenny Williams, *Vogues in Villainy: Crime
and Retribution in Ante-Bellum South Carolina* (University of South Carolina Press, 1959). State studies which cast light on social history include
Rosser W. Taylor, *Ante-Bellum South Carolina* (University of North Carolina Press, 1942); Guion Johnson, *Ante-Bellum North Carolina* (University
of North Carolina Press, 1937).

The most exhaustive study of Calhoun is Charles M. Wiltse's three-volume
biography (Bobbs-Merrill, 1944–1951). A vigorous defense of Calhoun's political theory is August O. Spain, *The Political Theory of John C. Calhoun*
(Bookman Associates, 1951). Richard N. Current's "John C. Calhoun, Philosopher of Reaction," *Antioch Review*, III (June, 1943) gives a new interpretation. The publication of the Calhoun papers was begun in 1959 by the
University of South Carolina Press under the editorship of Robert P. Meri-
wether. Until the papers are published, a convenient selection is John M.
Anderson (ed.), *Calhoun: Basic Documents* (Bald Eagle Press, 1952). Other
useful biographies include: John D. Wade, *Augustus Baldwin Longstreet, a
Study of Culture in the South* (Macmillan, 1924); Linda Rhea, *Hugh Swinton Legaré, a Charleston Intellectual* (University of North Carolina Press,
1934); Charles S. Sydnor, *A Gentleman of the Old Natchez Region: Benjamin L. C. Wailes* (Duke, 1938); Harvey Wish, *George Fitzhugh: Propagandist of the Old South* (Louisiana State University Press, 1942); and
Fayette Copeland, *Kendall of the Picayune* (University of Oklahoma Press,
1943).

Stanley Elkins' *Slavery: A Problem in American Institutional and Intellectual Life* provides a good historiographical introduction to discussions of
slavery. It is also an effort to attack the subject of the Negro slave from a new
angle. Three scholarly studies illuminate the Negro's religious life: Leonard
L. Haynes, *The Negro Community within American Protestantism, 1619–
1844* (Christopher Publishing House, Boston, 1954); Haven P. Perkins, "Religion for Slaves: Difficulties and Methods," *Church History*, X (September,
1941); and Benjamin H. Mays, *The Negro's God* (Chapman & Grimes,
1938). W. F. Allen, C. P. Ware, and L. McK. Garrison, *Slave Songs of the
United States* (New York, 1867), was a pioneer collection. More modern efforts are Newman I. White, *American Negro Folk Songs* (Harvard, 1928),
and Miles Mark Fisher, *Negro Slave Songs in the United States* (Cornell,
1953), an analytical study. Leon F. Litwack, *North of Slavery: The Negro in*

*the Free States, 1790–1860* (University of Chicago Press, 1961), discusses the fortunes of the free Negro outside the South. Carter G. Woodson, *The Education of the Negro Prior to 1861* (Putnam, 1915), overestimates the incidence of literacy, but provides a good introduction to the subject.

Contemporary materials of more than ordinary interest are: the files of the *Southern Literary Messenger* and *DeBow's Review*; George C. Eggleston, *Recollections of a Varied Life* (Holt, 1910); Charles Frazer, *Recollections of Charleston* (New York, 1854); Ezra Ripley, *Social Life in Old New Orleans* (New York, 1912); Josiah C. Nott and George R. Gliddon, *Types of Mankind* (Philadelphia, 1854); Lester B. Shippee (ed.), *Bishop Whipple's Southern Diary, 1843–1844* (University of Minnesota Press, 1937); Chancellor Harper Sims, *The Story of My Life* (New York, 1895); Susan D. Smedes, *Memorials of a Southern Planter* (Baltimore, 1887); the novels of William Gilmore Simms; and Mary C. Simms Oliphant *et al.* (eds.), *The Letters of William Gilmore Simms* (5 vols., University of South Carolina Press, 1952–56); *The Writings of Hugh Legaré* (Charleston, 1846); Reuben Davis, *Recollections of Mississippi and Mississippians* (Boston, 1891); Hinton Rowan Helper, *The Impending Crisis* (New York, 1857); Frederick Law Olmsted, *A Journey in the Seaboard States* (New York, 1859), *The Cotton Kingdom* (New York, 1862), and *A Journey in the Back Country* (New York, 1863). Carter G. Woodson (ed.), *The Mind of the Negro as Reflected in Letters Written During the Crisis, 1800–1860* (Association for the Study of Negro Life and History, 1926), should be read by everyone with more than a superficial interest in the subject. Frederick Douglass' *Life and Times, Written by Himself* (Hartford, 1881), is a great document.

### 18. The Civil War and Intellectual Life

For sentiments regarding peace and war on the eve of the conflict, see Merle Curti, *Peace or War: The American Struggle, 1636–1936* (Norton, 1936), ch. 2. Edward H. Wright, *Conscientious Objectors in the Civil War* (University of Pennsylvania Press, 1931); Albert A. Moore, *Conscription and Conflict in the Confederacy* (Macmillan, 1924); and Ella Lonn, *Desertion during the Civil War* (Appleton-Century-Crofts, 1928), discuss various phases of opposition to the war. Bell I. Wiley, *Southern Negroes, 1861–1865* (Yale, 1938); Joseph C. Carroll, *Slave Insurrections in the United States, 1800–1865* (Chapman & Grimes, 1938); Herbert Aptheker, *American Negro Slave Revolts* (Columbia, 1943); and Benjamin Quarles, *The Negro in the Civil War* (Little, Brown, 1953), treat the subject of the Negro's ideas from differing angles.

George W. Adams, "Confederate Medicine," *Journal of Southern History*, VI (May, 1940,) is a competent study. More comprehensive, however, is H. H. Cunningham's *Doctors in Gray: The Confederate Medical Service* (Louisiana State University Press, 1958). Stephen B. Wells, "Confederate Textbooks," *Report of the United States Commissioner of Education, 1898–1899* (Washington, 1900), I, ch. 22, is useful. Richard B. Harwell, *Confederate Music* (University of North Carolina Press, 1950), records the impetus to music which secession provided. Mary Elizabeth Massey, *Ersatz in the Confederary* (University of South Carolina Press, 1952), discusses shortages and makeshifts behind the lines in the South. Bell I. Wiley, *The Plain Folk of the Confederacy* (Louisiana State University Press, 1943), is a readable and informative account. W. Pearson (ed.), *Letters from Port Royal, written at the Time of the Civil War* (W. B. Clark Co., 1906), and the *Reports of the National Freedmen's Relief Association* (New York, 1863–1865), are illuminating. Interesting material on intellectual life in the South during the war may be found in George C. Eggleston, *A Rebel's Recollections* (New York, 1876); Thomas W. Knox, *Camp-Fire and Cotton Field* (New York, 1865); Basil L. Gildersleeve, *The Creed of the Old South* (Johns Hopkins, 1915); T. C. DeLeon, *Four Years in Rebel Capitals* (Mobile, 1890); A. J. H. Duganne, *Camps and Prisons* (New York, 1865); William J. Jones, *Christ in the Camp, or Religion in Lee's Army* (Richmond, 1888); William Watson, *Life in the Confederate Army* (London, 1887); and Wirt Gate (ed.), *Two Soldiers: The Campaign Diaries of Thomas J. Key, C.S.A., and Robert J. Campbell, U.S.A.* (University of North Carolina Press, 1938). Frank Moore (ed.), *Songs and Ballads of the Southern People, 1861–1868* (New York, 1886), is helpful.

Chester F. Dunham, *The Attitude of the Northern Clergy toward the South, 1860–1865* (Gray Co., Toledo, 1942), is an example of the type of monograph needed in many areas before it will be possible to understand the role of intellectuals in great social crises. See Lewis Vander Velde, *Presbyterian Churches and the Federal Union* (Harvard, 1952) and Rena M. Andrews, *Archbishop Hughes and the Civil War* (University of Chicago Press, 1935). Emerson D. Fite, *Social and Industrial Conditions in the North during the Civil War* (Macmillan, 1910), has a chapter on education. Earle D. Ross, *Democracy's College; The Land-Grant Movement in the Formative Stage* (Iowa State College, 1942), is an excellent treatment of the Morrill Act and the movement leading to it. George Worthington Adams, *Doctors in Blue: The Medical History of the Union Army* (Abelard-Schuman, 1952), is a scholarly treatment. A useful study is Patricia Jahns', *Matthew Fontaine Maury and Joseph Henry: Scientists of the Civil War* (Hastings House, 1961). Anthony Trollope, *North America*, edited by Donald Smalley and

Bradford Allen Booth (Knopf, 1951), is an interesting account of a visit by a European traveler during the war. Richard G. White, *National Hymns: How They are Written and How They are Not Written* (New York, 1861), recounts the story of the effort to secure a suitable national hymn by means of a competition. Arthur C. Cole has an informative discussion of war propaganda in *The Irrepressible Conflict, 1850–1865*. Frank Freidel, "The Loyal Publication Society: a Pro-Union Agency," *Mississippi Valley Historical Review*, XXVI (December, 1939), is an able paper. The coverage of the war in the northern press has been the subject of several recent studies: Bernard Allen Weisberger, *Reporters for the Union* (Little, Brown, 1953); Louis Morris Starr, *Bohemian Brigade: Civil War Newsmen in Action* (Knopf, 1954); and J. Cutler Andrews, *The North Reports the Civil War* (University of Pittsburgh Press, 1955). Still useful are two briefer treatments, Hairlah Babcock, "The Press in the Civil War," *Journalism Quarterly*, VI (March, 1920), and Thomas F. Carroll, "Freedom of Speech and of Press during the Civil War," *Virginia Law Review*, IX (May, 1923).

Bell Irvin Wiley has discussed the soldiers' lives in his *Life of Johnny Reb* (Bobbs–Merrill, 1952), and *Life of Billy Yank* (Bobbs–Merrill, 1952). For northern soldiers' reading, see William F. Yust, "Soldiers' Reading in the Civil War," *The Outlook*, CXX (October 23, 1918); Philip Jordan (ed.), "William Slater's Forty Days with the Christian Commission, a Diary," *Iowa Journal of History and Politics*, XXXIII (1935); the *Reports of the United States Christian Commission* (Philadelphia, 1863–1865); Lemuel Moss, *Annals of the United States Christian Commission* (Philadelphia, 1868); and such reminiscences as *Memorials and Letters of the Rev. John R. Adams, D.D.* (privately printed, 1891); Frank Wilkeson, *Life of a Private Soldier* (London, 1896); Mason W. Tyler, *Recollections of the Civil War* (Putnam, 1912); and John D. Billings, *Hardtack and Coffee* (Boston, 1888). The Reverend H. Q. Butterfield, *United States Christian Commission, a Delegate's Story* (n.p., 1863), is an interesting account.

The discussion of intellectuals' interpretation of the impact of the war on literature, science, and thought is based on the Smithsonian *Collections*; the *Proceedings* and *Transactions* of the National Academy of Science, the American Philosophical Society, and the American Academy of Arts and Sciences, the *American Journal of Science*, the *Annual of Scientific Discovery*, the files of the *Atlantic Monthly, Hunt's Merchants Magazine, Harper's Weekly, North American Review*, the *Independent*, and other periodicals. Thomas J. Pressly, *Americans Interpret Their Civil War* (Princeton, 1954), discusses some early analyses of the war. Robert A. Lively, *Fiction Fights the Civil War* (University of North Carolina Press, 1957), is an entertaining analysis of historical fiction about the war.

The exhaustive researches of James Finney Baxter in *The Introduction of the Iron Clad Warship* (Harvard, 1933), set a high standard for the history of technology. The wide variety of types of material that cast light on the Civil War period can only be illustrated by such sources as *The Works of Charles Sumner* (12 vols., Boston, 1874); the Emerson *Journals*; W. C. Ford (ed.), *A Cycle of Adams Letters, 1861–1866* (2 vols., Houghton Mifflin, 1920); Elizabeth Cady Stanton, *Sixty Years and More* (European Publishers Co., 1896); Horace Bushnell, "Our Obligation to the Dead," in *Building Eras in Religion* (Scribner, 1881); Charles Loring Brace, *The Races of the Old World: A Manual of Ethnology* (New York, 1863); and Albert B. Paine, *Thomas Nast, His Period and His Pictures* (Macmillan, 1904).

### 19. The Nature of the New Nationalism

The sources and character of Lieber's nationalism are discussed in Merle Curti, "Francis Lieber and Nationalism," and Frank Freidel, *Francis Lieber, Nineteenth-Century Liberal*. Other expressions of the nationalistic impulse may be explored in Frances A. Harmon, *The Social Philosophy of the St. Louis Hegelians* (Columbia, 1943), and Kurt F. Leidecker, *Yankee Teacher: The Life of William Torrey Harris* (Philosophical Library, 1946). John Burgess developed Lieber's general position in "The American Commonwealth," *Political Science Quarterly*, I (1886). Earle D. Ross, "Northern Sectionalism in the Civil War Era," *Iowa Journal of History and Politics*, XXX (October, 1932), is useful to the special student. Two excellent books explore to some extent the intellectual overtones of the reconciliation between North and South: Paul H. Buck, *The Road to Reunion* (Little, Brown, 1937), and C. Vann Woodward, *Reunion and Reaction: The Compromise of 1877 and the End of Reconstruction* (rev. ed., Doubleday, 1956). The nationalist interpretation of the Civil War is discussed in Thomas J. Pressly, *Americans Interpret Their Civil War*. The Centennial evoked much nationalistic writing, typical of which is Frederick Saunders, *Our National Centennial Jubilee* (New York, 1877). Wallace Evan Davies, *Patriotism on Parade* (Harvard, 1955) examines patriotic organizations.

For Morse's position on the Negro, see *An Argument on the Ethical Position of Slavery in the Social System* (New York, 1863). Charles Wesley, "The Concept of Negro Inferiority in American Thought," *Journal of Negro History*, XXV (October, 1940), demonstrates the continuity of the racial theory of the antebellum proslavery argument in subsequent discussions of the Negro. Jacobus tenBroeck, *The Anti-Slavery Origins of the Fourteenth Amendment* (University of California Press, 1951), is a careful and scholarly study. Helper's views were expressed in *La Nojoque: A Question for a Continent* (New York and London, 1867) and *Negroes and Negroland* (New York, 1868). Hampton M. Jarrell presents a sympathetic discussion of one southern leader in *Wade Hampton and the Negro: The Road Not Taken* (University of South Carolina Press, 1949). George R. Bentley's *A History of the Freedmen's Bureau* (University of Pennsylvania Press, 1955) is an excellent study. Henderson H. Donald, *The Negro Freedman: The Life Conditions of the American Negro in the Early Years after Emancipation* (Abelard-Schuman, 1952), takes a gloomy view of the Negro's qualification for freedom. John Hope Franklin's *From Slavery to Freedom: A History of American Negroes* (2nd ed., Knopf, 1956) and La Wanda Cox and John Cox, *Politics, Principles and Prejudice* (Free Press, 1963) present a different picture. Samuel R. Spencer, Jr., *Booker T. Washington and the Negro's Place in American Life* (Little, Brown, 1955), is a readable essay. Also useful is Basil Mathews, *Booker T. Washington, Educator and Interracial Interpreter* (Harvard, 1948). Rayford W. Logan, *The Negro in American Life and Thought: The Nadir, 1877–1901* (Dial Press, 1954), contains considerable discussion of intellectual history. A valuable local study is George Brown Tindall, *South Carolina Negroes, 1877–1900* (University of South Carolina Press, 1952).

E. Merton Coulter, in *The South During Reconstruction* (Louisiana State University Press, 1947), discusses the effects of reconstruction on cultural and intellectual life. For a somewhat later period, chs. 6 and 16 of C. Vann Woodward, *Origins of the New South* (Louisiana State University Press, 1951), treat the mind and spirit of the South. For contrasting views of the impact of reconstruction on southern education, see Edgar W. Knight, *The Influence of Reconstruction on Education in the South* (Teachers College, Columbia University, 1913); Henry L. Swint, *The Northern Teacher in the South, 1862–1870* (Vanderbilt University Press, 1941); William K. Boyd, "Educational History in the South since 1865," *Studies in Southern History and Politics* (Columbia, 1914); W. E. Burghardt Dubois, *Black Reconstruction* (Harcourt, Brace & World, 1935); and Horace Mann Bond, *The Education of the Negro in the American Social Order* (Prentice-Hall, 1934). Jessie Pearl Rice, *J. L. M. Curry, Southerner, Statesman and Educator* (King's Crown, 1949), is informative. Arthur Benjamin Chitty, Jr., *Reconstruction at Sewanee: The Founding of the University of the South, and its First Administration, 1857–1872* (University of the South Press, 1954), is a charming and brief account of the early years of that institution. Willard Range, *The Rise and Progress of Negro Colleges in Georgia, 1865–1949* (University of Georgia Press, 1951), is a well-documented study of Negro higher education. Valuable biographies of "New Departure" leaders are Joseph Frazier Wall, *Henry Watterson, Reconstructed Rebel* (Oxford, 1956); Isaac F. Marcosson, *"Marse*

*Henry"*: *A Biography of Henry Watterson* (Dodd, Mead, 1915); and Raymond B. Nixon, *Henry W. Grady, Spokesman of the New South* (Knopf, 1943). Among contemporary materials, Frances L. Butler, *Ten Years on a Georgia Plantation* (London, 1883); *The Proceedings of the Trustees of the Peabody Education Fund* (Boston, 1874–1881); and *Proceedings of the John F. Slater Fund* (Baltimore, 1883–1885, and Hampton, Virginia, 1886), are major sources.

There are several valuable general treatments of the immigrant in American history, such as Marcus L. Hansen, *The Immigrant in American History* and Carl Wittke, *We Who Built America*, which are cited in the general bibliography. The late nineteenth century is discussed with compassion in Oscar Handlin's *The Uprooted: The Epic Story of the Great Migrations that Made the American People* (Little, Brown, 1951), and in pertinent chapters of *Boston's Immigrants: A Study in Acculturation*. Dumas Malone, "The Intellectual Melting-Pot," *American Scholar* (Winter, 1935), is suggestive. Theodore C. Blegen, *Norwegian Migration to America* is excellent. Carl Wittke has brought together a great deal of material in his *The Irish in America* (Louisiana State University Press, 1956), which is mainly concerned with the period of the mid-nineteenth century. Edward N. Saveth's *American Historians and European Immigrants, 1875–1925* (Columbia, 1948) reveals the influence of immigration on historical scholarship. Edward George Hartmann's *The Movement to Americanize the Immigrant* (Columbia, 1948) is detailed and interesting. The Catholic role is discussed in Joan Bland, *Hibernian Crusade: The Story of the Catholic Total Abstinence Union of America* (Catholic University of America Press, 1951); John Tracy Ellis, *The Life of James Cardinal Gibbons, Archbishop of Baltimore, 1834–1921* (2 vols., Bruce, 1952); James H. Moynihan, *The Life of Archbishop John Ireland* (Harper & Row, 1953); and Colman J. Barry, *The Catholic Church and German-Americans* (Bruce, 1953). The attitudes of the immigrants on public issues are the subject of Florence E. Gibson, *The Attitudes of the New York Irish towards State and National Affairs, 1848–1892* (Columbia, 1951); Carl Wittke, *The German-Language Press in America* (University of Kentucky Press, 1957), a general study which concentrates heavily on the period between 1848 and about 1890; and Arlow William Anderson, *The Emigrant Takes His Stand: The Norwegian-American Press and Public Affairs, 1847–1872* (Norwegian-American Historical Association, 1953). An excellent discussion of nativism is John Higham's *Strangers in the Land: Patterns of American Nativism, 1860–1925* (Rutgers, 1955). For a different approach, see David B. Davis, "Some Themes of Counter-Subversion: An Analysis of Anti-Masonic, Anti-Catholic, and Anti-Mormon Literature," *Mississippi Valley Historical Review*, XLVII (September, 1960). Barbara Miller Solomon's *Ancestors and Immigrants: A Changing New England Tradition* is an excellent regional study.

Theodore C. Blegen has provided a choice collection of immigrant letters home in *Land of Their Choice: The Immigrants Write Home* (University of Minnesota Press, 1955). Other excellent expressions of immigrant thought and feeling are M. E. Ravage, *American in the Making* (Harper & Row, 1938); Jacob Riis, *The Making of an American* (Macmillan, 1901); and Mary Antin, *From Platzk to Boston* (W. B. Clarke and Co., 1899) and *The Promised Land* (Houghton Mifflin, 1912). Herbert Spencer, in *Essays, Scientific, Political, and Speculative* (Appleton-Century-Crofts, 1892), III, develops his thesis regarding the effect of assimilation. The problem is discussed from other angles by H. P. Bowditch, *The Growth of Children* (Boston, 1872), and John W. Draper, *Thoughts on the Future Civil Policy of America* (New York, 1865). For Depew's position, see John D. Champlin (ed.), *Orations, Addresses, and Speeches of Chauncey Depew* (10 vols., Austin and Lipscomb, 1910), III.

One of the best of the many biographies and quasi-autobiographies of Indians is Frank B. Linderman, *American: The Life Story of a Great Indian, Plenty-Coups, Sioux Chief* (John Day, 1936). The movement for Indian reform can be followed in the reports of the Commissioner for Indian Affairs, the proceedings of the Lake Mohonk Conference, and the reports of the Indian Rights Association. Helen Hunt Jackson's relation to the movement is competently discussed in Ruth Odell, *Helen Hunt Jackson* (Appleton-Century-Crofts, 1939). Also quite interesting is Helen Hunt Jackson's own major plea, *A Century of Dishonor* (Harper & Row, 1881). The most detailed study of Indian policy during this period is Loring B. Priest, *Uncle Sam's Step-Children: The Reformation of the United States Indian Policy, 1865–1887* (Rutgers, 1942). For a briefer treatment, see William Thomas Hagan, *American Indians* (University of Chicago Press, 1961). Katherine C. Turner discusses an interesting facet of the subject in *Red Men Calling on the Great White Father* (University of Oklahoma Press, 1951).

The social and economic ideas of western farmers are discussed in John Hicks, *The Populist Revolt* (University of Minnesota Press, 1931). A provocative treatment is contained in Richard Hofstadter, *The Age of Reform, from Bryan to F.D.R.* (Knopf, 1955). Pessimism and loneliness on the one hand, and an exuberant faith in the future of the West on the other, were reflected in many of the frontier folk songs. See especially Theodore C. Blegen, *Norwegian-Emigrant Songs and Ballads* (University of Minnesota Press, 1937) and *Grass Roots History* (University of Minnesota Press, 1947); Hamlin Garland, *Son of the Middle Border* (Macmillan, 1925) and *Prairie Songs* (Stone and Kimball, 1895); and Ole Rölvaag, *Giants in the Earth* (Harper & Row, 1929). The development of the more settled western areas is discussed in Lewis Atherton, *Main Street on the Middle Border* (Indiana University Press, 1954), and Merle Curti, *et al.*, *The Making of an American Community: A Case Study of Democracy in a Frontier County* (Stanford, 1959).

Marie Sandoz, *Old Jules* (Little, Brown, 1935), is an unusually vigorous and vivid account of what frontier conditions did to a Swiss medical student. An interesting account of the first schools in Minnesota may be found in the *Journal of the National Education Association*, XXII (January, 1933). See also Solon Buck (ed.), *William Watts Folwell: The Autobiography and Letters of a Pioneer of Culture* (University of Minnesota Press, 1923). Everett Dick, *The Sodhouse Frontier, 1854–1890* (Appleton-Century-Crofts, 1939), has an excellent account of the development of schools in this region. William J. Trimble, *The Mining Advance into the United States* (*Bulletin of the University of Wisconsin*, no. 638, 1914), devotes two chapters to the characteristics of mining society and the introduction of educational and religious agencies into the mountain West. A more recent and fuller account is Everett Dick, *Vanguards of the Frontier* (Appleton-Century-Crofts, 1940), which treats intellectual developments in the Northern Plains and in the Rocky Mountain country.

Walter P. Webb, in *The Great Plains* (Ginn, 1931), gives an artistic and valuable account of the literature and the "mysteries" of the Great Plains. John A. Lomax has been the great pioneer in the collection of cowboy songs, and his *Cowboy Songs and Other Ballads* (Macmillan, 1938), is a fine collection. Joe B. Frantz and Julian E. Choate, *The American Cowboy: The Myth and the Reality* (University of Oklahoma Press, 1955), discusses the cowboy as an historical phenomenon, and also as a figure in fiction and folklore. Robert Taft, *Artists and Illustrators of the Old West, 1850–1900* (Scribners, 1953), presents a fine body of neglected material. For examples of Mormon social philosophy, see John A. Widtsoe (ed.), *Discourses of Brigham Young* (Deseret Book Co., 1925). The Mormons are discussed from varying points of view in Nels Anderson, *Desert Saints: The Mormon Frontier* (University of Chicago Press, 1942); Thomas F. O'Dea, *The Mormons* (University of Chicago Press, 1957); and Ray B. West, *Kingdom of the Saints: The Story of Brigham Young and the Mormons* (Viking, 1957).

Josiah Royce's *California from the Conquest of 1846 to the Second Vigilance Committee* (Houghton Mifflin, 1886) is written with charm and insight. Constance Rourke has told the story of San Francisco theatricals in *Troupers of the Gold Coast* (Harcourt, Brace & World, 1928). John Swett's *Public Education in California, its Origin and Development, with Personal Reminiscences* (American Book, 1911) contains a mass of information. So does L. P. Brockett's *Our Western Empire* (Bardley, Garretson and Co., 1882). John W. Caughey's *Hubert Howe Bancroft, Historian of the West* (University of California Press, 1946) fills a gap in American historiography. Major John Powell's *Exploration of the Colorado River of the West and its Tributaries* (Washington, 1875) is a classic. Wallace Stegner's *Beyond the*

*Hundredth Meridian: John Wesley Powell and the Second Opening of the West* (Houghton Mifflin, 1954) is a readable and scholarly study. Clarence King, *Mountaineering in the Sierra Nevadas* (Boston, 1871), is excellent reading. Raphael Pumpelly, *My Reminiscences* (Holt, 1918), is fascinating. John Muir's articles in *Scribner's Monthly* and the *Century* in the 1880s did a great deal to interest eastern readers in the scenic beauty and scientific significance of the Far West. Edmund Pearson, *Dime Novels, or Following an Old Trail in Popular Literature* (Little, Brown, 1929) is popular but informative, and Albert Johannsen, *The House of Beadle and Adams and its Dime and Nickel Novels* (2 vols., University of Oklahoma Press, 1950), is a useful study.

## 20. Business and the Life of the Mind

Several excellent studies survey the ideas and values of the businessmen of the period. Irvin G. Wyllie has examined the rags to riches myth in *The Self-Made Man in America* (Rutgers, 1954). Edward C. Kirkland's *Dream and Thought in the Business Community, 1860–1900* (Cornell, 1956) is a well-balanced treatment. The essays in William Miller (ed.), *Men in Business: Essays in the History of Entrepreneurship* (Harvard, 1952), discuss the ideas and social origins of business leaders. Edward C. Kirkland has discussed recent changes in historians' attitudes toward businessmen in "The Robber Barons Revisited," *American Historical Review*, LXVI (October, 1960). Other enlightening discussions may be found in Allan Nevins, *The Emergence of Modern America, 1865–1878* (Macmillan, 1927); Arthur M. Schlesinger, Sr., *The Rise of the City, 1878–1898* (Macmillan, 1933); Lewis Mumford, *The Brown Decades* (Harcourt, Brace & World, 1931); Dixon Wecter, *The Saga of American Society* (Scribner, 1937); Van Wyck Brooks, *New England: Indian Summer* (Dutton, 1940); Stewart Holbrook, *The Age of the Moguls* (Doubleday, 1953); and Edward C. Kirkland, *Industry Comes of Age: Business Labor, and Public Policy, 1860–1897* (Holt, 1961).

*The Autobiography of Andrew Carnegie* (Houghton Mifflin, 1920) is interesting and informative. Robert Green McCloskey has a pungent discussion of Andrew Carnegie in *American Conservatism in the Age of Enterprise: A Study of William Graham Sumner, Stephen J. Field, and Andrew Carnegie* (Harvard, 1951). Rowland Gibson Hazard's granddaughter, Caroline Hazard, edited three volumes of his writings, *Economics and Politics* (Houghton Mifflin, 1889), *Freedom of the Mind in Willing* (Houghton Mifflin, 1889), and *Causation and Freedom in Willing* (Houghton Mifflin, 1889). Other valuable biographical studies are William Croffut, *The Vanderbilts and the Story of Their Heritage* (Bedford, Clark and Co., 1886); Bouck White, *The*

*Book of Daniel Drew* (Doubleday, 1910); Bliss Perry, *Life and Letters of Henry Lee Higginson* (Little, Brown, 1921); Louise Ware, *George Foster Peabody, Banker, Philanthropist* (University of Georgia Press, 1951); Hal Bridges, *Iron Millionaire: Life of Charlemagne Tower* (University of Pennsylvania Press, 1952); Thomas C. Cochran, *Railroad Leaders, 1845–1890: The Business Mind in Action* (Harvard, 1953); Allan Nevins, *Study in Power: John D. Rockefeller, Industrialist and Philanthropist* (2 vols., Scribner, 1953); Richard Lowitt, *A Merchant Prince of the Nineteenth Century: William E. Dodge* (Columbia, 1954); Alfred D. Chandler, *Henry Varnum Poor: Business Editor, Analyst, and Reformer* (Harvard, 1956); Julius Grodinsky, *Jay Gould: His Business Career, 1867–1892* (University of Pennsylvania Press, 1957); and W. A. Swanberg, *James Fiske: The Career of an Improbable Rascal* (Scribner, 1959).

The material on higher education is extensive. G. Stanley Hall, *Life and Confessions of a Psychologist* (Appleton-Century-Crofts, 1923), tells the story of the great educator's relations with the founder of Clark University. Daniel C. Gilman, *Launching a University* (Dodd, Mead, 1906), is especially useful. Carl Becker, *Cornell University: Founders and the Founding* (Cornell, 1943), is a graceful study. Philip Dorf has intelligently discussed Cornell's philanthropy in *The Builder: A Biography of Ezra Cornell* (Macmillan, 1952). Hugh Hawkins, *Pioneer: A History of the Johns Hopkins University, 1874–1889* (Cornell, 1960), is a model study. The ideas of David Starr Jordan are discussed in detail in Edward McNall Burns, *David Starr Jordan: Prophet of Freedom* (Stanford, 1953). Walter P. Rogers, *Andrew D. White and the Modern University* (Cornell, 1942), emphasizes social forces. Henry James, *Charles W. Eliot* (2 vols., Houghton Mifflin, 1930), is a formal biography which should be supplemented by Eliot's own writings, edited by William A. Neilson, *Charles W. Eliot, the Man and His Beliefs* (Harper & Row, 1926). Thorstein Veblen's *The Higher Learning* (Huebsch, 1918) is penetrating. Elsa P. Kimball, *Sociology and Education* (Columbia, 1932), traces the influence of Spencer and Ward on educational thought. Arthur B. Chitty, Jr., discusses the early years of the University of the South in *Reconstruction at Sewanee: The Founding of the University of the South and its First Administration, 1857–1872* (University of the South Press, 1954). The most succinct account of the conflict between the classical and utilitarian conceptions of education is that by R. Freeman Butts, *The College Charts Its Course* (McGraw-Hill, 1939). Matthew Arnold's influence is discussed in Seymour C. Link's *Matthew Arnold's "Sweetness and Light"* (George Peabody College for Teachers, *Abstracts of Contributions to Education*, No. 209, Nashville, 1938). Jacob Bigelow, *Modern Inquiries: Classical, Professional, and Miscellaneous* (Boston, 1877), is of basic importance. The views which James Jackson Jarves held concerning the status and function of the arts in the United

BIBLIOGRAPHY 863

States are engagingly presented in *Art-Hints* (New York, 1856), *The Art Idea: Sculpture, Painting and Architecture in America* (New York, 1866), and *Art Thoughts* (New York, 1870).

Ellis P. Oberholzer, *A History of the United States since the Civil War* (5 vols., Macmillan, 1917–1937), III, discusses Dudley Field and legal ethics. Mark Hopkins, *Lectures on Moral Science* (Boston, 1870); Josiah G. Holland, *Every-Day Topics* (Scribner, 1876); Jonathan Harrison, *Certain Dangerous Tendencies in American Life* (Boston, 1880); and Henry Cabot Lodge, *Early Memories* (Scribner, 1913), are useful. *The Autobiography of Charles Francis Adams* (Houghton Mifflin, 1918), and, of course, *The Education of Henry Adams* (Houghton Mifflin, 1918), are outstanding.

Quentin Anderson, *The American Henry James* (Rutgers, 1957), examines James in a context of American ideas. Leon Edel has begun what promises to be a definitive biography with *Henry James: The Untried Years, 1843–1870* (Lippincott, 1953). Henry Lubbock (ed.), *The Letters of Henry James* (2 vols., Macmillan, 1920), should be read by any serious student. Other useful evaluations of James are J. B. Beach, *The Method of Henry James* (Yale, 1918); Van Wyck Brooks, *The Pilgrimage of Henry James* (Dutton, 1925); and C. P. Kelley, *The Early Development of Henry James* (University of Illinois Press, 1930). William Dean Howells' novels, especially *The Rise of Silas Lapham*, are important. Edwin H. Cady, *The Road to Realism: The Early Years, 1837–1885, of William Dean Howells* (Syracuse University Press, 1956), and *Realist at War: The Mature Years, 1885–1920, of William Dean Howells* (Syracuse University Press, 1958), is the most thorough biography. A useful study of Howells' social ideas is Robert Lee Hough's *The Quiet Rebel: William Dean Howells as a Social Commentator* (University of Nebraska Press, 1959). Henry Nash Smith and William M. Gibson (eds.), *Mark Twain-Howells Letters: The Correspondence of Samuel L. Clemens and William D. Howells, 1872–1910* (2 vols., Harvard, 1960), repays reading. Walter F. Taylor, *The Economic Novel in America* (University of North Carolina Press, 1942); Edward C. Cassady, "The Business Man in the American Novel" (unpublished doctoral dissertation, University of California, 1938); and Robert L. Shurter, "The Utopian Novel in America, 1865–1900" (unpublished doctoral dissertation, Western Reserve University, 1936), are useful critical-historical studies. Martin S. Peterson, *Joaquin Miller, Literary Frontiersman* (Stanford, 1931) provides background material on *The Destruction of Gotham*. Two excellent and stimulating discussions of the reputation of businessmen, differing in approach, are Edward C. Kirkland, *Business in the Gilded Age: The Conservatives' Balance Sheet* (University of Wisconsin Press, 1952), and Sigmund Diamond, *The Reputation of the American Businessman* (Harvard, 1955).

Rollo Ogden, *Life and Letters of Edwin Lawrence Godkin* (2 vols., Macmillan, 1927), has much useful material. Alan Pentleton Grimes, *The Political Liberalism of The New York Nation, 1865–1932* (University of North Carolina Press, 1953), analyzes the political views of *The Nation*. A modern biography of Godkin is much to be desired. For Bryce's relation to Americans, see H. A. L. Fisher, *James Bryce* (2 vols., Macmillan, 1927), ch. 13, and Albert Shaw, "James Bryce as We Knew Him," *American Review of Reviews*, LXV (March, 1922).

### 21. The Delimitation of Supernaturalism

Henry Steele Commager's *The American Mind: An Interpretation of American Thought and Character Since the 1880's* (Yale, 1950), is an excellent introduction to the recent intellectual history of the United States. Henry F. May, in the early chapters of his *The End of Innocence: A Study of the First Years of Our Own Time, 1912–1917* (Knopf, 1959), provides a stimulating survey of late nineteenth-century American culture. The introduction to Perry Miller (ed.), *American Thought: Civil War to World War I* (Holt, 1954), is an incisive commentary on the dominant ideas of the period's intellectuals.

Arthur M. Schlesinger, Sr., has written a superior brief account of religious developments during the waning years of the century, "A Critical Period in American Religion, 1875–1900," *Proceedings of the Massachusetts Historical Society*, LXIV (June, 1932). Ambrose W. Vernon gives a broad view of theological currents in *The Cambridge History of American Literature*, III, ch. 16. Frank H. Foster, *The Modern Movement in American Theology: Sketches in the History of American Protestant Thought from the Civil War* (Revell, 1939), is compact and readable. Francis P. Weisenberger's *Ordeal of Faith: The Crisis of Church-Going America* (Philosophical Library, 1959) is a useful attempt at a synthesis, emphasizing the conflict of science and religion. Valuable studies of particular religious denominations in the period are Aaron Ignatius Abell, *American Catholicism and Social Action: A Search for Social Justice, 1865–1950* (Hanover House, Doubleday, 1960); Robert D. Cross, *The Emergence of Liberal Catholicism in America* (Harvard, 1958); Thomas T. McAvoy, *The Great Crisis in American Catholic History, 1895–1900* (Regnery, 1957); James Arthur Muller, *The Episcopal Theological School, 1867–1943* (Episcopal Theological School, 1943); Lefferts A. Loetscher, *The Broadening Church: A Study of Theological Issues in the Presbyterian Church Since 1869* (University of Pennsylvania Press, 1954); and Arnold Crompton, *Unitarianism on the Pacific Coast: The First Sixty Years* (Beacon Press, 1957). Daniel D. Williams, *The Andover Liberals: A Study in Ameri-*

*can Theology* (King's Crown, 1941), and Thomas Le Duc, *Piety and Intellect at Amherst College, 1865–1912* (Columbia, 1946), are scholarly discussions.

Bernard Weisberger, *They Gathered at the River,* and William McLoughlin, *Modern Revivalism: Charles Grandison Finney to Billy Graham,* are informative discussions of popular religion. Gamaliel Bradford, *Dwight L. Moody: A Worker in Souls* (Doubleday, 1927), stresses psychological factors. Paul D. Moody, *My Father: An Intimate Portrait of Dwight Moody* (Little, Brown, 1938), is naturally sympathetic. Maud B. Booth, *Beneath Two Flags* (Funk & Wagnalls, 1889), and Ballington Booth, *From Ocean to Ocean* (J. S. Ogilvie, n.d.), are sympathetic accounts of the Salvation Army. F. de L. Booth-Tucker, *The Social Relief Work of the Salvation Army in the United States* (J. B. Lyon and Co., 1900), gives the main outlines. Several studies cast light on the important influence of urbanization and industrialism: Samuel P. Hays, *The Response to Industrialism, 1885–1914* (University of Chicago Press, 1957); Aaron Ignatius Abell, *The Urban Impact on American Protestantism, 1865–1900* (Harvard, 1943); Henry F. May, *Protestant Churches and Industrial America* (Harper & Row, 1949); Ray Ginger, *Altgeld's America: The Lincoln Ideal versus Changing Realities* (Funk & Wagnalls, 1958); and Blanche Housman Gelfant, *The American City Novel* (University of Oklahoma Press, 1954).

Anthony Comstock's own defense of himself may be found in *Frauds Exposed* (J. H. Brown, 1880), and *Traps for the Young* (Funk & Wagnalls, 1883). Heywood Broun and Margaret Leech, *Anthony Comstock* (Boni, 1927), is a sophisticated and journalistic account. Mary A. Bennett, *Elizabeth Stuart Phelps* (University of Pennsylvania Press, 1939), is a well-organized and competent biography. Lew Wallace, *My Autobiography* (2 vols., Harper & Row, 1906), gives the story of the writing of *Ben Hur.* Earl Barnes, "Theological Life of a California Child," *Pedagogical Seminary,* II, (1892), is a pioneer child-study report. Winfred E. Garrison, *The March of Faith* (Harper & Row, 1933), emphasizes social forces. Simon Newcomb, *The Reminiscences of an Astronomer* (Houghton Mifflin, 1903), is good reading and informative. A. Trevor Barker has edited the *Complete Works of H. B. Blavatsky* (Rider and Co., London, 1933–1936). C. E. B. Roberts, *Mysterious Madame, Helena Petrovna Blavatsky* (Harcourt, Brace & World, 1931), is a vivid account. Ella Wheeler Wilcox tells of her interest in spiritualism and theosophy in *The Worlds and I* (Doubleday, 1918). Lyman P. Powell, *Mary Baker G. Eddy, A Life Size Portrait* (Macmillan, 1931), meets Christian Scientists' approval. Norman Beasley, *The Cross and the Crown* (Little, Brown, 1952), is a popularization. Less sympathetic studies are E. F. Dakin, *Mrs. Eddy, the Biography of a Virginial Mind* (Scribner, 1929), and Ernest Sutherland Bates and J. V. Dittemore, *Mary Baker G. Eddy* (Knopf, 1933). For the mental healing movement in the Episcopal church, see Elwood Worcester, *Life's Adventure* (Scribner, 1932).

The summary of Frederick L. Bronner's doctoral dissertation, "The Observance of the Sabbath in the United States," *Harvard Summaries of Ph.D. Theses* (Harvard, 1938), is the best brief account of the subject. Stow Persons, *Free Religion: An American Faith* (Yale, 1947), is a definitive monograph. Sidney Warren has discussed opposition to organized religion in his *American Freethought, 1860–1914* (Columbia, 1943). Clarence Cramer has provided an able biography of Robert Ingersoll, *Royal Bob: The Life of Robert Ingersoll* (Bobbs-Merrill, 1952). Eva Ingersoll (ed.), *The Letters of Robert Ingersoll*, (Philosophical Library, 1951), is a fine collection. The reception of the new position of Pasteur, Koch, and Lord Lister on bacteria and infection may be studied in the *Medical Record*, edited by G. G. Shrady. Dr. Henry Gradle, a Chicago physician and pupil of Koch, published in 1883 *Bacteria and the Germ Theory of Disease*, a pioneer discussion of the subject in the English language. Brief accounts of developments in the field of bacteriology can be readily found in the *United States Department of Agriculture Yearbook* for 1899.

The impact of the philological studies evoked a massive literature. Examples are Charles A. Briggs, *Whither?* (Scribner, 1889); Washington Gladden, *Who Wrote the Bible?* (Houghton Mifflin, 1891); Llewelyn J. Evans, *Biblical Scholarship and Inspiration* (R. Clarke and Co., Cincinnati, 1891), and William N. Clarke, *Sixty Years with the Bible* (Scribner, 1909). The religious novel is discussed in *The Nation*, XLVII (October 25, 1888).

Andrew Dixon White, *A History of the Warfare of Science with Theology in Christendom* (2 vols., Appleton-Century-Crofts, 1896), and John William Draper, *History of Conflict between Religion and Science* (Appleton-Century-Crofts, 1874), are pioneer works that still repay reading. *The Autobiography of Andrew D. White* (Macmillan, 1905), is an important book, but throws less light on White's career than one might wish. Donald Fleming's *John William Draper and the Religion of Science* (University of Pennsylvania Press, 1950) is an excellent biography. Edward A. White, *Science and Religion in American Thought: The Impact of Naturalism* (Stanford, 1952), is a Christian interpretation. Samuel P. Langley, *The New Astronomy* (Ticknor and Co., 1888), was an influential popularization of recent developments. Simon Newcomb's *Reminiscences of an Astronomer* is not too technical for the lay reader. Henry Adams, *The Education of Henry Adams*, speculates on the implications of the second law of thermodynamics for mankind. The work of Willard Gibbs is discussed in Lynde P. Wheeler, *Josiah W. Gibbs: The History of a Great Mind* (Yale, 1952); J. G. Crowther, *Famous American Men of Science* (Norton, 1937); and in Muriel Rukeyser,

*Willard Gibbs* (Doubleday, 1942). *The Physical Papers of Henry August Rowland* (Johns Hopkins, 1902) is a scientific classic. The development of evolutionary theories in geological thought can be followed conveniently in George P. Merrill, *The First Hundred Years of American Geology.*

Every student of this period is much indebted to Bert J. Loewenberg for his scholarly and brilliant work on the reception of evolutionary theories in the United States. His extensive research has been admirably summarized in "The Reaction of American Scientists to Darwinism," *American Historical Review,* XXXVIII (1933), and "Darwinism Comes to America," *Mississippi Valley Historical Review,* XXVIII (1941). The first chapter of Richard Hofstadter's *Social Darwinism in American Thought* (rev. ed., Beacon Press, 1955), is another brief account of the reception of Darwinism. Some of the essays in Stow Persons (ed.), *Evolutionary Thought in America* (Yale, 1950), are important.

Daniel C. Gilman, *Life of James Dwight Dana* (Harper & Row, 1899), is old but still useful. A. Hunter Dupree's life of Gray, *Asa Gray, 1810–1888* (Harvard, 1959), is a distinguished contribution. For Gray's relationships with Darwin, see Asa Gray, *Darwiniana: Essays and Reviews Pertaining to Darwin* (New York, 1876); the *Calendar of the Letters of Charles Robert Darwin to Asa Gray* (Historical Records Survey, Boston, 1938); and Jane Loring Gray (ed.), *The Letters of Asa Gray* (2 vols., Houghton Mifflin, 1893). Edward Lurie's *Louis Agassiz: A Life in Science* is excellent. George Frederick Wright's position may be followed in his *Man and the Glacial Period* (Appleton-Century-Crofts, 1892) and *Story of my Life and Work* (Bibliotheca Sacra Co., 1916). *The Autobiography of George Le Conte* (Appleton-Century-Crofts, 1903) is an important contemporary source. Milton Berman, *John Fiske: The Evolution of a Popularizer* (Harvard, 1961), discusses in detail Fiske's attempt to reconcile evolution and theology. Particularly informative are Fiske's *Excursions of an Evolutionist* (Houghton Mifflin, 1893), and *A Century of Science* (Houghton Mifflin, 1899). J. S. Clark, *The Life and Letters of John Fiske* (2 vols., Houghton Mifflin, 1917), and Ethel Fisk, *The Letters of John Fiske* (Macmillan, 1940), contain a great deal of relevant material. Ira V. Brown's *Lyman Abbott, Christian Evolutionist: A Study in Religious Liberalism* (Harvard, 1953) emphasizes Abbott's role as a popularizer of ideas. Chauncey Wright, *Philosophic Discussions* (Holt, 1877), is a brilliant book; Wright's *Letters* (C. W. Sever, 1878) are excellent. There is no adequate life. Charles M. Schuchert and Clary M. LeVene have prepared a documented biography of O. C. *Marsh, Pioneer in Paleontology* (Yale, 1941). David Lowenthal, *George Perkins Marsh: Versatile Vermonter* (Columbia, 1958), is a well-rounded and thorough biography. Also useful is H. F. Osborn, *Cope: Master Naturalist* (Princeton, 1931).

### 22. Impact of Evolutionary Thought on Society

Thoughtful and informative general discussions of the intellectual ramifications of evolutionary theory are available in Richard Hofstadter, *Social Darwinism in American Thought*; Stow Persons (ed.), *Evolutionary Thought in America*; the introduction to Perry Miller (ed.), *American Thought; Civil War to World War I*; Henry Steele Commager, *The American Mind: An Interpretation of American Thought and Character Since the 1880's*, and Henry F. May, *The End of American Innocence*.

Psychology has been a relatively neglected field of intellectual history. The best general discussion is still John W. Fay, *American Psychology before William James* (Rutgers, 1939), though it is technical and little concerned with the impact of the general intellectual and social milieu. Edward L. Thorndike, "Darwin's Contributions to Psychology," *University of California Chronicle*, XII (1909), and James R. Angell, "The Influences of Darwin on Psychology," *Psychological Review*, XVI (May, 1909), are precise and enlightening, though the problem needs a great deal more probing. G. Stanley Hall, *Life and Confessions of a Psychologist* (Appleton-Century-Crofts, 1923), and Carl E. Seashore, *Pioneering in Psychology* (University of Iowa Press, 1942), are important. A. A. Roback, *History of American Psychology* (Library Publishers, 1952), is reliable on some subjects. Both scholars and general readers will be rewarded by Chauncey Wright's *Philosophic Discussions* and his *Letters*. Ralph Barton Perry has a discriminating account of James's contributions to psychology in *The Thought and Character of William James* (2 vols., Little, Brown, 1935). See also *In Commemoration of William James* (Columbia, 1942). John L. Child's *Education and the Philosophy of Experimentalism* (Appleton-Century-Crofts, 1931) is a lucid exposition of the new conception of human behavior and its implications for education, but Dewey's *Human Nature and Conduct* (Holt, 1922) and *Reconstruction in Philosophy* (Holt, 1920) are indispensable. Fiske's position can be found in brief in "The Scope and Purport of Evolution," in *A Century of Science and Other Essays* (Houghton Mifflin, 1899). For a fuller statement, see *Outlines of Cosmic Philosophy* (Boston, 1872) and *The Destiny of Man* (Houghton Mifflin, 1884). Edward Livingston Youmans "Observations on the Scientific Study of Human Nature," in *The Culture Demanded by Modern Life* (Appleton-Century-Crofts, 1867), sets forth an interesting program. Concepts of mind and of human nature are discussed in cultural perspective in Merle Curti, "Human Nature in American Thought," *Political Science Quarterly*, LXVIII (September, December, 1953).

Octavius B. Frothingham, *The Religion of Humanity* (Putnam, 1877), is

still readable, but Stow Persons' *Free Religion: An American Faith* is definitive. Morton G. White, *Social Thought in America: The Revolt Against Formalism* (Viking, 1949), analyzes the ideas of several pragmatists or
near-pragmatists. Edward C. Moore is concerned with the internal problems
of philosophy in his *American Pragmatism: Peirce, James and Dewey* (Columbia, 1961). Philip P. Wiener's *Evolution and the Founders of Pragmatism*
(Harvard, 1949) is a superior study of the influence of evolutionary ideas on
early pragmatists. Peirce's writings are available in Arthur W. Burks, Charles
Hartshorne, and Paul Weiss (eds.), *The Collected Papers of Charles Sanders
Peirce* (8 vols., 2nd ed., Harvard, 1960). James Feibleman has systematically
surveyed Peirce's thought in *An Introduction to Peirce's Philosophy* (Harper
& Row, 1946). Murray G. Murphey traces the chronological development of
Peirce's thought in *The Development of Peirce's Philosophy* (Harvard, 1961).
Much more convenient than the *Collected Papers* is Philip P. Wiener (ed.),
*Values in a Universe of Chance: Selected Writings of Charles S. Peirce*
(Doubleday, 1958). Ralph Barton Perry, *The Thought and Character of Wil-
liam James*, is the standard biography. James first clearly expounded his prag-
matic philosophy in *Pragmatism, a New Name for Old Ways of Thinking*
(Longmans (David McKay Co.), 1907) and in *The Will to Believe, and
Other Essays in Popular Philosophy* (Longmans (David McKay Co.), 1898).
See also the *Essays in Radical Empiricism* (Longmans (David McKay Co.),
1922), *A Pluralistic Universe* (Longmans (David McKay Co.), 1909), and
*The Varieties of Religious Experience* (Longmans (David McKay Co.),
1902). A number of James's important books are available in modern print-
ings. There is an engaging essay on Santayana by Morris Cohen in the third
volume of *The Cambridge History of American Literature*. The most complete exposition of Santayana's thought is *The Life of Reason* (5 vols., Scribner, 1905–1906). Santayana's autobiography, *Persons and Places* (2 vols.,
Scribner, 1944–1945), is very readable. Edmund Montgomery, a neglected
thinker in his own times, has received attention in two recent studies, I. K.
Stephens, *The Hermit Philosopher of Liendo* (Southern Methodist University Press, 1951), and Morris T. Keeton, *The Philosophy of Edmund Montgomery* (University Press, Dallas, n.d.).

Sidney Hook's *John Dewey* (John Day, 1939) is a good brief introduction.
Morton G. White, *Origin of Dewey's Instrumentalism* (Columbia, 1943), is
one of the most important of the vast number of discussions of Dewey available to the student and scholar. In the last resort, there is no better approach
to Dewey than through his own books. In addition to the works already cited,
important books are *Essays on Experimental Logic* (University of Chicago
Press, 1916), *The Theory of Inquiry* (Holt, 1938), *Democracy and Education*
(Macmillan, 1916), *The Public and Its Problems* (Holt, 1927), *Liberalism*

*and Social Action* (Putnam, 1935), and *Art as Experience* (Minton, 1934). Some of Dewey's writings are available in inexpensive paperbacks.

Louis H. Sullivan, *The Autobiography of an Idea* (American Institute of Architects, 1924), and *Kindergarten Chats and Other Writings* (Wittenborn, Schultz, New York, 1947); Ralph Adams Cram, *My Life in Architecture* (Little, Brown, 1936), and *Convictions and Controversies* (Marshall Jones, 1935); Frank Lloyd Wright, *Autobiography* (Longmans (David McKay Co.), 1943), and Frederick Gutheim (ed.), *Frank Lloyd Wright on Architecture* (Duell, Sloan & Pearce, 1941), reveal the diverse social philosophies held by leading American architects. Hugh Morrison's *Louis Sullivan* (Museum of Modern Art, 1935), and Henry-Russell Hitchcock's *The Architecture of H. H. Richardson and His Times* (Museum of Modern Art, 1936) are important individual studies. Lewis Mumford, *The Brown Decades: A Study of the Arts in America, 1865–1955* (2nd ed., Dover, 1955) discusses Sullivan and Wright.

Fiske's ideas on history are developed in his *American Political Ideas Viewed from the Standpoint of Universal History* (Harper & Row, 1885) and in E. N. Saveth, "Race and Nationalism in American Historiography: The Late Nineteenth Century," *Political Science Quarterly*, LIV (September, 1939). W. Stull Holt has edited some of the correspondence of H. B. Adams in *Historical Scholarship in the United States* (Johns Hopkins, 1938). Valuable and detailed background information is available in David D. Van Tassel's *Recording America's Past: An Interpretation of the Development of Historical Studies in America, 1607–1884* (University of Chicago Press, 1960). Ernest Samuels has published two volumes of his excellent biography of Henry Adams: *The Young Henry Adams* (Harvard, 1948), and *Henry Adams: The Middle Years* (Harvard, 1958). Elizabeth Stevenson's *Henry Adams: A Biography* (Macmillan, 1955) is an excellent one-volume study. Useful collections of Henry Adams' letters are W. C. Ford (ed.), *The Letters of Henry Adams* (2 vols., Houghton Mifflin, 1930–1938); Harold Dean Cater (ed.), *Henry Adams and His Friends* (Houghton Mifflin, 1947); and Newton Arvin (ed.), *The Selected Letters of Henry Adams* (Farrar, Straus & Cudahy, 1951). The best study of Henry Adams as an historian is William H. Jordy, *Henry Adams: Scientific Historian* (Yale, 1952). Timothy Paul Donovan, *Henry Adams and Brooks Adams: The Education of Two American Historians* (University of Oklahoma Press, 1961), is a valuable contribution. Henry S. Commager's essay on Henry Adams in the *Marcus W. Jernegan Essays in American History* (University of Chicago Press, 1937) is both brilliant and unusually judicious. Roy Nichols, "The Dynamic Interpretation of History," *New England Quarterly*, VIII (June, 1935), is masterly. Arthur F. Beringause, *Brooks Adams: A Biography* (Knopf, 1955), is scholarly and well written. Thornton Anderson, *Brooks Adams: Constructive Conservative* (Cornell,

1951), examines Brooks Adams as a conservative critic of American society. No serious student should miss Brooks Adams' *The Degradation of the Democratic Dogma* (Macmillan, 1919).

In addition to Turner's own writings, see the splendid essay by Fulmer Mood in *The Early Writings of Frederick Jackson Turner* (University of Wisconsin Press, 1938); Fulmer Mood, "The Development of Frederick Jackson Turner as a Historical Thinker," *Transactions of the Colonial Society of Massachusetts*, XXXIV, (1938–1941); Avery O. Craven's keen essay in the *Marcus W. Jernegan Essays in American History*; Merle Curti's treatment in Stuart Rice (ed.), *Methods in Social Science* (University of Chicago Press, 1931); and the critically searching papers by George W. Pierson, especially "The Frontier and Frontiersmen of Turner's Essays," *Pennsylvania Magazine of History and Biography*, LXIV (October, 1940). Ray A. Billington is preparing a biography of Turner.

James Harvey Robinson, *The New History* (Macmillan, 1921), is a landmark. Cushing Strout discusses Beard and Becker competently and dispassionately in *The Pragmatic Revolt in American History: Carl Becker and Charles Beard* (Yale, 1958). Burleigh Taylor Wilkins' *Carl Becker: A Biographical Study in American Intellectual History* (Harvard, 1961) is rewarding. The essays in Raymond O. Rockwood (ed.), *Carl Becker's Heavenly City Revisited* (Cornell, 1958) are uneven, but some are particularly perceptive. Charlotte W. Smith, *Carl Becker: On History and the Climate of Opinion* (Cornell, 1956), is a detailed analysis of Becker's writings. Howard K. Beale (ed.), *Charles A. Beard: An Appraisal* (University of Kentucky Press, 1954), contains valuable essays. Also useful is Bernard C. Borning, *The Political and Social Thought of Charles A. Beard* (University of Washington Press, 1962).

For economics, a first-rate introduction is Thorstein Veblen, "Why Is Economics Not an Evolutionary Science?" *Quarterly Journal of Economics*, XII (July, 1898), and *Theory of the Leisure Class* (Macmillan, 1899). A significant treatment of Veblen is that by Wesley C. Mitchell in *A Quarter Century of Learning, 1904–1929* (Columbia, 1931). This may be supplemented by Joseph Dorfman's outstanding study, *Thorstein Veblen and his America* (Viking, 1934).

More studies of particular disciplines are needed. Two works that prepare ground are L. L. and Jessie Bernard, *Origins of American Sociology: The Social Science Movement in the United States* (Crowell, 1943), and Fay Berger Karpf, *American Social Psychology, Its Origins, Development and European Background* (McGraw-Hill, 1932). Harry Elmer Barnes and Howard Becker, *Social Thought from Lore to Science* (Holt, 1925), a monumental repository of information, is useful for American thought during this period. The discussions of Sumner and Lester Frank Ward in Richard Hofstadter's *Social*

*Darwinism in American Thought* are perceptive brief treatments. There is no satisfactory life of Sumner, though Harris E. Starr, *William Graham Sumner* (Holt, 1925), is useful. Both the general reader and the student will find Sumner's own writings very readable. A. G. Keller, *Reminiscences of William Graham Sumner* (Yale, 1933), is a book by a devoted disciple. Ward's best statement of his thought is *The Psychic Factors of Civilization* (Ginn, 1892). Samuel Chugerman, *Lester F. Ward, the American Aristotle* (Duke, 1939), is the best secondary account yet available. Robert Green McCloskey takes a critical view of Sumner's thought in his *American Conservatism in the Age of Enterprise.*

The theory of Social Darwinism can be readily followed in Richard Hofstadter, *Social Darwinism in American Thought.* Major statements of the theory appeared in the *Popular Science Monthly,* VI (February, 1875), VIII (March, 1876), and XI (September, 1877). John Fiske, *Edward Livingston Youmans* (Appleton-Century-Crofts, 1894), is a readable, though not always accurate account. Responsibility toward their employees on the part of employers is advocated in an editorial by Youmans, *Popular Science Monthly,* XXII (June, 1886). C. A. Henderson, "Business Men and Social Theorists," *American Journal of Sociology,* I (January, 1896), is an important article. See also Henry Emory, *Some Aspects of War* (Government Printing Office, 1914), and the articles by Woodrow Wilson in *Atlantic Monthly,* LXXVI (November, 1895) and LXXXII (October, 1899). For efforts to refute Social Darwinism, see George Nasmyth, *Social Progress and Darwinian Theory* (Putnam, 1916), and Eric Goldman, *Rendezvous With Destiny: A History of Modern American Reform* (Knopf, 1952). For Kropotkin's American connections, *Kropotkin's Revolutionary Pamphlets* (Vanguard, 1937), is useful.

The new spirit in legal thinking is exemplified in Oliver Wendell Holmes, Jr., *The Common Law* (Boston, 1881), a pioneer work of great importance. Mark de Wolfe Howe (ed.), *The Holmes-Pollock Letters* (2 vols., Harvard, 1941), is superb reading. Max Lerner has edited a useful selection of Holmes' speeches, essays, letters, and judicial opinions in *The Mind and Faith of Justice Holmes* (Little, Brown, 1943). Mark de Wolf Howe, *Justice Oliver Wendell Holmes: The Shaping Years, 1841–1870* (Harvard, 1957), is excellent. See also R. D. Dugdale, *The Jukes: A Study in Crime, Pauperism, and Heredity* (Putnam, 1877).

Carl Resek, *Lewis Henry Morgan, American Scholar* (University of Chicago Press, 1960), is a superior brief study, but should be supplemented by Bernhard J. Stern, *Lewis Henry Morgan, Social Evolutionist* (University of Chicago Press, 1931). Morgan's *League of the Iroquois* is available in an inexpensive modern edition (Corinth Books, 1962). Revealing letters are available in Leslie White (ed.), *Pioneers in American Anthropology: The Bande-*

*lier-Morgan Letters, 1873–1895* (University of New Mexico Press, 1940), and George P. Hammond and Edgar F. Goad (eds.), *A Scientist on the Trail: Travel Letters of A. F. Bandelier, 1880–1881* (Quivira Society Publications, Berkeley, 1949).

## 23. Professionalization and Popularization of Learning

Ideals of scholarship and research in relation to American society can be followed in James B. Angell, *The Old and the New Ideal of Scholars* (Ann Arbor, 1905); Carl Snyder, "America's Inferior Position in the Scientific World," *North American Review*, CLXXIV (January, 1902); Charles S. Slichter, "Recent Criticisms of American Scholarship," *Transactions of the Wisconsin Academy of Science, Arts, and Letters* XIV (1903). Paul Shorey, "American Scholarship," *The Nation*, XCII (May 11, 1911); A. Lawrence Lowe..l, *At War with Academic Traditions in America* (Harvard, 1934); T. Atkinson Jenkins, "Scholarship and Public Spirit," *Proceedings of the Modern Language Association*, XIX (1914); Charles P. Steinmetz, "Scientific Research in Relation to Industries," *Journal of the Franklin Institute* (December, 1916); and Raymond F. Bacon, "The Value of Research to Industry," *Science* (December 18, 1914), are important papers. The impact of German scholarship is discussed from various points of view by Charles F. Thwing, *The American and the German University* (Macmillan, 1928); J. M. Coulter in the *University of Chicago Record*, VIII (February, 1904); Basil Gildersleeve, "Classical Studies in America," *Atlantic Monthly*, LXXVIII (1896); Edward A. Ross, *Seventy Years of It* (Appleton-Century-Crofts, 1937); John W. Burgess, *Reminiscences of an American Scholar* (Columbia, 1934); and Richard T. Ely, *Ground Under Our Feet* (Macmillan, 1938). James Harry Cotton, *Royce on the Human Self* (Harvard, 1954), is technical but reveals the influence of German thought on a major philosopher. Bernard Edward Brown, *American Conservatives: The Political Thought of Francis Lieber and John W. Burgess* (Columbia, 1951) is a useful review of the ideas of two political thinkers. Thomas Le Duc's *Piety and Intellect at Amherst College, 1865–1912* (Columbia, 1946) shows quite specifically the influence of German scholarship on one academic institution.

The development of higher studies can be followed in Nicholas Murray Butler, *Across the Busy Years* (2 vols., Scribner, 1939); Samuel E. Morison (ed.), *The Development of Harvard University since the Inauguration of President Eliot, 1869–1929* (Harvard, 1930); *A Quarter Century of Learning, 1904–1929* (Columbia, 1930); G. Stanley Hall, *The Life and Confessions of a Psychologist*; and Daniel C. Gilman, *Launching a University*

(Dodd, Mead, 1906). Edward McNall Burns, *David Starr Jordan: Prophet of Freedom* (Stanford, 1953), is an excellent piece of scholarship. Maurice M. Vance, *Charles Rutland Van Hise: Scientist Progressive* (State Historical Society of Wisconsin, 1960), is a thorough biography of an important University of Wisconsin president. Informative studies of particular institutions include Merle Curti and Vernon Carstensen, *The University of Wisconsin: A History, 1848–1925* (2 vols., University of Wisconsin Press, 1949); John Tracy Ellis, *The Formative Years of the Catholic University of America* (American Catholic Historical Association, 1946); Nora Campbell Chaffin, *Trinity College, 1839–1892: The Beginnings of Duke University* (Duke, 1950); James Gray, *The University of Minnesota, 1851–1951* (University of Minnesota Press, 1951); George Wilson Pierson, *Yale College: An Educational History, 1871–1921* (Yale, 1952); R. Gordon Hoxie, *et al.*, *A History of the Faculty of Political Science*, Columbia University (Columbia, 1955); and Hugh Hawkins, *Pioneer: A History of the Johns Hopkins University, 1874–1889*. Carson Ryan, *Studies in Early Graduate Education* (Carnegie Foundation for the Advancement of Teaching, 1939), may be profitably consulted.

Abraham Flexner, *I Remember* (Simon and Schuster, 1940), contains valuable information on the improvement of professional education, especially in the field of medicine. Helen Clapesattle, *The Doctors Mayo* (University of Minnesota Press, 1941), is an excellent study. Donald Fleming, *William H. Welch and the Rise of Modern Medicine* (Little, Brown, 1954), is a deft, brief biography, but does not entirely replace Simon and James T. Flexner, *William Henry Welch and the Heroic Age of American Medicine* (Viking, 1941). Kirtland Wright, *Geography in the Making: The American Geographical Society, 1851–1951* (American Geographical Society, 1952), is exceptionally well-informed. Herman Ausubel has examined the presidential addresses of the American Historical Association in *Historians and Their Craft* (Columbia, 1950). Louise Fargo Brown, *Apostle of Democracy: The Life of Lucy Maynard* (Harper & Row, 1953), is sympathetic.

The reports of the foundations are the chief sources for their activities. Ernest V. Hollis, *Philanthropic Foundations and Higher Education* (Columbia, 1938), and Leonard P. Ayres, *Seven Great Foundations* (Russell Sage Foundation, 1911), are sympathetic. For government-sponsored research see A. Hunter Dupree, *Science in the Federal Government to 1940* (Harvard, 1940), and Gustav A. Webber, *The Bureau of Chemistry and Soils* (Johns Hopkins, 1928), *The Bureau of Entomology* (Brookings Institution, 1930), and *The Bureau of Labor Statistics* (Government Printing Office, 1922), provide an introduction to the specialized researches.

For accounts of the university extension movement, see *Bureau of Education Bulletin* for 1912, 1914, and 1920; W. S. Bittner and Herbert F.

Mallory, *University Teaching by Mail* (Macmillan, 1923); and A. L. Hall-Quest, *The University Afield* (Macmillan, 1926). A somewhat pessimistic contemporary essay by George H. Palmer appeared in the *Atlantic Monthly*, LXIX (March, 1892). Ruth Frankel, *Henry M. Leipziger, Educator and Idealist* (Macmillan, 1933), competently tells the story of an interesting career. Owen Pence, *The Y.M.C.A. and Social Need* (Association Press, 1939), and Grace H. Wilson, *Educational Philosophy of the Young Women's Christian Association* (Teachers College, Columbia University, 1933), are competent studies.

David Mead, *Yankee Eloquence in the Middle West: The Ohio Lyceum* (Michigan State College Press, 1951), discusses fifteen popular lyceum lecturers. Joseph E. Gould, *The Chautauqua Movement* (State University of New York Press, 1961), is brief and incomplete, and should be supplemented by Ellwood Hendrick, *Lewis Miller, a Biographical Essay* (Putnam, 1925); Leon H. Vincent, *John Heyl Vincent, a Biographical Sketch* (Macmillan, 1925); and John H. Vincent, *The Chautauqua Movement* (Chautauqua Press, 1886). The brief sketch in the useful bibliography of Chautauqua publications prepared by Arthur E. Bestor, Jr., *Chautauqua Publications* (Chautauqua Press, 1934), is excellent. Gay Maclaren, *Morally We Roll Along* (Little, Brown, 1938), and Marion Scott, *Caravan* (Appleton-Century-Crofts, 1939), are delightful accounts of experiences in the later commercial circuit Chautauqua. Charles F. Horner, *Life of James A. Redpath* (Barse and Hopkins, 1926), is hardly an adequate biography. Kermit Vanderbilt, *Charles Eliot Norton, Apostle of Culture in a Democracy* (Harvard, 1959), is an interesting discussion of Norton's efforts to effect a working synthesis of culture and democracy.

Sidney Ditzion, "Social Reform, Education and the Library, 1850–1900," in *Library Quarterly*, IX (April, 1939), is a careful piece of research on an important subject. J. C. Croly, *The History of the Woman's Club Movement in America* (Henry G. Allen and Co., 1898), is a storehouse of information on this subject. *The Life Stories of Undistinguished Americans as Told by Themselves* (James Pott and Co., 1906) should not be overlooked by any student of the ideas of the plain people. Richard B. Kenna, *The Private Correspondence School Enrollee* (Columbia University, 1940), and John S. Noffsinger, *Correspondence Schools, Lyceums, Chautauquas* (Macmillan, 1926), may be consulted for commercial correspondence schools. Raymond H. Shove, *Cheap Book Production in the United States, 1870 to 1891* (University of Illinois Library, 1937), is better on the quantitative than the qualitative aspects of the subject. Although there is much scattered material on publication in the *Publishers' Weekly*, United States Census *Reports*, and the autobiographies of publishers, the whole subject needs further investigation. James H. Wellard, *Book Selection* (Grafton and Co.,

1937), is useful. The best brief account is that by Arthur M. Schlesinger, Sr., *The Rise of the City, 1878–1898*. For the dime novel, see Edmund Pearson, *Dime Novels, or following an Old Trail in Popular Literature* (Little, Brown, 1929), and Merle Curti, "The American Tradition and the Dime Novel," *Yale Review* (Summer, 1937). Edward W. Bok tells the story of the *Ladies' Home Journal* in *The Americanization of Edward Bok* (Scribner, 1920). Samuel S. McClure, *My Autobiography* (Stokes, 1914), is an important and readable firsthand account of a muckraking magazine. Lincoln Steffens, *Autobiography* (2 vols., Harcourt, Brace & World, 1931), and *Letters*, edited by Ella Winter and Granville Hicks (Harcourt, Brace & World, 1938), are full of good material. The best secondary studies of the muckraking movement are Cornelius C. Regier, *The Era of the Muckrakers* (University of North Carolina Press, 1932), and Louis Filler, *Crusaders for American Liberalism* (Harcourt, Brace & World, 1939). Oliver Carlson and Ernest S. Bates have written a more or less psychological analysis of Hearst in *Hearst, Lord of San Simeon* (Viking, 1932). See also Don Seitz, *Joseph Pulitzer* (Garden City, 1924), and James W. Barrett, *Joseph Pulitzer and His "World"* (Vanguard, 1941).

J. A. Hill, "Illiteracy," *Supplementary Analysis and Derivative Tables* (U.S. Twelfth Census, *Special Report*, Government Printing Office, 1906), and the U.S. Commissioner of Education's *Report for 1916*, II, are convenient sources of information. The scientific movement in education is discussed in James E. Russell, *The Scientific Movement in Education* (Teachers College, Columbia University, 1927), and in I. L. Kandel (ed.), *Twenty-Five Years of American Education* (Macmillan, 1924.)

Robert J. Graf, "Public Lectures in New York, 1851–1876: A Cultural Index of the Times" (unpublished dissertation, University of Chicago, 1941), should stimulate similar studies. Sidney Ditzion's *Arsenals of a Democratic Culture: A Social History of the American Public Library Movement in New England and the Middle Atlantic States from 1850 to 1900* (American Library Association, 1947), is a scholarly study which breaks new ground. William S. Learned, *The American Public Library and the Diffusion of Knowledge* (Harcourt, Brace & World, 1924), is competent. The discussion of the Sears, Roebuck book lists is based on David L. Cohn, *The Good Old Days* (Simon and Schuster, 1940), ch. 4. Further work in this field is needed.

### 24. Formulas of Protest and Reform

The reform impetus is discussed from various points of view in a number of excellent and wide-ranging recent studies: Daniel Aaron, *Men of Good Hope: A Story of American Progressives* (Oxford, 1951); John Chamberlain,

*Farewell to Reform* (Liveright, 1932); Harold U. Faulkner, *The Quest for Social Justice, 1898–1914* (Macmillan, 1931); Sidney Fine, *Laissez Faire and the General Welfare State: A Study of Conflict in American Thought, 1865–1901* (University of Michigan Press, 1956); Eric Goldman, *Rendezvous with Destiny: A History of Modern American Reform* (Knopf, 1952); Samuel P. Hays, *The Response to Industrialism, 1885–1914*; Richard Hofstadter, *The Age of Reform, from Bryan to F.D.R.* (Knopf, 1955); Henry F. May, *The End of American Innocence: A Study of the First Years of Our Own Time, 1912–1917*, and David W. Noble, *The Paradox of Progressive Thought* (University of Minnesota Press, 1958).

There is no better introduction to the ideas of protest and reform than the outstanding writings of principal reformers: Henry George, *Progress and Poverty* (Robert Schalkenbach Foundation, 1940); James B. Weaver, *A Call to Action* (Iowa Printing Company, 1892); Edward Bellamy, *Looking Backward, 2000–1887* (Houghton Mifflin, 1887); and Henry D. Lloyd, *Wealth Against Commonwealth* (Harper & Row, 1894). Charles A. Barker's biography, *Henry George* (Oxford, 1955), is a definitive study. Arthur E. Morgan, *Edward Bellamy* (Columbia, 1944), and Sylvia E. Bowman, *The Year 2000: A Critical Biography of Edward Bellamy* (Bookman Associates, 1958), are based on solid research. Anna George de Mille, *Henry George: Citizen of the World* (University of North Carolina Press, 1950), is an intimate portrait by George's oldest daughter. The best available biographical study of Lloyd is Caro Lloyd, *Henry Demarest Lloyd, 1847–1903* (2 vols., Putnam, 1912). Reminiscences and autobiographies of importance include Gregory Weinstein, *The Ardent Eighties* (International Press, 1928); Helen Rand Thayer, "Blazing the Settlement Trail," *Smith Alumnae Quarterly* (April, 1911); Jacob Riis, *A Ten Years' War* (Houghton Mifflin, 1900); Vida D. Scudder, *On Journey* (Dutton, 1937); Frederic C. Howe, *The Confessions of a Reformer* (Scribner, 1925); Lincoln Steffens, *Autobiography* (2 vols., Harcourt, Brace & World, 1931), and Ray Stannard Baker's autobiography, *American Chronicle* (Scribner, 1945). Amos Warner, *American Charities* (Crowell, 1894, and many revised editions), is a standard work.

Theories of reform through currency control and taxation revision are expounded in W. H. Harvey, *Coin's Financial School* (Coin Publishing Co., 1894); Ignatius Donnelly, *The American People's Money* (Chicago, 1895); William Jennings Bryan, *The First Battle* (W. B. Conkey Co., 1896); and George's *Progress and Poverty*. Chester McA. Destler, "The Influence of Edward Kellogg upon American Radicalism, 1865–1896," *Journal of Political Economy*, XL (June, 1932), is a valuable study. Sidney Ratner, *American Taxation, Its History as a Social Force in Democracy* (Norton, 1942), chs. 9 and 10, and Elmer Ellis, "Public Opinion and the Income

Tax, 1860–1900," *Mississippi Valley Historical Review*, XXVII (September, 1940), are useful. Henry George, Jr., *The Life of Henry George* (Doubleday and McClure Co., 1900), gives some account of the mayoralty campaigns. The mayoralty campaign of 1886 is discussed in Allan Nevins, *Abram S. Hewitt: With Some Account of Peter Cooper* (Harper & Row, 1935). *The Philosophy of Henry George*, by George H. Geiger (Macmillan, 1933), and *The Single Tax Movement in the United States*, by Arthur N. Young (Princeton, 1916), present contrasting interpretations of the Henry George program. The influence of George is exemplified in Brand Whitlock, *Forty Years of It* (Appleton-Century-Crofts, 1915), and Mary Fels, *Joseph Fels, His Life-Work* (Huebsch, 1916).

Among the books written during the reform era that portray the ideas of the Progressive movement, the following deserve special mention: Robert M. La Follette, *A Personal Narrative* (Robert M. La Follette Co., 1911); Herbert Croly, *The Promise of American Life* (Macmillan, 1912); J. Allen Smith, *The Spirit of American Government* (Macmillan, 1907); Walter Weyl, *The New Democracy* (Macmillan, 1912); Theodore Roosevelt, *The New Nationalism* (Outlook Co., 1913); Woodrow Wilson, *The New Freedom* (Doubleday, 1913); William O. Foulke, *Fighting the Spoilsmen* (Putnam, 1919); Carl Schurz, *Reminiscences* (3 vols., Macmillan, 1907–1908); Everett P. Wheeler, *Sixty Years of American Life* (Dutton, 1917); Charles H. Parkhurst, *Our Fight with Tammany* (Scribner, 1895); and George Vicker, *The Fall of Bossism* (Philadelphia, 1883). The conservation movement is discussed in Charles H. Van Hise, *The Conservation of Natural Resources* (Macmillan, 1910); Gifford Pinchot, *The Fight for Conservation* (Doubleday, 1910), and *Breaking New Ground* (Harcourt, Brace & World, 1947); and Alpheus T. Mason, *Bureaucracy Convicts Itself* (Viking, 1941).

Though their emphasis is mainly on politics two recent histories provide excellent perspective on the Progressive movement: George E. Mowry, *The Era of Theodore Roosevelt, 1900–1912* (Harper & Row, 1958), and Arthur S. Link, *Woodrow Wilson and the Progressive Era, 1910–1917* (Harper & Row, 1954). Charles Forcey, *The Crossroads of Liberalism: Croly, Weyl, Lippmann, and the Progressive Era, 1900–1925* (Oxford, 1961), is an admirable discussion of the democratic nationalism expressed in the influential *New Republic*. Interesting studies of particular geographical manifestations of Progressivism are Russel B. Nye, *Midwestern Progressive Politics: A Historical Study of Its Origins and Development, 1870–1950* (Michigan State College Press, 1951); George E. Mowry, *The California Progressives* (University of California Press, 1951); Robert S. Maxwell, *La Follette and the Rise of the Progressives in Wisconsin* (State Historical Society of Wisconsin, 1956); and William D. Miller, *Memphis During the Progressive Era, 1900–*

*1917* (American History Research Center, Madison, Wisconsin, 1957). For contrasting treatments of Populism, see Richard Hofstadter, *The Age of Reform*; Eric Goldman, *Rendezvous with Destiny*, and John D. Hicks, *The Populist Revolt: A History of the Farmers' Alliance and the People's Party* (University of Minnesota Press, 1955). Cornelius C. Regier, *The Era of the Muckrakers* and Louis Filler, *Crusaders for American Liberalism*, are the leading studies of the muckraking crusade. Frank M. Stewart, *The National Civil Service Reform League* (University of Texas, 1929), and Clifford W. Patton, *The Battle for Municipal Reform: Mobilization and Attack, 1865–1900* (American Council on Public Affairs, 1940), are competent and give the main facts.

Arthur S. Link, *Wilson* (3 vols., Princeton, 1947–1960) is a well-documented and thorough biography. John Morton Blum's brief essay, *Woodrow Wilson and the Politics of Morality* (Little, Brown, 1956), is perceptive and stimulating. Other valuable studies of Wilson are William Diamond, *The Economic Thought of Woodrow Wilson* (Johns Hopkins, 1943), and the essays in Earl Latham (ed.), *The Philosophy and Policies of Woodrow Wilson* (University of Chicago Press, 1958). John Morton Blum, *The Republican Roosevelt* (Harvard, 1954), is a well-written and interesting analysis of Roosevelt's personality. Carleton Putnam has published one volume of a projected multivolume biography, *Theodore Roosevelt: The Formative Years* (Scribner, 1958). Elting E. Morison (ed.), *The Letters of Theodore Roosevelt* (8 vols., Harvard, 1951–1954), is a superior collection. Other significant biographical studies are Eric F. Goldman, *Charles J. Bonaparte, Patrician Reformer: His Earlier Career* (Johns Hopkins, 1943); Edward A. Fitzpatrick, *McCarthy of Wisconsin* (Columbia, 1944); Charles Madison, *Critics and Crusaders* (2nd ed., Ungar, 1959), a composite biography of a number of reform leaders; Alpheus Thomas Mason, *Brandeis: A Free Man's Life* (Viking, 1946); Walter Johnson, *William Allen White's America* (Holt, 1947), and *Selected Letters of William Allen White, 1899–1943* (Holt, 1947); Belle Case La Follette and Fola La Follette, *Robert M. La Follette* (Macmillan, 1953); C. Vann Woodward, *Tom Watson, Agrarian Rebel* (Holt, 1955); and Paul W. Glad, *The Trumpet Soundeth: William Jennings Bryan and His Democracy, 1896–1912* (University of Nebraska Press, 1960).

For the beginnings of the National Association for the Advancement of the Colored People, the Urban League, and similar groups, see the annual reports and bulletins of these organizations, and Ray Stannard Baker, *Following the Color Line* (Doubleday, 1908), and W. E. B. DuBois, *Dusk of Dawn* (Harcourt, Brace & World, 1940). See also M. A. de Wolfe Howe, *Portrait of an Independent, Moorfield Storey* (Houghton Mifflin, 1932).

An excellent summary of the arguments for and against woman suffrage may be found in T. V. Smith, *The American Philosophy of Equality*, ch. 3. Charlotte Perkins Gilman, *This Man-Made World* (Charlton Co., 1914), is especially significant. For the later aspects of the woman's rights campaign, see Doris Stevens, *Jailed for Freedom* (Liveright, 1920), and Carrie Chapman Catt, *Woman Suffrage and Politics* (Scribner, 1928). Francis Willard, *Glimpses of Fifty Years* (Woman's Temperance Publishing Association, 1892), has useful material. For the Anti-Saloon League, see Peter Odegard's *Pressure Politics* (Columbia, 1928). Mary Earhart's *Frances Willard: From Prayers to Politics* (University of Chicago Press, 1944); Josephine Goldmark, *Impatient Crusader: Florence Kelley's Life Story* (University of Illinois Press, 1953); and Katherine Anthony, *Susan B. Anthony: Her Personal History and Her Era* (Doubleday, 1954), are significant and informative biographies.

Robert H. Bremner, *From the Depths: The Discovery of Poverty in the United States* (New York University Press, 1956), is a well-documented and interestingly prepared study of changing attitudes toward the poor. Frank J. Bruno, *Trends in Social Work, 1874–1956: A History Based on the Proceedings of the National Conference of Social Work* (2nd ed., with chapters by Louis Towley, Columbia, 1957), is a valuable record by authors involved in the history they discuss.

For anarchism, socialism, and the labor movement, the literature is extensive. The socialist movement is discussed in detail in Howard H. Quint, *The Forging of American Socialism: Origins of the Modern Movement* (University of South Carolina Press, 1953); Ira Kipnis, *The American Socialist Movement, 1897–1912* (Columbia, 1952); and David A. Shannon, *The Socialist Party of America: A History* (Macmillan, 1955). The essays in Donald Drew Egbert and Stow Persons (eds.), *Socialism and American Life* (Princeton, 1952), stress the period since 1917. Walter B. Rideout, *The Radical Novel in the United States, 1900–1951: Some Relationships of Literature and Society* (Harvard, 1956), has a judicious discussion of socialist novels. Other interesting materials include Morris Hillquit, *History of Socialism in the United States* (5th ed., Funk & Wagnalls, 1910), and *Loose Leaves from a Busy Life* (Macmillan, 1934); *The Voice and Pen of Victor L. Berger* (*Milwaukee Leader*, 1929); Charles Edward Russell, *Bare Hands and Stone Walls* (Scribner, 1933); James H. Maurer, *It Can Be Done* (Rand School Press, 1938). Ray Ginger, *The Bending Cross: A Biography of Eugene V. Debs* (Rutgers University Press, 1949) is one of the competent recent biographies. McAllister Coleman, *Eugene V. Debs* (Greenberg, 1930), is still of some interest. Henry David, *The History of the Haymarket Affair* (Holt, 1936); Emma Goldman, *Living My Life* (2 vols., Knopf, 1931);

and Alexander Berkman, *Prison Memoirs of an Anarchist* (Mother Earth Publishing Co., 1912), are the best introduction to anarchistic ideas in the United States. Richard T. Ely, *The Labor Movement in the United States* (T. Y. Crowell, 1886), reveals the insights of one reformer. The writings on the labor movement by John R. Commons and Selig Perlman are significant. Florence Calvert Thorne, *Samuel Gompers: American Statesman* (Philosophical Library, 1957), discusses Gompers' ideas. Philip Taft, *The AF of L in the Time of Gompers* (Harper & Row, 1957), is scholarly and well documented. Revealing contemporary writings are Samuel Gompers, *Seventy Years of Life and Labor* (2 vols., Dutton, 1923); *The Autobiography of Mother Jones* (Charles H. Kerr, 1925), and *Bill Haywood's Book* (International Publishers, 1929).

Bellamy's *Looking Backward*, available in many editions, should be supplemented by his *Equality* (Appleton-Century-Crofts, 1897), and *Bellamy Speaks Again* (Peerage Press, 1937). Although James Dombrowski's *The Early Days of Christian Socialism* (Columbia, 1936), is still useful at many points, it has been in the main replaced by Charles H. Hopkins, *The Rise of the Social Gospel in American Protestantism, 1865–1915* (Yale, 1940); Aaron Ignatius Abell, *The Urban Impact on American Protestantism*; Henry F. May, *Protestant Churches and Industrial America*; and Aaron Ignatius Abell, *American Catholicism and Social Action: A Search for Social Justice, 1865–1950*. Washington Gladden, *Recollections* (Houghton Mifflin, 1909), and his various writings, especially *Applied Christianity* (Houghton Mifflin, 1886) and *Christianity and Socialism* (Eaton and Mains, 1905), are important. W. D. P. Bliss, *Encylopedia of Social Reform* (Funk & Wagnalls, 1897; rev. ed., 1908), is a mine of information. Charles M. Sheldon, *In His Steps* (Thompson and Thomas, n.d.), has gone through many editions. Herron's writings include *The Message of Jesus to Men of Wealth* (Revell, 1891), *The Christian Society* (Revell, 1894), *Between Caesar and Jesus* (Crowell, 1899), and *The Day of Judgment* (Charles H. Kerr, 1904). Rauschenbush's most important contributions are *Christianity and the Social Crisis* (Macmillan, 1907), *Christianizing the Social Order* (Macmillan, 1912), and *A Theology for the Social Gospel* (Macmillan, 1917). D. R. Sharp, *Walter Rauschenbush* (Macmillan, 1942), is adequate.

### 25. The Conservative Defense

Valuable discussions of the conservative defense may be found in Charles E. Merriam, *American Political Ideas: Studies in the Development of American Political Thought, 1865–1917* (Macmillan, 1920), and Edward R.

Lewis, *A History of American Political Thought from the Civil War to the World War* (Macmillan, 1937). Richard Hofstadter, *Social Darwinism in American Thought*, discusses conservative Darwinian theorists. Henry F. May, in *The End of American Innocence*, surveys the conventional, conservative culture of the late nineteenth century. David Spitz, *Patterns of Anti-Democratic Thought* (Macmillan, 1949), presents a critical analysis of antidemocratic ideas, concentrating on the twentieth century. A very useful general account is still to be found in W. J. Ghent's *Our Benevolent Feudalism* (Macmillan, 1902). C. Vann Woodward, *The Strange Career of Jim Crow* (Oxford, 1955), discusses the development of racial discrimination in the South in the late nineteenth century.

Writings of special significance are Theodore Woolsey, *Communism and Socialism, in their History and Theory* (Scribner, 1880); Andrew Carnegie, *The Empire of Business* (Doubleday, 1902); William Graham Sumner, *What the Social Classes Owe to Each Other* (Harper & Row, 1920), and *Folkways* (Ginn, 1906); and Mark Hopkins, *The Law of Love and Love as Law* (Scribner, 1868). Robert Green McCloskey, *American Conservatism in the Age of Enterprise*, discusses Carnegie, Sumner, and Justice Field. Thornton Anderson, *Brooks Adams: Constructive Conservative*, emphasizes Adams' conservatism. Charles A. Beard called attention to Laughlin's misrepresentations of John Stuart Mill's thought in the *Virginia Quarterly*, XV (Autumn, 1939).

On the cult of the elite, consult Elbert Hubbard's writings in *The Philistine* (1895–1915); Robert Shafer, *Paul Elmer More and American Criticism* (Yale, 1935); Louis J. A. Mercier, *Le Mouvement humaniste aux États-unis* (Hachette, 1928); Frederick Manchester and Odell Shepard (eds.), *Irving Babbitt, Man and Teacher* (Putnam, 1941); and More's and Babbitt's own writings, especially *Shelburne Essays* (Houghton Mifflin and Putnam, 1914–1919), *The New Laokoon* (Houghton Mifflin, 1910), and *Democracy and Leadership* (Houghton Mifflin, 1924). Agnes Repplier, "The Cost of Modern Sentiment," in *Counter Currents* (Houghton Mifflin, 1916) and "Consolations of the Conservative," in *Points of Friction* (Houghton Mifflin, 1920), are charming expositions of social conservatism.

Irvin G. Wyllie, *The Self-Made Man in America*, critically examines the rags-to-riches idea. The literature of the cult of success is voluminous. Examples are L. U. Reavis, *Thoughts for the Young Men and Young Women of America* (S. R. Wells, 1871), and Harriet Beecher Stowe, *The Lives and Deeds of Our Self-Made Men* (Boston, 1889). For Thayer, in addition to his own writings for boys, see *Unfinished Autobiography of William Makepeace Thayer* (n.d., n.p.). Herbert R. Mayes, *Alger: A Biography without a Hero* (Vanguard, 1928), gives the story of Alger's life and the cult he promoted. The official biography of Conwell is that by Agnes R. Burr, *Russell H. Con-*

*well and His Work* (Winston, 1927). A critical account is the one by W. C. Crosby in the *American Mercury*, XIV (May, 1928). Margaret Connolly, *The Life Story of Orison Swett Marden, 1850–1924* (Crowell, 1925), is the only biography thus far. Dixon Wecter's *The Hero in America*, (Scribner, 1941) is bright and well documented. Excellent discussions of the businessman's reputation are available in Edward G. Kirkland, *Business in the Gilded Age: The Conservatives' Balance Sheet*, and Sigmund Diamond, *The Reputation of the American Businessman*.

The beneficence of capitalism was upheld in the writings of John Bates Clark; see his "The Society of the Future," *The Independent*, LIII (July 18, 1901). Thorstein Veblen's criticism of Clark in *The Place of Science in Modern Civilization and Other Essays* (Huebsch, 1919) is a brilliant analysis. James L. Boswell summarizes Patten's ideas in *The Economics of Simon Nelson Patten* (Holt, 1934). Rexford G. Tugwell's "The Life and Work of Simon Patten," *Journal of Political Economy*, XXXI (April, 1923), and Scott Nearing's *Educational Frontiers* (Seltzer, 1925) are appreciative tributes by former pupils. Frederick W. Taylor's *Principles of Scientific Management* (Harper & Row, 1911) is the classic in the field. B. F. Copley's *Frederick W. Taylor, Father of Scientific Management* (Harper & Row, 1923) is an appreciative study. For a brief account of Ivy Lee, see *Literary Digest*, CXVII (June 9, 1934) and CXVIII (November 17, 1934).

The best brief account of the foundations is Frederick P. Keppel, *The Foundation, Its Place in American Life* (Macmillan, 1930). The best source for contemporary criticisms is the *Final Report of the Commission on Industrial Relations* (Washington, 1915). Truxton Beale (ed.), *The Man versus the State: a Collection of Essays by Herbert Spencer* (Kennerley, 1916), contains evaluations of Spencer's social philosophy and its applicability in 1915 by Nicholas Murray Butler, William Howard Taft, Elihu Root, Henry Cabot Lodge, Harlan Stone, and others.

## 26. *America Recrosses the Oceans*

The history of the sentiment for intervention in Europe in behalf of liberty is dealt with in several studies: Eugene P. Link, *Democratic-Republican Societies, 1790–1800* (Columbia, 1942); Merle Curti, *Austria and the United States, 1848–1852* (*Smith College Studies in History*, XI, no. 3, 1926), and "Young America," *American Historical Review*, XXXII (October, 1926); and J. Fred Rippy, *America and the Strife of Europe* (University of Chicago Press, 1938). The most recent general treatment is Edward McNall Burns, *The American Idea of Mission* (Rutgers, 1957).

The idea of a glorious overseas commercial destiny is analyzed, with documentation, in Charles A. Beard, *The Idea of National Interest* (Macmillan, 1934). For expansionist ideas, see Albert K. Weinberg, *Manifest Destiny*, Frederick Merk, *Manifest Destiny and Mission*, and Richard Hofstadter's essay, "Manifest Destiny and the Philippines" in Daniel Aaron, ed., *America in Crisis* (Knopf, 1952). For Doheney's early interest in Mexico, see United States Congress, *Senate Document*, IX, 66th Congress, 2nd session, 1920. The position of the press on the Cuban crisis is discussed in Joseph E. Wisan, *The Cuban Crisis as Reflected in the New York Press* (Columbia, 1934).

The somewhat uncritical biography by W. D. Puleston, *The Life and Work of Captain Mahan* (Yale, 1939), should be supplemented by Mahan's autobiography, *From Sail to Steam* (Harper & Row, 1907). The best account of navalism is Harold and Margaret Sprout, *The Rise of American Naval Power, 1776–1918* (Princeton, 1938).

Anti-imperialism and pacifism are discussed in Merle Curti, *Bryan and World Peace* (*Smith College Studies in History*, XVI, April–July, 1931), and "Literary Patriots of the Gilded Age," *Historical Outlook*, XIX (April, 1928). See also Fred Harrington, "Literary Aspects of Anti-Imperialism," *New England Quarterly*, X (December, 1937), and "The Anti-Imperialist Movement in the United States," *Mississippi Valley Historical Review*, XXII (September, 1935). Edward McNall Burns, *David Starr Jordan: Prophet of Freedom*, (Stanford, 1953), discusses the political and social ideas of a leading anti-imperialist, and H. C. Peterson and Gilbert C. Fite, *Opponents of War, 1917–1918* (University of Wisconsin Press, 1957), concerns the public's attitude toward groups who opposed World War I.

The ideological background of Wilson's foreign policy is traced in Harley Notter's competent study, *The Origins of the Foreign Policy of Woodrow Wilson* (Johns Hopkins, 1937). See also Robert Endicott Osgood, *Ideals and Self-Interest in America's Foreign Relations: The Great Transformation of the Twentieth Century* (University of Chicago Press, 1953), for an analysis of the ideological bases for foreign policy. Arthur S. Link's biography *Wilson* (3 vols., Princeton, 1947–1960), gives some attention to Wilson's ideas, and Harry N. Scheiber, *The Wilson Administration and Civil Liberties, 1917–1921* (Cornell, 1960), provides a brief, informative summary. For the growth of the idea of the American obligation to police disorderly areas see, in addition to the studies by Beard and Weinberg already cited, Dwight Miner, *The Fight for the Panama Route* (Columbia, 1940).

The ideas and values involved in American relief efforts in Europe, both during and after the war, are discussed in Herbert Hoover, *An American Epic* (3 vols., Regnery, 1959–1961), and in Merle Curti, *American Philanthropy Overseas* (Rutgers, 1963).

For the impact of World War I on American intellectual life, see Merle Curti, "The American Scholar in Three Wars," *Journal of the History of Ideas*, III (June, 1942); Guy Stanton Ford, *On and Off the Campus* (University of Minnesota Press, 1938); Frederic P. Keppell, "American Scholarship in the War," *Columbia University Quarterly*, XXI (July, 1919); Park R. Kolbe, *The Colleges in War Time and After* (Appleton-Century-Crofts, 1919); Andrew F. West, *The War and Education* (Princeton, 1919); and Sidney Kaplan, "Social Engineers as Saviors: Effects of World War I on Some American Liberals" in *Journal of the History of Ideas*, XVII (June, 1956). James R. Mock and Cedric Larson, *Words that Won the War* (Princeton, 1939), gives the main outlines of the war propaganda.

## 27. Prosperity, Disillusionment, Criticism

The tendency of many in the 1920s to ascribe to the war much that seemed to characterize the decade is illustrated in the sprightly book by Frederick Lewis Allen, *Only Yesterday* (Harper & Row, 1931), and in Mark Sullivan's impressionistic volume, *The Twenties* (Scribner, 1935). For a longer-range perspective, see Preston W. Slosson, *The Great Crusade and After, 1914–1928* (Macmillan, 1928). For an examination of isolationist ideas, see Selig Adler, *The Isolationist Impulse: Its Twentieth Century Reaction* (Abelard-Schuman, 1957). Also, see Arthur S. Link's perceptive analysis "What Happened to the Progressive Movement in the 1920's?", *American Historical Review*, LXIV (July, 1959), and Henry May's *The End of American Innocence* (Knopf, 1959), and "Shifting Perspectives on the 1920's," *Mississippi Valley Historical Review*, XLIII (December, 1956).

American attitudes toward Europe and European criticisms may be followed in Francis P. Miller and Helen Hill, *Giant of the Western World* (Morrow, 1930); Frank Crane, "The New Internationalism," *Current Opinion*, LXXVII (September, 1924), and LXXVIII (March, 1925); Struthers Burt, "Furor Britannicus," *Saturday Evening Port*, CC (August 20, 1927); J. L. Chastenet, *L'Oncle Shylock ou l'imperialisme americaine à la conquête du monde* (Paris, 1927); Georges Duhamel, *America the Menace* (Houghton Mifflin, 1931); C. E. M. Joad, *The Babbitt Warren* (Harper & Row, 1927); J. F. C. Fuller, *Atlantis, America and the Future* (Dutton, 1926); and Frederick C. Barghorn, *The Soviet Image of the United States* (Harcourt, Brace & World, 1950).

An informative study of the Red Scare is found in Robert K. Murray, *Red Scare; A Study in National Hysteria, 1919–1920* (University of Minnesota Press, 1955). Nativism and the restriction of immigration are analyzed in

John Higham, *Strangers in the Land: Patterns of American Nativism, 1860–1925* (Rutgers, 1955), and Oscar Handlin, *Race and Nationality in American Life* (Little, Brown, 1957), ch. 5. For the wave of "one hundred percentism," consult Bessie L. Pierce's admirable study, *Public Opinion and the Teaching of History in the United States* (Knopf, 1926); Howard K. Beale's well-documented and forthright investigation, *Are American Teachers Free?* (Scribner, 1936); Norman Hapgood (ed.), *Professional Patriots* (A. and C. Boni, 1928); and James M. Beck, *The Constitution of the United States* (Doubleday, 1922). The reaction against "super-patriotism" is reflected in Harold Stearns, *America and the Young Intellectual* (Doubleday, 1928); and Harold Stearns (ed.), *Civilization in the United States; an Inquiry by Thirty Americans* (Harcourt, Brace & World, 1922). Henry S. Harrison, "Last Days of the Devastators," *Yale Review*, n. s. XVII (September, 1928), is a good introduction. Matthew Josephson, *Portrait of the Artist as an American* (Harcourt, Brace & World, 1930); Gerard Crittenden, *Reflections of an Ex-Patriate* (Longmans (David McKay Co.), 1931); and Warren I. Susman, "A Second Country: The Expatriate Image," in The University of Texas *Studies in Literature and Language*, III (Summer, 1961) are pertinent.

For belles-lettres several books are important: Oscar Cargill, *Intellectual America, The March of Ideas* (Macmillan, 1941); Alfred Kazin, *On Native Grounds* (Harcourt, Brace & World, 1942); and Frederick J. Hoffman, *The Twenties. American Writing in the Postwar Decade* (Viking, 1955). Malcolm Cowley (ed.), *After the Genteel Tradition* (Norton, 1936), and Malcolm Cowley, *Exile's Return: A Literary Odyssey of the Nineteen Twenties* (rev. ed., Viking, 1951) are valuable. Maxwell Giesmar's *The Last of the Provincials: The American Novel, 1915–1925* (Houghton Mifflin, 1947) contains discriminating criticism, and Joseph W. Beach, *American Fiction, 1920–1940* (Macmillan, 1941), and Percy Boynton, *America in Contemporary Fiction* (University of Chicago Press, 1940), are academic in their approach. Frederick J. Hoffman, Charles Allen, and Carolyn F. Ulrich have done good spade work in *The Little Magazine: A History and a Bibliography* (Princeton, 1946). American painting is considered in relation to social, intellectual, and economic developments in Milton W. Brown, *American Painting from the Armory Show to the Depression* (Princeton, 1955).

For the critical attitude toward democracy, the following books may be consulted: William McDougall, *Is America Safe for Democracy?* (Scribner, 1921); Henry L. Mencken, *Notes on Democracy* (Knopf, 1926); and Irving Babbitt, *Democracy and Leadership* (Houghton Mifflin, 1925).

In addition to the materials already cited on the philosophy of success and prosperity, extensive use was made of the files of the *Delineator, Woman's Home Companion, Ladies' Home Journal, Saturday Evening Post.*

*American Magazine,* and *True Story Magazine.* E. W. Howe, *The Blessing of Business* (Crane and Co., 1918), and *Ventures in Common Sense* (Knopf, 1919); Garet Garrett, *The American Omen* (Dutton, 1923); J. G. Frederick, *The Great Game of Business, its Rules, its Fascination* (Appleton-Century-Crofts, 1920); Walter B. Pitkin, *The Psychology of Achievement* (Simon and Schuster, 1930); and Thomas Nixon Carver, *The Recent Economic Revolution in the United States* (Little, Brown, 1926), illustrate the business philosophy of the decade. William E. Leuchtenburg, *Perils of Prosperity, 1914–1932* (University of Chicago Press, 1958), contains stimulating analyses. An important study of economic ideas during the decade is James Warren Prothro, *The Dollar Decade: Business Ideas in the 1920's* (Louisiana State University Press, 1954). See also Morrell Heald, "Business Thought in the Twenties: Social Responsibility," *American Quarterly,* XXX (Summer, 1961), for a different emphasis. Thomas C. Cochran, *The American Business System* (Harvard, 1957), provides a scholarly analysis of the development in the twentieth century of business as a culture. Otis Pease discusses the advertising industry's attempts to sell in quantity in *The Responsibilities of American Advertising: Private Control and Public Influence, 1920–1940* (Yale, 1958). James T. Adams, *Our Business Civilization* (A. and C. Boni, 1929), has many interesting observations; and Robert and Helen Lynd, *Middletown, A Study in Contemporary American Culture* (Harcourt, Brace & World, 1929), is an important study. Two useful reports are those by Robert D. Kohn, "The Significance of the Professional Ideal," *American Academy of Political and Social Science Annals,* CI (May, 1922), and Harold F. Clark, *Life Earnings in Selected Occupations in the United States* (Harper & Row, 1937).

For a widely held business view of education, see the *Saturday Evening Post,* CIXCIII (April 16, 1921). For education in general, consult the *Bulletins of the Bureau of Education.* Two approaches to the structure and functions of institutions of higher education are D. A. Robertson, *American Universities and Colleges* (Scribner, 1928), and Abraham Flexner, *Universities, English, German, and American* (Oxford, 1930). For efforts to break the "lockstep," see R. L. Duffus, *Democracy Enters College* (Scribner, 1936). A comparable study for the arts is R. L. Duffus, *The American Renaissance* (Knopf, 1928). Richard Hofstadter and C. DeWitt Hardy have a fresh treatment of this period in *The Development and Scope of Higher Education in the United States* (Columbia, 1952).

The foundations are discussed from varying angles in Edward C. Lindeman, *Wealth and Culture* (Harcourt, Brace & World, 1935), Frederick A. Ogg, *Research in the Humanistic and Social Sciences* (Appleton-Century-Crofts, 1928); and Abraham Flexner, *Funds and Foundations: Their Policies*

*Past and Present* (Harper & Row, 1952). For accounts of the contributions of specific foundations, see Raymond B. Fosdick, *The Story of the Rockefeller Foundation* (Harper & Row, 1952); Howard J. Savage, *Fruit of an Impulse: Forty-Five Years of the Carnegie Foundation, 1905–1950* (Harcourt, Brace & World, 1953); and Raymond B. Fosdick, *Adventures in Giving. The Story of the General Education Board* (Harper & Row, 1962).

The materials on publishing are abundant. Noteworthy studies include Douglas Waples and Ralph W. Tyler, *What People Want to Read About* (University of Chicago Press, 1931); William S. Gray and Ruth Monroe, *The Reading Interests and Habits of Adults* (Macmillan, 1929); the relevant chapters in President's Research Committee on Social Trends, *Recent Social Trends in the United States* (2 vols., McGraw-Hill, 1933); R. L. Duffus, *Books, Their Place in a Democracy* (Houghton Mifflin, 1930); and E. Haldeman-Julius, *The First Hundred Million* (Simon and Schuster, 1928).

Ray Ginger, *Six Days or Forever? Tennessee v. John Thomas Scopes* (Beacon Press, 1958); Norman F. Furniss, *The Fundamentalist Controversy, 1918–1931* (Yale, 1954); Maynard Shipley, *The War on Modern Science* (Knopf, 1927); and Stewart C. Cole, *History of Fundamentalism* (Richard R. Smith, 1929), discuss aspects of the conflict between religion and science in this period. For a stimulating discussion of religion, see Herbert Wallace Schneider, *Religion in Twentieth Century America* (Harvard, 1952). The response of the Protestant churches to social problems is treated in Robert Moats Miller, *American Protestantism and Social Issues, 1919–1939* (University of North Carolina Press, 1958); Paul A. Carter, *The Decline and Revival of the Social Gospel: Social and Political Liberalism in American Protestant Churches, 1920–1940* (Cornell, 1956); and Donald B. Meyer, *The Protestant Search for Political Realism, 1919–1941* (University of California Press, 1960). For an analysis of the Catholic reply to social issues, see Aaron I. Abell, *American Catholicism and Social Action: A Search for Social Justice, 1865–1950* (Hanover House, Doubleday, 1960); and for a discussion of Catholicism in the twentieth century, with particular emphasis on immigration, see the essays in Thomas T. McAvoy (ed.), *Roman Catholicism and the American Way of Life* (University of Notre Dame Press, 1960). Gaius G. Atkins, *Religion in Our Times* (Round Table Press, 1932), and Halford E. Luccock, *Contemporary American Literature and Religion* (Harper & Row, 1934), are thoughtful books. See especially *Recent Social Trends, Middletown,* and, on a less serious level, E. Haldeman-Julius, *The Big American Parade* (Stratford Co., 1929). For an account of Freudianism and its impact on thought, see Oscar Cargill's richly illustrated study, *Intellectual America: The March of Ideas* (Macmillan, 1941). Robert A. Millikan, *Science and the New Civilization* (Scribner, 1930), is a popular essay by a distinguished physicist with religious sympathy. Joseph Wood Krutch, *The Modern Temper* (Harcourt, Brace & World, 1929), is a keen account of the psychological conflicts of the decade. See also the sociological analysis by Caroline Ware in *Greenwich Village, 1920–1930* (Houghton Mifflin, 1935).

On the impact of the machine on thought there is a plethora of material in the periodicals of the decade. Ralph Borsodi, *This Ugly Civilization* (Harper & Row, 1929); Lewis Mumford, *Technics and Civilization* (Harcourt, Brace & World, 1934); Irwin Edman, *Adam, the Baby, and the Man from Mars* (Houghton Mifflin, 1929); *The Contemporary and his Soul* (Cape and Smith, 1931); and Guy Stanton Ford, "Science and Civilization" in *On and Off the Campus* (University of Minnesota Press, 1938), represent a variety of views. Cargill's *Intellectual America* is highly useful at this point.

Edgar Dale, *The Content of Motion Pictures* (Macmillan, 1935), is based on an extensive investigation.

Stuart Sherman, *Americans* (Scribner, 1922) and *The Genius of America* (Scribner, 1923); and John Dewey, *The Public and Its Problems* (Holt, 1927) and *The Quest for Certainty; A Study of the Relation of Knowledge to Action* (Minton, 1929), represent different reactions to similar problems.

## 28. Crisis and New Searches

In his vividly written *Since Yesterday: The Nineteen-Thirties in America* (Harper & Row, 1940), Frederick L. Allen recaptures much of the mood of the decade. Robert and Helen Lynd, *Middletown in Transition* (Harcourt, Brace & World, 1937), shows how the depression accentuated cultural conflict in Muncie, Indiana. Charles and Mary Beard, *America in Midpassage* (Macmillan, 1939), is based on an extensive investigation of firsthand materials and is an illuminating interpretation. *The American Spirit*, also by Charles and Mary Beard (Macmillan, 1942), is helpful, and Harold Stearns (ed.), *America Now: An Inquiry into the Civilization of the United States* (Scribner, 1938) is an interesting anthology. David A. Shannon has collected informative writings of the depression in *The Great Depression* (Prentice Hall, 1960). Dixon Wecter, *The Age of the Great Depression* (Macmillan, 1948), is valuable and contains useful bibliographies.

*Depression, Recovery, and Higher Education, a Report by Committee Y of the American Association of University Professors* (McGraw-Hill, 1937), is an authoritative report. Walter Kotschnig, *Unemployment in the Learned Professions* (Oxford, 1937), includes a discussion of this problem in the United States. *The Schools and the Depression, a State by State Review* (prepared for the Joint Commission on the Emergency in Education, Washington, D. C.) paints a grim picture. The "Spasmodic Diary of a Chicago School-teacher," *Atlantic Monthly*, CLII (November, 1933), records the plight of unpaid Chicago schoolteachers. George S. Counts, *Dare the School Build a New Social Order?* (John Day, 1932) and *A Call to the Teachers of the Nation* (John Day, 1932), stimulated much discussion in educational circles. Edmund deS. Brunner and Irving Lorge, *Rural Trends in Depression Years* (Columbia, 1937), ch. 7, traces the influence of the depression on rural schools.

A brief introduction to government aid to learning and the arts is Robert C. Binkley, "The Cultural Program of the W. P. A.," *Harvard Educational Review*, IX (March, 1939). Also useful are Daniel M. Fox, "The Achievement of the Federal Writers' Project," *American Quarterly*, XIII (Spring, 1961), and Ray A. Billington, "Government and the Arts: The W.P.A. Experience," in the Winter, 1961 issue of the same periodical. Hallie Flanagan, *Arena* (Duell, Sloan and Pearce, 1940), and George Biddle, *An American Artist's Story* (Little, Brown, 1939), are firsthand accounts of the Theater and Art Projects. Grace Overmyer, *Government and the Arts* (Norton, 1939), is an informal discussion.

Robert Cantwell has reported on an analysis of the predepression period in the lives of fifty creative artists, *New Republic*, XCIV (April 27, 1938). Malcolm Cowley summarized the social impact of the depression on creative writers in *The New Republic*, CL (November 8, 1939). In *The Angry Decade* (Dodd, Mead, 1947), Leo Gurko has written with both liveliness and thoughtfulness of the literature of the 1930s. Walter B. Rideout, *The Radical Novel in the United States, 1900–1954*, provides helpful insight, as does Daniel Aaron, *Writers on the Left* (Harcourt, Brace & World, 1961). See also the studies by Cargill and Kazin already cited.

Readable accounts of scientific developments and thought may be found in George W. Gray, *The Advancing Front of Science* (McGraw-Hill, 1937); Harold Ward (ed.), *New Worlds in Science. An Anthology* (McBride, 1941); and Bernard Jaffe, *Outposts of Science* (Simon and Schuster, 1935). Thomas H. Morgan, a great figure in the field of genetics research, has written a clear exposition, *The Scientific Basis of Evolution* (Norton, 1935). See also Richard Goldschmidt, *Ascaris: The Biologist's Story of Life* (Prentice-Hall, 1937). A popular summary of the work in extrasensory perception may be found in two articles in *Harper's Magazine*, CLXX (January, 1935), and CLXXIII (November, 1936). Robert A. Millikan, "Recent Findings in Cosmic Ray Researches," *Scientific Monthly*, XLIII (November, 1936); Edwin Hubble, "Problems of Nebular Research," *Scientific Monthly*, LI (November, 1940); and Arthur K. Solomon, *Why Smash Atoms?* (Harvard University Press, 1940), are popularizations by distinguished authorities.

The impact of new currents of thought in the philosophical field is reflected in John Dewey, *Logic: The Theory of Inquiry* (Holt, 1936); George H. Mead, *Mind, Self, and Society* (University of Chicago Press, 1936); Ernest Nagel, *Principles of the Theory of Probability* (University of Chicago Press, 1939); I. A. Richards, *The Philosophy of Rhetoric* (Oxford, 1936); C. K. Ogden and I. K. Richards, *The Meaning of Meaning* (Harcourt, Brace & World, 1936); Alfred Korszbski, *Science and Sanity* (Science Press, 1934); and the writings of Kenneth Burke, including *Permanence and Change* (New Republic, 1935), and *Attitudes toward History* (New Republic, 1937).

On educational thought, see Merle Curti, "Totalitarianism and American Education," *Educational Forum*, VI (November, 1941); George S. Counts, *The Social Foundations of Education* (Scribner, 1934) and *The Prospects of American Democracy* (John Day, 1938). Lawrence A. Cremin, *The Transformation of the School: Progressivism in American Education, 1876–1957* (Knopf, 1961), is an important study of reform in education. Neo-Thomism is expounded by Robert Hutchins, *No Friendly Voice* (University of Chicago Press, 1936) and *The Higher Learning in America* (Yale, 1936). John U. Nef has interpreted contemporary American culture from the Hutchins-Adler-Barr point of view in *The United States and Civilization* (University of Chicago Press, 1942). For an incisive criticism of the Hutchins position, consult Harry D. Gideonse, *The Higher Learning in a Democracy* (Holt, 1937).

On the impact of Marxism, see Sidney Hook, *Toward an Understanding of Karl Marx* (John Day, 1933) and *From Hegel to Marx* (Reynal and Hitchcock, 1936); Lewis Corey, *The Decline of American Capitalism* (Covici, 1934); Granville Hicks (ed.), *Proletarian Literature in the United States* (International Publishers, 1936); and the files of *The Marxist Quarterly*, and *Science and Society*. Eugene Lyons has discussed fellow travelers and front organizations with some animus in *The Red Decade, the Stalinist Penetration of America* (Bobbs-Merrill, 1941). See also Wilson Record, *The Negro and the Communist Party* (University of North Carolina Press, 1951). David A. Shannon, *The Socialist Party of America: A History* discusses the Socialist party from 1901 to 1952. For the reaction against Marxism, see Granville Hicks, "The Failure of Left Criticism," *New Republic*, CIII (September 9, 1940) and *Where We Came Out* (Viking, 1954); Alfred Bingham, *Insurgent America: The Revolt of the Middle Classes* (Harper & Row, 1936); Sidney Hook, *Reason, Social Myths and Democracy* (John Day, 1940); and James Burnham, *The Managerial Revolution* (John Day, 1941). Lawrence Dennis, *The Coming American Fascism* (Harper & Row, 1936) and *Dynamics of War and Revolution* (Weekly Foreign Letter, New York, 1940) are expositions by America's leading intellectual fascist. Raymond Gram Swing, *Forerunners of American Fascism* (Messner, 1934), and Max Lerner, *It is Later than You Think* (Viking, 1938), sounded danger signals.

The literature of the philosophy of the New Deal is extensive. *The Public*

*Papers and Addresses of Franklin D. Roosevelt* (9 vols., Random House, 1938–1941) states the official position. Roosevelt's ideas, personality and policies are treated comprehensively in Arthur M. Schlesinger, Jr., *The Age of Roosevelt* (3 vols., Houghton Mifflin, 1957–1960). General treatments are: Stuart Chase, *The Economy of Abundance* (Macmillan, 1934); Mordecai Ezekiel, *Jobs for All Through Industrial Expansion* (Knopf, 1937); Charles A. Beard, *The Open Door at Home* (Macmillan, 1934); Edwin G. Nourse, *America's Capacity to Produce* (Brookings Institution, 1934); and Maurice Leven, *America's Capacity to Consume* (Brookings Institution, 1934). Howard M. Bell, *Youth Tell Their Story* (American Council on Education, 1938), is based on interviews. National Resources Planning Committee, *Research, a National Resource* (Washington, 1938), is important. See also Eric F. Goldman, *Rendezvous With Destiny* and Charles A. Madison, *Leaders and Liberals in 20th Century America* (Ungar, 1961). Alvin Johnson, *Pioneer's Progress* (Viking, 1952), is an informative autobiography of an influential liberal. An interesting point has been made by Lewis S. Feuer, "Travelers to the Soviet Union 1917–1932: The Formation of a Component of New Deal Ideology" in *American Quarterly*, XVI (Summer, 1962).

Winston Sanford, *Illiteracy in the United States* (University of North Carolina Press, 1930), is useful. Edgar Dale, *The Content of Motion Pictures* (Macmillan, 1935), presents an unfavorable view of the influence of movies on youth. For a contrasting view, see Raymond Moley, *Are We Movie Mad?* (Vanguard, 1937), and Mortimer Adler, *Art and Prudence* (Longmans (David McKay Co.), 1937). Douglas Waples, *People and Print; Social Aspects of Reading in the Depression* (University of Chicago Press, 1937), is based on elaborate investigation. Charles H. Compton, *Who Reads What?* (Wilson, 1935); Robert Cantwell, "What the Working Class Reads," *New Republic*, LXXXIII (July 17, 1935); Hickman Powell, "Collier's" in *Scribner's Magazine*, XI (February, 1935); and Margaret MacMullen, "Pulps and Confessions," *Harper's Magazine*, CLXXV (June, 1937), are all informative. See also *These are Our Lives. As Told by the People and Written by Members of the Federal Writers' Projects of the Works Projects Administration in North Carolina, Tennessee and Georgia* (University of North Carolina Press, 1939). The Beards have a fine discussion of the radio in *America in Midpassage*, 643 ff.

The challenge of totalitarianism and the reinterpretation of democracy occasioned a wealth of writing. The titles cited here are highly selective. Henry Cabot Lodge, *The Cult of Weakness* (Houghton Mifflin, 1932); Lewis Mumford, *Faith for Living* (Harcourt, Brace & World, 1940), and Archibald MacLeish, *The Irresponsibles* (Duell, Sloan & Pearce, 1940), are stirring tracts. William A. Neilson (ed.), *The City of Man* (Viking, 1940), is a notable collection of statements of democratic faith. Edward M. Earle, *Against This Torrent* (Princeton, 1941), and Charles A. Beard, *A Foreign Policy for America* (Knopf, 1940), state the interventionist and noninterventionist views. Harold Fields, *The Refugee in the United States* (Oxford, 1938), does not deal fully with the contributions of refugees to our intellectual life, but is suggestive. Donald Peterson Kent, *The Refugee Intellectual: The Americanization of the Immigrants of 1933–1941* (Columbia, 1953), is a valuable study of the problems of assimilation of refugee intellectuals. See also Maurice R. Davie and others, *Refugees in America. Report of the Committee for the Study of Recent Immigration from Europe* (Harper & Row, 1947).

### 29. *American Assertions in a World of Upheaval*

Useful studies of the problems of ideology of World War II, of morale, civilian and military, and of loyalty, include Arthur Derounian, *Under Cover* (World, 1943), a firsthand report of subversive groups before and after Pearl Harbor; Pendleton Herring, *The Impact of War, Our American Democracy Under Arms* (Holt, 1941); William F. Ogburn (ed.), *American Society in Wartime* (University of Chicago Press, 1943); Francis J. Brown and Joseph S. Roucek, *One America* (Prentice-Hall, 1945); Melvin Gingerich, *Service for Peace: A History of Mennonite Civilian Public Service* (Mennonite Central Committee, 1949), the story of Mennonite conscientious objectors; Morton Grodzins, *Americans Betrayed; Politics and the Japanese Evacuation* (University of Chicago Press, 1949); and Dorothy Swaine Thomas, *Japanese American Evacuation and Resettlement*, (3 vols., University of California Press, 1946–1954). Of special importance, both from the methodological standpoint and from that of findings, is S. A. Stouffer's *The American Soldier: Adjustment During Army Life* (3 vols., Princeton, 1949).

Pierce Butler (ed.), *Books and Libraries in Wartime* (University of Chicago Press, 1945), and I. L. Kandel, *The Impact of the War upon American Education* (University of North Carolina Press, 1949), are informative about the agencies of intellectual life during the war. Useful also are M. M. Chambers, *Opinions of Gains for American Education from Wartime Armed Services Training* (American Council on Education, 1946); T. R. McConnell and M. M. Wiley (eds.), "Higher Education and the War," *Annals of the American Academy of Political and Social Science*, CCXXXI (1944); and J. H. Miller and D. Brooks, *The Role of Higher Education in War and After*.

Alfred Cohn's *Minerva's Progress* (Harcourt, Brace & World, 1946) is a thoughtful essay on the agencies of intellectual life. William Miller's *Book Industry* (a report of the Public Library Inquiry of the Social Science Research Council, Columbia, 1949) is a significant analysis of the book trade in the postwar years; other volumes in the report of the Inquiry are also pertinent. For a study of an influential columnist, see David Weingast, *Walter Lippmann: A Study in Personal Journalism* (Rutgers, 1949).

For an attack on the instrumentalist and pragmatic emphases in education and the defense of a required "core" and of "permanent" values, see Jacques Maritain, *Education at the Crossroads* (Yale, 1943); Alexander Meiklejohn, *Education Between Two Worlds* (Harper & Row, 1943); Robert M. Hutchins, *Education for Freedom* (Louisiana State University Press, 1943); and Mark Van Doren, *Liberal Education* (Holt, 1943). Lawrence A. Cremin, *The Transformation of the School: Progressivism in American Education, 1876–1957* is also useful. The argument for the humanities is ably developed in Loren C. McKinney (ed.), *State University Surveys the Humanities* (University of North Carolina Press, 1945). Contrasting views appeared in Sidney Hook, *Education for Modern Man* (Dial, 1946); Howard Mumford Jones, *Education and World Tragedy* (Harvard, 1946); James E. Conant, *Education in a Divided World* (Harvard, 1948); and the report of President Truman's Commission on Higher Education, *Higher Education for Democracy* (Harper & Row, 1948). Paul Blanshard, *American Freedom and Catholic Power* (Beacon Press, 1949), and James M. O'Neill, *Religion and Education Under the Constitution* (Harper & Row, 1949), present conflicting positions on church and state relations in education.

Studies of contributions of intellectuals to the war effort are included in Francis Biddle, *Artist at War* (Viking, 1944); Paul M. A. Linebarger, *Psychological Warfare* (Washington Infantry Journal Press, 1948); Daniel Lerner (ed.), *Propaganda in War and Crisis: Materials for American Policy* (Stewart, 1951); and Charles A. H. Thomson, *Overseas Information Service of the United States Government* (Brookings Institution, 1948).

James Finney Baxter's *Scientists Against Time* (Little, Brown, 1948) is an objective, clear, and readable account of the mobilization of scientists in the war effort. Irvin Stewart has written a sober, detailed account of the Office of Scientific Research and Development, *Organizing Scientific Research for War* (Little, Brown, 1948). For a detailed, objective account of medical advances, see *Advances in Military Medicine* (2 vols., Little, Brown, 1948). Henry de Wolfe Smyth offered the first official report of the application of atomic fission to warfare in his factual *Atomic Energy for Official Purposes* (Princeton, 1946). John Hersey's *Hiroshima* (Knopf, 1946), is a straightforward account of the experiences, during and after the explosion, of a group of citizens in that Japanese city. Public reactions to the atomic bomb have been completely reported in Leonard S. Cottrell and Sylvia Eberhart, *American Opinion on World Affairs in the Atomic Age* (Princeton, 1948). Good introductions to the extensive literature on the problems of atomic control are Ansley J. Coale, *The Problem of Reducing Vulnerability to Atomic Bombs* (Princeton, 1947), and James R. Newman and Byron S. Miller, *The Control of Atomic Energy* (McGraw-Hill, 1947). The reports of the Atomic Energy Commission are, of course, indispensable. Thoughtful discussions of the implications of the new scientific developments for the future of society include Vannevar Bush, *Science the Endless Frontier* (American Council on Public Affairs, 1946), and the same author's *Modern Arms and Free Men* (Simon and Schuster, 1949); *Physical Science and Human Values* (Princeton, 1947), a report of a symposium in which leading philosophers and scientists took part; Norman Cousins, *Modern Man is Obsolete* (Viking, 1945); and the reports of the Conference on Science, Philosophy, and Religion in Their Relation to the Democratic Way of Life, especially that of the seventh conference, Lyman Bryson, *et al.* (eds.), *Conflicts of Power in Modern Culture* (Harper & Row, 1947).

### 30. Dialogues in Our Time

The problem of communication has been widely written about on several levels. The more technical discussions include Leo Bogart, *The Age of Television: A Study of Viewing Habits and the Impact of Television on American Life* (Ungar, 1956); W. Y. Elliott (ed.), *Television's Impact on American Culture* (Michigan State University Press, 1957); David K. Berlo, *The Process of Communication; An Introduction to Theory and Practice* (Holt, 1960); and Joseph T. Klapper, *The Effects of Mass Communication* (Free Press, 1960). James B. Conant has developed his position on the possibility of a lay understanding of the sciences in *Modern Science and Modern Man* (Columbia, 1953), while J. Robert Oppenheimer has discussed the relations between science and the wider culture of our time in *The Open Mind* (Simon and Schuster, 1955).

Reactions to the Cold War, evidences of espionage and subversion, and McCarthyism are discussed from varying points of view in William F. Buckley, Jr. and L. Brent Bozell, *McCarthy and his Enemies* (Regnery, 1954); Richard Rovere, *Senator Joe McCarthy* (Harcourt, Brace & World, 1959); Samuel A. Stouffer, *Communism, Conformity and Civil Liberties; A Cross-Section of the Nation Speaks its Mind* (Doubleday, 1955); and Morton Grodzins, *The Loyal and the Disloyal* (University of Chicago Press, 1956). Sidney Hook's *Heresy, Yes—Conspiracy, No!* (John Day, 1953) sharply delineated several aspects of the limitations of civil liberties in nonconformist and conspiratorial situations. Edward Shils, in *Torment of Secrecy* (Free Press, 1956), discusses critically the background and consequences of the American security police. David Fellman's scholarly lectures, *The Limits of Freedom* (Rutgers, 1959), analyze key court cases involving the right to communicate and the right to talk politics, while Henry Steele Commager's *Freedom, Loyalty, Dissent* (Oxford, 1954); Elmer Davis' *But We Were Born Free* (Bobbs-Merrill, 1954); Zechariah Chafee's *The Blessings of Liberty* (Lippincott, 1956); and John W. Caughey's *In Clear and Present Danger: The Crucial State of our Freedoms* (University of Chicago Press, 1958) are eloquent defenses of the civil liberties in crisis situations.

Firsthand accounts of espionage, subversion, and personal experiences in the Communist movement and indictment of the party are too numerous to list. Representative examples, however, include James Wechsler, *The Age of Suspicion* (Random House, 1953); Wittaker Chambers, *Witness* (Random House, 1952); Granville Hicks, *Where We Came Out* (Viking, 1954); Herbert Philbrick, *I Led Three Lives* (McGraw-Hill, 1952); James Burnham, *The Webb of Subversion* (John Day, 1954); G. Bromley Oxnam, *I Protest* (Harper & Row, 1954); and Norman Thomas, *The Test of Freedom* (Norton, 1954).

Explanations of McCarthyism include Loren P. Beth, "McCarthyism" in the *South Atlantic Quarterly* (April, 1956); Paul Bixler, "McCarthyism, Communism and Intellectual Freedom," *Antioch Review* (September, 1954); James Rorty and Moshe Decter, *McCarthy and the Communists* (Beacon, 1954); Edward J. Heffron, "McCarthy," *Commonweal* (October 31, 1952); and Richard Hofstadter, "The Pseudo-Conservative Revolt," *American Scholar* (Winter 1954–1955).

Writings on the Radical Right include Barry Goldwater, *The Conscience of a Conservative* (Victor Publishing Co., Ky., 1960); Alan F. Westin, "The Deadly Parallels, Radical Right and Radical Left," *Harper's Magazine* (April, 1962); William Buckley Jr., *Up From Liberalism* (McDowell, 1959); and Daniel Bell (ed.), *The New American Right* (Criterion, 1955). The relations between the Radical Right and the New Conservatism are discussed with balance and common sense in Clinton Rossiter's *Conservatism in America; The Thankless Persuasion*.

It is hard to select representative titles from the extensive literature that is concerned with military security and foreign policy. Hans Morgenthau, *In Defense of the National Interest* (Knopf, 1951), is a brilliant essay which distinguishes between utopianism, legalism, sentimentalism, and neoisolationism in recent American foreign policy. William W. Kaufmann, Gordon A. Craig, Roger Hilsman, and Klaus Knorr, in *Military Policy and National Security* (Princeton, 1956), probe the complexities of the problems. George F. Kennan, in *Realities in American Foreign Policy* (Princeton, 1954) and *Russia, the*

*Atom and the West* (Harper & Row, 1958), develops ideas which attracted a good deal of attention. Perhaps the best brief introduction to the wide ranging aspects of the problem are the essays in *Daedalus* in the Fall, 1962, issue. Studies focusing on atomic power and foreign policy include Henry Kissinger's *Nuclear Weapons and Foreign Policy* (Harper & Row, 1957) and *The Necessity for Choice* (Harper & Row, 1961), a reappraisal of his earlier thesis on limited war. The extreme positions are represented in the writings of Edward Teller, *Our Nuclear Future* (Criterion, 1958) and *The Legacy of Hiroshima* (Doubleday, 1962), on the one side, and, on the other, Ralph E. Lapp, *The Voyage of the Lucky Dragon* (Harper & Row, 1958) and *Roads to Discovery* (Harper & Row, 1960); Lewis Mumford, *In the Name of Sanity* (Harcourt, Brace & World, 1954); and the essays in John C. Bennett (ed.), *Nuclear Weapons and the Conflicts of Conscience* (Scribner, 1962). Thomas E. Murray, a former member of the Atomic Energy Commission, takes a middle ground in *Nuclear Policy for War and Peace* (World, 1960). Relations between the civilian and military authorities are critically discussed by Arthur Ekirch, Jr., *The Civilian and the Military* (Oxford, 1956), and may be checked against Walter Millis and others, *Arms and the State* (Twentieth Century Fund, 1958); Samuel P. Huntington, *The Soldier and the State* (Harvard, 1957); W. W. Kaufmann (ed.), *Military Policy and National Security* (Princeton, 1956); and G. C. Reinhardt, *American Strategy in the Atomic Age* (University of Oklahoma, 1955), a bold blueprint for thawing the Cold War. Useful introductions to the extensive literature on space exploration include Heinz Haber, *Man in Space* (Bobbs-Merrill, 1953), and Wernher Von Braun, Fred L. Whipple, and Will Ley (eds.), *The Conquest of the Moon* (Viking, 1953).

On the philosophical and religious side of the search for absolutes, Jacques Maritain's *Christianity and Democracy* (Scribner, 1945), *The Person and the Common Good* (Scribner, 1947), and Reinhold Niebuhr's *The Children of Light and the Children of Darkness* (Scribner, 1944) and *Pious and Secular America* (Scribner, 1958), present authoritative defenses of absolute values. See also the essays of Brand Blanshard and George E. Thomas in *Changing Patterns in American Civilization* (University of Pennsylvania Press, 1949). Able presentations from a more liberal standpoint include Arthur E. Murphy, *The Uses of Reason* (Macmillan, 1943), and Morris R. Cohen, *Studies in Philosophy and Science* (Holt, 1949). F. Ernest Johnson edited a book of essays, *Patterns of Faith in America Today* (Harper & Row, 1957), which place the main religious positions in an historical context. Will Herberg, *Protestant, Catholic, Jew* (rev. ed., Doubleday, 1960), emphasizes the impact of American culture on three great religious systems. Also worthy of attention is John J. Kane's *Catholic-Protestant Conflicts in America* (Regnery, 1955),

and John Cogley (ed.), *Religion in America* (Meridan Books, 1958). Msgr.
J. T. Ellis, *American Catholics and the Intellectual Life* (Heritage, 1956), and
Thomas O'Dea, *American Catholic Dilemma; An Inquiry* (Sheed, 1958), discuss the ferment in some Catholic circles over the failure of American Catholics to contribute to scholarship and the creative arts in terms commensurate
with their numerical position.

The New Conservatism has evoked a considerable body of writing. The
best overall introduction is Clinton Rossiter's *Conservatism in America, the
Thankless Persuasion*, with an extensive bibliography. Also important are
Russell Kirk, *The Conservative Mind; from Burke to Santayana* (Regnery,
1953) and *A Program for Conservatives* (Regnery, 1954). Francis Wilson,
*The Case for Conservatism* (University of Washington Press, 1951), and
John J. Hallowell, *The Moral Foundations of Democracy* (University of Chicago Press, 1954), rest their intellectually sophisticated arguments on classical
thought. Less ordered but lively are Peter Viereck's *Conservatism Revisited*
(Scribner, 1949) and *Shame and Glory of the Intellectuals* (Beacon Press,
1953). Walter Lippmann's *Essays in the Public Philosophy* (Little, Brown,
1955) should be included even in a brief list of books on the New Conservatism.

For any discussion of democratic thought in the 1950s a good taking off
point is Edward S. Mason (ed.), *The Corporation in Modern Society* (Harvard, 1960), a collection of essays by lawyers and social scientists exploring in
compact form the impact of the corporation on decision-making in many
spheres and the influence of the corporation on almost every aspect of American life. The thesis that the corporation is here to stay, must be lived with,
and has a good deal to be said for it characterizes Adolph A. Berle's *The
Twentieth Century Capitalist Revolution* (Harcourt, Brace & World, 1954);
David E. Lilienthal's *Big Business: A New Era* (Harper & Row, 1953); and,
in some respects, John Kenneth Galbraith's *American Capitalism: The Concept of Countervailing Power* (Houghton Mifflin, 1952). Such widely read
popularizations as Vance Packard's *The Hidden Persuaders* (McKay, 1957)
and *The Status Seekers* (McKay, 1959), and Martin Mayer's *Madison Avenue
USA* (Harper & Row, 1958) emphasize the pervasive and often unrecognized
influence of public relations counsels, advertisers, and other manipulators of
opinion. In addition to Charles Frankel's *The Case for Modern Man*
(Harper & Row, 1956) other books restating and recasting familiar democratic ideology in new contexts include Lewis Mumford, *The Transformation
of Man* (Harper & Row, 1956); Arthur M. Schlesinger, Jr., *The Vital Center*
(Houghton Mifflin, 1949); William Kornhauser, *The Politics of Mass Society*
(Free Press, 1959); and Samuel Lubell's *The Revolt of the Moderates*
(Harper & Row, 1956). C. Wright Mill's books, especially *White Collar* (Ox-

ford, 1951), *The Power Elite* (Oxford, 1956), and *The Sociological Imagination* (Oxford, 1959) are provocative and keen criticisms of the erosion of democracy under the influence of corporation executives, high military brass, and key politicians. Richard T. Rovere's *The American Establishment and Other Reports* (Harcourt, Brace & World, 1962) makes some of the same points with wit and urbanity. Also relevant to an understanding of the dialogues about democracy is Daniel Bell's *The End of Ideology, on the Exhaustion of Political Ideas in the Fifties* (Free Press, 1960), which argues that traditional idea systems, including Marxism, are unable to explain the social behavior of our time.

The implications for democratic theory and action of changing patterns of thought in race relations can be followed in Louis Lomax, *The Negro Revolt* (Harper & Row, 1962); James Baldwin, *Nobody Knows My Name* (Dial, 1961); Lawrence Dunbar Reddick, *Crusade without Violence: A Biography of Martin Luther King, Jr.* (Harper & Row, 1959); Merrill Proudfoot, *Diary of a Sit-In* (University of North Carolina Press, 1962); Harry S. Ashmore, *Epitaph for Dixie* (Norton, 1958); and Thomas D. Clark, *The Emerging South* (Oxford, 1961), chs. 12–17. The more comprehensive studies and commentaries on minorities include Arnold and Caroline Rose, *America Divided: Minority Group Relations in the United States* (Knopf, 1948); Carey McWilliams, *A Mask for Privilege* (Little, Brown, 1948); Robert M. MacIver (ed.), *Unity and Difference in American Life* (Harper & Row, 1947); and Louis Ruchames, *Race, Jobs, and Politics: the Story of FEPC* (Columbia, 1953). E. Franklin Frazier, *The Negro in the United States* (Macmillan, 1949), and Maurice R. Davie, *Negroes in American Society* (McGraw-Hill, 1949), are useful. Like ethnic relations, the status of women received attention from writers. Mary R. Beard presented a forceful defense of the larger role of women in society in *Woman as a Force in History: A Study in Traditions and Realities* (Macmillan, 1946); and Ferdinand Lundberg and Marynia Farnham attacked feminism in their somewhat dogmatic and sensational *Modern Woman: The Lost Sex* (Harper & Row, 1947). Rainwater Lee, *et al.*, in *Workingman's Wife* (Oceana Publications, 1959), deal with a neglected aspect of the matter.

Max Lerner's *America as a Civilization* (Simon and Schuster, 1957) is the most important overall synthesis published in the 1950s. The quality of American civilization is discussed from several points of view in *America and the Intellectual* which comprised a special issue of *Partisan Review* in 1953. Joseph Wood Krutch edited a series of essays under the title *Is the Common Man too Common?* (University of Oklahoma Press, 1954), which might well be read with Leo Gurko's defense of the "middlebrow" in *Heroes, Highbrows, and the Popular Mind* (Bobbs-Merrill, 1953). In addition to titles already mentioned, the issues involved in the general concept of mass culture are treated with greater and lesser degrees of sympathy in Gilbert Seldes, *The Public Arts* (Simon and Schuster, 1946); Eric Larrabee (ed.), *Mass Leisure* (Free Press, 1948); George Soule, *Time for Living* (Viking, 1955); and Bernard Iddings Bell, *Crowd Culture* (Harper & Row, 1952). Thoughtful discussions of the quality of American civilization also include Richard Chase, *The Democratic Vista* (Doubleday, 1958); David Riesman, *Individualism Reconsidered* (Free Press, 1954); Howard Mumford Jones, *One Great Society: Humane Learning in the United States* (Harcourt, Brace & World, 1959); and Joseph Wood Krutch *The Measure of Man* (Bobbs-Merrill, 1954). Jacques Barzun's *The House of Intellect* (Harper & Row, 1959), is witty, salty, and biased.

Central to the question of the quality of American civilization in our time is the kind and amount of education available to American youth. Some of the widely read and discussed books include Arthur E. Bestor, Jr., *Educational Wastelands* (University of Illinois Press, 1953) and *The Restoration of Learning* (Knopf, 1955); James B. Conant, *The Citadel of Learning* (Yale, 1946), *The American High School Today* (McGraw-Hill, 1959), and *The Child, the Parent and the State* (Harvard, 1959); Admiral H. C. Rickover, *Education and Freedom* (Dutton, 1959); Fred M. Hechinger, *An Adventure in Education* (Macmillan, 1956); and Paul A. Woodring, *A Fourth of a Nation* (McGraw-Hill, 1957). Evan Hunter's *The Blackboard Jungle* (Simon and Schuster, 1954) dramatized the issue of juvenile delinquency and the schools. Among the contributions to educational philosophy especially noteworthy are Robert M. Hutchins, *The Conflict of Education in a Democratic Society* (Harper & Row, 1953); Theodore Brameld, *Patterns of Educational Philosophy* (World, 1950), and *Toward a Reconstructed Philosophy of Education* (Dryden Press, 1956). John W. Gardner's *Excellence: Can We Be Equal and Excellent Too?* (Harper & Row, 1961) is a searching discussion.

Much scholarly as well as popular attention was given in the postwar period to the so-called "image of America" entertained by peoples overseas, and this image, often fragmented and biased but sometimes perceptive, is important not only for an understanding of the quality of American civilization at mid-century but also for an understanding of international cultural relations. Representative titles are James Burnham (ed.), *What Europe Thinks of America* (John Day, 1953); André Siegfried, *America at Mid-Century* (Harcourt, Brace & World, 1955); Franz M. Joseph (ed.), *As Others See Us* (Princeton, 1959); Raymond-Léopold Bruckberger, *Image of America* (Viking, 1959); and "American Influences Abroad," *Antioch Review* XXII (Summer, 1962). The other side of the coin has long received much attention, but Cushing Strout's *The American Image of the Old World* (Harper & Row, 1963) is of special interest.

# Index